DISCARD

THE
INTERNATIONAL ENCYCLOPEDIA
OF
EDUCATIONAL TECHNOLOGY

Advances in Education

This is an internationally acclaimed series of Pergamon educational reference works. Each volume in the series is thematically organized and aims to provide comprehensive and up-to-date coverage of its own specialist subject area. The series is being developed primarily from the well-received *International Encyclopedia of Education* using the latest electronic publishing technology for data capture, manipulation and storage of text in a form which allows fast and easy modification and updating of copy. Where appropriate a number of other volumes have been specially commissioned for the series. Volumes that are not derived from *The International Encyclopedia of Education* are indicated by an asterisk.

DUNKIN (ed.)
The International Encyclopedia of Teaching and Teacher Education

KEEVES (ed.)
Educational Research, Methodology, and Measurement: An International Handbook

LEWY (ed.)
The International Encyclopedia of Curriculum

POSTLETHWAITE (ed.)
The Encyclopedia of Comparative Education and National Systems of Education

PSACHAROPOULOS (ed.)
Economics of Education: Research and Studies

REYNOLDS (ed.)*
Knowledge Base for the Beginning Teacher

THOMAS (ed.)
The Encyclopedia of Human Development and Education: Theory, Research, and Studies

TITMUS (ed.)
Lifelong Education for Adults: An International Handbook

WALBERG & HAERTEL (eds.)
The International Encyclopedia of Educational Evaluation

WANG, REYNOLDS & WALBERG (eds.)* 3 volumes
Handbook of Special Education: Research and Practice

A Related Pergamon Journal[†]

International Journal of Educational Research

Editor: Herbert J Walberg, University of Illinois at Chicago, Illinois, USA .

[†]Free Specimen copy available on request.

NOTICE TO READERS

Dear Reader

If your library is not already a standing/continuation order customer to the series **Advances in Education**, may we recommend that you place a standing/continuation order to receive immediately upon publication all new volumes. Should you find that these volumes no longer serve your needs, your order can be cancelled at any time without notice.

ROBERT MAXWELL
Publisher at Pergamon Press

THE
INTERNATIONAL ENCYCLOPEDIA
OF
EDUCATIONAL TECHNOLOGY

Edited by

MICHAEL ERAUT
University of Sussex, Brighton, UK

PERGAMON PRESS
OXFORD · NEW YORK · BEIJING · FRANKFURT
SÃO PAULO · SYDNEY · TOKYO · TORONTO

U.K.	Pergamon Press plc, Headington Hill Hall, Oxford OX3 0BW, England
U.S.A.	Pergamon Press, Inc., Maxwell House, Fairview Park, Elmsford, New York 10523, U.S.A.
PEOPLE'S REPUBLIC OF CHINA	Pergamon Press, Room 4037, Qianmen Hotel, Beijing, People's Republic of China
FEDERAL REPUBLIC OF GERMANY	Pergamon Press GmbH, Hammerweg 6, D-6242 Kronberg, Federal Republic of Germany
BRAZIL	Pergamon Editora Ltda, Rua Eça de Queiros, 346, CEP 04011, Paraiso, São Paulo, Brazil
AUSTRALIA	Pergamon Press Australia Pty Ltd., P.O. Box 544, Potts Point, N.S.W. 2011, Australia
JAPAN	Pergamon Press, 5th Floor, Matsuoka Central Building, 1-7-1 Nishishinjuku, Shinjuku-ku, Tokyo 160, Japan
CANADA	Pergamon Press Canada Ltd., Suite No 271, 253 College Street, Toronto, Ontario, Canada M5T 1R5

Library of Congress Cataloging-in-Publication Data

The International encyclopedia of educational technology
edited by Michael Eraut.—1st ed.
p.   cm.—(Advances in education)
Includes bibliographies and indexes.
1. Educational technology—Dictionaries.   I. Eraut, Michael. II.
Series.
LB1028.3.1567   1989
371.3'07'8—dc19   89-3006

British Library Cataloguing in Publication Data

The international encyclopedia of educational
technology.—(Advances in education)
1. Educational Technology
I. Eraut, Michael. II. Series
371.3'07'8

ISBN 0-08-033409-1

Database design and computer composition by Maxwell Data Management Ltd., Derby

Printed in Great Britain by BPCC Wheatons Ltd, Exeter

Contents

PART 3   MEDIA POTENTIAL, UTILIZATION, AND IMPACT

[†] deceased

PART 4   INSTRUCTIONAL DEVELOPMENT

[†] deceased

[†] deceased

PART 5   **DISTRIBUTION AND ORGANIZATION OF KNOWLEDGE AND RESOURCES**

Preface

Thirty years ago, in 1959, the term *educational technology* had yet to be introduced. However, the contributory streams of educational television, programmed learning, and audiovisual instruction had already begun to bubble with innovatory excitement. Ten years later, in 1969, there was an embryonic field of study with a few research units and academic qualifications already carrying the *educational technology* label. A fourth contributor, computer-based learning had arrived on the scene, and integrating concepts such as learning resources, instructional development, and systems approach were beginning to be explored. By 1979 these concepts had been well-researched, if not fully exploited, yet the field was far from unified and its organization still reflected particular media traditions and subcultures. Distance education was a major concern and nonformal education was also attracting increased attention. Now, in 1989, it can be seen that further integration is coming through technological convergence. What is now called *information technology* is both integrating media for learning, as in interactive video, and transforming simple telephone lines into interactive information networks. It is no longer possible to regard computing, video, and telecommunications as separate areas of technical development.

The time then is particularly ripe for taking stock of developments in educational technology. Practitioners need to know what has been happening across the whole field and it is particularly important that the developers of new learning systems and resources do not neglect the knowledge and know-how that has been built up over the last thirty years. They rightly perceive much earlier work as having been technologically limited, but they themselves are in danger of becoming conceptually limited even to the extent of repeating some of the mistakes of the early pioneers. The purpose of this *Encylopedia* is to meet the current need for educational technologists to broaden and consolidate their knowledge base by providing state-of-the-art reports which cover the whole field of educational technology.

A further characteristic of the *Encyclopedia* is its international orientation. Authors come from 14 different countries, though authors from the United States (48 percent) and the United Kingdom (27 percent) still form a significant majority. This reflects partly the decision to keep the whole *Encyclopedia* in English, and partly the difficulty for many third world experts in finding time and library facilities. All authors were asked to adopt an international perspective and many were chosen because they had the knowledge and experience to do so. Some articles were specially commissioned to redress the balance by presenting specifically regional or developing country perspectives. Overall, there are very few articles that are not relevant to the particular needs and concerns of any individual nation.

1. The Origins of the Encyclopedia

This *Encyclopedia* has a parent, the 10-volume *International Encyclopedia of Education*, which was published in 1985. Now well-established in major academic libraries, it was awarded the 1986 Dartmouth Medal for an outstanding reference work by the American Library Association as well as being selected by Choice as an Outstanding Academic Book of 1987. However, its size made the price high for many individual users and educational technology units to purchase their own copies, and its alphabetic mode of organization meant that the hundred or so entries on educational technology were widely distributed.

The use of advanced computer technology enabled the publisher to issue the *International Encyclopedia of Education* with far greater speed and accuracy than would have been possible with traditional editorial and printing techniques. For example, in the past it was necessary to complete pagination of the text before indexing could commence. In contrast, with computer database publishing techniques it is possible to key in the index terms at the same time as the article. The appropriate page numbers are then automatically generated for printing in the index. Furthermore, it is not necessary to keyboard the articles in any strict order. These techniques have made it possible to retrieve and update the educational technology articles for this volume with enormous savings in editorial and keyboarding time. Another important feature of the parent encyclopedia is its availability, since 1988, on a single compact disc (CD-ROM).

For this *Encyclopedia*, articles have been organized thematically rather than alphabetically. Relevant articles from outside the original Educational Technology section have been added, 11 new articles have been specially commissioned, and many others have been substantially revised. Moreover, each of the five parts has an Editor's introduction explaining the scope of its ideas and the range of applications covered. The offspring has taken on a life of its own. Indeed when one surveys the list of contents, one can see that the *Encyclopedia* has now become more than a substantial work of reference. It provides the equivalent of several authoritative books—a "series" under a single cover—with the additional advantages of cross-referencing and a common index. There are extensive and fully verified bibliographies for all entries to help the reader pursue a particular topic, and there are comprehensive subject and author indexes for easy access.

2. Boundaries, Foci, and Structure

Like most fields of study, educational technology does not have obvious natural boundaries. Nor is there a single uncontested, internationally recognized definition. Much of its claimed territory is also inhabited by people who do not seek their occupational identity within the educational technology community. Thus, the criteria for including articles in this volume have been essentially pragmatic. The topics selected represent areas of knowledge that are either taught on at least some educational technology courses or used by practising educational technologists; most will qualify under both these criteria. Those who consider that the Editor has set the boundaries too wide may find, on reading and reflection, that the "marginal entries" are more relevant than at first they thought. Those who find the boundaries too narrow will still, it is hoped, be able to consult the parent encyclopedia or other volumes in the series.

The only aspect of the educational technology literature which has been deliberately omitted has been writing about educational futures. There is always a danger that the potential use of educational technology will be constrained by current patterns for the organization and delivery of learning. Thus, it is important for educational technologists to suggest alternative patterns, especially when the rapid development of new technology is challenging our imaginative capacity to realize its potential. However, such futuristic thinking, vital though it is, does not fit easily within an encyclopedia which seeks to provide authoritative reviews of current knowledge. The Editor's policy has been to restrict reviews to established knowledge and theorizing about established knowledge. More speculative thinking has therefore been excluded, left to books where single authors have the scope to expand their arguments about current trends and future possibilities, and to project their imaginations forward into alternative scenarios.

Otherwise the *Encyclopedia* aims to cover the major content interests of all those people who call themselves educational technologists and to make it easy for them to find what they want. It has avoided adopting a single view of educational technology in order to gain greater coherence: that would be highly desirable in a textbook but inappropriate for an encyclopedia. Thus, access by educational technologists across the field, with different needs and specialisms and different national backgrounds, has been the prime consideration in deciding both the structure of the *Encyclopedia* and the titles of individual articles.

The conceptual framework for the *Encyclopedia* is represented in Fig. 1. This shows the five main parts and their interrelationships. Part 1 is set apart from the other four because it is about the development and organization of Educational Technology as a Knowledge Field and Occupation. Thus, it sets the historical and organizational context for the more detailed articles in the other four parts. New articles have been added on specifically Asian and European perspectives to balance the number of British and American authors. Part 2 covers Technical Developments in information technology and the media which affect both Media Potential, Utilization, and Impact (Part 3), and the Distribution and Organization of Knowledge and Resources (Part 5). These parts are also interrelated with Instructional Development (Part 4), which many consider to be the heart of educational technology. Making resources available for teaching and learning requires knowledge from all three parts: instructional development know-how (Part 4), using knowledge of media potential and impact (Part 3) to create resources for organization, and distribution (Part 5) to the user. The last three parts are also rather larger than the first two, and therefore have been subdivided into four or five sections.

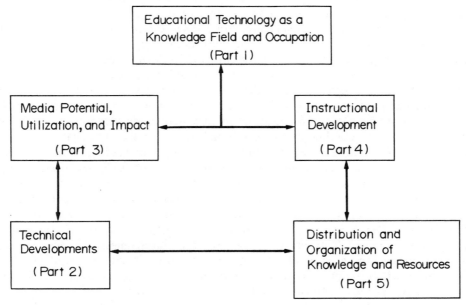

Figure 1
Schematic representation of the *Encyclopedia*

3. The Content of the Five Parts

Part 1 sets the scene for the *Encyclopedia* as a whole by providing answers to the following central questions:

(a) How did the term *educational technology* arise?

(b) For whom does it provide an occupational identity?

(c) How are educational technologists trained, and for what kinds of job?

(d) For what kinds of organizational settings are educational technologists employed?

(e) What do educational technologists do?

(f) To what degree can educational technology be described as a distinctive field of knowledge?

The answers to some of these questions are not clear-cut, because there are strong national traditions which affect occupational labels and how people classify and categorize knowledge. In a field like educational technology these labels are not static but changing. Thus, one could find two people performing what looks like the same job, one of whom claimed to be an educational technologist while the other did not. The difference might be attributable to their nationality, their age, their training, or even the employing organization, and it would probably affect how they perceived their job and their relationship with colleagues. This poses particular problems for anyone trying to take an international perspective.

The Editor has contributed an opening article on *Conceptual Frameworks and Historical Development*, which examines the origins and development of the term *educational technology* and some of the key ideas that have been associated with it. Questions concerning educational technology as an occupation and field of study are addressed next in articles on *Field of Study, Personnel, Training,* and *Professional Associations*. Educational technology units are reviewed under *National and International Centers, Local Centers, Higher Education Support Services,* and *Higher Education Consultancy,* and these are followed by an article on *Media Program Administration*. These units are largely concerned with educational technology in general rather than one specific aspect of it, with coordinating different areas of expertise, and with instructional development. More specialized units or subunits, for example those concentrating on such matters as computer-based learning, television production, graphic production, broadcasting, or the organization of learning resources are covered in later sections under the appropriate headings. Finally, two articles review educational technology from *Continental European Perspectives,* and *Asian Perspectives*. These indicate some different ways of looking at the field, and show how the Anglo-American initiatives and literature have influenced, but not determined, the way in which educational technology is perceived and organized in these other parts of the world.

The Technical Developments part opens with an important article on the *Economics of Educational Technology*. This examines the costs and effectiveness of large-scale educational technology programmes whose aim is to improve educational productivity. The review covers within-school programmes and out-of-school programmes on five continents, and includes some of the most ambitious attempts so far to harness the potential of educational technology to nontraditional patterns of delivery, that is, not only through recognized teachers working in schools. Whether its conclusions will be significantly affected by changes in the technology itself must remain a matter for conjecture for some time yet.

The rest of Part 2 provides authoritative reviews of current developments. *Computer Technology and Telecommunications* and *Videodisc Technology* provide introductions for the nonexpert to the fundamental technology, while new or revised articles on *Information Storage and Retrieval, Videotex and Electronic Mail,* and *Interactive Video* cover three areas of particularly rapid change. Developments in more familiar technologies are covered by articles on the *Distribution and Reception of Television Programs, Audio Production and Distribution,* and *Audiovisual Equipment* which are supplemented by short specialist articles on *Microforms* and *Time-compressed and Time-extended Speech.* Another important area to be discussed is the design of *Learning Environments* for optimum use of new technology. Finally, there is a specialist article on *Information Technology for Disabled Students,* which indicates how far new technology has transformed learning possibilities for that particular group.

While Part 2 deliberately concentrates on the hardware aspects of new technology, Part 3, Media Potential, Utilization, and Impact, is about the design and use of software and the potential-for-learning of different forms of media and learning resources. This is the largest part of the *Encyclopedia* and has been divided into four separate sections.

The Computers section contains five articles describing the different ways in which computers have been used to support teaching—*Computer-assisted Learning, Computer-managed Learning, Computer-managed Testing, Computer-assisted Counseling,* and *Computers in the Curriculum*—and two articles reviewing the degree and kind of penetration achieved by microcomputers into schools and adult education. Three of the seven articles in this section are new.

Film, Television, and Video opens with an article on the changing *Role of Film, Television, and Video.* Then two entries on the *Use of Television in the Classroom* and the *Use of Film in the Classroom* are complemented by one on *Video Production as a Learning Activity.* Four specialist articles on microteaching are followed by a review of *Video Recording in Educational Research.* There is no attempt to provide anything resembling a production manual for aspiring producers, for that would be well beyond the scope of an *Encyclopedia,* and a separate but related section on Broadcasting can be found in Part 5.

The next section, on Simple Media, is included for a number of reasons. First, it is mainly concerned with resources which teachers can produce and find for themselves, though some of the more complex examples will continue to be produced commercially. Second, their use does not depend on complicated or expensive equipment. Third, their potential for enhancing learning is considerable, and there is a danger that they will be forgotten as attention is focused on newer and more glamorous technologies. This makes it of particular relevance to those engaged in teacher training and/or units for producing and distributing learning resources. The coverage is split between articles on production and articles on utilization, and some include both. Three articles on *Graphic Production, Photographic Production,* and *Reprography* are followed by three on presentation—*Overhead Transparency Projection, Bulletin Board Displays,* and *Boardwork.* Flexible use of simple resources is emphasized in entries on *Printed Materials in the Classroom* and *Sound Resources in the Classroom,* and slightly more complex equipment is discussed under *Language Laboratories.* A general article on *Media Utilization* reviews evidence on the classroom use of both simple and complex media. The final article on *Simulation and Gaming* sits a little uncomfortably in this section, but it is a thorough review of an important and growing area of education that is directly accessible to teachers without any need for special technological support.

The fourth and final section of Part 3 is devoted to Distance Education. This is a relatively small section as many of its concerns are dealt with elsewhere under Technical Developments (Part 2), Instructional Development (Part 4) and Broadcasting [Part 5(b)]. The articles here include *Children's Television* and *Mass Media in Adult Education*, neither of which is mediated through formal educational institutions. A general article on *Distance Learning Systems* and specialized articles on *Self-directed Learning in Distance Education* and *Telephones in Education* conclude the section.

Part 4 on Instructional Development is comprised of five small but interrelated sections. General Approaches to Design and Development indicates the range of contexts in which designers work, the different models that guide or describe the design process, and differing conceptions of what design is essentially about. The Editor's introduction to these issues is followed by two reviews: the first covering those conceptions of design that influence the field of curriculum, and the second examining the range of systems approaches advocated by instructional technologists. This leads naturally to Needs and Objectives, beginning with processes for assessing needs and selecting objectives for adult education and for schools. Then a long article on *Specifying and Using Objectives* reviews the literature, discusses practical concerns, and clarifies some of the major issues of public debate. Finally, the research on *Taxonomies of Objectives* is surveyed and their purpose and use are explained.

The section on Instructional Design is concerned less with procedures than with assembling available knowledge for the benefit of the designer. Thus, it summarizes important areas of research and introduces different ways of thinking about the learning process which a designer has to consider. Three articles on the analysis of instruction show a move from the simple behavioural models of the 1960s to a much more complicated cognitive approach, while similar trends towards more complex interpretations of the design problem can also be found in the four articles concerned with media research.

The section on Individualized Learning Systems opens with two general articles introducing the wide range of approaches found in higher education and in schools. Many of these are then given more detailed treatment in the four subsequent articles. At one end of the spectrum is the *Mastery Learning Model* whose applications include *Programmed Learning* and the *Keller Plan*, while at the other end is *Self-planned Learning*.

The final section, Evaluation, is necessarily selective because evaluation has become a burgeoning field in its own right, and occupies a companion volume to this *Encyclopedia*. The four articles were chosen for their particular relevance to instruction developers. Thus, a short introductory article on *Formative and Summative Evaluation* is followed by three specialist reviews on *Program Evaluation, Evaluation of Learning Resources*, and *Criterion-referenced Measurement*.

Part 5, Distribution and Organization of Knowledge and Resources, is comprised of four sections. Three represent organizations and traditions that have not been linked together as closely as they should: (a) the curriculum development/textbook publishing tradition which has typically distributed resources directly to schools, (b) the educational broadcasting tradition which represents another mode of mass distribution of packaged knowledge, and (c) the library tradition which has emphasized individual-user access to knowledge and diversity rather than uniformity. The fourth and last section looks more generally at knowledge organization and knowledge use in our society.

Curriculum Packages and Textbooks ranges wider than its title implies. The analysis of *Curriculum Development* in a number of countries examines how knowledge is officially selected, recommended, or approved for dissemination in schools and colleges, while the review of *Curriculum Implementation* highlights the significance of the mediation process and the gap between rhetoric and reality. The *Role of Textbooks* and *Curriculum Packages* are examined, and the consequences for transnational influences on the curriculum are discussed.

Educational Broadcasting is covered by seven regional articles. These reflect not only regional preoccupations but some of the special concerns of their authors. Thus, issues raised in one region may be equally significant for others where the authors have given them less attention. Taken as a whole, they constitute a thorough and authoritative review of educational broadcasting worldwide. They are supplemented by an eighth, newly commissioned article which examines *Transnational Influences in Broadcasting*.

Libraries and Resource Centers is also a substantial section. Five articles look at functions, roles, and policies of different types of library—school, public, college and university, film, and special, while a sixth examines the role of *Libraries in Adult Education*. Three further articles look at the *Processing of Library Materials*, the *Storage and Handling of Learning Resources* other than books, and *Learning Centers*.

Finally, there are six articles concerned with Knowledge Organization and Knowledge Use. The first three cover *Knowledge Industries and Knowledge Occupations*, the expanding area of research on *Knowledge Utilization*, and the more familiar topic of *Knowledge Diffusion in Education*. These provide important perspectives on the work of educational technologists that are only rarely given the attention they deserve. A short article on the *Educational Resources Information Center* (ERIC) is followed by a review of *Copyright* which highlights issues raised by educational technology and discusses recent changes in national laws. The section concludes with a new article on *Electronic Publishing*, a rapidly developing area that promises to challenge many of our current assumptions about the distribution and organization of knowledge and resources.

4. How to Use the Encyclopedia

The Encyclopedia is designed to serve two main purposes: reference book and textbook. A user with a specific topic or question already in mind will find it useful to proceed either via the list of Contents at the beginning of the book or the Subject Index at the end. More general questions are best pursued through the Contents, more specific questions through the Subject Index. On the other hand, a user wanting a more general review of a large segment of the field would do better by starting with the introductions to each part. These give useful overviews and sufficient guidance on the contents of individual entries to assist the reader in deciding where to go next.

Further assistance is provided by a list of references at the end of each article which the reader will find useful in locating further reading. In addition to the Subject Index at the back of the book, there is an Author Index covering all authors cited, and a full list of contributors and their affiliations.

5. Acknowledgements

Robert Maxwell conceived the idea for the parent encyclopedia, while Torsten Husén and Neville Postlethwaite took on the enormous task of finding Section Editors and guiding it through its development. Together with Barbara Barrett, the Editorial Director at Pergamon Press, they were largely responsible for initiating and overseeing that remarkable work. Many entries in this *Encyclopedia* were originally commissioned and edited by other Section Editors, to whom I am especially grateful. They also assisted me with my own section, as did Donald Ely and colleagues at the University of Illinois and the University of Indiana. To all of them I am profoundly grateful, and also to Joan Burks and Debra Rosen who were responsible for the more detailed work at Pergamon Press.

I also received help from the "invisible college" of friends and colleagues across the world who were always reacting with suggestions, encouragement and advice; and support from the University of Sussex, particularly from my secretary Margaret Ralph, who transformed so many edited manuscripts into new copy on top of her normal duties.

Finally, I should like to thank the Authors, without whose expertise, enthusiasm, commitment, and forbearance this *Encyclopedia* would never have been produced.

June 1989

MICHAEL ERAUT
Brighton, UK

Part 1

Educational Technology as a Knowledge Field and Occupation

Part 1

Educational Technology as a Knowledge Field and Occupation

Introduction

The first Part of the *Encyclopedia* is probably the most controversial because it concerns people's knowledge base and occupational identity. These vary between nations more than many people realize, and there are cultural as well as economic factors involved. The approach adopted has been to take the United States as the main starting point, because it is there that the knowledge base and occupation of educational technology have been most clearly delineated. Other national perspectives are then related to that framework, both within articles and through separate articles by British, Dutch, and Japanese authors. Care has been taken, however, to present the diversity of viewpoint that exists and not to regard the mainstream tradition of educational technology in the United States as standard or orthodox.

1. Educational Technology as a Knowledge Field

Outsiders usually expect a knowledge field to have a core of generally accepted theories and approaches, even though there may be greater diversity of perspective at the frontiers and in areas of detailed application. However, in the area of applied social sciences, where education surely belongs, acceptance of a theory or approach is more likely to indicate acknowledgement of its importance rather than its truth. What is more generally agreed is a map of the field in which competing theories and approaches occupy salient positions and command the support of recognized experts. Fields of study are divided not only into specialisms but also into factions. Moreover, the differences between such factions are more likely to be based on philosophy, ideology, and methodology than on evidence alone. The argument is about what is important, what is appropriate, and how the evidence is to be interpreted and judged. Disagreements about criteria tend to rule out the resolution of disputes between factions by purely empirical arguments. Within a given approach, however, the expansion of the knowledge base relies on empirical evidence, and in the long term empirical evidence, as well as ideology, plays an important part in sustaining the reputation of an approach.

Some educational technologists will argue that this portrait of educational research is true but unsatisfactory. The role of educational technology is to develop the application of the behavioural sciences to education. These are perceived as more like the natural sciences, less faction-ridden, less ideological, and built on a solid and growing platform of empirical research. There is a strong body of opinion within the social sciences which supports this view and another which opposes it. These are often referred to as the positivist and interpretative paradigms.

The positivist paradigm has played an important part in the field of educational technology. It is strongly research-based and incorporates two major research traditions. The experimental tradition is rooted in behavioural psychology and is associated with small-scale experiments under controlled conditions. The correlational tradition forms the basis of much educational research and is associated with large field samples and the use of statistical techniques to ascertain the relative significance of various personal and situational factors. In both traditions the purpose of theory is to explain, generalize, and predict. Hence, the positivist paradigm is associated with strong knowledge claims.

The interpretative paradigm starts from a different view of theory. Theories are not part of some natural truth waiting to be discovered, they are invented by people in order to interpret and make sense of their world. Empirical evidence affects whether people find a theory adequate for this purpose, but so also do other considerations. The purpose of a theory is not to provide a causal explanation of a situation or sequence of events but rather to add to the understanding of it. Moreover, it is expected that the individuals' understanding of any given social situation will differ according to their role, interest, and knowledge; so it is important for a person's own understanding to know how other people perceive the situation. Hence, there is a strong emphasis on qualitative methods and case study research, though not to the exclusion of quantitative data. Knowledge claims in this paradigm tend to be rather weaker than those in the positivist paradigm because they are believed to be more situationally and culturally specific.

Within the field of educational technology, both paradigms can be found in abundance, however, their distribution is not even. Positivist approaches are stronger in instructional design, and interpretative approaches in utilization. Positivist approaches are more readily found where there is political power and in large-scale developments, whereas interpretative approaches are found where there is little power and the enterprise is small-scale and local. Positivist approaches are stronger in North America, interpretative approaches are stronger in Europe. Positivists believe in expertise, interpretativists in wisdom.

Of immediate relevance is the format in which knowledge about educational technology is to be displayed. The positivist approach is well-suited to a textbook, a handbook, or a research paper, where knowledge is expected to be presented with considerable coherence and authority. Interpretative literature can then be properly excluded or marginalized as lacking validity or introducing too great a degree of complexity. The interpretative approach, on the other hand, is well-suited to a multiauthored book, presenting a range of perspectives on a particular theme or to a single lengthy case study. The editor of an encyclopedia has to adopt an interpretative stance towards its domain, because a positivist approach would exclude large areas of knowledge from what at least some people regard as "the field". An interpretative approach includes positivist literature, because it presents potentially useful evidence and ideas even when one does not agree with all its premises and conclusions. This more eclectic stance is particularly important in an international encyclopedia where the greater variation in cultural background and situational circumstance puts the positivist concept of generalizability under considerable credibility stress (Stewart 1985).

2. Educational Technology as an Occupation

An international perspective becomes even more important when educational technology is considered as an occupation. While many countries have learned societies with an annual conference and one or two journals, only in the United States can there be said to be an association with an agreed definition statement, standards, and a high proportion of formally trained members. But even in the United States there are groups of working educational technologists with allegiances to associations other than the Association for Educational Communications and Technology. Moreover, while formal training in educational technology is well-distributed in English-speaking nations, it is relatively scarce elsewhere. This is not due to wealth or time-lag; it is simply that educational technology is not perceived as a distinctive occupation in Japan or most of Europe. This does not prevent those nations from acknowledging, or indeed contributing, knowledge of the kind found in this *Encyclopedia*. It merely prevents them doing so with the same conceptual and occupational assumptions. Thus, considerable caution is needed when treating educational technology as if it is a universally recognized knowledge field and occupation. Even in English-speaking countries the boundaries are extremely permeable and it would be unwise to alienate those many contributors to the field who do not choose to call themselves "educational technologists" by even hinting that this may make them "second class citizens".

3. Further Issues Concerning Educational Technology as a Knowledge Field and Occupation

The above discussion provides some background to Part 1, and explains some of the decisions taken by the Editor. For example, the Editor has deliberately chosen not to develop a series of definitions to provide guidelines for the whole *Encyclopedia*. His attitude throughout has been to explain how people *do* use terms, not to dictate how they *should* use terms. To have done otherwise would have resulted in conflict with many authors. Moreover, an interpretative stance was essential were the Editor not to imply some kind of transatlantic hegemony over the field. On the other hand, precisely because it is only in certain countries that educational technology is regarded as a distinct field, the topics in this Part are attractive only to scholars within, or in close contact with, English-speaking countries.

Part 1 is mainly comprised of ten articles from British and American authors. Though they give numerous references to work in other countries, their own national frameworks still affect how these are interpreted. This transatlantic dominance is somewhat redressed by two contrasting articles in which distinguished European and Asian scholars compare and contrast these first ten articles with the situations pertaining in continental Europe and Asia.

Molenda's (1986) review of the educational technology section of the parent encyclopedia drew attention to subtle differences between the British and American perspectives. In particular he criticized British authors' acceptance of existing institutional relationships between teachers and technology, which he contrasted to American authors who, following Heinich (1984), tend to regard such relationships as the major obstacle to realizing the potential of new technology. This accompanies greater optimism about what educational technology could do for education, if only the educators and their political masters were prepared to reconsider their structures and assumptions. These issues are of wider significance than simple binational comparison, and require examination in greater depth.

Heinich was correct to emphasize the need to reconsider the institutional structures of education. This has been a major concern of some educational planners during the 1970s and 1980s. Hitherto, large-scale structural innovations have been mostly outside the compulsory years of schooling or in areas of developing countries where traditional structures of schooling were not yet fully established. These are reported elsewhere in this volume. What has been omitted is that section of the educational technology literature which is primarily speculative and futuristic. The best of this literature is imaginative and stimulating, the mediocre is merely embarrassing; but it is not well suited to an encyclopedia seeking to provide reliable reviews of current knowledge.

Another reason for excluding the more speculative literature is that it repeatedly makes claims for educational technology which are regarded by the Editor as extravagant. While endeavouring to include a wide range of opinion and thus avoid implying a single orthodoxy, the Editor must nevertheless protect less informed readers from articles claiming that the established knowledge base for educational technology is much greater than can be properly substantiated. There is also a tendency for this literature to ignore aspects of radical change that are likely to be of crucial importance—the learning group and the social context in which it is situated, the perceived benefits of different kinds of knowledge, the relationship between generations, and the role of learning in particular cultural settings. Without collaborating with other social scientists who could contribute to these valuable contextual perspectives, the speculations of educational technologists are likely to be seen as somewhat naive.

4. Overview of Part 1

The opening article, *Conceptual Frameworks and Historical Development*, has been contributed by the Editor. It traces the historical and intellectual roots of the term *educational technology*, and its evolution since the 1950s. The viewpoint is that of an independent insider presenting the range of "conceptual frameworks used or advocated by people describing themselves as educational technologists". Early developments are attributed to the intersection of two main strands of work: audiovisual education as reflected in the work of Finn, Hoban, and later Heinich and Ely; and programmed instruction as promulgated by Skinner, Lumsdaine, and Glaser. The dominant metaphors were *applied learning theory* and *product development*. Then the onset of more generic terms like *learning resources*, *individualized learning*, and especially the *systems approach* introduced a period of consolidation when people from a wide range of backgrounds were able to work together for a common purpose. One allied field of research which did not influence educational technology at a conceptual level as much as may have been desirable was mass communications. But an interactionist concept of educational technology, deriving from the work of Moore, Flechsig, and Papert, is increasingly seen as offering a challenge for the future. The article thus presents an intellectual history of educational technology in which the origins of the various conceptual frameworks that have characterized the field are traced. The frameworks themselves are examined for their underlying assumptions and their implications for research, development, and implementation.

This article is complemented by Ely's analysis of educational technology as a *Field of Study* which includes a useful analysis of contributory disciplines. There then follow two interrelated articles, also by Ely, on *Personnel*, and *Training*. His analysis of personnel is based on the typology introduced by the Association for Educational Communications and Technology (AECT) in the United States to which he himself contributed. The typology comprises three dimensions: nine task groups or functions, three levels of responsibility, and four employment contexts, the latter being: instructional programme development, media product development, media management, and training of educational technologists. The training article focuses on the highest level of responsibility, that of the generalist or specialist with qualifications in educational technology. This includes an international survey of training programmes and some indication of their content. Some major training issues are then discussed: the definition of the field, recruitment of personnel, the question of core competences, the balance between theory and practice, and issues relating to certification of personnel and accreditation of programmes.

Hitchens, a former Secretary of AECT, examines the origin and role of *Professional Associations* in general and their development in the particular field of educational technology. Some ten attributes of a profession are described, then used to measure the progress of AECT in professionalizing educational technology. The most notable achievements are the journals and meetings for communication amongst members, standards, training, a code of ethics, leadership, and links with other professions.

The other major source of leadership in educational technology comes from the *National and International Centers*. Hug's article divides these into college and university units; government centres, units, and agencies; professional associations and nongovernmental organizations; units located within business and industry; corporations selling educational technology services; and international centres. Several of these centres will be discussed further in Part 5, which focuses on the distribution and organization of knowledge and resources. Hug is one of the few authors to mention the industrial sector which now accounts for more than half the annual output of higher degree programmes in educational technology in the United States (Molenda 1986). The scant attention given to the industrial sector in this volume stems from the clear focus on education of the parent encyclopedia. Thus, in spite of the considerable overlap between training technology and educational technology, no attempt has been made to cover specifically industrial applications.

Hug also writes on *Local Centers*, which he defines as below the level of national, regional, or state centres but above the level of the individual school—at least in the North American context. Similar functions may be performed at other levels in other countries, for whom most of the article is still highly relevant. Apart from management and administration, local centres are usually involved with information services and media production. Some also engage in instructional development. Besides the perennial question of funding, many of their difficulties concern communication with school administrations. Thus, major problems arise from lack of common terminology, uncertainty about roles, and always being perceived as an add-on function to a school system whose basic stucture remains unquestioned. Issues for the future are likely to relate to cooperation and networking between centres and the impact upon them of high technology. Local educational technology centres are rarely researched, and probably more vulnerable as a result.

Most of the services performed by local centres for groups of schools are also needed in higher education, where they are normally the responsibility of an educational technology unit. These are discussed by Moss under the heading *Higher Education Support Services*. Their clients are departments, individual teaching staff, the central administration, and even, in some cases, students. Moss distinguishes two main functions of such units. One is to provide hardware and software services, and to produce learning materials under commission. The other is to offer consultancy, training, and advice on general issues arising from the teaching–learning process. In both functions the right balance between proactive and reactive approaches can be difficult to achieve, but it is crucial for the organization, staffing, and operation of units.

Hewton's article *Higher Education Consultancy* points out that educational technology units are but one type of provider. His survey of organizational arrangements encompasses both different types of consultancy units and the varied backgrounds of the consultants themselves. He gives an analysis of consultancy models and their relationship to instructional development, organizational development, and faculty development. Issue-based consultancy is suggested as an approach that is particularly well-suited to the higher education context, where consultants often have to negotiate their roles with considerable care. The impact and style of consultancy are highly dependent on the organizational context, where the question of who the principal clients are has political as well as ethical significance. The article therefore has implications for educational technologists outside the higher education sector for whom relationships with a range of clients are also a constant cause for concern.

This group of articles on educational technology organizations concludes with a further contribution from Hug on *Media Program Administration*. The article is included in this part because it is largely concerned with the role of educational technologists. Hug discusses leadership and administration in terms of establishing programme purposes, written policies and procedures, and in-service programmes. The evaluation of media programmes is followed by a discussion of future trends that is largely focused on mergers between different types of service.

Plomp and Pals begin their article on *Continental European Perspectives* by explaining that the concept of educational technology as a distinctive profession and field of study which predominates in North America and the United Kingdom, does not exist in continental Europe. However, similar tasks and concepts can still be found under other labels. Plomp and Pals list three conceptions of educational technology from the US/UK literature: ET1 based on products, ET2 based on processes, and ET3 based on problem-solving or systems. An elegant diagram shows how and where each of these three approaches can be found in Europe and a survey of leading European institutions is classified in a similar manner. Ely's typology of personnel can be usefully applied in Europe, but is rarely supported by any organized system of training. Leadership comes mainly from the national or state institutes.

Sakamoto's review of *Asian Perspectives* gives special attention to Japan, Korea, India, China, Singapore, Malaysia, and the Philippines. India, Korea, and the South East Asian countries recognize educational technology as a distinct field of study, with a strong emphasis on audiovisual education. Japan, however, more closely resembles continental Europe in not regarding educational technology as a separate field and in emphasizing on-the-job training rather than off-the-job training. All the areas covered in North America are also found in Japan, many in considerable depth. Their network of local centres, for example, is particularly strong. Other Asian countries rely mainly on national and regional centres, though in China the most notable feature is their strong and still expanding commitment to distance education.

5. Further Treatment of these Issues

Many of the themes discussed in this opening section will be picked up again later. In particular these deal with more specialist areas of expertise in much greater detail. Readers are therefore urged to make liberal use of the Contents pages and indexes in order to get the maximum benefit from the *Encyclopedia*.

Bibliography

Heinich R 1984 The proper study of instructional technology. *Educ. Commun. Technol. J.* 32: 67–88
Molenda M 1986 Book review of the *International Encyclopedia of Education. Int. Rev. Educ.* 32: 355–63
Stewart A 1985 Appropriate educational technology: Does "appropriateness" have implications for the theoretical framework of educational technology? *Educ. Commun. Technol. J.* 33: 58–65

Conceptual Frameworks and Historical Development

M. R. Eraut

Educational technology came into existence as an occupational category during the course of the 1960s. Prior to that time people were engaged in jobs and activities which are now regarded as pertaining to educational technology, without being labelled as educational technologists, and to some extent this situation still persists in the 1980s. The occupational history is so short that an account of how various occupations and patterns of thinking were brought together to create the field of educational technology is essential for understanding the contemporary situation. Indeed the conceptual frameworks which evolved during the 1960s still provide the basis of what is taught as educational technology today, even though they have undergone considerable modification.

In order to establish a boundary for discussion, this article will confine itself to conceptual frameworks used or advocated by people describing themselves as educational technologists. Most of these frameworks are often treated as occupationally specific, although this is rarely the case. Many have been imported and adapted, and some are still shared with other occupations. There is also a more philosophical line of thinking which examines the idea of educational technology in the context of knowledge claims in general, the impact of the social and natural sciences, and the nature and historical significance of technology. This proceeds with only token attention to the occupational niches taken up by people calling themselves "educational technologists". However, this apparently disinterested pursuit of philosophical argument may also serve important political purposes. Educational technologists can be viewed as an interest group whose conceptual frameworks are intended not only to guide and describe practice but also to gain political or academic credibility. Thus, claims about the effectiveness and utility of educational technology serve an important political purpose in attracting resources and sponsorship, and claims about the theoretical foundations of educational technology play an important part in justifying its academic status, for which criteria related to disciplined and research-based study usually count for more than those related to utility.

1. Early Developments

Entrants to educational technology during the 1960s usually came by one of two routes—audiovisual education or programmed learning. Each was associated with a number of possible conceptual frameworks, which practitioners adopted according to the nature of their job, their training, and their personal preference. However, whilst programmed learning could be viewed as theory driven in its initial stages, audiovisual education

found it difficult to formulate any theoretical basis for its practice. In contrast, audiovisual educators could easily link their expertise to the accumulated professional experience of classroom teachers while programmed learning specialists tended to criticize teachers with a detachment that did little to promote mutual understanding.

Most audiovisual specialists saw themselves solely as practitioners: advisers to teachers, trainers of teachers, and providers of learning resources for use by teachers. In so far as they had a theoretical base it consisted of two assumptions: (a) that stimulus richness and variety would enhance attention and motivation, and (b) that degree of abstraction was a critical variable in learning. Dale's Cone of Experience, with "direct purposeful experience" at the base and "verbal symbols" at the apex, was probably the most frequently cited conceptual model (see *Media Selection*). Although there were always provisos about appropriateness, quality, and effectiveness, it was generally believed that the more audiovisual materials used the better, and that students needed to spend a significant amount of time in contact with "the real world" or with lively mediated representations of it, for example motion pictures. Neither of these assumptions is theoretically tenable today, but they are not without merit as "rules of thumb".

Communication theorists have shown that there is a limit to the amount of information that can be received and processed at any one time, and that multiple-channel communication can be disadvantageous (Travers 1970). The average classroom, however, remains a long way from media saturation. The conclusion seems to be that, in using audiovisual materials to enhance richness and variety, basic principles of message design such as simplicity, clarity, and logical organization need to be carefully observed.

Similarly, the notion of "authentic reality" inherent in Dale's Cone of Experience has been undermined by perception theorists' demonstration that much of what is seen and heard is framed by preexisting cognitive/perceptual schemas. It is not just experience but its interpretation that is crucial. Nevertheless, the problem of abstraction is still recognized by developmental psychologists who stress the role of concrete–operational experience for young children and distinguish between concrete, iconic, and symbolic modes of representation (Bruner 1966). The audiovisual specialists' concern with "real experience" can also be reformulated in terms of the sociology of knowledge, with attention being focused on the tensions and barriers to learning which arise from the gap between school knowledge and knowledge that has currency in the students' lives outside school.

11

How then did the move towards educational technology begin? One of the key individuals was Dr James Finn who became president of the Division of Audiovisual Instruction, the United States media specialists' professional association, in 1960. His seminal paper "Technology and the Instructional Process" (Finn 1960) examined the possible relations of technology with education but set this in the context of a general discussion of the role of technology in society. His main argument was that many areas of society in the United States were being transformed by technology, and that it was inevitable that education would eventually undergo a similar transformation. Moreover, although technological change might be led by changes in instrumentation, it was never limited to that. The transformation would involve organizational and cultural changes so radical that it was impossible to predict them. At that time two major trends were discernible but they led in opposite directions: one was the trend towards mass instructional technology as exemplified by the new prominence of television; the other was a trend towards individualization of which programmed learning provided a new example. The concept of programming was central to both these trends.

Underneath Finn's mantle of social prophet was some hard political advice. Recent highly publicized experiments in instructional television had by-passed the audiovisual specialists, and this could happen again with teaching machines, "How many of us", he asked "will go overboard and sink with the old concepts that will be absorbed or outmoded and tossed to the sharks by the new technology?" The concept of audiovisual education may go "down the drain, or it may not, depending on whether or not it can be redefined acceptably". Referring to teaching machines, he then added:

> It is my position that the audio-visual field is in the easiest position to help integrate these mechanisms properly into the instructional process. They are not primarily audio-visual; they are primarily technological. The audio-visual field, I think must now suddenly grow up. The audio-visual specialists, are, of all educational personnel, the closest to technology now; we have, I think, to become specialists in *learning technology*—and that's how I would redefine audio-visual education. (pp. 393–94)

Significantly, the Department of Audiovisual Instruction (DAVI), published a major sourcebook *Teaching Machines and Programmed Learning*, edited by Lumsdaine and Glaser, that very same year. It was the second major book in the field and, apart from a shortened version of Finn's paper, was written entirely by psychologists. Finn explained the reasons for DAVI sponsorship in a foreword:

> the audiovisual professional, as a technologist of the teaching profession, must relate to fields like psychology exactly as the medical doctor relates to his basic sciences.

The editors' concluding remarks suggested that psychologists were now ready to play their part:

> It seems to us that the numerous contributors whose writings have produced this volume have reflected one dominant idea. This is the concept that the processes of teaching and learning can be made an explicit subject matter for scientific study, on the basis of which a technology of instruction can be developed. . . . As we learn more about learning, teaching can become more and more an explicit technology which can itself be definitively taught. (pp. 563–64)

> The basis for consistent improvement in educational methods is a systematic translation of the techniques and findings of the experimental science of human learning into the practical development of an instructional technology. To achieve the full benefits inherent in this concept, instructional materials and practices must be designed with careful attention to the attainment of explicitly stated, behaviorally defined educational goals. Programmed learning sequences must be developed through procedures that include systematic tryout and progressive revision based on analysis of student behavior. (p. 572)

This introduces two new concepts, which were to be of seminal importance. First, there is the concept of instructional technology as applied learning theory. Secondly, there is the idea of product development through the systematic testing and revision of learning materials. Though familiar in industry it appears that the idea of product development was rediscovered in education almost by accident:

> An unexpected advantage of machine instruction has proved to be the feedback to the programme. (Skinner 1968 p. 49)

Linking the two concepts gives the idea of scientific research leading to technological development which gradually evolved among psychologists between 1954 and 1964. Indeed, associations between science and technology, research and development, and psychology and education provided an attractive platform for expanding psychological research during the 1960s, without the precise nature of the linkages and dependencies needing to be agreed.

At least three different perspectives on this issue can be discerned in the psychological writings of the period.

(a) Technology is seen as the direct application of the findings of instructional scientific research. Laboratory-derived procedures need only minor modification to fit them for general use in education. The psychologists' expertise is paramount (Skinner 1958).

(b) Technological research and development is needed to combine findings from learning research with other forms of knowledge. Research and development centres are needed to accomplish the often major modifications that are required to put theory into practice (see *Knowledge Diffusion in Education*). These should be run by a partnership of psychologists and educators (Hilgard 1964, Glaser 1965).

(c) Science and technology proceed in parallel. Each is capable of contributing to the other, especially if mutual communication is improved. Education is not just the straightforward application of learning theory, and psychological research has generated no more than "islands of knowledge and understanding within the science of learning" (Melton 1959).

The third perspective uses the term technology descriptively, much as social anthropologists would use it, but the first two perspectives use the term prescriptively with an aspirational futurist connotation. Thus, Melton would describe current educational practice as technologically primitive, while Skinner and Hilgard describe it as nontechnological.

On the whole, these psychologists saw educational technology being developed within the educational sector, though very closely linked to training technology in the industrial and military sectors. However, Finn et al. (1962) saw it coming mainly from the outside:

> ... Education, as a sector of national life, has, for the most part, been cut off from technological advances enjoyed by industry, business, military establishments, etc. The American educational enterprise exists out of technological balance with great sectors of the society. As such, it can be viewed as a relatively primitive or under-developed culture existing between and among highly sophisticated technological cultures.

He was overtly sceptical about the psychologists' claims that a science of learning was almost developed (Finn 1968).

Many writers confuse these different meanings of the term educational technology or simply choose the one that best suits their argument. For easy reference, they have been depicted in Fig. 1.

The descriptive categories (a) and (b) have been expanded to include educators' common concerns with disseminating practices developed in one place and thought to be improvements on tradition. Box (d) includes both the psychological perspectives described above, the "strong" applied science of Skinner and Lumsdaine, and the weaker "technological research and development" perspectives of Hilgard. Box (c) could also have been subdivided between those who extrapolate from existing trends (the prophets) and those who have advocated redesigning the educational system from a new set of "first principles" (the utopians), but this is probably too fine a distinction for current purposes.

Lumsdaine (1964) made a widely quoted distinction between educational technology 1, the application of physical science and engineering technology to the design of instructional devices [corresponding with Box (a) in Fig. 1], and educational technology 2, the application of the behavioural sciences to create a technology of learning (corresponding with Box (d) in Fig. 1]. However, he somewhat marred the discussion with the implication that a technology was dependent upon rather than interdependent with its "underlying" sciences—an unfortunate misapprehension when technological developments such as paper, ink, and movable type are discussed which preceded scientific understanding of the phenomena by several centuries. More significant for the future, perhaps, was Lumsdaine's generic definition of a programme:

> An instructional program is a vehicle which generates an essentially reproducible sequence of instructional events and accepts responsibility for efficiently accomplishing a specified change from a given range of initial competences or behavioral tendencies to a specified terminal range of competences or behavioral tendencies. (p. 385)

This goes beyond the idea of a programme as a reproducible presentation to the idea of a programme as guaranteed learning, with the programmer accepting responsibility for student learning whenever the conditions meet the original specifications. This concept of a validated learning package neatly combined the scientists' need for reproducibility with the technologists'

	Imported into education and adapted	Developed within the educational sector
Description and dissemination of good current practice	(a) Use of existing devices, mainly developed outside education (Audiovisual education)	(b) Currently used teaching techniques and educational practices (Teacher as educational technologist)
Prescription for and prediction of future practice	(c) Wholesale use of post-industrial instruments, techniques, and organizational patterns (Educational futures)	(d) Results of massive investment in research and development (Technological research, applied science)

Figure 1
Conceptions of educational technology

practice of empirical development to meet specified criteria, and provided the cornerstone for several important future developments.

Finn also identified programming as a central concept, but for a different reason. In noting that programming was common to several new technological developments—both in mass communication and in individualized learning—he perceptively added:

> The heartland is programming. He who controls the programming heartland controls the educational system. (Finn 1960 p. 393)

Moreover, the economics of programme production demanded thinking about learning resources on a larger scale, for only then could the high production costs of television or the high development costs of programmed learning be justified. At the same time, however, people began to be aware that utilization of programmes might be an even greater problem than design (Miles 1964). The concept of "systems" became increasingly dominant during the mid-1960s and assumed a central role in the emergent field of educational technology.

2. The Systems Approach

The term "system" appeared fairly regularly in the early writings on educational technology referred to above, but did not immediately become widely adopted as a central conceptual framework. The Oxford English Dictionary gives it two main types of meaning:

> An organized or connected group of objects; a set or assemblage of things connected, associated, or interdependent, so as to form a complex unity; a whole composed of parts in orderly arrangement according to some scheme or plan.

> A set of principles, etc.; a scheme, method.

The physical, biological, and social sciences used it only in the first sense, but the influential new field of systems engineering began to use it in the second sense as well. The fields having the most immediate impact on the thinking of educational technologists were those of man–machine systems, management, and systems engineering.

The central concept of thinking about man–machine systems was that it made little sense to design machines without also thinking about their human operators or to design human jobs without considering whether some tasks were more appropriately delegated to machines than others. It was the system as a whole which needed to be optimized. These ideas were developed in military and industrial contexts where the use of machines was taken for granted, and resulted in the coordination of the previously separate fields of personnel selection, training, and equipment design. Its attractiveness to educational technologists was that it addressed one of their most pressing problems: the respective roles of classroom teacher and mediated instruction. This recurrent issue was raised in dramatic form by early experiments with closed-circuit television and programmed instruction. The consequence, as Heinich (1968) persuasively argued, was the need for media specialists to reconceptualize their role. Decisions about the use of machines and materials needed to be made at the curriculum planning stage rather than the classroom implementation stage, according to Paradigm 2 rather than Paradigm 1 in Fig. 2.

Hoban (1965) added a further strand to the reconceptualization process when he emphasized the need for a management of learning perspective:

> When we consider the part machines play in education, we are forced into a consideration of man/machine systems. When we consider man/machine systems, we are forced into a consideration of technology.... technology is *not* just machines and men. It is a complex, integrated organization of men and machines, of ideas, of procedures, and of management. (p. 242)

> The central problem of education is not learning but the management of learning. .... No matter which of the new educational media is introduced, the situation into which it is introduced is transformed by the introduction. Acceptance of management of learning as a central problem of organized and institutional education would, at least, permit the admis-

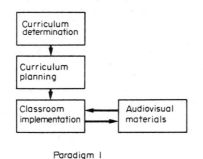

Paradigm 1

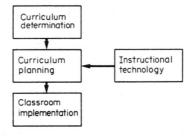

Paradigm 2

Figure 2
Two paradigms for educational technology

Source: Heinich R 1968

sion of a wider range of alternative procedures, techniques, and methods in teaching—without threatening or substantially altering the critical functions of education, teaching, or learning. (p. 244)

By this time systems thinking had become an important aspect of the field of management. The initial influence came not from engineering but from biology, where Bertalanffy (1950) first formulated his theory of open systems. The theory was taken up and further developed by organization theorists during the 1950s and early 1960s (Griffiths 1964), and their prime concern was not with designing new systems but with analysing and improving existing systems, not with man–machine systems but with social systems. In particular, the systems concept drew attention (a) to an organization's interaction with its environment, and (b) to the interplay between and coordination of its various subsystems. For educational technologists intimately concerned with the problem of change, this kind of understanding was crucial, and so was the growing body of research on innovation which followed it. This particular strand of systems thinking had relatively little influence for some considerable time, because it was overshadowed by the impact of the systems engineers.

Systems engineering (sometimes described as operations research) evolved during the Second World War as a field concerned with the design of large-scale technical systems. Its reputation was based on successes in the military and aerospace sectors but it also found increasing application in sections of industry. Ramo (1973) defined it as follows:

The systems approach is a technique for the application of a scientific approach to complex problems. It concentrates on the analysis and design of the *whole,* as distinct from the components or the parts. It insists upon looking at a problem *in its entirety,* taking into account all the facets and all the variables, and relating the social to the technological aspects. (p. 15)

Ramo illustrated his argument with a telling comparison between telephones and automobiles. The telephone system was designed as a system from the outset and provided a closely integrated network of people and equipment that handled a wide range of demands with considerable efficiency. The automobile system was never designed as an integrated system, its subsystems (e.g., roads, repair, manufacture, insurance, parking, etc.) were uncoordinated and it was extremely inefficient. Media specialists had no difficulty in identifying the "audiovisual system" with the latter, for it suffered from an equally frustrating lack of coordination between such aspects as hardware manufacture, building design, teacher training, and software production and distribution. The message was to "think big" and throughout the 1960s it was felt that systems engineers were waiting in the wings, itching to redesign the United States educational system from scratch.

Ramo's use of the term "technique" was significant because what began as an approach to the design of

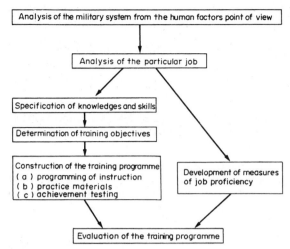

Figure 3
Steps in the development of training

Source: Crawford M P 1962 p. 314

systems rapidly evolved in the educational context (and indeed many other contexts) into a system of design, thus transforming the meaning of the word "system" from its first dictionary definition to its second, from a mode of conceptualizing an organization to a set of design principles (see *Systems Approaches to Instructional Development*). The first definition led to what Andrews and Goodson (1980) later described as integrated models of instructional design, while the second led to task-oriented models.

Integrated models derived also from general systems theory and continued to stress communication feedback, large-scale planning, and interaction between subsystems. They advocated a problem-solving approach with exploration of many alternatives and a design team with a diverse range of talents. Their most obvious disadvantage was that it was only rarely possible to mobilize the necessary finance, political support, and human talent. A series of experimental institutions and projects—Oakland Community College, Oklahoma Christian College, Project PLAN, Oakleaf School, the Open University, Televised Primary Education in the Ivory Coast, IMU Mathematics in Sweden, and many others—captured the imagination of educational technologists and nurtured their ambitions. Most of them, however, had no opportunity to work on this scale, and could only use systems analysis to choose innovation strategies for smaller scale efforts.

Task-oriented models attempted to list all the design tasks that had to be performed and tended to stress specific steps and linear progression through them with only occasional feedback. An early example from the United States Army is given in Fig. 3. The similarity with Tyler's model of curriculum development is immediately apparent, and it requires only slight modification to incorporate the models for designing programmed instruction which were also evolving in the early 1960s. Variations on this theme mushroomed throughout the 1960s and 1970s and models of this kind soon became a central part of the conceptual frameworks of educational technologists. They had three main advantages.

(a) Although insisting on detailed specification of objectives and preordinate evaluation, these models still allowed considerable flexibility of interpretation.

(b) The tightly coupled objectives–evaluation framework gave sufficient sense of a scientific approach to remain attractive both to psychologists and to politicians concerned with accountability.

(c) The product orientation and often implicit promise of a multimedia approach gained the allegiance of media specialists.

3. Consolidation

The period between 1967 and 1972 can be regarded as a period of consolidation. Educational technology became a recognized term and people began to accept it as an occupational definition which covered a range of jobs in all sectors of education. The early conceptual frameworks were tried, developed, and modified according to three main types of criteria. (a) Did they provide a credible rationale for a newly emerging field? (b) Did they define a distinguishable set of activities as being primarily the concern of educational technologists? (c) Did they create a boundary for the occupation that was politically defensible?

The first official endorsement of a field called educational technology may well have been the establishment in the United Kingdom of a National Council for Educational Technology in 1967. This followed the report of a committee on Audiovisual Aids in Higher Scientific Education, which only used the term "educational technology" in its concluding section. The United Kingdom Association for Programmed Learning promptly added "Educational Technology" to its title in 1968, while in the United States it was the Department of Audiovisual Instruction of the National Education Association which changed its name to Association for Educational Communications and Technology in 1970. This coincided with the publication of a major report by a Commission on Instructional Technology appointed by Congress, and anticipated the creation of a National Center for Educational Technology within the National Institute of Education in Washington, DC. UNESCO held a conference on Training Programmes for Educational Technologists in June 1970, and the International Bureau of Education published an important bibliography of educational technology later that year (Huberman 1970). Though the first periodical, *Educational Technology*, had been founded in the United States as

early as 1960, it was some time before the second journal, *Programmed Learning and Educational Technology*, added the term in 1967.

As official recognition grew, the problem of defining educational technology became even more acute and is still the subject of lengthy debate (Mitchell 1978). The definition produced by the National Council for Educational Technology (NCET) in the United Kingdom when it first met in 1967 was:

Educational technology is the development, application, and evaluation of systems, techniques, and aids to improve the process of human learning. (NCET 1969)

This shrewd compromise has stood the test of time because it allowed all the appropriate interest groups to identify with it without appearing too threatening to the others. The United States Commission on Instructional Technology showed a similar concern for reconciling the aspirations of educational technologists with the beliefs and expectations of educators and politicians:

Instructional technology can be defined in two ways. In its more familiar sense, it means the media born of the communications revolution which can be used for instructional purposes alongside the teacher, textbook, and blackboard. In general, the Commission's report follows this usage. In order to reflect present-day reality, the Commission has had to look at the pieces that make up instructional technology: television, films, overhead projectors, computers, and the other items of "hardware" and "software" (to use the convenient jargon that distinguishes machines from programs). In nearly every case, these media have entered education independently and still operate more in isolation than in combination.

The second and less familiar definition of instructional technology is more than the sum of its parts. It is a systematic way of designing, carrying out, and evaluating the total process of learning and teaching in terms of specific objectives, based on research in human learning and communication, and employing a combination of human and nonhuman resources to bring about more effective instruction. The widespread acceptance and application of this broad definition belongs to the future. Though only a limited number of institutions have attempted to design instruction using such a systematic, comprehensive approach, there is reason to believe that this approach holds the key to the contribution technology can make to the advancement of education. It became clear, in fact, as we pursued our study, that a major obstacle to instructional technology's fulfillment has been its application by bits and pieces. (Tickton 1970 pp. 21–22)

More useful perhaps for current purposes is the much longer definition statement produced by the Association for Educational Communications and Technology (AECT) in 1972, which included a rationale for the field of educational technology, a description of what people in the field do, and a discussion of its social and professional context (Ely 1972). The rationale section identified the uniqueness of the field with three major concepts and their synthesis into a total approach. These were "the use of a broad range of resources for learning, the emphasis on individualized and personalized learning, and the use of the systems approach". The development of each of these concepts during the consolidation period is discussed below.

The concept of resources for learning was a useful expansion of the earlier term, audiovisual materials, because it incorporated printed resources and could also be interpreted as including environmental resources (school trips and visits) and resource people (visitors). Although some resource production was integrated with curriculum development in the manner envisaged by Heinich's Paradigm 2 (see Fig. 2), most of it remained only loosely coordinated with the curriculum. Hence the teacher retained a major role in the selection of learning resources, and considerable attention was given to resource management, distribution, and utilization. Indeed the teacher was often referred to as a manager of learning resources (Taylor 1970), an idea suggesting that every teacher was an educational technologist (Fig. 1 Box b) and that teacher education, therefore, was the highest priority (Witt 1968). Resource production was assumed to be a shared responsibility. Some would be produced by commercial firms, some would be produced by locally based educational technologists, and some would be produced by the teachers themselves, preferably with technical and advisory support from educational technologists.

The associated term *resource centre* also came into common currency, combining a number of functions now considered essential for the teacher's role as a manager of resources. Thus a teachers' resource centre was a place where teachers could select from a collection of existing resources, make multiple copies of a resource, produce their own resources, or even commission others to produce resources for them. Similar facilities could also be envisaged for pupils for whom the term *learning centre* or *pupils' resource centre* was sometimes used.

The resources concept raises the issue of the respective roles of educational technologists and librarians, and in most countries there is now a long history of interprofessional discussion and mutual accommodation. It has become increasingly common for simple audivisial materials to be stored in libraries and for pupils to have access to them there, while production facilities are usually found in educational technology units. Arrangements for storing complex software such as film or videotape and for managing the audiovisual equipment used in classrooms are much more varied, with reprographic equipment often being lodged with the administration (see *School Libraries/Resource Centers*).

Attention to individualized learning was not a new concept, but the idea was given a considerable boost by the advent of programmed learning. Earlier initiatives such as the Dalton and Winnetka plans were revived and redeveloped under the influence of behavioural psychologists to incorporate tightly specified student assignments, programmed learning sequences, and criterion-referenced tests. Most of these systems individualized only the pace at which students could learn but some such as the IMU in Sweden or Project PLAN in the United States introduced assignments of different levels of difficulty, the latter backed by a computer-based record-keeping and advisory system. Later, terms such as mastery learning, modular instruction, audiotutorial systems, and personalized systems of instruction (PSI) came to be associated with this line of development, and these are discussed in Part 4(d) on Individualized Learning Systems. On the whole, mastery learning and PSI came to be associated with extremely specific objectives and repetition of units by students who failed to get high scores on criterion-referenced tests, while modular instruction and audiotutorial systems allowed a looser interpretation of the systems approach and put more emphasis on the use of nonprint media. Some systems incorporated short tutorials and even some group teaching into what remained basically individualized systems.

Another approach to individualization was the introduction of Dial Access Information Retrieval Systems (DAIRS), which allowed students to dial up audiotapes from remote learning carrels or even from their dormitories. This can be seen both as an extension of the library and as an extension of the language laboratory for private study. Some installations have incorporated a video facility, but most institutions found even audio facilities too expensive. Very little is heard of DAIRS today but the concept remains attractive and it awaits further technological development before its potential can be more fully realized.

Computers have proved to be more powerful and flexible devices than DAIRS for delivering individualized learning. During the period under discussion, 1967–72, computer-assisted learning (CAL) was also confined to a few experimental facilities, but the technology has developed much faster and the advent of microcomputers has greatly enhanced the chance that the average child in the average school will gain access to such a facility. Moreover, while DAIRS is only an improved delivery system for existing types of programme, CAL demands radical changes in programming techniques if its potential is to be properly exploited (see *Computer-assisted Learning*).

The third key concept in this first AECT definition statement was the systems approach, whose origins have already been discussed. By this time some of the more flagrantly overambitious claims on its behalf had been dispersed by the criticisms of, among others, Travers (1968) and Oettinger and Mark (1969), and its main area of application was instructional design. However, the boundary between instructional design and curriculum development was not at all clear, particularly in higher education where there was no established professional group of curriculum specialists and in those school systems where curriculum development was already associated with the production of learning

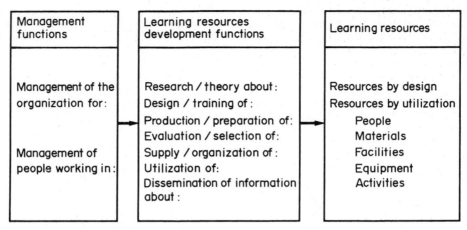

Management functions	Learning resources development functions	Learning resources

Management of the organization for:
 	
Management of people working in:
	Research / theory about :
	Design / training of :
	Production / preparation of:
	Evaluation / selection of:
	Supply / organization of :
	Utilization of:
	Dissemination of information about :
		Resources by design
		Resources by utilization
		  People
		  Materials
		  Facilities
		  Equipment
		  Activities

Figure 4
The domain of educational technology

Adapted from Ely 1972

materials, for example, in the United Kingdom. The situation was usually resolved by subject specialists retaining control and using whatever kind of consultancy assistance was available, or, in the case of large projects, by whoever was able to acquire the necessary support and finance.

Ely's description of what educational technologists do in practice was organized round the concept of learning resources (see Fig. 4). It is important to recognize that neither of the other two concepts, individualized learning and systems approach, could have served this purpose because significant numbers of practitioners would then have been excluded. However, the term "resources" is used in a very broad sense that includes both people (human resources) and settings (the resources of the organization and its environment). This usage is similar to that of economists and planners, but wider than the educators' meaning which generally refers only to materials and equipment. Thus, educational technologists could negotiate local meanings in their own work settings, according to what they felt was feasible and appropriate.

A slightly modified form of Fig. 4 (with the first two boxes headed educational management functions and educational development functions) provides the basis for AECT's (1977) current definition of educational technology.

4. Educational Technology and Mass Communications

The field of mass communications has grown up in parallel with that of educational technology with contributions from an equally wide range of perspectives. As with educational technology, three distinct types of knowledge are involved: social science knowledge (psychology, sociology, and linguistics); engineering knowledge; and production/design knowledge from practising broadcasters, journalists, advertisers, and publishers.

The main area of overlap with educational technology has been educational broadcasting and closed-circuit television, where work has usually been undertaken by mixed groups of educators and broadcasters. The broadcasters have usually been trained outside education and neither they nor the associated educators often describe themselves as educational technologists. This is not surprising when educational broadcasters are employed by broadcasting organizations whose main interest lies outside education, and whose criteria for success derive (a) from the aesthetic criticism of their peers, and (b) from their ability to attract and hold audiences (not to instruct captive audiences). Thus, it is only when instruction is seen as the main purpose of a broadcast that a television or radio producer is likely to identify with the field of educational technology. This occurs most often with closed-circuit television systems, with certain adult education programmes, and with large educational broadcasting systems that are specifically designed to make a major contribution to the delivery of instruction (as in the Ivory Coast). This more integrated perspective on mass communication and educational technology has been promoted in many Third World countries by international organizations such as UNESCO and the World Bank which have sponsored a large number of important initiatives.

Many of the concepts employed by producers of motion pictures, still pictures, sound, and graphics are common to those working inside and outside education (see *Graphic Production*; *The Role of Film, Television, and Video*; *Photographic Production*), and the same is true for engineers. However, the social scientists' contributions to mass communication have been less widely used in education. Although communication models were frequently cited by media specialists during the formative period of educational technology, they were discussed only in the most general terms. However, the development of research in related fields suggests that communication theory concepts could have more direct application today. Since communication theory models have as many variants as systems models, a composite model is presented in Fig. 5 to show the main features of this approach.

Traditional educational technology research focused primarily on the interaction between message characteristics and subsequent receiver action, and was thus dependent on the constructs available for describing them. Receiver characteristics were also considered, first in terms of prior learning alone, then later (but not too successfully) in terms of "learner attributes". Neither simple media distinctions nor the simple "types of learning" classifications of the behavioural psychologists have provided adequate descriptions of messages, and this is now recognized as a much more complex problem to which linguistics, visual communication semiotics, cognitive psychology, and the relevant content specializations also have to contribute. Similarly, the "decoding" of messages is now seen as dependent on the receiver's idiosyncratic cognitive structure and cognitive strategies, which are only beginning to be adequately portrayed by cognitive psychologists (and then only in certain limited content areas). Receiver actions have also to be understood as part of their ongoing interaction within their environment in which some messages and some actions are given greater priority than others. So receiver behaviour cannot be interpreted in terms of the communication system alone.

Even in culturally familiar settings the sender often lacks appreciation of the receiver's environment and encodes the message in some inappropriate way or misinterprets the feedback he or she receives, and this problem is magnified as the cultural gap between senders' and receivers' environments widens. The often unconscious influence of the senders' attitudes and beliefs is being increasingly researched, as also is the influence of the politics of the senders' environment on message selection. Then, finally, there is the question of control over the communication system as a whole. Whose interests does it serve and to what extent can any of the available channels be described as responsive or interactive? (see *Transnational Influences in Broadcasting*).

The enormous range of research that is now relevant to the work of educational technologists is likely to remain a major problem for a field with a strong commitment to improving professional practice (Hawkridge 1981), especially since the links between such theories and the practices of message or system design are so very complicated. Yet there is an equal danger that if such research is ignored, the impact of existing practice will become too strong and "educational technology will only confer a *rational cover* for already existing conventions" (Ahlström et al. 1975). The opposite danger, that of "scientism", is rapidly receding as the monolithic early influence of behavioural psychology diminishes, but it could arise again if some other branch of social science were to begin to exaggerate its knowledge claims.

5. The Interactionist Concept of Educational Technology

Flechsig (1975) defines a fourth, interactionist, concept of educational technology as a necessary addition to three which have already been discussed—the teacher's tool concept, the mass communication concept, and the systems concept:

> This fourth concept is characterised by the principle that learners take over the control over their learning processes, whereas the three other concepts—explicitly or implicitly—locate the control functions within the teacher or the teaching system. (p. 8)

Thus, unlike the systems concept, which he identifies with values such as "achievement" and "efficiency", the interactionist concept could be associated with "emancipatory education" and the "democratization of society".

Ten years earlier, Lewis and Pask (1965) had argued that "although learning can be approximated as goal-directed adaptation...a complete specification must entail the possibility of *creating*, as well as satisfying, goals" (p. 217). However, it was Moore's conception of an educational environment with which Flechsig most readily identified. Moore began by using the term "autotelic responsive environment" to describe his computer-controlled "talking typewriter". An autotelic activity is defined as something one engages in for its own sake and not for obtaining some external reward (an explicitly anti-Skinnerian concept) and a responsive environment is one which satisfies the following conditions:

(a) It permits the learner to explore freely.

(b) It informs the learner immediately about the consequences of his actions.

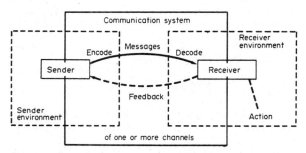

Figure 5
A composite communication model

(c) It is self-pacing, i.e., events happen within the environment at a rate determined by the learner.

(d) It permits the learner to make full use of his capacity for discovering relations of various kinds.

(e) Its structure is such that the learner is likely to make a series of interconnected discoveries about the physical, cultural, or social world. (Moore 1968 p. 419)

The much admired work of Seymour Papert (1980) clearly belongs in this same direction.

Later, Moore expanded his ideas still further when he added a "perspectives principle" to the autotelic principle and the productive principle [implied in condition (e) above] for the design of what he now called "clarifying environments". The perspectives principle, which he derived from the symbolic interactionist theory of Mead, stated that learners should have a chance to take at least four roles in each learning situation: agent, patient, significant other, and generalized other. For example they might create a goal (agent), achieve a goal defined for them by someone else (patient), advise another learner (significant other), or become part of an audience for another learner's presentation (generalized other). This principle can be considered as reinterpreting the principle of learner control for a democratically oriented social context. It suggests giving special attention to the social organization of groups of children engaged in group projects or working with computers, and it also assigns an important role to simulations and games.

The interactionist concept is also fundamental to new developments in information technology. It is now relatively easy to store knowledge and make it available to possible users, but difficult to make much of it accessible, in the sense of finding it, understanding it, and appreciating its significance. Thus, the physics section of a library is available for inspection by all who enter, but little of it will be accessible to someone without any scientific background. Then there is the additional question of how to find knowledge of whose existence one is not even aware. Hence the problem of how different users can interact with stored knowledge is a major concern of cognitive scientists, information scientists, and educational technologists alike. Travers (1973) argued along similar lines when he wrote:

Educational technology needs to become preoccupied with the development of rich and interesting environments in which children can make real decisions about what to explore. It needs to bring out the importance of significant intellectual relationships between people and the significance of intellectual interaction. It needs to encourage self-initiated exploration. (p. 990)

Returning to the political aspect of Flechsig's conception, Boguslaw (1973) has noted that the systems approach was originally developed for use with nonsocial systems where the goals were formulated by people outside the system itself. However, in any social system there are people within the system who may wish to participate in defining the system's objectives, or at least their own personal objectives, and their concerns cannot easily be ignored. The implications for educational technology are twofold. Concerning personal objectives, Azuma has argued as follows:

An important problem we have to recurrently rethink during this coming decade is the proper balance of the two approaches which we have seen in technological development over the two preceding decades. One is the effort to improve the effectiveness of mastering externally defined learning tasks, the other is an orientation towards providing a learning environment wherein learning is intrinsically motivated and self-directed. (Azuma 1977 p. 3)

Concerning wider participation in defining the system's objectives, there will be value issues which cannot be resolved by arguments concerned only with efficiency or effectiveness. Under these conditions, Boguslaw suggests:

It may be possible to define one task of the systems designer as essentially similar to the task of a labor arbitrator in industry—that of working out acceptable tradeoffs and compromises; of dealing with the realities and prospects of power; and defining objectives acceptable, if not completely satisfactory, to all parties involved. (Boguslaw 1973 pp. 182–83)

This broker role is inherently attractive to those with little power who wish to stimulate the process of educational change. However, compromises based on the realities of power will not always be compatible with one's personal values, and reluctant agreements are not always implemented. Educational technology necessarily involves social and political processes which cannot be understood in purely technical terms, and like other professionals, educational technologists need to clarify and attend to their own and other interested parties' values (Greene 1968, Hoban 1977, Travers 1973).

Bibliography

Ahlström K G, Lindblad S, Wallin E 1975 *Notes on Educational Technology.* Steering Group on Educational Technology, Council for Cultural Cooperation, Council of Europe, Strasbourg

Andrews D H, Goodson L A 1980 A comparative analysis of models of instructional design. *J. Instruct. Dev.* 3(4): 2–16

Association for Educational Communications and Technology (AECT) 1977 *Educational Technology; Definition and Glossary of Terms.* AECT, Washington, DC

Azuma H 1977 The third decade of educational technology. *Educ. Technol. Res.* 1: 1–4

Bertalanffy L von 1950 The theory of open systems in physics and biology. *Science* 111: 23–29

Boguslaw R 1973 Systems concepts in social systems. In: Miles R F (ed.) 1973 *Systems Concepts.* Wiley, New York, pp. 177–90

Bruner J R 1966 *Toward a Theory of Instruction.* Harvard University Press, Cambridge, Massachusetts

Crawford M P 1962 Concepts of training. In: Gagné R M 1962

Psychological Principles in System Development. Holt, Rinehart and Winston, New York, pp. 301–42

Ely D P (ed.) 1972 The field of educational technology: A statement of definition. Report of AECT Committee. *Audiovis. Instr.* 17(8): 36–43

Eraut M, Squires G (eds.) 1971 *An Annotated Select Bibliography of Educational Technology.* National Council for Educational Technology, London

Finn J D 1960 Technology and the instructional process. In: Lumsdaine A A, Glaser R (eds.) 1960 *Teaching Machines and Programmed Learning: A Source Book.* Department of Audiovisual Instruction, National Education Association, Washington, DC, pp. 382–94

Finn J D 1968 The emerging technology of education. In: Weisgerber R A (ed.) 1968 *Instructional Process and Media Innovation.* Rand McNally, Chicago, Illinois, pp. 289–327

Finn J D, Perrin D G, Campion L E 1962 *Studies in the Growth of Instructional Technology I: Audiovisual Instrumentation for Instruction in the Public Schools, 1930–1960: A Basis for Take-off.* Department of Audiovisual Instruction, National Education Association, Washington, DC

Flechsig K-H 1975 *Towards a Critical Appraisal of Educational Technology Theory and Practice.* Steering Group on Educational Technology, Council for Cultural Cooperation, Council of Europe, Strasbourg

Glaser R 1965 Toward a behavioral science base for instructional design. In: Glaser R (ed.) 1965 *Teaching Machines and Programmed Learning: A Source Book*, Vol. 2: *Data and Directions.* Department of Audiovisual Instruction, National Education Association, Washington, DC

Greene M 1968 Technology and the human person. In: Witt P W F (ed.) 1968 *Technology and the Curriculum.* Curriculum Conf., Columbia University, 1967. Teachers College Press, Columbia University, New York

Griffiths D E 1964 Administrative theory and change in organizations. In: Miles M B (ed.) 1964 *Innovation in Education.* Teachers College Press, Columbia University, New York

Hawkridge D 1981 The telesis of educational technology. *Br. J. Educ. Technol.* 12: 4–18

Heinich R 1968 The teacher in an instructional system. In: Knirk F G, Childs J W (eds.) 1968 *Instructional Technology: A Book of Readings.* Holt, Rinehart and Winston, New York

Hilgard E R 1964 A perspective on the relationship between learning theory and educational practices. In: Hilgard E R (ed.) 1964 *Theories of Learning and Instruction.* 63rd National Society for the Study of Education (NSSE) Yearbook Part 1. University of Chicago Press, Chicago, Illinois

Hoban C F 1965 From theory to policy decisions. *Audiovis. Commun. Rev.* 13(2): 121–39

Hoban C F 1977 Educational technology and human values. *Audiovis. Commun. Rev.* 25(3): 221–41

Huberman M 1970 Educational technology: A bibliography. *Bull. Int. Bur. Educ.* 177: 263–309

Lewis B N, Pask G 1965 The theory and practice of adaptive teaching systems. In: Glaser R (ed.) 1965 *Teaching Machines and Programmed Learning: A Source Book.* Department of Audiovisual Instruction, National Education Association, Washington, DC

Lumsdaine A A 1964 Educational technology, programmed learning and instructional science. In: Hilgard E R (ed.) 1964 *Theories of Learning and Instruction.* 63rd National Society for the Study of Education (NSSE) Yearbook Part 1. University of Chicago Press, Chicago, Illinois

Lumsdaine A A, Glaser R (eds.) 1960 *Teaching Machines and Programmed Learning: A Source Book.* Department of Audiovisual Instruction, National Education Association, Washington, DC

Melton A W 1959 The science of learning and the technology of educational methods. *Harvard Educ. Rev.* 29: 96–106

Miles M B (ed.) 1964 *Innovation in Education.* Teachers College Press, Columbia University, New York

Mitchell P D 1978 Educational technology. In: Unwin D, McAleese R (eds.) 1978 *The Encyclopedia of Educational Media Communications and Technology.* Macmillan, London, pp. 307–32

Moore O K 1968 Autotelic responsive environments and exceptional children. In: Weisgerber R A (ed.) 1968 *Instructional Process and Media Innovation.* Rand McNally, Chicago, Illinois, pp. 418–64

Moore O K 1969 Some principles for the design of clarifying educational environments. In: Goslin D A (ed.) 1969 *Handbook of Socialization Theory and Research.* Rand McNally, Chicago, Illinois

National Council for Educational Technology (NCET) 1969 *Towards More Effective Learning.* The Report of the National Council for Educational Technology 1967–1968. Councils and Education Press, London

Oettinger A G, Mark S S 1969 *Run, Computer Run: The Mythology of Educational Innovation.* Harvard University Press, Cambridge, Massachusetts

Papert S 1980 *Mindstorms: Children, Computers and Powerful Ideas.* Basic Books, New York

Ramo S 1973 The systems approach. In: Miles R F (ed.) 1973 *Systems Concepts: Lectures on Contemporary Approaches to Systems.* Wiley, New York, pp. 13–32

Skinner B F 1958 Teaching machines. *Science* 128: 969-77

Skinner B F 1968 *The Technology of Teaching.* Appleton-Century–Crofts, New York

Taylor G (ed.) 1970 *The Teacher as Manager: A Symposium.* Councils and Education Press, London

Tickton S G (ed.) 1970 *To Improve Learning: An Evaluation of Instructional Technology.* Bowker, New York

Travers R M W 1968 Directions for the development of an educational technology. In: Witt P W F (ed.) 1968 *Technology and the Curriculum.* Curriculum Conf., Columbia University, 1967. Teachers College Press, Columbia University, New York

Travers R M W 1970 *Man's Information System: A Primer for Media Specialists and Educational Technologists.* Chandler, Scranton, Pennsylvania

Travers R M W 1973 Educational technology and related research viewed as a political force. In: Travers R M W (ed.) 1973 *Second Handbook of Research on Teaching: A Project of the American Educational Research Association.* Rand McNally, Chicago, Illinois, pp. 979–96

Weisgerber R A (ed.) 1968 *Instructional Process and Media Innovation.* Rand McNally, Chicago, Illinois

Weisgerber R A (ed.) 1971 *Developmental Efforts in Individualized Learning.* Peacock, Itasca, Illinois

Witt P W F 1968 Educational technology: The education of teachers and the development of instructional materials specialists. In: Witt P W F (ed.) 1968 *Technology and the Curriculum.* Curriculum Conf., Columbia University, 1967. Teachers College Press, Columbia University, New York

Field of Study

D. P. Ely

Educational technology is firmly established as a field of study. Institutions which offer training programs in, for example, instructional development, educational communications, and educational resources use many labels to describe the field. Current efforts to describe the field are reflected in position papers of professional organizations and curricula of training programs. Beyond these sources, interpretations of the field are largely inferential and based on the performance of individuals in the field and published accounts about various aspects of the field. Such sources often lead to conclusions based on earlier definitions of the field which focused on the mass media rather than on the processes of instruction and learning, the current emphasis. As new technologies and learning strategies have appeared, educational technology has added and integrated them to bring about new dimensions to an ever-changing field. This article traces the evolution of educational technology as a field of study by highlighting the contributing disciplines and changing content which constitute the field.

1. A Brief History

In North America, educational technology was first recognized as a field of study with the establishment of the audiovisual education curriculum at Indiana University in 1946. Separate courses had been offered in the 1930s but no comprehensive program had been organized until L. C. Larson inaugurated the Indiana graduate program. An emphasis on the selection, use, production, evaluation, and management of audiovisual media provided the substance of courses at Indiana and other North American universities which used the Indiana curriculum as a model. The 1960s saw the introduction of communication concepts thus giving the field a process orientation with concerns for the "sender–message–channel–receiver" aspects of communication being grafted onto the audiovisual roots. Academic programs called "audiovisual communications" and "instructional communications" began to appear.

About the same time, the results of B. F. Skinner's research in operant conditioning were manifest in the programmed instruction movement which was embraced by the budding field of educational technology. Learning psychology was incorporated into many educational technology curricula. James D. Finn was probably the first person to label the field "instructional technology" when, in 1961, he organized a department at the University of Southern California.

In the United Kingdom, programmed instruction marked the inauguration of educational technology as a field of study. The audiovisual movement had been growing through the National Committee for Audio Visual Aids in Education and the Educational Foundation for Visual Aids but did not embrace the communication or learning psychology developments as did the North American practitioners. The Association for Programmed Learning (and Educational Technology) was organized in 1962 and became the focal point for educators and trainers who espoused the tenets of the new behavioral psychology applied to the instructional process.

The changing nature of the field was confirmed in 1970 when the Department of Audiovisual Instruction (of the National Education Association) in the United States became the Association for Educational Communications and Technology. The Council for Educational Technology in the United Kingdom was started in 1968, then established in its present form in 1973.

The expanding use of computers in education during the 1970s was compatible with most of the new technologies and procedures which had characterized the growth of the field since the Second World War. Thus, instructional applications (computer-based education), management applications (computer-managed instruction), and information applications (database retrieval systems) came naturally into educational technology.

Even as educational technologists are insisting that their major concern is with the design, development, and evaluation of instruction, there are practitioners contemplating ways in which videodiscs, videotex, and new computer systems can find their place in the field.

2. The Nature of a Field

A field of study is much less rigorous than a discipline. A discipline is usually defined as an organized body of knowledge which is constantly tested and changed by research. Disciplines are more often found in the sciences although the term covers the social sciences and humanities as well. Fields are usually found in areas of applied study—the professions. Fields often draw on disciplines for basic substance as engineering draws on physics and mathematics, and medicine on biology and chemistry. A field, such as educational technology, is an amalgam of several fields and disciplines. It uses those concepts, theories, procedures, and tools which help it to accomplish its basic purpose: the design and implementation of learning systems.

There are signs that a field has become a legitimate entity. Formal programs of study with curricula which are substantially congruent from institution to institution is one such sign. Another is the creation of associations where individuals who are engaged in common practice can share ideas and explore new research findings. An outgrowth of the associations is usually a journal through which information can be shared among practitioners in diverse locations. Continuing demand for personnel who are being trained in the academic programs is another indicator that a field exists and is performing a valuable societal function.

For a field to become a profession, additional criteria need to be met (Finn 1953). Quality control of graduates through certification of individuals or accreditation of academic programs by agreed-upon standards; establishment and enforcement of a code of ethics; and an organized body of intellectual theory constantly expanding by research all constitute some of the requirements for a profession. In some parts of the world, educational technologists claim to belong to such a profession.

3. Contributing Fields

Educational technology is a field made up of elements of other fields. There is very little content which is unique. It has taken elements of cognitive psychology, perception psychology, measurement, evaluation, communications, management, media, and systems engineering and arranged these elements synergistically to a point where the whole is greater than the sum of its parts.

Stakenas and Kaufman (1981) have graphically shown how scientific knowledge is used and transformed by educational technology into tools for instruc-

tion and learning. They have grouped the contributing fields into the "behavioral sciences," "management sciences," and "physical sciences." The "techniques" derived from the "principles" become curricular topics in academic programs (except for the engineering area). The "artifacts" are the tangible outcomes created by practitioners in the field. Table 1 shows how contributing fields are used in educational technology as a field of study. Educational technology, in its broadest sense, is concerned with all these elements as they contribute to the design and use of effective learning systems.

Short's (1981) study of graduate educational technology programs in the United States indicated emphasis on materials production and utilization/application at the master's level; on management/administration at the post-master's level; and on research, instructional development, theory, evaluation, and instructional systems design at the doctoral level. Each of these content areas draws from the behavioral, management, or physical sciences.

4. Preparation for Career

Educational technology as a field of study appears to lead to placement within the field. Sink's (1980) study of about 1,000 1979 graduates of educational technology

Table 1
Development sequence and scientific areas that contribute to educational technology

Development sequence	Behavioral sciences	Management sciences	Physical sciences
Principles	Learning Perception Cognition Motivation Measurement	Systems approach Management Cybernetics Macroeconomics Microeconomics	Optics Mechanics Electricity Circuits Chemistry
Techniques based on scientific principles	Programmed learning Learner analysis Task analysis Reinforcement scheduling Message design Test construction	Needs assessment Systems analysis Systems design Cost-effectiveness analysis	Optical engineering Communications engineering Chemical engineering Electrical engineering
Artifacts produced by applying scientific principles	Learning materials and activities that satisfy the conditions of learning	Management by objectives Systematically designed learning systems	Devices for transmitting, e.g., television, radio, telephone Devices for storing and retrieving, e.g., computers

Source: Stakenas R G, Kaufman R 1981 *Technology in Education: Its Human Potential.* © Phi Delta Kappa Foundation

programs in the United States indicates about 90 percent placement with the greatest numbers being placed in management/administrative, instructional development, and media production positions. These three major categories represent distinct categories in which educational technologists often seek employment (AECT 1977). The Association for Educational Communications and Technology (AECT) has published a list of competencies required for instructional development specialists and material design and production specialists (*Instructional Innovator* 1980). These competencies have been used by many educational technology academic programs to plan courses and curricula. The composite list is a fairly good representation of the content in the field of educational technology. Another view eschews the body of knowledge approach to the field (McCormick 1976) and opts for description of the educational technologist's role as a more valid statement of its content.

5. Beyond Content

The field of educational technology has established its credibility in the academic community and in the marketplace. The field will continue its identity struggle in the fashion described by Hawkridge (1976): "The time is now coming when educational technology should take its place as a specialized branch of educational research and development, retaining its identity but cementing ties with other fields instead of rivalling them."

The critics will no doubt continue to raise their voices. Lewis (1980) suggests how to handle the criticism. He suggests making "a preliminary statement of what educational technology is seeking to do, and why society (a) needs such a profession now, and (b) is likely to go on needing it in the future. The statement should also make a preliminary attempt to justify any assertions made about societal needs; and to say why such needs cannot (for the present time at least) be satisfactorily met in ways *other than* the establishing of a new profession."

The field may show signs of ambivalence in its many settings but there appears to be more uniformity of opinion now than ever before as to the content and approach of educational technology. It is a field which has come of age and will find its place among the twentieth-century movements in education.

Bibliography

Association for Educational Communications and Technology (AECT) 1977 *Definition of Educational Technology*. AECT, Washington, DC

1953 Professionalizing the audio-visual field. *Audio-Vis. Commun. Rev.* 1(1): 6–17

Hawkridge D G 1976 Next year, Jerusalem! The rise of educational technology. *Br. J. Educ. Technol.* 7: 7–30 *Instructional Innovator* 1980 Competencies for instructional development specialists. Competencies for materials design and production specialists. 25(9): 27–31

Lewis B N 1980 The professional standing of educational technology. *International Yearbook of Educational and Instructional Technology 1980/81*. Kogan Page, London, pp. 20–36

McCormick R 1976 Educational technologists: Knowledge retention and role change. *Br. J. Educ. Technol.* 7: 75–84

Short R 1981 *An Analysis of Instructional Technology Graduate Degree Programs in US Colleges and Universities*. Farmland Industries, Kansas City, Missouri

Sink D L 1980 Employment trends for media graduates. *Instr. Innovator* 25: 36–37

Stakenas R G, Kaufman R 1981 *Technology in Education: Its Human Potential*. Phi Delta Kappa, Bloomington, Indiana

Personnel

D. P. Ely

Increased use of the concepts of educational technology in education and training programs worldwide has led to the creation of a new genre of personnel. New methods and techniques of educational practice, often derived from adoption of new media and technologies, have brought about new specialists who are not teachers, supervisors, or administrators, but educational technology professionals. These new professionals do not always work in the classroom, on the university campus, or in the training department of an organization. They may be concerned with production of instructional media, the dissemination and distribution of learning resources, or with the design, development, and evaluation of courses and curricula. To understand the scope of personnel who are within the domain of educational technology, it is helpful to know the functions they perform, the levels of service, the locus of employment, and the nature of the positions they fill.

1. Functions

The job responsibilities of educational technologists are as wide and varied as the number of titles which are used to identify individuals serving in this field: television producer, instructional developer, film librarian, evaluator, curriculum developer, learning resource center director, and audiovisual specialist—to name just a few. To bring order out of this jumble, the concept of function is useful. Function is used to refer to a group of interrelated activities engaged in by an educational technologist to achieve a particular outcome or purpose. These outcomes or purposes may involve data, people, things, or combinations thereof. Seldom, if ever, is a job composed entirely of one function.

The functions of educational technology personnel were studied extensively in the United States by the Jobs in Media Study (Wallington et al. 1971). Detailed task analyses were made of personnel who were employed in a variety of positions related to the field of educational technology. By clustering the tasks in logical groupings, nine functions were established. Later modification of these functions by the Definition and Terminology Committee of the Association for Educational Communications and Technology (AECT) yielded more comprehensive descriptions of each function which now serve as the basis for planning training curricula, establishing certification requirements, and preparing job descriptions. The functions are (AECT 1977, Chisholm and Ely 1975):

(a) Organization management—to plan, establish, and maintain policies and procedures for operating a program or agency related to educational technology.

(b) Personnel management—to hire, interact with, supervise, and terminate personnel.

(c) Research—to generate and test theory related to educational technology.

(d) Design—to translate theoretical knowledge into instructional specifications.

(e) Production—to create instructional products based on specifications.

(f) Evaluation/selection—to examine and judge the worth, quality, and significance of instructional products and programs.

(g) Logistics—to acquire, store, retrieve, distribute, and maintain information in all formats.

(h) Utilization—to bring learners into contact with instructional products and programs.

(i) Utilization/dissemination—to bring learners and others into contact with information about educational technology.

Each function includes a cluster of competencies and each competency, in turn, is composed of many tasks (Chisholm and Ely 1975 p. 166). For example, the design function can be divided into six competencies, one of which is analyzing learner characteristics. Tasks associated with this competency then include diagnostic testing, learner interviews, reviewing student records, and meeting with parents.

It is unlikely that one professional person would perform all functions and all the competencies and tasks within each function. Some people may specialize in one function; others may acquire a few competencies in all functions.

2. Levels of Training and Responsibility

Many of the tasks within each function are performed at various levels of sophistication. There are three basic levels of responsibility: (a) aide, (b) technician, and (c) specialist and/or generalist. Each level is determined by the amount of instruction required to fulfill the tasks. For example, an aide would perform relatively low-level tasks in which the procedures are completely specified. Almost everything the person needs to know is part of the job assignment and can be learned on-the-job. The technician has received training in a specialty, such as photography or electronics, but not necessarily at the tertiary level. The specialist or generalist is usually professionally prepared and has completed graduate work in the field of specialization, such as television or computers, or in a broader aspect of educational technology, such as instructional design and development or management of media programs. The concept of differentiated staffing is evident in many multistaff educational media and technology programs. Each level serves a distinct purpose and personnel who fill the positions have different types of preparation and experience.

2.1 Aide Level
Aides usually have no specific training in educational technology. They learn on-the-job. They may serve in such positions as clerks, secretaries, and delivery people. They perform according to standards set by a supervisor.

2.2 Technician Level
Technicians usually provide services or create materials according to specifications established by others. The technician is responsible for a product or service as long as all the tools are made available. Technicians can have such titles as graphic artist, television camera operator, or electronics maintenance repair person. Training usually comes from formal study in a technical or vocational curriculum and from on-the-job experience.

2.3 Specialist or Generalist Level
Specialists, as the label implies, emphasize one aspect of educational technology and usually complete advanced study beyond the baccalaureate degree. Typical specialists are television producers/directors, computer-based education personnel, and audiovisual media designers.

Generalists choose to prepare themselves broadly so that they might manage or coordinate the work of an educational technology organization. They tend to study at the graduate level to gain competencies in most of the functional areas of the field. They usually do not specialize in one aspect of the field but may possess more competencies in management than other functions.

It is important to note that aides, technicians, specialists, and generalists can be employed in all of the nine functional areas. There are tasks at each level. The combined performance of staff at all levels provides the output of any educational technology program. Not all tasks are performed by people at each level; sometimes one person tries to handle all functions at several levels. The success of such an effort depends upon individual competencies and time available.

3. *Locus of Employment*

Educational technology is a young field. Its practitioners carry a wide array of job titles. There are three categories of positions which include most of the personnel who operate within the field: (a) instructional program development, (b) media product development, and (c) media management. Some educational technologists teach in academic programs preparing people for the field.

3.1 *Instructional Program Development*

Positions in this category primarily emphasize the functions of design, research, evaluation/selection, and utilization. They include such generic positions as curriculum supervisor, media consultant, instructional developer, and staff developer. Employers who seek instructional program development personnel are school systems; colleges and universities; training departments in business, industry, military, and health organizations; and other agencies which use instruction as a vehicle for education and training.

3.2 *Media Product Development*

The production function is the major focus of personnel who work in this area. Some minor aspects of research, evaluation/selection, and utilization are usually included. Individuals who are employed in this area have such job titles as graphic artist, photographer, cinematographer, computer programmer, and television director. People who work in media product development are often employed in the same settings as individuals who perform instructional program development and media management functions. In such cases they usually work as a member of an instructional development team or a media support services staff. In some cases, media product development competence is acquired through short-term contracts with freelance personnel or with organizations and agencies that specialize in media production.

3.3 *Media Management*

Positions in this category fall primarily within the functions of organization and personnel management, logistics, and utilization dissemination. Some aspects of research, evaluation/selection, and utilization are also included. Some of the titles of persons who serve in this category are: director of learning resource center, film librarian, audiovisual director, and instructional materials manager. Sink (1980) reports that 40 percent of the 1979 graduates of educational technology programs in the United States were employed in management positions.

The settings for media management personnel are largely in the schools, colleges and universities, libraries, and training departments of companies and governmental agencies. There are some aspects (tasks) of management that are required for the successful operation of instructional program development and media product development projects.

3.4 *Trainers of Educational Technologists*

The growth of educational technology has brought about more formal training programs. These programs offer new career opportunities for people who have had experience in the field and want to help prepare others. The study of Sink (1980 p. 37) indicated that 12 percent of 1979 educational technology graduates entered programs as trainers or professors of future educational technology personnel.

4. *The Nature of Positions*

There still remains some confusion regarding educational technology personnel. Some organizations require personnel possessing the competencies in one or more of the functional areas noted earlier but often they do not know that such people are being trained. Other employers may hire educational technology personnel to handle specific media production tasks and discover that the new employees have instructional program development competencies. The broad nature of educational technology calls for specificity in job description and professional training which will ensure an appropriate match of the people and jobs. A case study analysis of educational technology job profiles as seen through roles and competencies was made by Leedham and Berruer (1979) for UNESCO.

Another problem stems from the misperception of employers regarding the level of personnel needed. Some organizations who seek personnel with technical competencies but hire more highly trained specialists or generalists are often disappointed because the more highly trained person feels the need for a technical level person to handle routine matters. On the other hand, a person who is engaged at a technician level and is expected to perform as a specialist does not have the requisite competencies to achieve the higher level tasks within a functional area.

Leedham and Berruer (1979) mention the problem of status among educational technology professionals. They note the "lack of identity between vocational roles and the public service sector" (p. 21). The misperception of what educational technologists do, and the assumption that communication media are the major products, lead some employers and the general public to think that the people who serve in this field do not play a significant role in the instructional process.

As the field grows and matures, so will develop the understanding of those who employ educational technologists.

Bibliography

Association for Educational Communications and Technology (AECT) 1977 *The Definition of Educational Technology*. AECT, Washington, DC

1975 *Media Personnel in Education: A Competency Approach*. Prentice-Hall, Englewood Cliffs, New Jersey

Leedham J, Berruer A 1979 *Status of Staff Employing Modern Educational Techniques*. UNESCO, Paris

Sink D L 1980 Employment trends for media graduates. *Instructional Innovator* 25 (9): 36–37

Wallington J et al. 1971 *Jobs in Instructional Media*. Association for Educational Communications and Technology, Washington, DC

Training

D. P. Ely

Professional preparation of educational technologists began in the late 1940s, partly stimulated by the successful use of audiovisual training aids during the Second World War. Colleges and universities in the United States offered the first formal graduate programs leading to master's degrees and later, doctoral degrees. Other countries followed, but about 20 years later. The formal training of educational technologists occurs at two levels: generalist/specialist, and technician. This article discusses the preparation of generalists and specialists. Technicians are usually trained in specific vocational areas such as graphic arts, photography, television production, and computer programming. They later apply these skills to education-on-the-job. The location of training programs worldwide, the content of the curricula, and issues pertaining to professional education of educational technologists are discussed.

1. Training for What?

As educational technology has become a more integral part of teaching and learning at all levels of education and in other settings, the demand for specialized personnel has accelerated. Schools, universities, industrial training programs, open universities, medical education, international educational planning programs, and educational broadcasting are representative types of organizations which seek educational technology personnel. The general functions of such personnel include management, instructional development, media production, evaluation, and research.

Some positions seek generalists who are competent in many functions and move freely from one responsibility to another. Many of the educational technology managers are generalists. In some cases specialists are required to handle specific functions in depth such as instructional design, product development, or evaluation. Most educational technologists are prepared to serve a wide range of responsibilities pertaining to systematic instruction.

There appears to be a continuing need for educational technology personnel as new technologies enter the education and training arena. Professional education programs preparing such people currently exist and are growing throughout the world.

2. The Location of Educational Technology Training Programs

Virtually all programs are located within higher education institutions. They are not uniform in designation. A sample reveals such program titles as: educational media, instructional systems technology, educational communications, instructional technology, and learning systems. Some departments are located within faculties of education, others are independent. Some offer special emphasis within departments of educational psychology or communications. Some are aligned with library and information science. Still others use an educational technology label to cover one specialization such as computer-based education. There is little order among professional training programs. An extensive search is often required to find them.

The greatest number of educational technology programs are to be found in the United States. From 1955, when there were 50 programs, the number increased to 193 programs in 1980 (Short 1981). In 1981, Harvard University and Stanford University announced new programs in the field. The largest enrollment is at the master's level. There are more part-time students than full-time students. Short (1981) determined that there were 788 full-time and 469 part-time faculty in 1980 with the largest percent of full-time faculty holding the professor's rank and a doctoral degree. Moore (1981) studied the most influential educational technology programs in the United States and determined that the top five were at Indiana University, Syracuse University, Michigan State University, the University of Southern California, and Florida State University. A complete list of United States graduate programs appears in the annual edition of the *Educational Media Yearbook*.

Professional training programs in the United Kingdom are found in 24 institutions. The nature of these programs varies. Some are diploma programs, some are postgraduate programs approved by the Council for National Academic Awards (CNAA), others grant bachelor's, master's, and doctoral degrees. Programs of study are described in *Courses Leading to Qualification in Educational Technology*, which is updated and published annually by the Council for Educational Technology for the United Kingdom. Some of the innovative professional training programs have come from Scotland. The CNAA Diploma in Educational Technology at

Jordanhill College of Education and the Diploma in Educational Technology at Dundee College of Education were the first professional training programs to be offered to part-time students at a distance. Each institution has made the modules available through local sources.

Beyond the programs in educational technology in the United States and the United Kingdom are several educational technology courses in Australia and Canada. Major programs in Australia are located at Macquarie University in Sydney, the University of Melbourne, Salisbury College of Advanced Education in Adelaide, South Australia, and the Western Australia Institute of Technology in Perth. Canada's major programs are located at Concordia University in Montreal, the Ontario Institute for the Study of Education, Toronto, the University of Alberta at Edmonton, and the University of British Columbia.

Europe has pockets of interest in training for educational technology, but the programs are not generally self-contained. They are associated with departments of pedagogy, computer science, or other cognate areas. An exception is the program in Applied Instructional Science at the Twente University of Technology in the Netherlands which began an undergraduate program in 1981. There are programs at the *Ecole Normale Supérieure* at St. Cloud in France, the University of Tübingen in Germany, and the Department of Education of the *Eötvös Lorand Tudomanyegyetem* in Budapest.

Various countries in Latin America have made efforts to build academic programs in educational technology but there appear to be only a few in operation. The University of Trujillo in Peru has a department of educational technology, the *Universidad Nacional de Lujan* in Argentina offers courses, and several Brazilian universities have basic programs. The Departmente de Technologia Educativa y Educacion Permanente in Cordoba y Laprida is an Argentine government organization which trains educators in all aspects of educational technology, especially the production of nonconventional learning materials.

It is more difficult to determine the existence of programs in Asia and Africa. However, programs in Central and Eastern Asia are described by Sakamoto at the end of this section.

3. Content of Training Programs

Since most of the training programs in educational technology are on the graduate level, they tend to build on undergraduate studies, most frequently teacher education. The trend is shifting away from the teacher education base as more educational technology personnel are being employed in nonschool settings. Most academic programs provide new content which is not dependent upon previous studies. Persons who have good preparation in mathematics and psychology seem to have a head start.

The content of academic programs changes as one goes further into a training program and seeks advanced degrees. Most of the individuals who enter the field spend most of their time acquiring the basic vocabulary, concepts, and procedures of practitioners. There is some formal way of acquiring competencies in each of the nine functional areas stated by the Association for Educational Communications and Technology (AECT) in the United States (1977). Thus, courses, experience, and independent study in organization management, personnel management, research and theory, design, evaluation, logistics, utilization, research, and utilization/dissemination constitute the bulk of most curricula. Short (1981) found that the major emphases of masters' programs in the United States were materials production and utilization/application. All programs included in his survey offered at least one course each in management, production, and utilization. Curricula in other countries appear to follow the same pattern. Other high-frequency offerings include management, selection, instructional development, instructional systems design, and evaluation. Cognate areas most frequently used by educational technology are educational psychology (learning, instructional, and developmental), statistics, communications (theory and applied areas—radio, television, and film), computer science, and library and information science.

In the United States there has been a strong movement to prepare educational technology personnel for elementary and secondary schools through library science programs. The term "school media specialist" has been frequently used rather than educational technologist. The programs, largely at the graduate level, merge competencies of school library (resource center) management and some of the nonprint media competencies such as production, utilization and, to some extent, evaluation. Many of the programs are competency based and require demonstrated minimal performance before degrees are awarded. This American trend has not spread widely to other countries, but several programs in Canada and Australia appear to be moving in that direction.

In an attempt to bring about some uniformity of the training programs, national efforts have been initiated in the United States and the United Kingdom to develop standards for professional training programs. In the United States the Association for Educational Communications and Technology has developed a list of competencies for: (a) instructional development specialists; (b) material design and production specialists; and (c) media management specialists. In the United Kingdom, the Council for Educational Technology explored core competencies for educational technology personnel. These documents have become basic planning tools for determining the content of new curricula in educational technology in many institutions.

4. Issues in Professional Training

As any field grows and matures, fundamental questions are raised regarding the training of future professionals. Finn (1953) insisted that one major criterion for a profession is "a period of long training...before entering into the profession." As today's professionals consider that criterion, certain issues seem to be paramount. They center on (a) the definition of the field; (b) recruitment of personnel; (c) core competencies; (d) theory/practice balance; and (e) certification of personnel and accreditation of academic programs.

4.1 Definition of the Field

As the field rapidly evolved from audiovisual education through educational communications to educational technology, there has been no consistency in its definition. A series of statements regarding the definition were published by AECT in 1963 and 1972. The most recent and comprehensive (1977) seems to have taken hold in North America but there is not wide agreement on it from all concerned parties. Until there is conceptual agreement, professional training programs will vary according to the definition they value. If it is oriented toward media and their application, one type of curriculum will emerge; if the systems design definition is accepted, then another type of curriculum will be developed. The issue has not been resolved.

4.2 Recruitment of Personnel

Many educational technologists stumble into the field through participation in innovative teaching and learning activities. There is no natural and logical route from any undergraduate program to a graduate program in educational technology. There is not much active recruiting of new personnel into training programs. Most people are steered by individuals who are already practitioners or by circumstances which lead to a career change such as from teaching to educational technology. The lack of knowledge regarding professional training programs and the technical image often turn potential practitioners away. There appears to be sufficient demand for personnel worldwide, so more active recruiting of candidates should be considered.

4.3 Core Competencies

There is probably no other question which can create such disparate answers and feelings as, "What essential knowledge must all educational technologists possess?" Translated to academic training programs, this question means identification of those core competencies which all individuals who enter professional training programs must acquire. There is no agreement among programs or official statements of professional associations which provide guidance. Short (1981) reports courses in management, production, and utilization at all 193 master's programs in the United States. The content of these courses would have to be examined to determine consistency from institution to institution. The list of competencies compiled by the AECT (*Instructional Innovator* Dec. 1980) provides some agreement among professionals in the United States. There may be more agreement than is realized, but the basic question still goes unanswered.

4.4 Theory/Practice Balance

The field of educational technology began with a practical orientation. The early emphasis on the media of communication in a teaching/learning environment and the continuing acceptance of new technologies tends to perpetuate the image of practice. However, with the establishment of academic programs came the need for theoretical bases. Individuals were asking, "What medium should be used and why?" The psychology of learning was obviously closely related to the use of communication media. Theories were borrowed or adapted from psychology, communication, and psychometrics programs and found their way into educational technology curricula. Graduates of programs were expected to perform practical tasks in the real world of education and training and they wondered about the value of theory. There seems to be more agreement among academics about theory for advanced graduate studies, though the basic conflict has not been resolved in any widespread fashion. Some institutions are known to have programs which are more practical in curricular offerings while others are more theoretical. Each program will probably continue to determine its own balance.

4.5 Certification of Personnel and Accreditation of Programs

Another criterion for a profession is the standards established for entry into the profession (Finn 1953). Each country has control mechanisms at the national or state levels to ensure that academic programs prepare people according to specific standards. These standards have not yet touched the field of educational technology to any great degree. Some exceptions are the Council for National Academic Awards (CNAA) validations in the United Kingdom. In the United States, about 30 states have established certification requirements for educational technology personnel working in the public schools. The Association for Educational Communications and Technology (AECT) has attempted to implement an association-oriented certification program but has not been successful. Accreditation of academic programs in educational technology is usually covered by institution-wide approval by regional academic accrediting associations or sometimes by the National Council for the Accreditation of Teacher Education if the program is housed within a faculty of education which prepares teachers. Without published standards for academic programs it is possible for any institution to claim a legitimate academic program in the field and for an individual to declare himself/herself as an educational technologist. The approach of benign self-regulation may be sufficient until there are abuses of current procedures.

Bibliography

Association for Educational Communications and Technology (AECT) 1977 *The Definition of Educational Technology*, AECT, Washington, DC

Courses Leading to Qualification in Educational Technology. Council for Educational Technology, London

Educational Media Yearbook. Libraries Unlimited, Littleton, Colorado

Finn J D 1953 Professionalizing the audio-visual field. *Audio-Vis. Commun. Rev.* 1: 6–17

Instructional Innovator 1980 Competencies for instructional development specialists, and competencies for materials design and production specialists. 25 (9): 27–31

International Yearbook of Educational and Instructional Technology, 1980–81. Kogan Page, London

Moore D M 1981 Educational media professional's perceptions of influence and prestige in the field of instructional technology: A national survey. *Educ. Technol.* 21: 15–23

Short R 1981 *An Analysis of Instructional Technology Graduates Degree Programs in United States Colleges and Universities*. Farmland Industries, Kansas City, Missouri

Professional Associations

H. B. Hitchens

A professional association is an organization of individuals with a common background in a subject—medicine, law, engineering, and so on, whose chief purpose is to expand knowledge in their professional field or to establish professional standards which will improve the way in which individuals practice their profession. There are an increasing number of professional associations involved in the development of educational technology and the introduction of the products of today's technological society into education, and they have a set of functions that are held in common with all professional associations. They have grown up mostly in the industrialized countries, but there are emerging groups in most regions of the world who find it useful to band together in order to accomplish more by associating themselves professionally, than they can accomplish as individual professionals.

1. Defining a Profession

A profession can be simply defined as a person's occupation, if it is not commercial, mechanical, agricultural, or the like. The traditional professions have been the law, medicine, and clergy. There is a substantial literature on the characteristics of a profession which was first linked to the emergence of educational technology by Finn (1953). The definition later adopted by a committee of the Association for Educational Communications and Technology comprised ten characteristics.

(a) *An organized body of intellectual theory, constantly expanding by research*. This is a fundamental and very important characteristic. A systematic theory must constantly be expanded by research and thinking within any profession. Alfred North Whitehead said, "...the practice of a profession cannot be disjoined from its theoretical understanding or vice versa... The antithesis to a profession is an avocation based on customary activities and modified by the trial and error of individual practice. Such an avocation is a Craft..." (Price 1954).

(b) *An intellectual technique*. This is the manner in which an individual searches for solutions to problems. Intellectual technique serves as a bridge between theory and practical application.

(c) *An application of that technique to practical affairs*. Practical application involves making ideas and processes result in tangible products. For example, a person actually performing a scientific experiment is making a practical application of intellectual technique.

(d) *A long period of training and certification*. Specialists and technicians in the profession have undergone long periods of training. Training issues include the nature and content of professional education, certification standards, admissions standards and practices, and job placement.

(e) *A series of standards and a statement of ethics which is enforced*. Codes of ethics indicate how members of a profession should behave. Sets of standards specify guidelines for the tools and the facilities used by people in a profession. Merely stating standards and publishing codes of ethics do not guarantee anything—professionalization requires that the standards and the code of ethics be universally followed.

(f) *The ability to provide its own leadership*. Enough leadership must be present to ensure that the present status of the profession is attended to and that the members of the profession are looking to the future.

(g) *An association of members of the profession into a closely knit group with a high quality of communications among the members*. A strong organization for the people in the profession is needed to help implement and develop the other characteristics—standard setting, a code of ethics, leadership, and training. A strong association is needed to achieve vigorous enforcement of practices, standards, and ethics.

(h) *Acknowledgement as a profession.* The members of the profession must believe in it and be conscious of their membership of it; they must form an association and must make public statements that ensure they achieve some recognition as a professional group.

(i) *Professional concern for responsible use of its work.* Using the intellectual technique for practical application is not enough; the members of the profession must exercise a responsibility for the practical work they do. As a group they must be concerned about the uses to which their work is put in society. They must examine the values for which their profession stands and take positions on societal issues that are affected by its work.

(j) *An established relationship with other professions.* Since there is probably more than one profession operating within the general field of educational technology, the professional group must acknowledge its relationship with those other professional groups.

2. The Origins of Professional Associations

Professional associations and learned societies have manifested themselves primarily in the industrialized countries. Tocqueville (1969) observed this phenomenon in the United States in the nineteenth century.

> Americans of all ages, all conditions, and all dispositions constantly form associations. They have not only commercial and manufacturing companies, in which all take part, but associations of a thousand other kinds, religious, moral, serious, futile, general or restricted, enormous or diminutive. The Americans make associations to give entertainments, to found seminaries, to build inns, to construct churches, to diffuse books, to send missionaries to the antipodes; in this manner they found hospitals, prisons, and schools. If it is proposed to inculcate some truth or to foster some feeling by the encouragement of a great example, they form a society. Wherever at the head of some new undertaking you see the government in France, or a man of rank in England, in the United States you will be sure to find an association.

Professional associations are nonprofit-making, cooperative, voluntary organizations. Academic credentials, an accrediting examination, or a license may be a prerequisite for membership, but is not always. Membership is usually composed of individuals who seek an exchange of ideas and discussion of common problems within the profession.

Today's professional associations were preceded by scientific or learned societies. Such scientific societies have always been preeminent agencies for collecting and diffusing knowledge. They originated in Europe during the Renaissance. The first known scientific society seems to have been the Academia Secretorum Naturae founded in Naples in 1560. In the next century the Royal Society was founded in London (1662). This was the leading scientific society serving the American Colonies before 1776. The oldest American scientific society, in continuous existence since its founding in Philadelphia by Benjamin Franklin in 1743, is the American Philosophical Society. In the middle of the nineteenth century in America, many of the leading professional groups still in existence today were founded: the American Statistical Association in 1839, the American Psychiatric Association, 1844, the American Society of Civil Engineers, 1852, and the National Education Association, 1857.

Before the mid-1800s most American scientists were generalists whose interests ranged over the whole field of human knowledge. From the latter half of that century, science became increasingly specialized and men devoted more and more time to particular aspects of a broader subject. This lead to a demand for scientific and technical societies of a specialized character.

Educational technology was one of several specialized groups which developed under the auspices of the National Education Association between the First and Second World Wars. The Association for Educational Communications and Technology of the United States grew as a part of the National Education Association into an autonomous organization in the last quarter of this century.

Though professional associations stress their roots in the learned societies, their functions also include the pursuit of their members' interests in ways that sometimes resemble the trade associations. A trade association can be defined as a nonprofit-making, cooperative, voluntary organization of business competitors designed to assist its members and its industry in dealing with mutual business problems in several of the following areas: accounting practice, business ethics, commercial and industrial research, standardization, statistics, trade promotion, and relations with government, employees, and the general public.

The history of the trade associations demonstrates their antiquity. The ancient empires of China, Egypt, Japan, and India contained trade groups operating for the benefit of their members, as did Rome, whose groups set wages and prices and fostered apprentice training. During the Middle Ages, European craft and merchant guilds increased in number and power and developed strict regulations and many member services. Merchant guilds were associations of merchants and traders formed originally for protection and increased profit. Craft guilds were made up of artisans and craftsmen producing consumer goods who set quality standards for their work. Both groups set up monopolies with severe entrance requirements and limited the training of apprentices.

In the eighteenth century the rising tide of invention with the Industrial Revolution doomed the efforts of the old guilds to oppose economic and social change and they gradually declined. However, in America, trade associations were found to be necessary as early as the mid-eighteenth century. The New York Chamber of

Commerce, the oldest trade association still in existence in North America, was formed by 20 merchants in 1768. The New York Stock Exchange was formed in 1792. National trade associations were not formed, however, until the second half of the nineteenth century.

3. Functions of Professional Associations: A Case Study of the Association for Educational Communications and Technology (AECT)

A description of the above association serves as a good example of the development of the functions of a professional association. The AECT had its origins in the National Education Association's Division of Visual Education, which began in 1923 in the United States. Until recently, the AECT was called the Department of Audiovisual Instruction (DAVI); and the change in name reflects the development of the field from visual education to educational technology. The following account is organized under headings that characterize the major functions of most professional associations.

3.1 Communications with Members and the Field

The association's *Journal of Educational Communications and Technology* (formerly AV *Communication Review*) is more than 20 years old and highly regarded in the field. *Instructional Innovator*, the association's journal of practical applications of media and technology to instruction, is widely read by both members and nonmembers. In addition, the AECT maintains communications with its members through other, nonperiodic publications and through an annual convention and regional meetings.

3.2 Ethics

The AECT has a code of ethics along with procedures for the review of the behavior of its members. This is considered a hallmark of professional responsibility.

3.3 Standards

The AECT has devised standards for school (kindergarten through grade 12) media programs; newly revised standards for the cataloging of nonprint materials; standards for learning resource programs in two-year colleges; technical standards for audiocassettes; and standards for media training in teacher education programs and advanced programs in educational media.

3.4 Leadership

Leadership is evident through the standards of the association as well as through participation in joint groups such as the Educational Media Council and the Joint Council on Educational Telecommunications. The AECT was chosen by the National Center for Education Statistics to develop a handbook of definitions and terminology for educational technology. In 1977, the AECT, as the representative of the United States, hosted the International Council on Educational Media. The association develops the leadership capabilities and responsibilities of individual members through national and regional leadership seminars. Leadership is also a goal of the association's special foundation, the Educational Communications and Technology Foundation.

3.5 Training

Training is performed mostly through colleges and universities for which the association has developed standards for training programs. Additionally, some training seminars are conducted at the association's annual convention and at regional meetings and workshops. It is currently developing continuing education programs for its members by offering courses and certification. Task competencies for media management, instructional program development, and media product development have been identified and will serve as the basis for training and certification programs.

3.6 Cooperation with Other Associations

Cooperation with other associations pervades the forgoing activities. Most standards (such as the standards for school media programs) have been developed in conjunction with other associations. Some of the workshop and seminar activities are developed with other associations. The AECT assists states in the formation of certification programs. The development of a Handbook of Definitions and Terminology for Educational Technology directly involved 19 other education and media organizations. Finally, the participation of the AECT in consortia and joint councils shows its commitment to interdependence with other associations related to education and technology. As technology plays an increasing role in education and instruction, the interaction between the AECT and other associations will inevitably increase and lead to a concerted attempt to improve education through the application of technology.

4. Professional Associations of Educational Technology Worldwide

Around the world, the professional associations with a primary focus on the field of educational technology number approximately 60. The 40 associations in the United States with a clearly identified relationship to educational technology range from a concern with student development in media, such as the American Student Media Association, through organizations that focus on particular media of communication, such as the Association for Educational Data Systems and the Biological Photographic Association, to organizations that are primarily concerned with behavioral change, such as the National Society for Performance and Instruction and the International Visual Literacy Association.

In Canada, there is a national Association for Media and Technology in Education in Canada (AMTEC). The United Kingdom numbers at least seven organizations which are readily identifiable, preeminent among them being the Association for Educational and Training Technology. India also has several. Australia has the Australian Society for Educational Technology (ASET); Japanhas the Japan Audio-Visual Education Association (JAVEA); Brazil has the Brazilian Association of Educational Technology; Uruguay has the Inter-American Association of Broadcasters. Finally, Spain formed a new national Association of Educational Technology in 1982.

The field of educational technology is growing worldwide, with thousands of active professionals organized loosely in professional associations which are sometimes national and sometimes international in scope. The history of the professions demonstrates that working cooperatively in associations ensures regular growth of the academic and intellectual field at the same time as it provides professional people with an opportunity to develop their roles and improve their contribution to society.

Bibliography

Association for Educational Communications and Technology 1977 *Educational Technology: Definition and Glossary of Terms.* Association for Educational Communications and Technology, Washington, DC
Educational Media Yearbook. Libraries Unlimited, Littleton, Colorado
Finn J D 1953 Professionalizing the audio-visual field. *Audio-Vis. Commun. Rev.* 1 (1):6–17.
International Yearbook of Educational and Instructional Technology. Kogan Page, London
Lieberman J K 1970 *The Tyranny of the Experts: How Professionals are Closing the Open Society.* Walker, New York
Price L (ed.) 1954 *Dialogues of Alfred North Whitehead. Recorded by Lucien Price.* Little, Brown, Boston, Massachusetts
Tocqueville A C H M de 1969 *Democracy in America.* Doubleday, Garden City, New York

National and International Centers

W. E. Hug

The *International Yearbook of Educational and Instructional Technology* for 1986/87 listed some 1,000 centers which promote and offer services in educational technology. This list is undoubtedly incomplete but it does indicate an extremely wide dispersal of activity. Practically every country has at least one center, and more than 20 countries have more than 10 such centers. Most but not all of these centers can be considered as having some influence at the national level, and many are primarily national rather than local in the audiences they serve.

Centers of activity with a national impact can be grouped into five main types: (a) research and teaching units in colleges and universities; (b) governmental centers, units, and agencies; (c) professional associations and nongovernmental organizations; (d) units located within business or industry; and (e) proprietary corporations whose major purpose is the sale of educational technology services. Some centers have a wide range of activities while others tend to be more specialized, providing services such as television and film production, development of computer courses, or general support of institutional instruction. The more highly developed centers deploy people with a variety of specialized skills, including instructional designers, subject matter experts, educational psychologists, script writers, graphic artists, and editors.

1. College and University Units

Most colleges and universities have centers of educational technology or media service centers to support their instructional programs.

A second function assumed by some such centers is the training of educational technology personnel. Major training centers have an important national role, and several of them have international reputations. Such centers will also have a significant research and development role and obtain funding from a range of governmental agencies, charitable foundations, industry, and business. Some centers, particularly in the United States, may contract for projects that frequently have little bearing on the instructional programs. Colleges and universities producing research in the new educational technologies, like videodiscs programmed with computers, may be producing training programs for industry or the military. Others have outside support for the applications of educational technology directly related to the educational programs of the institution. For example, in the United Kingdom, the University of Bath was supported by the British Petroleum Company, in the design of an instruction program for business studies. In this respect centers for educational technology resemble many other university-based research units. Their research role enhances the quality of their advanced teaching, and probably also their reputation with colleagues in other fields.

Universities also house a significant number of more specialized research and development centers, which have no formal training or consultancy function. These will usually focus on a specific area within educational technology such as information science, television, or computer-based learning. The PLATO laboratory at the University of Illinois and the Centre for Mass Communications Research at the University of Leicester are well-known examples.

2. Governmental Centers, Units, and Agencies

The first distinction to be made under this heading is between centers which provide services within the governmental sector and agencies which the government has set up to coordinate, promote, provide, or even regulate educational technology activities in the nation as a whole. The most prominent centers in exploiting the use of educational technology within government have tended to be those concerned with the dissemination of government information and those concerned with the training of military personnel. The latter, in particular, have been prominent in the development of educational technology in the United States and the United Kingdom.

The organizational mechanisms devised by governments to coordinate, promote, or provide educational technology services are remarkably varied. National production facilities are most common in the area of broadcasting, with the United States being a significant exception. Film, however, is supported in a variety of ways. Only some nations have national film production agencies, the National Film Board of Canada being one of the best-known examples. The Federal Republic of Germany and the Netherlands have central scientific film institutes to produce and distribute research films and films for higher education. New Zealand has a national film library, while the British Film Institute is best known for its archival and educational functions.

Many governments, for example in the Federal Republic of Germany, the Netherlands, and the People's Republic of China, also support national audiovisual centers which may or may not include any responsibility for film or broadcasting. Singapore has moved its Division of Educational Technology into its Curriculum Development Institute, while India has a Center for Educational Technology within the National Council for Educational Research and Training. Japan has an office for audiovisual education within the Ministry of Education, and Israel has a National Center, supporting pedagogic centers at the regional level, located within the Ministry of Education and Culture.

National institutions are most prominent in the United States in the area of libraries and information science. In addition to the famous Library of Congress, there is an associated National Information Center for Educational Media (NICEM), a National Commission on Libraries and Information Science to provide policy advice to government, and a nationally coordinated network of 16 Educational Resources Information Centers (ERIC) (see *Educational Resources Information Center (ERIC)*).

The most all-embracing national center for educational technology is probably the Institute for School Equipment and Educational Technology of the Soviet Union Academy of Pedagogical Services (Kerr 1982) which undertakes basic research, media production, and instructional design on a substantial scale. This contrasts with the very small Council for Educational Technology in the United Kingdom, where, in keeping with the decentralized character of the school system, a government-financed but independent council with a core of administrative staff provides leadership in the field, advises central and local government, and gets additional finance for special separately approved projects (Hubbard 1981).

3. Professional Associations and Nongovernmental Organizations

Professional associations play a particularly important role in the dissemination of knowledge about educational technology. The majority of journals in the field are published by such associations. Their membership also comprises a larger number of professionals working outside higher education than many comparable organizations. Membership is largely confined to a single country with the exception of strong Canadian participation in organizations in the United States and European and Commonwealth participation in the United Kingdom-based Association for Educational and Training Technology.

Nongovernmental organizations range from a quasigovernmental consortium, such as the Agency for Instructional Television (AIT) which serves the United States and Canada, through trade associations like the Canadian Book Publishers Council, to special interest groups like Action for Children's Television. Charitable foundations such as Ford in the United States and Nuffield in the United Kingdom have also played a particularly significant part in the development of educational technology.

4. Units Located within Business or Industry

Educational technology is being applied in business and industry in ever-increasing ways. In fact, many training programs in business and industry use a higher degree of educational technology than do schools, colleges, and universities. Sometimes the degree of specialization is also highly advanced, especially where complicated simulations or computer-based training are involved. Several units located within business or industry have national reputations outside their parent companies and contribute to conferences and journals on a significant scale.

5. Corporations Selling Educational Technology Services

Apart from the educational equipment and publishing industries and the more commercially oriented higher education centers, there are several firms which develop educational technology programs for business, industry, education, and government. The largest of these firms employ a wide range of technologists—instructional designers, writers, editors, graphic artists, test and measurement specialists, and printers. These proprietory companies generally use consultants as subject matter experts because of the wide variety of their clients. A significant proportion of the training in the United States military is designed by proprietory corporations, but few other countries have a similar degree of private sector involvement. However, it is common for such firms to design training or assist in its development within the industrial and commercial sectors of a number of countries. Other services frequently provided by proprietory corporations include cost-effectiveness studies of training; evaluation of techniques like testing procedures, analyzing jobs and duties, producing training manuals, and evaluating trainers; and serving as consultants to personnel producing training materials.

6. International Centers

International centers of activity include the various United Nations agencies, several nongovernmental organizations, an increasing number of regional organizations and national institutions whose prime purpose is to provide aid and develop international links. Within the United Nations, UNESCO's Division of Structures, Content, Methods, and Techniques of Education has a major responsibility for educational technology; but significant units also exist within the International Labour Organization (ILO), the Food and Agriculture Organization (FAO), the World Health Organization (WHO), and a number of smaller United Nations agencies (Dieuziede 1976). A number of nongovernmental and regional organizations are linked to UNESCO through membership of the International Film and Television Council. This council of about 40 organizations includes among its members the regional broadcasting organizations for Asia (ABU) and Europe (EBU) and the International Council for Educational Media (ICEM). ICEM promotes worldwide contacts among media professionals and has also assisted UNESCO in a series of comparative studies on the administration of audiovisual services in advanced and developing countries.

Other nonregional centers of international activity include professional associations such as the International Association for the Study and Promotion of Audio-visual Methods and confederations of associations such as the International Federation of Library Associations and Institutions (IFLA). The Center for Educational Research and Innovation (CERI) of the Organisation for Economic Co-operation and Development (OECD) also has an important educational technology program.

At the regional level, the UNESCO regional centers in Bangkok and Dakar have strong educational technology programs. The Arab League Educational, Cultural, and Scientific Organization (ALECSO) established an Arab States Educational Media Center in Kuwait in 1976, and the South East Asian Ministers of Education Organization (SEAMEO) established a Regional Centre for Educational Innovation and Technology (INNOTECH) in 1970.

National Agencies with an international brief include both those specifically concerned with educational technology, such as the Japanese Council of Educational Technology Centers which provides consulting assistance throughout Asia, and educational technology divisions within larger organizations such as the United States Agency for International Development (AID) and the British Council.

Bibliography

Dieuzeide H 1976 Education and training for development: Towards united technologies in the UN? *International Yearbook of Educational and Instructional Technology 1976/77.* Kogan Page, London
Educational Media Yearbook. Association for Educational Communications and Technology (AECT)/Libraries Unlimited, Littleton, Colorado
Hubbard G 1981 Educational technology in the United Kingdom. *Educational Media Yearbook 1981.* Libraries Unlimited, Littleton, Colorado
International Yearbook of Educational and Instructional Technology. Kogan Page, London
Kerr S T 1982 Innovation on command: Instructional development and educational technology in the Soviet Union. *Educ. Commun. Technol. J.* 30: 98–116

Local Centers

W. E. Hug

Local centers for educational technology are considered as units below the national, regional, or state level and above the level of the individual school. In North America, local centers have a variety of titles—learning resource center, district media center, media/library services—and are usually located in the system's administrative offices. In Europe, some of the functions of such centers may be found in other units. The various states in Australia set standards for resources and educational technology but do not mandate local centers. The functions and activities described herein are more typical for local centers in North America than for other parts of the world, because in North America local centers are more abundant, tend to be discrete administrative units, and have a clearer mission.

The purpose of these centers for educational technology is to promote learning through the systematic identification, development, and utilization of a full range of human, material, and physical resources. To fulfill this mission the center usually establishes a division of labor that brings to bear knowledge about the nature of the learner, the teacher, the system, the media, and people's perceptual systems, as well as methodological problems such as sequencing of instruction. Such centers employ an eclectic, pragmatic philosophy to accomplish their purposes.

1. Functions and Activities

Four functions are generally visible in well-developed local centers—management and administration, instructional development, information services, and media production.

1.1 Management and Administration

Management tasks include developing a philosophy of service, setting goals and priorities, developing a long-range plan, and evaluating programs and personnel. Most local centers have advisory committees that assist in these activities. These committees are usually composed of persons who represent the user population—students, teachers, principals, administrators, and members of the community.

Administration includes duties that ensure that plans and services developed by management are implemented. Typical tasks include supervising production, circulation of machines and materials, and maintaining work flow.

An important activity associated with management and administration involves working with the individual schools and the community since they provide both resources and support for local centers for educational technology. These activities point to the leadership role expected of management and administrative personnel.

1.2 Instructional Development

The close relationships between educational technology and instructional development are discussed in other articles. Here it may be noted that many local educational technology centers engage in at least some instructional development activities, especially those located in the affluent suburbs of large cities. Typically they will stress the systems approach to instructional development, rather than cognitive approaches.

1.3 Information Services

Local centers for educational technology have a broad view of the critical nature of information, and are intimately concerned with making it more widely available in the most appropriate and useful form. This concern, allied to rapid changes in information technology, has led to the merging in many districts of what had previously been two distinct forms of activity: media services and library services (see *School Libraries/Resource Centers*). In districts where these services are still separate, it is usual for the media center to handle the more complex nonprint materials such as 16mm motion pictures and videocassettes, and to provide technical assistance with the associated equipment. This responsibility may extend to reprographic equipment and even to word processors.

Local centers are likely to be the agency for district participation in television distribution systems and information networks, and for maintaining links with regional centers, where they exist.

Still another important aspect of information services is machine distribution and maintenance. Media equipment includes 35mm slide, overhead, 8mm and 16mm film, and video projectors. Also common are microform readers, record players, public address systems, audio and video recorders and players, cameras, and speech compressors. Local centers usually maintain records on such equipment so that they can estimate maintenance costs and project costs for needed replacements as machines are retired.

Professionals working in information services of local centers also play a consultative role, helping teachers and students utilize the various pieces of communication equipment and the accompanying software. These professionals frequently conduct workshops and assist individuals to use media in the most appropriate and effective way. The services usually include alerting teachers and other educational professionals to new materials on the market and recently acquired materials. Local centers encourage other school personnel to preview materials before use as well as to preview materials for purchase.

1.4 Media Production

Local centers usually have much more sophisticated production facilities than the individual schools. For example, many have both television and radio production capabilities.

Many educational systems use their local centers to print, duplicate, and distribute curriculum materials in many formats. These centers frequently have the capability of typesetting, editing, mimeographing and spirit duplicating, visualizing, offset and letterpress printing, and binding. Word processing is also common in preparation of printed materials in local centers. Some centers have the ability to create covers for books and to make posters and other items through processes like silkscreen reproductions.

Most local centers have the capacity to produce a variety of photographic materials. These usually include producing black and white and color negatives and prints, color 35mm slides, overhead transparencies, 8mm and 16mm motion pictures, microforms, and filmstrips.

Original artwork is rarely produced in the individual schools; however, such work is common in local centers. Graphic artists create original illustrations, design graphs and charts, make posters and signs, design and layout materials for reproduction, and create computer graphics.

Production of audio materials includes creating masters for reel to reel and cassette tape playback units, audiotape duplication, and programming for single and multiple screen programs.

2. Types of Local Center

A full range of centers exist from those having developed all functions to those engaging in only a few activities under a single function. Some systems perform functions normally associated with local centers in different administrative units. For example, the printing of educational materials is sometimes carried out in a department of curriculum development within the system. Other centers provide little if any material support yet maintain a professional staff to work with schools in developing functions associated with local centers. In centers with limited functions, the most frequently promoted services include: circulation and maintenance of a film library, a professional collection of books and periodicals for use by central-office staff and teachers of the system, a production facility, and a circulation and maintenance system for media and machines not commonly found in schools. In addition, local centers with limited services usually provide technicians who can make repairs on communication equipment for schools.

Coordinators or directors of fully developed local centers frequently hold the position of assistant or associate superintendent of schools and function in the highest governing bodies of the educational system. Such coordinators manage all functions of local centers while other administrators are responsible for specific functions commonly grouped in divisions. The staff may include a wide array of personnel such as instructional designers, test and measurement experts, writers, editors, graphic artists, photographers, and computer programmers. Well-developed centers usually have budgets which permit hiring consultants and purchasing services that are not provided for in the local center. For example, a college specialist in social studies might be employed to help produce a series of units for the high-school curriculum.

At the opposite extreme, the most minimal center might have a clerk who is responsible for a few activities, such as acquiring and circulating a collection of books for use by the professional staff of the school system. This individual's immediate supervisor might be a secretary. In somewhat more developed local centers the coordinator operates at the level of a subject supervisor or consultant which is considered a level between building-level principals and assistant and associate superintendents.

The separation of activities associated with print media from those activities associated with nonprint media is becoming less and less common in North America. National and international associations have recommended the merger of both functions into local centers under one administrative unit as have state, province, and national legislations. Under these more comprehensive units the personnel, material, and physi-cal resources can develop the broad functions that describe information and educational technology.

3. Problems in Local Center Development

In North America, the pattern has been to merge separate departments within the system. For example, an audiovisual distribution system, a systemwide professional library, and a department for media production would be combined into a local center for educational technology. These mergers obviously resulted in power struggles in many instances and a shift in policy by the governing body of the educational system.

Another problem that local centers face is the lack of understanding of center operations by teachers and school administrators. "The greatest misfortune...is the lack of acceptance, understanding, and respect on the part of teachers and administrators" (Shapiro 1979 p. 26). Similar findings were reported in studies made in Houston, Texas, and in a study conducted by the Massachusetts Institute of Technology (Mugnier 1979 p. 19–23).

Perhaps an even greater problem is a lack of general understanding of the concept of educational technology on the part of most school personnel. Various centers tended to define educational technology in a way that reflected their restricted view. Time has helped correct this problem with the assistance of over 300 colleges and universities in North America preparing professionals in educational technology.

More recently, funding has become a major problem. As inflation raises the costs of machines and materials, and as wage levels rise, less and less money is available to support local centers. This tends to be less of a problem in well-developed centers that have carefully articulated their services with the educational programs of their constituent schools, the reason being that such centers are considered a critical rather than an auxiliary service that teachers could do without.

4. Issues in Local Centers

Many issues exist, some of which may be resolved by professional organizations while others may be resolved by forces outside the educational system. Some may never be resolved. Issues involve terminology used in the field, role and training of personnel in local centers, cooperation and networking among information services agencies, censorship, role of national and international organizations, high technology, and school organization.

4.1 Terminology

At least two basic issues exist with regard to terminology: the use of certain terms and the number of synonyms that exist. For example, professionals trained in educational technology think first of technology as a process or technique for accomplishing some task. On the other hand, educators and the public at large think of hardware—satellites, telephones, and assembly lines. Another example is the use of the term media. The profession defines media as "all of the forms and channels used in the transmittal process" (AASL/AECT 1975 p. 109). However, other education professionals as well as members of the community think of newspapers and television when they think of media; they see mass media and media as one and the same.

4.2 Role of Personnel in Local Centers

Most personnel managing local centers are educated in departments of educational technology in colleges of education. These personnel tend to view themselves as specialized educators. On the other hand, library schools also produce personnel serving in local centers. They tend to think of themselves as specialized librarians. Compounding the issues raised by these two points of view is the school administrator's lack of understanding of the role and technical operations of local centers. The academic preparation of administrators makes little mention of principles of management as they are applied in the operation of local centers.

These different views create a basic issue. What constitutes legitimate activity in local centers for educational technology?

In the United States the personnel situation is further complicated by the uncoordinated nature of accreditation and certification procedures. The National Council for the Accreditation of Teacher Education (NCATE) accredits college of education programs preparing professionals to work in local centers. Programs found in library schools are accredited by the American Library Association (ALA). To complicate matters, both programs in colleges of education and in library schools must undergo approval by the individual states where the programs exist. Each of these three groups—NCATE, ALA, and state departments of education—exist for somewhat different purposes and have different expectations. This situation creates a number of issues that tend to block efforts to bring into clear focus the role of local centers.

The fact that each of the states requires the professionals working in local centers to have state certificates in order to practice also creates several problems. One problem relates to the great variation in the requirements among the states. These variations create difficulties with the reciprocity of certificates when a professional moves from one state to another or when local center personnel are trained in an out-of-state institution. Another problem is the length of time involved in effecting the changes in state legislation that are needed to keep abreast of the rapidly changing role of local centers.

4.3 Cooperation and Networking

Local centers are expected to cooperate with other information agencies such as public libraries and to participate in information networks. Issues that surround cooperation and networking include overcoming psychological and legal barriers, funding, and planning.

Psychological barriers are directly tied to attitudes of local center staff as well as personnel in other information agencies. Too many reasons for not cooperating seem to overpower perceived benefits. In addition, making available vast databases poses copyright and royalty problems. Funding and planning also raise numerous issues as to who should do what and who should pay for what. Center personnel agree that cooperating and networking have enormous benefits yet most are individually afraid to become involved.

4.4 Censorship

When selection, circulation, and withdrawal of material in local centers is influenced by political, religious, or other groups, the centers are being censored. Extreme examples exist. Groups have requested that the Bible be placed on an adult reading list, and some dictionaries have been banned in Texas because they contain "bad words." Because most material has the potential of being offensive to someone, objections frequently come unexpectedly and quickly bring out differences within the community at the expense of local centers.

Local centers should have a written policy statement on procedures for selecting, circulating, and withdrawing materials. When censors come, they should put their concerns in writing, and the local center should follow an established procedure in each case. Unfortunately, the basic issue may never be resolved. What are the ultimate criteria for determining content of materials found in local centers and who should be responsible for applying these criteria?

4.5 High Technology

Developing technology will change many basic routines for everyone in increasingly dramatic ways. The use of computers to access information from the growing number of databases and the capacity of videodiscs to store information are changing basic concepts of information storage and retrieval. Personal computers are bringing these resources directly into the home and changing the way people shop, compose, copy, scan newspapers, and conduct research. Using videodiscs and microcomputers can reduce the proliferation of formats, access enormous collections of still and moving images, reduce costs, and increase flexibility in using educational materials. When this technology is in place, it may change the role of local centers in dramatic ways. Implications for collections development and for storage and retrieval are a case in point. In the future any student, teacher, or administrator may have easy access to most films, telecasts, filmstrips, records, tapes, books, magazines, or other media.

When this occurs, local centers may no longer need to maintain collections of materials and machines for circulation. Will these centers become expert in programming computers to access materials from videodiscs for individual schools? Will local centers expand their instructional design and curriculum production efforts? Will personnel in local centers play a leadership role in conceptualizing what schools will ultimately develop? Will they become "resource thinkers" rather than "resource warehouses"? Or, will they be eliminated since the new technology is available to everyone?

4.6 School Organization

Largely because schools are organized around the concept of a class directed by a teacher, more cost-effective educational systems have failed to develop. Theoretically, as local centers produce more and more autotutorial materials, a greater number of the programs associated with the traditional classroom should be replaced. This would mean that local centers would receive increased budgets and savings accrued from expenditures in local schools. This trade-off is common in business and industry and is one reason why educational technology is increasingly more popular in those sectors.

The issues that develop from these concepts relate to how traditional structures can be replaced to allow for development. This is where power, control, and school organization become critical to realizing the potential of both local centers and high technology.

5. Research and Local Centers

What research is produced or utilized in local centers for educational technology depends upon the operation of the center. If a large part of a particular center's activity is devoted to creating educational programs, then much of the research discussed becomes important. In addition, research in the area of management becomes more and more useful as local centers expand into complex organizations.

Research that is concerned with the program of a local center for educational technology tends to draw broadly from more general educational research. The reason for this is that any research that assesses the effect of the school and district environment on learning has implications for the local center. Several studies have demonstrated that the presence of a local center improved the instructional program. Some research shows that an important function of local centers is the integration and articulation of center services and the local curriculum. The way media are introduced in teaching and learning activities appears critical.

Another body of research concerns user services and how they impact on clients of local centers. This research studies policies and procedures that improve or hamper user satisfaction. They also analyze statistical data for the purpose of making local center operations more cost effective and for justifying their existence.

The quality of research conducted by local centers tends to be uneven and sometimes misleading. For example, countless studies have tried to demonstrate that one media is better than another—programmed instruction is better than a lecture, television is better

than printed messages. Again, the various media have different capacities which probably make all media better for some messages and worse for others (see *Media Selection*).

The widespread use of instruments for planning and evaluation constitutes another body of research. Several schemes are used nationwide, and many states have produced procedures and instruments for evaluating centers for educational technology on several levels. Some states require specific procedures and services from schools and districts for accreditation.

Although the research is not as abundant as everyone would like, it does provide a useful body of information for helping centers to improve their contributions to the educational program. One critical need is to improve the quality of research in and about local centers. The development of doctoral programs in educational technology has greatly contributed to reaching this goal. Also needed is research that concentrates on the effect of the presence or absence of services offered by local centers.

6. Literature on Local Centers

The literature that details operations of local centers generally falls into one of three categories—management and administration, production, and instructional design and development. Materials devoted to center administration tend to provide guidelines for particular operations such as planning, acquisitioning, budgeting, production, reference, storage and retrieval, evaluation, research and development, and maintenance. Materials on production tend to provide references for various production techniques, such as all of the ways to produce overhead transparencies. Materials on instructional design tend to be a set of prescriptive procedures for creating and validating an instructional sequence.

Media Programs: District and School (ALA/AECT 1975) provides guidelines for functions and operations of local centers for educational technology. This book presents a set of national guidelines useful to states developing standards of their own. As a result of this work, many states have publications that present guidelines or set standards for local centers. Many books are currently on the market that provide assistance in the details of center operations, including Brown et al. (1972), Brown et al. (1983), Erickson (1968), and Chisholm and Ely (1976). However, some tend to be oriented toward school libraries while others are oriented toward audiovisual materials.

The literature dealing with production is vast since it deals with all aspects of all media. The most useful general reference is *Planning and Producing Audiovisual Material* (Kemp 1980). This work presents a philosophy and techniques for using media, summarizes research in the design of material, and provides easy-to-follow, well-illustrated guides for producing most media appropriate for local centers. More detailed advice on production and instructional design can be found in later sections of this *Encyclopedia*.

Bibliography

American Association of School Librarians (AASL)/Association for Educational Communications and Technology (AECT) 1975 *Media Programs: District and School*. AASL/AECT, Chicago, Illinois

Brown J W, Lewis R B, Harcleroad F F 1983 AV *Instruction: Technology Media and Methods*, 6th edn. McGraw-Hill, New York

Brown J W, Norberg K D, Srygley S K 1972 *Administering Educational Media: Instructional Technology and Library Services*, 2nd edn. McGraw-Hill, New York

Chisholm M E, Ely D P 1976 *Media Personnel in Education: A Competency Approach*. Prentice Hall, Englewood Cliffs, New Jersey

Erickson C W H 1968 *Administering Instructional Media Programs*. Macmillan, New York

Hug W E 1975 *Instructional Design and the Media Program*. American Library Association (ALA)/Association for Educational Communications and Technology (AECT), Chicago, Illinois

Kemp J E 1980 *Planning and Producing Audiovisual Materials*, 4th edn. Harper and Row, New York

Mugnier C 1979 Views on school librarianship and library education. *Sch. Libr. J.* 26: 19–23

Shapiro L L 1979 Celebrations and condolences: A time of reckoning for the school library. *Sch. Libr. J.* 26: 13–18

Higher Education Support Services

G. D. Moss

This entry describes the varying nature of teaching support services available in higher education, ranging from the advice given to teaching staff on their teaching problems, to the design and production of specific teaching resource materials. The organization and management of such support services are examined with the intention of relating their characteristic features to their function. Then the attitudes of teaching staff towards support services are discussed, and the costs of such services and the problems of staffing service centres are examined. Finally, the potential future of educational technology units in higher education is briefly considered.

1. Role Definition

There are two clearly defined roles which have been assumed by teaching support services and educational technology units in higher education (Hewton et al. 1975).

On the one hand are those support units which seek to further the professional development of the staff of the institution in relation to their role as teachers. Such units offer consultancy, training, advice, and resource support on general issues faced by the teaching staff arising from the teaching–learning process. These might include recommendations on the optimum uses to be made of various teaching strategies such as small-group tutorials, lectures, games and simulations, and problem-solving activities (Moss and McMillen 1980). They also offer guidance to staff on issues which are directly related to the teaching–learning process, but which are not an immediate part of it; such as student counselling, student assessment, and the psychology of how students learn. Some offer direct guidance to students on learning problems (Gibbs 1981).

The second major group of support activities are usually referred to as educational technology, instructional resources, or audiovisual services. Their early development is charted by Mackenzie et al. (1970), who also draw attention to the differing conceptions of educational technology. In particular they distinguish between the use of technology in education, as evidenced by increasingly complex audiovisual equipment and computers, and the idea of developing a technology of education which is concerned with the broader aspect of the systematic design, production, and evaluation of learning systems, regardless of whether those systems employ audiovisual equipment or not.

Regardless of their philosophy of educational technology, most centres bearing that name are usually well-equipped with closed-circuit television, audio, photographic, cine-photographic, graphic, and reprographic facilities. As well as having the capacity to design and produce learning resources, many of them are also involved in their presentation either to large classes or to individual students in learning centres. The latter are often associated with the provision of multimedia library facilities.

In many institutions around the world, teaching service units take on the dual role of consultant–adviser on teaching–learning problems and specialist producer of learning resources. It is therefore not possible to identify the precise role of the unit from its name. For example, the Institute of Educational Technology at the Open University of the United Kingdom is a specialized research and evaluation unit which contains no large-scale production facilities for audiovisual aids (although these may be designed and evaluated there) while the Centre for the Advancement of Learning and Teaching at Griffith University in Queensland, Australia, has extensive audiovisual support facilities.

Widespread development of educational technology units is much less marked in the Third World nations. While Ronchi (1980) reports on 16 specific centres for educational technology in Argentina, only three of these are in higher education. Oliveira (1980) states that educational technology has had "little impact" on graduate-level education in Brazil. This may be because the emerging nations take a much more global view of the role and potential benefits of educational technology in their educational systems. This has resulted in major programmes related to staff training for curriculum development such as that reported by Rojas (1980) for Panama and Venezuela.

This centralization of effort is also reflected in the Arab world where Al-Araby (1977) stresses the need to establish "one central institution to offer services, disseminate information, and send consultants to all Arab countries which request assistance".

Soremekun (1979) describes the development of educational technology units in Nigerian universities on a pattern similar to that in the United Kingdom, the major constraints on development being adequately trained personnel, traditional bureaucratic practices, and financial restrictions.

2. Organization and Management of Service Units

2.1 Organization

In higher education in the United Kingdom, the central service unit is separate from the teaching department in its organization within the institution. Usually the head of the unit is an academic member of staff. Of the 44 service units in the United Kingdom, 27 of their heads have academic status (Stephen and Daniels 1976). The heads manage the centres, and are usually responsible to a management committee set up by the institution. Policy issues and requests for resources (both staff and financial) are handled by such committees. If the head of the centre is not academic then he or she is usually on an academically related salary scale with only a minority of centres being run by heads on an administrative salary scale.

The separation of the service units from the teaching departments was an essential feature of their development. The traditional user of such services is prepared to go to "neutral" ground for advice and assistance, but would probably be less prepared to do so were the centre part of a specific teaching department or faculty. However, this fundamental reason for being seen to be a separate organization has often resulted in the service unit being left outside of the main institutional decision-making and resource-allocating procedures which are largely faculty based. Thus, in the most recent survey, only 16 of the 44 United Kingdom universities' heads were members of the senate of their institution, and only 14 of them have representation on faculties (Stephen and Daniels 1976).

A further problem in both the developing and the developed countries is that the centralized unit may well be replicating facilities which some departments have had for many years. For example, it is quite common to find science departments which have photographic and sometimes even graphic facilities. In times of plentiful financial resources this does not present a problem, but when resource provision becomes a limiting factor, then antagonisms may arise within the institution as to the most cost-effective way of providing a particular service. Significantly, these areas of dispute tend to centre around technical services and technical personnel. However, it is not only the need for cost-effective services which is affecting the centralization of educational technology facilities. The pace of change is such that non-specialists find it increasingly difficult to keep abreast of recent developments. Information technology, computer-assisted learning, and interactive video systems (Copeland 1983) are obvious areas where specialist technical support is essential.

However, it is also quite possible that within specialist subject teaching areas, specific audiovisual provision may be made on site. For example, the widespread use of video distribution systems in science teaching laboratories and specialized facilities for language teaching.

2.2 Personnel

In a central service unit fulfilling all of the roles outlined above, the staff are likely to have very varied backgrounds and qualifications. Indeed one feature of the service units that stands out when they are compared with the teaching departments is the variety of expertise and experience demonstrated by the former.

Staff involved in consultancy and advice work are likely to have a minimum qualification of a subject specialist first degree, and probably a higher degree or other qualification related directly to education. They may well be involved in their own research areas and such staff are probably closest to the academic stereotype of the teaching departments. However, they are also likely to be specialists in and advocates of a variety of pedagogical techniques.

Staff involved in the design and production of learning materials, particularly of audiovisual materials, are likely to have a less academic, more technical background and may well have joined the unit from the commercial world. This is particularly true of the technical staff needed to operate and maintain the production equipment. Problems may be generated here by their status (usually equivalent to technical staff in teaching departments) which in many cases does not truly reflect the creative nature of their work.

Finally, the centre may be involved in the storage, retrieval, and presentation of nonbook materials or multimedia materials in a library context. Where this is the case then the organizational skills of library and information science are essential.

Clarke (1982), identifies four levels of expertise (professional and managerial, skilled technical, technical, and unskilled) which are essential for the operation of an audiovisual production unit, while Tucker (1979) prefers to group staff according to their job role. Certainly it is not possible to define a managerial structure which is common to all such service units. Perhaps the classification of Collier (1981) into managerial, production, and academic staff is the only one which can be universally applied.

3. Models of Operation

In general there are two models of operation which may be adopted by central service units; the prescriptive model and the reactive model. Staff development activities are both prescriptive (as when short training courses or seminars are offered to teaching staff) and reactive (as when the service unit is approached by an individual member of teaching staff with a specific teaching problem). In contrast, the role of the educational technology units, in terms of the production of teaching materials, is largely that of reacting to the teaching needs of the staff. However, such units are prescriptive in specifying the audiovisual hardware systems (such as video replay standard, nature of tape–slide facilities, etc.), which are employed in the host institution.

The forms of audiovisual support given by centralized educational technology units may relate to the acquisition of equipment and materials, the production of learning materials, and the storage and presentation of learning materials.

Centralized acquisition of materials and equipment is an important role for the educational technology centre since the variety of equipment on the market can bewilder the enthusiastic amateur as well as the average faculty teacher. Centralized purchasing of major items of equipment such as television monitors, videocassette recorders, slide projectors, and audio recorders, can result in substantial financial discounts. However, there are many additional benefits, since standardized equipment allows the centre to hold a limited stock of clearly defined spare parts and accessories—even replacement equipment if necessary—which can be used to maintain the operational state of the teaching equipment in the institution. Centralized purchasing also ensures that the amateur purchaser is not "seduced" into buying an item which is less than ideal for his or her needs, thanks to the pressure from the salesperson. This particular activity is even more relevant in institutions in developing countries where the supply of equipment and materials may be less regular than in Western Europe.

The production of learning materials may range from the generation of slides or overhead projector transparencies from artwork and other sources, to the preparation of tape–slide programmes, 16mm cine films, educational videotapes, and so on. A typical production centre is likely to have at least one graphic artist experienced in preparing diagrams and captions for photography or in preparing associated worksheets and handouts for reprography. The graphic artist, is in many ways the "eye of the needle" since he or she is essential in providing additional pictorial material and

high-quality captions and displays. Very few of the teaching staff in higher education have the graphic skills necessary to produce high-quality artwork themselves.

Even a small centre will also possess a photographic suite equipped to prepare slides and prints and to offer specialist location camerawork when necessary. When this is combined with relatively simple audio recording facilities then the institution has the capacity to produce handouts, slides, tape–slide programmes, audio cassettes, and so on for a relatively modest cost. This probably represents the type of facility which is easiest to install and operate, both in terms of cost and specialist labour (see *Photographic Production*).

However, when the problems of 16mm cine and videotape production are considered, then both cost and essential expertise become significant factors. A typical medium-size educational technology centre is able to offer colour videotape recording facilities, either on location or in a studio situation. The basic cost of video cameras, recorders, editing suites, time-based correction facilities, production quality monitors, etc., is likely to be in the region of £60,000–£120,000 at 1987 prices. In addition, such equipment requires specialist maintenance and trained operators if it is to provide a reliable service. Such operators are likely to have good technical qualifications in further or higher education as well as extensive production experience. This is a vitally important consideration, often ignored by institutions in the Third World which have acquired prestigious technical facilities, but have no-one to operate them.

Once learning materials have been produced then the central service unit may be responsible for their presentation. In its simplest form of presentation, staff from the centre may equip and service teaching rooms with appropriate projectors, screens, and related audiovisual hardware. This would be directly related to the presentation of materials, such as tape–slide programmes or films, to large groups of students in lectures. While this may seem a fairly obvious consideration, it is surprising to find many modern teaching rooms to be poorly designed in this respect (see *Learning Environments*). An alternative presentation arrangement may be via the encouragement of self-study provision, either in the teaching departments, in the centre itself or in the institution library. Harris and Kirkhope (1978) report on the use of largely print-based study packs in the library of the University of Bath and found that these were well-received by students who used them as support resource material for essays and related course work. The educational technology centres become more involved when institutions adopt multimedia self-instructional systems in special learning libraries. Gabb (1978) and Roach and Hammond (1976) both report successful adaptations of the audiotutorial approach (Postlethwait et al. 1972) in which audiovisual media are employed alongside self-instructional booklets and related laboratory activities. In both cases students were particularly appreciative of the self-paced aspect of the course and the qualities of the audiovisual support materials (see *Individualized Instruction in Higher Education*).

Clearly, where there is extensive audiovisual support for a course so that the audiovisual materials are closely integrated as part of the learning experience, then more is needed than technical proficiency in production. The project must be overseen by a producer/designer who is able not only to coordinate production of materials within the centre, but also to liaise with members of the teaching staff and identify the particular needs of the course involved. Ideally, the producer will have had teaching experience in higher education. This close cooperation between the subject teacher and the media specialist is already marked in the area of tape–slide, film, and television production and is likely to be emphasized even further during the development of computer-aided learning materials (Rushby 1979) .

It can be seen therefore that the interaction of a central educational technology centre with a subject teacher can vary from the straightforward supply of a simple teaching aid, such as a slide, to the coordinated production of multimedia learning packages. The development of distance learning systems requires a still more complex level of interaction (see *Distance Learning Systems*).

4. Resource Implications

In terms of recurrent annual expenditure, central service units in universities in the United Kingdom consume from 0.5 to 1.5 percent of the overall annual costs of the institution. This figure covers staff salaries and recurrent consumable and maintenance costs, but excludes capital equipment costs. One feature of the high operating costs is related to the necessity to employ specialist staff at all levels. Academic staff involved in training and consultancy work are likely to have previous experience as subject specialist teachers in higher education, and are therefore well-placed in the salary scale. Specialist technical support in the area of graphics, photography, and television in particular, may only be secured if the salaries paid are competitive with those of the world of commerce. These factors, together with the high maintenance costs incurred by using sophisticated projection and recording equipment, can often result in the overall operating costs being considerably higher than those incurred by similar-sized teaching departments.

One significant factor which is often neglected, is the need for an educational development fund and resources to enable faculty to get part-time release for working on new courses and developing learning resources. At the Tertiary Education Institute of the University of Queensland, the budget of the institute is sufficient to allow it to "sponsor" educational developments within the university on a regular basis, and similar arrangements can be found in many North American universities.

5. The Future

It would be nice to think that the development of centralized teaching support services was determined only by the effectiveness of the services offered. Sadly this is not the case at present when much of the provision in this area is being reduced for reasons of political and financial expediency. However, it is worthwhile to try and identify current developments which are likely to have a significant impact in higher education beyond the 1980s. On the technical side, advances in microcomputer and video technology will see the development of self-instructional systems with extensive interactive facilities, and this is likely to be paralleled by the introduction to libraries of new forms of information technology. On the instructional side, new research into student learning styles and study techniques is likely to influence the ways in which teaching courses and learning materials and experiences are designed. To what extent service units are influenced by the technological changes (and attempt to produce teaching materials to fit the new systems) or the developments in our knowledge of how students learn (and attempt to produce teaching materials to fit the learners) remains to be seen.

Bibliography

Al-Araby S A 1977 Educational media for the Arab World: The Arab States Educational Media Centre. *Aspects Educ. Technol.* 11: 45–49

Clarke J 1982 *Resource Based Learning for Higher and Continuing Education.* Croom Helm, London

Collier G 1981 *Teaching and Learning Support Services.* Vol. 1: *Higher Education.* Council for Educational Technology, London

Copeland P 1983 The Cavis system: A new level of interactive video. *Br. J. Educ. Technol.* 14 (1): 59–65

Gabb R G 1978 Student rating of the components of a successful self-instructional course. *Program. Learn. Educ. Technol.* 78: 284–90

Gibbs G 1981 *Teaching Students to Learn: A Student-centred Approach.* Open University Press, Milton Keynes

Harris N D C, Kirkhope S M 1978 Uses of, and students' reactions to, study packs as self-instructional material in the library. *Program. Learn. Educ. Technol.* 15: 262–70

Hewton E, Becher T, Parlett M, Simons H 1975 *Supporting Teaching for a Change: A Report.* Nuffield Foundation, London

Mackenzie N I, Eraut M, Jones H C 1970 *Teaching and Learning: An Introduction to New Methods and Resources in Higher Education.* UNESCO, Paris

Moss G D, McMillen D 1980 A strategy for developing problem-solving skills in large undergraduate classes. *Stud. Higher Educ.* 5: 161–71

Oliveira J B A 1980 The status of educational technology in Brazil. *Program. Learn. Educ. Technol.* 17: 210–17

Postlethwait S N, Novak J, Murray H T 1972 *The Audio-tutorial Approach to Learning, through Independent Study and Integrated Experiences*, 3rd edn. Burgess, Minneapolis, Minnesota

Roach D K, Hammond R 1976 Zoology by self-instruction. *Stud. Higher Educ.* 1: 179–96

Rojas A M 1980 An innovative project in educational technology: The Panama–Venezuela project. *Program. Learn. Educ. Technol.* 17: 239–45

Ronchi R 1980 Educational technology in Argentina. *Program. Learn. Educ. Technol.* 17: 201–09

Rushby N J 1979 *An Introduction to Educational Computing.* Croom Helm, London

Soremekun E A 1979 Factors affecting the development and use of educational technology in Nigerian universities. *Br. J. Educ. Technol.* 10: 217–28

Stephen K D, Daniels V A 1976 *Central Service Units in UK Universities.* Council for Educational Technology, London

Tucker R N 1979 *The Organisation and Management of Educational Technology.* Croom Helm, London

Higher Education Consultancy

E. Hewton

A consultant is normally defined as a person who is consulted or asked for advice; the person or persons asking for advice or consulting being described as clients. Educational consultancy services provide access to consultants for advice about educational matters; and in higher education they are usually focused on teaching and problems relating to teaching. Such services are provided by appointing one or more full-time or part-time consultants, and may be integrated with, or distinct from other teaching support services.

This article is in four parts: (a) who are the consultants? (b) what is their role? (c) who are the clients? and (d) the organizational context.

1. Who Are the Consultants?

It is not possible to quantify the number of consultants practising in higher education, and identification would not, in any case, be easy for not all roles bear the title "consultant" and many of those acting within the broad rubric of teaching support services would regard consultancy as part of their job.

It is apparent from a number of surveys and discussions—for example, Nuffield Foundation (1975), Commonwealth Secretariat (1978), Greenaway and Harding (1978), Teather (1979), Eraut et al. (1980), Matheson (1981)—that consultancy, in one form or another (often linked with staff development), is now common in many institutions in the United Kingdom, the United States, Canada, Australia, New Zealand, and several Third World countries. It would seem that consultants are usually attached to units carrying any one of the following titles: educational development unit; centre (or institute) for educational technology; teaching and learning support service; advisory centre for university education; office for research in academic methods; educational research and resources unit; centre for advancement of learning and teaching; centre for study of higher education; higher education advisory and research unit; instructional development unit; university instructional methodology and development committee, and so on (Commonwealth Secretariat 1978).

But who are the consultants and what qualifications and training do they have? Consultancy in higher education probably originated with efforts to supply efficient media services to faculty. Units set up for this purpose mainly attracted staff from outside higher education and

recruited, for instance, television producers and media technology specialist designers. These specialists found that it was not possible to give straightforward technical answers to many complex teaching problems and they were forced to explore wider curriculum problems with their clients. As a result, some units began to employ "educationalists" from educational departments within the institution itself or academics, from other disciplinary backgrounds, who had demonstrated a particular interest in teaching and learning. This change occurred at the same time as interest in staff development was growing, and appointments were often made with this dual responsibility in mind.

Another source of recruitment was from the field of research into higher education. Some students completing their doctorates, or research fellows, previously employed by nationally funded curriculum projects, were employed for their specialist skills or knowledge acquired during their research.

As well as full-time "experts" or "specialists", many institutions involved ordinary members of faculty on a part-time, and sometimes on a purely departmental, basis to work in a consultancy role with their colleagues. Initial short-term contracts of this kind were sometimes extended into longer term involvement.

The role of consultants and consultancy units has been analysed by various writers. MacKenzie et al. (1970) discussed the part which consultants might play in course development; McMillan (1975) considered consultancy as an essential part of instructional improvement; Swain (1979) sought to identify the qualities and skills of the expert consultant; and Boud and McDonald (1982) and Hewton (1982) considered the problems which face consultants and the possibilities open to them.

It is clear from this work that consultancy involves expertise of various kinds including: a wide knowledge of research and practice in education, psychology, social psychology, and sociology; familiarity with a range of methods (quantitative and qualitative) used in the sciences and social sciences; knowledge of the various strategies available for influencing people in order to bring about change; political skills; and the ability to sustain a consultancy programme—often with minimal support and resources and sometimes against considerable resistance.

Specific training for consultants in higher education is seldom provided. The consultant learns on the job and through experience. Workshops and conferences, sometimes held for staff developers, may have something to offer the consultant, and some higher degree courses in educational technology or curriculum development may cover some aspects of the consultant's job (see, for instance, Council for Educational Technology 1982 or Eraut et al. 1980). But apart from this there is very little in the way of formal training.

2. The Role of the Consultant

Consultancy involves a working relationship between a consultant and a client or client group which directs their joint efforts towards the identification of the client's problem and a collaborative attempt by both parties to find and apply solutions to that problem. The nature of the consultancy process thus depends upon the kind of relationship established and upon the type of activities which flow from it. An important issue is the extent to which the client participates in the problem-solving process and the amount of reliance that is placed upon the consultant for providing direction, advice, and resources presents a range of possibilities. At one extreme the consultant acts as an expert, calling upon theory and research to dispense solutions, the client participating only in the sense of supplying information regarding the problem and obtaining the resources necessary for implementing the suggested changes. At the other extreme the consultant plays the role of facilitator, or "process helper", and seeks to maintain a very low profile encouraging the client to reflect carefully upon the nature of the problem and the possible alternative solutions available. A mixture of the approaches is likely to occur in practice.

Boud and McDonald (1982) suggest a number of possible models.

(a) The "professional service" model in which the consultant brings to bear "organizational and technical expertise" onto a problem defined by the client.

(b) The "counselling model" in which the consultant provides the conditions under which clients explore the problem and attempt to understand for themselves how best to deal with those which have been identified.

(c) The "colleague model" in which educational development takes place as a result of the collaboration of peers, each taking equal responsibility and each having the same stake in the outcomes.

(d) The eclectic approach in which the consultant draws upon each of these models and acts flexibly according to the demands of each situation.

The work of the consultant can be extremely varied. Eraut (1981) provides some concrete examples. In connection with the improvement of teaching skills, for instance, he points to the presentation of research findings on teaching, and to faculty interested in this field. By treating teaching almost as if it were part of the research role it is accorded a certain academic respectability. Another approach is the presentation, by a consultant, of videotaped recordings of teaching for discussion by a group of faculty. An alternative, again using the television camera, involves teachers agreeing to record and review with the consultant their own performance in a real or simulated classroom situation. This approach includes "microteaching" in its various forms (see *Conceptual and Theoretical Bases of Microteaching*). Other approaches suggested by Eraut involve groups of faculty in the discussion of teaching and learning problems and in course evaluation or institutional research.

Gaff (1979) classifies the work under three headings: instructional development, faculty development, and organizational development.

> The instructional developer helps a faculty member, or a team of teaching faculty, to specify measurable cognitive and affective objectives of student learning, design learning activities and materials relevant to the objectives, measure student accomplishment and revise the instructional sequence and procedures in light of the evaluation. (p. 237)

The roots of this approach lie in the fields of "curriculum and instruction, learning theory, educational media, and technology and system theory".

In the context of the second work category (faculty development), the consultant calls upon a range of disciplines in the social sciences. The activities in which the consultant may become engaged in this sphere include: providing knowledge about higher education; offering help and guidance in the improvement of "teaching skills"; providing "feedback about...teaching behaviour"; helping faculty towards "affective" development by examining their own attitudes, values and assumptions"; creating situations whereby teachers improve their "awareness of other disciplines and the community"; encouraging attention to "learning rather than teaching".

The intellectual roots of organizational development are found primarily in "organizational theory, organizational change and group dynamics".

> Discussions, workshops and consultation are provided to help those persons responsible for operating the organization to (a) clarify their attitudes, (b) identify various leadership styles and develop those consistent with their personalities and the needs of the organization, (c) clarify and establish organizational goals, (d) plan and conduct meetings effectively and expeditiously, and (e) manage conflict among individuals in a creative and productive manner. (p. 240)

Gaff also points out that an important element of this approach is the development of policies which support teaching improvement.

A detailed analysis of a participative approach which draws upon all three approaches mentioned above is provided by Hewton (1982). He describes the formation of working parties (or task groups) supported by consultants. The approach involves subject departments or course teams in a problem-solving exercise. The department or team identify a particular issue of concern to the group which may be to do with, for instance, teaching problems, assessment, allocation of teaching resources, and monitoring of course developments. A working party, usually of five or six members of the department or course team, is set up and is led by a member of the group. The consultant is attached to the group and works out with members a more detailed statement of the problem and the most appropriate means of investigating it. The collection of evidence, its analysis, and the eventual recommendations for action become the joint responsibility of the group as a whole. The approach seems to fit with the preferred way of working of lecturers who normally enjoy a great deal of autonomy.

3. Who Are the Clients?

In most instances, consultancy is offered primarily to teaching faculty as individuals, as course teams, or in the context of their departments' work. The offer is usually made in a policy statement or brochure and advertised through newsletters, bulletins, or internal mail. Consultants will also generally try to establish a network, involving those teachers interested in the improvement of teaching and learning, through which the consultancy services available may become more widely known and understood.

The consultant is, in effect, an outsider required by a brief to become involved in the working practices of an institution and its members. The role is essentially interventionist and this raises the important question—who is the client?

The consultant may be appointed temporarily by an institution to carry out a specific task and to advise on such matters as, for instance, curriculum policy, the organization of support services, or the efficiency of the teaching and learning process. In this case the consultant will normally have little problem in identifying the client. Usually a fee will be earned and, in large measure, the work, consultancy period, and requirements for reporting will be set out in a contract. The client will normally be the senior management in the institution concerned.

More often, however, a consultant is appointed by, and to, an institution and holds a brief which requires work to be directed towards the improvement of teaching and learning within the institution. Interpretation of this general brief can lead in various directions, as has been shown in the previous section. However, requests for consultation will normally come from departments, course teams, or individuals. If this is the case, the consultant will wish to make sure that the role is not regarded as, what Boud and McDonald (1982) call, "a private detective for management". Indeed, as Eraut (1981) notes, consultants in the course of their work often unearth a great deal of sensitive information which might prove useful to management—perhaps in stopping or modifying certain courses, or perhaps in making tenure or promotion decisions. The consultant may sometimes be faced with requests for information of this kind and such requests will bring to the fore the important question—who is the client?

Another important issue is whether students should be regarded as the consultant's clients. Hopefully they will benefit through their teacher's involvement in consultancy activities, in the course of which they may be interviewed or otherwise asked to make their views known. In this sense, however, they are a resource used in the problem-solving process. If they become more directly involved in the consultancy relationship, complications can occur. There is in such a relationship, the seeds of an alliance between students and consultants; possibly even of collusion against teaching faculty. Such a position is hardly justified if it contributes to a worsening of relationships between students and staff. It may also be performing a disservice to students by encouraging them to blame poor teaching for their difficulties rather than concentrating their efforts upon improving their own learning strategies.

Direct student counselling is another matter. Many institutions in higher education employ student counsellors who deal with, among other things, specific problems of teaching and learning which cause stress to students. This often leads the counsellor into discussing specific courses, teachers, or assessment techniques and as a result student counsellors sometimes seek to extend their role into academic consultancy or at least to work in close collaboration with the educational consultancy unit.

Although the question—who is the client?—clearly has an ethical dimension it is also one which has a pragmatic answer. If consultants are to create and maintain relationships of trust and confidence with individuals and groups of faculty within the institution, they must establish a reputation for scrupulous neutrality and integrity. Confidentiality must at all times be respected. Those *with* whom they work must be those *for* whom they work: the client is thus always the member of faculty or group that seeks the consultation. Information obtained in the course of the enquiry is theirs. To avoid any problems which might arise through uncertainty in this respect, some writers such as House (1976) and Boud and McDonald (1982) argue for explicit arrangements, possibly resulting in a written agreement, to be worked out as soon as possible. Such agreements will normally specify who should receive reports and what form they should take. In this connection, the consultant may wish, from time to time, to publish the results of the work either as a contribution towards research in the field or to make known to a wider audience or potential clientele, an expertise in this kind of work. It would generally be agreed that publication of this kind should first receive the consent of the clients concerned.

Failure to observe this code of practice will almost certainly result in the collapse of the consultancy process within the institution. Loss of confidence and trust in consultants will mean that they will no longer be consulted.

4. *The Organizational Context*

The knowledge which potential clients have about consultants and their work, the access which they have to consultants and vice versa, the status of the consultants and their authority to intervene in the working lives of others, the resources which can be commanded by the consultants or their clients and the approaches which they can legitimately use: all of these are affected, to a greater or lesser extent, by the nature and climate of the institution in which the consultancy process takes place. The main factors involved relate to both the structure of the organization and to the kinds of political and interpersonal processes which take place within it.

Structural influences include size, specialization, physical location of units, means of communication, and formalization of rules and procedures. March and Simon (1958) stress the importance of "information-handling processes" in innovation in organizations generally, and House (1976), dealing with innovation in school systems, emphasizes the importance of organizational structures which offer the possibility of face to face contact, and information about, and access to, new ideas.

Although there are bound to be exceptions and special cases, it would seem likely that competent and experienced consultants located centrally in a relatively small institution with a good communication system, having access to all departments, and not hindered in making contact with potential clients by formal procedures and protocol should find that at least the preliminary stage of their work is less difficult than consultants situated on the periphery of a very large campus with few opportunities to meet faculty, and facing a highly segmented, specialized, and rule-bound community.

But structural influences tend to merge with, and will generally be dominated by, political, ideological, and interpersonal factors. Organizational style, climate, or culture are areas of increasing interest to those concerned with innovation generally and consultancy in particular. The way in which authority is administered, the kinds of rewards and sanctions used, the way power is distributed amongst various groups and individuals, the norms and values subscribed to by members, or the degree of cohesiveness or divisiveness found within the organization are all factors which will, in one way or another, affect the work of the consultant. For instance, some organizations are extremely bureaucratic whereas others operate more on collegial lines: the consultant may find advantages or disadvantages in either case. The bureaucracy, with its strictly defined hierarchy of authority and formalized rules and procedures, stands in contrast to a collegial system in which authority is based upon knowledge and expertise, and decision making is shared through a network of committees. The former style of organization will probably require the consultant to work through formal channels of authority and generally from the top down. The support of senior management is essential and without it the consultant will probably have neither access nor influence. But once gained, senior management backing will normally be of considerable help to the consultant. In the collegial system, however, the consultant will probably have unhindered access to any individual or group but then faces individuals with considerable autonomy. Support from the institution as a whole through policy statements, formal briefing, and the availability of resources will be of limited value if the autonomous subject specialists or departments remain unconvinced of the need for consultancy. There is no authority which can require them to collaborate with the consultant.

The consultant will also generally find a climate of opinion which is either conducive to, or set against, the free discussion of teaching and learning matters. If regular and open debate on such matters is a normal part of the department's or the institution's activities, the consultant will find a more receptive clientele than in a situation in which such matters are seldom discussed and in which research or administration take a higher priority.

Eraut (1975) and Startup (1977) have also pointed to the importance of the reward structure. To what extent will the increased attention to teaching and learning implied by collaboration with an educational consultant result in the furtherance of an individual's career or the enhancement of promotion prospects? In most institutions the answer would seem to be—very little; it may even result in detriment if, for instance, disciplinary research is neglected as a result.

There are, however, few hard and fast rules about organization which consultants might use to promote their cause. Organizations and their departments differ considerably from one to another. In these circumstances, consultants must carefully study the organization to which they are attached in order to establish an ongoing consultancy practice: a view expressed strongly by Berg and Östergren (1977) and Hewton (1982).

There are now sufficient consultancy posts and units in institutions for it to become a career for some academics and researchers and for it to be reaching the stage of developing its own set of approaches and code of ethics. In this sense it might perhaps be regarded as an embryo profession. So far, however, there have been few systematic attempts to provide training schemes specifically for consultants in higher education and although there is much literature on the subject of consultancy generally, more analysis of its practice in higher education is needed.

In the early 1980s, in the climate of financial cutbacks in higher education in many countries, consultancy services could possibly be seen as relatively easy targets for reductions in expenditure. This would be regarded by consultants as a short-sighted policy and it might be argued that consultancy, if used wisely, could assist in improving efficiency and helping to explore a range of alternative strategies which could be considered as possible solutions to the problems of contraction.

Bibliography

Bennis W G, Benne K D, Chin R, Carey K (eds.) 1976 *The Planning of Change*, 3rd edn. Holt, Rinehart and Winston, New York

Berg B, Östergren B 1977 *Innovations and Innovation Processes in Higher Education*. National Board of Universities and Colleges, Stockholm

Boud D, McDonald R 1982 *Educational Development through Consultancy*. Society for Research into Higher Education, Guildford

Commonwealth Secretariat 1978 *Improving University Teaching: A Survey of Programs in Commonwealth Countries*. Commonwealth Secretariat, London

Council for Educational Technology (CET) 1982 *Courses Leading to Qualifications in Educational Technology*. Council for Educational Technology, London

Eraut M 1975 Promoting innovation in teaching and learning: Problems, processes and institutional mechanisms. *Higher Educ.* 4: 13–26

Eraut M 1981 *Problems of Change in University Teaching: The Role of Teaching Support Units*. Center for the Study of Higher Education, University of Arizona, Tucson, Arizona

Eraut M, Connors B, Hewton E 1980 *Training in Curriculum Development and Educational Technology in Higher Education*. Society for Research into Higher Education, Guildford

Gaff J G 1975 *Toward Faculty Renewal: Advances in Faculty, Instructional and Organizational Development*. Jossey-Bass, San Francisco, California

Gaff J G 1979 The United States of America: Towards the improvement of teaching. In: Teather D C B (ed.) 1979 *Staff Development in Higher Education: An International Review and Bibliography*. Kogan Page, London, pp. 232–47

Greenaway H, Harding A G 1978 *The Growth of Policies for Staff Development*. Society for Research into Higher Education, Guildford

Hewton E 1979 A strategy for promoting curriculum development in universities. *Stud. Higher Educ.* 4: 67–75

Hewton E 1982 *Rethinking Educational Change: A Case for Diplomacy*. Society for Research into Higher Education, Guildford

House E R 1976 The micropolitics of innovation: Nine propositions. *Phi Delta Kappan* 57: 337–40

MacKenzie N I, Eraut M, Jones H C 1970 *Teaching and Learning: An Introduction to New Methods and Resources in Higher Education*. UNESCO and the International Association of Universities, Paris

McMillan J H 1975 The impact of instructional improvement agencies in higher education. *J. Higher Educ.* 46: 17–23

March J G, Simon H A 1958 *Organizations*. Wiley, New York

Matheson C 1981 *Staff Development Matters: Academic Staff Training and Development in Universities of the United Kingdom 1961–1981*. Coordinating Committee for the Training of University Teachers, University of East Anglia, Norwich

Nuffield Foundation 1975 *Supporting Teaching for a Change: A Report*. Group for Research and Innovation in Higher Education, Nuffield Foundation, London

Schein E H 1969 *Process Consultation: Its Role in Organization Development*. Addison-Wesley, New York

Startup R 1977 *The University Teacher and his World: A Sociological and Educational Study*. Saxon House, Farnborough

Swain R 1979 How to recognise the real thing: Professionalism and expertise in teaching development. *Impetus* 11: 12–20

Teather D C B (ed.) 1979 *Staff Development in Higher Education: An International Review and Bibliography*. Kogan Page, London

Zaltman G, Florio D H, Sikorski L A 1977 *Dynamic Educational Change: Models, Strategies, Tactics, and Management*. Free Press, New York

Media Program Administration

W. E. Hug

Media programs vary from level to level. In the United States media programs exist at the school, system, region, state, or province levels. Also, programs differ from school to school, from system to system, and so on. For example, a school may have completely decentralized learning resources with collections of materials and equipment being found in the individual classrooms. Other schools may have all materials and equipment controlled in a central location, and many schools have combinations of the above. Intermediate centers at district or regional level provide programs that complement the individual schools and provide services such as the inservice training of teachers in media selection and use, centralized cataloging and processing, circulation of more expensive items like films, models, and other items that are not economical for schools to own. With regard to state media programs Mahar wrote,

Certification, standards, supervision, research, statistics, the supervision of information, and cooperation for school library development are the major categories of state department of education responsibilities. (1960 p. 1)

Today the role is very much the same. However, because of the mergers of services—school libraries, media, television production, and so on—the concept of the school library has greatly expanded and this is reflected in the change of media program titles. Another major role of state departments of education is the certification of media professionals working within the individual states.

1. Leadership and Administration

A key role of media program administrators relates to their ability to develop a staff that is confident in its expertise and aware of how its roles contribute to the media program and how the media program contributes to the educational program and the community. In order to help staff achieve these qualities, administrators (a) make clear the purposes of the media program and its relationship to the educational program; (b) develop written policies and procedures that set standards for operations and services; (c) provide an inservice program that promotes cooperation and professional development; (d) develop an inservice program for users—students, teachers, and administrators; (e) evaluate media program staff using agreed-upon criteria on a regular basis; and (f) protect the media program staff from unreasonable demands and criticism.

1.1 Media Program Purposes

All media programs, regardless of level, should have a written mission statement. The mission should clearly communicate to users as well as the public-at-large. Mission statements are usually printed at the beginning of publications, describing the media services available in a particular unit. Also included are lists of services provided and directions for obtaining these services. Some centers provide users with catalogs of materials and machines available and include a mission statement at the front of the document.

Purposes are also communicated by media programs to the level above and/or below. For example, in local centers at the district level, communication links need to be made with the state or province as well as with the individual schools. This is accomplished in a variety of ways both formally and informally. Formal links include newsletters, advisory boards, scheduled meetings of various interest groups, and task forces organized to study problems in operations, adjust services, and so on. Informal links are also important. These should include frequent visits among personnel on the various levels where information is solicited and shared. Each level should feel that other levels approve of and support their operation because their existence is necessary for the operation of individual units.

Media program personnel must become aware that all contacts with users are important since they result in user perceptions of the media program. Skill in interpreting the media program is critical and needs careful monitoring since user satisfaction is the ultimate test of success.

1.2 Written Policies and Procedures

A valuable tool for communicating internally as well as with the user community is a written statement of operational policies and procedures. Policies are usually formulated with the assistance of advisory boards on the various levels. The documents produced should detail specific steps to an operation, specify conditions under which the operation takes place, and contain a standard to judge the value of each operation. Examples of operations that should be included are acquisitions, production, reference, storage and retrieval, personnel and program evaluation, research and development, maintenance, and distribution.

1.3 Inservice Programs

A common pattern is for national units to provide inservice media programs for state and province media departments, for state and province departments of education to provide inservice programs for districts, and for districts to provide inservice programs for local schools. As in many other operations, inservice programs provide a communication link as well as an opportunity to acquire new skills and to improve existing capabilities. Determining what inservice programs are needed and can be provided requires information from many sources. Formal and informal communication with media program staff and users should disclose many needs. This can be supplemented by user surveys and questionnaires.

Materials selection and use are familiar topics provided by school and system inservice media programs. A rapidly expanding area for inservice programs involves high technology—microcomputers, word processing, videodiscs, and sophisticated production techniques. Common workshops provided by states and provinces for their district level media programs focus on accreditation, legislation, national programs, and future trends. State and province media programs frequently provide inservice education at annual conventions within the state or province as well as at national conventions. In addition to information sharing, these inservice activities frequently highlight model programs within the state or province. This is also true on the national level; that is, many local programs throughout the nation are highlighted at national professional conventions and occupy many sessions on these programs.

Inservice activities provided by the system to individual schools tend to be more skill-development oriented. Activities like programming microcomputers, mastering techniques for producing various media, making computer graphics, and selecting educational games are more common. These activities may be designed for different classes of users—students, teachers, administrators—throughout the school year.

2. Evaluation of Media Programs

Many schemes are available for evaluating programs that have been developed by the states and provinces, by individuals working in colleges and universities, and by national organizations. One of the most recent systems was produced by the American Association for Educational Communications and Technology (AECT) entitled *Evaluating Media Programs District and School* (1980). These procedures provide for an internal as well as an external assessment. The document provides guidelines and forms for making a school and district profile and for evaluating media program goals, budget, staff, services, collections, and facilities. Questionnaires are included to collect the opinions of students and teachers. After all the information is gathered, it is synthesized into a written plan of action which includes a narrative summary of the evaluation, major goals for each operation, specific objectives for improvement, and activities that will assist in attaining each objective.

Any evaluation scheme must be guided by a written mission statement. Once this has been prepared and accepted, evaluators have a way to look at specific operations which also have missions. For example, the mission of budgeting procedures is to contribute to the effectiveness of the media program it supports. If these procedures cause undue paperwork and time delays, the procedures are not fulfilling the mission. A usual procedure for assessing the budget for the media program is to look at past, current, and future needs. Most recommend that a separate budget be established for the media program which facilitates certain operations and planning. The basic question is whether or not budgeting procedures contribute to the effectiveness of a particular media program.

In North America uncertified personnel (e.g., clerks, secretaries, technicians, photographers) are separated from certified personnel—personnel holding a certificate which permits them to practice in the schools of a particular state or province. The data collected in personnel evaluations usually form a duty profile. Conferences with supervisors include a discussion about the appropriateness of the time spent on various tasks, how work flow might be improved, and a plan to help individuals realize personal and professional objectives.

Questions asked of each operation again relate to the goal of each. For example, the goal of reference services is to provide the information a user needs at the time he or she needs it. A goal of maintenance is to have all equipment in working order. Evaluation procedures collect information in order to assess whether or not these goals are met. In the first case, what percentage of users obtained the information for which they came? Are users satisfied with the information they receive? In the second case, how many times have users needed but failed to receive equipment because too many machines needed repair? Is machine failure in the classroom too common?

3. Future Trends

Both the nature of the media program and the role of administration are changing. Perceptions of the contributions of media programs are expanding to include more and more operations and services. Media program administrators are quickly moving away from being preoccupied with warehousing materials and machines and toward being key educational leaders.

As more and more individual efforts merge into a consolidated effort, stronger and stronger units develop.

This, in turn, is rapidly changing the nature of media program administration. This point is illustrated in a recent national survey (Hug 1982). Questionnaires were mailed to media program administrators in the 50 states in order to assess the consequences of mergers on six different levels—state departments of education, state professional organizations, training programs in colleges and universities, regional media services, district media services, and media programs in individual schools. Personnel on all six levels were firmly convinced that their units were greatly strengthened as a result of consolidation.

Merging services and departments involving various aspects of educational technology—audiovisual services, library, television production, graphic productions, and so on—changed media programs in six important ways:

(a) the merged units believed that they greatly increased their political influence and consequently became more competitive with other units;

(b) merged programs were able to provide much broader services which were greater than the sum of the individual units;

(c) professionals on all levels thought that their professional image improved as a result of merger;

(d) consolidation was believed to make operations more efficient;

(e) merging decreased and in many cases eliminated power struggles among the independent units;

(f) many believed that mergers resulted in a clearer role for both personnel and program.

As consolidation occurs, administrators play a more important role in the school, district, and state or province. Administrators are becoming more active in the programs where their units exist and are expanding their contributions as they better understand the units they support. Instead of being buried in the routines within the media program, administrators are beginning to understand the more subtle aspects of the total effort.

Bibliography

Association for Educational Communications and Technology (AECT) 1980 *Evaluating Media Programs District and Schools*. AECT, Washington, DC

Hug W E 1982 Perceptions of mergers among library/media technology professionals. *J. Res. Dev. Educ.* 16 (1): 1–5

Mahar M H 1960 *State Department of Education Responsibilities for School Libraries*. Macmillan, New York

Marks J R, Stoops E, King-Stoops J 1971 *Handbook of Educational Supervision: A Guide for the Practitioner*. Allyn and Bacon, Boston, Massachusetts

Continental European Perspectives

T. Plomp and N. Pals

Educational technology (ET) as a distinctive profession and field of study has developed mainly in English-speaking countries. This does not mean that ET does not exist (as a whole or in part) in continental Europe but rather that it often appears under other labels. Thus, in order to discuss a European perspective, it is best to use a conceptual framework which links European theory and practice to those Anglo–American perspectives. Three concepts of ET will be presented.

1. Conceptual Framework

The first concept, ET1, centres on the use of newer (often audiovisual) media to aid teaching and learning. ET is conceived of as hardware to support these processes both at classroom level and for mass instruction; it is a *product concept* (Romiszowski 1981) or *hardware concept* (Davies 1971) of ET.

The second concept, ET2, is the process or the technique for designing software, or instructional materials, or programmes to support learning; programmed instruction is a well-known example. ET2 is characterized by a stepwise procedure: define objectives, decide method, develop resources, test, evaluate, and implement. The starting assumption is that the development of a piece of instruction (educational software) is needed, or at least desired. This approach to ET is called the *process concept* (Romiszowski 1981) or *software concept* (Davies 1971).

The third concept, ET3, is the problem-solving concept of ET, (see also Romiszowski 1981). This concept, often also called the *systems approach* to ET, represents a holistic approach: a problem has to be analysed in its context and approached with an eye to the many factors which are determining it and can play a part in the solution. It is important to point out that ET1 and ET2 are included in ET3 because they can serve as valuable

means in attaining certain goals or objectives. Institutions involved in ET in one or more of its meanings may have as their mission one, or generally a combination, of the following functions: educational problem solving, curriculum development, instructional design, courseware development, courseware production, and courseware distribution. (Courseware is used in a broad meaning to include all sorts of curricular or instructional printed material, audiovisual media, computer software, etc.) The relative importance of these functions within the three concepts of ET is summarized in Fig. 1. For ET1, the emphasis is on courseware production and distribution, for ET3 on educational problem solving, while for ET2 the design and development functions are the most important.

2. Field of Study

If Ely's criteria for a field of study are used, it cannot be said that ET in its broadest meaning is a field of study in most European countries. The criteria of having curricula which are substantially congruent from institution to institution, or of having professional associations of educational technologists, or journals on ET are not met in the continental European countries. However, this does not mean that there is no use of educational technology. On the contrary, many people in the non-English-speaking countries of Europe are working in the field of educational technology in one of its previously mentioned meanings, but their work and their institutions are labelled with names which reflect the educational tradition of their country, as can be seen from the following examples (see also Fig. 2).

3. Institutes Involved in ET

Many countries in continental Europe have institutes working in the field of educational technology, a few of which will be cited to illustrate the broad range of activities. Further examples can be found in the *Yearbook of Educational and Instructional Technology*, published biannually by Kogan Page. An emphasis on ET1, especially audiovisual media in education, is found in France in the Centre Audiovisuel École Normale Supérieure (St. Cloud); in the Federal Republic of Germany in several institutes (at the state and federal level) for the study and production of audiovisual materials (e.g. Institut für den wissenschaftlichen Film, Göttingen); in Hungary in the National Centre for Educational Technology; and in the Netherlands in the Foundation for Film and Science and the National Institute for AV-Media (NIAM). The International Council on Educational Media (ICEM) holds most of its meetings in Western Europe.

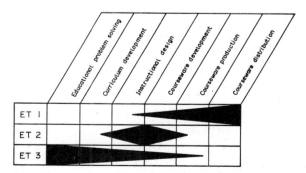

Figure 1
Relative importance of some functions within the different educational technology fields

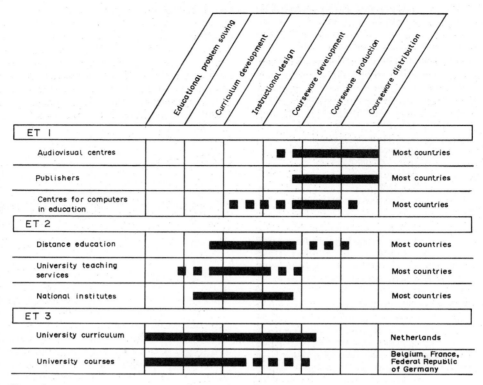

Figure 2
Overview of types of institutions concerned with aspects of educational technology

Another example of ET1 is the use of computers in education. In almost every European country, institutions with special interest in this application can be cited, for example, the Centre for Education and Information Technology (Enschede, Netherlands) and the Central Organization for Programmed Learning and the Computer in Education (Augsburg, Federal Republic of Germany). Many of these institutions have no audiovisual media tradition, but were created recently as a consequence of the rapid development of the new information technologies.

The Federal Republic of Germany has some institutes, like the Gesellschaft für Pedagogik und Information (Paderborn) and the above-mentioned Augsburg institute, where a tradition in programmed learning has been continued into the development of computer-assisted instruction using comparable design techniques. The same holds in Belgium for the Laboratoire de Pédagogie Expérimentale at Liège.

With respect to ET2, there is great interest in instructional design and development in almost all European countries, but it is seldom known as educational or instructional technology. This interest in instructional design and development usually has its origin in the university departments of education or pedagogy (as they

are often called). Examples include the Institute for Science Education (University of Kiel, Federal Republic of Germany), Laboratoire de Pédagogie Expérimentale (University of Liège, Belgium), Laboratory for Didactics (University of Ghent, Belgium), and the École Polytechnique Fédérale (Chaire de Pédagogie et Didactique, Lausanne, Switzerland). The interest in instruction and curriculum development in these institutes is often combined with a research interest in teaching methods, educational innovations, evaluation, and/or the use of media in education. They often have a teaching function as well. Teaching support services in higher education are also frequently involved in instructional development (e.g., in the Netherlands).

The use of technology in distance education is studied and practised at INREF, the Institut National de Récherche en Éducation et Formation in Paris, which is also active in other domains; the Central Institute for Research into Distance Study at the Open University in Hagen (FRG); and in the Netherlands by the Teleac Foundation for Adult Education in Utrecht, via broadcasting and multimedia presentations, and at the Open University at Heerlen.

The approach conceptualized in ET3 underlies the programme of the Department of Education of Twente University of Technology in the Netherlands (Plomp and Verhagen 1983). It is also recognizable in the programme of the Centre for Educational Technology at Liège, and to some extent at the University of Paris VII, and the University of Paderborn (FRG).

This overview illustrates that in continental European countries many aspects of ET are in evidence, though seldom under this name. This means that ET as a field of study or a knowledge domain has not developed in Europe in the same way as in the USA and the UK. But in national and regional institutions and in universities and teacher training colleges many people are working in a technological way on improving education. They are involved in media, didactics, production, and distribution (mostly audiovisual media, but also computer applications), and in instruction and curriculum development.

4. Personnel

On page 25 of his article, *Personnel*, Ely distinguishes three levels of training and responsibility: (i) aide, (ii) technician, and (iii) specialist and/or generalist, depending on the level of sophistication of the tasks and the amount of instruction required to fulfil the tasks. In continental Europe we can distinguish task levels which are quite similar to the Anglo–American. In Fig. 3 a rough indication is given of the kind of people who are involved in the different ET functions, and the type and level of their training. As there are hardly any recognizable training facilities for educational technology, most people are trained on the job. Film directors, for instance, are trained in art colleges with hardly any emphasis on educational film making.

As soon as such people get jobs in educational media institutes they have to adopt an ET way of thinking and working.

Because of the lack of ET training facilities, it is almost impossible to identify a common knowledge base for a certain function. However, the educational problem solvers, developers, and designers in continental Europe almost certainly use a great deal of Anglo–American literature on ET in their work.

5. Conclusions

In continental Europe, many people work in the field of ET in one of the meanings defined here, but only a few call themselves educational technologists. There are no curricula which are congruent from one institution to another; there are no European associations; European journals on educational technology are confined to hardware-oriented journals on computers and audiovisual media in education, and national journals like *Schul Praxis* in the Federal Republic of Germany. So Ely's criteria for ET as a field of study are far from being met.

Many European countries, especially smaller ones, have national institutes whose mission is within the field of what in English-speaking countries would be called educational technology. Various examples can be given, such as the Foundation of Curriculum Development (Enschede, Netherlands), the Film and AV Media Education Service (Flemish Ministry of Education, Brussels), and the National Institute for Educational Media (Copenhagen). In the Federal Republic of Germany we

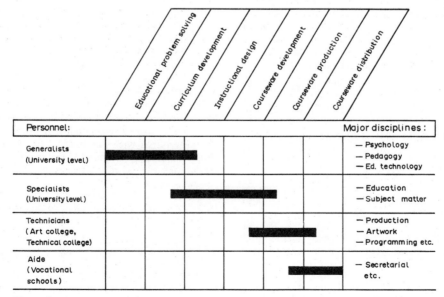

Figure 3
Indication of specialism and training of personnel in continental European institutions

find the same on state level, for example, the Landesinstitut für Lehrerfortbildung, with activities ranging from curriculum development to courseware distribution.

The examples presented here illustrate that educational technology is well-developed in countries such as the Federal Republic of Germany, France, Belgium, and the Netherlands, but rooted in the tradition of the national educational culture and structure. However, the development of a coherent European scene of educational technology in the near future is unlikely, mostly because of the lack of information exchange in European journals and associations. On the other hand there is a positive development: almost all countries are heavily involved in the introduction of the computer and other new technologies (ET1) in education. This is apparent in the many national plans, national and regional institutes for research and development, and pilot projects in this domain. As these activities are not typical for continental European countries, they might have a positive effect on the future development of a distinctive continental European perspective on educational technology, perhaps even an international one.

Bibliography

Association for Educational Communications and Technology (AECT) Task force on Definition and Terminology 1977 *Educational Technology: Definition and Glossary of Terms*. Association for Educational Communications and Technology, Washington, DC

Davies I K 1971 *The Management of Learning*. McGraw Hill, London

Plomp T, Verhagen P 1983 An educational technology curriculum emphasizing systematic, scientific problem solving. *Educ. Commun. Technol.* 31: 239–45

Romiszowski A J 1981 *Designing Instructional Systems*. Kogan Page, London

Asian Perspectives

T. Sakamoto

The concept of educational technology was originally introduced to Asian countries in the 1960s from the United Kingdom and the United States. At that time the use of audiovisual media in education, and the application of behavioural sciences to educational processes were the two major features of educational technology. Other concepts identified by Eraut—mass communications, systems, and interactionist—have also been more or less accepted in Asian countries. Educational technology as a field of study and the scientific areas contributing to educational technology are regarded similarly in Asia as in Euro–North American countries.

1. Concepts of Educational Technology in Asia

Figure 1 shows an example of the structure of educational technology in Japan in the late 1960s (Sakamoto 1969). Since that time the approach to educational technology has been understood in a variety of ways, but the following three components tended to be included in the approach to educational technology in Japan by the late 1980s (Sakamoto 1987):

(a) to pursue an optimal combination of the components both in the teaching–learning processes and in the instructional management processes;

(b) to develop and use the technologies, media, and systems that are most useful for implementing these optimal combinations; and

(c) to organize the technologies, media, and systems as a science of technology concerning instruction and management for instruction.

In other Asian countries, educational technology is often considered theoretically as educational communication technology and as a systematic approach to educational processes. For example, Bonilla, Director of the Curriculum Development and Educational Technology Centre, Technological University of the Philippines, states that "it implies a disciplined and systematic approach to the organization of resources for learning". In practice, however, educational technology is more often treated as the application of media and programmed learning to teaching–learning processes. Bonilla points to two distinct meanings of educational and training technology: (a) hardware approach as teaching aids and (b) software approach as learning aids. He then integrates these two into hardware and software approaches which "correspond to the systematic and integrated approach and applies behavioural science to the problem of both teaching and learning".

In India, Shah (1984), President of the Indian Association for Educational Technology wrote, "In India, we started off with programmed learning and then turned our searchlight with an enlarged focus to cover educational technology". He listed the studies on educational technology in South Gujarat University, Surat, as follows:

(a) An inquiry into the effectiveness of systems approach in curriculum planning;

(b) an inquiry into the relative effectiveness of linear-style book format programmes and multimedia programmes;

(c) the development and testing of a multimedia package on effective questioning in the context of microteaching;

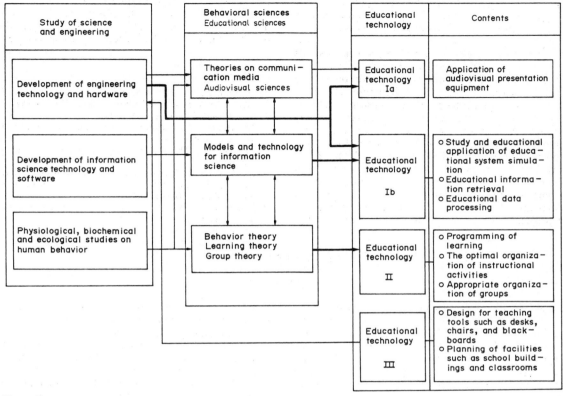

Figure 1
Educational technology in Japan

(d) the development of a self-instructional training package for nonformal education facilitators;

(e) the evolution of a strategy for developing teaching skills in secondary school teachers;

(f) an inquiry into the effectiveness of media with reference to classroom ethos;

(g) an inquiry into the effectiveness of a motion film in improving cognitive behaviour in English;

(h) an inquiry into the effectiveness of radiovision as a partial substitute to educational television (ETV); and

(i) the development and evaluation of radiovision as an instructional system.

In the People's Republic of China, educational technology is called *electrifying education*. In practice this means audiovisual education, though the theory behind it, which is emphasized in several textbooks, is that communication theory, information theory, and control theory should be integrated in educational technology. The focus of discussion in China in the late 1980s is the change of the name *electrifying education* to *educational communication technology*.

In Malaysia and Singapore, educational technology is mainly centred on audiovisual aids, while in the Republic of Korea, the concept has been extended beyond audiovisual education to include the use of microcomputers in teaching.

2. Academic Societies and Professional Associations

There are many academic and professional societies and associations for educational technology in Asian countries. In Japan, for example, the Japanese Society of Educational Technology (JET) was established in 1984, to function as a coordinating body for educational technology research groups. The first national joint conference of educational technology societies was held in 1985.

In addition to JET, the Japanese Society of Science Education, the Japanese Society for the Study of Audiovisual Education, the Japanese Society for the Study of Educational Radio and Television, the Society of Computer-Assisted Instruction in Japan, the Technical Group on Educational Technology in the Japanese Institute of Electronics and Communication Engineers, and the Society of Educational Methods are academic societies for specialists working in various educational technology fields.

Several professional associations are also active in promoting educational technology, such as the Japanese Association of Educational Technology (JAET), the Japanese Association of Educational Information, the Japanese Council of Educational Technology Centre, the All Japan Association for Audiovisual Education in Schools, and the All Japan Association of Broadcast Education.

Activities in the academic societies are research-oriented, while activities in the professional associations are practice-oriented, but they have no function as workers' unions or guilds for controlling and protecting the jobs, quality, and rights of educational technologists. Many researchers, teachers, and people from media industries participate as members or observers and attend the conferences to study educational technology and exchange information and experiences.

In 1986, JAET and the Japanese Council for the Promotion of Educational Technology held the International EDUTEC Conference with the American Educational and Communication Technology in Tokyo.

In the Republic of Korea, the Korean Society for the Study of Educational Technology (KSET) was organized in 1985. The aims are: (a) to conduct research on educational technology; (b) to link practice with theory; (c) to consult; and (d) to innovate and reform education by using educational technology.

In India, the Indian Association for Programmed Learning was set up in 1967 and became the Indian Association for Educational Technology in 1981. Its major objective is to undertake and coordinate research and training in the field of educational technology. It also organizes inservice training and extension work, and disseminates information about educational technology.

In China, the Chinese Research Society for Electrifying Education and the Chinese Association for Higher Foreign Language Electrifying Education are national organizations, and the North East Three Provincial Association for Electrifying Education and North West Five Provincial Association for Electrifying Education are interprovincial ones. Each province, city, and so on also has its own association. The total number in the early 1980s was about 40. Their main activities are meetings and the exchange of information.

3. Educational Technologists and Training

The functions of educational technologists are wide and varied, and include organization management, personnel management, research, design, production, evaluation/selection, logistics, utilization, and utilization/dissemination.

Imae et al. (1985) conducted a survey on the skills and characteristics required of specialists in educational technology. They received 563 (35.4 percent) replies from 1,589 members selected from academic societies connected with educational technology, and found by the factor analysis method that five areas of competence are required for specialists in educational technology: instructional design and research, media production and equipment operation, research, educational systems development and management, and basic knowledge of education. Primary areas of competence for specialists in schools and education centres were "instructional design and research" and "media production and equipment operation". However, the primary competence for specialists in universities and research institutes was "research" with the remaining four factors being equally weighted.

In Japan, special jobs for educational technologists are not always clearly defined, because educational technologists as a vocational professional group are, in the 1980s, still not generally recognized. However, there are some specialists in educational technology for various fields. Advisory teachers and superintendents in educational technology fields design educational software and instruct teachers how to design, implement, and evaluate instruction. Specialists for media product development produce educational radio and television programmes, audiovisual educational materials, and computer-assisted instruction (CAI) courseware. They sometimes operate equipment or write computer programmes. Some develop hardware such as CAI systems, display equipment, and interface devices. Others manage audiovisual libraries and deliver educational software nationwide. Some members of the Japanese Society of Educational Technology are professors or researchers in universities, colleges, and institutes, who teach and investigate educational technology. Their academic backgrounds range from education, psychology, sociology, and linguistics to mathematics, physics, chemistry, electronics, information sciences, control engineering, and systems engineering.

There are no departments of educational technology in Japan, and no formal degrees for educational technology. Students, however, can study educational technology in graduate and undergraduate courses in universities, and write dissertations in the field of educational technology. Even in these cases their degrees will be in education, literature, engineering, science, or philosophy. Students can also study educational technology in doctoral degree courses: educational systems technology in the system science course at Tokyo Institute of Technology; educational information in the educational psychology course at the University of Tokyo; and educational technology in the human sciences study course at the University of Osaka.

Training for educational technology practitioners is usually not undertaken in Japanese universities, though technical specialists for graphics, photography, and broadcasting are trained in the arts faculties in some universities and special colleges. Those graduates are not always recruited to television production and other industries, because most of their personnel are trained on the job. Teachers are trained in educational technology at some universities and colleges of education as preservice training and at educational centres as inservice training.

Japan, however, is exceptional, for in many other Asian countries educational technology is formally and systematically taught in universities and colleges. In the Republic of Korea, for example, many universities have established, or are planning to establish, departments of educational technology or centres for the use of educational technology in teacher education and training. Educational technology courses are included in all teacher education and training programmes, with all students in teacher training colleges taking educational technology as one of eight common courses.

In India, the University Grants Committee recently set up four educational media research centres (EMRCs) and four audiovisual research centres (AVRCs). The EMRCs (Jamia Millia Islamia in New Delhi, Gujarat University in Ahmedabad, Poona University, and the Central Institute of English and Foreign Languages, CIEFL, in Hyderabad) conduct research and development on the use of audiovisual media and also teach students. For example, Jamia Millia Islamia offers a postgraduate diploma course for research and development in educational technology. The AVRCs are at Osanmia University (Hyderabad), Roorkee University, Anna University (Madras), and Jodhpur University. Some EMRCs organize workshops for academics and produce educational television (ETV) programmes which are broadcast through the INSAT–IB or Doordarshan networks.

The National Council of Educational Research and Training (NCERT) is also engaged in improving the quality of school education in India, through research and development, training, extension, and dissemination. The NCERT established a centre for educational technology in 1973, which later became the Central Institute of Educational Technology (CIET). It is responsible for production of ETV programmes for primary school children, training of personnel nominated by the six states covered by INSAT, and setting up of the state institutes of educational technology (SIET), which also produce ETV programmes. The CIET and SIETs investigate the use of educational television and video programmes in school and community education settings. The NCERT plans to equip its four regional colleges of education as regional centres of educational technology, so they can organize advanced level teacher education courses as part of four-year undergraduate programmes and special short cycle inservice programmes.

The Computer Literacy and Studies in Schools (CLASS) project was launched in 1984 in 250 secondary schools and expanded to an additional 500 secondary and upper-secondary schools in 1985. A total of 1550 teachers were trained in 17 resource centres in 1984–85. Out of 50 resource centres only four (two under the NCERT and two under the Technical Teacher Training Institutes) are located in the traditional teacher education institutes. The rest are located in the computer science departments of Indian institutes of technology, colleges of engineering, and universities (APEID 1985b).

In Malaysia, educational technology departments or units have been established in all universities and teachers' colleges. In general they teach educational technology to students, provide for other departments or faculties, and conduct staff development in educational technology. They are well-equipped with the educational hardware and software necessary for training educational technology personnel.

The educational technology course is compulsory in three universities, but optional in the other two. In the teachers' colleges, a course on instructional systems technology is centrally prescribed by the Teacher Education Division of the Ministry of Education and is compulsory for all student teachers. A one-year specialist course in educational technology is offered at the Specialist Teachers' Training Institute. The Educational Media Service of the Ministry of Education, which is responsible for the provision of educational radio and television programmes for Malaysian schools, helps to implement some of the optional courses.

The University of Sains Malaysia has two similar inservice programmes in educational technology for graduate and nongraduate teachers: one at diploma level, the other a certificate course. In addition, many schemes for teacher training in educational technology are being implemented in Malaysia.

In the Philippines, the Curriculum Development and Educational Technology Centre of the Technological University of the Philippines provides two courses for graduate students: the Master's degree in Educational Technology, which tends to be technician-oriented, and the MA in Educational Technology, which is more researcher-oriented.

In preservice teacher education, Principles of Teaching and Educational Technology is a compulsory subject for all education students taking Bachelor's degrees in elementary or secondary education. In other teacher education institutions, educational media is an elective subject. However, the curriculum for the MA in Education includes educational media courses such as audiovisual aids, radio, television and education; and graduate students can work for an MA in education specializing in educational media.

In China, 22 higher education institutes are training four kinds of personnel: teachers in the Departments of Electrifying Education in normal universities, editors for electrifying education materials, researchers for electrifying education, and administrators for electrifying education. There are three levels of qualification: a two- to three-year general course, a four-year undergraduate course and a two- to three-year Master's course. The main subjects covered include theories of electrifying education, audiovisual materials, educational television, computer education, material production, research methods, administration, photography, audiovisual psychology, educational communication, electrifying technology, computer programming, and speech.

In 1983, the first faculty of educational communication and technology was approved by the Ministry of Education at South China Normal University, where it runs a Master's course in electrifying education. After that two other Master's courses in electrifying education were set up, at the North River University and at Beijing Normal University.

In Japan, media specialists and media technicians are often not formally trained in universities and colleges. Usually graduates are recruited from various other fields to work on educational technology in broadcasting stations, media production, and education. But in many other Asian countries jobs in educational technology fields are commonly taken by personnel with qualifications in educational technology.

In Singapore, for example, the Department of Educational Technology (DET) of the Curriculum Development Institute of Singapore (CDIS) has personnel with professional qualifications in educational technology. A number of officers in the DET have received training in courses relevant for the work of media producers; and most of them obtained Master's degrees or diplomas in educational technology in the United Kingdom or the United States.

In the Philippines, job descriptions of educational technologists are clearly defined, and any qualification in educational technology is usually beneficial for obtaining such a job.

4. Educational Technology Centres

Local centres of educational technology in Asian countries have functions such as management and administration, instructional design and development, training, consulting, information services, and media production.

In Japan audiovisual libraries or centres are found everywhere. Service centres provide films, video, and other audiovisual materials for teachers and community workers. Educational technology centres have also been set up in most teacher training colleges. These are primarily research centres, but sometimes also conduct services for faculty members in the universities and colleges. In the Tokyo Institute of Technology, the Centre for Research and Development of Educational Technology was established in 1971 to conduct research work in educational technology. In 1986, the Centre for Educational Computing was established by the Ministry of Education, Science, and Culture and the Ministry of International Trades and Industries for promoting the educational use of microcomputers in schools.

In other Asian countries, most of the teachers' centres and educational technology centres in universities and colleges provide services to faculty members for producing educational materials and assisting research.

In China, the Ministry of Education set up the Department of Electrifying Education and the Central Electrifying Educational Library in 1978, to promote the national policy of electrifying education. In 1979 the Central Radio and TV University was established which had by its 10th year one million students and 610,000 graduates. In 1985 the National Committee of Education decided to separate the Department of Electrifying Education and the Central Electrifying Education Library and to set up the Central TV Normal Institute. Under the recognized system, audiovisual education is now conducted, under the control of the National Committee of Education, in these three organization systems. The Electrifying Educational Library System had established 29 provincial libraries; 438 county libraries; and 2,253 city, town, or village libraries by 1985. They provide services, training, production of audiovisual materials, and research on educational technology. Under the Radio TV University system, 35 provincial television universities; 540 county branches; 1,168 city, town, and village branches; and 30,000 fundamental classrooms have been established, teaching large numbers of students using educational technology. Furthermore, by 1985, 809 universities and higher education institutes had electrifying centres or rooms. Their functions are to conduct research on educational communication technology, the production of audiovisual materials, staff development, and teaching students. The number of personnel working in audiovisual education was 101,799 in 1985. Among them 52,746 (44,993 in elementary and secondary 7,743 in higher education) are full-time and 49,503 (48,836 and 667) are part-time, excluding personnel in Radio TV Universities. In 1986 a satellite was set up for inservice teacher training and continuing and adult education.

In Singapore, the National University of Singapore has a Centre for Educational Technology; Nanyan Technological Institute has an Educational Technology Unit; the Institute of Education has educational technologists in the Department of Pedagogical Studies; and Ngee Ann Polytechnic has an Educational Technology Centre. They provide staff development and support services for using media, for preparing teaching materials, and for conducting research work.

In most Asian countries distance teaching is considered a useful means for teaching workers and those who have had no chance to study. Thus the application of new advanced technology to distance education is, in the 1980's, one of the most important educational topics (APEID 1986) in China, India, the Philippines, Japan, Indonesia, Bangladesh, Fiji, Thailand, and Hong Kong. Another topic of growing importance in some Asian countries, such as the Republic of Korea, Singapore, India, China, and Japan, is the use of microcomputers in education. These and other topics regularly appear on the agenda of the main international centre for the region, the Asian Centre for Educational Innovation and Development (ACEID), situated in Bangkok, in the UNESCO Regional Office for Education in Asia and the

Pacific (ROEAP). ACEID carries out the Asian Programme of Educational Innovation for Development (APEID) and holds a seminar on educational technology every year in Tokyo. Topics covered there have included media production, computers in education, computers in teacher education, and the application of advanced technology in distance teaching. ACEID also provides an important information service on educational innovation in the region.

Bibliography

Asian Programme of Educational Innovation for Development (APEID) 1985a *Computers in Education: An Outline of Country Experiences.* UNESCO/ROEAP, Bangkok

Asian Programme of Educational Innovation for Development (APEID) 1985b *Final Report of the Fourth Asian Seminar on Educational Technology in Tokyo—The Third Programming Cycle of APEID Activities.* Japanese Commission for UNESCO

Asian Programme of Educational Innovation for Development (APEID) 1986 *Final Report of the Fifth Asian Seminar on Educational Technology in Tokyo.* Japanese Commission for UNESCO

Imae K, Hirata K, Shimizu H, Kitaoka F, Nakatsu N, Nishinosono H 1985 Competencies required of specialists in educational technology. *Educ. Technol. Res.* 8:11–18

Sakamoto T 1969 Broadcasting education as a branch of educational technology. In: *Television and Further Education of Employed.* Publishing House of Polish Radio and Television, Warsaw

Sakamoto T 1987 Educational technology in Japan. *Educ. Technol. Res.* 10

Shah G 1984 Whither educational technology? In: Adiseshiah M, Shah G (eds.) 1984 *Educational Technology.* Indian Association for Educational Technology

Part 2

Technical Developments

Part 2

Technical Developments

Introduction

This Part of the *Encyclopedia* is not written for technologists but for educators who need to gain some understanding of recent technical developments. For this reason it is probably the least specialist section in its approach. Its purpose is to survey important areas of technology which affect patterns and modes of teaching and learning, to describe their significant characteristics, and to review factors affecting their further development and educational use. In most cases the discussion stops short of any detailed analysis of utilization because that is picked up in subsequent sections of the *Encyclopedia*.

The opening article, *Economics of Educational Technology*, is rather different from the rest of the Part. Its purpose is to provide a framework for thinking about the economic aspects of introducing new technology into education, especially that technology which could be introduced on a large scale as part of a major policy initiative. There is a long tradition in educational technology of reporting new developments in single institutions without much attention to cost factors and their dependence on scale of application. Whilst essential for exploring the potential of new developments, this tradition has not provided good guidance on educational futures. There is clearly a need to estimate the costs and benefits of large-scale application in addition to performing small-scale feasibility experiments, and sometimes that consideration leads to different approaches to utilization. The same arguments apply when some of the crucial differences between developing and developed countries are considered, for both qualitative and quantitative factors affect advantages and limitations of introducing new technology.

Orivel distinguishes between "within-school" and "out-of-school" applications of educational technology, giving greatest attention to radio and television. He concludes that for a variety of reasons within-school educational technology has not dramatically improved the cost-effectiveness of educational services compared with traditional teaching. There are some examples of positive cost-effective impact where the teaching staff is underqualified, however, the main area of success from an economist's viewpoint has been in out-of-school projects, both in equivalency programmes and in nonformal education.

While some of the findings may change in the future if comparative costs fall and media potential rises, that change will need to be demonstrated by the kind of analysis that Orivel has provided if policy makers are to take note.

The wide range of technologies for distributing television signals is reviewed by Miller's article on *Distribution and Reception of Television Programs*. This covers traditional broadcasting, microwave transmission, cable networks, distribution by cassette or disc, and transmission via satellite. In each case advantages and limitations are examined together with channel capacity, initial and recurrent costs, and transmission and reception costs.

Television distribution systems are now being used for data and text transmission in addition to television programmes. This forms part of Copeland and Scott's review of the rapidly changing area of *Videotex and Electronic Mail*. This article examines how both television transmission and telephone systems have been used for data transmission in addition to their original purposes. The broadcast system is commonly referred to as Teletext and the interactive telephone-based system as Viewdata. The relative cheapness of adapting existing facilities such as television sets, microcomputers, and telephones has led to a rapid growth in this mode of communication. The implications for education are only just beginning to be explored, so there is no applications article included in the *Encyclopedia*.

Computer Technology and Telecommunications is now the most significant of the technical areas that affect education. Not only is the direct use of computers becoming more pervasive as they become cheaper, more user-friendly, and more common, but computers are increasingly involved in the delivery of a range of mediated messages, not only text but still and moving pictures as well. Their growing influence is apparent not only in the use of computers in education, which is covered in Part 3(a), but also in such developments as *Interactive Video*, and *Information Storage and Retrieval* (both covered in this Part), and *Electronic Publishing* [Part 5(d)]. Kubitz provides a layperson's guide to bipolar and MOS (metal-oxide-semiconductor) technology and their incorporation into processors, various forms of storage, software issues, user workstations, and communications between machines and users. The latter heralds a discussion of the relationship between computer technology and telecommunications, where political as well as commercial considerations are of increasing importance.

One of the areas most affected by computerization is that of *Information Storage and Retrieval*. Lancaster summarizes the principles of off-line information retrieval systems before describing the advent of on-line retrieval systems. He then concludes by discussing the organization needed to exploit the use of machine-readable databases.

Microforms are also used for information storage. Minor's article shows that they still have some advantages for storing large printed documents. More recently, however, the limelight has been captured by videodiscs. Schipma reviews recent developments in *Videodisc Technology*. Several alternative technologies are described, of which laser reflective technology has now emerged as the leader, spawning digital audiodiscs or compact discs as an audio by-product and CD-ROM as a new form of data storage for computers. While the cost of replication has steadily decreased, the cost of making a master copy is still too high for local, small-scale production to be feasible.

Linking videotapes or videodiscs to a computer which can both interact with the user and control the presentation has given rise to *Interactive Video*. Copeland's survey of this new approach begins by explaining the technical aspects and the parallel development of videotape and videodisc systems. The tape system lends itself to cheap, locally produced programmes, while disc systems are more suited to large-scale distribution. A brief discussion of interactive video production is followed by accounts of several applications. Significant use in the commercial and military sectors has not yet been matched in education. However, there have been a series of specially funded projects to explore the educational potential of interactive video. Two independent research studies have reported significant learning gains but longer study times for interactive programmes than for less interactive or noninteractive versions.

Snell's survey of *Audio Production and Distribution* points out not only that educational equipment is dominated by developments in consumer electronics but also that in sound, unlike video, the quality of modern equipment designed for home use often meets the standard required by broadcast professionals. He reviews the increasing quality of cassette technology and the additional quality of the digital audiodisc. More relevant for education, however, is the rapid access time provided by discs. Most educational users, however, will continue to use cassettes until discs can be edited and locally produced. Foulke's brief article on *Time-compressed and Time-extended Speech* highlights an earlier development in audio technology whose potential has yet to be explored.

The dominance of the commercial world applies equally to other forms of *Audiovisual Equipment*. As Crocker points out, very few types of equipment were specifically designed for educational use. The most notable examples are the overhead projector and the audio-card (as in a Language Master). His review of equipment issues covers performance criteria, lamp technology, maintenance, and standardization. The *Learning Environments* in which equipment is used are surveyed by McVey. Though beginning with a section on the ergonomic aspects of seating and desk design, he concentrates primarily on the design of teaching spaces. This covers room shape and size, acoustics, illumination, colour, thermal factors, sound systems, and display systems.

Part 2 concludes with a new article by Vincent on the rapidly developing field of *Information Technology for Disabled Students*. Most attention has been given to improving communication rather than curriculum supplementation. Vincent reviews the technical developments which support communication by visually handicapped, physically handicapped, and deaf students, and the design of work stations for their use. Finally, he discusses the important issue of access to appropriate software.

Economics of Educational Technology

F. Orivel

The production of educational services is a sector where the relationship between inputs and outcomes is much less clearly identifiable than in most other sectors of production of goods or services. What is the effect on educational results of a better qualified teacher, a lower pupil–teacher ratio, or educational media such as audio-visual aids, television programs, or computers? There is some evidence on these questions, but it is very often contradictory or inconclusive. These uncertainties are due to the variety of educational outcomes (cognitive and affective, internal and external, immediate and long term), and to the difficulty of measurement of most of them, in spite of some significant progress, at least in the measurement of cognitive achievements.

Most educational systems or educational institutions do not consider as a major and central objective the optimal use of inputs to maximize their outcomes, not only in public educational systems, but even in supposedly competitive private institutions. The survey carried out by Bowen (1980) among American colleges and universities leads to the conclusion that in higher education institutions, both private and public, unit costs are determined quite simply by the amount of money that can be raised from diverse sources: it is the "revenue theory of cost." The analysis of the relationship between expenditures (or costs) and outcomes (quantitative and qualitative) is basically inconclusive. It seems that the variance of costs is much higher than the variance of outcomes, which would mean that a certain number of institutions could have the same results with less resources. But on the other hand, the author argues that in its present trend, American higher education tends to be underfinanced and that the quality is declining.

These apparently contradictory results mean two things: there is a likely relation between available resources and academic excellency, but the right inputs remain to be specified. The provision of better educational services, leading to better educational results, requires more resources, and is therefore more expensive. But more expensive educational services are not necessarily better ones if the right inputs have not been clearly identified.

Traditional teaching takes place in classrooms with a teacher facing students. The teacher has the main role, and the basic additional input is the use of textbooks. The concept of new educational technologies is applied to systems where the traditional system is either enriched, or completely redesigned, in order to provide a substitute for the traditional system. Such a substitute is essentially covered by the concept of distance education.

An important aspect of both enrichment in traditional schools and distance education is that they were not originally introduced to improve the cost–effectiveness ratio of educational systems. Enrichment is aimed at improving school performances, fighting against failures, dropouts, repetition rates, and so on. Distance education objectives are mainly to provide access to education to excluded segments of the population: sick or handicapped people, mothers raising children, working people, adults who did not have the opportunity of studying while they were children, people living in remote areas, etc. The introduction of distance education for such target audiences was motivated principally by equity rather than economic considerations.

The situation in the late 1980s is entirely different. Most countries, especially the poorest, are facing dramatic budgetary difficulties which have stopped the expansion of public resources allocated to education (Eicher and Orivel 1979). This shrinking of resources for education accelerated in the second half of the 1970s and raised serious problems in satisfying a growing demand for educational services. More generally, after a quarter century of rapid expansion of public resources allocated to education (1950–75), public authorities and public opinion are increasingly concerned with the idea of a "good" use of these resources, which explains the growing popularity of the concept of a "cost–effectiveness ratio" applied to educational services. This concept may be used for traditional teaching as well as for the so-called new educational technologies. Up to 1970, studies and data on the costs of these new educational technologies were very scanty, and usually based on inadequate or noncomparable methodologies. Rapid progress has been made during the 1970s, both methodologically and empirically, especially through the pioneering work of D. T. Jamison. The results of these efforts to measure costs are such that one tends to have more evidence on cost comparisons (between traditional teaching and new educational technologies) than on results and outcomes.

In the first section of this entry, a description of the field of educational technology is provided, along with some tentative taxonomies; in the second and third sections, the economics of the two main uses of this technology, namely within and out of school, are examined; and finally, in the fourth section, some additional information is given on a medium-by-medium basis.

1. Taxonomies of Educational Technology

As shown above, the two great objectives of new educational technologies were the improvement of school performances and the expansion of access to education of excluded groups. For an economist, the emphasis is rather on the potential changes in the productivity of educational services, namely to provide more or better services for a given budget, or to provide similar services at a lower cost.

Fortunately, this first dichotomy between new educational technologies is particularly adequate to fit with economic analysis. The introduction of new media within schools does not significantly modify the labor input (teaching staff) that exists in traditional teaching. One cannot expect, as a consequence, dramatic changes in terms of cost reductions. The typical case is characterized by a slight increase in costs, and potential changes in results, which are more likely when the former level was low than when it was already high or satisfactory.

The second objective, however, opens large possibilities of changing the share of the labor input. The costs of a centralized production of didactic materials, printed or broadcasted, may be shared by a large number of users, and as the fixed part of costs tends to be higher than in traditional systems, a large audience may substantially reduce the unit costs, as shown in Fig. 1, where FC is the total fixed cost, VC the per student variable cost (or marginal cost), and where the index t refers to traditional teaching and n to new educational technology. It appears clearly from Fig. 1 that above a certain number of students in the system (N_o), the unit costs in distance education are lower than in traditional teaching.

This cost behavior suggests the taxonomy of new educational technologies given in Fig. 2. From an economic perspective, the differences between the two basic models are significant. The pupil–teacher ratio (it would be more correct to say pupil–labor ratio) in distance education is much larger, and that means that the cost of labor is lower than in traditional teaching; as a result, it usually more than compensates the additional costs of supplementary teaching inputs. (Distance education systems may be followed by working adults, and therefore

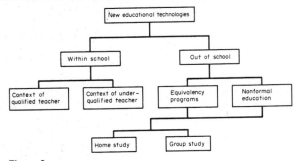

Figure 2
Taxonomy of educational technologies

have a reduction effect on forgone earnings, i.e., on private costs.) Finally, most of the study time is spent at home, and that reduces transportation and boarding costs.

2. Within-school Applications of New Educational Technologies

Two main objectives have pushed the introduction of new educational inputs in the context of schools. The first is to improve school performances in a context of relatively qualified teachers, in order to help at least a certain number of students who tend to fail through lack of motivation, family support, or adequate cultural background (language mastering, etc.). This model appears mostly in developed countries, where thousands of such projects have been implemented in the twentieth century. Tons of evaluation literature, poor and good, have been produced, but most are inconclusive on the effectiveness of such programs. The economic analysis of these projects has been dramatically neglected. In spite of the fact that the most costly programs, with motivated teachers, reinforced pedagogical teams, and access to a great variety of didactic supports, are likely to have measurable positive impact on school performances, there has not been a serious attempt either to relate these effects to costs, or to measure productivity changes. One of the pioneering countries in this field, Sweden, is experiencing a rapid decline in such use of educational technologies, as shown by Brusling (1982). This may be due, as Brusling argues, to new approaches in pedagogical ideologies, the use of technological devices being associated with an outdated Skinnerian and behaviorist theory, and to the development of more "participation-group-animation" types of pedagogical approach, in which hardware-type didactic inputs are used minimally. But another interpretation could be linked with the economic failure of these technologies, unable to demonstrate adequately any productivity increase. As a consequence, the tightening and shrinking of educational budgets in most countries, developed countries included, is rapidly killing these innovations.

The second objective is to improve school performances in a context of underqualified teachers, either

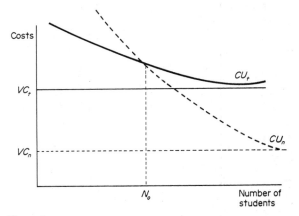

Figure 1
Unit costs in traditional teaching (CU_t) compared to distance education (CU_n)[a]

a Note: $FC_t < FC_n$

Table 1
Cost effectiveness of some within-school educational projects

Project	Units for measuring N[b]	Value of N at time of study	Cost function in 1978 US$ at 7.5 percent discount rate	Average cost for given N in 1978 US$	Project impacts on		
					Pedagogical quality	Access	Cost per enrollment
Brazil Maranhão FMTVE[a]	Number of students reached per year	1976 N = 13,000	TC(N) = 1,551,000 + 116N	235.3	Improvement	Improves access to disadvantaged groups	Between traditional public schools and private
Brazil Ceára Educational tele. project[a]	Number of students reached per year	1978 N = 19,800	TC(N) = 971,000 + 87N	136.6	No effect	No effect	Slight decrease
Mexico Radioprimaria[b]	Number of students reached per year	1972 N = 2,800	TC(N) = 57,500 + 139.2N	160.0	No effect	Improves geographical access	38 percent decrease
Mexico Telesecundaria[c]	Number of students reached per year	1972 N = 29,000	TC(N) = 842,700 + 204.1N	235.7	Slight improvement	Improves geographical access	40 percent decrease
Ivory Coast PETV[d]	Number of students reached per year	1980 N = 700,000	TC(N) = 4,500,000 + 200N	206.4	Slight improvement	No effect	10 percent increase
Senegal PTS[e]	Number of students reached per year	1980 pilot project N = 400 Possible extension 140,000	TC(N) = 2,100,000 + 120N	135.0	Slight improvement	No effect	8 percent increase

a Arena A, Jamison D T, Oliveira J, Orivel F 1977 Economic analysis of educational television in Maranhão, Brazil. Mimeo (French and English). UNESCO, Paris. Also available in Portuguese (ABT–Av Erasmo Braga 255 grupo 401, Rio de Janeiro) and in Spanish in the *Revista de Centro de Estudios Educativos* 1978, 8(1): 121–40. An updated version by Oliveira and Orivel (1980) has been published in two languages (English and French), with a comparison of a similar system, the Ceára Education Television system b Jamison et al. 1978, Chap. 6 (on Mexico's *Radioprimaria*) c Jamison et al. 1978, Chap. 11 (on Mexico's *Telesecundaria*). See also Mayo et al. 1975 d Eicher and Orivel 1980 e Orivel 1981

69

underqualified in general, or underqualified in specific fields. This case is more common in developing countries, where shortages in qualified teachers have been, and sometimes still are, particularly acute. From an economic point of view, the introduction of one or several audiovisual aids is supposed to compensate for the lack of teacher qualification, but in turn, such teachers ought to be paid less than regularly qualified ones. Unfortunately, this last assumption has been rarely verified, except in a couple of Brazilian projects (Maranhâo, at least in the beginning of the project, and Ceâra—see Table 1).

The two main media used in this context are television and radio. The focus was first placed on television (as in projects in the Samoa Islands, El Salvador, Mexico, Brazil, Ivory Coast, Niger, and Senegal) and later on radio (Nicaragua, the Philippines, and Thailand). As can be expected, radio is much cheaper than television and the risk of a negative productivity effect is much lower. The majority of these projects have shown a positive impact on school performances and on access to education of previously excluded children. The question of cost effectiveness is less clear, except that it is more likely to be positive with radio than with television.

Several of the above projects have already been closed (Tele-Niger, Samoa Islands, Ivory Coast). The Senegal pilot project will probably not be expanded, and the future of the Nicaraguan Radio Math is uncertain. In most cases, these closures are not due to a negative cost–effectiveness ratio, but to various sociopolitical factors. Even when financial difficulties have been emphasized, as in the case of Ivory Coast, they were actually minor compared with sociopolitical issues.

Table 1 summarizes some of the cost studies carried out on these systems and provides some evidence, mostly on within-school projects, where the basic auxiliary medium is television (except for Mexico's *Radioprimaria*). The cost–effectiveness performances of these projects is not clearly demonstrated. Except in Mexico, where the costs are lower for similar results, the four other cases do not bring decisive improvements: a slight gain in school performances is obtained at the expense of a slight increase in unit costs. The results are somewhat better in Latin America than in Africa for two reasons: (a) supplementary costs of television are lower than in Africa because this technology is entirely mastered by local resources, while in Africa costly expatriate specialists have to be hired; (b) the labor qualification substitution is better obtained in Latin America, while in Africa such a substitution has not taken place.

Subsequent similar projects, based on radio instead of television, have been tried in Nicaragua (Radio Math), in the Philippines, and in Thailand. Radio is much cheaper than television (Jamison and McAnany 1978, Perraton, Jamison, and Orivel 1982), and above a rapidly reached audience threshold, unit costs tend to be negligible. As a consequence, when significantly positive performances appear, as is clearly the case in these three projects, one can reasonably assume that one has a positive cost–effectiveness ratio (Suppes, Searle, and Friend 1980).

The main conclusions we can draw from these economic evaluations are the following:

(a) Within-school educational technology has not dramatically improved the cost–effectiveness ratio of educational services compared with traditional teaching.

(b) Radio is more likely to be cost effective than television, especially when carefully designed curricula are implemented.

(c) The labor qualification/media substitution, which assumes that underqualified teachers supported by media will be paid less to compensate media costs, is in most contexts unrealistic. Sometimes the opposite occurs: in the Ivory Coast, PETV's teachers have been promoted to higher salaries.

(d) The high death rate of within-school media projects is often due to teachers' rejection. This rejection may be explained by the rigidity of broadcast systems, and also by the fact that after some years of implementation, the underqualified teachers have assimilated the content of broadcast programs, and feel able to teach by themselves, without this now useless and constraining tool. Such an evolution may be seen as an unexpected result of this system, i.e., a successful inservice training of teaching staff.

(e) From an economic and organizational perspective, such a result implies that such projects should be conceived of as temporary institutions, using part-time external consultants (media specialists or curricula designers) instead of a full-time permanent staff.

3. Out-of-school Applications of New Educational Technologies

This field is the most promising area of the economically successful introduction of technology in education. While within-school technology is tending to decline, there is a rapid expansion of out-of-school systems, both formal and nonformal. There is a large variety of such systems, from simple and long-established correspondence courses to sophisticated multimedia projects, such as the now-famous Open University (UK), and in between, numerous nonformal educational projects in the field of hygiene and health habits, agricultural information, family planning, literacy and numeracy campaigns, etc. Several classifications of these systems are possible, according to the type of media used, the audience, the mode of studying, and the level of education, as shown in Fig. 3.

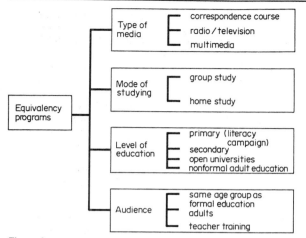

Figure 3
Classification of out-of-school use of educational technology

3.1 Type of Media

From an economic point of view, the differences in costs between the simplest correspondence course and a sophisticated multimedia system are larger than the differences in effectiveness. The marginal productivity of each additional medium is therefore decreasing. But many authors argue that even if the additional impact of the last medium is lower than its costs, it may have significant external effects. For instance, in most open universities, the broadcasting of television programs is frequently considered by students as less important than printed material, in spite of the fact that it is substantially more expensive. But the broadcasting of these television programs generates useful external effects: large audiences, respectability, advertising possibilities, international recognition, and exports of didactic material and pedagogical expertise.

3.2 Mode of Studying

In contexts where the majority of the target audience owns a receiver for the broadcasted programs at home, the reception may take place on an individual basis (home study) but when this is not the case, the project has to organize a group study system, and to provide the receivers and the space. Very often the broadcasting is done early in the morning or late in the afternoon, when regular classrooms are available. But there are many alternatives to classrooms, such as a church or under a tree. Group study generally requires the presence of a monitor or "animateur," and is therefore more expensive than home study. On the other hand, group study provides more assistance, both from the monitors and from the peers (peer tutoring), and stimulates the motivation of students more efficiently. There is relatively little evidence on the respective cost effectiveness of both systems, and the choice is very often dictated by

contextual constraints (for example, finances, distance, existence of qualified monitors).

3.3 Level of Education

Since it radically reduces the face-to-face component of traditional teaching, distance education is more likely to succeed with students able to show some autonomy in the learning process. As a consequence, young children are less able to follow these types of courses than older children and adults. In practice it is difficult to enroll in such systems children below the age of 15. From an economic perspective, this is approximately the age from which forgone earnings can be estimated as private costs. (This limit is actually lower in rural areas, and higher in developed countries, where the working age may begin at 16 or 18.) Furthermore, for young children, the formal school system plays an additional role, which one could call a "child care" role, provided at no cost by the formal system as a by-product. This service would no longer be free under a home-study distance education system, and the economic advantage of a larger pupil–teacher ratio in distance education would be lost for children who still need the permanent presence of an adult, teacher or nonteacher.

Nevertheless, in developed countries the rapid development of microcomputers and the fact that many households possess these microcomputers as well as video recorders will increase the possibilities of individual instruction, young children included. However, the most appropriate level of education for distance education is clearly the university level, at which students have a solid basic background and can study by themselves. The second clear field of distance education is in nonformal education aimed at adults (permanent education, lifelong education, etc.). Secondary education, especially at the senior level, and literacy programs for illiterate adults may be provided through distance education, but more easily with a system of group study than with a system of home study, in order to provide some minimal supervision and assistance (from the peers and/or from the monitor).

3.4 Audience

The audience of distance education systems may theoretically be composed of the same age groups as formal systems for equivalent programs, as they were originally considered as equivalency programs, aimed at pupils who have missed the formal system for reasons such as sickness, social background, excessive private costs, distance, motherhood, etc. Distance education is a substitution system, some sort of second best to give a second chance to people excluded for nonacademic reasons. It is still exceptional to have a distance education system considered as a normal, regular, and fully competitive alternative to traditional schools or universities. Primary-school teachers are another common audience for distance education projects, especially in developing

Table 2
Cost effectiveness of 10 out-of-school educational projects

Project	Units for measuring N	Value of N at time of study	Cost function in 1978 US$ at 7.5 percent discount rate	Average cost for given N in 1978 US$	Project impacts on		
					Pedagogical quality	Access	Cost per enrollment
South Korea Air Correspondence High School (ACHS)	Student enrollments	20,000	$TC(N) = 51,500 + 42.8N$	68.4	ACHS students do less well on tests but evidence suggests that this is because they start at a much lower level than regular high-school students	Improves access for students who must work to support themselves	The ACHS cost per enrollee is about 24% of the $250 annual cost of the regular high schools
Kenya inservice teacher training	Subject equivalent per year	1977 N = 790	$TC(N) = 165,850 + 114.8N$	324.7	Improvement	Improves access in rural areas	Though comparisons are difficult, can be considered high
Israel Everyman's University	Course enrollments (18 courses required for bachelor's degree)	8,000 in 1978 (26,000 in projected steady state)	$TC(N) = 5,286,500 + 81.7N$ (fixed costs are long-term steady state operation)	324.0 (284.0)	No evidence	Improves access for geographically and other disadvantaged groups	n.a.
Dominican Republic *Radio Escuela* Santa Maria	Student enrollments	20,000	$TC(N) = 187,000 + 10.7N$	20.0	Test results suggest that Radio Santa Maria students score as well as students in traditional adult schools even though they start further behind	Improves access in rural areas	Costs are about half those of traditional adult education for equivalency

Project	Measure	N	Total cost function	Cost	Quality	Access	Cost comparison
Brazil *Telecurso Secundo Grau*	Student enrollments	40,000	$TC(N) = 5,632,100 + 53.4N$	194.2	Improvement	Improvement	Between 25 and 67% of alternatives
Chinese Television University	Student full-time equivalent	186,000	Not available	Not available	No evidence	Strong improvement in urban areas	Clear indication of reduced cost
Brazil Minerva *Madureza* project	Number of subject equivalence a year	1977 N = 177,000	$TC(N) = 907,120 + 19.7N$	24.8	No evidence	Slight improvement from both geographical and social point of view	Between 0 and 50% decrease, according to the alternatives
Brazil Bahia *Madureza* project	Number of subject equivalence a year	1977 N = 8,000	$TC(N) = 437,900 + 12.6N$	67.4	Rather lower than other systems of preparation to *Madureza* exams	No effect	Between 50% and 1150% increase, according to the alternatives
Malawi Correspondence College	Number of students reached per year	1978 N = 2,800	$TC(N) = 132,000 + 117N$	160.0	Pass rates lower than in traditional schools, but students enter much less well prepared	Increases fractions of cohort enrolled; improves access in rural areas	The cost is 62% that of day secondary schools and 23% that of boarding schools
Mauritius College of the Air	Number of course enrollments	1976 N = 12,000	$TC(N) = 143,800 + 1.98N$	14.0	Probably improved quality in remote schools	No effect	Project costs are in addition to the sum of $77 per student per year which was given to the schools in which it was used

a Source: Jamison and Orivel 1982

countries where they are often underqualified. Such systems allow the retraining of these teachers without formal meetings in a single place, thus avoiding potentially high transportation costs.

Table 2 provides cost information on 10 distance education projects. It does not include several other available case studies, such as the Open University, the French *Télé-Enseignement* or the Brazilian Logos II for inservice teacher training. In these three cases, as in 8 out of 10 cases in Table 2, costs per student and per graduate are lower than in equivalent formal systems, with similar results. The proportion of fixed costs within the total cost is important, often exceeding 50 percent and reaching 90 percent in the case of Everyman University in Israel. The importance of fixed costs in the projects reviewed here should be seen in conjunction with what is to be observed in traditional education where, for the most part, fixed costs and administration costs are the same thing, the latter, however, being less "fixed" on the whole than production costs in media-based projects. The administration component is only slightly sensitive to marginal changes in system size (the same administrative unit being able to cope with an increase of up to, for example, 20 percent in system size without having to increase its staff, and probably not needing to reduce its staff if system size is marginally reduced by, for example, up to 20 percent). On the other hand, a significant change in size necessarily involves a strengthening (or paring down) of the administration. Not only are the fixed costs of traditional education systems fixed only within a certain range, but they are also proportionally very low, administration costs rarely exceeding 10 percent of the total. This statement must however be corrected for certain institutional contexts. When teacher legislation does not allow the employing authority to relocate or dismiss teachers when reductions in staff are called for, labor costs tend to become almost a fixed item, which is possible only when it is the taxpayer who bears the bulk of education system costs (a private school without pupils would be obliged to dismiss its teachers).

Going back to the case of media systems, fixed production costs are real fixed costs. If a film costing $100,000 is seen by 1,000 pupils, the fixed production cost per pupil is $100; it if is seen by 10,000, the cost falls to $10 per head; if it is shown to 100,000 the cost is as low as $1; and if the number of viewers rises to 1,000,000 the cost per head falls to a negligible 10 cents.

This cost structure means that enrollment levels are of particular importance. For an equivalency program to succeed it must be assured of an appropriate minimum number of students over a long enough period. To take one clear example, the Kenyan project has probably reached a stage where it no longer has enough students to justify its continuation; the Bahia project probably never will, if we take into account the alternatives in Brazil, such as Minerva or *Telecurso*. It is, of course, impossible to set a precise figure for the minimum number of students as this varies from project to project. But

at the level of secondary education, projects with fewer than 10,000 students per year are generally at risk, and this figure may be a good enough estimate for general postsecondary education. Specialized vocationally oriented projects whose audience is dispersed and working may sometimes be justified with far fewer students. In this type of project, seen quite often in teacher retraining, the closest conventional alternative would show particularly high unit costs, due mainly to:

(a) the need to assemble the participants in a single place, necessarily at a distance from where some of them reside;

(b) the need for participants to abandon their usual employment temporarily, and therefore to receive payment equal to their normal salaries;

(c) the additional cost of accommodation for nonresidents;

(d) possible cost of family accommodation, if the training course is a prolonged one, or the alternative psychological cost produced by the separation.

Under these circumstances the cost of the closest alternative is likely to be very high. In Kenya, for example, it was shown that the system could be economically justified if there were 2,000 enrollments for certificates.

In any event, the general figure of 10,000 should not be regarded as a magic threshold. The threshold will actually depend on four factors:

(a) the level of study (primary, secondary, higher, adult);

(b) the choice between radio and television;

(c) the cost of the closest alternative;

(d) the degree to which the capital–labor substitution is extended.

These factors are linked. It is in adult education that the costs of the closest alternative are likely to be highest and where it is easiest to go much further ahead with capital–labor substitution, since adults are more capable than young children of studying alone with the media, unassisted by a teacher. In this type of situation, a relatively modest number of students, say in the vicinity of 2,000, will justify a well-defined radio or radio-correspondence project economically. On the other hand, at the primary and secondary levels, where the teacher is crucial, many more pupils are necessary (several tens of thousands, usually) before a positive cost–effectiveness ratio can be obtained, especially when television is the medium used. For these reasons it is important to look closely at the pupil target groups in a media project. Since many projects are experimental, or quasiexperimental, they involve small numbers of pupils, by definition, so that unit costs prove relatively high, since fixed costs must be spread over a small number of users.

Projects that use television have higher unit costs. But television makes only a small difference to total costs where, despite the use of media, projects still rely to a great extent on teachers (as in the two Mexican examples). An additional factor is that television costs vary greatly depending on whether the system utilizes an existing network at its marginal cost during off-peak times, or whether it operates its own transmitter and its own network of ground relay transmitters. For out-of-school distance teaching projects it is impossible to use television unless numbers of the intended audience already own receivers.

Most of the projects studied here are less expensive than equivalent traditional methods of education, especially if we take into account the fact that many of them are aimed at adults in employment who, by studying part time at a distance, avoid a loss of earnings while they study. This cost in salary would either be borne by the individual, who agrees to undergo training or retraining on a nonsalary basis (rare), or, as is more often the case, by the employer, who continues to pay the trainee's salary but must find a replacement and therefore disburse two salaries on a single occupied work slot. For many such students these equivalency program systems are the only available way of studying. There was, however, substantial variation among projects in the extent to which they were cost saving, as compared with traditional education. Since the costs of both electronic and printed media are declining relative to the cost of teacher time, cost advantages for distance teaching can be expected to increase in the future.

Equivalency program projects seem to have a clear and positive impact on educational equity, in terms of making quality education more widely available and of making access to any education at all possible for previously excluded groups.

The majority of projects in developing countries are relatively unsophisticated if one compares them to certain multimedia systems used in the developed countries (the Open University, for instance). This simplicity has proved a sound choice. It is clear that a systematic quest for programs of high artistic quality would have swung the cost–effectiveness ratio to the negative side, something particularly true of television-based systems. All the school television projects described here, except *Telecurso*, are the work of absolutely minimal production teams, perhaps 10 times smaller than similar professional groups in the high-income countries. The achievement of professional standards while maintaining a good cost–effectiveness ratio would be possible only if enrollments were far more numerous. In most cases, television personnel have gained their experience on the job, so that a certain amateurism is a feature of the production studios. If, instead of making do with modest local talent, reliance had been placed on a large complement of technicians from high-income countries, it is likely that, in the absence of a significant increase in enrollments, the cost–effectiveness ratio would again have been an inverse one.

4. Further Comments on the Economics of Some Specific Media

Several means have been introduced in conventional schools to improve the quality of teaching services. A common belief among educators is that the reduction of the number of pupils per teacher is the most appropriate solution to improve the quality of their teaching. From an empirical point of view, this point remains today highly controversial. Most studies do not show significant changes in student performances associated with class size. Some others tend to show that some slight improvements can be reached when the average number of students goes from 40 to 20, and more substantial improvements below, especially around 10, but this solution is clearly impractical in most developing countries because of its cost implications.

One word should be said concerning the provision of textbooks. It is not a new medium, but its cost–effectiveness ratio remains remarkable. In a school context where a substantial proportion of pupils have no access to textbooks (essentially for economic reasons), the free provision of textbooks has a relatively small effect on the per student cost (in the range of 1 percent) and a significant impact on cognitive performances (a 10–20 percent improvement in test scores is not exceptional). A review is given below of the potential impact of the newer media used in classes, that is, radio, television, language, laboratories, and computers.

4.1 Radio

Radio is by far the cheapest means to reach a wide audience. A study on Malawi (Perraton, Jamison, and Orivel 1982) has shown that to provide relevant information and training to farmers, an hour of contact by radio is 3,000 times cheaper than face-to-face communication. When radio sets are widespread, the use of radio for informal educational programs is certainly appropriate. But it can also be used for in-class direct teaching in some fields, such as mathematics, when primary teachers are unsufficiently qualified, or for the retraining of teachers themselves. Finally, radio can be used for distance teaching systems, especially for equivalency programs (late secondary and postsecondary levels). This last point will be expanded below.

4.2 Language Laboratories

The introduction of language laboratories in school institutions in most developed countries has produced rather disappointing results. Their pedagogical impact is usually not statistically significant and the per student costs tend to be high. The hourly student cost is, for instance in the case of France, around US\$4 (Orivel In press), of which half is due to the language laboratory itself, and half due to additional teaching staff, because the class has to be divided into two groups (the majority of classes being between 20 and 40 students). Furthermore, the utilization of these language laboratories follows the traditional school rhythm, instead of intensive periods of learning during a short period of time. This means usually 1 hour every 2 weeks, which tends to be too long an interval between two sessions to produce significant results. Very likely, the utilization of language laboratories will tend to encourage free access by students and a more intensive rate of utilization. It is also possible that language-teaching computers will be developed for autonomous learning (see the paragraph below on computer-assisted instruction).

4.3 Television

Great expectations were placed on the introduction of television programs in education. A wide range of experience has been gained around the world with uneven success. Today, the feelings of decision makers in educational systems concerning the advantages of using television in formal education are rather mixed. It is therefore necessary to try to clarify what we have learned from these experiences and what we can predict for the future.

(a) *The question of the costs and quality of television programs*. Table 3 shows, for 12 educational projects using television programs, the yearly number of program hours produced and the average cost of production of a one-hour program. Of course, some of these figures are out of date, but the most surprising overall result is the very large variability of the cost of a unit of output.

The nature of the programs produced in these different projects may vary considerably. In the case of Stanford University, it is a live production of a professor giving a lecture; while in the case of the Open University, one has sophisticated programs with professional standards similar to the British Broadcasting Corporation (BBC) programs (the television unit in the Open University is part of the BBC staff). In between, there are a variety of television productions, managed either by nonprofessional television people, mainly retrained teachers, or by semi-professional or professional televi-sion specialists. Using professional television criteria, it is possible to find a close relation between the unit costs of these different television programs and their technical quality. But the relation between the cost and/or the quality of educational television programs and their pedagogical impact is much less close. In any case, even if it were possible to show that technically good programs have a better pedagogical impact, there is no chance that the differences of impact may have the same range as of costs (1 to 300). This means that with a given budget constraint, it is rational to sacrifice some technical quality in favor of other educational material (especially books).

(b) *Computer-assisted instruction*. The recent development of microcomputing systems has raised great expectations. Nevertheless, their introduction in the educational systems has to be carefully evaluated. In spite of a rapid decline of the costs of the hardware, the costs per student remain relative high: most projects show hourly per student costs around US$4, and as long as the software costs cannot be shared by a great number of students, it is unlikely to have a positive cost–effectiveness ratio in the context of most developing countries in the near future, except for some specific reasons, namely: (a) the teaching of computer science should rapidly be undertaken, to avoid the building of a new gap between developed and developing countries in a strategic field; and (b) the teaching of foreign languages may very soon become cost effective with computers. That does not mean that developing countries themselves should invest in the development of this material, but they should be ready to use, at a relatively low marginal cost, what is implemented in this field in richer countries.

5. Conclusion

The economics of educational technology is a new field within educational sciences, but has already produced

Table 3
Quantity and costs of different television programs[a]

Project	Number of hours of programs produced per year	Cost of a 1-hour program (US$ 1980)
El Salvador	333	5,665
Hagerstown (USA)	1,440	1,450
Telesecundaria (Mexico)	1,080	925
Korea, Republic of	n.a.	3,220
Stanford (USA)	6,290	175
Open University (UK)	288	18,150
Ivory Coast (formal)	201	25,900
Ivory Coast (nonformal)	17	51,200
Telecurso (Brazil)	75	53,800
Ceâra (Brazil)	300	2,750
Maranhâo (Brazil)	525	1,815
Senegal (TSS)	49	16,600

a Source: Evans and Klees 1976, formal Ivory Coast; Klees 1977, nonformal Ivory Coast; Klees 1980, *Telecurso*; Oliveira and Orivel 1980, Maranhâo and Ceâra; Orivel 1981, Senegal; Jamison et al. 1978 all others significant results which will probably affect the design of innovative educational projects. The shrinking of educational budgets, especially from public sources, makes the need for a better use of educational resources more urgent. The cost–effective allocation of educational resources means that one of the clear objectives of educational technology is the improvement of the productivity of the educational sector, and not only the improvement of school performances, regardless of its costs.

Within-school introduction of educational technology, to enrich traditional teaching, has been and still is the most common area of educational media. Nevertheless, this type of use has not produced dramatic changes in educational productivity (either negative or positive). In a context where the teaching staff is underqualified, especially in certain fields such as mathematics or foreign languages, the support of broadcast media may have a positive cost–effective impact, relatively often with radio, and sometimes with television.

But the main area where educational technology has been successful from a cost–effectiveness point of view is in the framework of out-of-school projects, for both equivalency programs and nonformal education, where the labor/media substitution has significantly taken place. In such projects, fixed costs are higher than in traditional teaching but variable costs, thanks to a larger pupil–teacher ratio, are lower, and when a large enough number of students are registered in the system to share the fixed costs, total unit costs are lower than in traditional teaching. Case studies on such systems have shown that most are indeed cost effective, in spite of the fact that this was not their original objective. This often unexpected result could therefore be achieved more demonstratively if this objective became more explicit, as will probably be the case with growing budgetary constraints. Optimization of media combination remains to be assessed, but after centuries of face-to-face teaching without any significant productivity change, education is now entering a new age, in which technology will play a growing role.

Bibliography

Bowen H R 1980 *The Costs of Higher Education: How Much do Colleges and Universities Spend per Student and How Much Should They Spend?* Jossey-Bass, San Francisco, California

Brusling G 1982 Essor et déclin de la technologie de l'éducation en Suède. *Perspectives* 12(3): 7

Eicher J-C, Orivel F 1979 *L'Allocation des ressources à l'éducation dans le monde.* Office des Statistiques, UNESCO, Paris

Eicher J-C, Orivel F 1980 Cost analysis of primary education by television in the Ivory Coast. *The Economics of New Educational Media*, Vol. 2. UNESCO, Paris

Evans S, Klees S 1976 ETV *Program Production in the Ivory Coast.* Academy for Educational Development, Washington, DC

Guillin M, Orivel F 1984 *Critères technico-économiques pour la mise en oeuvre des média dans les institutions d'éducation* [also English transl.]. UNESCO, Paris

Jamison D T, McAnany E 1978 *Radio for Education and Development.* Sage, Beverly Hills, California

Jamison D T, Orivel F 1982 The cost effectiveness of distance teaching for school equivalency. In: Perraton H (ed.) 1982 *Alternative Routes to Formal Education.* Johns Hopkins University Press, Baltimore, Maryland

Jamison D T, Klees S, Wells S 1978 *The Costs of Educational Media: Guidelines for Planning and Evaluation.* Sage, Beverly Hills, California

Klees S 1977 *Cost Analysis of Non-formal ETV Systems: A Case Study of the Extra-scolaire System in the Ivory Coast.* Academy for Educational Development, Washington, DC

Klees S 1980 Cost analysis of Telecurso. In: Araujo J G, Oliveira J B (eds.) 1980 *Telecurso Ilè Grau.* ABT, Rio de Janeiro

Mayo J, McAnany E, Klees S J 1975 The Mexican Telesecundaria: A cost effectiveness analysis. *Instruc. Sci.* 4: 193–236

Oliveira J B, Orivel F 1980 Socio-economic analysis of two systems of educational television in Brazil in the States of Maranhâo and Ceâra. *The Economics of New Educational Media*, Vol. 2. UNESCO, Paris

Orivel F 1981 *La Télévision scolaire du Sénégal: Evaluation économique et perspectives.* DEDPH Discussion Paper No. 81–50. World Bank, Washington, DC

Perraton H, Jamison D T, Orivel F 1982 *Mass Media for Agricultural Extension in Malawi.* International Extension College, Cambridge

Suppes P C, Searle B, Friend J 1980 *The Radio Mathematics Project in Nicaragua 1976–77.* Stanford University Press, Stanford, California

Distribution and Reception of Television Programs

P. Miller

In educational television, program distribution is the middle link in a chain that begins with the design and production of educational programs, and ends with the students actually using the programming individually or in groups, in homes, schools, and other educational settings (see *The Role of Film, Television, and Video*; *Use of Television in the Classroom*). The purpose of this article is to examine the various methods of delivery used to distribute educational television programming, and to offer a general analysis of the factors that determine which method is most appropriate for particular educational applications.

For 50 years, open-air broadcast transmission has been the most prevalent means of distributing educational television programs. More recently, educational programming has also been delivered through videotape, videocassette, and videodisc distribution; and through cable, microwave, and satellite transmission. Each of these technologies possesses specific strengths as a distribution medium. Each also suffers from a number of limitations (see Table 1). The distribution method most appropriate for a particular application or educational setting depends on the number and location of viewers to be served, the scheduling needs of viewers, the need for single versus multiple channel transmissions, the need for interactive versus one-way communication, and the funding and transmission facilities available to participating institutions and organizations.

1. Broadcast Distribution

In television broadcasting, television stations transmit program signals on electromagnetic frequencies called carrier waves. Each television station transmits audio and video signals on assigned carrier frequencies, and each station's assigned frequencies correspond to a single television channel on the tuner of a conventional television receiver. During a broadcast, the television station's carrier wave radiates from a transmitting tower, carrying the program information through the air at the speed of light. At reception sites, the program signals are received through television antennae attached or built into conventional television receivers. When a television receiver is tuned to the correct frequency, the receiver's electronic circuits recreate the original program sound and picture from the audio and video information impressed on the carrier waves.

The exact range of a broadcast television signal depends on the strength of the signal, the height and location of the transmitting tower, and the degree to which the signal is blocked by natural or human obstructions. In the United States, a typical very high frequency (VHF) television signal has an effective range of about 40 miles. Within that 40-mile radius, most homes and educational institutions can receive the signal without the use of special antennae or signal amplifiers.

Table 1
General comparison of television distribution technologies

	Transmission facility costs	Reception facility costs	Multi-channel	"Live" real-time) transmission	Two-way audio and video transmission	Signal coverage area (approx.)	Easy access for educators	Data/text transmission
Broadcast	High	Low	No	Yes	No	30–50 miles[a]	No	Yes
Broadband cable	Low[b]	Low	Yes	Yes	Yes	Normally local	Yes	Yes
Microwave (ITFS)	Moderate	Moderate	Yes	Yes	Yes	25 miles[a]	Yes	Yes
Video-cassette	Low–moderate[c]	Low–moderate	Does not apply	No	No	Does not apply	Yes	Yes
Video-disc	High[c]	Low–moderate	Does not apply	No	No	Does not apply	Yes	Yes
Fixed service satellite	Very high	High	Yes[d]	Yes	Only at extra cost	One-fifth to one-third of Earth's surface	No	Yes
Direct broadcast satellite	Very high	Low–moderate	Yes[d]	Yes	No	One to four time zones	No	Yes

a Signal range can be extended by installing "repeater" or "translator" facilities in fringe reception areas, or by installing sophisticated antenna equipment at reception sites   b The cost is only low when educational institutions transmit programming over channels leased from or provided by commercial cable television systems   c These costs include the cost of the equipment used in mastering and duplicating tapes or discs   d Most communication satellites are capable of transmitting 12 or more television channels. However, because satellite "transponder time" is very expensive, most educational television services have been limited to single-channel transmission

1.1 Strengths of Broadcasting as a Distribution Medium

Broadcasting is most effective as a means of "scattering" live or prerecorded program signals over a broad geographic area. Because program transmission is "open", a broadcast program can be received by any television set within the transmitting station's coverage area. Reception-site costs are normally confined to the cost of a television receiver and a consumer-grade television antenna.

In Europe and North America, basic television reception equipment is widely available, making broadcast transmission an effective means of delivering programming to large, general audiences. In the United States, for example, television sets are found in 98 percent of all homes and 86 percent of the nation's public schools. (Corporation for Public Broadcasting 1979 p. 32). In nations where television receivers are not as generally available, broadcasting can still be an efficient means of delivering programming to those who have sets. There are substantial audiences in many urban areas, and even remote or scattered sites are sometimes most easily reached by this method.

As Table 1 indicates, broadcast television transmission can also be used to deliver text and data signals. In most cases, the text and data information is encoded into the "vertical blanking interval"—an unused portion of the television signal. Televised text services that use this broadcast method are currently operating in France, Canada, the United Kingdom, the Federal Republic of Germany, and the United States. Like all broadcast services, these televised text services are limited by the one-way nature of broadcast transmission (as contrasted with the two-way, interactive communication possible with wire, cable, and some types of microwave transmission).

1.2 Limitations of Broadcasting as a Distribution Medium

Many of the limitations of broadcast distribution stem from two related considerations—cost and channel scarcity. In many industrial nations, competition for television channel assignments is keen, and educational and commercial groups frequently find themselves competing for the same channel slots. In some nations, educational groups are also forced to compete for broadcast time on television stations that are responsible for delivering entertainment and information programming to more general audiences (Perry 1977 p. 267). Even in countries where a sufficient number of television frequencies are set aside for educational use, the high cost of equipping (US$500,000–$5,000,000) and operating television broadcast facilities discourages individual schools and universities from forming and operating independent television stations, and encourages the centralization of educational broadcast services through regional and national television networks.

In locations where a national, regional, or local educational broadcast service is available, problems of cost and channel scarcity generally limit program distribution to one-way transmission over a single television channel. Usually, single-channel transmission requires broadcasters to adhere to fixed, inflexible program schedules—schedules that are often too rigid to meet the varied needs of the students and teachers who comprise the viewing audience. In at least one survey, teachers have identified fixed broadcast schedules as the most significant hindrance to the classroom use of educational television programming (Corporation for Public Broadcasting 1979 p. 18).

Broadcast transmission is also constrained by problems of signal privacy. By their nature, broadcast signals are "open" transmissions that can be received by any television set located within the transmitting station's coverage area. This often makes broadcasting an inappropriate method for distributing sensitive program material, or for delivering programming that is intended for a narrow, specific audience.

Finally, although broadcast transmission can provide an effective means of delivering programming to large audiences located within a defined geographic area, broadcast transmissions are limited by the restricted range of terrestrial television signals. In some instances, a broadcast station's coverage area can be expanded by increasing the power of its transmitter, or by building repeater or repeater stations. However, each of these alternatives increases the costs associated with transmitting broadcast signals—costs that already work to limit the use of educational television broadcasting in many regions of the world.

1.3 Applications of Broadcast Distribution

In its 50 year history, broadcast television has been used to deliver instructional programming to schools and universities, to bring "master teachers" into a nation's classrooms, to distribute informational and instructional programming to general audiences, and to deliver college and professional education courses to adult learners. Thus broadcasting is a proven method of program delivery.

For the most part, international experience confirms that television broadcasting is best-suited as a means of distributing programming to large numbers of students or general viewers. Although start-up and operating costs are generally high, the actual transmission cost for broadcasting one hour of educational programming to 5,000 students can be less than US$0.01 per student (Jamison et al. 1978). However, when the audience for an educational program is relatively small, or when students and teachers require the sort of flexible access to programming that fixed broadcast schedules cannot provide, broadcast transmission becomes a much less efficient and cost-effective means of program distribution.

2. Broadband Cable Distribution

Cable television systems fall into two general categories: closed-circuit cable systems designed to serve school or industrial needs, and community cable systems designed to deliver entertainment and information programming to more general audiences. In both systems, television signals are transmitted to reception points through coaxial or fiber-optic cables. While a 400 MHz coaxial cable can carry between 50 and 60 television channels, a single fiber-optic cable can carry 200 or more television channels.

In North America, community cable systems initially developed as community antenna television (CATV), a service that gathered-in broadcast signals through a large local antenna, amplified and filtered the signals at a central technical facility, and distributed the signals to subscribers through special trunk, feed, and drop cables. By 1960, there were approximately 650 of these local CATV systems in the United States, each providing up to 12 television channels to homes and schools in communities too remote to receive adequate television service using ordinary home antennae.

Over the next two decades, technical and regulatory changes combined to increase the number and type of services available through community cable systems. By 1972, advances in cable technology allowed cable systems to carry 30 or more television channels on a single coaxial cable. By 1976, many cable systems in the United States were using their expanded channel capacity to offer program services delivered by communications satellites. In the 1970s, a series of rulings by the Federal Communications Commission also required many United States cable systems to provide channels for educational use, to construct television production facilities for local use, and to equip their technical plants with the capacity for interactive (two-way) video communication. Although these requirements have since been overturned in the United States courts, they prompted initial experimentation with the local production of cable programming, and encouraged growing numbers of schools to explore the educational uses of community cable systems.

With these changes, modern cable systems have become much more than simple retransmission services for broadcast television signals. Today, cable systems employing fiber-optic or dual coaxial cables are using 100 or more television channels to deliver programming received through satellite reception dishes, programming produced by cable company employees, programming produced by citizen and school groups, and interactive video, text, and shop-at-home services. Some community cable systems have also installed "institutional networks"—special closed-circuit loops that interconnect schools and other public buildings for program distribution and interactive voice/video communication.

Since the early 1950s, school and university systems have also designed and built their own internal cable systems. Like early CATV systems, many of these closed-circuit networks are actually "master antenna" systems that retransmit programming received through a central antenna or satellite reception dish. Some newer systems are also equipped for interactive voice/video communication, and for transmitting live or prerecorded programming from television studios or videotape facilities. On all closed-circuit cable systems, program signals are amplified and routed at a main technical facility, and distributed to classrooms and lecture halls through coaxial or fiber-optic cables.

2.1 Strengths of Broadband Cable as a Distribution Medium

As an educational medium, cable's greatest assets are its flexibility and availability. A single 400 MHz coaxial cable can carry between 50 and 60 television channels; hundreds of voice, radio, and data signals; or any combination of television, voice, radio, and data channels. Fiber-optic cables offer two to ten times the channel capacity of coaxial cable, and the same ability to combine various types of signals.

In the United States, cable is rapidly becoming a widely available transmission medium. According to various industry estimates, there were approximately 5,700 community cable systems operating in the United States in 1983, delivering program signals to more than 29 million homes (Knowledge Industry Publications 1983). Most cable systems built since 1972 are equipped with television production studios, and many systems make channel space and production equipment available to educational groups for little or no charge (provided that appropriate provisions are written into the franchise agreement between the local community and the cable company). Reception-site costs are generally low, particularly when the franchise agreement requires the cable company to provide schools with cable drop lines and television converter boxes free of charge.

On closed-circuit cable systems, and on community cable systems that feature educational access channels or closed-circuit institutional networks, educators often exercise complete control over the selection and scheduling of television, voice, and data transmissions. With this control, and with access to multiple-cable channels, schools and educational television agencies are generally able to transmit programming at times that are convenient for both teachers and students. Additionally, with multiple-channel transmission, educational groups are able to deliver programming to audiences that are too small or specific to be served through single-channel broadcast distribution. In communities with newer cable systems, schools may also arrange to receive educational television services delivered over communications satellites, to experiment with the educational uses of two-way cable communication, and to isolate or scramble program signals to create private communication channels.

2.2 Limitations of Broadband Cable as a Distribution Medium

Cable television is limited by the restricted transmission range of most cable systems, by the age and channel capacity of many existing cable systems, and by the experimental nature of much modern cable technology. Although most community cable systems are equipped to bring distant broadcast and satellite signals into their franchise areas, few are capable of transmitting signals beyond their local areas. Additionally, over 50 percent of the cable systems currently operating in the United States are older, 12-channel systems that are already saturated with television signals, and that are often reluctant to commit scarce channel space to educational uses. Although channel availability is generally not a problem on most modern cable systems, these high-capacity cable systems employ technology that has often proven difficult to obtain, activate, and operate. This is particularly true for the equipment used in data, two-way, and pay-per-view transmissions.

Although several European, Asian, and Latin American nations offer limited levels of cable television service, community cable remains primarily a North American phenomenon (Grandi 1978 p. 50). Outside Canada and the United States, educational institutions that would like to take advantage of cable distribution must usually plan and build their own closed-circuit systems. Even in the United States, where community cable systems are widely available, many remote and sparsely populated areas remain unwired, and pending federal legislation may soon work to limit the number and type of free or inexpensive educational services that communities can require from private cable operators.

When schools, colleges, and universities build closed-circuit cable systems, construction costs can also be a limiting factor. The cost of installing cable ranges from US$8,000 per mile in rural areas to $12,000 in urban areas, and can be as high as $80,000 per mile where underground wiring is necessary. Equipment costs for technical (head-end) facilities on closed-circuit systems range from $100,000 to over $2 million, with the exact cost determined by the channel capacity of the system and the degree to which the facility is equipped for program production, satellite reception, and two-way signal transmission.

2.3 Applications of Broadband Cable Distribution

Cable television has been used to deliver continuing education programming to adult viewers, to transmit data and text information, to receive programming broadcast by distant educational television stations, to deliver college and professional education courses, and to provide flexible transmission schedules for instructional programming distributed to schools and colleges. In an advanced application of cable technology, students and teachers in Higashi Ikoma, Japan, interact over an experimental fiber-optic cable system funded by the Ministry of International Trade and Commerce. Using cameras and microphones located in their homes, students in Higashi Ikoma are able to see and speak with teachers conducting classes from a school or cable studio (Murata 1981 p. 149). In the United States, schools in California, Pennsylvania, and several other states are experimenting with similar types of two-way cable communication (Moss 1978 p. 160).

In Spokane, Washington and many other United States communities, educational groups use multiple-cable channels to transmit programming produced by students, and to deliver instructional programs at times that meet teachers' individual needs. Many United States cable systems also receive and retransmit the Appalachian Community Services Network (ACSN), an educational television service carried over a cable-serving satellite. In some communities, students view ACSN programming in their homes in conjunction with courses offered by local colleges and universities. A number of United States cable systems also carry the American Educational Television Network (AETN), a satellite programming service that delivers professional education courses to paying viewers; and the Cable–Satellite Public Affairs Network (C-SPAN), a satellite service that transmits live coverage of the United States House of Representatives to schools and homes.

In Cambridge, Massachusetts, the Massachusetts Institute of Technology (MIT) operates a closed-circuit cable network that accommodates television transmission, two-way video communication, and high-speed data transmission. The system employs approximately two miles of trunk cable, and connects over 1,000 campus locations for interactive communication. Through a special microwave interconnection, MIT is also able to transmit signals through the closed-circuit system operated by nearby Harvard University. A number of United States public schools operate similar closed-circuit cable systems. In Hagerstown, Maryland, the school system has distributed television programming over a closed-circuit cable system since 1956. The system was built with the assistance of the local telephone company and accommodates the simultaneous transmission of six television channels to 45 schools (Jamison et al. 1978 p. 179).

Through these experiments and established services, cable has proven to be a flexible, high-capacity, and relatively inexpensive means of distributing educational television programming to audiences within individual communities or limited geographic areas. As more community and closed-circuit cable systems are linked through microwave and hard-wire interconnections, cable may also become an effective means of transmitting television programming to wider audiences. In the United States, Pennsylvania State University currently uses a microwave interconnection to deliver educational programming to 240 of the state's 300 community cable systems. Finally, as cable technology matures, wideband cable distribution will likely emerge as the most efficient means of delivering educational services that involve two-way voice/video and high-speed data communication.

3. Microwave Transmission

In several respects, microwave transmission is similar to television broadcasting. In both transmission systems, program signals are impressed on electromagnetic carrier waves. Both systems are also "over-the-air" transmission media—distribution methods that send signals through the air, rather than through wires or cables. In both systems, program signals are sent from transmitting towers, and received through antennae attached to conventional television receivers.

There are also some important differences between the two transmission systems. Unlike broadcast signals, microwave signals are limited to line-of-sight transmission. Buildings or natural obstructions that come between the microwave transmitter and receiving sites will block the signal, necessitating the purchase and installation of relay or translator stations. Microwave systems also require a special antenna and downconverter at each reception site. The antenna is specially designed to receive relatively weak microwave signals, and the downconverter transforms the microwave signals into a VHF television signal that can be displayed on a conventional television receiver. Because this special reception equipment is relatively expensive (US$1,500–$2,000), it is not usually found in homes. As a result, microwave transmission is not normally an effective means of delivering educational programming directly to the general public.

To minimize line-of-sight obstructions, microwave transmitting towers are usually located on a hill or building top, and receiving antennae are usually located on a roof, a freestanding tower, or a rooftop tower. In most locations, receiving antennae must be installed with the asistance of a professional engineer. A typical microwave signal has a range of 20 to 25 miles.

In the United States, the federal government has set aside 28 microwave channels for the transmission of educational television, radio, and data signals. These instructional television fixed service (ITFS) channels fall in the 2500–2690 MHz band (as compared to the 54–108 MHz band reserved for VHF television broadcasting). Currently, there are approximately 100 operating ITFS systems licensed to schools, universities, and other formal educational organizations. Most ITFS operators use their channels to deliver live and prerecorded program signals to outlying buildings from a central transmitting facility. In the United States and other nations, government, commercial, and educational groups have also used microwave relay networks to deliver programming to cable television systems and broadcast television stations.

3.1 Strengths of Microwave Transmission as a Distribution Medium

Compared to broadcast transmission, microwave is a relatively economical means of "over the air" program delivery. Equipment and construction costs for a four-channel microwave transmitting facility are approximately US$250,000, as compared with $1 million or more for a full power, single-channel broadcast television station. However, this immediate cost advantage is somewhat offset by the extra cost of equipping receiving sites. Equipment and installation fees for the dish antenna, downconverter, and associated hardware needed at each reception site total approximately $2,000. In locations that require a freestanding antenna tower, reception equipment and installation costs can exceed $20,000.

Multiple-channel transmission is another advantage of microwave distribution. In the United States, ITFS licensees can operate up to four channels in a single service area. With two or more channels at their disposal, educational organizations can provide programming on flexible and varied transmission schedules. Additionally, in regions where microwave frequencies are reserved for educational use, educational groups generally exercise full control over the channels. As a result, these groups are usually free from the competition for transmission time that often accompanies broadcast transmission. With control over multiple microwave channels, many educational groups have also been able to experiment with the microwave transmission of data and two-way voice/video services.

Microwave transmission is also a proven method of program delivery. In the United States, educational microwave systems have been in operation since 1961, when the Federal Communications Commission (FCC) authorized the Plainedge, New York school system to operate an experimental ITFS system. Full authorization for ITFS came on July 25, 1963, when the FCC voted to reserve microwave frequencies for educational use. Governments and educational groups in Ethiopia, India, and several other nations also operate or have experimented with various forms of educational microwave service. In some locations, microwave relay networks have proven to be more economical than cable or broadcast transmission for the delivery of television programming to remote or underdeveloped regions (Jamison et al. 1978).

3.2 Limitations of Microwave Transmission as a Distribution Medium

Like all over-the-air transmission systems, microwave transmission systems operate on assigned carrier frequencies. In regions where governments have reserved microwave frequencies for educational use, the availability of channel assignment is generally not a problem. However, in countries or regions that do not allocate a specific range of frequencies for educational use, educational groups must often compete with groups that plan to use microwave channels for other types of over-the-air transmission. Even in the United States, where the government has set aside educational channels in the microwave bandwidth, educational groups must often compete with one another for channel assignments in crowded urban areas, and the government is continually pressured to reassign microwave frequencies for commercial use. This pressure has already resulted in the reassignment of three of the original 31 ITFS channels, and in a proposal for further channel transfers that received initial approval from the FCC in 1983.

As mentioned earlier, cost can also be a limiting factor in microwave distribution. Although microwave transmission facilities are less expensive than broadcast facilities, the $250,000 needed to build and equip a multichannel microwave transmitter represents a substantial sum to many schools and educational organizations. In several locations, educational groups have overcome this problem by sharing construction and operating costs, or by leasing transmission time on existing educational microwave systems.

Although microwave is an over-the-air transmission medium, microwave transmission systems actually operate as closed-distribution networks. In many nations, it is illegal for unauthorized sites to receive or retransmit microwave signals. With most educational microwave systems, signal piracy has not been a problem since very few unauthorized homes or buildings have been willing to spend $2,000 for the reception equipment needed to intercept microwave signals. Unfortunately, this also works to the detriment of educational groups that operate microwave distribution systems, since it prevents them from delivering programming directly to home viewers (except when the microwave signals are received and retransmitted by community cable systems or broadcast television stations).

The restricted (20 to 25 mile) range of terrestrial microwave signals is also a limiting factor. To extend their coverage area, many microwave installations employ a series of terrestrial relay stations. Each relay station receives microwave signals from the main transmitter or another relay station, and retransmits the signals on channels that can be received by nearby reception sites or the next relay station. Studies of relay systems in Ethiopia and India place construction and equipment costs for microwave networks at $4,000 to $6,000 per mile (Jamison et al. 1978 p. 105).

3.3 Applications of Microwave Transmission

Educational microwave systems have been used to extend instructional television service to rural areas, to transmit "live" teacher workshops and training sessions, to accommodate the transfer of computer information over hundreds of data circuits, and to provide continuing educational courses to professionals at their work sites (Curtis and Biedenbach 1979). In the United States, public and private school systems use ITFS channels to deliver instructional programs to schools on flexible transmission schedules. In San Francisco, New

York, and several other major metropolitan areas, the Catholic Church uses ITFS to deliver educational programming to parochial schools, and to transmit religious instruction and general information to individual parishes.

Medical and graduate schools have also made use of microwave distribution. In the United States, the Indiana University School of Medicine uses an ITFS network to provide continuing education courses to health care centers in 19 cities (Curtis and Biedenbach 1979 p. 39). Recently, a number of medical and graduate institutions have also used ITFS systems to conduct seminars that feature video/voice interaction between the transmitting and receiving sites. In many medical and educational applications, the microwave signals received by participating institutions are retransmitted to classrooms over closed-circuit cable networks.

In a final analysis, microwave transmission can provide an effective means of distributing flexible schedules of instructional programming to reception sites located within a 20 to 25 mile radius of the transmitting station. Like cable television systems, many microwave systems offer the flexibility of multichannel distribution and the capacity for two-way communication. In the past, microwave relay systems have also been used to deliver television programming to remote television stations. However, many of these terrestrial microwave networks may soon be replaced by more cost-effective satellite relay systems.

4. Videocassette and Videodisc Distribution

In videocassette and videodisc distribution, cassette or disc copies of television programs are distributed to schools through the mail or private parcel delivery services. In videocassette distribution, the programs are copied at cassette duplication centers—public or privately owned facilities that are specially equipped to make multiple videocassette copies from a master videotape. Most of these facilities duplicate copies in real time (a program that is 30 minutes long requires 30 minutes to duplicate, a program that is 60 minutes long requires 60 minutes to duplicate, and so on). To make copies, technicians place the master tape in a videotape playback machine, and the playback machine sends program signals from the tape to one or more recording videocassette recorders (VCRs). With the necessary number of VCRs, duplication facilities can record 1,000 or more cassette copies at a time.

With videodiscs, the duplication procedure is very different. Like audiodiscs (records), individual videodiscs are stamped from a master disc. The cost of transferring a one-hour program produced on videotape or film to a master disc is approximately US$3,000. However, this high transfer cost is balanced by the relatively low cost of stamping individual disc copies. Most commercial facilities charge $5–$10 for stamping copies from a master disc, as compared to $20–$40 for duplicating videocassette copies of the same program. As a result, videodisc duplication can offer considerable cost savings over videocassette duplication—as long as enough disc copies are made to offset the high cost of preparing the master disc. In 1982 videocassette duplication remained the more economical alternative for 100 copies or less; but videodisc duplication offered a definite cost advantage when 500 or more copies were pressed.

Videocassette recorders are very versatile machines. Schools can use VCRs to play back programs obtained through a videocassette distribution service, or to record and replay programs delivered by broadcast, cable, microwave, or satellite transmission. In recent years, many schools and television production facilities have also used videocassette equipment to record and edit their own television programs, and to duplicate and distribute copies of programs to television transmitting facilities (see *Video Production as a Learning Activity*; *The Role of Film, Television, and Video*).

Unlike the VCR, the videodisc player (VDP) is currently a playback-only machine. As a result, schools can only use videodisc players to play back discs pressed at mastering plants. Schools cannot use disc players to record program signals delivered through cable or over-the-air transmission, or to record and edit their own video productions. However, disc players do offer a number of search, storage, and playback features that are not available on VCRs.

4.1 Strengths of Videocassette and Videodisc as Distribution Media

With many types of cable and over-the-air distribution, individual programs are transmitted as part of larger blocks or daily schedules of educational programming. Often, this results in considerable transmission waste. At reception sites, teachers and students select and tune into programs that meet their individual needs, and tune-out the rest.

With videocassette and videodisc distribution, teachers and students receive only the programs that they request. Additionally, once they receive cassette or disc copies of programs, teachers and students are able to use the programs at their convenience, free from the constraints of fixed transmission schedules. With cassette or disc copies, teachers and students are also able to preview and review programs, and to select and playback sections of programs that are particularly relevant to specific topics or subject areas. Through the addition of microcomputer or microprocessor equipment, teachers can also program cassettes and discs to play segments in a predetermined sequence, or to search out and play segments on the basis of a student's responses to questions embedded in the program.

With videocassette distribution, the relatively low cost of duplication facilities is also an advantage. A small-scale videocassette duplication facility can cost less than US$30,000. Equipment costs for larger duplication centers range from $100,000 for a facility capable of duplicating 25 tapes simultaneously, to more than $2 million for a facility capable of duplicating 1,000 or more tapes

at a time. In many United States locations, educational television agencies operate small-scale duplication facilities as a supplement to their regular broadcast service.

With both videocassette and videodisc distribution, reception site costs are also relatively low. In the United States, Japan, and many European countries, the small-format videocassette recorders found in schools and homes cost from $300 to $1,000. Optical videodisc players, the disc player format most appropriate for school use, cost from $600 to $3,000, with the exact cost determined by the sophistication of the microprocessor built into the player. Program signals from videocassette recorders and videodisc players can both be played on conventional television receivers.

Because of their low cost, and because they can perform a variety of useful tasks, videocassette recorders have become standard items in the media inventories of many school and university systems. According to a survey conducted by the Corporation for Public Broadcasting, over 90 percent of all United States secondary schools are equipped with some type of video recording equipment (Corporation for Public Broadcasting 1979 p. 9). In the United Kingdom, officials for the British Broadcasting Corporation (BBC) also report that "nearly all" secondary schools have video recorders (Alexander and Barnes 1981 p. 96). In contrast, videodisc players have not yet enjoyed widespread acceptance in the educational market. However, many observers feel that sales to schools and universities will increase rapidly once educators became aware of the disc's potential as a teaching tool, and once a sufficient supply of instructional programs becomes available for school use (Sigel et al. 1981).

Because cassettes and discs can both be delivered through the mail, distibution does not require the construction of expensive terrestrial or satellite transmission systems. With direct mail delivery, cassettes and discs also offer considerable program privacy. Both cassettes and discs are easy to store and catalog, and both are free from the problems of channel availability, spectrum scarcity, and limited signal range that afflict other types of program transmission.

4.2 Limitations of Videocassette and Videodisc as Distribution Media

In many areas of the world, problems of equipment incompatibility force television agencies that distribute programming on cassettes or discs to duplicate programs in a confusing variety of forms and formats. Currently, the world market is crowded with at least five incompatible videocassette recording formats, and at least six different videodisc formats. In the late 1980s, the half-inch Beta and VHS videocassette systems (systems that use half-inch wide tape) dominate the consumer VCR market, but videocassette recorders that use three-quarter inch tape are still used in many schools and television production studios. In the videodisc market, the leading formats are the capacitance electronic disc (CED) and the video high density (VHD) systems, which use a stylus to read the information encoded on the disc; and the optical format system, which uses a laser beam to read the information encoded on the disc.

Format incompatibility is a particular problem for educational television agencies that distribute programs on videocassettes. Although many schools have now committed themselves to the Beta or VHS format, others continue to use videocassette machines that use three-quarter inch tape or some other incompatible type of half-inch or quarter-inch tape. Because no single video-cassette format is clearly superior for school use, and because manufacturers continually introduce new formats, the problems caused by cassette equipment incompatibility will probably persist indefinitely. With videodiscs, equipment incompatibility may not prove to be as severe a problem, since many analysts feel that the optical disc player has already proven itself the superior format for educational and instructional applications.

Videodisc distribution is limited by the inability of videodisc players to record programming, and by the high cost of the equipment needed to prepare and duplicate discs. Videodiscs are duplicated at a handful of highly sophisticated facilities located in Europe, Japan, and the United States. Educational television agencies must first produce a program on film or videotape, and then send it to a disc duplication facility for master preparation and pressing. This process can take two months or more at some disc duplication plants, and some duplication facilities have reportedly experienced severe problems with quality control (Sigel et al. 1981 p. 55).

In developing nations, the shortage or absence of cassette and disc equipment in schools is also a problem. Even in industrial nations, where videocassette equipment is widely available, the home video market has not yet grown to the point where videocassette or disc distribution can serve as an effective means of delivering educational programming to the general public. With videodiscs, the shortage of disc equipment in schools is directly related to the short supply of educational disc programming. As mentioned earlier, many schools seem reluctant to purchase videodisc equipment until they can be sure that the supply of educational disc programs is sufficient to justify their investment. Finally, because videocassette and videodisc distribution systems are designed to deliver prerecorded packages of programming, neither system is well-suited to the various sorts of live and two-way communication possible with many types of cable and over-the-air transmission methods.

4.3 Applications of Videocassette and Videodisc

In the United States, Canada, the United Kingdom and other industrial nations, many films and television distributors are beginning to make their educational programming available to schools on videocassettes and discs. In most cases, disc or cassette copies of programs are available for less than half the cost of film prints. Many distributors also provide or sell schools the right

to videorecord programs that are delivered through cable, broadcast, microwave, or satellite transmission. These videorecording rights are particularly important to secondary school teachers, who generally have the most difficulty working with fixed transmission schedules (Alexander and Barnes 1981).

Compared to most other television delivery systems, per-program costs for cassette and disc distribution are relatively high. With cable and over-the-air distribution systems, systems that are capable of serving many reception sites with a single transmission, distribution costs for a one-hour program can be lower than US$0.10 per receiving site (Jamison et al. 1978). With cassette and disc duplication systems, distribution costs generally range from $10–$40 per program hour (Van Der Drift 1980). However, these higher per-program costs are balanced by the relatively low cost of building or renting cassette and disc distribution facilities, and by the flexible access to programming that cassette and disc distribution provide.

5. Satellite Distribution

Satellite communication as it is known today, began in 1963, with the launch of a small satellite known as Syncom II. Unlike earlier communications satellites, Syncom II was placed in a geostationary orbit, 22,300 miles (35,970 kilometers) above the equator. At that height, and with its orbiting speed synchronized to the earth's rotation, Syncom II appeared to remain fixed in the sky. As a result, Syncom made a relatively easy, steady target for communication signals transmitted from the earth's surface. The signals would reflect off the satellite and bounce back to earth, where they could be received by large dish antennae located hundreds or thousands of miles from the original transmitting station.

Since Syncom II, private companies, national governments, and international satellite organizations have launched over 100 geostationary satellites. Currently, most satellites used for communications purposes fall into two categories: fixed service satellites that deliver signals to large reception dishes located at known, fixed points; and direct broadcast satellites that deliver signals to small reception dishes located at individual homes, schools, and businesses. Like Syncom II, fixed service and direct broadcast satellites function as orbiting relay stations, receiving and relaying signals sent from transmitting stations on the earth's surface. Most fixed service satellites transmit signals in the frequency bandwidth known as the C-band (4–6 GHz). Most direct broadcast satellites transmit signals in the Ku band (12–14 GHz). Both types of satellite are powered by batteries and solar cells.

Most communications satellites are capable of transmitting various combinations of television, telephone, radio, and data signals. Some satellites are used primarily for telephone, radio, or marine communication.

Others are used for transmitting television coverage of international news and sporting events, or for distributing data signals to schools and businesses. In the United States, fixed service satellites are also used to deliver program services to community cable systems, and to interconnect the television stations affiliated with the Public Broadcasting Service.

5.1 Strengths of Satellite as a Distribution Medium

Satellites have one clear advantage over other transmission systems—they have tremendous signal range. The exact signal coverage area (or "footprint") of a communications satellite depends on the transmitting power, transmitting frequency, or orbital location of the satellite. In theory, a communications satellite positioned above the equator can transmit signals to one-third of the earth's surface. As a result, a single satellite can deliver television signals to several nations at one time, or to all or most of a nation's homes, schools, and universities. Through relay systems, satellites can also be interconnected to create global communications networks.

With their extensive signal range, communications satellites can also reduce the need for expensive terrestrial distribution systems. As mentioned earlier, satellite distribution has already begun to replace microwave and land-line transmission as the most economical means of delivering national program schedules to local broadcast stations and community cable systems. Theoretically, any home or school can also purchase a satellite reception dish, and use it to receive signals directly from communications satellites. With direct broadcast satellites, prices of a dish plus a decoder start from $1000.

Fixed-service satellites, the satellites that currently carry most television transmissions, require a reception dish that is too expensive ($5,000–$50,000) to install in most homes and schools. As a result, signals from fixed service satellites are usually received through reception dishes located at terrestrial transmission facilities, and then retransmitted to homes and schools through broadcast, cable, or microwave distribution.

Most direct broadcast and fixed service satellites are capable of transmitting multiple television channels. Using current technology, fixed service satellites can receive and retransmit 20 to 30 television channels. Direct-broadcast satellites, which must transmit stronger signals, generally have about half the channel capacity of fixed service systems. As mentioned earlier, both systems are capable of transmitting various combinations of television, telephone, text, radio, and data signals. With both direct broadcast and fixed-service transmission, signals can also be scrambled or encoded to create private communications channels. Two-way satellite transmission is possible, but it requires that participating sites have access to expensive satellite "uplink facilities."

5.2 Limitations of Satellite as a Distribution Medium

The primary limitation to satellite distribution is cost. Construction and launching costs for a modern communications satellite range from US$75 million to $100 million, and yearly rental fees for a single satellite channel (or "transponder") can cost as much as $13 million. Hourly television transmission costs range from $500 per hour in off-peak periods, to $10,000 or more per hour in high-use periods.

These high costs pose special problems for developing nations. To date, no developing country has been able to generate by itself the capital and technical expertise necessary to build and launch a geostationary satellite, and few have been able to finance the full-time rental of transponders on satellites operated by other nations (Rice and Parker 1979). As a result, most developing nations that are planning satellite communication services must turn to Intelsat, the 102 nation consortium that operates a global satellite system. Compared to most commercial carriers, Intelsat's transmission rates are relatively low. However, the channel space reserved for television transmission on Intelsat satellites is limited, and transmission time is in high demand (Mahony et al. 1980).

Satellite transmission is also limited by problems related to orbital reservations and spectrum allocation. At meetings of the International Telecommunications Union (ITU), developing nations have charged industrial countries with appropriating the best orbital slots for themselves, leaving little room for new satellites designed to improve communications in rural and agricultural regions. Developing nations have also pointed out that the frequency bandwidth used to transmit fixed-service satellite signals is already overcrowded in many regions, and that the Ku band used for direct broadcast satellites is filling-up rapidly. Some nations have argued that spectrum and orbital slots should be set aside to ensure sufficient satellite service to developing areas, particularly as the ITU considers opening up new orbital paths and frequency bands for satellite transmission. This plan has been opposed by the United States and some other industrial nations, who feel that spectrum slots should not be set aside until countries develop definite plans for building and launching satellite systems.

Satellite transmission is further limited by a number of other technical and cost considerations. For example, although fixed service satellites have been tested through 20 years of general use, direct broadcast satellite technology remains experimental. Japan and Canada have tested prototype direct-broadcast satellite services, but neither nation has proved conclusively that this method is technically and economically viable as a television delivery system. As mentioned earlier, the power required to transmit direct-broadcast satellite signals limits the number of channels a single direct-broadcast satellite can receive and retransmit. Even with fixed-service satellites, which have the capacity for 20 or more television channels and two-way voice/video communication, high transponder rental costs usually limit educational television agencies to one-way transmission over a single satellite channel. Consequently, satellites are not normally used to deliver instructional programming on flexible transmission schedules, or to transmit instructional services that include interactive voice/video communication.

For some time the United States and the Soviet Union were the only two nations capable of placing satellites in geostationary orbit. This gave both nations a head-start in satellite communications, and precluded true competition in the satellite market. However, the European Space Agency completed several launches in 1983 and 1984. Along with the potential of lower cost launches from the United States space shuttle, this new competition promises to reduce the high cost of placing communications satellites in orbit, and to provide more nations with the opportunity to initiate and operate satellite communications systems. Eventually, increased competition and technical improvements also promise to increase the channel capacity and lifespan of communications satellites, and to decrease the cost of the earth stations used to transmit signals to communications satellites.

5.3 Applications of Satellite Transmission

Fixed service satellites have been used to deliver health and occupational education programs to remote towns and villages, to transmit adult education and school programming to rural regions, and to distribute professional education and college telecourses to local television stations and community cable systems. From 1971 to 1974, the United States used their Applications Technology Satellites (ATS) to conduct a number of experiments in the satellite delivery of educational programming to remote and mountainous regions in Hawaii, Alaska, and the continental United States. Several of the experiments also tested text and two-way audio transmission over the ATS system (Cowlan and Foote 1975). In 1975 and 1976, India used the Applications Technology Satellite to deliver educational television programs to approximately 2,500 villages. The satellite signals were delivered to community viewing sites in each village, and the programming included instruction in agriculture, health, science, and family planning. In 1977, the United States and Canada used the Communications Technology Satellite (CTS) to transmit programming between universities and health centers in the two countries. Indonesia, Brazil, Australia, and several other nations have also planned or established experiments in the delivery of instructional programming over fixed service satellites (Polcyn 1981).

In 1978 and 1979, Japan and Canada established experiments that tested the educational applications of direct broadcast satellites. In the Japanese test, the NHK television network used direct broadcast satellite to deliver school and special education programming to rural areas. In the Canadian experiment, the Canadian

Department of Communications used four transponders on the Anik B satellite, a satellite which transmits signals in both the C and Ku bands, to broadcast educational programming directly to schools and homes. The broadcasts were received in Ontario and British Columbia through 1.2 and 1.8 meter dish antennae—antennae that are expected to be mass-produced for $300 (Mahony et al. 1980 p. 64). According to current projections, the Federal Republic of Germany, France, the United Kingdom, and the United States will also have operating direct broadcast satellite services by 1985.

For the most part, international tests confirm that satellite distribution can serve as an effective means of delivering television programming to remote and rural regions. Spurred by the success of early experiments, some educational planners have envisioned a global education system based on the satellite transmission of television, voice, and data signals. Citing the apprehension that many nations have displayed toward international education projects, other analysts predict satellite education systems that are more national in nature (Polcyn 1981 p. 242). For the near future, both national and international projects will continue to be limited by the high cost of sending and receiving satellite signals.

Like other over-the-air transmission methods, satellite transmission becomes more cost-effective with the more reception sites served. Although construction and transmission costs are generally higher for satellite systems than for broadcast or microwave systems, satellites can potentially serve a far greater number of reception sites. Governments and educational television agencies that are considering satellite distribution must first determine whether the number of reception sites will be high enough to offset high satellite transmission costs, and whether the reception sites might be better or more economically served through some other type of program distribution. When there are a high number of reception sites, and when the sites are scattered across a wide geographic area, satellite distribution is generally cost-effective. When the intended viewing audience is located in a limited number of reception sites, or when the sites are located in a limited geographic area, other distribution methods may offer a less expensive and more flexible alternative.

Bibliography

Alexander J, Barnes H 1981 The BBC's provision of education material in the United Kingdom. *Educational Media Yearbook*. Libraries Unlimited, Littleton, Colorado, pp. 94–99

Arnove R F (ed.) 1976 *Educational Television: A Policy Critique and Guide for Developing Countries*. Praeger, New York

Corporation for Public Broadcasting 1979 *Uses of Television for Instruction 1976–77*. National Center for Education Statistics, Washington, DC

Cowlan B, Foote D 1975 *A Case Study of the ATS-6 Health, Education and Telecommunications Projects*. Agency for International Development, Washington, DC

Curtis J A, Biedenbach J M (eds.) 1979 *Educational Telecommunications Delivery Systems*. American Society for Engineering Education, Washington, DC

Grandi R 1978 Western European broadcasting in transition. *J. Commun.* 28(3): 47–51

Jamison D T, Klees S J, Wells S J 1978 *The Costs of Educational Media: Guidelines for Planning and Evaluation*. Sage, London

Knowledge Industry Publications 1983 *The Home Video and Cable Report* 13(26): 3

Mahony S, Demartino N, Stengel R 1980 *Keeping PACE with the New Television*. VNU, New York

Moss M L 1978 Experiments in interactive cable TV: Research on community uses. *J. Commun.* 28(2): 160–67

Murata T 1981 Development of communication technology in Japan: The HI-OVIS Project. *Videodisc/Videotex* 1(3): 149–53

Perry W 1977 *The Open University*. Jossey-Bass, San Francisco, California

Polcyn K 1981 The role of communication satellites in education and training: The 1990s. *Programmed Learning and Educational Technology* 18: 230–43

Rice R E, Parker E B 1979 Telecommunications alternatives for developing countries. *J. Commun.* 29(4): 125–36

Sigel E, Schubin M, Merrill P, Christie K, Rusche J, Horder A 1981 *Video Discs: The Technology, the Applications, and the Future*. Van Nostrand Reinhold, New York UNESCO 1977 *The Economics of the New Educational Media: Present Status of Research and Trends*. UNESCO, Paris

Van Der Drift K D J M 1980 Cost effectiveness of audiovisual media in higher education. *Instr. Sci.* 9: 355–64

Waniewicz I 1972 *Broadcasting for Adult Education: A Guidebook to Worldwide Experience*. UNESCO, Paris

Videotex and Electronic Mail

P. Copeland and A. Scott

Videotex is the generic term for information systems which involve the transmission of "display" text and "pixel" graphics and their reception on an adapted television set. Videotex was first developed as a method of low-cost information delivery into homes, to be available through the use of microcomputers and appropriate additional equipment. Broadcast videotex (teletext) differs in scope from interactive videotex (viewdata). Both are now established in several countries and used for educational purposes. Figure 1 shows some of the categories of videotex in public and private use.

Electronic mail is used here as a generic term for information systems in which plain-text messages are transmitted to a central computer for storage and later interrogation by the addressee of the message. It includes both public messaging (bulletin boards) and closed-group messaging (computer conferences). The use of electronic mail requires either a "dumb terminal" or a microcomputer to be connected to the telephone network via a modem, which translates the data into a form suitable for transmission through the telephone service. Where a microcomputer is used, the same equipment can also be connected to videotex services.

School use of on-line facilities has been concerned with finding educational applications of electronic mail and videotex systems, and with access to commercial database systems for bibliographic or full-text searching (see *Electronic Publishing*).

1. Videotex

Videotex transmission is achieved either by broadcast signal or by telephone network. Broadcast videotex, or teletext is available in the United Kingdom as the Ceefax service of the British Broadcasting Corporation (BBC) and as the Oracle service of the Independent Broadcasting Authority (IBA). Both provide a news and sports headline service and the IBA service carries advertisements.

Videotex transmitted via telephone line is available to public subscribers in the United Kingdom (Prestel), France, and Canada. In addition, private viewdata systems provide internal communications to multisite firms or connections between firms and their regular customers.

1.1 Teletext

The one-way nature of teletext means that the user can select information only from the limited amount being transmitted. A fixed number of "pages" are continuously broadcast one at a time and in sequence. Access can be marginally improved by broadcasting copies of most-used pages at more frequent intervals and by spreading the topics covered across pairs of television channels; but users have found that any significant increase in the number of pages results in unsatisfactory delays.

Selection of a given page is achieved by the user entering the number of the page required on a keypad; each page received by the apparatus is checked against this number and, when a match is found, is displayed. Some

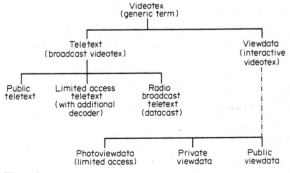

Figure 1
Categories of videotex in public and private use

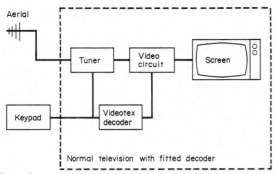

Figure 2
Teletext

pages may have more than one screen of information. These further screens are automatically displayed when they arrive in the cycle, without further request.

The United Kingdom Ceefax and Oracle services transmit the information as a train of pulses embedded in four unused lines of the 625 horizontal lines used in the UK standard television picture. All the viewer needs in addition to normal television equipment is a videotex decoder (usually fitted inside the set) and a keypad, as shown in Fig. 2.

A sequence of about 500 pages gives a typical access time of about 7 seconds. Ceefax and Oracle services are provided free to viewers, being financed out of licence fees (BBC) or advertising (Oracle). Besides news and sports information they also broadcast share prices and other financial information, weather forecasts, and subtitles which can be used in conjunction with normal viewing as a service for the deaf and hard of hearing. Difficulties in providing subtitling for the large amounts of broadcast material have largely restricted these services to films and to repeat broadcasts, though experiments have been carried out on the automation of subtitling.

1.2 Viewdata

The two-way nature of interactive videotex (viewdata) means that the user has access to thousands of pages of information stored in several computers. These are in communication with each other but may be geographically dispersed.

Interactive videotex systems are sometimes described as "paged databases" because a "chain" or "tree" structure is used to provide information to an enquirer a screenful at a time. The enquirer accesses the information being sought by selecting page numbers from a series of menus. The system invented by Sam Fedida, and pioneered by British Telecom as "Prestel", uses characters designed to be legible on an ordinary (625 line) domestic television set.

There are 25 lines of 40 characters on each page, and considerable use is made of colour. Access to data is via a series of menus. Although helpful to the new user, these can become frustrating in large databases where

the choices of options on each menu do not exactly match the specific query the user is making. Access can be speeded up by publishing a directory of the most-used page numbers, or using keywords to direct searchers to particular menus.

In practice, using the normal telephone network, the user dials, or the viewdata device automatically dials the local service computer. The television set displays a welcoming message in the form of a videotex page and asks the viewer either to use the index available or to key in directly the page number required. In addition to a normal telephone and a modem, the user needs either a microcomputer or an adapted television and telephone interface/keypad (see Fig. 3).

There is a growing number of small-scale information providers supplying a more limited number of pages than the large public systems such as Prestel and the French paged-database system, Teletel. These interactive videotex services are based either on small computers, supplying services direct to the public or to particular trades, or on large mainframe computers, supplying private viewdata systems to multisite companies.

With the UK Prestel service there is (a) a connecting charge and (b) a local telephone charge for the time the user is connected to the computer. In addition, the information provider (who may be a sub-contractor of Prestel) may levy a charge for each page accessed. For school users these page charges are absorbed in a special education subscription, as they can be a significant component of Prestel usage costs.

Pages available include public service information provided by government agencies and local authorities, financial information, flight schedules, news and encyclopedias. Access is provided to a "teleshopping" service and to "home banking" facilities, and several information providers allow orders to be submitted through the Prestel system and charged to the user's credit card. There is also a more general "mailbox" system which allows Prestel users to send messages to each other, and also to telex users.

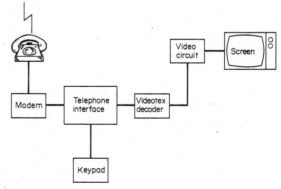

Figure 3
Viewdata terminal

The development of videotex interface units for microcomputers has allowed the extension of the videotex concept in a number of ways including:

(a) a teletext adapter enabling the capture of broadcast videotex information by a microcomputer, and its immediate use as data in a computer programme;

(b) the downloading of computer programmes;

(c) the provision of facilities to edit and create viewdata pages on a much cheaper basis than was previously possible;

(d) the pre-preparation of searches so that telephone call costs can be minimized; and

(e) the ability to capture viewdata pages for use in local viewdata displays and systems.

1.3 Videotex Systems

Many different implementations of the videotex concept have been developed, and recent advances have included "encrypted teletext" broadcast between television images, on the same channels and alongside normal teletext, but only accessible to viewers who subscribe to the service and are issued with a special decoding device; "radio teletext", where teletext data similar in nature to that broadcast alongside television images is transmitted on a given radio frequency; and high-resolution viewdata, capable of transmitting images of photographic quality.

2. Electronic Mail

Electronic-mail systems provide users with opportunities to communicate with each other by storing messages in a large central computer system, and to access data or services provided on that system.

Because messages are retained by the central facility until requested by the person receiving the message, it is possible to exchange information without both parties being logged on to the computer system at the same time. It is also possible, using the telephone system (and a "modem" to translate data signals to transmittable form), to access the central computer from any distance, so the communicating parties can be in different parts of the country or even in different countries.

Like viewdata systems, electronic-mail systems often provide access to databases containing information provided either as a commercial venture or as a public service by government or professional organizations. Some companies, with significant data-access or messaging needs set up private systems for their own exclusive use. Others act as "information providers" and reach the market through "host" agencies, which provide customers with access to a variety of data, access and communications facilities.

Electronic-mail systems evolved from telex and other typewriter-based systems, and tend to use 80 characters to a line. Because of the practice of adding new lines to the bottom of the screen, moving existing data up the

screen and deleting the top line, these largely monochrome systems are sometimes known as "scrolling" databases. Access to data is often by means of a search phrase which has to be entered in the system's "query" language. Some systems also provide access by keyword search or by a limited menu structure.

Using a microcomputer as a terminal to an electronic-mail system enables mail to be prepared off-line prior to logging on and sending the messages, and incoming messages can be captured onto disc and printed later: this considerably reduces telephone and central computer usage.

Electronic-mail systems enable one to send a message to several named addressees simultaneously, so the use of mailing lists coupled with off-line preparation can be significantly cheaper than conventional bulk mailing.

It is also possible to organize or join a "computer conference" about a given topic. The use of such conferences is particularly appropriate where geographically separate experts need to reach a consensus rapidly, as would be the case, for instance, in disaster relief organizations. They have also been used effectively by collaborating institutions to enable the joint development of courses and teaching materials.

3. Educational Applications

3.1 Videotex

Research has been carried out in the United Kingdom since 1981 in a number of aspects of the educational use of videotex systems including:

(a) the use of teletext for the distribution of texts and diagrams to accompany educational broadcasts;

(b) the use of teletext to distribute computer programmes;

(c) the use of Prestel as an information source for careers information and courses being offered;

(d) the use of Prestel as a medium for instruction; and

(e) the use of Prestel for the distribution of computer programmes.

The Council for Education Technology in the United Kingdom conducted field trials to investigate the potential of Prestel as a learning resource (Thomson 1981) and to compare Prestel and the Times Network System (formerly The Times Network for Schools; hereafter "TTNS") TTNS as educational facilites. It was recognized in these studies that cost was a major disincentive, particularly to primary schools; these and other studies have recognized that backup resources in terms of staffing, training and finance are critical in obtaining the best educational use of communications technology. On a more optimistic note, the increasing use of Prestel for careers and course information in the secondary and tertiary sectors, and the provision of "gateways" through Prestel to educationally-oriented services such as NERIS (National Educational Resources Information Service), and to university and polytechnic "clearing-house" information indicates a continuing commitment to the educational use of viewdata systems. It is also a focus for research in the provision of distance learning and individualized learning packages.

3.2 Electronic Mail

In the United Kingdom the most significant factors in establishing the potential for educational uses of electronic mail have been the provision of low-cost subscriptions by TTNS and the Department of Trade and Industry's initiative in supplying free modems to a large number of schools in early 1986.

Research into the field conducted in the late 1980s is focused on the use of electronic mail

(a) to assist in the administration of Local Education Authorities (school districts);

(b) by practitioners and specialists to establish and maintain networks of contacts to exchange "professional" information;

(c) to distribute training materials to colleagues and institutions, or as a component in distance learning systems;

(d) to publicize careers and course information and to facilitate polytechnic and university "clearing" procedures;

(e) to provide pupils with opportunities to develop skills as information providers and information retrievers; and

(f) to establish international networks of pupil, school, and teacher contacts useful in modern-language teaching and in educating for international understanding.

3.3 Pupils as Information Providers

A significant area of application of both electronic-mail and viewdata systems is the opportunity for pupils to practice "information provider" skills. Software which enables even small microcomputers to act as information hosts has been used effectively by schools to provide viewdata services on limited topics to anyone with appropriate equipment to log on to the system. Swadelands School in Kent (United Kingdom), for example, provides information about weather satellites and health education through its SWAFAX databases. The structure is determined and the pages of data designed and updated by the pupils. Elsewhere in the United Kingdom pupils have been designing teletext news magazines and interactive viewdata services for school staff.

The Times Network provides similar facilities for the construction of viewdata-style databases to be embedded in its electronic mail system. Pupils in Derbyshire and in Rotherham have helped construct databases of local information for teachers to consult when designing school visits. Pupils have also used TTNS to set up databases of information to provide information about their local area for use by corresponding schools abroad.

4. Future Developments

The ease with which information can be prepared and sent into videotex systems will be a major factor influencing their future success. Many automated facilities are now available for information input and graphic design, but they do not yet match in sophistication the current capabilities of word processors or computer-aided design systems. The videotex systems are beginning to overcome the limitations of the coarse graphics which were necessary to ensure legibility on the television sets for which they were originally designed. Now that many videotex users are employing either microcomputers or dedicated viewdata terminals, research is under way to establish "photovideotex" services which provide much more detailed and sophisticated imaging capacity.

Although electronic mail and interactive videotex still retain their own distinct styles, there is a growing convergence of services: data-oriented systems such as Prestel provide limited message-exchange facilities and access to telex; and message-oriented systems such as Dialcom are providing access to an increasing number of databases. In 1988 the merger of TTNS and Prestel Education in the United Kingdom, to form a single new subscription service for the education sector—Campus 2000—may prove to be the first of many such combinations.

The major factor in encouraging the use of any communications system is the "critical mass", the number of existing users of the system; a related factor in encouraging the use of database systems is the amount of data contained in the system, and thus the likelihood of finding an answer to any particular enquiry.

The UK Dialcom electronic-mail system, BT Gold, has 70,000 users, with the potential to exchange messages with other Dialcom system users worldwide. Teletel in France, is seeking to achieve this critical mass by providing Minitel terminals to the majority of telephone users, and totally replacing the telephone directory/enquiry system with a database queried directly by the user.

An alternative strategy to achieve a larger number of potential users, and to provide users with access to a greater range of services, is to link two systems together via a "gateway" by means of which one system's central computer can exchange messages at very high speed with the central computer of another system. The use of such gateways reduces the need for a user to subscribe to several systems, thus potentially reducing customers' overall costs; it also removes the need to deal with several different log-on codes and disciplines.

Recent developments in this area have been an agreement between competing electronic-mail systems to provide channels for their customers to exchange messages with each other's customers, significantly increasing the number of potential contacts; the development by British Telecom of the "Message Handling System" to support such exchanges and the establishment of gateways between commercial and university-based systems. General developments in communications technology, and increasing standardization will bring two particularly significant benefits to educational users: easier access to contacts in other countries, and the ability to transmit and receive more complex images for teaching purposes.

Bibliography

Alber A F 1985 *Videotext/Teletext: Principles and Practice*. McGraw Hill, New York

Carter C, Monaco J 1986 *Learning Information Technology Skills*. Council for Education Technology, London

Copeland P 1981 The educational significance of electronic media. In: Black D (ed.) *Aspects of Education Technology*, No. 15, *Distance Learning and Education*, Kogan Page, London

Emms J, McConnell D 1988 An evaluation of tutorial support provided by electronic mail and computer conferencing. In: Mathias H, Rushby N, Budgett R (eds.) 1988 *Aspects of Educational Technology*, No. 21: *Designing New Systems and Technologies for Learning*, Kogan Page, London

Firth R J 1982 *Viewdata Systems: A Practical Evaluation Guide*, National Computing Centre, (NCC), Manchester

Gilman J 1983 *Information Technology and the School Library Resource Centre*, Council for Educational Technology, London

Kaye A 1988 On-line services for schools: An appraisal. In: Jones A, Scrimshaw P (eds.) *Computers in Education 5-13*, Open University Press, Milton Keynes

Martin J 1982 *Viewdata and the Information Society*. Prentice-Hall, Englewood Cliffs, New Jersey

Megarry J 1985 *Inside Information: Computers, Communications and People*. BBC, London

Read G A 1981 *The Cyclops Project*. Open University Press, Milton Keynes

Sigel E (ed.) 1983 *The Future of Videotext*. Kogan Page, London

Smith D 1988 *New Technologies and Professional Communications in Education*, Occasional Paper No. 13. National Council for Educational Technology, London

Somekh B, Groundwater-Smith S 1987 *Take a Balloon and a Piece of String : A Report on the UK/USA Schools Project*. NUT, Cambridge Institute of Education, Cambridge

Thomson V 1981 *Prestel and Education : Report of a One-year Trial*. Council for Educational Technology, London

Vervest P 1985 *An Introduction to Electronic Mail and Message Handling*. Frances Pinter, London

Computer Technology and Telecommunications

W. J. Kubitz

Computer technology refers to the applied science aspects of the design and construction of computers, as opposed to the application of the resulting computers to specific problems. In the case of the hardware, the electronics which perform the logical and storage operations associated with a computer, the underlying scientific knowledge comes from physics and chemistry (and photography, itself the application of the others). For the architecture (the overall structure of the units which perform the logical operations) as well as for the software (the logical instructions stored in the computer) the underlying science is drawn primarily from mathematics. Great advances have taken place in the application of these three sciences to the design and construction of computers since the 1960s. These advances have resulted in major decreases in the size, power consumption, and weight (all by a factor of roughly 100,000), while at the same time (and as a consequence of the former), the reliability has increased by this same factor and the speed of operation has increased by a factor of 10 to 100, all for a comparable number of active electronic elements used in the computer. In addition, decreasing cost has made possible a 10- to 1,000-fold increase in the amount of primary storage (memory) associated with a computer in this same time frame. These impressive changes in such a short period of time (20 years) are a direct result of improvements in integrated circuit technology and, at present, the end of such improvements is not in sight.

The largest single contribution to all of the above changes is the decrease in the size of the individual circuit elements used in making computers. This has allowed designers to put an extremely large number of circuit devices (transistors) on a single small piece of silicon (a chip). In the late 1980's, between 500,000 and 1,000,000 devices can be put onto a square chip which is 350 mils (1 mil = 0.001 inch) on a side. The chips themselves can be mass produced with the resulting low cost. The individual transistors are used in combination to form circuits which perform logical (decision) operations and these in turn are combined to form a computer.

There are two classes of electronic circuits employed in computers: digital and analog. The former are a special case of the latter wherein only two values (of voltage or current) are used rather than a continuous range of values, as is the case for analog circuits. Digital circuits are thus simpler than analog circuits from an electronic point of view and therefore smaller. Being smaller, many such circuits can be put in a rather small space. This, along with the fact that only two easily distinguishable signal values are allowed, makes possible the construction of extremely complex but compact

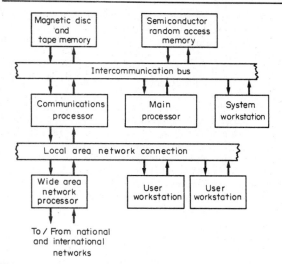

To / From national
and international
networks

Figure 1
Basic structure of a modern digital computer

units built from simple basic circuits with a reasonable expectation that they will function correctly. This cannot be done with analog circuits because they are larger and thus require more space. In addition, maintaining the correct signal values for a multitude of signal levels is simply not possible if large numbers of circuits must be used as in a computer. In general, analog computers are inherently very much less flexible in use than digital systems, so are nowadays restricted to highly specialized applications. Of course all digital computers contain some analog circuits but these are a minority of the total. The remainder of this discussion will be restricted to digital computer technology and the underlying digital electronics that make highly reliable, extremely small, but very powerful computers possible.

The basic structure of a modern digital computer is shown in Fig. 1. This figure is drawn in such a way that it represents a range of possible present-day computing configurations. All computers have at least one processor (called main here), some memory (called random access memory or RAM here), and some means of entering information into and retrieving information from the computer (embedded in the user workstation here).

The user workstation is the part of the computer that a person sees and might consist of such devices as keyboards, displays, and printers of varying degrees of sophistication. The user workstation is an area of extremely rapid development at the present time. In the usual arrangement nowadays there is an internal communication link called a bus which ties the various subunits of the computer together. Computers can be tied together in networks. At the lowest level, local area networks (LANs) enable a number of computers on the same site to share use of expensive peripherals such as

graph plotters or laser printers. At the next level, computers (or LANs) can be tied together in wide area networks (WANs), communicating via wire or radio transmission nationally and internationally.

Besides the essential primary RAM, it is common to have additional storage called secondary storage in the form of magnetic discs and tape. These units supply lower cost and larger amounts of storage but are slower in terms of their response to a demand for data. Notice that this use of magnetics is the single exception to an otherwise all-electronic, solid-state processor and memory configuration, excluding mechanical parts.

The communications processors handle the formatting and transfer of data between the various networks and spare the main processor this burden.

In simple computers, the main (and only) processor would handle all of the tasks that must be performed. In more complicated computers there might be a large number of processors used to perform various tasks. The communications processor shown in Fig. 1 is an example.

The system workstation is just a workstation connected directly to the computer. In a simple system it would be the only workstation, but in a more complicated arrangement it would be the system console used for start-up and system operation monitoring but probably little else.

The next section discusses digital electronic technology. Ensuing sections then discuss each of the elements in Fig. 1 along with current trends. The final section discusses the major problems facing computer technologists at the present time.

1. Electronic Technology

There are two types of electronic devices used to construct digital circuits: bipolar devices and unipolar [or metal-oxide-semiconductor (MOS)] devices. The term bipolar refers to the fact that the operation of these devices depends on two types of electrical conduction mechanisms whereas the unipolar device operation depends on only one. A clear explanation of the difference in operation is beyond the scope of this article and the reader is referred to any introductory digital circuits text. Here it is the difference in the capabilities of the circuits made from these different types of device that is important. Bipolar circuits are faster but cannot be as tightly packed on a chip as can the slower but denser MOS circuits. This means that large, high speed computers ("number crunchers" mainframes) are constructed of bipolar devices. Here the basic building blocks are less complex (fewer devices per chip) and we say that these bipolar circuits have a lower level of integration. At the slower end, the microcomputers (as found in personal computers) are implemented in MOS technology which has a high level of integration (many devices per chip). In between these two extremes there are many intermediate forms usually called minicomputers. Current minicomputers are mixtures of bipolar and MOS technologies as needs dictate.

Both bipolar and MOS technology have increased in level of integration but MOS has remained ahead. Similarly, both have increased in speed as size was reduced, but bipolar has remained ahead. Bipolar technology also has a higher power dissipation than MOS technology. This is a problem as more and more devices are squeezed onto a chip. Circuits have passed through several eras of density from SSI (small scale integration), through MSI (medium scale integration), to LSI (large scale integration). Current efforts are aimed at achieving VLSI (very large scale integration) which corresponds roughly to 1,000,000 devices on a chip. This level will be achieved more quickly with MOS technology than with bipolar.

As mentioned earlier, innovations in physics, chemistry, and photography have all contributed to decreasing the size of devices. The devices (bipolar or MOS transistors) are made in and on the surface of the silicon chips. The depth the transistor goes into the chip is a physics/chemistry problem and the lateral dimensions on the surface of the chip are a photographic problem. Early size reductions were primarily in the lateral dimensions and more recently in the depth dimension. As the size of the devices is reduced, they use less power (produce less heat), operate faster, and can be placed in a given area at higher and higher densities. As more and more parts of a computer are placed onto a single chip, where all devices and connections are made simultaneously, there are fewer chances that connections will fail (if initially good) and the reliability of that part of the computer increases. The results of reducing the size of devices as described above are indeed fortuitous in that all of the changes are in the desired direction—smaller, faster, cooler, more reliable and, of course, cheaper. Nevertheless, there are some problems, and these are discussed later.

The smallness of the technology is often specified in terms of the minimum feature size, the smallest controllable lateral dimension on the chip. In the late 1980s, standard devices are in the 2 to 3 μm range (1 μm = 10^{-6} meter) and special devices are around 1 μm. Still smaller devices have been fabricated in the laboratory. Dimensions in the depth direction are in hundreds of angstroms (1 Å = 10^{-10} m); and there is only one layer of devices across the surface of the chip, although the devices themselves are constructed by means of putting down a sequence of layers, the last of which are the layers interconnecting various parts of the circuits. It is rather hard to grasp such small dimensions. The chips have sides of about one-quarter of an inch (250 mils). If there are 250,000 devices in a 250 × 250 mil chip, each device will use about 0.25 mil² of area. Thus 40 to 50 such devices would occupy an area equivalent to the cross-section of a human hair, which has a diameter of 3 to 4 mils.

The seeming obsession with reducing the feature size as opposed to simply using larger chips results from the fact that, in practice, chips are limited to about 250 to 350 mils on a side if one is to have a reasonable chance that the chip will not contain a fatal defect. This is because the material defects are essentially randomly scattered across the surface of the silicon wafers on which the chips are made. These wafers are currently in the range of 4 to 5 inches in diameter and 100–300 chips can be obtained from each wafer. It is desirable to have as many of the chips as defect-free as possible in order to offset the manufacturing cost. Thus, the chip size must be limited to a value which will produce a reasonable yield of good chips from each wafer.

It has been observed (by Gordon Moore of Intel Corporation) that the number of devices per chip has doubled each year over the 1965–1980 period. This "law" held more or less until the early 1980s when it slipped somewhat. Moore also observed that the person-years taken to design and layout (the process of placing the devices in the proper position on the chip) chips has doubled every year. This doubling of human effort has become a serious problem and is a result of the increasing complexity of the chips. A similar problem has been encountered by software designers working on very complex programs. Considerable research effort is being directed at this time toward finding methods for managing this complexity. This is discussed in more detail in later sections.

2. Processors

As mentioned previously, processors vary in size over a considerable range. The size variation is not just one of physical size but, more importantly from a computing point of view, one of word size and speed. The word is the amount of data that can be processed at one time and the size of a word is measured as word length in bits. A bit is a *BI*nary digi*T* and corresponds to a physical element in the computer that can represent one of the two states *ON* or *OFF*. These two circuit states are the two distinguishable signal levels mentioned earlier. Thus, longer word length means more bits and more circuitry and a larger machine. Word lengths vary from 4 to 60 bits. Large mainframe machines have word lengths of 32 to 60 bits, minicomputers 16 to 32 bits, and microcomputers 8 to 32 bits. The longer the word length, the more information can be contained in a single word. An n bit word has 2^n possible values; 10 bits can represent the range 0 to 1023 in base 10. Thus, it takes about $2\frac{1}{2}$ bits to represent one base 10 digit.

In addition to longer word length, large mainframe machines are constructed using the faster bipolar technology with its inevitable lower scale of integration. These machines are designed for high performance: high speed and high precision (word length). Large machines are found wherever large numerical calculations must be performed or where large amounts of data must be managed. Sometimes the entire processor may be used to perform computations on a single problem but at other times it might be idle much of the time unless time sharing is used to allow it to switch rapidly between many small tasks. The concept of time sharing evolved from the need to efficiently use large machines by allowing many users to sit at workstations and use the machine at the same time (the machine actually switches between users so fast, hopefully, that they are unaware of it). Time sharing was necessary because there were no small machines and individuals could not afford their own computers. This has changed completely with the advent of small affordable machines and the time-sharing concept has evolved into the networking concept described earlier. In networking, users and machines are linked together in a hierarchical way.

Occupying the middle range in size are the minicomputers. Originally these evolved as lower cost, lower performance machines for users who could not afford and/or did not need the performance of large machines. With time, they have grown more powerful and are now available in 16 and 32 bit sizes. Now, so-called "minis" have the power to carry out all but the largest and most sophisticated operations and have replaced "main-frames" for the vast majority of uses. Usually they are employed clustered together in various configurations, to share jobs and peripherals. Their construction uses a combination of bipolar and MOS technology. The increasing scale of integration has allowed them to maintain their price advantage while extending their word length and performance.

At the bottom of the scale are the microcomputers constructed primarily of single chip microprocessor components implemented in MOS technology. Because of the mass production of these very complex parts, the cost is low. This low cost has reached the point where individuals (or at least households) can afford to own their own computer. The cost of the electronics in these systems is really minimal but the electromechanical parts (keyboard, tape drive, disc) are relatively expensive and will remain that way since the mechanical arts are at a much more advanced state of evolution and are not likely to discover major cost reducing methods. Many companies (including the largest, IBM) are now in the personal computing business and that is a sign that there is money to be made. The microcomputers have evolved from 4-bit processors to 32-bit processors. The increasing scale of integration has allowed the single chip computer to move into the area traditionally occupied by minicomputers, and it is beginning to compete with low end mainframes.

The current problems and trends for large, medium, and small machines are quite different. Large machines are already built with the fastest technology that is known (and works). Thus, the problem in high-performance computing is how to increase the performance when the machine cannot be made faster. The answer has always been to use more machines working together. The problem is that no one has been able to devise a scheme in which all of the machines can be kept busy all of the time. As more machines are added, the performance for, say, n machines falls well below n times the performance of one machine. Part of the problem lies in how to connect the machines together; connecting every machine to every other machine is usually too expensive. Another problem is how to organize the machines. Two commonly discussed schemes are single instruction stream (all processors do the same thing) multiple data stream (on different data) or SIMD; and MIMD (multiple instruction, multiple data). Here, the various processors may be performing different operations on different data. This is clearly more complicated than the SIMD case. The theoretical ways of connecting machines together is limited only by the imagination; the practical ways by cost and whether any benefit can be derived. Another problem with multiprocessor schemes is that there is little or no software to support such parallel machines and not enough is known about how to produce it. These machines need a programming language that supports parallel operations.

A different approach to improving the performance of large machines is to change to an entirely new technology. Josephson junction technology, for example, was vigorously pursued for a time by IBM. Josephson junctions are superconducting devices and must be operated at liquid helium temperatures (around $-270°C$). They can be used to construct logic circuits and they have a very fast switching speed (the time it takes to change from 0 to 1 or 1 to 0). The speeds are in the picosecond range ($1ps = 10^{-12}$ s) as opposed to the tenths of nanoseconds range ($1ns = 10^{-9}$s) for conventional devices. However, there are serious thermal problems to be overcome and the increasing speed of more conventional approaches has decreased its advantage, so it is no longer clear that this technology will ever have commercial application. More recently there have been major advances in the use of a different semiconducting material as a basis for building computer circuits. Rather than using silicon, gallium arsenide is used. This material is more complex and more difficult to use, but has an intrinsic speed advantage over silicon and, if the manufacturing complications can be overcome, offers the promise of circuits that are substantially faster than those possible using silicon.

Another problem in large machine design is that of inventing new architectures for specialized problems such as the management of large information retrieval data banks or those arising in the field of artificial intelligence. The architecture of a machine is the way in which the various electronic units are connected together and specification of what these units do. Most computers are similar in their basic structure. It appears that certain types of problems could be solved much more efficiently if a different structure, one especially suited to the problem, were used. With very large scale integration, it may now be possible to economically produce such specialized designs.

The current trends in the design of medium size machines are directed toward networking these machines together and providing configurations that result in highly reliable systems. Networking is desirable because a number of medium size machines are often used within a single organization to perform similar operations but at different physical locations. There is then a need for communications between the machines in order to share data. Highly reliable systems are important because medium size machines are commonly used in real-time applications such as process control or online transaction processing. In these environments it is important that the computer systems never "go down" (cease functioning) because of undesirable consequences (physical or financial damage). Networking is usually accomplished by means of some scheme such as a ring network, a closed loop of coaxial cable to which the machines are attached. Highly reliable systems are implemented by duplicating all the elements shown in Fig. 1 and connecting them in such a way that at least one complete system always exists no matter which parts fail. Reliable software is a major problem in these systems and research continues in this area.

The effort in the field of small computers at this time is directed toward networking many machines together for reasons similar to those given above, and toward putting a more and more powerful processor onto a single chip (64 bits currently). In addition, considerable effort is going into putting the nonprocessor functions of a computer (the peripheral circuits) onto chips. Although considerable attention has been given to the miracle of a processor on a chip, little attention is given to the fact that the processor chip cannot be used without a large number of SSI and MSI chips surrounding it when a working computer is implemented. A large number of peripheral chips are now becoming available and this should greatly reduce the number of chips needed and thus the cost.

3. Storage

Storage in a computing system is organized in a hierarchical manner. Closest to the processor is fast random access memory (RAM). It is semiconductor memory and must be fast to keep up with the speed of the processor. It is random access in that any storage location (containing a word) may be read or written in any order. The RAM itself is often hierarchical with a smaller, faster bipolar memory being located closest to the processor (particularly when the processor is bipolar) and a somewhat slower but larger, lower cost MOS memory being connected to the faster bipolar memory. In addition to RAM, Read Only Memory or ROM is used. This comes in a variety of forms such as EPROM (erasable programmable ROM) which can store control or applications programmes. From the point of view of the processor ROM is identical to RAM in terms of speed and ease of reading its contents.

At the next level in the hierarchy is located the secondary storage (the RAM being the primary storage). This consists of magnetic disc storage. Disc storage can only be sequentially accessed and a given piece of information can only be reached by traversing past other data that occur earlier. Thus, it is slower than RAM, but it is much cheaper on a cost per bit basis. The disc mechanism itself is very expensive but one unit can provide up to half a billion bytes (1 byte = 8 bits) of storage. With the increasing use of smaller, lower cost computers there has been a need for small low cost disc units. In response to this, smaller disc units have evolved. Lowest cost are the "floppy" disc units. These units accept a flexible disc medium which can be inserted into or removed from (removable media) the disc drive. There are at least three sizes now, the floppy disk at 8 inches diameter, the minifloppy at $5\frac{1}{4}$ inches and the microfloppy at $3\frac{1}{2}$ inches. The next step up is a fixed media disc (usually called a Winchester) or a removable cartridge disc. These have capacities in the 10 to 50 MB range. At the top in terms of capacity are the large removable media drives in the 500 MB range mentioned above. These units use disc packs that consist of several individual discs mounted together on a single spindle.

Above the secondary storage level is the archival storage level. This region of the hierarchy is most commonly satisfied at present by magnetic tape, and is the region most in need of improvement. Magnetic tape is a serial access medium and is relatively slow. From an archival point of view it has two main deficiencies: it has a low capacity for an archival medium and its storage life is only about two years without rewriting. For short-term archiving it is very good; for long term it is poor. Various other archival schemes have been attempted including using tape cartridges, burning holes in thin metal films with a laser, writing onto MOS chips with an electron beam, and so on, but no satisfactory archival storage method has yet been found. Note that archival storage may acceptably be read-only after initial writing. The great hope in this area is the optical digital disc which can store 10^{10} to 10^{11} bits. It is read-only and is written (once) by a laser diode which evaporates a metal film from the inner surface of a phonograph-record-like plastic sandwich, similar to the home optical video disc. The reason that video discs are in use whereas the digital discs are not is that virtually no errors are tolerable in the digital case whereas a rather large number of errors are tolerable in the video case.

Two other memory technologies deserve mention: magnetic bubbles and charge-coupled devices (CCDs). Both of these have suffered the same fate in competition with MOS RAM. The density of MOS RAM has increased so fast that there is no place for either of these technologies in most computing systems. Both are serial access memory technologies and, for the same cost, RAM is clearly more desirable. Thus neither CCDs nor bubbles have found a large market. The CCD technology has become important for solid state imagers (solid state television cameras, for example) and bubbles are used in certain applications where their nonvolatility is important. Nonvolatile memory retains its stored information without electrical power being supplied. This is important in some applications and is a property of all magnetic storage.

Currently available semiconductor RAM chips are at the 256k bit level (actually 262,144 or 2^{18} bits). The present effort is then directed toward the next generation 1 M bit chips (containing 1,048,576 or 2^{20} bits). The 64k and the 256k chips were produced with some difficulty and it is reasonable to assume that the 1 Mb chips will be even more difficult to produce. Bipolar memory chips will also grow in size but will continue to lag a generation or two behind their MOS rivals. At the higher densities, power dissipation in the chip becomes a bigger problem and a technology called CMOS (complementary MOS) gains in importance. MOS transistors may be of two types—P channel or N channel. Ordinary MOS uses only N channel devices and is often called NMOS. Complementary MOS uses both types in a complementary way in which one of them is always off. The result is that the circuit does not consume any power except when it is in transition from on to off, or off to on. Because of this, the power dissipation is much lower. Unfortunately, more devices are required to implement a given logic circuit so this technology is not as dense as NMOS. Some density may have to be sacrificed to control heat in the future.

Disc technology is a highly refined technology at this point and little should be expected in the way of major improvements. However, surprises do occur. The recent increase in disc storage density has been due to the development of thin film heads. The heads are the devices that ride close to the moving magnetic surface and write onto or read from it. Heads are now made with extremely small dimensions by using methods developed for semiconductor technology. The heads have parts that have μm dimensions and the head to surface spacing is also in the μm range. Because of these small dimensions, disc units must be almost dust free. Disc density has also been improved by better magnetic materials coating the disc.

As mentioned, however, one hope for a solution to the archival storage problem is the optical digital disc.

4. Software

Software is not always considered to be a part of computer technology but it certainly should be. Software accounts for 80 to 90 percent or more of the cost of moderate to large computing systems. Although hardware complexity has been increasing rapidly, it was traditionally kept relatively simple in order to obtain high reliability. The hardware can usually execute only a limited number of simple instructions. However, the programmer is free to combine these instructions into sequences that can become extremely complex. For a time, intricacy in programs was considered to be clever and a sign of great intellect. However, it often turned out that even the programmer who wrote the software originally could not decipher how it worked after six

months, without extraordinary effort resulting in much wasted time. It is relatively easy to make software very complex. This complexity problem, faced some years ago by software people, is now being faced by hardware designers. Studies show that programmers can produce five to ten working (debugged) lines of code per day. Similarly, integrated circuit designers average five to ten working devices per day. Humans can cope with only a limited complexity. The solution to managing complexity is to use what is called a hierarchical, structured approach. Hierarchical implies the decomposition of a complex problem into simpler ones in a systematic way until, at the lowest level, the subproblem is manageable. Structured means that strict rules and formats are enforced on the designers. Cute and clever methods are forbidden and clarity is stressed even at the expense of efficiency. The result is software or hardware that is more apt to be correct the first time and, if not, is much easier to test and correct afterwards. This programming methodology is usually referred to as structured programming. Early programming languages did not include statements which enforced structured programming, however, more recent languages do (as do more recent versions of old languages).

Programming languages provide human-understandable names for instructions that the computer can execute. The computer itself translates the instructions into a form that ultimately controls what the electronic circuits do. The translation may take place as each instruction is executed (by an interpreter), or an entire program may be translated prior to any execution (by a compiler). BASIC is an example of a language that is interpreted, and FORTRAN one that is compiled. Newer languages like PASCAL and ADA were designed to include structured programming statements such as IF–THEN–ELSE. Older languages such as COBOL or FORTRAN did not have these although structured programming statements were added to FORTRAN in a later version, FORTRAN 77.

The other major software encountered by a user is the operating system. This program resides permanently in the computer and performs the task of data and program management. It performs such diverse tasks as swapping between time-sharing users, locating needed data, and loading a program into storage and noting where it is. It manages the hardware and all the other software. Operating systems are large and complex programs on large machines. Very small machines have a very simple operating system.

A long-term dream of some people in the software world is to develop a universal language that incorporates all of the best features of other languages (and, of course, none of the disadvantages). Most languages were designed for specific users—FORTRAN for numerical computations and COBOL for business computations. IBM developed PL/1 as one attempt at a universal language and it is very good but is very complex and can run only on large machines. More recently, the all-purpose language ADA was developed by the United

States Department of Defense (who also developed COBOL). Its utility is still unclear as ADA compilers are just beginning to appear. BASIC was originally designed as a simple beginners language, but the advent of the cheap microcomputer resulted in its wide adoption. It is still by far the most commonly used language in spite of its lack of structure.

The major software issues in the 1980s were: What are the ideal structured programming constructs to incorporate into a language? How does one know whether a program is correct or not? What is the best working and support environment for software development? There is also substantial effort being made in the area of databases (the management of large data banks), languages to support graphics, and languages which support parallel tasks (concurrent operations). A new discipline of software engineering has emerged representing the application of the engineering concepts of hierarchical decomposition and structuring to software. Proving programs to be correct is a formidable task and progress has been made on only the simplest of programs. Improving the working environment and design tools available to programmers is thought to be a crucial step in raising their productivity. The human interface to computers has traditionally been abysmal, and considerable effort is now being expended in this area as discussed in the next section. The major problem in the graphics area is that computer graphics are very hardware- and software-specific and there was a total lack of standardization until very recently, with the adoption of GKS, the Graphical Kernal System, in the early 1980s. The management of software complexity continues to be the single largest problem in the software world.

5. The User Workstation

The most neglected part of computers traditionally has been the human interface. There is now a considerable effort to improve this part of a computer system. The problem has basically been one of cost. The input/output (I/O) devices for a computer are necessarily electromechanical since the computer is electrical and the human is mechanical. Electromechanical devices, as mentioned before, are expensive. The only way to reduce the cost is through high volume production and that means volume such as one has for, say, television sets or electronic games. With the electronics of computers so cheap, in the mid-1980s it was possible to introduce the mass production of personal computers. Once this process took hold, prices fell and quality improved.

The user workstation in Fig. 1 includes all I/O such as keyboards, color cathode ray tube (CRT) displays, printers, plotters, and graphic tablets. It is important to realize that the workstation can itself be a computer system as shown in the top part of Fig. 1. In fact, each of the components of the workstation may contain a processor and memory. Thus the complete workstation can consist of a computer (processor, primary and secondary

memory), plus the I/O devices and a communications processor.

Keyboards have been around a long time and vary greatly in quality but, other than that, the only major deficiency is in the character set and the layout of the characters on the keys. There is a need for standardization here, and, in addition, there is a need for the addition of a significant number of extra characters. It would be useful if the keyboard characters could be redefined (English to Arabic for example) at will by the user but there appears to be no inexpensive way to do that. Printers have progressed considerably and small dot matrix printers can display a variety of characters as well as simple graphics. There are also laser xerographic printers available and eventually these may dominate the field. It is important to realize that the user workstation should be able to handle multiple fonts and at least simple graphics. The other element essential to the workstation is some kind of reasonably high resolution display capable of text and graphics. The CRT serves this function and will continue to do so for the indefinite future. Along with the CRT there must be some kind of pointing device and one of the best (though cumbersome) is the graphic tablet with some kind of stylus. The tablet allows the user to enter freehand drawings and to point to items on the CRT screen. The CRT display and tablet must have sufficient resolution (say at least $800 \times 1,000$ dots) and this is now on the verge of being affordable. As pointed out earlier, the problem in the user workstation part of the system is not what is possible but what is affordable. What is affordable will change rapidly as volume production increases.

The trends in the workstation area are as follows: higher resolution for CRTs, tablets, and printers; color for CRT displays; the addition of voice output and limited voice input; and, from a system point of view, the integration of both text and graphics in a single workstation environment. There is a long way to go to create an environment with which a human is truly at home, but considerable progress is finally being made. The proliferation of workstations in the home and office will create the needed volume.

The workstation can be linked to other workstations and other computers over networks and this is discussed in the next section.

6. Communications Between Machines and Users

Communication between machines and users is a complex problem which is just beginning to be solved. The electronic technology for making any desired interconnection exists and is not a limitation. The problem is economic, political and, in the case of the recently evolved local area networks, one of competition between several incompatible systems.

There are many ways to classify intercommunication systems. Systems may be tightly coupled as in the multiprocessor systems discussed earlier, or loosely coupled.

The kinds of systems involved in communication networks are loosely coupled—the nodes (machines and/or people) are some distance apart and information to be sent from one node to another is put into some format called a message and then placed on the network. A message may be sent point to point or it may be broadcast to all (or a group of) other nodes. Information identifying the sending and receiving nodes is transmitted as part of the message.

At the lowest level in the network hierarchy there is the computer's system bus as shown in Fig. 1. The bus carries words (all bits in parallel) to and from the various parts of the computer. At the next level there is the local area network which ties user workstations together with each other as well as to larger local computers and data banks which are shared among users. There are a number of competing schemes for implementing this level and no best solution, let alone a standard, has evolved. As a result, a definition has been proposed by the International Standards Organization (ISO), the Open System Interconnection (OSI) scheme. A network at this level would exist within one building, or a group of buildings. Physically, coaxial cable would be used and the cable would normally be a single line with taps (the nodes) or a closed ring with taps. Fiber optics can be used when cost effective.

At the next level there would be a connection to a national network. This level would allow communication within and between cities. At present there is no common network for all users, primarily because the telephone companies failed to implement one, not entirely because of their own failing (see below). There are a number of private data communication networks which have been operating for some time of which the Department of Defense ARPA Net is the oldest. At the national level there are a number of different ways to carry the messages across the country. A major distinction is space versus terrestrial. Space communication uses satellites and is the most recent method available. It is particularly good for broadcasts since one satellite can send a signal to a very large area. Most cable television signals are broadcast by satellite for example. Terrestrial methods include wires such as the telephone lines into homes, coaxial cable such as the cable that brings cable television into the home, and point to point microwave radio as used by the telephone company. In addition, broadcast radio and television could be used in the broadcast mode to transmit information other than, and/or in addition to, normal programming as is done in teletext systems.

One would think that the telephone system could be used directly to satisfy the need for data communications at the national level but this is not the case at the present time. The fundamental technical problem is that the telephone system is primarily an analog system designed to carry voice. The telephone companies of the world have a vast investment in plant and equipment designed for this purpose. The problem with an analog system is that it does not carry digital signals at all well.

Thus, while the greatest need is for digital transmission, the system is not designed to handle it. The problem is that voice transmission requires a relatively narrow band of frequencies (typically 5kHz) and so telephone networks were originally designed to carry signals of such a bandwidth. The consequences for data transmission would be that digital signals could only be sent at a maximum rate of 5 kilobits/sec. Obviously more sophisticated electronics would enable data to be sent at a faster rate, but if cabling and switchgear had been designed merely to cope with the lower rate, errors and loss of data would result. The newer parts of the telephone system—the satellites and some microwave stations—can handle digital signals but the local exchanges were not designed to handle them and a tremendous (indeed, the largest) investment must be made there in order to convert to an all-digital system. If the telephone companies were starting now they would build an all digital system. Unfortunately, the world, now all digital, was all analog when they started. Thus very expensive and lengthy redesign is only now being undertaken in the late 1980s. In the meantime, schemes for transmitting digital data on an analog network have been devised.

The failure of the telephone companies to offer adequate digital transmission led to the start-up of competing common carriers who specialized in offering these services much to the chagrin of the telephone company who saw potential revenues slipping away. At present there are a number of successful carriers specializing in digital data transmission services. The telephone companies have wasted considerable energy and money fighting these competitors, mostly as a delaying action. Until recently, they also fought anyone who attempted to connect non-telephone-company equipment to their system, again mostly as a delaying action until they could get their own house in order. Why did this strange situation arise? In addition to the technological reasons given earlier, in the United States there was an additional political problem. In 1956 AT and T (the Bell System) agreed to stay out of the computer business in an antitrust consent decree. The fear at the time was that the fledgling computer industry would be annihilated by the telecommunications giant. In the ensuing years Bell took the agreement far too literally and simply failed to take adequate steps to convert the system to a digital system and to design and build computers into the system. The result was that they were unprepared for the rapid increase in demand for digital service. In retrospect, by 1956 the consent decrees should have been challenged in court. The telephone companies are in a catch-up program to modernize their system and their offerings to users. The Bell System has now been split up with a separate nonutility subsidiary (American Bell) offering a variety of computing type services and equipment to the public in the competitive marketplace. In the meantime the regulated monopoly part of the company must continue to convert to an all-digital world. The competition is already great with such giants as IBM (through Satellite Business Systems) in operation and the government itself (through the Post Office) beginning to offer communication services.

The advent of low cost digital technology has thrown the traditional means of communications into disarray. The heart of the problem is that voice, data, pictures, mail—any form of communication—can be easily handled at high speed by digital systems. Thus, the traditional distinct markets dominated by the telephone company, the post office, and the commercial broadcast industry have disappeared. Who should do what? At present the best high bandwidth channel into homes is the cable television system. Not all homes have it and it often does not provide two-way communication or connections to a national network. The telephone link to homes is low bandwidth. Thus, at present there is no suitable data link to homes or most businesses.

Once a nationwide digital transmission system is established, it will be easy for computers and users to communicate over the system. Such a system will be able to handle voice transmissions, facsimile transmissions, data, and text with equal ease. It will be possible for groups to communicate with each other in a conference way. The technology to accomplish facsimile transmission and teleconferencing exists now but the transmission system to handle it at reasonable cost does not.

7. Current Problems in Computer Technology and Telecommunications

The major problem in computer technology is how to manage complexity in both software and hardware. The problem exists at all levels from design to testing. Hopefully, the hierarchical structured design approach supplemented by adequate computer-aided-design systems will alleviate this problem.

The continuing challenge in digital electronics is how to make the devices smaller and put more functionality on a chip. This will require using shorter wavelength radiation such as X-rays for chip exposure, and a better understanding of how very small devices behave; at very small dimensions, the devices behave differently. To lower the power dissipated on the chip, the signal levels must be lowered and interference from electrical noise will become more of a problem.

There is a paradox in putting more and more functionality on a chip: the chip becomes less and less general purpose and therefore useful to a smaller and smaller market. This means smaller volume for higher design cost. Thus, very complex chips may be uneconomical to manufacture. The solution to this problem is to automate the design process to the point where custom designs can be made economically. Considerable effort is being directed toward this goal by researchers around the world.

The major problem in the telecommunications area is the lack of a general purpose digital network at the national and international level.

There is another general problem that exists in the computer business which is both detrimental and a blessing: lack of standardization. The field has been and continues to be a rapidly evolving field and better ways of doing things are found almost daily. Thus, standardization would stifle innovation, the life-blood of the computer revolution. However, the lack of standardization means that computer systems are incompatible in almost every way. Neither hardware nor software from one system will work on another system. While this may be a competitive advantage, it represents an incredible waste of effort and time spent on conversion. The trouble is that no one knows which way is best.

The largest changes that will be apparent to the user in the future will be the proliferation of small computer systems, the improvement in the quality and availability of software, and the improvement in digital transmission networks.

Bibliography

Kubitz W J 1980 Computer technology: A forecast for the future. In: Lancaster F W (ed.) 1980 *The Role of the Library in an Electronic Society*. Proceedings of the 1979 Clinic on Library Applications of Data Processing. University of Illinois Graduate School of Library Science, Urbana–Champaign, Illinois

Information Storage and Retrieval

F. W. Lancaster and D. Shaw

The term "information retrieval," as commonly used, refers to the searching of some body of literature in order to identify items that deal with a particular topic; the term is synonymous with "literature searching." An information retrieval system is any device that allows the characteristics of a set of documents to be matched against a search strategy. Such systems have existed for many years, although only in card or printed form before the 1940s. The major breakthrough in information retrieval was the development, in the 1940s, of systems that broke away from the linear organization of indexing entries (a severe limitation of earlier forms) and allowed a truly multidimensional approach to the representation and searching of subject matter. These early "coordinate" indexing systems, as developed by Batten and Cordonnier (the optical coincidence or "peek-a-boo" principle), Mooers (edge-notched cards), and Taube (the Uniterm system), were the immediate predecessors of modern computer-based systems. Indeed, all systems developed since then may be regarded as successively more sophisticated and more automated versions of the two basic systems of file organization produced first by Batten (one record per class or index term) and by Mooers (one record per document). These systems became known as "coordinate" indexing systems because they allow the searcher to manipulate the file in order to discover which documents are common to two or more classes existing in the system (i.e., coordinate or intersect document classes to discover members held in common).

1. Off-line Systems for Information Retrieval

The use of telecommunications networks to access databases on-line is now commonplace, but off-line systems were first applied to information retrieval as early as the 1950s. The first major systems for information retrieval by computer were implemented by the US Armed Services Technical Information Agency (ASTIA) [later known as the Defense Documentation Center (DDC) and now known as the Defense Technical Information Center (DTIC)] in 1959–1963, the US National Aeronautics and Space Administration (NASA) in 1962, and the US National Library of Medicine in 1964. During the same general period of development, a number of smaller, more specialized systems were implemented by other government agencies.

All of these were off-line, batch processing systems, and had basically the same characteristics. In a system of this general type the computer plays a somewhat minor role, most of the processing being done by people. The database of such a system is constructed as a result of the human analysis and indexing of documents, which involves the examination of a document to determine its subject matter (conceptual analysis) and the representation of this subject matter by index terms selected (usually) from a prescribed list (i.e., a controlled vocabulary). The document representation or surrogate thus created is made machine readable and stored in a database that can conveniently be searched. In an off-line system the document representations are usually stored sequentially on magnetic tape.

The output side of the operation is similar to the input side. Once a request for information is made to the system, it is conceptually analyzed by an information specialist, that is, the specialist tries to determine the exact subject matter needed. Having established this, the specialist constructs a search strategy, which is a formal representation of a request in much the same way that the index surrogate is a formal representation of a document. The search analyst, like the indexer, must use only terms selected from the database. This may mean terms from the controlled vocabulary or "natural language" terms occurring in the text stored in the database (titles, abstracts or even, in some cases, complete text). There is one important difference between the representation of the document (surrogate)

	Terms								
	a	b	c	d	e	f	g	h	.... n
1	x		x	x			x		
2		x	x					x	
3	x		x		x	x			
4	x	x						x	
5		x		x				x	
6	x			x		x	x		
⋮									
n									

Documents

Figure 1
The document-term matrix

and the representation of the request (search strategy). The former may consist solely of a list of terms, without display of relationships among these terms, but the latter is likely to include both index terms and a prescribed set of relationships among them. In fact, it is customary to construct a search strategy as a formal algebraic expression, using the operators (AND, OR, NOT) of Boolean algebra. Thus, a search strategy may look something like the following:

(A *or* B *or* C *or* D *or* E) *and* (F *or* G *or* H) *and not* I

where the letters represent index terms selected from a controlled vocabulary. Boolean strategies are not essential (i.e., alternative approaches are possible) but they are still the most common form of search strategy.

In an off-line, tape-oriented system the search strategy is matched sequentially against each and every document representation in the file; all representations that satisfy the logical requirements of the strategy are retrieved and printed. Because a computer can handle many searches at once, it is customary to hold searches until a group has been accumulated. The entire group or batch of searches are then run at the same time; hence the term batch processing.

The computer plays a comparatively minor role in the typical off-line retrieval system because it merely effects a match between search strategy and file of document representations and plays no direct part in the indexing operation, the vocabulary control activities, the construction of searching strategies, or in interaction with requesters. It is these "intellectual" operations that govern the performance of an information retrieval system, whether manual or mechanized.

1.1 Indexing

The search file or database, which forms the heart of any retrieval system, may be regarded as a document-term matrix as illustrated in Fig. 1. The indexing operation involves the assignment of terms to documents or (another way of looking at it) the assignment of documents to classes, each class being labeled with a particular index term. Two of the four major factors that control the performance of any information retrieval system are fixed at the time of input, by the assignment of terms to documents (or documents to classes), and by the size of the classes existing in the system. The size of the document classes is determined by the specificity of the vocabulary used in indexing. A specific vocabulary will allow the formation of many small classes while a nonspecific vocabulary will allow the formation of only a small number of large document classes.

A computer-based retrieval system may also provide access through the terms used in the documents themselves, in addition to or in place of access by indexer-assigned terms from a controlled vocabulary. Access through the vocabulary used by the document authors is referred to as "natural language" or "free text" searching. This approach requires less work in the creation of the database, as human indexers are not needed to review each document. However, more work is required for document retrieval, as the searcher must anticipate various synonyms for the desired topics and also avoid retrieving unwanted material due to homographs or other ambiguous representations. Computer software for free text searching expands on the Boolean operators to include: searching for specific strings of two or more words; proximity operators for locating words in the same sentence; and truncation allowing searches for word stems.

Researchers continue to investigate machine-based and machine-assisted indexing. Limitations in computer programs to process natural language texts have hindered the former, but automated support for human indexers is now used by several database producers.

1.2 Retrieval

Once the indexing characteristics (assignment of documents to classes and size of the classes thus created) are fixed, only two major variables remain to affect the performance of the retrieval system. These occur at the output end of the retrieval operation. One of these is the quality of the information requests made to the system (i.e., the degree to which they actually reflect the true information needs of the user) and the second is the quality of the search strategy prepared to interrogate the system (i.e., the degree to which this strategy reflects the true information needs of the requester and covers all possible approaches to retrieval).

A search is conducted by matching the search strategy against the database. Conceptually, this database may be regarded as nothing more than a stored matrix, as in Fig. 1, in which document records are associated with controlled vocabulary and/or free text index terms. A document record is retrieved when the index terms associated with it match the index terms specified in the search strategy. This is true whatever form of system, manual or mechanized, is used to effect the match. It is

clear that, once the indexing process has assigned documents to classes, a particular search strategy will retrieve the same set of documents whatever mechanism is used to effect the match and whatever method is used to associate document records with index terms. In other words, retrieval hardware and methods of file organization have no direct influence on the effectiveness of a retrieval system although they may have a profound influence on its cost effectiveness and on the speed with which searches are conducted.

2. Advantages and Disadvantages of Computer-based Systems

The computer offers significant advantages over other approaches to information retrieval. A computer-based system: (a) can provide multiple access points to documents conveniently and economically, (b) allows processing of very large files, (c) will conduct many complex searches simultaneously, (d) will allow the conduct of complex searches involving many terms in various logical relationships, (e) will provide a printout capability and can be used to produce a high quality printed bibliography, (f) can produce electronic and microform output, (g) will yield various types of management information, and (h), perhaps most important of all, will generate machine-readable databases that can easily be shipped to and used by other organizations.

Although computer-based systems do have significant advantages over less sophisticated systems, those operated in an off-line, batch processing mode also have several limitations. First, the system is virtually always searched in a delegated mode. The person who has the real need for information has no opportunity to conduct his own search, but delegates this responsibility to an information specialist. This creates the danger that the requester will not be able to describe precisely what he or she is looking for. Likewise, there is a danger that the information specialist will misinterpret the information need of the user, especially true with off-line systems and their long response times. Cost and response-time limitations tended to restrict the use of such systems to one type of information need only: the situation in which the user is involved in a relatively long-term research project (for whom rapid response is not critical) and needs a comprehensive search of the literature. For this type of requirement the off-line system is quite effective. However, such a system is of little value for the user who does not need a comprehensive search but "a few good papers" and needs them right away.

Another significant disadvantage of the off-line system is that it is noninteractive. That is, the search analyst, in preparing a search strategy, cannot interact directly with the database. Instead, the searcher is operating virtually "blind," having to think in advance of all the terms and term combinations that might retrieve documents relevant to a particular request. If the strategy is defective in some way, the searcher will not know this until a printout of results is obtained, perhaps some days later. This is not a "natural" way of conducting a literature search. Much more natural is the way normally employed in the searching of printed indexes: a particular approach is tried and, if this does not work out, another is substituted. One approach may lead directly to another because one subject heading may refer to another, or because in browsing among the citations under one heading, the searcher may think of other possible terms. This type of heuristic searching is possible because the searcher can obtain immediate "feedback" from the tool used. But an off-line system does not give immediate feedback and provides no real interaction and browsing capabilities. Search strategies are "one shot" efforts and cannot be developed heuristically.

3. On-line Retrieval Systems

On-line retrieval systems avoid all the major disadvantages of the off-line systems noted above. An on-line system can be used in a nondelegated search mode, most systems responding to most commands and search strategies within seconds, and the search strategy can be developed as a result of a "conversation" between the user and the system. A typical search in an on-line system can be done in a matter of minutes and the end result may be a list of retrieved citations, the texts of documents or numeric data. Thus, an on-line system can be used in the type of search in which the user needs a few relevant citations but needs them right away. Moreover, an on-line system provides some capability for browsing.

The term "on-line," as applied to information retrieval, means that the searcher is in direct communication with some database and with the computer on which it is loaded. The searcher communicates with the system by means of a terminal, which may be a simple typewriter or video display terminal or a microcomputer. The terminal may be physically far removed from the computer on which the database is loaded, perhaps several thousand miles away, with the communication taking place by means of telephone lines.

On-line retrieval systems are frequently referred to as "interactive" or "conversational." Other adjectives that may be applied include "real-time" and "time-shared." Real-time operation implies that the computer receives data, processes it, and returns results quickly enough for these to be used in some continuing task being conducted by the system user. Applied to information retrieval, real-time implies that the computer responds quickly enough to interact with a user's heuristic search processes. Time-sharing refers to the ability of a computer to share its processing time among one or more completely independent activities. An on-line, time-shared system will operate via a number of independent, concurrently usable terminals, giving each terminal user processing time when he needs it and creating the illusion (most of the time) that he is the sole user of the computer facilities.

Experimental work on on-line information retrieval began in the early 1960s. Early work was conducted at the Massachusetts Institute of Technology (MIT), the System Development Corporation (SDC), and at the Lockheed Missiles and Space Co.

It was not until the 1970s, however, that on-line information retrieval came into its own. Since 1970, most off-line systems have been converted to an on-line mode of operation. By the early 1980s several thousand databases were accessible on-line. Many are scientific and technical in nature but others exist in the social sciences, in business, and in current affairs.

The major application of on-line systems in the information services area is in the conduct of retrospective searches. On-line systems also provide current awareness listings, matching user interest profiles against database updates. This service is known as *selective dissemination of information* (SDI), and was originally developed in the early 1960s for use with off-line retrieval systems. On-line systems also support information services in cooperative cataloging, the provision of union catalogs, in interlibrary lending activities, and in question answering.

4. The Growth of Machine-readable Databases

The emergence of the machine-readable database may be the single most important development to take place in the provision of information services. The MEDLARS database of the National Library of Medicine, begun in 1964, was the first to be made widely available. Since then, several thousand have emerged and are now being used in the provision of information services on a worldwide basis. Some are general in scope, covering entire scientific disciplines, while others are highly specialized. Some contain numerical, physical, chemical, or statistical data rather than bibliographic citations (i.e., they are databanks rather than databases). Other databases contain the full text of encyclopedias, journals, textbooks, newspapers, or other publications.

Many machine-readable databases, and most of the largest ones, exist essentially as a by-product of the preparation of printed publications. The reason for this is that most of the major indexes, many newspapers, and some other works are now photocomposed, under computer control, from a machine-readable file. The publishers, who may be regarded as the wholesalers of information, have been eager to have their databases exploited by others. Six major developments in the provision of information services from machine-readable databases have occurred since 1964:

(a) *Networking and other cooperative arrangements.* Beginning in 1965, the National Library of Medicine made its MEDLARS database available for use by libraries and other centers. A network of MEDLARS centers was established throughout the United States and beyond. Several of these centers had their own computer facilities and were thus able to offer a retrospective search service, and in some cases selective dissemination of information, for a designated group of users. Others, without suitable computer facilities, merely acted as search formulation centers, the actual searches being run on computer facilities elsewhere in the network. Somewhat similar network arrangements were made by other agencies, including the Educational Resources Information Center (ERIC), and various information systems existing within the United Nations [see *Educational Resources Information Center (ERIC)*].

(b) *Leasing arrangements.* Several databases were made available through leasing, allowing an individual organization to acquire a database and process it on its own computer facilities in order to provide retrospective and/or selective dissemination of information services. But it is relatively expensive to lease a large database and this type of arrangement is likely to appeal only to fairly large companies, a fact which led directly to the next development.

(c) *The scientific information dissemination center (SIDC).* The scientific information dissemination center is a retailer of information that acquires a number of different databases from the information wholesalers, through licensing agreements, and offers service from these databases to any organization or individual willing to pay for such service. By spreading the licensing and processing costs over many users, the scientific information dissemination center is able to keep the cost for a selective dissemination of information profile, or for a single search, to a reasonable level. Moreover, the scientific information dissemination center provides a convenient single source through which a user can obtain service from a number of different databases. Many scientific information dissemination centers were set up in the United States, and elsewhere, in the 1960s and 1970s. Most were in academic centers but some were provided by national libraries or other government agencies (for example, in Canada and Australia).

(d) *On-line access.* With the widespread conversion of systems to an on-line mode of operation a number of databases are now available for remote access directly from the database producer. That is, the producers of the database load it on their own computer facilities and sell access to it via remote on-line terminals. Examples of on-line access provided by database producers are H W Wilson's WILSONLINE as well as the National Library of Medicine's MEDLINE and related databases.

(e) *The on-line retailer.* The on-line retailer of information services operates in much the same way as the scientific information dissemination center except that the emphasis is on retrospective search rather than selective dissemination of information and its services are available on-line. The on-line retailer acquires a number of databases through licensing agreements, loads these on its own computer, and sells on-line access to them. Such organizations provide a convenient single source through which service from a number of different resources can be obtained. Three major on-line retailers

in the United States are the Orbit Information Technologies Corporation (formerly System Development Corporation), Dialog Information Services, and Bibliographic Retrieval Services. In Europe a somewhat different pattern has emerged. The Commission of the European Communities (CEC) has established an international on-line network, Euronet, to improve access to information. Computers in the various CEC countries are linked by the network, thus permitting shared on-line access to a wide range of information resources. The information access system within Euronet is known as DIANE (Direct Information Access Network for Europe).

(f) *Distributed databases.* Technological developments, notably microcomputers and associated storage devices such as CD-ROM, make it possible for an individual or institution to act as a lessor of databases. In such cases the database may be considered as the electronic equivalent of a subscription to an indexing service or an encyclopedia. The database and search software are leased from the database producer, who may also provide the requisite hardware. Some arrangements provide a quarterly update of the distributed database, with reduced charges for on-line access to the more recent information.

4.1 Concerns about Access

The increasing number and variety of databases have sparked concerns about who will be allowed to use these resources. Today the most common form of access is through on-line retailers, with charges incurred for on-line time and royalties to the database producer for each item retrieved. Especially in public libraries there are differences of opinion as to whether these costs should be borne by the user for whom the search is done, or by the institution as part of its provision of information service. This concern is somewhat abated with the increasing use of distributed databases, which, like printed indexes, provide access to many topics at a fixed cost.

Another area of interest is when searches should be delegated to information specialists (intermediaries) and when they should be done by the person who needs the information (termed the "end user"). The development of easier-to-use retrieval software and increasing the use of microcomputers and telecommunications networks for other purposes are developing a more sophisticated clientele for information retrieval. The user who needs "a few good papers" may well conduct his own search, but exhaustive retrieval requires the skills of an experienced information specialist.

5. Conclusion

In a brief survey of this kind only major developments can be covered. Some further trends, however, should at least be mentioned. Most existing systems operate by means of a controlled vocabulary, that is, a limited set of terms, frequently a thesaurus, that must be used by both indexers and searchers. However, other systems have operated successfully on natural language for the past 20 years, and there seems to be a continuing shift in this direction. Most natural language systems allow searches to be performed on any words contained in abstracts or, sometimes, the complete text of documents. Much research has been performed on "completely automatic" systems, that is those in which human intellectual processing is replaced by computer processing. While many experimental systems exist, there are no information services of any significant size operating in a completely automatic mode. Work continues on research to develop more "user cordial" online systems, systems that would obviate the need for the human intermediary. The application of artificial intelligence to information retrieval is an area of increasing interest. Finally, as more and more text becomes available in machine-readable form, including text of reference "books," journals and newspapers, the emergence of a completely paperless publication/communication environment becomes increasingly feasible. Paperless systems, including the potential of new publication

forms and the impact of such developments on libraries, are dealt with elsewhere by Lancaster (1982).

Bibliography

Borgman C L, Moghdam D, Corbett P K 1984 *Effective On-line Searching.* Marcel Dekker, New York
Harter S P 1986 *On-line Information Retrieval: Concepts, Principles and Techniques.* Academic Press, Orlando, Florida
Lancaster F W 1979 *Information Retrieval Systems: Characteristics, Testing and Evaluation,* 2nd edn. Wiley, New York
Lancaster F W 1982 *Libraries and Librarians in an Age of Electronics.* Information Resources Press, Washington, DC
Mathies M L, Watson P G 1973 *Computer-based Reference Services.* American Library Association, Chicago, Illinois
Meadow C T, Cochrane P A 1981 *Basics of On-line Searching.* Wiley, New York
Smith L C 1980 Artificial intelligence applications in information systems. *Annu. Rev. Inf. Sci. Technol.* 15: 67–105
Sparck Jones K 1974 Progress in documentation: Automatic indexing. *J. Doc.* 30: 393–432
Vickery B C 1970 *Techniques of Information Retrieval.* Archon, Hamden, Connecticut

Microforms

B. B. Minor

Microforms are media for the storage in miniature of printed and other graphic materials. Microforms in several film-based formats are widely used in school systems and institutions of higher learning for record-keeping, for the storage and dissemination of educational information, and for making available materials that are no longer obtainable in the original form. Microforms as a means of delivering instruction are less widely used, though a number of projects in the 1970s reported positive results and acceptance by students at a variety of educational levels. More recent efforts have involved the integration of microfiche with computer-based education or with other technologies.

1. Microform Formats

Produced in either sheet or roll film, microform formats used in education include both black and white and color microfiche, microfilm jackets, and 35 mm roll film. Ease of access and relatively straightforward handling have made the sheet microforms more popular, although it is more expensive to produce the original microfiche master than it is to produce the traditional roll film. Three types of film are available: silver halide, which produces the highest quality image and is generally recommended for archival use; diazo, which is less expensive, simpler to process, and also produces a high-quality image, but tends to fade with exposure to light; and vesicular, which is also less expensive, and is considered satisfactory for day-to-day use and reproduction in both microfiche and paper formats.

A standard size microfiche—a 105 × 148 mm sheet of film—can contain as many as 96 frames, or pages, on a single fiche at 24 × reduction for viewing on a standard microfiche reader. Color microfiche typically hold 60 35 mm slides on a standard sheet, and should be viewed on a neutral tint screen. In some cases, color slide fiche are issued with audiotape cassettes, and at least one unit—the Revox Audiocard—will move the fiche automatically in response to signals on the control strip of the tape (Williams and Fothergill 1977 p. 21).

Jackets, which are transparent plastic holders with channels for the insertion of either 16 mm or 35 mm film, are used primarily where updating or corrections will be required. A 105 × 148 mm jacket will hold up to 60 frames of 16 mm film in five channels, and a narrow opaque strip is provided across the top for writing or typing a title or other identifying information.

Available on open reels, in cartridges, or in cassettes, 35 mm roll film is used for the micropublication of newspapers and periodicals, as well as the recording of rare books, manuscripts, and other archival materials. The relatively low reductions (12 × to 20 ×) and ability to handle the large formats of the original newspapers make this a desirable format for such use.

2. Advantages and Disadvantages

The major advantages generally cited are the economy, that is, the low cost of microforms as compared with print media, and compactness for storage. In addition, local or specialized materials can be produced in small numbers less expensively, some resources that would otherwise be unavailable can be made available on microfilm, and wear and tear on originals, as well as their loss, can be avoided by the use of microfilmed copies. It may be noted that, although adult users of libraries and library personnel have not accepted microforms gracefully (Raikes 1982), children who have used them in their classes and school projects have responded favorably to microform editions of traditional children's literature and other materials (Burchinal 1974). Research on the use of microfiche by visually impaired persons indicates that the microform in the same large print format as a printed page is more easily read, perhaps due to the elimination of glare from the page by using a backlit screen (Connor 1981). In any case, large print microfiche or regular fiche combined with a reader with a high magnification lens can be used to provide a wider variety of reading and/or instructional materials for this group at a much lower cost than the traditional paper copy (Connor 1978). The portability and economy of using microfiche to provide medical students with individual copies of color clinical visuals have also been cited as advantages, although the lack of a really satisfactory inexpensive portable reader was seen as a disadvantage (Glickman 1978).

The need to buy and maintain equipment, which may or may not be satisfactory, obviously offsets some of the economy of microform publications. Reader printers to produce paper copy blown back up to the original size are considerably more expensive, though usually not needed in as large numbers as the simple readers. Specialized cameras for recording and producing microforms are expensive enough to warrant considering centralized cooperative services or the use of commercial services, while simple duplicating equipment may be within the price range of an individual school or college.

3. Recordkeeping

Reports on the use of microforms for keeping student and other school records emphasize the compactness, efficiency, ease of retrieval and updating, and file security, and the advent of computer output microfilm (COM) in records administration was hailed as a "highly compatible marriage of the data-storing advantages of microfilm and the data-manipulating capabilities of the computer" (Renner 1978 p. 310). Specific cases described include the production of some 250,000 transcripts each year using five microfiche reader printers at the University of Minnesota, Minneapolis, St. Paul (Microfiche speeds... 1979); an increase in staff productivity and morale in proportion to the decrease in paperwork when Temple University made the transition from paper to microfilm (Microfilm/microfiche... 1978); the use of fiche jackets at Florida State Junior College, where film is added or removed for making corrections or updating, and color coding indicates the type of file (Cusack and Hart 1981); the reclamation

of 29,087 square feet of space and several hundred thousand dollars in filing equipment for the storage of records back to 1890 in the Dade County Schools, as well as faster access, faster service, and greater security (Dade County Schools 1981); and the capability of providing privacy and accessibility in an office with many part-time student workers, as well as file security when copies of records are needed by counselors and branch campuses at the College of the Redwoods (Systems in action 1982). At Southern Illinois University, microforms are used not only in the library, but in four vice-presidential areas, business offices, academic departments, and service areas to store records, solve problems, and communicate information (Lillard 1981).

4. Academic Libraries

A major effort to improve user acceptance of microforms has been mounted at Princeton University, where the collection comprises current materials including subscriptions to periodicals, college catalogs, telephone directories, Supreme Court records and briefs, and United States and foreign government documents, as well as materials available only in microform, for example, back issues of newspapers, dissertations, and out-of-print books and journals. Cataloging and storage problems are described by Raikes (1982), as well as facility changes, staff training, and efforts to improve reader attitudes toward the medium.

Many academic libraries are turning to COM to replace card catalogs which have become far too large and unwieldy with the information explosion, and to generate various union catalogs with other libraries to facilitate resource sharing through interlibrary loan. This format has another advantage: it is light and portable enough to enable the library to make the catalog accessible in several different locations (Folcarelli et al. 1982 p. 148).

A rich source of information for educators, the ERIC (Educational Resources Information Center) database makes available research reports and other educational resources on microfiche. The ERIC microfiche collection is currently available in more than 700 libraries and information centers throughout the world, and individual copies of these fiche are also available through the ERIC system [see *Educational Resources Information Center (ERIC)*].

5. Instructional Applications

Despite Burchinal's optimism in 1974, when a number of projects that had been funded in elementary and secondary schools were reporting effectiveness in the delivery of instruction and enthusiastic acceptance by both students and teachers (Burchinal 1974), the use of microforms in the instructional area has not expanded widely (Williams and Fothergill 1977, Lane 1978).

A description of the use of microfilm in the White Plains, New York, public schools in the early 1970s cites use in the high school as "in class" and independent study tools; having an active role in the media center; elementary school pupils reading children's books in microform editions; and teachers using the ERIC collection to update their methods, learn about new research, and complete graduate study requirements (Cohen 1973).

Williams and Fothergill (1977) provide examples of a variety of applications, ranging from the use of microfiche to make resource materials available for secondary and tertiary students and to provide materials for individually guided study, to the filming of archival materials for elementary and secondary school children to use in studying local family history, to distributing materials that would be prohibitively expensive in the regular format to part-time law students, to encouraging reading by teenagers through a cassette and microform introduction to fiction books and biographies in the school library.

In an overview of instructional uses of microforms in the United Kingdom, United States, and Australia, Lane (1978) briefly describes programs integrating microfiche into systems of computer-assisted instruction at the Orange Coast and Golden West Community Colleges in Southern California, and for training personnel at IBM (International Business Machines) in Poughkeepsie, New York, as well as an advanced interactive programmed learning system using microfiche that was designed and built in the Kodak Research Laboratories in Rochester, New York. She also notes that microfilm can be used to project a larger than normal image for children with visual problems and slow readers in the primary grades, that special programs have been generated to use microfilm with children suffering from dyslexia; and that microfilm readers have been adapted for use by quadraplegic students (pp. 73–74).

An unusual use of microfiche was the Fiche Flash, which was created and produced by the Educational Service Staff of the Minneapolis Star and the Minneapolis Tribune (Minnesota) when challenged to devise a way to help children make meaningful use of the hour they spend on the school bus. Primarily a pictorial selection of the daily news on microfiche for display in small hand-held viewers, the Fiche Flash included current news, historical events, brain games, and children's interpretations of the news. The fiche were produced each morning in time for the ride to school, and sent to the media center at the end of the ride for use by other children (Interchange 1980).

A study conducted by the United States Navy investigated the feasibility and cost effectiveness of replacing the traditional color sound/slide programs for individualized, self-paced instruction with color microfiche/audiocassette packages. Positive reactions were reported by 20 instructors and 20 trainees at the Basic Electricity and Electronics School in Orlando, Florida, who reviewed four sound/microfiche programs and compared this medium with their experience using sound/slide programs (Rizzo 1977).

An example of the integration of microforms with computer technology is provided by Pratt (1979), who describes a computer-assisted learning facility at Portsmouth Polytechnic in England, which incorporates a front-end processor controlling communication between the terminal user and the mainframe, and the accessing and displaying of invariant information held on microfiche at the appropriate terminal.

Another approach to such integration is the microterminal/microfiche system developed for the United States Air Force to provide access to the appropriate test materials on microfiche and record the student's answers in a computer-based instructional environment. An evaluation of the system indicated that students preferred the microterminal to other means of test administration, and that the use of microfiche for the presentation of test items did not affect the students' ability to perform (Kottenstette et al. 1980).

In summary, the enthusiastic acceptance of microforms as an instructional medium in the late 1960s and early 1970s has been overshadowed by the development of other technologies. However, the advantages of low cost and compactness have led to investigations of the integration of microforms with other technologies, and the substitution of microforms for printed materials in programmed instruction or for slides in slide/audiocassette learning packages. The flexibility of microforms as a projected medium has also led to investigations of their effectiveness with visually handicapped students and efforts to adapt their use for the physically handicapped.

Bibliography

Burchinal L G 1974 Uses of microfilm in educational institutions. *J. Micrographics* 7(3): 107–12

Cluff E D 1980 *Microforms*. Instructional Media Library, Educational Technology Publications, Englewood Cliffs, New Jersey

Cohen A J 1973 The use of microfilm in the White Plains, New York, public schools. *J. Micrographics* 7(1): 3–7

Connor A 1978 Building bridges for the visually handicapped through micrographics. *J. Micrographics* 11(6): 349–51

Connor A 1981 A comparison of traditional large type and microfiche as reading modes for low vision students. *J. Micrographics* 14(11): 32–8

Cusack J B, Hart J L 1981 Microfiche file system meets demands of a junior college. *Office: Magazine of Management, Equipment, Automation* 94(4): 141–42

Dade County Schools 1981 District reclaims filing cabinet space. *Am. Sch. Univ.* 54(1): 62–63

Folcarelli R J, Tannenbaum A C, Ferragamo R C 1982 *The Microform Connection: A Basic Guide for Libraries.* Bowker, New York

Glickman J 1978 The initial introduction of color microfiche as supplement to the Boston University School of Medicine curriculum. *J. Micrographics* 11(6): 370–72

Interchange. 1980 *Reading Teacher* 33(6): 712–15

Kottenstette J P, Steffen D A, Lamos J P 1980 *Microterminal/ Microfiche System for Computer-based Instruction: Hardware and Software Development*. University of Denver, Denver, Colorado ERIC Document No. ED 196 416

Lane N D 1978 Microforms: Tools for learning. *Australian Society of Educational Technology Yearbook, 1978*. University of Adelaide, Adelaide, South Australia ERIC Document No. ED 171 308

Lillard S 1981 Micrographics beyond the library. *J. Micrographics* 14(7): 23–25

Microfilm/microfiche in student records. 1978 *Coll. Univ.* 53: 656–57

Microfiche speeds transcript service. 1979 *Am. Sch. Univ.* 52: 54–55

Pratt S J 1979 A microfilm-based CAL facility. *Comput. Educ.* 3: 235–40

Raikes D A 1982 Microforms at Princeton. *Microform Rev.* 11: 93–105

Renner D L 1978 Some considerations for microfilm utilization of postsecondary educational records administration. *J. Micrographics* 11(5): 309–12

Rizzo W A 1977 *Demonstration and Evaluation of a Microfiche-based Audio/Visual System*. Naval Training Equipment Center, Training Analysis and Evaluation Group, Orlando, Florida ERIC Document No. ED 140 809

Systems in action. 1982 *Administrative Management* 33(4): 73–74

Williams B J S, Fothergill R 1977 *Microforms in Education*. Working Paper 13. Council for Educational Technology, London, pp. 31–44

Videodisc Technology

P. B. Schipma

Videodiscs are a storage medium developed as a consumer product but now showing considerable penetration into the information marketplace as an information storage and retrieval mechanism. The early 1980s proved to be a shakedown period for four competing technologies, of which one has emerged as a worldwide de facto standard, while another remains in the running in the Japanese marketplace. From 1985–87 there was a rapid increase in the same technology as applied to audio storage (compact discs), and another revolution is forthcoming in data storage and mixed media storage. Indeed, the technology of reflective laser optical discs is now, to a great extent, independent of the type of information recorded on the disc, so the term *videodisc* pertains more to historical derivation than to current applications. Further, since the information market is small in comparison to that of consumer entertainment, information products based on this technology are stepchildren of the mass entertainment market developments.

1. Videodisc Technology

The storage of video images on a rotating platter similar to a phonograph record is not a new idea, and attempts to produce such a device date from the 1920s. However, not until the mid-1970s were such techniques commercially viable. The major technological barrier was that of bandwidth, the amount of information to be presented in a given signal. Analog audio recordings must present information equivalent to the human hearing range (from about 50 hertz to 20,000 hertz) in real time, requiring a bandwidth up to 60 kilohertz. A video recording must contain much more information: each of the 375 raster scans that comprise a television picture requires a bandwidth of about 0.5 kilohertz, and the picture must be refreshed 30 times per second to be perceived as continuous. The total bandwidth required is approximately 5 megahertz, more than 80 times as large as that for audio information. It is important to note

that the waveform of an analog signal can be stored as numerical values if the sampling rate is high enough (just as one can draw a circle with a group of dots); such encoding is called *digital*, and its importance to this discussion will become clearer below. Many different techniques have been attempted for packing all this information on tracks analogous to those of a phonograph record: laser optical (reflective), laser optical (transmissive), capacitive (grooved), and capacitive (grooveless). While all of these systems have enough storage density to hold the large amount of information required for the production of video images, the mechanisms vary in the extent to which they can be adapted for use in information storage and retrieval systems.

1.1 Laser Optical (Reflective)

This technology was developed by Phillips (Netherlands) and is marketed under the trade name Laserdisc. Several companies, such as MCA and IBM, have been members of marketing consortia for these products. Currently, the major partners are Phillips, DuPont, and Sony. 3M is a major producer of material for manufacturing discs, and the disc players are manufactured by several additional companies. Each of 54,000 concentric tracks on a 300mm (12in.) diameter disc contains 1/30 second of analog video material, or one television frame, so one side of a disc, played at 1,800 rpm, holds a half-hour of continuous signal (there are also extended-play discs that pack more tracks per frame and rotate at varying speed depending on how close to the center of the disc the reading is taking place). The signal is encoded in pits that are about a micron in length. The pits are in a layer of metal that has a thickness of one-fourth the wavelength of the laser light used to read the disc. This metallic layer is coated on a stiff metal substrate and the whole is overlaid with a clear plastic. When the laser beam encounters a pit, the signal is cancelled out by destructive interference; in the absence of a pit it is reflected and can be detected by a photo-diode.

Servomechanisms are used to keep the laser beam properly positioned. By using pits of varying length, a frequency modulated (FM), or analog, signal can be generated; the mere presence or absence of pits can be used to encode binary (0 or 1) information, which is a digital signal.

The equipment necessary to coat a very thin layer of metal on the substrate and to position precisely millions of pits thereon, is very expensive and requires clean room conditions (a speck of dust, or a human hair, is large compared to the size of the pits). However, once the master has been made (the pits are generated by ablating the metal layer with a high-powered laser), copies can be stamped out in much the same fashion that phonograph records are made. Thus, though the mastering is expensive, replicates are very inexpensive (total cost is about one-fourth that of videotape for equivalent amounts of program material). It is this low-cost replication that has made reflective laser optical discs a de facto standard.

1.2 Laser Optical (Transmissive)

Also using a laser beam to read the disc, the transmissive method developed by Thomson-CSF (France) reads through the disc. The spots that modulate the laser beam in this case need only be opaque to the laser light rather than requiring a specific depth so as to cause destructive interference. A singular advantage of the transmissive optical disc is the potential for embedding multiple signal layers on a single thick disc. By focusing on one plane within such a disc, only that layer would be read, so it would be possible to make a single disc containing two, four, or even eight layers, permitting playing times of up to four hours. However, the precision required to implement this technology proved to be very costly, the expected market did not develop, there was intense competition from laser reflective technology, and Thomson-CSF has abandoned further development. A similar technology is in limited use in the United States, marketed by McDonnell-Douglas for industrial videodisc use.

1.3 Capacitive (Grooved)

The grooved capacitive or CED disc, developed by RCA, is the videodisc technology most similar to that of a phonograph record. A stylus, tracking in a groove, provides a modulated signal as it encounters deformations of the bottom of the groove. Mechanical styli do not have adequate response time for sensing the high density of shape changes (in effect, bumps) needed for a video signal, so a capacitive stylus is used. This disc can be thought of as one plate of a capacitor, with the stylus being the other. One plate moves up and down (the height of the groove surface with its deformations) and the other remains constant (the stylus). This induces a continuously modulated capacitive value which can be sensed by a piezoelectric crystal and used to generate a signal.

The CED disc was the most aggressively marketed of the technologies to the consumer market. RCA invested large amounts of money in building and selling players, and in manufacturing discs. However, consumer acceptance was low and, after several years of severe losses, RCA abandoned the product line.

1.4 Capacitive (Grooveless)

The VHD (video high density) system of Japan Video Corporation (JVC) was the fourth technology variation. Also based on capacitive technology, this system provides stylus tracking via a tracking signal encoded within the disc and read by a servomechanism rather than by use of grooves. While this requires more sophistication in both the disc and the player, it permits random access to any track. In both capacitive systems, more than one television frame is stored on each track.

The VHD system has made a modest penetration into the consumer marketplace in Japan. However, JVC, despite repeated announcements of intent to market in the United States and Europe, has not done so, and VHD remains a uniquely Japanese product.

2. Expansion of Laser Reflective Technology Applications

The shakedown of technologies occasioned by consumer acceptance has made laser reflective technology the clear-cut winner in the international arena. Though the installed base is small in relation to that of video cassette recorders (VCRs), for example, it is large enough to support player and disc manufacturing facilities. More importantly, companies with investments in the technology began to look for other applications of the basic laser reflective methodology. One of these was the digital audio disc (DAD) or compact disc (CD). Compact discs are smaller than videodiscs (120mm or 4¾in. in diameter), but use the same basic recording and reading methodology. Moreover, consumers were already used to buying stored audio information in prerecorded form. While CDs compete against an established technology, that of phonograph records, videodiscs had to compete against an emerging technology, VCRs. These had a significant additional feature, their local recording capability, and won the match hands down. Before CDs were announced as consumer products, the principal companies, Sony and Phillips, having learned from the plethora of competing technologies in the videodisc arena, jointly promulgated a worldwide standard format. The results have been phenomenal. Compact discs are the fastest growing consumer product ever known.

Though CDs use laser reflective technology, with pits cut by a laser on a master which is then pressed for replication, the signal itself is generated in a digital fashion rather than by frequency modulation. Pits denote the presence (1) or absence (0) of information and represent sampling of the original analog signal at a very high time rate. Sophisticated electronics (in effect, a computer) are required in the player to regenerate the signal from the sampling and, since every bit must be detected, sophisticated error detection and correction algorithms are required as well. However, electronics technology has proceeded at an extremely rapid pace, and all the code necessary to perform these functions is now easily stored on an inexpensive chip. Information is stored redundantly to provide data for error correction (it is said that a 0.22 caliber bullet can be fired through a CD with no loss of signal capacity), but even so, 75 minutes of audio information can be stored on one CD.

The phenomenal success of CD has spawned two additional applications, CD-ROM (compact disc/read only memory) and CD-I (compact disc/interactive). CD-ROM uses the same technology to store data for use by a computer, and one disc holds 550 million characters of information (compared to the 360 thousand characters stored on a typical computer floppy magnetic disk). Because the market penetration of CDs has been so high, the cost of players has dropped precipitously (to less than $100 in 1988), and only a few chips have to be changed to have a player read a CD-ROM instead of a CD. It is therefore expected that CD-ROM will cause a revolution in computer storage of information.

CD-I was targeted as a consumer product to become available in 1989. CD-I discs store audio, computer data, graphics, still photographs, and motion video (i.e., videodisc-like information) all on the same medium. So videodiscs have come full circle. The successful transition from analog to digital signal encoding, coupled with application for an acceptable consumer product, has brought the technology to maturity. Rather than referring to videodiscs, this article shall henceforth refer to the basic technology of laser reflective optical discs, which have now reached a multitude of applications all deriving from the original videodisc application. Laser discs are currently produced in 300mm (12in.), 200mm (8in.) and 120mm (4¾in.) sizes, the latter typically being called a compact disc. If the information on the disc is frequency-modulated analog video information, the disc can be called a videodisc; if the information is digitally encoded, it can represent audio, character, graphic, or video information. In all cases, laser recording and reading are present, and the discs are replicated through a mechanical pressing process. Local writing devices are also available, and many laboratories are working on erasable optical discs, but those technologies are beyond the scope of this article.

3. Optical Disc Attributes for Information Storage and Retrieval Uses

The basic technology can be used to play television programs, movies, and similar continuous material. The signal from an optical disc is typically better than that obtained from 8mm or ½in. videotape recorder/players, but discs are playback only devices, requiring prerecording at the manufacturing facility. Though the materials cost is inherently lower than tape, the lack of recording

capability made VCRs the device of choice in the consumer market for video products. However, in the audio market, where people are used to buying prerecorded material, discs are far outstripping tape systems. Since information comes in a variety of forms, and since the single technology permits storage and retrieval of all of them, optical discs are rapidly becoming a major medium for information storage and retrieval. There are several attributes of optical discs that support this development.

3.1 Storage Density

An optical disc holds a tremendous amount of information in a small volume. The difference between discs and all other media becomes most pronounced for digital data. A 300mm videodisc holds 1 hour's worth of motion video, and a videotape cassette, which is not a great deal more voluminous, can hold 8 hours of video. But a 120mm disc can hold 550 million characters of data (and the 300mm disc, encoded the same way holds 2 billion characters), which is the equivalent of 1000 books. Even the state-of-the-art computer storage device, the magnetic disk, pales in comparison. A magnetic disk with 550 million characters of storage has 80 times the volume of a CD, costs 100 times as much and requires a player that costs 15 times as much.

3.2 Archival Quality

The information stored on an optical disc is encoded by physical alteration of the disc, not by magnetic or electronic alignments. Thus the information is stable for decades. The discs, protected by a layer of plastic, are extremely rugged. Most importantly, since reading is via a laser light system, there is no contact and no wear. Information can be played millions of times with no deterioration. Though optical discs have not been available long enough to measure lifespan, accelerated testing has indicated that usable lifetimes of 25 to 50 years are likely. The major physical degradation likely to be experienced (other than cutting or breaking through misuse) is separation of the protective coating from the information layer, caused by permeation of various chemicals through the plastic layer.

3.3 Repeatable Play or Freeze-frame

Because a disc is a rotating medium, it is possible to play the same track repeatedly merely by keeping the read head stationary. With videotape this is very difficult, since the tape has to be continuously moved forward and then back one frame, making maintenance of synchronization a problem. Since information storage and retrieval is frequently dependent upon the ability to repeatedly transfer the data from one track, this is an important feature of optical discs.

3.4 Random Access

Probably the single most important attribute for information storage and retrieval is that of random access. Unlike tape, which is a linear medium, discs do not require that you read through the first half of the material to get to the middle; you merely position the head over the middle track (or whichever one is desired). Because the storage density is so high, and the medium is read optically, such positioning does take some time; typically, the seek time to a specific track is of the order of $\frac{1}{4}$ to $\frac{1}{2}$ second—considerably longer than for magnetic disk. This has to be taken into account when designing information retrieval systems that rely upon optical media, but can be overcome.

4. Applications

Optical discs are now being used for all aspects of information storage and retrieval. At the simplest end is linear material, either audio or visual (music and movies) in which the disc is merely played from beginning to end. Most players have the capacity to select randomly from various segments of the disc; for example, the typical CD player permits the choice of any of up to 20 musical "cuts" on a disc, in any order. In the video arena, considerable use has been made of this selection capability in the design of training and educational discs. By controlling the player with a microcomputer, extremely complex and variable training sequences can be generated from the material on a single disc.

It is also possible to consider each of the video images stored on an optical disc to be a separate entity rather than as one frame of a motion picture. Thus, large pictorial collections can be stored on disc, and an individual picture can be retrieved (via random access) and viewed for an indefinite period of time (via freeze-frame). There are many commercial applications of this use, such as art collections, photographs of homes for real estate sales, and so forth. In each of these applications, the limitation of utility lies in the resolving power of television, which is fairly low. An A4 page of typewritten text, for example, is barely legible when displayed on a television screen. However, page dissection with sophisticated computer algorithms can be used to overcome this problem, as can high definition television monitors.

The major applications of information storage and retrieval relate not to audio or video, but to computer-readable text (although image information such as drawings and medical images do constitute an information resource worthy of treatment). Most information retrieval is conducted by computers reading large databases of character information. With the advent of digital storage on optical discs, this most important problem also entered the realm of application on discs. Since storage density is so high, and since the widespread use of consumer products has reduced the price of the technology, huge information collections are now being stored on optical discs for use by anyone who has a personal computer. Doctors can have the most recent literature at their fingertips, lawyers can study the most recent decisions of interest to them, financiers can have years worth of stock market quotations immediately available, and so forth. The person who could earlier afford only a book can now afford a library, thanks to optical disc technology. An information revolution is under way, spurred by this phenomenal technology.

Bibliography

Bowers R A (ed.) 1986 *Optical/Electronic Publishing Directory 1986*. Learned Information, Medford, New Jersey

Broadbent K D 1976 Review of the MCA disco-vision system. *Inf. Disp.* 12(2): 12–19

Broussaud G 1978 The videodisc: General considerations and a look at some areas of application. *Rev. Tech. Thomson-CSF* 10(2): 655–80

Gunther G 1978 The optical videodisc. *Bull. Am. Soc. Inf. Sci.* 5(2): 39–40

Hendley T 1985 *Videodiscs, Compact Discs and Digital Optical Disks*. National Centre for Information Media and Technology (Cimtech), Hatfield

Lambert S, Ropiequet S (eds.) 1986 *CD ROM: The New Papyrus*. Microsoft Press, Hagerstown, Maryland

Marsh F E 1981 *Videodisc Technology*. Department of Energy, Oak Ridge, Tennessee

Mathieu M 1977 A random access system adapted for the optical videodisc: Its impact on information retrieval. *Soc. Motion Picture TV Eng. J.* 86: 80–84

Roth J P (ed.) 1986 *Essential Guide to CD/ROM*. Meckler, New York

Schipma P B 1981 Videodisc for storage of text. *Videodisc/Teletext* 1(3): 168–72

Schwerin J B 1986 *Compact Disc Read Only Memory Standards: The Book*. Learned Information, Oxford

Interactive Video

P. Copeland

Interactive video can be defined as the presentation of video and audio information according to the response input made by the viewer. The presentation of images and sound is via a television monitor, which is usually part of a self-contained user-station with microcomputer, video source, and input device. The source of video can be one of several devices such as videodisc, videotape or compact disc. The response input can be achieved using one, or a combination of several devices, such as numeric keyboard, alphanumeric keyboard, touch-screen, light pen, mouse, trackerball and/or voice recognition systems.

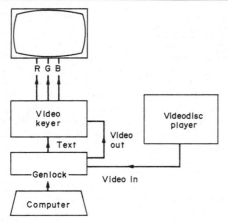

Figure 1
An interactive videodisc system

1. Technology

The concept of interactive video, from a technical perspective, became established in the late 1970s (Bennion and Schneider 1975, Copeland 1983, Hallgren 1980). The availability of the personal computer facilitated experiments in controlling videotape and videodisc players. In the case of tape, various interface units became available to enable industrial VHS and U-Matic format tape players to be controlled via the output ports of microcomputers. The accuracy of video-segment retrieval varied according to the level of sophistication of the control techniques employed. Simple systems proved unreliable over continued use, due to the inaccuracies introduced by stretch and mechanical handling. More sophisticated systems avoided these problems by recording an absolute address on the tape for each second or part of a second. Such techniques provided reliability, accuracy, and relatively fast retrieval of video-taped sequences. However, the added sophistication tended to increase the cost.

Interactive videotape is now popular for small-scale implementation of interactive video where production of programmes takes place in-house and/or the number of user-stations is small.

In contrast, interactive videodisc has become popular for the large-scale implementation of interactive video and for situations where the cost of its unique attributes can be justified. Its applications encompass training, education, information delivery at museums and exhibitions, and special applications such as surrogate travel.

Three formats of videodisc currently exist:

(a) the VHD system introduced by JVC of Japan, based on a capacitance technique;

(b) the Laserfilm system introduced by McDonald Douglas in the United States, using a disc of photographic film; and

(c) the LaserVision system introduced by Philips in the late 1970s, using optical laser technology.

The LaserVision system is to date the most popular choice of system for interactive videodisc applications. Unlike videotape systems, LaserVision videodisc players have electronic addressing and retrieval capability built in. Control of the videodisc via a microcomputer is thus easily achieved, usually via the RS232 communications port. Such control enables full exploitation of the unique characteristics of videodisc via the software programme running on the microcomputer. A typical system configuration is shown in Fig. 1.

The microcomputer communicates with the videodisc player to achieve the retrieval of video segments, search and still-frame functions, switching on and off of the two audio channels, and various features such as fast/slow reverse play. The communication is usually two way to allow the videodisc player to send status information back to the computer.

The remaining signal paths allow either the output from the computer, or the output of the videodisc player, or both to be displayed. This last requirement is the most difficult to achieve technically since it requires the timing signals of both video sources to be synchronized to within a close tolerance. This requirement is facilitated by the genlock unit which receives an incoming signal and synchronizes its associated display system with the external source. The images of the two systems can then be mixed or "keyed" to achieve a videodisc picture overlaid with computer text or diagrams.

The LaserVision videodisc player utilizes 12 in. diameter optically read videodiscs, but alternative formats to the 12 in. diameter disc have been developed using the smaller 5 in. diameter compact disc. Originally used for CD audio, this format has now been adopted for CD-ROM (compact disc read only memory) CD-I (compact disc interactive) and CD-V (compact disc video).

The CD-ROM and CD-I systems offer similar characteristics to the larger format optical disc, but either the quality of video, or the amount of movement seen in the display, will be considerably reduced in the short term due to the high digital-to-analogue transfer rate required to present moving pictures. Various techniques are being investigated to overcome this limitation, but their commercial implementation is not considered imminent.

2. Interactive Video Production

The stages in the development of interactive video have been identified by Griffiths (1985) and are shown in Table 1.

Analysis of case studies by Bayard-White (1985) shows that up to 25 percent of project costs can be attributed to the stages of preproduction. The complexity of interaction and level of content detail involved, is directly related to this cost.

Table 1
Stages in the design and development of an interactive video programme

Analysis	— determination of the objectives of the programme enabling their ordering and the allocation of a priority rating. The content is identified and delimited.
Design	— production of a content map, interactive and production scripts, and flowcharts for logic checking.
Production	— shooting and editing of the video elements, generation and integration of graphics, and computer screens.
Interaction	— generating the control program and branching structures; debugging and testing.
Field trials	— trial of the production with a representative sample of the intended audience (in the case of videodisc—preferably using a check disc).
Evaluation	— analysis of the results of the trial, possibly using automatically compiled data.
Revision	— incorporation of the conclusions of the evaluation.
Validation	— establishing the level of success the programme achieves with a large sample of users.

The editing of interactive videodisc production is often referred to as premastering, and this phase of development is particularly demanding both technically and in terms of production complexity. Videodisc master tapes have to adhere to a mastering specification laid down by the disc replication agencies. Particularly significant is the need to ensure that motion sequences which are likely to be used on still-frame, carry identical picture information for each of the two fields that constitute a TV picture frame. For this reason, material not produced originally on film is often electronically processed using field correlation or field doubling techniques.

Once a videodisc has been produced, its presentation is programmed using either a conventional computer language such as BASIC, C, or PASCAL, or a special interactive video, or Computer-based Training (CBT) authoring language. The benefit of using a computer language is the flexibility it offers in terms of user and videodisc control. The benefit of using a special authoring language is the speed at which material can be authored by personnel unfamiliar with computer programming languages. A rather different approach is provided by "hypermedia", a generic term for a new brand of systems which can combine text, graphics, and video information into a single database with access software to allow cross-references to be made. The approach is pedagogically different, not tutoring the learners but providing them with an extensively annotated, cross-referenced and illustrated electronic encyclopedia.

3. Selective Applications

The applications of interactive video have been most evident in the area of training. Organizations with a large geographically distributed workforce needing information and skills to be up-dated on a regular basis, were the first to apply the technology. In the United Kingdom, Lloyds Bank installed 1,500 interactive video stations in 1985–86 and used programmes to teach skills ranging from cashiering to services information. IBM installed 1,500 touch-screen stations in their dealerships across Europe to provide dealer training coupled with customer support information. In the mid-1980s other networks were installed in the United Kingdom in the banking, manufacturing, retailing, and telecommunications industries.

A similar pattern of implementation exists in the United States, but here the military is potentially the largest single user of interactive video having ordered approximately 50,000 stations over a three-year, staged-delivery period for project Electronic Information Delivery System (EIDS).

The United States has demonstrated some unique medical and specialized applications of interactive video. Most notable of these was the use of interactive video to help teach the skills of cardiopulmonary resuscitation (Hon 1982). In this application, the student practised resuscitation techniques using a manikin which was equipped with special sensors. The student was guided via the television presenter to lift the neck to the appropriate position, and administer mouth to mouth resuscitation and heart massage. Inappropriate or incorrect actions were signalled to the microcomputer via the sensors and the videodisc responded with appropriate advice.

Another application by the same developer, used interactive video to teach welding. In this, a light pen held against the television screen, becomes the welding rod and responds with remarkable similarity to the real device. The user is thus able to "create" a weld on-screen and observe this happening in real time.

One of the early special demonstrator projects of interactive video was the Movie Map project developed at the Massachusetts Institute of Technology (Lippman 1980). In this project the streets and buildings of Aspen, Colorado were filmed. Using two videodisc players, the user was subsequently able to "move" through the town, stopping and turning by using a joystick or touch-screen monitor.

To date one of the most ambitious interactive video projects has been the BBCs Domesday project (Gove 1988). Conceived to mark the 900th anniversary of the Domesday Book, the project involved the development of a special LaserVision player and the gathering of data by children in over 50 percent of United Kingdom schools. Two videodiscs hold data and pictures relating to life in the United Kingdom in 1986. The computer programme and databases are stored as LV-ROM (LaserVision read only memory) and down-loaded from the videodiscs on start-up. The user is then able to "move" across the United Kingdom using a trackerball, and "zoom" through maps of decreasing scale to locate a given region. Pictures and information relating to that region can be selected and statistical options, such as graphs and charts, can be presented. Primarily an educational application of interactive video, the Domesday product has also been marketed to companies and organizations who can utilize the demographic information it contains.

The first educational videodisc specifically published for use in United Kingdom schools was *The Interactive Science Laboratory*. This disc contains experiments on distillation, chromatography, electrolysis, and AC circuits and provides users with the opportunity to "experiment" with expensive or dangerous apparatus. Using the keyboard, touch-screen, or mouse, the user manipulates equipment into place, selects values and parameters, and is given the feel of conducting the experiment and experiencing the results.

A further series of eight interactive videodiscs, specifically produced for schools, form the IVIS project (Plummer 1986). This project has been sponsored by the UK Department of Trade and Industry and administered by the National Interactive Video Centre, London. Topics covered by the discs include teacher training, French studies, geography, design processes, environmental science, mathematics, and social behaviour.

4. Research

Little formal educational research has been conducted on interactive video to date. However, two independent studies of the effects of increasing interactivity (Schaffer and Hannafin 1986, and Copeland 1987) both reported increases in learning gain. Both studies also reported that the fully interactive version of the programmes took longer to complete than the less interactive and non-interactive versions.

The format of the interaction for both experiments took the form of video segments with embedded questions which provided feedback for correct and incorrect answers and branching to alternative video segments. Both studies suggest that considerable opportunity exists for investigating the effects of varying the nature and type of interaction facilitated by interactive video. Laurillard (1987) examined the feasibility of using existing video cassette material for interactive video and found students enthusiastic, but reticent in using the

control facilities provided. The study by Copeland (1987) included an analysis of the way programmes were viewed including the extent to which students made use of the interactive features available. He concluded that the extent to which users have the skills needed to use interactive video programmes may influence their potential effectiveness. This may explain the fact that many early interactive video programmes are simple to use, relatively didactic in structure, and assume no previous experience of interactive video. As the experience of the user-base increases, it is likely that more sophisticated interactive techniques will be used.

Less formal studies in interactive video have centred on its use in certain contexts. Hills (1986) examines the issue and potential of interactive video for educational applications. Bayard-White (1985) presents a number of case-studies which illustrate the potential and problems of introducing interactive video for training. Doughty and Lent (1984) examine the criteria relating to the cost-justification for interactive video. The implementation of the IVIS project mentioned earlier promises more detailed evaluation of interactive video in education and a full report of the project will be available from the NIVC in due course.

Research into interactive video potentially shares the problems of noncomparability and multivariable complexity that have existed for some years within the general field of media research. Hannafin and Garhart (1985) identify some of the research criteria that apply, and Copeland (1987) attempts a rationale for monitoring achievement, attitudes towards, and usage factors associated with, interactive video programmes.

Bibliography

Bayard-White C 1985 *Interactive Video Case and Studies Directory*. National Interactive Video Centre, London

Bennion J L, Schneider E W 1975 Interactive Videodisc Systems for Education. *Journal of SMPTE* 84(12): 949–53

Copeland P 1983 An interactive video system for education and training. *Br. J. Educ. Technol.* 14(1): 59–65

Copeland P 1987 Interactive video: Rationale, use, and evaluation. Ph.D. thesis, University of Sussex

Doughty P L, Lent R M 1984 Case studies of the cost justification of interactive video applications in key industries. In: *Interactive Video in Education, Proc. Sixth Ann. Conf. of the Society for Applied Learning Technology* (SALT), pp. 43–53

Gove P S 1988 BBC advanced interactive video and the Domesday discs. In: Mathias H, Rushby N, Budgett R (eds.) 1988 *Aspects of Educational Technology, 21: Designing New Systems and Technologies for Learning*. Kogan Page, London

Griffiths M G 1985 Interactive video at work. *Program. Learn. Educ. Technol.* 23(3): 212–18

Hall W 1988 The use of Interactive Video in undergraduate teaching. In: Mathias H, Rushby N, Budgett R (eds.) 1988 *Aspects of Educational Technology, 21: Designing New Systems and Technologies for Learning*. Kogan Page, London

Hallgren R C 1980 Interactive control of a videocassette recorder with a personal computer. *Byte* 5(7): 116–134

Hannafin M J, Garhart C 1985 *Research Methods for the Study of Interactive Video*, Conference Paper for the Association for the Development of Computer-Based Instructional Systems, Philadelphia, Pennsylvania

Hills L 1986 *Interactive Video in Education.* Scottish Council for Educational Technology, Glasgow

Hon D 1982 Interactive training in cardiopulmonary resuscitation. *Byte* 7(6): 108–38

Laurillard D (ed.) 1987 *Interactive Media.* Ellis Horwood, Chichester

Lippman A 1980 Movie-maps: An application of the optical videodisc to computer graphics. *Computer Graphics* 14(3): 32–42

Miller, Rockley L 1987 GE/RCA puts full motion video on CD. *Videodisc Monitor.* 5(4): 1

Pals N, Verhagen P W 1988 DIDACDISC: Development and evaluation. In: Mathias H, Rushby N, Budgett R (eds.) 1988 *Aspects of Educational Technology,* 21: *Designing New Systems and Technologies for Learning.* Kogan Page, London

Plummer B 1986 *Interactive Video in Schools: The IVIS Project.* National Interactive Video Centre, London

Schaffer L C, Hannafin M J 1986 The effects of progressive interactivity on learning from interactive video. *Educ. Commun. Technol. J.* 34(2): 89–96

1986 *The Interactive Science Laboratory.* Futuremedia Ltd., Bognor Regis

CD-ROM, CD-I, CD-V, Technical Paper, October 1986, Philips, Eindhoven

Audio Production and Distribution

R. Snell

The technical base for sound production and distribution has now changed from the more cumbersome tape recorders and gramophones to easy-to-use cassettes. In the late 1980s it is beginning to change once more, this time to digitally recorded sound on compact discs. The pace of change will be determined by technical progress and by the market in consumer electronics. However, the gap between professional equipment and home equipment has already narrowed sufficiently for professional quality to be a realistic standard in education. This article briefly describes these technical changes, then moves on to review equipment and techniques for production (recording and processing audiomessages) and distribution (replication, playback, and broadcasting).

1. The Technical Base

1.1 The Influence of Consumer Electronics

The audio equipment used in education has been increasingly influenced by developments in consumer electronics. Whereas the gap in technical quality between "home video" and broadcast television is still very wide, modern sound equipment designed for home use often meets the standards of broadcasters, and is indeed used by them.

While sometimes less rugged than broadcast or educational/industrial hardware, consumer audiovisual equipment is as reliable, when used within its limits. Competition results in an enormous range of facilities and the large production runs in countries chosen for low overheads ensure the lowest possible costs. For example, the educational user considering the purchase of a heavy-duty mono-tape player with built-in amplifier and speaker will find a glossy stereo system with the same total power, two speakers, AM/FM radio, and twin cassette decks costing about the same. The former will be tough, easy to service and should remain in the catalogues for several years; the latter will be better for music playback, will have extra features which may be

useful, and will be available for 6 or 12 months before the model is changed.

1.2 The Compact Cassette

The recorder has always been a key component in audio production and distribution, and the compact cassette invented by Dutch Philips for office dictation recording has now advanced to the point where it equals the performance of the open-reel studio tape recorders of the 1970s. Indeed, portable cassette recorders are now used by news broadcasters. By combining the use of proprietary noise-reduction systems (such as Dolby B or C) with metal-particle tapes used in the latest consumer cassette recorders, the most demanding music can be stored with scarcely any loss. Since quality per se no longer limits the use of cassettes, ruggedness and editing facilities are more important factors in selecting equipment for instructional use.

1.3 Digital Recording

Computing technology or digital electronics is used in modern systems which will challenge the position of the Philips cassette. One example is the compact disc which stores up to 75 minutes of stereo sound to a standard well beyond that of the best broadcasts. The 12 cm plastic disc is a cut-down version of the laser-scanned optical videodisc pioneered by Philips in the early 1970s. Optical scanning gives zero degradation in use, infinite life, in theory, and the ability to access any part of the disc within 1–2 seconds. With the potential for accurate indexing included in the digital data format, the system is ideal for music and sound-effects libraries. Developed and established for recorded music, the compact disc has more recently been adopted for other kinds of digital data-storage.

The main limitation for education is the cost and complexity of recording onto the disc. When simple means of recording onto laser discs are perfected, their use in foreign language teaching and other areas needing quick access should follow.

The other more recent digital recording system to note is R-DAT, or rotary head digital audio tape. This uses the mechanical principles of home-video cassettes, but scaled down to a cassette which is much smaller than the Philips system. Again designed for home recording, the quality is sufficient for broadcast mastering, and the early production models are already being used in this way.

2. Production

2.1 Capture: Microphones and Other Sources

Live recording of natural sounds, speech, and music are still the hardest to capture because the range of intensity, or "dynamic range" is very much greater than that of the available hardware. Figure 1 compares the $10^{12}:1$ range of the human ear with the microphone and the magnetic recorder. It is simpler to express this range in terms of powers of 10 with a constant of 2 to take account of the fact that pressure rather than intensity is measured. The dynamic range of the ear thus becomes 12 bels, or more conveniently, 120 decibels (dB), and that of a standard audiocassette recorder $100:1$ or 40 dB. The latter only became suitable for prerecorded music or live speech when improved tapes and proprietary noise-reduction systems increased this to 60–70 dB. The digital systems can accommodate an even wider dynamic range, as Fig. 1 shows, but this is not useful for speech recording because of the limitations of distribution and playback.

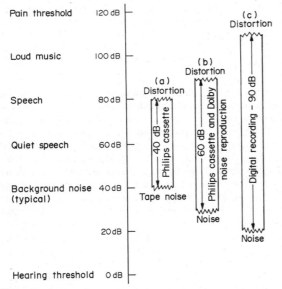

Figure 1
Comparison of recording systems with actual sound levels.
(a) Philips cassette, standard version; (b) New Philips cassette with noise reduction; and (c) Digital recording

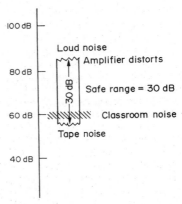

Figure 2
Limits of playback system in noisy room

Very cheap mass-produced "electret condenser" microphone modules are built into the simplest cassette recorders. Sold as small hand-held units they cost a few dollars and can give very accurate recordings. The dynamic range is adequate for speech recordings under controlled conditions. However, under interview conditions, where sound levels vary widely, a more costly microphone may be needed. The problems of background noise and echo can be solved by using miniature microphones clipped to the speaker's clothes, or more directional models aimed at the speaker. In both cases low-cost versions are satisfactory for speech.

2.2 Sound Control and Mixing

Given that sounds can be captured with the required frequency and dynamic range, it becomes necessary to combine (or mix) them and balance their different intensities, or levels. Also, the playback situation will usually impose severe constraints on dynamic range. Thus, tape recorders in language laboratories often require carefully controlled levels of sound because they lack noise-reduction circuits. Likewise, the sound level in a classroom is limited by the power of the playback system but still has to exceed the background noise (see Fig. 2). Even with the advantages of ideal acoustics and experienced speakers, broadcast and professional studios still need both compressors to reduce the overall dynamic range to match the worst-case listening conditions, and limiters to ensure that the distribution medium (the radio transmitter, the disc, or the tape recording) is not overloaded. The better quality portable cassette machines include such features, which are valuable for instructional recording, and good quality compressor/limiters made for the amateur and semiprofessional sound recording market can be bought for between $100 and $200. A wide range of such semiprofessional sound equipment is now available, much of which is suitable for educational sound production. For example, the "portastudio" or "mini-studio", which combines a four-to six-channel mixer with a good quality multitrack cassette recorder, is used in the music departments of many schools and is equally useful for speech.

Editing is now usually done by copying from cassette to cassette, but the best results still require an open-reel tape and a razor blade. Such equipment is now made for the semiprofessional market at modest prices.

Both solid-state and magnetic-disc digital storage for computing is ideal for sound editing and production. Hitherto, high cost has restricted its use to broadcast and professional work, however, the falling prices of digital electronics and the large market base for consumer and semiprofessional audio equipment should make the technology accessible to educational users by the early 1990s.

3. Distribution

3.1 Master Recordings

As a rule, master recordings should be at least a grade higher in quality than the copy. For example, a chrome or "high bias" cassette with Dolby noise reduction is a suitable master for a language laboratory or other player which uses normal tape without noise reduction. For music, an open-reel master or metal-particle cassette is worthwhile. Digital recording of masters is now the norm for the recorded music industry and it should come within the budget of all educational users in the longer term.

3.2 Replication

The compact cassette is replacing the black vinyl gramophone record as a source of music for economical domestic playback. High-speed, high-quality cassette duplication is well-established, but the hardware is expensive and tricky to maintain. When large "print" runs are needed, such existing facilities should be used wherever possible. Smaller and simpler cassette copy systems which can make between three and 10 copies per pass from a cassette master come within the budget range of the larger institution, but they do not equal the quality of the professional equipment and are not recommended for music. For more limited areas of use, the twin hi-fi cassette deck with its double-speed copy feature can be useful, and costs little more than the single deck. Portable radios with twin cassette decks can combine the copying function with good quality broadcast recording for small-scale operations.

3.3 Playback to Groups

A number of points need to be noted when playing back recordings to groups.

(a) If ambient noise levels are high, the equipment may not have the power to overcome this.

(b) If the reverberation or echo is excessive, speech will lack clarity and articulation regardless of the equipment and recording quality. Carpets, curtains, and other soft furnishings reduce echoes.

(c) Corner placement of the loudspeakers increases reverberation, so for clearest speech they must be placed away from corners and walls. For music, however, the corner placement of speakers may be better. A high position is best for both speech and music, to ensure that the speakers are in the direct line-of-hearing of all the listeners. Conversely, low-level positioning dissipates high frequencies and loses clarity.

(d) Clear middle frequency and treble from medium and small loudspeakers is most important for clarity of speech. Large loudspeakers with a good bass response for music are generally neither louder nor clearer in the registers that matter for speech. Separate bass and treble controls on the amplifier/player are useful as the bass can then be reduced to maintain clarity in nonideal rooms.

(e) For speech reproduction, dedicated educational products are still the most suitable, but for music, a portable stereo system with speakers that can be separated and placed at the right height is the best choice where budgets are limited.

3.4 Playback to Individuals

Here the range of cassette players, radios, and radio cassette players is wide and very good value. Rugged players with simple controls should be chosen for library and other public-access areas. For personal use, miniature battery-operated cassette players costing as little as $20 are adequate for speech, and their mechanisms can be as reliable as the more expensive models.

3.5 Broadcasting and Narrowcasting

The developments in regional sound broadcasting in some countries have brought new opportunities for the distribution of educational programmes, and even the most basic production and editing facilities discussed are suitable, given the right content and operational skills.

On a smaller scale, legislation allowing local transmitters to be set up for special events such as festivals has been enacted. This is in effect very local broadcasting. On the smallest scale, induction loop broadcasting allows AM radio transmitters to cover a defined area such as a university or hospital campus without a full public-transmitting licence. The signals can be picked up on a normal AM radio covering the 500 to 1,000 kilohertz medium waveband. Costs of the transmission equipment are in the region of hundreds rather than thousands of dollars.

4. Conclusions

The capability of professional programme production is no longer the privilege of the large institution. Developments in consumer hi-fi and semiprofessional recording have seen to this. Just as the results from the modern camera depend more on the skills of the photographer than on the equipment, so this new audio production hardware can give fully professional results in competent hands. Playback hardware has never been better,

and costs are also very low. In the near future video playback will be available in units of similar size but the costs will, of course, be greater.

Bibliography

Kirk D 1980 *Audio and Video Recording*. Focal Press, London
Watkinson J 1988 *The Art of Digital Audio*. Focal Press, London

Time-compressed and Time-extended Speech

E. Foulke

Time-compressed speech is recorded speech that is reproduced in less time than that required for its original production. If the time spent in reproducing recorded speech exceeds the time required for its original production, it is called time-expanded speech. When recorded speech is compressed or expanded in time, its word rate is changed. For example, if an oral reader requires 1 minute to read a paragraph containing 175 words, and if a tape on which the reader's speech has been recorded is reproduced in 4 minutes, the word rate of the reproduced speech will be 350 words per minute (wpm), and it will have been compressed in time to 50 percent of the original production time. Speech that is moderately compressed or expanded in time remains comprehensible, and listeners can perform some tasks more effectively or efficiently if they can change the word rate of recorded speech or the time in which it is reproduced.

1. Methods for the Compression and Expansion of Speech

1.1 Compression

There are several methods for compressing speech. The simplest is the speed-changing method. If a record or tape of speech is played at a faster speed than the speed at which it was recorded, the speech will be compressed in time and its word rate will be increased. However, when speech is compressed in this manner, voice pitch is raised, voice quality is distorted, and the listening experience afforded by such speech is not very satisfying, especially after prolonged listening.

Another method is now available for compressing recorded speech in time without distorting the pitch and quality of a speaker's voice. It is called the sampling method. When this method is used, not all of the original recording is reproduced. Instead, brief samples of the original recording are periodically discarded and the resulting gaps are closed. The missing samples are briefer than even the briefest sounds. Thus the ear cannot detect their absence, and no speech sound is ever entirely discarded.

As an illustration, imagine that a tape containing speech recorded at 15 inches per second (ips) has been cut into $\frac{1}{2}$-inch segments, and that these segments have been numbered consecutively. Now if all of the even-numbered segments are thrown away and the odd-numbered segments are joined, the resulting tape will be only half as long as the original tape, and if it is reproduced at the recording speed of 15 ips, only half as much time will be needed to play it. The pitch and quality of the speaker's voice will be preserved, but the rate at which words occur will be doubled. Each of the discarded segments of tape will contain 1/30 second (33 ms) of the original recording. When discarded samples are only 33 ms long, their absence will not be noticed by listeners. All that will be noticed is an increase in the speaker's word rate. The feasibility of compression by sampling was first demonstrated in just this way by Garvey (1953). But the required tape splicing is so tedious and time consuming that, if no other way could be found to sample recorded tapes, the sampling method would have no practical value.

However, in 1954, Fairbanks and his colleagues at the University of Illinois demonstrated a successful electromechanical speech compressor (see Fig. 1). A compressor of the Fairbanks' type operates as follows: the tape loop (1) traveling in the direction shown by arrow (7) passes over erase head (8) and recording head (9). The tape loop (1) then goes over idler (2), down around the rotating head assembly (10), between the tape drive capstan (5) and pressure roller (6), around tension adjusting wheel (3) and back to erase head (8) where it started. When the compressor is in operation, material on the tape is erased at erase head (8) in order to record cleanly at the record head (9). The recorded tape passes the rotating head assembly (1) in the direction shown by arrow (7). The tape moves faster than the rotating head assembly, so that speech recorded on the tape is picked up by any one of the four heads (A, B, C, D) in the assembly over which it is passing. At the instant when A leaves contact with the tape, head B contacts the tape. Everything recorded on the tape wrapped around the rotating head assembly between heads A and B will not

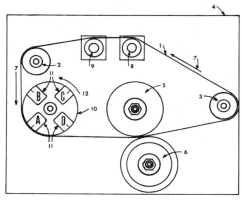

1. Tape loop
2. Idler wheel
3. Tension adjusting wheel
4. Mountin plate
5. Capstan
6. Pressure roller
7. Direction of tape loop travel
8. Erase head
9. Record head
10. Rotation head assembly
11. Playback heads
12. Direction of rotating head assembly when compressing

Figure 1
Detail drawing of Fairbanks' compressor (from Fairbanks et al. 1959)

be scanned or played back by either A or B and therefore will be discarded.

A computer may be used to compress speech by the sampling method (Duker 1974 Chap. 4). However, although there has been a dramatic reduction in the cost of computers, this is still a rather expensive method, which is only be employed to produce specimens of compressed or expanded speech for use in research.

The processes carried out by the computer can also be carried out by solid-state, electronic circuits designed specifically for that purpose. With the introduction of transistors, and more recently, of integrated circuit chips, it has become feasible to make electronic speech compressors that are relatively inexpensive and small enough to be incorporated in conventional cassette recorders or record players. Several satisfactory speech compressors are now commercially available.

1.2 Expansion

Recorded speech may also be extended in time with a resulting reduction in word rate. In the case of the speed-changing method, this is accomplished by playing a tape or record at a slower speed than the speed at which it was recorded. In the case of the sampling method, it is accomplished by repeating speech samples periodically instead of discarding them periodically. Electromechanical speech compressors, computers,

and electronic speech compressors are all capable of expanding speech in time.

2. Comprehension of Time-compressed and Time-expanded Speech

The word rate of trained oral readers is, on the average, 175 wpm (Johnson et al. 1963). Those who first explored applications of speech compressed by the sampling method hoped that it would enable the equivalent of speed reading, and that with proper training people might be able to comprehend at a faster rate by listening to recorded speech with a word rate of 1,000 wpm or faster. The results of experiments concerning the relationship between *word rate and listening comprehension* soon made it clear that this hope would not be realized, and that only moderate compressions in time would be feasible. The relationship between word rate and listening comprehension is affected by factors such as the age, intelligence, and educational background of listeners, and their familiarity with the content of the speech listening (Foulke and Sticht 1969). However, this relationship is fairly well described by the results of an experiment by Foulke (1968). He found that as word rate is increased, listening comprehension does not decline much until a word rate in the neighborhood of 275 wpm is reached. Thereafter, comprehension declines rapidly. At a word rate of 350 wpm, performance on the multiple-choice test used to measure listening comprehension was no better than the performance that would be expected if answer choices were made randomly.

The results just presented were produced by experimental subjects who had not been trained by listening to time-compressed speech. It is conceivable that with appropriate training, listeners could acquire the ability to comprehend speech presented at a very fast word rate. However, although a few experimenters have been able to demonstrate statistically significant improvements in the comprehension of time-compressed speech with training (Orr and Friedman 1968), these improvements were not large enough to have any practical value.

Researchers have not paid much attention to time-expanded speech. However, the results of an experiment conducted by Woodcock and Clark (1968) suggest that speech which has been expanded in time by the sampling method is less comprehensible than unexpanded speech.

3. Conclusions

Time-compressed speech has not enabled the dramatic improvement in listening efficiency sought by early investigators. However, moderately compressed speech can bring about a useful improvement in listening efficiency if its applications are chosen with care. Few useful applications of time-compressed speech have been found, but it has not received much attention from researchers, and there are possibilities that await evaluation.

Bibliography

Duker S (ed.) 1974 *Time-compressed Speech: An Anthology and Bibliography in 3 Volumes.* Scarecrow, Metuchen, New Jersey

Fairbanks G, Everitt W L, Jaeger R P 1959 *Recording Device.* (Patent No. 2,886,650). United States Patent Office, Washington, DC

Foulke E 1968 Listening comprehension as a function of word rate. *J. Commun.* 18: 198–206

Foulke E, Sticht T G 1969 Review of research on the intelligibility and comprehension of accelerated speech. *Psychol. Bull.* 72: 50–62

Garvey W D 1953 The intelligibility of speeded speech. *J. Exp. Psychol.* 45: 102–08

Johnson W, Darley F L, Spriestersbach D C 1963 *Diagnostic Methods in Speech Pathology.* Harper and Row, New York

Orr D B, Friedman H L 1968 Effect of massed practice on the comprehension of time-compressed speech. *J. Educ. Psychol.* 59: 6–11

Woodcock R, Clark C R 1968 *Influence of Presentation Rate and Media on the Comprehension of Narrative Material by Adolescent Educable Mental Retardates.* IMRID *Reports and Papers* No. 5(7), pp. 1–27

Audiovisual Equipment

A. H. Crocker

The audiovisual equipment considered in this article is that used in education or training. However, since education has only a minority share of the market, most of this equipment has been primarily designed for use in the home or in professional entertainment. Two rare examples of the development of specialist educational equipment are covered. Then the performance needs for various applications in education are discussed, with special reference to the development of projector lighting systems in Europe and the United States. Some aspects of maintenance are explored, and a brief treatment of standardization issues concludes the article.

1. General

Most audiovisual equipment which is used in education was not designed for educational use, although some has been specially adapted from equipment primarily designed for other uses. By far the largest proportion was designed only for entertainment purposes, either for use in the home or for professional entertainment in theatres or cinemas.

Audio cassette recorders, analogue audiodisc record players, digital audiodisc record players, slide projectors, video cassette recorders, 8mm motion picture film projectors are all examples of audiovisual equipment which has been designed for private use in the home. The professional entertainment industry has been responsible for the development of 35mm and 16mm motion picture film projectors, although initially 16mm was aimed at the hobbyist with film stock exclusively of the safety film type. Today it is possible to find models of audio cassette recorders, analogue and digital audiodisc record players, and certain types of slide projector which the respective manufacturers will claim were designed for education. However, all of them make use of components and subassemblies which would not be available if the home-use models were not in commercial production. Also, the stock material—recording tape, film, and so on—that is used for education

programmes only exists because the large home-use market has enabled high volume production to bring down unit costs.

2. Market Shares and Costs

It is not difficult to see the reasons for the lack of special equipment for education use when a study is made of the relative sizes of the home-use and education markets. Taking audio cassette recorders as an example, out of the total volume of sales in Western Europe, only about $2\frac{1}{2}$ percent goes into institutional education. Comparable figures for some other categories of equipment are: slide projectors 8 percent, video cassette recorders 1.7 percent.

The costs of researching, designing, and developing audiovisual equipment are very high and high volumes of production with correspondingly high sales are necessary in order to recover those costs within a reasonable period. With the rapid advances that are being made in modern technology, development costs have to be recovered before they render a model outdated and therefore unattractive in the market place. The volumes of sales which are taken by education alone fall far short of that which is required to enable development costs to be recovered in what manufacturers generally consider to be a reasonable time.

3. Special Educational Products

Only one of the many pieces of audiovisual equipment in use in educational situations today was developed from a very early point as an educational device. This is the overhead projector. The first overhead projector was built by a British company and the concept was subsequently developed for economic production under a contract with the United States Navy. This was in the early 1940s, when the United States Navy had a large training programme to mount in as short a time as possible. It was considered that the overhead projector concept would be highly effective as a visual aid. Without this one large user having funded this development from which the modern overhead projectors have all evolved in one way or another, it is doubtful that education would be able to buy overhead projectors at anywhere near the prices found today: and they would probably not perform as well as they do.

One other type of educational audiovisual learning aid which was conceived as a solution to a genuine problem is the audio card, the first of which was manufactured by the Bell and Howell Company of the United States and called by them "Language Master". However, this device was only economically possible because of the previous development for other purposes of magnetic tape recording.

The Language Master had its origins in Chicago in the mid-1950s with a group of teachers, psychologists, and doctors who were trying to find ways to teach some handicapped children to speak. These children rejected normal human contact, but loved to play with mechanical toys. From this discovery, the idea of a talking picture card grew and a friend of one of the group, who was an engineer, agreed to make a prototype machine which would record and play back a strip of recording tape glued to a card. Trials of the machine, using cards prepared by the teachers, showed that a solution to their problems could well have been found. They then approached a local manufacturer, Bell and Howell Company, to develop the machine so that it could be manufactured as economically as possible and in a form that would be safe and effective to use. The company developed the card and the method of bonding the tape to it, as well as many course packs of card programmes. Many other course packs have since been developed and published in the United Kingdom.

The Language Master, and all its variants which subsequently were produced by other companies, became successful products in the education market. However, in comparison with audio cassette recorders they are expensive: this is due to low-volume production compared with the production of cassette recorders. So far as it is possible to compare these two types of equipment which employ an essentially similar technology, an audio cassette recorder is about half the price of a Language Master with a comparable performance level.

The standards body, International Electrotechnical Commission (IEC), has recognized the value of the audio card by publishing the International Standard IEC 574-14. This ensures compatibility of cards and recordings between card players and recorders from different manufacturers.

4. Performance

Audiovisual equipment is required at a range of levels of performance to suit different applications. A level of performance that suits one type of use may not suit another type of use, or, if it does, it may be unacceptably expensive for that other use. The size of group and conditions of use are especially important. Equipment in a classroom may be needed for presentation to a group of 40 students while a lecture theatre may contain an audience of several hundred. Alternatively, the equipment may be required for use by just a single student, or a small group of up to 10 students. All types of application call for good quality of performance, but different levels of sound output and of light output are needed in each case, for comfortable listening and to provide correct levels of picture brightness on suitably sized screens.

Gaining larger amounts of sound power output is not a significant problem because, if necessary, booster amplifiers and external loudspeakers may be used with small, low-power equipment. However, increases in light output from projectors are more problematic. Fortunately for the user in education, the home user and the professional entertainment user have also been demanding more and more light to get satisfactory pictures in critical conditions. Thus the development of projectors has followed two separate paths. For home use there is the need for small equipment that is readily portable and easy to store away. For professional use, small size is of less importance, but the performance requirements are more stringent. In home-use equipment, the efforts to produce more light were satisfied by the development of high current, compact filament lamps which operate at a low voltage. The professional equipment has developed from carbon-arc illumination involving large-size lamphouses to more compact enclosed discharge lamps.

5. Lamp Technology

The original quest for more light from portable home-use projectors was partly satisfied by the use of higher power lamps. For these filament lamps to operate efficiently in projection equipment, the area of the filament structure in the plane at right angles to the optical axis of the projector needs to be as small as possible. The problems of electricity arcing across parts of the filament and of the very high temperatures at which filaments operate both limit the bunching of the filament coils. In countries, such as those in Europe, where the mains supply is in the range 220–240 volts, the problems are greater than where a mains supply of 100–130 volts is used such as in North America and parts of Japan. For direct mains voltage operation, higher power lamps could originally only be used where the mains supply was in the lower range. During the 1940s, 1950s, and part of the 1960s, it was very common in Europe for projectors using high-power lamps, 750 to 1,200 watts, to be operated with separate step-down transformers because only 100–120 volt lamps were available. Eventually, lamp technology advanced to allow 220–240 volts 750 and 1,000 watt lamps to be acceptably reliable and models of projectors were introduced for direct mains operation in Europe and other higher mains supply areas. However, mains voltage high-power lamped projectors produced significantly less light output than the corresponding models using 100–120 volt lamps.

European lamp manufacturers therefore continued the quest for more light and greater reliability of lamps.

The successful development and marketing of the low-voltage halogen lamp was a milestone in the quest for light. Lamps of 12 and 24 volts with powers of 100, 150, and 250 watts have compact and robust filaments; the use of quartz or fused silica glass for the bulbs enabled the manufacture of smaller and robust bulbs; and the addition of a trace of a halogen gas, iodine or bromine for example, to the bulb filling at a high pressure retards degradation of the filament in use. Of course, a transformer needs to be built into the projector to supply the lamp and this increases projector weight, but this has generally been accepted as a beneficial trade-off, aided by the use of lightweight alloys and plastics in general projector construction.

The light from a projector lamp, due to the structure of its filament, is emitted predominantly in two directions, "backwards" and "forwards". The light emitted "backwards" is returned through the gaps in the filament, or past one side of the compact low-voltage filaments, by a reflector. However, the resulting beam emitted forwards by the lamp and reflector combination is divergent. This would result in an excessive loss in light because only a small part of the beam would pass through the film frame and into the projector's objective lens. So condenser lenses are placed in front of the lamp to make the beam convergent, bringing it to a focus in the objective lens. In still projectors, a heat filter glass also has to be placed between the lamp and the film gate to avoid burning the film. Each of these optical elements, condenser lenses and heat filter, absorb light, and further lines of development were followed to try to overcome these losses.

Larger, alternative-shaped reflectors and dichroic coatings marked the next milestone in lamp development. By suitable combined design of lamp and reflector, it is possible to obviate condenser lenses by producing a convergent beam from the lamp and reflector combination. To overcome the problems of excessive heat at the film gate, a special dichroic coating was used on the reflector. A dichroic coating is in some ways similar to "blooming" put on high-quality photographic lenses. By very carefully controlling the thickness of the coating, a surface can be applied to the glass which will reflect visible light, but not infrared light (heat). The heat passes through the dichroic reflector to be absorbed by the structure of the lamphouse in the projector. Dichroic reflector lamps of modern design emit very little light directly forward from the lamp itself, most of the forward travelling beam having been produced by reflection. Originally these lamps made with integral reflectors were called "cold light" lamps: not really a true description, but the light from them is certainly less hot than it would be if a conventional silvered or aluminized reflector were used.

Some projectors using halogen lamps and dichroic reflectors were made with the reflector as an integral part of the projector. However, it was found that the user had some difficulty in locating the lamp accurately in the reflector and that the dichroic coating was insufficiently durable for the reflector to outlast two or so lamps. Because of this, the general pattern has been for integral reflector lamps to be produced that are factory aligned with a new reflector fitted to each new lamp. This has led to high lamp replacement costs. More recently, dichroic coatings have been applied in ways that give better durability; and it is expected that a return may be made to having the reflector as an integral part of the projector if the problems of accurate fitting of replacement lamps can be overcome.

In many ways, there have been remarkably close parallels in the developments of lamp systems for professional entertainment equipment which is also used for educational purposes when permanently installed in the lecture theatre projection rooms of large educational institutions. The reduced emphasis on weight and size has permitted the use of high intensity, enclosed arc lamps which need a special control gear to supply starting and running electrical power feeds. This control gear can be of such weight and size as to render its application to portable equipment unattractive.

The light from an arc lamp has a different kind of spectral response compared with that of a filament lamp which varies in amplitude continuously over quite a wide spectrum and is strong in the infrared region; light from an arc lamp consists of a series of high-amplitude emissions which vary sharply over its spectral range. An arc lamp's output is quite high in the ultraviolet region, but low in the infrared, so heat problems are less troublesome.

Since professional entertainment projectors, including those used in education, are operated by technicians rather than teachers, the problems of accurate alignment of lamps with reflectors are easily overcome. Therefore, arc lamps usually do not need to be supplied with integral reflectors. However, some types, known as "Marc" lamps, are integral with reflectors because they are intended for portable equipment where higher light outputs are essential. However, the projectors are more expensive than other portable models and the lamps themselves, in relation to their operating lives, are much more expensive than filament lamps or the types of arc lamp used in professional projectors of the installed type.

6. Maintenance

To most educators, maintenance of audiovisual equipment is a major problem. The reasons for this are many, although perhaps only a few apply to each individual situation. Probably the greatest problem related to maintenance is the cost of repairing and servicing equipment. Often, budgets make no specific provision for preventive maintenance or repair. Either it is omitted completely, or it is combined with other "general" items of expenditure which are later given priority. Thus when a budget looks likely to overrun, it is often the maintenance and repair of audiovisual equipment that is cut back or even cut out completely.

The maintenance and repair of low-cost home-use type equipment presents its own peculiar problems. It is quite usual for the cost of the labour needed to isolate and rectify a faulty small component to approach or even exceed the purchase price of the equipment. The faulty component is likely to cost but a few pennies, but the designated repair procedures will mostly call for the total replacement of major subassemblies. The subassembly which has the fault can usually be identified rapidly and then changed in just a few minutes, so saving the costly time of a service technician. However, this relies on the technician or service facility having the necessary replacement subassembly immediately available. If the subassembly is not in stock, the technician will be tempted to spend more time in order to identify the faulty component itself, because there may be a suitable replacement ready to hand. The alternative is to order the subassembly and put the job aside perhaps for only a day or two or possibly for several weeks. All the time, the frustrated user will be getting less enamoured of audiovisual equipment.

The manufacturers of some home-use audiovisual equipment have gone to further extremes in their "repair" policies. If the equipment is still within its warranty period, a new replacement will be provided. After the warranty has expired, a new replacement will be offered at a discount off the list price. In the latter case, if the particular model is discontinued and all stocks are exhausted, but the faulty equipment is less than, say, five years old, the nearest equivalent in current production may be offered at a discount. After a period considered by the manufacturer to be a reasonable expected operating life, any faulty equipment will be rated as "beyond economical repair" and returned to the owner. Of course, this kind of repair policy will only be firmly adhered to by manufacturers and their own service facilities. However, commercial service agencies will need to follow the policy in many cases because subassemblies and special replacement parts will eventually cease to be available from the manufacturer.

Equipment that is fully repairable will often have a purchase price considerably greater than that of a "throw-away" model of comparable performance. Also, it will need preventive maintenance; oiling, cleaning, and adjusting, every 200 to 1,000 hours of operation. Higher performance, professional types of equipment will be designed as repairable and, if given good treatment and correct regular maintenance, should serve for many years. However, where high performance equipment is not really needed, the cheaper throw-away models can be more cost-effective than repairable versions of equipment with similar performance levels. Also, low-cost equipment which is replaced, say, every year or two, gives users the chance of taking advantage of advances in technology as they come to the market.

Whatever types of equipment are purchased, it is of the utmost importance that allowance is made in budgets for expenditure on equipment maintenance and repair, or replacement as appropriate.

7. Standardization

Standardization is a multilevel concern and needs to be approached sensibly and logically. The top level at which certain types of standardization should be applied should be as high as it is possible to make it. It should certainly encompass as much of education as possible, and should be worldwide wherever this can be achieved. The lowest level of standardization can be at the organizational or at the institutional level, according to how the equipment is issued, stored, maintained, and repaired.

Standardization at the top level should be concerned solely with the compatability of software. It is highly desirable that there should be the possibility of a full interchange of educational programmes of all types between departments within an institution; between institutions within an area or region, or subject area; between areas and regions; and between countries. It is of great importance that programmes made on tape, disc, film, or any medium should have the widest possible market not only to give the benefits of good programmes to as many students as possible wherever they may be, but also to spread the costs of production of the original programme over many copies in order to reduce unit costs and enable producers to recover their costs quickly. In this way, the producers of good and successful programmes will be able to apply their valuable skills to more productions for the overall benefit of education and those educated.

The lower levels of standardization should be concerned with the compatibility of interfaces between equipment. This is of tremendous importance when using individual items of equipment connected together in a system. A system in this sense can be as simple as connecting together two tape recorders in order to make a second copy of a recording. Simpler still, there is the purchase of a loudspeaker from one company to use with another manufacturer's amplifier or disc record player.

Standardization on actual models of equipment can bring considerable benefits at the levels at which maintenance and repair and the issuing of equipment are organized. Maintenance difficulties will be eased by the need to hold fewer special replacement parts and subassemblies in stock and by service technicians becoming more familiar with the equipment and being able to work with greater efficiency. Also, the users will become more familiar with the equipment if they do not have to bother themselves with an unnecessarily wide range of models. This should lead to more effective use and a smaller number of user-initiated faults and failures.

Standardization should be constantly under review by those who have the responsibility of decision making. Standard procedures, systems, and so on, should be followed sensibly and logically. Standardization should not be used as a means of keeping back advances in technology. Every so often, the considerable inconvenience of a change of standard, for example changing to another type of video cassette, can give longer term benefits. These benefits may include better performance, lower costs, easier use, a wider choice of available programmes, and greater versatility of application.

Bibliography

Educational Products Information Exchange (EPIE) *EPIE Products Reports*. EPIE Institute, PO Box 839, Water Mill, New York 11968, USA
Training & Educational Systems Testing (TEST) Bureau, Technical Reports on Audio Visual Equipment. TEST Bureau, Vauxhall School, Vauxhall Street, London SE11 5LG, England
Wyman R 1976 *Mediaware: Selection, Operation and Maintenance*. Brown, Dubuque, Iowa

Learning Environments

G. F. McVey

A learning environment consists of all those physical–sensory elements such as lighting, color, sound, space, furniture, and so on that characterize the place in which a student is expected to learn. This surround should be designed so that learning may proceed with minimum stress and maximum effectiveness. Thus it should promote sensory comfort and high auditory and visual acuity; and its dimensions and physical layout should accommodate scheduled activities, allow for people's sense of personal space, and promote desirable patterns of social interaction and communication.

In addition to supporting human functioning, the learning environment must accommodate the equipment, tools, and materials that are used in education and training. The introduction of these media, be it chalkboard, computer terminal, video, or film display, inevitably alters the nature of the environment. When media is prudently integrated into the learning environment, it may be effectively employed in ways that are coordinated with basic human sensory processes. However, when media technology adds glare, noise, or excessive heat to the learning situation, it vitiates the design of that environment and interferes with those same processes.

Consequently, guidelines are required that will enable the facility designer to create learning environments that recognize both how the human senses function and how instructional media operate. The educator also needs to be aware of ways of managing both the equipment and the physical surround to effectively promote his/her educational objectives. Thus, the facility designer, through prudent design, and the educator, through effective media utilization, create the learning environment.

To aid the educator and facility designer in these efforts, a number of handbooks emerged in the late 1960s that focused on the design of educational facilities in general (CEFP 1969) and educational facilities for specialized media use (Green 1966). Their recommendations were subsequently incorporated into architectural standards (DeChiara and Callender 1980) and influenced the construction of a large number of facilities.

While such standards have proven to be a useful starting point, it is generally agreed that they need to be supplemented by information contained in the more "people specific" human factors engineering handbooks and ergonomic texts, and by the personal experience of facility designers and consultants. As Hunt and Bernotat (1977) noted:

...the ergonomist is concerned both with improving the health and well-being of the individual human and with improving the efficiency of the system of which the individual is a part. The improvement of man–environment combinations involves altering the machine and the environment; this part of the ergonomist's work has been called "fitting the job to the man."

Designing the environment so that it complements the way people function is extremely important since unlike conventional architectural design where "form follows function" when it comes to human operations, "function follows form"—that is, the anatomical form and physical and mental capabilities of the human learner.

1. Seating and Desk Design

Proper seating and desk design are important factors in determining a student's relative comfort and effectiveness as a perceiver, recorder, and processor of information. Furthermore, there is evidence that improper seating may result in improper skeletal development in children between the ages of 11 and 16 (CCSE 1938). Since chairs need to accommodate the body dimensions of those who use them, most schools need a variety of chair sizes to serve their student population. In fixed work stations, such as audiovisual/television carrels, video display terminal stations, and operational control rooms, where a chair has to accommodate a varied user population, pneumatically adjustable chairs are recommended.

A chair's seat pan should be contoured so that an individual's weight is distributed primarily in the buttocks area. It should be slightly padded (about one inch) and covered with a porous textured fabric. The seat and frame parts which come in contact with its occupant should be made of wood or some other thermally non-conductive material. It should be equipped with a padded backrest that provides support in the lower back (lumbar) area. Chairs that swivel are recommended for large group lecture halls and conference rooms.

Research has shown that access and egress to seating areas in lecture halls is dramatically improved when seats are spaced a minimum of two feet apart, and four feet front to back (McVey 1979). This last dimension also allows for the provision of an 18 inch writing surface. A five-star pedestal and casters provide stability and ease of access and egress in carrels and conference settings. The design of the note-taking, reading, and working surface is also a contributory factor in an individual's operational comfort and effectiveness. Horizontal writing and reading surfaces force students to bend

forward excessively, setting up stresses in their skeletal and visual systems which can cause digestive, respiratory, visual, and postural problems (Harmon 1951). Proper reading and writing posture is promoted by tilting the whole surface 15 degrees from the horizontal for note-taking tasks, particularly when viewing informational presentations at the front of the room. Inclining the desk top 30 to 45 degrees places reading and viewing materials at a comfortable inclination. Horizontal work surfaces, of course, are best for three-dimensional manipulative tasks.

The coordination of seating, viewing, and work positions is important to those whose learning activities involve using computer terminals, microfiche readers, or video monitors in carrels. Recommendations based on recent research, especially those of Diffrient et al. (1974), are summarized in Fig. 1.

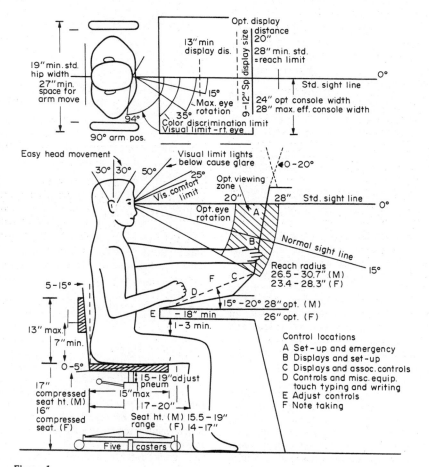

Figure 1
To show the coordination of seating, viewing, and work positions for learners (after Diffrient et al. 1974)

2. Room Characteristics

2.1 Room Size and Seating Configuration

The size of a teaching–learning space should be such that it accommodates the programmed number of occupants and provides additional space for its intended activities. If these intended activities include extensive media use, then additional space should be provided both for the set up and use of equipment, and for whatever empty floor space is needed to keep viewers from being seated too close to the display surface, that is, the projection screen, television monitor, and so on. The following are recommended room sizes:

(a) Large group media
    presentation room
    (auditorium)............................12 ft^2 per person
(b) Media classroom
    lecture (with 18″ tables).......25 ft^2 per person
    demo style (with tablet
    armchairs) ....15 ft^2 per person
(c) Media conference room
    (circle shaped table).............30 ft^2 per person
    (U shaped table) ....35 ft^2 per person
    (rectangle or boat shaped
    table) ....30-40 ft^2 per person
(d) Audiovisual/television/
    computer assisted instruction
    carrels ....15-30 ft^2 per person

Seating capacity and configuration are major factors in determining room size. As noted by Menell (1976):

> Generally speaking, a 20 × 32 foot room will seat about 49 people theatre style, 24 people classroom style, 18 people at a U-shaped table, and 15 people at a conference table.

The theater style seating arrangement is generally recommended for lecturing, orientation activities, and media presentations. A U-shaped seating arrangement also allows for effective media presentation (with smaller groups), but promotes more social interaction and discussion. A rectangular conference seating arrangement promotes interaction with the locus of authority generally vested with those seated at each end of the table. The circular seating pattern promotes more uniform social interaction among the group.

2.2 Room Shape and Viewing

A room's shape is a major factor contributing to a space's aesthetic character, its overall sense of perceptual appropriateness, and the kind of social interaction pattern which its planners desire to promote among its occupants. In rooms planned for extensive media use, the configuration of a room and its viewing area can be one of the most significant factors contributing to the effectiveness of the display system, the viewer's comfort, and the strength and clarity of the instructor's voice.

The basic dimensions for medium and large media presentation rooms should be 2:3 (width to length) with

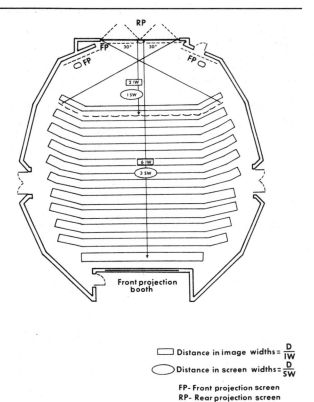

Figure 2
Viewing parameters = distance and horizontal angles

seating contained in a fan-shaped area beginning at a distance two times the width of the projected image (1w for rooms employed for multi-image display systems) and extending to a distance of six times the projected image width (3w for multi-image rooms). The viewing area is fan-shaped to improve horizontal sight lines. The boundary for the viewing area is shown in Fig. 2 as a line extended out 30° from the far side of the screen. Such a wide viewing sector assumes the use of a well-designed display system.

2.3 Ceiling Height

One of the structural features of a room which often reduces the potential effectiveness of a display system is its ceiling height. Given that a projection screen must be large enough to display images of adequate size and yet be placed high enough from the floor so that sight lines are unobstructed, it stands to reason that the eight-foot high ceilings often found in schools or training centers are not acceptable for media presentation purposes. To determine the ceiling height appropriate for a room, one should divide the room length by six and add four feet to that measurement. The resultant elevation will permit the installation of a projection screen of adequate size and still offer most viewers unobstructed sight lines. In

Table 1
Activities and recommended reverberation times

Speech recording and broadcast	0.4–0.6 seconds
Elementary classrooms	0.5–0.9 seconds
Motion picture presentation	0.6–1.2 seconds
Lectures and other activities using sound amplification	0.6–1.2 seconds
Musical comedy	1.0–1.4 seconds
Drama	1.0–1.4 seconds
Opera	1.2–1.6 seconds
Piano recital	1.2–1.6 seconds
Voice and violin recital, string quartet, chamber orchestra	1.4–1.8 seconds
Symphony orchestra (contemporary works)	1.3–1.6 seconds
Symphony orchestra (Brahms, Wagner)	1.8–2.0 seconds
Liturgical choral music, organ	1.8–3.0 seconds
Medieval liturgical works	4.0–8.0 seconds

many cases, a conventional classroom can be modified to properly accommodate a projection screen by eliminating an eight-foot section of the dropped ceiling at the front of the room. Doing so, however, will make it necessary to modify the lighting and air ventilation service of that portion of the room.

In large group media rooms and auditoria, ceiling height is usually not a problem. In fact, projection screens are often placed too high from the floor causing uncomfortable vertical viewing angles and poor image quality for those sitting in the front and side row seats below. Viewing comfort and accuracy are promoted when sight lines to informational displays do not exceed angles of elevation or depression of 25 degrees. Keeping the bottom of the projection screen four feet from the floor (or three and one-half feet in rooms with inclined or stepped floors and a lecture stage) is also recommended for these special purpose rooms, regardless of their ceiling heights. Proper screen placement is an important determinant of visual comfort and projection quality and also allows the instructor direct interaction with the presentation on the screen.

2.4 Room Shape and Acoustics

A room's shape affects its acoustics. The orientation of a room's walls, ceiling, and floor should be such that sound is reflected from the front of the room toward the back. To accomplish this, side walls should be nonparallel (splayed). In large group media rooms and auditoriums, floors should be stepped or inclined. The ceiling section over the instructor should also be inclined toward the audience in such a manner that the speaker's voice is projected forward, although it should also be reflected slightly downward so that the instructor will have no difficulty hearing himself or herself. A room's shape should be such that sound is propagated throughout but in a diffused fashion. Consequently, concave curved walls are usually not recommended since they tend to refocus reflected sound waves.

The character of each room surface should be consistent with the general acoustical treatment of a space.

The ceiling above the lecture stage should be sonically reflective. If reflecting panels (acoustical clouds) are used, they should be no smaller than eight feet wide, or else they will not reflect the lower sound frequencies. While it is generally recommended that the front half of the space be acoustically reflective, it is also recommended that the rear half of the room be acoustically absorptive so that sound waves will not be reflected back toward the front of the room. This condition can usually be accomplished by putting acoustical tiles on the rear one-third of the ceiling, and acoustical carpet or other sound absorptive material on the rear and side rear walls.

Installing carpeting on the floor area usually completes the acoustical treatment of a room while adding a welcomed bit of texture and color to the space. In a large auditorium that is used for a variety of activities involving groups of varying numbers, the addition of upholstered chairs may be required to keep the room's reverberation time near a desired constant. A room's reverberation time affects the intelligibility and aesthetics of sounds and words and limits the type of audio activities appropriate to the room. Table 1 shows the recommended reverberation times for different audio activities.

Other major features affecting a room's acoustical acceptability include its sonic isolation from neighboring spaces and the general background noise level produced by its architectural support systems, for example, lighting and air conditioning. It is generally recommended that media rooms be so constructed and insulated that there is at least a 45 decibel noise reduction between adjoining spaces.

The regulation of background noise levels can be readily achieved by various conventional architectural procedures. Total quiet is rarely if ever recommended

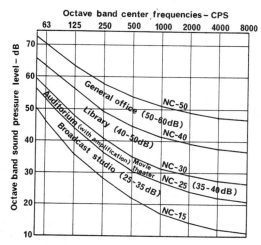

Figure 3
Recommended noise criteria for rooms shown by NC (noise criteria) curves and average dB level

since a certain amount of diffused noninformational ("white") noise is needed to mask distracting, activity-associated sounds. On the other hand, one does not want too much background noise for it will interfere with the strength and intelligibility of sound signals emanating either from the lecturer or from some audio program source. Figure 3 shows the background noise levels (noise criterion curves) recommended for different instructional and program support spaces.

2.5 Sound Systems

Voice and program amplification systems can contribute to the effectiveness of large group instruction and the use of audiovisual materials. A good sound reinforcement system should have sufficient power, good sensitivity, low distortion, and smooth frequency response. Ideally, reinforced sound should appear to emanate from where the lecturer is standing or, in the case of an audiovisual presentation, from the informational display area (e.g., the projection screen). Certain room shapes are best served by particular types of sound systems. A high-level centralized system is usually recommended for large lecture halls and auditoria which have adequate ceiling height and appropriate acoustical shaping. Column speaker systems are generally recommended for rooms having very wide horizontal and narrow vertical dimensions. Distributed systems consisting of many individual speakers mounted in the ceiling are usually recommended for the following situations: (a) rooms having inadequate ceiling height; (b) large "open plan" flexible classrooms; (c) rooms having high background noise levels; (d) rooms where most of the listeners do not have a good sight line to the program source.

Another type of sound system gaining popularity for use in specialized media rooms is the stereophonic sound system: a set of acoustically balanced and properly located high fidelity speakers can reproduce the quality and give the spatial separation desired for the playback of stereo recordings. To perceive the stereophonic spatial effect faithfully, the listener should be centrally located between the two speakers at a distance (from each of them) equal to their distance relative to each other.

3. Illumination

Educational spaces require lighting that produces a pattern of brightness from room surfaces that is aesthetically pleasing, and that promotes good depth perception. They also require enough illumination on major and supplementary task areas such as chalkboards, tackboards, desks, and other work surfaces to allow students to complete their visual tasks in comfort and with a high degree of visual efficiency. Control of all sources of illumination is imperative, particularly in rooms where media is used. Such control includes audiovisual blinds or opaque drapes over windows, dimmers for incandescent fixtures, and individual

switching for fluorescents. The following are recommended illumination requirements for instructional settings:

(a) Illumination level—general classroom activities require 300–500 lux; critical visual tasks (art work, etc.) 1,000 lux; audiovisual activities, variable from 0–300 lux.

(b) Reflectances—desk tops should be matte finish with a reflectance of 30–50 percent; floors of natural wood or light-colored tile or carpet with a reflectance of 30–50 percent. Classroom chalkboards should be green (with a reflectance not exceeding 20 percent), grey, or black. Auditorium chalkboards should have a reflectance not exceeding 10 percent; walls should have matte finish with 40–60 percent reflectance; ceilings should be matte finish with 70–90 percent reflectance.

3.1 Brightness Contrast Ratios (BCR)

The BCR of large adjoining areas under moderate to high illumination levels should fall somewhere between 1:1 and 3:1 with the task area being brighter than its surroundings. For smaller adjoining areas under low light levels, the acceptable BCR will range between 3:1 and 10:1 (Kaufman 1981). Lighting informational display areas so that they are brighter than their surround has resulted in significant increases in viewing time and significant reductions in distraction time (LaGuisa and Perney 1974).

3.2 Glare

Glare, a luminous condition that brings about discomfort and/or a reduction in visual acuity, is caused by either an unduly bright source of light in the visual field or from reflectances off a specular surface (Kaufman 1981). Most glare in the classroom can be eliminated or reduced by the following methods:

(a) Shades or drapery should be provided for all classroom windows which have outside exposure.

(b) Bright fixtures should be equipped with some directional or diffusing device.

(c) All lighting should be located so that its major transmission does not fall within a zone measured 45° above the student's line of sight.

(d) Glossy or specular surfaces should be avoided in the classroom.

Glare has recently surfaced as a major problem in environments that employ television monitors, computer terminals with cathode ray tubes (CRT), microfiche readers, and other visual display units (VDU). Recommendations for improving the situation range from the use of indirect lighting, equipping existing fixtures with directional louvers, and covering display screens with antiglare filters (NIOSH 1981).

3.3 Flicker

All light sources which produce noticeable and discomforting flicker should be either modified or eliminated from the classroom. Typical sources of flicker include: excessively bright lights; excessively bright motion picture projection; defective lamps; the ends of fluorescent lamps, and excessively bright television picture tubes.

3.4 Color Rendition

Since all types of illumination reproduce colors differently, lighting (incandescent or fluorescent) selection should consider the color appearance and color rendering qualities. There are several recommendations that can be followed to gain the best color rendition for a given situation:

(a) Incandescent lights should be used on dimmers for low levels and in specialized media presentation rooms.

(b) Cool white or warm white fluorescent should be used for general classroom lighting.

(c) Deluxe warm white fluorescent or incandescent should be used for reception areas where natural looking skin tones are desired.

(d) High color rendition fluorescent can be used for special graphic and visual arts rooms.

3.5 Fluorescent Versus Incandescent

Since research indicates that one can expect relatively little difference in visual acuity and fatigue with either fluorescent or incandescent lighting, the choice between these two lighting systems should be based on factors other than visual performance. It should be noted that indirect lighting systems employing either fluorescent or high-intensity discharge lamps (HID) have gained favor with a number of facility designers in their VDU workplace projects. Claims range from greater visual comfort and acuity at lower illumination levels, energy savings, and reduced glare at the terminals.

4. Windows

The windowless classroom eliminates the glare and extreme brightness contrasts caused by many window exposures. Other advantages frequently cited are the elimination of outside noise and visual distractions and better thermal control. Other benefits include safeguarding the building and students from vandalism and air pollution—factors currently plaguing urban-center schools. According to Larson (1965) children do not experience ill effects from windowless classrooms. In fact, their capacity to learn may be increased due to better mental concentration. Still, these proposed advantages must be weighed against the psychological factors that cause many students and their teachers to prefer classrooms with windows that allow them to maintain contact with the world outside the school. Perhaps the solution is a compromise where both types of rooms are integrated into the school's design and scheduled for complementary activities, that is, windowless rooms to be used for large group classrooms and auditoria, laboratories, gymnasia, study carrel areas, visual aids viewing rooms, and the like; and windowed rooms to be used for action-oriented activities, seminar and small group discussions, office spaces, reception areas, and so on.

5. Color

When used properly and combined with the right kind of illumination, color can be an effective tool for the facility designer and the classroom teacher. It has relatively predictable behavioral concomitants both as a surface treatment and as an illuminant. Different colors evoke different physiological awareness levels and emotional/attitudinal responses (Birren 1969), as well as producing different psychospatial effects which can be used effectively by the facility designer in his or her treatment of the school interior, and by the classroom teacher in the arrangement of displays and decoration of the school's or training center's work and study environment. Recommended colors for various surfaces are given below:

(a) Rooms to be action-oriented should be decorated in pastels of the warmer colors (yellow, orange, etc.) and those planned for quiet activities in pastels of the cooler colors (blue, green, etc.).

(b) Boldly saturated colors, particularly blues and reds are stressful, and should be avoided for general wall treatment, especially on surfaces which may be used as backgrounds for visual displays.

(c) Chalkboard green, grey, or beige are visually neutral and should be used for end walls which are planned as backgrounds for visual displays or projection screen locations.

(d) Bold colors, particularly red and blue, should be confined to art work, wall murals, display exhibits, and the like, where exaggerated feelings of depth or autonomic arousal are specifically desired.

(e) The use of color coded stripes (up to five different colors) on walls can help people locate the areas they seek in large and complex educational facilities.

6. Thermal Factors

The nature of the thermal exchange between people and their surroundings is a major factor affecting mental alertness, level of comfort, and effectiveness with which they complete their tasks. Consequently, the learning environment must be designed with thermal conditions that promote study and work:

(a) Air temperature should be kept constant within a range of 68–74°F.

(b) Relative humidity (RH) should be kept within a range of 30 to 60 percent in classrooms and 50 percent, constant, in computer areas.

(c) Air velocity should be kept within 15–25 feet per minute for low activity rooms and 25–50 feet per minute for rooms programmed for greater activity.

(d) Outside air in quantities of 10–25 cubic feet per minute should be provided for each student.

(e) The room's ambient temperature should be uniform ($\pm 2°F$) at working height throughout the room within one foot from exterior walls.

(f) The room should be serviced by automatic control systems, integrated thermostats, and automatic timing devices for day–night operations.

(g) Air conditioning is recommended where possible, particularly for schools which operate year round.

(h) Separate and additional cooling is required for special purpose media spaces, such as projection rooms, television and audio studios, and computer rooms.

7. Display Systems

One of the most important components of the learning environment, and particularly of spaces used extensively for media presentations, is the display system. Display systems range in sophistication from a basic setup which typically includes a television monitor, a couple of projectors, and a matte white screen, to highly complex front and rear projection multimedia systems. They can be as simple to operate and maintain as microfiche viewers or as complex as light-valve television projectors or plasma displays hooked up to an interactive computer program. In all cases they require the same basic environmental considerations if they are to serve the function for which they were designed.

7.1 Characteristics of Effective Display Systems

A good display system

(a) provides high legibility of individual characters and meaningful groups of symbols, for example, words are easily recognizable;

(b) affords easy detectability of weak signals at all display range scales and at long and short viewing distances;

(c) provides comfortable and accurate viewing at any required viewing angle;

(d) allows minimum fall-off in image brightness at all viewing angles;

(e) provides appropriate brightness–contrast, resolution, and minimal image distortion;

(f) elicits highest possible observer accuracy and response time in performing visual functions;

(g) gives no apparent flicker for any of the viewers;

(h) affords effective viewing within entire operating range of ambient illumination;

(i) responds with minimal equipment delay to user's request for display, as in information retrieval systems;

(j) permits display parameters (e.g., brightness and contrast) to be adjusted by user;

(k) gives audio signals of sufficient strength and fidelity to provide accurate and comfortable hearing for all users;

(l) affords audio localization complementary to image location;

(m) provides properly coded display controls for ease and accuracy of operation;

(n) provides equipment and components—capable of being maintained by in-house technical staff;

(o) can be readily provided with software.

7.2 Front and Rear Screen Projection

The two projection systems commonly employed in education and training facilities are front and rear screen projection. In a front projection (FP) system, an image is produced by reflection off an opaque screen. Screen

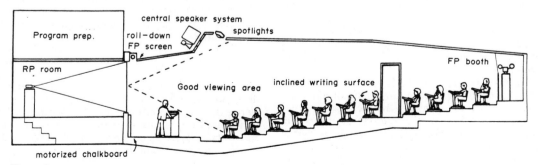

Figure 4
Preferred media lecture room design

types include "matte," "beaded," "lenticular," and "aluminum foil." The matte screen is recommended for general classroom and auditorium use. Beaded screens are often recommended for rooms with narrow viewing sectors and where higher image brightness is required from standard projection equipment. Fixed, perforated lenticular screens are standard equipment for motion picture theaters and the aluminum foil screen is used for special situations involving high ambient illumination and low brightness television projection.

In a rear projection (RP) system, an image is produced by transmission through either a vinyl, plexiglass, or glass translucent screen. This type of projection system has found favor in training centers where media presentations generally occur in rooms with high ambient illumination.

Since front and rear screen projection systems have different features relative to image quality and functionality they are both quite often recommended for installation in specialized media presentation rooms (see Fig. 4).

8. Outdoor Study Areas

While outdoor study areas are quite often desired by students, in general, they are characterized by too much glare, noise, thermal discomfort, and uncomfortable seating to be recommended for extended instruction and when verbal communication and information display are required. If such areas are to be of functional value, then their design should include the following features (Cannon and Kapeliz 1978):

(a) windbreaks and sound-deflecting walls for noise control;

(b) tree and shrub plantings for visual privacy;

(c) comfortable outdoor seats with backrests;

(d) rotundas for small group work;

(e) contiguity with indoor work areas; and

(f) scale appropriate to user groups.

If these areas are also to be used for media presentations, then provisions should be made for sound reinforcement, electrical power, and projection systems.

9. Conclusion

The topics and recommendations discussed here are a few of the environmental and human factors which affect student comfort and media utilization. When such factors are prudently integrated into a learning environment's design they have gained acceptance and appreciation from students and teachers alike (McVey 1979). When such factors have not been included in a facility's design, consequences have been human discomfort, poor performance from audiovisual equipment and subsequent disenchantment with instructional technology.

Bibliography

Bennett C 1977 *Spaces for People: Human Factors in Design.* Prentice-Hall, Englewood Cliffs, New Jersey

Birren F 1969 *Light Color and Environment: A Thorough Presentation of the Facts on the Biological and Psychological Effects of Color.* Van Nostrand Rheinhold, New York

Cannon R, Kapeliz Z 1978 Learning environments. In: Unwin D, McAleese R (eds.) 1978 *Encyclopedia of Educational Media Communications and Technology.* Macmillan, London

Canter D V 1975 *Psychology for Architects.* Wiley, New York

Consultative Committee on Secondary Education (CCSE) 1938 *Report of the Consultative Committee on Secondary Education.* CCSE, His Majesty's Stationery Office, London

Council of Educational Facility Planners (CEFP) 1969 *Guide for Planning Educational Facilities.* CEFP, Columbus, Ohio

DeChiara J, Callender J H (eds.) 1980 *Time–Saver Standards for Building Types,* 2nd Edn. McGraw-Hill, New York

Diffrient N, Tilley A R, Bardagjy J C 1974 *Humanscale 1/2/3: A Portfolio of Information.* MIT Press, Cambridge, Massachusetts

Fanger P O 1970 *Thermal Comfort: Analysis and Applications in Environmental Engineering.* Danish Technical Press, Copenhagen

Green A (ed.) 1966 *Educational Facilities with New Media.* Association for Educational Communications and Technology (AECT), Washington, DC

Hall E T 1966 *The Hidden Dimension.* Doubleday, New York

Harmon D B 1951 *The Coordinated Classroom.* AIA File No. 35-B. American Seating Co., Grand Rapids, Michigan

Hawkes R J, Douglas H 1970 Subjective acoustic experience in concert auditorium. *Architectural Res. Teach.* 1(2): 34–35

Holt J C 1970 *What Do I Do Monday?* Dutton, New York

Hunt D P, Bernotat R 1977 *University Curricula in Ergonomics.* Forschungsinstitut für Anthropotechnik, Meckenheim

Kaufman J E (ed.) 1981 IES *Lighting Handbook,* Vols. 1, 2. Illuminating Engineering Society of North America, New York

Kryter K D 1970 *The Effects of Noise on Man.* Academic Press, New York

LaGuisa F F, Perney L R 1974 Further studies on effects of brightness variations on attention spans. *J. Illuminating Eng. Soc.* 3: 249–52

Larson C T 1965 *The Effect of Windowless Classrooms on Elementary School Children.* University of Michigan, Ann Arbor, Michigan

McVey G F 1979 User assessment of media presentation rooms. *Educ. Commun. Technol. J.* 27: 121–47

Menell J 1976 Training facilities and equipment. In: American Society for Training and Development (eds.) 1976 *Training and Development Handbook: A Guide to Human Resource Development,* 2nd edn. McGraw-Hill, New York

NIOSH 1981 *Potential Health Hazards of Video Display Terminals.* NIOSH Publication No. 81–129, DHHS, Washington, DC

Sommer R 1969 *Personal Space: The Behavioral Basis of Design.* Prentice-Hall, Englewood Cliffs, New Jersey

Van Cott H P, Kinkade R G (eds.) 1972 *Human Engineering Guide to Equipment Design.* United States Government Printing Office, Washington, DC

Yerges L F 1969 *Sound, Noise, and Vibration Control.* Van Nostrand Rheinhold, New York

Information Technology for Disabled Students

A. T. Vincent

In 1985 a group of students at a college for blind girls in the United Kingdom sat their General Certificate of Education (GCE) O' level examinations. As in previous years, they produced their answers in braille using the 40-year-old Perkins Brailler (a mechanical braille embosser). To the casual observer nothing had changed, but a more detailed investigation revealed that information technology (IT) had been introduced through linking the brailling devices to microcomputers that could translate the braille to text for subsequent marking (Schofield and Vincent 1986). This is one of many developments where information technology has been introduced to meet the needs of disabled students. This article looks at some selected IT developments for students with sensory and physical disabilities. The presentation will concentrate on applications and experiences, with only sufficient detail of the related technologies to provide a general understanding. Of necessity, the coverage will be limited; further information can be found in books dedicated to this topic including Hawkridge et al. (1985), Goldenberg et al. (1984), Behrmann (1984), Hope (1987), and Vincent and Vincent (1985).

1. What Can IT Offer?

Recent developments in technology create the most promising possibilities yet available for solving or mitigating the problems of disabled people. Yet, paradoxically, the technology which offers this potential can also widen the gap between those with and without a disability. For example, the growing use of computer-assisted learning (CAL) may disadvantage a disabled student for whom access to a computer is not possible.

Many of the early attempts to use microelectronics and microcomputers for disabled students have focused on the breaking of communication barriers. These barriers may exist because a physically disabled student cannot write, a deaf student cannot hear, or a blind student cannot read text. These are fundamental problems in giving students full access to the curriculum, and they have motivated many developers to seek ways in which IT can overcome them. In some cases this has required the development of special devices based on microprocessors; in others, the adaptation (often through software) of devices that are normally used by non-disabled people.

The use of IT to supplement the curriculum has not received the same degree of attention. There are examples such as CAL in the teaching of braille, interactive video for sign language, and other applications. This limitation may be explained to some extent by the longer development time for software that is used directly for teaching or training.

It is necessary also to consider the user–machine interface problems that have been created by the introduction of computers into education. These require both manual dexterity to operate a keyboard and visual acuity to read from a visual display. Much of the software developed for use in schools has a high degree of graphical output, which poses special problems for blind students. The graphics are difficult to convert to another medium and, even if a conversion can be made, the visual concepts may still be difficult to learn. Hence although the computer can help to overcome some barriers it can also introduce others.

The more recent introduction of WIMP (windows, icons, mouse, and pull-down menus) environments provides easier access to application programs for sighted users, but it has created problems for blind people. Screen reading techniques, using synthetic speech, developed to date, provide access only to serial or single screen visual presentations. Further research and development is now needed to develop enabling software for a WIMP environment (Edwards and O'Shea 1986).

2. IT and Communication Problems

The following sections look at some of the communication problems of students with sensory and physical disabilities, and some of the IT devices that have been introduced in an attempt to overcome them. In some cases the use of the device has been successful, in others it has not. Often lack of success is due less to the inadequacy of the device than to underestimating the degree of initial assessment, training, and support that is necessary. There is no doubt that the implications of introducing IT go far beyond the provision of hardware.

2.1 Visually Disabled Students

Developing communication skills is of prime importance for visually disabled students but, as Napier (1974) indicates, there is a need to consider also special subject adjustments and the acquisition of alternative skills. The most difficult educational problems for blind and partially sighted students are associated with reading and writing. They cannot depend on speech and hearing for all educational activities, and there have been numerous developments to overcome communication problems caused by loss of sight.

Access to the written word for blind students is possible through braille, audio recording, or sighted readers. For normal use, braille is very similar to speed writing, with wordsigns and contractions of symbols being commonly used to cut down bulk. There are 64 combinations of 6 dots (a braille cell) that can be used for different meanings depending on context. However, even in a contracted form, braille is bulky (its volume compared to text being increased by a factor of 15 to 20). In addition, there is a significant time factor for the conversion of braille to text, even with skilled braille transcribers, though this has been significantly reduced by the introduction of automated transcription systems. A typical microcomputer-based system is the one developed by the University of Warwick Research Unit for the Blind (Gill 1982b), the BITS system. A preliminary report (in a personal communication from D Crosby 1983) on the use of the BITS system in an educational environment indicated that it had several applications, including the preparation of examination papers and general work for students. As the system includes a word processor for text entry, it is possible to produce print copies simultaneously for partially sighted students.

Audio recording of textbooks has made an important contribution for several years. Although the audio cassette has the advantage of containing large amounts of text in a small volume, it has the disadvantage of being in a linear format. However, advances in tape players to provide indexing, variable replay speeds, and pitch compensation at high speed have considerably improved access. The advent of compact discs offers an even greater potential for fast and efficient access to audio material.

The introduction of the Optacon heralded a new era for blind people as it was one of the first attempts to provide a sighted reader. The "sight" is provided by a miniature camera passing over a line of text. As the camera passes over each letter, the image is simultaneously reproduced on a tactile array (approximately $1\frac{1}{2}$ ins. $\times$ 1 in.) of vibrating miniature rods and "read" by the index finger. The Optacon has played a significant role in two extensive school programmes: one in Italy (outlined by Testa and Venturini in a presentation at the World Optacon Conference, California, September 1980), and the other in the United States, funded by the Federal Government. By the end of 1983, 9,462 Optacons were in use worldwide.

More recently, there have been developments concerning the *recognition* of characters rather than image conversion, as with the Optacon. For example, the Kurzweil Reading Machine (KRM), developed in the United States, can "read" a book to a blind person by automatically tracking over the pages, reading the characters optically, assembling the characters into text and converting the text to synthetic speech. The system is based on Optical Character Recognition (OCR) methods. As a table top device, the KRM can be found in numerous libraries.

The magnification of text enables many partially sighted people to read more easily. The development of Closed Circuit Television (CCTV) for this purpose offers great potential because of the technical options available, including: variable magnification, black and white reversal, colour, and movable viewing tables (horizontal and vertical). Further developments include the use of a miniature fibre optic camera and a flat, neon matrix, low resolution screen that combine to produce a portable device. An example is the Viewscan, which is included by Gill (1984) in a review of aids for the visually handicapped. CCTV methods can be used for diagrams or text but this is not generally true for braille transcription and OCR methods. The tactile diagram is an invaluable aid for blind people, but skill and time are required to produce the master from which plastic sheet thermoform copies can be produced. The stereo copying system produced by Minolta can convert a black and white drawing to an embossed form on special paper. The paper has a layer of microcapsules which expand on the absorption of light energy. The absorption takes place at points, lines, or in areas that are drawn or photocopied in black on the special paper.

Gill (1982a) points to the lack of research on computer-generated graphics displays for the blind, and indicates the need for a more scientific approach to the optimum design for blind users. He reports that the majority of research has concentrated on the generation of audio displays, although there are examples of page braille displays.

Note-taking and reading are possible with a number of "paperless" braille devices. A common feature is an electronic keyboard for entering braille characters, a cassette system for the storage of the braille, and an electromechanical braille display. The units are generally small and portable, providing a compact information storage and retrieval system. In the San Diego Unified School District, an evaluation (Doorlag and Doorlag 1983) of one "paperless" braille device, the Versabraille, indicated that students using cassette-braille were able to read and write faster than with paper braille.

2.2 Physically Disabled Students

Many physically disabled students can write only very slowly. Notetaking is a problem and, as Foulds (1982) reports, limits the use of a scratch pad or rough notebook in subjects such as mathematics. Drawing presents even more problems because of the high accuracy that may be required in, for example, science and mathematics. Loss of speech prevents or slows down verbal communication; in combination with the loss of ability to write, the handicap is very severe in an educational environment.

One of the information technology developments that has been successfully adapted for students who are unable to produce written material is the word processor. This has the advantage of being able to store text which can be edited and printed. However, word processors are normally used with a QWERTY keyboard which may be difficult or impossible for someone who has restricted motor control of their hands. A great deal of research and development has taken place already to see how normal multikey access can be replaced by simpler arrangements, even to the point of a single switch. The addition of alternative keyboards often requires the development or modification of word processing software.

The numerous options available for modifying or changing the keyboard input to a word processor include: (a) modifying the existing keyboard, (b) replacing the keyboard by an alternative keyboard, or (c) providing an alternative to the keyboard. These options are considered, for example, by Watts et al. (1985) in relation to their research in this area.

(a) *Modification of the existing keyboard.* One of the simplest modifications for a student with a hand tremor but who can span a normal keyboard is a software modification to change or remove the auto repeat facility on keys. This is often combined with keyguards to guide a finger to a single key. This arrangement can be operated with a head-pointer, mouthstick, typing stick, or similar device. However, problems can still arise if two or more keys have to be pressed simultaneously. Some keyboards may have a shift and/or caps lock which can overcome this limitation.

(b) *Replacement of the existing keyboard.* The limitations of a modified standard keyboard can be overcome with an "expanded keyboard". This type of keyboard may be physically larger, have a built-in keyguard and, more importantly, incorporate features such as single finger operation, variable "anti-tremor" delays and variable auto repeat speed. Ideally, it can directly replace a standard keyboard without any modification to the application software.

(c) *Provision of an alternative to a keyboard.* Alternatives to a keyboard are numerous (see Sect. 5 for references) and can be as simple as a single switch (foot, eye, suck/blow, etc.) The selection of a single switch input immediately implies changes (hardware or software) to provide for the variety of normal inputs from a QWERTY keyboard. One method is to provide a screen presentation of characters or groups of characters (referred to as a *menu*) in the form of a matrix of rows and columns, or as a branching tree structure. The selection of characters (equivalent to typing on a keyboard) is made with a single switch and they are then transferred to the main application program. In designing a system, two approaches can be made. Firstly, the menu software can reside alongside the application software. Secondly, the menu software can reside in a separate processor (possibly a second microcomputer). The latter has the advantage of giving access to software that could not be modified to incorporate a menu feature.

Head and Poon (1983) describe the MAC-Apple which is a communication program for the Apple II microcomputer that enables the user (operating a switch or keyboard) to select letters and/or words. Words are selected from preprepared word lists. MAC-Apple incorporates word processing facilities and column arithmetic. A free drawing facility is available to produce simple line diagrams. This communication program can also be used to directly replace another microcomputer keyboard.

WORDSCAN is an example of a computer-based communication system for single switch users. It was developed for a UK school for the physically disabled. Its initial evaluation and enhancement have been reported (Fowler et al. 1985). A precursor to WORDSCAN is SENTENCE SCAN which can be used by younger pupils. Its use by a boy who has severe dyskinetic cerebral palsy has been reported by Millar (1985). She goes on to argue that these new tools for reading and writing must be firmly integrated into the curriculum.

Word processing is also possible with a device that was initially developed for the "electronic office"—the Microwriter. The main advantages for this commercially available device is that it is portable, battery operated, has a complementary metal-oxide semiconductor (CMOS) memory (retains text when switched off), and a keyboard which fits the shape of one hand. There are five main keys plus a sixth (control key) which is operated as an alternative for the thumb position. In order to generate characters for text entry and control commands for editing, combinations of the keys are pressed. For example, pressing the five main keys generates the letter *p*. The keys do not have to be pressed simultaneously as the input monitors between the first key pressed and the last released. This does enhance its potential use for physically disabled students. For a severely disabled person, there is a Scanning Microwriter which can be used with a single switch.

The BITSTICK is another example of a commercially available device that has proved to be suitable for physically disabled students. BITSTICK is a computer-aided design (CAD) system that is controlled from a joystick that features zoom control. Although designed to produce sophisticated diagrams, its use as a drawing aid has proved to be possible even with young children.

For physically disabled students who are also unable to speak, numerous devices now have a speech output. Portable units are available which are programmed with a limited number of words or phrases that can be recalled with a single keystroke. The Vocaid is such a device. It has a touch-sensitive matrix of 36 squares for which there are several overlays that provide different vocabularies. Experiences with the Vocaid in the United States are reported by Eulenberg and Rosenfeld (1982). Stanford University has been involved in the development of the Versatile Portable Speech Prosthesis (VPSP), designed for people who are speech handicapped but linguistically capable. A prototype system has been described [*Communication Outlook* 2(3) August 1980] which allows the user to create an unlimited vocabulary that can be accessed via a single switch, joystick, or keyboard.

2.3 Deaf Students

The learning problems of deaf students cannot be described only in terms of their degree of hearing. Factors such as language acquisition and the ability to interact with the social world are part of this complex communication handicap. One distinction that can be made between deaf people is those who are profoundly deaf (no usable hearing), and those who are partially deaf (some usable hearing, with or without a hearing aid). The difference can be related to how an individual uses alternative modes of communication. Another distinction is between those people who are prelingually and postlingually deaf.

Information technology has been used for hearing disabled students for the visual presentation of what is being said in, for example, a lecture or a television programme. Two approaches have been used: firstly, the presentation of accurate syntactical English in a summarized form; secondly, a verbatim transcription. An example of the former was reported at the British Open University (Hales 1976, Hales 1978). An "interpreter" listens to the original speech and dictates through a sensitive microphone link to a typist who uses a microcomputer to produce the text on a screen that is available to the student.

A similar system has been used for the real-time captioning of live television in combination with teletext (Independent Television's Oracle system). The verbatim system has been the subject of a great deal of research. For example, software has been developed that can take the output of shorthand machines (Palantype in the United Kingdom and Stenotype in the United States) and convert it to text in real-time. The automatic conversion is difficult because the output from the shorthand machines is phonetically based. However, the techniques have improved to the point where such verbatim displays are used in classes at the National Technical Institute for the Deaf in the United States, and for the captioning of television programmes in the United States and the United Kingdom.

Several projects were established in the UK under the Government's Microelectronics Education programme (MEP). For example, at the University of Bristol, the Computer-Assisted Teaching of Communication to Handicapped Users Project (CATCHUP) has developed a reading scheme for profoundly deaf children using an interactive picture language on a microcomputer to teach the use of English syntax. Sentences or questions can be built in rebus form and so interact with the computer or the pupils' peers in a similar way to using speech. Further examples are described by Dyke (1985).

Visispeech is a device for displaying vocal patterns. It is used at the Elmfield School, Avon, by students of all ages to encourage consistent and good quality voicing. It can display voice patterns of both teacher and student simultaneously. The system was developed by the Royal National Institute for the Deaf.

At the California School for the Deaf an authoring system has been developed to enable teachers with no knowledge of programming to devise special lessons for their students. The system is called BLOCKS 82. Teachers use simple English commands, and peripherals such as a graphics tablet, to develop CAL material. They can keep track of student progress and devise lessons using a built-in management system.

3. Access to Computer Software

Microcomputers and microprocessor devices are capable of giving special assistance to disabled individuals. Examples have been given already of how they can help to overcome communication problems. However, microcomputers in particular are being used more widely in education for CAL, programming, data analysis, information storage and retrieval, and so forth. The question arises how access can be provided so that these aspects of the curriculum can be made available to all students regardless of disability. There are two approaches that can be considered in relation to the application software. Firstly, special software can be written that is customized for a particular requirement (e.g. speech output or single switch input) and a particular application. Secondly, access can be provided to standard software. The latter must be the ideal provided that the quality of the access is high enough.

Consider a word processing program that uses option menus. Normal access is gained by scanning a menu of up to 10 options by eye and pressing a key to select the required option. This visual method is not suitable for a blind student but access could be provided by directing (typically through operating system commands) the screen output to a speech synthesizer or braille display. This would have the advantage of not having to modify the standard software but the disadvantage that all of the options would have to be spoken or brailled every time that the menu appeared. There is no doubt that alternative menu methods can be programmed to give efficient access; however, this immediately implies customized software.

Vanderheiden (1982) argues that disabled individuals should have access to standard software. He indicates that the provision of transparent access to microcomputers usually requires some type of hardware intervention. Examples have already been discussed of alternative keyboards and keyboard emulators for physically disabled students that give this type of access. In a similar way it is possible to provide a braille input. However, the input to a computer is relatively simple in comparison with the output. Programs that are designed to produce a line-by-line output (as with teletype access on-line to a mainframe computer) do not present much difficulty; but there are significant problems where output is normally to a screen. There can be a high degree of redundancy in the display (as with the menu example); the screen may be updated in any and variable positions; or cursor movements (positioning on the screen) may be involved. The translation of static or dynamic screen information into another medium requires intelligent decisions to be made in reforming or filtering information that appears on the screen.

As Knox (1983) indicates in his discussion of the case for standard packages or made to measure software, much time and effort is required for the latter approach. The time and effort will vary significantly depending on the software application and the alternative input or output medium. In general terms, it would seem that changing the input medium to a microcomputer can be readily achieved for a wide range of needs without special application software. The change of the output medium is more complex and requires that efficiency as well as access is considered before a choice between standard or special software can be made. In both cases cost has to be considered. With standard software there is likely to be an additional hardware cost for every user whereas with customized software, the cost of development is likely to be high and the final individual cost will depend on the number of potential users.

Whether standard or customized software is used, the hardware interface for the user will, in most cases, be the same. For example, a physically disabled student who uses a single switch in place of a keyboard may be linked either directly to a microcomputer with customized software or indirectly via a second microcomputer or microprocessor to standard software.

In general, it is the input and/or output device that may have to be replaced for a disabled individual. The main devices are the keyboard, screen, or printer which are common to many microcomputer configurations. The replacement of the keyboard for physically disabled students has already been considered. Further suggestions are made by Gowans (1982) in his state-of-the-art report on alternatives to keyboards. A hearing disabled student will generally be able to use a microcomputer without modification although there would be limitations if speech or sound output were used. In the case of the latter, the redirection to a printer would be possible. For a blind student a variety of options can be considered.

Synthetic speech has been a popular replacement for visual displays for blind people. It has the advantage of being relatively low cost and capable of handling an unlimited vocabulary in real-time. However, speech is a relatively slow medium and care must be taken to remove all redundant speech. Braille is another alternative as both hard copy on paper or in a refreshable form (electromechanical pins that can transiently represent braille cells). An electronic braille keyboard can be used. For partially sighted students, screen or character enlargement is an alternative. These options are discussed in more detail by Ashcroft (1984) and Ruconich (1984).

In 1984, the Office of Special Education and Rehabilitation Services (US Department of Education), in conjunction with the White House, took the initiative to begin a process of bringing computer manufacturers, developers and consumers together to address the question of access and use of standard computer and computer software by persons who have disabilities. A Design Considerations Task Force was established. Initial guidelines have been issued on 'access to information technology by users with disabilities' (NIDRR and GSA 1987).

4. Workstations for Disabled Students

Ideally, application software should be accessible to any user with special needs through any hardware interface with the minimum of inconvenience. One approach in this direction has been the development of workstations that provide an integrated hardware and software environment.

A project at the Hereward College of Further Education in the United Kingdom where several students have been provided with personal workstations is described by Firminger (1983). Each workstation consists of a standard microcomputer plus extra devices and software selected on the basis of an assessment of the students' needs. A word processor is a common feature, and there is software to enable graphs, graphics, and calculations to be produced. In collaboration with the University of Warwick (Pickering and Stevens 1984) an experimental interface is being designed with a word processor, calculator, and graphics display forming an integrated "electronic notepad".

At Concordia University in Canada, a workstation has been developed for student programmers taking an introductory course on computers and computing for the physically handicapped. It uses standard hardware, except for a purpose-built braille display unit (Grossner et al. 1983). The workstation includes a standard American Standard Codes for Information Interchange (ASCII) keyboard with programmable function and cursor-control keys, a visual display unit (VDU) that assists interaction between blind and sighted users, a synthetic speech output, a 20-character braille display, a printing device for hardcopy output in character or braille formats, a modem for connection to a remote computer, plus the software to integrate these devices. Fundamental to the work at Concordia has been the philosophy that "a workstation intended for a blind programmer should enable the use of any program written for or by sighted programmers" (Grossner et al. 1983 p. 9).

In the United Kingdom, a workstation approach has been adopted by the Computing and the Blind project at the Open University since 1979. The initial objective was to design a system that could be used by blind students studying at home. In 1982, eight schools joined the project. They were equipped with identical workstations based on the BBC microcomputer with a Perkins Brailler and a touch-sensitive keyboard (with embossed overlays) as alternative input devices, synthetic speech output, VDU, and printer. All of the hardware was relatively low cost and commercially available including the adaptation to the Perkins Brailler (Spragg 1984). The software developed for the project included the teaching of braille, braille transcription, programming (Vincent 1983), and wordprocessing (Vincent and Turnbull 1984).

Figure 1
A computer workstation for blind pupils and students developed at the Open University, Milton Keynes
© Crown Copyright Reserved

5. *Sources of Published Information*

This article has given examples of the use of some information technology developments to meet the needs of disabled students. The late 1980s have seen many developments in this area which are beyond the scope of this article. However, an attempt has been made to show examples of what has been and now is possible with information technology. It is therefore appropriate to include further references to hardware and software developments in this area. Sources of published information include:

(a) *Aids to Communication in Education—Switches and Interfaces* (1985). ACE Centre, Ormerod School, Oxford.

(b) *Special Education Catalogue* (1985). Techmedia, Loughborough.

(c) *Electronic Aids for those with Special Needs* (1984). Handicapped Persons Research Unit, Newcastle upon Tyne Polytechnic.

(d) Voice output for computer access by the blind and visually impaired (1983) *Aids and Appliances Review* Nos. 9 and 10. Carroll Center for the Blind.

(e) Braille and computers (1984) *Aids and Appliances Review* No. 11. Carroll Center for the Blind.

(f) *International Survey of Aids for the Visually Disabled* (1984). Research Unit for the Blind, Brunel University.

(g) *International Software/Hardware Registry*. Trace Research Center for the Severely Communicatively Handicapped, Madison, Wisconsin.

(h) *Equipment for the Disabled: Communication* (1987). Oxfordshire Regional Health Authority, Oxford.

(i)   Trace Center Reprint Service (1987-1988). *Information on Communication, Control, and Computer Access for Handicapped Individuals*. Trace Research Center.

Bibliography

Ashcroft S C 1984 Research on multimedia access to microcomputers for visually impaired youth. *Educ. Vis. Hand.* 15(4): 108–18

Behrmann M (ed.) 1984 *Handbook of Microcomputers in Special Education*. College-Hill Press, San Diego, California

Doorlag D M, Doorlag D H 1983 Cassette braille: A new communication tool for blind people. *J. Vis. Imp. Blind.* 77(4)

Dyke R G 1985 Microtechnology and the hearing impaired pupil. *Primary Contact* Special Issue No. 3. Didsbury School of Education, Manchester

Edwards A D N, O'Shea T 1986 Making graphics-based programming systems usable by blind people. *Interactive Learning Int.* 3(2)

Eulenberg J B, Rosenfeld J 1982 Vocaid—A new product from Texas Instruments. *Commun. Outlook* 3(3)

Firminger J 1983 Assessing IT for severely disabled students: New developments at Hereward College. *NATFHE J.* 8(7)

Foulds R A 1982 Applications of microcomputers in the education of the physically disabled child. *Excep. Child.* 49(2): 155–62

Fowler J R, O'Neill M J, Wheeler C S 1985 The development of a micro-based communication system through field evaluation. Paper presented at the conference on The Computer as an Aid for those with Special Needs, Sheffield 17-19 April

Gill J M 1982a Computer generated graphics displays. In: Raviv J (ed.) 1982 *Uses of Computers in Aiding the Disabled*. North-Holland, Amsterdam

Gill J M 1982b Microcomputer aids for the blind. *Comput. Educ.* 42: 21

Gill J M 1984 Aids for the visually handicapped. *Micropro. Microsys.* 8(10): 516–19

Goldenberg E P, Russell S J, Carter C J, Stokes S, Sylvester M J, Kelman P 1984 *Computers, Education, and Special Needs*. Addison-Wesley, Reading, Massachusetts

Gowans J 1982 Alternatives to keyboards. *Micro. Printout.* pp. 76–80

Grossner C P, Radhakrishnan T, Pospiech A 1983 An integrated workstation for the visually handicapped. *IEEE Micro.* 3(3): 8–16

Hales G W 1976 Communicating with the deaf by conventional orthography: The case for a non-verbatim approach. *Br. J. Audio.* 10 83–86

Hales G W 1978 Some problems associated with the higher education of deaf and hearing-impaired students in an open system. Doctoral thesis, The Open University, Milton Keynes

Hawkridge D, Vincent T, Hales G 1985 *New Information Technology in the Education of Disabled Children and Adults*. Croom Helm, London

Head P, Poon P 1983 Communication in an educational setting. *Learning to Cope '83: An Educational Computing Special*. Educational Computing, London

Hope M 1987 *Micros for Children with Special Needs*. Souvenir, London

Knox R 1983 Packages or purpose built. *Spec. Educ.: For. Trends* 10(1)

Millar S 1985 New tools for reading and writing. *Primary Contact*, Special Issue No. 3. Didsbury School of Education, Manchester

Napier G D 1974 Special subject adjustments and skills. In: Lowenfeld B (ed.) 1974 *The Visually Handicapped Child in School*. Constable, London, pp. 221–277

National Institute on Disability and Rehabilitation Research (NIDRR), General Services Administration (GSA) 1987 *Access to Information Technology by Users with Disabilities: Initial Guidelines*. NIDRR, GSA, US

Pickering J A, Stevens G C 1984 The physically handicapped and work-related computing: Towards interface intelligence. *Proc. Second Int. Conf. Rehabilitation Engineering* Ontario June 17-22 1984. Rehabilitation Engineering Society, North America, Bethesda, Maryland, pp. 126–28

Ruconich S K 1984 Evaluating microcomputer access technology for use by visually impaired students. *Educ. Vis. Hand.* 15(4): 119–25

Schofield J, Vincent A T 1986 Information technology and braille examinations: An automated approach. *Program. Learn. Educ. Technol.* 23(2): 150–55

Spragg J 1984 Interfacing a Perkins Brailler to a BBC micro. *Micropro. Microsys.* 8(10): 524–27

Vanderheiden G 1982 Computers can play a dual role for disabled individuals. *Byte* 7(9): 136–62

Vincent A T 1983 Talking BASIC and talking Braille: Two applications of synthetic speech. *Comput. Educ.* 45: 10–12

Vincent A T, Turnbull S D 1984 Word processing for blind people. *Micropro. Microsys.* 8(10): 535–38

Vincent B, Vincent T 1985 *Information Technology and Further Education*. Kogan Page, London

Watts P, Smullen J, Brown D N 1985 Computer access for non-keyboard users. Paper presented at the conference on The Computer as an Aid for those with Special Needs, Sheffield 17-19 April

Part 3

Media Potential, Utilization, and Impact

Part 3

Media Potential, Utilization, and Impact

Introduction

This Part of the *Encyclopedia* progresses from considering technical developments to reviewing the use of technology in education. Its central concern is with the potential of media for enhancing the quality of education. What can the various media do, how can they best be used and what is their likely impact? Media have many attributes, some more relevant to one context, some to another, and mediated materials can be designed to exploit these attributes in different modes and for different purposes. Hence, there can be no simple, generalized, unequivocal answers to questions about media potential. Nevertheless, it is important to examine critically questions relating to the design, utilization, and impact of media-assisted learning, and to give them a prominent place in educational technology research.

The articles that follow are not designed for specialists in the topics under review. The space is too short for that, so those seeking a more detailed treatment are referred to more substantial books in the bibliographies. Rather, they are aimed at generalist educational technologists, at those whose specialism lies elsewhere, at people concerned with designing curricula or learning packages, and at teachers who seek to use various media to enhance the quality of the learning experiences they provide for their students. No designer of learning materials or user of media can realize the full potential of media without understanding their characteristics and knowing something about the accumulated experience of other designers and users. So reviews of the kind that follow offer an extremely valuable resource. Given their purpose and format, however, these reviews concentrate on media characteristics, modes of use, trends, and issues. They do not attempt to duplicate the kind of practical advice given in production manuals. The field is already well-served by such manuals and by some excellent standard texts, and it would be neither feasible nor appropriate to seek to emulate them.

The articles in this Part have been grouped into four sections: Computers; Film, Television, and Video; Simple Media; and Distance Education. Some overlap is unavoidable as computers, for example, are used in interactive video (reviewed in an article of that name in Part 2), in many simulations, and also, increasingly, in graphic production. However, computers and video are still recognizably different domains with their own publications, associations, and networks. More than most areas of educational technology, they are strongly influenced by specialist expertise outside the field of education which determines the nature of their equipment and strongly influences production standards and norms. Specialists within educational computing or educational television tend not to be conversant with other areas of educational technology, thus adding to the separateness of these domains. Whether this situation will persist remains an interesting question, for the technological interdependence of these media is increasing rapidly. Since media production requires a diversity of talents, it may be better to develop teams with complementary expertise than to expect a new generation of educational technologists who can combine several different styles of thinking and working into a single persona. The problem is how best to combine the knowledge developed in the different subfields of educational technology without losing the aesthetic qualities inherent in the best current production. This covers not just the relationship between different media specialisms but also the relationship between the media knowledge reviewed here and the instructional development knowledge reviewed in Part 4.

The relationship between media knowledge and instructional development knowledge becomes even more critical when distance education is considered. Not only do many distance learning systems combine video resources with single media, but they also tend to be more systematically developed than most other learning systems. The articles in the Distance Education section discuss the nature of distance education and different forms of provision, as an important aspect of media potential, utilization, and impact. Instructional development issues are left for fuller treatment in Part 4, and the distribution of media resources in curriculum packages, through libraries by publications, or through broadcasting is discussed in Part 5.

1. Computers

The first five articles in this Section are primarily concerned with elucidating the potential of computers for education, making conceptual distinctions, and describing some fundamentally different modes of use. The last two articles review their application in the schools and adult education sectors, their impact, and some of the problems of implementation.

Rushby opens the section with a conceptual review of *Computer-assisted Learning* (CAL), which he distinguishes from computer managed learning by its ongoing interaction between computer and student. The term *computer-assisted instruction* is avoided because it is only appropriate for CAL modes in which the locus of control rests firmly with the computer. Rushby suggests that this applies only to the "drill and practice" and "tutorial" modes. The learner has considerable influence in the "simulation" and "modelling" modes, and still more when the computer is used for an "interactive knowledge-based system" or for general "information seeking". Rushby also looks at methods of use which he classifies according to group size (class, individual, or small group) and additional equipment (input devices, audiovisual presentation, and access to a larger computer). An implementation section focuses on the design, testing, and production of CAL packages.

Finally, Rushby reviews peripheral hardware, computer software, and overall costs and benefits.

McMahon's companion article on *Computer-managed Learning* (CML) distinguishes three main aspects of the process. First, data has to be acquired and entered into the computer which includes both standard student data and a more detailed assessment of their knowledge and achievement. This data is often obtained by tests specially designed for the purpose, which are usually diagnostic pretests and posttests for each instructional unit. Second, information is fed back to the teacher and/or the student, often incorporating a detailed analysis of performance. This is usually accompanied by instructions or advice on what to do next. Such advice is based on predetermined sets of rules called routing systems. Third, CML systems normally provide records or reports for subsequent use. While CML systems hitherto have been largely based on mastery learning principles, McMahon suggests that pedagogies other than individually prescribed instruction could also be supported by appropriate CML.

Two short specialist articles follow. Leclercq reviews *Computer-managed Testing* and Thomas reviews *Computer-assisted Counseling*. The testing applications cover the management of item banks; the preparation of test material by selecting and printing out stored items according to each new brief; the administration of tests to students at a keyboard, possibly interactively or including presentations on linked audiovisual presentation devices. Testing is also used as an integral test scoring and data processing part of a CML system. Counselling applications range from routine administrative and information-providing tasks to on-line assistance to clients. Counsellors may also use computers for their own training, where the simulation mode is particularly useful.

Salomon's article on *Computers in the Curriculum* uses his long experience in media research to address two fundamental issues. What unique functions can computers serve? How can the use of the computer be integrated into the curriculum and daily school activities? Salomon's analysis of computers as media is based on four dimensions: the information or content presented, the symbolic modalities, the activities pursued by students, and the relations that are possible between the learner and the technology. He argues that the uniqueness of the computer lies in its capacity to combine several attributes into a fully integrated communication pattern, and to establish a highly interactive relationship with each learner. The computer is able to amplify cognitive, communicative, and instructional functions, but there is no evidence to support the suggestion that it can enhance mental abilities. Successful integration of computers into the curriculum will depend on curriculum designers taking into account their unique contribution at three different levels, those of goals and objectives, pedagogical thought, and learning experiences. Ideally, the fields of educational computer and curriculum design should be in a reciprocal relationship with each affecting the other.

The pace of change in the computing field is so rapid that both the applications articles were newly written for this *Encyclopedia*. Smith begins his review of *Microcomputers in Schools* by reminding us how their sudden arrival on the scene preceded any proper analysis of their educational role. Moreover, it was accompanied by a boom in the home computer market, the result being that some students knew more about computers than their teachers, while others had no experience at all. In many Western countries, the computer soon became an important status symbol for schools but uneven purchasing and access created problems of social equity and gender equity. There has also been a major debate about the relative priority of computer studies as a specialist, vocationally oriented subject, computer literacy as a new component of general education, and the use of computers as an aid to teaching ordinary school subjects. Against this background, major problems in introducing computers into schools have included teacher training, the variety and changing nature of the hardware, the low level of access in all but the richest schools, and the aptly described "software famine". For less developed countries, which cannot afford to make costly mistakes, the problems are even greater. Smith also points out that instructional modes of CAL have become less dominant as patterns of use have diversified throughout the 1980s. However, this has accentuated the timelag between the practices of the enthusiastic pioneers and reliable independent evaluations of the benefits to learners.

Graebner's companion review of *Microcomputers in Adult Education* reflects the greater range of learning contexts in the adult sector and the relative scarcity of documentation. She draws attention to the major impact on thinking about adult education of the post-industrial model of nonformal education and decentralized learning. Even though progress towards this kind of provision has been slow, it has been closely linked in many people's minds with the introduction of information technology. However, the greatest regular use probably occurs in the more formalized, though increasingly flexible, computer-based training programmes of large companies. Other new initiatives have occurred in training projects supported by the European Commission's Social Fund. Aimed at disadvantaged groups, provision of experience with new technology is a mandated requirement. Although largely dominated by vocational training, often to meet the increasing number of jobs requiring work with computers, adult education also provides a context for experimenting with more learner-controlled uses of computers in accordance with its long-established emancipatory tradition. Finally, Graebner reviews some significant areas of development: advanced computer-based training; information storage and retrieval; distance learning, electronic mail, and improved communications; and support for individual adult learners, especially those with disabilities or other special needs.

2. Film, Television, and Video

The opening article by Wagner discusses *The Role of Film, Television, and Video* in our society, as technical and economic changes create new patterns for the production, distribution, and utilization of moving picture images. Film and television production are converging, and already it is not uncommon for material to be shot on film, edited on videotape, and then distributed in both media. The arrival of interactive video brings a totally new dimension, allowing not only user participation but user control as well. The increasing quality of low-cost equipment enables consumers to become producers, so there is a wide range of possible relationships between the producers and the consumers of video material. While the pessimists see a greater centralization of media power, the optimists stress the increased access to production facilities and even to communication networks of less powerful, less wealthy, and minority groups. Unfortunately, education is in a weak position, having neither the power to influence future developments nor a clear rationale for how video materials can best be used to improve the quality of learning.

The rest of the section is more specifically concerned with contemporary practice. The reviews, for example, of *Use of Television in the Classroom* and *Use of Film in the Classroom* necessarily dwell on programmes in common use. However, as Rockman and Burke point out in their survey of developments in educational television in several countries, practice has never been static. Both articles note the variety of roles which film or television may be expected to play, for example, enhancing quality, extending children's experience, demonstrating model behaviour, improving effectiveness, equalizing opportunity, providing motivation, and developing affective education. Each article then draws attention to factors affecting the successful use of video resources in the classroom. Rockman and Burke discuss viewing conditions, teacher knowledge and attitudes, and instructional design while Hammond also discusses audience variables, raising issues of prior experience, visual literacy, cognitive structure, ability level, and cognitive style. Hammond concludes with general advice on the use of film and a summary of the advantages and disadvantages of the medium. Rockman and Burke prefer to use four case studies of television series to illustrate a range of contemporary approaches to the design and use of video resources in the classroom. Both emphasize the importance of integrating the design of video messages with that of ancillary material and classroom activities.

Turner's article on *Video Production as a Learning Activity* adds a new dimension to Wagner's theme of the consumer turned producer, for he transfers the focus from access to communication networks to what is learned from being involved in production. In media studies, for example, learners come to understand how the medium is manipulated when they have to make their own programmes. Moreover, participation in video production is such a powerful motivating force that it often leads to the significant development of pupils' communication and social skills. This is especially true for children with specific learning or behaviour difficulties. The learning of academic content is also enhanced when it becomes the focus for a class or small-group video production. Finally, it is increasingly recognized how much people learn from seeing themselves perform, whether in sport, in the performing arts, or in developing interpersonal skills. Self-recording now plays an important part in several areas of professional education, not least in teacher training.

This brings us to microteaching, the subject of the next four articles. Perlberg introduces the process of microteaching and examines its *Conceptual and Theoretical Bases*, contrasting the pragmatic approach of Allen with the behaviour-modification approach of McDonald. Common to all approaches are the ideas of starting teacher training in a controlled laboratory setting, getting early practice in "safe" situations, and adopting an analytic approach to teaching. There is, however, still much argument about the procedures to be followed and the particular teaching skills to be developed. Perlberg argues that transfer to regular classroom situations tends to be taken for granted, when it could be aided by a developmental approach. Newly acquired skills can be integrated in the laboratory setting as trainees progress from short lessons with a small group to longer lessons with a large group.

MacLeod's review of the *Effectiveness of Microteaching* concludes that the only unanimous finding is that participants enjoy and value the experience. Many comparative studies are apparently favourable but small sample sizes, large within-group differences, and variations in procedure from one study to another make it difficult to draw any clear conclusions. There is considerable debate about the validity of the criterion measures of teaching effectiveness. MacLeod also extends Perlberg's analysis to include cognitive approaches to microteaching which emphasize the development of teacher self-awareness and thinking.

Two important aspects of many microteaching procedures are *Feedback* and *Modeling*. These form the subjects of two further articles by Levis and MacLeod. Feedback may be provided by video or audiorecording, accompanied by comments from peers and/or pupils and/or a designated supervisor. Self-evaluation guides can also be used. Evidence suggests that some form of focus is essential for good feedback, almost regardless of mode, and that the affective dimension cannot be ignored. Research also shows that modelling plays an important part in the acquisition of teaching skills during microteaching, in accordance with Bandura's theory of social learning. Perceptual modelling using video is slightly favoured over symbolic modelling using print, but both have positive effects. This can be enhanced by dissemination training and, in such cases, it is suggested that feedback is less important.

At this stage, it is useful to note that the analysis of teaching into sets of skills, so fundamental to most microteaching procedures, is only one approach to the questions of "What is effective teaching?" and "How can it best be developed?". More detailed discussions of these issues can be found in *The International Encyclopedia of Teaching and Teacher Education*, a companion volume in this series.

The section concludes with Leinhardt's review of *Video Recording in Educational Research*. She distinguishes between using videotape as an audiovisual data source for analyzing teacher–student interactions, and using it as a record for subsequent review and discussion. While the former is associated with process–product studies and evaluation research, the latter is used in research on teacher thinking and decision making. Yet another approach is used by ethnographic researchers. Leinhardt surveys techniques under four main headings: entrance into the setting; the time-frame; the audio and visual points of focus; and the general orientation or perspective of the recording. Finally, she discusses the possible effect of introducing recording agents and equipment on the validity of the record.

3. Simple Media

This third section could be described as residual, that is, it contains all those media which cannot be classified as computers or video. It does, however, have coherence. With little exception the media in this section are simple to use and simple to produce. While more sophisticated means of production are sometimes justified, many of the materials can be produced simply and effectively by the teachers themselves. Moreover, much of the quality of such materials resides not just in their design but in the pedagogic thinking that underpins it. The impact of these simple media is even more dependent on the skills of the classroom teacher than the more complex and expensive computer-based and video materials.

The first three articles, *Graphic Production*, *Photographic Production*, and *Reprography* are closely related. The authors review the range of techniques available for producing and copying print, graphic, or photographic materials. These materials may be projected (e.g. slides), displayed (e.g. posters), or distributed (e.g. worksheets) for individual study or group discussion. Sometimes the work is entirely original. Often materials are developed from existing materials by copying, labelling, redesign, or reassembly into a form that is more appropriate for classroom use. Dayton's article on *Graphic Production* focuses on design, illustration, lettering, and assembly, with a concluding section on computer graphic systems. Burbank and Pett's entries on *Photographic Production* and *Reprography* concentrate more on the production techniques used by media service units, and their relative advantages and disadvantages. Many of these services can also be found in school offices or staffrooms (reprographic), or art or science departments (photographic). Much of the photographic work involves copying and titling, while reprography also covers the production of overhead transparencies from opaque originals.

Moldstad's article on *Overhead Transparency Projection* also gives some attention to production, but its main focus is on utilization. The overhead projector is one of the easiest media for the teacher to use without training, though even an hour's training would greatly improve most teachers' practice. Its flexibility, ease of updating, and association with didactic modes of presentation make it especially popular in upper-secondary and higher education. Moldstad's survey covers equipment, patterns of use, and relevant research.

Two further methods of communication to large groups, *Bulletin Board Displays* and *Boardwork*, are covered by Tyo. In spite of their common usage, these media are little researched. So Tyo has to rely on logic, commonsense, and generally accepted pedagogic and aesthetic principles. His advice covers the construction of various types of display facilities and boards, the pedagogic purposes they can serve, and the design of the messages they carry.

Flanagan faces similar problems in reviewing *Printed Materials in the Classroom*. She reminds us of the wide range of printed materials found in classrooms and the variety of pedagogic purposes they can serve. In addition to many kinds of book—picture book, textbook, workbook, reference book, topic book, "paperback"—there are pamphlets and worksheets, and source materials like newspapers, documents, and magazines.

Sound is a medium which has suffered unnecessarily from the advent of television, yet it offers great potential and flexibility. Technical developments were reviewed in Part 2. Here simpler formats are reviewed by Trowbridge in *Sound Resources in the Classroom* and more complex ones by Higgins in *Language Laboratories*. Trowbridge adopts the perspectives of a teacher and a headteacher when he discusses the provision and organization of equipment and surveys a large number of applications and techniques. He also includes an introductory section on effective listening. Higgins examines the growth and decline of the language laboratory, while speculating on its possible revival with the enhanced potential for interactivity provided by microcomputers and the arrival of interactive video.

Moldstad's review of *Media Utilization* is primarily concerned with research on the levels of utilization of different media in the classroom. This includes film and television but not computers. Though somewhat dated, the pattern is revealing; and some of the reasons given reflect less on media potential than on the availability of media resources and the traditional nature of many teachers' pedagogic preferences. There are, as might be expected, differences between levels of education and between subjects.

The section concludes with Megarry's review of *Simulation and Gaming*, located here because most simulations and games are still based on simple media although the use of computer-based materials is growing. These should be seen as expanding the repertoire rather than replacing many simpler materials. Megarry carefully distinguishes, with the aid of several examples, between games, simulations, simulation games (which belong to both categories), and role playing. She then discusses their impact on motivation and learning, their tendency to take up a great deal of teacher time in preparation and even in classroom use, as well as other benefits and limitations. Further sections cover classroom preparation and use, the adaptation and design of games, evaluation, and a guide to the literature on materials and techniques.

4. Distance Education

The term *distance education* is used to denote learning contexts where the learner is distant from and rarely, if at all, meets his or her "main" teacher. Access to supplementary local tuition would not prevent a student from being described as a distance learner, provided the tutor did not assume the role of "manager" of that student's learning. However, supported self-study programmes of the kind organized by many schools and colleges would be excluded, because the learning is managed by teachers who are regularly visited by the students concerned. The term "independent study" is commonly used to describe such situations. Apart from children's television, the subject of the first article, distance education for children of school age is relatively rare outside remote rural areas. Indeed, a number of experiments to develop distance learning systems for school age children were later abandoned as too expensive to sustain. With adults, however, the use of distance education is still increasing, and new developments continue to be reported in all parts of the world.

Rainsberry's review of *Children's Television* has been included here, because it is primarily concerned with the use of the medium, and the nature of the programmes. More policy-related issues are discussed in Part 5(b) on Educational Broadcasting. Rainsberry examines the wide range of television programmes designed to educate children as well as entertain them, focusing on some of the most common formats. He discusses the work of some agencies specifically concerned with children's television and reviews the relevant research. Rainsberry argues that what the research does not adequately reveal is the importance of aesthetic factors in determining both the quality and the impact of programmes.

This theme is also noted in the following article on *Mass Media in Adult Education*. Robinson and Groombridge's review ranges from contexts where the learning process is almost incidental, as with many arts and documentary programmes, to those where it is precisely planned by a process of instructional design. In this latter case, discussed in some detail in Part 4, audiovisual media usually form part of a multimedia learning system or package in which the major instructional burden is carried by printed materials. Sometimes nonprint materials are used in a supplementary role or to convey some essentially audio or visual content. However, often their role is primarily motivational or catalytic, providing human contact, opportunities for feedback, a sense of learning community, and a common experience for learners to discuss when and if they meet each other. Local tutors may also be helped by such materials. The article also includes, as its title may suggest, some reference to the use of mass media in adult learning contexts other than those concerned with distance education.

Kaye's article on *Distance Learning Systems* is clearly central to this section. He examines the rationale for distance education, the evolution of more complex multimedia systems from simple correspondence courses and the main characteristics of effective distance learning systems. Areas given special emphasis are institutional structures for developing and delivering distance education, factors affecting the design of teaching materials, and the skills needed by students to gain the most benefit from distance learning. These skills and important motivational aspects of distance learning also figure prominently in Burge and Frewin's entry on *Self-directed Learning in Distance Education*. They examine issues of openness and student autonomy in distance education courses, raising the possibility of more student-centred courses and greater learner participation in course decisions.

The Section concludes with Robinson's review of *Telephones in Education*. This article mainly focuses on distance education, but it is timely to consider whether some of the practices she describes could not also play a useful role in more traditional learning systems. As practices such as teleconferencing become more familiar, their pattern of use may change. Meanwhile, the use of telephones for communication between computers is rapidly rising. This is noted in the articles on *Videotex and Electronic Mail* (Part 2) and *Microcomputers in Adult Education* [Part 3(a)].

Computers

Computer-assisted Learning

N. J. Rushby

One of the consequences of the rapid growth of computers in education is that the terminology has become confused and confusing. Different people use the term "computer-assisted learning" (CAL) to mean a number of different things all concerned with the use of a computer to learn about something. For the purposes of this article, however, a more precise definition is required.

First, it must be made clear that the concern of this article is with learning with the aid of computers, rather than learning about computers. However, this distinction is rather blurred because the aid of computers must be enlisted to learn about them as objects, and because in learning about some other subject with the aid of computers, something is inevitably learned about the computers themselves.

Within the overall field of learning with the aid of the computer, distinction should be made between the use of the computer to manage learning by supporting the assessment, routing, recordkeeping, and reporting functions, and the more intimate intervention in the learning process itself. Computer-managed learning (CML) is discussed in the next article, while computer-assisted learning (CAL) is examined below.

Again, the distinction between CAL and CML is rather blurred, for some computer-assisted learning materials can help with assessment, keep records, and advise learners on their route through their course of study. Similarly, some CML systems take advantage of the assessment function to provide feedback which assists the students to learn.

Distinction might also be made between computer-assisted learning (CAL) and computer-assisted training (CAT) on the grounds that the aims and methods of training are rather different from those of education. However, both are concerned with learning, and in practice there are more similarities than differences between the two. Most of the knowledge and skills of CAL are equally appropriate in training.

Fundamentally, all that computers do, whether they are used for scientific calculations, weather forecasting, banking, or training, is to process information by moving it from place to place, combining it, and comparing it according to a set of prespecified rules called a "program". This is true both for very large computers and for small, personal, microcomputers. Thus, although the advent of microcomputers has brought quantitative changes to CAL, it would be misleading to assume that CAL only started when microcomputers became widely available. The first research in CAL dates back to the late 1950s, and the principles, developed since that time, are applicable to all sizes of computer.

Computer-assisted learning therefore, is concerned with the use of computers to mediate in the flows of information in the learning process. These may be flows between the learner and the factual information that he or she must absorb, feedback from the learner on his or her progress, information about a model with which the learner is working, or flows between the learner and his or her tutor or studies advisor. This provides a framework for looking at CAL in more detail, for several different methods and modes of CAL can be identified by considering the way in which the computer is used to mediate the information flows.

1. CAL as a Learning Medium

The process of learning is typically supported by a variety of media to provide information and to help the learner to organize his or her growing knowledge. Each different medium has its own strengths and weaknesses so media are selected to match specific learning problems and blended so that the weaknesses in one are overcome by the strengths of another.

The main strength of the computer as a learning medium is its ability to process information very quickly and accurately. The set of rules (the computer program) which specifies the way in which the information is to be manipulated can be very complex, yet the processing can be completed so quickly as to appear almost instantaneous to the learner. This makes it possible for the computer to accept and act upon a variety of different kinds of response from the learner and to provide information in textual, graphical, and animated form. The computer can control and coordinate information from other pieces of equipment, for example a slide projector or videodisc player; and based on the learner's progress through a piece of structured material, it can make sophisticated decisions as to what course to follow next.

This gives it an ability to adapt and respond to the learner's needs, difficulties, and progress which is very much greater than that of a book or videotape, but which is still less than that of a real tutor. Although it may be less impersonal than a tape/slide, it should not be regarded as a substitute for another human being.

Its weaknesses arise from its technology. The real cost of computing equipment continues to fall, it continues to get smaller and more sophisticated, but it will still be some time before a really cheap, fully intelligent, pocket size, ubiquitous CAL system is developed. So, in adding CAL to the toolkit of learning media it is necessary to be aware of its particular strengths and weaknesses.

2. Modes of CAL

Within this medium of CAL, there are a number of modes, shown in Fig. 1, which in practice overlap somewhat and are often used in combination. Each of these will be described in turn.

2.1 Drill and Practice

Perhaps the simplest form of CAL uses the computer to present the learner with a series of exercises which he or she must complete by giving some response—an answer. The computer processes that response (according to the rules embodied in its program) to determine whether or not it is "correct". It may then provide the learner with some feedback about the answer in the form of a congratulatory message if it was right, or a corrective comment if it was wrong, with perhaps a noncommital

message if the computer was unable to recognize the response. The exercises are specified in advance in their complete form or as templates which can be filled out according to a set of rules.

Computer-assisted learning offers a means of providing endless drill and practice without repetition, at a pace that can be controlled by the learner. It is possible to arrange that the nature of the exercises depends on the learner's progress. Thus, as he or she learns and his or her accuracy and speed improve, the exercises can become more difficult or conversely, if the learner makes too many mistakes, they can be made easier. Systematic mistakes can be detected and the computer can adapt the pattern of exercises to rectify this weakness. This ability to tailor a drill and practice session to the progress of each learner, combined with helpful feedback, can lead to more effective learning.

2.2 Tutorial

The lay image of CAL is of serried ranks of students, each seated in front of a computer keyboard and screen, all learning in their own way and at their own pace. There is an assumption that each student is participating in some sort of tutorial where he or she is taken on a journey through the learning material via a dialogue in which information is presented and feedback is elicited through a process of question, answer, and challenge.

In its simplest form, this tutorial dialogue bears a close resemblance to the programmed learning sequences found in print and on teaching machines in the 1960s. It is reasonable to ask what the computer can add to the material apart from illuminating the text. If that were all, then there could be little benefit in using the computer; a book would be better. However, programmed texts present a number of problems, particularly in determining whether the student has really mastered the current step and in deciding how to branch to the next step. Self-assessment may require the student to make difficult judgments and the routing may involve complex decisions based on his or her performance and progress through the material to date. This responsibility may make the student's work more, rather than less, difficult.

As in the drill and practice mode discussed earlier, the computer can be used not only to present the learning information but also to determine the student's needs and preferences, and to decide how to branch through the structured material. Thus, the material can be made more complex without adding to the student's burden.

In order to construct the CAL tutorial, the teachers (as a part of the production team) must set out the dialogue that they themselves might have with learners under various conditions, and decide upon the criteria which determine how they would adapt the pace and direction of their students' learning. These rules are then embodied in the computer program so that the computer can deliver an analogue of the real tutorial. Clearly, there must be some simplifications, because a real tutor does not slavishly follow preset rules as a computer must, but

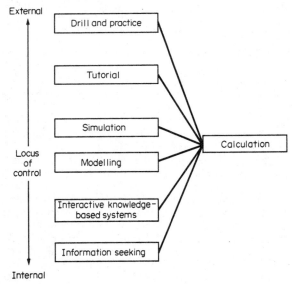

Figure 1
Modes of CAL

can also make use of insight, inspiration, and intelligence. However, in topics where it is reasonable to assume that most of the students will follow a few well-trodden routes through the material, this mode can be an effective way of learning.

Since the computer can only follow prespecified rules, it is difficult to arrange for it to exhibit very sophisticated intelligence and so present any real challenge to the human tutor. But, advances in artificial intelligence have led to programs which can handle very complex structures of rules and inferences, and can assist in the process of decision making. Such "expert systems" can be used to help fault diagnosis in very large systems like oil production platforms or to help doctors identify viral infections from a mass of symptoms and test results. If the program's decision-making process can be made transparent, and if the program is prepared to explain its "reasoning" and to answer any questions the student wants to ask, then the expert system can be turned into a very powerful tutorial system. However, until the early 1980s, the programs needed to support expert systems were orders of magnitude larger and more complex than those required to automate a programmed learning text. Although such systems had been developed during the 1970s, they required large (and expensive) computer facilities and so they remained in the research laboratory. It was not until the advent of the microcomputer-based expert system that artificial intelligence began to fulfill the promise that it had shown many years earlier.

Artificial intelligence ideas and tools can provide not only a representation of the knowledge to be acquired by the student, but also a model of the learning process which allows the computer tutorial to adapt to the learner's needs in a heuristic way. This is much more like the behaviour of a human tutor than the deterministic prespecified instruction inherent in the earlier forms of computer-mediated tutorials. The appropriate style—deterministic or heuristic—must be chosen to suit the particular learning situation.

2.3 Simulation

Both the tutorial and drill and practice modes of CAL operate by providing information in a structured way, according to rules specified by the author/tutor. Another facet of learning involves the student studying real-life systems or phenomena. Sometimes this is quite feasible, but there are some learning experiences which are too time consuming, too expensive, too difficult, or too dangerous. Among the many examples could be included: the study of genetics through Mendel's breeding experiments, the experience of running a small business, experiments in urban planning, and the operation of a nuclear reactor. Many simulations are already used in education and training, to provide surrogate experiences when an investigation of the real-life system is impractical. The simulation may be supported by a laboratory system, which must be constructed beforehand and may require expensive equipment. Or it may be based on printed materials, rather like a board game,

with a (possibly complex) rule book and a referee. In this case, the effective management of the simulation, the interpretation of the rules and the necessary calculations, may be difficult in the time available.

The computer can be used to emulate a real-life system by following a set of rules (a program) which approximates the behaviour of the real system. The quality of the approximation is governed by the author of the simulation who can specify the rules as being simple or complex. It may be educationally desirable to provide various levels of approximation within the same simulation package, so that it can be used to show the effects of increasing experimental error or to give a feeling for the accuracy of the simulation.

The advantage of a CAL simulation over the use of other equipment and media, is in the flexibility and control which the computer can bring. The computer is a general purpose information processing machine which is transformed into a machine to carry out a specific task by the program within it. Thus, with different programs the same computer can simulate different systems. As it runs the simulation, it can also mediate between the student and the analogue of the real-life system, guiding him or her towards experiences which are likely to be helpful and providing some tutorial assistance where necessary.

There is a concomitant danger that the style of the tutorial dialogue will become too prescriptive, thus combining with limitations of the simulation to limit the student's exploration of the analogue and pre-empt his or her results. The essence of the simulation is that the student should be able to ask the question "what happens if. . .?" and be able to find the answer.

The main difficulty with all simulations, whether they use a computer or not, is in their credibility and in the transfer of learning to real life. Thus, although the simulation can be useful as a simplified learning experience (for example, by allowing the experimental error to be controlled), it should not be regarded as a total surrogate for experience of the real-life system or phenomena. Part of the credibility problem with computer-based simulations lies with the interface between the student and the computer. The student must control the simulation by entering data on a keyboard, or through other devices such as touch screens, light pens, joy sticks, or roller balls (these are described briefly below). Except in a few cases, these are very different from the means that he or she would use to control the real-life system, and can form an artificial barrier to learning. However, the experience has generally been that the problem can be ameliorated by introducing other factors, such as time pressure, which increase the sense of realism.

2.4 Modelling

This mode of CAL is similar to the simulation mode in that both help the student to learn by working with an analogue of a real-life system or phenomena, expressed as a set of rules within the computer. However, whereas in a simulation, the analogue is specified by the tutor, in modelling it is the student who must construct the analogue. In effect, the student must "teach" the computer the rules, so that it can emulate the real-life system in given circumstances and correctly predict the behaviour of the real-life system in new circumstances. The student learns through this process and demonstrates his or her mastery of the learning through the final model.

As with simulations, the technique of learning by modelling is not unique to CAL; it is possible to devise systems of rules or equations which describe the behaviour of the system to be studied, and to test these models in new circumstances, without using a computer. However, the computer provides a convenient way of checking the model, performing the calculations, and following through the set of rules, as an impartial referee.

The student must be provided with some means of teaching or programming the computer. This may be a general purpose computer programming language or a language developed specifically for this purpose, perhaps specifically for modelling in a specific subject area. Such specialization can reduce the learning effort needed to master the programming language; effort which might be considered "wasted" since it does not contribute directly to the main learning.

The problem of credibility is not so acute since the student is consciously working with the analogue and is trying to determine the underlying rules for its behaviour. For the same reason the problem of transferability is less. The mismatch between the real-life system and the student's analogue is not so much a barrier as a topic for investigation, so that the student can determine the inaccuracies and inadequacies. Then, if time allows, he or she can modify and refine the analogue so that it is a closer approximation.

2.5 Interactive Knowledge-based Systems

The preceding distinction between simulation and modelling for imperative analogues of real-world systems has a parallel in interactive knowledge-based systems (IKBS). These two modes may thus take an alternative approach. The imperative analogue comprises a set of (often mathematical) rules or equations which are used as instructions to the computer to govern the behaviour of the system. The IKBS comprises a descriptive model of the knowledge relating to a particular topic, system, or situation.

This can be explored by the learner, perhaps with an expert system providing tutorial guidance and explanation, or by means of asking questions which will lead to an understanding and assimilation of the knowledge. Alternatively the learner may use the IKBS to model his or her own knowledge of the topic, building and testing his or her own knowledge base. The best way to learn a subject is to teach it, and this use of an IKBS provides an opportunity for the student to "teach" the computer about the topic.

2.6 Information Seeking

The last of the six major modes of CAL uses the computer as a mentor and guide through a range of learning resources which might, but need not, be themselves based on a computer. The power of the computer to store, retrieve, and process information is used to help the student as he or she browses through the material, responding to questions about related information, retrieving items which are needed, summarizing statistical data, and suggesting possible lines of investigation that may be of interest.

This is also the least well-developed mode since it requires very substantial computing resources to cope with the large quantity of information that people are accustomed to using in libraries and resource centres and finding out from other people. Further, if it is to act as an effective mentor it must have some artificial "intelligence" at a higher level than is currently feasible in classroom systems. In its unintelligent form, where all the routes through the materials are prespecified and selected according to what is known about the student, the mode degenerates to the computer-managed learning (CML) routing function.

2.7 Calculation

In the early days of computers, before their full potential for general information processing was realized, they were regarded principally as calculating engines. It was natural to use them as sophisticated calculators to relieve some of the numerical labour involved in learning, in the numerical sciences and in statistics. It was noted earlier that, in practice, most CAL packages use components of several modes (for example simulation may be supported by some tutorial material) and calculation facilities are often to be found in packages which are predominantly drill and practice, tutorial, or simulations. A number of the larger, general purpose CAL systems provide the student with a "calculation mode" which he or she can select in the middle of a tutorial sequence to help work out some numerical results.

The mode could sensibly be widened to include other ways in which the computer can process information so as to relieve the student's work load and help him or her to reach through to the underlying ideas. Thus, the computer might be used to retrieve data from a large database and to prepare analyses and summaries.

As with the use of simulations, care must be taken to ensure that the computer does not replace too much of the activity. Although the calculation and other information processing is often an unnecessary nuisance because it takes time and can obscure the underlying facts and ideas, it may be that the student must understand the processing and be able to carry it out without the computer. If the calculation is always carried out by the computer then the student will lose out on valuable practice in circumstances where he or she is motivated by seeing it as a part of a larger process leading to a desired result. However, once he or she has had adequate practice, further repetition is tedious and demotivating, and could sensibly be undertaken by the computer.

2.8 Locus of Control

In Fig. 1, the various CAL modes are arranged along the dimension of a locus of control. Thus although the tutorial and drill and practice modes have certain similarities of style, they may be distinguished by the measure of control that the student has over his or her learning. In drill and practice the student must follow preset routes through the exercises devised by the tutor: in the tutorial mode he or she has rather more, and the tutor has rather less, control. A similar distinction can be drawn between simulation and modelling. At the top of the figure the locus of control is strongly external to the student—the tutor is in control; at the bottom, it is internal to the student—he or she is in control and the tutor takes on a facilitating rather than a prescribing role.

3. Methods

Distinction can also be made between different methods of using CAL materials in teaching and learning, all of which are familiar in other contexts with other media.

3.1 Computer-assisted Teaching

The CAL package can be used as a class demonstration, under the control of the teacher, either as the main focus of the lesson or to illustrate various points that may arise. This is similar to the laboratory demonstration or the use of a videotape (or filmstrip) with the whole class. The lesson may require some preparation by the students and the demonstration will be accompanied by group discussion. Clearly, this method works best with simulations and modelling; the more individualized modes of drill and practice, tutorial, and browsing, do not lend themselves to large group work, although there are some notable exceptions in primary education.

Logistically, the method requires only one computer equipped with several large displays so that the whole class can see the screens clearly. The computer may be operated by the teacher or by a chosen student.

The relatively modest requirement of a single computer makes it attractive where the availability of equipment is limited. Perhaps unfortunately, teachers aspire to a better provision of equipment and thence to more individualization of learning, and this has tended to mask the appropriate use of the method.

3.2 Individual Learning

What may be lost when a student participates in a CAL programme is the social aspect of learning, the opportunity for students to learn by face-to-face discussions with each other and with their tutor. It has often been criticized as an impersonal and dehumanized method of learning.

In part this is a reflection of the deterministic style of some tutorial material which resembles illuminated programmed instruction with the pages being turned by the computer. Some materials do not take appropriate advantage of the flexibility in response matching and branching offered by the computer and the resulting packages appear mechanistic. This problem can be reduced in material based on artificial intelligence techniques where the heuristic approach can give the impression of a conversation with a more human tutor. The fundamental criticism of isolated learning remains.

3.3 Small Group Learning

The use of CAL with small groups offers many of the advantages of the classroom teaching and individualized methods while avoiding their disadvantages. A group of two or three (perhaps as many as five or six) students work with the CAL package discussing the course of their joint learning, their inputs to the package, and the resulting output. The dialogue between the students is equally important as their dialogue with the computer which serves to stimulate their discussions and confirm (or contradict) their conclusions. Unlike the classroom demonstration, each member of the group has a good opportunity to influence what happens so that the learning is tailored to the individual members of the group; and unlike the totally individualized method of using CAL, the interpersonal aspects of learning are preserved and brought to the fore.

However, there are some instances, for example in drill and practice exercises, for which the small group method is inappropriate. As with the different CAL modes, each of these three methods has its strengths and weaknesses and should be selected with care.

3.4 Convergent Technologies

There is one additional and key factor which sets the computer and CAL apart from the other instructional equipment and media. This is its ability to control other pieces of equipment and hence the presentation of material through these media. In this respect, the computer is much closer to a real-life teacher (who of course can also control the computer!) than to the audiovisual equipment previously found in the classroom. Figure 2 shows the computer at the centre of a range of other equipment such as a videodisc, a random access slide projector, and so on, which it can control to show sequences of materials selected according to the student's immediate needs in combination with other material presented through the computer display.

In some cases, these additional facilities serve to improve the quality and ease of the computer-controlled presentation or of the students' responses to the system. In others, particularly in the combination of videocassette or disc and the computer, the result is qualitatively different, amounting to a new way of learning.

The result of this convergence between computer and video—"interactive video"—can be seen from three viewpoints. The video viewpoint is that it provides a

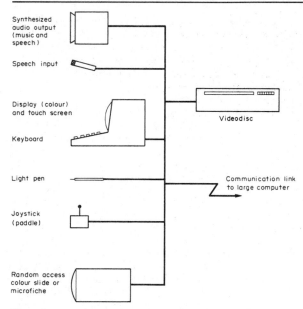

Figure 2
Some possible components of a CAL system

Labels in figure:
Synthesized audio output (music and speech)
Speech input
Display (colour) and touch screen
Keyboard
Light pen
Joystick (paddle)
Random access colour slide or microfiche
Videodisc
Communication link to large computer

way of resequencing and controlling video material, thus making that medium more flexible. The CAL viewpoint is that it provides a method of including very high resolution, animated, colour graphics in CAL packages by substituting pictures of the real thing for simplified diagrams.

The third viewpoint is that interactive video is a new medium in which the whole is greater than, and different from, the sum of its parts. By the early 1980s it had become clear that interactive video offered a range of new styles of learning and was likely, with artificial intelligence, to change the future face of computer-assisted learning (see *Interactive Video*).

4. Implementation

4.1 Overall Design

The detailed design of a CAL package follows from the overall instructional design of the system of which the package is one component. It has already been shown that CAL provides a new set of learning techniques which can be added to the instructional designer's toolkit to complement those using other media. The computer can be used to mediate in the flows of information in places where its ability to process information quickly and accurately, and to offer a measure of adaptability and interactivity with the learning materials are advantageous. Something of its limitations has also been seen in that it cannot (as yet) emulate the intelligence or intuition of a human tutor, although in some well-defined areas it can exhibit sufficient artificial intelligence to conduct an adequate teaching dialogue.

From a knowledge of the possibilities and limitations of CAL, its various modes and methods, the instructional designer can specify the role that the computer is to play in the whole system and move to a detailed description of the CAL package itself.

It should be recognized that this type of structured planning is the exception rather than the rule and that learning materials are more often designed piecemeal. A strategy which can be adopted for the initial study and introduction of an unfamiliar learning technique such as CAL, is to use noncritical material which is supplementary to the main course. This gives safeguards against failure with untried ideas, but results in components which have been "added on" to an existing course and which may not use the new medium to best effect. The assembly of disparate components, designed at different times, perhaps with different aims and different philosophies, may also lead to problems of incompatibility.

4.2 Detailed Design

The outline instructional design determines:

(a) the detailed objectives of the package;

(b) the method to be used;

(c) the CAL mode to be used;

(d) the relationships between the package and other components of the systems.

The next stage is to determine the interaction between the student (or students) as he or she progresses through the package and then to design the dialogue—what will be shown on the computer display, what responses the student is expected to make, and the consequences of this input. At this point the design starts to divide into three areas:

(a) the learning sequence;

(b) the presentation of information on the computer display and through any other media controlled by the computer;

(c) the processing of the student's responses.

The first of these will not be discussed in any detail since the design of learning sequences is not unique to CAL; this is a specific application of general principles. Clearly, the CAL mode (drill and practice, tutorial, simulation, modelling, IKBS, or information-seeking) will be reflected in the sequence; for example, the student will progress through a tutorial sequence from some appropriate starting point to an appropriate finishing point, while his or her progress through a CAL simulation may be repetitive as he or she works through the simulation a number of times, trying different conditions and answering a number of different questions about its behaviour in different circumstances.

Early examples of CAL, written in the 1960s and 1970s, were predominantly text oriented because of the limitations of the computer terminals of that time.

Although there were some terminals that could display simple diagrams, it took some time to draw these on the screen and the equipment was expensive. With the advent of microelectronics, the cost of terminals that could display graphics, first in monochrome and then in colour, fell dramatically and the speed at which material could be presented on the display screen increased. Thus there has been a progression of styles of presentation, from text printed on a typewriter-like terminal, through text displayed as a series of "pages" on a display screen, to text mixed with black and white or colour graphics with the possibility of animation. Unfortunately, with a few notable exceptions, most designers of CAL packages failed to appreciate how to use these new facilities appropriately so that typical displays were packed with text, diagrams were used in a haphazard fashion, and the student became confused by the plethora of information on the screen.

Although the computer display screen cannot be regarded as an electronic equivalent of a page in a book, useful guidelines can be derived from the graphics design of printed material.

First, the amount of information displayed at any one time should be kept to a minimum, consistent with maintaining a smooth flow through the learning sequence. It is very tedious to follow a dialogue which is displayed as a sequence of very short passages, or even as individual sentences. One way of avoiding this problem is to treat the screen as a dynamic display to which additional material can be added. If there must be a long text passage, then it can be built up in a series of steps with a pause after each. This gives the student a chance to read and digest each step without feeling pressured by a stream of text, written on the screen much faster than he or she could possibly read.

Where large quantities of text are required then it may be preferable to present them in the form of printed notes or perhaps on slides or microfiche. Printed notes have the advantage that the student can refer back to them whenever he or she pleases; this is not always easy to arrange within a computer program.

More recent CAL materials make extensive use of graphics on the principle that one colour diagram is worth a thousand words of text—particularly when the diagram is animated. Again the screen is used as a dynamic display with specific areas being used in a consistent way to show text and pictures. As the dialogue progresses, parts of the display can be erased or overwritten with new material. However, it is helpful to maintain a consistent style so that the diagrams and text always appear in the same places on the display.

The student should always know what is expected of him or her and what options are available to control progress through the learning sequence. These options may include the facility to go back and review earlier material, to end the sequence, to carry out some calculations, to change some of the parameters in a simulation, to list the available options, and so on. There have been some attempts to standardize these options and to provide a uniform list of commands that the student can use as he or she works through the package. Like all standards in the areas of education and computing, this idea has not been widely adopted except within sets of packages produced by specific teams using their own specific standards.

The third area is the design of the student's side of the interaction. The student must be able to respond to what is displayed by the computer, either by typing messages on a typewriter-like keyboard, or by indicating a position on the display. Some systems also provide for limited speech recognition and can be set up to respond to standard commands spoken into a microphone.

From the student's point of view, the simplest form of response is for him or her to indicate a particular position on the display screen. This can be touch sensitive so that the computer can detect when and where the screen is touched. Or the student can point at the screen with a light pen. Again the computer can detect when and where the pen is pointed. An alternative method is for the student to position a cursor on the screen, by using a joy stick control, a rolling ball, or a series of buttons. When the cursor is in the desired position, then a switch is depressed to identify it.

Those familiar with computers often take keyboard input for granted, but in doing so they make assumptions about the student's ability to type. As long as the input is kept very short, one or a few characters at the most, then there is unlikely to be any great difficulty, but if longer responses, perhaps sentences, are required, then the student's lack of keyboard skills may interfere with his or her learning. Single key depressions may suffice to select one option from a menu, or to pick one answer in a multiple-choice question. If the responses "yes", "no", "help", "stop", and so on cannot be provided by a set of special keys, they can be obtained by typing only two, three, or four characters. The difficulties become more severe when constructed responses are needed. The student may need extra time to hunt and peck his or her way through a long response and spelling mistakes are more likely. Constructed responses also present technical problems for the recognition of unexpected words and syntax. Here again, artificial intelligence techniques may be needed to work out the meaning.

The student's side of the dialogue must be designed with care to ensure that he or she has the maximum freedom of expression, and that no matter what input is made the package will respond in a sensible way.

4.3 Formative Evaluation

In the usual model of instructional design the pilot materials undergo a formative evaluation to determine how well they meet the original educational objectives. They can then be improved in the light of this evaluation. Evidence for the evaluation may be gathered from pre- and post-tests, from interview data, and from observations of the students using the material. In a

CAL package the computer can be used to record the flow of information between the student and the learning material, and to carry out various analyses of the student response data. The problem is not so much one of collecting sufficient information for an evaluation, but one of deciding which information is relevant and which analyses are appropriate. Some examples of drill and practice and tutorial packages are sufficiently adaptive that they can, in effect, carry out a continuous formative evaluation and modify their material according to the needs of each individual student.

It has been shown that a CAL package may be made up of a number of components including, and usually centred on, a computer program. Some or all of these components may need to be changed in the light of the evaluation. Of these, the computer program is often the easiest to change; there is no need for substantial retyping to insert, delete, or amend passages of print-based material, for new photographic slides, or for editing of video sequences. Modifications to the program (the set of rules which control the processing) can be made quickly and tried out immediately, so that the iterative process of evaluation and adaptation can be repeated a number of times before the package is completed.

4.4 The Production Team

The production of a CAL package has a number of similarities with the production of video-based material. Both require a variety of specialisms, including:

(a) subject knowledge;

(b) instructional design;

(c) graphics design;

(d) programming.

While some smaller packages may be conceived, designed, and produced by individuals, it is more usual for this to be done by a team involving one or more subject specialists, an educational technologist, a graphics designer, and a computer programmer. It may also be helpful to include a student who has previously studied the material, for while teachers are familiar with the teaching problems it is the students who are closest to the learning problems. Some groups also include an independent researcher to evaluate the materials.

Clearly the size and nature of the team depends on the kind of CAL package that is being produced. Three broad groups can be identified:

(a) *The "home movie" package.* This is a package produced quickly and at a minimal cost to meet the immediate needs of a single teacher. In many cases it will be produced by the teacher himself or herself and it is unlikely to be very polished or accompanied by well-developed supporting materials. It is analogous to the home-produced worksheet run off on a spirit duplicator.

(b) *The "inhouse" production.* This is a development of the previous type, where more resources have been devoted to producing a package which will meet the needs of a group of teachers, each of whom may have contributed to the design. The package is more polished and more robust so that it does not rely on the presence of its author to use it effectively. There will be more supporting materials probably in the form of student notes and worksheets.

(c) *The published package.* This is a package which has been designed and produced for general use. It is carefully developed and polished to meet a particular teaching need, or topic in the syllabus, and is supported by equally well-developed materials such as teachers' and students' notes, worksheets, and supplementary reading. Such packages are analogous to textbooks and are increasingly published in a similar way to school texts.

5. The Computing Aspects

A detailed description of the computing equipment needed to support CAL can be found elsewhere in this encyclopedia. It is appropriate here to discuss how this equipment relates to CAL and to say a little about the programming languages which can be used to specify the way in which the computers should process the information.

5.1 Hardware

It has already been shown that the computer can be used to control other pieces of equipment in the learning environment. Fig. 2 shows some (but by no means all) of the "accessories" that might be involved in an elaborate complex. This does not imply that all of this equipment is, or should be, involved; again there must be an informed decision as to what is appropriate in different circumstances. The prime consideration in each case is the way in which the different pieces of equipment contribute to the overall interaction with the student. Thus, some of them: (a) the display screen; (b) the random access colour slide or microfiche display; (c) the videodisc; and (d) the synthesized audio output are concerned with the presentation of information to the student. Each has different characteristics. The computer display can produce straight text mixed with simple pictures which may be animated. More complex graphics require complex programs. These are time-consuming to write and it may be far easier to record these on a videodisc or random access videocassette. Colour slide and microfiche are relatively cheap to produce and can reproduce fine detail, but cannot provide animation.

Each of the above provides visual information; audio output can be achieved through random access audio tape or cassette players or, more recently, by synthesized speech or music. Since it can take an appreciable time to locate a desired sequence at random on an audiotape or cassette, speech synthesis is attractive and is now financially practical, with the falling cost of microelectronics. Audio output can, of course, also be provided by the videodisc.

As yet, most CAL materials only use visual information, perhaps supplemented by some audio. The possibility of using the other senses of touch, smell, and taste under computer control has not been exploited.

The other pieces of technology shown in Fig. 2 are concerned with input by the student to the system. These are the keyboard, the light pen, the joystick, and speech input; and they are discussed above in the section on implementation.

5.2 Software

The computer hardware, the metal, glass, and plastic components of the computer system, makes up a general purpose information processing machine which must be organized to carry out a specific function by means of a set of instructions called a program. The set of programs for different functions is collectively termed the computer "software". In broad terms, each CAL package, be it a tutorial, a simulation, or a package for browsing, will require a separate set of instructions or program to specify precisely how the information is to be processed and how the interaction will proceed.

Now, sets of instructions can be nested: in other words, one set of instructions can be used to turn the computer into a machine which is able to work with a further set of instructions. The computer can be thought of as an onion with the hardware at the core and the software represented by the layers of skin. The basic, electronic computer is a completely general purpose information processing machine which is transformed into successively more specific machines by the successive layers of software. Each layer forms the input data for the program layer beneath, and provides successively more sophisticated facilities for the interaction between the student and the computer.

Some of the inner program layers are supplied by the manufacturers of the computer system: the outermost layers must be written specifically for the CAL task, using the facilities provided by those beneath. Different circumstances and different tasks are best satisfied by different underlying layers and starting points. The producers of CAL programs typically use one of two alternative approaches. The first is to write the programs in a general purpose programming language such as BASIC, FORTRAN, or PASCAL. The programming language is itself a software layer which provides a general range of facilities for arithmetic and logical operations suitable for solving a range of information processing problems. The advantage of this approach is that the same language, with the same facilities, is likely to be available on many different computers and so the CAL program can be transferred and used with other hardware without great difficulty. The disadvantage is that the language aims to provide a range of facilities but is not specifically designed for CAL. Thus, although the author

achieves everything he requires, many of the facilities are not in the most convenient or obvious form, so that writing the programs requires rather more knowledge and programming skill.

The alternative approach is to use one of the many special purpose CAL author languages. This is an alternative software layer which provides special facilities deemed to be of use to the CAL author. The language may include such facilities as:

(a) the organization of the output into display frames (similar to those used in programmed instruction texts);

(b) the matching of student input with anticipated responses allowing for misspellings;

(c) the keeping of student records.

In contrast with the use of general purpose languages, CAL author languages facilitate the programming of instructional dialogues by nonspecialists, but can present problems for transferability and may not provide adequate facilities for the complicated calculations needed in simulations. Consequently, they are most likely to be used for the tutorial or drill and practice modes of CAL, while general purpose languages are favoured for programming simulations and browsing. The modelling mode of CAL requires the student to write his or her own program. To do this a general purpose language or a simplified programming language designed specifically for the task, and offering a restricted range of facilities, may be used.

6. Costs and Benefits

Like all other ways of teaching and learning, CAL involves some costs in the form of resources to introduce it, to develop or acquire materials, and to operate it in the classroom. In return, it offers some benefits. The cost benefits of CAL should now be examined and related—briefly—to other media.

The costs of using CAL are readily identifiable and are comprised of people costs and equipment costs. Both of these may be divided into the costs of producing the materials and the cost of delivering it to the students. In common with other forms of resource-based learning, CAL shifts the bulk of the people costs from the delivery (recurrent) budget to the production (capital) budget. The time expended by the team of teachers, graphics designers, and programmers (described above) will depend on the kind of material being produced. Clearly, more resources will be needed to develop a highly polished publishable package, than to produce the CAL equivalent of a teacher's own worksheet. Different projects have reported figures varying between 30 and 600 hours to produce one hour of student learning.

While the top end of this range seems an alarming figure, it is comparable with the resources needed to produce video-based material, or to write and publish a good textbook. The production team also need access to good computing facilities to write and test the CAL programs, but the costs of these are small in comparison with the real costs of the production team.

The costs of the computing equipment needed to support the delivery of the material are more significant since, depending on the method used, one computer is required for each class, student, or small group of students. However, as the costs of providing computing power continue to fall, this becomes less of an impediment. It has been seen that the computer is likely to be only one of a number of components of the package and so the overall costs of learning, which may include print- and people-based costs, may not be affected so dramatically. Particularly, the time spent by teachers in supporting the learning may be spent in different ways but does not seem to be much reduced. The teacher's role changes from being a prime provider of information, to a facilitator of learning and a producer of packaged materials. It appears that time saved in the classroom is often spent in developing new materials or in improving existing materials.

Thus the costs of introducing CAL are dominated by the cost of producing the learning materials. Clearly, these are constant and so the cost per student can be reduced, perhaps to an insignificant amount, by spreading the production costs over a large student population.

The benefits are less readily established. It is fairly easy to conduct comparative tests in which comparable groups of students learn by CAL and by "traditional" means. These are likely to show that CAL is marginally better (or at least not worse) than traditional learning, for attaining the same objectives. However as was seen above, CAL offers not only different ways of learning things, but ways of learning different things. So, if CAL is to be used appropriately, it should be used to achieve those objectives which are more suited to this medium than the others. Statistical evaluations can only be an attempt to compare unlike with unlike.

When other media are looked at, it is found that although the costs can again be identified, that is not always done. While cost figures for learning through technology (for example CAL or video) are apparent, the costs of classroom lecturing or practical work tend to be hidden and discounted. Similarly, the benefits of "traditional" methods are less well-researched and less questioned. This makes any comparison which seeks to demonstrate that CAL is quantitatively better or worse than another medium rather difficult.

There is a further hidden cost associated with the introduction of CAL. Any innovation is accompanied by additional resources needed to help to develop new materials and to acquire the equipment needed to support their development and classroom use; some is hidden in the form of opportunity cost but is a real barrier to change nevertheless. While general problems of innovation are covered in the Part 5 entries on *Curriculum Implementation* and *Knowledge Diffusion in Education*, particular note should be made of the importance of training when introducing CAL. The recent rapid development of CAL has given rise to a situation in which most teachers are unaware of its possibilities and limitations. In contrast to almost all other learning media, most teachers have no experience of learning themselves through CAL. Therefore if CAL is to be used effectively, efficiently, and appropriately, there must be a substantial investment in both inservice and preservice training courses. However, the return in terms of new and more relevant learning experiences can justify these costs.

Bibliography

Feurzeig W 1985 Algebra slaves and agents in a logo-based mathematics curriculum. *Instr. Sci.* 14: 229–54

Fielden J, Pearson P K 1978 *The Cost of Learning with Computers: The Report of the Financial Evaluation of the National Development Programme in Computer Assisted Learning.* Council for Educational Technology, London

Rushby N J 1977 *An Introduction to Educational Computing.* Croom Helm, London

Rushby N J (ed.) 1981 *Selected Readings in Computer Based Learning.* Kogan Page, London

Sleeman D, Brown J S (eds) 1982 *Intelligent Tutoring Systems.* Academic Press, New York

Tawney D 1979 *Learning Through Computers.* MacMillan, London

Yazdani M 1984 *New Horizons in Educational Computing.* Ellis Horwood, Chichester

Computer-managed Learning

H. F. McMahon

The ultimate purpose of computer-managed learning (CML), or computer-managed instruction (CMI) as it is often designated, is to enhance learning by providing automated management of elements of the individual student's learning environment. Computer-managed learning systems are usually conceptualized and implemented as aids to teachers in their task of controlling and managing the content, pace, sequence, and method of learning of the students in their charge. More rarely, CML systems attempt to place the locus of control of learning closer to individual students, thus using the computer to enhance the students' power to understand and develop their own learning according to their own purposes.

The facilities provided by a fully fledged CML system are usually organized around three major sets of functions. Firstly, the computer is able to capture data about the learner, to generate and mark objective tests being used for diagnostic or assessment purposes, to accept the results of tests marked subjectively by teachers, and to analyse the performance of these tests. Secondly, the computer is able to provide feedback to the individual student on test performance and, acting on decision rules provided by the course developer, to steer or route the student through an individualized curriculum. Thirdly, the computer is able to store and update records of each student's performance on the course and report in summary form on the general progress of students to the teacher or trainer, course developer or administrator.

This article will consider in turn each of these sets of functions, give illustrations of the way they have been exploited in CML-based learning systems, point towards unresolved problems and issues underlying their use, and conclude with a projection of some trends in the development of CML systems.

1. Data Capture, Testing, and Test Analysis

For management of learning to take place, the manager has to have information, both current and cumulated over time, about the learner. In the more straightforward applications of CML systems, most of the information typically comes in the form of students' performance on objective tests which are marked by the computer. An objective testing procedure is used as the information-gathering phase of a learning cycle which begins when the student either selects or is directed to study an element of the curriculum, one of the modules of a modularized course. The student, having partially or fully completed the study of the module, then takes either a diagnostic or an assessment test covering the objectives of the module studied. The results of the test are entered into the computer which then marks the test according to instructions provided by the test or course designer. The computer provides feedback on the test performance to the student, identifies revision tasks, updates the information stored in the student's profile record and then completes the cycle by advising or prescribing the next module for study. This basic cycle, or some refinement of it, underpins all applications of CML.

More often than not step by step repetition of this cycle is used to manage the progress of students through a series of mastery tests presented in a strictly linear sequence along the lines of a Keller Plan course. In this type of application of CML it is the behaviourist model of learning which is used to guide the specification of behavioural objectives of successive study modules, the systematic design of learning tasks, the choice of curriculum content, the establishment of criteria for demonstrating mastery of objectives, the character of feedback giving knowledge and reinforcement of results, and so on.

While most CML applications seem to limit themselves to this method of acquisition of data about students' learning, via the results of performance testing in the cognitive domain, a significant number of applications seem to be premised on cognitive models of student learning and, as a consequence, tend to extend data capture about students and their learning into the realm of the subjective and into the affective and psychomotor domains. The most common practice here is to use the CML system to record the results of diagnostic and assessment procedures which involve the teacher in making subjective judgments about the internal states of the learner as a processor of information and active constructor of knowledge, to recognize and store these subjective judgments in the form of essay and project grades and marks, classifications of level of student motivation, judgments of students' intellectual capacity to tackle more or less complex tasks, their level of physical handicap in relation to the demands of the learning task, and so on. A further step taken in some CML system applications is to allow for the entry (and subsequent use in routing decisions) of the subjective judgments of students on matters such as their currently preferred learning style, choice of vocational goal, or level of confidence in understanding. The most sophisticated CML systems are able to build very large and very detailed profiles of students containing all or almost all of those items of information deemed by the course designers to be of relevance in course management decisions. A student record in such a system might well contain a complex mix of information including demographic descriptors of the student, records of performance in courses taken in previous years, records of performance in diagnostic tests in the current course, standard measures like reading level or mathematical ability, a profile of the student's preference for course objectives, learning style or choice of tutor, and coded judgments of the teacher about the level of motivation, degree of supervision required, level of cognitive ability, or stage of cognitive development of the student.

The actual process used in collecting all this information about students and their learning varies from application to application. Options for data capture techniques include the direct transfer of student data from existing central administration files to student records in the CML system, the use of optical mark cards or form readers and direct entry via the keyboard either by ancillary staff, the teacher, or the student. In educational or training institutions with well-established computer-based record systems it makes sense to use electronic data transfer from these files to the CML student files, especially when large numbers of students or long records are involved. In other situations, the CML course organizer may well find the use of specially designed optical mark cards or forms the most efficient method for establishing student files. During the course itself, it is probable that the bulk of data entry will be in batch format, with the sets of cards or forms being processed from time to time as they are presented by students and teachers.

Increasingly there is a tendency towards making use of direct keyboard entry. As the cost of intelligent terminals falls, and keyboard familiarity spreads among students and teachers, more and more CML systems designers are taking seriously the provision of user-friendly routines for data collection from the keyboard itself. As this trend develops the procedures for direct entry are being made less dependent on specialist computing knowledge. One further and increasingly significant form of data capture is for data acquisition to take place during the individual student's study of a computer-assisted learning (CAL) package. In this case significant information in summary form is automatically accumulated while the student works at the terminal on a CAL program which has been designated as one of the study modules in the course. This data is then transferred by the computer from the temporary student file in the CAL program to the permanent student file in the CML system. In this way the boundaries between CAL and CML are being broken down. A further refinement occurs when the CML system is able to generate tests automatically and to present them for student completion in an interactive mode. Testing takes place at the computer terminal and test results are transferred directly to the CML files. Using this technique allows the course designer to employ much more sophisticated testing techniques than are feasible with preprinted off-line testing.

All CML systems worthy of the name provide a set of test analysis facilities. Almost invariably it is the results of diagnostic and assessment tests which form the core of data interrogated during the automatic processing of management decisions, so it is vital that these tests should be as effective as they possibly can be. The course designer must be able to answer questions about the validity and reliability of each complete test and any criterion-related subsections within tests, about the levels of facility and discrimination of individual test items, about the effectiveness of distractors in multiple choice questions, and so on. Most CML systems provide statistical tools for the analysis of both norm-referenced and criterion-referenced tests.

2. Feedback and Routing

It is possible to divide CML system designers into two groups: those who see the teacher manager as the prime beneficiary of the system, and those who see the individual student as the person upon whom the system is centred and for whom the system exists. For the latter group a CML system is of little purpose unless at the very minimum it provides feedback to students on their test performance. Typically, CML systems used in this way will provide the student with an item by item breakdown of their performance on objective tests. The marks gained are presented for each item in turn and automatically generated comments are printed. Sometimes these comments are limited to cryptic statements of "correct" or "incorrect". More often, course designers provide detailed statements which attempt to provide remedial learning, for example, by indicating why the particular distractor chosen by the student in an objective test item is incorrect.

A second level of feedback can be generated if the test has been structured so as to examine the student's competence in a number of different areas of knowledge or levels of skill. Test items can be coded so that the student score on that item is allocated to a number of subsections, each of which can measure understanding of some significant content area or give an indication of competence in some particular cognitive skill. Feedback comments can then be generated on the basis of student performance on these subsections of the test.

A third level of feedback is brought into play if the computer makes reference to the student's personal records during the comment generating process. Test scores can be cumulated across several tests, current performance can be compared with past performance, trends identified, and prospects deduced. Feedback generated after this kind of analysis can be extremely helpful to students as they try to place their current performance in the context of their own and other students' progress throughout the course as a whole. This is especially important if students are working at their own pace. If the computer keeps records of the dates of completion of learning tasks and submission of assessments and assignments, then the feedback comments can reflect the course designers' wishes in relation to the students' progress through the course, congratulating those on schedule and encouraging or sanctioning those falling behind a reasonable rate of progress.

Many CML systems restrict the course designer to feedback of the type indicated above, feedback which allows the student to look backward at past performance. However, the more sophisticated CML systems provide an extra dimension for feedback by allowing for the processing of decision rules provided by the course designer, which produce recommendations or prescriptions for what the student should do next. They route or steer the student, perhaps on a unique path, through the individualized curriculum.

These decision rules can be quite simple and at face value quite straightforward. For example, in a Keller Plan course one of the rules would look like this:

If:
(a) The student has failed to reach mastery on this test, and
(b) This is the second attempt to master this test

Then:
Direct the student to a tutorial with the course tutor.

However, they can be much more sophisticated, with reference being made by the computer to a large number of items of information in the student record. For example, in a distance education course, a decision rule could take a form something like this:

If:
(a) Today's date is 1st March, and
(b) The student's cumulated average test score to date in the study of X is greater than 70 percent, and
(c) The student has expressed a wish for more face-to-face contact, and
(d) The student is not housebound, and
(e) The student lives less than 10 miles from North campus

Then:
Invite the student to join the seminar for advanced study of X at North Campus.

Not all CML systems allow the level of sophistication of routing implied by the second of these two examples, although most would provide facilities which would allow something approaching the first.

The simplest routing systems are usually found in purpose-built CML systems, designed to be used in one specific application only. In these systems routing rules are built into the computer programs in an unchangeable form. An instance of this practice is the case where the system designer has, for example, conceptualized the course in the form of a Keller Plan: as a set of performance tasks, sequentially related in terms of prerequisite requirements, and optimally studied in a predetermined and prescribed order. In this type of application the teachers who find themselves acting as tutors on this course have no room for manoeuvre in their management roles, and the student even less. The designer's model of the content, the student, and the method of study is clear, and so the routing rules are straightforward.

If, however, the course designer has a more complex or less well-defined model of course content, a broader conceptualization of the factors influencing decisions about the individualization of feedback to students, and the intention to employ a wide variety of teaching and learning methods, then that designer needs the kind of freedom for feedback design offered by so-called context-free CML systems, in which routing rules of high complexity can be constructed along the lines shown in the second example above.

Whether simple or complex, routing decisions are constructed before the students take the course, and for this reason they can quickly add up to firm statements about how this learner with these characteristics should learn within this domain. Little or no research exists which has managed to develop models of knowledge, learner, and learning to a degree which would justify decision rules being seen as anything more than hypotheses about how student learning might best be advantaged. Routing is still an art, even though it is embedded in high technology.

3. Recording and Reporting

Computer-managed learning systems are nothing if they do not include a comprehensive reporting system. This function, often given only cursory attention by system designers, is the key to management success. Reports need to be generated to support the teacher manager in a very wide range of managerial tasks. For example, when students are first registered on the course, reports will be needed by the teacher manager on the students' entering profiles, on their programmes of studies, on the identity of groups or classes to which they have been assigned, and so on. While the course is running, reports will be required on any changes in group assignment, attendance, or resource allocation. In addition, reports which summarize student performance in profile form will be required by teachers on a regular basis. For example, past and current test scores, lists of objectives successfully mastered, identification of the currently allocated assignments with dates of allocation and deadlines for completion are all items of information required by teachers in relation to both individual students and to sets of students organized in administrative groups.

The teacher will also require reports on students who are likely to be needing special attention, for example, those who are experiencing difficulty in achieving objectives or those who have a history of procrastination in previous courses. As the course moves towards completion there will be a need for reports which present the results of formal assessment procedures, perhaps in the form of final grades, percentage, or percentile scores.

One form of report which features rarely in CML systems, but which can be extremely helpful to the busy teacher, is the type which alerts the course teacher to management tasks to be carried out immediately. For example, in a distance education course this might include a list of students to be contacted by phone for an explanation of late submission of an assignment, a list of students who were asked to attend for a tutorial during the following week, or a reminder that the marks for a particular essay or project are needed by a certain date.

Most CML systems have in the past been oriented towards the production of reports in hard copy format. Reports in this medium are certainly useful, but increasingly it will be found that management information in report form will be presented to course developers, teachers, and administrators by display on video terminals. Since this trend applies also to the presentation of feedback to students, both students and their teachers will be regularly signing on to the CML system. In these circumstances a computer-based bulletin board and person-to-person message system can be a very attractive feature in a CML system, especially where student numbers are high or opportunities for regular face-to-face contact with individuals or small groups of students are infrequent.

4. *Problems and Issues*

Computer-managed learning systems can bring major benefits to those involved in their use. The system provides continuous feedback to students on how they stand within the learning or training programme. Learning strengths and weaknesses are diagnosed and suggestions made for remediation of difficulties and enrichment of learning. The students' metacomprehension, their ability to comprehend the status of their own learning endeavour, is enhanced and students are able to proceed in a responsible fashion towards goals appropriate to their individual needs. Teachers for their part are relieved of lower level management tasks which are automated by the CML system. Their knowledge of students is greatly enriched by purposeful reporting of information relevant to decision making, and their capacity to control complex and rapidly changing procedures for the individualization of learning is greatly enhanced. Their freedom from involvement in the processing of large amounts of clerical work allows more time for human interaction. Administrators have rapid access to information on course registration, student progress, and resource use which better informs a range of administrative decisions. Lastly, curriculum developers and course designers have continuous access via the CML system to vital information for formative and summative evaluation of their innovations.

These are some of the benefits of careful implementation of well-designed systems. However, there are problems—and some of them are considerable.

One danger underlying all applications of CML is the potential for mismatch between the underlying management philosophy of the CML system users and the facilities for management offered by the CML system. It must be said that at the moment CML systems in general are dominated by a goal-oriented management philosophy which incorporates behaviourist models of learning. Developers are often forced by the system's characteristics to use a heavily structured, tightly controlled, and clearly specified syntax of knowledge. Epistemological analysis of the content area has to lie within the purview of the course developer so that knowledge is cut and very thoroughly dried before the student is allowed near it. Few CML systems allow designers to adopt deliberately loose representations of the knowledge domain, or to promote in teachers and students the "fuzzy logic" of ordinary human judgment.

Closely related to this first problem area is the issue of locus of control of learning. Designers of mechanistic learning systems tend to be prescriptive in their dealings with students. If the system is designed through the application of scientific principles, then the presumption follows that routing decisions are necessarily right and should therefore be prescriptive. The control of learning and specification of correct knowledge lies with the course designer, represented on the ground by the teacher who allows the CML system to hold sway in the classroom. Many teachers and many students with justification resent this concept and practice in learning situations. Context-free CML systems which allow the implementation of this view of learning, but which also allow implementations where control of learning is passed across to students and knowledge is represented as problematical are more likely to be widely useful in education.

The declared purpose for CML is often the goal of individualization of learning. But in practice this often amounts to little more than the individualization of pace of study. Computer-managed learning systems certainly can bring very considerable savings in learning and training times to achieve specified objectives. As yet there are relatively few instances of CML use where content, sequence, and method or style of learning are tailored to the needs of the individual student.

In CML, course designers are required to build and almost invariably succeed in building paths for the student to move through the domain of knowledge. This is done preordinately, prior to the educational encounter. At the same time, the same designers while succeeding in their goal of relieving the teacher of routine clerical and administrative tasks, often fail to define, or even to loosely describe the role that the teacher should take in the CML environment. This combination of high prior definition of the role of the machine, and poor support in developing the complementary role of the teacher, can lead to dissatisfaction among teachers and students.

5. *Trends*

Several trends in CML are discernible at the moment. One is the rapid proliferation of systems. As the concept of CML spreads, more and more systems incorporating different mixes of the various facilities and functions described above are being produced. The best systems are very good indeed, but some are very shoddy. The former are the systems produced for mainframe computers and backed with large development investment over several years from public or private funds. Unfortunately these systems are expensive and perhaps for that reason a number of new systems have appeared recently on small personal computers. They are cheap, but they can also be nasty in the sense that they provide a very limited set of facilities which constrain the user to one particular manifestation of learning management. However, it is unlikely that this situation will last for very much longer. Within the next few years the power and capacity of cheap microcomputer systems will have reached the stage where CML systems based on these machines will be able to match existing mainframe systems, but at much lower costs.

A second trend is towards the marketing of single application systems, for example, a system for the management of the introductory reading curriculum, or a system for the management of career guidance, or a system for the management of mathematics training for craft trainees. The product on the market will be the whole curriculum package, and not just the empty all-purpose computing system yet to be filled with content, tests, feedback comments, and routing decisions.

A third trend will be for general purpose CML systems to move in conception towards general purpose communication systems. General purpose database management packages will be linked to general purpose report production and word-processing systems via general purpose decision tables or rule processing. The communication technologies of the commercial office and the public classroom will converge.

A fourth trend will be the gradual merging of CAL and CML. Interactive CAL packages will increasingly feature along with classroom study, lectures, tutorials, library and laboratory work as modules in individualized curriculum. Teachers and course designers may continue to distinguish between them, but students will not.

A fifth trend will be for research in CML to gradually shift its focus from the computer system towards the individual learner. When CML impacts on a traditional curriculum it transforms it from end to end. Large and problematical issues underpin the changes wrought. To date the literature on CML has concentrated on the analysis of the development task rather than the explanation of how students learn in situations where computers are being used to manage the learning environment. A key question for investigation follows from the fact that many teachers are, without the aid of computers, real "experts" in the management of learning. Computer-managed learning systems attempt to automate this expertise and deploy it in a way which allows students to become experts in the management of their own learning in their own right. Are CML systems really "expert" systems in embryos?

Bibliography

Baker F B 1978 *Computer Managed Instruction: Theory and Practice.* Educational Technology Publications, Englewood Cliffs, New Jersey

Lawless C 1980 New chips but old problems. In: Evans L, Winterburn R (eds.) 1980 *Aspects of Educational Technology, Vol. 14: Educational Technology to the Year 2000.* Kogan Page, London, pp. 308–13

McDonald B, Atkin R, Jenkins D, Kemmis S, Tawney D 1977 The educational evaluation of NDPCAL . *Br. J. Educ. Technol.* 8: 176–89

McMahon H 1981 Progress and prospects in computer managed learning in the United Kingdom. In: Rushby N J (ed.) 1981 *Selected Readings in Computer Based Learning.* Kogan Page, London, pp. 55–70

Mitzel H E 1974 *An Examination of the Short-range Potential of Computer-managed Instruction.* Conference Proceedings, November 6–8, National Institute of Education

Computer-managed Testing

D. A. Leclercq

As their capacities and speed increase and their costs decrease (on average by about 20 percent each year), computers are coming to play an increasingly significant role in the preparation, administration, and scoring of tests. In the past, a clear distinction has been drawn between computer-assisted learning (CAL) and computer-assisted testing on the one hand, and computer-managed learning (CML) and computer-managed testing on the other. In the first group, the computer's role was only to help the teacher who remained the primary decision maker. In the second group, the computer software was extended to provide a self-contained instructional and/or testing experience for the student. However, a range of new applications combines features from both approaches so that the demarcation between them is becoming increasingly blurred.

1. Item Pools

Item pools can themselves be stored as computer files. Classification of the items based on taxonomies or catalogues of instructional objectives, on the "universe" of possible questions (Hively et al. 1968), and/or on psychometric and technical characteristics (such as item difficulty, format, etc.) can be conveniently organized by a computer. The computer is helpful in managing and updating such pools and can retrieve items appropriately for test instruction purposes.

Ways in which the computer can use an item bank for test construction to serve specialized purposes have been described by a number of writers. These special topics include "multiple matrix sampling" (Shoemaker 1973), "quasi-parallel tests with defined characteristics" (Choppin 1978, Wright and Stone 1979), and "individualized tailored testing" (Wood 1969, Leclercq 1980).

2. Preparation of Test Materials

Advances in computer-controlled printing techniques, specifically including laser printers, make it possible for items which include complex drawings or pictures to be reproduced inexpensively on paper from computer files. Using the computer to print test forms is of special interest to the examiner who wants to scramble the order of questions in a test, or the order of alternative responses in multiple-choice questions. The resulting variations of an original test constitute an effective way to minimize cheating by students, and the computer is adept at unscrambling what it has previously scrambled. The computer can also provide another kind of quasiparallel test in which the phrasing of the questions is fixed but the numerical values included are generated at random.

3. Test Administration

An individually administered interactive criterion-referenced test can be conveniently administered by a computer. A decision algorithm applied repeatedly during the testing sequence determines the sequence of questions to be asked, and perhaps the point at which testing may be discontinued (Weiss 1982). In interactive testing situations, the computer can be programmed to control a variety of peripheral devices so that test items can be displayed on a cathode ray tube (a television or monitor), on slides, or via sound recordings, and so on. The videodisc has excited considerable interest as a storage medium for test material since it can handle still and motion pictures, sound, and digital information, and has a very large capacity.

4. Data Processing and Test Scoring

Even when the testing is not individualized and adaptive, computers are regularly used to process test data. Various techniques are used to facilitate the introduction of student test responses directly into the computer system without the need for a keypunching stage. These include optical mark-sense sheets, bar-code reading, and direct optical character recognition. In these areas, educational testers are benefiting considerably from technology originally developed for other purposes.

A major advantage of the computer scoring of test protocols is the possibility of computing numerous and complex scores and indices and of providing detailed and individualized feedback. For instance, students can receive comments on each category of questions or on each individual question including recommendations for subsequent learning activities. Teachers can receive individual results detailing, for instance, which students have mastered which objective (Cooley and Glaser 1969). Some special modes of test response, such as intervals or fractiles (Hardy 1981) imply sophisticated scoring formulas for which the computer is the only convenient solution.

5. Integrated Packages of Computer-managed Learning and Testing

Computer-managed testing is often integrated into systems of computer-managed learning. Many formal activities in the classroom can be managed by a computer, for example in the "Individually Prescribed Instruction" system (Glaser 1977) where each student follows at his or her own pace a curriculum according to the mastery learning approach. The computer assesses students' achievement after each learning sequence and prescribes the next learning activity in which each student is to engage.

Bibliography

Choppin B H 1978 *Item Banking and the Monitoring of Achievement.* (Research in Progress Series No. 1.) National Foundation for Educational Research, Slough

Cooley W W, Glaser R 1969 The computer and individualized instruction. *Science* 166: 574–82

Glaser R 1977 *Adaptive Education: Individual Diversity and Learning.* Holt, Rinehart and Winston, New York

Hardy J L 1981 Computer-based feedbacks to improve estimation ability. In: Lewis R, Tagg E D (eds.) 1981 *Computers in Education: Proc. of the IFIP TC-3 3rd World Conf. on Computers in Education, Lausanne, Switzerland, July 27–31, 1981.* North-Holland, New York

Hively W, Patterson H, Page S 1968 Defined system of arithmetic tests. *J. Educ. Meas.* 5(4): 275–90

Leclercq D A 1980 Computerised tailored testing: Structured and calibrated item banks for summative and formative evaluation. *J. Eur. Educ.* 15: 251–60

Shoemaker D M 1973 *Principles and Procedures of Multiple Matrix Sampling.* Ballinger, Cambridge, Massachusetts

Weiss D J 1982 Improving measurement quality and efficiency with adaptive testing. *Appl. Psychol. Meas.* 6(4): 473–92

Wood R 1969 The efficacy of tailored testing. *Educ. Res.* 11: 219–22

Wright B D, Stone M H 1979 *Best Test Design.* MESA Press, Chicago, Illinois

Computer-assisted Counseling

R. M. Thomas

The use of electronic computers to aid or replace human counselors is still in its pioneering stages. Until recently, limitations of computer technology have hampered progress both in exploring the potential of computers for counseling services and in extending computer services to a wide audience.

The limitations have included high computer costs, a shortage of programs for counseling purposes that could be used by personnel with minimal training, and the relatively large size of sophisticated computer installations. However, recent advances in the computer field have been rendering such limitations a thing of the past.

The most dramatic advance has been the development of relatively inexpensive microcomputers which are not much larger than a small typewriter and are readily programmed to perform a wide range of functions at the hands of personnel with relatively little training. As a result, the prospect of a rapid early increase in the application of computers in counseling appears to be strong.

The following review describes a number of roles for computers: performing administrative and clerical tasks; collecting information; giving information; making counseling decisions; conducting research; and educating counselors. The article closes with observations about computer use from the perspective of counseling ethics.

1. Performing Administrative and Clerical Tasks

Computers are well suited to carrying out a variety of the clerical functions typically related to counseling services—keeping track of clients' appointments, calculating costs for services, maintaining expense accounts and inventories of such supplies as tests, and storing records of clients' backgrounds and counseling sessions. The fact that a computer can store large quantities of information in a small space permits the counselor to eliminate file cabinets of clients' records. A magnetic tape or a plastic "floppy disk", less than 9 centimeters wide, can hold the equivalent of several hundred pages of information. A further advantage is that an extra copy of the information can be produced in a matter of seconds, so that the loss of one set of records does not mean the information itself has been lost. A counselor's notes about a client can be typed into the computer either from a remote terminal or directly, as in the case of a microcomputer installed in the counselor's office. When the information is needed later for review by the counselor, it can either be read from a television screen or printed out in the form of a report or letter.

2. Collecting Information

A typical early stage in the counseling relationship is that of collecting information about the client's background. The counselor can perform this function through a direct interview with the client or else can conserve time by having a computer conduct the intake interview. Either the client can fill in a printed questionnaire, which is then typed into a computer by a secretary, or the client can directly use the keyboard on the computer to type answers to questions that appear before him or her on a television screen. Not only does the computer-administered intake interview save the counselor's time, but the collected data are complete, in a standard form, objective, legible, and already stored.

Computers can also serve in test administration. As one option, the answers the client gives on a printed test can be coded to be read and scored by the computer, and then a report of the results can be printed on paper or displayed on a television screen. As another option, the test itself can be stored in the computer rather than being printed on paper, so that the client takes the test by using the typewriter keyboard on the computer to answer questions that appear on the screen. The ability

of the computer to combine graphic with verbal information allows the creation of test items that merge pictorial and written material in a wide variety of patterns (Pellegrino et al. pp. 231–36).

The testing functions commonly carried out by computers are not limited to test administration and scoring. A large quantity of test items can be stored on a computer, and then selected questions can be drawn out of this item bank to compose a particular test (Edwards 1980 pp. 9–15).

3. Giving Information

In many forms of counseling, one of the responsibilities of the counselor is to furnish information to the client. This is particularly true in educational and vocational guidance. The client is told the results of aptitude and interest tests he or she has taken and is informed of schooling and job opportunities that appear to suit his or her pattern of abilities and interests. Likewise, a person who suffers a physical or social handicap may profit from learning about the nature of the disorder and about suitable ways of reacting to it. While counselors have traditionally provided these types of information either orally or in the form of pamphlets, the service can be offered as readily by a computer. Not only can the computer furnish the information, but the client seated at a keyboard can interact with the computer by posing questions about the material and having them answered on the visual-display screen or by voice simulation. In cases in which educational or vocational guidance consists primarily of test interpretation and giving the client schooling and job information, a computer can conceivably replace the counselor altogether.

Computers can also facilitate the task of giving information about clients to other professionals. If a client moves to another city or is referred to a specialist for medical treatment or occupational therapy, the record of the case need not be copied and sent by mail. Rather, it can be transferred over telephone lines from one computer to another, thus providing a copy of the record both in the original counselor's file and at the new location, with the transmittal being instantaneous.

4. Making Decisions

When decision making is conceived of as a two-step process (generating alternative solutions to a problem, then determining which of the alternatives will be the best), then a computer can become a potential decision maker. For making common types of counseling decisions it is required that the computer contains (a) clusters of symptoms or information about the client and his living environment—past or present—that suggest the causes of his problem and (b) types of treatment that counselors have in the past found to be effective with clients displaying identical or similar conditions. Usually these two sets of variables—the symptoms and the treatments—are linked together with a theory about the nature of humans and the reasons why they think, feel, and act as they do. However, for the purpose of arriving at a decision about counseling treatment, it is sufficient to have two sets of variables in the computer: (a) clusters of pertinent characteristics of the client and his environment and (b) types of treatment—without the theoretical foundation. The theory has played its role by determining the form of the program that has been entered into the computer, that is, by determining what information about clients is significant and how this information is related to treatment. The most critical technical problem in this plan for substituting a computer for a human decision maker therefore, is to ensure that the program offers a true picture of the relationship between the data about the client and the treatment. In essence, the counseling theory underlying the computer program needs to be correct. However, which of the diverse counseling theories available today is most suitable, and for what kinds of counseling cases, continues to be a much-disputed matter. Thus, the problem of producing such programs has yet to be solved.

Nevertheless, the potential for the computer to make sophisticated diagnoses and prescriptions appears high, as advances in the medical profession have demonstrated. Computers, once they are filled with quantities of data derived from research on large numbers of cases, are conceivably capable of manipulating the variables in more complex and accurate ways than are human counselors. In short, the technical problems of providing the means of substituting computers for counselors in making clinical decisions are likely to be solvable in the future.

However, the technical problems are not the only issue. Many people in the field of counseling believe that the human element in the counseling relationship is essential to the success of counseling, at least in cases that require more than the information giving that educational and vocational counseling so often involve. Relationship therapists or relationship counselors, in particular, contend that it is the presence of a sympathetic, supportive human that enables the client to work through problems. The human relationship, rather than a particular theory, is the catalyst that effects the improvement in the client's condition. For cases in which this is true, the computer cannot substitute for the counselor, but can only assist the counselor by providing analyses of data on which to base clinical decisions. With the rapid growth of interest in computer technology in all facets of modern societies, it can be expected that more research on these issues will be carried out in the near future. As yet, the question of the extent to which computers can do the job of counselors is incompletely answered (Altemose and Williamson 1981 pp. 356–63).

While the general question of computer versus counselor has not been solved, a growing quantity of evidence suggests that computers can function efficiently in the realm of vocational guidance. Illustrative of developments in this area are the Canadian CHOICES program that matches individuals' interests and abilities to occupations (Wilson 1979 pp. 13–15) and the SIGI (System of Interactive Guidance and Information) program (Katz 1980 pp. 34–39) in the United States. In the SIGI version, students interact with a computer to examine their own values, identify options, interpret information, develop decision-making strategies, and plan actions.

Progress is also being made in the computer-based selection of candidates for educational and occupational roles, as illustrated by the British Royal Air Force program for assessing potential pilots and aircraft controllers (Hunt and Burke 1987 pp. 243–45).

5. *Conducting Research*

Up to the present, perhaps the most profitable use of computers in the field of counseling has been for conducting research. As the following examples suggest, computers have served the needs of counseling research in a variety of ways.

The scholar who wishes to survey the professional literature on a topic need no longer pore over the contents of individual journals nor inspect bibliographical lists. Instead, seated at the keyboard of a computer terminal in a library, he or she can enter topics of interest and the computer will search a specified range of journals from the recent past and will quickly print abstracts of relevant articles—frequently hundreds of them—from the journals.

In regard to specific varieties of research projects, investigators have constructed computer programs to represent several types of human personality, have put these simulated personalities into problem situations, and have then applied simulated forms of therapy in order to estimate what success such forms might achieve if used with real people displaying similar personality traits (Loehlin 1968). Other researchers have experimented with computers in carrying out behavioral therapy, as in desensitizing people who suffer anxiety when facing tests in school (Donner and Guerney 1969 pp. 1–13). Colby (1973 pp. 254–60) found that computer games improved the speech skills of autistic children. Cory (1977 pp. 551–64) compared the relative effectiveness of computerized tests versus paper-and-pencil tests for predicting how well workers would perform on the job. Crawford (1980 pp. 119–14) developed an automated behavioral-rehabilitation system for the mentally retarded, a system that assesses the client's condition, selects a treatment program, and documents the treatment plan.

In addition to such investigations that directly use computers as essential elements of their methodology, a host of other researchers employ computers simply for making rapid and accurate analyses of complex statistical data.

6. Educating Counselors

One of the most promising developments in counselor-education programs has been the use of computers to simulate cases which counselors might meet in their practice. In the typical program, the counseling student is presented with the opening of a case on the computer monitor's screen, such as the opening remarks of a client at interview. The student types his or her response onto the keyboard, and the computer then shows, on the screen, the sort of client reaction that such a response would likely elicit. The simulated interview continues in this same dialogue pattern, demonstrating to the student the kinds of client reactions this interview approach would be likely to evoke in a real counseling situation (Colby 1975).

Other computerized training systems do not engage the student in dialogues with simulated clients but, instead, pose questions for the student at different stages of a described case and ask the student to say what he or she would do in the case. Typical questions are "What test would you use at this point?" and "What do you believe are the significant symptoms in this case?" An example of such case simulation is a program designed by Chan et al. (1987 pp. 210–17) for evaluating the clinical problem-solving skills of students in a rehabilitation-counseling program.

Computers have also been used for teaching counseling theories by having counseling students compare their handling of hypothetical cases with the approaches of the "great therapists" in the field of psychotherapy. The computer program calls for students to simulate dialogue with a client via the computer keyboard, then compare their responses with those of classic therapists (Halpain et al. 1987 pp. 255–59).

7. Computers and Counseling Ethics

Experiments with the substitution of computers for counselors have brought forth objections that such a practice violates professional ethics. For example, Weizenbaum, as the author of a computer program named Eliza that simulates the counselor's role in nondirective counseling, has contended that people interacting with such a program begin to attribute human qualities to the computer as they participate in a dialogue with the machine (Lester 1977 p. 63). They come to think that the computer actually does understand them. And even though such clients may gain benefit from the encounter, Weizenbaum considers such an arrangement a fraud and thereby unethical. Lester, in

reply to Weizenbaum's criticism, has contended that it becomes a fraud only if the clients are not informed about the nature of the system. Lester has suggested, in addition, that "ethics are subjective. It might be considered unethical to withhold a treatment modality that might benefit people who would use it, were it available" (Lester 1977 p. 64). It seems likely that the morality of devising machines to perform counseling will continue to be a matter of dispute as computer technology provides increasingly sophisticated devices for replacing human functions.

Bibliography

Altemose J R, Williamson K B 1981 Clinical judgment versus the computer: Can the school psychologist be replaced by a machine? *Psychol. Sch.* 18: 356–63
Chan F, Parker H J, Lam C S, Mecaskey C (1987) Computer case management simulations: Applications in rehabilitation education. *Rehabil. Couns. Bull.* 30: 210–17
Colby K M 1973 The rationale for computer-based treatment of language difficulties in nonspeaking autistic children. *J. Autism Child. Schizophr.* 3: 254–60
Colby K M 1975 *Artificial Paranoia: A Computer Simulation of Paranoid Processes.* Pergamon, New York
Cory C H 1977 Relative utility of computerized versus paper-and-pencil tests for predicting job performance. *Appl. Psychol. Meas.* 1: 551–64
Crawford J L 1980 Computer support and the clinical process: An automated behavioral rehabilitation system for mentally retarded persons. *Ment. Retard.* 18: 119–24
Donner L, Guerney B G 1969 Automated group desensitization for test anxiety. *Behav. Res. Ther.* 7: 1–13
Edwards J S 1980 Computer-assisted testing. *J. Res. Dev. Educ.* 14(1): 9–15
Halpain D R, Dixon D N, Glover J A (1987) The great therapists program: Computerized learning of counseling theories. *Couns. Educ. Superv.* 26(4): 255–59
Hunter D R, Burke E F (1987) Computer-based selection testing in the Royal Air Force. *Behavior Research, Methods, and Computers* 19(2): 243–45
Katz M R 1980 SIGI: An interactive aid to career decision making. *J. Coll. Stud. Pers.* 21: 34
Lester D 1977 *The Use of Alternative Modes for Communication in Psychotherapy: The Computer, the Book, the Telephone, the Television, the Tape Recorder.* Thomas, Springfield, Illinois
Loehlin J C 1968 *Computer Models of Personality.* Random House, New York
Pellegrino J W, Hunt E B, Abate R, Farr S (1987) A computer-based test battery for the assessment of static and dynamic spatial reasoning abilities. *Behavior Research, Methods, and Computers* 19(2): 231–36
Wilson D 1979 Want to know what career may be right for you? Just ask CHOICES! *Can. Vocat. J.* 15(2): 13–15

Computers in the Curriculum

G. Salomon

With the decrease in computer costs and the development of more, better, and more diversified learning materials designed for personal computers (courseware), there has been an impressive growth in the use of computers in schools all over the world. The early years of unqualified enthusiasm accompanied by naive explorations of computer usages have given way to a more thoughtful examination and development of the uses of computers in the curriculum. This process is guided by two major questions: What *unique* functions can computers serve in education? How can the use of computers be *integrated* into curricula and daily school activities? The first question stems from the growing impression and from research findings which indicate that computers can profoundly contribute to the educational process only under particular conditions and only when some unique attributes of theirs are capitalized upon. The second question is raised as an antithesis to the widespread usage of computers as a technology and curriculum that have become independent of all other school curricula and activities; computers, it is felt, ought to be an integrated part of the ongoing life in school much like the pencil and the book. The present article is devoted to these two questions.

1. Unique Attributes of Computers in Curricular Use

Computers must be seen as part of the wider category of instructional technologies. Each technology—whether books, television, pocket calculators, or microscopes, has some unique attributes which, given appropriate modes of usage, might "make a difference" in learning. However, the unique attributes of technologies ought to be integrated into some more general, multidimensional map, so that each technology and each technological use in instruction could be placed vis-à-vis that of other technologies.

Such a map would entail at least four dimensions along which one could align various technologies and point out their unique attributes. The first dimension of such a map would be *information*, that is, the particular content that a technology can present to or elicit from the learner. The second dimension concerns the *symbolic modality*, or symbol system of information presentation: word, picture, number, space, tone, and so on. There is a close link between the informational dimension and the symbol-system: certain contents are better suited to certain modes of symbolic representation and certain symbol systems are better suited to represent certain contents. As there is a strong link between technologies and symbol systems (television is better suited to deal with concrete spatial and figural Gestalts, whereas print is better suited to deal with abstract, linear, and discrete symbols), there is also a link between technology and content: television is well-suited to represent ongoing dynamic but concrete events, whereas print is better suited to represent abstract and formal knowledge.

The third dimension pertains to the kinds of *activities* a technology requires or affords: viewing, reading, measuring, testing hypotheses, reconstructing, and the like.

The fourth dimension pertains to the *relations* that become possible between the student user and the technology. This dimension entails such issues as whether the technology and its use place the student at the receiving end or whether the student participates in the process of information generation; whether the communication with the student is one-sided or interactive; whether the information and activity are individually tailored, and the like.

All other instructional technologies are restricted to particular kinds of symbol systems and hence to a limited range of contents. Computers, on the other hand, are not limited to either one. They are tools that allow a large variety of contents and symbolic modes—ranging from printed word to dynamic scheme, from graph to musical notation, and from realistic picture to dance-notation. Their uniqueness lies in their informational capacity to present the learner with a whole dynamic simulated world in a capsule ("microworld"), enabling the learner to directly interact with a domain of knowledge hitherto inaccessible.

Another kind of uniqueness is the variety of alternative symbolic modes of representation that computers allow, whereby the same information can be represented in different modes. Even more importantly, computers differ from other technologies in the variety and kinds of activities that they afford—ranging from responses to questions as in drill and practice programs, to autonomous hypothesis testing in simulations; from discovery-like activities via game playing to rigorous, logical planning as in programming; and from writing and revising to categorizing and calculating. No other technology known to us allows such a wide variety of contents, symbolic modes, and learning activities.

Last, computers allow the development of partner-like interactive and individualized relations with the user which no other technology (save a human teacher) can. The most impressive distinctiveness of computers is manifested in the *combination of attributes*, as when learners are given the opportunity to interact with computerized microworlds by means of, say, a discovery-like activity based on a science simulation where information—both computer and student generated—can be represented in a variety of symbolic modes. Add such features as immediate and informative feedback, the explicit "mirroring" of students' own underlying logic, and the personally tailored guidance that is now possible, and a unique combination becomes evident.

Computers differ from most other technologies in still another sense. They are not only interactive instructional devices but also useful tools that extend in many important ways our mental capacities (see, for example, Bolter 1984). As such, they amplify learners' capacities, allowing them to carry out tasks like hypothesis generation and testing, using expert logic that no other device or method affords. Furthermore, they serve as possible models for certain kinds of thinking that learners could use to discover powerful ideas with, as well as emulate, internalize, and use as newly acquired mental tools (Papert 1980).

This raises the more general question of whether computers could serve not only as superb instructional devices but also as unique cultivators of mental skills and strategies. Scholars have often suggested that such activities as programming could, potentially, develop in students procedural logic, planning ability, clarity of thinking, and self-regulation. Unfortunately, most research to date has not succeeded in providing persuasive evidence that such effects are forthcoming (see, for instance, Pea and Kurland 1984). One possibility is that despite the uniqueness described above, no computer-afforded activity can, under normal conditions of usage, cultivate mental abilities. The computer is thus to be seen as an important *amplifier* of cognitive, communicational, and instructional functions, but not as a technology capable of affecting the functions it amplifies. An alternative possibility is that the cultivation of mental abilities is possible and that computers could accomplish, in this respect, a rather unique function, provided that certain—as yet unknown—conditions are met. Much current research and thoughtful considerations are devoted to the study of such conditions (see, for example, Perkins 1985).

Given computers' diversity, it becomes evident that neither the computer itself, nor even a particular kind of software in and of itself, are likely to affect learning in any profound way. Research clearly shows that while software and activities that realize computers' unique attributes are a necessary condition, much still depends on the particular way computers come to be used. For example, learning to use word processing has not been found to affect the quality of essays written nor students' ability to write, unless accompanied by a whole writing curriculum. If computers are to accomplish unique instructional functions, let alone to cultivate abilities, they must become fully integrated into school curricula. It is to this that the article turns next.

2. The Integration of Computers into the Curriculum

Computers, as Taylor (1980) has pointed out, can serve as tutors, tutees, and as tools. Until recently most usages of computers in the schools were relatively limited to their functions as tutors in computer-assisted instruction (CAI). They served also, although to a lesser extent, as tutees, as when students learned to program in mainly the languages of BASIC or LOGO. Serving in these capacities, computers were treated as separate and independent tutors and tutees, segregated from all other school activities. Such modes of computer use have led to disappointments as no profound changes in either students' achievements or in curricular design and teaching have been witnessed. Presently, there is a growing desire to capitalize on computers' unique attributes

and to fully integrate them into regular learning activities in the three capacities described by Taylor. The difference now is that these three capacities become part and parcel of various curricula.

What is the nature of this integration and how is it accomplished? The integration of computers into a curriculum means that these two components affect each other reciprocally. The designers of a curriculum take into consideration computers' unique possibilities, whereas the use of computers comes to serve the curriculum rather than its own purposes. More specifically, this reciprocal relationship takes place on at least three levels: the level of goals and objectives, the level of pedagogical thought, and the level of instructional contents and activities.

Concerning the first level, there is a change in the goals towards which computers come to be used. While in the initial days of computer use activities such as programming were self-serving, increasingly more computer activities are now designed to serve curricular goals. For example, LOGO is now often taught as part of a mathematics curriculum and comes to serve the attainment of that curriculum's goals. Similarly, curricula are now designed taking into consideration that computers are not just new means to old goals, but can serve rather novel ones as well. Perhaps the best manifestation of integration on this level is in the design of new curricula which were impossible in the past and for which the computer is best suited, for example, ecological programs that afford, for the first time, first-hand experience in the manipulation of complex and interrelated ecological variables. The world of ecology can now be symbolically recreated in all its complexity, enabling the design of a suitable curriculum.

Such changes need to be accompanied by a change in pedagogical thought manifested by a growing acceptance of the computer as a technology that allows more independent exploration, more personally tailored activities, more team work, and significantly less didactic instruction (see, for example, Wilkinson 1983). This implies a gradual change in the perception of the teacher's role—from information delivery to learning management, and from an authoritative source of information to a guide of self-propelled exploration. Similar changes take place with respect to the computer; it is gradually perceived as a tool to be placed in the hands of active students rather than as tutor that instructs a relatively passive student-responder.

Reciprocal changes of goals and of educational thought are reflected in instructional contents and activities, the level at which the integration of computers and curricula is actually realized. Here, the integration appears as the incorporation of computer microworlds into the curriculum: the student encounters new contents in ways that simulate the world outside (e.g., exploratory simulations of outer space). The integration is also reflected in the introduction of novel, often unique kinds of student activities with computer tools such as intelligent electronic spreadsheets that allow new modes of interaction with academic materials. Rather than have a drill-and-practice program accompany a curriculum as an independent add-on, we begin to see exciting instructional games, intelligent tools, and problem-solving programs that are central parts of a curriculum. The result of this integration is that computers become used all the time, by all students, for a variety of purposes, and in a variety of capacities. Computers, much like microscopes in the study of biology, affect what is taught and how.

It ought to be emphasized that the role of computers in curriculum, based on the realization of their unique attributes, is still in its infancy. Organizational, psychological, philosophical, and financial hurdles are still to be overcome. Moreover, wholesale and hasty integration of computers into well designed and tried curricula may in some cases be more harmful than helpful. Not everything possible is necessarily also desirable. The research and the accumulation of experiences may ulti-

mately show us how best to reap the potential advantages of computers in education.

Bibliography

Bolter J D 1984 *Turing's Man: Western Culture in the Computer Age*. University of North Carolina, Chapel Hill, North Carolina

Papert S 1980 *Mindstorms: Children, Computers and Powerful Ideas*. Basic Books, New York

Pea R D, Kurland D M 1984 On the cognitive effects of learning computer programming. *New Ideas in Psychology* 2: 137–68

Perkins D N 1985 The fingertip effect: How information-processing technology shapes thinking. *Educ. Res.* 14(7): 11–17

Taylor R P (ed.) 1980 *The Computer in the School: Tutor, Tool, Tutee*. Teachers College, New York

Wilkinson C A (ed.) 1983 *Classroom Computers and Cognitive Science*. Academic Press, New York

Microcomputers in Schools

D. Smith

Since 1960 the computer has evolved from a number-crunching "mathematical engine" to form the basis for a vast range of devices. The pace of this evolution has been startlingly rapid in the 1980s, for the advent of the microcomputer has elevated the computer from having only a marginal role in education to becoming a major educational medium. This has paralleled the evolution of the computer in the world at large from its former limited role in big business to its new status as a "primary work tool" (Pogrow 1983).

This same brief period has been a time of great dynamism and of dramatic changes in the ways in which education is conceived and organized, both as a process and as a system. The sheer diversity of ways in which the new information technologies (NITs) are used in school systems throughout the world means that it is not possible to give a comprehensive overview of school computer applications in any one country, much less internationally. This article outlines some of the general trends and patterns that have characterized the introduction of microcomputers to schools—in what is without doubt one of the most significant developments in the history of educational technology.

Distant horizons have a habit of remaining obdurately distant, and the situation regarding computers in schools is no exception to this rule. The general picture is of slow but gradual progress towards the institutionalization of the technology in schools throughout the world. However, there have been a succession of false summits, and it seems reasonable to suggest that the final objective is nowhere in sight, though there is at least a growing sense of where it might be.

1. The First Wave

Computers have not suddenly appeared overnight on the educational scene. It could even be argued with some justification that the possibilities and dangers inherent in intelligent machines were grasped to some extent by nineteenth-century writers such as Samuel Butler before the computer was ever invented. It is certainly chastening to read the essays of the early pioneers anthologized by Taylor (1980) and to realize that a few brave souls on both sides of the Atlantic were using computers in schools as long ago as the early 1960s. Indeed, many of the current modes of computer application in schools were laid down, if not in the practice, then at least in the "thought experiments" of these early days.

Despite the efforts of the pioneers and widespread government-sponsored experimentation during the 1970s (for example, the United Kingdom's National Development Programme for Computer Assisted Learning and similar experimental programmes in France, Denmark, and elsewhere), the complexity and expense of mainframe-based hardware and software technologies were severe constraints to the incorporation of computers into school-based education. Those few schools which were active in the field at this time either acquired obsolete early generation hardware "junked" by industry, or else used "dial-up" links with remote mainframes. Despite these limitations, pioneers such as Sylvia Charp in Philadelphia were able to institute a wide range of mainframe-based services and facilities. Some schools even managed to teach programming successfully using postal services to carry card decks and printout, but these were the exceptions rather than the rule. For most schools, nonadministrative computing was simply not a realistic proposition until the end of the 1970s.

2. The Microcomputer Phenomenon

The present prominence of the computer and related technologies in schools may be related to three factors. One is undoubtedly the emergence during the late 1970s of a generation of small relatively cheap microcomputers and all the commercial interest which went with the "Silicon Valley" phenomenon. The second factor was a realization that the new technologies were going to be part of life, and that citizens of the future would need to deal with them and their consequences. The third was a search for technological solutions in the context of the relative economic decline of many Western industrialized countries. The combined effect of these factors was an immense pressure on schools to obtain computers, almost irrespective of any planned educational role for them.

The rationale behind the adoption of computers in schools has sometimes seemed to have more in common with Melanesian cargo cults than any planned expansion of the school curriculum. As Cerych (1985) observed, "...the almost mythical importance attached to the computer in education may or may not have an adequate rational justification but there is no doubt that it reflects a sociological phenomenon which is unique in the history of the relationship between education and technology." Perhaps the nearest recent parallel is the panic response to the Soviet Union launch of Sputnik, which fuelled a significant and influential drive to renew curriculum in science and technology in the United States and elsewhere.

In many countries, the arrival of the computer in the classroom seems to have preceded analysis of its probable educational role. This was in marked contrast with the general technological assessment which was occurring at the end of the 1970s. The French Nora and Minc Report (1978) alerted the government to the "Informatization of Society," and similar policy reviews were undertaken by most advanced societies. The problem was translating general awareness of a major trend in industrial technology into specific patterns of classroom activity. The situation was often clouded by the complexity of government intervention. Thus the first major UK initiative to supply schools with computers was undertaken by the Department of Trade and Industry rather than by conventional education agencies.

In the confusion of the early days, it was often parents, anxious for the future of their children in the face of a flood of alarmist journalism and political rhetoric, who were most influential in obtaining computing equipment for schools. A buoyant market was created for home computers, sustaining the pressure on schools to keep up with developments in the home. The result was a flood of equipment for which there was very little

immediate application, and yet which was clearly expected to achieve educational and economic miracles.

Questions of equity have been significant social and educational issues in this context. Where resource provision has depended on parental or other "unofficial" efforts, it has often been the case that the gulf between advantaged and disadvantaged social groups has been emphasized rather than diminished. In the United States, adjacent school districts have varied enormously in terms of the levels of resourcing which have been possible, and it remains difficult for schools to use computers for the benefit (however tangible) of a small minority of students when a majority of parents have combined to acquire the equipment.

Gender equity has also become a major issue. There is strong and widespread evidence that girls are less motivated than boys by current generations of educational software, and indeed by the general climate of the "computer culture" in schools. In the United Kingdom there is evidence of an absolute decline in the numbers of suitably qualified young women applying for specialist courses in computer science at university level—a trend which must be regarded as deeply disturbing. The causes of these apparent gender effects are almost certainly complex, but one thing that has already become apparent is that the evolution of "girl-friendly computing" must assume a high priority in the evolution of curriculum.

One field where the computer and related technologies have been instrumental in removing rather than creating inequities is in the education of those with special needs. From the earliest days of computing, many students whose educational attainment was inadequate in conventional environments were found to benefit from computer-assisted learning. Although there has been a tendency to accept this fact as a form of classroom miracle, the computer is now a major tool of remedial education. More generally, computers have assumed a vital role in the education of learners with physical and/or mental handicaps (Rostron and Sewell 1984). There are numerous anecdotal and more systematic accounts of specific applications of computers in the general field of special needs education, and there is no doubt that this area of educational computing will continue to grow and develop.

The complexity of the situation was further increased by confusion about what it was that the computers were actually expected to achieve. The realization of Turing's vision of a "universal machine", able to emulate any other machine, has been both the strength and weakness of the computer as far as education is concerned: strength because of the vast array of roles which NITs have been able to assume within the educational process; weakness because this multiplicity of actual and potential applications has rendered it extremely difficult to relate educational computing to a specific theoretical context.

The conceptual foundations for classroom applications of new technologies have been disappointingly sparse. Formal understanding of computer-based educational technologies has not developed at a pace commensurate with the rate of evolution of practice, and one side-effect of the mushroom growth of classroom computing has been a situation described for the United Kingdom (Sage and Smith 1983) as "theoretical impoverishment". In a recent European Commission report (1985) "lack of solid theoretical foundation for teaching/learning and the appropriate use of media, in particular computer-aided learning" was included among its list of "obstacles to the introduction and appropriate use of IT".

There exists an unresolved division of opinion within the teaching profession about the most effective use of what remains a scarce resource. From the earliest days, some have seen the computer itself as the object for study, and there has been a corresponding growth of courses in computer literacy, computer studies, computer awareness, and so on. Others saw the proper role of the computer as a teaching or learning tool (the two are unfortunately not synonymous), and sought to apply classroom computers in roles appropriate to this conception. Making the computer and related technologies the objects of computer literacy or computer science programmes has the practical merit of sidestepping the underresearched issue of an optimal pedagogic role for the computer, and this is the line taken by a substantial proportion of countries wishing to introduce the computer into their educational systems.

3. Teacher Training

The education and training of teachers has been a source of major problems from the earliest days of the current era of educational computing. Quite apart from the fact that the lack of theoretical underpinning and a shortage of real practical experience in the classroom have made it extremely difficult to know what teachers ought to be trained to do, there is the embarrassing fact that computing expertise of any kind is highly saleable. Competent computer personnel can often earn more than competent teachers, and there is a constant drain of computer-trained teachers out of educational systems which can ill afford to lose them.

There has been a gradual evolution in teacher training provision, from the crash programmes of "emergency" awareness training (such as was associated with the original Computers in Schools programme in the United Kingdom), to more strategically designed longitudinal staff development programmes such as that contained in the French *Cent Mille Ordinateurs* plan or the Netherlands NIVO programme. The process has not, however, been at all easy in any country. The pressures on teacher educators (in training systems which were already, in many instances, under considerable stress from political demands for financial stringency) were enormous. Not only did they have to come to terms with the basic operation of the new technologies, but they were faced with the need to exercise professional judgments (for example

in course design) for which their own training and experience left them unprepared. Training of trainers remains a major strategic priority.

4. The Hardware Problem

The 1980s have seen great changes in the relative costs of very powerful computing equipment. Those who bought the first generation of microcomputers obtained primitive equipment with very little memory (as little as 4 kilobytes) and an extremely limited range of peripheral equipment. The situation changed rapidly. The power of microcomputers increased by leaps and bounds, the relative price plummeted and the range of choice expanded dramatically, but the instability of the market was a problem. A host of incompatible systems made buying decisions difficult, and the natural tendencies of national government programmes to favour indigenous technologies sometimes led to long-term difficulties. The school systems which were first into the microcomputer era are left with technical and management problems associated with the likely replacement costs of established hardware: equipment which was acquired over a very short period of time is likely to reach the end of its lifetime over a similarly brief timespan.

The situation in the late 1980s is relatively stable. The plethora of manufacturers associated with the immature market of the early 1980s has contracted. Microcomputers with 8 bits are being supplanted by powerful and versatile 16-bit machines. At the same time, the variety of peripheral devices available to schools has blossomed amazingly. It is now possible to interface school computers with devices ranging from printers, through telecommunications equipment, to videodisc players. The educational potential is clearly enormous, but for reasons outlined already, rather ill articulated. This contrasts with the subtlety and sophistication of the commercial pressures seeking to exploit education as a market for every new development in software and hardware technologies.

The growth of national support and acquisition programmes, the contributions of the wider community (including parents and industry), and other factors have combined to bring about a relatively high level of resourcing in some school systems, and in fact the level is remarkably uniform throughout the developed world. Hardware resource levels are typically about two computers per primary school and between ten and twenty per secondary school, though considerable variations exist, for example, in the case of countries such as Italy and Japan where national development strategies have specifically targeted the upper-secondary phase of education.

In terms of classroom availability, however, gross statistics may disguise or even distort reality. Taking the case of primary schools, resource availability levels in the United Kingdom suggest that there is one microcomputer for every 107 primary children (DES

1986). That represents a maximum individual accessibility of 14 minutes per child per week. But this assumes total and random availability of the computer throughout the school week—an improbable state of affairs. More realistically, individual access is likely to be measured in terms of a discrete number of key depressions per child per week. The situation is further clouded by the tendency to install compact networks of computers in specialized computer laboratories. This has the effect of limiting the availability of hardware. Consequently, the true impact of resourcing levels cannot be inferred from national statistics based crudely on head-counting.

5. The Software Famine

As teachers began to develop ideas about extending the curricular role of the computer, the discrepancy between software supply and demand developed into something of a crisis. The vacuum was filled by the mushroom growth of what has often been described as a "cottage industry". The slow but sure development processes of established computer projects were swept aside by a flood tide of amateur software, much of it written by people with only scant regard for basic principles of educational design and fundamentally ignorant of even the most elementary tenets of modern computer science (Self 1985). The result was a large quantity of low-quality material, which Kurland (1983) described as:

> . . . often poorly conceived, "buggy", difficult to use, difficult to integrate with the rest of the curriculum and designed without sufficient regard for the range of needs and abilities of students. . . the vast majority of software produced for schools is amateurish, unimaginative, or both.

There are clear indications from many countries that the supply of software is a major bottleneck, obstructing wider application of the computer. Different countries have tried to approach this problem in different ways, commensurate with indigenous resource provision and national educational philosophies. This is clearly an immense undertaking, and one in which commercial software producers have been reluctant to become too heavily embroiled. In fact, the United Kingdom educational market has seen the gradual withdrawal rather than the extension of commercial involvement, and similar patterns have been observed elsewhere.

The reasons for the widespread software famine are complex, but one major difficulty lies in the costs of producing high-quality materials on a large enough scale to provide a "critical mass" within the curriculum. Estimates vary on this subject, but figures such as 300 person-hours development input per student hour of courseware have been put forward. Melmed (1982) examined the costs of producing software to provide 30 minutes computer contact per US student per day over 12 years of schooling. He estimated a cost of about $250,000 per package, a package lifetime of 4–6 years and an annual replacement cost of about $96 million (at then current costs). Not even the most lavish national development plans seem to contemplate spending on anything like this scale.

6. Electronic Imperialism?

Developing countries have been beset by equity problems related to the dominance in the computer world of a small number of highly developed nations. For example, there were until recently few examples of good educational software offering a user interface written in Arabic or other non-Roman scripts. This tended to mean that students were obliged either to be, or to become, competent in a language such as English before they were able to engage in any sort of computer-mediated learning activity. The potential cultural drawbacks of such a situation are obvious and have done little to promote the application of computers in schools in many countries.

Third World countries in general have experienced a growing demand for computers. The reasons are clear enough. First, there is the way in which computers have pervaded modern business and government administration. Second, there is the recognition that in the modern world, information is power, and that that power is increasingly dependent on the use of the computer. Third, and no less important, is the awareness on the part of Third World educators that the computer is potentially an immensely powerful medium for development. The balancing act facing these countries involves advancing in a controlled way whilst resisting the blandishments of salespeople and educators offering inappropriate models. It will be important in the next few years for those responsible for education in developing countries to avoid institutionalizing the errors made in other societies.

7. The Classroom Revolution

Despite their limitations, early generation computers were spectacularly good at the orderly processing of serially structured data. It was therefore possible to conceptualize the computer as a device for delivering ordered and preordained sequences of stimuli to learners. This related well to the needs of programmed learning. A movement grew up around well-articulated educational theories supporting a pedagogy which was apparently ideally suited to the new technology. The computer offered a means of delivering "pure" stimuli according to a specifically targeted teaching strategy. As both software and hardware technologies advanced, experience with computer-based programmed learning and its derivatives grew. By the time that the microcomputer came onto the scene, there were approaching 30 years of cumulative experience and wisdom associated with a conception of the computer as a highly structured stimulus environment. In the early days, therefore, the dominant style of software available for school use reflected this body of expertise, which has come to be particularly, if rather inappropriately, associated with the labels *computer-assisted instruction* or *computer-assisted education* (O'Shea and Self 1983).

Some teachers were, of course, delighted with this state of affairs. Having acquired computers, schools often had only the haziest ideas about what should be done with them. Drill-and-practice software constructed on programmed learning principles offered ways of automating activities which were often found boring by teachers and pupils alike in conventional classrooms. Some of this software was undoubtedly highly effective in meeting its stated objectives. The operation of a powerful Hawthorne effect and the possibility that computers were in some unexplained way intrinsically motivating (Lepper 1985) often led to dramatic improvements in student attitudes. In many applications, programmed-learning based software appeared to be well justified, but there was never sufficient computer-assisted learning (CAL) software of this kind to provide cost-efficient coverage of more than a small fraction of the curriculum of a limited range of subjects, notably mathematics, certain science subjects, and some aspects of language drill teaching.

This was not too much of a problem when both computers and educational software were in such limited supply that their very appearance in the classroom was in itself a remarkable event: one can go for a long time with very few programmes if one only has weekly access to a computer. Teachers throughout the world have therefore tried to extend and develop the range and quality of learning experiences which the computer can offer to their students. There is now a vast range of computer-mediated learning materials for school use: so vast, indeed, as to defy simple classification. It can be fairly stated that the past few years have witnessed a classroom-based practitioner-led revolution to the extent that current information technology applications in schools are far ahead of the attempts of bureaucrats to regulate them or for academics to understand them.

There have been numerous attempts to categorize or classify classroom computer applications, but none of them has been practically useful. Computers are used in schools in almost as many roles as they are in society at large—which is, perhaps, just as it should be. Setting aside the use of computers in school administration, the division between teaching *with* computers and teaching *about* computers remains. The point of balance of this division in curricular terms is, interestingly, about the point of transition between the primary and secondary phases of schooling. So far, the bulk of investment has been at the secondary level; in Japan, for instance, only very few primary schools have microcomputers, compared with 81 percent of upper-secondary schools (Shafroth and Sakamoto 1985). The main thrust of secondary level applications tends to be towards information technology education.

The greatest diversity of application, however, is probably to be seen in primary phase schools, particularly in the United Kingdom and United States. At this level, there has been a rapid move away from the use of the computer as a surrogate teacher towards a much more open-ended style of application. Packages such as adventure games, or utilities such as spreadsheets, word processors, database management systems, and so on are not narrowly pretargeted towards specific cognitive, behavioural, or affective objectives, but are to varying degrees plastic, in the sense that they may be moulded to the service of a variety of objectives determined by teachers, or even by students.

One consequence of this diversity of application is a gradual reconceptualization of the computer itself. The device is seen less as a delivery system than a complex textual medium, analogous with television. The focus of research is gradually slipping from "what is the computer doing to children" to "what are children doing with the computer". One significant context for this attention is the use of the programming language LOGO. This LISP derivative was developed by Papert and others (Papert 1980) and is currently established as the most popular single item of software in the primary phase in the United Kingdom, Japan, and elsewhere. It is argued that LOGO helps children to take control of the construction of their own knowledge, and the rationale for the use of LOGO in the curriculum owes much to the epistemological work of Piaget. It is not, however, without its critics (Layman and Hall 1987).

The new view of the role of the technology has stimulated attempts to reconsider the management and organization of the learning environment. There has been a trend towards a reallocation of the physical and intellectual control of learning processes, and recognition that knowledge and expertise are distributed differently in computer-based and conventional classrooms. Above all, the advent of the computer has been a seed-crystal which has accelerated long-established processes of development of pedagogy. The microcomputer has changed the centre of gravity of the learning environment, and it is not yet clear where the new equilibrium will be established.

8. Curriculum Development and the School Computer

Irrespective of the dominant conception of the educational role of the computer, there has been remarkably little progress towards reconceiving the school curriculum in the light of opportunities and insights focused around the new technologies. The absence of any obvious direction along which computers and related technologies clearly *ought* to aim has so far been beneficial in stimulating a widespread search for new applications, rather than the acceptance of a single line of attack. But many of the major curricular issues remain untackled. Japan has subjected the concept of "information ability" to rigorous scrutiny, and other countries are also approaching the problems of curriculum evolution in a similarly analytic way.

Progress is undoubtedly hindered by a lack of research into all aspects of computer application in schools. Sheingold et al. (1983) targeted six types of issue for attention in their research agenda:

(a) access to computers;

(b) new roles (of teacher and student) in response to computers;

(c) integration of the computer into elementary classes and curriculum;

(d) quality and quantity of software;

(e) preparation of teachers for using computers; and

(f) effects and outcomes of instructional uses of computers.

In the United Kingdom, Sage and Smith (1983) also listed "areas for concern". But few of these agenda items have been tackled in any systematic way. The quality of research undertaken in the 1990s will determine the durability of what comes to be built on the foundations laid in the 1980s. The prospects are very exciting indeed.

Bibliography

Cerych L 1985 Problems arising from the use of new technologies in education. *Eur. J. Educ.* 20: 223–32

Department of Education and Science 1986 Results of the survey of microcomputers etc. in schools—Autumn 1985. *Statistical Bulletin 18/86*. Department of Education and Science, London

European Commission 1985 *Opportunities for IT Based Advanced Educational Technologies*, Final Report for the Commission of the European Community, Vol 1, Executive Summary. European Commission, Brussels

Kurland D M 1983 *Software for the Classroom: Issues in the Design of Effective Software Tools*, Center for Children and Technology Technical Report No. 15. Bank Street College, New York

Layman J, Hall W 1987 LOGO: *A Cause for Concern*. Paper given at CAL87 conference, Glasgow, April 1987

Lepper M R 1985 Microcomputers in education: Motivational and social issues. *Am. Psychol.* 40: 1–18

Melmed A S 1982 Information Technology for US Schools. *Phi Delta Kappan* 63: 308–11

Nora S, Minc A 1978 *L'Informatisation de la société: rapport à Monsieur le Président de la République*, 5 Vols. La Documentation Française, Paris

O'Shea T, Self J 1983 *Learning and Teaching with Computers*. Harvester, Brighton

Papert S 1980 *Mindstorms*. Harvester, Brighton

Pogrow S 1983 *Education in the Computer Age: Issues of Policy, Practice, and Reform*. Sage, Beverley Hills, California

Roston A, Sewell D 1984 *Microtechnology in Special Education*. Croom Helm, London

Sage M W, Smith D J 1983 *Microcomputers in Education: A Framework for Research*. Social Science Research Council (SSRC), London

Self J 1985 *Microcomputers in Education: A Critical Appraisal of Educational Software*. Harvester, Brighton

Shafroth C, Sakamoto T 1985 A comparison of microcomputer use in Japanese and US schools. *Educ. Technol. Res.* 9: 43–49

Sheingold K, Kane J H, Endreweit M E 1983 Microcomputer use in schools: Developing a research agenda. *Harvard Educ. Rev.* 53: 412–32

Taylor R P (ed.) 1980 *The Computer in the School: Tutor, Tool, Tutee*. Teachers' College Press, New York

Microcomputers in Adult Education

C. Graebner

Previous articles have examined a range of approaches to the use of computers in education. All of them are potentially relevant to adult education, and have been used to enhance adult learning by somebody somewhere. However, there are many factors specific to adult education which determine its use of information technology; and it is the interaction of these factors with a slowly developing body of evidence about the potential of computers for enhancing adult learning that this article seeks to explore. These factors include: (a) the constraints of organization, structure, and funding; (b) the educational appropriateness of the various computer-supported learning strategies to the existing range and styles of provision; and (c) the potential of computers for extending the diversity of what we understand as organized education for adults.

1. Adult Learners and "Post-industrial" Educational Technology

The classic scenario for the future of adult education is based on a post-industrial model which assumes that advances in educational technology will make varied learning resources widely available. For example:

IT will have sufficiently wide field [sic] of application in education that it may have the eventual effect of removing formal education from its position at the centre of our knowledge (and eventually, the assimilation of this information with existing knowledge and understanding of the relationships within this growing knowledge structure) could be carried on outside, as well as inside, educational establishments, with the support of IT-aided learning systems. (GB Cabinet Office 1986)

Recurrent elements of this scenario are: the decentralization of learning, through the growth of workplace learning, open learning, home-based learning, etc; and the blurring of distinctions between formal and informal education and enhanced opportunities for lifelong education.

At first sight, this seems a promising scenario for the development of recurrent education on an individual basis, but how is this implied transformation of educational management and resourcing to be achieved? One model is based on a market, in which learners pay for learning opportunities at full cost-prices, and provision comes from a mixture of private companies and public institutions, whose activities would have to be self-financing. Another model sees an expansion and/or reorganization of current subsidized public provision. An example is a recent US proposal for downloading resources for community education through satellite links.

United Kingdom policy has tended towards a mixed economy with a growing market emphasis, confining public subsidies to special projects and start-up costs. Thus the late 1980s have seen some progress towards decentralization of post-compulsory education with two national schemes, the Open Technical Education initiative and the Open College, attempting to extend the Open University's successful distance learning model to a broader market. The materials offered through these schemes are essentially vocational, geared and sometimes priced to employers' needs rather than those of independent learners. Moreover, the Open College emulation of Open University practice does not extend to integrating distance learning support into the package; though centres are encouraged to offer their own add-on support and charge the consumer accordingly. The Open College is expected to become self-financing within a short time, and the Open Technical Education initiative was focused on development projects. Neither has put a major emphasis on computers. However, a network of regional centres equipped for computer-based open learning is now being developed in connection with the Open College scheme. These are essentially local initiatives, in some cases with areas of specialization in software and hardware to match local industrial needs, especially those of small- and medium-sized enterprises which cannot support in-house computer-based training. Workplace open learning schemes, as opposed to in-house training for specific work roles (such as that offered by Jaguar cars), are of marginal significance in the United Kingdom.

2. Areas of Use

The take-up of computer-based resources for adult learning is currently strongly differentiated by client group. Access to computer-assisted education is greater for employees of large firms than for those of small firms, or individual adults who have to rely on public educational provision for experience or access.

Developing a full-fledged programme of computer-based training requires a substantial investment which can only be justified where economies of scale in training can be achieved. However, the adoption of computer-based training can also reduce costs through facilitating "embedded" training which reduces absence from work, allows existing staff to provide tuition, and existing computer facilities to be used. One disadvantage is that these tend to lead to nontransferable formats, which can limit possible economies of scale.

Multimedia computer-assisted learning is well-established in the in-house training schemes of large firms in the United Kingdom, including customer relations and interpersonal skills training using interactive video, while building societies and insurance firms regularly commission computer-based training materials for purposes such as acquainting staff with changes in commercial practice. A successful example of a broad-based embedded computer-based training project has been the British Association of Travel Agents MSC-funded project which in its first phase delivered training in on-line travel booking procedures directly to the workplace through the Prestel viewdata system.

At local level, publicly funded training for adults using information technology has generally centred on the acquisition of skills in the most common business applications such as database, spreadsheet, wordprocessing, and in traditional programming languages such as BASIC and Pascal, while the availability of subject-specific educational software for the further education market is not widely reflected in the curriculum of general adult education classes.

One area of innovation has been in small-scale vocationally biased technology projects, often funded through the European Commission's Social Fund, and aimed at disadvantaged groups such as women and ethnic minorities in areas of high unemployment. For example, the Belgian Prodidac scheme offers young unemployed people training in working as a software project team, designing and coding software for the educational market. (New technology experience is mandatory for all training schemes supported by the European Social Fund.)

Microcomputers have come to be perceived as a valuable tool in providing emancipatory learning for adults with limited educational experience; apart from topic-specific software for this group, such as that provided by the Adult Literacy and Basic Skills Unit in the United Kingdom, microcomputers offer confidence-building through the use of general-purpose software—for example, adult literacy groups gain from learning word-processing to present their writing in a "professional" format. Again, despite the significance of the computer for the educationally disadvantaged, scarcity of resources for software development and access to hardware is an obstacle to full realization of its educational potential.

3. Relevant Roles for the Computer

There is a long tradition in adult education of learner-centred provision, in which the personal goals and development of learners are accorded the highest priority. This conflicts with the assumption underlying most computer-based training, which offers individualization of opportunities for learning but not individualization of goals. Programmes are necessarily predicated on objectives which are defined in advance, reached by prescribed or predictable routes, and whose attainment can be checked. Research on computer-based training has generally shown positive responses from learners, yet areas of particular significance for adult students, such as the development of individual and group goals have not been taken into account.

However, computers can also offer support for discovery and emancipatory modes of learning, particularly significant for the independent adult learner. This does not necessarily entail the one-to-one interaction with the computer typical of computer-assisted training. Bostock and Seifert (1986) testify to the value of introducing simulation software into group learning, for example as a substitute for an experiment in studying population dynamics or plate tectonics, or a stimulus to team work and discussion through the simulation of a national economic system.

From this point of view the failure of adult education to establish its own distinctive software base need not be seen as significant. With appropriate staff development, general-purpose software can be deployed to support groups and individual learners through a range of activities. A database used to record and analyze plant distribution data by a centre's ecology group might also be used for a bibliography by a history class or for record keeping by tutors.

On the computer literacy front, ready availability of a wide range of sophisticated software for microcomputers is leading to stress on applications at the expense of programming, and one of the major debates has been over the relevance of programming to a definition of computer literacy for the general public. Current developments in microcomputers emphasize a user-centred approach which is arguably convergent with the student-centred approach of adult education.

Increased processing power in microcomputers has brought advances in simplicity of presentation—for example, menu-driven software which offers the user reminders of the range of choices available at any time, and on-screen tutorial and help systems built into complex programmes such as wordprocessors and spreadsheets. The Apple Macintosh system, widely used for educational purposes in the United States, established an early model for supportive and consistent user interfaces based on graphics and menus. With the development of a new generation of more powerful business machines capable of sophisticated graphics, this style is beginning to influence the presentation of business software.

Similarly, opportunities for users to tailor applications for themselves have increased—preferred formats for reports, and graphic presentations of information can readily be developed within sophisticated wordprocessing and datahandling programmes. Fourth generation languages offer a task-specific set of high-level commands which allows users without a technical background to specify applications to suit their own needs.

Thus, the greatest enhancements which microcomputers can offer adults as independent learners may be relatively indirect:

(a) as an aid to communication and presentation of ideas;

(b) as a resource for research and information retrieval;

(c) as a source of contact with other learners and support for distance learning through computer-mediated communications systems; and

(d) as a means of improving educational information and advice systems for adults.

Development of computer use in adult education may be indirectly supported by the spread of functional computer literacy which follows the integration of computer-based tasks into nonspecialized employment, and by the permeation of information technology into other sectors. Public access is clearly significant: the availability of free local telephone calls has been a considerable stimulus to the development of electronic communications in the United States and Canada, while in Europe the provision of free terminals to launch the French telephone service's Minitel information system has produced a flourishing subculture of information providers, contact groups, and addicts.

4. The Potential of New Educational Resources

4.1 Advanced Computer-based Training and Interactive Video

The most exciting recent developments in computer-based training are in multimedia training materials, combining text, graphics, and animation with television-quality moving pictures. The key technology is interactive video-pictorial information stored on a high capacity optical—or laser—disc, and accessed by computer software. Interactive video can present action and movement—whether advanced manufacturing processes or human interactions—with the immediacy of film, but with the possibility of pausing, freezing, replaying sequences, and interposing textual commentary or questions. One application area of particular interest to adults is training in interpersonal skills—negotiating skills, counselling techniques—where interactive video can be used to re-present live or simulated situations for reflection and analysis (see *Interactive Video*).

However, interactive video development is necessarily focused in areas where a large homogeneous audience with access to standard equipment can be assumed. For example, interactive video plays a major part in the workplace training programme established by the retail chain B & Q to address training problems of a largely part-time workforce operating on scattered sites. Each store has an interactive-video workstation available to staff on an open-access basis. All the learning materials are accessible with a simple menu interface, including informational videos on specific products provided by manufacturers, along with the company's own interactive programmes covering areas such as customer relations and store operations.

A quite different example of the capacity of interactive video to meet a common learning need is a project funded by the European Community to help adults with learning difficulties master the skills involved in travelling by public transport.

4.2 New Media for Information Storage

Other forms of mass storage are increasing the opportunities for resource-based learning. Compact discs, familiar from audio use, can be used to store large amounts of data, and are becoming established as a format for reference works such as the *Whole Earth Catalogue*, the *British Oxford English Dictionary*, and even the parent of this *Encyclopedia*, The *International Encyclopedia of Education* (see *Information Storage and Retrieval*). The next edition of the *Grolier Cyclopaedia* (1989) will move into a new dimension, incorporating sound as well as graphics through the multimedia technology of interactive compact disc (CDI).

Depending on the flexibility of the retrieval software, computerized indexing and cross-referencing can significantly extend the types of information retrieval and comparison available through traditional reading of a linear text, thus stimulating investigative types of learning activity. However, for such resources to be used effectively, training in information handling skills needs to be incorporated into the adult learning repertoire.

With improvements in storage media and in scanning methods for transferring printed text directly into computer memory, the quantity and quality of learning resources on-line is set to increase rapidly. One line of development is likely to be publishing on demand, to replace bulk production, warehousing, and shipping of learning resources (see *Electronic Publishing*). This would offer tutors and students the flexibility of calling up a document on-line, and printing copies locally as required, allowing for course planning to be more responsive to students' emerging needs and to current developments in their field of study.

4.3 Video Conferencing

Participation in face-to-face continuing education is constrained by time and distance. Computer-based communication can provide some interaction across distance, and electronic mail in particular provides some interaction across time. Live interactive video probably comes closest to simulating face-to-face learning situations as it offers instant feedback between group members and retains some of the nonverbal communication of classroom situations.

Unfortunately, the demands of effective video conferencing exceed the data-transmission capacity of telephone lines and most existing public data networks. However, this can be overcome by using satellite transmission or a high-power optical-fibre network. Satellite transmission has been used for some time in the United

States for the dissemination of video learning materials and for two-way video-conferencing in applications such as professional updating for engineers. The launch in 1989 of a European Direct Broadcasting satellite with channels dedicated to educational use (Olympus) will create an international exchange in learning materials. Again, professional updating in rapidly changing areas such as information technology, including the use of video, is seen as a major application.

The Livenet system, developed by London University in collaboration with British Telecom, provides fibre-optic video and data links between seven colleges, so that lectures delivered to a live audience at one site, accompanied by text, diagrams, and microscope slides, can be shared by students at all colleges. Linked with a communications satellite, the system has also been used to deliver an international conference on tropical child health-care linking participants in London, Harare, and Baltimore, including visual demonstrations of techniques such as oral rehydration and growth monitoring. The availability of remote visual information, including X-rays, has special significance for distance learning in the medical professions, an area currently under development in many of the European health services.

Japanese universities are making use of video links in teacher education (Boyd 1988). At Okayama University, a permanent link with a local school enables a lecturer to illustrate teaching styles to students by selecting an ongoing class for remote observation.

5. Innovative Approaches to Adult Learning

Irrespective of specific technological innovations, some computer-based learning activities can be seen to carry implications of organizational or social change, and may extend or challenge our received conceptions of adult learning.

5.1 Computer-mediated Communications in Adult Learning

Time-independent or time-shifted learning involves innovation in the management of learning interactions. The core facilities for learning support are electronic mailboxes and file transfer facilities. For example, in a mid-career updating course on computer-based information systems in business, produced in 1988 and run by the University of Victoria in Canada for students scattered over a 2,000 mile area, course members use electronic mail to keep in touch with tutors and course administrators (and each other) and upload their course assignments for marking and return by the tutor. In the United Kingdom, national electronic-mail networks for education are well-developed, with a Joint Academic Network serving higher education, and the Times and Prestel networks serving schools. There is, however, no specific niche for the adult learner. Around the Times Network's electronic-mail service a good deal of innovative educational activity has developed, much of it providing relevant models for adult learning support in general: teachers have access to a national professional database including careers and curriculum information, and on-line educational events such as news-gathering simulations for schools and more recently on-line training in computer communications for educators have been organized. The system avoids the one-way dissemination model by offering opportunities for teachers to set up local discussion or information exchange groups and to contribute project materials to the main database. There are signs that the remit of the Times Network will be extended to include adult education establishments (see *Videotex and Electronic Mail*).

However, a specialized class of communications software, known as "conferencing" software has developed from its original base in business organizations to accommodate unified and highly structured distance learning environments. The central concept is that of a shared electronic "space" functioning as a meeting place ("conference table" or "seminar room") for a dispersed student group and their tutor. Typically, group members exchange their (electronic) comments and responses on a chosen discussion theme over an agreed period of time, with the tutor playing a facilitating role. Rather than modelling face-to-face teaching encounters (as would two-way video, for instance), conferencing systems aim to simulate the variety of interactions available to students in face-to-face learning institutions. In the commonly used architectural metaphor, the electronic "virtual campus" includes libraries and resource centres, coffee bars or common rooms for social exchanges, and allows for the creation of secluded spaces where groups can pursue private conversations or collaborative work projects.

In the education world, the most influential system has been the CoSy conferencing system developed at the University of Guelph in Ontario, a system which is available for microcomputer as well as large installations. This is the system which has been used in the first mass-enrolment experiment, the British Open University's Introduction to Information Technology course, introduced in 1988, which provides conferencing facilities to over 1,300 students and tutors.

The range of learners currently supported by computer conferencing includes:

(a) the international business clientele of new technology and business management courses (Western Behavioral Sciences Institute, California; Connected Education, New York);

(b) postgraduate students (Ontario Institute for Studies in Education);

(c) Open University students in nontechnical subjects: archaeology students (working from study centres) and home-based Humanities Foundation Course students at the Open University of Jutland (Denmark); and

(d) small business enterprises in rural Denmark, who are provided with advice and support through computer conferencing links (University of Aarhus).

In the United Kingdom, the Arkleton Trust's Rurtel computer conferencing network, based on the Guelph CoSy system, links the regional development agency for the Scottish Highlands, the Workers' Educational Association, local training schemes, and individual subscribers. Information exchange has been the main activity, but Rurtel has also experimented with course delivery, linking a pilot group of participants into a University of Guelph course on electronic communications media.

By removing constraints of time as well as space, computer-mediated conferencing offers a great enhancement of opportunities for recurrent education. Educators monitoring activity in their course conferences have found that students log on to the system at most hours of the day and night, seven days a week. Enthusiasm for the social contact and practical help available through conferencing is unanimous, though computer-mediated tutorial discussion remains problematic.

Where—as frequently happened in the Open University experiment—certain seminar members remain "silent", their engagement cannot be verified by non-verbal cues, as would be possible in face-to-face situations. In conference exchanges discussions are carried out through participants preparing their contributions "off-line" before transmittal to the participants. This being a new medium of discussion, students and tutors lack a set of established conventions for interacting, and this appears to be a significant inhibiting factor in joining or developing an intellectual exchange.

Some of the most successful computer-mediated communications courses follow face-to-face group building activities, and it may be that computer-mediated communication will be found most effective as a supplement, rather than a substitute, for other forms of exchange. One method of establishing a supportive structure for students and tutors is to develop a centrally-defined range of conference areas each with a determined life-cycle, oriented towards specific tasks and supporting a different learning function. The range of group interactions which can be fostered within a context of informal social interchange is considerable. Thus, activities on a typical postgraduate education course at the Ontario Institute for Studies in Education may encompass plenary seminars, small-group seminars, learning partnerships, and group projects.

At this stage, substantial further research is needed into the processes by which proficiency in conferencing can be developed in order to maximize the benefits to distance-learning students.

Despite these reservations, computer-mediated communications must be seen as one of the most promising resources for distance education. Kaye and Mason (Harasim 1988), writing from the vantage point of the Open University's experience of computer-mediated communications, and in terms which acknowledge many of the traditional desiderata of adult education, refer to:

the breaking down of conceptual distinctions between distance education and place-based education, primarily because of the opportunities which computer-mediated communications provides distance learners for discussion, collaborative work and the development of autonomy in learning, and also because of the potential for building a sense of community amongst them.

5.2 Informal Learning Opportunities

The availability of on-line information and communications networks extends the range of sites for learning activities, and the diffusion of informal computer-based learning through the community. The greatest advantages are in rural areas where conventional learning opportunities are restricted. An influential initiative has been the establishment in Vemdalen, Sweden, in 1985, of a multipurpose information technology resource centre, the "Telestuga" or "electronic village hall", serving the remote Härjedalen area. In the first 18 months of its existence, the centre involved 15 percent of the town's population, adults and children, in activities ranging from computer-based learning and formal information technology training, to watching satellite television. The inclusion of business services and other income-generating projects promised to make the centre self-financing (FAST 1986).

An urban example of the information technology resource centre is the Technothèque at Liège (Belgium), which offers activities at all levels, from public demonstrations and a technical library, to access to advanced computer-aided engineering and design facilities for commercial and industrial users, and support for professional user groups.

In the United Kingdom the British library's PIRATE project (Public Information in Rural Areas Technology Experiment) has sited microcomputers in publicly accessible places in small towns, mainly with local information resources, but also with some software. Local public libraries have begun to add access to microcomputers and educational software to their computer-based public information services.

Some progress has also been made in using computers to improve educational advice and information services for adults. ECCTIS, a national course and credit transfer information system for adults seeking to enter higher education, is available both on-line and on CD-ROM, while the Training Agency's locally based Training Access Points pilot schemes offer information on a wide range of local training opportunities, from terminals sited in public places such as local JobCentres.

5.3 Addressing the Diversity of Adult Learning Needs

The adult sector of education, more than any other, is characterized by the diversity of its clients. However advantageous this may be from an andragogical standpoint, it can exacerbate resourcing problems. In the case of computer-based learning, the concensus emerging among education providers is for a plurality of media reflecting the diversity of learning styles and needs. Thus within one course, a student might use computer-assisted learning, communications, video or audiotape, and paper-based materials. Hence, one major strand in the European advanced open-technology programme, DELTA, is the specification of a multipurpose computer-based learning environment for independent learning, at the level of hardware and user-interfaces. A second strand is investigating learner models (see below).

At the level of software design, responsiveness to the needs of the individual learner can be improved by incorporating artificial intelligence strategies. For example, a predictive wordprocessor (Mindreader) builds up its own profile of a writer's vocabulary, and is thus able to anticipate the conclusion of many words, achieving a saving in keystrokes which is particularly valuable for writers with literacy problems or physical disabilities. The thrust of development in artificial-intelligence based learner support is towards teaching software which maps the patterns of a learner's responses, identifies problem areas, and offers remedial input.

Such facilities can, in principle, be provided by linking computer-based learning materials with an expert system equipped with a knowledge base on characteristics of the adult learning process. As with many expert systems implementations, this raises controversial questions about the adequacy of the knowledge modelling process, the specific conceptualizations of learning on which it is based, and how or whether these conceptualizations would be accessible to the learning provider (or to the individual learner). Megarry (1988) argues, for instance, that computers "are only just beginning to tackle human expertise. The process has been handicapped by the lack of an agreed theory of human learning, let alone a prescriptive theory of instruction" and that therefore ". .it is more prudent to use the computer system to model the knowledge base and to give the learner freedom to choose how to interact with it". Additionally, intelligent tutoring software involves very high initial development overheads, and is thus unlikely to percolate into nonspecialized learning situations.

The style of knowledge base which could satisfy these demands at a worthwhile level—a multimedia customizable resource bank—is currently developing in the form of hypertext software and hypermedia learning environments. The appeal of these for adult educators is twofold: they extend the range of independent learning by allowing transparent access to applications software and information sources which may be remote as well as local, and are characterized by an openness which corresponds well to the ethos of adult learning. (Users have the opportunity to extend or modify the knowledge base by constructing new links between elements, thus blurring the distinction between producers and consumers of educational materials.) In many areas of education, the fluidity of electronic information is coming to be seen as a challenge to the central values of originality and individual ownership of knowledge. Adult education, with its tradition of collaborative work and shared knowledge, is well-positioned to take advantage of this aspect of electronic information, and to offer mainstream education an alternative to individualistic models of learning.

One area where sophisticated responsive software has unambiguous promise is in work with adults whose personal disabilities—physical or perceptual problems, learning difficulties, or some combination of these factors—have excluded them from mainstream educational opportunities. While their individual problems and learning requirements are extremely diverse, and require careful diagnosis, these students share a need for software which supports them in working independently towards their educational goals. The computer as tutor can be invaluable in developing confidence and missing skills; it can offer instant feedback and confirmation of success, experience of control over a limited environment, reliable and patient repetition of points, and privacy for making experiments and mistakes. At the same time, the development of common computer-based skills can contribute significantly to educational and social integration—particularly where computer-mediated presence in the wordprocessed letter or the contribution to an electronic discussion makes personal disability invisible. However, in a market climate, resources for materials and innovative schemes for educationally disadvantaged adults are likely to remain scarce (see *Information Technology for Disabled Students*).

Bibliography

Bostock S, Seifert R (eds.) 1986 *Microcomputers in Adult Education.* Croom Helm, London

Boyd G 1988 The impact of society on information technology *Br. J. Educ. Technol.* 19(2): 114–22

Forecasting and Assessment in Science and Technology Programme (FAST) 1986 *Proc. Conf. Social Experiments with Information Technology of the Commission of the European Communities.* Odense, January 13–15 1986, Reidel, Dordrecht

Harasim L (ed.) *Online Education: Perspectives in a New Medium.* (in press)

Information Technology Advisory Panel 1986 *Learning to Live with IT.* Cabinet Office, London

Megarry J 1988 Hypertext and compact discs: The challenge of multimedia *Br. J. Educ. Technol.* 19(3): 172–83

Winder R 1988 *Information Technology in the Delivery of Distance Education and Training.* Peter Francis, Soham

Film, Television, and Video

The Role of Film, Television, and Video

R. W. Wagner

This article examines three main issues: the increasing prominence of moving picture images in our society; the impact of technological change on the production and distribution of those images; and the significance of new kinds of relationship between producer and consumer.

One major change is that definitions of "film," "television," and "video" have begun to overlap. "Film," or "cinema," continues to be identified with large screen (35mm–70mm) theater systems as well as nontheatrical and classroom systems (S8mm–16mm); and with collective audiences in schoolrooms, auditoria, and theaters. "Television" is equated with network, studio, and national broadcasting systems, including cable and satellite transmission. The term "video" while used interchangeably with television, is becoming more applicable to mobile, flexible, creative electronic productions, and is also distinguished from mobile, flexible motion picture productions usually made on 16mm film. The technical distinctions, however, seem to blur.

What the world is, or seems to be, at any given moment is increasingly dependent upon what people see and hear in the form of mediated experiences. The ubiquity of film and television, in particular, is changing the very nature of knowledge or, at least, the process of cognition. What was once easily identified as "fiction," or "fact" or "education" or "entertainment" has now become more difficult to distinguish. Everywhere in the world people are becoming more dependent upon these captured images, and there are some who already feel uncomfortable witnessing a "live" event without also being able to view it in close-up, from several angles, with immediate playback in slow-motion or in freeze-frame form. Much of what is happening in a kaleidoscopic world is so rapid, abstract, and changing that the only way to understand it seems to be through the encapsulization, reorganization, and interpretation found on some kind of photoelectronic screen.

The result is the production and delivery of an increasing amount of everyday information for business, military, government, science, arts, humanities, and education through photoelectronic imagery found in industrial plants, business offices, barracks, laboratories, community centers, classrooms—and in homes. Such uses expand the traditional pattern of film and television production to match the requirements of a greater variety of specific audiences or learners, emphasizing modular structure, operational simplicity, accessibility, adaptability to related but different media systems, and interactive qualities to engage the viewer directly in the teaching–learning process. The latter attribute, in particular, makes the consumer or "prosumer" of mediated message systems a part of the image-making process itself since he or she may alter the rate and succession of images at will, thus changing the nature of the production itself.

At the same time the use of conventional film and television production and distribution methods continues to be important in educational systems everywhere. In 1981 in the United States, the 16mm film was still the medium preferred by teachers in fields such as home economics, agriculture, career guidance, science, and technological areas, and more than a million 16mm sound film projectors were in use in schools, colleges, universities, churches, and industrial training programs. The 35mm and 16mm film systems remain among the most standardized technologies while electronic systems are typically incompatible. However, in the late 1980s videocassettes became the common denominator in instructional and home media environments.

Forecasts vary about the state of media technology in the year 2000, but it should be remembered that, with the exception of photography, all of the "new" photoelectronic media of communication have been fully developed only within the span of a single human lifetime. In the perspective of history, modern-day humans are still the primitives, writing on the walls of modern-day caves, creating lights and sounds with media that are still being invented.

1. Film, Television, and Video

As new technologies develop, dire predictions of the demise of earlier forms also appear. However, photography did not replace painting; the motion picture did not replace the book; television did not kill radio or the film. No medium has ever destroyed any other medium, but rather has brought about shifts in the functions of each. In the 1980s more print materials were being produced than ever before, radio was very active in every part of the world, and while the number of large-budget motion pictures was down, thousands of low-budget films of all types were being produced, and videotape formats of several kinds were used to produce both professional and amateur video productions. Yet 8mm film is still used in learning systems, 9.5mm is still used by a few amateurs in Europe, and 9.75mm is in wide use in educational and informational programs in the People's Republic of China.

In 1981, 41 percent of all television programming in the United States originated on film. In "prime time" (2000–2200 hrs) this reached 80 percent due to the heavy use of feature films and films made specifically for television. Both television and film studios are being built around the world, and film processing laboratories are still doing work for both film and television industries. The Finnish Broadcasting Corporation began operating a 16mm color laboratory in 1979 capable of processing three million meters of film per year, primarily for television news. In Denmark in 1983, television film was still being processed, although most news for television was on tape or ENG—Electronic News Gathering.

In addition to great advances in electronic technology, photographic innovations continue to be made. In 1982, Eastman Kodak introduced a 35mm color negative film with an exposure index of 1000, making it possible to make pictures under nearly any existing light conditions. The Fuji Corporation introduced an improved 8mm film that year, and similar developments were seen in motion picture cameras, lenses, lighting equipment, and sound recording and playback systems.

Films are extensively used at Disney's Experimental Prototype Community of Tomorrow (EPCOT), in Florida, including a 3-D animation production with twin 70mm projectors which throw images onto a 55-foot screen. Another exhibition uses five interlocked projectors and 100 screens of different dimensions, forming a 195-foot master mosaic—each screen being controlled by a microprocessor which makes it possible to move each individually in several positions in 30-degree increments. The entire audience may also be rotated 180-g on a moving platform, bringing the viewers from a film experience to a "live" performance instigated by the preceding motion picture. "Zones of smell" are also included, using a powerful airgun to deliver and exhaust appropriate odors to supplement the visual experience. The Canadian and the People's Republic of China pavilions both use two complete 180° projections with films of large format. The French display, also using large format films, was transferred to videocassette for synchronous, digital editing purposes.

Such combinations of film and video technology are improving the quality and efficiency of audiovisual productions. This is especially true in film-to-tape and tape-to-film transfers, utilizing high-definition electronic systems with scanning specifications of 60 fields per second with 1,125 scanning lines interlaced 2:1. The trend is for producers to use motion picture technology for original productions, especially on location—that is, in the field—because of its flexibility and convenience, and then transfer the photographic images to videotape for editing and postproduction work. The result is transferred to film where 16mm or 35mm prints are required.

While the present television and video transmission standards of 525 lines (in the US, Canada, Mexico and Japan) and 625 lines (in Europe and elsewhere) are not adequate to reproduce either the vertical or horizontal high resolution of 35mm and 70mm film, high-definition video for home reception is an expected development before the end of the century. This would make possible large-screen television originating on either film or videotape, with a 1,125-line system producing detailed images such as scientific or mathematical information and print as well as fine art work and graphics, projected on large classroom screens as well as on small theater screens.

An interesting aspect of the synergism between film and videotape is the apparent resurgence of the "kinescope" and "telecine"—early forms of recording and playing back a television program on film before the advent of videotape. Improvements in this process, the continued use of film for original production, and a vast backlog of film-based material has resulted in the growth of telecine usage in postproduction facilities. In the London area in 1983, over 60 such telecines were operative in addition to 50 in use throughout the British Broadcasting Corporation (BBC) (Moralee 1983 p. 218).

A "teleproduction" of the twenty-first century may begin with a camera crew shooting with electronic cameras where the images are formed on nonsilver halide surfaces composed of organic implants embedded in the material itself. In 1982 Eastman Kodak developed such a photographic film with a magnetic coating on the nonsensitive side which provided machine-readable information for nearly every postproduction situation, coded for immediate, detailed identification of every kind. Combination cameras, designed with the best attributes of cinema usage and the best of electronic camera features will be digital, have no moving parts, use diffraction, rather than refractive optics, and be greatly reduced in bulk, weight, and complexity. If the shots are made on location, or in the field, the actors, special effects, and computer-generated animation may be added in the postproduction studio and colors will not only be corrected, but added or subtracted with precision, and the final editing will be electronic. The final master copy will be transferred to film using a laser scan or an electronic beam to produce prints for conventional screening situations. For worldwide release first-run showings, the master videotape will be transmitted to special theaters or to homes by Direct Broadcast Satellite. Copies will be available in several formats of videotape (assuming that no universal standard appears), or videodisc, or in the form of solid-state information chips or cubes which, when ultimately accessible in volume, may be had at a cost which would make illegal duplication uneconomic.

"Electronic cinema," a term popularized by film-maker Francis Ford Coppola (*Apocalypse Now* and *One From the Heart*), begins with the keying of the script into a word processor, making possible almost instantaneous print-out of the many changes in a motion picture or television script. An "electronic storyboard" is developed by transferring sketches of each scene to a videodisc. A similar "audio sketch" is made of the actor's dialogue, the sound effects, and the music which are also added to the videodisc, providing a complete previsualization of the total production which makes possible changes and improvements in direction, lighting, performance, camera set-ups, sound, editing, and other elements *before* the actual production begins.

It was predicted by the supervisor of Coppola's Electronic Cinema Division at his Zooetrope Studio that:

> The next important development would be to enable our illustrators to draw straight onto the system with a light pen, and then connect that to the script via a word-processing unit. Eventually, we'll have a giant database, so that you can point with a light pen to a section of the script, and if you're a financial guy, the system will give you the budgetary information; if you're an editor, it can call up the relevant images; if you're a designer, you can recall your blueprints and dimensions. Our ultimate aim is high-definition video, which will take the film out of filmmaking altogether. (Bygrave and Goodman 1981 p. 43)

Preproduction planning, testing, and prototyping is not new to the field of educational and instructional film production, much work in this dimension having been done in industry and military audiovisual programs during the Second World War and afterwards in universities. This also included psychometric testing on sample audiences of intended learners and experimental work on nearly every aspect of film production. What is new is the application of computer-based visual, audio, and word-processing systems which make multiple-factor analysis easier and quicker to accomplish. Whether such methods will be affordable in education is questionable; the cost of maintaining and replacing the high technology involved in computer-based production is often not included in production cost statements.

This raises the interesting and very real possibility that "high" technology will not completely replace "low" technology, the latter being more "appropriate" than the former in many educational settings throughout the world. What Ivan Illich refers to as "convivial tools," as contrasted with those which may be used only by experts, would include simple spring-driven 16mm cameras and half-inch and quarter-inch videotape equipment in cassette forms in systems small enough to combine both recorder and camera with a two-hour tape capacity and instant playback format. By 1964

Eastman Kodak had developed a combination electronic quarter-inch camera and playback system using videotape cassettes.

The accessibility of such equipment will put the means for image production into the hands of more people, professionals and amateurs alike, than ever before in history. The implications of this development for teaching and learning are treated in a later section in terms of producer–consumer synergism.

The question of the relationship between film, television, and video production seems most reliably answered by observing that both photographic and electronic forms will continue to exist and improve in increasingly intricate and mutually supportive combinations. But the principles of communication and the central importance of the design of such productions for educational, informational, and entertainment purposes will be of continuing concern, regardless of the specific and changing photoelectronic technologies involved.

2. Design in Film and Television for Education

"Design" may be defined as the thoughtful, artful, organic application and creative control of a learning experience. It provides a flexible but purposeful framework for a film or television production which, while carefully planned with the nature of the learner and the instructional objectives clearly in mind, will stimulate and energize the learner's own imagination, judgment, and abilities whether the material or content be in the cognitive, psychomotor, or affective domain. An ideal educational production would be one which would serve in this capacity for both teacher and learner, providing a rich experience which could be shared. That many entertainment programs, both film and television, are experienced in this way by large segments of the population, young and old, is a fact which should be studied by designers and producers of educational media.

After more than 60 years of film research, however, there is very little evidence that much of it has been either really helpful, or widely applied. Many studies have been taken from behavioral science models, most deal with cognitive processes, and new research methodologies which explore the affective domain have yet to be developed by educational researchers. The effects of the public media have been widely reported and much publicized, usually with negative conclusions, but little of such information has been employed to improve the design and production of film and television programming either for theaters, broadcast, or for educational productions. A singularly grim picture of the future of instructional design and development is painted by some educational media specialists:

> What can we expect in the area of designing instruction? Unfortunately, I see little of profound importance occurring in the next few years. It would appear that we are continuing to plow the same worn ground in learning theory. While research on lateral specialization of the brain holds some promise, I personally doubt it will have a major near-term

influence on how we design instruction....Similarly, our models of the instructional development process show little prospect of soon leading us to any brave new world. Almost no significant conceptual advances have occurred in these models in the last few years and I predict none in the near future. (Hortin and Teague 1983 p. 29)

Educational systems continue to lag behind other sectors of society for well-identified academic, economic, and political reasons. Large-format film and television, for example, are infrequently found in educational settings. On the contrary, classrooms and school auditoria are typically inadequate if not deplorable even in the simplest 16mm seating, auditory, and projection requirements. "Spectator comfort" has been a principal concern of the CSTCF—the *Commission Supérieur Technique du Cinéma Françâis*—for at least a decade, and the Society of Motion Picture and Television Engineers has published long-established standards for film and television viewing situations, but the recommendations of such internationally recognized bodies seem to be ignored by educational administrators in designing learning environments (see *Learning Environments*).

The media are changing the nature of such environments, including the home, and the function of the teachers as well. Teachers are referred to as "providers" in the Canadian Teledon cable system. A new abbreviated way of writing is required for the print messages in teletext material on the television tube, raising questions of legibility, rate of delivery, vocabulary level, and other issues once thought to be only the province of print. "Visual literacy" is coming to have a meaning that must include reading as well as visual abilities. The essential function of print is thus subsumed in the total design of what have been classically characterized as media which have undermined the young learner's ability and interest in the book.

The design of educational materials is affected by the parsimony of television messages, including the commercials, as well as by the longer, multi-episode television series and miniseries. Such design must take into account the likelihood of individual ownership of visual materials in the form of videotapes and videodiscs. This will make possible the random accessing and comparative personal viewing of film and television programs which were formerly only available in group settings.

Good design in educational productions has always included the elements of organization, amplification or enhancement of the subject, simplification, and dramatization. Today, media designers are also concerned with the elements of flexibility, modularity, and interaction with the viewer or learner.

Open systems such as videotex add other dimensions to the educational potential of the electronic media. For example, when using the Prestel system in the United Kingdom, and Antiope in France, a consumer–learner is hooked up to telephone lines or coaxial cable linked to a television receiver with which he or she can interact with or instruct the machine by using a calculator-type keyboard. In Columbus, Ohio, the Warner QUBE system provides 30 channels with five response buttons making possible, through connection with a home computer, interactive exchanges between the studio and the viewers including political polling, game shows, and credit courses at three educational institutions in the area. This system however, once extended to several other cities, has been found economically unviable, and interactive programming was greatly reduced by 1984. A more sophisticated interactive experiment is found in a community in Japan where all households on the system have direct, interactive cable communication with respondents in all other households in the system. While presently mostly used for person-to-person communication, the potential for the use of film, videotape, and videodisc materials in these settings may begin to be realized as respondents on these interactive systems explore ways to visualize as well as verbalize their messages. Visual contact through built-in cameras or videophone systems linked to disc, tape, or film playbacks could produce, in homes and schools, the effect now found in teleconferencing in industry and business settings and in some university or public broadcast systems (see *Videotex and Electronic Mail*).

Highly creative imagery may be eventually fed into such a system, including some poetic and personal visions in the form of the modern equivalent of the family photographic album, the "snapshot," or the "home movie." References may also be drawn from on-shelf videotapes or videodiscs, selected through random access, to illustrate a point; to stimulate those to whom the message is directed to say: "I *see* what you mean!"

3. Image Consumer as Producer

From time of birth all people are image consumers absorbing verbal, visual, and auditory signs and symbols as part of their cultural heritage. But people also continually process such information through their own perceptual system, altering these messages and reproducing them in terms of what they are and what they know. Thus, a great number of factors external to any specific film or television display come into play as part of its effect on any given set of viewers.

The classic transaction between the image maker (communicator) and image consumer (receiver) is immensely enhanced through technology which makes it possible for the viewer to change a given message, not only psychologically but also physically, and to do this instantaneously while a program is in progress. Interactive cable networks offer viewers multiple choices on many issues including what and when certain programs are preferred, which should be cut off before completion, polling of opinion on public matters, and the like, thus making it possible to receive, collate, and report such reactions on the screen within five seconds, as in the case of the Warner-Amex QUBE system once found in several cities in the United States.

More direct involvement in production has been possible with 8mm film, home videotape recording equipment, and public broadcast access to the facilities for the creation and public exhibition of film and to works by individuals or civic groups. Thus in the former "Challenge for Change" program in Canada and the present "Public Access" cable channels in the United States, programs conceived and produced by nonprofessionals with the help of experienced broadcast personnel have been put on the air.

While professional producers will always be required, there is a growing involvement of nonprofessionals in the image-making process. A large part of this development has been due to the advent of what Illich refers to as "convivial tools" which, as he defines them,

> . . . are those which give each person who uses them the greatest opportunity to enrich the environment with the fruits of his or her vision. . . . Tools foster conviviality to the extent to which they can be easily used, by anybody, as often or as seldom as desired, for the accomplishment of a purpose chosen by the user. The use of such tools by one person does not restrain another from using them equally. They do not require previous certification by the user. Their existence does not impose any obligation to use them. They allow the user to express his meaning in action. (Illich 1973a p. 67)

This concept is supported by the fact that students are becoming involved in the design and construction of learning materials, from books to films. Amateur videotapes of disasters and other happenings are beginning to appear with more regularity on both local and network news in the United States and elsewhere. Local cultural and ethnic groups are expressing themselves in their own idiom—the Navajo Indians of the American southwest, and the natives of Liberia and Zambia reflecting their own cultural values in film and video forms. The Innuit of northern Canada have their own television station, and the Aboriginals of Western Australia their own radio broadcast facility.

The case for local production is expressed by the chairman of the public service commission of New Guinea:

> It is a political reality that television will come to Papua, New Guinea. Certainly I have no wish to deprive my fellow countrymen of the value of good television broadcasting, [but]. . .we should be doing everything humanly possible to ensure that our television programmes should have a preponderance of locally-made material, scripted and filmed *by* our own people *for* our own people. (Lohia 1982 p. 5)

The same opinion is reflected by the Secretary-General of the South Pacific Commission:

> I think the greatest need is for the recognition of Pacific cultures, the recognition of the need for Pacific content in radio, television, and film programmes, and hence a need for Pacific professionals in the industry. (Bogutu 1982 p. 6)

In 1982 at the 21st International Congress of the *Centre Internationale de Liasion des Ecoles de Cinéma et de Télévision*, representatives of national film and television schools from more than 30 nations passed a resolution that students of cinema and television production should be trained and educated to communicate not only with audiences of theatrical films and broadcast television, but also for purposes of education, information, and national development. It was declared necessary to combine the study of film, television, and video along with other related communication technologies in courses of study. It was also agreed that the education and training of film and television personnel in the developing countries should receive the support of established training centers who should help such countries to organize their own film and television centers to educate their own producers, and determine the introduction of the appropriate technologies of communication to meet the objectives of their national development (Camre and Giese 1982).

Such developments appear to be predictive of the future of the film and television producer and the role of the media. It does not seem to restrict, but rather expand, the responsibility of the professional even as production opportunities become more available to the nonprofessional, since participation in the image production process makes it more collaborative, democratic, and personal as people begin to speak directly to other people through audiovisual imagery.

4. Futures in Media

Forecasting, regarded with suspicion in most academic circles, is a central concern in the communication industry. The Rand Corporation, for example, developed the "Delphi" technique (informed opinion polling), one of many methodologies being used to reduce bias and the "crystal ball" effect in futuring. For film and television production such futuring is regarded as essential for its existence.

A Delphi study conducted in 1979–80, in 20 countries involving 80 authorities, 21 percent of whom were from universities and international communication institutes, 21 percent from governments and international organizations, 19 percent from aerospace and telecommunications industries, and others from various research organizations, predicted with more than 50 percent agreement, that by the year 2000: there would be continual and rapid growth in the tele-informational services including videotext and videoconferencing; and direct broadcast satellite services in homes for under 100 dollars (US 1979) in the countries associated with the OECD—the Organisation for Economic Co-operation and Development.

Industrialization and the construction of megastructures in space would be counterbalanced by "a lack of significant progress in achieving unified international, social, political, and economic cooperation in telecommunications or space applications. Global cooperation was thus expected to continue on an ad hoc, piecemeal basis". The summarizer of the report concludes that there would be: "A prosperous and information-rich society, one that risks information overload for its citizenry and in which individual privacy may be endangered by universal data bases and electronic monitoring" (Pelton 1981 p. 189).

A similar Delphi study conducted in 1981 at Indiana University, exploring the question of the future of film and video specifically in education, reported the consensus of 56 experts in the production of instructional media, including the following predictions: there will be more emphasis on planning and evaluation as part of production development; media designers and producers by 2001 will be skilled in both technology and instructional design, and will work as teams of technical, creative, and educational specialists; and media design will become more creative, flexible, and interactive with programs being produced with specific objectives for specific learners in both formal and informal learning environments. Referring to the latter, this report stated that "a major portion of the instructional media of 2001 will be used in the home; an increase in leisure time will result in a greater demand for instructional materials for the general public; the home market will be the driving force for the development of instructional hardware and software; and that the development of the home market will make possible the mass distribution of instructional media at low cost" (Dayton 1982 pp. 236–37).

The role of commercial producers of educational media is seen as "critical" by some educators because "Teachers don't know enough about designing varied forms of instruction" (Hortin and Teague 1983 p. 28). Interactive cable, educational conferencing by satellite, high-definition video and videodisc, and even "talking toys" are identified as being the significant media of the future. On the other hand, there seems to be little emphasis on advances in matters of instructional design and development although considerable research may be devoted to these areas.

The evidence on the future of the role of media, as in other forecasting, is mixed, but it appears that an immense quantity of photoelectronic production will be needed to satisfy the requirements of entertainment, instruction, and education in the decades ahead to meet a sustained growth in the number of persons having access to such media. In this process the rivalry between film and television technologies will become obsolete as they merge and become interrelated with the microcomputer, telephone, and other communication technologies (Mareth 1983 p. 717).

The historic fear of the negative influence of film and television may also be demystified as more consumers and groups of consumers become aware of the ways in which these media are constructed and as they continue to gain access to the means of production. A French communications expert at a UNESCO conference in Paris expressed this recent optimistic vision: "I do not know what type of happiness is given to people without television, but I know all the pleasure I have to get all the knowledge of this world by pushing just a button, and I feel very lucky to have this strange window 24 hours a day in my living (sic)" (Flipo 1982 p. 82–42).

Production of photoelectronic media of the future must be based on designs that take into account their uses in "24-hour living" environments in a proliferation of forms including videodisc, tape, film, cable television, satellite transmission, 360° screens to be seen by thousands of viewers at one time, and screens the size of a wrist watch for an audience of one.

More and better trained designers and producers are needed, including professional groups utilizing "high" technologies, as well as local, indigenous individuals and groups who will continue to make useful and successful productions using less expensive "low" technologies. Producers of all types will need to have some form of continuing education to keep up with rapidly shifting technology and the changing needs of education and society. Producers, working with educators, will need to participate in media futuring, although the predictions referred to in earlier citations mention technologies which, for the most part, are already in place, and there are very few surprises in these forecasts. There will be a continual increase in the number and kinds of photoelectronic productions and, in an information-rich world society, there will always be some groups and individuals who will be more and better informed than others. Worldwide communication systems being implemented by international corporations may or may not equalize educational opportunities for all. Quantity of production and multiplication of delivery system forms does not mean a quantum leap in the improvement of quality, unless educators, teachers, administrators, designers, and media producers place the highest priority on the development of a world population of verbally and visually literate human beings. This requires massive administrative, financial, and human resources devoted to the design, production, and utilization of all forms of these proliferating photoelectronic media for the purpose of teaching the world the things which must be known to relieve the pressing personal, national, and international problems shared by all, and to improve the quality of entertainment, education, and life itself in the twenty-first century.

Bibliography

Bogutu F 1982 Address to the 21st International Congress of the Centre International de Liaison des Ecoles de Cinéma et de Télévision. *Proceedings of the Congress.* Australian Film and Television School, Sydney

Bygrave M, Goodman J 1981 Meet me in Las Vegas. *Amer. Film* Oct: 38–43

Camre H, Giese S 1982 *Bridging the Gap: Towards a Policy and Strategy for Film and Television Training in the Developing World.* Danish National Film School, Copenhagen

Dayton D K 1982 Future trends in the production of instructional materials: 1981–2001. *J. Educ. Technol. Commun.* 29(4): 192–99

Flipo E 1982 IFTC intervention during the NGO's meeting. IFTC *Letter of Information* 82(9): 82–42

Harwood A M 1983 Cable television, and satellite broadcasting. BKSTS *J.* 65: 192–98

Hortin J A, Teague F A (eds.) 1983 Thoughts from the field of educational technology. *Educ. Considerations* 10(2)

Illich I D 1973a *Tools for Conviviality*. Perennial Library, New York

Illich I D 1973b Convivial tools. *Sat. Rev. Educ.* 1: 62–64

Journal for the Society of MPTV Engineers 1981 90(9): 1004

Lohia R R 1982 Implications of the introduction of television in Papua New Guinea. *Proceedings of the Congress of CILECT*. Australian Film and Television School, Sydney

Mareth P 1983 Film and video: A producer's viewpoint. *J. SMPTE* 92(7): 716–17

Moralee D 1983 Telecine: Bridging the gap between film and tape. BKSTS *J.* 65: 218–22

Pelton J N 1981 The future of telecommunications: A Delphi survey. *J. Commun.* Winter: 177–89

Use of Television in the Classroom

S. Rockman and R. Burke

This article deals mainly with the systematic use of instructional television programs in elementary and secondary classrooms. Other uses are treated elsewhere. A historical introduction leads to a discussion of roles for classroom television and hence to patterns of use. The presentation of some specific examples is then followed by a brief concluding section.

1. Introduction

Many countries that adopted classroom television in the late 1950s and early 1960s had already had some experience with classroom radio. Educators had seen the benefits of using electronic mass media to bring stimulating materials from the world at large into the classroom. Television broadcasters, like their radio predecessors, saw school programming as a good opportunity to render an important and necessary public service. Yet what seemed to be a mutually satisfactory relationship was in many instances an uneasy alliance. Educators were concerned mainly with pedagogical values, whereas broadcasters, focusing on the medium, were concerned mainly with entertainment and audience appeal.

The pattern of development was markedly different in North America and Europe. North American initiatives were primarily local and usually ambitious. Encouraged by the extravagant claims of proponents of new media, school administrators looked on television as a means of improving curricula, of upgrading teachers, and of bringing about significant changes in educational practice. Teachers, on the other hand, often looked on classroom television as an imposition from above and as a threat to their long-cherished sense of autonomy. They resented the implication that their teaching was somehow deficient, and they found repugnant such terms as "follow-up teacher" or "receiving teacher." They further resented the inflexible broadcasting schedules, which made little allowance for individual needs.

Many teachers, along with administrators, were appalled by the quality of most of the early programs. Television had been promoted as a "window on the world," a "magic box," and so forth, but in fact it offered too many programs of "talking heads"—teachers standing in front of chalkboards, giving conventional lectures in a conventionally didactic manner.

By the late 1960s, however, educators and broadcasters started moving in more productive directions. Each group made greater efforts to understand the other's point of view, with the result that classroom television became, often, a product of cooperation and integration, built from creative tension rather than from antagonism and mistrust.

The quality problem was less marked in Europe, where production was in the hands of national broadcasting agencies. However, the development of classroom television was quite slow. There was little pressure on teachers to use the television programs available; and many education authorities were apprehensive of the cost of progressively equipping all their schools. Although a minority of teachers were enthusiastic from the outset, many were unwilling to adapt their teaching to accommodate the new medium. They felt unsure of themselves in handling it, and scheduling was a major source of difficulty in most secondary schools.

The producers, meanwhile, had been experimenting with pilot schemes and were learning what television could most usefully and effectively provide for the classroom. In the United Kingdom, where the term used was always educational rather than instructional broadcasting, the first television programs were almost exclusively directed to the enrichment both of children's experiences and of their teachers' resources. In the secondary schools, which were their first target, both the British Broadcasting Corporation (BBC) and the independent television companies endeavored by means of a varied output in such subjects as geography, science, current affairs, and drama to add a dimension of their own to the teacher's work. In spite of the difficulties of timetabling and the priority generally given by teachers to their own basic courses and television often being referred to as a frill, these enrichment programs acquired a faithful and appreciative clientele sometimes of considerable size. Talking heads were an infrequent source of complaint, and programs were valued for the skilful application of studio techniques, a wide ranging use of film, and a generally high standard of performance.

In the primary schools the flexibility of the curriculum made it easier for teachers to adopt television as a stimulus to their work and as a springboard for interesting new projects. The visual element soon became immensely popular, making conspicuous contributions over a wide field of general knowledge, in music and in remedial work. Eventually some series attracted audiences in 70 or even 80 percent of junior and infant schools.

In contrast to developed countries, developing countries have seen the emergence of different problems as they have attempted to use television in classrooms. Since the early 1970s, developing countries have devoted enormous resources to education. Because of the expense of developing a traditional Western school system, administrators turned to technology in an effort to do more with fewer teachers and at the same time to take advantage of the economies of scale associated with broadcasting.

Although more planning has been done in recent years, at first many groups rushed in too quickly. Weaknesses in curriculum and instructional planning became widely evident in short order. Plans to provide universal quality education through television in a few years were unrealistic, and the several attempts to do so were unsuccessful. What took a century in Europe and North America could not be done in a year or two.

The belief that television would reduce educational costs was also mistaken. Television still required the presence of a teacher for its most advantageous use. It was an addition to the system and often improved neither the quality nor the quantity of classroom instruction.

Problems similar to those in developed nations also emerged. The teachers who had training, especially at the high-school level, found television programs to be inconsistent with their teaching values and styles. Administrative mandates were not sufficient justifications for the use of television; poorly developed curricula led to teachers' rejection of materials. Television was superimposed on the educational system without respect for the nature of the system.

Television should not be blamed for the failures. A medium that promised everything—a solution to all of education's problems, a cure for an ailing society, economical and political benefits—was not capable of living up to expectations. It is less productive to blame the medium than to change the expectations.

Classroom television can be highly beneficial to education and society in nations with widely diverse political, economic, and educational systems. In order to succeed, television must do only what it does best.

2. Roles

Educators who have chosen to adopt classroom television have usually done so for one or more of the following reasons:

2.1 Improvement of Quality

Ideally, the television programs represent the best educational efforts of curriculum specialists, program designers, audiovisual artists, and broadcasting specialists; the programs incorporate the best, most up-to-date thinking in the field; and the content is presented in an attractive and stimulating format.

2.2 Television as a Catalyst

Classroom television can also stimulate educators to reconsider curricular options, to evaluate methods of pedagogy now in practice, and to see new relationships among discrete curricular areas. It provides a source of ideas for teachers and can catalyze their development of more varied, more motivating, and more contemporary practices. Classroom television has helped to facilitate the rapid dissemination of new curricular ideas, many of which remain long after their parent projects or programs have been abandoned.

2.3 Television as a Means of Extending Children's Experience

Television in the classroom is truly what UNESCO has often called it: "a window on the world." The programs allow students to transcend the boundaries of space and time, and to see society in new and diverse ways. The rural child sees life in the city, and the urban child sees life in the country; various patterns of consumption and economic structure, alternative religious forms, cultural patterns, and sexual role models become available.

2.4 Television as a Means of Introducing Affective Education

Television has been instrumental in introducing affective education into elementary classrooms. Television programs that provide shared, relatively universal experiences have given teachers and students the opportunity to examine their feelings about themselves and their environment. Similar opportunities arise in secondary social studies and humanities. Developing a national identity is an important goal of television in newly independent countries; and television can also be used to encourage and strengthen diverse cultural and religious traditions.

2.5 Television as a Means of Equalizing Educational Opportunity

Educational inequality is a persistent problem in most countries, from both economic and sociocultural viewpoints. A broadcast signal, however, is not limited to wealthy school districts or to new schools. For young children, in particular, the impact of programs developing basic skills has been encouraging, and similar programs for older students are now being created.

Presenting black faces in all-white schools and white faces in all-black schools provides useful role models of all races to facilitate interracial acceptance and understanding. But what school television can do best in equalizing educational opportunity is to provide instructional presentations so universal that they become specific to every viewer and are effective regardless of sex, race, ethnic background, or economic condition.

2.6 Television as a Means of Improving Efficiency and Productivity

Productivity in education means significantly more than the ability of fewer teachers to teach more students. It means better preparation of students to be effective and fulfilled members of the community at large. When school television adds to the number of possible approaches to instruction, stimulates improved class interactions, initiates and reinforces cognitive learning, or motivates better classroom behavior, it is providing better, more efficient education.

To increase productivity requires finding the right mixture of school television and classroom teaching. By using school television economically—that is, by examining the variety of available utilization and programming options and by choosing wisely—educators can effect improvements in the patterns and results of instruction with minimal increases in cost. Television is not seeking to replace teachers, only to assist them in reaching their desired goals.

2.7 Television-based Instructional Systems

In several countries, the main vehicle for achieving some of these goals has been a television-based instructional system. Such systems are distinguished, not by their format or purpose, but by their mode of development. The program designers are commited to a method of development that incorporates a student needs assessment, a lesson design, formative evaluation, product revision, summative evaluation, and the revision of objectives and strategies. Their product may include not only television programs but also any printed supplementary materials, such as teacher's guides or student workbooks, designed to complement the curriculum directly. The programs are viewed in the classroom on a regular, long-term basis, and should then result either in a measurable difference between the students who receive instruction by television and those who do not, or in some attributable change over time in learning gain, attitude, or behavior. Otherwise further revision is needed.

3. Patterns of Use

Classroom television must be seen as more than a television program. Complex interactions between the program, people, and their environment all contribute to instruction. To describe the process, it is perhaps easiest to begin with utilization.

3.1 Viewing Conditions

In some cases, the unit of instruction is the television program alone. Individual viewers learn by themselves. But in most cases, the instructional unit is the television lesson. A teacher spends a few minutes preparing the class, with a series of questions for discussion or independent thought, or a review of previously taught concepts, vocabulary words, or other advance organizers. Then the class attends to the television set and views the program with the teacher. Teachers viewing prerecorded tapes on classroom playback equipment are able to stop and start the tapes, illustrating and reinforcing teaching points throughout the viewing period.

After the viewing, teachers use a variety of techniques—structured discussions, the teaching of related content, written exercises and tests—to continue the lesson. Any activity that reinforces and extends the content will be valuable to students. Sometimes homework, testing, or a long-term project is part of the lesson.

The classroom environment influences the use and the effectiveness of school television. The television receiver must be visible to all students and in good working order; the conditions for transmission and reception or playback must provide a usable signal. The time of day may also be important. Television is a change of pace in a lecture-and-workbook classroom; it may be especially welcome in the late morning before lunch, just after lunch, or in the late afternoon.

Accumulated research evidence suggests that the degree to which the television program becomes part of the traditional classroom process and the degree to which it is treated like other instructional materials, can significantly effect learning. Conversely, the degree to which teachers diminish the perceived value of the program—for example, by leaving the room when it is on or by ignoring its content after viewing—will determine how credible students find the program.

To use classroom television successfully, one must take into account the nature of the interacting variables: the personal characteristics of teachers and students, the interpersonal relationships within the school and the class, the program itself as designed and produced, and the environmental conditions under which it is viewed.

3.2 Teacher

Teachers vary greatly in their ability (and willingness) to develop comprehensive lessons for a television program; often they depend on a teacher's guide for the program. Often they take cues from their students and form opinions about the program based on students' reactions to it; a program that holds the attention of the students may be seen as successsful even if its content is weak.

Teachers vary also in their attitudes towards television and other technologies in the classroom. If television is presented to them as a means of replacing them or reducing their autonomy, they will use it with great reluctance. However, if television lessons are designed to help meet the learning goals of the classroom, teachers will be quick to adopt and use them. The attitude of administrators also greatly affects the willingness of teachers to use television and the degree of emphasis they place on it. The support system for teachers—

administrative, technical, student, and parent attitudes—also contributes to successful school television utilization.

Students take cues from their teachers and treat television as they do. However, even if the students bring a positive attitude to the viewing, the program may change their attitude. The program must be at the appropiate developmental level, must treat the content and the viewer with intelligence, and must appeal to the viewer.

Attention to the television program is a serious concern. While distractions to the viewer at home are common and inconsequential, attention to the program at school is a neccessary, though insufficient, condition for learning. Moreover, inattention by a few students can easily escalate if they do something that distracts the teacher and other students.

3.3 Instructional Design

Research into the nature of viewing and of the viewing audience has led to some understanding of how television works best. The attributes of television programs that contribute to their appeal, salience, interest, and educational value must be insured in the design and production of the programs. The technical resources on command include music, movement, sequencing, format, and character appeal. To make the most of these, researchers may often cooperate with designers and producers to create successful programs.

The instructional design of school television programs must also take viewing conditions into account. If the program is to require no follow-up from the teacher, it should include factors that promote immediate student learning, for example, advance organizers, repetition, and so on. However, if the teacher is to be an integral part of the lesson, the role of the program can be:

(a) to introduce the content for the teacher to elaborate later and to drill the students on;

(b) to provide background material for a lesson the teacher will deliver;

(c) to reinforce and review ideas already covered in class;

(d) to provide salient illustrations that will stimulate class discussion and discovery.

These pedagogical functions should be taken into account in the design and production of school television programs.

4. Examples

4.1 United States: ThinkAbout

One well-documented classroom television project is the "ThinkAbout" series developed by a consortium of American states and Canadian provinces. The state and provincial education and television agencies received unlimited and unrestricted use of the materials for seven or more years in return for their financial and intellectual support. This series was initiated, developed, and produced over a six-year period by the Agency for Instructional Television and consists of sixty 15-minute programs for students 10 to 12 years of age.

The project's initial focus was presenting various general problem-solving skills in realistic settings as a means of improving the way students learned and studied. Over the course of the project's development period, the focus shifted towards the reinforcement of already-taught skills in language arts, social studies, and mathematics. The programs illustrated the application of these subject matter skills in out-of-school situations. The general problem-solving theme remained in many of the programs but with less emphasis than originally planned. The curriculum was developed in conjunction with teachers and subject matter specialists and extensively verified with classroom teachers.

The design of the programs moved along this path as a result of the influence of the consortium of states and provinces funding the project. The representatives of these funding agencies were, for the most part, middle level administrators of their state or provincial education or television agency who met regularly during the development and production phases to review programs and reflect on the project's activities. The problem-solving curriculum appeared to them as a drastic departure from the traditional emphasis on subject matter skills and as possibly too advanced for teachers to easily adapt and use in the classroom. The political pressure from the funders resulted in a modification of the curriculum, in a change meant to make the instructional materials more accessible to, and usable by, fifth- and sixth-grade teachers.

The television programs themselves are short, realistic dramas that set up a plausible problem for students but end before the problem has been resolved. This approach gains the attention of students by the appeal of the "real-life" drama, and motivates them to finish solving the problem in the classroom. Extensive formative evaluation helped instructional designers identify appealing dramatic segments and salient teaching points. Programs were revised during production based on the feedback provided by representative teachers and classrooms.

The pattern of classroom use is as follows: the teachers focus students' attention on the topic or theme of the program and often relate the theme to ongoing classwork in a specific curriculum. The class and the teacher then view the program together. Following the viewing the teacher directs a discussion of the program, its theme, and the application of ideas presented in the program to activities in school and out. The discussion often takes a spiraling route, at first a recapitulation of the events in the program to be sure everyone understands what has been seen, followed by a generation of alternative hypotheses or solutions to the problem. This is followed, in turn, by relating the problem and its theme to classwork currently underway. Seatwork assignments and long-term class activities are included in the teacher guide but do not seem to be used frequently.

In use, many teachers find 60 programs to be more than they can comfortably fit into their schedule, especially since they commonly use more than one television series. Thus, alternative utilization patterns have emerged. Rather than using the series at a two-per-week rate over the course of a school year, some teachers, with the cooperation of their broadcasting agencies or with access to videocassette recorders, use the first 30 programs for the fifth grade and the second 30 for the sixth grade. A more common pattern, especially in areas where the use of videocassette machines is the norm, is the selection and viewing of individual programs or groups of programs on a common theme when convenient. In this manner the correlation of the programs with course material is more precise and, because of the foresight and planning required, the television program is very likely to be well-integrated into the lesson.

Evidence from research associated with the "ThinkAbout" project shows very modest changes in problem-solving abilities, a result due to several factors. First, measurement of problem-solving skills is an emerging and exploratory effort with few valid and reliable measures; second, the research design desired by the consortium militated against finding strong experimental-control group differences; and third, the modification of the curriculum placed less emphasis on problem-solving skills, which remained the overall goal of the series. Nevertheless, research evidence indicates the widespread appeal and use of the material. The modified curriculum in problem solving—an organized curriculum heretofore not present in more than a handful of classrooms—was adopted and used successfully by a wide variety of teachers who differed greatly in background, teaching style, and subject matter emphasis. The series continues to be in wide use as of its fourth year.

4.2 Canada: Eureka!

Television Ontario (TVO) has taken a different approach to the development and use of a school television series. TVO is a provincial organization responsible for many aspects of intraprovince communications including elementary and secondary classroom television. In contrast to the curriculum development efforts of the Agency for Instructional Television (AIT), which had to find common agreement across state, provincial, and national borders, TVO starts with a centrally adopted curriculum statement and a relatively homogenous population.

To help define educational needs that can best be served by television, discipline-specific advisory committees were formed. These committees periodically commission needs ascertainment surveys of the membership of professional organizations and other teachers of a subject. These surveys explore what is taught (both core and optional topics within the established curriculum) and what is difficult to teach (especially among the core

topics). In exploring the themes that seemed especially difficult to teach, survey results often point to the lack of curriculum support materials for those topics.

The discipline advisory committee and TVO staff review the material that is perceived as difficult to teach and partition out those concepts that television would find difficult to do (or that a teacher could do better), and those concepts that are undergoing a change in curricular emphasis and should not be tackled at present. The remaining concepts become a ranked list of priorities.

Two or three practicing teachers who teach the subject well work with a TVO producer and writer to develop program materials that can engage teachers and students, remediate the curriculum deficiency, and match the established provincial curriculum.

The "Eureka!" series was developed to meet the needs of seventh- and eighth-grade science teachers, usually science generalists, who were having difficulty teaching certain physics topics. The high priority curriculum needs identified by the needs ascertainment survey were all central to the students' understanding of physics and could be directly taught as independent single concepts. The content for short models developed by the TVO team was then validated by university faculty and made into single-concept, 5-minute units in full cell-animation. Within this 5-minute unit there were several potential stopping points built in, so that a teacher could have discussion with the class on one aspect of the content, clarify the material, and raise issues for continued focus before continuing the program. This design practically demands the use of videocassettes and about 90–95 percent of the use is with the teacher-controlled tape unit. This design also permits the teacher to use the single concept program, follow it with an experiment or book work exercise, and then the class (or individuals within the class) can view the program again.

While the material is designed for in-school use, its highly appealing animation format makes it useful in other contexts. TVO presently uses the programs as fillers between science programs during the evening broadcasts. The material is widely used and evaluation data are currently being collected to explore its impact.

4.3 United States: Freestyle

The "Freestyle" series is a well-documented project initiated from a strong federal perspective. These 13 half-hour-long programs were designed to aid children's career development and reduce restrictions on career selection based on sex and social stereotyping. These programs are "prosocial" in their goals and are directed more towards attitude change than towards classroom-related knowledge or behavior. Nevertheless, these materials found their widest use and greatest impact in the classroom.

This television project was conceived as a major federal initiative to meet broad social goals and its creation was undertaken by a consortium of independent television education, university, and research organizations.

Much background research and formative evaluation led to the selection of themes included in the project's curriculum. The mix of educators and "Hollywood" production personnel led initially to great confusion over the amount of instructional content and the degree to which it would be emphasized. A strong executive producer was able to get the production process under control, striking a balance between education and entertainment, with a tilt toward the latter.

The programs were designed with a strong dramatic format and were structured to balance the highly entertaining material with the social modeling needed to meet educational goals. While initially scripted as half-hour programs, the design called for a dramatic high-point about half-way through the program. In this format, a single program could be divided in two in order to more easily fit classroom time periods. Thus, a half-hour program useful in the broadcast schedule for at-home viewing, could be seen in two parts within the same week in a classroom.

As the project was being developed, the influence of the funders and the conflicting demands placed on the producer led to a modification of the project's goals. Rather than give equal focus to racial and gender stereotyping, the emphasis was placed on sexual bias and stereotyping. It was thought that a single major issue could be more easily handled through the format selected.

During its first year of availability, a major study of the series impact was conducted on its use at home and in school. Using a best-case model in the schools, the researchers noted impressive changes in attitudes towards nontraditional sex-role behavior. This best-case model studies the programs under ideal rather than normal conditions of use. Little flexibility is permitted in the manner and amount of viewing and postviewing activities. Teachers used a warm-up activity to introduce the viewing of the lesson, followed the class viewing with extensive discussion, and used prepared printed materials for short- and long-term follow up.

The impact of the series was reduced under at-home conditions and when the emphasis in classrooms was reduced. The setting in which the programs were used and the importance attributed to the instructional nature of the programs seem to have greatly influenced the impact of the series.

The series was widely broadcast to homes and schools during its first year, but its availability diminished rapidly over the next two. It is no longer available since, under the commercially based system of production, the rights to the material were obtained only for three years.

4.4 United Kingdom: "Scene"

For the 15-year-old school student in the United Kingdom there are some 15 to 20 broadcasts available in any week of the school year. Over half of these are concerned with the main curricular subjects—mathematics, the sciences, English, history, geography, modern languages. The remainder cover such areas as career guidance, the arts, and social studies. In the latter class the most popular and successful is "Scene," a weekly transmission of documentary or dramatized programs for teenagers, providing material for discussion, investigation, and written work.

The introduction and early development of this series is described in some detail by Kenneth Fawdry (1974) who was Head of the British Broadcasting Corporation (BBC) Schools Television at that time, and an account by the producer, Ronald Smedley, has also been published (Marland 1972). Some of the broadcasts are on very controversial topics, and several were specially commissioned scripts from well-known contemporary playwrights. Most are presented from the teenager's angle, with a special thought for the nonintellectual student who is impatient to leave school at 16.

The two descriptions which follow cannot represent the diversity of themes encompassed by "Scene," but they can give some indication of the producer's approach to the audience and of the reactions at the viewing end.

"The Last Bus" tells in dramatized form how a group of high-spirited, irresponsible teenage boys board the last bus home, pick a quarrel with the bus conductor, beat him up and, as an afterthought, steal his purse. There were a few fellow passengers and, though mildly protesting, none of them came to the victim's aid. The driver, a West Indian, froze to his seat, fearing the consequences to himself and to his family's precarious existence if he should intervene and himself be mugged in consequence.

A BBC schools' liaison officer reported, after watching the broadcast with a large class of 45 adolescents: "I am convinced they really lived through the whole incident: they had been caught up in those feelings of devilment, arrogance and hatred that presumably account for many acts of teenage aggression."

Then the scene abruptly changed. The presenter of the program turned investigator and cross-examined each of the passengers as they made excuses for their inaction. Finally the bus conductor himself showed more magnanimity than the youths deserved, saying that he understood these pranks that got out of hand; he had helped in youth clubs and the like.

Not all the viewing classes appear to have understood this inquisitorial ploy; but, by the crude measuring rod of excited comments and questions afterwards, the program was a spectacular success. Another visiting BBC officer wrote: "This . . . arresting, provocative but simple story line is a certain way of getting through to this kind of child, who has little reading ability, is bored with traditional teaching. . . . It may be the nearest they will get to any depth of thought on current social issues."

The following week's broadcast, "The Sentence of the Court," told what happened to the boys and showed the ringleader, very much deflated, in a borstal prison, while a probation officer and a borstal governor were interviewed about their work and spoke frankly about the difficulties and shortcomings of the system of punishment and rehabilitation of which they were a part. This well-devised program did not have the impact of "The Last Bus," but enabled the thoughtful viewer to ponder further the problems of teenage violence and its consequences.

The second recent broadcast which also made a considerable impression, "James is our Brother," is a study of a mentally handicapped boy. The program starts with his first unassisted journey home from school—catching the right bus, paying his fare, changing buses, getting off at the right stop—a landmark of achievement in James' struggle to cope with the outside world. Then his brothers and sisters describe life at home with James, and through copious film inserts he is seen gradually surmounting his difficulties, establishing a modus vivendi among his peers, and finally entering for the Olympics for the Disabled and receiving a bronze medal from the Duke of Edinburgh. By now he is articulate enough to speak for himself and describes his conquest of the problems of everyday life ("They don't take the mickey any more; they don't laugh"), and he proudly shows the press photograph of himself with the Duke.

The audience reaction may be judged from a selection of the postcard reports sent by viewing teachers to the producer of the series:

Very good because it portrays life from the point of view of the mentally handicapped person, particularly the last conversation with James. They greatly admired the interviewer's sympathetic handling of James. . . .

The programme was excellent. . . . Many of the class were very moved. They had been able to appreciate James' gallant attitude to life and his philosophical acceptance of being "different." They noted the maturity of his brothers' attitude, and this led on to discussion led by two pupils who had mongol chlidren in the family. . . .

This outstanding programme . . . ought to be a part of every school's compulsory studies. . . .

In one school, a class composed a letter to the local council asking for a hostel to be built in the area, and in another school a group of girls decided to offer to help at a nearby school for severely subnormal children.

A BBC schools liaison officer visited a class of 35 boys and girls of good intelligence and watched the taped programme with them. "The atmosphere was electric. . . . Everyone laughed a lot with James and some of the girls and Hazel (their teacher) were close to tears several times. . . ." Immediately afterwards the teacher got everyone to write down their instant reactions. "Feelings of anger, sadness over the whole situation predominated. . . . The boys were very articulate in expressing their anger at those who laugh at mongols. . . . A group of girls said they didn't realize how human the mentally handicapped feel." They then built up a character study of James and were surprised to find that his qualities and his attitudes were very much like their own. The officer's report goes on to commend the teacher's versatile and imaginative handling of "this superbly moving programme."

4.5 Comparisons

Of these four projects, the first three were all developed from carefully researched bases of information and direction. They differed in the way they related to the educational mission of the schools. "Eureka!" illustrates the closest fit with the existing curricula of schools and was designed to be integrated closely with existing instruction. "ThinkAbout" attempted to extend the curriculum slightly by introducing and organizing problem-solving skills (many of which were being haphazardly taught in the classroom). This infusion of new curriculum material succeeded because it built on the familiar, and on the related skills in basic subject areas taught universally in the schools.

"Freestyle," in contrast, attempted to deal with a social problem through instruction. Its initiative was from a federal source in a nation where state and local agencies have the responsibility for education. While the focus of this series is certainly important to the United States (and other nations), it is not seen as important to schools.

These three projects also used an instructional design process through which the programs and related print materials could be developed, evaluated, and revised. In some cases the political process imposed itself, but with the best intention—that of getting the series used.

All three had the highest of production values, and the expectations for the projects were supported with large budgets. As a result, all were seen as highly appealing to students and teachers and obtained, at a minimum, an initial use in large numbers of classrooms. The continued use, however, was based on the programs' perceived utility in assisting teachers to reach their stated instructional goals.

The fourth example, "Scene," differs somewhat from the other three, being a continuing miscellany of programs not necessarily related to any special syllabus or project. Replacing a current affairs series, "Spotlight," of some years' standing, "Scene" was easily integrated into the nationwide service of broadcasts to schools whose general policy is laid down by an Educational Broadcasting Council representative of the whole educational spectrum. Within these policy lines, program proposals are examined and accepted, modified or rejected by committees of educationalists appointed by the Council. They are normally subject to no other political pressures.

School producers have access to all the resources of the BBC and, subject to a modest but not illiberal budget, can go where they please for scriptwriters, presenters, actors, and production facilities. There are periodical postal surveys of audience size, and reactions to the programs are communicated by panels of reporting teachers and by visiting BBC liaison officers (called Education Officers), extracts from whose reports have been given above.

Teachers receive printed notes indicating the aim and content of each program and the proposed treatment of the topic, together with some follow-up suggestions. Broadcasts may be fitted into an existing scheme of work but are often used as a starting point for discussion and to prompt initiatives like those described in the forgoing account of "James is our Brother."

In 1981, the "Scene" broadcasts were seen off air or on videotape, regularly or selectively in 48 percent of British secondary schools. A number of the broadcasts have been repeated in the BBC's evening schedules for the general audiences by virtue of their human interest and the excellence of their production.

5. Concluding Observations

It is clear from previous experience that classroom television is not simply another audiovisual teaching device. It is too powerful and pervasive for that. The technology that supports it can, if desired, be used to support distance learning systems, adult education programs, the promotion of national identity, and the fostering of national culture. It can also be used, and in some countries has been used, for political purposes that do not always benefit education. Undoubtedly, classroom television serves education best when planners, curriculum specialists, teachers, and television programmers work together to capitalize on the strengths of the medium and to diminish its weaknesses.

Classroom television is often thought of in the context of conventional broadcasting, but surely, within this century, it will benefit from such new technologies as cable television, direct broadcast satellite, videodiscs, and videocassette recorders. These will compensate for the inflexibility of broadcast program scheduling, which educators have sometimes found inconvenient.

Television is an expensive medium; in few instances has it reduced the cost of instruction. As Wilbur Schramm (1977) has noted in *Big Media, Little Media: Tools and Technologies:*

> One conclusion that emerges strongly is that systems, built around the broadcast media in particular, can be used with favorable economic results to extend and expand learning opportunities. In this case the media cost is not merely an add-on to the normal cost of instruction, as supplementary media instruction might be, but can be compared directly with the cost of doing the same thing by conventional means.... If we can assume then, that favorable cost ratios can be expected from using media to do something that would otherwise have to be done by conventional means, what can we expect of the costs of simply adding media to ongoing class instruction? This is clearly an add-on cost, to be justified, if at all, by its contribution to quality of instruction, unless it makes possible a reduction of some kind in present costs.

Many would argue that several television programs in this supplementary category do indeed contribute a significant additional quality, but the extra cost is difficult to justify unless it is distributed over a large number of classrooms.

As educators and broadcasters feel increasing economic pressures, they are increasingly likely to look for less expensive methods of obtaining classroom television programs. One method is coproduction, either among the states or provinces of one or two countries or among several countries. This can reduce the cost of the programs to each coproducer, and at the same time generate large enough audiences to justify the investment. Another method is the structured instructional use of entertainment programs—to increase students' motivation to read, to improve their comprehension of a foreign language, to complement social studies activities, and so on. Such use must involve assignments and interventions, either by teachers or teacher surrogates (e.g., aides or parents). Both the viewing of the program and some follow-up activity must be required, and the focus must remain on education rather than entertainment.

Finally, some promising directions for future research must be mentioned. The effectiveness of television as a teaching device is no longer in doubt. Indeed, it has been verified so thoroughly that comparisons between the television classroom and the so-called traditional classroom are no longer interesting. Yet much remains to be learned about some elements of the learning situation.

While little research has been done in diversifying formats and production techniques, those of the Children's Television Workshop and other groups in the United States, Canada, Western Europe, and Japan have shown how differences in those elements, differently combined, variously affect students' learning and attitudes. In addition, developmental studies have shown how comprehension and learning vary with age. As children pass from one stage of cognitive development to another, their ability to perceive and use the content and organization of television programs grows more sophisticated.

Instructional design is now more important than ever in the production of classroom television. This greater importance has led to an increase in formative research, designed to improve the programs as they are being developed. More time and money are being spent to determine the needs and abilities of audiences before production and to test-run scripts, parts of programs, and whole programs in classrooms throughout production. Thus it is possible to revise one or a few programs in a series, if necessary, rather than the entire number.

Bibliography

Arnove R F (ed.) 1975 *Educational Television: A Policy Critique and Guide for Developing Countries.* Praeger, New York

Bates T, Robinson J (eds.) 1977 *Evaluating Educational Television and Radio.* Proc. of the Int. Conf. on Evaluation and Research in Educational Television, Milton Keynes, 9–13 April 1976. Open University Press, Milton Keynes

Carlisle D (ed.) 1978 *Patterns of Performance: Public Broadcasting and Education 1974–1976.* Corporation for Public Broadcasting, Washington, DC

Dorr A 1986 *Television and Children: A Special Medium for a Special Audience.* Sage, Beverly Hills, California

Fawdry K 1974 *Everything but Alf Garnett: A Personal View of BBC School Broadcasting.* British Broadcasting Corporation (BBC), London

Johnston J, Ettema J 1982 *Positive Images.* Sage, Beverly Hills, California

Marland M (ed.) 1972 *"Scene" Scripts: Seven Television Plays from the BBC School TV Series, "Scene", by Michael Cahill,*

Keith Dewhurst, Rex Edwards, Donald Eyre, Bill Lyons, Alan Plater, Fay Weldon. Longman, London

Schramm W L 1977 *Big Media, Little Media: Tools and Technologies for Instruction.* Sage, Beverly Hills, California

Sloan K R 1980 *Thinking Through Television: The First Six Years of the Skills Essential to Learning Project.* Agency for Instructional Television, Bloomington, Indiana

Wood D N, Wylie D G 1977 *Educational Telecommunications.* Wadsworth, Belmont, California

Use of Film in the Classroom

M. F. Hammond

Edison believed that the invention of motion pictures would have a great impact on education—films would be used to motivate, enrich, and instruct students. Nearly a century later, film is a medium that has had little real impact on education and, with the increasing use being made of the various forms of television, it seems destined never to achieve those hopes of Edison.

Nevertheless, film does have a place in the educational process and deserves to be accepted as a valuable tool for instruction, either as a discrete unit or as a component of a multimedia methodology of instruction at all levels of education. Provided due attention is paid to patterns of classroom use, to desired educational and curricular objectives, and to salient learner characteristics, the medium of film has considerable potential for promoting learning.

Three stages can be identified in the process of communicating messages and each is subject to considerable variation: (a) the nature of the messages, comprising both their content and structure (design variables); (b) the manner in which they are conveyed (utilization variables); and (c) the learning capacities of the recipients to whom they are directed (audience variables). This article is primarily concerned with utilization variables but, in order to provide an appropriate context, design variables and audience variables are also briefly discussed.

1. Design Variables

Film is a visually based language that shares the same basic principles of all languages. As written language is dependent on a balance between sender and receiver through a matching of encoding and decoding in a supporting general environment, so too is film.

The similarity in the structuring of film and writing may be demonstrated through a listing of some of the elements of each.

(a) Elements of film—finding an idea, movement, sequence, lighting, colour, sound, editing.

(b) Elements of writing—invention, prewriting, organization, audience, point of view, tone, diction, rhythm, style, editing, purpose.

In the relationship between the coding systems of sender (film maker) and receiver (learner/audience) with respect to films, there exists a very intricately woven structure of symbols. The structure is concerned with the symbols of the content of the message and the symbols arising from the syntax of the medium itself. This symbolic structure will be significantly affected by the function of the film which may be: (a) instructional, leading to gains in knowledge; (b) motivational, designed to affect or restructure attitudes and personal values; or (c) demonstrational, leading to changes in skill performance.

2. Audience Variables

Important learner characteristics, which need to be considered by both film makers and film users, include prior experience of film, general visual literacy, cognitive structure, ability level, and cognitive level.

2.1 Prior Experience with Film

With the world of the learner in most Western countries being very involved with television, learners of all ages have varying degrees of prior experience with the film format. While film on television is not the same experience as film in a theatre, auditorium, or classroom, the learner has nevertheless learnt something of the structure and syntax of film which affects the way in which film is dealt with in the instructional setting.

2.2 Visual Literacy

Visual literacy refers to the set of skills which enables the individual to use and understand visual material for volitional communication with others. Being analogous to verbal literacy it has the components of both reading and creating content. Just as verbal language has a vocabulary, grammar, and syntax, so have visuals. Only the visually literate can make full use of a highly visual technology.

Students throughout the contemporary educational situation are generally more successful in dealing with visual messages than previous generations and thus many visual sequences that adults find interesting are boring to young learners and complicated visual sequences that are intelligible to children are beyond the comprehension span of some adults.

Visual literacy calls for the abstraction of visual images using a classificatory skill that is based upon innate cognitive styles. It is also dependent upon the differentiation of the visual attributes of objects from other objects; younger children tend to overgeneralize, while adults tend to overdiscriminate.

2.3 Cognitive Structure

Most instructional strategies through primary and secondary education now take account of Piagetian stages of cognitive development. This has changed the sequencing of much curriculum material as far as the use of concrete and abstract material is concerned.

Consideration of the stages and paying attention to the social and cultural background of learners will assist in making reasoned selections of films and techniques for their use. A typical learner cannot handle abstraction until about puberty so the structuring of both the visual and verbal components of film need to take this into account.

The range of learning experiences that an individual has had shapes their cognitive structure and the flexibility of their schemas to accommodate and assimilate new material.

2.4 Ability Level

Learners have a range of abilities within themselves just as they do among themselves. About 40 percent of learners prefer acquiring knowledge from looking and reading and 30–40 percent prefer listening, with the balance preferring combinations of the senses. All operate at different levels of skill with spatial abilities and hence may display a range in capacity to interpret the visual elements of film.

In addition to this are the differences in intelligence, or ability to cope with reality, which affect a learner's capacity to see relationships between things or events and then the ability to deduce correlates.

With film building into a complex structure of information there is a call for much learner seeking of relationships so that comprehension and interpretation might occur.

2.5 Cognitive Style

Cognitive style may be interpreted as an individual's typical way of processing information. The most reported styles are (a) field-independent in which the individual tends to analyse the individual elements making up a situation, focusing on items in an analytic way, separating items from their contexts; (b) field-dependent in which the individual focuses upon the whole in a global way, overlooking individual elements (c) reflective in which the individual proceeds with information in a slow, deliberate way with high levels of accuracy; (d) impulsive in which the individual works on hypotheses and judges quickly with low levels of accuracy; (e) levelling/sharpening which represents the degree to which a learner merges new stimuli with earlier ones that are stored in memory; and (f) rigidity/flexibility which relates to the readiness to review and change judgments. The attribute of cognitive style is directly related to the structural elements of film when effects such as zooming, type of shot, and frame composition are considered.

2.6 Summary

Usually the film maker can only make general estimates of the characteristics of his or her audience. However, the class teacher will be much better informed and can use this information both in selecting and in planning how to use each film. When making such plans, the teacher will need to theorize that interpretation of visual material does not have the use of visual short-term memory in the way that verbal content utilizes iconic storage. Hence memory strength for any visual object is a function of attention. Moreover, while recognition of information in pictorial memory is a fairly high-speed associative task that is reasonably accurate, it is linked to an individual cognitive structure and the arrangement of individual schemas.

3. The Viewing Experience

With film requiring specialized facilities for its use in the learning situation, attention needs to be paid to factors that may affect its effectiveness.

3.1 Methods of Projection

Film may be shown by (a) front projection using a projection booth or positioning the projector within the learning space; (b) rear projection in which the film is back-projected onto an opaque screen using a mirror in the projector to reverse the image; or (c) transferring it to videotape and using closed-circuit television (CCTV). The use of the second and third techniques permits the use of a wide range of learning situations as they are less affected by the level of illumination within the area.

It seems that the rear projection method leads to greater acquisition of information if that information is dependent upon sound and vision. Depending on the balance of perceiver reliance on sound and vision, CCTV gives second best acquisition of knowledge.

The success of rear projection may be accounted for by factors such as screen brightness, sharpness of image, and steadiness of image.

In the case of front projection, it seems that perceivers prefer to have the projector behind them and not between them and the screen.

3.2 Physical Environment for Film Presentation

It would appear that while projection in the classroom is a practical method of film use, it is also marginally better than auditorium projection if instructional gain and learning activity is considered.

The ambient light may be just sufficient for note taking before there is deterioration in image interpretation.

The audience should not span an area greater than 30° from the centre line, nor be more than 12 screen widths from the screen. Increasing the size of the projected image does not necessarily improve the effectiveness of instructional illustrations.

3.3 Colour or Monochrome

While learners indicate a preference for colour over black and white versions of the same film, they do not learn significantly better from the colour version. Colour is often justified on the basis that a colour presentation provides the learner with more information cues and stimulation and consequently enhances learning.

Colour cues may add to the information density of a film but the consequence may be that the learner's capacity to process the information is overloaded. This may bring attenuation of some of the relevant incoming sensory data and/or focus attention on some of the irrelevant sensory data leading to distraction from essential information.

It seems that when specific abilities are considered, there are differences in perceivers' learning. Colour facilitates the learning of task-relevant information for high spatial aptitude students but tends to inhibit learning for the low spatial aptitude students.

3.4 Viewer Participation

The participation of the viewer, through overt or covert responding to questions inserted before or after a section of film, leads to greater learning. This gain is likely to be the result of an interaction between practice, increased motivation, and sustained attention. Vigilance theory would suggest that an individual will be more alert if constantly expected to respond and thus attention may be sustained.

Note taking during a film or the use of study guides leads to either no difference or a decline in knowledge acquisition. Dividing the attention to different tasks may lead to interference with retention. Questions and restatement of important points during the running of a film would appear to favour acquisition and retention.

4. Use of Films in the Classroom

To maximize the instructional gains that may come from the use of films, it is necessary for the teacher/instructor to follow a set of orienting and follow-up activities: (a) the students should be prepared for what they will see—there should be an indication of the objectives for the screening; (b) most films will contain material that is extraneous to the needs of the instructional unit—the learners should be told what sections are relevant to the objectives; (c) there should be an indication of the learning strategies that need to be followed which depend on how the information is to be used, for example, as specific facts or as basic concepts; (d) giving a list of significant incidents in the film assists the learners' cognitive processing of the material—advance organizers facilitate accommodation and

assimilation; (e) the new information within the film should be related to past learning through pre- and post-projection activities to assist in moving the information from short-term to long-term memory; (f) key drawings of significant incidents can be introduced to assist in associative recall; and (g) the students should be encouraged to group major points into an organized summary that provides a conceptual structure for further development.

5. Purposes of Film Use

Film may be chosen to perform a range of tasks. It may be used as: (a) a direct instructional tool: a film may be produced to teach a concept, a set of facts, or a skill and be quite self-contained to achieve that goal; (b) a supplement to other forms of instruction: a film may be used to provide an alternative means of communication to supplement, support, or give examples of material that is being principally communicated through another medium; (c) a means of enrichment or lateral extension: a film may be selected to provide learners with extra experience of a topic or material or to extend their views and ideas that may, for example, be limited because of geographical or ethnic constraints; (d) in combination with other media: to provide a total multimedia learning package as exemplified by audiotutorials and independent study kits; or (e) a focus of study in itself: the medium of film can be treated as an area of curriculum study in the same way as traditional subjects.

6. Advantages of Films in Instruction

(a) Films can be used to communicate directly and effectively with learners who have minimal reading skills. Concepts that may be inaccessible to a student through reading may be conveyed to the learner by the combination of words and pictures.

(b) Films can overcome some psychological barriers to communication that may exist in other media through the use of dramatization of events or concepts.

(c) Learners can be given perceptual experiences that are not possible through most other media—for example, microphotography, photomicrography, telephotography, animation, time lapse, superimposition—by changing time and space boundaries.

(d) Action can be presented as it occurs, as it will occur, or as it might have happened through the use of editing techniques.

(e) Films can be used to teach or evaluate analytical skills and abilities in learners.

(f) Use of films can be made to equalize experience or awareness in a group of learners through the ability to provide common input.

(g) Films can be used for group or individual learning.

7. Disadvantages of Films

(a) Relatively expensive equipment is required for projection of films.

(b) Films are made in a variety of gauges—8mm, Super-8, 16mm, 35mm, 70mm—which call for a range of projection facilities.

(c) A special environment is required with minimal ambient light or preferably an absence of light for the use of films.

(d) Films depend on set ratios of screen size, focal length of lens, and strength of illumination for optimal user comfort and gain.

While a film producer/director may have gone to great lengths to construct a film, in most cases the conditions of viewing are out of the control of the producer. He or she cannot accommodate to the physical environment or the psychological structure of the audience. The best that can be done by the user is to consider both the characteristics of film as a medium of communication and the possible characteristics of the audience for whom the film is intended. To do less is to demean both the audience and the craft of film making; to do more is generally unrealistic in terms of cost efficiency.

Bibliography

Ausburn L J, Ausburn F B 1978a Cognitive styles: Some information and implications for instructional design. *Educ. Commun. Technol. J.* 26: 337–54

Ausburn L J, Ausburn F B 1978b Visual literacy: Background theory and practice. *Program. Learn. Educ. Technol.* 15: 291–97

Berry C, Unwin D 1975 PLET monitoring: A selected bibliography of production and audience variables in film and television. *Program. Learn. Educ. Technol.* 12: 54–70

Cohen P A, Ebeling B J, Kulik J A 1981 A meta-analysis of outcome studies of visual-based instruction. *Educ. Commun. Technol. J.* 29: 26–36

Hefzallah I M 1985 Visual primacy, reality and the implying image in motion pictures and television. *Int. J. Instructional Media* 12(13): 157–66

Heidt E U 1977 Media and learner operations: The problem of a media taxonomy revisited. *Br. J. Educ. Technol.* 8: 11–26

Marchant H 1977 Increasing the effectiveness of educational films: A selected review of research. *Br. J. Educ. Technol.* 8: 89–96

Moskow M, Ledford B 1986 A theoretical treatment and review of advance organizer media research. *Int. J. Instruct. Media* 13(2): 131–40

Salomon G 1979 *Interaction of Media, Cognition, and Learning.* Jossey-Bass, San Francisco, California

Teather D C B 1974 Learning from film: A significant difference between the effectiveness of different projection methods. *Program. Learn. Technol.* 11: 328–34

Teather D C B, Marchant H 1974 Learning from film with particular reference to the effects of cueing, questioning, and knowledge of results. *Program. Learn. Educ. Technol.* 11: 317–27

Unwin D 1979 Production and audience variables in film and television: A second selected bibliography. *Program. Learn. Educ. Technol.* 16: 232–39

Wilkinson G L 1976 Projection variables and performance. *Audio-Vis. Commun. Rev.* 24: 413–36

Winn W 1982 Visualization in learning and instruction: A cognitive approach. *Educ. Commun. Technol. J.* 30(1): 3–25

Worth S 1974 The uses of film in education and communication. In: Olson D R (ed.) 1974 *Media and Symbols: The Forms of Expression, Communication and Education.* National Society for the Study of Education, Chicago, Illinois

Video Production as a Learning Activity

P. Turner

Video production can be viewed as a learning activity whenever the making of a video recording is an integral part of the learning process. Students are involved in programme preparation and this activity has at least equal learning value to the consideration of the replay. In some circles this application of the video recorder is called "process television".

1. Video Recording and Learning Activities

In an educational application, the video recorder, like the film projector before it, is used most frequently to replay moving pictures and associated sound as an uninterrupted programme to large groups of pupils. It has become an essential tool of the teacher but in consequence is less responsive to the needs of individual students. The alternative of providing programmes on open access to permit students to control the replay, and in consequence the pace of learning, has also become well-established.

In all too many educational institutions these two applications comprise the total educational demand for the most versatile item of technology available in the classroom. This article examines uses of the video recorder beyond these fairly obvious tasks and specifies the educational benefits observed by teachers working with students in the activities concerned.

Video recording can be used to permit a study of the medium itself. Although television, like radio, began life as an essentially ephemeral means of communication, the development of magnetic tape recording permits deliberate care in broadcast preparation and provides the opportunity for analysis of the end product. Students, at each stage in the education process, should be provided with the opportunity to consider the nature, role, and effects of broadcast communication.

Once camera equipment is available for use with the video recorder, the learning activities available to the student expand beyond the confines of both the classroom and the broadcasters' programme schedules. It is possible to use video recordings made by students to encourage the retention of information, to develop communication skills, and to help overcome learning, behaviour, or social problems. Routines may be developed to improve or enhance performance in professional or artistic activities. In all these enterprises the student gains learning benefits from active rather than passive involvement with video recording.

2. Video Production and Television Studies

The skills associated with discrimination in television viewing do not develop through neglect. Children in many countries spend more hours watching television than they spend in the classroom. The Bullock Report on language learning in the United Kingdom cited an average of 25 hours per week for pupils aged 5 to 14, that is, 1,300 hours per year compared with 900 classroom hours (Department of Education and Science 1975 p. 3). Thus it would be reasonable to expect that schools should promote those skills needed for effective viewing and listening. Unfortunately, some teachers share the belief of many parents that children watch more television than is good for them and, in consequence, television studies has no place in the classroom (Murdock and Phelps 1973). Pupils do need guidance, however, if they are to become a discriminating audience aware of quality in concept, content, and presentation. They need to learn to analyse their own reactions to the attitudes implied in television news and current affairs reports in order to form independent judgments. The best television studies achieve these objectives.

Unfortunately, the teacher of television studies cannot possess the subject in a way that is possible in the traditional classroom subjects. Masterman (1980) suggests that information in television studies should be "transmitted laterally from the medium to the pupil rather than hierarchically from the teacher". This is best achieved if pupils are given practical experience of those processes necessary for the creation and composition of a television programme. For this to be achieved, camera and recording apparatus needs to be made available to the television studies teacher.

Pupils placed in the position of a television camera operator discover the selective nature of the television image while the pupil vision mixer and director learn how picture choices affect the programme balance. Group editing exercises can be used to give pupils direct

experience of programme construction and to illustrate, in a practical way, the use of editing to change programme bias. The physical experience of television production can promote understanding in a way that no amount of viewing can achieve. This, together with consideration of selected prerecorded material can ensure that the broadcasters of the future have an educated audience.

3. Video Production and Specific Learning of Academic Content

All education establishments have a proportion of students who fail to understand particular concepts or who do not master particular skills or techniques. In most institutions, little can be done to help those who cannot reach the recognized standard. At school level, it may be possible to employ remedial specialists to help some pupils overcome problems of literacy or numeracy but this seldom extends to other subject areas.

One solution is to involve such students in making video programmes on appropriate topics, thus providing a concrete experience in subject areas where previously information was available only in abstract form. This produces educational gains unlikely to be made when using traditional methods of teaching or learning. Perhaps, when a student prepares a programme for others, this produces greater motivation and the concentration necessary to arrange ideas in logical sequence results in a greater retention of information. When recall is necessary, the student associates the information with the making of the programme as well as its audiovisual content.

A student required to produce a video recording in a particular academic discipline has to translate the information collected through reading and research into a form that can be presented on a medium not designed for the expression of abstract ideas. It is necessary for that student to recognize relationships between the concepts involved, distinguish between significant and supporting data, and organize the whole in logical form. To complete the preparation, it is necessary to identify examples and illustrations and to support the main threads of the argument in a way which can be presented to camera in concrete form. The organization and transformation of information collected from various sources into a single work, expressed in a new format, tends to reinforce learning in a way not always possible when book extracts are transposed into student writings.

If, instead of working alone, the student is part of a working group, producing a video recording as a combined effort, there is additional benefit from the group discussion that is essential to the preparation of the programme. This provides an opportunity for individual students to gain knowledge as ideas of others are considered and information selected before being arranged to form a programme sequence. In class discussion, where the teacher takes the leading role and where those with least understanding seek passive obscurity, misconceptions often remain hidden in the minds of particular students. In video recording the enthusiasm generated by the activity encourages the passengers in traditional group discussion to contribute, and this may reveal gaps in their knowledge or understanding. The resulting group discussion gives opportunity for those with the most accurate information to lead, and thus engenders learning in weaker students.

The practical tasks of arranging material and preparing a video recording help students to develop appropriate techniques for gathering and presenting information, which leads to an improvement in the written presentation required by most academic institutions. Thus, although television communication may seem to be an alternative to the written form, it does much to promote the skills needed for writing.

4. Video Recording as a Means for Communication

Although teachers have always expressed concern about the need for pupils in their charge to develop communication skills, in practical terms this has meant a heavy concentration upon the need to develop effective written communication techniques. Little has been done to relate this verbal communication to the visual communication encouraged in art and design subjects. More significantly, almost nothing is done to promote effective spoken communication or to develop greater understanding and appreciation of nonverbal communications.

There is considerable recent evidence to support the opinion that ignoring other modes of communication can narrow children's understanding and perhaps even disturb their self-image (Ornstein 1977). The appreciation of pupils' abilities and achievements is vital if a teacher and pupil are to cooperate in constructive learning, and such association is only possible with the mutual respect which should be established without denigrating the child's existing skills.

The development of video recording provides new openings for the exercise of those neglected communications talents not traditionally developed in the classroom. The medium provides opportunity to link together all other forms of communication. The recorded television image preserves nonverbal communication and shows it in relation to visual and verbal communication, the whole supported by patterns of sound.

Once pupils have mastered the skills used in the studio for the operating of cameras, sound and vision mixers, and the video recorder, they can begin to explore the communications possibilities of the medium. Although much of their early work may be attempts to copy favourite broadcast programmes, once they respond to carefully graded challenging topics selected by the teacher, they are usually able to develop original ideas into original programmes.

In the early stages, many of the pupil groups produce programmes which lack the formality of story board, script, or rehearsal. The children themselves quickly realize that these things are necessary to give proper form to their ideas. They will begin to undertake research from written sources within the school and to consider the accuracy of the information conveyed within their programmes. Perhaps for the first time they will feel the motivation to prepare and produce recorded communication of a high standard.

The motivation seems to come from three areas:

(a) the novelty of the medium and equipment associated with the work;

(b) the opportunity for a new start;

(c) the aura which surrounds the television industry in general.

The work done with pupils in schools using video recording indicates that there are definite educational gains in this activity which can be observed. As a significant part of the work involves close cooperation with others within the group, children begin to improve listening skills. Progress in oral communication, not only in relation to quantity but also the quality of pupils' contribution in class discussions, becomes evident. Even the least able sometimes provide the beginning of an idea which leads to a successful project. This helps these children to gain confidence and as a result there is a definite improvement in the construction and purposefulness of their oral contributions. In group discussion, one pleasing feature is that no contribution seems to be dismissed out of hand. Each is carefully evaluated by the group and anything of value incorporated in the project.

The resulting programme can be analysed and compared with the output of broadcasting stations. As with written composition, it is only through personal contact with the structure and grammar of the means of communication that appreciation of quality can be developed. In consequence, it is important for all pupils at some stage in their education to have access to facilities that will permit them to experience television communication through video recording.

5. Video Production and Special Needs: Children with Specific Learning or Behaviour Difficulties

Once facilities for video recording are made available, it is often those pupils suffering from specific learning difficulties in written communication who gain most benefit. Although a proportion of such students are of above average intelligence, they come to regard themselves as educational failures because their difficulties make it harder for them to succeed in any subject needing effective written communication, for example, history, geography, economics, and so on.

Although such pupils may fail to express ideas effectively in a written form, this does not mean that they lack thoughts worthy of expression. Frequently, the harsh treatment their work receives encourages them to reduce their written responses and so minimize the possibility of errors.

If this cycle of failure is to be reversed, the children need to develop confidence in their ability as communicators. Video recording offers an opportunity for them to succeed using new skills and in a new medium. Although some work can be done using small portable video equipment, it is best to employ a multicamera system for this purpose. Not only does this add to the sophistication of the programme-making possibilities, but it also ensures that each member of a teaching group of economic size can be employed upon a meaningful task. There are additional benefits in working as a team for pupils who have developed particular personality disorders, perhaps as a result of their learning difficulties. It is significant that by using the video communications technique, a large number of pupils who have failed with written English, feel an urge to produce written documents as a basis for a communications exercise.

In schools where this work has been introduced, children with definite antischool attitudes display new enthusiasm. Frequently, their attendance figures improve and they want to continue after school or even return to do this work during occasional holiday periods. They become anxious, perhaps for the first time, to complete assignments. This increased motivation appears to have some beneficial effects upon their relationships with school staff in general and their attitude to other school subjects and activities.

Some of the work done with remedial departments in schools has included children who exhibit particular behaviour problems. In some cases, for example, disruptive pupils have been included in a television communications group. These pupils, given definite tasks, begin to work with the teacher because of their enthusiasm for the medium. This feature was noted by some teachers involved in the Schools Council Communication and Social Skills Project (Lorac and Weiss 1980) and in the work done by Surrey teachers using the county's transportable video system.

There is also some evidence to suggest that hyperactive children involved in this type of activity do not seek to become a disruptive centre of attention as in the classroom. In many cases they begin to control their outbursts and to contribute to the group activity. In work done within the remedial department at Millfield School in the United Kingdom (Turner and Atkinson 1971, Turner 1973), it was noted that such pupils cannot control the situation because of the three separate areas of activity. It is possible to contribute from in front of cameras, behind cameras, and in the control room, but no single place is responsible for the complete content of the programme. There is also the change in the teacher/pupil relationship, reported by

Lorac and Weiss (1980), where they become partners in the activity. Each of these factors may produce conditions where the hyperactive child feels that there are benefits in cooperation rather than conflict with the teacher.

It was also in the remedial department at Millfield that mildly autistic children were involved in activity behind cameras and permitted to progress until they volunteered for roles in front of cameras often requiring spoken responses. The pace of such development was set by the child and frequently the first appearance before cameras required action but not speech.

To date, insufficient research has been done in this field, perhaps because few of the educational establishments working with behaviour disorders have finance available for a television studio installation.

6. Video Production and Social Skills

Social skills can be identified as those activities and attitudes that encourage effective interpersonal relationships within groups. For an individual to succeed, it is necessary to show considerable flexibility; adapting to the need for changes in role emanating from changes in composition, the external influences, or the intentions of the group.

As a part of the activities in communication using video recording, it has been of considerable interest to note the development of social skills. Although in most instances this has been a by-product of the work of the class, there is some evidence to suggest that the most lasting benefits are social.

The creation of a video recording is essentially a collaborative exercise with each group member accepting a changing role. The pupil, for example, who takes the lead in planning, is not necessarily the leader in execution. Alternatively, outstanding acting ability may not prove to be crucial to the quality of a particular section of the completed tape. Throughout the exercise, changing requirements will place differing pupils in a position of importance for a time and relegate others from leadership to a supporting role. The essential requirement, if the activity is to be successful, is for the group to pool expertise rather than for particular members to assume authority.

Video recording activities help pupils to develop the social ability needed to organize information collected through personal research, and to use this information as a basis for a script. Pupils develop the skill needed to present ideas in the persuasive manner necessary to influence group decision making. They learn to accept modification of their ideas and even rejection of their proposals. Their experience as programme makers help them to appraise their own performance and that of others. In general, as reported by Lorac and Weiss (1980), pupils involved with this work show increased self-confidence and develop a new awareness of their abilities and strengths.

7. Video Recording for Performance Modification

It is very difficult to modify existing performance while a student is satisfied with the present level of competence. Any attempt to modify skills performance, for example, is in reality an attempt to modify an established behaviour pattern. Frequently the self-image of the student is deceptive, with the student clinging to the belief that the performance is adequate. This acts as a barrier to further progress or improvement. Video recording can produce an almost immediate benefit by confronting the student with the recorded image and producing circumstances where student and teacher can agree on the need for change. Once this need has been accepted, the performance faults can be considered in detail before teacher and student begin to work together to produce the desired performance improvements.

The most obvious application of this type of video recording technique is in sports training. The majority of sports schools and clinics use this system as a regular part of the programme to eliminate faults in athletic performance, bowling action, or golf swing, for example.

In the performing arts, drama, music, and dance for example, the same technique can be employed to improve individual performance. The video recorder captures the true image, without mirror reversal, and yet provides an immediacy as yet unequalled by other technology.

In the development of interpersonal skills too, the use of video recording has distinct advantages for those with difficulties. The recording of "mock" interviews, for example, can prepare students seeking employment for facing their first interview panel. Although the result is somewhat artificial, it can be used to help candidates to avoid the more obvious mistakes.

In all these learning activities the camera and recorder act as a third eye; observing performance and permitting the student to learn through the careful evaluation of a replay of that performance. The recorded material is not required to communicate concepts nor does the programme need a formal structure.

8. Video Recording and Professional Training

Agencies responsible for the initial training of students for employment in those learned professions demanding the precise exercise of particular skills, find considerable benefit in the application of the video recorder as a tool within that training. The skills of the student can be developed and improved through observation of their own recorded performance, together with analysis by their peer group, under the direction of an experienced tutor. It may be necessary also, to compare student performance with that of a highly regarded practitioner within the particular profession. In many respects this work is a very special application of performance modification.

The use of video recording for teacher training has become highly developed within the process of microteaching, and a similar approach is also used in the training of medical staff including doctors and surgeons, priests, industrial executives, and sales personnel.

In many professions, as practitioners gain advancement, new skills become essential. These may be those most closely associated with management, including an ability to talk to large groups, to act as chairman during discussion sessions, or to provide counselling services for junior staff. All these skills may be developed through careful analysis of recorded performance as part of inservice training. Surrey County Media Resources Centre in the United Kingdom has developed video programmes for school-based inservice training for several of these skills areas.

In the education service, an experienced teacher can often benefit from further regular consideration of classroom performance. This encourages continual evaluation of established assumptions, teaching techniques, or patterns of behaviour to ensure that classroom method does not become an unquestioned routine. This exercise, a form of responsive evaluation, is conducted with the assistance of an experienced colleague. The video recording of the teacher's performance is analysed, with each aspect being the subject of a neutral question from the evaluator. (The absence of direct criticism is an essential feature in the technique and makes it more acceptable to experienced staff.) Together, teacher and evaluator isolate areas which would benefit from modification to the teaching approach and perhaps agree a course of action involving particular targets (Fuller and Manning 1973).

This technique is the subject of a video programme produced by Surrey County Media Resources Centre and published through Drake Educational Associates, and was also used by Chris Day (1981) for his work on classroom-based inservice teacher education. Day describes the video recording as "a means of enabling the researcher and teacher to discuss reflectively their view of events. Though these events were inevitably selections from reality viewed from different standpoints, they were at least selections common to both researchers and teacher". If responsive evaluation is to be used for the advancement of classroom techniques, it can only be against such shared experience.

Bibliography

Day C 1981 *Classroom-based In-service Teacher Education: The Development and Evaluation of a Client Centred Model.* University of Sussex Education Area, Occasional Paper 9. University of Sussex, Brighton

Department of Education and Science (UK) 1975 *A Language for Life.* Report of the Committee of Enquiry Appointed by the Secretary of State for Education and Science under the Chairmanship of Sir Alan Bullock. Her Majesty's Stationery Office, London

Fuller F F, Manning B A 1973 Self confrontation reviewed: A

conceptualisation for videoplayback in teacher education. *Rev. Educ. Res.* 43: 469–528

Lorac C, Weiss M 1980 *Communication and Social Skills.* Wheaton, Exeter

Masterman L 1980 *Teaching about Television.* Macmillan, London

Murdock G, Phelps G 1973 *Mass Media and the Secondary School.* Macmillan, London

Ornstein R E 1977 *The Psychology of Consciousness*, 2nd edn.

Harcourt Brace Jovanovich, New York

Turner P 1973 *Television in the Service of a School.* Educational Foundation for Visual Aids, London

Turner P 1980 Television in the hands of pupils. In: Utz P (ed.) 1980 *Video User's Handbook*, Instalment 3. Prentice-Hall, London

Turner P, Atkinson C R M 1971 *An Experiment in Closed-circuit Television at Millfield School.* Educational Foundation for Visual Aids, London

Conceptual and Theoretical Bases of Microteaching

A. Perlberg

Microteaching is a laboratory training procedure aimed at simplifying the complexities of regular teaching–learning processes. The trainee is engaged in a scaled down and focused situation—scaled down in terms of class size and lesson length and focused on teaching tasks such as practice and mastery of specific skills such as lecturing, questioning, or leading a discussion; mastering specific teaching strategies; flexibility in instructional decision making; alternative uses of curricula, instructional materials, and classroom management.

The short lesson is recorded on an audiotape or videotape recorder and the trainee can see the replica immediately after the lesson. When hardware is not available, a supervisor can record in writing the basic verbal and nonverbal interaction as feedback for the teacher. Pupils are asked to fill in rating questionnaires evaluating specific aspects of the lesson and at times can also provide oral feedback. The trainee's own analysis of the lesson based on the authentic feedback from the various sources helps in restructuring the lesson, which is taught to a new group of pupils either immediately or a few days later.

The restructuring cycle continues until mastery is achieved. The trainee can also choose to view or listen to, either before the first teaching experience or thereafter, a recording of a model teacher practicing a particular teaching–learning skill. The above description pertains mainly to the original microteaching model developed at Stanford around 1960.

It is important to note that during the initial stages of its inception and development, microteaching, like many other educational innovations, was not based on solid theoretical conceptualization and research evidence. It was described rather as an "idea" (Allen and Ryan 1969). As a result, developers and practitioners around the world, in teacher education and other related fields adopted the basic idea, but took the liberty of modifying the original model and adapting it to their ideologies, concepts, needs, and constraints. Some adaptations were quite different from the original model and in some cases the basic concept of an intensive laboratory experience was missed.

1. Historical Background

To understand the lack of a unified theoretical conceptualization of microteaching on the one hand, and the rationale for some of its components on the other hand, one has to examine the background from which it originated. Allen, one of its main developers, states that: "Microteaching was born out of the frustration of liberal arts graduates who felt that there was nothing they could possibly learn from teacher education" (Allen and Ryan 1969, Allen 1980). The Stanford group which developed microteaching responded to a wider feeling of frustration and dissatisfaction the world over, by the public at large, educators, and even teacher educators, with the traditional models of teacher education (Joyce 1975). In the United States, during the 1950s and 1960s, schools and teachers came under attack for failing to help children master reading, writing, and arithmetic and to teach science and other subjects adequately. There was an increasing demand that teachers be held accountable for the achievement of their pupils. Teachers, in turn, blamed teacher education, claiming that their preservice and inservice training had not provided them with the skills necessary for ensuring student achievement at the level being called for (Gage and Winne 1975).

The traditional models were criticized for being heavily slanted towards verbal and cognitive input, which was described at times as superficial and much to say about nothing. The theoretical studies were not integrated with the practical experiences and even the experiential part, practice teaching, was criticized as ineffective. Concurrently, educational researchers admitted that half a century's research on teaching and learning did not have much impact on classroom interaction. Gage (1963) claimed that the holistic macro approach to research on teaching had failed, and that educators should adopt the methods used by scientists who tried to understand complex phenomena by breaking them into micro elements.

The 1960s and early 1970s were not, however, the only times of criticism. Through extensive governmental and foundation resources, American teacher educators were encouraged to innovate and were ready to adopt any innovation based even on intuitive professional judgement, with the hope of substantiating it later on. Microteaching was one of these innovations which was practiced first and only at the later stage started the process of its theoretical conceptualization.

2. The Debate over Theoretical Conceptualization

The original Stanford group which developed microteaching was very heterogeneous in ideologies and beliefs about education and psychology and the debate over the theoretical conceptualization has gone on since the inception of the idea. Ivey and Authier (1978) reflected on this issue stating that: "In the early phase of experimentalism and research, conceptual frameworks and theoretical constructs were deliberately omitted in the search for a method which consistently showed results—a system that worked as needed rather than one which was theoretically sophisticated." On the other hand, McDonald (1973), the second principal developer of microteaching, subscribed to a theoretical point of view that "teacher education programs should be conceptualized as behavior modification systems, designed to modify complex behavioral repertoires which are adaptable to a variety of learning problems." He viewed microteaching as an excellent example of behavior modification technique. For McDonald microteaching was devised as a procedure for facilitating behavioral control. Further, it was used as a way of creating a more effective experimental paradigm which for the first time made it possible to use sophisticated experimental designs in learning studies. The purpose of these teaching studies was to assess the relative effectiveness of modeling and reinforcement variables in facilitating the acquisition of teaching behavior. These were some of McDonald's hopes and aspirations. Looking back, however, a decade later, he stated that "microteaching remains an unstudied technique. The literature that purports to be research on it is deplorable...much of what has been written about microteaching is promotional and even misleading...more disappointing is the fact that the original conception and rationale for microteaching has been lost sight of—a point significant in the context of a discussion of behavior modification in teacher education" (McDonald 1973).

Even after more than two decades of microteaching, Allen still sees McDonald's emphasis as misleading (Allen 1980). He agrees, however, that there is still a need for a vigorous research program to substantiate the many claims made on its behalf and adds that microteaching has been pretty well accepted as having a de facto face validity, "Its high level of acceptance both in the United States and abroad has been based not so much on research evidence as upon the satisfaction level of the teacher education staff, the teaching candidates, and the school personnel involved in its use. It is a harsh reality that this affective evidence is more important than many research findings." Allen's assertion about

the wide acceptability of microteaching is supported by the large numbers of publications, books, and research reports published on microteaching and related areas in many countries (see references), and by its acceptability to international organizations such as UNESCO as an important vehicle to improve teacher education.

In a review of the literature on microteaching, Copeland (1982) states that there appears to be a considerable research base supporting the inclusion of microteaching as a prestudent teaching laboratory experience in teacher education, and that participation in microteaching appears to assume initial acquisition of related technical skills of teaching to be associated with shifts in participants' attitudes: "Further, skills acquired during microteaching may be used in student teaching classrooms subsequent to training if the nature of these classrooms support such use."

In the absence of a unified theoretical conceptualization in the early 1980s, microteaching could be viewed as an eclectic laboratory training technique. Its components are based on different theories, concepts, empirical evidence, professional judgments, and notions. The following discussion examines its different components.

3. The Components of Microteaching

3.1 The Teaching–Learning Laboratory

Learning by doing and intensive experiential involvement are the basic principles on which the teaching–learning laboratory is based. While learning takes place throughout life by trial and error, or by guided experience, it is widely agreed that it is desirable that practice in simulated situations in laboratory settings should precede practicing and learning through real life situations. This concept has been accepted in the professional training of scientists, engineers, and other professions, and has been accepted for thousands of years in the training of armed forces, through war games and more recently in the training of astronauts. Drawing on research and empirical evidence as to how people change and learn in social settings, scientists in applied psychology, and other behavioral sciences have developed the concept of the "training laboratory" in behavioral sciences.

In providing a theoretical and empirical rationale for early field experiences in teacher education, Webb et al. (1981) state that the learning process pattern that emerges from psychological investigation is one that

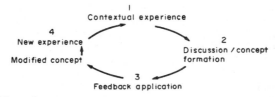

Figure 1
Cyclical pattern of teaching

centers on the significance of the learner and his or her concerns. The pattern contrasts verbal or symbolic input to the learner, with experience in the learning context by the learner. The contrast reveals that verbal teaching alone or verbal teaching prior to learner contextual experience will be less productive than teaching in accordance with the cyclical pattern illustrated in Fig. 1.

Probably the most often-voiced complaint of graduates of teacher education programs is that we perpetuate a discrepancy between the real world of teaching and the verbal theoretical world of preservice training. The building of a personally meaningful concept of teaching (which includes attitude, knowledge, and skills) is facilitated by early and frequent contact with classroom, pupils, administrators, professional teachers, and parents—the real environment of education. The contextual experience is a necessary preliminary to concept formation and, hence, skilled teaching.

Even though Webb's rationale refers to early field experiences, the teaching–learning laboratory could be viewed as an early simulated field experience, and Webb's rationale applies to the laboratory experience as well. Moreover, the laboratory is a safe practice ground and it should precede teaching in the field, especially in early field experiences.

3.2 Safe Practice Ground

Safe practice ground is another concept embedded in any laboratory. The ability to experiment, to try out, explore, and fail without being penalized or hurting someone is one of the main justifications for the teaching–learning laboratory. In the traditional teacher education models, supervised student teaching, whether before the theoretical studies or after them, has always been a source of tension and anxiety to the neophyte student teacher. In many instances, not only the student teacher but the learners in the classroom suffered. Administrators, cooperating teachers, students, and their parents objected to excessive use of regular classrooms for student teaching. This is one reason why laboratory schools, attached to schools of education, which were very common in the past, have diminished in recent years. The moral obligation of teacher education towards the school system and their neophyte student teachers is to provide them with a safe practice ground before going out into field experience.

The concept of a safe practice ground is supported also by knowledge from theories of learning and change and empirical experience in clinical supervision, clinical psychology, and other related areas. Anxious learners tend to protect themselves by defence mechanisms, are not flexible, and resist change and learning. Moreover, in many instances excessive anxiety may cause frustration and fixation of undesirable behaviors. Equipping neophyte teachers with a degree of mastery in teaching skills and strategies will enable them to benefit more, both during their early field experiences and their student teaching. A safe practice ground is important not only to the neophyte teacher, but also to experienced teachers. They, who are supposed to be secure, safe, and confident, are also subjected at times to tension and anxiety, especially when facing new situations and unpredictable developments. This natural phenomenon has been one of the main obstacles to the introduction of innovation. Experience has shown that the microteaching laboratories have been safe practice grounds even for experienced teachers, participating in professional development programs. They can try out these new instructional strategies and curricula in a relatively secure atmosphere. While stressing the importance of a safe practice ground, it is essential to remember that the concept of "safe" is a relative one. Even in a microteaching laboratory participants experience a certain amount of tension and stress as a result of feedback. This phenomenon is inevitable and even essential and will be discussed later at greater length.

3.3 The Micro Element and Teaching Skills

Underlying the micro element is the supposition that before attempting to understand, learn, and perform effectively the complicated task of teaching, one should master the components of the task. By focusing the training on a specific task and reducing the complexities of the situation, it is possible to concentrate the training process and assure greater effectiveness in the learning process. Moreover, effective learning is achieved in general, when the learner moves from the simple task to the more complex one. The above concept is supported by ample theoretical and empirical evidence, in the areas of learning, teaching, and training in different settings and, in particular, the systems approach and task analysis.

Scaling down the class size and lesson length from the macro to micro provides more effective initial learning conditions. It stands to reason that the neophyte teacher could cope and learn more easily during a short lesson to a small class rather than plunging into a real classroom of 40 children and teaching them for 50 minutes.

Another aspect of the micro element is the focus on particular teaching skills. Gage (1963) was quoted above, stating that for better understanding and investigation of the complexities of teaching–learning interactions we should move from the macro to the micro situation. Allen and McDonald have applied the same concept to training and have developed the concept of "technical skills of teaching." The initial list of technical skills of teaching developed was by no means exhaustive and other skills were added during the years. The competency-based teacher education (CBTE) or performance-based teacher education (PBTE) movement, which developed at the end of the 1960s, has contributed greatly to the identification and development of a wider range of classroom interactive skills in the cognitive, affective, and motoric domains. It should be stressed at this point that the original concept of technical skills of teachers was not clear, and many practitioners have adopted only the Stanford list of teaching skills or even only part of that list. In many instances, this was done because of lack of time and resources or for logistical reasons. Some practitioners assumed that there will be a transfer from practice in certain skills to other skills. Focusing training on a partial list of skills and in many instances minute technical skills has contributed greatly to the alienation of many teacher educators and especially those subscribing to humanistic values from the whole concept of the microteaching laboratory.

It could not be emphasized more strongly that the list of required skills to be practiced in a laboratory should include a wide range of classroom interaction skills in all domains, that is cognitive, affective, and motoric. Moreover, many practitioners of microteaching laboratories assumed that mastery of particular skills in a microlesson will enable the teacher to use them automatically when necessary in regular classroom interactions. However, the macro, whole lesson is not the sum of its micro elements, as the group is not a simple sum of its members. The macrolesson is a phenomenon in itself. Using classroom interactive skills in a regular classroom situation requires training and preparation in teaching a microlesson as well as in the particular skills. Therefore, the right sequence in a teaching–learning laboratory should be from mastery of simple subskills, to skills, clusters of skills, and interaction strategies; from skills in isolated domains to interaction between domains; from the use of a particular strategy of interaction to flexibility training and the use of multistrategies; and finally, from a short lesson to a small group to longer lessons to larger groups.

3.4 The Feedback Element

Another cardinal element of microteaching and the teaching–learning laboratory is feedback. When microteaching was developed at Stanford, it coincided with the initial developments of portable, relatively inexpensive videotape recorders. The Stanford group took advantage of this innovative tool and used video recordings extensively as the main source of feedback. Since then, microteaching has been associated around the world with video recorders. As will be discussed later, video recording is still probably the most powerful available source of feedback (Perlberg 1984). On the other hand, it should be stressed emphatically that the microteaching laboratory does not depend on the availability of video recorders or any other electronic hardware. Allen and Ryan (1969) were aware of the misconception of coupling microteaching with video recorders and have tried to correct it. Since this notion was deeply rooted and disturbed the dissemination of the basic concept in developing countries, UNESCO initiated a special report in microteaching and allied techniques which could be implemented in

developing countries without hardware or with inexpensive hardware, such as portable tape recorders (Perlberg 1975).

3.5 The "Modeling" Element

The use of recorded "models" of master teachers demonstrating particular classroom interactions is another important element in the microteaching laboratory. McDonald (1973), who was one of the developers of microteaching, has investigated the role of "modeling" in learning even before the inception of microteaching. Both McDonald and Allen drew also on Bandura's work on the role of models, learning by observation and imitation. There is abundant theoretical and empirical evidence which testifies to the wide range of learning situations and behavioral changes which take place as a result of observation and imitation. Basic and applied research in that area is part of the wider field of behavior modification and other behavioristic approaches.

It is interesting to note that the "modeling" element and the skills training through reinforcement techniques, became the main cause for rejecting the whole concept of microteaching and tagging it as a behavioristic–mechanistic approach which negates humanistic concepts in education. However, humanists ignored the fact that learning by observation and imitation is hardly new in education. This apprenticeship concept which was practiced as early as the guilds, and is still practiced, is based on the modeling concept. Socialization processes are based on learning by observation and imitation, teacher education has used similar approaches since early days by sending neophyte teachers to observe "master teachers." Our daily behavior, in general and professionally, is shaped to a great extent by the bad and good models we have had. The study of history and philosophy of education has put great emphasis on the "great master teachers" exemplars who became our models.

In the microteaching laboratory, this widely used learning method was systematized. Instead of a general, diffused observatory, the "model" enabled focused observation. The models are recorded and thus it is possible to observe again and again in a systematic manner, a wide variety of master teachers, all of which facilitates more effective learning. It is interesting to note that "modeling" which was considered by many to be a mechanistic and low-level imitation process could be viewed also as involving high-level cognitive processes. McIntyre et al. (1977) suggest that even Bandura's concept of social learning theory "is more cognitively oriented than is often realized." Here again the ways models are used are important. Providing one model only and directions to follow it produces imitation. Providing several models and creating a learning environment which facilitates evaluation and requires flexibility and in-depth decision making could be described as a highly cognitive process.

4. Towards a Unified Theoretical Conceptualization of Microteaching

As stated above, microteaching is still in the process of developing a unified theoretical conceptualization. Whether such a unified theoretical basis can be achieved is still to be seen. Until then, the fact that it is an effective eclectic technique can be accepted. Its components are based on a wide range of theories and available empirical evidence which justify its use in the future and call for further research and development.

Bibliography

Allen D W 1980 Microteaching: A personal review. *Br. J. Tech. Ed.* 6: 147–51

Allen D W, Ryan K A 1969 *Microteaching*. Addison-Wesley, Reading, Massachusetts

Borg W R, Kelley M L, Langer P, Gall M 1970 *The Mini Course: A Microteaching Approach to Teacher Education.* Collier Macmillan, London

Brown G 1975 *Microteaching—A Program of Teaching Skills.* Methuen, London

Center for Educational Research and Innovations (CERI) 1975 *The International Transfer of Microteaching Programs for Teacher Education.* Organisation for Economic Co-operation and Development, Paris

Copeland W D 1982 Prestudent teaching laboratory experiences. In: Mitzel H E (ed.) 1982 *Encyclopedia of Educational Research,* 5th edn. Free Press, New York

Educational Resource Information Center (ERIC) National Institute of Education, Educational Resource Information Center, Washington, DC

Falus I, McAleese W R 1975 A bibliography of microteaching. *Program. Learn. Educ. Technol.* 12(1)

Gage N L 1963 Paradigms for research on teaching. In: Gage N L (ed.) 1963 *Handbook on Research on Teaching: A Project of the American Education Research Association.* Rand McNally, Chicago, Illinois

Gage N L, Winne P H 1975 Performance-based teacher education. In: Ryan K (ed.) 1975 *Teacher Education.* 74th Yearbook of the National Society for the Study of Education, Part 2. NSSE, Chicago, Illinois

Ivey A E, Authier J 1978 *Microcounseling: Innovations in Interviewing, Counseling, Psychotherapy, and Psychoeducation.* Thomas, Springfield, Illinois

Joyce B 1975 Conceptions of man and their implications for teacher education. In: Ryan K (ed.) 1975 *Teacher Education.* 74th Yearbook of the National Society for the Study of Education, Part 2. NSSE, Chicago, Illinois

McDonald R J 1973 Behavior modification in teacher education. In: Thoresen C E (ed.) 1973 *Behavior Modification in Education.* 72nd Yearbook of the National Society for the Study of Education, Part 1. NSSE, Chicago, Illinois

McIntyre D I, MacLeod G H R, Griffiths R (eds.) 1977 *Investigations of Microteaching.* Croom Helm, London

Perlberg A 1975 *Recent Approaches on Microteaching and Allied Techniques Which can be Implemented Easily in Developing Countries.* UNESCO, Paris

Perlberg A 1984 When professors confront themselves: Towards a theoretical conceptualization of the use of video self-confrontation in improving teaching in higher education. *Higher Educ.* 12: 31

Perrott E 1977 *Microteaching in Higher Education: Research, Development and Practice.* Society for Research into Higher Education, Guildford

Trott A J (ed.) 1974 *Microteaching Conference Papers.* Association for Programmed Learning and Educational Technology, London

Turney C, Clift J C, Dunkin M J, Trail R D 1973 *Microteaching: Research, Theory and Practice: An Innovation in Teacher Education Especially as it Relates to the Australian Context.* Sydney University Press, Sydney

Webb C, Gehrke N, Ishler P, Mendoza A 1981 Theoretical and empirical bases for early field experiences in teacher education. In: Webb C et al. (eds.) 1981 *Exploratory Field Experience in Teacher Education.* Association for Teacher Education, Washington, DC

Effectiveness of Microteaching

G. R. MacLeod

Questions about the effectiveness of microteaching depend upon the aims of particular microteaching programmes and these aims are dependent upon the models of participant learning underlying the programme. From the literature, four distinct but sometimes overlapping models may be discerned.

From the original Stanford programme, two models emerge. First, there is the apparent "easy pragmatism" of the first programme as represented in the writing of Allen and Ryan (1969). Here microteaching is seen within a general training paradigm, where concepts from psychology like modelling and reinforcement are freely borrowed, the emphasis is upon "what works", and the criteria for success are skill acquisition and measures of general teaching effectiveness. This is very clearly the "model" adopted by many microteaching programmes.

The second model from the Stanford programme is that of behaviour modification (McDonald 1973). The focus of such a programme would be on the application of modelling, on detailed response analysis, and on the use of contingency reinforcement principles, whilst the criterion for success would be in terms of specific behaviour change. Few microteaching programmes have operated according to these principles and by 1973, McDonald wrote that "Many users of micro-teaching did not see the relevance of behavior modification procedures" (p. 72) and that "The most undesirable consequence of the promotion of micro-teaching was that the role of behavior modification...was obscured" (p. 73).

The third approach to microteaching is one derived from the social skills training model of Argyle (1970) and applied in a microteaching context by Brown (1975). Teaching skills, like other social skills, are seen as analogous to perceptual and motor skills, and the foci of a training programme therefore relate to the selection of aims, the selective perception of relevant cues, motor response (or practice), and feedback and correction. Criteria for success are again to be found in performance.

The fourth approach encompasses a series of cognitive models which place greater emphasis on participants' thinking about their teaching. Represented here is the work of Fuller and Manning (1973), and of Bierschenk (1974) in which emphasis is placed upon incongruity between intent and action as revealed by videotape, upon the dissonance which this creates, and the subsequent intentional behaviour change which this produces. A model which focuses less on the motivational aspects is that proposed by MacLeod and McIntyre (1977), in which attention is drawn to the heavy information-processing demands imposed by the complexity of classroom environments, to the cognitive strategies which teachers use to cope with that complexity, which suggests that teaching skills should be reconceptualized as "ways of thinking" rather than as "ways of behaving", and that the effectiveness of microteaching should be assessed in terms of whether it provides "for the development and induction of functional and adaptive cognitive structures" (p. 262). Recent increased interest in describing and mapping teachers' thinking about teaching (e.g. Shavelson and Stern 1981) suggests that more emphasis in microteaching research ought to be devoted to cognitive processes and outcomes as criteria of effectiveness. This is described in Perlberg's and MacLeod's entries in this Section.

1. Attitudinal Outcomes of Microteaching

Perhaps the most consistently reported outcome of research on microteaching is that participants find it a valuable and enjoyable activity. For example, a recent course evaluation by MacLeod involving over 100 preservice teacher-education students found that over 95 percent of them rated microteaching as interesting, practical, relevant, and useful. Similar favourable assessments from both pre- and in-service participants have been reported frequently. Amongst teacher educators, reactions to microteaching were, at least initially, mixed. Although many immediately accepted and implemented the innovation, others questioned the assumptions implicit in the practice of microteaching. In particular, doubt was cast upon whether the complex and dynamic art of teaching could readily be dissected into component parts or skills. However, over time, microteaching seems to have won acceptance as an integral part of teacher-education programmes and to have received favourable and widespread acceptance (Turney 1977).

2. Performance Outcomes of Microteaching

The major gap in research on microteaching is a lack of firm evidence as to whether microteaching training affects subsequent classroom performance. This is not because the question has not been asked but rather because the modes of answering have been unsatisfactory or only partial rather than conclusive. Three main research approaches to the question may be discerned: a correlational one, in which relationships between performance in microteaching and performance in subsequent classroom teaching are sought; a preexperimental approach in which participants' teaching performance before and after microteaching is assessed; and a true experimental approach in which the classroom performance of previous microteaching participants is compared with the performance of a control group which has not experienced microteaching.

A series of correlational studies, showing substantial relationships between microteaching performance and subsequent classroom performance has appeared (Brown 1975). These may be interpreted as suggesting that microteaching does affect classroom performance, or, equally plausibly, as providing a simple indication that those participants who can demonstrate skilled performance in microteaching can also do so in a classroom setting.

The preexperimental approach is represented in the work of Borg (1972). In this study a group of inservice teachers were videotaped in their classrooms to allow a precourse evaluation of skill usage. The group then undertook a microteaching course and were videotaped again one week after the course, four months later, and 39 months later. It was shown that classroom performance immediately after microteaching is marked by greater skill use than before microteaching, that there is no significant regression in skill use after four months, and that after 39 months, performance remained significantly superior to premicroteaching performance in 8 of 10 skill-related measures. Unfortunately, the design of such studies does not permit one to conclude that the observed changes are a consequence of microteaching, for several possible rival explanations of the results are possible.

A series of true experimental studies of microteaching has been carried out, but the results of these have been mixed, with some reporting that microteaching does have effects on subsequent teaching performance, and some finding no differences between the effects of microteaching and control treatments. This section reviews a set of three negative outcome studies, and a set of three positive outcome studies, and concludes that no firm conclusions as to the effectiveness of microteaching can be drawn, not primarily because of the mixed results but rather because of the difficulties inherent in carrying out such research.

One of the negative outcome investigations was that by Copeland and Doyle (1973). They compared the effects of a six-week microteaching treatment (focusing on three questioning skills) with the effects of a control treatment not related to microteaching or to the three teaching skills. The criterion measures of skill performance were derived from two audiorecorded 15-minute discussions taught by the 14 participants during a practice-teaching period occurring seven weeks after the experimental treatments. Instructions for these criterion discussions were designed not to sensitize trainees to the fact that the major interest was skill acquisition. The reported outcome of this study was that microteaching did not have a significant effect on classroom performance. However, inspection of the reported data indicates that individual differences among the seven subjects in each group are very substantial, and a partial reanalysis of the data (MacLeod 1981) reveals that significant differences in favour of the microteaching group may be produced by controlling for overall frequency of questioning.

Two further studies involving Copeland (1975, 1977) report that the main effects of microteaching on subsequent classroom performance are not significant. However, the second study does show two significant interaction effects involving microteaching training, and this suggests that microteaching training may lead to skill acquisition but not necessarily to subsequent skill performance (see *Modelling in Microteaching*). In both studies, group sizes were again small, and some effort was made to control for large within-group differences in the second study but not in the first. Thus, the fact that the experimental group's mean rate of higher order questioning in the criterion lesson was twice the rate of the control group was shown to be statistically nonsignificant and due in large part to a single extreme score in the experimental group.

An experimental study finding positive outcomes of microteaching was that by Raymond (1973). Raymond compared the classroom skill performance of a group who had received microteaching skill practice with a group who had not. It was found that the microteaching group did differ significantly from the control group on two of the three skill criteria, and on four other measures of teacher behaviour.

One of the comparisons in a complex but elegant and carefully controlled experimental investigation by Levis et al. (1974) was between a group participating in a normal school experience programme and a group undertaking a microteaching programme in a school setting. All participants in the study were given identical skill training. At the end of the training programme, all participants taught a 10-minute lesson to a class of five pupils and measures of skill acquisition were derived from this. On two of the three criterion skills the microteaching group significantly outperformed the school experience group.

Butts (1977) compared a group of students receiving microteaching practice of questioning and responding skills with a group of students who did not receive such practice. On a pretest, there were no systematic differences between the groups; on a posttest, 15 of the 16 criteria favoured the microteaching group, and these differences were statistically significant for the questioning skill components.

Apart from the obvious difficulties of synthesizing diverse and different outcomes, several other difficulties of interpretation arise from this sample of investigations of the outcomes of microteaching.

First, it is clear that the term microteaching is used by different investigators to label different sets of activities, and this in turn means that the relevant control or comparison treatments also differ across investigators. Thus, in the studies by Copeland, the comparison was between trainees receiving skill instruction, practice, and feedback and those who did not, whilst in the study by Levis and his associates all trainees received the same skill instruction but differed in the type of practice subsequently undertaken and perhaps also in whether they were explicitly asked to practise the relevant skills.

Second, it is clear from some of the studies reviewed here that small sample sizes and large within-group differences can minimize the power of the analyses to detect between-group differences. Several possible remedies to this difficulty are possible but it is perhaps significant to note that two of the positive outcome studies did pretest the participants on skill performance. In the case of Butts, the pretest was used to match subjects across the two groups; in the case of Levis et al., the pretest was used to determine whether adjustment to posttest scores was required.

Third, the criteria to be used in assessing outcomes of microteaching do pose difficulties. In the Copeland investigations, a clear assumption was that skills acquired in microteaching should become part of a teacher's habitual repertoire of classroom skills. This implies that samples to be used as criterion measures need to be adequate measures of subsequent teaching behaviour, and it is by no means clear that this has been achieved (Shavelson and Dempsey-Attwood 1976). An alternative approach has been to ask trainees to use in a criterion lesson the skills they have acquired (Peterson 1973). This not only leads to an obvious reduction in generalizability of results but also implies that trainees in control of "no microteaching" treatments should be as familiar with the required skills as those in the "microteaching" treatment. Only the Levis et al. study provided identical skill training for all participants. However, even in that study a criterion problem arose in that outcomes were assessed on the basis of an audiorecorded microteaching lesson, a format which might be seen as favouring a microteaching group over a nonmicroteaching group.

Fourth, greater consideration must be given to evaluating the likely value or validity of the outcomes of experimental studies of the effectiveness of microteaching. An implicit assumption seems to have been that microteaching is a teacher-education technique which has the same aims and functions as other teacher-education techniques, and thus experimentation comparing microteaching with some other technique has been viewed as an appropriate way of assessing effectiveness. However, if the assumption is not a justifiable one, then the value of experimental research of this kind must be questioned.

3. Conclusions

Despite some 20 years of research effort, the only definitive conclusion which can be drawn about the effectiveness of microteaching is that participants are seen to enjoy and value the experience. It seems clear that microteaching enjoyed almost faddish popularity in the late 1960s and early 1970s and that this produced a plethora of studies on isolated aspects of microteaching from which only few useful generalizations may be formed. It is also clear that there has been no recent sustained research programme which has attempted to draw both upon these generalizations and the lessons learned in the execution of that research.

Simple verdicts on the effects of microteaching on subsequent teacher behaviour are unlikely to be reached. Microteaching, like any other teaching method, is complex, in terms of the variety of components it uses, the aims it attempts to achieve, and the theoretical models which underlie these aims. Assessment of success is further complicated by the difficulty of specifying criteria for achievement of some of the less tangible aims and by the sheer cost and practical difficulties involved in mounting meaningful long-term research in this area. Nevertheless, microteaching is itself a costly endeavour and there is a clear need for research-based study of its effects so as to allow judgments as to its effectiveness. It is apparent that much experimental research on microteaching has been sterile, providing only a situation-specific evaluation of a particular and local set of training components. This has prevented any meaningful accumulation of research results into a coherent pattern. The remedy for this problem lies in ensuring that research on microteaching is derived from, or allows for, the testing of coherent and generalizable theory. Only then will coherent and generalizable results emerge.

Bibliography

Allen D W, Ryan K A 1969 *Microteaching*. Addison Wesley, Reading, Massachusetts

Argyle M 1970 *Social Interaction*. Methuen, London

Bierschenk B 1974 *Perceptual, Evaluative and Behavioral Changes Through Externally Mediated Self-confrontation:* *Explorations and Experiments in Microsettings*. School of Education, Malmö

Borg W R 1972 The minicourse as a vehicle for changing teacher behavior: A three year follow-up. *J. Educ. Psychol.* 63: 572–79

Brown G A 1975 Microteaching: Research and developments. In: Chanan G, Delamont S (eds.) 1975 *Frontiers of Classroom Research*. National Foundation for Educational Research, Slough

Butts D C 1977 An assessment of microteaching in the context of the graduate training year. In: McIntyre D I, MacLeod G R, Griffiths R (eds.) 1977 *Investigations in Microteaching*. Croom Helm, London

Copeland W D 1975 The relationship between microteaching and student performance. *J. Educ. Res.* 68: 289–93

Copeland W D 1977 Some factors related to student teacher classroom performance following microteaching training. *Am. Educ. Res. J.* 14: 147–57

Copeland W D, Doyle W 1973 Laboratory skill training and student teacher classroom performance. *J. Exp. Educ.* 52: 16–21

Fuller F F, Manning B A 1973 Self-confrontation reviewed: A conceptualization for video playback in teacher education. *Rev. Educ. Res.* 43: 469–528

Levis D, Thompson H, Mitchell J 1974 An assessment of alternative techniques to practice teaching and an examination of selected variables within a microteaching format. Paper presented at the South Pacific Association for Teacher Education Conference, Adelaide

McDonald F J 1973 Behavior modification in teacher education. In: Thoresen C E (ed.) 1973 *Behavior Modification in Education*. University of Chicago Press, Chicago, Illinois

McIntyre D I, MacLeod G R, Griffiths R (eds.) 1977 *Investigations of Microteaching*. Croom Helm, London

MacLeod G R 1981 Experimental studies of the outcomes of microteaching. *South Pac. J. Teach. Educ.* 9: 31–42

MacLeod G R, McIntyre D I 1977 Towards a model for microteaching. In: McIntyre D I, MacLeod G R, Griffiths R (eds.) 1977 *Investigations in Microteaching*. Croom Helm, London

Peterson T L 1973 Microteaching in the preservice education of teachers: Time for a re-examination. *J. Educ. Res.* 67: 34–36

Raymond A 1973 The acquisition of nonverbal behaviors by preservice science teachers and their application during student teaching. *J. Res. Sci. Teach.* 10: 13–24

Shavelson R, Dempsey-Attwood N 1976 Generalizability of measures of teaching behavior. *Rev. Educ. Res.* 46: 553–611

Shavelson R J, Stern P 1981 Research on teachers' pedagogical thoughts, judgments, decisions and behaviour. *Rev. Educ. Res.* 51: 455–98

Turney C (ed.) 1977 *Innovation in Teacher Education: A Study of the Directions, Processes, and Problems of Innovation in Teacher Preparation with Special Reference to the Australian Context and to the Role of Cooperating Schools*. Sydney University Press, Sydney

Modelling in Microteaching

G. R. MacLeod

Modelling, or learning by observation, has long been an integral component of learning to teach. In microteaching too, modelling has played an important part in preparing trainees for their practice of teaching skills. As Allen and Ryan (1969) describe it, the original rationale for the inclusion of modelling in microteaching was the very pragmatic one that skill learning was likely to be enhanced if trainees were able to view a demonstration of a particular teaching skill prior to their practice of that skill. This article reviews research on the effects of modelling on skill acquisition and relates the outcomes to Bandura's (1977) theory of social learning.

In Bandura's conceptualization, learning by observation is said to occur principally through the informative function of modelling influences, and is governed by four component processes: attending, retention, motor reproduction, and motivation.

Attending refers to the observer's selective perception of the significant features of the model, while retention refers to the maintenance in permanent memory of a symbolic form of the patterns which have been attended to in the model. According to Bandura it is an advanced capacity for symbolic representation which enables humans to learn much of their behaviour by observation, with the symbolic codes allowing for the retention of large quantities of information in easily stored form. It is also this capacity to create symbols which serves to distinguish modelling or learning by observation from simple imitation.

Motor reproduction refers to the translation of symbolic representations into actions or their use as guides for actions, whilst motivation refers to the rewardingness or nonrewardingness of enacting the modelled behaviours. Thus, in Bandura's model, the processes of attending and retention refer to acquisition of behaviour or skills, motor reproduction refers to performance, whilst motivation refers both to acquisition and to performance.

1. Research on Positive and Negative Models in Microteaching

Studies comparing the effects of positive and negative models have been reported by Allen et al. (1967), Koran et al. (1972) and Gilmore (1977). All three studies found the use of positive models to be the more effective, but the first two studies also indicated that negative models were significant aids to skill acquisition. However, Koran and his colleagues note that their positive models included a greater amount of more explicit information than did the negative models, whilst the definitions of treatments in the Gilmore investigation indicate that this was also the case in his study. Thus, differences between treatments may be attributed to the different quantities of skill-related information provided by the different models, this being an interpretation consistent with Bandura's contention that modelling operates primarily through the information it conveys. The second difficulty in interpreting the results of these studies is that the labels "positive" and "negative" may be used to refer to very different treatments in different investigations. Thus, a negative model may be one which portrays the absence of criterion behaviours, or few of the criterion behaviours, or inappropriate use of the crite-

rion behaviours, or, perhaps, exemplification of the behaviours to be avoided. Perhaps the major conclusion to be drawn from these investigations is that modelling in microteaching can have significant effects on skill acquisition.

2. Research Comparing Written and Audiovisual Models

The issue of the medium used for model presentations has received considerable research attention, and is an important area because of the cost implications of its outcomes.

A common theme in the research has been the comparison of symbolic modelling (written) with perceptual modelling (film or videotape), and a frequently used method has been to use a transcript from the film or videotape sound track as the symbolic model, thereby making the information content of the rival treatments more comparable. This was the procedure followed by Koran (1971) who reported that both treatments produced significant changes in a criterion of generating written questions whilst a control treatment had no such effects. Phillips (1973) compared the effects of a treatment involving the provision of a written handout and discussion, with a treatment involving these same components but with the addition of a videotape model. It was found that both treatments had an effect on subsequent questioning behaviour, but that there was no significant difference between the treatment effects.

A group of studies which lend some support to the superiority of perceptual over symbolic models are those by Orme (1966), by Young (1967), and by Koran (1969). It is noteworthy that these studies tend to involve more complex experimental designs than those which find no significant differences. Thus, although the results of these investigations are more difficult to interpret unequivocally, it is also likely that the power of the analyses is greater than in those with simpler comparisons.

In summary, these studies of modelling media again indicate strong effects of modelling in microteaching and seem to indicate a slight favouring of perceptual over symbolic models. If information content of these models is similar, then these results may be attributable to the greater motivational or attention-drawing value of perceptual models. As Bandura (1977) puts it, people "rarely have to be compelled to watch television, whereas oral or written reports of the same activities would not hold their attention for long" (p. 40).

3. Research on Focus in Modelling

> Observers who code modeled activities into either words, concise labels or vivid imagery learn and retain behavior better than those who simply observe . . . (Bandura p. 26)

Most uses of modelling in microteaching involve trainees in more than simple observation or unguided reading. In general some kind of cueing, coding, or labelling is involved, with this focus either being provided for the trainees in the model itself, or being acquired by the trainees through practice in the use of prespecified codes or labels. A useful review by Griffiths (1976) indicates the wide variety of focusing devices and observer activities which have been undertaken alongside modelling in microteaching, ranging from a brief "peep" on the sound-track of a film, through verbal labels, and the use of rating or observation schedules by the trainees, to the use of testing and immediate feedback on the trainees' recognition of skill components.

The available evidence suggests that where cues or other focusing devices are provided during viewing, this adds significantly to the effectiveness of modelling procedures (McDonald and Allen 1967, Claus 1968). These devices may be seen as increasing the information value of models by providing for trainees the symbolic representations of criterion behaviours which are required for, and maximize the efficiency of, retention. Thus, the provision of focus seems to enhance the relative effectiveness of the modelling process.

Of greater theoretical and practical import are those studies in which the focus in modelling is provided through some form of discrimination training whereby trainees learn to code and label appropriate and inappropriate behaviours, and the effects of this treatment are then compared with a conventional microteaching treatment which includes trainee practice of the skill. It has been asserted that "practice is necessary for skills acquisition" (Trower et al. 1978 p. 71), with this assertion being supported by reference to the acquisition of motor skills. However, the evidence arising from studies of the acquisition of teaching skills through modelling with discrimination training suggests that practice may not be as essential as has been supposed.

Peterson (1973), for example, compared the effects of a full microteaching treatment involving modelling, discrimination training, individual practice, videotape feedback, and further practice, with a treatment involving modelling, discrimination training, and limited group practice. Seven weeks after these treatments, trainees were asked to prepare a lesson using the 12 skill components previously identified. No significant differences between the groups were found on any of the criteria.

In contrast to the Peterson study, which provided modelling and discrimination training for both groups, an investigation by Wagner (1973) compared a microteaching treatment (with practice and videotape replay, but without modelling) with a discrimination training treatment. It was found that while the microteaching treatment failed to produce significant overall changes in teaching behaviour, the discrimination training was highly effective in changing teaching behaviour, such that on two of the three behavioural criteria, the discrimination training group significantly outperformed the microteaching group.

Further studies which suggest that modelling with discrimination training may be sufficient for skill acquisi-

tion are those by MacLeod et al. (1977) and Batten (1978). An ongoing study by Pegg (1985) reaches similar conclusions in regard to skill acquisition, but further demonstrates that a modelling/discrimination training component can be as favourably received by trainees as the practice/feedback component of microteaching.

4. Conclusions

The studies reviewed here, together with those in the following article, indicate the powerful role which can be played by modelling procedures in microteaching. Further, the outcomes of the research seem entirely consistent with Bandura's social learning theory. The research is of particular interest in suggesting that modelling with discrimination training may lead to skills acquisition without a skill practice component being required, an outcome consistent with Bandura's distinction between acquisition and performance. Thus, modelling has been shown to be a significant component of microteaching but its role as a possible substitute for microteaching requires further investigation.

Bibliography

Allen D W, Ryan K A 1969 *Microteaching*. Addison Wesley, Reading, Massachusetts

Allen D W, Berliner D C, McDonald F J, Sobol F T 1967 A comparison of different modelling procedures in the acquisition of a teaching skill. ERIC Document No. ED 011 261

Bandura A 1977 *Social Learning Theory*. Prentice-Hall, Englewood Cliffs, New Jersey

Batten H D 1978 Factors influencing the effectiveness of microteaching in a teacher education programme. Ph.D. thesis, University of Stirling, Scotland, 1978. *Aslib Index to Theses* 28(2): 5515

Claus K E S 1968 The effects of modelling and feedback variables on higher order questioning skills (Doctoral dissertation, Stanford University, 1968) *Dissertation Abstracts International* 1969 29: 2133A (University Microfilms No. 69–207)

Gilmore S 1977 The effects of positive and negative models on student–teachers' questioning behaviour. In: McIntyre D I, MacLeod G R, Griffiths R (eds.) 1977 *Investigations of Microteaching*. Croom Helm, London, Chap. 10

Griffiths R 1976 The preparation of models for use in microteaching programmes. *Educ. Media Int.* 1: 25–31

Koran J J 1971 A study of the effects of written and film-mediated models on the acquisition of a science teaching skill by preservice elementary teachers. *J. Res. Sci. Teach.* 8: 45–50

Koran J J, Koran M L, McDonald F J 1972 Effects of different sources of positive and negative information on observational learning of a teaching skill. *J. Educ. Psychol.* 63: 405–410

Koran M L 1969 The effects of individual differences on observational learning in the acquisition of a teaching skill (Doctoral dissertation, Stanford University, 1969) *Dissertation Abstracts International* 1970 30: 1450A–1451A (University Microfilms No. 69–17,435)

McDonald F J, Allen D W 1967 Training effects of feedback

and modeling procedures on teaching performance. Technical Report No. 3, Center for Research and Development in Teaching, Stanford University, California

McIntyre D I, MacLeod G R, Griffiths R (eds.) 1977 *Investigations of Microteaching*. Croom Helm, London

MacLeod G R, Griffiths R, McIntyre D I 1977 The effects of differential training and of teaching subject on microteaching skills performance. In: McIntyre D I, MacLeod G R, Griffiths R (eds.) 1977 *Investigations of Microteaching*. Croom Helm, London

Orme M E J 1966 The effects of modeling and feedback variables on the acquisition of a complex teaching strategy (Doctoral dissertation, Stanford University, 1966) *Dissertation Abstracts International* 1966 27: 3320A–3321A (University Microfilms No. 67-4417)

Pegg J E 1985 The effect of practice on the acquisition of teaching skills. Doctoral dissertation, University of New

England, Armidale

Peterson T L 1973 Microteaching in the preservice education of teachers: Time for a reexamination. *J. Educ. Res.* 67: 34–36

Phillips W E 1973 Effect of a video-taped modeling procedure on verbal questioning practices of secondary social studies student teachers. Fairmont State College, West Virginia, ERIC Document No. ED 079 967

Trower P, Bryant B, Argyle M 1978 *Social Skills and Mental Health*. Methuen, London

Wagner A C 1973 Changing teaching behaviour: A comparison of microteaching and cognitive discrimination training. *J. Educ. Psychol.* 64: 299–305

Young D B 1967 The effectiveness of self-instruction in teacher education using modelling and video-tape feedback (Doctoral dissertation, Stanford University, 1967) *Dissertation Abstracts International* 1968 28: 4520A (University Microfilms No. 68–6518)

Feedback in Microteaching

D. S. Levis

The microteaching training format developed at Stanford consists of a three-phased sequence. In phase 1 (modelling), opportunity is provided for trainees to observe a model teacher who emits the teaching behaviours to be learned. In phase 2 (practice), trainees are given an opportunity to practise the same behaviours. In phase 3 (feedback), trainees are reinforced for those instances of the desired behaviour they have emitted. This phase is considered necessary because the teaching behaviour emitted may not have been sufficiently reinforced during the modelling and practice phases.

Research studies have attempted to measure the general effectiveness of microteaching as a means of developing teaching skills and to investigate the modelling, practice, and feedback variables operating within the observational learning model on which microteaching is based. This article focuses upon the feedback phase.

1. Feedback

Feedback refers to the communication of information about performance to the learner. Research evidence in different fields of the behavioural sciences has shown that feedback can be effective in motivating and facilitating behavioural change. There is little contrary evidence to the general conclusion that learning is enhanced by frequent, immediate, and positive feedback.

Behaviouristically oriented theorists have attributed the effects of feedback largely to reinforcement. Informing the learner that a given action is successful gratifies the cognitive, affiliative, and ego-enhancing drives and increases the probability of the action recurring.

The advantages of feedback may also be argued on the grounds of its cognitive effects on learning. According to Ausubel and Robinson (1969 pp. 299–300),

information about performance "confirms appropriate meanings and associations, corrects errors, clarifies misconceptions and indicates the relative adequacy with which different portions of the learning task have been mastered. As a result of feedback, the subject's confidence in his learning products is increased, his learnings are consolidated, and he is better able to focus his efforts and attention on those aspects of a task requiring further refinement".

Perlberg (1976) provides a psychological explanation for feedback based largely on cognitive dissonance theory (Festinger 1957). He argues that the feedback receiver or person confronting himself identifies discrepancies between actual and desired performances. This discrepancy creates tension, dissatisfaction, or anxiety, any of which activate a motivating force leading to their reduction. Perlberg sees feedback and self-confrontation as complementary processes. A person confronts himself or herself when he or she receives feedback messages through different sources. These messages do not have to be channelled through mediators. A person may perceive a discrepancy between his or her intentions and the respective outcome with or without the aid of others. When this occurs, he or she develops a need or drive to eliminate the discrepancy. According to Perlberg (1976 p. 17) "The degree of importance attached to the elimination of the discrepancy is a function of the intensity of the need created by the discrepancy and the availability and awareness of opportunities and resources through which he can satisfy these needs."

Essential to all the above conceptualizations of feedback is the necessity of highlighting important elements of the feedback process. Unless accompanied by appropriate shaping behaviour or some kind of focusing, feedback has not been found to change behaviour significantly.

2. Feedback in Microteaching

The research literature in the period 1963 to 1975 indicates that there was considerable interest in the effects of the feedback component in the microteaching process. While a number of studies consistently supported the advantages of providing accurate feedback information to trainees, there was a lack of congruence in the findings of studies which systematically varied feedback treatments.

Three major areas of research interest were (a) the effects of videotape and audiotape feedback, (b) the effects of supervisor influence during feedback, and (c) the relative effects of modelling and feedback.

2.1 Videotape and Audiotape Feedback

The development of microteaching coincided with the development of portable videotape recorders and cheap, compact audiotape recorders. It was not surprising, therefore, that they should be regarded as powerful tools in bringing about behavioural change by providing accurate feedback and that they should be used extensively in microteaching settings as adjuncts to critiques by supervisors, peers and pupils, and as a basis for the trainee's self-evaluation.

The videotape recorder has commonly been considered to be the major source of feedback. Because of its capacity to reproduce the teaching immediately and in a complete, objective, and reliable manner, it has been seen as providing a common frame of reference for supervisor and trainee to focus on specific behaviours emitted during the practice phase, and helping to depersonalize criticism, thus making trainees less defensive and more amenable to behavioural change.

In a most comprehensive review of the literature on feedback and self-confrontation via videotape replays, Fuller and Manning (1973) draw attention to some of the potentially harmful effects of this form of feedback. From Fuller and Manning's detailed analysis and discussion of the problem, various important principles emerge: (a) videotape feedback can be a stressful, anxiety-producing experience: objective representation of the self can be more anxiety producing if the subject is already anxious; videotape representation of self involves a selectivity and focusing on self which makes such a feedback experience more arousing emotionally, and different from other representations of self; (b) initial exposure to videotape replays causes intense self-focus on physical cues; (c) for videotape feedback to be successful, it should be done in situations where the subject feels basically secure; moderate rather than extreme dissonance has been found to be more effective in bringing change in nonattitudinal matters; and (d) when subjects are given videotape feedback of themselves, it produces less discrepancy between their self-concept and the way in which others see them, and increases their accuracy of self-perception and of self-appraisal.

A review of the literature of microteaching reveals that videotape feedback has been perceived mainly as a means of providing accurate information; its potentially disruptive effects have been largely unexplored. One possible explanation for this is that stressful, anxiety-producing experiences are most likely to occur when videotape feedback focuses on the self. In the typical microteaching setting, the focus is on the trainee's application of previously modelled teaching skills. This focus on the technical skills of teaching tends to avoid direct confrontation with self and its potentially stressful effects.

That videotape feedback is more effective in producing behavioural changes than other forms of feedback has been more often assumed than tested. While several studies have supported its effectiveness in microteaching settings, a number of studies have found no significant difference between videotape feedback and feedback without videotape for the development of teaching skills. In general, it would seem that research and application of videotape feedback within microteaching contexts have not been sufficiently penetrating and critical to comprehend its advantages and disadvantages and to optimize its potential.

Studies which have compared videotape and audiotape feedback have produced conflicting results, suggesting that the effectiveness of the type of feedback may depend substantially on the nature of the skill being practised. Feedback on the performance of predominantly verbal skills might be more effectively mediated by audiotape, while feedback on skills with visual elements would benefit from the use of videotape. Fuller and Manning report the findings of Poling (1968) and Yenawine and Arbuckle (1971) that videotape replays have been found initially to be more threatening than audiotape replays. They suggest that videotape playback should be used for initial arousal and individual playback and that audiotape feedback be used for group feedback and long-term practice.

2.2 Supervisor Influence During Feedback

While the role of supervision during feedback sessions has received attention, empirical evidence regarding optimal supervisory styles and modes is inconclusive.

Griffiths (1976) identified three broad conceptualizations of the supervisory role within a microteaching context: (a) an approach to supervision related to the behaviourist theory of shaping in which the trainee attempts to approximate the teaching behaviour of a model and the supervisor provides feedback information as to the degree of success the trainee has achieved in performing the modelled behaviour; (b) formulation of the supervisor's contribution in terms of a counselling role addressed to the trainee's current psychological state; and (c) a supervisory approach which focuses on cognitive variables in the critique situation so that the trainee is viewed as a processor of information and the supervisor as a facilitator in this process. In the absence of empirical evidence on the differential effectiveness of these conceptualizations of the supervisory role, the professional literature has tended to promote an eclectic approach based on a listing of possible and overlapping supervisory tasks.

Research studies on the effects of supervisory influence during the feedback phase tend to cluster around two major concerns: (a) the effects of supervisor discussion based on videotape or audiotape feedback compared to supervisor discussion without playback facilities; and (b) the differential effects of source of feedback.

While a number of studies have supported the proposition that a combination of a trained supervisor and playback facilities provides a powerful means of feedback, a sufficient number of studies have produced non-significant differences to raise doubt about the need for playback facilities during critique sessions.

In relation to source of feedback two questions arise: firstly, whether other participants in the microteaching programme, such as peer observers or pupils, are as powerful a source of feedback as the supervisor; and, secondly, whether playback facilities permit the trainee to self-monitor his or her feedback and obviate the need for supervisory feedback.

Research evidence almost unanimously supports the view that feedback not accompanied by some form of focus will have little effect in changing behaviour. The importance of supervisory feedback within the microteaching format is supported by a number of studies. It appears that conferences led by trained supervisors serve the purpose of providing focus; however, a factor which also emerges is that it is not so much the presence of a supervisor, but the kind of person he or she is and the procedures he or she follows, that are important. There is also empirical evidence to suggest that self-analysis, supported by a self-evaluation guide to focus trainee attention, is a viable alternative for feedback involving supervisor-led discussion. Studies which have investigated feedback from pupils to trainees or from pupils and peers to trainees, have shown a disruptive effect on trainee behaviour, and pointed to the need for the supervisor to boost the morale of a trainee faced with critical feedback.

2.3 Relative Effects of Modelling and Feedback

A considerable body of microteaching research investigated the relative effects of the modelling and feedback phases of the microteaching format, in an effort to determine the most effective combination of these two variables. Studies by Bandura and McDonald (1963), Claus (1969), Salomon and McDonald (1970) and Resnick and Kiss (1970) showed that modelling procedures alone had a significantly greater effect on trainee behaviour than feedback alone.

McDonald and Allen (1967) compared different combinations of modelling and feedback procedures. Their comprehensive series of studies investigated the combination of symbolic models (involving such written materials as transcripts of teaching and oral or written descriptions of teaching skills) or perceptual models (involving visual or auditory models presented either live or on film, videotape, or audiotape) with a feedback process which included reinforcement and discrimination training on relevant cues. The treatment which consistently gained the highest scores combined symbolic and perceptual modelling and prompting and confirmation feedback conditions.

On the basis of their studies, McDonald and Allen (1967) were impressed by the comparative effectiveness of complementary modelling and feedback procedures and suggested the possibility that feedback could be reduced in scale if powerful modelling were available.

Bandura (1965 p. 313) argued that modelling procedures are most effective in transmitting new response patterns, whereas feedback is an efficient method of "strengthening and maintaining responses that already exist in the behavioural repertoire of an organism". Modelling is regarded as an acquisition variable, while feedback functions as a performance variable. Modelling enables trainees to acquire a skill; feedback helps them to adapt the skill to their own personality and to teaching situations other than those demonstrated by the model.

Another study which lent support to the comparative importance of modelling was the investigation by Salomon and McDonald (1970). In this study, the investigators found, as they had predicted, that without any prior conception of the criterion behaviour, the videotape replay of a lesson only gave trainees information about how far their behaviour departed from their own predispositions about a skill, so that subsequent behaviour was unlikely to be productively changed. The implication of this finding is that if trainees know through careful modelling what behaviours are expected of them, feedback sessions are more useful because they are able to compare their performance with the criterion, assess the extent to which it departs from the desired behaviour, and thus effect necessary changes.

A study by Resnick and Kiss (1970) found that, if responses and stimulus occasions have been adequately discriminated in advance of practice, subjects can apply the discrimination to their own behaviour and learn to self-edit their practice of teaching skills. The investigators concluded that prepractice discrimination training offered the possibility of doing away with costly feedback procedures, because the trainee's reliance on outside feedback would be substantially reduced.

3. Summary

The preceding overview of theory and research relating to feedback in microteaching provides evidence for the following conclusions:

(a) The provision of immediate accurate feedback regarding a particular teaching behaviour enhances the subsequent performance of that behaviour.

(b) Unless accompanied by appropriate highlighting, focusing or cueing, feedback will not change behaviour significantly.

(c) When accompanied by powerful modelling procedures, the effects of feedback tend to be less significant.

(d) Studies which have compared various feedback treatments in microteaching settings have produced inconclusive results. Research findings tend to favour the use of videotape playbacks as a basis for critique sessions. However, there is evidence to show that initially they may have disruptive effects on learning, and that for some verbal skills and for long-term practice they may not be as effective as the use of audiotape playbacks. Results tend to favour the presence of a trained supervisor to provide focus, reinforcement, and morale boosting during feedback sessions; however, there is also evidence to show that trainee self-analysis can be effective if supported by cueing devices, such as self-evaluation check lists.

Bibliography

Ausubel D P, Robinson F G 1969 *School Learning: An Introduction to Educational Psychology.* Holt, Rinehart and Winston, New York

Bandura A J 1965 Behavioral modification through modeling procedures. In: Krasner L, Ullman L P (eds.) 1965 *Research in Behavior Modification.* Holt, Rinehart and Winston, San Francisco, California, pp. 310–40

Bandura A J, McDonald F J 1963 The influence of social reinforcement and the behavior of models in shaping children's model judgment. *J. Abnorm. Soc. Psych.* 67: 601–7

Claus K E S 1969 Effects of modelling and feedback treatment on the development of teachers' questioning skills, Technical Report No. 6. Stanford Center for Research and Development in Teaching, Stanford University, California (ERIC Document No. ED 033 081)

Festinger L 1957 *A Theory of Cognitive Dissonance.* Row, Peterson, Evanston, Illinois

Fuller F F, Manning B A 1973 Self-confrontation reviewed: A conceptualization for video playback in teacher education. *Rev. Educ. Res.* 43: 469–512

Griffiths R 1976 Preparing tutors for microteaching supervision. *Ed. Media Int.* 1: 11–15

McDonald F J, Allen D W 1967 Training effects of modeling and feedback procedures on teaching performance, Technical Report No. 3. Stanford Center for Research and Development in Teaching, Stanford University, California (ERIC Document No. ED 017 985)

Perlberg A 1976 Microteaching – present and future trends. *Educ. Med. Int.* 1976(2): 13–20

Perlberg A 1983 When professors confront themselves toward a theoretical conceptualization of video self confrontation in higher education. *Higher Educ.* 12: 633–63

Perlberg A 1984 When professors confront themselves: The use of video self-confrontation (VSC) in improving university teaching. In: Zuber-Skeriff O (ed.) 1984 *Video in Higher Education,* Kogan Page, London

Poling E G 1968 Videotape recordings in counseling practicum: Environmental considerations. *Couns. Educ. Superv.* 7: 348–56

Resnick L B, Kiss L E 1970 Discrimination training and feedback in shaping teacher behaviour. Paper presented to annual conference of the American Educational Research Association (ERIC Document No. ED 039 175)

Salomon G, McDonald F J 1970 Pretest and posttest reactions to self-viewing one's teaching performance on videotape. *J. Educ. Psychol.* 61: 280–86

Yenawine G, Arbuckle D S 1971 Study of the use of videotape and audiotape as techniques in counsellor education. *J. Couns. Psychol.* 18: 1–6

Video Recording in Educational Research

G. Leinhardt

Since the early 1960s, videotape has been a popular tool in educational research and training. This article covers one aspect of videotape use, that of its role in research. Videotape, as it is used in training, will be only briefly mentioned. The article covers the following: equipment, historical uses, summary of current use and techniques, examples of use in current research, and issues of intrusion, reliability, and validity.

1. Equipment

Video recording systems usually comprise a recording unit, a camera and a monitor. These three pieces of equipment can be used in a variety of configurations. For example, cameras can be visible or hidden, recording units can be near to the camera or in a console-type control room. The camera can have a built-in wireless, or a wired microphone. The equipment may be permanently mounted in experimental classrooms, or settings where there is frequent videotaping, or portable equipment may be used which can be carried to specific sites.

2. Historical Use

The most prominent early use of videotape was in the development of teacher-training materials. Essentially there were two basic approaches. Tape was used to model appropriate behaviors by developing microlessons on such topics as tutorials, questioning, topic introducing, and so on. Staged instructional packets with a small number of students served as the model. Tape was also used as a feedback device for teachers who self-critiqued or worked with a supervisor in watching their own performance in the classroom. These techniques are most successful when the trainee has his/her attention focused on a few specific behaviors (Biberstine 1971).

3. Current Use

By 1982, videotape was no longer an exotic gimmick in research, but an integral part of many studies. This is because the equipment has become commonplace, relatively lightweight, highly portable, and robust. Videotape provides a semipermanent, very complete, audiovisual record of events. The instant replay permits it to be used as a stimulus for recall, as well as an artifact of an action sequence that can be coded from multiple perspectives. The tape can be scored and rescored, so observer reliability and training is greatly simplified.

Videotape is used most frequently in the following types of studies: process–product or evaluation research as an audiovisual data source of teacher–student interactions (Cooley and Leinhardt 1980, Leinhardt et al. 1981); research on the cognitive processes and decision making of teachers (Peterson and Clark 1978); ethnographic microlevel studies of student and teacher behaviors (McDermott 1977); and laboratory studies of situational interactions, such as task persistence. In the first type of research, videotape is used instead of an in-class observer. Information is used in real time, but a permanent record is constructed. In the second type of research, the tape is the stimulus that prompts the production of the data to be actually used, as well as providing a validity check on action. In the third type of research, tape is used to document a short event that is representative of a larger system of actions. A small segment of videotape is intensely analyzed and studied in slow motion so that the implications of the microlevel actions for macroevents can be explored. In the last type of research, the tape is used as an unobtrusive recorder of events. Examples of each of the types of studies will be briefly described.

Videotape is used in process–product studies by sampling a small portion of instructional time (one to six hours), and coding the videotape with respect to teacher–student interactions. The purpose of process–product research is to explain or predict student outcomes using student inputs and instructional processes as predictors. Videotape is used to help capture important characteristics of the instructional process. Literally thousands of codes can be used. However, some basic elements seem to permeate the majority of the literature: teacher affect, instructional content, managerial content, questioning style, initiation, interruption, and feedback. These codes can be estimated by time or even sampling procedures. The codes may be used singly or collapsed and used to form a core measure of teacher instructional behaviors (Cooley and Leinhardt 1980). Information obtained in this way should be no different from that which would have been obtained if in-class observers had been used. The advantage is increased precision and reliability due to recoding potential.

Videotape is used in a quite different way in research on teachers' thinking. In this type of research the videotape serves the role of an unbiased record and acts as a stimulus to produce data for future analysis. The purpose of such research is to understand the nature of teachers' information processing, decision making, problem solving, or execution of plans. The teacher is taped for some period of time (usually one class). The tapes are analyzed by the researcher for key points, either regarding decisions, lesson objectives, or alterations in routines. The tape is played back, in part or in whole, to the teacher fairly soon after the occurrence and the teacher is questioned with respect to his or her thoughts during activity sequences. It is the responses to these questions that are analyzed. Versions of this work have been carried out in Australia, the United Kingdom, the United States, Canada, France, the Federal Republic of Germany, and Belgium. It is a relatively new field and has not yet produced major results. However, it is an interesting convergence of process–product studies and studies of teacher attitude and background. In this research videotaping makes the work possible and plays a significant role (Bennett 1978, Calderhead 1981, Clark and Joyce 1981).

Ethnographic work that examines the context and content of classroom actions uses videotape in a third way. In these studies, videotaping is done over many months and an exemplary slice is taken and analyzed in tremendous detail. In the work of McDermott (1977), for example, a very small piece of a teacher-directed reading lesson is analyzed. The tape is slowed down and many aspects are studied: the body position of all actors, the changes in those positions, voice inflection, eye contact, culturally consistent and clashing behaviors. This microlevel analysis is used to support the description of a more global reality. The tape is a vehicle for showing the consistency of that reality from life success or failure at one end, all the way to unconscious eye contact or aversion at the other. Here again, the videotape plays an especially significant role because it is possible to replay any part or to observe any section in slow motion. It should be noted that film has better resolution (at much greater cost) in extreme slow motion (McDermott 1977).

Videotaping has largely replaced filming in laboratory settings. In these situations the subjects are usually unaware of the fact that they are being taped. The tape is analyzed by examining their behaviors while interacting with people or things, or responding to unexpected situations. One of the more common types of studies involves motivational or task persistence research. Another type of laboratory usage involves constructing scenarios that show confederates engaging in a scripted behavior. The tape is then used as a stimulus.

4. Techniques of Use

This article now turns to techniques of use of videotape. Four issues will be discussed: the entrance into the setting; the time frame of the videotape segment; the audio

219

and visual point of focus; and orientation. For simplicity it will be assumed that lightweight portable cassettes are in use.

Whenever possible, entrance should be gradual. Ideally, observers should be in the classroom for a week prior to taping, and several days before taping the observer should bring the equipment to the classroom and briefly explain it (15 to 20 minutes). Finally, two to three tapings should be made (or one long one), in order to minimize the effects of the taping process. In large-scale studies it is sometimes too costly to spend very much time on the entrance process. Often as little as half a day, or even one hour of preparatory time is given, in which the children and adults can see the equipment—the recorders and the teacher wired up for the various sound devices. In these cases the effects of entrance are felt or seen on tape, and estimates will have to be made of the degree to which the teacher and the students are responding artificially.

The observer/taper role must be clearly defined, regardless of setting. The role can range from no communication at all to almost the participant observer level. There are advantages to each approach. No communication assures a minimum of camera stares and sneaked looks. However, because it looks natural does not mean it is. A more complete involvement of the observer/taper assures more sincere cooperation of students and teacher.

The second issue is time frame. Videotape reels are either 40 or 60 minutes long; cassettes are as long as six hours. Most classroom lessons last either 40 or 60 minutes. There is a question as to when the tape should be started. Should it start with the class bell? In this case some of the tape may be taken up with the children coming in, settling down, and getting started. Or should the tape start with the beginning of the lesson? If the tape starts with the beginning of the lesson, or the main instructional segment, then the density with which this activity seems to take place is inflated because extraneous material has been deleted from the estimate. It is essentially a sampling problem. If a researcher's interest lies in taping a particular lesson, a certain amount of time prior to and after the lesson should be taped as well. If the researcher is interested in getting a feel for the dynamics of the classroom and naturally occurring activity structures, then the tape should run on a randomly sampled time basis, not limited by period boundaries.

The third issue is audiovisual focus. Present technology does not easily permit multiple audio sources, although these will soon be available. The best system currently available is to wire the main actor (teacher) with a small wireless mike, and to film using a camera which has a mounted directional mike with a wireless override. When the teacher is giving a lesson, the camera mike can be used; when the teacher is interacting, the wireless mike will pick up both teacher and student. Switching from one to the other only involves plugging and unplugging a camera mounted jack.

Similarly, there are few devices for multiple visual focuses. It is possible to insert the overlay of the class in a frame that is primarily focused on the teacher, by using several cameras, and it is possible to use multiple audio pickups. However, this type of work is best done in a laboratory setting. Multiple cameras are more intrusive. It seems that one camera and one audio system is optimal. The camera operator should be focusing on either a geographic area, following individual children; or following the teacher, and then catching people as they come into the view of the individual on target. There is no way the camera can capture the whole class all of the time. It must focus on one element or another which restricts the information available to coders and to analyzers later on. Some tapes focus exclusively on a group of children, and other tapes focus exclusively on a teacher. Some tapes focus on a teacher and then scan the children at regular intervals, which is a reasonable system for understanding what is going on in the classroom (Cooley and Leinhardt 1980).

The last issue is orientation. This is related to visual focus, but refers to the point of reference rather than what is on the tape. The camera can act as the eyes of an actor in the class; for example, if the camera is to take the position of a child, it can be shot over the shoulder of a child. The audio focus would be on the individual that the child was looking at, probably the teacher. For other types of research, such as stimulated recall, the camera can focus from the perspective of the teacher.

5. Reliability and Validity of Videotaping

Regardless of the positioning, or the care taken in familiarizing the subjects with the equipment, videotaping is intrusive. The question is, is the taping process so disruptive that the record produced is neither reliable nor valid? Taping is an event that teachers and children prepare for (even if they don't know when it will happen); however, a teacher that is punitive and loud cannot suddenly change for the camera because the students will not follow. What has been seen to happen is that major elements in the normal routine are accidentally left out because of nervousness. Such changes in behavior are rare and do not usually happen on the second or third taping. Taping can and does produce changes, but these changes are not likely to reverse the basic ordering of teachers along a single dimension. Good teachers tend to look a little better than usual—poor teachers look a little worse. Thus, the representativeness of taping can be questioned to some extent, but it is an area in which little research has been carried out.

The coding of videotape is far easier than in-class coding. Thus, interobserver reliability can be raised to very high levels and can be maintained by systematic checks of coders' tapes (Cooley and Leinhardt 1980) and recoding when necessary. The potential for validity is raised by having reliable coding and frequent taping. Videotaping is, in some cases, the only way to carry out a study; in such cases, issues of whether taping is more or less obtrusive are moot. As taping becomes more popular, it is likely that more rigorous techniques for studying the effects of taping will be forthcoming.

Bibliography

Adams R S, Biddle B J 1970 *Realities of Teaching: Exploration with Video Tape.* Holt, Rinehart and Winston, New York

Bennett S N 1978 Recent research on teaching: A dream, a belief, and a model. *Br. J. Educ. Psychol.* 48: 127–47

Biberstine R D 1971 The utilization of videotape equipment in teacher education. *Contemp. Educ.* 42: 217–21

Calderhead J 1981 Stimulated recall: A method for research on teaching. *Br. J. Educ. Psychol.* 51: 211–17

Clark C, Joyce B 1981 Teacher decision making and teaching effectiveness. In: Joyce B R, Brown C C, Peck L (eds.) 1981 *Flexibility in Teaching: An Excursion into the Nature of Teaching and Training.* Longman, New York

Cooley W W, Leinhardt G 1980 The instructional dimensions study. *Educ. Eval. Policy Anal.* 2: 7–25

Leinhardt G, Zigmond N, Cooley W W 1981 Reading instruction and its effects. *Am. Educ. Res. J.* 18: 343–61

McDermott R P 1977 Social relations as contexts for learning in school. *Harvard Educ. Rev.* 47: 198–213

Peterson P L, Clark C M 1978 Teachers' reports of their cognitive processes during teaching. *Am. Educ. Res.* 15: 555–65

Simple Media

Graphic Production

D. K. Dayton

Within the realm of educational technology, graphic production refers to the creation of visual educational materials. It is an applied art. Typical products include:

(a) An overhead transparency which shows the plot of an algebraic equation.

(b) A poster which illustrates actions to be taken in the event of a fire.

(c) Art for a slide presentation on the development of the human embryo.

(d) An illustrated pamphlet describing how to conserve energy in the home.

While these products vary considerably in form, the basic processes by which they are produced are quite similar. A common approach to the graphic production process is illustrated in Fig. 1.

1. Design

The first step in the graphic production process is design. Good design creates visual materials which

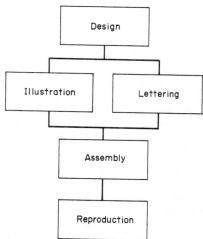

Figure 1
The graphic production process

clearly communicate their intended message to the intended audience. Factors such as aesthetics are important, but are secondary considerations when compared to effective communication.

At the beginning of the design process, the graphic artist consults with the client to determine the objective and content for each visual, the audience for whom the visuals are intended, the format in which the final product will appear, and any special circumstances affecting the production or use of the visuals.

Using this information, the artist often produces a rough sketch to show how the visuals will appear in their final form. At this point the artist should consider a number of visual design principles.

(a) Clarity—when producing education materials, the most significant principle of visual design is clarity. The purpose of the visual must be obvious to the intended audience. Audience characteristics such as reading level and previous experience should be considered.

(b) Simplicity—one of the most effective ways to insure clarity is through simplicity. Unnecessary or distracting details should be eliminated and, if possible, each visual should be restricted to a single idea.

(c) Emphasis—when visuals are complex, the key elements within the visual should be emphasized to draw the viewer's attention. Methods for emphasis include the use of labels, contrasting colors, or enlarged elements.

(d) Harmony—in order for the key elements to be emphasized, the background elements must not draw attention to themselves. Unless a particular element is to be emphasized, the use of contrasting sizes, type styles, colors, or drawing styles should be avoided.

(e) Organization—the way in which the elements of a visual are organized can have a significant effect on the efficiency with which the information in the visual is perceived. The organization of a visual

223

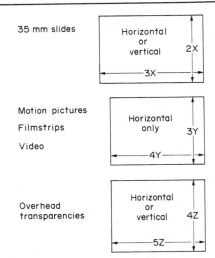

35 mm slides — Horizontal or vertical — 2X / 3X

Motion pictures / Filmstrips / Video — Horizontal only — 3Y / 4Y

Overhead transparencies — Horizontal or vertical — 4Z / 5Z

Figure 2
Aspect ratio of common media formats

should be obvious and consistent with cultural practices.

(f) Legibility—textual elements within visuals must be legible. Simple type styles which are large enough to be easily read under a variety of conditions are best.

(g) Balance—visual materials with elements arranged in an unnatural or unbalanced manner can distract viewers. The arrangement of visual elements should appear in balance.

(h) Unity—the separate elements of a visual should create the final effect of one meaningful unit. The unity of a visual can be increased by moving the elements closer together. Other techniques include the use of overlap, borders, or a common background.

Early in the design process, the graphic artist should determine the format for the final product. This information is critical if the produced visuals are to conform comfortably to the characteristics of the medium. For projected media, the most significant of these characteristics is the aspect ratio, which is the ratio of the height to the width of the projected image. The aspect ratios of common projected media are illustrated in Fig. 2. The size of the art may vary as long as the aspect ratio is maintained.

2. Illustration

The illustration step involves the creation or manipulation of pictures to be included in the final product. Common sources for pictures include original or reproduced photographs, as well as original, reproduced, or manipulated art.

The form of an illustration can have a significant impact upon the ease and cost of production. For example, a color photograph is usually more expensive to reproduce than a simple black-and-white drawing. In this case, the two factors affecting production costs are the use of continuous tone art and the use of multiple colors. When cost is a major consideration, illustrations should be limited to line drawings (see Fig. 3) and to one or two colors.

Photography provides one of the most common sources of art for graphic production. Usable photographs may be available from existing resources within the organization or may be acquired from external photographic archives. However, original photographs usually have to be taken or commissioned by the artist or client. Before pictures are taken, the artist should determine if the final product is to be in color or black-and-white, and whether a transparency or print is best. Color transparencies are commonly used in the production of slides, films, or filmstrips, whereas black and white prints are most common for print materials. Most photographic originals are continuous tone and may need to be converted to line art. This is most commonly done by using a dot screen to convert the photograph to a dot pattern, but can also be accomplished using other specialized photographic techniques.

Existing art provides an abundant source of illustrations. Since the creation of original art can be time consuming, it is common practice to reuse illustrations from other sources such as books, periodicals, and handouts. However, care should be taken to ensure the resulting product conforms to copyright regulations. Often such drawings can be reproduced photographically or on a copy machine and then used intact or modified to meet the needs of a particular visual.

Clip art services provide copyright-free, readymade illustrations. Usually such services provide sheets or booklets of general topic line drawings which have a common theme such as sports, media, or educational scenes. The purchase price of these materials includes reproduction rights.

Often, however, it is difficult to find an existing illustration which meets the exact requirements of a planned visual. In such cases it becomes necessary to manipulate existing art. Common manipulation techniques include clipping illustrations from a variety of sources and assembling them in a single visual, tracing a continuous tone illustration to convert it to a line drawing, or tracing a key element from one illustration and drawing the other elements of the visual freehand. An extensive, well-organized picture file will greatly facilitate this process.

Original art is often the only option for the artist. For additional information on specific art techniques refer to Kemp (1980) or Minor and Frye (1977).

While almost any art medium can be copied, some illustrations are easier to reproduce than others. Where cost or production techniques limit flexibility, continuous tone art should be avoided in favor of line

Continuous tone

Line

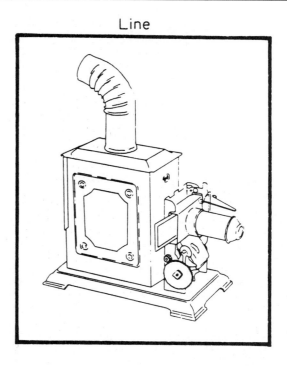

Figure 3
Line versus continuous tone art

drawings. Thus pen and ink drawings will usually be much more appropriate than pastel or shaded pencil drawings.

A variety of drawing instruments and aids are available to assist in the illustration process. A visit to the nearest art supply store should provide insight into the range of possibilities.

3. Lettering

Type is an important component of most educational materials. The type may be as simple as a label or caption, or as extensive as the printed text of a pamphlet. For the purpose of this article, type will be considered in two categories—text type and display type. Text type is relatively small (less than 14 pts.), usually appears in columns, and accounts for the bulk of most printed materials. Display type is larger (14 pts. and up) and is used for headings, labels, or any application in which the type is designed to attract attention. Many typesetting systems are designed to set either text or display type, not both. Thus many graphic production facilities will require more than one typesetting system.

Phototypesetting refers to a process in which the type font is a photographic negative. Light is used to print an image of the type characters on photographic paper which must be chemically developed before the type becomes visible. These typesetting systems range from the cumbersome and inexpensive to the efficient and ultraexpensive. The more sophisticated versions incorporate a standard typewriter keyboard and a microcomputer system so that the text can be entered and edited prior to being printed. Systems can be purchased which handle text type, display type, or both.

A variety of strike-on lettering devices exist which use the pressure of a raised character against an inked ribbon to create the type image. These devices range from common typewriters to more sophisticated versions which offer a variety of type sizes and styles, as well as a range of other options. While most are intended to set text type, the quality of some systems permits the type to be photographically enlarged and used for display purposes. In addition, several relatively inexpensive strike-on systems are now available which use large plastic, disc-shaped fonts to set display type on transparent adhesive tape which can easily be adhered to art.

Mechanical lettering systems offer a relatively inexpensive method of producing quality type. Most systems either use a stencil through which a tracing pen is inserted, or a grooved template in which the point of a mechanical scriber traces out the shape of the letter. Such systems are designed primarily for creating display type and require some skill on the part of the artist.

Dry transfer type is a system by which the artist uses a burnishing tool to transfer letters to the finished art from large translucent sheets. The material is available in a wide variety of sizes and styles, but is intended primarily for display purposes. While the process is relatively inexpensive for small quantities of type, application is tedious and alignment can be difficult.

Artists with limited resources or exceptional talent should consider hand lettering as an option. Carefully executed hand lettering can equal or surpass the lettering quality of some of the mechanical systems. The use of guidelines and a consistent style is recommended. A variety of style manuals are available to aid artists in the development of their hand lettering technique.

4. Assembly

Assembly is the positioning of visual elements for reproduction. When preparing materials to be printed, the resulting product is frequently called a paste-up or a mechanical. However, the same step can also result in the assembly of slide flats, filmstrip flats, mounted pictures, or displays.

A variety of adhesives are available for use during the assembly process and selection of a specific adhesive will depend upon the intended use of the product. Under varying circumstances the artist may use an adhesive that is permanent, removable, or temporarily repositionable.

Rubber cement is one of the most common and flexible adhesives available and can result in either a permanent or removable bond. In addition, several manufacturers provide a special "one-coat" version which remains tacky and repositionable for months after application.

Units which do a lot of paste-up work often use waxers which apply narrow strips of melted wax to the back of the art. Wax bonds are repositionable, but adhere reasonably well when burnished properly.

Dry mounting provides another common tool for the assembly process. In this case a sheet of heat-sensitive material is placed between the two surfaces to be adhered and a dry mount press is used to apply heat and pressure. The system also provides an excellent means of laminating visual materials for protection from moisture or dirt. Other common adhesives include sprays, tapes, and glues.

A major concern of the assembly process is the proper alignment of the visual elements. A variety of tools assist the graphic artist with this task. The most common of these are the drawing board, T-square, triangle, and ruler.

5. Reproduction

Reproduction is the conversion of visual products from intermediate to final forms. It is the most diverse of the production steps, with each process having its own specific requirements and procedures.

For example, an assembled thermal overhead transparency master must be approximately 8×10 inches and should consist of carbon-based images on white paper. It is reproduced by laying a sheet of thermal

transparency film on the master and inserting it in a thermal copier.

On the other hand, if a diazo transparency is required, the master must have an opaque image on a translucent or transparent base. The transparency is made by exposing the master to ultraviolet light in contact with diazo film. The film is then developed in ammonia fumes.

If the desired product is a 35mm slide, the art may be in color and of any reasonable size, but it must conform to the 2:3 aspect ratio. In this case, reproduction requires a 35mm camera, a copystand, and appropriate lighting.

Other reproduction processes will have requirements and procedures which are as diverse as the examples given. Readers are also referred to Kemp (1980) as well as Minor and Frye (1977).

6. Graphic Production Facilities

Graphic production facilities vary, depending upon the size of the staff and the types of products which are produced. However, certain features are typically found in all units. Basic drawing tools, a good working surface, and one or more lettering systems are essential. Also needed are storage space for supplies, a papercutter, a sink, and an assortment of specialized reproduction devices. Most units also offer some photographic facilities such as a darkroom, process camera, and

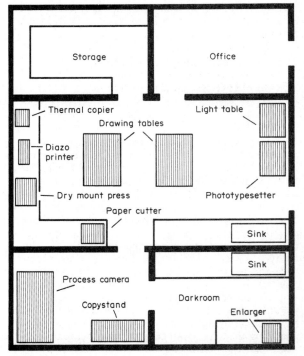

Figure 4
Graphic production unit: typical floorplan

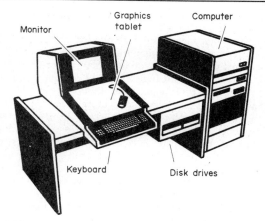

Figure 5
Computer graphics console

copystand. A typical floor plan for a graphics production unit is shown in Fig. 4.

7. Computer Graphic Systems

Computer graphic systems which have radically changed the way visuals are produced have been developed in the 1980s. By letting the computer assume most of the tedious handwork, graphic artists can easily quadruple their productivity while consistently producing high-quality art.

These systems typically consist of a keyboard for entering information or computer commands, a graphics tablet for entering and manipulating drawings, a monitor for viewing the drawings, a computer for processing the information, and one or more disc drives for data storage (see Fig. 5). Once a visual is designed at the console, the information is sent via telephone lines or on a floppy disc to a computerized camera for reproduction into slides, overhead transparencies, or camera-ready art.

While such systems are available, their price may place them beyond the grasp of smaller production units. However, where production volume is great, such systems can be cost-effective.

Bibliography

Dayton D K 1981 Computer-assisted graphics. *Instructional Innovator* 26(6): 16–18
Fleming M, Levie W H 1978 *Instructional Message Design: Principles from the Behavioral Sciences.* Educational Technology, Englewood Cliffs, New Jersey
Kemp J E 1980 *Planning and Producing Audiovisual Materials,* 4th edn. Harper and Row, New York
Minor E, Frye H R 1977 *Techniques for Producing Visual Instructional Media,* 2nd edn. McGraw-Hill, New York

Photographic Production

L. Burbank and D. W. Pett

Photography plays an important role in the development of instructional materials, and most organizations involved in the production of these materials have a photographic unit. Typical projects can be as varied as making a black-and-white print for reproduction in a training manual and producing master slides for a filmstrip that will be duplicated and distributed in large quantities.

The size of the organization, the demand for photographic services, and the amount of work that is done in-house or sent out to commercial agencies determine the scope of activities in a photographic unit.

Some units are very narrow in the range of services they provide, while others carry out a broad spectrum of activities. For example, the Mayo Clinic in Minnesota, with a staff of about 30 persons, turns out a quarter of a million slides and 100,000 black-and-white prints each year, serving the needs of staff training, patient education, record keeping, medical school programs, and, to a limited extent, public relations.

This article can only include a general discussion of the major types of silver photographic processes used in the development of instructional materials; however, the bibliography includes a number of sources that provide the reader with more detailed information.

In most photographic departments work can be grouped under the following headings:

(a) Original photography: pictures taken of live subjects or inanimate objects.

(b) Copying: reproducing continuous tone or original line pictures and screening negatives or prints.

(c) Titling: making titles for slides or filmstrips.

(d) Processing: developing and printing black-and-white negatives, color negatives, and reversal color materials.

(e) Slide and filmstrip duplication.

1. Original Photography

Original photography for instructional purposes consists of taking indoor and outdoor pictures of people, places, and things that can be photographed in different ways using a variety of equipment, materials, and techniques.

The choice of camera equipment depends on the final product and on the photographer's preferences. The same criteria can be applied to film choice and processing methods. For original photography and for copying continuous tone originals, four kinds of films are commonly used.

(a) Color reversal films for making slides or display transparencies.

(b) Color negative films for making prints on paper or on color print film for slides or large transparencies.

(c) Black-and-white continuous tone negative films for making prints on paper or film. These films can also be reversal processed to make slides from original subjects, artwork, or photographs.

(d) Black-and-white direct positive films for making slides from original photographs or artwork.

Any of the basic texts on photography discuss cameras and their operation, film choice, processing, and the various techniques that can be used to produce effective photographs.

Good photographs for instruction have the same characteristics as good photographs for advertising or public relations. They attract and hold one's attention, and communicate their message clearly. This means selecting visual elements that contribute to message clarity. Distracting elements should be avoided. Careful organization of the visual elements is necessary, keeping in mind the design principles of balance, harmony, simplicity, unity, emphasis, and clarity. After the photographer has selected and organized the visual elements, then good photographic techniques are needed for optimum impact and communication. Techniques such as careful lighting, correct film choice, and appropriate special effects must be considered.

The photographer's creativity can greatly contribute to the success of a picture, and therefore it is important that he or she be involved at the planning stage in the design of instructional materials. The photographer must also understand the instructional goals so he or she can contribute ideas that will result in more effective photographs. Good equipment and materials are necessary to create good photographs, but the thought behind the picture and the techniques used are most critical.

2. Copying

Copying is an important activity in any photographic unit that is involved with developing instructional materials. In fact, it was found in a sampling of photo laboratories that about 60 to 70 percent of the total work volume included some type of copying.

2.1 Color Copying

Consistent quality in copying is achieved by establishing standards in lighting techniques, exposure, and choice of film. Most color copying is done to a 35mm slide format; however, larger format cameras are sometimes used for special purposes.

An ideal camera for copying on 35mm is the single lens reflex camera with a macro lens for close-up work. Supplementary lenses can also be used, but a macro lens is more convenient, as is a built-in exposure meter. For all copying, the best way to determine exposure is to use a standard gray card that reflects 18 percent of the incident light. In every case, tests should be run to standardize the camera, film, and lighting used.

Many good color films are available. Because each film varies in color rendition and contrast, the choice of a particular color film is based on desired results, personal or client preferences, and the ultimate use of the picture. Ordinarily, it is best to use the same type of film throughout a specific project. This is especially true if duplicates are to be made.

Most color copying for slides is done on indoor color reversal film, but if electronic flash or daylight photofloods are used as a light source, then daylight color reversal film should be used. If large quantities of duplicate slides are needed, it is economical to shoot the originals on color negative film and have the copies printed on color print film.

It is advised when copying flat artwork or pictures from books that a polarizing filter be used over each light and on the camera lens. When these filters are rotated correctly, they act to polarize the light in such a way that reflections are reduced and color saturation is improved. The filters over the lights must be turned so they polarize the light in the same direction, and the filter on the lens should be rotated for maximum polarizing effect. This effect can be visually checked by placing a shiny nonmetallic object on the copyboard and rotating the camera polarizing filter to the point where reflections are minimized.

Two problems frequently occur when making copies. First, more visual information may be included in the final photograph than is seen through the viewfinder, unless a specially designed camera is used. Careful testing of each copy setup will show the photographer what to expect. A second problem concerns reflections. Reflections are critical when photographing celluloid overlays or when a sheet of glass is being used to keep the copy flat. Polarized light sources and a polarizing filter on the camera lens do help, but this does not always solve the reflection problem. Painting the area around and above the copystand with flat black paint can help to eliminate reflections. In addition, care should be taken to ensure all overhead lights are turned off. Shiny metal parts on the camera can also reflect. A black card placed in front of the camera with a hole for the lens to point through, will usually eliminate these unwanted reflections.

2.2 Black-and-white Continuous Tone Copying

Black-and-white continuous tone copying uses similar lighting and exposure techniques to color copying. If slides are required, direct positive films are available which, when conventionally processed, result in positive slides. Black-and-white continuous tone negative films can be reversal processed to obtain positive slides. The reversal processes, though somewhat more time consuming and expensive, produce extremely high-quality results.

2.3 Black-and-white Line Art Copying

Line art is any drawing that is composed of just blacks and whites with no intermediate gray tones. Copying line art is similar to color or black-and-white continuous tone copying in terms of lighting techniques, exposure, and other standardization considerations. However, line art copying involves a variety of materials, and which material is used depends upon the original to be copied, the quantities of copies needed, and the ultimate use (see Fig. 1).

The conventional line art copy process involves either a large format (8 × 10 inch) or a small format (35mm or 4 × 5 inch) camera that is used for making negatives on high contrast lithographic film. The process includes making an exposure in the camera and then processing: develop, stop, fix, wash, and dry. These negatives can be used as slides if exposed in a 35mm camera, or as overhead transparencies, in the case of an 8 × 10 inch camera. Any size negative can be used to make a print on film to use as a positive transparency. Negative or positive transparencies can be colored, using a variety of methods to differentiate parts of the visual or to make them more attractive. In addition, the negatives can be printed on paper to produce a positive that can be used for publication purposes or for display.

Line art can also be copied on direct positive film which produces positive 35mm slides or overhead transparencies and is processed in standard lithographic film chemistry. This film, pre-exposed during manufacturing, is reduced in density as exposure is increased, resulting in a high quality positive transparency (35mm or larger) that can be colored or used as it is.

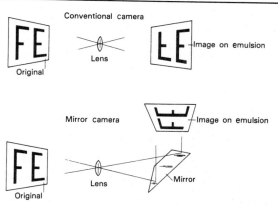

Figure 2
Comparison of conventional and mirror cameras

Positive films are also useful when several copies of an existing line negative or positive are needed. By contact printing on positive film, a duplicate of the original negative or positive can be produced without going through the regular negative-to-positive (or positive-to-negative) process. This saves considerable time, however, if many copies are needed, it would be more economical to go through the conventional negative-to-positive process because direct positive films are more expensive than are negative films. The direct positive process is also excellent for making prints of a line paste-up on paper; however, the image will be wrong-reading unless a camera with a mirror is used to reverse it (see Fig. 2).

If such a camera is not available, then line art, such as a paste-up, can be copied in conventional cameras using diffusion transfer reversal (DTR) materials. The process is relatively simple. An exposure of the line art is made on DTR negative material in a suitable camera such as an 8 × 10 inch camera. Then the negative and a paper-receiving sheet are processed in a unit that brings them into contact so that both come out of the machine sandwiched together. While they remain in contact, for about 30 seconds, a negative image develops and a positive image is transferred to the receiver sheet. The receiver sheet is peeled away from the negative, which is discarded, revealing a positive, right-reading image. In addition, this process can be used for making overhead transparencies by using a film receiver sheet instead of paper. Diffusion transfer reversal is similar to the "instant" processes which will be discussed later. It should be noted that either the negative or the positive produced from the line art copy process can serve as an excellent master for making additional copies of colored transparencies by the diazo process.

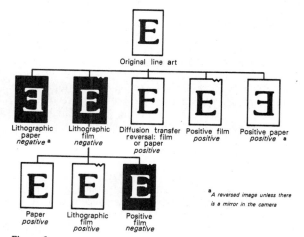

Figure 1
Line art copy processes

2.4 Screening Continuous Tone Photographs

When continuous tone photographs are to be printed, it is necessary to convert the continuous tone picture to a dot pattern by using a screen. The reason this conversion has to be done is because the printing process represents shades of gray in dots of varying sizes (see Fig. 3). Small dots represent light grays, larger dots represent middle grays and still larger dots represent dark grays and the color black. The number of dots per inch is related to the quality of the image: that is, the greater the number of dots per inch, the finer the quality of the reproduction. Therefore, 133 to 150 dots per inch will result in higher quality reproduction than 65 to 85 dots per inch which gives a coarser reproduction of a photograph (Eastman Kodak Company 1976). The quality of reproduction also depends upon the type of printing or duplicating process used. A high quality printing system and plates can reproduce 133 to 150 dots per inch; however, electrostatic duplicating and offset processes that use inexpensive plates use screens in the range of 65 to 100 dots per inch.

There are two ways to screen a continuous tone photograph. The most common technique involves copying the original photograph onto a sheet of lithographic film through a dot screen, which is placed over the film (see Fig. 4). The second way involves special films with the dot pattern incorporated into the emulsion. Because both of these methods are complex and they depend upon the type of printing, paper, and equipment being used, the screening is usually done by a printer.

If high quality reproduction is not necessary, then screened prints, instead of negatives, can be used. Their advantage is the ease with which they can be incorporated into camera-ready copy that is sent to the printer. To obtain screened prints, the original negative is enlarged onto high contrast paper, and an exposure for a print is made (in the usual way) through a dot screen placed over the paper. The result is a screened print with light areas of the original represented by small dots, and dark areas represented by large dots. Use of screened prints is most practical when the reproduction is 100 or fewer dots per inch.

Screened negatives or prints are expensive to produce,

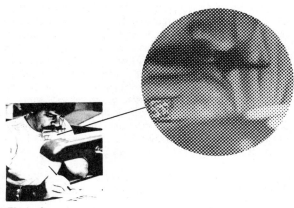

Figure 3
Screened print

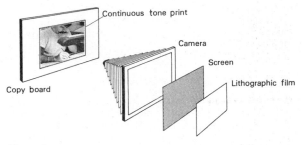

Figure 4
Screening process

and therefore many photographs are being reproduced as simple posterized illustrations. A simple posterization (see Fig. 5) involves the following procedure:

(a) Make a high contrast positive on lithographic film from an original continuous tone negative.

(b) Then, use the high contrast positive to make a high contrast negative on lithographic film.

(c) Make the final paper print from the high contrast negative.

On the final print, light grays are reproduced as white and dark grays are reproduced as black, resulting in a line copy that is suitable for printing without going through the screening process. Imaginative variations of this technique can be used to produce eye-catching color posterizations (Eastman Kodak Company 1973).

3. "Instant" Films

A wide variety of "instant" films are available when high quality black-and-white or color pictures are needed in a very short time. The films range in speed from ASA 50 to ASA 10,000. Formats include rolls and packets and in the case of color, 8×10 inch separate negative–positive units.

Most instant films produce a positive print and are processed in the camera by a process similar to diffusion transfer reversal. As the negative image develops, a positive image is transferred to a receiver sheet which becomes the final print. Some materials result in a positive print and a negative from which additional prints can be made. Special purpose materials are made for oscilloscope trace video recording, for making positive transparencies, and for high contrast photography.

4. Titling

Making title slides, or slides that consist largely of words or line art, is becoming an increasingly common activity in most photo laboratories concerned with producing instructional materials.

Slides that have clear or colored words against a colored background or an appropriate pictorial background are produced with slide duplicating equipment

Figure 5
Continuous tone (reproduced as a halftone) and a simple posterization

that allows for making multiple exposures on one frame (see Fig. 6). For example, to make a slide with white lettering on a colored background, the following steps are necessary.

(a) Lettering (or line art) is prepared in the proper proportion, that is 2:3 for slides and 3:4 for filmstrips.

(b) Then it is photographed on lithographic film with a 35mm camera, or a larger format camera depending upon the slide duplicating equipment to be used. The film is processed, resulting in a high contrast negative (clear letters on a black background).

(c) The resultant negative is placed on the slide duplicator and, with color film in the camera, an exposure is made of the lettering. The negative is removed and a second exposure is made of colored light without advancing the film. This is done by putting a filter of the desired background color over the lens.

The same procedure is followed when making title slides with colored letters on a colored background except that a colored filter is used for both exposures, that is, when photographing the lettering and the background. Table 1 from *Technical Photography* (1981) lists some typical color combinations. A similar procedure is used to produce lettering on a pictorial background: one exposure is made of the lettering that has already been copied in the proper position on lithographic film, and a second exposure is made of the background slide or transparency.

5. Processing

Processing is an area of photography that can use a great percentage of a photographic laboratory's resources. The types of photo materials most often produced characterize the four general processing areas as:

(a) Black-and-white negative or positive film processing.

(b) Black-and-white printing.

(c) Color reversal and color negative film processing.

(d) Color printing.

Decisions on black-and-white processing have to be made on whether processing is done in-house or at an outside laboratory, and on whether to use conventional or automated methods. Most black-and-white photographic instructional materials are processed in-house because the materials and equipment for film or paper processing are relatively inexpensive, and needed skills can be easily learned. Also, stabilization processing of resin-coated papers has greatly simplified the making of prints, while significantly reducing the amount of time needed to turn out high quality work. The primary advantage of doing black-and-white processing in-house is increased quality control with reduced cost and time.

More complex decisions are related to color processing. Usually, many of the photographic departments that produce instructional materials can process a small volume of reversal films if the laboratory has reasonable temperature control of the environment and the water, plus personnel that have the necessary skills which are not difficult to acquire. Even so, a number of factors

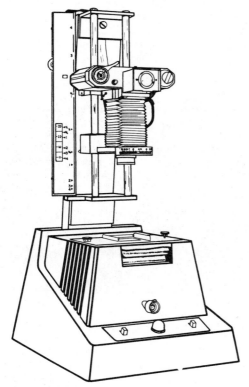

Figure 6
Typical small volume slide duplicator

must be considered when deciding whether color processing will be done in-house. These include:

(a) the volume of work to be done;

(b) the facilities (rooms and equipment) that are available;

(c) the skills of the personnel, and how much training will be necessary;

(d) the proximity of commercial laboratories;

(e) the required completion time.

Processing a few rolls of color film each day is not much more complicated than developing black-and-white negatives. However, when dozens of rolls, or hundreds of feet of film are used in a day, developing is done in batch processors or in automatic film processing machines. The batch or automatic methods require greater technical skills and a larger cash investment in facilities. Therefore, many photographic departments with large volumes prefer to send their film to commercial laboratories for processing. This decision is particularly appropriate when the laboratory is nearby so the job time is minimized. In many places, facilities are limited and technical expertise is not readily available, and the nearest commercial laboratory is a great distance

away. In this instance, the processing decisions are based on compromise: all the work that is not needed immediately is sent out, and only a small volume of rush jobs are done in-house.

Color prints on paper and large format photographic color transparencies are not extensively used in instruction. The reasons are the high cost of such materials, and because 35mm slides can adequately serve most instructional purposes. The number of color prints that will be needed in most photo laboratories can be best handled at a commercial laboratory that specializes in the making of prints. However, high quality color prints can be produced in 6 minutes at room temperature, with a minimum of technical skill needed, due to recent developments in one-step color print processing. The photo color transfer (PCT) process is used when a few prints are needed in a short time. Although this process is basically simple, an understanding of color filters and their use in color correction, plus the ability to judge color quality, are necessary requirements.

6. Slide and Filmstrip Duplication

For instructional purposes, it is often necessary to produce duplicate slide sets or to produce filmstrips or microfiche from an original set of slides. For optimum quality, the original slides should be consistent in density and contrast and should all be taken on one type of film.

6.1 Slide Duplication

Basically there are two methods for making duplicate slides. One method involves copying the slides on color negative film and then printing them on color negative print film. This method is used when large quantities of duplicate slides are needed, and it is usually done at an outside laboratory that specializes in this type of work. The other method is to copy the slides on reversal film, and it is used when small quantities are needed.

A wide variety of slide duplicating equipment is available for copying slides. The expensive slide duplicators are more versatile than the inexpensive models, and they have features that facilitate accurate positioning of the slide in relation to the copy camera. Also, some units allow for the production of special effect slides and the combining of multiple images on one slide.

Table 1
Typical color combinations for use on title slides

Filter for lettering	Filter for background	Results
Green	Red	Yellow on red
Red	Green	Yellow on green
Blue	Green	Cyan on green
Green	Blue	Cyan on blue
Blue	Red	Magenta on red
Red	Blue	Magenta on blue

Two basic problems in slide duplication are (a) maintaining color accuracy and (b) controlling contrast. The best way to be assured of high quality duplicates is to produce high quality originals, that is, to choose film that matches the lights being used, and to carefully control lighting and exposure so as to maintain detail in the highlight and shadow areas of the picture. Taking some pictures with tungsten lights and others under fluorescent lighting results in color variations that will be emphasized in duplication. Color correction filters can be used to correct for these variations in the original slides, but this process is time consuming and therefore expensive. Even when lighting is carefully controlled, there will be an increase in contrast between the original and the duplicate unless contrast control methods are used. The best method is to use film that has a low contrast emulsion that is specifically designed for making high quality duplicates.

It is important that the slides to be duplicated or converted to a filmstrip format should not be handled anymore than is absolutely necessary. It is a good practice to make two originals: one that will be used for editing and formative evaluation, and another that is stored in a cool, clean, dry place and is used just for duplication.

6.2 *Filmstrips*

Filmstrips can be made from original artwork using a single frame 35mm camera. However, most filmstrips are produced from a set of original slides. When slides are expected to be converted to a filmstrip format, a 3 : 4 proportion has to be maintained. Therefore, an artwork size of 6 × 8 inches is ideal because it is easily filed, and lettering that is one quarter inch high will meet legibility standards. Because the proportion of a standard 35mm slide (double frame) is 2 : 3 and the proportion of a filmstrip (single frame) is 3 : 4, a small area on each side of a slide is lost when converting to a filmstrip format, so making slides with important information near the edges should be avoided if the final format is to be a filmstrip (see Fig. 7).

Filmstrips are usually done at commercial laboratories either by the negative–positive method, or the reversal method. When the negative–positive method is used, each original slide is copied, in sequence and in single frame format, on 35mm color negative film. Color and density corrections are made at this time. This negative film is then printed on color print film resulting in an "answer print" for customer or client approval. At this point, if there are no changes and the answer print is approved, multiple copies are printed on color print film from the negative, and the required number of filmstrips is produced.

If the reversal method is used, then each original slide is copied, in sequence and in single frame format, on color reversal film. Density corrections are made at this time by varying the exposure according to the density of the original. Color corrections usually are not made when this method is used. After reversal processing, the resultant filmstrip is ready for approval and if no

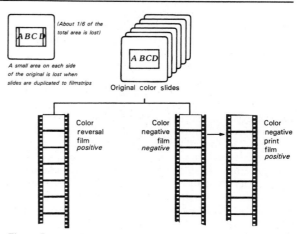

Figure 7
Slides to filmstrip process

changes are necessary, the required number of copies is made. In other words, each filmstrip is made from the original slides. Assuming that the original slides are consistent in color quality, this is an inexpensive method of making a few filmstrips. One filmstrip is about one-tenth of the cost of a filmstrip produced by the negative–positive method. However, if more than 20 filmstrips are needed, it is more economical not to use the reversal method. The exact cost figures will vary depending on the number of frames in the filmstrip and the specific laboratory doing the work.

6.3 *Microfiche*

Slides can also be duplicated in microfiche formats. From 56 to over 100 slides can be reproduced on one microfiche. These are ideal for individual study and are being used for that purpose in some medical schools. Original slides are sent to a laboratory that specializes in duplication onto microfiche.

7. *Organization and Management*

Managing a photographic unit within an organization involves many decisions related to the structure, budget, facilities, and personnel of that organization. These decisions must be carefully considered if high quality instructional materials are to be produced within appropriate time and budget limitations.

There are many ways a photographic unit can contribute to an organization. In schools or in other educational settings, photographic units frequently have not only the responsibility of developing instructional materials, but also have other responsibilities such as producing photographic materials for public relations, publications, or even sports. Meeting multiple responsibilities can, however, interfere with the task of designing and producing effective instructional materials. One way to prevent this from happening is to assign design and production material services to a unit that is directly concerned with better teaching and learning, such as "instructional resources," "learning resources," or "curriculum and instruction" (see Fig. 8). Within these departments, such production services as audio, graphics, photography, motion picture, video, and reprography can be coordinated. In a small unit, all phases of design and production may be handled by one or two production generalists, and in a larger unit specialists are employed for specific production tasks.

Budget is an important consideration for a production unit. The overall budgeting patterns of the parent organization determine whether funds come from appropriations, from direct charges to individuals or departments, or from some combination of the two. How funds are allocated is not as important a consideration as initiating and maintaining a system for determining the costs of projects. This system should include direct costs of personnel, supplies and amortization of equipment as well as indirect costs such as overheads.

Facilities—rooms and equipment—are another important consideration when setting up and operating a photographic service. Photographic units have unusually high demands for electrical power, temperature control, and adequate water supply, and this reality must be remembered when facilities are built or renovated. Space needs to be allocated and arranged in such a way that work can flow in a logical order with minimal disruption. Equipment should be purchased at a reasonable cost and at the same time be able to handle the required work volume efficiently. Maintenance is a prime consideration when purchasing equipment. Equipment parts and technical expertise must be readily available if production delays are to be avoided. Geographical area can determine the availability of parts and maintenance; what is an ideal equipment choice for one location may be a very poor choice for another location. This is why working closely with technical representatives of major manufacturers of photographic equipment can be very helpful when planning and setting up a photographic unit.

The selection of personnel is most critical when organizing or managing any photography unit. Photography is involved with such things as cameras, lights, film, and chemicals, but more importantly, it is involved with people. The staff must know processes and techniques, and be able to work creatively with subject matter specialists and with clients. Selection of employees must be on the basis of their aptitudes and skills. Professional growth experiences such as opportunities to upgrade skills and to develop competencies in new technologies must be provided. In a recent study (Dayton 1981), a group of production experts agreed that the basic aspects of working with clients and designing effective visual instructional materials are not likely to change very much in the future; however, the processes and technology will change. For example, silver-based photographic processes will probably be replaced by nonsilver-based processes by the year 2000, there will be an increase in "instant" and rapid processing of film and prints, and electronic technology will have a greater impact on the production of photographic images. Therefore, the need to upgrade personnel through training programs in the new technologies is rapidly growing.

8. Summary

A wide variety of products can be produced from a range of photographic materials. Selection of materials and processes depends upon the desired results, the available equipment and materials, and the technical skills and knowledge of the production staff. Also, many approaches must be examined to determine the best production methods. All these activities must be carried out within an administrative framework and in facilities that promote the development of high quality instructional materials.

Bibliography

Craven G M 1982 *Object and Image,* 2nd edn. Prentice-Hall, Englewood Cliffs, New Jersey
Dayton D K 1981 Future trends in the production of instructional materials; 1981–2001. *Educ. Commun. Technol. J.* 29: 23–49
Eastman Kodak Company 1973 *Creative Darkroom Techniques.* Eastman Kodak, Rochester, New York
Eastman Kodak Company 1976 *Halftone Methods for the Graphic Arts.* Eastman Kodak, Rochester, New York
Frair J, Ardoin B 1981 *Effective Photography.* Prentice-Hall, Englewood Cliffs, New Jersey
Hattersley R 1977 *Photographic Printing.* Prentice-Hall, Englewood Cliffs, New Jersey
Horenstein H 1977 *Beyond Basic Photography: A Technical Manual.* Little, Brown, Toronto, Ontario
Kemp J E 1980 *Planning and Producing Audiovisual Materials,* 4th edn. Harper and Row, New York
Langford M J 1973 *Visual Aids and Photography in Education: A Visual Aids Manual for Teachers and Learners.* Hastings House, New York
Minor E, Frye H R 1977 *Techniques for Producing Visual Instructional Media,* 2nd edn. McGraw-Hill, New York
Stroebel L D 1972 *View Camera Technique,* Rev. edn. Hastings House, New York
Sturge J M 1977 *Neblette's Handbook of Photography and*

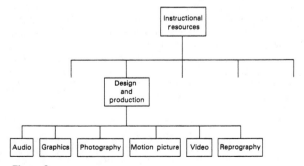

Figure 8
A possible administrative structure

Reprography: Materials, Processes, and Systems, 7th edn. Van Nostrand Reinhold, New York

Swedlund C 1974 *Photography: A Handbook of History, Materi-* *als and Processes*. Holt, Rinehart and Winston, New York

Technical Photography 1981 Vol. 13 (11) (issue devoted to Copy Photography)

Reprography

L. Burbank and D. W. Pett

Reprography is defined as reproducing flat originals (printed matter, documents, or pictures) by silver and nonsilver photographic techniques. Since reproduction of such materials by silver photographic means has already been covered in the article on photography, this article will just deal with nonsilver processes that are commonly used in educational settings: diazo (or dye line), thermal, and electrostatic.

Offset duplication will also be discussed because it is the most widely used process for reproducing printed educational instructional materials, reports, and tests. Plates used in offset duplication can be produced by either silver or nonsilver photographic processes. It should be noted here that, whatever reprographic technique is used for educational purposes, copyrighted materials should not be reproduced without permission.

Before discussing each of the reprographic techniques, it is important to distinguish between two types of originals that are usually reproduced: continuous tone and line art. Continuous tone originals are made up of several different shades of gray or color. Common examples are black-and-white or color photographs, color slides, pastel and wash drawings. Line art is any drawing that is composed of just blacks and whites, no grays: if shading or texture is desired, it is accomplished with black-and-white lines or with screen overlays. Typical examples include pages of type, line drawings, and simple photographic posterizations. Another example of line art is the halftone. Because some processes will not reproduce continuous tone images well, the image has to be converted to a halftone or screened image that consists of various size dots, or some other pattern, to reproduce light grays as small dots, or thin lines, and dark grays as larger dots, or heavier lines.

1. Diazo

The diazo or dye line process is based on the sensitivity of diazonium salts to light. When exposed, these decompose into a colorless by-product so no image is formed. The remaining unexposed salts chemically combine with couplers to form a colored image. This process takes place in an alkaline state. The result is a positive from a positive original or a negative from a negative original.

There are many variations of the diazo process; however, two are of particular importance to the educational market.

1.1 Dry Diazo

(a) *Process*. Diazo film, paper, or cardstock is coated during manufacturing with diazonium salts and a coupler. In use, the sensitized material is exposed to ultraviolet light through an original, and then developed in ammonia fumes to reproduce a colored image of the original. The color of the image depends upon the particular couplers used.

(b) *Procedures*. The sensitized material is exposed to ultraviolet light through an original with an opaque image on a transparent or translucent base. The original can be india ink or dark pencil on clear or translucent plastic or on tracing paper. Continuous tone or line images on film or translucent paper are ideal originals. Images produced on film by the thermal or electrostatic processes are also suitable. Other diazo transparencies can be used as originals if their colored image will block ultraviolet light.

The light source for exposing diazo materials should be high in ultraviolet, and rotary units or flat exposing boxes are usually used for this purpose. Development can be done in a large jar or in a special developing machine. If a large jar is used, a sponge is placed on the bottom of the jar and soaked with ammonium hydroxide. To develop, the top is briefly opened to insert, and later to remove, the film or paper. Development takes from one to several minutes, depending upon the type of diazo materials being used. The disadvantages of using the jar method are the exposure to ammonia fumes, which are unpleasant, and that it is a slow process. There are, however, developing machines that heat the ammonia so the warm fumes rapidly develop the image, and these units greatly reduce the amount of ammonia fumes that escape into the air (see Fig. 1). When large quantities of diazo prints need to be produced, machines can be used that combine exposure and development operations in one unit.

(c) *Characteristics and uses*. Dry diazo coatings are made in several colors on film, paper, and cardstock. Diazo films come in a wide variety of colors with black or colored images on different colored bases. Papers are commonly available in blue, brown, black, and red. Cardstock is made in many color combinations including brown or black on a white base, red or blue on an aluminum-colored base, and black on a bronze base. For special purposes, diazo coatings are also made on translucent paper bases and on cloth.

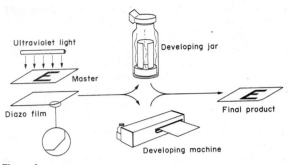

Figure 1
The diazo process

Diazo images produced by the dry diazo process are characterized by bright colors and excellent reproduction of fine detail. Contrast varies from medium to high depending upon the type of materials used. The emulsion speed of diazo materials is very slow; therefore, a lot of light is needed for exposure which limits their use largely to contact printing. The shelf life of diazo materials varies greatly depending on storage conditions. Six months is about average shelf-life under normal conditions. In a cool, dry environment, shelf-life will be longer, and in a warm, moist environment the materials will deteriorate very rapidly. Image permanence after exposure and development also depends upon the storage conditions. If materials are exposed to light during storage, the colored dyes will fade, so they should be stored where excessive light will not reach them. Optimum storage for diazo materials is in a dark, cool, dry place; there it is estimated they will last 50 or more years.

The dry diazo process is primarily used for the reproduction of architectural and mechanical drawings. In education, it is also used for the production of overhead transparencies, the reproduction of documents and illustrations for instructional booklets, as well as the creation of covers for booklets or reports.

1.2 Moist Diazo

(a) *Process.* The moist diazo process quickly and easily reproduces multiple colors on one piece of film or paper. This is done by moistening the exposed materials with different color coupling developers. Because the film or paper is coated only with diazonium salts, it is possible to apply colored couplers to create an image in several hues on one piece of film.

(b) *Procedures.* The type of original required, and the exposure procedure for moist diazo film or paper, is the same as for the dry diazo materials. However, development is done not in ammonia fumes, but by applying the moist developer to the image by wiping, spraying, or by dipping the materials into a tray of developer. As with the dry diazo method, when large amounts of moist diazo prints of one color are needed, it is best to use a machine that does both exposure and development in one unit.

(c) *Characteristics and uses.* Moist diazo film is coated on both sides, and therefore it should be developed on both sides. This results in brighter colors and color combinations because the two sides can be developed with different color developers. The most common color coupling developers are black, blue, brown, red, and yellow. The contrast, speed, and storage characteristics of moist diazo materials are similar to dry diazo materials. Moist diazo is primarily used in educational settings to produce overhead transparencies.

Other diazo processes are used in document and microfilm reproduction, and for diazo-sensitive lithographic plates for offset printing. Also, diazo reversal materials are available when the final product must be a reversal of the original.

In summary, a wide variety of diazo materials is available. Because these materials have a low sensitivity to light, they are generally limited to contact printing from transparent or translucent originals. Within this limitation, however, they have many uses in the production of educational materials.

2. Thermal

(a) *Process.* The thermal process makes copies on film or paper. It is a one-step process that uses heat to cause a chemical change in a sensitized coating. An original, with an infrared-absorbing image, is placed in contact with sensitized film or paper and exposed to an infrared light source. Where infrared radiation is absorbed, a sufficient amount of heat is created to induce a chemical change in the coating resulting in a colored image (see Fig. 2).

(b) *Procedures.* Making a thermal copy is a simple and fast procedure. The only control is a speed selection dial which determines the lightness and darkness of the copy. Slow speeds provide more exposure, that is, the copy comes out darker, and fast speeds provide less exposure. The selected speed depends upon the heat-absorbing quality of the original image and also on the type of thermal material used. For example, materials with a thick base require longer exposure time than materials with a thin base.

An original for the thermal process must absorb infrared radiation. Carbon and metallic images such as those made with pencil, india ink, and most printing

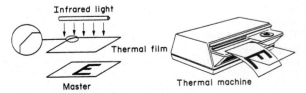

Figure 2
Thermal process

inks work well. So do electrostatic copies and line photographs. Images drawn with most ballpoint or felt-tip pens cannot be used because they do not absorb infrared. However, electrostatic copies can be made of these images and used to produce thermal copies.

(c) *Characteristics and uses.* A variety of thermal materials are available, including paper and films that produce a black image on a clear or colored background (base) or a colored image on a clear base. Also, some materials produce a negative image which is a clear image on a black or colored base.

The thermal process is not suitable for reproducing continuous tone or finely screened halftones. It is excellent, however, for reproducing line copy and, depending upon the specific materials and equipment used, it can do a good job of reproducing coarsely screened halftones. This process is not suitable for copying fine lines because fine lines do not absorb sufficient infrared radiation to cause a chemical change in the sensitized coating. Also, large dark areas do not reproduce well. In addition, thermal copies cannot be made from pages in a book or magazine unless paper copies are first made by the electrostatic process which are then used to make thermal transparencies. Because of the relatively poor quality of thermal paper copies compared to electrostatic copies, the production of thermal paper copiers has greatly decreased as electrostatic copiers have become increasingly available.

Under normal storage conditions, the shelf-life of thermal materials is excellent. Since heat forms the image, it is important that the sensitized materials be protected from heat before copies are made, as well as in storage. Also, prolonged exposure on a hot overhead projector will cause the overall transparency to darken.

In education, the thermal process is primarily used for the production of overhead transparencies. Most of these thermal transparencies are of poor quality because of the selection of originals. For example, typewritten pages, which are frequently used as originals, do not meet legibility standards. The typing is too small to be read at a distance, and typed words do not sufficiently absorb infrared to produce a good image. A properly adjusted typewriter using a carbon ribbon and producing a quarter inch letter height will give good results. In summary, when the original consists of reasonably heavy lines, or lettering, that absorbs infrared radiation, then the thermal process is capable of quality reproduction that compares favorably with high-contrast photographic methods.

3. *Electrostatic*

(a) *Process.* The electrostatic process is based on the fact that an electrostatic charge can be made photosensitive. Xerography and electrofax are two copy methods that work on this principle. In both methods, an image is projected on an electrostatically charged surface and where light strikes, the charge is dissipated, resulting in an electrostatically charged image. In xerographic

machines, an image is formed on a plate or drum and toner is applied that adheres to the image area. The toner is then transferred to a paper or plastic receiver sheet, where heat fuses the image (see Fig. 3). In a typical xerographic machine, this process takes place very rapidly. The electrofax process uses a paper coated with zinc oxide in place of a plate or drum. This paper is charged then exposed, toner is applied, and the image is fused.

(b) *Procedures.* Machine operating procedures for either the xerographic or the electrofax process are relatively simple. Depending upon the type of machine, it is usually loaded with roll or cut paper. The original is either fed into the copier or it is placed on a glass platen and the cover is closed. A start button is pushed to activate the unit and in a few seconds the copy is delivered. Multiple copies can be made in most machines by simply setting a number counter to the quantity needed. In addition, some electrostatic copiers have the capability of making reduced or enlarged copies.

Xerographic copies were first made using a large process camera and the steps of charging the plate, exposing, applying toner, transferring and fusing were all done manually. This is still done in some places, especially when the versatility of a camera is needed to produce copies in varying sizes.

(c) *Characteristics and uses.* The electrofax process is limited to making copies on specially coated materials, but xerography can be used to make copies on any good quality bond paper, cardstock, self-adhering labels, heat-resistant plastic, all of which come in several colors. It is critical to emphasize the importance of using heat-resistant plastic to make overhead transparencies.

Electrostatic processes are excellent for reproducing line copy, but they do not reproduce continuous tone materials very well unless a white dot screen is placed over the original, converting it to a halftone. Already screened materials, such as a picture from a magazine, can be reproduced reasonably well depending upon the

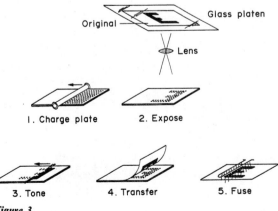

Figure 3
Electrostatic process

type of copier. Most dark colors reproduce quite well; however, very light colors, especially light blue, may not reproduce at all. If the background color of an original is not white it may be recorded and show up as gray.

Until the mid-1970s, the electrostatic process was thought of and used only when a few copies of an original were needed. However, recent developments in technology have resulted in machines that can quickly turn out many high-quality copies in a short period of time. The cost is comparable to offset duplication unless hundreds of copies are required. Educators primarily use electrostatic reproduction for duplicating small quantities of handout materials, tests, and reports. Overhead transparencies are also made using this process, but these do not, as yet, match the quality of thermal transparencies.

Color copiers are available that reproduce full colored originals, and color slides, on paper or on heat-resistant plastic. However, the cost is high and there is limited demand for such copiers in the education market.

4. Offset Duplication

Offset duplication is a lithographic process. Lithography, developed in the late 1700s, literally means "stone writing" because a grease crayon is used to produce an image on a flat stone. The stone is then wiped with water which is repelled by the greasy image, but not by the nonimage areas. Ink is rolled on the stone and it is attracted to the greasy image and repelled by the damp wet areas. Paper is placed on the stone and pressure is applied to transfer the ink, and therefore the image, to the paper.

The term "offset" is used because the image is not directly transferred to paper. From a plate or master, the image is offset or transferred to a roller called the blanket cylinder, which comes in contact with the paper, producing a right-reading image. When reproduction is

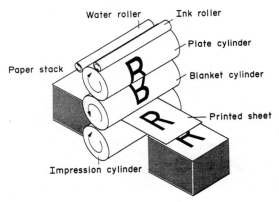

Figure 4
The offset duplication process

done on a small machine, using paper no larger than 14 × 17 inches, it is called offset duplication; however, when larger machines are used this same process is usually called offset printing (see Fig. 4).

Plates or masters for offset duplication come in various types and sizes.

(a) *Direct image plates*. These plates are prepared by typing or drawing directly on a paper surface with special ribbons, in the case of typing, or with oil-based inks, lithographic crayons, or ball-point pens that are made specially for this purpose. There are several different kinds of direct image paper plates and, depending on the type, 100 to 1,000 copies can be run.

(b) *Electrophotographic plates*. Electrophotographic plates, based on the electrostatic concept, can be made by either the xerographic or electrofax process. Such plates are typically used in "quick printing" operations because they can be produced rapidly and require a minimum of technical skill. These inexpensive plates are particularly useful for medium quantity runs of up to 1,000 copies.

(c) *Silver emulsion plates*. These plates are either paper or plastic depending upon the quality of reproduction necessary. Plastic plates are used when higher quality is needed such as when reproducing fine line originals or halftones. Typically, the silver emulsion plates are exposed in a special camera that handles both exposure and processing. Runs of up to 10,000 can be made with the plastic plates.

(d) *Diffusion transfer plates*. A diffusion transfer negative is exposed in a camera and a positive image is transferred onto a paper or metal plate. A paper plate will give runs up to about 2,500 copies and metal plates will run up to 25,000 copies.

A variety of sensitized metal plates are available, but these are mainly used for offset printing, not duplication.

Reprography is an integral part of any production unit, especially one serving instructional needs. Because a variety of reprographic processes are available, the preparation of originals and the products produced will vary greatly depending upon the process selected.

As in photographic production units, a reprographic unit, especially one that is involved in the development of instructional materials, should be administratively related to "instructional resources," "curriculum and instruction," or some other department that is concerned with the improvement of the teaching–learning process. Decisions on the facilities and types of equipment to purchase or lease will depend upon the particular unit's needs, the scope of the operation, and the availability of materials and maintenance. Personnel should be technically competent, but more importantly, they have to understand the various reprographic processes and the role each one can play in instruction.

Bibliography

Adams M J, Faux D D 1977 *Printing Technology: A Medium of Visual Communications.* Duxbury, North Scituate, Massachusetts

Cogoli J E 1967 *Photo-offset Fundamentals.* McKnight and McKnight, Bloomington, Illinois

Eastman Kodak Company 1976a *Basic Printing Methods.* Eastman Kodak, Rochester, New York

Eastman Kodak Company 1976b *Graphic Design.* Eastman Kodak, Rochester, New York

Hawken W R 1966 *Copying Methods Manual.* American Library Association, Chicago, Illinois

Kemp J E 1980 *Planning and Producing Audiovisual Materials,* 4th edn. Harper and Row, New York

Langford M J 1973 *Visual Aids and Photography in Education: A Visual Aids Manual for Teachers and Learners.* Hastings House, New York

Minor E, Frye H R 1977 *Techniques for Producing Visual Instructional Media,* 2nd edn. McGraw-Hill, New York

Sturge J M 1977 *Neblette's Handbook of Photography and Reprography,* 7th edn. Van Nostrand Reinhold, New York

Overhead Transparency Projection

J. A. Moldstad

Since its appearance on the instructional scene around the early 1940s, overhead transparency projection has steadily increased in use and recognition as one of the most flexible and effective methods of visual communication. The design of the overhead transparency projector enables a transparency to be placed on a flat horizontal stage. Then a lens–mirror system projects the image upward over the instructor's shoulder onto a projection screen behind the instructor, thus the name overhead transparency projector (see Fig. 1).

The most prominent feature of this projector is that the operator normally sits or stands facing his or her audience. Use of a short focal-length lens system enables a large image to be projected on the screen behind the operator requiring only limited space at the front of the classroom.

Initially overhead transparency projectors were designed specifically to enable instructors to project $3\frac{1}{4} \times 4$ inch lantern slides from science demonstration tables located in the front of the classroom.

Experimental use during the Second World War by various military organizations resulted in gradually enlarging the 5×5 inch platen to 7×7 inch and seemingly standardizing on 10×10 inch (250×250 mm) formats. Recently however, increasing numbers of producers are also manufacturing stage sizes $11\frac{1}{4} \times 11\frac{1}{4}$ inch (285×285 mm) and even larger for projection of X-rays and other special uses.

Although other types of projectors already available for instructional purposes provided projected images of acceptable quality, the overhead transparency projector has been widely acknowledged as having unique advantages which make it especially useful as an aid to the modern-day instructor.

1. Ease of Operation

The instructor faces his or her audience when using the overhead transparency projector and has complete control over the pacing of the presentation. Functionally, both the operation of the projector and the feeding of transparencies are within the operator's control. This gives the instructor freedom to gear the presentation to audience response and questions and also provides the option of quickly adding or deleting visual materials as time and discussion dictate.

The overhead projector's high wattage lamp and short projection distance enable it to be used effectively

Figure 1
Bell and Howell Specialist® overhead projector model 389B with 14″ triplet lens and instant lamp changer system GP 564

in a lighted room since it can flood the screen with about 2,000 lumens of light. This makes it especially useful in situations where note taking is desired and where light control conditions normally prohibit adequate projection of visual images.

Although generally acknowledged as far more functional than just an electric blackboard, it nevertheless serves as an important substitute for chalkboard presentations to large audiences since the 10 × 10 inch platen is large enough to write on and such writing can be projected on a large screen so that images are perfectly legible for class groups in the hundreds. Also, an attachable cellophane roll enables the instructor to have written materials and diagrams prepared before class-time to simply roll into place on the platen as desired.

Because the standard overhead projector weighs between 15 and 25 pounds and has only three adjustments—off–on switch, focus, and image height adjustment—it is within the operating capability of even the least mechanically inclined.

Since only the projection lamp or cooling fan can burn out, repair and maintenance is of minor consideration; certain models have quick-change lamp devices which enable the user to replace a burnt-out lamp without disrupting the presentation.

2. Software Availability

Obviously, projection equipment is only as useful as the available software. The 1980 National Information Center for Educational Media's *Index to Transparencies* lists 5,800 entries of commercially available transparencies; many are prepared in color and include special overlays so as to provide additive data, accent special oral or visual cues, and even simulate motion.

Perhaps the single most appealing feature of the overhead projection system is the ease, versatility, and low cost of preparing personal visuals to supplement those commercially available.

Commercial manufacturers have perfected reliable, simply operated mechanical systems—thermal, diazo, and xerox—whereby instructors can transfer a master (drawing, typing, tracing, or photograph) into a usable overhead transparency in a matter of seconds.

Special lettering, coloring, and commercial art materials are also available to assist instructors in creating their own transparencies without extensive training or art abilities.

Of special note is one simple and inexpensive method of producing a color or black-and-white transparency from printed pictures in selected current periodicals, called the "picture transfer" or "lifting" process (Kemp 1980 pp. 210–11). It involves causing inks from black-and-white or colored pictures printed on clay-based paper to adhere to specially prepared acetate, thus making a projectable transparency. The picture and the specially treated acetate are sealed together by either heat

or pressure. They are then submerged in water with a mild detergent which dissolves the clay coating and soaks the paper, freeing it from the ink which now clings to the acetate. By peeling off the paper, only the ink remains attached to the acetate. After washing and drying the acetate, a clear spray is applied to the inked side to protect it.

Unfortunately, the original printed picture is destroyed, but in its place is a usable transparency—often comparable to an expensive color photographic transparency. A second limitation is that the resulting transparency is obviously the same size as the original picture; thus, if enlargement or reduction of the original is required, this "lifting" process is not suitable.

Although the primary objective of the overhead transparency projector is to project two-dimensional transparent materials, certain opaque or translucent objects may also be projected. Opaque objects such as leaves, shells, blocks, coins, compasses, magnets with iron filings, and so on, project as silhouettes and have important instructional uses. Other objects which are themselves transparent or translucent, such as protractors, meters or rulers, and even transparent containers of colored liquids can be placed on the projector platen and shown in enlarged form on the screen.

Special tachistoscopic attachments can be combined with the basic overhead projector to provide specially timed sequences useful in speed reading, word recognition, mathematics drill, and so on. A special polarizing attachment makes possible simulated motion, as in showing the flow of fluids through an engine's cooling system.

3. Utilization Suggestions

While this projection system requires minimal instructor training to operate, the effectiveness and creativity of presentations are usually enhanced when certain utilization procedures are practiced.

(a) Before the audience is assembled, the instructor should center the first transparency on the stage, turn on the light switch and focus the image on the screen and then walk to each end of the last row of the audience seating area and see if the projected image is clearly visible. All visuals should be checked for lettering or drawing deficiencies which may make them unreadable from the back of the room.

(b) For most normal classroom situations where there is a flat rather than an inclined floor, it is suggested the instructor sit beside the overhead projector and present the visual materials in this position to assure that the body does not obscure the projected image on the screen.

(c) On all overhead projectors, the projection head can be tilted upwards, thus focusing the projected image high enough on the screen to enable the audience to have an unobstructed view. This suggests use of a tilted screen (usually about 15° declination) so as to correct for image distortion called "keystoning."

(d) Audience attention should be focused on specific cues in the visual itself by using any pointer-type object to directly touch the transparency on the projector's platen rather than moving back to point out such visual cues on the projection screen itself. This avoids the danger of having your body obstruct the projected image for certain viewers.

(e) The projector should only be turned on when using a transparency and it should be turned off when use of the visual is completed.

(f) Emphasis can be added to visual cues on transparencies by circling or underlining key points with a grease pencil or coloring pen.

(g) The audience should be given time to study the visual materials projected on the screen using progressive disclosure or additive overlays when the situation or content suggests such action.

(h) Judicious judgment should be used in selecting visual or written materials which enhance overall instructional objectives.

(i) It should be remembered that humorous cartoons and creative visuals are audience pleasers.

4. Research on Extent of Use and Effectiveness

The adoption and use of the overhead transparency projector for varied types of group instruction has been a most encouraging phenomenon. In many United States public schools, colleges, and universities it is not uncommon to find this projector and stand considered a permanent fixture of every classroom. Such is also the case in many developed countries and certain schools in Third World countries.

A recent study in the Springfield, Oregon schools revealed that the overhead transparency projector was the most frequently used projector in both the junior-high and senior-high schools and second behind the filmstrip projector in use in the elementary schools (Laird 1978 p. 24).

In a 1981 study of media utilization by the faculty of the School of Education at Indiana University (Bloomington, Indiana), Librero reported that next to the chalkboard, overhead projection was the second most frequently used audiovisual medium, with 71.2 percent of the faculty using it in their classes during the 1980 fall semester (Librero 1981 p. 124).

Faculty teaching undergraduate courses estimated that they employed the overhead transparency projector an average of 10.6 percent of their class time and those

teaching graduate courses estimated use at 8.3 percent of their class time (Librero 1981 pp. 81–83).

Notwithstanding this rapid adoption, this author has been able to locate but one decision-oriented piece of research designed to study the effective integrated use of overhead transparencies as compared to the traditional lecture–discussion approach.

At the University of Texas, Chance and two other instructors of engineering descriptive geometry studied what effect the additional use of 200 specially prepared transparencies would have on student learning. In comparing this instructional approach (transparencies plus current practice) with their traditional lecture–discussion approach covering identical content, the researchers arrived at the following conclusions: (a) the groups having the added use of the transparencies did significantly better on mean final course examination scores and final course grades (at 0.05 level of confidence); (b) the three faculty members unanimously agreed on the desirability of using these transparencies in their teaching; (c) use of the transparencies resulted in an average saving of 15 minutes per class period; and (d) students reported overwhelming preference for instruction using transparencies (Chance 1960).

The overhead projector with accompanying transparencies has proven so versatile for creative teachers that it has given rise to an extensive literature; booklets of transparency masters; and numerous films, filmstrips, and slide sets on utilization and production of overhead transparencies.

Bibliography

Bathurst L H Jr, Klein B 1966 *A Visual Communications System Utilizing Thermofax Infrared Processes*. Brown, Dubuque, Iowa

Chance C W (ed.) 1960 *Experimentation in the Adaption of the Overhead Projector Utilizing 200 Transparencies and 800 Overlays in Teaching Engineering Descriptive Geometry Curricula*. United States Office of Education, Dept. of Health, Education and Welfare, Washington, DC (University Microfilm No. 61-2610)

Kemp J E 1980 *Planning and Producing Audiovisual Materials*, 4th edn. Harper and Row, New York

Laird N R 1978 Which media do teachers use most? *Audiovisual Instruction* 15(6): 23–25

Librero F 1981 A descriptive analysis of audiovisual media utilization by the faculty of the School of Education at Indiana University (Bloomington) (Doctoral dissertation, Indiana University, Bloomington, Indiana) *Dissertation Abstracts International* 1982 42: 2984A–2985A (University Microfilms No. 8128073)

National Information Center for Educational Media 1980 *Index to Educational Overhead Transparencies*. National Information Center for Educational Media, University of Southern California, Los Angeles, California

Schultz M J 1965 *The Teacher and Overhead Projection: A Treasury of Ideas, Uses and Techniques*. Prentice-Hall, Englewood Cliffs, New Jersey

Wyman R 1969 *Mediaware: Selection, Operation, and Maintenance*. Brown, Dubuque, Iowa

Bulletin Board Displays

J. H. Tyo

Ever since primitive humans scratched drawings of the hunt on the walls of their caves, they have used their environment to proclaim their presence. In today's world of electronic telecommunications the "wall newspaper" still retains its original charm and fascination. Properly prepared, it captures attention with a sense of urgency and immediacy and, above all, relevance.

In the world of education, the equivalent to the wall newspaper is the bulletin board display, without which it might appear that the business of information flow would grind to a halt. Display boards are everywhere, visually pleading, promising, announcing, introducing, advertising, and even educating. They are a part of our world of communications, but without the glamor of the more technologically sophisticated media. Nevertheless, displays are worthy of serious study as they are often the most accessible form of communication, and they are certainly the most familiar!

1. Bulletin Boards

A successful bulletin board is one which compels attention in the presence of competing stimuli. It is usually displayed where people meet and congregate, in lobbies and passageways and other channels of traffic where many things clamor for attention. Therefore, in planning a board the intelligent approach is to make a blatant attempt to capture and hold attention by every means possible, such as with bright colors, flickering lights, moving figures, unusual shapes, and other deviations from the normal environmental background. However, it is one thing to capture attention, but another thing to hold that attention, so there should be substance to the message. The analogy to a newspaper may be helpful. The front page captures the attention with a big, bold headline, a banner which is instantly comprehended. Then there are smaller headings promising more information, headings which in the newspaper trade are called "leads" because they lead the reader into the body of the item or article. Now that the reader is hooked, the information is conveyed, the message delivered. Another similarity between a bulletin board and a newspaper is that both should be current. Yesterday's newspaper has little value, and the messages and notices on bulletin boards should be removed and replaced when their life is over.

In planning a bulletin board, the intended audience, often called the "target audience", should be specified. This seems to be a reasonable, commonsense approach. Yet all too often bulletin boards are made up by people who satisfy their own sense of design and taste, irrespective of those for whom the message is intended. Consider the reading ability of the intended audience; will they understand all of the vocabulary being planned? Will the main message be at their eye level? Will the

message be perceived as important and relevant to the people whose behavior is to be affected?

Also, the conditions under which the message will be displayed to the audience need to be considered. It makes a difference in the design of a board if it is to be placed where seated people can see it, as in a waiting-room, bus station, clinic, and so on, or if the people are quickly (or slowly) walking by as in a hallway, corridor, or even on a street. In short, bulletin boards, as all communication media, need to be designed to influence a specific behavior of a specific audience under specific conditions.

1.1 Types of Bulletin Board

There are two general types of bulletin board: the pin-up board and the poster board. Most people are familiar with the common pin-up board. It is a place to pin up messages, announcements, schedules, help wanted pleas, articles or services for rent or sale or wanted, and similar miscellaneous messages. Even a pin-up bulletin board can be organized, however, for more effective communication. Permanent or temporary partitions or dividers can be fastened to the board to set off sections on which related items can be attached. Usually the divisions are vertical, but other applications may call for horizontal sectioning.

As an example of an administrative context, consider a bulletin board which might be found in an airline operations area where air crew members report for duty. The vertical sections might be labeled and used for such information as weather reports, time schedules, maintenance reports, personnel duty rosters, navigation hazards, radio frequency changes and so on, and in each section there might be many items. However, crew members would know where to look for information which was of vital interest to them. Imagine the chaos if all of the above mentioned notices were pinned up at random. Most people do respond to a logical organizational system, both in attaching messages in the appropriate sections and in quickly locating the sections to read which are of interest to them.

Also in the category of pin-up boards is the thematic board. This type of board is generally under control of one person, such as a teacher, who can decide to organize the items on the board so that they are all related according to a predetermined theme. Thus a teacher might ask for small or large group contributions of items for a thematic display. Examples might be agencies of the United Nations, or types and appearance of clouds, or basic nutritional food groups, or agricultural accidents; the range is unlimited. As items are brought in they are fastened in some sort of pattern to make the point of the theme. Group participation contributes to a sense of satisfaction and belongingness.

In contrast to the pin-up board is the more highly structured poster board, so called because it resembles the poster in the unity of its design, and because the items displayed are not so much collected as assembled and/or produced. The message is clear and direct, and simplicity and boldness contribute to instant comprehension.

The poster board type of display is generally designed and executed by one person. It is made for one location, for one purpose, and for a specific period of time. When poster boards are obsolete because their message is no longer cogent they should be renewed or even left blank for a period. Familiarity breeds staleness which leads to selective blindness to the message. The environmental space occupied by a poster board will continue to attract attention when it is renewed regularly with fresh, vital displays.

1.2 Design Principles

It is possible to improve the impact and effectiveness of poster board visual displays by attending to a few basic principles of graphic design. These principles are the stock-in-trade of commercial designers who influence the behavior of millions. There is no reason why an educational communicator cannot use the same principles on a display for a school lobby, or a convention, or a classroom.

The first element to consider in design is space. This is usually defined in two dimensions by the edges of the display board, which is traditionally a rectangle. But other shapes are possible, such as the square and the circle. These are formal shapes, and there are variations here too, such as trapezoids, triangles, and ovals. Boards can also be informally shaped at the discretion of the designer, and "free form" displays are a welcome relief from the traditional rectangle.

Within the spatial boundaries of the board is the area which carries the design elements. This area can be used to advantage if it is not cluttered with "information overload." Advertisers have learned the appeal of "white space," which is open space between message and the boundaries. Simplicity is a design element, and it is achieved by restraint. Self-control should be exercised not to fill up space simply because it is there.

Space can be used to convey a feeling of similarity or difference. When elements (words, symbols, shapes) are placed on the board, similarity can be suggested by a formalized balance, in which an equality is expressed. Also working to suggest the sameness between elements is repetition of numbers of elements and a unity in terms of their size, shape, color, texture, and so on.

Differences, on the other hand, can be conveyed in the use of space by informal balance or lack of balance, by inequality, and by deviations from what is normal.

Another tool of the display designer is line, which can be formal, uniform, and conventional, or informal, of varying width, and with eccentric patterns. One designer described such an unconventional line pattern as "a point taking a walk." Lines lead the eye with almost hypnotic compulsion; the eye therefore travels to where the designer wants it to look. One of the lessons which a designer of displays needs to learn is that the display is seen from a distance, and so lines must be bolder than they would be if they were viewed from close up. Always evaluate a display from the intended viewing distance, which could well be several meters, and strengthen the elements accordingly.

Color is another tool of the message designer. Much has been written about the symbolic meaning of color in various cultures, and the designer who wishes to use color effectively should know what colors "mean" in his or her own environment. If there is a universality of color communication it has probably more to do with color contrast ("clashing" or "harmonizing") than with the moods culturally associated with hue. A guiding principle in regard to color is that most of the rules which are taught regarding color harmony can be ignored when designing a poster board display. Colors are not chosen for their decorative value, or so that the resulting display will harmonize with the existing room colors. On the contrary, colors should be chosen with only one criterion in mind: they should attract attention. Vibrating color combinations which do not in fact harmonize with the milieu but which "catch the eye" should be the goal. Communication, not decoration, is the guiding factor.

The size and shape of elements on the display can also be controlled by the designer to achieve the emphasis required. Once again the aim is to attract attention, to invite further inspection, and then to deliver the message. The trick is to use size and shape creatively, and this can be accomplished through a deliberate manipulation of the relative sizes of the symbols and elements of the display. Proportions can be exaggerated, distorted, caricatured. Heads can be too large for bodies, perspective can be twisted, the world turned inside out and upside down. At the same time emphasis is directed to the deviate element: that which is out of step with the rest, such as small things which loom unusually large, or large things miniatured. Reality is discarded in favor of simplification and abstraction, and the passer-by looks, stops, smiles, and moves in closer.

While it is true that most board displays are two-dimensional, the surface can hold three-dimensional materials, adding yet another tool of design. The element of texture can add impact to a display, especially if the texture is related to the message. For example, the words on an agricultural display could be made out of appropriate grains or seeds, glued onto a background. A method must be found of adhering the objects to the background, a problem that can be solved by experimenting with various glues and cements.

Consider the effect of using some of the following materials to make letters, numbers, symbols, and shapes: white, fluffy cotton; woolly, colored yarn; old, new, and textured rope; small pebbles, stones, marble chips, sand; assorted or uniform beads; sea shells in all their shapes and colors; glass, broken, bits of smashed mirrors, dishes; wood strips such as balsa and pine; leaves from trees, or palm fronds; nuts, nutshells; tweed, plaid, metallic, rough, or shiny cloth; copper, steel, insulated, bare, or solder wire; aluminum foil, tinfoil; plastic, lucite, plexiglass; cork, tree bark, grass, straw; chain, belting; wire or plastic, colored or plain screens; corrugated, rough, or smooth cardboard.

The list is endless, but it should be sufficient to stimulate the creative imagination of a display.

1.3 Construction of Bulletin Boards

The main requirement of a permanent bulletin board which has temporary displays is that provision must be made for attaching materials quickly and easily, and then removing them without damage to the surface. A porous surface is indicated, and the best seems to be sheet cork, attached to a stiff backing, like plywood. When pins are removed from a cork surface the holes close up. It is usual to frame the board with wood or metal edges, but if the backing is stiff enough such a frame is not necessary. It is conventional, however, probably from its inheritance from a framed picture.

Substitutes for cork might be insulating building board, such as used for interior walls. This goes by such trade names as Cellotex, Homosote, and so on. Not at all satisfactory are the plaster boards, such as gypsum-filled sheet rock wall boards, which do not hold pins or staples. A panel of soft wood such as pine or balsa is a satisfactory expedient, but holes will show when pins are removed. One solution is to cover the surface with a fabric such as burlap, natural or colored.

The board may be fastened vertically to a wall or even on posts or trees. It may be supported on an easel, or suspended from the ceiling by chain, rope, or wire. Two boards can be hinged together to make a free-standing partition, and multiple surfaces can be provided by having three or more boards hinged together so that they may be folded flat for transport.

The actual fasteners have been called pins, and indeed common household pins are excellent for bulletin boards. They can be made even more unobtrusive by cutting off their heads with a wire cutter. The heads serve no useful purpose on a display, and may even be distractors. A type of pin on which the head is the chief part is the so-called map tack. It has a ball-shaped end, and comes in many colors, so that locations, routes, and so on can be pin-pointed on a map or any other display. Draftsman's thumb tacks are often used but their heads are really too large for this purpose. There are various kinds of commercial pins available for bulletin boards, commonly called push pins with metal and colored plastic tops. They too call attention to themselves, so much so in fact that they are often removed by acquisitive collectors. Office staplers are often used to attach paper to boards, and the staples are certainly easy to attach, but sometimes so difficult to remove that the paper is simply torn away, leaving the redundant staples cluttering up the board.

2. Exhibits

An exhibit usually consists of more than one display, organized systematically to communicate a theme. Exhibits can be temporary as for a fair, or permanent as in a museum. They may be open, inviting audience participation, or closed, behind glass, to protect valuable, delicate, or dangerous objects. But in all cases the same design principles discussed earlier regarding displays apply to an exhibit, or expanded display, with the added element of a multiplicity of stimuli to consider. The traffic pattern needs to be carefully planned so that each display receives its share of attention.

Imagine a series of displays, all dealing more or less with the same theme, but each important enough to warrant separate exposition to its public. These displays could be arranged along the four walls of a large hall. Such an arrangement will in fact exhibit the displays, yet there is no assurance that the public will view the displays in the optimum sequence, nor that the viewers will not be overwhelmed with the sight of so many displays before them. This exhibit can be improved by ensuring that each display is seen in isolation from its neighbors and in some predetermined sequence. The solution is to set up a series of free-standing or suspended displays in a zig-zag pattern, with a marked entrance at one door of the room, a definite path to follow, and an exit at another door. Temporary barriers can be set up to form the pathway, such as furniture, screens of bamboo or cloth, drapes over pipes, potted plants, and so on. The zig-zag pattern enables the designer to arrange displays so that each viewer sees one display at a time, then turns the corner of the pathway to be confronted by a new display, and so on.

The question naturally arises as to how to make each exhibit different, to elicit a positive response from the viewers. Variety is the answer, variety in all aspects of the display. Sizes, shapes, lines, colors, textures, all should vary so that although there may be a recurrent theme unifying the entire exhibition the audience is treated to a banquet of visual delights.

Nor is there any reason to be limited to a static display. Human beings are fascinated by motion, and if movement can be legitimately introduced into the displays, the attraction will be strong. Simple movements can be produced using a toy motor and a dry battery with the operating mechanism hidden behind the display. A rotating table can carry toys, symbolic figures, models, captions, and so on from front to back, again with a screen to hide the back half of the revolution. A phonograph turntable may turn too rapidly for such a display, so commercial store-window turntables may need to be obtained, or one may be built specifically for the purpose. One expedient is to use a carousel-type slide projector as the operating mechanism, since this slightly jerky movement can be tolerated for many moving displays. In order to operate continuously, it is necessary to connect the two operating leads on the remote control wire so that the slide change switch stays closed.

Taping a cardboard disk onto a slide tray provides an operational turntable. Alternately, one can fasten a wide cardboard collar to the slide tray and turn the projector onto its side to make a vertical-rotating cylinder, to which one can fasten cartoons, captions, photographs, and so on. These can then be seen in turn through a cut-out window.

The kind of motion which attracts the most attention is a live demonstration or, second to that, a motion picture recording. These can cause special scheduling problems if the flow of visitor traffic has to move past all of the exhibits in an orderly way. Unless they are quite short they may be better separated from the exhibit as special events; though this has the disadvantage of distracting attention away from the exhibit itself.

Bibliography

Kemp J E 1980 *Planning and Producing Audiovisual Materials*, 4th edn. Harper and Row, New York
Minor E, Frye H R 1977 *Techniques for Producing Visual Instructional Media*, 2nd edn. McGraw-Hill, New York

Boardwork

J. H. Tyo

Boards within the context of education provide a dynamic adjunct to personal, human verbalization. A board can serve as a "group memory" revealing and holding ideas and concepts, with the attributes of immediacy, flexibility, and an almost hypnotic attention-holding power, and can also be used to organize the flow of ideas, structuring and shaping the linear flow of words from the speaker's mouth.

Choosing the best available board surface on which to write, draw, or display depends on what is available, what has to be accomplished, and how it will be received. Boards of various types fit different teaching and demonstration situations and the modern communicator–educator will profit from a knowledge of the wide variety of boards which have been developed.

1. Blackboards or Chalkboards

The blackboard is probably the most ubiquitous visual aid in the world, although the dark slate and composition surfaces of old are now being slowly replaced by the softer colour green and the word "blackboard" is itself being replaced by "chalkboard." Blackboards absorb light and do not reflect enough for easy reading. Also, there is a high contrast between the blackboard and the surrounding white or light-colored walls. It is now some time since an experiment first found that adults and children could read 10 percent faster from a yellow–cream board with dark-blue ink than from a traditional blackboard with white chalk (Seymour 1937 pp. 259–68); but blackboards are still common in most countries of the world.

One of the great advantages of the chalkboard is its dynamic quality. As the lecturer develops points, key words, phrases, diagrams, cartoons, symbols, and so on can be written or printed, and with a quick pass of an eraser, they can be removed.

However, there are occasions when the speaker does not want to take class time to write on the chalkboard because such writing per se serves no useful purpose. Then it is helpful to have the material already prepared on the board before the class assembles. Prewritten material may distract attention, so it may be advisable to conceal it or cover it. Concealment is possible when the board can be turned round on an easel so that only the back is visible or when some system of sliding boards allows one board to conceal another. The most flexible arrangement is that found in some lecture rooms which have four chalkboard surfaces on a roller system with two surfaces visible at any one time. This allows the upper surface to be visible for reference while the lecturer writes on the lower surface. Two further surfaces remain concealed at the back and a small movement will reveal one line of writing at a time. In ordinary classrooms the progressive disclosure of prewritten material can be achieved by covering the chalkboard surface with strips or sheets of paper attached with pressure-sensitive tape so that they can be removed by the teacher as required.

In using a chalkboard, certain principles can be applied to improve communication. Legibility is of prime importance, yet many teachers make letters which are too small and weak to be seen from the back of the room. Letters should be made bold and at least 10 cm high. New pieces of chalk should be broken in two so that a firmer grip can be used. A new piece of chalk may break anyway, so by using half pieces embarrassment is avoided. If the chalk is turned frequently in the fingers when writing, an even width of lines is ensured. Lines should be kept level, and should not be so high as to require reaching nor so low as to require squatting. A good practice is to walk while writing, so that the relative position of body and chalkboard remains constant.

Chalkboard use can become more effective by the simple expedient of varying the color of chalk used. Roots of words can be given emphasis by contrasting color, mathematical equations can reveal their relationships by the judicious use of colors, headings can stand out, and so on in practically every subject field. Not all colors are equally legible from a distance, so legibility checks from the back of the room should be performed by the teacher or lecturer. Many teachers make good use of pointers to direct attention. A simple wooden or cane pointer makes a better attention director than the reaching arm, because the user can keep eye contact with the audience and his or her body doesn't obstruct the view of part of the audience. Also, by tapping on the board, audio emphasis can be added.

There are other aids which can make chalkboards more effective, most of which can be improvized by anyone wishing to become a better communicator. Circles, for example, are always difficult to draw freehand, so an adjustable chalkboard compass may be used. It is usually made of wood, with a maximum radius of about 50 cm. The pivot point has a rubber tip to prevent damage to the board, and there is a holder on the other leg for chalk. If such an instrument is not available, a meter stick or similar strip of wood can serve as a circle-maker. A series of holes large enough to accept a piece of chalk can be drilled along the length of the stick. The hole at the end should be smaller, the diameter of an ordinary pencil. With the eraser-end of a pencil serving as a pivot, circles of various diameters can easily be drawn with chalk held in selected holes. An even simpler expedient would be a piece of string tied to a pencil, held with the eraser end on the chalkboard, with a piece of chalk tied to the other end of the string a suitable radius away.

Music teachers who are forever drawing the five lines of the musical staff, surely a tedious task, will appreciate a simple wire or wooden holder for five short pieces of chalk suitably spaced. One pass of this ingenious device makes five nicely parallel lines.

Straight lines are drawn quite easily with the aid of a straight-edge about a meter long. This simple device is available commercially, but any light-weight straight piece of wood will do as well, especially if a small block of wood is fastened on the center to serve as a handle.

Sometimes teachers and lecturers find that they need to draw certain shapes many times over for their presentations. These shapes could represent geographical features, scientific apparatus, or geometrical figures, for example. Much time and human energy can be saved by making a stiff cardboard pattern or template of the desired shape. This template can be held flat against the chalkboard and a chalk outline traced. The template can be external, that is, a cardboard piece cut to the desired shape, or internal, in which a hole is cut in a piece of cardboard, the hole being the shape which is traced.

Usually the tracing of the shapes is done before the class or group assembles so as not to waste class time in drawing on the chalkboard. However, sometimes it is an effective attention-gaining procedure if the teacher draws a required, fairly elaborate shape right before the eyes of the audience. One way of accomplishing this feat of apparent skill is by the use of a previously prepared pattern. The required shape is first drawn or traced onto a piece of tough, lightweight paper. Then, with a sharp needle or nail, a series of small round holes are made in the paper about 2 cm apart along all the lines of the drawing. Before the class assembles, this paper pattern,

or "pounce" as it is often called, can be held flat against the chalkboard. The lines can then be gently patted with a chalk-filled eraser; small dots of chalkdust will be deposited through the holes onto the board, making a faintly visible outline. During the course of the presentation, the lecturer merely connects the dots with bold chalk lines, performing what appears to be a skillful exhibition of drawing. The paper pounce pattern can be preserved for future use by giving it a coat of shellac or by spraying it with clear plastic or even hair spray.

2. White Boards

A white board is a board covered with special nonabsorbent white plastic, and instead of chalk, special felt-tip color markers are used. The colors are brilliant and they dry instantly. However, their main attraction is the ease with which the colors can be erased. A quick rub with a piece of cloth or paper tissue and the color wipes off without a trace. In addition, there is no dust and the color markers write silently. These erasable color markerboards have one disadvantage—the special marking pens must be the only kind used. Ordinary felt-tipped marking pens may leave a nonerasable, permanent record of this disadvantage.

For institutions wishing to change over from chalkboards, an erasable marker surface in sheet form can be obtained. It has a pressure-sensitive adhesive backing which can be adhered to any smooth, flat surface. As before, one must have an assured supply of the special felt-tip erasable markers for this system to be operational. These markers are more expensive than chalk and they "dry out" if stored for too long.

3. Magnetic Boards

As the name implies, the magnetic board makes use of the principle of magnetic attraction as a means of actively displaying materials on a vertical surface. Materials placed on the board stay precisely where they are placed, yet can be freely moved around to show relationships, and can be easily removed and replaced.

The board itself is a ferrous metal plate of iron or steel, usually in the form of a thin sheet or screen attached to a rigid backing. If a fine mesh screen is used, it is generally covered with a sheet of thin plastic. If it is a thin sheet of galvanized steel, it can be painted with chalkboard paint and serve double duty as a regular chalkboard with the added attraction of being able to hold small magnets. Also, it can have permanent images or diagrams painted on its surface, such as airport runways and taxiways, street intersections, musical staffs, sports fields, and so on. Actually, the name "magnetic board" is a misnomer, as the board itself is not magnetized, but it provides a surface onto which magnets will adhere. Therefore, small magnets are cemented or taped onto the back of objects which are part of a communications process, then placed on the surface of the board.

If commercial "magnetic boards" are not available, it is possible to make one out of readily available materials. Any thin sheet of galvanized iron or steel will suffice, such as might be obtained from a tinsmith. Use the thinnest gauge which can be obtained as the sheet will be fastened to a rigid sheet of plywood or hardboard by screws or brads to make a board of the desired size. Such a metal board would have an unattractive appearance, so it is usual to give it a coat of paint or enamel. First the surface of the bare metal must be "etched" to receive paint. This is done by coating the surface with a common acid—household vinegar—for a few minutes. Photographic short-stop (acetic acid) can also be used. The acid is then drained off and washed thoroughly with soap and water. A good quality white enamel will make an attractive-looking surface, which may also serve as a board for the new-style "dry-ink" markers. Or the white surface could be used as a projection screen. Another alternative is to coat the etched metal with black or green chalkboard paint, again extending the magnetic board's usefulness.

Readymade alternatives to the sheet of galvanized iron or steel could be an auto mechanic's oil-drip pan, or even a baker's cookie or biscuit sheet. There are probably other utilitarian sheets of metal available, such as advertising signs, whose use in this capacity will occur to the imaginative and ingenious media producer.

Small magnets in the shape of bars or discs may be purchased in many stationery shops and school supply houses. These small magnets may then be fastened to the backs of a host of small objects, ranging from light cardboard labels and shapes, to actual objects. For a temporary or one-time lecture or demonstration the magnets can be affixed with small pieces of pressure-sensitive tape. However, for permanence, it is better to use one of the modern casein glues. Although most of these small magnets are familiar to almost any school child, new varieties are appearing on the market with remarkable holding power. These are the so-called "super magnets," made of cobalt. Then there are flexible magnetic tapes about 25 mm wide, with self-adhesive backing. These can be cut with scissors to appropriate lengths and fastened to visuals to convert them to magnetic pieces.

When ordering magnets from a distant city or country, it must be remembered that they cannot be sent by air. Sending magnets by air is prohibited by the International Air Transport Association (IATA) in case they disrupt electronic communication and navigation systems.

One compelling application of the magnetic board is to show positional situations. Examples might be in teaching games such as backgammon or chess to large groups. The vertical magnetic board would have the appropriate field pattern glued to it and the individual pieces would have small magnets glued to their bases. Pieces could then be moved as the game progressed, visible to all. On a more serious level, the same technique could be used to plan military maneuvers, the logistical movement of crops and commodities, or sports strategies.

4. Cloth Boards

The cloth board is also known as a felt board, a visual board, a flannel board, or a flannelgraph. Basically, it is a rectangular piece of woolly, fuzzy material such as flannel, felt, burlap, or wool attached as a surface on a stiff backing. The simple operational principle on which it depends is that another piece of woolly, fuzzy material will stick to it when pressed firmly against it. When a vertical board covered with suitable cloth material is placed in front of an audience, a speaker or presenter can attach visual symbols which are glued to a similar small piece of adhering cloth. Thus, the presenter with a previously prepared supply of visuals can actively illustrate his or her talk as he or she smoothly and effortlessly places the visuals on the board, moves them to other positions, removes them, and replaces them as the presentation requires.

Hence, the cloth board can be a dynamic, exciting adjunct to what otherwise would be a verbal-only presentation. It is a technique which is especially useful in areas without electricity and can readily be used with audiences of up to 160 people. It is also an inexpensive teaching device, suitable for audiences of all ages and at all levels of economic status and literacy.

The cloth board is one type of board which is almost always locally produced. Therefore, it may be useful to consider how many materials can be adapted for use in making and using cloth boards.

First, there is the backing. Stiffness, lightness, and an adequate size are the major criteria. Materials most often used for backing include heavy cardboard, plywood, hardboard, pressboard, wallboard, Bristolboard, and a variety of other building board products with such trade names as Cellotex, Homosote, and so on. The backing can be a single panel or two panels hinged together. In this configuration, one panel could be a chalkboard and the other a cloth board. The backing can be supported on an easel, on a table, or suspended by a rope from above. In all cases it should be firm so that distracting movement will not occur.

The covering for the backing can be a felt-like material such as flannel, cotton outing, suede, burlap, turkish toweling, or even billiard-table felt. If possible, neutral-or light-colored materials should be used. The cloth can be adhered to the backing in a variety of ways using such adhesives as wallpaper paste, wheat paste, rubber cement, animal glue, or casein glue. Alternatively, the cloth can be mechanically attached by tacks or staples, or laced on the backside with string or thread. The main requirement is to have the cloth absolutely flat and taut. Wrinkles prevent objects from adhering.

Now to consider the other half of the cloth-board system—the pieces of material which will stick to the surface of the board. These pieces can be made out of the same material as the board itself, or they may be entirely different. Any material which adheres to the board will do. Common sandpaper works well, as do blotting paper and pieces of thin plastic foam or foam rubber. All of these materials can be cut with scissors to produce the needed visuals. For primary grades, geometrical shapes are used in an active mode in teaching shape recognition, and animal forms can be used to illustrate stories. But the use of the cloth board is not limited to objects made of adhering materials. Pieces of these same materials can be adhered by glue to the backs of other visual materials, greatly extending the range of applications. Many lightweight objects, so backed with a small piece of material, will make good cloth-board figures. Paper flash cards for vocabulary or spelling drills, or mathematical symbols, or foreign language drill, all of these work well on the cloth board. Magazines provide sources of cut-outs which can form the supportive part of a presentation. In fact, any piece of colored paper, stiff cloth, plastic, or balsa wood makes an excellent piece for cloth board use when backed with a small piece of adhering material such as the sandpaper referred to above.

The effective use of a cloth board can be greatly enhanced by the observance of a few basic principles.

4.1 Organization of Ideas

The main ideas to be presented should be decided upon prior to a lecture or lesson. Generally many presenters become enamored of the technique of the cloth board and lose sight of the logical progression of ideas. The cloth board is an adjunct, not the main attraction. It is wise to limit one presentation to a few main ideas, which may be illustrated, restated in different ways, and repeated with variety.

4.2 Visualization of Main Ideas

Note that it is not wise to have a constant stream of visuals, each on the board for only a few seconds. Instead, a visual "theme" symbol should be decided upon and it should remain on the board while other supporting visuals are added and subtracted, smoothly and deliberately, at crucial points of emphasis, such as to introduce a new character, or a change of action or place. Use can be made of color contrast, size contrast, and position contrast. Also, the principle of deviation can be used to gain emphasis. (All fish are going in the same direction except one; all girls are wearing brown dresses except one in a green dress, etc.) Visualization of ideas comes with practice, and quick pencil sketches made while giving an initial, practice talk can provide the basis for more developed visuals. When using words, remember that legibility is more important than elegant style. To be seen at a distance of 10 meters, letters should be at least 3 cm high.

4.3 Sequencing

A cloth board presentation should be smooth and professional. To prevent fumbling through a pile of visuals, the pieces can be arranged in sequence beforehand, in an orderly stack. The presentation can be rehearsed with a friend listening and watching from the maximum distance. The presentation can then be revised if necessary.

4.4 Presentation

Usually an audience is enthralled at the way the "story" unfolds before their eyes and ears. Therefore, it is a good idea not to draw attention to the technique by excessive smoothing, straightening, and adjusting of the visuals once they have been placed. Visuals should not be thrown on the floor as they are removed, but unobtrusively placed face down on a pile, and the visual should not be left on the board after its point has been made. A blank cloth board is preferable to a visual left on after its function is over. Then the stage is set for the next attention-gaining visual.

The presenter should not stand in front of the board, but slightly to one side, reaching up only to manipulate a visual. This enables the speaker to direct the attention of the audience alternately from the board to himself or herself.

5. Hook'n Loop Boards

A technological invention which was developed for the fastener industry had an unplanned happy application in the area of boardwork in communications. Basically, a nylon fabric material was developed in two matching, but different surfaces: one has nylon fibers in the form of tiny loops and on the other surface the nylon fibers are formed with tiny hooks on the ends. When these two pieces of fabric are mechanically pressed together, the hooks engage the loops and the two interlocked pieces of fabric are thus fastened tightly together. To separate them requires quite a strong mechanical pull. Thus was born a modern alternative to zippers, snaps, buttons, and other methods of fastening clothing and other fabrics and materials. A trade name for these hook'n loop fasteners is "Velcro," and they now have a wide use in the garment industry. An unusual application is in space capsules and stations. Interior walls are lined with loop fabric, and objects the astronauts and cosmonauts use have small pieces of the hook fabric cemented to them, so that in a zero gravity environment, objects will stay where they are placed on the walls. Meanwhile, back on earth, educators found a use for this new material in the form of boards which had a certain advantage over chalkboards, magnetic boards, and cloth boards— the ability to hold remarkably heavy objects on a vertical surface, with the capability of being pulled off, repositioned, or replaced at will during a presentation.

Commercial hook'n loop boards can be purchased in a variety of sizes and colors, together with matching rolls and sheets of nylon hook material, which can be cut and cemented to the backs of objects for use in lectures, demonstrations, lessons, and so on.

The loop material itself can also be purchased in rolls from school supply companies and adhered by the user onto sheets of rigid backing, such as plywood. Because of the special heavyweight applications of this board, the loop material should be firmly fastened to the backing. Ordinary cements and glues may not have sufficient holding power to keep the material fixed to the backing, so one solution is to use the "contact" cement which is normally used to adhere plastic laminates to counter tops.

Because of the remarkable holding power of hook'n loop materials, the hook fabric which is attached to objects need only be a small patch, two or three square centimeters in area. The hook material may be purchased in rolls about 2 cm wide, with a self-adhesive backing so that small pieces may be cut off and adhered to the required objects. But for heavy objects, such as tools, bottles, dishes, and the like, the self-adhesive bits of hook fabric may not suffice. The solution is to buy pieces of hook materials without a self-adhesive backing, cut off small pieces, and cement them to the heavy objects with some of the modern "super-glues," made of cyanoacrylate, observing the cautions which attend the use of this adhesive.

As is the case with other boards, permanent features can be painted, taped, stapled, or cemented onto the board, leaving the rest of the board free for the positioning of objects in relation to the permanent background. For example, in teaching traffic control to harbor pilots and controllers, the outlines of docks, jetties, harbor entrances, etc., could be permanent features and model ocean liners, tankers, and other marine traffic could be relatively heavy objects with loop patches cemented to their backs, and moved about by the instructor. Once in place, the object will not slip nor change position, yet can be plucked off with a firm pull by the demonstrator, then repositioned or replaced with another object.

Although the main attraction of hook'n loop boards is their ability to hold relatively heavy objects, lightweight objects can also be used. One caution, however, is to be careful not to damage the object when pulling it from the board. Flimsy articles such as labels and dimensional letters should first be mounted on heavy cardboard to prevent such an occurrence. Hook'n loop boards are thus a solution to the problem of demonstrating rather heavy objects, such as tools, machine parts, books, art objects, and so on, limited only by the ingenuity and imagination of the communicator.

Bibliography

Kemp J E 1980 *Planning and Producing Audiovisual Materials*, 4th edn. Harper and Row, New York
Minor E, Frye H R 1977 *Techniques for Producing Visual Instructional Media*. McGraw-Hill, New York
Satterthwaite L L 1977 *Graphics: Skills, Media and Materials: A Laboratory Manual*, 3rd edn. Kendall–Hunt, Dubuque, Iowa
Seymour W D 1937 Experiment showing the superiority of a light-colored blackboard. *Brit. J. Educ. Psychol.* 7: 259–68

Printed Materials in the Classroom

C. C. Flanagan

Printed materials are one of the oldest and most widely used forms of educational resources. They include books, pamphlets, magazines and newspapers, and single sheets. Printed materials can be distinguished from other forms of media by the fact that they are composed of leaves or sheets (made chiefly from paper) on which information is displayed in rows of characters or symbols. Visual material such as line drawings, half-tones, graphs and the like may be interspersed within these rows as well. Some printed materials are only a single sheet in length, while others contain a number of sheets that are folded, stitched, glued, tied, bound, or stapled together along one side to form a sort of packet. Printed materials can be issued in single or multiple copies; the production of multiple copies is accomplished by means of either the printing or the photoduplication processes. However, printed materials are frequently combined with other forms of media to form multimedia packages, which may be either locally or commercially produced (Beswick 1975). In the United Kingdom, facsimiles of historical documents are often combined with other related materials to create integrated packages for use in the teaching of history.

1. Advantages and Disadvantages

In an instructional setting, printed materials fulfill a dual function: as a medium of communication and as a medium of instruction. The advantages of printed materials in these two modes are several. Printed materials permit a reader to skim their contents and to react spontaneously to them by making marginal comments or underlining. They can be produced in multiple copies, and can thus be used for independent study. They will tolerate delays in completion; a reader can stop, put the material away, and return later to the point of termination. Because they allow a reader to return again and again to the same point, print materials facilitate the study of difficult or complicated concepts. They are easily portable, and do not require expensive or complicated machines in order to be consulted. If produced in a loose-leaf or ring binder format, they can be quickly and easily revised and updated. Most importantly, they are a familiar format to teachers and students alike. At the same time, however, printed materials possess some disadvantages. They cannot present motion materials effectively; as a result, their ability to engage all of our senses for a total learning experience is quite limited.

They are also difficult to revise and update if produced in a hardbound format.

2. Books

A book is a written or printed work, produced and issued as an independent unit, and generally more than 50 pages in length. It may be composed solely of printed material, or it may contain a mixture of visual and textual elements. If the visual material functions merely to decorate or enhance the text, the book is called an illustrated book. If the illustrations carry the essence of the book's meaning, however, it is termed a picture book. Types of books commonly found in today's classrooms are picture books, textbooks, workbooks, paperback books, and reference books. Before beginning any course of instruction involving books, students need to become familiar with the parts of a book. These include the cover (binding and spine), the preliminary materials (title page, copyright, dedication, preface, table of contents, lists of illustrations or tables, introduction), the body (main text and illustrations), and the supplementary materials (appendix, bibliography, glossary, footnotes, and index). Students also need to learn how to use a book, which implies understanding the book's structure, the kinds of information it contains, and how to retrieve information from it.

2.1 Picture Books

Picture books are a special type of modern book in which visual and textual material are of equal importance. They are of two kinds: true picture books and picture storybooks. In true picture books, illustrations appear on nearly every page and are closely synchronized with the text. Examples include alphabet books, counting books, shape and color recognition books, and books designed to help identify abstractions or concepts such as time, distance, mass, or size. In picture storybooks, text and illustrations form a unified presentation, with both being used to tell a continuing story and convey changes in mood, setting, and plot and character development.

In selecting picture books, three elements should be considered: the text, the illustrations, and the graphic presentation. The traditional criteria of literary analysis (setting, point of view, character development, plot, theme, and style) are used in the evaluation of picture-book texts. Illustrations may be judged by whether their style is appropriate to the mood of the text, whether they are accurate and authentic in detail, and whether they form a harmonious unit with the textual material. Criteria advocated for the evaluation of a book's graphic presentation include consideration of the appropriateness and effectiveness of its size, cover and jacket design, type face, paper quality, and arrangement of printed and visual material (Cianciolo 1973).

Traditionally, picture books have been designed for use with young children, but recently picture books intended for young adult and even adult readers have been produced. With young children, picture books can be used to aid in concept or object recognition, to develop vocabulary and language skills, to build cultural or literary awareness, and to answer questions about the world around us. Picture books can be used with all ages to convey information, to aid in the socialization process, to challenge the imagination, to develop understanding and appreciation of the graphic arts, and as a source of pleasure and enjoyment.

2.2 Textbooks

Textbooks are books that are designed to present the basic principles or aspects of a given subject for use as the basis of instruction; they can, in fact, be considered as an entire course of study in print. They are highly organized, they contain a summary (often simplified) of a specific body of knowledge, and they usually contain learning activities or suggestions for further study. Although these attributes have contributed markedly to the improvement of modern instruction, they have also provoked severe criticism. Because textbooks are designed to summarize a subject, it is said that they do not encourage in-depth learning. Because they are so highly structured, they may tend to ossify a subject, encouraging rote learning rather than creative inquiry. Because textbooks must be used by many different types of students, they often are not responsive to the needs and abilities of individual learners. Textbooks have also been criticized for the inclusion of racial, ethnic, and sexual stereotypes at odds with our changing multiethnic and multicultural society (Fitzgerald 1979). Much current research involving textbooks, therefore, focuses on the identification of inappropriate, insensitive, or outdated material.

Although some of the criticisms leveled at textbooks can be traced to content or structural limitations, others are the result of inappropriate or insensitive applications. Because of this, teachers have a special responsibility to understand the nature of their textbooks and to use them creatively and effectively.

Five basic patterns characterize contemporary textbook utilization. The traditional pattern is to use textbooks as a source of homework assignments, either for reading or various types of exercises. Related to this is the use of textbooks as a source of problems for students to work through on their own—a pattern common in mathematics instruction. Textbooks may be used as the primary source of instruction, allowing their content and structure to determine the nature and arrangement of the course. Two or more textbooks may also be used in conjunction with one another as the basis of instruction. A variation of this is the multitext approach, where a single text is replaced by a classroom collection containing a variety of textbooks. Students functioning in this mode must make use of the classroom textbook collection, but are free to choose the particular text they find most useful. Finally, textbooks can be used as supplementary materials, with reading matter or exercises from them incorporated where appropriate to expand upon or elucidate materials presented via other instructional means.

2.3 Workbooks

In the United States, workbooks are large paperbound books, usually produced on $8\frac{1}{2} \times 11$ inch pages and in ring binder or spiral bound format. They are closely associated with textbooks, and many American textbooks are sold together with an accompanying workbook. In the United Kingdom, worksheets or workcards are more common. These are smaller in size, often resemble a pamphlet in nature, and may be either locally or commercially produced. Worksheets and workcards may be linked to textbooks, reference books, or nonfiction books; they can also be used independently for practical activities (Ball 1980). Related to workbooks are laboratory manuals, which are similar in physical format to the American workbook, and are used principally in science education.

Workbooks, worksheets, and workcards are designed to provide a collection of objective exercises for the mastery of specific skills. They are highly structured; a typical format includes statements of behavioral objectives, instructions to the user, experiences and activities designed to facilitate skills mastery, and self-evaluation mechanisms. Laboratory manuals are also highly structured; their function, however, is to provide directions for carrying out a specific procedure or experiment. Thus laboratory manuals commonly include instructions to the student, statements of objectives to be accomplished, diagrams illustrating correct procedure, and space for recording the outcome of the process or experiment.

Since workbooks function as a source of exercises for skills mastery, the quality of the exercises they contain is critical. The value of workbooks can in fact be measured by the creativeness of the exercises they contain. Other useful criteria for the evaluation of workbooks include selecting workbooks that have been student tested, that encourage users to think about the skills they are trying to master, that can be used independently, and that are appropriate for use by students of varying needs, interests, and abilities.

Workbooks can be used effectively in a reinforcement mode, in a motivational mode, and to present bilingual or multilingual material. The reinforcement mode is the traditional approach, and involves the use of workbook activities to reinforce student learning of skills that have already been partly mastered. This is frequently seen in English studies classes, where workbook exercises are used to teach correct grammatical structures. The motivational mode incorporates exercises that can be completed successfully, but demand a certain amount of creativity, such as designing a machine to complete an absurd activity in order to convey the idea of the relationship between an object's form and its function. Finally, workbooks are well-suited to the provision of multilingual instruction. For classes composed of students speaking more than one language, workbooks can be designed that contain a single set of exercises accompanied by parallel instructions in two or more languages.

2.4 Paperbacks

Paperback books are similar to hardcover books except that their outer covering is made of a soft flexible paper material. They are of two kinds: mass-market paperbacks and quality paperbacks. Mass-market paperbacks are generally smaller in size and cheaper than hardbound books, and are distributed through mass-sales outlets such as grocery stores, chain stores, and news stands. Examples of mass-market paperbacks include sentimental romances, Westerns, adventure stories, mysteries, formula sports stories, and movie and television tie-ins. Quality paperbacks vary in size, but often approach the dimensions of hardbound books; in addition, they are more expensive than mass-market paperbacks. Quality paperbacks are distributed mostly through bookstores and mail-order book clubs and include reprints of classics and out-of-print titles, original works, collections of readings on issues or themes, anthologies of poetry or prose, and paperback editions of hardcover textbooks.

There are three patterns common to the instructional use of contemporary paperbacks. They are used in the teaching of reading, either as reading motivators or as resources for the development of specific reading skills. Mass market paperbacks have been found to be ideal reading materials for the reluctant reader because they seem less forbidding than hardbound books, they possess highly illustrated covers that are attractive to students, they are less expensive than other types of books, and they often deal with topics of more immediate interest to contemporary students (Fader 1976). Quality paperbacks can be used to sensitize students to contemporary world problems. Many of the quality paperbacks currently available deal with major social issues and concerns, such as the arms race, world peace, world hunger, drug addiction, consumer fraud, race relations, or environmental issues. Paperbacks dealing with topics such as these can form the basis of sensitive classroom discussion and analysis. Finally, both mass-market paperbacks and quality paperbacks are used as supplementary materials. Another instructional medium, such as a textbook, is used to present basic concepts or skills, while paperbacks furnish examples or illustrations of these concepts or skills in use.

2.5 Reference Books

Reference books are a form of book designed to be consulted for a specific piece of information rather than to be read through from cover to cover. They contain large numbers of facts organized for use, and may be arranged alphabetically, chronologically, or topically. There are two types of reference books: those which contain the needed information (encyclopedias, dictionaries, yearbooks and annuals, handbooks, almanacs, biographical tools, directories, atlases, and gazetteers) and those which tell the user where information can be found (indexes and bibliographies). Collections of reference books are found in school libraries or media centers (in schools having this type of centralized facility) and in classroom collections maintained by individual teachers. Reference books commonly found in a classroom collection include an unabridged dictionary, a general encyclopedia, an atlas, and a general almanac.

One of the aims of modern education is to help students improve their ability to find and use information. Teachers have an obligation, therefore, to see that students receive instruction in the effective use of reference books. Such instruction, which may be termed use of reference books, library or research skills, or use of information sources, is frequently presented jointly by the teacher and the school library media specialist. Instruction in the use of reference books involves helping students recognize the kinds of reference books available, the types of questions or information needs a person may have, and how to select the appropriate reference source for the question being studied (Katz 1978). Effective reference book utilization also entails study of the characteristics of a reference book, such as its purpose and objectives, how it is arranged, the nature of its entries, the types of study aids it provides, the cross-reference and index structure, the type of bibliographies provided, and any special features it may possess (Higgens 1980).

From the viewpoint of curriculum planning, instruction in the use of reference books should be presented systematically throughout a student's years of schooling. An ideal sequence would begin with picture dictionaries in kindergarten and the first year; selected handbooks, manuals, geographical dictionaries, and periodical indexes in the second and third years; abridged and unabridged dictionaries, general and subject encyclopedias, maps, atlases, and almanacs in the fourth and fifth years; yearbooks and biographical dictionaries in the sixth, seventh, and eighth years; and foreign language dictionaries, thesauruses, and specialized indexes in the ninth, tenth, eleventh, and twelfth years (Hart 1978). In such a system, instruction in the use of a particular type of reference book will be repeated and expanded in higher grade levels in order to reinforce student learning.

3. Pamphlets

Pamphlets are unbound independent publications, generally of less than 50 pages. They may be issued singly or in series. Pamphlet materials focus upon a single subject, but may vary widely in topic, size, and format. They may be issued by private businesses, government agencies, educational units, and social and professional organizations; they may also be home or locally produced. As instructional materials, pamphlets have several advantages. They are compact, they are usually less expensive than other types of printed materials, they are highly current, and they often treat topics that are too narrow or specialized to be dealt with in book form.

In schools having a central library or media center, collections of pamphlets relevant to the total school curriculum will be obtained by the library or media center and housed in a special pamphlet or vertical file collection. Individual teachers, however, frequently maintain their own collections of pamphlets for use as supplementary classroom materials. Examples of the types of pamphlets that might be included in either a library media center or individual classroom collection are: government publications; trade catalogs; college and technical school catalogs; annual reports of businesses, organizations, or government agencies; reprints of magazine or journal articles; transcripts of radio or television programs; newsletters from businesses, associations, government agencies, or chambers of commerce; and travel leaflets and brochures. Newspaper and magazine clippings or cuttings are often included here as well (Miller 1979).

4. Newspapers and Magazines

Newspapers and magazines are two forms of printed periodical publications. They are published in successive parts, at regular intervals, and are generally designed to be issued on a more or less indefinite basis. Newspapers are most apt to appear on a daily or weekly schedule; magazines at weekly, monthly, or quarterly intervals. Often a distinction is made between a magazine (meaning a general interest or popular publication) and a journal (denoting a more technical, specialized, or professionally oriented publication).

Modern newspapers and magazines contain a mixture of four types of material: informational and/or news materials, entertainment features (including works of fiction, illustrations, cartoons, and joke or humor columns), guidance materials (including opinion or advice columns and editorials), and advertising. Newspapers and magazines possess a number of features that make them ideal instructional materials. They are very current, and contain a vast amount of material on contemporary issues. They are economical, and readily available in multiple copies. They are a form of publication that is familiar to modern students. They are a never-ending source of bulletin board, display, or scrapbook material, and they provide valuable material for clipping or cuttings files (Heitzmann 1979).

Newspapers and magazines are used in the classroom in two different ways. One pattern is to teach about the publication; the other is to teach with it. Teaching about a newspaper entails a study of how a newspaper is produced and constructed, who is responsible for it, and what it contains. An introduction to the study of a newspaper includes analysis of the overall makeup of the paper, the structure of the front page, the role of the editorial page, the contents of the sports section, and the types and functions of advertising. Following this the concept of freedom of speech, the historical role of the free press, and careers in advertising, journalism, or communications may be studied. The introductory study of magazines follows a similar format: how a magazine is produced and financed, the objectives of magazines, how to read a magazine, the role of the editor and editorial content, magazine scope and contents, and the nature and functions of advertising.

Newspapers and magazines can be used to develop reading skills or to improve study skills; in addition, they can be integrated into the curriculum as one of a variety of instructional resources. Reading skills that can be developed via a systematic study of newspapers or magazines are: reading readiness, the comprehension of printed matter, the development of critical reading ability, the identification of propaganda, vocabulary and word identification skills, and reading rates (Cheyney 1971). Study skills that can be similarly expanded are: reading selection, outlining, summarizing, comprehension, understanding the sequencing of events, anticipating outcomes, proofreading, the ability to note and recall details, skimming, the interpretation of nonverbal material, locating information, the development of critical and evaluative thinking, and the development of an opinion or point of view. When used in the integrated mode, newspapers and magazines can provide resource material for the study of contemporary society or the identification of recurrent political issues; they can also provide raw material for creative writing or dramatics exercises (Rhoades and Rhoades 1980).

Bibliography

Ball S J 1980 Mixed-ability teaching: The worksheet method. *Br. J. Educ. Technol.* 11: 36–48

Beswick N 1975 *Organizing Resources: Six Case Studies: The Final Report of the Schools Council Research Centre Project.* Heinemann, London

Cheyney A B 1971 *Teaching Reading Skills Through the Newspaper.* (Reading Aids Series.) International Reading Association, Newark, Delaware

Cianciolo P J (ed.) 1973 *Picture Books for Children.* American Library Association, Chicago, Illinois

Fader D N 1976 *The New Hooked on Books.* Berkley, New York

Fitzgerald F 1979 *America Revised: History Schoolbooks in the Twentieth Century.* Little, Brown, Boston, Massachusetts

Flanagan C C 1981 *Books and Other Print Materials* (Instructional Media Library Vol. 1). Educational Technology Publications, Englewood Cliffs, New Jersey

Hart T L (ed.) 1978 *Instruction in School Media Center Use.* American Library Association, Chicago, Illinois

Heitzmann W R 1979 *The Newspaper in the Classroom.* (What Research Says to the Teacher.) National Education Association, Washington, DC

Higgens G 1980 *Printed Reference Material.* The Library Association, London

Katz W A 1978 *Introduction to Reference Work*, 3rd edn. (McGraw-Hill Series in Library Education.) McGraw-Hill, New York

Miller S 1979 *The Vertical File and Its Satellites: A Handbook of Acquisition, Processing, and Organization*, 2nd edn. (Library Science Text Series.) Libraries Unlimited, Littleton, Colorado

Rhoades L, Rhoades G 1980 *Teaching With Newspapers: The Living Curriculum.* (Fastback Series no. 149.) Phi Delta Kappa, Bloomington, Indiana

Sound Resources in the Classroom

N. E. Trowbridge

The use of sound resources depends on the ability of students to listen effectively. Because of their importance, the processes of listening are discussed first. They are interpreted in terms of mental activity, especially decision-making, carried out in response to things heard. Secondly, equipment and its organization to support the use of sound resources in classrooms are considered. Provision in classrooms is explored in the wider context of the overall pattern of resources in a school or college. Perhaps the most important section is the identification of applications for sound resources and the educational value associated with their use. The potential range of applications is very large and no attempt has been made to be exhaustive. The examples, however, relate both to class teaching and to the work of pupils organized for small-group resource-based learning. Finally, a selection of techniques is included. Because equipment designed for domestic use is often used in classrooms, teachers need to be aware of techniques that ensure the reliable achievement of adequate quality in sound recording, and the use of sound resources professionally in education.

1. Effective Listening

As the use of sound resources is introduced, so pupils need to be taught how to listen effectively. Listening to a voice coming from a loudspeaker is much more difficult than listening to a live teacher. There are no facial expressions or gestures, machines do not notice lack of understanding or lost attention, and they do not respond to the individual differences of pupils who use them. On the other hand, a machine does not get tired, bored, or exasperated, and will repeat recordings as often as required. It treats everyone the same, has no favourites, and makes no reports back to the teacher. A pupil has more decisions to make when listening to a recording. Effective listening is about decision-making and good practice is based on well-established habits that have to be learned. It is possible that intelligent machines of the future will be capable of discussing content and issues with listeners.

Experienced listeners using recorded sounds exploit the machine by stopping it to gain thinking time, winding back for a repeat, adjusting tone and volume controls for clarity, using the fast wind in either direction, and, if two recorders are available, copying extracts to a blank tape to isolate them from unwanted context.

A common mistake in listening is to assign the same importance to everything heard. Instead, decisions about relative importance are needed, so that attention is sharpened for some material, and other parts are tuned out mentally so freeing time for other things such as making predictions about what is coming and later checking these. It is important to make links between what is being heard, existing knowledge, and past experience, to make judgments about true/false, fact/opinion/fiction, logical/not logical, complete/incomplete, biased/unbiased, and so on, and to be alert for unstated content such as implications and a speaker's attitudes and hidden purposes. Selection, spotting and making sequences, and mental classification are all part of effective listening. Unconscious psychological editing is a common difficulty, and special attention is needed in order to notice everything rather than only those things expected or desired.

When recordings accompany text and/or pictures, as in educational television, the learning challenge is even greater because the interplay between the messages of the sounds and images takes many forms and these need to be understood.

Effective listening is not a subject but an interdisciplinary ability developed and used across subject boundaries, and in an ideal situation all teachers contribute to its development and monitor its application.

2. Equipment and Organization

Individual classrooms and units such as subject departments and year groups, cannot be effectively equipped without reference to the overall pattern of resources in the establishment. This is a most important planning principle. Continuity in meeting the needs of pupils across subject and age boundaries is essential. Compatibility between local resources and central facilities, such as a library or resources centre, is also essential, and unnecessary duplication of expensive facilities needs to be minimized.

2.1 Competing Formats

Compact cassettes, open reel tape, and discs are commonly used for sound recordings; computers synthesize speech and music, solid state storage on chips is developing, and there are other formats (see *Audio Production and Distribution*). Each carries sound recordings, but requires different equipment for these to be used. It is seldom possible and probably never desirable to equip individual classrooms with cassette recorders, open reel tape recorders, record players, radio receivers, and all the other audio equipment available. A more practical approach is to transfer all sound recordings to one format and to use in addition not more than one kind of specialist machine such as a card reader, when necessary. The most convenient carrier format at present is the compact cassette and it is easy to transfer sounds from other formats and off air to cassettes. When standardization on cassette machines is achieved, savings of money, space, organizational complexity, and the time needed to train teachers and pupils to use equipment safely and effectively are made. Access is needed, however, to facilities for copying recordings, and if the material is protected by copyright, clearance may have to be obtained (see *Copyright*). An additional advantage is that when sound recordings are held in libraries, the use of a standard format simplifies the problem of providing equipment for browsing and study, labelling and storage are less complex, and if required, high-speed cassette-to-cassette copying equipment can be made available.

2.2 Types of Equipment

Most educational needs can be met using equipment that is not too sophisticated or complex, and it is useful to aim at maximum simplicity in relation to the range of uses. This also tends to enhance reliability, reduce capital investment, and simplify training.

Amplifying loudspeakers can be connected to small cassette recorders/players when extra volume is needed, in halls and for participation lessons, for example. Alternatively, larger and more powerful cassette recorders and players are available.

Audio cassettes may be reused many times and it is good practice to erase old recordings completely before making a new one. This can be done in a few seconds using a bulk eraser. A powerful electromagnet is the main component in a bulk eraser, so it must be kept well away from collections of recordings. There is also a health risk if a bulk eraser is used close to the chest of a person fitted with a heart pace-maker.

In countries where educational radio is available, a good receiver and aerial system is important. There is a choice between having a radio with a tape recording socket to which any cassette recorder may be connected, or having a "radio/cassette recorder" unit. The latter is more convenient to use, but if a fault develops in the cassette deck, the least reliable component, the radio is lost while the unit is repaired.

Access to a record player and/or compact disc player is useful for making copies from disc to cassette, and access to a high-speed audio cassette copier speeds up the process of making multiple copies of recordings. Few classroom teachers use equipment such as audio mixers or radio microphone systems, but specialist educational sound equipment such as card readers, and, much more expensive, language laboratories are useful for some purposes. When a cassette recorder is fitted with a built-in microphone, a separate plug-in microphone is also advisable for it gives improved quality. Many built-in microphones pick up noise from the recorder's electric motor.

Mono sound and equipment is all that is needed for most educational applications in classrooms and halls, and stereo sound is normally appropriate only for specialist music teaching.

2.3 Levels of Provision

Sufficient equipment is needed to enable users to make full use of sound resources with a minimum of practical problems. Serious problems include: finding the store cupboard bare; discovering that the only equipment left is broken; having to book equipment that is needed every day; having to book too far in advance; having to carry equipment too far before it can be used. When there is sufficient equipment and it is appropriately organized, as described later, these problems disappear.

With a finite budget, a balance has to be decided on between the range of different machines and the levels of provision of each. A limited range, carefully selected, with high levels of provision of each machine, is more useful than many different machines all at too low a level of provision.

Sufficient copies of heavily used recordings are also needed, but by using audio cassettes as the carrier medium this is easily achieved.

2.4 Organization

Location of equipment is an important issue. It seldom makes sense to store all the audio equipment in one central place in a school. A balance between central storage, local storage, and long loan to teachers/classrooms is necessary.

Arrangements for maintenance and safety are necessary in the organization of resources. Elementary maintenance such as cleaning a recorder's heads, changing batteries, cleaning headphones, and simple safety checks, can be carried out by teachers, perhaps after a little training. Other arrangements are needed for repairs. It is also useful if guidance on the safe use of electrical equipment is available.

In larger establishments it may also be necessary to create a balance between services offered to teachers and those things they must do for themselves. Services offered in some schools include: making cassette copies of recordings from other formats; recording radio broadcasts; carrying and setting up equipment; and perhaps even the provision of studio facilities. Easy access to reliable facilities is required. When teachers have to do such things for themselves, easy access to reliable facilities is required, for example in a teachers' work room.

In software organization, it is often necessary to keep master recordings separate from those in regular use so that lost or damaged cassettes can be replaced by new copies. Audio material in reference libraries may be classified using the same system as for books, and boxes of cassettes on a given subject can be located on shelves next to books on the same subjects. This facilitates retrieval. More detailed information is given in the next section.

3. Educational Applications

The processes of making talking and other sounds permanent on tape and playing the resulting recordings have an almost unlimited range of educational applications. A small but varied selection is presented below. However, while reading these it is necessary to bear in mind the changing situation. As teachers continue to see their roles increasingly in terms of the management of learning, interrelationships between media become more important, especially in resourcing pupils to learn independently. For example, talk on tape links with photography in the production and use by pupils of talking photograph albums. This is another example of book/tape units introduced below and illustrates a developmental stage leading to the ability to exercise judgement when using television. Even more powerful, the capture of ideas on tape at talking speed, especially by pupils who write slowly, links with word processing during which the material is manipulated on screen and improved until it is ready to print. There is an obvious link between electronic mail, which is now in use by large numbers of pupils in primary and secondary schools and colleges in the UK, and word processing. As technologies continue to develop and make possible wider ranges of methods for teaching and learning, so it will become more important for educational technologists to identify, develop, and disseminate educational opportunities that spring from such interrelationships.

3.1 Presentations by Teachers

Teachers play recordings to classes at all age and ability levels and in connection with every subject on the timetable. Sometimes the pupils listen and at other times the purpose is participation. Sounds from the world outside school, and from within the school, are used in classrooms for many purposes, sometimes alone or, as in slide/tape, with other media. These are the most familiar applications of sound resources.

3.2 Diagnosis and Record Keeping by Teachers

Recordings made for diagnostic or record keeping purposes need to be short, because of the problem of finding sufficient listening time later. For example, as little as one minute recorded from a child's reading once every two weeks, provides a useful six minutes of material covering a 12 week period. Good writers generate plenty of permanent records of their progress, but audio evidence is often needed if justice is to be done to effective thinkers and talkers who are not so skilled at writing. It can also be valuable for a teacher to record parts of lessons for self-diagnosis of professional strengths and weaknesses.

3.3 Recordings by Pupils

For many pupils, writing is too slow and laborious to be a useful way of storing ideas, which explains the triviality of some essays and failure of some creative writing. Talking over a microphone can provide a way of capturing the products of a pupil's best thinking, and the recording can be a useful tool if written work is required as well. Such recordings can be made in busy classrooms, but it is important that nobody stands at the pupil's shoulder. Similarly, notes of continuous observations can be made by one or several pupils talking over a microphone. Pupils are also capable of self-diagnosis. Unexpected benefits can result when a pupil is allowed to make a short recording of his/her own reading aloud, and then to listen critically once or twice to the result.

3.4 Information Stores

Large numbers of people cannot read well enough to use appropriate reference books; and some information, such as bird song, cannot be written in books. Collections of reference cassettes give poor readers access to information and ideas, and good readers an alternative source. Book/tape units are also valuable. A short recording by a teacher guides pupils who use the book. Cassette library cases can be fixed to book covers using three strips of 12 mm wide transparent, self adhesive, double sided tape. The corners of the lid need to be snipped off with scissors or they catch on the cover.

3.5 Taped Fiction

Book/tape units are particularly useful, and give pupils the choice of listening to a story being read, following while listening, or reading the story. Alternatively, story tapes can be provided alone.

3.6 Work Tapes

Work tapes are the audio equivalent of worksheets and may give information, set assignments, or do both. A cassette can also be a component in a topic box to coordinate the use of the other materials in the box.

3.7 Consultation Tapes

During independent learning, if a teacher is consulted about a pupil's problem it is sometimes valuable to make an informal recording of the help given. This enables the pupil to study the help in more detail, and the same recording may also help other pupils, so reducing demands on the teacher.

3.8 Taped Course Work

When course work in tape recorded form is required, pupils have to be taught how to plan and organize short, concise recordings. Few will be longer than two or three minutes. If this is not done, the task of assessing the work becomes too time consuming.

3.9 Educational Broadcasts

Educational radio programmes should always be recorded when possible, to give teachers and pupils maximum control over their use and to enable a greater number of people to use them. It is also valuable to record the sound tracks of television programmes, when a video recorder is not available, to support follow-up work.

3.10 Changing the Medium

A useful enrichment task for clever pupils is to plan and record a teaching tape using the content of lessons delivered by the teacher. This is a challenging task, and successful results can be made available for use by other pupils. Similarly, a written article can be based on a tape recording, a recording can be based on information in books, and so on.

4. Techniques

Success in the classroom often depends on getting quite small details right. Some teachers, for example, lacked the confidence to use sound resources for years because nobody showed them how to remove an audio cassette from its box.

4.1 Making Speech Recordings

Never read from a script, for spoken language is quite different from written language being read aloud. In addition, script writing takes too long. Hold a plug-in microphone level with the tip of the chin. Speak over the sensitive end of the microphone, so no breath falls on it, and use a conversational volume level resisting the temptation to whisper. If the record level of the machine can be set manually, use this rather than automatic level control, for best quality. The main advantage is the extent to which background noises can be reduced on the recording. Useful recordings can be made in noisy places. In interviews, favour the voice of the interviewee, rather than attempt to move the microphone from person to person. For recording small-group discussions, sit in the smallest possible complete circle around the microphone. Everyone speaks over the microphone, and the ring of bodies forms an acoustic barrier that helps to compensate for the extra distance of the microphone from mouths.

4.2 Leader Tape

It should be noted that the first few centimetres of tape at each end of a cassette are transparent, and the rest is opaque and brown. The transparent leader tape is not magnetic and does not carry recordings. Before making a recording, wind the tape on until brown tape is over the record head, or the first few sounds will be lost.

4.3 Playing Recordings to a Group

Small equipment often has a loudspeaker that faces up to the ceiling. When the equipment can safely be placed on its side so that the speaker faces the listeners, this should be done.

4.4 Cleaning Erase and Record Heads

The surface of each head that comes into contact with the tape needs to be cleaned regularly at about monthly intervals, and more frequently in the case of heavily used cassette recorders. Head cleaning cassettes are not recommended for heavily used machines. Instead, one end of a cotton bud should be dipped into methylated spirit or clear industrial spirit, the surplus liquid squeezed out leaving the bud damp but not dripping. This should then be rubbed from side to side over the surface of each head in turn. The bud should then be turned as it picks up brown deposits. The dry end of a bud should be used to finish off.

4.5 Cleaning Headphones

Headphone ear pads get dirty very quickly and need frequent cleaning. It should also be noted that parasites such as head lice can be transferred from person to person on headphones.

4.6 Storing Audio Cassettes

Cassettes are too light to be treated as mini books and stored on edge on shelves. It is more successful to store them in boxes with the long transparent edge of each cassette's case uppermost to carry labels. A small shoe box, 18 cm by 11.5 cm cut down to 6 cm deep, holds 10 cassettes. This is a convenient size of container for shelf storage, and the boxes can be stiffened and made wipe clean by covering with plastic self-adhesive film. When stored with books, a box of cassettes on a given subject can be stored on a shelf beside books on the same subject, which simplifies retrieval. Cassette cases can also be fixed to book covers (see Sects. 3.4 and 3.5).

4.7 Protecting Recordings

On the long closed edge of a cassette there are two plastic flaps which are cut out on three sides and weakened on the fourth. Each flap protects one side of the tape when it is broken out. The result is that the "record" control on some cassette recorders will refuse to go down. A protected tape can be reused by sticking a strip of tape over one or both holes. It is important to tell and show users what happens when a recording has been protected. If this is not done, the "record" control is in danger of being forced down, which can bend or break its linkage.

4.8 Finding the Place

When a recorder does not have a digital counter, there is a simple method by which an index can be provided. When a recording needing an index has been made, record on the reverse side a voice counting slowly for the entire length of that track. Play the recording on the other side to each point that needs to be indexed, turn the tape over and note the number on the index track. When that place is needed again, find the number, turn the tape over and it will be at exactly the right place.

4.9 Copying Recordings

All that has to be done to copy a recording is connect two cassette recorders together, using a transcription lead, or one recorder to another source such as an open reel recorder, compact disc player, or audio output of a video recorder. For best results, record level should be set manually.

Bibliography

British Council, quarterly journal *Media in Education and Development*

Hayter C G 1974 *Using Broadcasts in Schools: A Study and Evaluation.* BBC Publications, London

Martin N 1976 Taped talk. In: Martin N, D'Arcy P, Newton P, Parker K (eds.) 1976 *Writing and Learning Across the Curriculum, 11–16 Years.* Schools Council, Ward Lock, London

Trowbridge N E 1974 *The New Media Challenge.* Macmillan, London

Trowbridge N E 1977 *Recorded Sounds* (slides with audio cassette recording). University of Reading, School of Education, Reading

Wilkinson A, Stratta L, Dudley P 1974 *The Quality of Listening: Report of the Schools Council Oracy Project.* Macmillan, London

Wilkinson A, Stratta L, Dudley P 1976 *Learning Through Listening* (3 audio cassettes, Teacher's Manual, book of spirit masters). Schools Council, Macmillan, London

Language Laboratories

J. J. Higgins

A language laboratory can be looked at either as a configuration of machines constituting a learning environment and heavily conditioning the types of learning activity that occur in it, or else as a relatively neutral carrier of software reflecting a diversity of approaches to learning. There is some evidence of a shift from the first to the second position since the early 1970s, and this article examines the background to that shift.

1. Hardware Development

The first use of the term "language laboratory" was by Ralph H. Waltz of Ohio State University in articles published in 1930, but the use of audio machinery as a language teaching aid goes back 26 years before that (Hocking 1964). The defining characteristic of the language laboratory is that it provides a bank of listening stations, each fed from a central source of recorded sound, and with each student isolated by headphones from overhearing or being overheard. An installation that provides this and nothing else is known as audio-passive (AP). If a microphone is added to this into which the student can speak so that student output is fed both to his or her own headphones and to a monitoring station manned by a teacher, this is called an audio-active (AA) installation. If each student position is equipped with a twin-track tape recorder, carrying the master program on the top track and the individual's responses on the bottom track, and permitting subsequent playback and comparison, this is called an audio-active-comparative (AAC) installation, and this is what the term language laboratory generally implies today. Most early labs were AA only, and the widespread use of AAC laboratories had to wait for the commercial development of the tape recorder in the early 1950s. Permanent laboratories of the 1950s and 1960s normally had forward-facing rows of built-in booths with underfloor wiring and transparent front panels, emphasizing the lockstep approach to class language teaching. The teacher's console has grown in complexity over the years. Modern consoles normally provide remote switching of the mechanical functions on the student machines (play and record, rewind, etc), monitoring of an individual, two-way conversation with an individual, group call, and some kind of conference facility, giving pairs or small groups of students a voice link.

Even though forward-facing ranks of booths make the most economical use of space, the modern trend is toward a different shape, with booths facing the outer walls and a central area left free for face-to-face activities. The monitor has no eye contact with the student when the booths are in use, so the learner's privacy and self-reliance are reinforced. Another recent development has been the use of "minilabs", usually based on cassettes rather than open-reel recorders, using light-weight components, and capable of being assembled on a trolley for transport from room to room. The term minilab used to be applied mainly to AA equipment, but the modern minilab is a full AAC installation.

The design and capabilities of the individual student's booth have remained remarkably stable since the early 1950s, although various devices have been used experimentally. Most laboratories come equipped with a screen and some projection equipment, but few institutions make much use of them, defeated by the need for room blackout and better resource management. (Exceptions to this can be found in France, where the visual element in audiovisual has always been stressed.) Some wealthy institutions, universities, or military training establishments, have equipped student booths with individual video monitors fed from a central video recorder. In the 1960s, Tandberg developed a repeater laboratory which provided a second tape recorder at each student position which constantly copied the last five seconds of the master programme on to an endless loop of tape. The student could press a button to secure unlimited repetition of a phrase he or she was unsure of, obviously a real boon in activities like phonetic dictation. However this was never put into full commercial development.

2. The Future

In its present form, the language laboratory cannot be anything but quasi-interactive. The programme recorded on tape is not modified by the learner's responses, and the student controls nothing except pace and amount of repetition. An ingenious application of a twin-track tape recorder has been proposed for a comprehension exercise: one starts with a recording on track one ending with a polar question, and continuing with two different recordings on the parallel tracks, each corresponding to one possible answer to the first question. This satisfied the hunger felt by teachers for some kind of branching. This is now being met in a different way by the combinations of tape recorders and microcomputers. By 1982, at least two companies, Atari and Tandberg, had language teaching products in which a computer input selects a segment of tape, permitting multiple branching. Neither machine was fully AAC in 1982, but the development of that facility is to be expected. However, recorded tape, whether open reel or cassette, is a serial medium, and branching to different parts of the tape is relatively slow. The language laboratory of the future will probably incorporate a tape for recording and comparison, but will rely on a laser-read disc, possibly a videodisc, to provide access to a large body of possible inputs (so-called random access). Innovative work on these lines has already begun, notably at Brigham Young University, Utah, with a videodisc project called *Montevidisco*, for learners of Spanish. The disc contains a simulation of a visit to a Mexican town, and permits real interaction since what the students see and hear is governed by the commands they enter or the answers they give to questions. Students also record utterances on to an audio cassette, for later monitoring (Gale 1983). For the time being the costs of the hardware are high, but they are likely to diminish as the domestic videodisc market expands.

3. Software

In the early days, audio aids were thought of almost exclusively as pronunciation aids, and most language laboratory material consisted of words, phrases, and passages for repetition. However, the 1940s and 1950s were the heyday of structural linguistics, behavioural psychology, and pattern practice methodology, and with all of these the language laboratory configuration was well in tune. Under these influences the staple diet of the laboratory became the "anticipation drill", which requires the student to respond to a cue, forming the response by analogy with an example. The response is given immediately before hearing the correct response (hence the "anticipation" of the name), and a pause then follows in which the correct answer can be repeated. A drill with all these elements (cue, student's response, correct response, and repetition) was called four-phase, and this was the normal pattern up to the mid-1960s. Since then, the three-phase drill (omitting the repetition) has become far commoner, since the repetition phase was seen to reinforce the boring and mechanical aspects of laboratory practice. Drills can be classified according to the relationship between each cue and response, for example, substitution drill (replacing one word with another given in the cue), replacement drill (replacing nouns with pronouns or similar changes), transformation drill (present to past, active to passive, etc), question and answer drill, and so on. No standard nomenclature was ever agreed upon, and it became apparent that such classification was irrelevant since the essential relationship was not that between cue and response but between example and response. Under the influence of two groups of people working on laboratory materials for English as a foreign language, one in Kursverksamheten in Sweden and the other in the British Council English Language Teaching Institute in London, it became established as a principle that the contexts for drills should be as rich and lifelike as possible. Each drill response should be a natural response to the same prompt in real-life conversation; the items in a drill should all refer to the same context or draw on the same body of data. Most published drills nowadays embody these principles. Earlier materials had often paid little attention to meaning, concentrating on form and word order (sometimes referred to as "fluency"). Dakin (1973) articulated a resistance to meaningless drills and illustrated how a semantic or problem-solving element could be built in to practice activities, but it is still the case that many laboratory drills can be executed correctly without the student understanding what he or she is saying.

4. Other Applications

Rehearsed dialogue has long formed a part of laboratory practice (Higgins 1969). Nowadays, one often meets "open dialogue" in which the student, after hearing a model, responds to the cues with data about himself or herself. Naturally such responses cannot be corrected on the tape, so the only feedback will come from sporadic monitoring by the teacher.

There has been a strong tendency recently towards using the laboratory mainly for listening activities, or to treat it as a kind of listening library. One activity that takes special advantage of the laboratory configuration is "jigsaw listening". Several different recordings (e.g.

three different accounts of a road accident) are dubbed to separate blocks of booths. Students sit at booths and make notes on what they hear. They must then find students who have heard the other recordings, compare notes with them, and discuss the solution to the task (e.g. assess blame for the accident).

Another important area of application is in oral examining, pioneered by the Association of Recognised English Language Schools in Great Britain. Using the laboratory can ensure common conditions for all candidates and remove much of the subjectivity and unreliability found in the assessment of oral interviews. Exercises in dictation and in both consecutive and simultaneous interpreting are also highly appropriate to the laboratory.

5. Conclusion

When the popularity of laboratories began to spread, they were given a great deal of commercial promotion and were often installed more for prestige than to answer felt needs. In the 1970s, there was an almost Luddite reaction. The profession abounds with tales of useless and abandoned laboratories, and with teachers who take pride in not using them. Coincidentally, much of the linguistic and learning theory underpinning the traditional laboratory drill was discredited. Notional approaches emphasize the variety of ways in which messages can be encoded, and communicative methodology deals with language which is not predictable. But there are signs of a renewal of interest as it is realized first that the machines are perhaps more flexible than was thought, and second, that some mastery of code and "fluency" in its old-fashioned sense are necessary to achieve adequate levels of communication.

Bibliography

Council for Educational Technology 1987 *Language Laboratories* USPEC, Information Sheet No. 4. Council for Educational Technology, London
Dakin J 1973 *The Language Laboratory and Language Learning*. Longman, London
Davies N 1974 The language laboratory: An annotated bibliography. *System* 1(2): 52–67
Gale L E 1983 Montevidisco: An anecdotal history of an interactive videodisc. *Calico J.* 1: 42–46
Hayes A 1980 *Language Laboratory Management*. British Council, London
Higgins J J 1969 *Guide to Language Laboratory Material Writing*. Universitetsforlaget, Oslo
Hocking E 1964 *The Language Laboratory and Language Learning*. National Education Association of the United States, Washington, DC
Stack E M 1971 *The Language Laboratory and Modern Language Teaching*, 3rd edn. Oxford University Press, New York

Media Utilization in the Classroom

J. A. Moldstad

From early times, teachers have relied upon various forms of visual and auditory aids to help them explain. The simple drawing in the sand and demonstrations with actual objects under study which primitive humans early on learned to employ have never been replaced. Teachers have simply expanded their repertoire of materials and teaching procedures to include some of the new aids as and when they have become available. Film, television, and most recently, microcomputers, videodisc, and satellite communication are the educators' new watch-words. But it is probably only teachers who work in relatively wealthy districts and are seriously committed to using audiovisual media that are significantly affected by this huge range of options.

Historically, some teachers have tended to be over-enthusiastic as each new aid has emerged, which has resulted in frequent disappointments as such heralded new technologies failed to solve all their problems. Even as astute an individual as Thomas A. Edison overestimated the value of the educational film he invented when he predicted:

> The only textbooks needed will be for the teacher's own use. Films will serve as guideposts to these teacher-instruction books, not the books as guides to the films. Pupils will learn from films everything there is in every grade from the lowest to the highest. . . . Films are inevitable as practically the sole teaching method. (Dale 1947 p. 183)

Sixty years of teacher experimentation with film and other "new media" proved otherwise. In 1964, John W. Gustad, Chairman of the National Education Association (NEA) Committee on Teaching of the Association for Higher Education surveyed results of numerous education innovations and concluded:

> At one time or another, radio, motion pictures, filmstrips, TV, language labs, and teaching machines have been hailed as the saviors of education. So have large classes, small classes, seminars, tutorials, independent study, years abroad, work study programs, mid-winter reading periods, and year-around operation. None of these is as bad as detractors assert or as good as zealots claim. Lacking an adequate theoretical framework in which to place these innovations, the pendulum continues to swing wildly from euphoria to cynicism. (Gustad 1964 p. 38)

Fortunately, most of today's teachers have learned from experience that there hasn't been nor will there ever be an instructional "panacea"! However, hundreds of research studies attest to the significantly greater student learning which can result when appropriate media are carefully integrated into each teacher's instructional program (Moldstad 1974 p. 390).

Rather than engaging in the precarious mental gymnastics of predicting the educational fall-out emerging

technologies may have on tomorrow's learners, this article will attempt a more mundane task—that is, to objectively report on the extent of use of various types of instructional media in common use in classroom instruction from the elementary school through higher education, and on the emerging trends and teacher preferences concerning the so-called "newer media" uses.

1. Extent of Classroom Media Utilization and Effectiveness

Teacher approaches to media utilization fall along a continuum. At one end are the instructors who feel secure in their familiar lecturing style. Many either do not know of or see no need for technological aids, other than the chalkboard and a few maps and wallcharts. A middle group employs one or more media types to supplement their classroom presentations whenever such materials seem capable of producing increased student learning or interaction. Such use is often sporadic; more in isolation than an integral aspect of a planned, learning process; and frequently hindered by problems of selection, inaccessibility, improper use, and logistical difficulties. At the other extreme of this continuum are the teachers who feel that through careful application of the principles of "systems design" they can make education more productive. This group includes both teachers who see themselves in the designer role and those who seek to use externally designed instructional systems. Such systems have been provided by various curriculum development agencies, but are usually print based with audiovisual materials being relegated to an optional or supplementary role. Moreover, in spite of considerable investment, the level of adoption has been disappointing; and the quality of implementation is generally regarded as unsatisfactory (see *Curriculum Implementation*).

Desirable or not, it is teachers in the middle of the continuum who are responsible for most of the reported media usage. In a 1970 report to the president and the Congress of the United States, Norman Kurland is quoted as follows:

> Instructional technology is today largely supplementary to the two primary media of instruction: the textbook and the teacher. Eliminate either of these and the educational system would be transformed. Eliminate all of technology, and education would go on with hardly a missed lesson. (Tickton 1970 p. 21)

If this was a fair evaluation of the significance of media in the 1960s, how does it hold for today? What recent research evidence is there upon which to base a fair assessment of the extent and use of instructional media in the 1970s and 1980s? Unfortunately, only a small number of such studies could be located for review by this writer, presumably because they just haven't been done.

The landmark United States status study entitled, *The State of Audiovisual Technology, 1961–1966* (Godfrey 1967), was the first extensive, systematic attempt to examine what a sample of school districts made of the use of audiovisual technology over a critical six-year period of ferment in instructional methodology. Base-line data were obtained from 2,927 school district administrators.

This monograph reported a relatively high incidence of use for all elementary grade levels but indicated use data varied with subject speciality in the secondary schools. Proportions of users of "any" audiovisual material ranged from a high of 95 percent for science to a low of 45 percent for mathematics. The traditional materials—films, filmstrips, and records—were by far the most popular media types preferred by elementary teachers. Generally, these same media preferences held true for secondary teachers; however, television pro-grams and the overhead transparency projector rivaled records for third place in areas of science and social studies instruction.

Throughout the analysis of teacher's preference and use patterns, these central themes persist:

Teachers in grades K-3 favored records, using them with rel-atively high frequency either as an integral part of their pro-gram or for supplemental enrichment. Teachers in grades 4–6, who present the widest range of subject matter, used the greatest variety of media and used them more frequently than any other group in the study. Teachers in grades 7–9 preferred films; teachers who span several grade levels, often as specialists in music or physical education, preferred records.

Science teachers used films on a fairly regular basis, often as an integral part of their course of instruction. Social stud-ies teachers also used films, but less regularly and more often as supplementary information. Language teachers tended toward one extreme or the other; either they used no lan-guage tapes at all or they used them intensively. English teachers used records occasionally but had not yet adopted a pattern of regular integrated use of any audiovisual materi-als. Mathematics teachers had only begun to experiment with audiovisual techniques.

The motion picture was still the primary audiovisual tool, but new materials were beginning to have an impact on instruction. Teachers who had not used films were using tapes and records to help them teach the spoken word. Emphasis on transparencies and programmed texts designed for mathematics may bring a similar upsurge of interest in audiovisual technology in that field. Already the mathemat-ics teacher was the "second best customer" for the overhead

projector, the instrument most akin to his cherished black-board. He was also attracted to programmed learning, per-haps because of its logical structure.

The lesson is there. A single all-purpose tool, no matter how versatile, cannot fulfill every instructional requirement. The teacher is a subject-matter specialist, and his use and evaluation of audiovisual technology is influenced by his view of his professional role. He will respond to techniques and materials which further his instructional goals. (Godfrey 1967 p. 74)

Unfortunately, this is the latest large-scale sampling study of the status of general media usage by teachers of pupils aged 4 to 18 conducted in the United States.

Since very little survey data regarding the utilization of audiovisual media by Canadian teachers had been available, the Media/Research Division of the National Film Board of Canada (Cruickshank 1975) conducted an investigation during the fiscal year 1974 to 1975 to ascertain the status of educational media utilization at all levels of education in Canadian educational institu-tions. The survey drew upon 1,600 teachers from throughout all the Canadian provinces.

The mean number of times each of the various audio-visual media formats were used during the 1974 to 1975 school year are shown in Table 1.

Media preference and usage findings for Canadian teachers are quoted below:

Elementary teachers are the most prolific in their use of material, using nearly twice as many items overall as secon-dary level teachers. University teachers, as expected, use least, perhaps reflecting the fewer number of contact hours with students.

Elementary teachers are also the most homogeneous group (if measured by the coefficient of variation of the indi-vidual formats). University teachers show the most variation in utilization rates.

The most common A/V medium at the Elementary level is 16 mm film followed closely by Filmstrips and Broadcast Television.

Secondary teachers use 16 mm film far more than any other item, followed to a much lesser degree by filmstrips and slides.

At the University level, 35 mm slide sets are the most used medium; 16 mm films are next and videotapes appear as a third choice. (Cruickshank 1975 p. 1, 3)

When further questioned concerning major purposes for use of instructional films and videotapes, Canadian teachers indicated that presenting "supplementary information" was the most frequently encountered pur-pose in 37 percent of all screenings. Secondary and uni-versity instructors used films and videotapes for "direct

Table 1

Use of principal audiovisual formats: Average number of times per year per teacher

	16mm film	Videotape	Television broadcast	8mm film	35mm filmstrip	35mm slide set	Audiovisual kits	Total
Elementary	16.2	2.9	14.4	1.7	15.3	4.4	4.0	59
Secondary	13.4	2.8	2.1	1.5	6.0	5.5	2.4	34
University	4.3	2.3	0.5	1.2	0.8	7.9	1.0	18

teaching" almost as frequently as for presenting "supplementary information."

When instructors were asked to indicate the number of 16mm films used per teacher per year in 23 specific teaching areas, an average of 15 or more films were used in 11 out of the 23 teaching specialties. Natural science teachers reported an average use of 35 films per year; sociology, 31; and history, 28.

Of the Canadian respondents, 40 percent encouraged students to use some form of audiovisual media while working alone. Nearly half (45 percent) of those who used filmstrips in their instruction allow students to work with them alone; 42 percent of those who use multimedia kits do the same; and 27 percent of the slide set users encourage independent use (Cruickshank 1975 p. 25–26).

While the Godfrey study and the National Film Board of Canada study are the two major North American efforts to ascertain the status of media use employing a nationwide sampling, several other localized research efforts present media utilization data which tend to fill in some of the gaps in this incomplete utilization pattern.

Project Discovery was one such study. This large-scale national demonstration project was conducted from 1964 to 1967. Its purpose was to find answers to the inevitable question: "What would happen if teachers had all the materials and equipment they could possibly use for instructional purposes?" Four project sites were selected in different sections of the United States, and chosen schools were saturated with audiovisual equipment and materials. The entire film and filmstrip library of Encyclopaedia Britannica Inc. and selected materials from Film Associates and the National Film Board of Canada were integrated into the centralized instructional materials collections in the library of each project building, thus totaling approximately 500 films and 1,000 filmstrips.

Bell and Howell Company supplied a 16mm motion-picture projector and a filmstrip projector for each classroom involved in this national study. Additional equipment was made available for individual and small group use within the instructional-materials centers and for students' home viewing.

A USOE funded research study of this demonstration project (Eboch 1966) revealed a marked increase in the utilization of media for instruction. In the one school where pre- and post-use data was available, film usage increased 140 percent during the first year of the project and filmstrip usage went up 220 percent. Mean yearly use per teacher across all participating schools was reported as 65 motion pictures and 37 filmstrips (Taylor and DiPaolo 1978 p. 17).

In responding to the question, "What special reactions or changes have you noticed in your students which you would attribute to the use of films and filmstrips this past year?" Eboch reported participating teachers' responses as follows:

88% of the teachers reported being able to convey more information; 92% reported the general information of students seemed to have increased; 81% indicated reading interests were stimulated; 85% felt discussion or oral expression was improved; 77% thought observation skills were increased; 52% thought critical judgment and independent study were improved; 78% noted vocabulary improvement. (Eboch 1966 p. 141)

In the late 1960s, a series of elementary-school visitations (Goodlad et al. 1970) to 67 schools in 13 major United States cities were undertaken to interview 260 teachers about their teaching practices. Regarding media utilization, the authors concluded that textbooks supported by text-like reading materials and workbooks dominated the teaching–learning process, and media utilization was found to be much less than expected. The researchers felt the media software and hardware were in short supply for an affluent society and were seldom seen in use—hardly ever by children individually and of their own self-directed volition. They concluded that the much-discussed "systems approach to instruction" was not characteristic of present practices and perhaps awaits the future along with the electric classroom (Goodlad et al. 1970 pp. 81–82).

A later study of media preferences (Laird 1978) showed a marked increase in teacher use of media. A group of 93 classroom teachers, representing a 20 percent random sample, answered survey questionnaires and were interviewed to find out the kinds of audiovisual materials and equipment they used and the approximate number of times they used them during the year. Results revealed that audiovisual materials and equipment played a major role in the education program of the Springfield, Oregon, school corporation.

During the 1976 to 1977 school year, these teachers reported using an average of 28 films per teacher per year. Their mean scores on the use of 24 kinds of audiovisual equipment ranged from 5 to 15 times per year. Most frequent equipment use at the elementary level was, in rank order, rear-projection filmstrip viewer, listening stations, classroom record player, cassette tape player, and special record player.

At the junior-high-school level, equipment most frequently used was, in rank order, the special record player, classroom radio, overhead projector, and silent filmstrip viewer.

Senior-high-school teachers reported most highly ranked usages as reel tape recorder, classroom radio, cassette tape recorder, and overhead projector.

The record player and associated audio playback equipment were in frequent demand throughout the school system; there was also evidence of very high use of the overhead projector at the junior and senior high levels (Laird 1978 pp. 23, 24).

During the past decade several studies have reported that a majority of school teachers seldom use media in their teaching. Multiple reasons are consistently given for this lack of use. In addition to inaccessibility of hardware, suitable software, and adequate projection conditions, fear, listlessness, and even burn-out have been cited as explanations for this less-than-enthusiastic acceptance and use of promising new technologies.

Goodlad's monumental study (Goodlad 1983b) involved an in-depth study of 1,016 classrooms, constituting a representative sample of 38 US elementary, junior- and senior-high schools. Analysis of the amount of time spent on various classroom activities revealed that:

teachers appeared to teach within a very limited repertoire of pedagogical alternatives emphasizing teacher talk and the monitoring of seatwork. Overall, three clusters of activities accounted for 60%, 59% and 54% of classroom time at elementary, junior, and senior high school levels respectively: preparing for and cleaning up after assignments; listening to teachers explain, or lecture; and fulfilling written assignments. (Goodlad 1983b p. 467)

Reporting on the remaining time category (psychomotor or physical practicing and performing) of high-school classes, Goodlad reports:

We estimated that, on the average, a total of approximately 12% of available class time was spent on a combination of observing demonstrations (1.7%), discussing (5.2%), simulation and role playing (0.2%), reading (1.9%), and activity involving the use of audio-visual equipment (2.9%). The general pattern was quite consistent for all three levels of schooling. (Goodlad 1983b p. 467)

Mean overall class-time percentages of activities involving the use of audiovisual equipment were found to be only 4.3 percent for junior-high classes and 6.0 percent for elementary classes (Sirotnik 1981 p. 44).

Such class-time use of data involving limited utilization of instructional technology is indeed both startling and disheartening, and tends to discredit the idea that instruction is moving toward more self-instruction and learning activities involving independent study and learner-initiated projects.

A similar national study of media usage by classroom secondary schools teachers in the United States and in American Overseas Schools was undertaken in 1978–79 (Gilbert and Hennigan 1979).

A randomly selected group of 1,152 secondary classroom teachers was drawn from a random sample of 150 schools (whose principals were members of the National Association of Secondary School Principals). Then, 10 percent of the teachers for each participating school were surveyed using a specially constructed Educational Media Questionnaire.

Analysis of data indicated that 86 percent of the teachers used media at least once a day and 14 percent used it on average more than three times a day. Fourteen percent indicated they did not use media. Of the teachers who responded, 95 percent reported that they valued media usage and the degrees of satisfactory value in teaching grew with increased frequency of media usage. No attempt was made to study what types of media received most common classroom usage.

Smith and Ingersoll (1984) sent a questionnaire to a random sample of 5,000 teachers and 1,000 administrators at all grade levels throughout the United States in an effort to ascertain the availability and use of both microcomputers and traditional materials in the schools. Audiovisual kits (defined as instructional packages containing filmstrips, tapes, or other audiovisual items along with printed materials) were found to be at least moderately available in 71 percent of the nation's schools. The percentage of teachers reporting use of the kits at least weekly was 26 percent with 11 percent indicating no use. Three-quarters of the users agreed that the "AV kits are an important supplement to classroom instruction" and the majority of teachers agreed that both the content quality and the technical quality had improved over the past few years.

Further probing the availability and use of pre-recorded videotapes in this same sample, the researchers reported 43.9 percent of teachers indicating that pre-recorded tapes were at least moderately available. In 1983, 9.3 percent of teachers reported at least weekly use, however, a high percentage (41 percent) answered that they never used them. Surprisingly, the relative use ratio of videotapes was found to be at the lowest level of all materials studied, perhaps because of the unavailability of video software and hardware in the smaller schools (Smith and Ingersoll 1984 p. 37).

In a 1984 study (Seidman 1986) 545 public school teachers in the Fort Worth, Texas public school system who were members of the Fort Worth Classroom Teachers Association responded to a media utilization inventory instrument designed to measure their frequency of use of 11 different media utilized during their classroom instruction. Seven response categories from "never used" to "every day" were provided.

The data analysis revealed some rather surprising findings, especially regarding computer and video utilization:

The two media that are the most recent and complex—computer and video—were utilized the least by Fort Worth school teachers, along with slide projection. Overall, 80 percent said they used computer programs a few times a year or less, or not at all; 79 percent reported that they never or infrequently utilized video tapes; and 90 percent never used 35mm slides, or a few times yearly or less. Other media that were seldom, if ever, employed by a majority of the respondents were audio tapes (65 percent), phonograph records (52 percent), models (51 percent), filmstrips (51 percent), and motion pictures (51 percent). Only overhead transparencies, pictures from books and magazines, and games and simulations were used once a month or more by more than half of the schoolteachers in the survey. Overall, overhead transparencies were the most utilized materials, with pictures from books and magazines second, and games and simulations third. (Seidman 1986 p. 20)

Results of the Fort Worth study are generally consistent with the many kindergarten through to the end of secondary school surveys of media utilization in teaching. While it must be noted that there exist model schools where instructional technology is skilfully and extensively used to increase learning and encourage student motivation, the composite data paint a clear picture: as a general rule school teachers do not use much of the media equipment and materials at their disposal. When they do, the simplest and most accessible are most often selected.

Rockman's (1985) survey of the growth and use of educational television in the United States presents quite a contrast to the findings of the Fort Worth study, as reported above by Seidman.

> Studies by the Corporation of Public Broadcasting and the National Center for Educational Statistics and by Quality Education Data, Inc., suggest that about 70% of the classrooms in this country have—and 55 percent *use*—television for instructional purposes. About 18.5 million students receive some of their instruction from television, and 14.5 million use it regularly as part of their classroom work. Classic school television series such as *Inside/Out* and *The Electric Company* each have more than three million regular viewers and these series were completed more than ten years ago. (Rockman 1985 p. 48)

A report on the accessibility and use of computers in United States school classrooms and computer laboratories (Levine et al. 1986) reported that in spring 1985 there were over one million in use. In 1987 the number may reach 1.7 million. Fifty-four percent of elementary schools now have five or more machines. Secondary schools with 15 or more computers jumped from 10 percent to 56 percent.

High school students averaged 90 minutes per week at the terminals while elementary youngsters were reported as spending only 35 minutes per week on the computer.

No in depth national analysis of computer use in schools is presently available, however, the United States Office of Technology Assessment (OTA) is reported as having such a study underway which will be published in 1988. Ideally such a national study should also include comparative data on the broad spectrum of instructional technologies now available to schools.

2. Media Utilization in Higher Education

There is little recent information on the extent of media utilization by professors in colleges and universities in the United States and elsewhere.

In 1980, a study (Oxford and Moore 1981) was undertaken to explore the instructional methodologies and media utilization in science-related courses in community colleges across the United States. A total of 1,275 courses offered in community colleges within six geographic areas were studied. The researchers reported preliminary results indicating that 441 (35 percent) of the 1,275 courses surveyed used the lecture approach over 50 percent of the time over the entire term. Instructors in only 3 percent of the courses (41) used media at least 25 percent of the class time. Noteworthy, however,

is the fact that when the media utilization rate was lowered to 5 percent of the class time to establish the category "high media," 508 (40 percent) of the 1,275 courses fell in this use category. The largest number of courses (475) or 37 percent were classified as "low lecture/low media" courses.

The highest percentage of courses in the "low media" usage categories were in the mathematics/computer science areas; social and behavioral sciences composed the largest percentage of the "high media" usage categories.

To discover the extent to which teacher educators in the United Kingdom were using educational technology, Bhushan conducted a questionnaire survey during April 1975. The 56 institutions responding represented a cross-section of teacher-training institutions in the United Kingdom. Major findings included:

> Amongst teacher educators in Britain, cine films and videocassettes or tapes are the most favoured educational technologies for teaching the theory of education. In most of the institutions the traditional lectures, seminars and discussions have been redesigned on the basis of modern research into behaviour to make them more effective. As teaching aids the educators preferred overhead projectors, tapes or tape–slide combinations and filmstrips.
> The use of simulation and games in education is gaining ground and about 50 percent of colleges have started to use them.
> 20 percent of the institutions report using language laboratories and a similar percentage use programmed textbooks. A few of them have also pointed out the use of individual assignment sheets.
> Computers for instructional use in teacher education are yet to be introduced. (Bhushan 1976 p. 87)

Reinforcing the Oxford–Moore finding concerning major dependence on the lecture approach, this United Kingdom study reported that structured lectures were being used by 71 percent of the instructors and almost all (69 out of 71) claimed these were self-developed.

Other findings of special interest included: (a) 62 percent of the institutions train teachers in objective-based lesson planning; (b) 55 percent train them in use of the overhead transparency projector; (c) simulation and games are used far more for teaching educational practice than educational theory; (d) microteaching was a generally accepted pattern of classroom behavior modification; (e) programmed texts have been tried and found wanting by over 25 percent of the sample institutions; and (f) the use of computer programs for instructional purposes is still very limited (Bhushan 1976 pp. 88–91).

Recognizing that little up-to-date research existed on the actual utilization of instructional technology by university professors, Librero (1981) studied frequency of use and media preferences of Indiana University School of Education professors. All these instructors were housed in the School of Education, Bloomington campus, and could take advantage of a wealth of film, television, computer-assisted instruction, multimedia kits, and so on, as well as an excellent library, curriculum center, and individual learning center.

All 129 faculty members who were teaching courses in this facility during the Fall Semester, 1980 to 1981 were sent questionnaires soliciting responses concerning their media use patterns and preferences. Ninety-four out of the 129 (72.8 percent) returned completed questionnaires indicating their utilization of 17 types of media classifications.

Major findings of this research included:

(a) The faculty used any and all of the 17 media classifications an average of 31.1 times per course during the semester studied. When the chalkboard was omitted, the average number of media uses was 20.2 times per course.

(b) The average amount of classtime the faculty reported for the top five media classifications was 32.2 percent for undergraduate classes and 23.9 percent for graduate classes.

(c) The three media most commonly used in both undergraduate and graduate instruction were, in rank order, the overhead projector and transparencies, 16mm projector and films, and 2 inch by 2 inch slide projector and slide sets. Charts and filmstrips ranked fourth and fifth for undergraduate instruction and 2 inch by 2 inch slides and videotapes held these respective ranks in graduate instruction.

(d) The faculty judged audiovisual media to be making significant contributions to their course offerings, with approximately 89 percent of the undergraduate faculty and 78 percent of the graduate faculty attributing either "extreme" or "moderate" significance to media contributions.

(e) The respondents considered themselves either "highly proficient" or "moderately proficient" in using 16 media types; however, 53 percent indicated they were "not proficient" in using computer-assisted instruction.

(f) Media predicted to be most in demand during the five years following the study were overhead transparencies, videocassettes, computer-assisted instruction, 16mm films, and videodiscs.

(g) Lack of time to preview and select appropriate media appeared to be the only major deterrent to greater use.

Lewis (1985) surveyed a sample of 254 full-time faculty members from 15 colleges and universities on their usage and opinions of computers, video technologies and audio technologies. Table 2 reports scores from 173 respondents, who described the level of use of computer, video and audio technologies in their courses during the previous two academic years (Lewis 1985 p. 59).

Many divergent views were expressed by these 173 faculty members, ranging from some who maintained there are *no* appropriate roles for information technologies in higher education to those advocating using technology to automate entire courses.

The majority were found to be ambivalent toward the use of electronic technology in instructional situations. They felt it has the potential to arouse student interest in many areas of learning, can visualize and clarify many complex concepts, assists in learning important perceptual motor skills, and provides opportunities for active and simulated experiments involving physical, social, and psychological phenomena. Lewis reported that: "while most faculty were guardedly optimistic about future possibilities of information technologies, many expressed deep reservations that technology encourages behavior antithetical to the goal of educating discerning citizens."

Passivity, poor reading and writing habits and preferences for predigested information are among the contemporary societal ills to which they see computer, video and audio technologies contributing. (Lewis 1985 p. 9)

However, Lewis reported that clear consensus emerged concerning what faculty wanted instructional technologies to do for them.

Faculty want infomation technologies to do things for them that they *cannot* do for themselves; technology should *not* be

Table 2
Levels of technology use for a variety of technologies, by number (N) and percentage of faculty respondents

	Technology Use					
	Non user		Moderate user		Heavy user	
	N	%	N	%	N	%
Computer (micro, mini, and mainframe)	57	33	53	31	62	36
Video technologies (all forms of television, videotape, satellites, video teleconferencing, videodisc, etc.)	42	24	85	49	45	26
Audio technologies (radio, audiotape, audio teleconferencing, etc.)	79	46	61	36	32	19

used to replace functions already performed satisfactorily! Faculty do not want to be replaced by technology, they want it to perform in a supplementary capacity. (Lewis 1985 p. 10)

Moldstad (1984 p. 72) summarized the 10 most frequent major deterrents reported in past studies as major obstacles to instructional use of information technologies. Lewis surveyed his higher education faculty members using an almost identical list and found the same universal obstacles cited: lack of funds, lack of access to hardware and requisite utilization facilities, insufficient incentives and rewards, lack of training, and inaccessibility to high quality software. The same problems have plagued instructors ever since the emergence of modern technological resources.

3. Conclusions

This limited review of status studies on the use of instructional technology might best be summarized by a statement from the 1973 Ford Foundation Report:

> The conditions of success and the use of things of learning are many, varied, imprecise, changeable and changing. (Armsey and Dahl 1973 p. 101)

Any broad generalizations concerning the availability and extent of use of hardware and software for classroom utilization presented by this author should be regarded as tentative and open to further question and study due to the following limiting factors. First, much of the research data collected and summarized here represents subjective instructor responses rather than actual researcher observations and tabulations and/or documented use records. Second, in the studies selected for review, school and teacher sampling varied from national random samples to smaller, localized teacher groups and were generally confined to the United States and Canada with few exceptions. Third, definitions of what constituted "accessibility" and "extent of use" varied from study to study as did individual researcher's definitions of the media categories. For example, certain unconventionally defined categories such as "audiovisual kits," "video technologies" and "activities involving use of audiovisual equipment" made meaningful comparisons of data between the media studies especially challenging.

Recognizing the dangers of generalizing from such varied databases and acknowledging the great diversity of media availability and use in individual schools, at different school levels, and among individual teachers in various content areas, the author offers the following broad generalizations concerning media use in the classroom.

First, elementary teachers appear to be the most extensive users of media, followed by junior-high/middle school and high school teachers. Higher education professors still appear to utilize media the least; however, recent technological advances simplifying the local production and reproduction of instructional software

(10 inch × 10 inch overhead transparencies, 2 inch × 2 inch sound slide sets, audio and video cassettes, and even computer software) has resulted in encouraging greater interest and use of instructional technologies by faculties of higher education institutions.

Second, most teacher respondents professed to the value of using media in their classroom teaching and the majority reported at least moderate availability of both media hardware and software for use in their classrooms.

Third, on average, data from actual observation and/or teacher questionnaires reported that all but a small percentage of teachers use some type of media at least once a day. However, such uses represent only a small percentage of the available classroom instructional time period, usually less than 6 percent according to Goodlad's and Sirotnik's analysis of kindergarten through to the end of secondary school data based on actual recorded classroom observations.

Great variation notwithstanding, the collective results seem to indicate that about 10–15 percent of teachers are enthusiastic, persistent media users; about 10–15 percent never or infrequently use any media other than the traditional textbooks, work books, and blackboard and wall maps; and the remaining 70–80 percent are convinced of its value but have not as yet incorporated media as an integral and substantive aspect of their instructional programs.

With the increased local capability of visual and graphic design, recording, and reproduction of instructional materials, instructors representing many academic disciplines previously without high quality teaching materials are now employing the new technologies as a means of in-house production of software meeting their specific curriculum objectives.

Fourth, to date research studies suggest that media which have traditionally been the easiest to access, produce, and use—recordings, pictures from books and magazines, games and simulations, overhead transparencies, and audiovisual kits—are still the most used media, especially in the elementary schools. However, recent reports document significant increases in the availability and use of the newer media of instruction—videotape, television, computers, and most recently videodiscs and interactive video—as tools for teaching both in the classroom and in learning laboratory centers.

The inconclusiveness of the data reported underscores the need for more reliable research on the increasing availability, effectiveness, and eventual institutionalization of both the more traditional media and the newly emerging technologies of instruction.

Educators throughout the world must accept the fact that educational technology still touches only a small fraction of instructional practice, but since the early 1960s, a significant increase in media usage as reflected by the literature and the studies reviewed here has occurred.

Bibliography

Armsey J W, Dahl N C 1973 *An Inquiry into the Uses of Instructional Technology.* Ford Foundation, New York

Bhushan A 1976 The use of educational technology in teacher education. *International Yearbook of Educational and Instructional Technology 1976/77.* International Publications Service, New York

Cruickshank L R 1975 Analysis of audio-visual acceptance and usage by Canadian teachers. Unpublished manuscript. National Film Board of Canada, Montreal

Dale E 1947 *Audio-visual Methods in Teaching.* Dryden Press, New York

Eboch S 1966 *Implementation of Research Strategies and Tactics for Demonstration of New Media.* (OE-5-16-016) US Department of Health, Education and Welfare, Office of Education, Washington, DC

Gibert R M, Hennigan T L 1979 Educational media usage by secondary classroom teachers. Unpublished manuscript, Northwestern State University of Louisiana, Natchitoches, Louisiana

Godfrey E P 1967 *The State of Audiovisual Technology, 1961–1966.* Department of Audiovisual Instruction, National Education Association, Washington, DC

Goodlad J I 1983a *A Place Called School.* McGraw-Hill, New York

Goodlad J I 1983b A study of schooling: Some findings and hypotheses. *Phi Delta Kappan* 64: 465–70

Goodlad J I, Klein M F et al. 1970 *Behind the Classroom Door.* Jones, Worthington, Ohio

Gustad J W 1964 On improving college teaching. *NEA J.* 53: 37–38

Laird N R 1978 Which media do teachers use most? *Audiovisual Instruction* 23(6): 23–25

Levine A et al. 1986 Something doesn't quite compute. *US News and World Report* 101(19): 78–79

Lewis R J 1985 *Faculty Perspectives on the Role of Information Technologies in Academic Instruction.* Corporation for Public Broadcasting, Washington, DC

Librero F 1981 A descriptive analysis of audiovisual media utilization by the faculty of the school of education at Indiana University (Bloomington). (Doctoral dissertation, Indiana University, Bloomington, 1981.) *Dissertation Abstracts International* 1982 42 2984A–2985A (University Microfilms No. 8128073)

Moldstad J A 1974 Selective review of research studies showing media effectiveness: A primer for media directors. *AV Commun. Rev.* 24: 387–407

Moldstad J A 1984 What we know about using communication technologies in education. In: Blume W T, Schneller P (eds.) 1984 *Toward International Tele-Education.* Westview Press, Boulder, Colorado

Rockman S 1985 Success or failure for computers in schools? Some lessons from instructional television. *Educational Television* 25(1): 48–50

Seidman S A 1986 A survey of schoolteacher's utilization of media. *Educational Technology* 26: 19–23

Sirotnik K A 1981 *What You See is What You Get: A Survey of Observations in Over 1000 Elementary and Secondary Classrooms,* A study of schooling in the United States, Technical Report Series, No. 29. Graduate School of Education, University of California, Los Angeles, California

Smith C B, Ingersoll G M 1984 Audiovisual materials in US schools: A national survey on availability and use. *Educ. Technol.* 24(9): 36–38

Taylor W D, DiPaolo A J 1978 Project discovery re-visited: Was it worth it? *Audiovisual Instruction* 23: 16–18,55

Tickton S G (ed.) 1970 *To Improve Learning: An Evaluation of Instruction Technology, Vol. 1.* Bowker, New York

Simulation and Gaming

J. Megarry

Although the theory of simulations and games can be traced back through history, their practical use in education today can be attributed to the work of an informal, international group of enthusiasts who have been active since the mid-1960s. Indeed, it is useful to speak of a simulation and gaming movement just as it was possible at one time to talk of a progressive education movement or a programmed-learning movement. The movement has produced many research studies as a by-product. But it is not research reports which have led to the increasing use of simulations and games in schools and colleges, it is more often the experience of participation. People usually try simulations and games because they have met enthusiasts. Their motivational power and educational potential have spread by word-of-mouth and by informal report.

The early publications on simulation and gaming date from the mid-1960s in the United States and the early 1970s in the United Kingdom. By the early 1980s most developed countries had a rapidly growing literature on the subject; many had national organizations devoted to its spread. Currently, there are half a dozen periodicals on simulation and gaming in the English language alone (Coombs 1980), directories listing thousands of educational simulation/games, conferences on the subject somewhere almost every month, and even an International Simulation and Gaming Association (founded in 1970).

The purpose of this article is to review the nature and impact of recent developments. The first section sets the scene with three thumb-nail sketches of simulations and games in action. Then the variety of activities embraced by these terms is discussed in a section on definitions and distinctions. A third section assesses the advantages and disadvantages of simulations and games, while later sections cover their preparation and use, adaptation and design, and evaluation. The final section gives sources of further information.

1. Simulations and Games in Action

Those who watch young children growing and learning are well-aware of the vital role of play in human learning. Of their own free will, children spend hours practising adult skills, rehearsing roles, and acting out fantasies. They play traditional games, sometimes improvized family games, sometimes formalized by boards, cards, or other props, often—and increasingly nowadays—displayed and paced by microcomputer. Such activities are often immensely serious; they may be pursued with intense concentration over sustained periods, and often children show great creativity in their play. There can be no doubt about its power to make learning flourish.

The aim of the simulation and gaming movement is to bring these characteristic features—intense motivation, personal involvement, and high-quality learning—into the classroom. This first section, therefore, tries to convey what a classroom is like when students are learning from simulations or games by briefly describing three examples.

CIRCUITRON is for learning about electric currents, RAILWAY PIONEERS teaches historical geography, and HUMANUS can be used to stimulate discussion of values in social subjects and also to promote communication skills. The three exercises have in common great flexibility of appeal; simple modifications make them suitable for a wide age range of students. Simplified versions of each have been used in primary schools and with remedial students. Other versions have been played with interest and benefit by university students and mature adults. This appeal to a wide age range is a common feature of simulation/games.

1.1 CIRCUITRON

A class of 12-year-olds is gathered around the benches in pairs, two pairs to each bench. This takes place in a science laboratory, but the "apparatus" consists of cardboard "pieces" and large boards with slots. The students take a handful of pieces representing batteries, bulbs, and switches out of a box and try to form them into a circuit. The students within each pair help each other, correcting each other's mistakes, or rearranging the pieces to score more points. Then the other pair check the circuit and try to score more from their own hands. Occasionally the teacher is called in as a referee, but mostly the students work intently—but far from silently—on their circuits. The scoring system reflects the difficulty of the circuits. No points are allowed for circuits which would not work in practice.

1.2 RAILWAY PIONEERS

The desks and chairs of a geography classroom are rearranged into five clusters. Around each a board of 15-year-old railroad company directors gathers. The aim is to try to cross the United States of America from East to West during the nineteenth century. The secretary has to record all the decisions, while the chairperson must if

necessary override the surveyor's ambitious route plans in the light of the treasurer's report about the balance sheet.

Arguments revolve around where to build track during the next round (three months), bearing in mind the way the building costs reflect the terrain, the need to connect towns in order to bring in revenue, the state of their bank balances after the last round, and the plans of the other companies. Once all the companies have made their decisions, the teacher draws a chance card and announces its message: flood damage means some companies have to repair their bridges, or perhaps Sioux Indians in the North have attacked railroad workers. The affected companies must amend their balance sheets, while the others start discussing their strategy for the next three months.

1.3 HUMANUS

This simulation takes place in a darkened room where student teachers can just about see each other's faces. All their attention is on the electronic and tape-recorded voice announcing the "voice print-out" of the group's survival computer, their lifeline to a hostile world after some global catastrophe. It poses the group with problems and sets time limits for its responses: How will they organize themselves? Will they admit a survivor? What message do they send to other survival cells?

HUMANUS feeds back the effects of the group's decisions and sets the next problem. During the exercise, the lecturer merely switches the tape recorder on and off, taking a few notes in preparation for running the discussion afterwards.

These three sketches are only intended as a brief introduction to the three exercises. CIRCUITRON was designed by Megarry (1977) and is described by Ellington et al. (1981); RAILWAY PIONEERS was designed by Walford (1969); and HUMANUS was adapted from an exercise called RALPH, devised by Benson (1971); both are described by Megarry (1975a, 1975b).

2. Definitions and Distinctions

The examples above illustrate some of the features of simulations and games. Before proposing formal definitions, it is worth noting three ways in which the educational use of the terms is distinctive. Outside the world of school and its playgrounds, children often play noncompetitive games with the object of creating laughter, movement, physical contact, and vertigo. Inside education, the term "game" usually denotes rule-bound and competitive games, often with an easily identified educational objective. However, this generalization does not apply to the way the term is used in interpersonal learning exercises such as theatre games or encounter games, or in transactional analysis.

Second, the priorities for educational simulation are quite different from those for mathematical modelling and simulation as used by academics and technologists for researching and predicting the behaviour of complex systems like the economy of a country or the spread of a forest fire. Ultimate realism and accuracy are not essential in an educational simulation—indeed they are sometimes counterproductive.

Third, there is no necessary connection between educational games and the mathematical theory of games in which choices are finite, pay-offs quantifiable, and "rational choices" identifiable. Although some educational games contain elements to which such notions can be applied, usually they are incidental.

A simulation is a working model of reality. Educational simulations are often simplified or accelerated representations which allow students to explore situations which would be too dangerous, expensive, time-consuming, or overwhelming to deal with "for real", like a nuclear reactor, a breeding experiment, or a general election.

A game is played by one or more players, competing and/or cooperating toward a definite objective, according to an agreed set of rules. These specify procedures for attaining the objective from the materials provided, and indicate a scoring system or method for identifying winners and losers.

A simulation game combines the features of a game (players, rules, and competition/cooperation) with that of a simulation (working model of reality). When the real-life situation to be simulated is competitive, simulation games tend to arise naturally.

Thus simulations and games represent two distinct, but not incompatible, categories whose overlap is the category of simulation games (see Fig. 1). The term simulation/game denotes any exercise in any of these categories—game, simulation, or simulation game.

Applying this terminology to the exercises described in the first section, CIRCUITRON is a formal game embodying both competition and cooperation which derives its rules from the laws of physics. It does not simulate physics. Indeed, part of the rationale of such a game is to avoid the real-life problems like run-down batteries and loose connections that can so easily provide an initial obstacle to learning. Many mathematical and word games belong in this same category. The competition built into them may be against another player, as in chess; against "Nature" or the player's previous best score as in a solitaire card game; or against a computer program as in computerized chess.

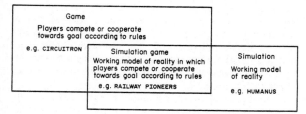

Figure 1
Simulation and game categories

HUMANUS is a simulation, albeit a highly structured one with a very compressed time scale. Nevertheless, participants readily make "that willing suspension of disbelief" and a powerful atmosphere of realism can be evoked with minimum props. Many other simulations are much more open ended. RAILWAY PIONEERS is a good example of an exercise which naturally turned out to be a simulation game. In order to simulate nineteenth-century American railroads accurately, Walford had to build in the element of competition between companies. Business games, war games, and many political simulations share these characteristics.

2.1 Caveats

The early literature on simulation/gaming was notable for its lack of consensus on the use of these terms; many writers were neither clear nor consistent in their own work, let alone in agreement with others. Some people seemed to think games were a special type of simulation, others that simulations were a special kind of game. Others again treated the distinction as if it were a matter of prestige, complexity, or plausibility. Many simply used the terms interchangeably. The confusion led to an extensive and largely arid academic debate.

Some writers preferred to avoid any competitive connotation for the term "game" and instead added a third overlapping category of "contests". On this model, RAILWAY PIONEERS would be placed at the intersection of a third overlapping rectangle and called a simulation game contest. Other authors, impressed by the importance of the range of case study techniques, have made this into another overlapping category, some showing it as a subset of simulations, others as intersecting with all simulation/games. Apart from the unwieldiness of the terms which result from these elaborate schemes, they also suffer from the crucial disadvantage that they do not enjoy wide currency.

The simple model in Fig. 1 is now well-established and will be used throughout this article. It is only intended to provide helpful groupings, not to imply watertight divisions between categories. Within each category, there is wide variation: games may be highly structured and competitive, or very open ended and strongly cooperative. Likewise, simulations may be very large scale, realistic, and compelling, or quite limited, abstracted, and low-key.

2.2 Role Play

Role play refers to a group of techniques in which participants are asked to accept a different identity, to try to think their way into someone else's situation and, perhaps, into their mind as well. Simulation/games often allocate different roles to the participants by issuing them with role cards bearing the name, age, and occupation of the person they are to represent. It might seem tempting to show role play in Fig. 1 as yet another overlapping rectangle, with role-playing simulation games like RAILWAY PIONEERS at the intersection of all three.

Such an extension of Fig. 1 might seem logically tidy, but it would be misleading: role play is a matter of degree, encompassing a spectrum even wider than simulation or gaming. Roles may be spelled out in great detail with extensive and convincing background material, so that participants are encouraged to take on other personalities vividly and sustain the performance over long periods. This is tantamount to unscripted acting; indeed there is no sharp boundary between such role play and improvised theatre. More commonly in educational role-playing exercises, roles will be sketched in outline only, and concerned more with prescribing function than personality. In RAILWAY PIONEERS the participants are expected to behave like a chairperson or a treasurer, but not to take on any particular personality for the purpose.

Finally, some exercises which are loosely described as role playing do not really ask participants to take on new roles at all, but merely to imagine themselves into a new situation and anticipate how they would respond to it. In HUMANUS, for instance, participants are expected to play themselves. This kind of simulation is sometimes called situation play to distinguish it from the kind of role-playing exercise where role cards are handed out with a new name, sex, age, and occupation for each person.

3. Advantages and Disadvantages

3.1 Motivation

The most consistent experience of teachers and trainers who use simulation/gaming is that their students find the experience motivating, enjoyable, or compelling, sometimes all three. This finding has withstood years of research and has tended to hold good irrespective of the type of exercise, subject matter, or age or stage of student. It does not even seem to break down when simulation/games are used frequently or repeatedly. It accounts for a large measure of their popularity with teachers as well as with students. Many teachers have seized with gratitude upon a technique which generates laughter, argument, even passion among students who tend to greet the most carefully prepared chalk-and-talk with an ill-concealed yawn.

The degree of involvement produced by a simulation seems to relate to its degree of realism, its duration, and to the initial attitudes and experience of the participants. Role-playing simulations can be particularly compelling, but they do require an initial commitment by the participants, and skilled supportive behaviour by the teacher. The motivational power of a game depends partly on how it challenges the players, partly on whether it appeals to their sense of fantasy or curiosity. The element of challenge often depends on the use of an appropriate difficulty level and scoring system. It is also important that the role of chance is not excessive, though most players prefer some random element in a game. In computer games, enjoyability seems to depend especially on the appropriate use of sound effects and animated graphics, player control over difficulty level and speed, and automatic computer score-keeping (Malone 1981).

Doubts have been voiced that games can be too motivating, that players are more concerned with winning than with learning, and that schools should discourage, not exacerbate, children's natural competitiveness. These are genuine concerns, but they lie outside the scope of this article. Many other educational practices encourage competition—notably sports days and examinations. Whether any such practices are harmless or unjustifiable is a matter for debate. Similarly, the problem of children and adults who become computer "addicts" goes far beyond the responsibility of simulation/gamers.

3.2 Learning

In discussing how effectively simulation/games promote learning, it will be necessary to distinguish the different roles they perform in different subjects. Nonsimulation games have been found valuable in mathematics, language teaching, and science as a palatable way of providing practice and consolidation of material already presented by other means. CIRCUITRON is a good example of this kind, where after the game has been introduced, pupils can use the game frequently, filling in short time-slots, perhaps alternating between game playing and using live apparatus. It is not intended that they discover the laws governing electric current flow from the game, merely that they use it for rapid revision, rehearsal, and remedial practice. Its considerable instructional effectiveness in this role has been demonstrated empirically (Megarry 1977).

A number of such studies have shown that games are an effective and efficient method of reinforcing student learning in science, language teaching, and mathematics. However, the laws of physics, grammar, and mathematics are all good examples of finite systems for which it is particularly easy to design games with rules which embody those laws. They also easily lend themselves to tests of student learning.

Most simulations and simulation games are intended to produce rather different kinds of learning. Teachers are sometimes as concerned with the process of learning as with its end product. To take an extreme example of this, in group work, tutors often use them to "heighten self-awareness", "work off tensions", or "increase empathy". Aims like these are very hard to assess "objectively" or quantitatively, other than by recording participants' comments after the exercises. These suggest that in the right hands, simulation/games can be very effective instruments of personal and interpersonal learning.

However, most of what is taught in secondary schools and colleges falls between these two extremes. Frequently simulation/games are used both because they lead to detectable improvements in the students' knowledge and skills after playing and also because the process undergone is considered to be valuable in itself. For example, most simulations involve at least some element of practising verbal skills. However much geography and history may be involved in RAILWAY PIONEERS, there can be no doubt about the vital role of discussion, negotiation, and persuasion.

In the course of many simulations, participants are obliged to draw on their knowledge from a variety of disciplines and bring it to bear on the problem in hand. This integrative quality makes simulation/games especially valuable in interdisciplinary studies in secondary and higher education. Problems like the routing of a motorway or the siting of a nuclear power station lend themselves naturally to role-playing simulation. They may be used at the start of a course, to arouse motivation and raise questions, or at the end, as a culmination and summary—or perhaps as both. The frequency with which participants recall incidents from such major simulations months, or even years, later does suggest that when they are successful, there is a peculiarly personal quality about the learning.

This section has asserted that simulation/games can assist learning, sometimes quite powerfully. Although its claims can be supported by evidence gathered since the early 1970s, naturally the method cannot guarantee success. There are some very badly designed simulation/games in circulation, just as there are poor audiovisual aids and bad teachers. In fact, the evidence is that participative exercises are particularly dependent on the qualities of the teacher running them. Compared with traditional methods, simulation/games are not only greater achievements when they go well, they are also probably worse disasters when they go badly. Nevertheless, on balance, there is little real doubt that simulation/games can promote learning as well as motivating it. The disadvantages of the technique are more in the heavy demands it makes on teachers and on the curriculum.

3.3 Heavy Demands

Adoption is difficult for any innovation which demands changes in the organization of the institution or variations in how teachers operate. Simulation/gaming does both. One major problem is that it is greedy for time. Many simulations need several hours to run to completion, and some take days. In an overcrowded syllabus, dominated by the pressure of outside examinations, this effectively rules them out for many teachers. Some exercises, whose designers seem oblivious of the demands of institutional timetables, require long unbroken periods. Enthusiasts justify the lengthy stretches of time by saying that there is a different quality of learning as a result. But unless they are able to convince the syllabus designers and examining bodies of this claim, many teachers will understandably feel that time simply cannot be spared for such luxuries.

The method makes other demands, too. Some of the

materials are expensive, many are difficult to store, some require a number of extra props or a rearrangement of the furniture, or a particular number of participants. Many simulation/games generate a good deal of noise, and this is often unpopular in schools and colleges run on traditional lines.

However, the greatest single obstacle to the widespread adoption of simulation/gaming is perhaps the demands it makes on the teacher. It takes time and energy for a teacher to select a suitable exercise and become familiar with it. It may take even more energy to rearrange rooms, classes, and other activities to meet its organizational requirements. Above all, both running the exercise and guiding the discussion afterwards may demand skills in which the teacher has not been trained, and may involve handling delicate situations of which she or he has no previous experience. Confidence is perhaps as important as skill in the running of such exercises. If keeping order is a concern of the teacher's, and disrupting it a sport for the class, some simulation/games provide unrivalled opportunities for chaos. When discipline is a problem, many teachers understandably "regress" to chalk-and-talk.

There is, of course, a positive side to the change in the teacher's role; some teachers are uncomfortable with the role of fount of all knowledge and source of all discipline. Some prefer a role in which they facilitate learning, rather than dispensing it. Some also prefer the illusion that constraints on behaviour come from the rules of the game, rather than from their personal or institutional authority. However, the belief that the introduction of such exercises in itself makes classrooms somehow more democratic is misleading (Megarry 1978). Examples of the skills which teachers need to prepare for, run, and follow up a simulation/game are considered further in the next section.

3.4 Other Pros and Cons

A wide variety of other claims and counterclaims are made about specific simulations and games. Some of the more important are summarized here. First, they can be especially useful when objectives include changing students' attitudes—a task on which traditional lessons and lectures have proved rather ineffective. It might seem that role-playing exercises would be especially valuable, but they can backfire all too easily, and should be treated with caution. For example, in experiments which try to combat prejudice against minority groups, notable success has been found with exercises which get the teacher to "discriminate" against an arbitrarily selected part of the class—for example, those with blue eyes, or with surnames in the first half of the alphabet (Christiansen 1979). However, some studies have shown that if students are encouraged to act out the role of oppressor, this can increase discriminatory attitudes however well-intentioned is the exercise and the discussion afterwards.

Another feature of simulations is the way in which they abstract from reality. While some simplification may be essential if students are to grasp the role of the United Nations, for example, there is a real danger that students emerge from a simulation with some misconceptions unless the discussion afterwards explicitly considers the ways in which the exercise was, and was not, realistic. Nevertheless, simulations can be very valuable in providing students who would never otherwise have to make decisions about, say, international relations, with vicarious experience. They also allow people who will have to cope with difficult or dangerous situations after training—like student teachers and airline pilots—to experiment with different approaches in a "safe" situation.

One problem which requires sensitive handling is presented by those few students who reject or dislike the technique. Whether or not they can voice or act on their distaste depends on the climate of the institution and their relationship with the teacher. However, it is obvious that most such exercises require much more active participation from the students than the average lesson or lecture. Students should not be forced or dragooned into playing roles. Quite apart from their rights as human beings—and in playing a role, each of us is obliged to disclose something of ourselves—the results are likely to be wooden and stereotyped. Even willing role players may, through inexperience, lack of preparation, or poor handling of the exercise, have difficulty in embracing their roles and mounting a convincing performance. However, a carefully structured process of introduction can overcome most, if not all, difficulties (van Ments 1983).

Great care should be taken over the specification and giving out of roles. Role allocation can be a creative opportunity for the teacher to cater for individual differences, or it can be a more dubious process in which the teacher's prejudices about the capabilities of different students (or of males and females) are reinforced and propagated. This reflects the fact that powerful techniques can be harnessed in positive or negative ways, and that the teacher's personal style and value system is the most important single influence on the students. Even in nonsimulation games, teachers will differ greatly in how they handle individual differences in ability and how publicly students' scores are proclaimed.

One disadvantage of many simulation/games is the unnecessary complexity of their rules and procedures. This is not only off-putting for the teacher, who has to master them all in order to act as a referee. It is also time wasting for the students, who are there to learn about politics or geography, not how to play games. Of course, some "irrelevant learning" is essential for the technique to work at all—just as students have to take some time to learn how to use a microcomputer before they can benefit from computer-assisted learning. But game designers are apt to get carried away with their own ingenuity; they should never forget that the cost of the "irrelevant learning" must be set off against the overall effectiveness. A game would have to be

extremely powerful to justify rules that take 10 minutes to read and an hour to understand.

4. Preparation and Use

The only firm rule for the teacher/facilitator who wants to use simulation/gaming is that there are no firm rules. Neither the suggestions below nor the rules stated by the designer are sacrosanct. A degree of improvisation is often desirable and sometimes necessary, according to how the classroom events unfold. Nevertheless, the following guidelines have been a useful starting point for many "first-timers".

4.1 Preparation

Careful preparation is essential, and a "dry run" helpful. The teacher will need a clear grasp of the administrative needs (time, numbers, arrangement of furniture, props, and so on) as well as a full understanding of the rules.

4.2 Introduction

Introducing the game requires special thought. Nothing is more boring and ineffective than reading out rules at length. A short demonstration, dummy run, or audiovisual sequence may help students to get the idea far more quickly and thoroughly. Computer-based games often benefit by having a built-in demonstration sequence, as long as it is easily by-passed once it is no longer appropriate.

4.3 Assigning Roles

Role allocation involves thorny problems (see previous section). The teacher should decide in advance whether to pre-empt role choices. In any event, participants should be given as long as possible to "feel" their way into their roles, and possibly some kind of warm-up exercise.

4.4 Observers

It is often useful to recruit observers from among the students at the start. It can be an excellent solution to the problem of the reluctant participant (see Sect. 3), since they take no part in the action. Research studies suggest that such observers seem to learn as much if not more than the participants. They may also perceive things which are not noticed by the teacher, who has many concerns and cannot be everywhere at once. In some simulation/games there is so much happening at the same time that an observer will be needed for each major group, or even to "shadow" key individuals. The use of a checklist identifying key questions may be useful to observers at the time, and will also help them to focus their reporting back afterwards.

4.5 Intervention

Intervention while the exercise is in progress should be avoided if possible. The whole point of an open-ended exercise is to allow students to make their own decisions and experience the consequences. In general, the teacher will use the time when the exercise is running to gather material for the discussion afterwards—issues, questions, perhaps verbatim quotes. Sometimes participants' direct questions about the rules or strategy are better deflected back to them. Nevertheless, there are bound to be occasions when intervention is unavoidable. If the exercise involves role play, the teacher should consider whether to intervene in a plausible role, rather than breaking in "as teacher". Role players could hardly be expected to sustain their roles for long if they were continually interrupted by an insensitive teacher.

4.6 Discussion

The discussion after a simulation is a vitally important part of the exercise. (By contrast, nonsimulation games may need little or no discussion, especially if used repeatedly.) However, in one-off simulations, empirical studies have shown that it is in the discussion afterwards that participants make sense of their experiences and much of the learning takes place. Neophytes often make the great mistake of becoming so engrossed in the simulation itself that they leave too little time for this vital stage, which can profitably occupy one-third to one-half of the time taken to run the simulation.

Although this concluding discussion is often called a "debriefing", it has little in common with the outpouring of military information that this term might suggest. There are up to four separate tasks which may be attempted:

(a) Participants and observers may want or need to talk about what happened.

(b) The teacher will want players to relate the simulation events to reality, and question how far the outside world is, or ought to be, like the model of it that was built into the simulation. This need is perhaps especially urgent in the case of a computer-based simulation, as the computer is often seen as having a kind of spurious infallibility.

(c) A wider ranging discussion of the similarities and differences between the exercise and the real world, and of their implications, may be appropriate.

(d) The teacher or the participants may want to stand outside the exercise and discuss its good and bad points, suggesting how it could be modified or extended.

All too many "debriefings" vacillate uncertainly between some or all of these tasks, perplexing would-be contributors in the process. In addition to the skills involved in running any group discussion, the teacher running a simulation/game discussion needs to combine clear thinking about the agenda with enough sensitivity to modify it in the light of the participants' responses.

4.7 Follow-up

Like any other teaching technique, simulation/games need to be integrated into the curriculum as a whole. Without appropriate follow-up activities, like films or field trips, a large-scale simulation is in danger of becoming a mere diversion from the main business of education. Used at the start of a course of study, however, such an exercise can provide a rich fund of shared first-hand experience on which subsequent lessons can draw freely.

5. Adaptation and Design

The process of designing an educational simulation/game is not very different from that of designing any game. There are surprisingly few original basic structures. The process of adopting or adapting the right structure to achieve a satisfying result consists of a large amount of trial-and-error together with a dash of inspiration. Whether the origins of the idea are in the bath or a dream, what determines whether it is any use or not is the hard work which follows in the classroom, trying out pilot versions, listening to guinea-pigs' reactions, polishing, and tidying up.

Although a number of authors have published ambitious flow charts purporting to give "a systems approach to designing games", there is little if any evidence that game designers operate like this. Nowadays, even educational technologists are beginning to admit that instructional objectives are often framed retrospectively if at all, rather than universally and in advance as they used to insist. In any event, it seems particularly unlikely that the designer of an open-ended exercise could start by defining objectives. Often it is not until the game has been played a number of times that the designer will be at all confident about what will happen, let alone what will be learned.

The sad truth is that after years of research since the beginning of the simulation and gaming movement, much more is known about how not to design a game than how to do it well. Two authors, Shirts (1976) and Megarry (1976), have identified 20 common mistakes in game design, summarized below. Many of these points apply equally to the design of simulations.

(a) Accept that design is not a linear process; the different parts interact.

(b) Game design involves many skills. A co-worker can be helpful, as long as he or she is constructive.

(c) Keep options for different structures open as long as possible; premature closure is a mistake.

(d) Do not attempt to define precise instructional objectives at the outset; at best they will change, at worst they will inhibit the design process.

(e) If the game is commissioned by a sponsor, do not accept what may be unrealistic and mutually incompatible demands.

(f) If the game is a simulation, do not get "straight-jacketed" by reality. Maximum realism is neither attainable nor necessarily desirable.

(g) Do not expect the same simulation to work well for education and for research; the criteria are different.

(h) Ensure that the use of chance factors is appropriate; although some random element may be desirable, never use chance as a substitute for careful design or to reduce player's autonomy.

(i) Ensure that players are encouraged to take responsibility for their own actions and decisions in the exercise. They should never feel that their decisions are pre-empted by stereotyped roles or "unreal" game constraints.

(j) If a game is worth developing, it is worth taking to completion; this means extensive testing and a teacher's manual which passes the "stranger test"— that is, the game can be run successfully by a stranger, without the designer's intervention.

(k) It is safe to assume that students will process only that information which is necessary for them to proceed. Too many games assume that information printed on the game materials will be learned by a process akin to osmosis.

(l) A scoring system should reflect the difficulty of the task, and should never be arbitrary nor merely reward speed.

(m) A satisfying game will teach and not merely test; a game which can only be played by those who have mastered its contents will attract few players.

(n) The structure of the game should have some relationship to its content.

(o) The game should make positive suggestions about how to introduce it to students for the first time.

(p) Many games can with benefit be differentiated into a graded series of games of increasing difficulty or complexity, rather than be presented as a single game.

(q) The scoring system should be a natural and integral part of the game, not added on as an afterthought like a car accessory.

(r) Success in a game should not be possible by use of cues which are irrelevant to the task—for example, matching the shape or colour of the card should not allow players to work out which quadratic equation belongs with which graph.

(s) Before a game is finalized, the quality of its physical props must be adequate to its task; too many games are let down by unwieldy equipment, undealable cards, illegible print, and so on.

(t) A well-designed game is a process as well as a product. The ideas and mistakes which contributed to that process should be shared, rather than passed off as an immaculate conception.

It is perhaps clear that designing a good educational simulation/game from scratch is a time-consuming and specialized business. Fortunately, although there are few really original structures for such exercises around, most can easily be adapted to work with different subject matter. Indeed some games, known as "frame games", are deliberately designed to be content-free; they are evaluated in Thiagarajan and Stolovitch (1979). Their use raises similar issues to that of computer software which is said to be "content-free". Even the humblest card game, like rummy, can be a surprisingly fertile source of games for use in different branches of science (Megarry 1975a, 1975b). Thus whereas game design may be a minority skill, adapting games is a much more promising approach, for which less dedication is needed.

One specific form of adaptation was alluded to in Sect. 2: whether the use of a computer would be of benefit. A game like CIRCUITRON may be successful in "manual" form, but it may nevertheless benefit from the use of a computer to relieve participants of all the games' routine administration—keeping scores, generating random "hands" of pieces, adjusting difficulty levels, and so on. In fact, the educational effectiveness of CIRCUITRON was found to be increased by being computer based, since the computer was able to give faster and more consistent feedback than was possible from teacher or peers. The contribution of the microcomputer to simulation/gaming is considered in depth by Walker and Graham (1979).

6. Evaluation

Since the early 1970s, educational evaluation has been going through a period of intense self-scrutiny and heated methodological debate. The evaluation of simulation/games is especially problematic. A traditional input/output model concerning itself with immediate and measurable end products is peculiarly inappropriate to assessing the effects and value of open-ended simulation/games. The unique course of each play of the game, the effect of a particular role play "performance", the extent of participants' input into each simulation—all these make nonsense of the rhetoric of replication, sampling, and the like.

Furthermore, few techniques can be more dependent on the skills, attitude, and personal style of the teacher. Again, the highly interactive nature of the activity makes the notion of "matching" classes on various criteria more than usually nonsensical. The social revolution effected by the creation of new classes specially for the experiment can confidently be expected to outweigh and disguise any differences between the teaching methods under test. It is a little like trying to compare the handling of badminton shuttlecocks in a howling gale.

Nevertheless, so strong was the grip of the psychometric tradition that a great deal of time and money was invested in fruitless comparative experiments purporting to discover which was "better", simulation/gaming or traditional methods. These were fruitless because, as argued above, the variability of simulation/games and of teachers' attitudes and skills in running them make consistent results unlikely. Hence it was scarcely surprising that Megarry (1978) reported that the results of over 150 such studies were "evenly distributed" between those that found games more effective, those that found games less effective, and those that found "no significant differences". More inappropriate still in these studies was the use of learning of factual material as the main criterion of effectiveness, when most simulation/games are designed to promote other kinds of learning like learning from personal experience, bringing about long-term changes in attitude, and developing new perspectives and conceptual frameworks. Such aims are not easily detected by conventional measurement techniques; and the use of simulations in conjunction with other teaching methods also makes measurement of their distinctive contribution difficult.

During the 1970s, a spate of new evaluation models were introduced that gave attention more to process than to outcome, and these would appear to be better suited for evaluating simulation/games (see *Program Evaluation*). Though there is no clear consensus about which model to use, some attention has at least been given to the use of observational evidence. For example, the results recorded by observers on suitable checklists (see Sect. 4.4) can be used both for debriefing and for evaluation. Another technique which has been taken up by game evaluators is the instructional interview in which a student's attitudes and understandings are probed by a tutor. Though not usually yielding statistical data this technique has been used to good effect by Piaget, by Bruner, and by clinical psychologists (see *Evaluation of Learning Resources*).

Of more immediate help to many teachers are the review columns of journals such as *Simulation/Games for Learning* and critical entries in one of the major directories (Stadsklev 1975, Horn and Cleaves 1980). Unfortunately, only well-known and published games are likely to find their way into such columns. Moreover, as with literary or theatrical criticism, no matter how scrupulously fair the reviewer and editor try to be, there are obvious dangers of bias or eccentricity. Review panels working from an agreed checklist are one possible way of mitigating this problem. It is a sad reflection on the poverty-stricken state of evaluation that such sources have nevertheless been a stronger influence on teachers' decision making about simulation/games than the results of empirical studies.

7. Further Information

Following the rapid growth since the beginning of the simulation and gaming movement, simulation/games have become widely established as a motivating and effective technique in a variety of subjects and with many different kinds of students. Readers interested in specific application areas in English-speaking countries should consult an appropriate resource list published by the Society for the Advancement of Games and Simulations in Education and Training (SAGSET) (various dates) or check abstracts of journals like *Simulation and Games* (USA), *Simgames* (Canada), *Simulation/Games for Learning* (UK), all of which carry articles and reviews.

Finally, here are some accessible books and articles giving short-cut introductions to the field. Of the many general texts, that by Taylor and Walford (1978) gives a good idea of the state of the art in the 1970s, especially in the United Kingdom and the United States. Many articles do likewise for various other countries, for example Diehl (1979) surveys the field in Australia. Contributed volumes are less easily digested but more useful on specific aspects; two American ones, edited by Boocock and Schild (1968) and Dukes and Seidner (1978), have stood the test of time. Two recent books by Milroy (1982) and van Ments (1983) provide valuable introductions to the theory and practice of role play; and Jones' (1980) primer is excellent on the simulation end of the spectrum. Other books cover related fields like war gaming (Wilson 1970) and theatre games (Barker 1977).

There is an extensive literature on using these techniques with adults, covering vocational as well as strictly educational applications. Megarry (1980) surveys the whole spectrum of techniques in teacher education, while others cover urban studies and town planning (Taylor 1971), library administration (Zachert 1975), health education (Hay 1981), and management and business education (Gray and Waitt 1982, Elgood 1981).

At the school level, many sources contain ideas for exercises in different subject areas, and some contain ready-to-use materials (e.g. Davison and Gordon 1978). For primary education, games to teach writing and mathematics are described by Kohl (1977); Brown (1982) advocates the adaptation of exercises intended for secondary education to promote international understanding in this age group. At secondary level, the sources are legion: simulation games may be based on Canadian history (Cavanagh 1976) or British (Birt and Nichol 1975). Geographical simulation games flourish in the United Kingdom (Walford 1969) and Canada (Wood 1976). Clarke (1978) describes their use to teach international relations and Benson (1971) in religious education. Mathematics and science are covered by contributions in Dukes and Seidner (1978) and by Ellington et al. (1981). Social subjects predominate in all the general texts, especially Boocock and Schild (1968) and Greenblat and Duke (1975); the latter collection also has articles about community education. Communication skills receive special emphasis from Jones (1980) and Davison and Gordon (1978).

However, most simulation gamers would agree that any interested newcomer would learn more from taking part in one simulation game than from reading all of the above.

Bibliography

Barker C 1977 *Theatre Games: A New Approach to Drama Training.* Methuen, London

Benson D 1971 *Gaming: The Fine Art of Creating Simulation/ Learning Games for Religious Education.* Abingdon Press, Nashville, Tennessee

Birt D, Nichol J 1975 *Games and Simulations in History.* Longman, London

Boocock S S, Schild E O 1968 *Simulation Games in Learning.* Sage, Beverly Hills, California

Brown M 1982 Simulation and gaming in the primary school. *Simul. Games Learn.* 12(4): 151–56

Cavanagh T K 1976 *Simulation Gaming in Canadian History.* Progressive Publications, Sherbrooke, Quebec

Christiansen K 1979 How the ABZ games work. *Simul. Games Learn.* 9(3): 107–16

Clarke M 1978 *Simulations in the Study of International Relations.* Hesketh, Ormskirk

Coombs D H 1980 Simulation/gaming journals: A review of the field. *Simul. Games Learn.* 10(2): 60–66

Davison A, Gordon P 1978 *Games and Simulations in Action.* Woburn Press, London

Diehl B J 1979 Current simulation gaming in Australia. *Simul. Games* 10(3): 265–74

Dukes R L, Seidner C J (eds.) 1978 *Learning with Simulations and Games.* Sage, Beverly Hills, California

Elgood C 1981 *Handbook of Management Games,* 2nd edn. Gower, Farnborough

Ellington H I, Addinall E, Percival F 1981 *Games and Simulations in Science Education.* Kogan Page, London

Gray L, Waitt I 1982 *Simulation in Management and Business Education.* Kogan Page, London

Greenblat C S, Duke R D 1975 *Gaming Simulation: Rationale, Design, and Applications: A Text with Parallel Readings for Social Scientists, Educators, and Community Workers.* Wiley, New York

Hay C 1981 Games and simulations in health education. *Simul. Games Learn.* 11(2): 68–74

Horn R E, Cleaves A (eds.) 1980 *The Guide to Simulations/ Games for Education and Training,* 4th edn. Sage, Beverly Hills, California

Jones K 1980 *Simulations: A Handbook for Teachers.* Kogan Page, London

Kohl H R 1977 *Writing, Maths and Games in the Open Classroom.* Methuen, London

Malone T W 1981 What makes computer games fun? *Byte* 6(2): 258–77

Megarry J 1975a A review of science games: Variations on a theme of Rummy. In: Dukes R L, Seidner C J (eds.) 1978 *Learning with Simulations and Games.* Sage, Beverley Hills, California, pp. 84–98

Megarry J 1975b Some notes on using HUMANUS with British participants. *SAGSET J.* 5(4): 151–56

Megarry J 1976 Ten further "mistakes" made by simulation and game designers. *SAGSET J.* 6(3): 87–92

Megarry J 1977 CIRCUITRON: An electric circuit game. In: Megarry J (ed.) 1977 *Aspects of Simulation and Gaming,* Kogan Page, London, pp. 47–53

Megarry J 1978 Retrospect and prospect. In: McAleese R (ed.) 1978 *Perspectives on Academic Gaming and Simulation.* Kogan Page, London, pp. 187–207

Megarry J 1980 Selected innovations in methods of teacher education. *World Yearbook of Education 1980: Professional Development of Teachers.* Kogan Page, London

Milroy E 1982 *Role-play: A Practical Guide.* Aberdeen University Press, Aberdeen

Shirts R G 1976 Ten "mistakes" commonly made by persons designing educational simulations and games. *SAGSET J.* 5(4): 147–50

Society for the Advancement of Games and Simulations in Education and Training (SAGSET) (various dates), Centre for Extension Studies, Loughborough, LE11 3TU, UK. Publishes many specialized resource lists, annual conference proceedings, quarterly journal *Simulation/Games for Learning* (formerly *SAGSET J.*)

Stadsklev R 1975 *Handbook of Simulation Gaming in Social Education,* Pt. 2: *Directory.* University of Alabama, Tuscaloosa, Alabama

Taylor J L 1971 *Instructional Planning Systems: A Gaming–Simulation Approach to Urban Problems.* Cambridge University Press, Cambridge

Taylor J L, Walford R 1978 *Learning and the Simulation Game.* Open University Press, Milton Keynes

Thiagarajan S, Stolovitch H D 1979 Frame games: An evaluation. *Simul. Games* 10(3): 287–314

van Ments M 1983 *The Effective Use of Role-play.* Kogan Page, London

Walford R 1969 *Games in Geography.* Longman, London

Walker D R F, Graham L 1979 Simulation games and the microcomputer. *Simul. Games Learn.* 9: 151–58

Wilson A 1970 *War Gaming.* Penguin, Harmondsworth

Wood C J B 1976 *Handbook of Geographical Games.* University of Victoria Press, Victoria, British Columbia

Zachert M J K 1975 *Simulation Teaching of Library Administration.* Bowker, New York

Distance Education

Children's Television

F. B. Rainsberry

Children's television covers the whole spectrum of programming in all its dimensions of storytelling, information, education, music, and light entertainment. This article surveys problems in the planning and production of television programmes for children and related issues which concern parents and professional leaders who work with children. A description of the kinds of agencies and international organizations which exist for the advocacy and promotion of better television for children is given. Rather than attempting an examination of research into children's television, certain issues concerning the nature of research in this area are raised for the reader's consideration.

1. The Spectrum of Children's Television

As was the case in radio programming, television for children has universally been scheduled as educational/instructional or entertainment/commercial programming. There is a certain contradiction in this persistent classification, since the distinction implies an adult judgment that education is a formal, institutional, and demanding enterprise and that entertainment implies some kind of escape from the duty to be educated; entertainment appeals to the viewer or listener as evoking only passive responses to the medium permitting relaxation rather than demanding any kind of energetic participation in the presentation. Children by nature do not make this distinction until later in their development since they seem to meet every event in their lives as a challenge to creative action. They rarely react passively to their environment if they are normal active children from any culture.

The distinction between educational television and television for the purpose of informal entertainment places the responsibility for programming in the hands of educators and general broadcasters respectively. Parental concern is focused largely on the area of entertainment programming because the programmes are received in the home and frequently without supervision.

Educational television is less controversial because it is used to implement or to enrich the school curriculum. Since the curriculum usually reflects the educational intentions, and the social and cultural values of governments and their people for the education of their children, there is much less likelihood of hostile public reaction. The only opponents are to be found among those who oppose the use of any medium other than the formal classroom with an emphasis on the three "R's"—reading, writing, and arithmetic. In this latter case, the only objection is met by putting heavy emphasis on information. In some countries, the emphasis will be on experiential content intended to evoke cognitive, affective, or creative responses from children. In other countries, the medium is employed for specific didactic purposes—political, cultural, or religious.

In the early stages of the development of educational television for children much emphasis was placed on the efficiency of television as a delivery system, often reducing the role of the teacher in the classroom to a secondary position. This phenomenon was most extreme in the United States where the Ford Foundation spent millions of dollars in several cities to demonstrate the effectiveness of television to present "master teachers" as models for the classroom teacher for the better instruction of children. At the same time a more centralized curriculum could be introduced ensuring more direct control over the process of education in the classroom. Extensive use of television to present "master teachers" extended from the elementary to postsecondary educational institutions. While research studies indicated for the most part that students learned as well from television as from direct teaching in the classrooms, students still indicated a preference for direct teaching. Perhaps the most satisfactory compromise arose in situations where the subject matter presented on television contained significant input from classroom teachers and where the television presentation gave the classroom teacher more time for individual instruction.

Today, educational television is seen as a complement to classroom teaching. The learner remains at the centre of the teaching–learning process and material presented on television is selected because it enriches the classroom presentation by means of carefully planned visual production. Educational personnel concerned with the use of television in the classrooms are increasingly learning to work with studio production personnel in order to gain the maximum benefits from the presentation. Creative educators recognize that the classroom as a medium of educational communication requires a certain ordering of subject matter in order to ensure that the maximum number of students experience the most intense learning. The television studio requires a completely different selection and ordering of material to achieve the same degree of learning. In both situations—the classroom and the studio—there are both social and aesthetic considerations which will contribute significantly to the motivation of the learner and to the meaningfulness of the learning experiences. Regardless of the medium of communication, its effectiveness in terms of education and human development will always be a function of concern for the viewer and the artistic presentation of the content or subject matter.

Many of the problems arising from the viewing of television can be resolved in terms of understanding how a television production is made. As long as very little is known about the organization and planning of a television show, it is difficult to criticize what programme fare is offered. If there is no awareness of the significance of human relationships presented in the sequence, and montage of camera shots, the correlation of set design with camera angles, or the social and cultural values of the production team which are reflected in the presentation, meaningful assessments of the impact of television on the individual, the family, and on society cannot be made. As well as the need to understand techniques of production, the viewer needs to know much more about the economic constraints on the producer. If commercial messages as a source of revenue are abandoned, is the public willing to pay for quality through taxation or direct licence fees? If research shows that violent action or an endless sequence of dramatic series flawed by over-idealized human relationships are much in demand by the public, does the broadcasting agency, private or public, turn its back on these demands? In the end, the ultimate challenge is to raise public consciousness about the importance of quality in television and film production.

2. Programme Formats for Children's Television

In every country of the world there are various formats for the presentation of programmes for children viewed out of school hours. In scheduling those programmes, age groupings are taken into consideration. Programmes for preschool children are presented during the morning or from mid-afternoon. The major grouping is for children aged 6 to 12 years. In North America and Australia children above this age are chiefly attracted to adult programmes while in Europe, Asia, and Africa there is a greater attempt to design programmes for

older children. In North America, the United Kingdom, and Australia there is considerable emphasis on "family entertainment" as a means of attracting large audiences. At the same time, teenagers are the smallest group of viewers. When they choose to watch, they tend to select programmes which are popular with adults.

Regardless of whether the programmes are for in-school or out-of-school purposes, programmes for the younger age group predominantly feature puppets, animation, or an ingratiating host/hostess. It is thought that puppets allow children some control over action which might otherwise be overwhelming or threatening. Young viewers enter the action as manipulators and participants are often able to enjoy human behaviour in a vicarious way. It is as though puppets enable them to distance problems which might otherwise seem irresolvable.

Animation has the added advantage of simple representation, rapid action, and often elements of nonsense or absurdity which provide wit and humour at a child's level when it is well-designed and executed. As in the case of puppetry, the simplified human characters enable the child viewer to relate in direct response and with immediate understanding.

Outstanding performers with easy and outgoing personalities enable children to enter the adult world in playful, creative, and challenging ways. By means of simple language, modulated speech, careful planning, and open physical gestures, great performers from every culture are able to command the undivided attention of young viewers.

Regardless of age level or of culture, programme planners and producers who do the best programmes for children of all ages are mindful of the totality of visual experience which evokes full responses from young viewers. The sensitive producer is aware that young viewers, as well as adults, will imitate or respond to the gestures of engaging personalities or action on the television screen. In the case of children, such "imitative" responses are the foundation of language. Language as gesture builds on imitative responses. The more satisfying and the more cumulative this social interaction becomes, the more fully a child achieves maturity and a deep sense of selfhood.

In contrast to this approach is the authoritarian view of some adults or professionals who claim to know what is good for children to see on television. In a single-minded fashion it is possible to see the experiential and creative dimension of television production reduced to information selected for child viewing because it confirms the conventional mores of adults with rigid views about child growth and development. They seek to present information regardless of the child's level of comprehension, neglectful of the aesthetic properties of television production, and ignorant of the dimensions of social communication. The result is inartistic television, boring programming, and rejection of the opportunity for creative responses. Such programming is common enough among countries in both the Old World and the New as well as the Third World.

Another simplistic approach to television is the campaign to eliminate all violence from children's programmes. Instead of trying to achieve some kind of ideal world in which there is no tension (and in which individuals lack any kind of self-identity!) the creative producer seeks to present the spectrum of human action in all its varied dimensions. Life is represented on an action–motion matrix with which a child is familiar. Beginning with the typical, predictable, and naive action story in a Western, children enjoy the very predictability of the sequence of events. They participate in the action much as they enjoy the rhythm of a nursery rhyme. Such simple experiences can be more complicated based on more significant human relationships. As children develop confidence in their responses to adults both on television, in their families, and among the members of their peer groups, they become ready for fuller dramatic experience in which they can cope with violence and other negative external forces which threaten those whom they love or respect. Here again the aesthetic factor becomes important as the producer enables the viewer to control his responses to the action of a drama by arranging lighting, camera shots, angles, and the sound so as to permit the right degree of aesthetic distance. Unnecessary violent action generates anxiety and uncontrollable tension resulting in feelings of fear, distrust, and insecurity. From this discussion it is possible to see how it is more important to differentiate between aggression or violence for its own sake and genuine dramatic action which focuses the viewer's attention on the realities of human behaviour in extreme situations.

Programme formats for children of the middle years (ages 6 to 12) are usually dramatic series or magazine programmes with a major host/hostess along with experts in various fields of activity, information, or entertainment. The major broadcasting networks produce dramatic series which they aim to distribute to other networks. These series packaged in 13, 26, or 52 episodes, well-planned and well-produced, are a boon to any broadcaster who does not have sufficient studio facilities to produce all the original programming required. A healthy interdependence exists in this area.

The magazine format permits variety in action, information, and participation. In some cases, young viewers contribute ideas for the magazine. Such a format allows for the presentation of public figures who are popular with children. Causes can be supported, clubs can be formed, and new information on subjects ranging from music to sports can be presented in an interesting way.

3. Agencies Concerned with Children's Television

Across the world there are agencies concerned with raising the quality and increasing the quantity of good programmes for children. The Prix Jeunesse International is held biennially in Munich for the exhibition of out-of-school programmes for children while the Prix Japon is held on alternate years in Japan for the exhibition of in-school or instructional programmes. Both agencies were founded in the 1960s and both have achieved a high level of prestige among broadcasters and educators concerned with the potential of television as a significant force in the creative growth and development of children.

In North America two major organizations exist for the purpose of improving television for children. Action for Children's Television (ACT) was founded in Newton, Massachusetts, in 1968 for the expressed goals of pressuring and persuading broadcasters and advertisers to provide programming of the highest possible quality designed for children of different ages. Action for Children's Television seeks to encourage the development and enforcement of guidelines relating to children and media and to encourage research, experimentation, and evaluation in the field of children's television. Action for Children's Television is a national organization dedicated to child-oriented television of high quality and free of commercial messages. The organization publishes a magazine, *Re-Act*, designed to inform concerned parents and the public about the world of children's television in the United States. Annually, the organization sponsors a national conference which focuses on issues of contemporary significance in the area of production and research into children's television. Since the broadcasting air waves in the United States are dominated by the major private networks, except for the educational television stations operating under the Public Broadcasting System, the relationship of ACT to the major networks is somewhat adversarial. However, since the early 1970s, mutual respect has developed between the two enterprises and ACT emerges as a significant force for quality in American children's television.

The Children's Broadcast Institute (CBI) was founded in Canada in 1974. Unlike the United States, Canada has a major publicly owned broadcasting network, the Canadian Broadcasting Corporation (CBC), along with two private networks. All of these networks carry commercially sponsored programmes although the CBC has the major responsibility to provide a balanced programme service to the whole country. While the concerns for quality in children's programmes are the same as in the United States and the rest of the world, the Children's Broadcast Institute has taken a somewhat different approach to the achievement of this goal than has Action for Children's Television. Instead of adopting an adversarial role, the CBI operates with a board of directors made up of representatives of both public and private broadcasting, the advertising agencies, the product manufacturers (of toys, cereals, and other goods consumed by children), and the major voluntary public service agencies concerned with the welfare of children. To avoid the excesses which prompted the necessity for and creation of an organization like ACT, the board of directors of the CBI aims to anticipate the excesses which may have negative effects upon children. Like ACT they exhibit children's programmes at a festival (every second year) and have established an award of merit for programmes of outstanding quality. They have conducted a series of workshops for parents and teachers who wish to learn more about the influence of television on children. In cooperation with the Canadian Radio and Television Commission (the national regulatory authority for broadcasting in Canada) they have published a handbook on children's television programming, which has been widely distributed and used by researchers, writers, producers, advertisers, and consumers of children's television. Every year in September as the autumn schedules of television programming appear, CBI sponsors Parents' Viewing Month featuring promotional messages urging parents to make television viewing a shared experience with their children.

In 1981, under the Ministries of Arts and Education for the Commonwealth of Australia, the Australian Children's Television Foundation was established as a national nonprofit organization to encourage the development, production, and transmission of high-quality children's television programmes. The policy is "to contribute to each child's sense of personal and national identity by presenting a diversity of faces, places, ideas, and values reflecting the rich multi-cultural heritage of Australia". The programme priorities emphasize children's drama, new formats for programmes, and diverse types of series for all age groups of children. The commonwealth and several state governments have financed the establishment of the Foundation with the understanding that it will not be reliant on government funds after 1985. The assumption was made that if only one Australian dollar per head of Australia's population was raised for the Foundation, its future would be secure.

The Foundation will undertake basic research into such problems as the role of television in the lives of disadvantaged and/or ethnic children, the economic needs of children's programming in Australia, the impact of advertising on children's values, monitoring worldwide trends in children's television, and the gathering and collating of information on programmes produced and televised from industry bodies, production companies, commercial and government research organizations, and pressure groups. The Foundation will also undertake the basic task of mass media education to help children understand and be selective in what they see, hear, and read—to cultivate a creative awareness of aesthetic values in film and television programmes.

The Foundation is a limited company with a board of directors and staff to implement its policies. Australia is the first major Western country to undertake such basic support for this development of high-quality programming in film and television for children. The Foundation may very well serve as a model for other countries with similar concerns for the welfare of children who are regularly exposed to television.

The comparison and contrast of these three organizations reflects the differences among three nations and their respective ways of licensing and controlling broadcasting. Each is effective in the environment in which they operate; and all three contrast greatly with organizations in countries where there is no commercial television, or where commercial television is very much secondary to the public enterprise. It is notable that among countries with a long cultural heritage there is a much greater impetus to use television to transmit the values and traditions of a nation which have been cherished for so long. The quantity of children's programmes is greater, although in some cases the quality leaves something to be desired, for example a greater concern to be didactic rather than creative in the presentation of programme content. In the Third World, television still suffers from lack of funds and the technical skill to do the best work. On the one hand, many of the leaders responsible for planning and production have a postcolonial mindset. On the other hand, simple productions featuring the most dynamic native traditions of the new nations have been produced. Such programmes are more refreshing than the slick but carelessly planned productions which sometimes emanate from the more dominant nations of the world. Support for the use of television for the creative growth and development of children in the less affluent countries of the world should not only entail the supply of adequate technical facilities; programme experts should work with creative production personnel to help them realize the creativity and vitality of traditions in Third World countries.

In September 1988 the OWL Centre for Children's Film and Television was established in Canada under the auspicies of the Young Naturalist Foundation. The centre is funded with a $4.25 million Founding Fund provided by the federal government of Canada and the government of the Province of Ontario. "The centre will provide a base where producers, writers and directors specializing in children's programming can strengthen their film-making skills and expand their creativity. It is hoped that this initiative will result in an increased variety of programming for young Canadians that will reflect Canada's cultural diversity and richness".

In addition to the basic programme service provided by the Canadian Broadcasting Corporation, ACCESS Alberta, TV Ontario and Radio Quebec, three new speciality channels have been added to the cable services. In Quebec, Le Canal Famille will provide recreational and entertainment programming of good quality and variety which will reflect society in a constructive manner. The channel will aim to reach 1.2 million francophone households in Quebec and will be transmitted by satellite to Eastern Canada.

Young People's Television (YTV) is scheduled on basic cable to provide a service for children and teens at times when there are presently no programmes for them. The schedule, from 7am to midnight, will be broken down as follows: 7am to 4pm, noncommercial; 4pm to 8pm, teens; 8pm to midnight, family. YTV plan to reach 3.7 million households across Canada (with the exception of Quebec). There will be a maximum of eight minutes per hour of sponsorships from advertisers in commercial messages.

A family channel is scheduled on Pay-TV. Its schedule is designed to enable families to share an emotional experience which will lead to discussion. Programmes are scheduled from 6am to 1am every day. The morning schedule is for preschool children with emphasis on music and play consistent with the aims of early childhood education. For the 6–12 year-olds, situation drama will be provided to encourage sharing and participation within the family. Classic Hollywood films for late-night viewing will follow. There will be no advertising but the channel will depend upon subscribers. The aim is to obtain 200,000 subscribers at the rate of $9.95 per month by the end of the first year of operation.

The Centre for Youth and Media Studies was created by a joint committee of the University of Montreal and the Charles R Bronfmann Foundation. Its mandate is to develop basic and applied research that will further an understanding of traditional media and new technologies for the benefit of young Canadians, be it for leisure, information, or educational programmes. The Centre views collaboration with practitioners in the field of youth and media, and with concerned individuals as essential. The mandate includes a research agenda, support for creative endeavour, and intervention in the public arena. The Centre also wishes to act as a forum to rally the talents and energies of those who share the goal of improving media fare for young people. In addition, the Centre is dedicated to research, to discovery and to quality in programming and research.

4. Problems with Research Concerning Children's Television

Most of the research into the impact of television on children has originated among behavioural scientists who seek cause–effect relationships between television viewing and child behaviour. Several elaborate studies have attempted to prove direct relationships between the viewing of violence on television and negative or destructive behaviour among children. Because of the specific focus of the study, and scientific ordering of the data, these studies tend to oversimplify the child's response to television programming. There is an exclusion of other existing forces which may affect the child's behaviour as much or more than the viewing of television.

Usually, those engaged in behavioural science are unaware of the techniques of television production and have little interest in creative endeavour. When an attempt is made to deal with subjects such as creativity, fantasy, and imagination, one is up against the problem of just what constitutes empirical evidence. How is it possible to categorize or classify a child's response to affection or to beauty manifested in colour, line, shape, or sound? What criteria can be employed to assess the importance of significant gestures in interpersonal communication?

Most scientific research into creativity fails to differentiate creative imagination from cognitive development. Most of the research literature neglects the factor of "play" as a response to the creative gestures of those who perform well for children on television.

Perhaps the most successful, long-term relationship between television production and research is to be found in the United States' Children's Television Workshop. Here, both the producer and researcher are committed to the fullest cognitive development of the young viewer. As psychologists, the researchers are readily able to measure a child's capacity for inference and for the assembly of vast quantities of information. The producers present these challenges to young viewers of this programme but very little study has been made of a child's capacity for social learning or creative expression. There is no question that the research which has been done is useful as far as it goes. The difficulty is that the somewhat narrow concern with the cognitive, physiological, neurological, and affective development of the child precludes the child's creative and social development.

The Prix Jeunesse International under the Society for the Promotion of International Youth and Television has undertaken research into children's television on a somewhat broader basis. In alternate years with the festival/contest, seminars are held to discuss current problems in the field of television for children and youth, for example, examination of criteria for the production of entertainment programmes, screen education (visual literacy), the child and the family in relation to television, and understanding prejudice—an examination of bias in the perception of "foreigners" on television.

Research studies have been related to specific children's programmes which have won prizes at the Prix Jeunesse. The studies are more sociological in character enabling the student or user of the research to see the implications of television for broad social issues in the world at large. In more recent years, the seminars have been based on the research studies making it possible to obtain firsthand reactions from producers, directors, administrators, and other professionals engaged in the production of television for children.

In spite of the efforts to correlate research, both formative and summative, to the planning and production of television programmes for children, research has had relatively little effect upon what the child sees on television. The reason for this phenomenon is that producers and directors as creative artists do not think in a scientific way. The scientist looks at the world of nature and society to classify and to reduce a vast range of particulars to single concepts. The artist looks at the same worlds to react, interact, and interpret in a unique but universal way so that all who listen, see, or feel may share in both the particularity of the artist's intense experience, while they, as spectators, can reorder their own perceptions of the world so as to have a new, fresh, and enlightened view. While the body of research in the behavioural sciences concerning child development is useful, of far greater importance is the continued consultation with writers, producers, teachers, artists, and recreation leaders in order to discover the nature of their success in the development of creative play among children and how they relate on a one-to-one basis with them. In the end, the greatest children's programmes, regardless of political, cultural, or social origin, have evoked creative ("playful") responses and have established meaningful aesthetic relationships with their young viewers.

Bibliography

Adler R P et al. 1977 *Research on the Effects of Television Advertising on Children: Review and Recommendations.* National Science Foundation, Washington, DC
Brown L K 1986 *Taking Advantage of Media: A Manual for Parents and Teachers.* Routledge and Kegan Paul, London
Canada Senate Special Committee on Mass Media 1970 *Report*, Vol. 3: *Good, Bad or Simply Inevitable?* Information Canada, Ottawa
Comstock G A, Rubenstein E A 1972a *Television and Social Behavior.* A report to the Surgeon General's Scientific Advisory Committee. 5 Vols. United States Government Printing Office, Washington, DC
Comstock G A, Rubenstein E A 1972b *Television and Social Behavior: An Annotated Bibliography of Research Focusing on Television's Impact on Children.* United States Government Printing Office, Washington, DC
Cook T D, Appleton H, Conner R F, Shaffer A, Tamkin G, Weber S J 1975 *"Sesame Street" Revisited.* Russell Sage Foundation, New York
Dorr A 1986 *Television and Children: A Special Medium for a Special Audience.* Sage, London
Halloran J D (ed.) 1976 *Mass Media and Socialization (International Bibliography and Different Perspectives).* International Association for Mass Communication. Kavanaugh, Leeds
Halloran J D, Brown R L, Chaney D C 1970 *Television and Delinquency.* Television Research Committee Working Paper 3, Leicester University Press, Leicester
Himmelweit H T, Oppenheim A N, Vince P 1961 *Television and the Child.* Oxford University Press, London
Kaye E 1974 *The Family Guide to Children's Television.* Random House, New York
Lesser G S 1974 *Children and Television.* Random House, New York
Liebert R M, Neale J M, Davidson E S 1982 *The Early Window: Effects of TV on Children and Youth.* Pergamon, New York
Melody W 1973 *Children's Television.* Yale University Press, New Haven, Connecticut
Meyer M, Nissen U 1979 *Effects and Functions of Television: Children and Adolescents.* A bibliography of selected research literature, 1970–78. Saur, Munich
Muller W, Meyer M (eds.) 1985 *Children and Families Watching Television: A Bibliography of Research on Viewing Processes.* Saur, Munich
Murray J P, Solomon G (eds.) 1984 *The Future of Children's Television.* The Boys Town Center, Communications and Public Service Division, Boys Town, Nebraska
Noble G 1975 *Children in Front of the Small Screen.* Constable, London
Prix Jeunesse International 1976 *Television and Socialization Processes in the Family.* A documentation of the Prix Jeunesse Seminar, 1975. Verlag Dokumentation, Munich
Rainsberry F B 1988 *A History of Children's Television in English Canada 1952–1986.* Scarecrow, Metuchen, New Jersey *Report of the Royal Commission on Violence in the Communications Industry*, Vols. 1–8. 1976. Publications Centre, Ministry of Government Services, Toronto, Ontario
Rogers F, Head B 1983 *Mister Rogers Talks with Parents.* Berkley Books, New York
Schramm W, Lyle J, Parker E B 1961 *Television in the Lives of Our Children.* Stanford University Press, Stanford, California
Surgeon General's Scientific Advisory Committee on Television and Social Behavior 1972 *Television and Growing Up. The Impact of Televised Violence.* United States Department of Health, Education and Welfare. United States Government Printing Office, Washington, DC
Ward S, Wackman D, Wartella E 1977 *How Children Learn to Buy: The Development of Consumer Information-processing Skills.* Sage, Beverly Hills, California
Wartella E 1979 *Children Communicating.* Media and Development of Thought, Speech and Understanding. Sage, Beverly Hills, California
Winick M P, Winick C 1979 *The Television Experience.* Sage, Beverly Hills, California
Winn M 1977 *The Plug-in Drug: Television, Children and the Family.* Viking Press, New York
Woolery G W 1983 *Children's Television: The First 35 Years 1946–1981*, Part I—Animated cartoon series, Part II—Live film and tape series. Scarecrow Press, Metuchen, New Jersey

Mass Media in Adult Education

J. Robinson and B. Groombridge

In this article the media refer to those means of communication that reach large numbers of people, namely national and regional newspapers, popular magazines, national and local radio, and television (by open transmission, cable system, or video recording). The material conveyed by these means of communication is described as the content or the programmes.

The most remarkable feature of the support these media give to adult learning is the multiplicity of ways in which it works. Any idea that it is always a didactic function is far from the truth. Occasionally the media do work didactically; but that function is generally far down the list of priorities.

The following sections illustrate some of the ways in which the media support adult learning.

1. By Broadening Understanding and Enlarging Interests Among the Adult Community as a Whole

This is a feature of the total content of the media: from topical news to long-term research reports; from ancient history to world geography; from immediate actuality to timeless imagination; from scientific discovery to aesthetic exploration; from intellectual challenges to feats of physical skill; from lighthearted satire to serious discussion; and so on. The content is continually variable—much of it will be unreliable and some may well be deliberately distorted. The degree of reliability of content will depend largely on who controls the various media and for what direct and indirect purposes. Certainly there needs to be an informed critical response to the media, and much of the content will then be seen to be not mindstretching, but rather mindcramping. However, overall and in most countries, whatever the political, social, and cultural control of the media, the total effect of news coverage, of articles, documentaries, and discussions, of stories, plays, and drama serials, of cartoons, sketches, and competitions, is to broaden the experience of the whole community, to stimulate a wealth of new interests, and to prepare the way for more systematic study.

Various aspects of this total effect were examined by Hoggart (1958), Williams (1958), McLuhan (1964), Scupham (1967), Groombridge (1972), and other writers on the media.

2. By Providing a Wider Acceptance of the Total Concept of Learning Continuing Throughout Life

By openly encouraging the development of new interests and the exploration of new areas of experience, the media constantly work either overtly or implicitly against the narrow but deeply ingrained view that learning is a matter only for children and for an elite group of young people. This is an immense aid to the agencies of adult education, who have a very difficult task changing this narrow view, to which popular opinion has been conditioned by centuries of associating education solely with child development. How quickly that popular opinion may change, so that resources for adult continuing education will be seen to be as necessary to a flourishing community, as are resources for schools and higher education—particularly during a period of galloping technology—will depend a great deal on the success of the media in encouraging this dynamic view of society and breaking down the old static model. This is perhaps the most vital of all the services that the media can perform for education as a whole (while not neglecting their services to children and young people). It is a service that is needed in every country, whatever the present level of educational provision, and a service that has not been sufficiently highlighted in most writing about the media and education.

3. By Encouraging Individuals into more Systematic Learning

For many years it has been recognized that magazine articles and radio and television programmes have stimulated interests in many readers, listeners, and viewers who have then pursued them in more systematic ways, by further reading and by joining classes, study circles, clubs, or societies. This happened at a more academic level when the British Broadcasting Corporation (BBC) in the United Kingdom and Sveriges Radio in Sweden developed their language courses and there was a boom in enrolment in language classes and study circles throughout the United Kingdom and Scandinavia; it happened when a number of universities and colleges in the United States offered credit courses carried partly by radio and television, and partly in newspapers; and it happened in Japan through broadcast and correspondence courses; in Kenya and Malaysia through teacher-updating programmes; and in many countries through the development of Open University-type projects. However, it has also been shown to work at the basic levels of adult literacy and numeracy, in the learning of a host country language by immigrant groups, and in basic parental education, in countries with as varied educational provision as the United Kingdom and Italy, India and Brazil. In most cases the media have performed this sensitive task by raising hopes and building confidence, and sometimes by providing confidential referral schemes, rather than by providing direct instruction. A similar service has happened at more practical levels, for example in the radio farm forums in Tanzania and in the SITE Experiment projects in village development in India.

Examples of several of these effects in Europe have been described in studies for the Commission of the European Communities (Kaye and Harry 1982).

4. By Publicizing Local Opportunities for Learning

This is a purpose related to the previous one, but distinguishable from it. It is a purpose particularly suitable for local journalism and local broadcasting and has been amply demonstrated in all parts of the world—especially where the local media are imbued with a strong sense of public service and community involvement, and not just with local commercial interests. The various forms that this publicity can take, including straightforward newspaper display and broadcast announcements, interviews with adult learners who are enjoying their courses, letters in the correspondence columns, phone-in enquiries on radio, telephone and postal enquiry services following such publicity, and many other imaginative ways, can now be illustrated in most countries that have local media. The service is not limited to local media. It can be found in national and regional broadcasting, in articles and enquiry services in women's magazines and journals devoted to special fields of interest, and in national newspapers from time to time.

5. By Providing Direct Learning Materials for Individual Learning

This introduces a directly didactic purpose for the first time in this summary, and it is not one to be ignored, especially when the learning materials are offered through several media, for example radio, television, and printed coursebooks, it is clear that the media can provide a direct learning experience of a very satisfactory kind. Perhaps the earliest clear evidence for this came from the broadcasting and correspondence courses for adults developed in the early 1960s by NHK, the Japanese Broadcasting Corporation. This was achieved through the foundation of the NHK Gakuen Correspondence High School in association with the education departments of the broadcasting corporation. It was discovered through surveys among adult students that those who were studying by broadcasts and correspondence showed a success rate in the high school examinations twice as high as that of the correspondence students alone, and that differential has continued over subsequent years. At about the same time the Chicago Television College recorded similar results for its television-based students. The same impression would have been conveyed by many broadcasting organizations in Europe from the modern language courses they had developed in a similar way—without the opportunity to assess them on examination results. Since then there is plenty of impressionistic evidence of such direct learning services in practical skills like cooking, dressmaking, home maintenance, and gardening: at least if continued demand and response is a fair indication of success. Inevitably it is more difficult to evaluate the success of such direct teaching services in basic education and community development in Third World countries, however, some projects have been evaluated and have shown encouraging results.

6. By Providing the Media Components in More Complex Multimedia Learning Schemes

The Open University in the United Kingdom is probably the clearest example of this mode of support, for, from its inception it was agreed that radio and television should be integral components of each course. While opinions vary among Open University students about the essential value of the broadcast contribution—and this, of course, varies from one course to another—there is no doubt at all that the university has been able to

include many courses that would not have been possible without the use of radio and television. In addition to their use in individual courses, the contribution that they make to general communication between staff and students and to enhancing the corporate life of the University can hardly be exaggerated, and now there are many Open University-type systems, in all parts of the world. Some of them manage without the involvement of the public media; but about half of them involve broadcasting to some degree, and some quite extensively.

The Allama Iqbal Open University in Pakistan, for example, already uses radio extensively, for practical instruction in vegetable growing and poultry farming, for updating teachers in curricula and methods, and for general education in mathematics, science, social science, English, and Urdu; and it is beginning to make use of television. The Universidad Nacional de Educacion a Distancia in Spain also uses radio extensively for university and professional courses for adults, and is planning to use television. The Universidad Nacional Abierta in Venezuela, the Free University of Iran, and the University of Mid-America, based in Nebraska, all use both media very widely. The Open Learning Institute in British Columbia has planned to make considerable use of cable television.

In addition to these single-institution systems, consortia schemes have developed in many countries and several of these have made use of the public media. Some examples of these are the California Educational Television Consortium, which links public television series with the state universities, the BBC's collaboration with the Trades Union Congress Education Department and the National Extension College, and the *Zeitungskolleg* in the Federal Republic of Germany, which collaborates with regional newspapers in the publication of academic articles and supports these with individual tuition.

Many detailed case studies of the use of broadcasting in open learning systems were collected for UNESCO during the 1960s and the 1970s. Schramm et al. (1967), Mackenzie et al. (1975), and Hawkridge and Robinson (1982) are a few examples of these.

7. By Providing Channels and Opportunities for Student Feedback and Learner Exchange

One of the great drawbacks of the public media in the learning process is the basically one-way nature of their communication. However, by arranging phone-in programmes on radio and television, extensive correspondence columns in newspapers and magazines, and programmes and articles prepared by students, it is possible to make the media available for the expression of direct feedback from the students and to allow the learners to discuss the content and the method of their courses among themselves. Most of the Open University type systems make provision for this as do many of the consortia systems. Inevitably it is a small minority of the learners who take advantage of this opportunity, and that fact has to be noted carefully in any interpretation of the views expressed. The fact that it can happen at all is an important encouragement to learner involvement. It is probable that the development of lightweight technology in recording systems, word processing, and fibre-optics will make the electronic exchange of learners' views much more extensive and available in the near future.

8. By Providing Learning Materials for Use by the Group Tutor or Class Teacher in Organized Adult Education

Both general content and specifically educational content may be useful for the group tutor and there is widespread use of both. They can be a rich source of discussion material and provide a welcome variation in class activity, whether in academic, social, or practical subjects. Broadcast programmes are normally used in recorded form, since they are unlikely to be broadcast at precisely the right time and the tutor will probably wish to see the programmes first. That is by no means strictly necessary and some of the most creative results have developed when tutor and students have responded to a programme together, following their respective preparation. Newspaper and magazine articles are likely to involve photocopying. Broadcast recording and photocopying both raise copyright issues in most countries. Some countries in Europe and Africa have virtually dismissed copyright where educational use is concerned; but in most countries it is still illegal to copy for group tuition use, unless prior permission has been given. In a number of European countries, copyright is previously cleared by the producing organization for educational use of educational content, but not for the use of general content. Copyright is a problem that will need to be resolved more universally in the future.

There is also the question of experience and training in the use of media material. Most tutors have had some direct training in the use of books, but few have been trained in the use of television, radio, and newspapers for direct learning purposes. Again some tutors take to it more readily than others, but in most countries there is a real need for more effective training in the use of the popular media.

9. By Encouraging Individuals to Offer their Services as Voluntary or Part-time Tutors in Adult Education

This is a purpose that has developed particularly strongly since the media became more widely used to serve educationally deprived groups such as nonreaders, the disabled, and immigrants with no working knowledge of the host country language. In all these situations the use of volunteer tutors working on a one-to-one basis in the learner's home or some other informal setting has proved to be of immense value. A basic training for such volunteers has usually been possible, but enough volunteers have not always come forward in the right places. The public media have been used very effectively to encourage the right kind of people to come forward for this work. So in the United Kingdom the referral service for adult nonreaders was also used as a confidential recruiting service for volunteer tutors. Similar methods have been used in other countries, and altogether it has been a surprising new bonus in media support.

10. By Providing Training Material for Voluntary and Part-time Tutors

Basic training has generally been available for these part-time tutors, but more often than not it is both uneven and largely improvised. In any specialized area there are likely to be very specialized skills involved, such as teaching reading, teaching a second language, teaching the skills of birth control and parenthood, and so on. It has been shown that the public media can help this training process considerably, by providing specialized, topical, nonpersonal training material that makes the work of the trainer much less arduous and the training process more successful.

In all these ways the media have shown that they can and do give valuable support to the whole range of adult learning, group learning, and individual learning, formal and nonformal. Every country can learn from others how these services can be extended, and there is immense scope for development in the future.

Bibliography

Groombridge B 1972 *Television and the People: A Programme for Democratic Participation*. Penguin, Harmondsworth
Hawkridge D, Robinson J 1982 *Organizing Educational Broadcasting*. Croom Helm, London
Hoggart R 1958 *The Uses of Literacy*. Chatto and Windus, London
Kaye A, Harry K (eds.) 1982 *Using the Media for Adult Basic Education*. Croom Helm, London
Mackenzie N I, Postgate R S, Scupham J 1975 *Open Learning: Systems and Problems in Post-secondary Education*. UNESCO, Paris
McLuhan H M 1964 *Understanding Media: The Extensions of Man*. Routledge and Kegan Paul, London
Schramm W L, Coombs P, Kahnert F, Lyle J 1967 *The New Media: Memo to Educational Planners*. UNESCO, Paris
Scupham J 1967 *Broadcasting and the Community*. Watts, London
Williams R 1958 *Culture and Society, 1780–1950*. Chatto and Windus, London

Distance Learning Systems

A. R. Kaye

Distance education, simply and somewhat broadly defined, is "education which either does not imply the physical presence of the teacher appointed to dispense it in the place where it is received, or in which the teacher is present only on occasions or for selected tasks". This French Government definition of the term *télé-enseignement* (Loi 71.556 du 12 juillet 1971) contains two basic elements: the physical separation of teacher and learner and the changed role of the teacher, who may meet students only for "selected tasks" such as counselling, giving tutorials or seminars, or solving study problems.

Distance education methods can be successfully used for catering to groups who, for geographical, economic, or social reasons, are unable or unwilling to make use of traditional (e.g., classroom-based) provision. In so doing, they can liberate the student from constraints of space, time, and age.

1. Principal Defining Features

In addition to the key element of physical separation of teacher and learner cited above, Holmberg identifies six main categories of description for the term (Holmberg 1981 pp. 11–13):

(a) the use of preproduced courses as the main basis for study;

(b) the existence of organized two-way communication between the student and a supporting organization, that is, the university, college, or school with its tutors and counsellors;

(c) the planned and explicit catering for individual study;

(d) the cost effectiveness of the educational use of mass communication methods when large numbers of students follow the same preproduced courses;

(e) the application of industrial work methods to the production of learning materials and to the administration of a distance education scheme (Peters 1973);

(f) the notion of distance study as a mediated form of guided didactic conversation.

The same characteristics will be found embedded in other definitions. For example, in discussing the planning and design of distance learning systems, Kaye and Rumble identify a number of key features, which, although not all found in every instance, contribute to the overall notion of a generalized distance learning system. Concerning students these are:

(a) an enlargement or "opening" of educational opportunity to new target populations, previously deprived either through geographical isolation, lack

of formal academic requirements, or employment conditions;

(b) the identification of particular target groups and their key characteristics (needs, age, distribution, time available for study, local facilities, etc.) to enable appropriate courses, learning methods, and delivery systems to be designed on a systematic basis.

Concerning the learning materials and teaching methods which characterize the courses, notable features are:

(a) flexibility in the curriculum and content of the learning materials through, for example, modular structures or credit systems;

(b) the conscious and systematic design of learning material for independent study, incorporating, for example, clearly formulated learning objectives, self-assessment devices, student activities, and the provision of feedback from students to learning system staff and vice versa;

(c) the planned use of a wide range of media and other resources, selected from those available in the context of the system, and suited to the needs of the students; these media may include specially prepared correspondence texts, books, newspaper supplements, posters, radio and television broadcasts, audio-and video-cassettes, films, computer-assisted learning, kits, local tuition and counselling, student self-help groups, lending-library facilities, and so on.

Finally, the following logistical and economic features are characteristic of distance learning systems:

(a) great potential flexibility compared to conventional provision in implementation, in teaching methods, and in student groups covered;

(b) centralized, mass production of standardized learning materials (such as texts, broadcasts, kits, and so on) in an almost industrialized manner, implying clear division of labour in the creation and production procedures;

(c) a systematic search for, and use of, existing infrastructure and facilities as part of the system (e.g. libraries, postal and other distribution services, printers, publishers, broadcasting organizations, manufacturers, etc.);

(d) potentially a significantly lower recurrent unit cost per student than that obtainable through conventional (classroom or equivalent) teaching arrangements and also potentially a considerably lower capital cost per student (Kaye and Rumble 1981 pp. 18–19).

The development of distance education methods in the recent past owes a great deal to the pioneering work carried out in the field of correspondence education. The print-based materials have remained but have been supplemented by modern communication media and personal contact. Thus distance education is often distinguished from correspondence study (Keegan 1980) by the notion of three-way teaching, combining "...the permanence of print, the reach of radio, and the intimacy of face-to-face study" (Young et al. 1980 p. 21). Slightly extending this definition, distance education can be equated with the combined, systematic, and flexible use of at least three major elements: print-based communication, broadcasting and/or other technologies, and face-to-face contact, in support of an independent learner.

Distance education methods imply major differences to intramural or classroom-based provision on three main dimensions: the learning experiences of the students, the nature of the teaching/learning materials, and the administrative and organizational structure of the providing institution. These three facets are briefly discussed below and are broadly relevant to the whole range of distance education provision, be it small, flexible, and localized, or large scale and highly centralized.

2. Learning at a Distance

Distance education methods cater *par excellence* for the individual learner studying independently. This entails, in most instances, high levels of motivation amongst the learners, and is a key reason for the fact that the great majority of distance education projects are aimed primarily at adults. Nevertheless, distance education provision does exist in some countries for school-age children unable (e.g. for geographical or health reasons) to attend classes. Examples, dating back for many years, can be found in Australia (radio plus correspondence tuition and personal contact), and in France, where the *Centre National d'Enseignement par Correspondance* was originally established during the Second World War to provide teaching, at a distance, to children unable to go to school. Most of its provision nowadays is aimed at adults.

In general, distance students are adults. They also tend to form very heterogeneous groups, compared to those following more traditional educational channels, so it is difficult to characterize the "typical" distance student. In a review of student characteristics at distance teaching universities in 10 different countries, the following features were highlighted (Kaye and Rumble 1981 pp. 35–38):

(a) an age range of 20–40 years;

(b) majority studying on a part-time basis;

(c) men generally outnumber women;

(d) study is primarily carried out at home;

(e) high levels of motivation;

(f) the majority of students are from less privileged social groups;

(g) students studying voluntarily (as opposed to those in compulsory inservice courses) tend to be from urban areas.

Concerning reasons for study, it is evident that the obtaining of examinations, diplomas, and degrees, and the acquisition and/or updating of professional and career-related skills rank very highly amongst a large proportion of students enrolled on distance courses (see, for example, Holmberg 1981 pp. 21–24).

The skills needed for study at a distance have some features in common with those required in any learning environment. However, certain skills are of particular importance in the distance learning situation. These include:

(a) setting of personal study objectives;

(b) development of personal confidence in the ability to study primarily on one's own;

(c) planning and organizing study time and study strategies;

(d) developing study skills in learning from the reading and analysis of self-instructional and other print materials, and, where appropriate, from listening to and viewing broadcasts, using audio- and videotape material, participating in group discussions, and undertaking practical work alone and/or in a group situation;

(e) making use of, and communicating with, a tutor—in writing, by telephone, or at face-to-face meetings. Tutors may play a range of different roles: counsellor, problem solver, provider of feedback, resource person, assessor.

The skills listed above are of particular importance because the distance learner does not benefit from the same levels and amounts of pacing, structure, and formal and informal contact with peers and teachers as a student in an intramural educational institution. However, distance students do have the advantage of being able to plan their study activities around a personal timetable in a relatively flexible manner, and this is one of the overwhelming reasons cited for enrolling on distance education courses, especially when employment and family obligations make other options impractical or inconvenient. Furthermore, it is evident that in well-planned and adequately financed distance education systems, the distance learner need not feel disadvantaged and may, in fact, be better served than many studying through more traditional channels.

The range of distance education situations and courses is now so diverse that it is impossible to make generalizations about study patterns and strategies adopted by learners. Even different students following the same course in the same institution will adopt and develop different approaches, according to their own tastes and interests. However, it is fair to say that in a large proportion of cases, the majority of the learner's time is taken up by individual study of specially pre-pared printed materials (which as the main "informa-tion channel" can be considered as analogous to a classroom presentation or lecture in a traditional con-text). Students may be provided with sets of learning objectives and related self-assessment questions and exercises, with model answers, against which they can check their understanding and progress. A much smaller proportion of time may be spent in viewing or listening to broadcasts or recorded audiovisual and audio ma-terial, often ideal for presenting real-life situations, or case-study or experimental material which cannot be clearly communicated in printed form. From time to time, either at the student's discretion, or by certain pre-determined dates, the student will submit written work to a correspondence tutor in response to preset assign-ments. Assignment modes may consist of multiple-choice tests, short answer questions, essays on set topics, or more extensive self-chosen projects or dissertations. The correspondence tutor may grade and comment on this work, and may also be able to meet the student to discuss it at a regular tutorial. In many instances, tuto-rial sessions at local study centres also exist to enable students to discuss general study problems and clear up difficulties in understanding. For example, the Lesotho Distance Teaching Centre, because of difficulties exper-ienced by students in studying at home, set up a net-work of local study centres where ". . . students could come once or twice a week, work in adequate comfort and good light by themselves at their courses and seek help from an 'elbow tutor' as they needed it" (Young et al. 1980 p. 71). Other opportunities for interpersonal contact also exist in many systems—ranging from infor-mally organized "self-help" groups established by stu-dents living in the same neighbourhood, to week-long residential contact programmes (such as the British Open University's "summer schools") which can pro-vide an opportunity for extended personal and group tuition and, for example, laboratory practicals and field work.

3. Distance Teaching Materials

Teaching materials designed for use in a classroom or other intramural learning environment are generally not suitable, and certainly not sufficient, for the distance learning situation. A standard school or college text-book, for example, is often designed to be used either as a source of reference, and/or as a basis for discussion and exposition by a teacher in a classroom situation. It is assumed that the student will be able to refer to peers, teachers, or other information sources (e.g. a library) when experiencing difficulties in following the material in the textbook. Audiovisual material for classroom use is also generally designed for a group situation with a teacher's presence assumed. Some of these materials may be suitable for use in group tutorials in a distance

education programme, but would probably not fit the situation of a distance learner viewing or listening to a broadcast in isolation, at home.

A number of criteria are of key importance in the design of materials for distance learning. Firstly, it is necessary to take a global approach to the range of media and materials that will be available within a given system, and decide on clear pedagogical functions and roles for each of them. For example, if radio is to be used only in a group situation at a local centre, say in the presence of an *animateur*, then the structure and objectives of the programme will be quite different from one made for individual listening in the home. An audi-otape for individual use will again have different func-tions to a radio programme for individual listening: a tape can be stopped, and replayed, or used in associa-tion with diagrams or experimental equipment. Sec-ondly, the organization of the materials needs to take into account the resources, capacities, and abilities, of both students and tutors. Prerequisite requirements for starting a course (i.e., knowledge and skills assumed by the course planners) need to be made explicit. Likely areas of difficulty need to be "signposted" to the tutors and perhaps covered by special guidance notes for tuto-rial and group work. Scheduling of course work should take into account realistic estimates of how much time a typical student is liable to be able to devote to study each week or month.

Materials designed for individual study—and in most cases these will be predominantly print materials—are prepared in a "self-instructional" format, namely: writ-ten and presented in a stimulating style (maybe a collo-quial style in some cultures); easily "accessible" to the student through the use of aids such as lists of learning objectives, concept maps, indices, glossaries, self-tests, and reviews; attractively designed, making good use of illustrations and of different typographical styles; "stu-dent active", containing opportunities for the student to test and monitor progress through activities, questions, and self-assessment exercises embedded in the text; flexi-ble, with some provision for alternative routes and bypasses through the material (without necessarily resorting to the complexity of a traditional branching programmed text).

A final important criterion of good quality distance-teaching materials concerns the care with which the dif-ferent media components are integrated with each other. Integration can be considered at two levels. Firstly, materials for tutors, *animateurs*, and other intermediaries in the system must complement and relate clearly to the materials provided for the students; this implies that items such as notes for tutors need to be developed in parallel with the students' course mater-ials. Secondly, when the individual student may be required to use material in several different media (say print, radio, and television), clear decisions need to be made as to how closely the different media are inte-grated within the segments of the course. Levels of inte-gration may vary from occasional cross-references, to a very tight structure which obliges the student, for example, to view a specific television programme before being able to proceed with the next section of text.

An example of an extreme form of integration of broadcast and print material is that developed by Radio ECCA, in the Canary Islands, and subsequently adapted for use on the Spanish mainland and in distance education projects in several Latin American countries. In the ECCA system

> ...every lesson is centred upon a "lesson master sheet". The teacher has a copy of the lesson master sheet in front of him while he broadcasts over the radio, and the student follows his own copy simultaneously in his own home.... The student is required to respond to the radio teacher by writing on the lesson master sheet during the course of the broadcast....a full set of master sheets comprises a student's text book. Exercises are included on the back of each master sheet...to be completed after the student has listened to the radio broadcast. (Cepeda 1982 pp. 213–14)

This degree of integration of print and broadcast materials is perhaps unusual in the field of distance education, but experience shows that it can be successful in a range of contexts.

4. Institutional Structures

A great variety of institutional structures can be found amongst distance education organizations. In many cases, structures are derived from those of conventional teaching institutions such as universities or schools, which in themselves vary from country to country. In other cases, broadcasting organizations, commercial correspondence colleges, or voluntary organizations, may have provided the original structure on which a distance institution has been built. More recently, there has been a growth in the number of projects which have involved collaboration between a number of institutions of different sorts, either on a long-term basis or for short-term campaigns.

However, regardless of the underlying institutional structure, a number of specific services to students need to be provided, organized, and administered:

(a) provision (acquisition, development, production), storage, and distribution of course materials;

(b) provision of educational support services (correspondence tuition, possibly telephone or other electronic communication, tutorial classes, study centres, counselling, etc.);

(c) maintenance of administrative and academic records and provision of administrative communication channels (e.g., for enrolment, fee payment, assignment data, etc.);

(d) in some instances, accreditation and the delivery of diplomas, certificates, and degrees.

The question of provision of course materials deserves particular attention in this context, because it is here that differences are perhaps greatest as compared to traditional educational methods, and where economies of scale are most noticeable (when large numbers of students use the same preproduced course materials). Some distance education projects use materials acquired elsewhere, that is, not produced in-house. However, even in this simplest model, the acquired materials may need adapting, translating, and reprinting or reproducing. The majority of projects develop their own teaching materials, both printed and audiovisual, either using their own full-time subject matter specialists and/or academic staff, and/or through the use of part-time consultants. Physical production of materials (printing, audiovisual production) may either be in-house, subcontracted, or carried out in collaboration with a production agency such as a publishing house, broadcasting organization, or a commercial audiovisual producer. Whatever the origin of the materials, they will require storage and distribution facilities, and the greater the variety or range of courses or materials on offer, the greater and more complex will these facilities need to be.

The overriding importance of these aspects of procurement, production, storage, and distribution calls for two comments which illustrate a clear-cut difference between distance and conventional educational provision. Firstly, it implies that distance education is "...an industrialized form of teaching and learning" (Peters 1973 p. 206). Rumble has pointed out that, in institutions such as distance-teaching universities which "...have to undertake directly a number of quasi-industrial processes...there is a need for a clear definition of the interrelationships between two broad areas, one of which is more in the nature of a business enterprise...while the other is more in the nature of traditionally conceived academic areas" (Kaye and Rumble 1981 p. 179). The industrial, or quasi-industrial, nature of the materials development and production aspects of distance teaching is certainly a reality in many of the large-scale centralized systems. Course development planning may start five or six years before the finished product is "launched"; orders need to be placed with suppliers and subcontractors; deadlines and production schedules drawn up and adhered to; personnel needs estimated; and contracts prepared. The constraints imposed by the production and distribution needs can lead to a situation of potential conflict between production demands and the working methods and values of the originators of the course materials—be they full-time academic staff employed by the institution, or outside consultants and lesson writers. This is related to a second main difference between traditional and distance education institutions: namely the changed role of the teacher in a mediated or distance learning system. A number of aspects contribute to this changed role:

(a) the need to develop skills in preparing mediated materials (print, audiovisual, etc.) both for individual use, and for use by tutors and learners in group situations; these are not necessarily the same skills as those required of a good face-to-face or classroom teacher;

(b) the loss of direct personal control of the teaching/learning process and the lack of direct feedback from students characteristic of the classroom situation;

(c) the need to work with other professionals (designers, producers, editors) in the preparation and production of materials, and the resultant requirement to submit one's work to scrutiny and comment.

These aspects are present regardless of the course creation models adopted in any particular institution—which may vary from that of an author and editor working together, to that of a large-scale course team of academics, editors, educational technologists, producers, and designers.

When, in addition to course provision, the other three service areas (educational support, records, and accreditation) are provided by the same institution, and the number of students is large, then the need to adopt industrial working methods already referred to becomes even more imperative. For example, computerized systems for organizing despatch of course materials, and for maintenance of tutor and student records may become a necessity; industrial-style management and control methods may need to be introduced to ensure efficient integration of the work in a range of different specialized areas.

However, many distance learning projects and schemes are decentralized and even localized, with different organizations being responsible for each of the categories of services listed above. Such projects can maintain a flexibility of operation which is often more difficult to achieve in large-scale and centrally controlled institutions such as the British Open University.

Neil has presented an institutional analysis of distance learning systems on the basis of the locus and nature of the control of four key areas: finance, examination and accreditation, curriculum and materials, and delivery and student support systems (Neil 1981 pp. 140–41). He quotes five models or types of institution based on this analysis:

(a) the classic centre–periphery model, such as the British Open University, with high levels of control in all four areas;

(b) the associated centre model such as Spain's Universidad Nacional de Educación a Distancia which works with over 50 associated centres each responsible for their own delivery and student support services;

(c) the dispersed centre model (e.g. Coastline Community College, California) which cooperates with a whole range of organizations and bodies in the community but retains a fair measure of central control over accreditation for many courses;

(d) the switchboard organization model, exemplified by Norway's recently created distance education institute (Norskfjernundervisning) which has essentially enabling, coordinating, initiating, and approving roles in the further development of the country's existing educational resources for distance students;

(e) the service institution model, for example the Deutsches Institut für Fernstudien (DIFF) at Tübingen which provides services to a range of distance teaching organizations (e.g. materials development, consultancy, evaluation), and has little control over any areas except in the creation and production of course materials.

5. The Extent of Distance Education

With Perraton, the main early developments of distance education (as defined in this entry) would be traced to the mid-1960s when "...a series of projects began in which attempts were made to link the three components of broadcasting, correspondence, and face-to-face tuition" (Perraton 1979 p. 14). There were a few isolated earlier examples of broadcasts linked to correspondence tuition (e.g. using radio in New Zealand in 1937, and the programmes of the Chicago Television College, which started in 1956) but since the 1960s there has been a very significant quantitative and qualitative increase in the number and range of distance programmes throughout the world. Much of this development has built on earlier experiences of correspondence tuition (e.g. the United Kingdom, Scandinavia, and the United States), correspondence plus face-to-face tuition (e.g. the very extensive programmes in existence in the Soviet Union since the 1920s), and the combined use of broadcasting and study groups (e.g. farm radio forums in Canada, India, and a number of African countries).

It is not possible within the scope of this article to provide a complete coverage of distance education projects worldwide. Firstly, the number and range of projects is so large: in a small country like the United Kingdom alone, over 70 distance education projects have started since 1970—ranging from the national highly centralized Open University, to decentralized and community-based projects and campaigns. Secondly, developments in communications technology are likely to bring about qualitative and structural changes in the design of distance education systems in the near future in a number of countries. These developments include applications of satellite communications (e.g. the University of the South Pacific, or the Open Learning Institute in British Columbia), of computers (e.g. the PLATO system in the United States), and the increasingly widespread availability of audio- and video-cassette/videodisc equipment. These developments are likely to

Table 1
Examples of distance education provision

Programmes not equivalent to formal education levels:

(a) Basic education	ACPO, Colombia
	Adult Literacy Project, United Kingdom
(b) Community education	Radio Learning Campaigns, Tanzania
(c) Agricultural extension	Radio Educative, Senegal
	Radio Farm Forums, Thailand
(d) Vocational	UNED, Costa Rica

Programmes equivalent to formal education levels:

(a) Primary	Radio ECCA, Canary Islands
(b) General secondary	Air Correspondence High School, Korea
(c) Technical secondary	Open University of Sri Lanka
(d) Higher	Everyman's University, Israel
	Open University, United Kingdom
	Polytechnic Institutes, Soviet Union
(e) Teacher training	Allama Iqbal Open University, Pakistan
	Correspondence Course Unit, Kenya

bring about major changes in the roles of both broadcasting and print-based communication in distance education, at least in the industrially advanced countries.

In the late 1980s distance education projects may be found in the majority of countries in the world at one level or another (see, for example, Daniel et al. 1982). The major part of this provision is concerned with adult education, which the Organisation for Economic Cooperation and Development defines as "organized programmes of education provided for the benefit of, and adapted to the needs of, persons not in the regular school or university system and generally older than 15". There appears to be no internationally recognized system for classifying adult education, but it is generally agreed that it covers both formal and nonformal curricula. Table 1 lists, purely for illustrative purposes, examples of the use of distance methods for a variety of adult education programmes. A number of the projects listed in the table emanate from institutions which also provide courses in other areas.

The examples listed form only a tiny fraction of existing provision, but detailed accounts of a wide range of projects can be found in a number of recent publications. Young et al. (1980) list over 120 projects in developing countries, excluding those only operating at

degree level. Rumble and Harry (1982) describe 9 institutions (from both developed and developing countries) which have been established in the 1970s to provide primarily degree-level programmes. MacKenzie et al. (1975) include case studies of postsecondary-level distance and open education projects drawn from 13 countries. Detailed accounts of eight basic education projects in Europe can be found in Kaye and Harry (1982). Finally, interesting samples of print materials taken from 30 or so distance education courses (from 10 different countries) may be found in the manual on writing for distance education prepared by the International Extension College (1979).

Bibliography

Cepeda L E 1982 Radio ECCA, Canary Islands. In: Kaye A R, Harry K (eds.) 1982 *Using the Media for Adult Basic Education.* Croom Helm, London

Daniel J F, Stroud M F, Thompson J (eds.) 1982 *Learning at a Distance: A World Perspective.* Athabasca University/ICDE, Edmonton

Holmberg B 1981 *Status and Trends of Distance Education.* Kogan Page, London

International Extension College (IEC) 1979 *Writing for Distance Education: A Manual for Writers of Distance Teaching Texts and Independent Study Materials.* IEC, Cambridge

Jenkins J 1981 *Materials for Learning: How to Teach Adults at a Distance.* Routledge and Kegan Paul, London

Kaye A R, Harry K (eds.) 1982 *Using the Media for Adult Basic Education.* Croom Helm, London

Kaye A R, Rumble G (eds.) 1981 *Distance Teaching for Higher and Adult Education.* Croom Helm, London

Keegan D J 1980 Defining distance education. *Distance Educ.* 1: 13–36

MacKenzie N I, Postgate R S, Scupham J, Bartram B (eds.) 1975 *Open Learning: Systems and Problems in Post-secondary Education.* UNESCO, Paris (also in French and Spanish versions)

Neil M W (ed.) 1981 *Education of Adults at a Distance.* Kogan Page, London

Perraton H D (ed.) 1979 *Alternative Routes to Formal Education: Distance Teaching for School Equivalency.* World Bank, Washington, DC

Perraton H D 1981 A theory for distance education. *Prospects* 11 (1)

Peters O 1973 *Die Didaktische Struktur des Fernunterrichts: Untersuchungen zu einer Industrialisierten Form des Lehrens und Lernens.* Tübingen Beiträge zum Fernstudium, 7. Weinheim, Beltz

Rumble G, Harry K (eds.) 1982 *The Distance Teaching Universities.* Croom Helm, London

Young M, Perraton H D, Jenkins J, Dodds T 1980 *Distance Teaching for the Third World: The Lion and the Clockwork Mouse.* Routledge and Kegan Paul, London

Self-directed Learning in Distance Education

E. J. Burge and C. C. Frewin

The 1970s and early 1980s have seen some major developments in the design, delivery, and administration of distance learning programs. Distance learning is defined here as learning activities designed by an educational institution and undertaken by a learner who chooses not to, or cannot, attend regular classroom instruction. The learning activities can be a mix of methods related to resources, settings, delivery systems, and program design. Types of resources include print, audiovisual, and computer-based materials and the learner might use these materials individually or in groups in home or work settings. Delivery systems have been enhanced by the use of various technologies. Administration has grown, especially in developing countries, through the establishment of distance education institutions (Daniel et al. 1982). Developments in the design of learning programs are not as consistently researched and documented as the aforementioned fields, especially as these developments relate to the learning processes undertaken by adult learners.

This article summarizes work in the design of learning processes in distance learning and indicates scope for developing self-directedness in distance learner behavior. An increasing number of adult educators are paying attention to the concept of self-directedness in learning because they recognize its contribution to critical awareness and constructive, creative thinking which in turn contribute to the further general development of the adult (see, for example, Nottingham Andragogy Group 1983).

The principles and procedures around which distance learning courses are designed (e.g. Jenkins 1981, Lewis 1981) have been developed from studies on learners and their interactions with course materials. Learners have been described from various perspectives, including their educational backgrounds, attitudes to study, perceptions of personal gain from courses, and methods for dealing with tutors and materials. Their interactions with course materials have been assessed in terms of levels of learning skills, use of information-processing styles and learning, selection of appropriate teaching models, kinds of interactions with resources and course learning guides, local personal and institutional support systems counselling strategies, and the impact of various audiovisual technologies on learning.

The principles and procedures derived from these studies enable a greater degree of quality control of course materials—an advantage which is not inherent in teacher changes in classroom situations. High-quality distance learning courses are characterized by academic rigour, high levels of learner interaction with materials, and sophisticated graphic design. Well-known examples of high quality learning materials are those from the Open University in the United Kingdom, but there are many other examples. Such materials are designed to lead students through a series of preplanned activities, often based on specific learning objectives and student assignments. This approach does not specifically encourage learners to develop self-directed approaches to learning.

However, this application of specific principles and systematic procedures has been accompanied by some questioning of the consistent use of an objectives-based, educational technology approach to learning design (Farnes 1976). Such an approach, it has been argued, can lead to unnecessary or inappropriate institutional controls over the learner's activity, which the learner can reject. Experience has shown that when distance learners are given options and some leeway to develop their own learning goals, they will take those opportunities, and under skilled guidance, show evidence of creative, relevant, and sound learning. Experience has also shown that many learners do not follow instructions strictly or sequentially. They tend, for example, to read and use printed materials selectively. Research has indicated that the use of highly specific learning objectives can inhibit incidental learning as well as initial intentional learning (Marland and Store 1982). This practical experience with what and how learners learn has been supported at a more theoretical level by the recognition of the general autonomy of the distance learner (Moore 1972).

Early responses to this problem of dealing with and even taking advantage of the autonomy inherent in distance learning have concentrated on increasing learner involvement and control in various ways. The self-pacing of distance learning is a traditional way of doing this. Pacing is usually controlled by the learner anyway, unless courses demand completion within a certain time period. The inclusion of experiential learning activities in courses has sometimes allowed choices for learners based on their own experience (Baume and Hipwell 1977, Fales and Burge 1984). Individual project work (Morgan 1983) can, with tutor guidance, allow learners considerable freedom and guided self-directedness. The design of different routes through a course (Melton 1982) can upgrade the levels of participation by learners in choosing how they will learn.

These design responses indicate new trends in distance learning, and recognize several important factors. First, adult distance learners can demonstrate high levels of initiative and responsibility while accomplishing learning. Second, the learners will respond to learning activities in accord with the demands of their individual situations—their relative isolation from the classroom allows them to do this. This response reduces the effective control of the tutor. Third, adult distance learners can become frustrated with a lock-step course process that is based on highly specific objectives. Adult learners will not easily tolerate learning activities which they see as tedious, repetitive, and irrelevant.

These factors contribute to the growing recognition for distance learning course design that adult learners can use more meaningful choices in what and how they learn (Taylor and Kaye 1986). A key issue in providing these choices is determining course structures and activities that will provide appropriate support and direction, and encourage freedom to choose the content and methods for their learning. Traditional distance learning courses have always allowed choices to be made concerning enrollment and self-pacing through a course.

New developments and adult education practices suggest that further choices can be designed around learning objectives, methods, styles of learning, and evaluation of learning.

The development of procedures to encourage learners to make these choices for increased self-responsibility and direction creates further concerns for course designers and tutors. These include the development of learners' skills and styles of learning, the identification of their attitudes to learning and teaching, and the provision of human and material resources needed for learning and psychological support (Morgan et al. 1982). Relating these factors to course design can directly affect the development of self-directedness, notwithstanding course structure and regular interactions with tutors and peers. If implemented, these factors will enhance the facilitative and guidance roles of the tutor, and develop collaborative rather than dependent relationships between tutor and learner. The factors can also be used to increase the degrees of peer learning and support among distance learners.

Another factor which will claim further attention will be that of the autonomy inherent in the distance learning situation. Adult learners can be encouraged to use time on their own for decision making and reflection about their learning, but their ability to do this will depend on their level of learning skill and on legitimate opportunities for this that are built into their courses.

These issues in developing self-directedness in distance learners are more directly discussed in literature relevant to classroom-based learning (Boud 1982). However, the next significant increment in the quality of distance learning course design will depend on their increased application to nonclassroom distance learning. The continuing development of a design perspective which centres on the learner, and on the application of adult learning principles to nonclassroom learning will help in the reduction of unnecessary levels of didactic teaching prevalent in many traditional distance learning courses.

Bibliography

Baume D, Hipwell J 1977 Adaptable correspondence courses for offshore engineers: A course that learns. *Teaching at a Distance* 9: 27–35

Boud C (ed.) 1982 *Developing Student Autonomy in Learning.* Kogan Page, London

Daniel J S, Stroud M A, Thompson J R (eds.) 1982 *Learning at a Distance: A World Perspective.* Athabasca University/ International Council for Correspondence Education, Edmonton

Fales A W, Burge E J 1984. Self-direction by design: Self-directed learning in distance course design. *Can. J. Univ. Cont. Educ.* 10: 68–78

Farnes N 1976 An educational technologist looks at student-centred learning. *Br. J. Educ. Technol.* 7: 61–65

Jenkins J 1981 *Materials for Learning: How to Teach Adults at a Distance.* Routledge and Kegan Paul, London

Lewis R 1981 *How to Write Self-study Materials.* Council for Educational Technology, London

Marland P W, Store R E 1982 Some instructional strategies for improved learning from distance teaching materials. *Distance Educ.* 3: 72–106

Melton R F 1982 *Instructional Models for Course Design and Development.* Educational Technology Publications, Englewood Cliffs, New Jersey

Moore M G 1972 Learner autonomy: The second dimension of independent learning. *Convergence* 5(2): 76–87

Morgan A 1983 Theoretical aspects of project-based learning in higher education. *Br. J. Educ. Technol.* 14(1)

Morgan A, Taylor E, Gibbs C 1982 Variations in students' approaches to studying. *Br. J. Educ. Technol.* 13(2): 107–13

Nottingham Andragogy Group 1983 *Towards a Developmental Theory of Andragogy.* University of Nottingham, Nottingham

Taylor E, Kaye T 1986 Andragogy by design? Control and self-direction in the design of an Open University course. *Program. Learn. Educ. Technol.* 23: 62–69

Telephones in Education

B. Robinson

Since the first experiments in the use of telephones as an educational medium in the 1950s there has been a rapid and accelerating growth in this field. The development of distance education systems, the growth of continuing education programmes for adults, increases in the costs of travel, and new technological developments, have all combined to point to the telephone as a potentially powerful educational tool. Since the early 1970s, teaching by telephone has been used in a number of distance education contexts, and in a variety of ways, with individuals, as well as with small and large groups.

Telephones offer two-way, interactive communication across distances. The means of providing the telephone link may be terrestrial wire or cable, high-frequency radio waves, microwaves, or satellite. Whatever the method used to provide the link, it means that people who use it can talk to each other, discuss, question, and interact with others beyond their immediate boundaries.

Although most familiar in its domestic form, the telephone also has other capabilities. By means of a telephone network, audio, video, and data information can be sent and received by individuals or large groups of people. As well as allowing conversation between two people at two different locations, a telephone network can also provide, as additional facilities, multipoint audioteleconferencing (conversation between people at a number of different locations, from 3 to over 100 in number), facsimile transmission of printed material, slow-scan transmission of graphic and photographs onto a television screen, data transmission, and computer conferencing.

1. Uses of the Telephone in Education

The use of telephones in education comes into what Schramm (1977) calls the category of "little media" as opposed to "big media". "Little media" (radio, tape recorders, telephone, film strips, slide transparencies, and other visual materials) are less complex and less costly to install and maintain than "big media" (instructional television, films, and computer-assisted learning). Hence, when resources are scarce, use of the "little media" invites reconsideration (Bates 1982). Telephones, in particular, provide a readily accessible network of communication in many countries, using existing and familiar technology.

Telephone communication can serve a number of functions in education and training: (a) it allows an immediate and interactive form of contact which can reduce the sense of isolation experienced by remote or off-campus students, and helps motivate them to persist with their studies; (b) it enables a distant student with a particular learning problem or query to get quick feedback (functional communication of this kind is difficult in circumstances where a letter takes two weeks to be delivered); (c) it provides access to courses previously unobtainable in remote areas; (d) it overcomes problems of travel and terrain; (e) when used as an instructional teleconferencing network, telephone communication can provide courses which are quicker, cheaper, and less onerus to prepare than their printed equivalent, for a wide range of subject matter and levels of study; (f) it is a means for separate institutions to share the teaching of jointly produced courses, as well as a convenient way of enriching courses by drawing in experts or guest speakers who would not otherwise be available; (g) it is flexible in terms of the groupings of participants it can join together.

The terms "teaching by telephone" or "tutoring" or "instructing" cover a variety of usage. They refer to:

(a) courses and students taught wholly or largely by means of an instructional telephone conferencing network with minimal accompanying printed material;

(b) courses taught on campus but "attended" by distant students via a telephone link;

(c) courses where parts are taught by correspondence materials, and part by group teleconferences;

(d) courses taught mainly through correspondence materials (perhaps with other media as well, such as television, radio, or audio cassette) and which offer supplementary tutorial support by means of telephone (either individual or group);

(e) courses where telephone communication is an integral part of the teaching event, for example, a live television presentation followed by students' telephoned questions, which are both asked and answered "on air";

(f) individual telephone calls (occasional or regular) to course writers or tutors from remote students with particular problems in understanding printed course materials;

(g) individual telephone calls to tutors from remote students needing advice or counselling in relation to educational problems.

The major use of telephones has been in higher education, particularly in North America. However, the number of countries using the medium in one form or another is growing. There are currently a number of institutions in Europe and Australia also using telephones for educational purposes. The following are examples of higher education institutions in the United States using telephones for educational purposes: the University of Texas Health Science Center, San Antonio; the University of Illinois; the University of Wisconsin-Extension (ETN); Chicago TV College; Learn/Alsaka Instructional Telecommunications Network; Regents Continuing Education Network, Kansas State University; and Kirkwood Community College, Iowa. In Canada, the following institutions are examples of users: Memorial University, Newfoundland; the University of Calgary; Athabasca University; Télé Université de Quebec; and the Open Learning Institute, British Columbia. In Europe, the University of Lund, Sweden; the Universidad Nacionale de Educación a Distancia (UNED), Madrid, Spain; the Open University of the United Kingdom, Milton Keynes, and Telekolleg, Deutsche Institut für Fernstudien (DIFF), University of Tübingen, Tübingen, FRG are examples of users. In Australia, the University of Technology, Perth; the Murdoch University, Western Australia. Other institutions include the University of the South Pacific, Suva, Fiji; the University of the West Indies, Jamaica; and the Universidad Estatal a Distancia, San José, Costa Rica are all higher education institutions known to be major users of telephones for educational purposes.

Telephone teaching has also been used at the pretertiary school level, though to a lesser extent. Such uses have included projects for widening the curriculum in rural schools in the United States, for teaching sick or disabled homebound children, for helping parents in remote communities to teach their handicapped children, and for inservice courses for teachers and school administrators.

Administrative meetings are held by teleconferences in an increasing number of distance teaching systems, particularly where an institution has a large regional network, or widely dispersed local centres. Teleconference meetings are held as additional meetings inbetween regular but infrequent face-to-face meetings involving travel, for committee or working group meetings on a regular basis, or for urgent meetings of people who would otherwise be difficult to assemble. Meetings by telephone are also used for conducting research projects when a team of researchers is scattered over several institutions or countries. It is now comparatively easy to arrange an international conference call bringing together experts from different countries for a seminar or for training purposes.

Telephones are also being used increasingly for "dial access" services, which allows users, particularly in continuing education, to dial an audiotape library for short information items (usually 2 to 4 minutes in length) stored in a central resource bank. It is one of the quickest ways to make specialized information accessible to large numbers of individuals, and topics range from medical up-dating on drugs to agricultural information, from child-care advice to money management.

2. The Technology

The ways in which the telephone is used for teaching vary between institutions not only because of the particular role it is assigned within a teaching system as a whole, but also because of the different kinds of equipment and technology available. The telephone systems run by different institutions are not necessarily technologically identical.

For one-to-one telephone tutoring, the public telephone system is commonly used with ordinary domestic telephone handsets. Students are usually at home, or less frequently, at a local study centre, and similarly for tutors. No equipment costs are involved in this form of use. Costs for the call are borne either by the teaching institution, or by the students, or by both (usually depending on the degree of costs involved in the particular country). It is widely reported that students are at first reluctant to telephone their tutors, so tutors are often encouraged to take the initiative in making contact. As might be expected, the quality of the line varies from country to country and according to the age and frailty of the particular telephone system. One-to-one tutorials with a regular tutor are used widely by (among others) the Open University of the United Kingdom and Athabasca University (Canada) where they are particularly appropriate for students studying self-paced courses. UNED (Madrid, Spain) runs a general educational advice service and a problem-solving tutorial service for mathematics students ("Consultel"). Although there is no special equipment involved, cost is still a factor in the provision and use of one-to-one telephone tutoring and differs from country to country. A survey conducted in 1983 (Observer Business News, Sunday 6 Feb. 1983) showed, for example, that telecommunications charges in the United Kingdom are currently among the cheapest in the world except for local telephone calls which are much higher than elsewhere and which, unlike most other countries, are charged according to duration of the call. Canada, by contrast, is one of the few countries which provides "free" local calls, but has very high charges for long-distance calls. An additional piece of equipment which may be added to the above is a loudspeaking telephone, an amplifying device which enables a small group of students at one location to hear and speak to the person on the other end of the line, and which leaves the hands free for taking notes or handling papers or worksheets.

Audioteleconferencing (a group telephone call) joins three or more locations into a common network which lasts only for the duration of the particular event. Audioteleconferencing has developed mostly in the United States (there are currently over 60 systems in operation and 170 organizations using teleconferencing regularly), to some degree in Canada, and to a much more limited extent elsewhere. There are two main types of audioteleconferencing system. In the first (sometimes referred to as "dial-up" networks), the conference call service is provided by the commercial or national telephone company. The company operator joins together up to about nine lines on request by means of a conference bridge. This enables all participants to hear each other via the public telephone service, usually from home using a domestic telephone handset or at a local centre using a loudspeaking telephone. Generally speaking (and this is true of the United States, Canada, and the United Kingdom at least) the quality of service and equipment is variable. Voice quality fluctuates, the bridging of lines is uncertain either because of technical difficulties or lack of operator expertise, and for technical reasons further loss of clarity occurs if loudspeaking telephones are used. While some teleconference calls work well technically, others do not. One frustration of teachers and students in using conference calls through the public network is the unpredictability of performance of the technology. Yet as is widely reported in studies done in several countries, the quality of the technology is a key factor in determining the success or failure of telephone teaching projects.

The quality of the system described above can be improved by the use of additional equipment. Improved conference bridges, capable of linking from 10 to over 100 locations simultaneously, enable very large conference calls to be held, and link the lines together more effectively. These bridges can be purchased and staffed by an institution, which then has more control over its use of telephone conferencing. Also, individual microphones and separate loudspeakers significantly improve the sound quality and make it easier for groups of people at different locations to talk to each other than when using loudspeaking telephones.

The second main type of audioteleconference system is a "dedicated" four-wire system (a permanently installed network to fixed sites, with lines exclusively available 24 hours a day to the institutions leasing them). This four-wire system provides much better quality transmission of sound than is possible on the usual two-wire system. It also enables a variety of subgroupings of locations to be patched together, as well as the joining in of a limited number of public telephone network lines. Examples of this kind of system are Wisconsin's Educational Telephone Network (ETN) and the more recently established network of Memorial University, Newfoundland (the only "dedicated" educational network in Canada). While relatively expensive to install initially, a telephone network of this kind can be financially viable to run where use and costs are shared with other users. For example, Memorial University's network installation was supported initially by a federal government grant and operating costs are shared by 40 different user organizations. Once an audioteleconference system is in place, teleconference lines can also be used for data transmission (often used for medical education courses or diagnosis at a distance), telewriting (handwritten graphics electrically transmitted to remote screens), or transmitting tones which will automatically call up photographic slides on projectors at participating sites. While interactive video is often seen as a desirable form of teleconferencing, the costs of it are generally very high. Audioteleconferencing has been found to be adequate for a number of communication tasks, either by itself or with additional graphics facilities.

Although satellites are more readily thought of in relation to television broadcasting, they do have other important audio and data applications. They do, for example, provide a standard long-distance telephone service at lower cost (and of better quality) than through terrestrial circuits. They make possible new opportunities for the development of education and training programmes through audioteleconferencing, either by themselves or in a hybrid media mix. The availability of satellites to Canada in the 1970s and the decision to designate some of their use for educational purposes have led to a variety of applications being developed for groups who were previously not able to participate in continuing education and training.

The possible educational applications of the Australian Domestic Satellite System (ADSS) are currently being considered and planned. For example, in the early 1980s the Tarcoola Schools project in South Australia conducted trials teaching remote schools by existing telephone lines in order to learn more about the teaching strategies needed when ADSS became operational in 1985–87. This system will be complemented by a terrestrial telecommunications network which, by 1990, should bring telephone facilities to 99.7 percent of Australia's population. This opens up considerable opportunities in Australia for the educational use of telephones at a more realistic cost than at present, for reaching currently inaccessible communities, and for providing an improved service for the School of the Air.

3. Examples from Three Institutions

How institutions make differing use of the telephone for education is illustrated in the following examples.

3.1 Wisconsin's Educational Telephone Network (ETN)

The Wisconsin ETN grew out of the idea that the boundaries of the University of Wisconsin should be the boundaries of the state. It was begun to meet the continuing education needs of medical doctors and held its first session in 1965, linking 18 locations. Since then it has become the largest and one of the most sophisticated telephone-based instructional systems in the United States. By means of a "dedicated" telephone network, it can now reach over 200 sites: rooms set aside in hospitals, course houses, libraries, and learning centres are fitted with microphones and loudspeakers, which, when a group is large, automatically become a public address unit at the location where a person is asking a question. ETN offers a range of continuing education courses of varying length in pharmacy, law, social work, education, and agriculture, and on topics ranging from bee-keeping to library management. These are mostly noncredit courses though some credit courses are also taught. The network can link up together very large groups of people (200 or so) or a number of smaller groups simultaneously. Courses are taught largely by means of the audio network, with minimal print support. At 23 sites (which form part of a second separate network, the Statewide Extension Education Network, SEEN), there is an electrowriting facility which enables line-drawn graphic materials to be transmitted via the telephone as they are being drawn by the instructor and received on a television monitoring screen. This has enabled courses with more complex visual content, for example engineering, to be taught. Many sites have local programme coordinators who help facilitate participation in interactive sessions and see to the smooth running of the programmes. The courses themselves are prepared and taught by the professional staff of the Extension Department, teaching staff from the 27 campuses in the state's university, and community members with specific expertise. Help and support is given by the ETN staff in designing and planning appropriate teaching formats. Over 30,000 students a year currently take part in some form of course.

3.2 University of the South Pacific (USP)

The University of the South Pacific is a regional university representing 11 countries and covering a geographical area of 11 million square miles (equal in size to the United States). Since 1974, USP has been making use of a satellite (ATS-1) to provide an audioteleconferencing system. The teleconferencing system links nine regional centres to the main campus in Suva, Fiji, often thousands of miles apart. Anyone using the system can (as in the Wisconsin network) talk to and hear everyone else, using push-to-talk microphones and loudspeakers. The system is used largely for extension (continuing education) courses. The main means of study are through print, audiotapes, and written assignments. The audioteleconferencing network has been used in four ways: (a) to provide tutorial assistance, either one hour once a week arranged for a student given a tutorial assignment, or at the request of the student, or scheduled at difficult points in the course; (b) to make use of structured teleconferencing as a direct teaching component of a course; (c) as a means of information exchange between the 11 different countries; and (d) as a communication network for administration between the main campuses. The university has recently added microcomputers at each site, and slow-scan video to three sites. Already projects are in progress to explore the teaching of courses by a different and wider mixture of media than before.

3.3 The Open University (UK)

This national institution provides distance learning courses for about 63,000 undergraduate and 30,000 continuing education students using a variety of media. The basis of a course is provided through print, together with a mixture of television, radio, audiocassette, videotape, computer-assisted learning, home experimental kits, and summer schools. Study of a course is supported by a network of local tutors who grade assignments and correspond with students, as well as holding face-to-face and telephone tutorials.

Telephone tutorials are used in support of the course materials, and are organized regionally, according to perceived need; students also have access to tutors on tutors' home telephone numbers. No course material is taught directly by telephone at present. Telephone tutorials are either one-to-one between tutor and student (sometimes schedules, sometimes spontaneous) or in small groups. Two kinds of small group arrangements are used. In the first kind, up to eight students are linked to their tutor by conference call. Usually all participants are home based, using domestic telephone handsets, or they can be linked in from a local study centre. In the second kind, a tutor is linked in to a small group of students (three to six) at a local study centre; the students use a loudspeaking telephone so that all can hear, and speak to everyone else. Sometimes more than one centre is linked into this grouping (a maximum of eight is possible) or it might be a mixture of individuals at home and groups at study centres. Characteristically, this is a small, interactive discussion group considering aspects of the course material provided by other media or current assignments. Lecturing by the tutor is discouraged.

This system uses the public telephone network (British Telecom); the bridging of lines to form a common network is usually done by the British Telecom operator, though two or three regional offices have now installed their own conference bridges to gain a better and more flexible service. A loudspeaking telephone in a small box form is the only additional piece of equipment, enabling a group of up to 10 students to participate.

Telephone conferencing is currently used for between 750 and 1,000 hours of tutoring per year and one-to-one tutoring is used considerably more. The main barrier to its wider use (apart from some user resistance) is the poor quality of the technology (lines, bridges, and loudspeaking telephones). British Telecom operated until 1983 as a monopoly, which meant that limited choice was available. A valuable addition to audioconferencing used since the late 1970s has been CYCLOPS, a two-way interactive telewriting device using television screens and light pens. This has enabled the use of two-way dynamic visuals, particularly on technology and science courses, as well as the use of prepared graphic material stored on audiocassettes. Although the Open University is considering setting up a "dedicated" teleconferencing network nationally (it already uses a small one for administrative meetings) it has so far been deterred by cost.

4. Effectiveness as a Teaching Medium

In reviewing the rather uneven research into the effectiveness of audio or telephone communication as a teaching medium, it is necessary to return to Schramm's conclusion that learning depends on how a medium is used rather than which medium is used. The research and evaluation studies cover a wide range of situations and include both field and laboratory settings. It is often difficult to draw firm conclusions because of research design problems. The studies, often done with very small samples, use diverse measurement methodologies and techniques which vary in reliability. Most of these studies evaluate in terms of user satisfaction, fewer attempt to measure learning gains because of the difficulties involved in a "real-life" situation. Also, many of the studies on teleconferencing were carried out with more primitive equipment than is used in the late 1980s.

In general, research shows that learning can take place as effectively, and in some cases more effectively, on courses taught by telephone as on courses taught by other means (the usual comparison is with face-to-face). No differences between face-to-face and telephone communication have been found for tasks involving information transmission, problem solving, and generating ideas. It seems that the tasks which most frequently occur in educational settings (giving and receiving information, asking questions, exchanging opinions, and problem solving) are tasks which can be done effectively by telephone. However, tasks such as getting to know someone, or persuasion, or negotiation are affected by the medium through which they are done. For example, people who have met face-to-face are judged more favourably than people who have met only by telephone. Broadly speaking, tasks in which interpersonal relationships are important are done less effectively by telephone, while those involving cognitive material are done as effectively. Though face-to-face meetings are generally reported as preferred, students rate the value of telephone teaching or tutoring highly when no other options are open to them.

Teaching by telephone is different from teaching face-to-face, and the teacher has to learn to manage the event effectively. Adaptation to the medium requires the teacher to adapt in a number of ways: in communicating with unseen participants without the usual visual cues to ease the transaction or provide feedback; in redesigning the format and content of the teaching materials and activities; and in accommodating to the changes in teaching role and the pacing of the event imposed by the medium. Teaching by telephone requires more structuring of the event, more preparation of support materials (such as agendas, worksheets, prepared reading) and more conscious planning to make use of the interaction the medium allows. On the larger instructional networks, the quantity and quality of interaction can be limited because of the size of the large groups involved. To compensate for this, use is made of local facilitators or animateurs to develop "off-air" on-site group discussions as part of a larger scale teaching event. Small-group tutorials are similarly reported as being more task centred and impersonal but, interestingly, demonstrate greater verbal participation by the students and less by the tutor than their face-to-face equivalent (possibly because of better preparation).

One of the key factors in developing effective telephone teaching (or tutoring or instructing) and in influencing the attitudes of participants is the kind of induction and training in the use of the medium offered to students and teachers. Teachers who feel inadequately prepared for an event which research shows to be more anxiety provoking on first encounter than face-to-face teaching, are unlikely to persist in the use of the medium or to adapt their teaching strategies effectively, even though the technology involved is user friendly (there is no complicated machinery to master before the participant can use it). Successful adaptation to communicating through the medium generally takes place fairly quickly (over the first few sessions). The development of appropriate teaching strategies takes longer as the teachers or tutors learn to make choices about suitable content and formats, or which media mix to use (for example, what combination of telephone, print, audiotape, videotape, slide transparencies), or what kind of visual or graphic support materials are needed and how to convey them. To this end a variety of briefing and training methods and programmes are being developed by different institutions to support tutors using the medium. In wide use are advisory booklets; audiotape examples of good and bad practice; simulated workshop sessions using the medium either for teaching purposes or to develop interpersonal and counselling skills; self-evaluation audiotapes and checklists; face-to-face workshops. For example, Athabasca University uses a workbook on interpersonal communications and counselling skills, together with tape feedback sessions of actual tutorials to help tutors with one-to-one telephone tutorials; the Open University of the United Kingdom uses a mixture of all the methods mentioned above including a handbook on small group and one-to-one telephone tutoring; Wisconsin's ETN uses a handbook and training programme to advise and support instructors in the planning and design of the courses to be taught by audio-teleconferencing. Experience suggests that teachers who are already effective face-to-face teachers are likely to make effective telephone teachers.

While providing a satisfactory means of teaching or tutoring for a wide range of subjects and groups, the medium of the telephone alone does impose some limitations in terms of the use of graphic or visual materials. Teaching strategies can, in many circumstances, circumvent this problem, for example, circulation in advance of diagrams (with grid or colour coding for easy reference), photographs, or worksheets. One-way graphics can be transmitted by the use of slow-scan video or facsimile transmission, or telewriting devices, but these are rather slow in use, and many teachers, particularly in science and mathematics, express the need for a simple, speedier chalkboard equivalent, preferably allowing two-way interaction. One such development which fills this gap is CYCLOPS, referred to earlier. At present this is installed at fixed study centre locations, but ideally (cost permitting) it would be home based for students, since it can also provide access to a computer.

Perhaps the best indicator of the effectiveness of telephone teaching or tutoring is the growing extent of its use. Telephone technology is not suitable as a means of mass instruction, in the way that radio and television are. To function as an interactive teaching system (one of its strengths as a medium) there is a finite number of locations that can participate. Teaching by telephone is more suitable for more limited groups and specialist needs in education and training. However, there are some cost advantages to this form of distance teaching. While recognizing the fact that all media are not functionally equivalent in terms of what they can do as a teaching medium, it is worth noting that the production of courses and training of staff to use telephone teaching systems can cost less than broadcast media such as television or print-based courses.

Bibliography

Bates A W 1982 Trends in the use of audiovisual media in distance education systems. In: Daniel J S, Stroud M A, Thompson J R (eds.) 1982 *Learning at a Distance: A World Perspective*. Athabasca University ICCE, Canada

Gough J E, Garner B J, Day R K (eds.) 1981 *Education for the Eighties: The Impact of the New Communications Technology*. Deakin University, Victoria

Lauffer S, Casey-Stahmer A C 1982 Telecommunications systems for education and training. *Educ. Media Int.* 3: 21–27

Parker L A, Olgren C H (eds.) 1980 *Teleconferencing and Interactive Media*. University of Wisconsin Extension Center for Interactive Programs, Madison, Wisconsin

Robinson B (ed.) 1982 *Tutoring by Telephone: A Handbook*. Open University Press, Milton Keynes

Ruggles R 1982 *Learning at a Distance and the New Technology*. Educational Research Institute of British Columbia, Vancouver, British Columbia

Schramm W 1977 *Big Media, Little Media: Tools and Technology for Instruction*. Sage, Beverly Hills, California

Part 4

Instructional Development

Part 9

Instructions: Development

Part 4

Instructional Development

Introduction

The term *instructional development* came into use at about the same time as *educational technology*. This was no coincidence as it was the addition of an instructional development strand which induced some media specialists and learning psychologists to redefine their work as educational or instructional technology. The process is fully discussed in the opening article of Part 1 on *Conceptual Frameworks and Historical Development*. This draws attention to Lumsdaine and Glaser's editorial conclusion to the first major sourcebook on programmed learning.

> The basis for consistent improvement in educational methods is a systematic translation of the techniques and findings of the experimental science of human learning into the practical development of an instructional technology. To achieve the full benefits inherent in this concept, instructional materials and practices must be designed with careful attention to the attainment of explicitly stated, behaviourally defined educational goals. Programmed learning sequences must be developed through procedures that include systematic tryout and progressive revision based on analysis of student behaviour. (Lumsdaine and Glaser 1960 p. 572)

This short quotation includes three seminal ideas. The idea of instructional technology as applied learning theory originated the subfield we now call *instructional design*. The emphasis on behavioural objectives provided a cornerstone for the systems approach which evolved during the late 1960s to become the dominant paradigm for instructional developers. The notion of systematic tryout and progressive revision has remained a central feature of instructional development theory, even if it has often been somewhat eroded by the extreme time pressures so often found in practice. Taken together, these ideas implied that learning programmes and resources needed first to be designed on the basis of principles established by scientific research, then subsequently to be further tested and developed in use until the desired objectives were reached.

It was no accident that this concept of instructional development closely matched the prevailing view of industrial innovation during the 1960s. At that time innovation was

301

thought to result primarily from what came to be called research and development (R and D). So it was natural that the new educational technology should seek to introduce instructional innovations in a similar kind of way. However, subsequent research has revealed this research and development approach to innovation to be oversimplified, particularly with regard to the human element. This is discussed in Part 5 in articles on *Curriculum Implementation, Knowledge Utilization*, and *Knowledge Diffusion in Education*. One of the significant changes in instructional development has therefore been the extent to which its approach has shifted over the past 25 years to take more account of human factors and implementation problems.

1. Instructional Development and Curriculum Development

These two terms are variously perceived as identical, totally separate, or overlapping. The Editor's view is that the terms are semantically distinct but refer to processes which often overlap a great deal. There are some situations where the characterization of a process such as *instructional development* rather than *curriculum development* is primarily a matter of tradition or personal preference; some where the term *instructional development* is more appropriate; and some where *curriculum development* is a better description.

The semantic distinction assumes that it is possible, indeed desirable, to separate curriculum decisions about what to teach from instructional decisions about how to teach. Yet few people in the field of curriculum development would be prepared to abdicate responsibility for teaching method; and few people in instructional development would be prepared to abdicate all responsibilities for decisions about what to teach, especially where decisions are incorporated into the process of formulating instructional objectives. In practice, decisions are made at different levels by different agencies. For example, a government or school district may approve a document as defining its "official curriculum", while further, more detailed decisions are made at institutional level, or effectively binding decisions are built into specifications for national examinations. Yet other decisions are incorporated into the design of learning materials, especially textbooks, and these preempt the instructional options of teachers whose style is textbook dominated, whether by choice or necessity.

At school level, four of the more common systems of decision making are as follows:

(a) The official curriculum is formulated in fairly general terms, leaving decisions about detailed content and teaching method to individual teachers or institutions. The preparation of the official curriculum is sometimes described as *curriculum development*. Its translation into a functional curriculum at local level may be called *school-based curriculum development* or *instructional development* according to the preference of those involved.

(b) A broadly defined curriculum, as in (a), is accompanied by a single approved textbook. This leaves room only for the development of ancillary learning materials and for variations in lesson planning. Neither of these activities would normally be called *instructional development*.

(c) A broadly defined curriculum, as in (a), is assessed by an external examination which preempts even detailed decisions about what to teach. This influences but does not determine the instructional strategy. The cooperative development of learning resources and teaching strategies could still be called *instructional development*, but would not normally be called *curriculum development*.

(d) A curriculum package of learning materials and teacher manuals advising on when and how to use them is officially sanctioned and disseminated to schools. Very little choice of either content or method is apparently left to the user. The process of developing such a package is commonly called *curriculum development*, but it is also sometimes referred to as *instructional development*. In the latter case it will almost certainly have been developed by people calling themselves *educational technologists*; and it is also likely that it will emphasize either self-instruction or audiovisual media.

In higher education, those countries with national curricula will normally conform with model (a) above, although occasionally (b) will also be found. Other countries approve higher education courses at institutional level, usually on the basis of a relatively simple course description. More detailed documentation is found wherever courses have to be approved by external agencies, for validation or for professional recognition. In all cases except (b), the detailed decisions about what to teach and how, are made by the department or the individual teacher. Thus the term *curriculum development* is rarely used in higher education, except in the context of preparing course proposals for external approval. *Instructional development* is the usual term used in North America for the systematic design of courses and course materials, while *educational development* is often preferred in the United Kingdom.

Where there is no accepted distinction between curriculum and instruction, the choice of whether to call a particular process *curriculum development* or *instructional development* will usually depend on other factors. One such factor is the training of the developers: were they trained in curriculum or educational technology? Another factor is political: the labelling of an activity can affect who controls it, an issue that is further discussed in the article on *Design Contexts and Processes*. Where teachers are involved in instructional development or curriculum development, it usually represents an expansion of their accustomed role. Not to be involved in curriculum development is less unusual, but not to be involved in instructional development implies having little influence on how one teaches in one's own classroom—a distinct contraction in the traditional role of the teacher that is likely to be viewed with considerable misgiving, if not with hostility.

2. Instructional Development and Instructional Design

Reigeluth (1983) draws a clear distinction between instructional design and instructional development, which he regards as consecutive stages in an instructional process. His dominant metaphor is taken from the building industry: design is the preparation of an "architect's blueprint", development is the process of constructing a building from that blueprint, implementation is the renter adapting the building for personal use. An alternative metaphor (not Reigeluth's), which places less stress on the product, is that of the theatre. The design is the script, the development is the production, and the implementations are the performances. However, neither the metaphors nor the stage-based distinction are convincing when one considers the following common approaches to development:

(a) A piece of instruction is designed in the form of a television script, then subsequently produced and sold with an additional user's manual to guide its implementation. This process involves two pieces of design, first the script and then the manual, and one piece of media production—two if the typographic design of the manual is included.

(b) A new course is designed for implementation by several teachers using already published books. They take the course design document and implement it without any intervening activity apart from normal lesson planning.

(c) A computer programme is prepared on-line, then tried out with learners and modified in the light of that experience before being sold for use on a larger scale. Here the trial involves small-scale implementation and formative evaluation, and the modification is effectively a second phase of design.

In every case the period between the first design and full implementation is occupied by some combination of the following: production; small-scale implementation; formative evaluation; and further periods of design. To describe each of the three situations as having a development phase after the design and before the implementation distorts rather than adds meaning to the account.

What most authors call *instructional development* is the total developmental process. This incorporates design, production, evaluation, and also an initial phase of developing the design brief. Developing the brief may involve needs analysis, situation analysis, and specifying aims and objectives, and is immediately followed by the design itself. Thus, instructional design is but one part, though sometimes a recurring part, of the total process of instructional development. It is also usual for *instructional development* to refer to a course of instruction or a whole instructional programme, not to a single media product. So, although media product development includes an element of instructional design, it would not often be called *instructional development*.

3. Structure of Part 4

It was concluded above that instructional development comprised a number of sub-processes: developing a design brief, design, production, and formative evaluation. Some of these may be repeated more than once as the embryonic ideas, prototype designs, or drafts of learning materials are tested and revised. For convenience, therefore, all but one of these four subprocesses has been made the subject of a separate subsection or cluster of articles. The exception is production, which was largely covered in Part 3. An overview section on General Approaches to Design and Development has been added at the beginning; and a specific area of application, that of Individualized Learning Systems, has been added towards the end. Since some aspects of developing a brief are included in the overview, the second section is devoted specifically to Needs and Objectives. Thus Part 4 contains five sections, each with its own cluster of articles:

(a) General Approaches to Design and Development

(b) Needs and Objectives

(c) Instructional Design

(d) Individualized Learning Systems

(e) Evaluation.

Though this division seems straightforward, two rather complex boundary problems have had to be resolved. The first concerns the extent to which the large body of general literature on teaching and learning should be cited or reviewed, as a full account of the many teaching and learning strategies which an instructional developer might need to consider would occupy a great deal of space. Fortunately, this particular problem can be avoided by referring readers to an earlier volume in this series, the *International Encyclopedia of Teaching and Teacher Education* (Dunkin 1987). However, a cluster of articles on Individualized Learning Systems has been included because this subject has always been a major preoccupation of many educational technologists.

The second boundary problem, which is briefly mentioned above, concerns the overlap between instructional development and curriculum development. This has been handled in a number of ways. Section (a) contains separate overview articles on the development process from both a curriculum specialist and an educational technologist. These are complementary rather than contradictory, as each field suffers from neglecting the issues which tend to preoccupy the other. Section (b) on Needs and Objectives covers material published in both fields, and all of its articles could have been found in either. The problems and difficulties of ascertaining needs and formulating objectives are now being increasingly recognized, so these four articles provide a useful and timely review. The final section, on Evaluation, also includes material common to both curriculum studies and educational technology, ranging from programme evaluation, through evaluation of learning materials to criterion-referenced measurement.

Only two sections, (c) and (d), contain relatively little material from the field of curriculum studies. The first reviews the substantial research base for instructional design to which designers can refer for some guidance, though not for any blueprints. This derives partly from instructional psychology and partly from media research, both central areas of concern for many educational technologists which have hitherto failed to gain more than peripheral attention from most curriculum specialists. This work is most frequently applied in the design of Individualized Learning Systems, which are given a section of their own. This area of application has been so much the province of educational technologists that it was considered appropriate to include it, even though there are no parallel sections on group teaching methods or systems based upon them. However, care has been taken to preserve a balance between highly structured individualized systems and those which seek to develop learner independence.

More detailed discussions of the five sections follow below, but first attention needs to be drawn to related articles in other sections of the *Encyclopedia*. Organizational and political aspects of instructional development are the principal focus of the article on *Curriculum Development* in Part 5(a), and they also appear in the article on *Higher Education Consultancy* in Part 1, while another article in Part 5(a) of particular relevance to institutional developers is that on *Curriculum Implementation*.

3.1 General Approaches to Design and Development

This Section comprises three articles surveying concepts and literature relevant to instructional design, curriculum design, and instructional development, recognizing that these are partially overlapping terms. Their purpose is to provide an overview of each of these fields that guides readers to relevant parts of the *Encyclopedia* and to potentially relevant areas of literature which lie outside its boundaries. In *Design Contexts and Processes*, Eraut describes the range of settings in which designers work and the widely differing scope of the design tasks in which they may be engaged. Factors determining the respective roles of teachers and specialist designers are discussed, and reference is made to the significance of personal qualities in affecting the character of a design. The design process itself is then examined by comparing and contrasting four "ideal type" approaches: the artistic, the scientific, the engineering, and the problem-solving. Each is discussed in its historical and scholarly context. The article concludes with a review of the many areas of literature where ideas relevant to instructional design may be found.

Klein contributes a parallel overview of *Curriculum Design*, which she defines as a set of interrelated decisions about the curricular elements. These elements normally comprise objectives, content, learning activities, and evaluation procedures, though some authors also include learning resources, time, space and environment, grouping, and teaching strategies. One essential characteristic of a good design is a high degree of internal consistency between the decisions for each element. These decisions should be properly grounded in three primary data sources: organized subject matter, students, and society. The main body of the article explores the relationship between different types of curriculum design and arguments about these data sources, and about the priority to be given to different aims and emphases. Some recent trends that do not quite fit the pattern are also discussed.

Diamond's review of *Systems Approaches to Instructional Development* explains variations on what has undoubtedly become the dominant paradigm for educational technologists. He describes the general characteristics of systems models as incorporating the following elements: an analysis of student needs and situational parameters (this includes some of Klein's "primary data sources"), specification of objectives (this also subsumes Klein's "content"), careful planning of instructional strategies and use of media, formative evaluation, and criterion-referenced assessment. The semantic differences with Klein create different expectations, although they are apparently concerned with similar matters. More significant, and in keeping with the distinctive nature of the fields of curriculum design and instructional development, is the fact that Klein's article is mainly concerned with differences between design products, whereas Diamond's is mainly concerned with differences between design processes. The Editor believes that the two are more closely connected than is commonly realized, partly for political reasons and partly because designers make more unexamined assumptions than they are prepared to admit. Empirical studies of these issues are conspicuously absent.

Diamond makes a useful distinction between two main types of systems model: classroom/product models for lesson planning and materials production; and comprehensive models for the design of courses and programmes. In Diamond's view the former are primarily the concern of the specialist instructional designer, using the knowledge base reviewed in sections (c) and (d) below, while the latter are the major concern of instructional developers. In discussing these comprehensive models, Diamond draws particular attention to project selection (also discussed in Part 1 under *Higher Education Consultancy*), needs assessment (see below), and the use of an "ideal design" stage to counter inherent conservatism. This last point corresponds to the notion of "alternative images" in Eraut's "problem-solving" ideal type; but otherwise it is the "engineering" ideal type which dominates most of the systems models.

3.2 Needs and Objectives

Adult education is typically less formalized and institutionalized than schooling or higher education. Thus a more direct relationship pertains between provider and potential students when it comes to the assessment of need. This makes it a good starting point for considering how needs may best be assessed. Pennington's review of *Needs Assessment in Adult Education* distinguishes three possible outcomes from a needs assessment study: an analysis of the target population and its key characteristics, the identification of areas of demand (topics) for educational programming, and the specification of areas of need. The systematic pursuit of these goals usually involves the collection of data from potential clients or their representatives, and Pennington describes five possible approaches to this task. The participation-demand approach tends to dominate but emphasizes existing clients and topic areas at the expense of new ones. The other four approaches—consulting educational experts, using key informants, holding a community forum, or conducting a community survey—also have advantages and limitations, so there is usually a trade-off between cost and validity. Finally there is the perennial difficulty of distinguishing between an "authentic need" and a "felt need", what others have referred to as the distinction between "needs" and "wants".

Instructional developers have tended to emphasize two of Pennington's goals: the analysis of the student population and the specification of areas of need. Typically, they pursue these goals in greater detail than either adult educators or curriculum developers, thus making the detailed specification of objectives a central feature of their approach. However, there is a danger that giving so much attention to the formulation of objectives will result in their selection and justification being taken for granted. Eraut's short article *Selecting and Justifying Objectives* points out that while curriculum theorists stress the derivation of objectives from primary data sources, as described in Klein's article on *Curriculum Design*, practice is often very different. Instructional developers typically use secondary sources such as current curriculum practices and well-known curriculum traditions.

Eraut argues that in order to justify an objective, both its feasibility and its desirability need to be established. Desirability arguments may be based either on expressed preferences (wants) or on evidence from primary sources. These latter arguments are of four main kinds. They may be based on occupational practice, what is said to be needed for work; on future roles in society such as citizen, community member, or parent; on gaining access to cultural and academic knowledge; or on the interests of students. None of these arguments are as simple and uncontroversial as their proponents often imply. Moreover, the many different types of justification make it virtually impossible to devise any rational approach to the selection of priorities. People cannot easily plan a school curriculum *ab initio*, they need to find a starting point in some current practice and then modify it until they are satisfied or can obtain sufficient agreement.

Eraut's much longer review of the literature on *Specifying and Using Objectives* traces the historical development of the concept of objectives and the distinctive meanings given to the term by Tyler, Bloom, Mager, and Gagné. In order to discern what kinds of objectives are being used or written about, various devices are recommended, particularly Krathwohl's characterization of three levels of specificity and the author's own density index (number of objectives per hour of learning). Also useful are Gronlund's distinction between minimum essentials and developmental objectives, and Eisner's distinction between instructional and expressive objectives. A section on the status of objectives looks at their structural status as part of a list, hierarchy, or concept-map; their logical status as indicators of behaviour and as intentions for a particular student; and their political status, with respect to who specifies them and who uses them. Classification into different types of objective is discussed in terms of Bloom's three domains, though also using classifications from a variety of other authors. Interaction between the cognitive and affective domains is discussed, as are objectives such as social skills which do not fit the domain pattern. Finally, arguments for and against using objectives are discussed for five different kinds of use—curriculum development, lesson planning, instructional design, evaluation, and communication to students.

Bloom's domain categories are also used to structure De Landsheere's review of *Taxonomies of Objectives*. First she introduces Bloom's cognitive domain and research into its assumptions, confirming the hierarchical nature of the lower levels, but suggesting that the relationship between the upper levels is more complex. Then she shows how Guilford's Structure of Intellect model can absorb the Bloom taxonomy. Although Guilford's model has been largely ignored by instructional developers it offers greater taxonomic possibilities than Bloom, is not confined to verbal modes of representation, and is logically more coherent. Bloom for example uses different classification principles between his major categories from those he uses in distinguishing subcategories. The third taxonomy reviewed at length, that of Gagné and Merrill, is not exclusively cognitive but attempts to integrate the domains under four main headings: emotional behaviour, psychomotor behaviour, memorization, and complex cognitive behaviour. More briefly described are the taxonomies of Gerlach and Sullivan, and of Block, and De Corte's adaptation of Guilford.

Discussion of the affective domain is limited to Krathwohl's taxonomy and De Landsheere's variation upon it. Both are recognized as being of only limited scope. More research is called for, but the concept of an affective domain is not questioned. While six taxonomies are cited for the psychomotor domain, four are regarded as being only of historical interest. Simpson's is found to be too abstract and general to be of practical use, leaving Harrow's as the best available.

3.3 Instructional Design

The literature on instructional design is of two main kinds: research and reviews of research, and manuals or guidebooks. While these used to be closely linked in the later 1960s, their respective paths have increasingly diverged. Today's researchers are generally agreed that the research base is insufficient to support any empirically grounded handbook of instructional design and many think that a science of instruction is unlikely to develop in the foreseeable future. Thus it was decided to focus this cluster of articles on reviews of research relevant to instructional designers with relatively little attention given to design manuals. However, the role of such guidebooks will be briefly discussed at appropriate points in this overview.

Resnick's review of *Instructional Psychology* explains how it has been transformed by the adaption of a more cognitive approach since the mid-1960s (p. 363). Three major trends have dominated this change of perspective. First, there was a shift towards studying more complex forms of cognitive behaviour, including those that formed part of the school curriculum. Second, much effort is being directed at finding ways to represent the structure of knowledge and at discovering the ways in which knowledge is used in various kinds of learning. Finally, today's assumptions about the nature of learning and thinking are interactional. It is assumed that learning occurs as a result of mental constructions of the learner. This requires the development of a new kind of instructional theory, one that takes explicit account of the personal theories, experiences, and mental processes of the learner.

The most thoroughly researched knowledge domain is probably that of reading, which Resnick reviews in considerable detail. She points out that there is now considerable evidence that: (a) reading involves both "bottom-up processes" like word recognition and "top-down processes" using syntactic and semantic information provided by the context; (b) inferences beyond the explicit information in the text are a normal part of reading; and (c) the prior knowledge of the reader is central, not only propositional knowledge but also more complex knowledge such as schemas for interpreting the text and knowledge of typical forms of discourse. Since virtually all school work involves reading, these findings are of very wide significance.

Resnick's review also covers mathematics and science, but the general conclusions are the same: the nature of the knowledge involved is both subject-specific and much more complex than that assumed by most instructional developers, and the constructivist view of the learner's role has enormous implications for how interventions to enhance learning are designed. However, there are still important issues concerning intelligence and aptitude and their cognitive correlates and components. Discussion of these leads on to questions of whether there are generalizable cognitive skills whose acquisition can be promoted by appropriate interventions.

Finally, Resnick (p. 372) assesses the current state of a prescriptive science of instruction. Most progress has been made in describing the state of knowledge to be achieved and the initial state in which the learner begins. However, the assessment of outcomes needs to be transformed by treating task performances as indicators of the understanding and knowledge that are the deeper goals of education, not as being themselves the main objectives of instruction. Resnick's position on this is directly opposed to those who advocate competency-testing and criterion-referenced measurement, but supports those educators who believe education is in danger of being supplanted by testing. This transformation in our approach to assessment is also feasible. The problem remains of deciding the appropriate instructional intervention for any given circumstance; and on this crucial question cognitive instructional psychology has been largely silent, and with good reason:

> As cognitive psychology has elaborated a theory of the human being as an active constructor of knowledge, a new view of learning has begun to emerge—one that describes changes in knowledge as the result of learners' self-modification of their own thought processes and knowledge structures. This in turn means that instruction must be designed not to put knowledge into learners' heads, but to put learners in positions that allow them to construct well-structured knowledge. To know what these positions are likely to be requires knowing more about the cognitive processes involved in learning than is known at present. As a richer picture of cognitive processes of learning emerges, in part from descriptive studies of knowledge transformations under various instructional conditions, the scientific basis for a more prescriptive theory of intervention will become available.

Resnick believes that most progress has been made in the area of characterizing the knowledge to be learned. In educational technology, this area has traditionally been called *task analysis* and it is reviewed in this section by Markle and Tiemann. They define task analysis as a stage in instructional development which follows the specification of objectives and precedes the design of instructional materials and procedures. Its purpose is to convert the list of valued outcomes established by the curriculum decision-making process into a complete specification of the skills and knowledge which students must acquire. Their opening historical survey points out that task analysis was first developed in the context of training technology where there were jobs that could be analyzed and master-performers that could be observed. Similar methods for deriving and validating task analysis do not exist in most areas of the school curriculum. Also, the major contribution of task analysis to training technology has been to challenge many traditional assumptions about what is taught and assessed. It seems that training, in spite of its purported practical orientation, rapidly regresses to the transmission of verbalized propositional knowledge instead of the practical know-how required to do the job. Task analysis provides a useful counteracting force. The immediate reaction of many educators to these arguments would be to assert that task analysis implies an undeniable vocationalization of the curriculum. However, that would indicate a failure to understand what Resnick's review was claiming, namely, that successful performance in those areas of the school curriculum which have been most thoroughly investigated by cognitive psychology requires many kinds of skill and knowledge besides that propositional knowledge which traditionally dominates the assessment systems and hence the public "success criteria" for schooling. Markle and Tiemann confine the second part of their review to four areas where research can offer a little guidance for the instructional designer: procedural tasks, committing knowledge to memory, mastering conceptual schemes, and problem-solving strategies.

At this point it is convenient to discuss the role of guidebooks or textbooks on instructional design. Some of these are virtually worthless, giving the impression of usefulness by describing design stages and providing numerous flow-charts and checklists, but ignoring all the difficult decisions where designer judgement is required. Others are genuine attempts to construct a grand theory of instructional design. For this the reader is referred to Reigeluth (1983) and Romiszowski (1981) mentioned in the opening article of Part 4. These articles cover the field very thoroughly and cannot be easily summarized, nor is this an appropriate place for a detailed critique, but readers should be aware of their status as knowledge. In the editor's view, they contain a large number of ideas that are useful to instructional designers and which experienced designers will want to use, but they do not constitute established knowledge. Designers will still need to establish the appropriateness of any ideas they find in this literature for their own particular tasks. The design theories presented in these handbooks have not been widely used in published instructional materials, and there is little sign that they are generating a new brand of significantly improved materials and procedures. More particularly they do not adequately take account of the more constructivist view of learning now favoured by many psychologists, nor of the growing volume of subject-specific research. Nevertheless, if more designers do not begin to tackle the issues presented by these guidebooks, the art of design will remain almost undiscussed and future progress will be limited.

As Resnick indicates, one of the best researched areas of school learning is that of reading, and the findings of this research have considerable significance for textbooks as well as for readers. Recent research on *Learning from Textbooks* is reviewed by Armbruster and Anderson, whose theoretical perspective is similar to Resnick's. First, they examine the characteristics of texts which affect learning: various forms of structuring, local coherence, and the focus and density of the content. However, in accordance with their interactionist perspective, they give equal attention to equipping students with cognitive strategies and study skills which will enable them to use texts more effectively. Second, they encapsulate the findings of these two areas of research into a checklist of questions for judging the instructional effectiveness of textbooks and teachers' manuals. The questions suggest criteria which good texts need to satisfy, and are thus of direct relevance to selectors and users of textbooks. These cannot easily be converted into guidelines for textbook writing, but nevertheless suggest issues that authors will need to resolve.

Further guidance to authors and designers is provided by Hartley's article on *Typographic Design*. This covers relatively obvious features of texts such as page size, spatial arrangement of type, typographic uses, and access structures. This research is not widely known by educators, who continue to produce large quantities of textual material with little consideration for typographic design.

The strong emphasis on textual materials in this section of the *Encyclopedia* is no accident, for it reflects the nature of formal education. While there is a growing emphasis on practical work in mathematics, science and technology, and on learning from the environment in science and social studies, issues of visual representation are still relatively neglected. However, both experiential learning and learning from pictorial representation are strongly affected by perceptual factors, and there is increasing evidence that visual imagery plays an important part in the thinking processes of mature adults. Fleming's article on *Perceptual Factors* suggests that the iconic and symbolic modes of representation develop in parallel from infancy to adulthood with imagery always playing an important part in thinking. This reverses earlier assumptions that the iconic mode was merely a route to the symbolic mode, which was in some way intrinsically superior. This shift in perspective accords with research showing that perception is so intertwined with other cognitive processes as to be virtually indistinguishable. Fleming chooses, therefore, to examine perceptual factors in association with related instructional goals, discussing the distinctive roles of visual and audio modes of representation as he proceeds. Most of his attention is devoted to visual and auditory attention (noticing and being interested in the appropriate objects or events), perceptual discrimination (seeing and learning what the expert sees and hears), and perceptual integration (parallel processing and synthesis of information). Though clearly vital for learning, these are not areas to which many instructional designers have given much attention. Rather briefer attention is given to equally important areas where there has been less research in the educational context: perceptual closure (judging and decision making), perceptual imagination (creating new ideas), and perceptual learning (adapting and performing).

Heidt's article makes a direct attack on the problem of *Media Selection*, another "black box" in many handbooks on instructional development. He detects six different approaches in the literature. Checklists of questions to be considered and assessments of the advantages and limitations of individual media, help to prepare the designer's brief but offer little help with the actual choice. One-dimensional taxonomies like those of Dale (based on abstraction) and Duncan (based on complexity) provide "rules of thumb" that are only partially valid; and cost-effectiveness algorithms seem to concentrate solely upon cost. More complete guidance is given by two-dimensional matrices setting media categories against instructional functions (Gagné) or types of objective (Sparks), with suitability ratings in the boxes, or by decision-making flowcharts like Romiszowski 's. However, except for certain areas of obvious commonsense, there is little empirical evidence to support any of these media selection models.

An alternative approach is to define the problem in terms of selection factors. Some 50 or so factors can be found in the literature, each of which is important under some sets of circumstances, but few can be quantified or prioritized. For convenience, Heidt groups them under six headings: task factors, learner factors, instructional management factors, technical factors, cost factors, and administrative factors. Significantly, only the first two of these were considered by the earlier articles in this cluster (the differences between theory and practice) though they do form part of Diamond's review of *Systems Processes to Instructional Development* [Part 4(a)]. Heidt concludes that the application and weighting of whatever factors are chosen as relevant still depends on the subjective judgement of the designer. Neither comparative media research nor aptitude–treatment–interaction research have made significant inroads on the problem.

The reason for this lack of progress in media research is attributed by Levie to its insistence on treating types of media as the significant variable. His article on *Media Attributes* argues that many types of media can produce several styles of message, each with different attributes; and it is these attributes, rather than the media themselves, which constitute the significant variables. His five classes of attribute are: sensory modality, visual, auditory, or tactual; symbolic modality, verbal or nonverbal; design cues and codes; forms of control characteristics; and interactive features such as response mode and type of feedback. Research is cited for each of these attributes, thus giving designers some guidance.

The overwhelming impression one gets from this cluster of articles is that instructional design is both an exceedingly complex task and one of vital importance. This will not be changed by the advent of new technology. The danger for educational technologists is that they seek to reduce design knowledge to deceptively simple courses and handbooks of little practical value. More might be gained by developing a tradition of design criticism than by continuing to search for grand generalizable themes. This would seem more appropriate for the relatively underdeveloped state of the research base.

3.4 *Individualized Learning Systems*

Individualized learning has been a major theme in the development of educational technology for two main reasons. First, because it has been frequently assumed that individualization was an intrinsically desirable educational goal, the only problem being how to deliver it within the manpower and resource constraints of a typical school system. This assumption has always underpinned the approach to learning of behavioural and cognitive psychologists, but is questioned by sociologists and social psychologists who draw attention to the powerful effects of groups on motivation and achievement. Second, individualized learning systems provide a context in which learning materials and procedures can be tested and revised until they are effective, using the product development process to which most educational technologists are committed. This process is more difficult to pursue in a group or class context where teacher and group variables significantly affect the interaction between learners and instructional resources. In theory, individualized learning systems allow the instructional developer to work directly with learners with only limited mediation by teachers. In practice, the research on implementation suggests this is far from being the case.

Boud's opening article reviews *Individualized Instruction in Higher Education* where the greatest variety of approaches can be found. He shows how an initial interest in programmed learning was broadened into several kinds of individualized learning systems, notably the Keller Plan (also reviewed in a separate article), the audio-tutorial approach, and various forms of modular instruction. There is also an increasing use of computers to support these activities. Parallel to this developing tradition of structured learning, there has developed a range of approaches to increasing student independence of which projects and learning contracts are notable examples. Finally, Boud reviews experience relevant to three vital issues: the transformed role of the teacher, the changed pattern of costing and staffing, and the problems of adopting and implementing new practices.

Bolvin follows with a brief review of *Individualized School Programs*. The characteristics he identifies as common to most such programmes can be grouped under three main headings: the organization of school time and the school environment; the resource base of well-structured curricula, instructional materials, and study plans; and a guidance system for assessing student readiness, assisting student choice, and providing feedback to students, teachers, and the system. He believes the system which has gone furthest in specifying organizational changes is probably the Individually Guided Instruction System developed by Klausmeier at Wisconsin. His assessment of the evaluation studies concluded that convincing evidence of individualized systems leading to improved student achievement has yet to be found. This view might well be disputed by the proponents of the various approaches. However, all of them agree that evaluation is more profitably directed towards improving the quality of programmes rather than comparing them with others before they have reached a mature stage of development.

Three articles on particular approaches to individualized instruction, which have been more thoroughly researched than most, cover *Programmed Learning*, the *Keller Plan*, and the *Mastery Learning Model*. Eraut begins by tracing the historical development of *Programmed Learning* and the way in which various assumptions about programmes and the programming process changed with increasing experience, research, and new innovations. His review of programme design includes such issues as frame size, lean programmes, response mode, feedback, and pacing. The pioneering approaches to developmental testing of materials are noted, as are the many forms of instructional systems which evolved out of the early programmed learning movement. Finally, there is some discussion of alternative paradigms like structural communication, the feedback classroom, and programmed tutoring.

The first and possibly best-known offspring of programmed learning was the *Keller Plan*, designed in the early 1960s by Skinner's friend and colleague, Fred Keller. Kulik's article describes the Keller system, also known as the Personalized System of Instruction (PSI), summarizes evaluations of it, and reviews the functions of its various components. Keller courses are mastery oriented and individually paced, rely on printed study guides to deliver instruction sprinkled with a few orienting motivating lectures, and use student proctors to mark the frequent quizzes immediately after completion. Comparative studies with conventional methods indicate that PSI courses are significantly more effective and preferred by the majority of students. Research reviewed on critical aspects of PSI relates to the mastery assumption, unit size, immediacy of feedback, amount of review, tutorial help, and student "engaged" time.

Mastery Learning Model is reviewed by Anderson and Block, well-known proponents of this movement to introduce individualized learning at school level. Although the idea of mastery learning underpins most of the individualized learning systems of the 1960s and 1970s, this particular movement originates from Bloom's advocacy in the late 1960s. Its major difference from most of the other systems is that it retains group-based teaching and teacher pacing. Instruction is only individualized when needed, namely, when students are experiencing difficulties, and even then it is seen as a temporary expedient. Thus, extra time has to be provided for some learners to enable them to reach mastery level along with the rest of their class. The theoretical justification is provided by Bloom's application of the Carroll Model which hypothesizes that aptitude affects the time taken to learn but not the level of learning that can ultimately be achieved. Traditional schooling keeps learning time constant and produces variable achievement. However, Bloom suggests varying the learning time in order to obtain a nearly homogenous level of achievement. This principle can be most easily realized in schools if group pacing is maintained by occupying students who mastered a topic early in enrichment tasks or even peer tutoring, while their slower colleagues catch up.

To implement a mastery learning programme, four basic tasks have to be accomplished: defining, planning, teaching, and grading. Defining mastery involves identifying objectives, designating and sequencing learning units, and developing mastery tests for each unit. Planning requires an original instructional plan, diagnostic tests and corrective plans for students who need further help, and a time-plan for their use. The teacher then has the formidable task of orienting students, managing the whole process, and delivering direct teaching whenever that is part of the plan. Grading should be based on summative tests alone, with 'A's being awards for performance at mastery level. A research review examines overall effectiveness, standard setting, the function of correctives, and effects on different types of students. The article concludes with some speculations on future developments and the need for further research.

Tough's review of *Self-planned Learning* stands in total contrast to the articles which precede it. Its primary concern is with learners gaining control of their own learning goals, whereas in most individualized learning systems goals are more tightly defined than in traditional education. Tough reminds us that only some 20 percent of the learning efforts of adults are planned by professional educators: self-planned learning is the norm. He discusses the optimum amount of teacher control, then reviews various approaches to providing support for self-planned learning in both noncredit adult education and recognized credit programmes. These include workshops, materials, networks, learning contracts, and self-help groups. Self-planned learning is most commonly found in adult education and higher education, but could be much more widely used in schools.

3.5 Evaluation

Evaluation has become a major field of educational activity which receives full treatment by Walberg and Haertel in the *International Encyclopedia of Educational Evaluation*, a future volume in this series. This Section is confined to four articles of particular relevance to educational technology, opening with Lewy's brief review of the distinction between *Formative and Summative Evaluation*. Though implicit in much of the pioneering work of the early 1960s, these terms were first introduced by Scriven in 1967. Formative evaluation rapidly became more popular among developers and was widely used for the improvement of their programmes and products. Summative evaluation retained the allegiance of researchers, then became increasingly important as a form of accountability. Scriven still believes that both types of study have unique and essential roles, and this is now generally accepted.

Worthen's article on *Program Evaluation* defines the term as "those activities undertaken to judge the worth or utility of a program in improving some specified aspect of an educational system" (p. 439). This includes both formative (improving the programme) and summative (deciding whether to continue the programme) purposes, but excludes evaluations of the system itself. Historically, programme evaluation originated with the importation of the experimental tradition then dominant in educational and psychological research. However, this primarily quantitative and comparative emphasis was increasingly criticized during the 1970s as newer qualitative approaches were developed. Worthen describes some of the more popular current approaches under five headings: performance-objectives congruence approaches, derived from Tyler; decision-management approaches, as exemplified by Stufflebeam's Context, Input, Process, and Product (CIPP) evaluation model; judgement-oriented approaches, including Scriven, Stake's Countenance model and Eisner's Connoisseurship model; adversarial approaches; and pluralist-intuitionist approaches such as those of Rippey, Parlett and Hamilton, MacDonald, and Stake's Responsive model. His conclusion after reviewing their strengths and weaknesses is that evaluation models provide essential stimulants to thinking about vital evaluation issues, but are less useful as prescriptive guidelines. To improve the quality of programme evaluations in the future, Worthen argues that we need a better knowledge base, more evaluations of evaluations, greater understanding of the political nature of evaluation, and more general use of a wider range of approaches and techniques within each individual evaluation.

Eraut notes four different ways in which *Evaluation of Learning Resources* is practised: panel or committee reviews, user surveys, intrinsic evaluation through methodical inspection, and field testing. As panel members and users have to derive their views from some combination of inspection and field observation, the number of methodologies is reduced to two. Accordingly, methods of intrinsic evaluation and of field testing are reviewed, and their practical application to each of these major evaluation purposes is discussed. These purposes are the selection or purchase of resources, planning how to use resources, and the improvement or modification of resources.

The final article, *Criterion-referenced Measurement* by Hambleton does not fit the pattern of the rest of the section. However, this is an important technical area for evaluations which seek to measure student achievement, and it plays a vital part in many individualized learning systems. It is included as a particular concern of many educational technologists, and to counteract the not uncommon assumption that the technical problems of measurement are largely confined to norm-referenced methods.

Bibliography

Dunkin M J 1987 *The International Encyclopedia of Teaching and Teacher Education*. Pergamon, Oxford

Lumsdaine A A, Glaser R (eds.) 1960 *Teaching Machines and Programmed Learning: A Source Book*. Department of Audiovisual Instruction, National Education Association, Washington, DC

Reigeluth C M 1983 *Instructional Design Theories and Models: An Overview of their Current Status*. Lawrence Erlbaum, Hillsdale, New Jersey

Romiszowski A J 1981 *Designing Instructional Systems*. Kogan Page, London

Walberg H J, Haertel G D *The International Encyclopedia of Educational Evaluation*. Pergamon, Oxford, in press

General Approaches to Design and Development

Design Contexts and Processes

M. R. Eraut

Several articles in this Encyclopedia address themselves specifically to the problems and concerns of those engaged in instructional design. Many other entries are clearly relevant. The purpose of this article is to provide an overview of thinking, writing, and practice in this field, and to refer the reader to other entries for more detailed treatment of specific issues and approaches. Thus the first section on definitions, settings, and tasks describes what tasks an instructional designer might find himself or herself doing in various institutional settings, and then goes on to discuss some further factors affecting the instructional design process. This process is itself examined in the second section, where different conceptions of the design process are compared and contrasted. Then finally the complex and multifaceted literature is surveyed with special attention to locating concepts and criteria that are potentially useful to instructional designers.

1. Definitions, Settings, and Tasks

No universally agreed definition of instructional design can be readily inferred from the literature. Indeed, two factors make such an agreement extremely unlikely. First there is considerable overlap with other terms, especially curriculum design, lesson planning, and production of learning materials. Second, the use of the term is significantly influenced by the context in which the author is working. In particular, those who engage in instructional design in schools, in higher education, and in industrial settings are accustomed to different parameters.

One common distinction is that between curriculum and instruction, in which it is generally assumed that decisions about what to teach—curriculum decisions—precede decisions about how to teach—instructional decisions. This assumption holds good in school settings where there is an agreed syllabus or curriculum specified primarily in terms of the content to be covered. Textbook writers, television producers, or teachers planning their lessons within the framework of such a predefined curriculum would then be engaging in instructional design. However, when a curriculum document specifies teaching activities or prescribes a particular teaching approach, the distinction between curriculum design and instructional design becomes more difficult to sustain. Usually this inclusion of advice on teaching within a curriculum document reflects the curriculum designers' wish to emphasize process objectives and the improvement of pupils' thinking skills. Sometimes, as in the arts, it reflects a concern for expressive objectives. Conversely, the exclusion of teaching advice from curriculum documents can be seen as sanctioning a highly traditional teacher-centred curriculum. Thus the distinction between curriculum and instruction is not without ideological connotations.

In a country like the United Kingdom, the political connotations are also significant. Teachers' claims to have the greatest weight in curriculum decision making rest not only on their professionalism but also on their intimate knowledge of the circumstances pertaining in their own classrooms. Within certain limits, this is arguing that curriculum decisions should not be made without knowledge of their probable instructional consequences. Where teachers are confident of retaining instructional control, they will argue that the separation of curriculum decisions from instructional decisions is impractical and unworkable. However, in countries where curriculum decisions are effectively out of the teachers' hands, their political interest will lie in maintaining a rigid distinction between curriculum and instruction in order to prevent further incursions onto their territory.

Another important distinction, particularly at school level, is that between the notion of an instructional designer as a specialist and that of instructional design as a normal part of every teacher's job. The specialist instructional designer will usually be engaged in the production of packages of learning materials for use by pupils and teachers, though some people who do this prefer to call themselves curriculum developers. The choice of label may depend on the background and training of the persons concerned and the kind of expertise they claim to possess, or it may simply reflect the

317

local tradition. The label which carries the greatest status and asserts the strongest claim on resources will usually be the most popular! Where instructional design is considered part of the teacher's job, it is usually associated with lesson planning and the presentation of simple learning aids. Its importance then becomes dependent on the teacher-training system and on the time and resources available for teachers to exercise this role. The literature on the specialist instructional designer can be found both under curriculum development and under educational technology, while the literature on the instructional design role of teachers is often incorporated into general books on classroom teaching.

In most universities, the situation is different yet again. The teacher is seen as a subject expert and therefore has more influence on the curriculum. Except on large introductory courses where departures from previous practice will need careful negotiation, teachers can usually shape their own courses to suit their own preferences and expertise with only minimal attention to the rubric which appears in the prospectus. While the curriculum or collectivity of courses is largely a departmental responsibility and is heavily influenced by the micropolitics of the institution, the individual course is the responsibility of the individual teacher. The term "course design" is accepted as normal, but "curriculum development" is rarely used in the higher education literature. Again there is a useful distinction to be made between the notion of the instructional-design specialist and that of instructional design as a normal part of the university teacher's job. However, the process of teaching is often seen primarily in terms of making the teacher's own subject expertise available to students. So the specialist instructional designer will always have a subordinate role, and the demand to make the nature of the subject expertise more explicit will be correspondingly less.

Many instructional design models were first developed in industrial and military settings, and metaphors derived from these settings strongly colour the literature. While in schools an instructional designer would normally take a curriculum document or an unwritten curriculum tradition as the point of departure and in universities he or she would start from the expertise of the professor, in industrial settings the job is the initial point of reference. Instructional design begins with job description and job analysis, and thus acquires an empirical base which is lacking in most educational settings (albeit a shifting base because jobs change and people change jobs). Indeed, one problem with some of the instructional design literature is that it treats educational problems as if a similar empirical base was available, thus ignoring the political and moral issues which suffuse educational decision making.

Even within these diverse settings, instructional designers may find themselves operating at different levels of intervention:

(a) a single classroom, where teachers, trainers, or professors, prepare their own instruction with or without the advice of an instructional designer;

(b) a single course in a single institution, taught by several teachers in several classrooms: this may be prepared by a course team, and it may, but need not, involve the production of learning materials, and a specialist designer may or may not be involved;

(c) a distance learning course, similar to (b) but with a more clearly defined end product and, usually, a more heterogenous student population;

(d) a course or learning package for use in several institutions. This will usually involve an instructional design specialist, but the tasks may be undertaken by a group of teachers without specialist support. There will normally be considerable uncertainty over the conditions of use, and teachers' manuals will often be included in the package;

(e) a programme of courses within a single institution;

(f) the most ambitious example would be the design of a new institution, but this is not, strictly speaking, instructional design.

Both the magnitude of the instructional design effort and the number of interested parties will be greatly affected by the level of intervention, as will the instructional design procedures. Yet this is not always made explicit in the literature. Hence it is important to exercise considerable caution in transferring advice intended for one kind of setting and one particular level of intervention to another.

A further factor affecting instructional design, which is rarely discussed at any depth, is the influence of personal factors. It is common to find certain types of expertise being recommended as relevant to, or even essential for, certain instructional design tasks; and the expertise is often described in formal terms with an emphasis on specialist qualifications. While such expertise is not unimportant, other skills of equal significance are frequently omitted; for example, ability to write with clarity and interest, ability to work in a team, and ability to get good feedback from students. Many other personal factors also influence instructional designs: authors' personal educational values, their wider interests and life experience, their often implicit image of what the product might look like, their career ambitions, and so on. While sometimes mentioned in passing, there has been little formal research on these important personal factors; yet they may well have a highly significant influence on design quality (Riley 1984).

2. Alternative Conceptions of the Design Process

Four alternative conceptions of the design process are discussed below: the artistic, the scientific, the engineering, and the problem solving approaches. These are often left implicit in the literature rather than analysed in any depth, partly because most designers work within traditions whose assumptions they do not usually question. Only some of these approaches are mutually incompatible, so many hybrids can be found.

Several traditions contribute to the notion of instructional design as an artistic process, though few of them would be happy with the use of the term "instructional". The first tradition is that of the teacher as artist, a metaphor particularly favoured in the humanities and in higher education. Indeed, one of the more original and interesting books about teaching in higher education is entitled *The University Teacher as Artist* (Axelrod 1973). Proponents of this tradition would argue that instructional design is indeed part of a teacher's role, and that the design process is one of forging a unique communication to fit each special set of circumstances. The teacher–designer is a performing artist, and, though prior planning is important, no two performances of the same teaching task can be, or should be, the same.

Specialist instructional designers, on the other hand, are often described as authors or producers. Taking written materials first, to what extent is it useful to regard the process of preparing a textbook or other learning materials as similar to that of writing a novel, a short story, a play, a newspaper column, or even an advertisement? If textbook writing is to be viewed as more than a purely rule-bound activity, then attention to its more creative aspects is surely overdue. Often it is only in the visual presentation of a textbook that an artistic contribution is formally acknowledged. Yet, whether it is acknowledged or not, writers of instructional materials are engaged in creating original communications; and more might be learned about instructional design by considering the writing process more carefully.

Perhaps the most glamorous task undertaken by instructional designers, if they admit to that designation, is that of producing motion pictures. Film and television producers see themselves as experts in their medium in a way that textbook writers do not. The prime requirement of audiovisual presentation is that it shall capture and hold the attention. Consequently producers tend to adopt the idioms of their commercial colleagues and of public entertainers and to accept their criteria for success. At one time, this commitment to standards derived from outside education was much lamented by educators, but experience with talking heads and amateur productions of low aesthetic merit caused many of them to change their minds. Children's Television Workshop has shown how commercial and instructional approaches can be fruitfully combined; and many European broadcasting networks have shown how creative producers can make educational programmes of considerable quality if their instructional brief is not too narrowly conceived (see *Use of Television in the Classroom*).

The fourth artistic tradition, already mentioned in passing, is that of graphic design (and photography might also be included). Apart from some evidence that the visual impact of printed material is indeed important, there must surely be some concern about the hidden visual education curriculum present in so many instructional materials. Moreover, shoddy learning materials are bound to affect the status accorded to those educational activities which use them.

What then are the implications of an artistic conception of the instructional design process? Clearly it affects the way the product is judged, an issue that is discussed in the next section. It could also affect the way the design process is researched into and talked about, as well as the way instructional designers are trained. More significantly still, by drawing attention to personal qualities and creativity, it suggests that these qualities should be given more attention when selecting instructional designers. Knowledge, qualifications, and experience alone will not suffice.

The notion of instructional design being a scientific process also has a long and complex ancestry. First, there is a long European tradition of pedagogy going back to Comenius and Herbart, whose *Science of Education* was first published in 1809. Though not without influence on textbooks, this tradition has operated mainly through teacher training with a consequent focus on the instructional design role of the teacher. Hence it was instructional psychology, particularly postwar behavioural psychology, that led to the introduction of specialist, scientifically trained, instructional designers. The early history of this approach is intimately linked to the development of programmed learning; and the idea of a "teacher-proof" learning package so effectively designed that teachers could be bypassed was popular for some considerable time. Indeed Skinner's seminal article "The science of learning and the art of teaching" (1954) set a tone of scientific optimism which was to pervade discourse about instructional design for the next 20 years. However, this optimism has now faded as pure behaviourism has been largely discredited among psychologists and supremely effective instructional packages have failed to appear and transform the educational scene. In many contexts, however, the design of learning materials remains a specialist task, and instructional designers are still looking for a scientific basis for their work. Where can they now look, and what sort of expectations should they have? Here it is perhaps useful to distinguish between macro- and micro-decisions in instructional design. Examples of macrodecisions would be whether to use an individualized learning system, or to make a television series, or to adopt an interdisciplinary approach, while microdecisions are concerned with the communication of particular ideas, or concepts, or the teaching of some specific skill.

Macrodecisions claiming a scientific justification tend to be based on empirical research studies of a comparative kind in which two different treatments, or media, or methods are compared. Such literature however rarely provides sufficiently clearcut advice. The reason, as Cronbach et al. (1981) have eloquently pointed out, is the large number of variables. Aim priorities vary both between contexts and over time, conditions vary, learners vary, and even the treatment itself varies. Only in a very limited sense is it helpful to group different television programmes under the generic level "televised instruction"; and even the same programme is handled differently from one classroom to another. There is much to be learned from studying these effects, but so far it appears unlikely that this knowledge will be systematically codifiable to a degree which allows the designer to substitute a set of decision rules for informed professional judgment.

With microdecisions, however, there has been considerable further development in "second generation" design theories based on instructional psychology. These are described and compared in an excellent book by Reigeluth (1983). Here the well known theory of Gagné and Briggs (1979) is set alongside the more purely behavioural theory of Gropper, and the algorithmic and rule-based theories of Landa and Scandura. The most completely developed theory is probably that of Merrill and Reigeluth, which combines a microlevel approach to the teaching of individual facts, concepts, procedures, and principles (Merrill's Component Display Theory, 1983) with an Elaboration Theory of Instruction (Reigeluth and Stein, 1983) that deals with the sequencing and structuring of such components into meaningful subject matter. The Reigeluth compendium does not include work outside North America, such as that of Romiszowski (1981) who tackles a wider range of knowledge-types.

In spite of this impressive array of instructional design theories, there is little empirical evidence to suggest that a system of decision rules for designers will be found which will guarantee effective instruction. However, these microtheories of instructional design also provide authors with a considerable repertoire of approaches to instructional analysis, which can be drawn upon whenever it seems appropriate. Their weaknesses stem partly from their neglect of peer-group effects and the social psychological aspects of teaching and learning, and partly from limitations in their approaches to knowledge representation (Eraut 1988). Their strength lies in their taking instructional design seriously at the microlevel, and even a cursory glance at commonly used textbooks suggests that their selective application could lead to some improvements.

These limitations in the scientific approach were becoming apparent to many designers in the late 1960s, when many practitioners supplanted it by an engineering approach (see *Conceptual Frameworks and Historical Development*). People soon found that programmes designed on "scientific principles" did not necessarily work first time; and the metaphor changed from science to engineering as designers found that they understood less and less about learning but could still improve their products by developmental testing. People began to describe programming as a process for specifying, designing, testing, and modifying instructional materials with psychological theory relegated to a supporting role. The research, development, and diffusion approach to educational innovation was born, and the systems approach was imported from engineering and adapted to instructional design.

Under the engineering approach, the teacher becomes a craftsperson who acquires his or her knowledge by absorption from a tradition during the course of his or her apprenticeship. If an instructional design role exists at classroom level then it is largely traditional in character. The specialist instructional designer is a technician who applies the techniques of specification of objectives, needs assessment, preassessment of students, and evaluation and revision, without understanding why some things appear to work and others do not. However, this process is not really instructional design at all. The emphasis has switched to instructional development, using the systems approaches outlined in the next article, while design has been relegated to the role of a black box in the middle of an otherwise empirically governed process of instructional development. Where the instructional design brief envisages nothing more than the marginal improvement or updating of an existing course, package, or programme, the black box can be filled by modification of an existing tradition, but where existing traditions are deemed to have failed, something new is clearly necessary.

It is in just such situations of radical change that the problem-solving approach has its greatest appeal. The advantages of a problem-solving approach are (a) that it recognizes the need for creativity as well as analysis, and (b) that it focuses effort and attention on what is thought to be the main source of difficulty. Moreover, there is a literature on problem solving and creativity of considerable relevance to the process of instructional design. Most problem-solving models begin, like instructional design models, with mapping the parameters, but then they give prime attention to research on creativity. This suggests that it is important to generate new ideas without criticizing them too early in the process; that procedures such as brainstorming will promote the invention of a diverse set of options; that images and metaphors are important sources of new ideas; and that practices like listing the advantages and limitations of each alternative can be useful in encouraging the fuller exploration of alternatives and discouraging premature closure on a particular approach. Clearly there is a significant difference, once the parameters have been outlined, between an ends–means approach through the further specification of objectives and a problem-solving approach in which a group of designers deliberately set out to generate and explore alternative images for the course, irrespective of whether the source of the image is an activity, a relationship, some subject matter, or a highly valued outcome (Eraut 1976).

Sometimes the problem to be solved is one of the designer's own making. Trying to achieve a range of outcomes whilst remaining faithful to the integrity of the content and promoting student motivation is usually a difficult task. Whenever a designer aims for something more ambitious than the norm, there is a premium on thinking of appropriate activities, structures, and sequences.

This kind of problem solving can also be used by teachers when they take on the instructional design role. Thus Clark and Yinger's (1977) "process model of teacher planning" has three empirically identified stages: problem finding, problem formulation and solution, and implementation followed by evaluation and eventual routinization. Problem finding, it can be argued, is the hallmark of creative instructional design without which the process degenerates into semibureaucratic routine.

The problem-solving approach to instructional design is somewhat analogous to the "deliberative" approach to curriculum development advocated by Schwab. Schwab (1971) argues that curriculum development is a practical art and that, as such, it will always require the eclectic use of several theories and a period of deliberation leading to experienced professional judgment. In essence, he is arguing on epistemological grounds that a scientific approach to curriculum development is impossible; and many of his arguments can be readily extended to the task of instructional design.

3. Literature Relevant to Instructional Design

The purpose of this section is to briefly survey those areas of the literature that are relevant to the instructional designer, referring where possible to other Encyclopedia entries. Pertinent concepts and criteria can be found in books on such general topics as aesthetics, communication theory, curriculum theory, educational psychology, and educational technology, but mainly the more specialist literature will be referred to.

Under the heading of aesthetics, the primary concern is with criteria for assessing the quality of a completed design. These can be found in aesthetic theory, in art criticism, in literary criticism, and even in phenomenology. The area has been partly explored by evaluators and curriculum specialists, for example Eisner (1979), and Willis (1978), but there is scope for considerable further research in this area. Children's literature is probably the only type of educational material for which there is a fully developed critical tradition. Factual writing receives far less attention from aesthetically oriented critics. Perhaps the convenient but deceptive distinction between affective and cognitive domains is a symptom of the problem?

Aesthetic criteria are more commonly found in the literature on designing audiovisual learning materials. In the field of graphic production, for example, aesthetic criteria such as harmony, balance, and unity are used alongside technical criteria like legibility with criteria like clarity and simplicity having both aesthetic and technical significance (see *Graphic Production*). Motion picture production also has a well-established critical tradition which combines aesthetic with technical considerations.

Aesthetic concepts can also be found in communication theory, where there has always been considerable concern both for media and for message design. Thus media research has tended to take two forms. Media selection has been approached first by comparative studies, then by decision models, then by aptitude–treatment interaction. Message design has been influenced at a practical level by research on specific media attributes, though it is possible at a more fundamental level to link it with the growing body of research on visual perception. All these aspects are discussed below in the Instructional Design section which includes articles on *Perceptual Factors*, *Media Selection*, and *Media Attributes*.

The same section also discusses structuring tactics in message design in articles on *Learning from Textbooks*, *Task Analysis* and *Typographic Design*. On the one hand these discuss such factors as logical organization and local coherence using terms such as frames, foci, links, and structures; while on the other they discuss various "signalling" devices for helping students to interact with messages at a metacognitive level, by questioning and guided exploration of their underlying structure. Such techniques include statements of objectives, reviews, inserted questions, advance organizers, conceptual maps, and patterned note making. Further ideas on this theme can also be found in the section on Individualized Learning Systems particularly in the article on *Programmed Learning*.

Reigeluth's compendium of instructional design theories and methods has already been mentioned. This covers the structuring and presentation of content at two levels, that of the topic or sequence of topics (which he defines as macrostrategies), and that of the individual concept or procedure (microstrategies). There is an interesting parallel to this in the growing body of literature on study skills and note-making, which increasingly emphasizes the link between the macro- and micro-levels of analysis.

Structuring at a more global level is discussed in the literature on Curriculum Design and on the teaching of specific subjects, which rarely penetrates to the level of detail expected by instructional designers. However, there is a fundamental division of opinion between those who see subject matter learning in terms of the gradual deepening of understanding of many interrelated concepts and ideas with students developing their own personal map of the subject as they progress; and those who see it in terms of the cumulative definition of precisely defined competencies. Proponents of the latter are likely to have a behaviourist orientation, favour individualized learning systems and a mastery learning model of instruction, and justify their position with arguments based on rationality and efficiency. Proponents of the former are likely to have a philosophical or subject specialist orientation, and to use epistemological arguments accusing the behaviourists of misrepresenting the nature of knowledge. Though the issue is often presented as an empirical question, it can only be treated as such if measurement criteria can be agreed. Yet this involves value judgments and cannot be reduced to a matter of operational definition. Careful probing will usually reveal that the argument has a deeper ideological basis.

In practice, designers can, if they wish, adopt an eclectic approach using structuring ideas derived from a variety of sources. What is often at issue is not just the subject matter but the form of assessment, and finding the right balance between intrinsic and extrinsic motivation. Research on motivation and on cognitive style suggests that some students would prefer a more behavioural approach while others would not. Some educators, however, argue that most students should be encouraged to become cognitively independent, "deep processors" regardless of their initial preferences. This, they would claim, is a more important educational goal than the relatively passive comprehension of predetermined objectives. However, other articles which survey recent psychological research, also indicate how psychology itself is moving from a behavioural to a cognitive emphasis in a manner that promises to narrow the gap between the psychological and the philosophical, subject-oriented approaches to instructional design.

Bibliography

Axelrod J 1973 *The University Teacher as Artist*. Jossey-Bass, San Francisco, California

Clark C M, Yinger R J 1977 Research on teacher thinking. *Curric. Inq.* 7: 279–394

Cronbach L J et al. 1980 *Towards Reform of Program Evaluation*. Jossey-Bass, San Francisco, California

Eisner E W 1979 *The Educational Imagination: On the Design and Evaluation of School Programs*. Macmillan, New York

Eraut M R 1976 Some perspectives on curriculum development in teacher education. *Educ. Teach.* 99: 11–21

Eraut M R 1988 What has happened to learning design? In: Mathias H, Rushby N, Budgett R (eds.) 1988 *Aspects of Educational Technology, No. 21: Designing New Systems and Technologies for Learning* Kogan Page, London

Gagné R M, Briggs L J 1979 *Principles of Instructional Design*, 2nd edn. Holt, Rinehart and Winston, New York

Merrill M D 1983 Competent display theory. In: Reigeluth C M 1983 *Instructional-Design Theories and Models: An Overview of their Current Status*. Lawrence Erlbaum DSS, Hillsdale, New Jersey, pp. 279–333

Reigeluth C M 1983 *Instructional-Design Theories and Models: An Overview of their Current Status*. Lawrence Erlbaum DSS, Hillsdale, New Jersey

Reigeluth C M, Stein F S 1983 The elaboration theory of instruction. In: Reigeluth C M 1983 *Instructional-Design Theories and Models: An Overview of their Current Status*. Lawrence Erlbaum DSS, Hillsdale, New Jersey, pp. 335–81

Riley J 1984 The problems of drafting distance education materials. *Br. J. Educ. Technol.* 15(3): 192–204

Romiszowski A J 1981 *Designing Instructional Systems*. Kogan Page, London

Schwab J 1971 The practical: Arts of eclectic. *Sch. Rev.* 79: 493–542

Skinner B F 1954 The science of learning and the art of teaching. *Harvard Educ. Rev.* 24(2): 86–97

Willis G (ed.) 1978 *Qualitative Evaluation: Concepts and Cases in Curriculum Criticism*. McCutchan, Berkeley, California

Curriculum Design

M. F. Klein

Curriculum design is the organizational pattern or structure of a curriculum. It is determined by decisions made at two different levels of development; a broad level which involves basic value choices and a specific level which involves the technical planning and implementation of curricular elements. At the broader level of decision making, curriculum design is influenced by the choice of the data source or sources which the developer chooses to emphasize. Three primary data sources historically have been used as bases for choices in making curricular decisions: organized subject matter, the students who are to experience the curriculum, and society (Tyler 1950). Although most scholars in curriculum advocate using a combination of all three data sources in order to insure a balanced curriculum, in practice one usually has a dominance over the other two. Even more often in practice, one data source is used to the exclusion of the other two. Which data source is chosen to be the primary or exclusive basis for making curricular decisions depends largely upon the values of the developer about what the curriculum ought to do for or contribute to the growth of students.

The pattern or structure of the curriculum is also influenced at a more specific technical level when decisions are made in relation to the curricular elements. The curricular elements usually referred to in a discussion of a design are objectives, content, learning activities, and evaluation procedures (Zais 1976). Some authors also include learning materials and resources, time, space and environment, grouping, and teaching strategies as curricular elements. These nine elements can be treated in different ways when developing curricula and through these different treatments, a variety of designs can be created (Goodlad 1979). Thus, at this technical level of development, a specific curriculum design is created by the ways in which the elements are treated and the interrelationships which occur among them.

Any preplanned or student-initiated curriculum has an inherent design whether the developer has dealt explicitly with the component parts and their interrelationships or merely made decisions about some of them on an unexamined basis. The challenge to curriculum developers is to make the necessary decisions so that the curriculum which is created has a high degree of internal consistency (Hunkins 1980). This results from a careful consideration of the elements involved in curriculum design. If the decisions made about each of the data sources and curricular elements are compatible, the curriculum will have internal consistency. When the curriculum possesses high internal consistency, it will have a greater potential for having the desired impact upon the students. If the data sources and curricular elements are not treated in a consistent manner and have no clearly defined relationships to each other, the design of the curriculum will be confused and the potential impact upon students will be lessened.

This article discusses how a curriculum design is created by devoting major or exclusive emphasis to each of the three primary data sources for decision making: organized subject matter, the student, and the society. Within the discussion of each primary data source, a description is included of how the nine curricular elements should be, and often are treated so that maximum internal consistency can be achieved within the design. Each section on a primary data source concludes with the identification of the strengths and weaknesses of that design. A brief discussion then follows of two curriculum designs which combine some aspects of those based on the three primary data sources: specific competencies and process skills. Two others are also included in the discussion: a newly emerging humanistic design and the core curriculum. The article concludes with an identification of general characteristics of design needed in any curriculum.

Decisions about curriculum design are, in part, value choices which should be made as a result of rational and logical deliberation. Each design will achieve different goals and meet different purposes for learning. Designs created on a theoretical level rarely exist in practice in a pure form (Zais 1976). The realities of schooling force changes and require compromises. Thus, conducting research to determine the best curriculum design to use is not feasible. Evaluative studies can be, and have been conducted to determine the impact of a particular curriculum upon the students. These studies, however, are not intended to help make decisions about other curricular designs which are created for different learning goals and purposes. This article, therefore, contains no research section, but does attempt to make clear the value positions involved and the deliberations to be conducted for each of the major designs.

1. Organized Subject Matter as a Data Source

Organized subject matter is the most commonly used data source for decisions to be made about curriculum design. It is used because it reflects humankind's collective wisdom and represents the cultural heritage of people. A study of the disciplines as an organized body of knowledge is thought to be essential to the continued progress of civilizations. Also, such a body of knowledge is considered to be a significant characteristic of an educated person.

A recent period in curriculum history in the United States illustrates the type of curriculum which results when organized subject matter becomes the dominant or exclusive source for curriculum design (Klein 1978). From approximately 1960 to 1970, large amounts of private and federal funds were made available for curriculum reform. Because of rather widespread dissatisfaction with the public schools, it was generally agreed that the curriculum of the public schools needed considerable revision and updating. One group contributing to the criticisms of the curriculum was scholars at the university level who taught the disciplines included in the public-school curriculum. As the new funding became available, the university scholars in these disciplines were looked to for leadership in developing the new curriculum. These scholars, of course, turned to their disciplines as the basis for revising the school curriculum.

Most of the curriculum projects from this era defined the content to be learned in terms of the structure of the discipline. The structure of the discipline is those concepts and processes which are necessary to an understanding of the discipline and essential to the study of it. Content not considered a part of the structure was eliminated, even though traditionally it had been included in the curriculum. The intent of the new curricula from this era was to assist students in learning to become, for example, young scientists and mathematicians. Students would engage in the processes central to the discipline and inquire into it using the basic concepts.

In using subject matter as the major data source, a logical organization of the content is emphasized. The selection and organization of the content, however that may be defined, is a major task in developing the design (Taba 1962).

Curricula are planned in advance for the students so that a logically organized body of content can be taught to them efficiently and effectively. Learning, however, can become a mechanistic process which emphasizes covering the desired content rather than developing understanding of it by the students (Taba 1962). Unfortunately, this often happens in practice.

Four variations in this curriculum design which uses organized subject matter as the primary data source have been developed. They are separate subjects, multidisciplinary, interdisciplinary, and broad fields. When the separate subjects are used, each one is treated as a discrete area of the curriculum. Thus, geography, history, and economics become offerings in the social science curriculum; geology, biology, physics, and chemistry are offered in the science curriculum and spelling, handwriting, and reading are offered at different times in the elementary-school curriculum. This variation of the design emphasizes the logical organization of each subject and no deliberate attempt is made to interrelate them (Hunkins 1980).

The multidisciplinary or correlated variation occurs

when several subject areas are coordinated for study, but are still taught as separate subjects (Hunkins 1980, Ragan and Shepherd 1977; Smith et al. 1957). For example, in a multidisciplinary variation, the literature of a country would be taught in conjunction with its history and geography. Students may be asked to write themes for composition classes on some aspect of that period of time. Through this approach, it is hoped that students will experience a greater degree of unity in their knowledge (Hunkins 1980, Zais 1976).

A third variation is the interdisciplinary approach. In this approach, a topic or concept is selected to which several separate subjects are related. Each separate subject is brought to bear upon the concept as an aspect of study. For example, the concept of energy might be studied from a physical science, economic, and historical perspective. Each discipline is seen as contributing an important, separate, but discrete part of the student's learning. It is thought that a comprehensive understanding of the concept can be gained only by studying the contributions of any discipline which relates to it. In this design the student has the opportunity to experience even greater integration of humankind's store of knowledge.

The fourth variation in the subject area is the broad fields (Hunkins 1980, Ragan and Shepherd 1977, Smith et al. 1957, Taba 1962, Zais 1976). In this one, the distinctions among the separate subjects are more blurred than in the previous three. Spelling, handwriting, and reading come together to form a language arts approach to help students become proficient in their native language. History, geography, economics, and sociology are combined in a social studies program to help students understand their social world. No attempt is made to emphasize the separate contributions of economics, history, or sociology to the study of the family, for example. It is hoped that this broad fields design assists the student in achieving a high degree of integration of the separate subjects and through integration, the content becomes more functional. A commonly recognized limitation of this approach, however, is a more superficial encounter with content (Hunkins 1980).

Within the separate subject design, decisions are made about the curricular elements to assure that the student learns the desired body of content. Objectives may be stated explicitly or they may be implicit within the selection and organization of other curricular elements such as content and activities. The objectives provide the direction for learning and the achievement for the learning process. They are often stated in behavioral terms in relation to the content to be learned and they are usually in the cognitive domain. Although in practice, most of the objectives are lower cognitive behaviors (often emphasizing recall of the content), behavioral objectives clearly can be written for the higher cognitive behaviors such as application, analysis, and evaluation. Objectives in the affective domain emphasizing values, beliefs, and attitudes also can be written within the separate subject design, but they are usually neglected in practice.

Content to be taught is selected and organized by scholars or the curriculum developer for the student and this is done prior to instruction. Two concepts are particularly important to the organization of content: scope and sequence. Sequence refers to the vertical organization of the content. Careful consideration is paid to the sequencing of the content so that the student progresses continuously in learning tasks through hierarchical or logical steps. Scope refers to the horizontal arrangement of content. The scope is carefully defined so content will be as meaningful and integrated as possible for the student and manageable within the length of time allocated (Zais 1976). Content may be concepts, generalization, ideas, processes, or skills within the subject area.

Materials are selected or developed which present the content to the student in a carefully organized form. The text is the most commonly used piece of learning material and it presents the content to be learned in a carefully designed sequential, logical order. The student has little or no role in selecting the materials to be used.

Learning activities are designed to relate directly to the explicit or implicit objectives or directions for learning. Activities are to foster the change in the behavior of the student as stated in the objectives or to keep the student focused on the intended directions for the learning process (usually learning a body of content). They are often of the traditional verbal type: reading, writing, and listening. Activities are planned so that students will be motivated to learn.

Teaching strategies are planned, often as an inherent part of the activities, with the same intent. The teacher uses appropriate methods to assist the student in learning the stated behavior and content in the behavioral objective, if used, or the defined body of content. One commonly used strategy is the diagnostic–prescriptive–evaluative one. In this strategy, the teacher diagnoses where the student is in his or her progress and what difficulties are being encountered, prescribes the next step in the learning sequence, and after the student has experienced the prescription, the teacher evaluates to determine if the student has learned what was expected. Lecture and discussion is another commonly used strategy. The teacher as an expert in the subject area uses methodologies, designed to impart his or her knowledge to the students.

Evaluation procedures are planned and developed to determine the extent to which the student has achieved the behavioral objectives or learned the body of content. Periodic determinations are often made. Emphasis is usually placed on a quantitative measurement and some curriculum scholars advocate measuring only observable behavior. Progress often is reported in terms of letter grades such as A, B, C, or F which presumably indicate some degree of achievement. A particularly close, direct relationship should exist among the behavioral objectives, content, learning activities, and evaluation procedures.

Much instruction occurs in a total group setting. When small groups are used, they are formed on the basis of where the students are in their learning and what the next sequential or logical steps are. A student is placed in a group with other students who are at a similar place in their progress toward some objective and an activity is planned or selected for them in relation to the next step in learning. Instructional groups are usually formulated by the teacher on the basis of his or her diagnosis of the students. The student stays in the group until he or she is ready for the next learning task. Often the group is kept together for some period of time since students of similar learning abilities are normally grouped together.

This type of grouping provides for some individualization to occur so that each student's needs can be better met. Another way in which individualization occurs is through the use of programmed materials and learning modules. These materials are designed for use by a single student so that a high degree of individualization occurs in the amount of time used and the pacing for each student. Each student progresses through the materials at his or her own pace. It is important to note that individualization primarily occurs in relation to time in this instance. In some cases students have options among materials, activities, and strategies. Individualization for objectives, content, and evaluation usually does not occur (see *Individualized School Programs*; *Mastery Learning Model*).

Time is viewed as a limited resource and students and teachers are expected to make maximum use of it. Teachers keep students actively engaged in the learning task and hold disruptions, routines, and socializing among students to a minimum. Time spent in classrooms is viewed as most valuable, although homework is often assigned at the older ages so that learning can continue beyond the confines of the school. Time is divided into blocks so that each subject area receives some special allocation.

The boundaries of space are usually those of the classroom, although special rooms may be used such as libraries, instructional materials centers, music or art rooms, and maths or science laboratories. The classroom space is organized so that large group instruction and small group work can occur.

Clearly, variations within the above description of curricular elements can occur within the organized subject matter design, and does so in practice. If the elements are to be internally consistent within the design, however, they all must be used to assist the student in learning the important content whether that has been defined from the separate subjects or broad fields.

The advantages often cited for using organized subject areas as a data source for curriculum design emphasize the logical organization of content and the fact that this is the traditional way of designing curriculum (Hunkins 1980, Saylor and Alexander 1974, Taba 1962, Zais 1976). Subject areas represent a systematic and efficient way to help students learn their cultural heritage. Knowledge of the subjects and the intellectual processes inherent within them form an essential foundation of

schooling. Also, there is a long historical tradition of designing curricula upon this foundation. Teachers are educated in this way and the most prevalent materials and resources for schooling are developed on this basis. Additionally, it is a convenient and easy way to administer curricula and schools.

The weaknesses of this design center upon six points. First, it compartmentalizes and fragments the knowledge to be presented to the student. This leads to rapid forgetting of the content and does not make it very functional for students. Second, it is removed from the real world of the students. The problems, events, and concerns they face on a daily basis are not adequately included in the curriculum. Third, it pays inadequate attention to the abilities, needs, interests, and past experiences of the students. This may cause a lack of fit for the content with the students and thereby reduce motivation for learning. Fourth, it is an inefficient arrangement for the students; one which is alien to the way students learn in a more natural setting. Fifth, it encourages a passive and somewhat superficial approach to learning. Coverage of content becomes more important than depth of understanding by students. It may include a narrow range of goals and neglect higher cognitive skills. Sixth, as the knowledge of humankind accumulates, new subjects must be created. They are added to the curriculum and this causes a proliferation of subjects in an already crowded curriculum. The curriculum is expected to be responsive, however, to some degree at least, to the problems encountered by the society and the students. This requires that new subjects be created such as driver education, drug education, and sex education. These are then treated as a body of organized subject matter for the curriculum.

2. *The Student as a Data Source*

A different curriculum design is created when the dominant or exclusive data source for decision making is the student. In this approach, the needs, interests, abilities, and past experiences of the students are chosen as the basis for making decisions about the curricular elements. Students are consulted, observed, and studied for cues to selecting and organizing the direction or purposes of learning as well as the content, materials, and activities. The subject areas become a means by which students pursue problems or topics derived from their interests. Although the curriculum cannot be preplanned in the logically organized way of the subject area design, there is advance preparation by the teacher so that the necessary resources are available and the necessary arrangements are made to enable the students to become and remain actively involved in the learning process. The student is consulted whenever choices must be made. Problem solving and other processes are prime emphases, not a body of predetermined content. This design involves much cooperation among the students and the teacher and is a highly flexible, personalized one. It is valued because students learn to direct their own education, an essential ability for lifelong learning (Saylor and Alexander 1974, Smith et al. 1957).

When the student is emphasized as the primary source for designing the curriculum, it is often called the emerging, activity, or experience-based curriculum. Free schools, alternative schools, open education, and the British infant schools use this curriculum design. Perhaps the most famous example of a school curriculum built upon this design is Summerhill in England (Neill 1960). In all of these examples, the student is valued as the dominant source to look to in making decisions.

To achieve this design, a different way of utilizing the curricular elements must occur. The concept of predetermined objectives, either explicitly or implicitly stated, is rejected and the purposes of the student or a group of students are used to direct the learning process. The purposes may develop out of a cooperative planning endeavor between the teacher and the student, however. There are no predetermined outcomes for the curriculum intended for all students (Macdonald et al. 1973).

Content is selected on the basis of interests, and by active involvement of the students themselves. Advocates of this design believe real learning occurs only when the student organizes the content for himself or herself and attaches some personal meaning to it. It is to be organized *by* the student; not by others *for* the student. The concepts of scope and sequence are minimized in curriculum planning, but the concept of integration is an overarching one. The student experiences a wholeness and unity in the learning process which is not possible in the subject area design.

Materials are defined broadly as whatever the student requires for learning. Texts are not highly valued since they organize content for students. Rather, a wide variety of materials is needed since the student must explore and organize for himself or herself.

Activities are planned and selected by the students, or students are consulted frequently by the teacher for any necessary prior planning of activities. The activities are likely to be ones in which students are very actively involved such as constructing, interviewing, locating their own materials, and organizing resources for learning. Activities are not designed to achieve specified predetermined outcomes, although they should help the student achieve his or her purposes for learning.

The teacher is expected to be a colearner with the student and to facilitate the learning process. There are no essential methods or strategies for a teacher to use in order to facilitate learning. The teacher helps the student in the learning process in any way possible as needed by the student.

Evaluation becomes a joint endeavor between the teacher and the student. Self-evaluation is also an important process. Evaluation of the process students engage in is as important, if not more so than evaluation of any product.

Grouping practices are highly flexible and groups are formed only as needed or desired. Instructional groups are based on common interests of students rather than on diagnosis of their abilities. Groups when formed are flexible, short term, and somewhat spontaneous.

Time is kept flexible and unstructured by the teacher. It is a resource which students are responsible for using for their own purposes. A fixed schedule is not kept or desired (Taba 1962). Time for learning is not viewed as restricted to the classroom and homework; learning what is important to the student occurs whenever time is available. Space is equally unstructured and undefined. The classroom is a central meeting place, but the learning process will require the use of many other places and resources within the school and community.

The advantages of a curriculum design based primarily upon the student are several. Learning is personalized, relevant, and meaningful when student needs, interests, abilities, and experiences direct it. Students are intrinsically motivated and do not depend upon an external system of rewards. It is an active process for students. Emphasis is upon development of individual potential and interests, and individual differences are fully met. Process skills are developed which enable students to cope more adequately with the demands of life (Hunkins 1980, Zais 1976).

A design based primarily upon the student has several disadvantages. First, some critics charge that such a design does not prepare adequately for life since it neglects social goals of education and the cultural heritage of humankind. Students experience a curriculum which does not assure learning outcomes common to all students. Second, the activities are often inadequately organized and do not assure that the curriculum will provide any defined scope or sequence to learning. A series of unexamined experiences may not produce intellectual abilities or any organized body of knowledge. Third, commonly available learning materials are not organized in this way and to accumulate the necessary resources can be very expensive. Fourth, the teacher is not prepared to teach in this spontaneous process. It makes heavy demands upon the most skillful teachers to stay abreast of the students' needs. Finally, this design contradicts the academic structure of schools and colleges and entrance to new institutions is made more difficult and complex.

The interrelationships among the curricular elements in the above design are looser and less strong than in the organized subject area design. In the design using the student as the data source, students are the prime decision makers, and control at least to some degree, the elements in the design. This is the essential point regarding this design. If the design is to be used with any validity, the student as a prime decision maker must be assured.

3. Society as a Data Source

Society is a third source which may be used as a dominant or exclusive basis for curriculum decision making. It produces a unique curriculum design which is valued as a way of understanding and improving society. Community schools often use this approach. Social-studies programs also sometimes use society as a primary data source.

Although explicit objectives may be used, they do not play as major a role in this design as when subject areas are used as a basis for decision making. There usually is a definite focus for the learning process for all students but definite outcomes are not prescribed in advance.

Content is derived from life in a society or societies. It may emphasize the functions of a society, the major activities of social life, or the persistent problems of students and humankind (Stratemeyer et al. 1957). Any subject area is used as it relates to the topic or problem under study. Problem-solving processes and human relations and social skills are major emphases rather than possession of a body of content.

Materials of great diversity are needed with community resources and original documents preferred rather than texts. Evaluation is likely to be a cooperative endeavor between students and teachers. It focuses upon resolutions of, or actions related to, the problems being studied and the processes engaged in during the study.

Activities would be a result of student and teacher planning. They would require the active participation of students in all phases of study. The teacher plays a more active role, however, in determining these than when the student is the primary data source. Teaching strategies would be those which have the teacher as a facilitator of the learning process more than as the authority and expert as in the subject area design. The teacher, again, would play a more direct role than in the student design, however.

Space would be broadly defined to include all the resources of the school and community which relate to the problem or topic under study. Time would be defined also as a general resource which students use as the study dictates. Artificial allocations of time would be minimized as much as possible. Grouping would be determined on the basis of student needs and desires as the study progresses and much use of committee work would be made.

The interrelationships among the curricular elements in this design are broadly defined. They are stronger and more direct than in the student design, but less strongly related when separate subjects are used as the primary basis for design.

The advantages of this type of curriculum design emphasize the unity and utility of content and the relevance to the student and society (Taba 1962). The subject areas are integrated and play a subordinate role to the topic being studied. Problem solving is emphasized and the content studied is in a functional form for the student. Thus, content is relevant and meaningful for the student. The student is actively involved in all phases of the study so there is considerable intrinsic motivation to sustain the study. In addition, the design

contributes in a significant way to the improvement of society.

The weaknesses cited are several. The scope and sequence of the curriculum are not clearly defined. This can contribute to superficial treatment of content. Also, the units of study can be fragmented for students. This would reduce the unity of content that students might achieve. Another weakness is a fear that the focus of study can indoctrinate students to existing conditions and thus prepare them for the status quo rather than improvement of society. It can also provide inadequate exposure to a cultural heritage through the lack of organized content used in the approach. Finally, it is criticized because of tradition. Teachers are not prepared to teach in this manner nor are the usual resources available to schools prepared for this type of study. It also is different to what parents and colleges normally expect.

4. Other Curriculum Designs

Two curriculum designs being advocated now appear to be a departure, or perhaps a combination of the traditional ones in that they cut across the three bases of decision making discussed above. They are specific competencies and process skills. A third one is being advocated which is similar to the student as a basis for a design but it is less clearly defined. A fourth design, the core curriculum, has been advocated in the past, but it is less clearly a unique design. These four are discussed briefly as follows.

The competency approach emphasizes specific behavioral objectives as defining what students need to learn. These are derived from any data source. Skills are usually emphasized and growth in the affective domain is neglected or underemphasized. An example of this approach is the current emphasis on the basics in the United States. In this, behavioral objectives spell out the specific competencies the student must possess to function adequately in the society. They also reflect the separate subjects. The specific curricular elements are likely to be treated as in the separate subjects design.

The second approach that cuts across traditional designs emphasizes processes which are not subject specific. The content of the curriculum is the processes which are considered to have maximum transfer to real life, not those basic to inquiry within a discipline. The affective domain of human behavior and personal development are highly emphasized. Values clarification, skills basic to the learning process (essential for lifelong learning), and problem-solving skills are examples of processes as content. Decisions made about the specific curricular elements are likely to be similar to the student as a primary source for curriculum design.

A new source for curriculum design has also been identified: the humanistic view of the person. This is, in part, a reaction against schooling based on the industrial, technological model as represented best in the separate subjects design. It is a search for new ways to conceptualize curriculum. Those who pursue this approach are referred to as the reconceptualists. Although limited progress has been made in the specifics of the design, it undoubtedly will be closer to the student as a source for design than the separate subjects and society.

A fourth and final design referred to often in the literature is the core curriculum. The most essential characteristics of this approach are the common learnings which all students are expected to achieve and the administrative arrangements for larger blocks of time than are customarily found. Beyond these two basic characteristics, the core curriculum can take on elements of any of the basic three described in the preceding sections.

5. Essential Characteristics of Curriculum Design

The preceding discussion identifies the importance of questions concerning design in the curriculum development process and highlights the fundamental nature of it. The design achieved must be the result of deliberate and enlightened decision making and should not occur as a result of omission and neglect. The design selected must match the intent or function of the curriculum. Curricula differ in their purposes or functions; the design should follow from this as a result of enlightened deliberations. Once the design has been decided upon, the curricular elements must be handled with considerable consistency. Decisions made about objectives and evaluation must be compatible with decisions made, for example, about materials and activities. Unless this consistency is present, the design will have gaps in it and the impact of the curriculum upon students will be lessened. This has important implications for the kinds of resources needed for schooling, the types of programs needed in teacher education, and the ways in which finances and personnel in school districts must be utilized.

The designs available for use in curriculum development must evolve as new demands are placed upon the schools. Older patterns of curriculum design must be improved and new ones must be developed as knowledge, societies, and students change. Curriculum design must not be perceived as, nor allowed to become, static and unchanging. Creativity and adaptability must be essential characteristics of existing and evolving patterns of curriculum design.

Within a given school, it becomes apparent that a balance is needed among curriculum designs. No single pattern is adequate for the entire curriculum of a school. Each design discussed in this article has particular strengths which can contribute in very significant ways to the education of students. Each also has weaknesses which can be compensated for by providing students with experiences in others. Most schools have goals toward which each of the designs could contribute in a unique way. It would be unnecessarily limiting to restrict the design of the total curriculum to only one. And yet, this is what usually occurs in practice. The challenge to each school is to make thoughtful and deliberate decisions regarding how each curriculum design can be used to make the best contribution to the diverse aims of education.

Bibliography

Goodlad J I 1979 *Curriculum Inquiry: The Study of Curriculum Practice*. McGraw-Hill, New York

Herrick V E 1950 The concept of curriculum design. *Toward Improved Curriculum Theory*. University of Chicago Press, Chicago, Illinois, pp. 37–50

Hunkins F P 1980 *Curriculum Development: Program Planning and Improvement*. Merrill, Columbus, Ohio

Klein M F 1978 *About Learning Materials*. Association for Supervision and Curriculum Development, Washington, DC, No. 8, pp. 1–45

Macdonald J B, Wolfson B J, Zaret E 1973 *Reschooling Society: A Conceptual Model*. Association for Supervision and Curriculum Development, Washington, DC

Neill A S 1960 *Summerhill: A Radical Approach to Child Rearing*. Hart, New York

Pinar W (ed.) 1975 *Curriculum Theorizing: The Reconceptualists*. McCuthan, Berkeley, California

Ragan W B, Shepherd G D 1977 *Modern Elementary Curriculum*. Holt, Rinehart and Winston, New York

Saylor J G, Alexander W M 1974 *Planning Curriculum for Schools*. Holt, Rinehart and Winston, New York

Smith B O, Stanley W O, Shores J H 1957 *Fundamentals of Curriculum Development*. Harcourt, Brace and World, New York

Stratemeyer F B, Hamden L F, McKim M G, Passow A H 1957 *Developing a Curriculum for Modern Living*, 2nd edn. Teachers College Press, New York

Taba H 1962 *Curriculum Development: Theory and Practice*. Harcourt, Brace and World, New York

Tyler R W 1950 *Basic Principles of Curriculum and Instruction*. University of Chicago Press, Chicago, Illinois

Zais R S 1976 *Curriculum: Principles and Foundations*. Crowell, New York

Systems Approaches to Instructional Development

R. M. Diamond

The systems approach to instructional development has been defined by Banathy (1968) as "common sense by design," a systematic way of analyzing a problem and solving it, while Twelker et al. (1972) describe the systems approach as "a management tool that allows individuals to examine all aspects of a problem, to interrelate the effects of one set of decisions to another, and to optimally use the resources at hand to solve the problem." Other terms used for basically the same process include systematic instruction (Popham and Baker 1970), and educational or instructional technology (Wittich and Schuller 1979). The term "instructional development" is itself often treated as synonymous with the systems approach.

Though terminology in this area is influenced by habit and fashion, it is still possible to identify a group of approaches to instructional development which most people working in the field would expect to find discussed under the general heading "systems approach." While these approaches differ on many specific points, they share a number of common features (Hannum and Briggs 1980):

(a) Planning, development, delivery, and evaluation of instruction are based on systems theory.

(b) Goals are based on an analysis of the environment of the system.

(c) Instructional objectives are stated in observable performance terms.

(d) Knowledge about the students is crucial for the success of the system.

(e) Considerable attention is paid to the planning of instructional strategies and the selection of media.

(f) Evaluation is part of the design and revision process.

(g) Students are measured and graded by their ability to achieve desired standards and criteria rather than by comparing one student with another.

A salient feature of instructional development using the systems approach is the use of a diagrammatic model of the development process. This is claimed to have the following advantages:

(a) It ensures that all key factors will be discussed, that all essential steps will be followed, and that this will be done in a logical sequence. It is, in effect, a management guide.

(b) It communicates effectively to all participants what will be done, how it will be done, and can be used to identify clearly their roles within the process.

(c) It can identify options and assist in decision making.

Though diagrammatic models share the common features outlined above, they also have significant differences. These can result from several factors.

(a) *Instructional setting.* Individuals working at the college or university level tend to have more flexibility in structure and content than do those at the primary and secondary levels or in industry and the military where both goals and time lines are usually firm and prestated. There are also differences in the structure of higher education in various countries that will either limit or expand the range of options open to the individual teacher or design team. The more central control, the fewer options; the more autonomy in the classroom, the less chance a cooperative approach has of success. If national or state examinations determine instructional goals, it is more difficult to question the assumptions and criteria on which those tests were based.

(b) *Who is involved in the development process?* Some models are designed for use by an individual teacher working on the improvement of his or her own teaching, a course, or a lesson. The majority, however, are structured to facilitate team involvement—one or more content experts (teachers) assisted by developers, evaluators, and media experts. In these instances, while content decisions usually rest with the teacher, it is the responsibility of others to coordinate the process, test assumptions, and ensure that options are explored, goals are reached, and quality is maintained.

(c) *Scope of the project.* While the systems approach can be used to design a single lesson, it can also be used to design a course, an entire curriculum, or a national educational system. The scope of the effort will determine which models will be most appropriate.

(d) *The author's perspective.* Most models clearly indicate the strength(s) and the biases of their author(s). Individuals with instructional technology backgrounds tend to place greater weight on media selection, production, and utilization; others will stress student characteristics, needs assessment, or perhaps in-depth analysis of the instructional objectives that are to be met. There are also significant differences between models designed by the pragmatist and those designed by the theorist.

Recognizing that differences do exist, it is up to the user or the using team to select and modify (when appropriate) that model which most directly meets their needs—the model that most closely meshes with what they must do and with the time and resources they have available to them. Model selection is critical since some tend to be impractical because they require too much time for completion or too many human and fiscal resources to be utilized. The systems approach is both effective and efficient but only when there is an ideal fit between the model and the project.

1. Characterizing Systems Models

Andrews and Goodson (1980), identified over 40 models with 14 common elements, and then compared the models not only on these elements but also by their origin, underpinnings, purposes and uses, and documentation. It was Andrews and Goodson's contention that "the educator who ultimately uses an instructional design model should know how and why the developer (author) arrived at the model so the designer can determine the suitability of the model for the desired goals." One of their principal distinctions was between integrated, task-oriented, and prescriptive models:

(a) Integrated models—those derived from general systems theory with numerous interacting elements. These models stress communication feedback and the predication of one action on other parts of the system.

(b) Task-oriented models—those that attempt to list all the necessary development tasks that must be performed. These models tend to stress the specific steps rather than the broader perspective of change.

(c) Prescriptive models—those that prescribe solutions. These models provide a series of "if—then" statements; that is, if the learning is of type "X," and the learner is of type "Y," then the following type of learning activity should be designed.

In a recent paper, Gustafson (1981) organized the models into four new categories recognizing that some models can exist as subsets of others and, therefore, that no hierarchy should or can be inferred:

(a) The classroom-focused models—these models assume that there is already a teacher, some students, a curriculum, and a facility, and that the scope of the project will be that teacher's classroom. In the models, emphasis is placed on selecting and adapting existing materials rather than developing new ones.

(b) The product-focused model—these models have one prestated goal—to produce one or more specific instructional packages.

(c) The system-focused models—these models have as their goal the development of an instructional system—this may include materials, equipment, a management plan, and, at times, an instructor training package. The instructional system, when complete, can then be implemented or disseminated to target locations.

(d) The organization-focused models—these models have as their goals not only improving instruction but also modifying or adapting the organization and its personnel to a new environment.

The relationships between these models are more easily understood if these four categories are merged into two—classroom/product models and comprehensive models. Thus the rest of the article devotes a separate section to each of the following types of model:

(a) Classroom/product models—those focusing on a single course or the design, field testing, and evaluation of a single instructional sequence. The models

are product oriented and focus on the "how" questions. How can an objective be met? How can a unit be designed? and so on.

(b) Comprehensive models—those dealing with entire programs of study (curricula educational systems, etc.). The models usually require the involvement of several individuals and deal with why a program exists and what should be in it.

Romiszowski (1981), in presenting a comprehensive model that included a number of other more specific models within it, identified several hundred questions that had to be addressed in defining, analyzing, and successfully solving an instructional development problem.

As noted previously, the key is to select the particular model or to decide to combine models so that the needs, resources, and priorities of a particular project are met as closely as is possible. The most successful projects have tended to be those that either used a broader/comprehensive model or selected elements from many different approaches. On the other hand, when a specific product is desired, any one of the many available classroom/product models may be effective.

Most instructional systems models have much in common and contain many of the same elements. Almost every model includes somewhere in the process the stating of objectives, a pre-assessment of students, the design and implementation of formal instruction, and evaluation which serves as the basis for revision. In addition, many also contain a needs assessment step early in the development process (see Fig. 1).

The key to success of the systems approach is the interrelationship of objectives to student performance. It requires that the evaluation criteria that are used to determine the success of the program mesh with objectives, and that revision is continued until a prestated level of student achievement is reached or until the objectives themselves change.

It should also be noted that, while most models appear to be extremely linear in their overall design (from step 1 to step 2 to step 3, etc.), this is somewhat deceptive. While ideally some actions should precede others and certain decisions should not be made until all relevant facts are known, this is often not possible. All of the data may not be available when the decisions are required, and data collected later in the project may tend to counter earlier information. Experience has indicated that, while the general flow is usually followed, the

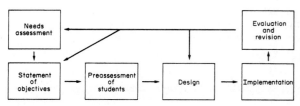

Figure 1
A general model

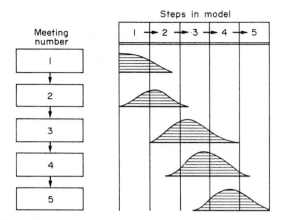

Steps in model

Meeting number

Figure 2
Work flow by meeting

sequence is never as cut and dried as it graphically appears (Fig. 2).

Since classroom/products models are usually the final portion of comprehensive models, any description of one must make reference to its relationship to the other.

2. Classroom/Product Models

From its very beginning, the systems movement in education was heavily influenced by the field of instructional technology, for it was this profession that first recognized the significant potential of the technique for the improvement of teaching and learning. It is, therefore, not surprising to find that many of the existing models have focused on the classroom, on the lesson, and on the design, production, and evaluation of instructional materials. These models tend to focus on objectives, design, and evaluation; and are usually elaborations on Fig. 1. Recent examples can be found in Briggs and Wager (1981), Gagné and Briggs (1979), Gerlach and Ely (1980), Kemp (1977), and Rowntree (1982). The model of the Instructional Development Institute, a consortium of American universities with high reputations in this field, is reported in Wittich and Schuller (1979).

More detailed discussions of these stages in the instructional development process can be found elsewhere in this Part.

3. Comprehensive Models

During the same years, 1962 to 1982, a second type of systems model was being developed, which focused more on course, curriculum, and program design and was usually structured for use by a development team. These models took more account of systems theory as a means for analyzing the complexities of practical situations, and were more than just systematic and logical. They covered broader issues than those which provided the focus for the classroom products models.

Early examples of such models include Hamreus (1968) and Mackenzie et al. (1970), while more recent examples are those of Diamond (1980) and Rowntree (1981).

These models as exemplified in Fig. 3 have the following characteristics:

(a) They focus on what and why as well as how; that is, basic assumptions about the content and structure of a program tend to be questioned.

(b) They place greater emphasis on needs assessment in both selecting the project and determining goals and objectives.

(c) While the teacher or faculty member has responsibility for content decisions, others (instructional developers, evaluators, media specialists) have the responsibility for coordination, quality control, and accomplishing certain tasks.

(d) Once an overall program/curriculum is designed, the entire development process is repeated for the major elements within that program.

(e) They delay producing a formal statement of instructional objectives until the overall goals of the program are known, the entering competencies and priorities of the students are identified, and the instructional content and sequence determined.

(f) They define and use evaluation in its broadest sense (including both formative and summative evaluation), and rely heavily on data collection and interpretation throughout the process.

(g) They tend to have two distinct phases: project selection and design, and production, implementation, and evaluation, with the classroom/product model being used for the second of two phases.

Since the second phase is generally identical to the classroom/product model, emphasis here will be on the earlier portion.

3.1 Step 1: Project Selection

Change itself is political and, unless a project is sensitive to the priorities of the academic community in which it is to be undertaken, its chance of survival is significantly reduced. Many excellent new programs have floundered simply because they did not have the support of the instructional staff who controlled the decision-making committees and functions. Diamond et al. (1975), identified five conditions that should be avoided if a project is to be successful:

(a) Projects where content expertise is lacking.

(b) Projects in schools or departments that are undergoing administrative change.

(c) Projects involving only one teacher or faculty member (when they leave the project, the project usually dies).

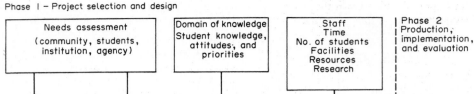

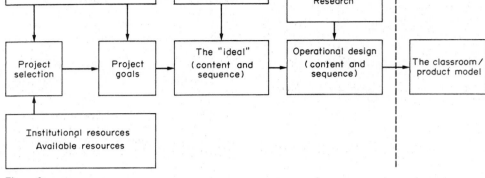

Figure 3
The comprehensive model

(d) Projects that do not have strong administrative support.

(e) Projects where what is expected is unrealistic in terms of time and existing resources.

In presenting a sequential process for project selection, they further identified five key areas of consideration:

(a) Needs and priorities (What problems exist? How important are they?).

(b) Administrative consideration (stability, long-term growth potential, etc.).

(c) Potential for success (commitment, quality of staff, realistic goals).

(d) Support agency resources (availability of staff and time).

(e) Political override.

In comprehensive models, needs assessment plays a vital role both in the process of deciding whether or not a project should be undertaken and in defining the instructional goals of the program. Needs assessment has been defined as a process "...identifying the gap between desired results and observed results" (Kaufman et al. 1981).

As noted previously, the systems theory can be, and often is, applied to each of the steps within a systems model. Such support models are described in more specialized articles later in this Part. Here attention will be drawn to Kaufman's recent analysis of needs assessment. Kaufman and English (1979) divided the needs assessment process into two broad categories: external needs assessment which focuses on those needs an individual has to have to be able to survive and be self-

sufficient outside of or beyond formal education, and internal needs assessment which deals with the needs within an organization (succeeding at a given job, passing a particular course, etc.). Kaufman et al. (1981) have, using the systems approach, developed a process that identifies the requirement for change from needs assessment data and links problem solving and planning to needs assessment information. Key elements in this system are an identification of: (a) what is; (b) what should be; (c) change requirements; (d) continuation requirements; (e) possible interventions; (f) selected interventions.

Needs assessment provides data that help not only to determine if a project should be undertaken but also to define the overall goals once it has begun.

3.2 Step 2: Designing for the Ideal

Once the project goals are identified, many models move directly into the statement of instructional objectives and the other elements within the classroom/product models. However, in Diamond's Syracuse model (1980), once goals are identified, an effort is made to identify the entering competencies, priorities, and attitudes of students, the domain of knowledge in the content area, and the specific competencies required either for success in the next course or in the profession if it is a job-related program. Then, once enough of this information is available, the design team is charged with designing the best possible program. They are asked, in effect, to forget what exists now and to structure the "ideal" program. If the faculty or teachers had "the best of all possible worlds," what would their instructional program look like? At this point in the process, the interrelationship of topics is developed, a flow of content evolves, and points at which there should be options, special content tracks, remediation, or exemption are identified.

Experience with this approach has shown that it has several specific advantages.

(a) It tests assumptions about structure and time. In many instances, teachers make assumptions about limitations on structure, time lines, etc., that are not accurate. They assume, without testing the system, that things must stay as they are.

(b) It tests assumptions about content. As a result, major changes in content often occur—new areas being added, traditional content being found no longer necessary and being dropped.

(c) It forces sensitivity to the needs and priorities of the specific student population that is being served.

(d) Teachers find the concept of designing the "best possible" program exciting and challenging.

3.3 Step 3: The Operational Design

Once the "ideal" version of the course or curriculum is complete, the design team then reviews the resources that are available (teachers, part-time instructional assistants, facilities, equipment, etc.), the time available for instruction, the number who must be taught, and what research says about teaching, learning, the use of technology, and so on. The original ideal design is then modified into what the team feels is realistic and possible. Once this is determined, the classroom/product model can be implemented (Phase 2).

It is important to stress, as with any system process, that the overall design is never static. It will change and be modified as new data become available, as priorities change, or assumptions about how long certain activities will take are proven wrong. The more flexible the design, the more chance a project will have of being successful.

4. Conclusion

The systems approach represents a process for solving an instructional problem. It is both effective and, when the particular model that is being used is appropriate for the project, efficient. It can provide education with a useful logic for improving what it does and how well it succeeds in meeting its own objectives. It can assist both teachers and administrators by bringing rationality into a system that has rarely defined where it is going, measured its effectiveness, or clearly established the criteria on which it is judged.

Bibliography

Andrews D H, Goodson L A 1980 A comparative analysis of models of instructional design. *J. Instr. Dev.* 3(4): 2–16

Banathy B H 1968 *Instructional Systems.* Fearon, Palo Alto, California

Briggs L, Wager W W 1981 *Handbook of Procedures for the Design of Instruction*, 2nd edn. Educational Technology, Englewood Cliffs, New Jersey

Diamond R M 1980 The Syracuse model for course and curriculum design, implementation, and evaluation. *J. Instr. Dev.* 4(2): 19–23

Diamond R M, Eickmann P E, Kelly E F, Holloway R E, Vickery T R, Pascarella E T 1975 *Instructional Development for Individualized Learning in Higher Education.* Educational Technology, Englewood Cliffs, New Jersey

Gagné R M, Briggs L 1979 *Principles of Instructional Design*, 2nd edn. Holt, Rinehart and Winston, New York

Gerlach V S, Ely D P 1980 *Teaching and Media: A Systematic Approach*, 2nd edn. Prentice-Hall, Englewood Cliffs, New Jersey

Gustafson K 1981 *Survey of Instructional Development Models.* ERIC Clearinghouse on Information Resources, Syracuse University, Syracuse, New York

Hamreus D G 1968 The systems approach to instructional development. In: Edling J V (ed.) 1968 *The Contribution of Behavioral Science to Instructional Technology.* Teaching Research Division of the Oregon State System of Higher Education, Monmouth, Oregon

Hannum W H, Briggs L J 1980 *How Does Instructional Systems Design Differ From Traditional Instruction?* University of North Carolina, Chapel Hill, North Carolina

Kaufman R, English F W 1979 *Needs Assessment: Concept and Application.* Educational Technology, Englewood Cliffs, New Jersey

Kaufman R, Stakinas R G, Wagner J C, Mayer H 1981 Relating needs assessment, program development, implementation, and evaluation. *J. Instr. Dev.* 4(4): 17–26

Kemp J E 1977 *Instructional Design: A Plan for Unit and Course Development*, 2nd edn. Fearon, Belmont, California, pp. 74–83

MacKenzie N, Eraut M, Jones H C 1970 *Teaching and Learning: An Introduction to New Methods and Resources in Higher Education.* International Association of Universities, UNESCO, Paris

Popham W J, Baker E 1970 *Systematic Instruction.* Prentice-Hall, Englewood Cliffs, New Jersey

Romiszowski A J 1981 *Designing Instructional Systems* Kogan Page, London, and Nichols Publishing, New York

Rowntree D 1981 *Developing Courses for Students.* McGraw-Hill, St. Louis, Missouri

Rowntree D 1982 *Educational Technology in Curriculum Development*, 2nd edn. Harper and Row, London

Twelker P A, Urbach F D, Buck J E 1972 *The Systematic Development of Instruction: An Overview and Basic Guide to Literature.* ERIC Clearinghouse on Media and Technology, Stanford University, Stanford, California

Wittich W A, Schuller C F 1979 *Instructional Technology: Its Nature and Use*, 6th edn. Harper and Row, New York

Needs and Objectives

Needs Assessment in Adult Education

F. C. Pennington

Adult education means many different things and there are few final answers respecting content, methods, or evaluation. Therefore it is more necessary in adult education than in other spheres of education to be clear about the needs of the learners, of the sponsoring organizations, and of society itself. Rigorous efforts to assess needs are increasingly being made in many countries. Some research has taken place in Europe but most of the published studies and manuals come from North America, some originating from educational institutions and some from management training, health-related, and welfare organizations.

Educators use the term "need" to imply or specify a discrepancy between an existing situation and some changed or desired set of circumstances. The term "needs assessment" suggests a systematic approach to measuring the discrepancy between the two. An educational need is a discrepancy that can be removed or reduced by administering a set of planned instructional interventions to those persons who have demonstrated a given discrepancy.

Adult educators conduct needs assessments as a basis for informed planning decisions. Careful planning using assessment data helps assure accountability to the adult learner, to the administration of the adult education agency, and to the taxpayers. Assessment data assist in the process of assigning priorities to the greatest areas of need.

A needs assessment often accomplishes three purposes: clientele analysis, identifying topics, and specifying areas of need. Analyzing characteristics and expectations of clientele to provide data for program and policy decisions is common to each of these purposes.

Clientele analysis data usually describe key characteristics of the target adult population. In larger studies, data describing participants in adult education activities are compared to characteristics of nonparticipants who could potentially be served. The characteristics typically examined include age, sex, education, marital status, occupation, recency of participation in a planned educational activity, and other variables correlated with participation in adult education activities.

The second purpose fulfilled in many needs assessments involves identifying areas of demand (topics) for educational programming. Adult education agencies rely on offering programs and services of sufficient interest to elicit active participation. To maintain programming viability, the agency must be sufficiently "market wise" to attract adequate resources that can be converted into programs that the adult consumer sees as beneficial.

The third major purpose involves specifying areas of need in specific circumstances. It involves systematic attempts to identify discrepancies between current and desired circumstances within the target population that can be reduced or eliminated through planned instructional activities. Data are collected and the magnitude of the need is measured or inferred.

The pursuit of all three of these subpurposes of needs assessment results in establishing the careful definition of a need, a gap or problem, the characteristics of those who have the need, the magnitude of the need, and the components and intensity of the current situation.

Individuals have educational needs which can relate to interpersonal relations or collective issues. However, it is not the collective group, agency, or community that has an educational need. The individual does the learning and applies what is learned to related collective concerns. It is important to keep this distinction in mind. It is especially important when the program's purpose is to benefit the quality of problem solving related to collective life. This distinction points out the importance of gathering needs assessment data from various persons and role perspectives in a group, agency, or community.

1. Characteristics of Needs Assessments

Needs assessments have several major characteristics. Most apply a systematic process of collecting data from persons who are affected by, or who can affect the discrepancy being investigated. In best practice, needs assessments are continuous. Needs of constituent groups are not fixed over time, but change as preferences and environments change. Continuous assessments make it possible to monitor changes to assure that data being used to make sure programming decisions are relevant to the need, the problem, and the client.

Needs assessments vary in scope and size. In some cases, data can be collected by making a few phone calls to key persons in a constituent group. Other studies can involve a variety of data collection techniques and include many persons. Needs assessment can be an ongoing part of an individual's job or can be a major study staffed by researchers skilled in assessment techniques.

Data collected in assessments can be subjective and objective. Adult educators are interested in the quality of opinions as well as quantitative indices inferring the magnitude of a situation. Users of assessment data will value different data and weight those data accordingly in their decisions. In most instances, a combination of data sources provides a reasonable basis for making programming decisions.

A pervasive characteristic of most needs assessments in adult education is the involvement of current or potential clients in the planning and implementation of the assessment activity. Assessment studies involving persons carefully selected for their role perspective on the situation being assessed can build support for the study, for the decisions made during the study, and for subsequent programs and services that follow the assessment. Adult educators feel more assured in selecting courses of action if representatives of persons who are required to carry out the action are brought into the assessment activity from the beginning.

2. Planning Needs Assessments

Needs assessment plans are developed to provide guidelines for addressing issues, determining methodologies, utilizing findings, and allocating resources for the project. A plan might include information about: purpose (Why is the needs assessment being done?), audience (Who will use the results of the needs assessment?), issues (What are the issues that the assessment should address?), resources (What resources are available for the assessment?), data (What kinds of data should be collected and what techniques will be used to collect the data?), sources (Where or from whom can the data be acquired?), analysis (How will the data be analyzed?), and utilization (How will the data be utilized?).

3. Techniques for Collecting Assessment Data

Techniques for assessing educational needs vary from the simple to the complex. Although the needs assessment process is defined as systematic, some techniques used in practice are hardly formalized or comprehensive in nature. This does not imply that the data from these techniques are not useful. Some less formal techniques for collecting assessment data include: intuitive feelings of experienced programmers; inferring need on the basis of currently successful programs; and requests from individuals or groups that educators assume are an indication of need.

Other techniques are more formal and involve some structure and planning. These techniques do not involve a great deal of face-to-face interaction between the person conducting the study and the client group assumed to have the need and include: (a) analyzing reports, publications, and records which summarize other assessment studies or provide statistical or other evidence that can serve as an indication of need; (b) using the observations of consultants and drawing on their perceptions, expertise, and experience; (c) assessing situations using structured observational techniques; and, (d) analyzing the results of tests and examinations.

Comprehensive approaches to needs assessments involve a complex set of techniques which are sometimes used in combination with those noted above. These comprehensive approaches include: (a) using groups and task forces; (b) carrying out formal surveys using written instruments, telephone surveys, or personal interviews; and (c) developing and utilizing systems or networks of contacts with the constituent group.

Though there is no one universally accepted model of the needs assessment process, it is possible to indicate some of the basic concepts and design characteristics of the commonly accepted needs assessment approaches. Each possesses inherent positive qualities as well as limitations.

3.1 The Participation–Demand Approach

This type of assessment draws its information from the records in adult education institutions about the individual requests for courses and the number of participants in such courses. The data provide a description of the interests and characteristics of those persons who are willing to undertake educational activities. The assumption of this approach is that relatively accurate estimates about existing educational needs can be based on a sample of persons who have actually shown interest in adult education.

The advantages of this approach are: it represents data of people who are most willing to take part in the provided educational service, the data are easily accessible, and there is no problem in transforming expressed needs into educational content.

The weakness lies in the assumption that the needs of a given population are represented by the interests of the participants of adult educational institutions. This assumption may not be valid, because the translation of needs into demand depends on the extent to which educational services are available, accessible, and accepted to clients and to the extent to which potential clients are aware of the services that may satisfy their needs.

3.2 The Educational Experts Approach

This environment process involves a committee generally composed of program planners, administrators, teaching personnel, and school board members who try to agree on the topics in which their prospective clients have interest and which they need to know. This approach draws on the wealth of experience of the adult education professionals and the data agreed upon can easily be translated into content and into particular teaching strategies to be used. A disadvantage can be that the professional teaching staff may rely heavily on either the participation rates in existing courses without contact with the nonparticipants or on the perceptions of the professionals alone about new educational content without any assessment of whether this new content meets the needs of the clients.

3.3 Key Informant Approach

The key informant approach is based on information from key persons in a community, who are in a position to know what their community's needs are. Key persons are selected by the researcher on the basis of prestige-rating questionnaires or selected by community leaders and public officials.

The obvious advantage of the key informant approach is that it is simple and inexpensive to conduct. If the information-gathering instruments are well-constructed, a fairly reliable impression of the community's needs can be obtained. The disadvantage of this method is that it depends on persons who may define existing needs in terms of their own perspective or that the selected key informants are not representative of the population. Thus, certain groups in a community which are not readily visible may go unnoticed and educational activities for those whose needs may be greatest are not undertaken.

3.4 Community Forum Approach

The community forum approach tries to include a broader cross section of the community in the needs assessment process than the key informant approach does. Information is gathered through public meetings to which the whole community population is invited and where a discussion around community-specific topics is stimulated.

Like the key informant approach this technique is simple to design, easy to conduct, and ensures wide participation of the community. Though the community forum includes a larger sample of the community, there is no guarantee that those attending are truly representative of the whole community and the information gathered may therefore be of restricted validity. This nonrepresentativity could lead to education programs that reflect only the interests of the already informed and vocal citizens in the community.

The community forum, like the key informant approach, provides data allowing quick access to the most obvious needs but which might be based on perceptions of only a few.

3.5 The Community Survey Approach

The community survey approach is the only systematic process by which data are collected directly from a sample of the entire population living in a community. The personal expression of needs by all adults serves as the basis for the establishment of new educational programs for the community.

The major advantage of this approach is that well-conducted surveys can give the most valid and reliable information on all needs existing in a community. Where the community is large, well-drawn probability samples are required. In all cases, the instrument construction and data-gathering procedures must be rigorous. From the data from such surveys it is possible to judge the utility of the other needs assessment approaches.

With the assistance of personal variables it is possible to break down the adult population into meaningful subgroups and identify the needs of each subgroup.

Participation rates of subgroups that are underrepresented in adult education (the elderly, those with low incomes and with low educational achievement) can be improved if more attention is paid to their specific needs.

The disadvantage of this approach is that surveys are much more difficult to conceptualize and undertake than any of the other needs assessment approaches outlined.

Each of the above strategies has an implicit theoretical orientation toward the definition of need and each varies in the degree of reliability and validity of the obtained measures and utilizes different measuring instruments. Information is mostly gathered through interview schedules or questionnaires. Interviews provide the best method for enabling the researcher to understand how and why the individual feels a need as he or she does. Questionnaires enable the researcher to reach a large number of people in a relatively short period of time.

The responses to needs perception questions are usually rank ordered by frequency. In this way the priority of needs can be identified. Different results from different approaches in needs assessment show that there is no one best source for the information to be used for planning.

Generally, those techniques which are simplest in design and the least expensive to administer have the disadvantage of producing less valid results. Those which can give greatest accuracy in measurement require a great deal of time, money, and training. The optimal goal of needs assessment for adult education should be to collect data from discrete and interrelated sources for purposes of comparison and utilization in program planning. What is to be avoided is the implication that the researcher can do objective needs assessment with generalizable instruments that can be applied in all situations in a standardized way.

4. Concluding Remarks

Though the concept of needs assessment has great relevance in the planning of adult education it is obvious that there are a number of problems with the concept of need which should be mentioned and which require further consideration: the difficulty of distinguishing an "authentic" need from a "felt" need; the fact that needs are probably infinite in number and cannot all be identified; there are often conflicting needs so that responding to one may undermine another; needs may not be conscious in the person having them but may nevertheless be real.

Although the needs assessment approaches assume that it should be possible to arrive at some kind of demand figures indicating how many adults will participate in adult education programs planned to respond to their needs, it is virtually impossible to offer such a figure with any confidence. Predicting the demand is far more difficult than undertaking a needs assessment.

Attitude surveys can give information about the motivational factors affecting adult participation in learning activities, can identify individuals who are seriously interested in further learning, and can supply supplementary data about the probable relevance of "felt needs" data. Assessing the patterns of participation and the reasons for nonparticipation (situational, institutional, and dispositional barriers) can provide better clues for the discrepancy between data concerning the stated need or interest of respondents about programs they would like and their subsequent participation rate.

It should be stressed that needs assessment studies do not necessarily produce sound "hard" data; rather, they are imperfect efforts for assessing, as yet, poorly understood concepts. It is impossible to plan without the type of data generated by such studies but much work remains to be undertaken to improve such studies before they can be used in a routine way.

Bibliography

Atwood H M, Ellis J 1971 The concept of need: An analysis for adult education. *Adult Leadership* 19: 210–12, 244

Coffing R T, Hutchinson T E 1974 *Needs Analysis Methodology: A Prescriptive Set of Rules and Procedures for Identifying, Defining and Measuring Needs.* Educational Resources Information Center (ERIC), Arlington, Virginia

Cross K P, Zusman A 1979 The needs of non-traditional learners and the responses of non-traditional programs. In: Stalford C B (ed.) 1979 *An Evaluative Look at Non-traditional Education.* National Institute of Education, Washington, DC

English F W, Kaufman R A 1975 *Needs Assessment: A Focus for Curriculum Development.* Association for Supervision and Curriculum Development, Washington, DC

Knox A B 1969 *Critical Appraisal of the Needs of Adults for Educational Experiences as a Basis for Program Development.* Teachers College Press, New York. ERIC Document No. ED 022 090

McMahon E E 1977 *Needs of the People and Their Communities and the Adult Educator: A Review of the Literature of Need Determination.* Educational Resources Information Center (ERIC), Syracuse University, Clearinghouse on Adult Education, New York

Mazmanian P E 1977 *The Role of Educational Needs Assessment in Adult Education and Continuing Medical Education Program Planning.* Educational Resources Information Center (ERIC), Arlington, Virginia. ERIC Document No. ED 155 371

Monette M L 1977 The concept of education need: An analysis of selected literature. *Adult Educ.* 27: 116–27

Nowlen P M 1980 Origins. In: Knox A B (ed.) 1980 *Developing, Administering, and Evaluating Adult Education.* Jossey-Bass, San Francisco, California

Pennington F C (ed.) 1980 *Assessing Educational Needs of Adults.* Jossey-Bass, San Francisco, California

Watson C D 1973 *Educational Needs Assessment, 1972.* Arkansas Department of Education, Little Rock, Arkansas. ERIC Document No. ED 084 293

Witkin B R 1975 *An Analysis of Needs Assessment Techniques for Educational Planning at State, Intermediate and District Levels.* National Institute of Education, Department of Health, Education, and Welfare, Washington, DC. ERIC Document No. ED 108 370

Selecting and Justifying Objectives

M. R. Eraut

It is not uncommon for the problem of selecting and justifying objectives to be concealed by the simple declaration that objectives are derived from aims. Since statements of aims and statements of objectives are usually produced for different purposes and different audiences, it would be naive to expect total consistency between the two. Moreover, the claim that objectives are simply derived from aims diverts attention from three critical issues with which curriculum developers have to contend. First, aims are not the only possible source of objective. In theory there is no limit to the number of places where people may find ideas for objectives. In practice, existing curriculum traditions probably serve as the major source. Second, there are no generally agreed or universally applicable procedures for deducing objectives from aims (Hirst 1973). Third, while aims may be used to justify the educational value of a particular objective, they often cannot determine the relative value of two alternative or competing sets of objectives, each of which appear consistent with the aims.

This article confines itself to three questions:

(a) What are the sources of objectives? From where can people get ideas for objectives they wish to consider for inclusion?

(b) How might the inclusion of an objective be justified?

(c) What guidance is available for tackling the problem of priorities?

1. Sources of Objectives

Hirst (1973) criticizes Tyler and others for failing to distinguish the sources of curriculum objectives from the grounds for their justification. The most frequently used sources are not Tyler's (1949) primary sources—the learners, contemporary life, subject specialisms, or even the philosophy of education—but secondary sources such as current practices and well-known curriculum traditions. So the process of formulating objectives is likely to be one of selecting goals from these practices and traditions and translating them into an appropriate linguistic form. Consultations with educators, parents, students, and the local community often provide useful information on preferences but seldom suggest any newer types of objective. However, there are occasional deliberate attempts to look beyond current practice and traditions; and some of these have had considerable impact. The curriculum reform movement of the 1960s sought to bring the curriculum into line with new views of academic knowledge by enlisting the support of eminent scholars. The planning of vocational courses seeks to reflect the changing structure of the job market. Social education is altered to include new conceptions of adult roles—that of women, for example. Even the curriculum traditions themselves get reconstructed and reconceptualized by great thinkers like Bruner and Freire. These occasions for fundamental curriculum change are fewer than many would like; and the rethinking of the curriculum is a worthy candidate for financial support. But it is also important to recognize when such rethinking is not taking place, so that tradition-based curriculum development is not hampered by the mistaken idea that all objectives have to be derived from primary sources—a task whose difficulty and complexity will be apparent from the ensuing discussion.

Many curriculum practices and traditions leave their objectives unstated and implicit, but there have also been many attempts to translate them into the language of objectives or to develop new courses with an objective-based approach. Hence there are many well-documented lists of objectives that can be used as secondary sources. Short subject-specific lists may be found in official curriculum documents, in textbooks, in examination syllabi, and in books on subject teaching. Longer lists may be found in the teaching manuals of individualized programmes, in the massive compilations of objectives

prepared under the auspices of the Russell Sage Foundation (Kearney 1953, French et al. 1957) and in the Instructional Objectives Exchange (Popham 1974). Using such secondary sources has three problems. They are variable in quality, their contextual or cultural specificity may not be immediately apparent, and selection from lists is likely to lead to a fragmented curriculum. These problems would be significantly reduced if such lists were used not as main sources but as supplementary sources after the first attempt at objective formulation had already been completed.

2. The Justification of Objectives

Leaving aside technical considerations such as clarity, the justification of an objective is based on two kinds of argument—feasibility and desirability (Bloom et al. 1981). Both are necessary. Feasibility arguments are normally based on evidence from practice, and they are often dependent on there being sufficient similarity of student population and interest for the transfer of experience to be valid. The criteria will be much tighter when mastery is being sought than when the objectives are of a more expressive variety; but even in the latter case it will still have to be argued that something of value is likely to occur. While feasibility arguments should not be used to prevent intelligent experiments, there is an equal danger that experiments will be treated as if they were bound to succeed.

Desirability arguments are of two main kinds: evidence of expressed preferences and arguments from basic values—the former concerns who thinks an objective is desirable, the latter concerns why it should be thought desirable. Techniques for collecting expressed preferences have been reviewed by Stake (1970), and their usefulness for selection is discussed below. The procedure is commonly referred to as needs assessment, but this designation is misleading because it takes an argument from basic values to establish that a preference is also a need. Pratt (1980) provides a useful summary of the issues involved in justification.

What, then, are the basic values on which arguments for the desirability or worthwhileness of an objective can rest? Combining a number of authors' suggestions gives four major categories in which such values may be said to reside—occupational practice, roles in society, cultural and academic knowledge, and the interests of the learners. Objectives relating to occupational practice can be justified in terms of national manpower needs, in terms of local needs for particular kinds of knowledge and skills, or an individual's need to be able to work with application. Sometimes these needs come into conflict as when doctors get sucked away from rural to urban areas or a subsistence farmer's education is based on the occupational requirements of industry. Often the technical problems of establishing occupational needs are greater than is commonly assumed. Job analysis techniques are well-developed only for lower level skills and tend to ignore important aspects of human relations. Manpower forecasting is a notoriously chancy activity. Thus arguments from occupational practice are likely to meet five major problems: (a) the large number of different occupations; (b) variations within the same occupation between different work contexts; (c) the changing nature of occupations; (d) the limitations of job analysis; and (e) uncertainty as to whether the student will spend any time in the occupation for which he or she is being prepared.

Roles in society include citizenship, membership of a local community, family life, and so on in addition to the occupational roles already discussed. This is controversial territory. First, there is considerable argument about what would be an appropriate role model. Second, there is evidence that most educational systems prepare students differentially according to their socioeconomic and cultural status—this is often a latent rather than an intended function of schooling. Then third, it is argued that many objectives in this area should not be taught in schools because they are the responsibility of the home, the church, or the local community.

Much that is found in the "role in society" category can also be subsumed under the heading of "cultural knowledge", a term to which curriculum thinkers are often attracted but whose implications have yet to be fully worked out. Thus it has been used both in the context of justifying attention to the arts and humanities and in the context of preparing students to live in a multicultural society. When one also considers many students' strong interest in youth culture, the potential for conflicting interpretations and priorities becomes even greater. Within the sphere of academic knowledge, arguments are better articulated but still not resolved. For example, there is considerable dispute as to whether generalizable and transferable thinking skills exist across disciplines; and even as to whether it is feasible to separate thinking processes from conceptual content within a discipline in the manner claimed by some curriculum theorists. Arguments from within a subject are likely to be based on notions of key concepts, on the position of an objective in some important learning hierarchy, or on induction into the ways of thinking in the discipline. Thus an objective's utility is defined in terms of its contribution to the further study of the subject. Otherwise some other form of justification would be invoked.

Arguments based on the learners' interests are of two main types. The motivational argument rests on what students are claimed to be interested in, while the needs argument rests on what is claimed to be in the children's interests. The two are combined if it is asserted that it is basic value for children to enjoy themselves or to have a wide range of interests. Otherwise the motivational argument is merely a means to ends which have to be justified on other grounds. Many authors have suggested lists of children's needs that can serve as basic values for curriculum justification. Pateman (1978) for example suggests eight: "to be able to survive; to get or stay healthy; to be able to work with application; to enjoy themselves; to have a sense of their own worth; to be able to relate to others; to understand the world in which they live; and to be able to participate in its major institutions." While some of these would be catered for under the other headings—occupational practice, roles in society, academic and cultural knowledge—they might receive a radically different emphasis in that other justificatory context. Moreover, Pateman suggests that some of these basic needs are virtually ignored in formal schooling. In spite of their prominence in educators' discussions about the aims of education, personal development objectives tend to get overwhelmed by more academic and vocational considerations.

Another area of need in the learners' interests category is the need to make the most of the educational process itself. This involves developing such skills as note taking, learning from books, working with others, preparing for and taking examinations, and so on. Even in higher education it is increasingly acknowledged that these skills should no longer be taken for granted but need to be incorporated into the formal curriculum.

3. Selecting Objectives: The Problem of Priorities

The wider the range of possible objectives considered—and many argue that it should be very wide indeed—the greater becomes the problem of selection. There are so many forms of justification that the value judgments involved in selection can never be resolved by reference to some single underlying principle. This does not prevent an appropriately designated group of experts or representatives from arriving at a compromise plan and gaining sufficient political support to get it adopted; but it does limit the degree to which issues can be settled by rational argument. Moreover, the technical problems of collecting evidence of people's preferences in order to guide such a debate are considerable. Stake and Gooler (1971) present a three-dimensional design for a study of people's educational priorities based on:

(a) the audiences whose preferences are being sought;

(b) different indicators of priority, namely—importance, time allocation, cash allocation, and vigour of efforts to remediate;

(c) a dichotomy between the "real"—what they think are the current priorities—and the "ideal"—what they would like the priorities to be.

This last dimension is particularly important in view of evidence that parents can be greatly mistaken about the "real", especially at the elementary level (Becher et al. 1981), and may therefore argue from premises that are demonstrably false. In practice, however, Stake and Gooler encountered three major obstacles. First, they found that teachers and citizens had a great deal of difficulty in thinking about the curriculum as a whole:

They appear to be devoid of the information needed to make judgments about the importance of the work of even a major subdivision of the curriculum, such as the science department or the athletic department. They do not know what the total effort to teach social responsibility is, and they feel most uncomfortable making even the crudest estimate of resources that might best be allocated to it.

Second, they found it impossible to give absolute priority information that was meaningful. It does not make sense to argue about the ideal allocation of time to mathematics without continual reference back to the status quo. Then, third, there is so much redundancy in the total education system that things are taught many times and in many ways. How can one assign a teaching time to an objective, when other objectives are also being taught at the same time?

These difficulties explain why planning a whole curriculum *ab initio* is rarely attempted. Instead piecemeal reform is found whenever someone can justify some change and mobilize the necessary support. Perhaps the most that can be expected is a series of attempts to narrow what Goodlad (1974) has called the "education gap" between the human race's noblest views of what it might become and the conventional wisdom that motivates current practice. But this is to assume that agreement can be reached on the nature of the gap, and that Goodlad's aspirational perspective can still command political support when the emphasis is shifting towards efficiency and effectiveness.

Within a single subject, the problem of selecting objectives becomes more manageable because people can at least conceptualize the task. However, rival forms of justifications still exist. "A" may be more feasible, "B" more enjoyable, "C" more immediately useful, and "D" more important for the development of advanced thinking in the subject. Moreover, it is not uncommon for a subject to be included because it is argued to be useful, but then planned as if utility were no longer an important criterion. The introduction of classification schemes for objectives has probably helped people to examine the emphasis and level of teaching in addition to the content balance. Though such schemes cannot

create new principles for choosing priorities, they can at least make it easier to recognize those that are already there; and they may even suggest some interesting alternatives. All this, of course, depends on the schemes being judiciously chosen and their limitations being recognized.

Bibliography

Becher T, Eraut M, Knight J 1981 *Policies for Educational Accountability*. Heinemann, London

Bloom B S, Madaus G F, Hastings J T 1981 *Evaluation to Improve Learning*. McGraw-Hill, New York

French W et al. 1957 *Behavioral Goals of General Education in High School*. Russell Sage Foundation, New York

Goodlad J 1974 Program development: Identification and formulation of desirable educational goals. In: Blaney J et al. (eds.) 1974 *Program Development in Education*. Education–Extension Centre for Continuing Education, University of British Columbia, Vancouver, British Columbia

Hirst P H 1973 Towards a logic of curriculum development. In: Taylor P H, Walton J (eds.) 1973 *The Curriculum: Research Innovation and Change*. Ward Lock, London, pp. 9–26

Kearney N C 1953 *Elementary School Objectives: A Report Prepared for the Mid-century Committee on Outcomes in Elementary Education*. Russell Sage Foundation, New York

Pateman T 1978 Accountability, values and schooling. In: Becher T, Maclure S (eds.) 1978 *Accountability in Education*. National Foundation for Educational Research, Slough, pp. 61–94

Popham W J 1974 Curriculum design: The problem of specifying intended learning outcomes. In: Blaney J et al. (eds.) 1974 *Program Development in Education*. Education–Extension Centre for Continuing Education, University of British Columbia, Vancouver, British Columbia

Pratt D 1980 *Curriculum: Design and Development*. Harcourt Brace Jovanovich, New York

Stake R E 1970 Objectives, priorities and other judgment data. *Rev. Educ. Res.* 40: 181–212

Stake R E, Gooler D D 1971 Measuring educational priorities. *Educ. Technol.* 11: 44–48

Tyler R W 1949 *Basic Principles of Curriculum and Instruction*. University of Chicago Press, Chicago, Illinois

Specifying and Using Objectives

M. R. Eraut

The term "objective" is frequently used by educators and laymen as a synonym for "goal". Sometimes it can be replaced by the word "aim" or "intention" without appreciable loss of meaning. However, the term "objective" has also come to acquire a more technical meaning, the significance of which is not so readily apparent to those unfamiliar with its use in the education literature. In this more specialized sense, the term "objective" normally refers to an intended and prespecified outcome of a planned programme of teaching and it is expressed in terms of what it is hoped the student will have

learned. The two usages are often distinguished by referring either to general objectives (goals) or to specific objectives (intended learning outcomes).

This more technical use of the term "objectives", with its associated demand for lengthy detailed statements of intended learning outcomes, is criticized by a number of writers on both practical and theoretical grounds. Thus to help the reader understand some of the controversies, as well as the development among some educators of a specialized terminology for communicating objectives, the article begins with a brief historical survey. This introduces different recommendations for the specification of objectives, with special attention to the notion of levels of specification and to various formulations of the concept of behavioural objectives. The ensuing discussion of problems associated with the status of objectives examines structural relationships between objectives, the logic of intentions expressed by an objective, and the political status of statements of objectives. The next section examines approaches to the differentiation and classification of objectives, but without going deeply into taxonomies of objectives as discussed by V De Landsheere in the final article of this Section. Then finally the uses and usefulness of objectives are examined in five contexts: curriculum development, lesson planning, instructional design, evaluation and communication with students.

1. Historical Development

The origin of thinking about objectives in a more technical manner is usually attributed to Bobbitt (1918) whose book *The Curriculum* was probably the earliest systematic treatise on curriculum theory. The circumstances were significant. Only five years previously, Bobbitt had been the first to expound principles of educational administration directly based on Taylor's (1912) theory of scientific management. Industrial language suffused the book while Bobbitt readily accepted Spencer's utilitarian approach to knowledge selection. Where Spencer (1860) had merely asserted that "the first step must be to classify, in order of importance, the leading kinds of activity which constitute human life", Bobbitt proposed to use Taylor's time and motion study techniques to make this a reality.

A similar position was advocated by Charters (1924) whose notes for curriculum construction began as follows:

First, determine the major objectives of education by a study of the life of man in its social setting. Second, analyse these objectives into ideals and activities, and continue the analysis to the level of working units.

Following this advice led Pendleton to list 1,581 objectives for English and Billings to find 888 important generalizations for social studies teachers. Hence the objectives movement was already collapsing under its own weight when its prevailing utilitarian ideology was eclipsed by the progressivism of the 1930s. Its revival by Ralph Tyler, a former student of Charters, was in a different context—that of diagnostic testing and evaluation—and with a different philosophy—one of individual development rather than utilitarian efficiency (Smith and Tyler 1942). Tyler's Eight-year Study was a cooperative venture with a group of progressive schools; one of its main purposes was to formulate educational objectives which involved pupils in thinking for themselves and applying their knowledge rather than merely memorizing it or performing routine exercises. This aspect of

the work was further developed by Tyler's former student, Benjamin Bloom, and a group of college examiners who eventually published two taxonomies of objectives, one for a cognitive domain and one for an affective domain.

Tyler's approach to curriculum development was based on reciprocal interaction between the formulation of objectives and the evaluation of their attainment (Tyler 1949). Evaluation was important for the improvement of educational programmes and proper evaluation required knowledge of what objectives the programmes were aiming to achieve. Thus objectives needed to be formulated with sufficient specificity to guide evaluation and subsequent attempts at course improvement in which the objectives themselves might be altered, both to include new possibilities and to remove that which was no longer considered feasible or of sufficiently high priority. For this purpose Tyler recommended that curriculum planners use behavioural objectives, in which both the content and the intended type of student behaviour are specified, and that course objectives be summarized in a two-dimensional matrix with content categories along one dimension and behavioural categories along the other.

It is sometimes forgotten that Tyler and the taxonomists defined objectives at a relatively general level, and it was Mager's (1962) influential book on preparing objectives for programmed instruction which more fully recaptured the spirit of Bobbitt. Moreover, like Bobbitt before him, Mager derived his position from the behavioural technology approaches of trainers in military and industrial settings.

First Mager (1962) argued that behaviour should be specified only in observable terms and outlawed the use of verbs like "know", "understand", "feel", or "appreciate" that were indicative only of unobservable internal states of mind. Second, he insisted that the standard of performance should be specified in minute detail and with a built-in assumption of mastery or near-mastery, for example 90 percent of the students should get 90 percent of the questions correct on a test covering addition and subtraction of two digit numbers. Then, third, to avoid any ambiguity he asked for the conditions of performance to be clearly identified. Given the emphasis on the nature of the terminal performance itself, objectives which satisfy Mager's criteria are sometimes referred to as performance objectives, though the term behavioural objective is still more usual.

Gagné (1965) was among many psychologists who welcomed Mager's operational definition because it would help to determine the particular type of learning required. Unlike Tyler who was concerned with providing general guidance to teachers and curriculum planners, Mager and Gagné were interested in instructional design, which at that time was seen in terms of the detailed planning of instructional events in accordance with the principles of behaviourist psychology. If the design did not always lead to programmed learning, it was still expected to yield something very like it.

Several authors took up Mager's guidelines on specifying observable behaviours and gave special attention to the action verbs whose incorporation into the statement of an objective was said to meet this requirement. More recently, however, Gagné and Briggs (1974), realizing that operational definitions of performance often conveyed little information about the kind of learning that had taken place, recommended the addition of a "learned capability" component to the specification of an objective. There would seem to be some contradiction between the focus on performance and the abandonment of operationalism implicit in the addition of the learned capability component.

Finally, it should be noted that it is possible for a planning group formulating objectives to pursue each of the four main dimensions noted in this discussion—content, behaviour, conditions, and standards—to varying degrees of specificity, and this issue is further discussed below.

2. Levels of Specificity and the Limits of Specification

Krathwohl (1965) has distinguished three levels of specificity and suggests that each is appropriate for a different purpose:

> At the first and most abstract level are the quite broad and general statements most helpful in the development of programs of instruction, for the laying out of types of courses and areas to be covered, and for the general goals towards which several years of education might be aimed or for which an entire unit such as an elementary, junior, or senior high school might strive.
>
> At a second and more concrete level, a behavioural objectives orientation helps to analyse broad goals into more specific ones which are useful as the building blocks for curricular instruction. These behaviourally stated objectives are helpful in specifying the goals of an instructional unit, a course, or a sequence of courses.
>
> Third and finally, there is the level needed to create instructional materials—materials which are the operational embodiment of one particular route (rarely are multiple routes included) to the achievement of a curriculum planned at the second and more abstract level, the level of detailed analysis involved in the programmed instruction movement.

The first level corresponds to what Taba has called a "platform of general objectives" though it may also apply to a specific programme within a school (Taba 1962). The second level corresponds to Tyler's and Taba's version of the term "behavioural objective", and is also the level at which the taxonomies were developed. Davies (1976) calls these "general objectives", a term which Taba reserves for Level 1.

While it is customary to describe levels of specificity in terms of language and purpose, the addition of a quantitative density dimension can also sometimes be helpful. Since objectives are usually formulated in groups or clusters, an index of density can be simply defined as

$$\frac{\text{Number of objectives in list}}{\text{Hours of learning which list is intended to cover}}$$

Thus, when working at Krathwohl's Level 1, a ministry of education lists 8 objectives for primary mathematics over the 5–9 age range, and about 600 hours of learning are involved, so the density is 8/600 or 1/75. Teachers planning a course of 100 hours using a Tyler matrix at Level 2 might well arrive at a list of about 20 objectives that would mean a density of 20/100 or 1/5. Then at Level 3 the objectives for an individual lesson, a self-instructional unit or a chapter in a book are likely to number between about 1 and 10 for a learning period of between 30 minutes and 2 hours, giving a density index that is usually greater than 1. The position is summarised in Table 1 below.

Another writer to identify three levels of objectives was Scriven (1967), though his perspective was primarily epistemological. His first level, entitled a "conceptual description of educational objectives", gives priority to conceptual structure and to student motivation. Then his second level, "manifestation dimensions of criterial variables", is concerned with the various ways in which a student's conceptual knowledge and understanding and his or her attitudes and nonmental abilities may be manifest or made observable. The third level provides an operational description of an objective in terms of how it is to be assessed. Thus Scriven's second and third levels correspond fairly closely to those of Krathwohl,

Table 1
Levels of specificity

Krathwohl Terms		Davies Terms	Level of application	Density[a]
1	General Goals	Aims	Institution Programme	less than 1/50
2	Behavioural Objectives (as in Tyler, Taba, Bloom)	General Objectives	Course Module Topic	$\frac{1}{2}$ to 1/20
3	Instructional Objectives (as in Mager, Gagné and Briggs)	Specific Objectives	Lesson Assignment	1 to 10

a Density = number of objectives/hours of learning

but the first level has quite a different character, being based on curriculum content rather than general goals.

Both Krathwohl and Scriven state that Level 1 statements of objectives can guide the development of Level 2 objectives and that Level 2 statements can guide Level 3. But this process is much more complicated than simple logical deduction. There is no defensible set of rules or procedures for deriving specific objectives from general objectives because (a) selection decisions are made which involve judgments about appropriateness and priority; and (b) the kind of analysis required goes beyond the existing state of philosophical and psychological knowledge (Hirst 1973).

Gronlund (1970) makes a useful distinction between *minimum essentials* and *developmental objectives*. While minimum essentials can be handled as Level 3 objectives, developmental objectives are so complex that:

(a) Only a sample of representative behaviours can be tested.

(b) Teaching is directed towards the general class of behaviour that the objective represents rather than towards the sample that is specifically tested.

(c) Standards of performance are extremely difficult, if not impossible to define; so it is more meaningful to talk of encouraging and directing each student towards the maximum level of development he or she is capable of achieving.

A more radical distinction is made by Eisner (1969) who argues for separate treatment for instructional and expressive objectives. While instructional objectives can be prespecified and mastered, expressive objectives are concerned with outcomes that cannot and should not be prespecified because some form of original response is being sought. An expressive objective may specify an educational encounter, situation, problem, or task but it cannot predict what will be learned from what is intended to be an idiosyncratic response. While more usually associated with art and literature, the term is equally applicable to essays and projects in which students are encouraged to develop personal perspectives and insights.

3. The Status of Objectives

3.1 Structural Status

An educational objective cannot be considered in isolation, either from its companion objectives or from objectives which are intended to come before or after it in some planned sequence. It is necessarily embedded in some structure of intentions, whether this is described explicitly in some plan or document or left implicit in the way the curriculum is organized. The list format which is commonly used to communicate sets of objectives is particularly ill-suited to conveying structural information. So quite different assumptions may inform the selection of a set of objectives from those which later guide the grouping and sequencing of those objectives for teaching purposes. There may also be considerable differences between the structure embedded in course materials, the structure in the mind of the teacher, and the structures developing in the mind of each student.

When compilers of objectives do give attention to structural assumptions, they frequently turn to the concept of a learning hierarchy. A group of objectives is said to constitute a learning hierarchy when it can be represented by a structure rather like a family tree, in which the achievement of each objective is dependent on the achievement of all the objectives connected to it on the level below. A hierarchy is usually developed by logical analysis, breaking down an objective into subobjectives until each step constitutes a clearly distinguishable learning task. Both the dependency claims of the hierarchy and the concomitant assumption that the level of analysis is appropriate may need to be empirically verified.

This notion of learning hierarchies, when combined with Carroll's (1963) suggestion that individual differences might be more appropriately attributed to rate of learning than to quality of learning, leads naturally to the type of individualized instruction that is commonly referred to as mastery learning. All knowledge within a mastery learning system is assumed to be essentially hierarchical in nature; instruction is individualized so each student can proceed at his or her own rate; and there is a built-in requirement for every student to master each unit before proceeding to the next. Hence the formulation and sequencing of objectives and the development of assessment instruments to indicate their mastery are an essential part of the strategy (Bloom et al. 1981).

The terms "terminal objective" and "enabling objective" are also associated with sequencing. A terminal objective represents the end of a learning sequence and needs to be justified in its own right; while an enabling objective situated in the middle of a sequence need only be justified in terms of its role in facilitating the achievement of one or more terminal objective(s). The distinction, though useful, is still an oversimplification because many objectives can be justified on both grounds and their description as "terminal" or "enabling" depends mainly on the time-scale adopted: the terminal objective of a lesson becomes an enabling objective in the context of a topic or course; and the terminal objective of a course becomes an enabling objective in the context of a student's subsequent life.

From the student's point of view, what probably matters most is an objective's position on the immediacy–remoteness continuum (Dressel 1976). Many objectives will appear to students both as conceptually remote, because they are far from what seems to be relevant in the community outside school, and as temporally remote because their utility lies far in the future. Perceiving links between their immediate objectives and possible ultimate goals can be crucial for some students' motivation. It has been suggested that objectives being communicated to students should be accompanied by individual rationales or justifications which relate them to more distant and more valued goals.

3.2 Logical Status

The logical status of an objective also deserves attention as it greatly affects the part it might play in planning and teaching. First, there is the distinction made by White who noted that the phrase "behavioural objective" can mean one of two things:

(a) objectives which themselves *consist in* pupils behaving in certain ways;

(b) objectives whose attainment is *tested by* observing pupils behaving in certain ways. (White 1971)

To state that no cognitive activity other than the repetition of memorized responses can be behavioural in sense (a) is not to claim that greater clarity cannot be achieved by giving close attention to the formulation of an objective; but it does imply that most educational objectives can be behavioural only in sense (b). Such objectives cannot wholly specify the ways in which they might be assessed, and no form of assessment can provide unambiguous evidence of their achievement. In practice, some forms of assessment are widely accepted as providing adequate evidence of the attainment of certain objectives, some have their adequacy disputed, and some are clearly unsatisfactory. If this were not the case, assessment would not be such a complex and elaborate field of study.

A second problem arises if one questions more carefully the notion of an objective being an intended outcome. In what sense is it intended? Is it expected to happen? Is its achievement specifically planned? Is it always explicit? Much of the writing about objectives seems to imply affirmative answers to all these questions, but observations of practice suggest a more cautious approach. Lists of objectives are often used to express aspirations rather than expectations and course documents often include a mixture of the two. More significantly, perhaps, an objective which is an expectation for one student may be an aspiration for another.

The term "emergent objectives" has been used to refer to objectives which may not even have been formulated in advance, but which, when the opportunity arises, are seen to contribute to important educational aims which tend to get neglected under the pressures of institutional expectations.

3.3 Political Status

The status of an objective is also affected by political factors. Who specifies them and with what authority? Who uses them and how strongly do they feel obliged to keep within the specifications? There are a large number of possible situations. For example, influences on objectives from outside school may be of any of the following kinds:

(a) external specification as part of a pattern of curriculum control;

(b) an external requirement for the school to formulate its own objectives, which may or may not be accompanied by a further requirement to have them formally approved;

(c) external specification as part of a system of external examinations;

(d) external specification as part of a package of curriculum materials which the school may choose or be obliged to adopt or adapt

(e) external comments by district officers, advisers, or inspectors.

Only in the first two uses will objectives necessarily be formally specified. However, evidence from curriculum implementation studies suggests that external specification of objectives alone has relatively little impact unless accompanied by sanctions or by other forms of specification such as textbook approval or external examinations. Congruence between externally specified objectives and classroom practice may be more readily explained by their sharing a common tradition than by hypotheses of cause and effect. Even when objectives have been internally specified, it must remain an empirical question whether they play a significant role in classroom practice. Accounts in the literature would seem to indicate that sometimes they do not.

4. Differentiation and Classification of Objectives

Advocates of using objectives in curriculum planning have been concerned not only with specificity and status but also with differentiation and classification. The connection between the two is clear: the more one specifies outcomes, the more responsible one becomes for seeing that an appropriate range of outcomes is considered. Otherwise the process of specification is likely to restrict the scope of the curriculum beyond the intentions of the specifiers. While reductions in curriculum scope are deliberately sought by followers of the "back to basics" movement, this was certainly not the intention of postwar curriculum theorists like Tyler and Taba, but quite the opposite. They perceived current practice as unduly narrow and used planning by objectives as a technique for broadening it.

Schemes for distinguishing between different kinds of objectives range from simple typologies to classifications involving two or three levels of differentiation. Table 2 compares Bloom's first level separation into three *domains* with the typologies of Taba and Gagné and Briggs.

Even at this first level, there is considerable interaction between separate categories of objective because all learning entails cognition of some kind and all human transactions involve values and attitudes. But this does not prevent simple typologies from being of assistance in the formulation and selection of a balanced set of

Table 2
First level differentiation of objectives

Bloom (1956)	Gagné and Briggs (1974)	Taba (1962)
Cognitive domain	Verbal information	Knowledge
Affective domain	Intellectual skills	Reflective thinking
Psychomotor domain	Cognitive strategies	Skills (basic, inquiry, social)
	Attitudes	Values and attitudes
	Motor skills	Sensitivities and feelings

objectives, provided that the structural status of the objectives and the delicate interplay between reasons and emotions are not forgotten. These considerations are equally important at the second level, that of taxonomies of educational objectives.

Although taxonomies are discussed in detail by V De Landsheere in the final article of this Section, their scope and assumptions will be given some attention in the sections below. Here, the purpose is to compare and contrast the taxonomies with other approaches to the classification of objectives. While, for convenience, the discussion is divided according to Bloom's three domains, the domain distinction is not taken for granted; and a fourth section is devoted to objectives such as social skills which have no obvious place in the Bloom classifications.

The main focus of this discussion is on general rather than subject-specific classifications, because there are so many subject-specific schemes in use. Several of these more specialised schemes can be found in the Bloom et al. (1971) handbook and the publications of groups, such as the International Association for the Evaluation of Educational Attainment (IEA), and the British Assessment of Performance Unit (APU) who are concerned with monitoring educational achievement at national level.

4.1 Classification of Cognitive Objectives

The traditional distinction in the *cognitive domain* has been between knowledge and skills, content and process, conceptual structure and critical thinking. Tyler called it content and behaviour. However, since terms like behaviour, process and skill have multiple meanings, many of which lie outside the cognitive domain, we prefer to use the terms *knowledge* and *cognitive operations* and to emphasise their interdependence. Thus knowledge is acquired, interpreted, transformed, used and even created by cognitive operations in such a manner that it is misleading to regard it as static or fixed.

Descriptions of knowledge are usually couched in such terms as facts, conventions, concepts, procedures, principles and theories; and these features may be depicted as loosely or tightly linked by some kind of network or conceptual structure. The loosest kind of link would be a metaphoric association of ideas while the tightest would be a learning hierarchy of the type discussed above. There are many gradations in between, as when several concepts are linked by their relevance to some common problem. Bloom's *taxonomy* is based on

cognitive operations and more readily understood if we adopt Alles's (1967) suggestion that the lowest level be renamed "recall and recognition" to avoid the semantic confusion caused by Bloom's idiosyncratic use of the term "knowledge". Research suggests that there is some justification for treating Bloom's lower four levels— recall and recognition, comprehension, application and analysis—as taxonomic, but not for including synthesis and evaluation in the same category (Madaus et al. 1973). Eraut (1975) has suggested a distinction between the lower three levels which concern cognitive operations with clearly delineated pieces of content and the upper levels where more generalised thinking skills are involved and selection of facts, concepts, theories and criteria is part of the desired behaviour. This draws attention to the possible substitution of Bloom's upper three levels by some alternative breakdown of generalised *thinking skills*, a procedure which was in fact followed by several contributors to Bloom et al.'s (1971) handbook. Klopfer, for example, substituted four categories under the general heading "Processes of scientific inquiry": observing and measuring; seeing a problem and seeking ways to solve it; interpreting data and formulating generalizations; building, testing and revising a theoretical model.

Ormell (1974) argues that "patching up" the taxonomy in this way will not prove satisfactory:

A much more radical reconstruction seems to be needed; which, (i) will relate to conceptual levels in subject areas, (ii) will not imply a single linear hierarchy of objectives and (iii) will include the ingredient of imaginative development from the beginning.

His first two criticisms would seem to be supported by the wide range of subject-specific classification schemes put forward by Bloom's own collaborators and other authors; and by their frequent abandonment of the single linear hierarchy principle. But it must also be recognized that much of this rethinking has been stimulated by the enormous impact of the taxonomy itself. Without it we might well not have the range of classification schemes available today.

Ormell's third criticism, however, would also apply to most of these newer subject-specific schemes. He argues that the taxonomy is implicitly based on materialist values: knowledge is treated as a commodity and imagination and personal meaning seem to have no place. Though not originally designed for classifying objectives, a model teaching-learning sequence suggested by

Parker and Rubin (1966) provides an interesting example of a much more interactive approach.

1. Processes which expose the student to a particular body of knowledge: formulating questions, reading, observing, listening, collecting evidence, discovering principles.

2. Processes which allow the student to extract meaning from the body of knowledge: analyzing, experimenting, reorganizing, consolidating, integrating.

3. Processes which enable the learner to affix significance to the knowledge: inferring generalizations, reconstructing, relating to other situations, testing for usability.

4. Processes which cause the learner to put his or her knowledge to functional use—to operate with it in different situations and to manipulate it through intellectual activity: solving a problem, creating a problem, clarifying a problem.

4.2 Classification of Objectives in the Affective Domain

Cazden (1971), writing about early language development, likens the relationships between the cognitive and affective domain to the linguistic distinction between competence and performance. Educators want students to be interested in what they are taught, to value it and to use it; and this major concern is identified with what many see as "the problem of motivation". Thus, many objectives in the affective domain can be appropriately described as socialization into the norms and values of educators. The terms most commonly used are "interest" and "appreciation", and the three lower levels of Krathwohl et al.'s (1964) *taxonomy*—receiving, responding and valuing—provide a useful analysis of the successive stages in the achievement of these aims. Though formal statements tend to confine their attention to socialization into school subjects, the hidden curriculum emphasises socialization into the norms and values of schooling in general. Educators seek not just good conduct but participation.

A second strand of the affective domain concerns the areas of moral education and social education. Here there is a delicate balance to be found between socialization of students into the norms and values of the local community and the nation and the development of the student's own personal value system. In any society, some values are broadly accepted, some are only accepted within certain subcultures, and others are regarded as deviant. This potential for conflict is ignored by the Krathwohl taxonomy which focuses only on the progressive internalization and development of students' personal value systems without paying attention to what might be considered as good and bad or right or wrong (Gribble 1970). Thus there is an inherent danger that sophistication and coherence will be valued for their own sakes. While it may reasonably be argued that cognitive excellence is necessarily based on the higher levels of the cognitive domain (at least within the academic arena), it is highly debatable whether a moral person needs to have a moral philosopher's understanding of value systems.

A third strand in the affective domain concerns feelings and sensitivities. While Kamii's (1971) use of the term "socio-emotional development" is clearly derived from the aim of socialization into schooling, other writers have talked about the education of the emotions. This discussion is most prominent in the context of the arts, but also becomes relevant in social studies, where the aim of developing empathy is likely to have a strong emotional component. Many psychologists, however, have argued that emotion is important in all types of learning and that it is particularly important in fostering creativity. There have been few attempts to analyze this aspect of education in terms of objectives, and most authors have argued that the language of objectives is inappropriate.

In conclusion, the interconnection between the cognitive and affective domains should be reemphasized. All cognitive operations both require and engender some form of affective response. The kind of valuing described in the socialization and personal development aims above, is strongly cognitive in many respects, at least as dependent on cognitive arguments about relevance as upon immediate emotional impact. It has been argued that feelings and emotions have a substantial cognitive component (Yarlott 1972); and many of the objectives discussed in section 4.4 below have strong affective components. Thus, the justification for the domain concept appears to be decidedly thin.

4.3 Classification in the Psychomotor Domain

Classification work in the psychomotor domain has been based more on physiology than on recognizable learning objectives. Thus Kibler et al.'s (1970) and Harrow's (1972) taxonomies set out different types of bodily movement and a range of perceptual and physical abilities. Even communication is classified physiologically into facial expressions, gestures, bodily movement, speech behaviour and the like. Since these movements serve such different purposes, one wonders how useful such general classifications can be. Eye-hand coordination in playing tennis is so radically different from eye-hand coordination in playing the piano that it is difficult to see what is gained from putting them in the same category.

The main exception to this physiological emphasis is the group of classification schemes based on the development of a physical skill. Seymour (1966), for example, distinguishes four stages:

1. Acquiring knowledge.

2. Executing the task in a step-by-step manner, with conscious watching and thinking-out of each step.

3. Transfer of control to the kinaesthetic sense, with consequent increase in the fluidity and rapidity of action, and freeing the eye for perceptual control.

4. Automatization of the skill.

A further stage involving the adaptation of a skill to new circumstances has also been suggested (Simpson 1966, Wellens 1974). The analysis is clearly relevant to such skills as driving a car or playing a simple tune on the piano, but cannot be applied to riding a bicycle or pole vaulting because the steps cannot be separately rehearsed. Again, subject-specific or even task-specific classifications are possibly more useful than general ones. The work of Harrow and Simpson seems primitive in comparison with Laban's analysis of dance or Flesch's analysis of violin playing. Moreover, the performing arts in general involve such a complex interplay between cognition, feeling and motor skill that thinking in terms of separate domains will often be quite inappropriate.

4.4 Social Skills and Other Objectives Outside the Bloom Domains

Taba (1962) included social skills in her typology of objectives but they do not seem to fit into any of Bloom's domains. The same would probably be true of sculpture, but since that already has a subject identity and a potential place in the timetable, the omission is less serious. Romiszowski (1981) suggests a fourth domain to include social, personal and interactive skills but this seems to be giving the domain concept rather more significance than it perhaps deserves. However, the skills he mentions are interesting because they go beyond the usual aim of getting on with people and include entrepreneurial skills such as leadership, persuasion, discussion and salesmanship.

The most elaborate exploration of the territory that lies outside school subjects is probably that of Raven (1977) whose approach to the concept of competence is refreshingly broad. He argues that the self-motivated competencies he advocates involve a major values component and are best thought of as motivational dispositions. They may also be regarded as personal skills. A few typical examples are: tendency to seek feedback, ability to recognise it and tendency to utilize it; ability to learn without instruction; and willingness to tolerate frustrations. Raven does not offer a classification scheme, but by drawing attention to objectives which are suggested neither by subject structures nor by classification schemes, he draws attention to important values and skills which might otherwise escape notice.

5. Arguments For and Against Using Objectives

When discussing the advantages and limitations of planning and working with objectives, it is important to specify the user, the context, and the type of use envisaged. Five main types of use will be distinguished—curriculum development, lesson planning, instructional design, evaluation, and communication to students. These different uses are often confused in the literature, with arguments for and against one type of use

being frequently applied to another. Moreover, it has not been unusual for authors to set up "straw-man" images of their opponents in order to demolish extreme statements while avoiding entanglements with more moderate positions [see, for example, the often quoted papers by Popham (1969) and Macdonald-Ross (1973)].

5.1 Using Objectives in Curriculum Development

Attention will be confined here to the use of objectives at Krathwohl's second level, leaving discussion of the use of highly specific objectives for the next section. In doing so, however, it must be remembered that most advocates of instructional objectives at the third level are agreed that prior specification at the second level is essential. But the converse is not true. Objectives may be used in curriculum development without any assumption that more detailed specification by teachers or by instructional designers will necessarily follow.

The principle arguments for using objectives for curriculum development purposes alone would appear to be (a) that they clarify the intentions of the developers and (b) that they focus attention upon the learner as well as the teacher. What the use of objectives cannot do is resolve disputes over what should be taught, though sometimes they may help to map out the issues. Objectives at the second level will never be devoid of ambiguity, and some educators are more skilful than others in using the language of objectives, so the question of whether or not objectives do indeed clarify intentions can only be answered in terms of individual cases.

Many authors have stressed that the clarification of teaching intentions is a difficult exercise involving considerable insight and delicacy of phrasing, and that it is incapable of totally satisfactory resolution. People who prepare curriculum specifications at district, regional, or national level need to understand these problems, if their use of objectives is not to do more harm than good. In particular, there is a tendency to issue lists of objectives which are specified at a mixture of different levels. This causes confusion for teachers seeking to translate curriculum documents into lesson plans and often leads to selective neglect of the more general, and seemingly more rhetorical objectives. A similar problem occurs when developmental or expressive objectives are treated as if they are competencies to be mastered, for this neglects the whole issue of quality performance.

At institutional level, however, the context of curriculum specifications is quite different because formal curriculum documents are only a small part of the communication between the teachers concerned. A statement of objectives then has a strongly indexical character in which its meaning is enriched by and partly dependent upon other communications which occurred before, during, and after its preparation. The advantages of using objectives will depend on whether the curriculum developers want to use them or merely feel obliged to use them; on whether they are genuinely seeking agreement as opposed to finding a form of words which maximizes the independence of individual teachers; and on whether intentions are easily communicated by other means, such as a common textbook or examination.

Above the institutional level, the political status of an objective is often critical. While some teachers are used to being told what to teach, others regard the formulation of objectives as the teachers' own responsibility. Normal practice varies greatly between one country and another, but in any country, attempts to alter the balance of power by changing either the locus or the extent of specification of objectives are likely to meet resistance. In practice, however, whether politically welcome or not, objectives may be misunderstood or even ignored by teachers. Even when the process of formulating objectives clarifies the intentions of a curriculum team or committee (and it is not unknown for it to lead to a deliberately vague compromise), the document that results does not necessarily convey those intentions adequately to teachers. This is not an argument against using objectives but rather one against placing too much reliance on them as a form of curriculum communication. The literature on curriculum implementation is replete with examples where misunderstanding or lack of sanctions or infeasibility have prevented externally specified curricula from being implemented as intended.

An important criticism from a theoretical rather than a practical perspective concerns not the use of objectives per se but approaches to curriculum development which assume that statements of objectives are adequate on their own in the first stage of curriculum planning. Several authors (see, for example, Stenhouse 1970/71), have argued for prime attention to content; others for an early consideration of assessment, which often counteracts the impact of objectives; and yet others for the early specification of certain crucial and often nontraditional learning experiences such as project work, community service, work experience, or artistic performance. Many of these other curriculum elements can be so important for a course that they need discussion prior to any detailed formulation of objectives. Moreover, when curriculum development is viewed as a problem-solving activity with a premium on creative imagination, an early emphasis on objectives may lead only to the reformulation of traditional practice at a time when more radical change is what is really needed (Eraut 1976). Thus, when the emphasis is on curriculum innovation, objectives may not be a starting point but a "late development of the curriculum maker's platform" (Walker 1971).

The argument against using objectives which has probably received the greatest support is that they are only appropriate for some areas of the curriculum. Eisner (1969) has eloquently argued against behavioural objectives in the arts, and their usefulness for describing higher level learning in the humanities (Stenhouse 1970/71) and social sciences (Eraut et al. 1975) has also been questioned. In all these cases it is the individuality and complexity of students' work which is said to limit the applicability of the language of objectives. Two major issues are at stake—the nature of the subject and the autonomy of the learner. Both have been and will long continue to be matters for debate among educators, though many would now agree that objectives are more helpful in some situations than in others. The principal problem lies in recognizing those situations in which the use of objectives is appropriate.

Given the problems of deriving, formulating, and justifying objectives, it is much safer if in the context of the education system as a whole objectives are regarded as means rather than ends. The courses and curricula that are planned constitute the means whereby students have to be guided towards a variety of ends; and the language of objectives provides one means of clarifying intentions during the planning process.

5.2 Using Objectives in Lesson Planning

The claim that highly specific objectives at Krathwohl's third level improve the quality of lesson plans and subsequent pupil performance is usually argued by asserting that good lesson planning is logically dependent on knowing what one is seeking to achieve; and that this necessarily entails having learning objectives. Both parts of this assertion have been challenged. To begin with the second—one counterargument is that teachers know what they are doing because they are working in a recognized teaching tradition. Provided that they can relate the content of their lessons to a topic on a syllabus, a chapter in a textbook, or a possible question in an examination, they do not need any separate list of course objectives. Once a tradition is clearly established, objectives become redundant. The use of objectives in such a context is less likely to be one of defining the course than one of inspiring teachers to move their students beyond the level of routine completion of textbook exercises or memorization of content, a purpose for which specifying beyond the second level is clearly inappropriate.

When more informal approaches to teaching are adopted, objectives are less likely to be implicit in textbooks, syllabi, and examinations. But then the first part of the assertion becomes more of an issue. Is good lesson planning logically dependent on knowing what objectives one is seeking to achieve? Sockett (1976) argues that objectives are totally inadequate as a description of a teacher's ends, because a teacher always has other equally important ends, to which his or her actions are directed: being fair to groups, getting students to ask questions, building up weaker children's confidence, developing interpupil discussion, and so on. Though one can argue that these "procedural aims" should be included as general course objectives, they need to be pursued over a long period. Such aims have a justifiably important influence on teaching, but cannot be converted into specific objectives for individual lessons.

Another criticism comes from Jackson (1968) whose interviews with teachers were judged as "outstanding" revealed that both their planning and their classroom responding were aimed not directly at the achievement of objectives but at creating productive learning conditions and securing student involvement. Since involvement in learning activities is logically necessary for learning, one might be permitted to modify the original assertion to argue that good lesson planning is dependent on having appropriate activities and strategies to achieve a high degree of student involvement. If that primary goal can be achieved then surely productive learning will follow. Where there is no established tradition, course objectives may be helpful in choosing between possible activities and in alerting a teacher to special opportunities. However, it is unreasonable to expect the teacher to be able to sustain a detailed knowledge of how each of 30 or more students is progressing towards each of a dozen or so objectives in every single lesson. Worse still is the possibility that it might distract the teacher from the primary task of securing involvement in learning.

A further argument against using highly specific objectives in lesson planning is that they overconstrain the teacher. Both Jackson and Sockett characterize good teaching as being strong on opportunism. Atkin (1968) suggests that higher order objectives are best pursued whenever the opportunity arises rather than according to preplanned schedules. For example, when students' questions lead to the discussion of some significant moral problem or issue, the teacher may see the opportunity for pursuing objectives whose introduction might have seemed artificial or nonproductive if the teacher had initiated them. Eisner's expressive objectives also resist very precise planning. In general, support for the use of specific objectives at Krathwohl's third level is now largely confined to situations where the teaching is highly directive and objectives are limited to the lower cognitive levels. Using general course objectives to guide lesson planning is quite a different procedure from allowing lesson planning to be dominated by the detailed specification of behavioural objectives; and there is little conclusive empirical evidence to support either practice. Until there is good evidence of how people who work with objectives plan or teach differently and of how this benefits their students, the use or non-use of objectives should remain a matter of personal preference.

5.3 Using Objectives in Instructional Design

The term "instructional design" commonly refers to the design of teaching and learning materials by a specially designated team, who may or may not include teachers who will be responsible for their implementation. Although some writers on instructional design appear to address ordinary teachers, there is little evidence that their recommendations get used by individual teachers who are not members of a design team.

The claim that using highly specific objectives at Krathwohl's third level improves the quality of instructional design is prominent in the literature. Indeed it is often taken for granted. Yet there is little empirical evidence to support this claim for learning systems other than those based on individualized learning. The detailed specification of objectives is an extremely time-consuming operation, which requires considerable skill if common pitfalls are to be avoided; and it is, perhaps, unlikely to be a good use of scarce personnel when there is an urgent need to create and try out new teaching ideas.

The more restricted claim that highly specific objectives are needed for individualized learning programmes based on mastery learning receives much stronger theoretical and practical backing. The advocates of highly specific objectives adopt a similar theoretical position to advocates of mastery learning; and designers of mastery-learning-based instructional systems consistently use highly specific objectives. It can be argued that designers could proceed directly from second level objectives to criterion tests, but this would ignore the detailed mapping of hierarchies of learning objectives which most designers working in this tradition recommend (see *Mastery Learning Model*).

5.4 Using Objectives in Evaluation

It is in the context of evaluation that the concept of objectives has been most continuously used and most elaborately evolved. Tyler's primary concern was with evaluation and the taxonomies were also developed for evaluation purposes. Arguments for and against using objectives in evaluation are treated at greater length elsewhere, so the discussion here will be brief.

One of the purposes of an evaluation, sometimes the main purpose, is to examine the realization of intention. To what extent have various people's intentions been realized in practice? People have many kinds of intentions but these usually include at least some that relate to student outcomes. Whether or not they are documented or made explicit, intended student outcomes can often be expressed either as objectives or in terms of performance on some task or in some anticipated situation. Thus an evaluation concerned with the realization of intention will usually need either to collect existing evidence of student performance (folders of work, test papers, etc.) or to devise some means of assessing what students have learned. If some differentiated comment on student performance is required, then this can be achieved by separate reports on each performance task or by using a list of objectives and commenting on the achievement of each. Classification schemes may be used to help set out the range of objectives, either at the data analysis stage or as an aid to constructing assessment instruments where these are deemed necessary (see *Criterion-referenced Measurement*).

The convenience of collecting student achievement data in this way and using them for improving the course by what is now called formative evaluation is what led to Tyler's model of curriculum development and it helps to explain the continuing popularity of that model with many evaluators (Bloom et al. 1981). However, formative evaluation normally requires more than just student performance data. Moreover, as recent disputes about performance contracting (Stake 1973) and careful studies of test performance (Cicourel et al. 1974) have revealed, the kind of cognitive behaviour which leads to a particular performance is not necessarily the same as that which was intended. Students interpret tasks differently and get tested in many different contexts. Even assigning an examination question to a particular level in Bloom's cognitive domain may depend on the assumptions made about the teaching prior to that examination. Thus the usefulness of information about objectives and their achievement is dependent on additional information about transactions and conditions which can assist in their interpretation. Even statements of objectives have to be seen in context because they are not absolute criteria but indications of people's attempts to express their intentions.

In case studies and small-scale evaluations, collecting qualitative contextual evidence to assist with the interpretation of achievement data is a feasible proposition. But the larger the scale of evaluation, the more diverse will be the programme being evaluated, until it becomes extremely difficult to collect sufficient contextual information to provide useful guidance for decision making. A further problem in evaluating large-scale educational programmes is that their objectives are usually negotiated as part of some political compromise, and are therefore ill-suited for bearing the brunt of a programme evaluation based on educational objectives (Cronbach et al. 1980).

Closely related to the use of objectives in evaluation is their use in the monitoring of student achievement and in accountability. In both cases objectives may be used as a guide to test construction or as an aid to data analysis. Their use, however, will not obviate the need for a careful demonstration of the validity of any assessment instruments. It will always need to be argued that an objective is an adequate statement of an intention and that a test item is an adequate indication of the achievement of an objective.

5.5 Using Objectives to Communicate to Students

There is much more empirical evidence on this issue than on other uses of objectives, presumably because it lends itself to short simple experiments. Several reviews of this research have been published (Hartley and Davies 1976, Faw and Waller 1976, Lewis 1981). The analysis is complicated by the existence of alternative methods for drawing learners' attention to what is expected of them. Hartley and Davies discuss pretests, overviews, and advance organizers as alternative attention directors; while Faw and Waller also included inserted questions. Most of the evidence reported is based on work with college students, some on work with high-school students and very little with other populations; and it has usually stemmed from situations where students learned from textual material rather than a teacher.

While several studies have shown that providing objectives enhances student achievement, an equal number have reported no significant difference (Lewis 1981). Some of the more favourable results can be "explained" in terms of increased learning time (Faw and Waller 1976). Alternative methods of guidance appear to have a similar impact—sometimes there are positive effects, sometimes there are none, but there are no reports of negative effects. On the whole the evidence for inserted questions seems to be the strongest, especially when applied to long passages of prose. However, the research is beset with methodological difficulties: when, for example, does an introduction become an implicit statement of objectives; and when does a statement of objectives become a form of coaching for a test? The general conclusion of reviewers is that giving a student clearer directions normally enhances his or her learning, but a statement of objectives is only one of several ways of doing it. Such additional guidance may only be necessary when the instruction was not well-designed in the first place.

Bibliography

Alles J et al. 1967 *Theoretical Constructs in Curriculum Development and Evaluation.* Ministry of Education, Sri Lanka

Atkin J M 1968 Behavioral objectives in curriculum design: A cautionary note. *Sci. Teach.* 35: 27–30

Bloom B S (ed.) 1956 *Taxonomy of Educational Objectives.* Handbook 1: *Cognitive Domain.* McKay, New York

Bloom B S, Hastings J T, Madaus G F 1971 *Handbook on Formative and Summative Evaluation of Student Learning.* McGraw-Hill, New York

Bloom B S, Madaus G F, Hastings J T 1981 *Evaluation to Improve Learning.* McGraw-Hill, New York

Bobbitt F 1918 *The Curriculum.* Houghton Mifflin, Boston, Massachusetts

Carroll J B 1963 A model of school learning. *Teach. Coll. Rec.* 64: 723–33

Cazden C B 1971 Evaluation of learning in preschool education: Early language development. In: Bloom B S et al. 1971 *Handbook on Formative and Summative Evaluation of Student Learning.* McGraw-Hill, New York, 345–98

Charters W W 1924 *Curriculum Construction.* Macmillan, New York

Cicourel A V et al. 1974 *Language Use and School Performance.* Academic Press, New York

Cronbach L J et al. 1980 *Toward Reform of Program Evaluations.* Jossey-Bass, San Francisco, California

Davies I K 1976 *Objectives in Curriculum Design.* McGraw-Hill, Maidenhead

Dressel P L 1976 *Handbook of Academic Achievement.* Jossey-Bass, San Francisco, California

Eisner E W 1969 Instructional and expressive educational objectives: Their formulation and use in curriculum. In: Popham W J, Eisner E W, Sullivan H J, Tyler L L (eds.) 1969 *Instructional Objectives.* (AERA Curriculum Evaluation Monograph 3.) Rand McNally, Chicago, Illinois, pp. 1–18

Eraut M R 1976 Some perspectives on curriculum development in teacher education. *Educ. Teach.* 99: 11–21

Eraut M R, MacKenzie N, Papps I 1975 The mythology of educational development: Reflections on a three-year study of economics teaching. *Br. J. Educ. Technol.* 6(3): 20–34

Faw H W, Waller T G 1976 Mathemagenic behaviours and efficiency in learning from prose materials: Review, critique and recommendations. *Rev. Educ. Res.* 46: 691–720

Gagné R M 1965 The analysis of instructional objectives for the design of instructions. In: Glaser R (ed.) 1965 *Teaching Machines and Programmed Learning*, Vol 2: *Data and Directions*. Department of Audio-visual Instruction, National Education Association (NEA), Washington, DC, pp. 21–65

Gagné R M, Briggs L J 1974 *Principles of Instructional Design.* Holt, Rinehart and Winston, New York

Gribble J 1970 Pandora's box: The affective domain of educational objectives. *J. Curric. Stud.* 2(1): 9–24

Gronlund N E 1970 *Stating Behavioral Objectives for Classroom Instruction.* Macmillan, New York

Harrow A J 1972 *A Taxonomy of the Psychomotor Domain.* McKay, New York

Hartley J, Davies I K 1976 Preinstructional strategies: The role of pretests, behavioral objectives, overviews and advance organizers. *Rev. Educ. Res.* 46: 239–65

Hirst P H 1973 Towards a logic of curriculum development. In: Taylor P H, Walton J (eds.) 1973 *The Curriculum: Research Innovation and Change.* Ward Lock Educational, London

Jackson P W 1968 *Life in Classrooms.* Holt, Rinehart and Winston, New York

Kamii C K 1971 Evaluation of learning in preschool education: Socio-emotional, perceptual-motor, cognitive development. In: Bloom et al. 1971 *Handbook on Formative and Summative Evaluation of Student Learning.* McGraw-Hill, New York

Kibler R J, Barker L L, Miles D T 1970 *Behavioral Objectives and Instruction.* Allyn and Bacon, Boston, Massachusetts

Krathwohl D, Bloom B S, Masia B 1964 *Taxonomy of Educational Objectives.* Handbook 2: *Affective Domain.* McKay, New York

Krathwohl D 1965 Stating objectives appropriately for program, for curriculum and for instructional materials. *J. Teach. Educ.* 17: 83–92

Laban R 1963 *Modern Educational Dance*, 2nd edn. MacDonald and Evans, London

Lewis J M 1981 Answers to twenty questions on behavioral objectives. *Educ. Technol.* 21: 27–31

Macdonald-Ross M 1973 Behavioural objectives: A critical review. *Instr. Sci.* 2(1): 1–52

Madaus G F, Woods E M, Nuttall R L 1973 A causal model analysis of Bloom's taxonomy. *Am. Educ. Res. J.* 10(14): 353–62

Mager R F 1962 *Preparing Instructional Objectives.* Fearon, Palo Alto, California

Ormell C 1974 Educational objectives: Bloom's taxonomy and the problem of classification. *Educ. Res.* 17(1): 3–18

Parker J C, Rubin L J 1966 *Process as Content: Curriculum Design and the Application of Knowledge.* Rand McNally, Chicago, Illinois

Popham W J 1969 Objectives and instruction. In: Popham W J et al. (eds.) 1969 *Instructional Objectives.* (AERA Curriculum Evaluation Monograph 3.) Rand McNally, Chicago, Illinois

Raven J 1977 *Education, Values and Society: The Objectives of Education and the Nature and Development of Competence.* H K Lewis, London

Romiszowski A J 1981 *Designing Instructional Systems.* Kogan Page, London

Scriven M 1967 The methodology of evaluation. In: Tyler R W, Gagné R M, Scriven M (eds.) 1967 *Perspectives of Curriculum Evaluation.* (AERA Curriculum Evaluation Monograph 1.) Rand McNally, Chicago, Illinois

Seymour W D 1966 *Industrial Skills.* Pitman, London

Simpson E J 1966 The classification of educational objectives: Psychomotor domain. *Illinois Journal for Teaching of Home Economics* 10: 110–44

Smith E R, Tyler R W 1942 *Appraising and Recording Student Progress.* Harper, New York

Sockett H 1976 *Designing the Curriculum.* Open Books, London

Spencer H 1860 What knowledge is of most worth? In: Spencer H (ed.) 1910 *Education: Intellectual, Moral and Physical.* Appleton, New York, pp. 1–66

Stake R E 1973 Measuring what learners learn. In: House E R (ed.) 1973 *School Evaluation: The Politics and Process.* McCutchan, Berkeley, California

Stenhouse L 1970/71 Some limitations on the use of objectives in curriculum research and planning. *Paedag. Eur.* 6: 73–83

Taba H 1962 *Curriculum Development: Theory and Practice.* Harcourt, Brace and World, New York

Taylor F W 1912 *Scientific Management.* Harper, New York

Tyler R W 1949 *Basic Principles of Curriculum and Instruction.* University of Chicago Press, Illinois

Tyler R W 1964 Some persistent questions on the defining of objectives. In: Lindvall C M (ed.) 1964 *Defining Educational Objectives.* University of Pittsburgh Press, Pittsburgh, Pennsylvania

Walker D F 1971 A naturalistic model for curriculum development. *Sch. Rev.* 80: 51–65

Wellens J 1974 *Training in Physical Skills.* Business Books, London

White J P 1971 The concept of curriculum evaluation. *J. Curric. Stud.* 3: 101–12

Yarlott G 1972 *Education and Children's Emotions.* Weidenfeld and Nicolson, London

Taxonomies of Objectives

V. De Landsheere

Originally, the term taxonomy (or systematics) was understood as the science of the classification laws of life forms. By extension, the word taxonomy means the science of classification in general and any specific classification respecting its rules, that is, the taxonomy of educational objectives.

A taxonomy related to the social sciences cannot have the rigour or the perfect branching structure of taxonomies in the natural sciences. In education, a taxonomy is a classification constructed according to one of several explicit principles.

The term "taxonomy of educational objectives" is closely associated with the name of B. S. Bloom. This is explained by the extraordinary worldwide impact of the *Taxonomy of Educational Objectives* first edited by Bloom in 1956. This taxonomy was enthusiastically received by teachers, educationists, and test developers because it offered easily understandable guidelines for systematic evaluation covering the whole range of cognitive processes (and not only the lower mental processes, as was too often the case in the past). This taxonomy had also a definite influence on curriculum development and teaching methods for the same reason: it emphasized processes rather than content matter, and helped determine a proper balance between lower and higher cognitive processes.

Bloom's taxonomy of cognitive objectives was soon followed by taxonomies for the affective and psychomotor domains. Within two decades, several taxonomies were developed by other authors and a great number of philosophical and empirical studies appeared on this topic.

A presentation of the main taxonomies so far published follows.

1. The Cognitive Domain

1.1 Bloom's Taxonomy

This taxonomy, which has inspired the majority of the other taxonomies, uses four basic principles: (a) the major distinction should reflect the ways teachers state educational objectives (methodological principle); (b) the taxonomy should be consistent with our present understanding of psychological phenomena (psychological principle); (c) the taxonomy should be logically developed and internally consistent (logical principle); and (d) the hierarchy of objectives does not correspond to a hierarchy of values (objective principle).

The taxonomy itself comprises six cognitive levels:

(a) Knowledge: recall or recognition of specific elements in a subject area. The information possessed by the individual consists of specifics (terminology, facts), ways and means of dealing with specifics (conventions, trends, sequences, classifications, categories, criteria, universals), and abstractions in a field (principles, generalizations, theories, and structures).

(b) Comprehension:
   (i) Translation: the known concept or message is put in different words or changed from one kind of symbol to another.
   (ii) Interpretation: a student can go beyond recognizing the separate parts of a communication and see the interrelations among the parts.
   (iii) Extrapolation: the receiver of a communication is expected to go beyond the literal communication itself and make inferences about consequences or perceptibly extend the time dimensions, the sample, or the topic.

(c) Application: use of abstractions in particular and concrete situations. The abstractions may be in the form of general ideas, rules of procedure, or generalized methods. The abstractions may also be technical principles, ideas, and theories which must be remembered and applied.

(d) Analysis: breakdown of a communication into its constituent elements or parts such that the relative hierarchy of ideas is made clear and/or the relations between the ideas expressed are made explicit. One can analyse elements, relationships, organizational principles.

(e) Synthesis: the putting together of elements and parts so as to form a whole. This involves arranging and combining in such a way as to constitute a pattern of structure not clearly there before.

(f) Evaluation: evaluation is defined as the making of judgments about the value of ideas, works, solutions, methods, material, and so on. Judgments can be in terms of internal evidence (logical accuracy and consistency) or external criteria (comparison with standards, rules...)

The content validity of the taxonomy is not considered as perfect by any author but, in general, they are satisfied with it: taken as a whole, it allows nearly all the cognitive objectives of education to be classified. Nevertheless, the taxonomical hierarchy is questionable and the category system is heterogeneous. De Corte (1973) has pointed out that the subcategories used are not always based on the same classification principle. He writes: "For knowledge, analysis and synthesis, the subcategories correspond to a difficulty scale of products resulting from cognitive operations. For comprehension, the subdivisions are specifications of operations and not of their products. For evaluation, the subcategories depend on the nature of the criteria chosen to formulate a judgment."

Gagné (1964) has also pointed out that some categories or subcategories only differ in their content and not by formal characteristics which affect their conditions of learning.

According to Cox (De Corte 1973), the agreement on classification among the users of the taxonomy ranges from 0.63 to 0.85. The lack of reliability must come from the vagueness of the concepts for which the authors of the taxonomy propose essential rather than operational definitions.

The taxonomy has been elaborated for evaluation purposes. It has also been very useful in developing blueprints for curriculum development. It helped in identifying and formulating objectives, and, as a consequence, in structuring the material and specifying assessment procedures.

When developing a test for a particular curriculum, the curriculum often only presents a theme (Bacher 1973). No indication is given about which behaviours of the theme are to be tested. The test constructor is left to guess about which behaviours are to be tested. Furthermore, the taxonomy of objectives movement could signal a renaissance of nineteenth-century faculty psychology. Instead of training separate mental faculties

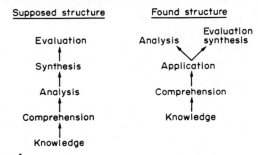

Figure 1
Schematic representation of an hypothesized perfect
hierarchy and of the hierarchical structure found by Madaus
et al. 1973

such as memory, imagination, and so on, one could artificially cultivate memory (knowledge in Bloom), application, analysis, synthesis, judgment, aptitudes.

Several authors are of the opinion that the taxonomy pays too much attention to knowledge, and not enough to higher mental processes.

It is not possible to use the taxonomy without reference to the behavioural background of the individual. There is an obvious difference between the individual who solves a specific problem for the first time and the individual who has met the same problem before. In both cases, however, the answer can be the same.

To test the validity of the hierarchical structure of the taxonomy, Madaus and his associates developed a quantitative causal model (see Fig. 1) to reveal not only the proportion of variance at each level explained directly by the preceding adjacent level, but also any proportion of variance explained indirectly by nonadjacent levels. The statistical techniques used were principal components analysis to identify the role of a factor of general ability g, and multiple regression analysis to measure the links between taxonomic levels. Hill (1984) has employed maximum likelihood estimation procedures, using LISREL, to list the hierarchical assumptions of the Bloom taxonomy, and has provided important evidence to support a hierarchical structure between the five higher-order categories.

In a pure hierarchy, there must be a direct link between adjacent levels and only between these two. As one proceeds from the lower to the higher levels in Bloom's taxonomy, the strength of the direct links between adjacent levels decreases and many links between nonadjacent levels appear. Knowledge, comprehension, and application are well-hierarchized. Higher up in the hierarchy, a branching takes place. On one side, analysis is found (even if the g factor is taken into account, analysis entertains an indirect link with comprehension). It is what Ebel (1973) calls the stage of content mastery. On the other side, synthesis and evaluation are found; they are differentiated clearly from the rest in that they are highly saturated in the g factor. This dependence increases if the material is not well-known

to the students, or is very difficult, or if the lower processes have not been sufficiently mastered to contribute significantly to the production of higher level behaviours.

Horn (1972) suggested an algorithm to classify objectives along Bloom's taxonomy. He notes that in lower mental processes, objectives content and problem cannot be separated. For instance, for the objective: "The student will be able to list the parts of a plant", there is no problem. The answer will be possible only if the student has it "ready made" in his or her memory. For higher mental processes, the problem is general, and can be formulated without reference to a specific content.

To quasioperationalize Bloom's taxonomy, Horn takes the level of complexity of the problem posed as a classification criterion. At each level, he considers the formal aspect and the content. Figure 2 presents Horn's algorithm.

Using Horn's algorithm, well-trained judges can reach a high interreliability in their classification of objectives.

Bloom's taxonomy is formulated in an abstract way. To help the users apply the taxonomy properly, Metfessel et al. (1970) suggested a list of verbs and a list of objects which, appropriately combined, give the framework for an operational objective at the different taxonomic levels.

Bloom is aware of the limits of the instrument to whose development he has contributed. What really matters to Bloom is that educators question as often as possible whether they have varied the cognitive level of the tasks, exercises, and examinations they propose, whether they stimulate their students sufficiently, and whether they really help them develop.

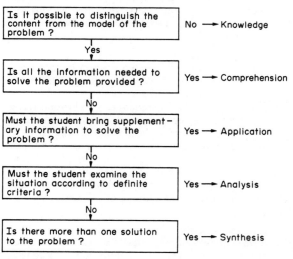

Figure 2
Horn's algorithm

354

1.2 Guilford's Structure of Intellect Model

To organize intellectual factors, identified by factor analysis or simply hypothesized, Guilford (1967) designed a structure of intellect (SI) model (see Fig. 3). This model was essentially conceived to serve the heuristic function of generating hypotheses regarding new factors of intelligence. The placement of any intellectual factor within this nonhierarchical model is determined by its three unique properties: its operation, its content, and its product.

Content categories are:

(a) Figural: figural information covers visual, auditive, and kinesthetic sense.

(b) Symbolic: signs that can be used to stand for something else.

(c) Semantic: the verbal factor.

(d) Behavioural: behavioural content is defined as information, essentially nonverbal, involved in human interactions, where awareness or attention, perceptions, thoughts, desires, feelings, moods, emotions, intentions, and actions of other persons and of ourselves are important.

Operation categories are:

(a) Cognition: awareness, immediate discovery or rediscovery, or recognition of information in various forms; comprehension or understanding.

(b) Memory: retention or storage, with some degree of availability, of information in the same form in which it was committed to storage, and in connection with the same cues with which it was learned.

(c) Divergent production: the generation of information from given information where the emphasis is upon variety and quantity of output from the same source; this category is likely to involve transfer.

(d) Convergent production: the area of logical productions or at least the area of compelling inferences. The input information is sufficient to determine a unique answer.

(e) Evaluation: the process of comparing a product of information with known information according to logical criteria, and reaching a decision concerning criterion satisfaction.

Product categories are:

(a) Units: relatively segregated or circumscribed items of information having "thing" character.

(b) Classes: recognized sets of items grouped by virtue of their common properties.

(c) Relations: recognized connections between two items of information based upon variables or upon points of contact that apply to them.

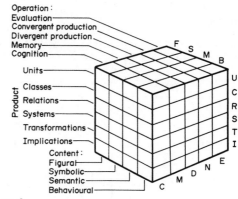

Figure 3
Guilford's Structure of Intellect Model

(d) Systems: organized or structured aggregates of items of information, a complex of interrelated or interacting parts.

(e) Transformations: changes of various kinds, of existing or known information in its attributes, meaning, role, or use.

(f) Implications: expectancies, anticipations, and predictions, the fact that one item of information leads naturally to another.

Each cell of Guilford's model represents a factor that is a unique combination of operation, content, and product. For instance, cell 1 (see Fig. 3) represents cognition of figural units.

Can Guilford's model be utilized to formulate or at least to generate objectives? First of all, it can be noted that the three dimensions of the model are hierarchical at least to a certain extent. Furthermore, Guilford has discussed the implications of his model for education. He thinks that it indicates clearly the kinds of exercises that must be applied to develop intellectual abilities. He remarks, in particular, that school, in general, overemphasizes cognition and the memorization of semantic units. It is important, says Guilford, to apply oneself much more to the exercise of the other products: classes, relations, systems, transformations, and implications.

The fact that Guilford compares his model to Bloom's taxonomy and acknowledges important similarities between both of them seems to confirm that Guilford does not exclude the possibility that his model may be used to generate and classify objectives.

Guilford's model can absorb Bloom's whole cognitive taxonomy (see Fig. 4). By its greater precision, the SI model may allow easier operationalization and, more generally, may offer greater taxonomic possibilities.

De Corte (1973) has adapted and transformed Guilford's model. The four dimensions of De Corte's general model of classification are: (a) the subject matter of specific content of a given universe of objectives; (b)

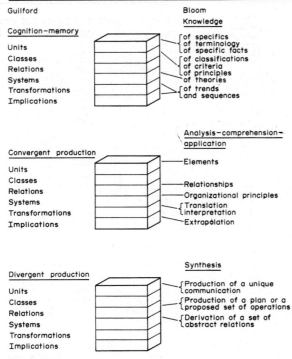

Figure 4
Parallelism between Guilford's model and Bloom's cognitive taxonomy

the domain of information to which the subject matter belongs (content in Guilford's model); (c) the product: the objectives are classified with respect to the formal aspect of the information they produce (products in Guilford's model); (d) the operation is defined as in Guilford's model.

De Corte focuses on this fourth category and develops Guilford's five operations into a seven category system. Cognition comprises receiving–reproducing operations: (a) perception of information; (b) recall of information; (c) reproduction of information and productive operations; (d) interpretative production of information; (e) convergent production of information; (f) evaluative production of information; (g) divergent production of information.

De Corte's system is of interest in that it develops Guilford's model in such a manner that it becomes a practical tool for the definition of the cognitive objectives of education. It seems to indicate how Bloom and Guilford's contributions could be integrated and be of use to education.

1.3 The Gagné–Merrill Taxonomy

Gagné proposes a hierarchy of processes needed to achieve the learning tasks assigned by objectives. Merrill designates the behaviour and psychological condition under which learning can be observed.

With Gagné's learning conditions, the push-down principle constitutes the basis of the Gagné–Merrill taxonomy. In the process of development, a person acquires behaviour at the lower levels before acquiring behaviour at the higher levels. Later, the conscious cognitive demand on the learner increases. Learners have an innate tendency to reduce the cognitive load as much as possible; consequently, a learner will attempt to perform a given response at the lowest possible level. The push-down principle states that a behaviour acquired at one level will be pushed down to a lower level as soon as conditions have changed sufficiently so that the learner is able to respond to the stimulus using lower level behaviour. It is rather surprising that this important principle is often neglected or even ignored in the literature related to the taxonomies of educational objectives.

The Gagné–Merrill taxonomy is an original formulation, integrating the affective, psychomotor, and cognitive domains.

The following is a condensed version of Merrill's presentation:

(a) *Emotional behaviour (signal learning)*. In the presence of every stimulus situation, students involuntarily react with physiological changes which they perceive as feelings. The direction (positive or negative) and the relative magnitude of this emotional behaviour can be inferred by observing the students' approach/avoidance responses in unrestrained choice situations.

(b) *Psychomotor behaviour*. A student is able to execute rapidly, without external prompting, a specified neuromuscular reaction in the presence of a specific stimulus situation. The observable behaviour is an overt skeletal–muscular response which occurs in entirety without hesitation. Psychological conditions of importance are the presence of a specific cue and the absence of prompts. Psychomotor behaviour may be further broken down into three constituent behaviours.

First, topographic behaviour (stimulus response) is where a student is able to execute rapidly without external prompting, a single new neuromuscular reaction in the presence of a particular stimulus cue. This can be observed as a muscular movement or combination of movements not previously in the student's repertoire. The important psychological conditions are the presence of a specific cue and the absence of prompts.

Secondly, chaining behaviour, where a student is able to execute, without external prompting, a coordinated series of reactions which occur in rapid succession in the presence of a particular stimulus cue, is observed as a series of responses, and occurs in the presence of a specified cue and in the absence of prompts.

Thirdly, skilled behaviour is where a student is able to execute sequentially, without external prompting, complex combinations of coordinated psychomotor chains, each initiated in the presence of a particular cue when a large set of such cues are presented. In some skills, cue presentation is externally paced while in other skills cue presentation is self-paced. This is seen as a set of coordinated chains, and occurs when there is a paced or unpaced presentation of a set of cues and an absence of prompts prior to or during the performance.

(c) *Memorization behaviour.* A student immediately reproduces or recognizes, without prompting, a specific symbolic response when presented with a specific stimulus situation. The observable behaviour always involves either reproduction or recognition of a symbolic response, and occurs under psychological conditions similar to those of psychomotor behaviour. Memorization behaviour can be broken into naming behaviour where a student reproduces or recognizes, without prompts, a single symbolic response in the presence of a particular stimulus cue; serial memorization behaviour (verbal association) which occurs in the presence of a particular stimulus cue, so that a student reproduces, without prompting, a series of symbolic responses in a prespecified sequence; and discrete element memorization behaviour (multiple discrimination) where a student reproduces or recognizes, without prompting, a unique symbolic response to each of a set of stimulus cues.

(d) *Complex cognitive behaviour.* The student makes an appropriate response to a previously unencountered instance of some class of stimulus objects, events, or situations. This can further be broken into classification behaviour, analysis behaviour, and problem-solving behaviour.

Classification behaviour (concept learning) is where a student is able to identify correctly the class membership of a previously unencountered object or event, or a previously unencountered representation of some object or event. It occurs when the student must make some kind of class identification, the important psychological conditions being the presentation of unencountered instances or noninstances.

Analysis behaviour (principle learning) is when a student is able to show the relationship between the component concepts of an unencountered situation in which a given principle is specified as relevant. The student must first identify the instances of the several classes involved in the situation and then show the relationship between these classes. The psychological condition of importance is presentation of a situation which the student has not previously analysed or seen analysed.

Problem-solving behaviour is when a student is able to select relevant principles and sequence them into an effective solution strategy when presented with an unencountered problem situation for which the relevant principles are not specified. Creativity and/or divergent thinking occurs when some of the relevant principles are unknown to the student and the strategy developed represents a new higher order principle. It can be observed when the student must synthesize a product which results from analysing several principles in some appropriate sequence and generalize new relationships not previously learned or analysed. The psychological conditions of importance are: an unencountered problem for which the relevant principles are not specified, and

which in some cases may require principles not previously analysed by the student or perhaps even by the instructor.

Without any doubt, Gagné–Merrill's taxonomy provides some order in the field of fundamental learning processes. However, it does not claim exhaustivity, and certain categories such as "process learning" and "problem solving" are rather vague.

D'Hainaut (1970) believes that Gagné does not give enough emphasis to the creative processes. Divergent thinking can be categorized under the heading "problem solving", but this category is perhaps too large.

Merrill and Gagné have made two important contributions to the definition of objectives. Their categories are expressed in terms of definite behaviour and the psychological conditions are considered, although these conditions are still to be integrated into an operational definition of objectives.

1.4 Gerlach and Sullivan's Taxonomy

Sullivan in association with Gerlach (1967) attempted to replace a description of mental processes in general terms (as in Bloom's taxonomy) by classes of observable learner behaviours which could be used in task description and analysis. Their model is empirical. After listing hundreds of learning behaviours, Sullivan has progressively grouped them into six categories, each headed by a typical verb. The six categories are ordered according to the increasing complexity of behaviours they represent, but the whole does not constitute a rigorous hierarchy and, for that reason, cannot be considered as a true taxonomy.

(a) Identify: the learner indicates membership or non-membership of specified objects or events in a class when the name of the class is given.

(b) Name: the learner supplies the correct verbal label (in speech or writing) for a referent or set of referents when the name of the referent is not given.

(c) Describe: the learner reports the necessary categories of object properties, events, event properties, and/or relationships relevant to a designated referent.

(d) Construct: the learner produces a product which meets specifications given either in class or in the test item itself.

(e) Order: the learner arranges two or more referents in a specified order.

(f) Demonstrate: the learner performs the behaviours essential to the accomplishment of a designated task according to pre-established or given specifications.

Gerlach and Sullivan consider their "taxonomy" as a check list helping to ensure that no important behaviour is forgotten when planning school activities. This may succeed, as long as "mastery objectives" (i.e., objectives

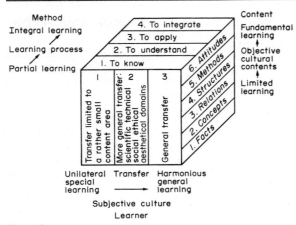

Figure 5
De Block's model of instruction

concerning a fully defined behaviour universe) are kept in sight. However, the six categories suggested do not cover creative productions and do not even make a clear place for transfer.

1.5 De Block's Taxonomy

De Block (1975) suggests a model of teaching objectives (see Fig. 5). He thinks that teaching pursues objectives in three directions: (a) from partial to more integral learning. Comprehension seems more desirable than rote learning (knowledge); in this perspective, mastery and integration are final objectives; (b) from limited to fundamental learning. Facts gradually become background data; concepts and methods come to the fore; (c) from special to general learning. The objective is thinking in a productive rather than in a reproductive way, taking initiatives, and being able to adapt oneself to a great variety of situations.

The combination of all subcategories yields 72 classes of objectives. De Block's system does not deal sufficiently with the criteria by which it is recognized whether an objective has been achieved or not. However, it can certainly help teachers to reconsider their activities, and to make their students work at higher cognitive or affective levels.

1.6 Conclusion to the Cognitive Domain

Not one of these taxonomies can be considered as entirely satisfying. Looking at highly nuanced classifications, only moderate reliability can be hoped for. If the system is reduced to a few operationalized categories, content validity decreases.

The taxonomy of Bloom and his associates has already been used successfully by hundreds of curriculum and test developers throughout the world. Furthermore, it has stimulated fruitful discussion and reflection on the problem of objectives. The several taxonomies that appeared after Bloom are useful to curriculum

developers, to test constructors, and to teachers planning their next lesson and preparing mastery tests for their pupils.

2. The Affective Domain

According to Bloom, the affective domain includes objectives which describe changes in interest, attitudes, and values, and the development of appreciations and adequate adjustment.

What are the main difficulties in the pursuit of affective objectives? Imprecision of concepts, overlap of the affective and the cognitive domains, cultural bias (Western culture still tends to consider feelings as the most secret part of personality), ignorance about affective learning processes, and poor evaluation instruments.

So far, the only significant taxonomy for the affective domain is the one published by Krathwohl et al. (1964), hence the brevity of this section when compared to the first.

2.1 Krathwohl's Taxonomy

The main organizing principles for the cognitive domain were "from simple to complex" and "from concrete to abstract". It soon appeared that these could not be used for the affective domain which dealt with attitudes, interests, values, and so on. After a long search, the authors discovered an ordering principle that was precisely characteristic of affective development: the degree of internalization, that is, the degree of incorporation of the affects within the personality. When the process of internalization is completed, the person feels as if the interests, values, attitudes, and so on were his or her own and lives by them. In Krathwohl's taxonomic terms, the continuum goes from merely being aware that a given phenomenon exists, and giving it a minimum attention, to its becoming one's basic outlook on life. The main organizing principles in Krathwohl's taxonomy are receiving, responding, valuing, organization, and characteristics.

(a) Receiving: "Sensitivity to the existence of certain phenomena and stimuli, that is, the willingness to receive or attend to them." Receiving consists of three subcategories that represent a continuum: (i) awareness; (ii) willingness to receive; and (iii) controlled or selected attention.

(b) Responding: "Behaviour which goes beyond merely attending to the phenomena; it implies active attending, doing something with or about the phenomena, and not merely perceiving them." Subcategories of responding are: (i) acquiescence in responding; (ii) willingness to respond; and (iii) satisfaction in response.

(c) Valuing: "It implies perceiving phenomena as having worth and consequently revealing consistency in behaviour related to these phenomena." The individual is motivated to behave in the line of definite values. Subcategories are: (i) acceptance of a value; (ii) preference for a value; and (iii) commitment.

(d) Organization: "For situations where more than one value is relevant, the necessity arises for (i) the organization of the values into a system; (ii) the determination of the interrelationships among them; and (iii) the establishment of the dominant and pervasive one." Subcategories are: (i) conceptualization of a value and (ii) organization of a value system.

(e) Characteristics by a value or value complex: "The values already have a place in the individual's value hierarchy, are organized into some kind of internally consistent system, have controlled the behaviour of the individual for a sufficient time that he has adapted to behaving in this way." Subcategories are: (i) generalized set and (ii) characterization.

The most striking feature of this taxonomy is its abstract, general character. Krathwohl is aware of the problem. The taxonomy deals with objectives at the curriculum construction level. This means that objectives as defined in the taxonomy are approximately midway between very broad and very general objectives of education and the specific ones which provide guidance for the development of step-by-step learning experiences.

For a short presentation of Krathwohl's taxonomy, G. De Landsheere (1982) tried to find a classification principle that would be easier to formulate in behavioural terms than internalization. He suggested a continuum of activity, or of personal engagement. De Landsheere's frame of reference was developmental psychology. He wrote: "An individual has really reached the adult stage if his behaviour has found its coherence, its logic and stability; he has developed at the same time a sound tolerance to change, contradiction, frustration; he is cognitively and affectively independent; he is, at the same time, able to abide by his engagement and feelings." Education is a long process leading to this ultimate balance.

De Landsheere suggests the following taxonomy:

(a) *The individual responds to external stimulation.*

(i) The individual receives: this is a rather amorphous stage. The individual encounters, for instance, beauty or ugliness without any reaction, like a mirror that would not reflect any image. This behaviour is hard to distinguish from the cognition (in Guilford's sense) that takes place before memorization. Only some manifestation of attention is observable.

(ii) The individual receives and responds to the stimulus: an observable reaction takes place. The individual obeys, manifests pleasure by his or her words or attitudes. At this stage, there is not yet explicit

acceptance or rejection that would reflect a deliberate choice.

(iii) The individual receives and reacts by accepting or refusing: now the individual knows what he or she wants or likes, provided things or events are presented.

(b) *The individual takes initiatives.* The individual tries spontaneously to understand, to feel, and then act according to the options available. Here the adult stage is reached. For instance, the individual lives a life in accordance with his or her values, feelings, beliefs, likings, but is also able to change his or her mind if convincing proofs or arguments are offered. This stage is parallel to evaluation in the cognitive domain.

The classification suggested by De Landsheere seems clearer than Krathwohl's taxonomy, but more limited. Objectives can be more easily operationalized, but the criticism of Krathwohl's work also applies here.

2.2 Conclusion to the Affective Domain

The situation in the affective domain remains unsatisfactory. Why does it appear that so much work is still to be undertaken in the field? Krathwohl has not succeeded in filling completely the gap in the theoretical framework and the methodology of educational evaluation in the affective domain. A more systematic attack on the problem of affective objectives is required, and, in particular, an inventory of existing studies, experiments, and evaluation instruments in the field should be undertaken. Indubitably, the affective domain will constitute a priority area in the field of educational research in the decades to come.

3. The Psychomotor Domain

Why is the psychomotor domain important? First of all, motion is a necessary condition of survival and of independence. Life sometimes depends on physical strength correctly applied, on agility, and on rapidity. Locomotor behaviour is needed to explore the environment and sensory-motor activities are essential for the development of intelligence. Some psychomotor behaviours such as walking and grasping, are also necessary for physical and mental health to be maintained. Dexterity is crucial for the worker, and also in civilizations giving a lot of time to leisure, corporal ability plays a considerable role in artistic and athletic activities.

Numerous taxonomies have been developed for the psychomotor domain. Some of them tend to be comprehensive, in strict parallelism with the taxonomies inspired by Bloom and Krathwohl for the cognitive and affective domains. Others have been developed for specialized fields and have, in many cases, a very technical character. Only six taxonomies which fall in the first category are presented in this article.

Ragsdale, Guilford, Dave, and Kibler's taxonomies are summarized very briefly for they are mainly of historical interest.

3.1 Ragsdale's Taxonomy

As early as in 1950, Ragsdale published a classification for "motor types of activities" learned by children. He worked with three categories only: (a) object motor activities (speed, precision): manipulation or acting with direct reference to an object; (b) language motor activities: movement of speech, sight, handwriting; (c) feeling motor activities: movements communicating feelings and attitudes.

These categories are so general that they are of little help in the definition of educational objectives.

3.2 Guilford's Taxonomy

Guilford (1958) suggested a simple classification in seven categories that is not hierarchical, and also does not seem of great utility for generating objectives. The seven categories are: power, pressure, speed, static precision, dynamic precision, coordination, and flexibility.

3.3 Dave's Taxonomy

Dave's classification (1969), although also rather schematic, can be considered as an embryo of a taxonomy. The categories are: initiation, manipulation, precision, articulation, naturalization (mechanization and internalization). The meaning of the first three categories is clear. Articulation emphasizes the coordination of a series of acts which are performed with appropriate articulation in terms of time, speed, and other relevant variables. As for naturalization, it refers to the highest level of proficiency of an act that has become routine.

3.4 Kibler's Classification

Kibler and his associates suggest a classification (1970) more developed than that of previous authors. The main frame of reference is developmental child psychology.

(a) Gross bodily movements: movements of entire limbs in isolation or in conjunction with other parts of the body (movements involving the upper limbs, the lower limbs, two or more bodily units).

(b) Finely coordinated movements: coordinated movements of the extremities, used in conjunction with the eye or ear (hand–finger movements, hand–eye coordination, hand–ear coordination, hand–eye–foot coordination, other combinations of hand–foot–eye–ear movements).

(c) Nonverbal communication behaviours: facial expression, gestures (use of hands and arms to communicate specific messages), bodily movements (total bodily movements whose primary purposes are the communication of a message or series of messages).

(d) Speech behaviours: sound production (ability to produce meaningful sounds), sound–word formation (ability to coordinate sounds in meaningful words and messages), sound projection (ability to project sounds across the air waves at a level adequate for reception and decoding by the listener), sound–gesture coordination (ability to coordinate facial expression, movement, and gestures with verbal messages).

3.5 Simpson's Taxonomy (1966)

Simpson's taxonomy can be divided into five main categories.

(a) *Perception.* This is the process of becoming aware of objects, qualities, or relations by way of the sense organs.

(i) Sensory stimulation: impingement of a stimulus upon one or more of the sense organs (auditory, visual, tactile, taste, smell, kinesthetic).

(ii) Cue-selection: deciding to what cues one must respond in order to satisfy the particular requirements of task performance, for example, recognition of operating difficulties with machinery through the sound of the machine in operation.

(iii) Translation: relation of perception of action in performing a motor act. This is the mental process of determining the meaning of the cues received for action, for example, the ability to relate music to dance form.

(b) *Set.* Preparatory adjustment of readiness for a particular kind of action or experience.

(i) Mental set: readiness, in the mental sense, to perform a certain motor act.

(ii) Physical set: readiness in the sense of having made the anatomical adjustments necessary for a motor act to be performed.

(iii) Emotional set: readiness in terms of attitudes favourable to the motor act's taking place.

(c) *Guided response.* Overt behavioural act of an individual under the guidance of the instructor (imitation, trial and error).

(d) *Mechanism.* Learned response has become habitual.

(e) *Complex overt response.* The individual can perform a motor act that is considered complex because of the movement pattern required. A high degree of skill has been attained. The act can be carried out smoothly and efficiently.

(i) Resolution of uncertainty: the act is performed without hesitation.

(ii) Automatic performance: the individual can perform a finely coordinated motor skill with a great deal of ease and muscle control.

Simpson suggests that there is perhaps a sixth major category: adapting and originating. "At this level, the individual might originate new patterns of actions in solving a specific problem."

The weakness of this taxonomy is to be found again in its very abstract and general formulation.

3.6 Harrow's Taxonomy

As operationally defined by Harrow (1972), the term "psychomotor" covers any human voluntary observable movement that belongs to the domain of learning. Harrow's taxonomy is the best available for the psychomotor domain, although some of the category descriptives are unsatisfactory:

(a) Reflex movements: segmental, intersegmental, suprasegmental reflexes.

(b) Basic–fundamental movements: locomotor, non-locomotor, manipulative movements.

(c) Perceptual abilities:
Kinesthetic discrimination: body awareness (bilaterality, laterality, sidedness, balance), body image, body relationship of surrounding objects in space.
Visual discrimination: visual acuity, visual tracking, visual memory, figure–ground differentiation, perceptual consistency.
Auditory discrimination: auditory acuity, tracking, memory.
Tactile discrimination.
Coordinated abilities: eye–hand and eye–foot coordination.

(d) Physical abilities: endurance (muscular and cardiovascular endurance), strength, flexibility, agility (change direction, stops and starts, reaction–response time, dexterity).

(e) Skilled movements: simple adaptive skill (beginner, intermediate, advanced, highly skilled), compound adaptive skill (beginner, intermediate, advanced, highly skilled), complex adaptive skill (beginner, intermediate, advanced, highly skilled).

(f) Nondiscursive communication: expressive movement (posture and carriage, gestures, facial expression), interpretative movement (aesthetic movement, creative movement).

In fact, Harrow does not describe her model in relation to a general, unique criterion (i.e., coordination), but simply looks for a critical order; mastery at an inferior level is absolutely necessary to achieve the immediate higher level in the hierarchy of movements.

This taxonomy has great qualities. First, it seems complete, not only in its description of the major categories of psychomotor behaviour, but also in terms of the subcategories within the different taxonomic levels. Furthermore, the author defines the different levels clearly. For each subcategory, she proposes a clear definition of the concept and indicates, where necessary, the differences from other authors who have written in this field. She also presents concrete examples.

Harrow's taxonomy seems to be of direct use to teachers in physical education. Level (c) is specially interesting for preschool and for elementary-school teachers. It contains a good example of a battery for testing the perceptive abilities of pupils, diagnosing difficulties, and proposing appropriate remedial exercises. The author underlines the dependence between the cognitive and psychomotor domains at the level of perceptual abilities. Several examples also show the great interrelation between the three domains. However, Harrow's hierarchy is not governed by a specified criterion, such as internalization or coordination. Moreover, the subcategories are not mutually exclusive.

3.7 Conclusion to the Psychomotor Domain

It seems that taxonomies in the psychomotor domain have not yet been given the attention they deserve. They should be tried in many varied situations and their relations with the other two domains should be carefully investigated.

4. Conclusion

The cognitive domain is the best developed. First, it is by nature favourable to the construction of logical models. Secondly, schools have traditionally been interested in cognitive learning, especially in the acquisition of factual knowledge which in turn leads to easy evaluation.

Compared with the cognitive domain, the affective domain is less developed. Only since about 1970 has the educational world been trying to change the situation (in the past, affectivity has sometimes been intensively cultivated, but nearly always in terms of indoctrination processes). Affects seem less observable than cognitive activities and in most cases are less susceptible to rigorous measurement.

One would think that the psychomotor domain would present fewer difficulties, but little systematic work has been undertaken. In most Western educational systems, physical and artistic education is comparatively neglected in the curriculum.

Despite certain weaknesses, the two taxonomies with which Bloom is associated, and Harrow's taxonomy dominate the field. The others should, however, not be neglected, since they supply further clarifications and suggestions.

At present, the taxonomy movement in education is of great value. Even though the instruments are so far imperfect, they stimulate educators to fruitful reflection. Half-way between the great ideological options and the micro-objectives, the taxonomies seem to relate philosophy and educational technology and practice. It is one of their great merits.

Bibliography

Bacher F 1973 La docimologie. In: Reuchlin M (ed.) 1973 *Traité de psychologie appliquée*. Presses Universitaires de France (PUF), Paris
Bloom B S (ed.) 1956 *Taxonomy of Educational Objectives: The*

Classification of Educational Goals, Handbook 1: *Cognitive Domain*. McKay, New York

Dave R H 1969 *Taxonomy of Educational Objectives and Achievement Testing. Developments in Educational Testing*, Vol. 1. University of London Press, London

De Block A 1975 *Taxonomie van Leerdoelen*. Standard Wetenschappelijke Uitgererij, Amsterdam

De Corte E 1973 *Onderwijsdoelstellingen*. Universitaire Pers, Louvain

De Landsheere G 1982 *Introduction à la recherche en éducation*. Thone, Liège; Armand Colin, Paris

De Landsheere V, De Landsheere G 1984 *Définir les objectifs de l'éducation*. Presses Universitaires de France (PUF), Paris

D'Hainaut L 1970 Un modèle pour la détermination et la sélection des objectifs pédagogiques du domaine cognitif. *Enseignement Programmé* 11: 21–38

Ebel R L 1973 Evaluation and educational objectives. *J. Educ. Meas*. 10: 273–79

Gagné R M 1964 The implications of instructional objectives for learning. In: Lindvall C M (ed.) 1964 *Defining Educational Objectives*. University of Pittsburgh Press, Pittsburgh, Pennsylvania

Gerlach V, Sullivan A 1967 *Constructing Statements of Outcomes*. Southwest Regional Laboratory for Educational Research and Development, Inglewood, California

Guilford J P 1958 A system of psychomotor abilities. *Am. J. Psychol*. 71: 164–74

Guilford J P 1967 *The Nature of Human Intelligence*. McKay, New York

Harrow A J 1972 *A Taxonomy of the Psychomotor Domain: A Guide for Developing Behavioral Objectives*. McKay, New York

Hill P W 1984 Testing hierarchy in educational taxonomies: A theoretical and empirical investigation. *Eval. Educ*. 8: 181–278

Horn R 1972 *Lernziele und Schülerleistung: Die Evaluation von den Lernzielen im kognitiven Bereich*, 2nd edn. Beltz, Weinheim

Kibler R J, Barker L L, Miles D T 1970 *Behavioral Objectives and Instruction*. Allyn and Bacon, Boston, Massachusetts

Krathwohl D R, Bloom B S, Masia B B 1964 *Taxonomy of Educational Objectives: The Classification of Educational Goals*, Handbook 2: *Affective Domain*. McKay, New York

Madaus G F, Woods E N, Nuttal R L 1973 A causal model analysis of Bloom's taxonomy. *Am. Educ. Res. J*. 10: 253–62

Merrill M D 1971 Necessary psychological conditions for defining instructional outcomes. In: M D Merrill (ed.) 1971 *Instructional Design: Readings*. Prentice-Hall, Englewood Cliffs, New Jersey

Metfessel N S, Michael W B, Kirsner D A 1970 Instrumentation of Bloom's and Krathwohl's taxonomies for the writing of educational objectives. In: Kibler R J, Barker L L, Miles D J (eds.) 1970

Ragsdale C E 1950 How children learn motor types of activities. *Learning and Instruction*. 49th Yearbook of the National Society for the Study of Education, Washington, DC

Simpson E J 1966 *The Classification of Educational Objectives, Psychomotor Domain*. University of Illinois, Urbana, Illinois

Instructional Design

Instructional Psychology

L. B. Resnick

Instructional psychology is concerned with the processes of learning educational subject matter and with the nature of interventions designed to enhance that learning. It is not so much a separate branch of psychology as a cluster of questions and concerns that have been addressed over the decades in different ways by psychologists with rather different training, different methods, and different perspectives on human learning and development. At its strongest, instructional psychology forms an integral part of the basic discipline of psychology, drawing some of the best scholars in the field to a concern with educational issues and enriching educational thought with theories and constructs rooted in an extended scientific system. Instructional psychology has undergone the same shifts in emphasis and approach as the rest of psychology as even a brief review of the history of the field reveals.

Led by Edward L. Thorndike, American instructional psychology in the 1920s and 1930s had a decidedly associationist cast. Educational subject matters were described as collections of "bonds" or associations to be learned, and there was much concern with the organization of practice to strengthen these associations. Some of this work survives in current "drill-and-practice" instructional programs, including those that are presented and managed by computers (see *Computer-assisted Learning*). Beginning in the late 1950s, instructional psychology in the United States took on a strongly behaviorist cast under the influence of B. F. Skinner (1957). This period gave birth to a number of technologies of education that are still in wide use (Glaser 1978). Perhaps best known as a direct product of behavioral instructional psychology is programmed instruction (Skinner 1968), which is an application of principles of shaping behavior and of "errorless learning" to the design of self-instructional materials (see *Programmed Learning*). Work on the development of programmed instruction has produced an extensive technology of task analysis which continues to be applied in instructional design. Two other behaviorally oriented educational approaches, mastery learning and

behavior modification, have also become familiar. Mastery learning (see *Mastery Learning Model*; *Keller Plan*) is a mode of instruction that builds on the cumulative nature of learning, by insisting that each curriculum segment be mastered by each student before a new segment is taught and by providing the time and instruction necessary for such mastery. Behavior modification (Kazdin 1981) is an application of principles of reinforcement to the maintenance of appropriate classroom behavior and attention to academic tasks.

Although these applications of an earlier period of psychological research continue to influence educational practice, research on the psychology of learning and instruction has moved in a new direction since the early 1960s. In English-speaking countries, human experimental psychology has become increasingly "cognitive"—that is, concerned with the nature of mental processing—and instructional psychology too has turned to direct study of the nature of mental processes in learning and ways of influencing them. This shift toward cognition has facilitated a convergence with major branches of Continental European psychology—especially the Gestalt school and the Piagetian or Genevan school—that had always been interested in the nature of thought and the structure of knowledge. In addition, partly through the influence of Bruner (1960), developmental psychologists have become more interested in instruction than had earlier been the case. The result of all these movements is a dynamic field of instructional psychology that is part of the mainstream of research on human cognition, learning, and development.

Three major trends within cognitive psychology have been particularly relevant to the development of instructional psychology. First, there has been a shift toward studying more and more complex forms of cognitive behavior, including those that form part of the school curriculum. Second, there has been a growing interest in the role of knowledge in human behavior, and much effort is now directed at finding ways to represent the structure of knowledge and at discovering the ways in which knowledge is used in various kinds of learning.

As a natural outgrowth of this interest, there is new attention paid to meaningfulness and understanding as a normal part of the learning process. Finally, today's assumptions about the nature of learning and thinking are interactionist. It is assumed that learning occurs as a result of mental constructions of the learner. These constructions respond to information and stimuli in the environment, but they do not copy or mirror them. This requires the development of a new kind of instructional theory, one that takes explicit account of the personal theories, experiences, and mental processes of the learner.

Several recent major publications (Anderson et al. 1977b, Klahr 1976, Glaser 1978, 1982, Lesgold et al. 1978, Snow et al. 1980) lend weight to this characterization of instructional psychology as a part of cognitive science. This article will illustrate the major trends and issues in the field by considering cognitive research in four broad areas of direct relevance to the school: reading, mathematics, science, and problem solving. In addition, it will describe an emerging body of research on aptitude and intelligence that may eventually change conceptions of these individual differences constructs. At the end of the article, some of the steps that may be necessary to link cognitive instructional psychology more directly to practical educational concerns will be discussed.

1. Reading

Reading is the instructional domain to which psychologists have attended for the longest time and in the greatest numbers. Until very recently, however, little systematic work was being done on processes of reading comprehension. Most research on reading was concerned with processes of word recognition, the early stages of reading acquisition, and difficulties in learning to read. Among psychologists, the microprocesses of word recognition are still studied extensively. Now, however, the issue whether to emphasize decoding or comprehension in instruction is giving way to research on how the various processes of reading interact, both in skilled performance and in acquisition (e.g., Lesgold and Perfetti 1981). At the same time, an extensive body of research and theory in reading comprehension is stressing the active, constructive, and inferential character of reading.

1.1 Processes of Word Recognition

How people access the meaning of the printed words that make up a text remains the most heavily studied topic in the psychology of early reading. There is now an extensive body of research on how skilled readers recognize words, and growing attention is being directed to processes of word recognition in children as they learn to read (Gibson and Levin 1975, Baron 1978a, Smith and Kleiman 1979). Some common problems permeate this work: the unit of processing in word recognition, the role of phonemic encoding

in reading, the automation of word recognition, and the influence of surrounding semantic and syntactic context on word recognition. Of these, research on automation and context effects have the most direct bearing on instruction and are therefore discussed briefly here.

What is the relationship between skill in word recognition and skill in deriving meaning from text? Although it is clear that there is more to reading than the sequential processing of individual words, there is also evidence that people who comprehend poorly have difficulty in recognizing words quickly and without special effort (Perfetti and Lesgold 1979, Frederiksen 1981, LaBerge and Samuels 1974). Fast or "automated" word recognition has been proposed as a necessary (although not sufficient) basis for reading comprehension, on the plausible assumption that limited working memory capacity is thus freed for higher level semantic processing. The general argument is that unless word recognition is automated up to some minimal level, other processes important to comprehension cannot proceed because too much time and/or too much attentional capacity is used up in word recognition. The apparent implication for instruction is that special training in fast word decoding should be offered to those having difficulty learning to read, but research clearly demonstrating the effectiveness of such training does not exist at the present time.

Several sources of evidence suggest that reading is an interactive process in which "top-down" information from the surrounding syntactic and semantic context, and "bottom-up" information from the visual stimuli combine to produce word recognition (Rumelhart and McClelland 1981). Oral reading errors, even in young readers, tend to be semantically and syntactically appropriate to the context. Long hesitations or misreadings occur at points where word changes in a text produce syntactic or semantic anomalies. People are faster at pronouncing a word in context than when the same word appears in isolation and faster at pronouncing words when the preceding context is congruous with the word than when it is incongruous. Finally, research on "lexical decisions" shows that even with isolated words as stimuli, people are faster at deciding if a letter string is a word when it has been "semantically primed" by prior presentation of an appropriate superordinate category name or a related word. Wherever more time might be needed for semantic processing, longer fixations tend to be found.

The documentation of "top-down" processes has led some theorists to propose that early reading instruction should not focus on the print–sound (grapheme–phoneme) code, but instead upon the use of context and meaning to make and test inferences about words (e.g., Goodman and Goodman 1979). However, research on the effects of code- versus language-oriented instruction generally tends to favor code instruction—at least in the first three years of instruction.

1.2 Reading Comprehension

The demonstration of context effects in word recognition accords well with the findings of an important body of recent research on reading comprehension that has fundamentally changed researchers' understanding of the reading process. Reading is now viewed as a constructive process in which inference by the reader and the reader's prior knowledge play a central role.

It is well-established by now that both immediate and delayed recall of texts typically includes material that is not actually in the text but is thematically related. This makes it clear that inferences beyond the explicit information in the text are a normal part of the reading process. However, the actual processes involved in making inferences and the way in which inference interacts with other processes of reading are only partially understood, and many questions are still unanswered. For example, efforts to establish whether inferences occur at the time of initially reading the text or at recall have yielded conflicting results. Research on inference processes has also been complicated up to now by problems in deciding what should be counted as an inference from the text, as opposed to a plausible construction by the reader in order to meet a real or perceived task demand.

Among factors that can affect the inferencing process, the structure of the text is critical. An analysis of the local coherence relationships—that is, the links between adjacent or nearly adjacent sentences—in a text provides the basis for the best developed and mostly extensively tested general model of reading comprehension by Kintsch and van Dijk (1978). The model takes as its material to be processed the set of propositions derived from the text. The reader's task in understanding a text is to construct a mental representation of the propositional structure of the text, in which all propositions are linked via shared arguments. If the text does not specify the links between propositions, the reader must supply these links through inference. The difficulty of building this representation is affected by features of the text, such as the explicitness of the links between propositions. It is also affected by characteristics of the reader, such as the amount of text material one is able to process in a given processing cycle and the amount that can be held in short-term memory and carried into the next cycle.

A potentially important instructional application of current work on text structure and inference processes is the development of a better theory of what makes a text easy or difficult to understand, that is, of "readability" (Klare 1976). Existing readability formulas largely disregard questions of meaning, structure, and connectedness in the text; in most cases scrambled sentences or paragraphs earn the same readability score as properly ordered text. Recent work is beginning to correct this problem. For example, extensions of the Kintsch and van Dijk model of text processing (Kintsch and Vipond 1979), have shown that the propositional density of the text (the number of propositions for a constant number of words), the number of different arguments (i.e., different concepts introduced), and the cohesiveness of the text (as defined by shared arguments between propositions) all affect readability.

A second major theme in research on reading comprehension is the role that readers' prior knowledge plays in allowing them to interpret and understand a text. Central to virtually all of the work on prior knowledge is the notion of a schema as a framework for interpreting the text (Rumelhart and Ortony 1977, Adams and Collins 1979, Schank and Abelson 1977).

Although schema theories vary in many potentially important details, they share general features. Schemata are general "prototypic" knowledge structures. They specify certain kinds of information that are required for the prototypic situation or relationship to be filled out or "instantiated." Reading comprehension proceeds, roughly speaking, by the reader's using the first part of the text to decide what schema is most likely to make sense of the text and then using that schema as a hypothesis for interrogating the text. This interrogation fills the schema's slots, thus completing the reader's mental model of the situation. The schema also serves as a filter that allows some information to be judged irrelevant and thus, presumably, not entered into the model.

Early work on schemata showed that passages that subjects report to be incomprehensible, and for which recall is very low, become comprehensible and recallable when readers are told in advance what the theme of the story is. More recent work shows that the kinds of schemata people are most likely to activate because of their own background and interests can also influence how a passage is understood (e.g., Anderson et al. 1977a, Waern 1977a, 1977b). Directions to adopt a particular perspective can also affect what is learned and remembered from a text and what is rated important; so can a story setting in which specific information is embedded. Individuals with high prior knowledge of a topic remember more propositions from a text on that topic (Chiesi et al. 1979), probably because prior knowledge aids readers in building and carrying in memory the propositions needed to make the text coherent.

A special kind of prior knowledge that is important in reading comprehension is knowledge of typical discourse forms. For example, several investigators have been exploring the ways in which highly schematized knowledge about "typical" sequences of events in narrative stories affects comprehension. Typical event sequences and the rules for generating them can be thought of as a "grammar" for stories (Stein and Trabasso 1982). A story grammar is, in effect, a schema for a well-formed narrative story. The story schema specifies the types of information which should occur and the types of logical relationships that should link the parts. Research has shown that people use knowledge of this schema in understanding stories. For example, people—especially children—have difficulty recalling stories in which information is given in orders other than those specified in the grammar. They also tend to recall story information in the order predicted by the grammar, even when the text from which they learn the story uses a nonstandard order. In remembering or retelling stories, certain categories of information that are central to the story are most likely to be recalled. If statements are added to the recall protocol that were not initially in the text, they are likely to fall into these same central categories. Some recent research suggests that the semantic content, rather than just form or placement of the information within the story, may be determining recall. As a result, investigators have begun to examine development of the children's social knowledge as relevant to story understandings.

Schemata apparently also play a role in the process of writing—a skill that is just beginning to receive attention from psychologists, often working collaboratively with teachers of English (Britton et al. 1975, Gregg and Steinberg 1980). This work is marked by attention to the processes as opposed to the products of composition and by a general view of composition as a schema-driven problem-solving process. For example, Flower and Hayes (1980) have been comparing the processes of expert and novice adult writers within the context of an information-processing model of composition. Bereiter and Scardamalia (1982) have been studying the difficulties that children have in switching from the interactive mode of language production that characterizes conversation to the written mode in which the writer must generate language in the absence of an immediately responding audience. Bereiter and Scardamalia have found that the tasks of searching for appropriate content and planning a piece of writing are more effectively performed by children for narrative story compositions than for other genres of writing. Since narratives are clearly the genre with which children have had the most experience, this finding suggests an important role for well-developed discourse schemata in the composition process.

The view of reading comprehension stressed here is too recent to have yet generated many instructional applications. However, a few efforts to teach reading "strategies" have been made. In addition, older lines of work on advance organizers, questions, and other adjuncts to texts may eventually be reinterpreted in light of today's more constructivist view of the reading process.

Various studies have shown that people adapt their reading to local features of the text. The evidence that skilled readers modify their processing to fit the demands of the reading situation has suggested the possibility of directly teaching reading strategies to less skilled people. A number of investigators have instructed subjects to use a particular strategy (e.g., imagining the situation, constructing elaborations of material in the text) during reading, and then have examined effects on comprehension and memory. It has become clear that, while various strategies can be evoked by experimental instructions, the likelihood of using them under normal reading conditions depends upon individuals' abilities to monitor their own comprehension as a basis for deliberately modifying processing (Brown 1980). This "metacomprehension" skill has been shown to be weak in poor readers. There have been a few attempts to directly instruct self-monitoring skills. These training efforts form part of a growing body of research on the possibility of improving general mental abilities through instruction (see Sect. 3). (Many of these efforts are described in Segal et al. in press, Chipman et al. in press.)

When texts are used to teach a particular subject matter, various devices can be used to make learning more likely (Rothkopf 1976). To some extent, today's work on the role of schemata in reading comprehension echoes an earlier line of work, introduced by Ausubel (1968) on the role of "advance organizers" in facilitating comprehension and retention of prose materials. A large body of empirical work has accumulated since Ausubel first proposed his theory on the effectiveness of advance organizers, and advance organizer research is still current. A recent review by Mayer (1979) helps to specify the conditions under which advance organizers can be expected to facilitate learning. Work on other adjunct aids, such as questions placed in various positions in the text, dates back to the early 1970s. Several reviews (e.g., Anderson and Biddle 1975, Faw and Waller 1976) document and summarize the considerable body of empirical work in the area. In recent work there is more careful attention than before to the structure of the text in terms of importance and subordination of relationships, density and distribution of information, and details of the relationships between texts and questions. There has also been an extension of the range of texts studies and the types of populations included (in particular, children and poor readers have been studied in addition to relatively well-educated adults). However, there seems to have been only slight progress in the direction of accounting for questioning effects in terms of cognitive processes. There has also not yet emerged an integrative account capable of linking questioning effects either to schema theories of reading or to general propositional models of reading such as Kintsch and van Dijk's.

2. Mathematics, Science, and Problem Solving

Since the early 1970s there has been a marked shift in the kinds of tasks studied by psychologists interested in human problem solving. Newell and Simon's (1972) landmark work described investigations that used puzzle-like tasks with well-defined structures. Today psychologists are studying loosely structured tasks whose solutions depend on a rich body of knowledge that problem solvers must bring with them from past experience. This shift within information-processing psychology has rendered much of the literature on problem solving relevant to the psychology of instruction because the tasks now studied are often part of school, university, or technical curricula. Among the instructionally relevant task domains now being investigated are a number of topics in mathematics and physics, along with work on the learning and teaching of general problem-solving skills.

2.1 Mathematics

Mathematics has become a prime topic in the cognitive psychology of instruction. This is partly because of its obvious importance in the school curriculum and partly because mathematicians' carefully formulated statements of the subject matter provide a well-defined arena for the study of psychological processes. Among the themes that characterize recent work on the psychology of mathematics are the relationships between computational skill and understanding, the role of mental representations in learning, and the ways in which new knowledge is constructed by learners. As in the field of reading comprehension, close associations and mutual influence exist between cognitive psychology and artificial intelligence. Resnick and Ford (1981) have provided a review of mathematics learning and instruction as studied by psychologists, and Begle (1979) has reviewed the empirical literature in mathematics education.

Calculation is traditionally at the heart of the elementary-school mathematics curriculum, and psychologists' interests in the learning and teaching of calculation dates back at least to Thorndike's (1922) work on the psychology of arithmetic. Until recently, however, studies of calculation aimed to establish the relative difficulty of various types of problems without attempting a psychological explanation of why some problems are more difficult than others. Since the early 1970s, cognitive psychologists have been testing detailed models of the processes involved in various kinds of computational problems. In the process, they have begun to explore how the understanding of number and computational skill are related.

Recent work has established quite clearly that even the most basic calculations can be analyzed as psychologically complex events. Groen and Parkman's (1972) study is the point of reference for most of this work. These investigators showed that a model for simple addition, in which a counter is set to the larger of the two addends (regardless of whether it is presented first or second) and then incremented a number of times equal to the smaller addend, best accounted for the pattern of reaction times for problems with sums up to 10. This has become known as the "*min* model," because reaction time is a linear function of the minimum of the two addends. With respect to children, the finding has since been replicated and the model slightly refined in studies that have extended both the populations and the range of problems (Svenson and Broquist 1975, Svenson et al. 1976). Groen and Resnick (1977) have further established that even when children are taught a simpler to learn (but less efficient to perform) procedure for addition, they are likely to invent the *min* procedure for themselves after a number of weeks of practice. This is reminiscent of the process that Krutetskii (1976) called

"curtailment," in which children (especially the more mathematically able) develop shortcut procedures that are more efficient than the ones taught. Counting models have been applied to other simple arithmetic tasks, such as subtraction and addition with one of the addends unknown.

Several investigations have established that when children make errors in extended calculations, they are likely to be systematically following incorrect algorithms rather than simply forgetting arithmetic facts (Menchinskaya and Moro 1975, Ginsburg 1977, Brown and Burton 1978). Systematic but incorrect arithmetic procedures have come to be called "buggy algorithms." Considerable recent effort has gone into explaining how these buggy algorithms arise (Carpenter et al. 1982). It is clear that they represent constructions or "inventions" by the learner; this makes them a particularly apt domain in which to study the interaction between computational skill and understanding of mathematical concepts. This effort complements the observations of correct invented calculation procedures described above.

Performance of mental calculation is a skill not explicitly called for in literate cultures. However, research on mental calculation helps to reveal more general aspects of arithmetic processes. There is evidence that when adults are required to do mental calculations, most attempt to perform them by imagining that the normal tools of calculation are present. Westerners go through steps much like those of written calculation (Hayes 1973), while expert Japanese abacus operators generate images of successive abacus displays (Hatano et al. 1977). Mental arithmetic performed the same way as written procedures, however, creates strains on short-term memory (Hitch 1978). It is therefore not surprising that adults who are expert at mental calculation do not attempt to mimic written procedures, but instead analyze numbers and their relationships in order to construct efficient mental strategies (Hunter 1968).

Story problems are one of the most difficult topics in the school mathematics curriculum. This topic also links mathematics with language understanding. For both of these reasons, story problems have attracted more attention from psychologists than most other topics in mathematics. Earlier work established some of the "structural variables"—such as position of the unknown and number of actions required—that render story problems difficult, but this research did not clearly relate difficulty to the mental processes involved in solution. Soviet research (Mikhal'skii 1975) has given quite detailed accounts of processing difficulties but has not linked them explicitly to problem structure. More recent work has focused on the semantic relationships expressed in stories and the cognitive processes by which they are interpreted.

The most extensive research has been done on simple addition and subtraction problems. Results of studies done in several countries (Riley et al. 1982, Carpenter and Moser 1982, Nesher 1981, Vergnaud 1981) have suggested that a limited number of basic story schemata (e.g., combination of quantities, changing a quantity by adding or removing from it, and comparing two quantities) are sufficient to characterize the situations described in such problems. However, there are no simple one-to-one relationships between words used in a problem and the schema of the overall story. These analyses suggest three basic sources of difficulty in solving story problems. First, children may not yet have a good command of some of the basic schemata. This seems to be particularly the case for comparison schemata, which cause difficulty as late as third grade. Second, a solution strategy that attends to surface cues (e.g., key words such as "more" and "fewer") will often produce wrong answers. A third source of difficulty lies in the complexity of establishing a mental representation for an unknown which is in other than the final ("result") position of a story.

Only scattered studies exist for more complex story problems, but those that have examined the semantic schemata underlying problems have found sharp differences in ease of comprehending different schemata. These findings seem to parallel the better developed findings for addition and subtraction. Several studies have also shown that skilled word-problem solvers are able to identify the underlying semantic schemata of algebra story problems (e.g., Krutetskii 1976, Hinsley et al. 1977) and use these structures to aid in problem solution. All of these findings are in contrast to a solution style that is sometimes recommended for teaching: sentence-by-sentence direct translation into equations, followed by solutions.

Other topics in mathematics are just beginning to receive attention from psychologists and other cognitive scientists. Most work on algebra (Shevarev 1975), largely descriptive in character, is based on extensive protocols of the behavior of individuals attempting to solve various kinds of problems. Greeno (1978) has developed computational models that match the essential characteristics of high-school students' performances as they construct geometry proofs or perform geometry constructions. These models highlight the role of strategic knowledge specific to geometry (e.g., looking for vertical and corresponding angles or for side–angle–side patterns) in problem solving. This kind of strategic knowledge is not now taught in most geometry courses. The Greeno geometry data has also been used as the basis for a computational program that acquires strategies of proof via practice on geometry problems (Anderson et al. 1981). This work constitutes one of the most complete cognitive theories of learning available at present and signals one of the most important agendas for cognitive–instructional psychology research for the near future: characterization of the processes of learning as well as of performance (see Anderson 1981 for a collection of "state of the art" papers in this area).

Mathematics educators favor the use of concrete representations of mathematical concepts in the teaching of arithmetic. While it is established that the use of concrete materials often enhances learning, little is known about the processes that underlie these effects. Requiring step-by-step mappings between operations in a written form and operations in a physical representation may enhance both written calculation skill and understanding of the mathematical principles that justify a written algorithm (Resnick 1981). Without this enforced mapping, however, children may simply learn an alternative means of calculation with the concrete materials. A parallel finding by Hatano (1982) shows that encouragement of mental imagery during abacus training is required if such training is to result in enhanced arithmetic performance without the abacus. Although some general principles for selecting representations for mathematics teaching have been suggested (Fischbein 1977), there is as yet very little psychological research that explores which kinds of representations are most effective.

2.2 Science and Problem Solving

Research on science learning and problem solving like that in mathematics is focused on the ways in which knowledge is organized and accessed and on the ways in which domain-specific knowledge and general strategies of problem solving interact. The bulk of psychological research on science learning has concentrated on physics. Several studies have shown a relationship between skill in solving physics problems and the kinds of knowledge structures possessed by the learner. For example, Chi et al. (1980) have shown that, when asked to sort and characterize physics problems, advanced graduate students in physics respond to the basic physics principles that can be abstracted from a problem. Undergraduates who have had only one course in physics, however, respond to the literal surface features of the problem. Larkin et al. (1980) have built computational programs that model the performance of novices and experts on problems in mechanics. The novice program begins by directly translating the verbal and diagrammatic information in the problem statements into algebraic formulas and then uses a "backward" (means–ends) strategy to work the problems. By contrast, the expert program uses information in its more extensive knowledge structure to build a "physical representation" of the problem and then works forward toward a solution. Other work on knowledge structures in physics is also pointing to the importance of specific knowledge about the domain in successful reasoning. In particular, there is an emerging body of work showing that students have strongly held and well-integrated beliefs about natural phenomena that can actually interfere with learning the modern scientific constructs taught in high-school and college courses (e.g., Viennot 1979, Gunstone and White 1981).

The question of when and how the ability to reason scientifically develops has concerned developmental psychologists as well as those more directly concerned with instruction in science. Several investigators have demonstrated that children's responses to reasoning tasks are governed by rules and that these rules appear in an ordered developmental sequence (Siegler 1978, Scandura 1977, Spada 1978). Siegler has shown that children unable to benefit from instruction that relied largely on feedback fail to encode (notice) certain key attributes. Teaching directed at increasing the encoding of these attributes can in some cases improve younger children's ability to benefit from the more general instruction.

There have been a number of efforts to teach general problem-solving skills—often in conjunction with mathematics, science, and engineering courses (e.g., Lochhead and Clement 1979, Tuma and Reif 1980). For the moment, evidence favors the teachability of domain-specific skills, but wide generalizability of taught skills has yet to be demonstrated. This is what might be expected in the light of the important role of domain-specific knowledge in problem solving that was noted above for physics. Nevertheless, strong arguments for continuing to explore the possibilities of teaching general strategies can be made (e.g., Simon 1980). Work toward the development of automated tutoring programs (e.g., Stevens and Collins 1980) is perhaps the best current instantiation of a widely shared intuition that problem-solving activity in the context of rich knowledge structures will probably best serve both the general strategy and the specific subject matter goals of instruction. These programs are intended to query learners in ways that force them to search their existing knowledge in order to answer questions for which answers are not immediately available. In the process, it is hypothesized, learners will acquire both more fully connected knowledge structures and an ability to use the querying strategies on their own.

3. Intelligence and Aptitude

For many decades the concepts of intelligence and aptitude, particularly as expressed in tests of mental ability, played a central role in those branches of psychology concerned with the theory and practice of education. In the years immediately preceding the 1970s, interest in intelligence research waned. Despite increased sophistication in psychometric methods, only limited progress was made in defining intelligence or in explaining the ability of intelligence tests to predict subsequent learning performance (Estes 1974). In addition, changing conceptions of the origins of intelligence and of the ways in which environmental encounters could modify the phenotype were calling the older views (which were rooted in a conception of genetically determined fixed intelligence) into question.

Recently there has been an intense revival of research on the nature of intelligence, and this research has had a decidedly new look (Resnick 1976, Sternberg and Detterman 1979, Snow et al. 1980). In the more recent work there has been (a) a focus on defining intelligence rather than perfecting technological instruments for prediction; (b) an assumption that the definition would require

characterization of intelligence and aptitudes in terms of cognitive processes or the actual processes of learning; and (c) an emphasis on how descriptions of individual differences in cognitive processing abilities might become the basis for adapting instruction to make it more effective for all individuals, rather than simply predicting success or failure in standard instructional situations (Glaser 1972). A useful distinction can be made between a "cognitive correlates" and a "cognitive components" approach to the study of intelligence (Pellegrino and Glaser 1979). The "correlates" approach uses an aptitude test as a criterion measure and seeks more elementary cognitive processes that are highly correlated with the test criterion. The "cognitive components" approach uses the test items as tasks to be analyzed in a search for the component processes of test performance itself. Research directly relating aptitude analyses to instruction has focused either on aptitude-treatment interactions (ATI) or on the possibility of training general learning strategies.

3.1 Cognitive Correlates of Aptitude

A major line of research seeks to identify basic cognitive processes that distinguish between high and low scorers on a particular aptitude test. The primitive processing parameters for study are drawn from the mainstream of basic research on cognitive processes, especially memory processes. This line of research was initiated by Hunt (1978), who suggests that verbal performance requires both the specific verbal knowledge that is called upon by the task and the exercise of certain mechanistic processes by which information is manipulated. According to Hunt's theory, individuals with less efficient mechanistic processes have to work harder at learning tasks involving verbal information. Over time this handicap produces relatively large individual differences in verbal skill and knowledge. The theoretical argument is buttressed by data from studies that have investigated the relationship between performance on laboratory information-processing tasks and scores on global measures of aptitude, such as IQ tests and college admission tests.

The most robust finding in this literature concerns differences in the time needed to access name codes in long-term memory. Code access is defined as the difference between the time it takes to decide whether two stimuli have the same name (e.g., $A = a$) and the time it takes to decide whether they are physically identical ($A \neq a$), or name identity time minus physical identity time ($NI - PI$). Summarizing the results of multiple studies there tends to be an increase in the $NI - PI$ difference as one moves from the high-verbal university students, to young adults not in a university, to normal elementary-school children, and finally to mildly retarded school children (Hunt 1978). However, a recent review of a number of studies on individual differences in code access (Carroll 1980) suggests that perceptual speed may underlie the apparent code access difference between high- and low-verbal individuals. The interpretation of code access and other processing speed differences is likely to be debated in the literature for some time.

Nevertheless, there seems to be enough evidence of individual and age differences in primitive parameters of mental processing to make plausible Hunt's notion that small differences in mechanistic processes could cumulate over time to produce considerable differences in verbal skill and knowledge.

3.2 Cognitive Components of Aptitude

Carroll (1976) and Simon (1976) first suggested the analysis of test items as cognitive tasks, and several research programs now focus on task analysis of traditional aptitude test items. Perhaps the most ambitious program in terms of the range of tasks studied is Sternberg's work on what he calls a "componential analysis" of intelligence (Sternberg 1977). Sternberg's analyses begin with a specification of the components hypothesized to be involved in the performance of a task. Several models are then specified, differing in the components called on, the sequencing of the components, the number of times each component needs to be executed, and the manner of execution (e.g., exhaustive or self-terminating searches). The models permit predictions of reaction time and error patterns under varying conditions of stimulus structure and task presentation. Empirical tests of models generated for verbal and pictorial analogies suggest that encoding the attributes of the elements in the analogy is a particularly important aspect of task performance.

Some studies have further analyzed the encoding process itself, with particular attention to what aspects of the stimuli are encoded. For example, Mulholland et al. (1980) showed that in geometric analogies, individuals analyze stimuli in a systematic serial manner, so that latency of responding is a function of both the number of elements that must be encoded and the number of transformations necessary on each element. They found a sharp increase in both reaction time and errors when multiple transformations on multiple stimuli had to be processed, suggesting that working memory limitations are important in analogy processing. For verbal analogies, studies by Pellegrino and Glaser (1980) and Sternberg (1977) have shown that individuals with high aptitude test scores specify more precisely the set of semantic features that relate the word pairs in an analogy, and that the extra time they spend on this process allows them to spend less time on subsequent decision and response processes.

Other test-like tasks that have been subjected to similar analysis include series completion syllogistic reasoning and transitive inference spatial abilities tasks such as mental rotation and visual comparison block designs and matrix tasks. One important finding to emerge from this work is that even on highly constrained test items, strategy differences between individuals can be important. An interesting case in point is Cooper's (1980) study of visual comparison, in which subjects split naturally into two quite different subgroups, one using a holistic and one an analytic comparison strategy. The two strategies produced very different patterns of latencies, and the subgroups responded in predictably different ways to variations on task instructions and stimuli.

Another emerging issue concerns the role of higher level "executive" and "control" processes in accounting for individual differences in test performance. Some of the evidence for individual differences in executive and control strategies comes from findings showing that high-aptitude individuals are more systematic in performing analogies, paper-folding, and vocabulary tasks (Snow 1980) than low-aptitude individuals. Increased attention to these higher level processes can be expected in future research on the components of intelligence. This trend is paralleled by growing attention to executive and control processes in the work on aptitude training described below.

3.3 Aptitudes and Instruction

It is commonly assumed that characterization of the cognitive processes that underlie ability and aptitude differences will permit better adaptation of instruction to individual differences. Two complementary approaches to adaptation can be identified: (a) matching instructional treatments to individual processing capacities, and (b) training of aptitude-like processes so that learners will be better able to benefit from ordinary instruction.

The scientific basis for aptitude matching as a strategy for adaptive instruction is the demonstration of an aptitude–treatment interaction (ATI)—that is, a finding that individuals with a particular aptitude profile progress further under one specified instructional treatment than another. Cronbach and Snow (1977) have provided an extensive review and critique of the ATI literature. Although the major interpreters of ATI research repeatedly stress the goal of reformulating traditional psychometric aptitude theory in terms of the cognitive processes that are implicated in aptitude test performance and in various instructional treatments, virtually all existing ATI research is limited to comparisons of rather grossly defined instructional treatments for populations characterized in terms of test scores. The mediating cognitive processes are not assessed in detail. The result is that only the most general conclusions can be drawn at this time about how to match treatments to abilities.

A recurrent finding is that structured treatments (tight sequencing, required responding, teacher control, instructions to process in a particular way, etc.) reduce the correlation between general intelligence and achievement. Low-intelligence students do better under these conditions, which are interpreted as reducing the burden of information processing for the learner. This kind of instruction sometimes—but not always—suppresses performance of the more able. Despite efforts to distinguish between fluid and crystallized intelligence in ATI experiments, no consistent pattern of differences has emerged. Nor have other more specialized abilities shown consistent patterns of interactions with various treatments, despite many experimental efforts. A cluster of cognitive styles and motivational traits have shown ATIs, but various inconsistencies and anomalies in the findings warn against too simplified a conclusion concerning personality and style factors. Instead, a renewed effort to analyze these variables and related cognitive style constructs in terms of cognitive process seems to be needed (Goodenough 1976, Messick 1976).

Interactions between instructional treatments and characteristics of learners can also be sought by describing learners not in terms of aptitude traits but of level of knowledge. Tobias (1976) has reviewed a number of studies of achievement–treatment interactions. These studies tend to show that individuals who enter a course of instruction with little prior knowledge of the field make the best progress under highly structured teaching (as in programmed instructional formats), while those with prior knowledge do as well—and sometimes better—when they only read the material. These results echo the findings (see above) showing that advance organizers and other adjunct aids tend to be of benefit only when students do not already have some information about the topic. They also set in an interesting instructional context the research described above on novice–expert differences in knowledge structures and processing.

There has been much recent interest in the possibility of teaching aptitudes or learning skills. A few of the aptitude training efforts are directly linked to information-processing analyses of intelligence test tasks. In these studies experimenters have taught knowledge and processing components identified in task analyses and/or specific algorithms for performing tasks such as series completion, syllogisms, or analogies. These studies show that performance on a class of tasks can be improved significantly by teaching their components. No effort has yet been made, however, to determine whether improved performance on the taught tasks also produces general improvement in ability, including transfer to other test-like tasks.

Until recently there was reason to be very cautious about expecting transfer from training on specific tasks. In work with retarded people, several investigators had been able to show impressive immediate gains in performance on memory tasks by simply instructing individuals to rehearse the items on the memory lists or to engage in verbal elaboration (e.g., Butterfield et al. 1973). In these studies, however, there was almost complete lack of transfer, even to only slightly modified tasks. More recently, emphasis in training studies has begun to shift to "superordinate" (Belmont et al. 1982) or "metacognitive" (Brown 1978) skills such as assessing one's own readiness for a test and apportioning study time or deciding when to use rehearsal, imagery, or self-interrogation strategies. After training, both

transfer and retention have improved. Efforts to train intellectual skills have also been made for nonhandicapped populations. For example, Dansereau et al. (1979) have developed a learning strategy program that includes strategies for comprehension and retention of text information, retrieval and utilization of information, and self-management of one's concentration and goal-setting behavior. Several interesting papers (Belmont et al. 1982, Brown and Campione 1980, Glaser and Pellegrino 1982) have suggested principles for developing general learning skills. These papers can best be thought of as outlining agendas for future research in the field.

The apparent promise of training that focuses on executive or self-control strategies accords well with theories of intelligence that stress general strategies rather than specific capabilities as the hallmark of those who learn more easily (e.g., Baron 1978b). Several investigators have proposed that the source of the ability to control one's own intellectual performance lies in social interactions in which an adult (acting in a formal or informal tutorial role) serves both as external controller and prompter and as a modeler of self-control strategies that the child can eventually manage alone (Wertsch 1978, Feuerstein 1979, Brown and Campione 1980). This view of the origins of intelligent self-monitoring is implicit in research efforts as divergent as shaping reasoning processes through computerized tutorial interactions (Stevens and Collins 1980) and characterizing social class differences in maternal teaching styles (Wood 1979).

At the beginning of the 1970s, psychologists were actively engaged in developing and assessing intervention programs designed to compensate for social class differences in educational opportunity. Today this is no longer a very active area of study, perhaps partly because early evaluations of preschool interventions had generally reported that increases in IQ or related general measures of intellectual functioning dissipated within a year or two after the intervention had ended. Recent evidence, however, suggests that early interventions may have more lasting benefits than previously had been thought. Reports on a 10-year follow-up of children who had participated in some of the American preschool programs of the 1960s show higher rates of school success for these children than for controls (Darlington et al. 1980).

4. Conclusion

A richly detailed picture of the ways in which people perform many of the tasks central to education is emerging as a result of the research described in this article. However, even a diligent search for instructional implications of these cognitive task analyses yields only the relatively general suggestions that have appeared in the course of this review. If prescriptions for instructional intervention were to be based entirely on studies that included direct instruction, the suggestions would have to be even more limited. There is, as yet, no applied cognitive technology of education to parallel programmed instruction, behavioral task analysis, or mastery learning. For the moment, cognitive instructional psychology must be characterized as a largely descriptive science, analyzing performance but not making strong suggestions for improving it. Can instructional psychology become a prescriptive science as well, able to guide processes of teaching as well as describe processes of learning?

Four components of a prescriptive theory of learning can be identified. These are: (a) description of the state of knowledge to be achieved; (b) description of the initial state in which the learner begins; (c) specification of interventions which can help the learner to move from his or her initial state to the desired state; and (d) assessment of specific and generalized learning outcomes. It seems fair to say that cognitive instructional psychology has focused most strongly up to now on components (a) and (b). The largest amount of research has been devoted to describing the processes of skilled performers in various domains. With the growing body of work on children and the various expert–novice contrastive studies that have been reported, however, considerable progress is now being made in building descriptions of initial and intermediate states of competence.

With respect to component (c), specifying the instructional acts that can help learners transform their initial states, cognitive instructional psychology has been largely silent. Some of the investigators cited here have offered broad suggestions, such as reducing memory demands during the early stages of teaching a concept, linking syntactic rules to the semantic justifications for procedures, or helping students to acquire and organize large amounts of domain-specific information. A few studies have directly investigated the effects of such instruction in some limited domain. However, most of the instructional prescriptions to be gleaned from cognitive psychology must be viewed as very general principles needing study and elaboration in multiple domains of learning. There is good theoretical reason for this silence. As cognitive psychology has elaborated a theory of the human being as an active constructor of knowledge, a new view of learning has begun to emerge—one that describes changes in knowledge as the result of learners' self-modification of their own thought processes and knowledge structures. This in turn means that instruction must be designed not to put knowledge into learners' heads, but to put learners in positions that allow them to construct well-structured knowledge. To know what these positions are likely to be requires knowing more about the cognitive processes involved in learning than is known at present. As a richer picture of cognitive processes of learning emerges, in part from descriptive studies of knowledge transformations under various instructional conditions, the scientific basis for a more prescriptive theory of intervention will become available.

With respect to assessment of specific and general outcomes [component (d) above] of learning, it appears that instructional psychology now has most of the necessary tools in hand. In theory at least, it is possible to use the descriptions of target and intermediate knowledge states, now being identified through cognitive task analysis, to create methods of measuring the success of instructional efforts. Rather than treating performance on a specified set of tasks as themselves the objectives of instruction, it should become possible to treat task performances as indicators of the understanding and knowledge that are the deeper goals of education. Considered from the laboratory, this point seems almost trivial because this is exactly how most cognitive research proceeds in interpreting behavioral data. But the job of building a technology of mental measurement aimed at describing the content of individual knowledge and the processes by which it is used is not a simple one. Work toward such a new approach to educational assessment would do much to make instructional psychology a more prescriptive science.

Bibliography

Adams M J, Collins A 1979 A schema-theoretic view of reading. In: Freedle R O (ed.) 1979 *New Directions in Discourse Processing*. Ablex, Norwood, New Jersey

Anderson J R (ed.) 1981 *Cognitive Skills and Their Acquisition*. Erlbaum, Hillsdale, New Jersey

Anderson J R, Greeno J G, Kline P J, Neves D M 1981 Learning to plan in geometry. In: Anderson J R (ed.) 1981

Anderson R C, Biddle B W 1975 On asking people questions about what they are reading. In: Bower G (ed.) 1975 *The Psychology of Learning and Motivation: Advances in Research and Theory*. Academic Press, New York, pp. 89–132

Anderson R C, Reynolds R E, Schallert D L, Goertz E T 1977a Frameworks for comprehending discourse. *Am. Educ. Res. J.* 14: 367–81

Anderson R C, Spiro R J, Montague W E (eds.) 1977b *Schooling and the Acquisition of Knowledge*. Erlbaum, Hillsdale, New Jersey

Ausubel D P 1968 *Educational Psychology: A Cognitive View*. Holt, Rinehart and Winston, New York

Baron J 1978a The word-superiority effect: Perceptual learning from reading. In: Estes W K (ed.) 1978 *Handbook of Learning and Cognitive Processes: Linguistic Functions in Cognitive Theory*, Vol. 6. Halsted, New York

Baron J 1978b Intelligence and general strategies. In: Underwood G (ed.) 1978 *Strategies of Information Processing*. Academic Press, London, pp. 403–50

Begle E G 1979 *Critical Variables in Mathematics Education: Findings from a Survey of the Empirical Literature*. Mathematics Association of America National Council on Teaching Mathematics, Washington, DC

Belmont J, Butterfield E C, Ferretti R P 1982 To secure transfer of training, instruct self-management skills. In: Detterman D K, Sternberg R J (eds.) 1982 *How and How Much Can Intelligence be Increased?* Ablex, Norwood, New Jersey

Bereiter C, Scardamalia M 1982 From conversation to composition: The role of instruction in a developmental process. In: Glaser R (ed.) 1982

Britton J, Bergess T, Martin N, McLeod A, Rosen H 1975 *The Development of Writing Abilities (11–18).* Macmillan, London

Brown A L 1978 Knowing when, where, and how to remember: A problem of metacognition. In: Glaser R (ed.) 1978 pp. 77–165

Brown A L 1980 Metacognitive development and reading. In: Spiro R J, Bruce B C, Brewer W F (eds.) 1980 *Theoretical Issues in Reading Comprehension: Perspectives from Cognitive Psychology, Linguistics, Artificial Intelligence, and Education.* Erlbaum, Hillsdale, New Jersey

Brown A L, Campione J C 1980 Inducing flexible thinking: The problem of access. In: Friedman M P, Das J, O'Connor N (eds.) 1980 *Intelligence and Learning.* Plenum, New York, pp. 515–29

Brown J S, Burton R R 1978 Diagnostic models for procedural bugs in basic mathematical skills. *Cognit. Sci.* 2: 155–92

Bruner J S 1960 *The Process of Education.* Harvard University Press, Cambridge, Massachusetts

Butterfield E C, Wambold C, Belmont J M 1973 On the theory and practice of improving short-term memory. *Am. J. Ment. Defic.* 77: 654–69

Carpenter T P, Moser J M 1982 The development of addition and subtraction problem solving skills. In: Carpenter T P, Moser J M, Romberg T A (eds.) 1982 *Addition and Subtraction: A Cognitive Perspective.* Erlbaum, Hillsdale, New Jersey

Carpenter T P, Moser J M, Romberg T (eds.) 1982 *Addition and Subtraction: A Developmental Perspective.* Erlbaum, Hillsdale, New Jersey

Carroll J B 1976 Psychometric tests as cognitive tasks: A new "structure of intellect". In: Resnick L B (ed.) 1976 pp. 27–56

Carroll J B 1980 *Individual Difference Relations in Psychometric and Experimental Cognitive Tasks.* University of North Carolina, Chapel Hill, North Carolina.

Chi M T H, Feltovich P, Glaser R 1980 *Representation of Physics Knowledge by Experts and Novices.* Learning Research and Development Center, University of Pittsburgh, Pittsburgh, Pennsylvania

Chiesi H L, Spilich G J, Voss J F 1979 Acquisition of domain-related information in relation to high and low domain knowledge. *J. Verb. Learn. Verb. Behav.* 18: 257–74

Chipman S F, Segal J W, Glaser R (eds.) 1985 *Thinking and Learning Skills: Research and Open Questions*, Vol. 2. Erlbaum, Hillsdale, New Jersey

Cooper L A 1980 Spatial information processing: Strategies for research. In: Snow R E, Federico P A, Montague W E (eds.) 1980 Vol. 1

Cronbach L J, Snow R E 1977 *Aptitudes and Instructional Methods: A Handbook for Research on Interactions.* Irvington, New York

Dansereau D F, Collins K W, McDonald B A, Holley C D, Garland J, Diekhoff G, Evans S H 1979 Developments and evaluation of a learning strategy training program. *J. Educ. Psychol.* 71: 64–73

Darlington R B, Royce J M, Snipper A S, Murray H W, Lazar I 1980 Preschool programs and later school competence of children from low-income families. *Science* 208: 202–04

Estes W K 1974 Learning theory and intelligence. *Am. Psychol.* 29: 740–49

Faw H W, Waller T G 1976 Mathemagenic behaviours and efficiency in learning from prose materials: Review, critique and recommendations. *Rev. Educ. Res.* 46: 691–720

Feuerstein R 1979 *The Dynamic Assessment of Retarded Performers: The Learning, Potential, Assessment Device, Theory, Instruments, and Techniques.* University Park, Baltimore, Maryland

Fischbein E 1977 Image and concept in learning mathematics. *Educ. Stud. Math.* 8: 153–65

Flower L S, Hayes J R 1980 Plans that guide the composing process. In: Frederiksen C, Whiteman M, Dominic J (eds.) 1980 *Writing: The Nature, Development, and Teaching of Written Communication.* Erlbaum, Hillsdale, New Jersey

Frederiksen J R 1981 Sources of process interactions in reading. In: Lesgold A M, Perfetti C A (eds.) 1981

Gibson E J, Levin H 1975 *The Psychology of Reading.* MIT Press, Cambridge, Massachusetts

Ginsburg H 1977 *Children's Arithmetic: The Learning Process.* Van Nostrand, New York

Glaser R 1972 Individuals and learning: The new aptitudes. *Educ. Res.* 1(6): 5–13

Glaser R (ed.) 1978 *Advances in Instructional Psychology*, Vol. 1. Erlbaum, Hillsdale, New Jersey

Glaser R (ed.) 1982 *Advances in Instructional Psychology*, Vol. 2. Erlbaum, Hillsdale, New Jersey

Glaser R, Pellegrino J 1982 Improving the skills of learning. In: Detterman D K, Sternman R J (eds.) 1982 *How and How Much Can Intelligence be Increased?* Ablex, Norwood, New Jersey

Goodenough D R 1976 The role of individual differences in field dependence as a factor in learning and memory. *Psychol. Bull.* 83: 675–94

Goodman K S, Goodman Y M 1979 Learning to read is natural. In: Resnick L B, Weaver P A (eds.) 1979 *Theory and Practice of Early Reading*, Vol. 1. Erlbaum, Hillsdale, New Jersey, pp. 137–54

Greeno J G 1978 A study of problem solving. In: Glaser R (ed.) 1978

Gregg L W, Steinberg E (eds.) 1980 *Cognitive Processes in Writing: An Interdisciplinary Approach.* Erlbaum, Hillsdale, New Jersey

Groen G J, Parkman J M 1972 A chronometric analysis of simple addition. *Psychol. Rev.* 79: 329–43

Groen G J, Resnick L B 1977 Can preschool children invent addition algorithms? *J. Educ. Psychol.* 69: 645–52

Gunstone R F, White R T 1981 Understanding of gravity. *Sci. Educ.* 65: 291–99

Hatano G 1982 Learning to add and subtract: A Japanese perspective. In: Carpenter T, Moser J, Romberg T (eds.) 1982

Hatano G, Miyake Y, Binks M G 1977 Performance of expert abacus operators. *Cognition* 5: 47–55

Hayes J R 1973 On the function of visual imagery in elementary mathematics. In: Chase W G (ed.) 1973 *Visual Information Processing.* 8th Carnegie Symp. on Cognition, Pittsburgh, Pennsylvania, May 19, 1972. Academic Press, New York, pp. 177–214

Hinsley D, Hayes J R, Simon H 1977 From words to equations meaning and representation in algebra word problems. In: Just M A, Carpenter P A (eds.) 1977 *Cognitive Processes in Comprehension.* Erlbaum, Hillsdale, New Jersey

Hitch G J 1978 The role of short-term working memory in mental arithmetic. *Cognit. Psychol.* 10: 302–23

Hunt E 1978 Mechanics of verbal ability. *Psychol. Rev.* 85: 109–30

Hunter I M L 1968 Mental calculation. In: Wason P C, Johnson-Laird P N (eds.) 1968 *Thinking and Reasoning*. Penguin, Baltimore, Maryland, pp. 341–53

Kazdin A E 1981 Behavior modification in education: Contributions and limitations. *Dev. Rev.* 1: 34–57

Kintsch W, van Dijk T A 1978 Toward a model of text comprehension and production. *Psychol. Rev.* 85: 363–94

Kintsch W, Vipond D 1979 Reading comprehension and readability in educational practice and psychological theory. In: Nilsson L G (ed.) 1979 *Perspectives on Memory Research: Essays in Honor of Uppsala University's 500th Anniversary*. Erlbaum, Hillsdale, New Jersey, pp. 329–62

Klahr D (ed.) 1976 *Cognition and Instruction*. Erlbaum, Hillsdale, New Jersey

Klare G R 1976 A second look at the validity of readability formulas. *J. Read. Behav.* 8: 129–52

Kruteskii V A 1976 *The Psychology of Mathematical Abilities in School-children*. University of Chicago Press, Chicago, Illinois

LaBerge D, Samuels S J 1974 Toward a theory of automatic information processing in reading. *Cognit. Psychol.* 6: 293–323

Larkin J H, McDermott J, Simon D P, Simon H A 1980 Expert and novice performance in solving physics problems. *Science* 80: 1335–42

Lesgold A M, Perfetti C A (eds.) 1981 *Interactive Processes in Reading*. Erlbaum, Hillsdale, New Jersey

Lesgold A M, Pellegrino J W, Fokkema S D, Glaser R (eds.) 1978 *Cognitive Psychology and Instruction*. NATO Int. Conf., Amsterdam, 1977. Plenum, New York

Lochhead J, Clement J (eds.) 1979 *Cognitive Process Instruction: Research on Teaching Thinking Skills*. Conf., Amherst, Massachusetts, 1978. Franklin Institute Press, Philadelphia, Pennsylvania

Mayer R E 1979 Can advance organizers influence meaningful learning? *Rev. Educ. Res.* 49: 371–83

Menchinskaya N A, Moro M L 1975 Questions in the methods and psychology of teaching arithmetic in the elementary grades. *Sov. Stud. Psychol. Learn. Teach. Math.* 14: 1–202

Messick S (ed.) 1976 *Individuality in Learning*. Jossey-Bass, San Francisco, California

Mikhal'skii K A 1975 The solution of complex arithmetic problems in auxiliary school. *Sov. Stud. Psychol. Learn. Teach. Math.* 1–100

Mulholland T M, Pellegrino J W, Glaser R 1980 Components of geometric analogy solution. *Cognit. Psychol.* 12: 252–84

Nesher P 1981 Levels of description in the analysis of addition and subtraction of word problems. In: Carpenter T, Moser J, Romberg T (eds.) 1982

Newell A, Simon H A 1972 *Human Problem Solving*. Prentice-Hall, Englewood Cliffs, New Jersey

Pellegrino J W, Glaser R 1979 Cognitive correlates and components in the analysis of individual differences. *Intelligence* 3: 187–214

Pellegrino J W, Glaser R 1980 Components of inductive reasoning. In: Snow R E, Federico P-A, Montague W E (eds.) 1980

Perfetti C A, Lesgold A M 1979 Coding and comprehension in skilled reading and implications for reading instruction. In: Resnick L B, Weaver P A (eds.) 1979 Vol. 1, pp. 57–84

Resnick L B (ed.) 1976 *The Nature of Intelligence*. Erlbaum, Hillsdale, New Jersey

Resnick L B 1981 Syntax and semantics in learning to subtract. In: Carpenter T, Moser J, Romberg T (eds.) 1982

Resnick L B, Ford W W 1981 *The Psychology of Mathematics for Instruction*. Erlbaum, Hillsdale, New Jersey

Resnick L B, Weaver P A (eds.) 1979 *Theory and Practice of Early Reading*, Vols 1 and 2, Erlbaum, Hillsdale, New Jersey

Riley M S, Greeno J G, Heller J I 1982 Development of children's problem-solving ability in arithmetic. In: Ginsburg H P (ed.) 1982 *The Development of Mathematical Thinking*. Academic Press, New York

Rothkopf E Z 1976 Writing to teach and reading to learn: A perspective on the psychology of written instruction. In: Gage N L (ed.) 1976 *The Psychology of Teaching Methods*. National Society for the Study of Education, Chicago, Illinois, pp. 91–129

Rumelhart D E, McClelland J L 1981 Interactive processing through spreading activation. In: Lesgold A M, Perfetti C A (eds.) 1981

Rumelhart D E, Ortony A 1977 The representation of knowledge in memory. In: Anderson R C, Spiro R J, Montague W E (eds.) 1977b pp. 99–135

Scandura J M 1977 *Problem Solving: A Structural/Process Approach with Instructional Implications*. Academic Press, New York

Schank R C, Abelson R P 1977 *Scripts, Plans, Goals, and Understanding: An Inquiry into Human Knowledge Structures*. Erlbaum, Hillsdale, New Jersey

Segal J W, Chipman S F, Glaser R (eds.) 1985 *Thinking and Learning Skills: Relating Instruction to Research*, Vol. 1. Erlbaum, Hillsdale, New Jersey

Shevarev P A 1975 An experiment in the psychological analysis of algebraic errors. *Sov. Stud. Psychol. Learn. Teach. Math.* 12: 1–60

Siegler R S 1978 The origins of scientific reasoning. In: Siegler R S (ed.) 1978 *Children's Thinking: What Develops?* Erlbaum, Hillsdale, New Jersey, pp. 109–49

Simon H A 1976 Identifying basic abilities underlying intelligent performance of complex tasks. In: Resnick L B (ed.) 1976 pp. 659–98

Simon H A 1980 Problem solving and education. In: Tuma D T, Reif F (eds.) 1980

Skinner B F 1957 *Verbal Behavior*. Appleton-Century-Crofts, New York

Skinner B F 1968 *The Technology of Teaching*. Meredith Corporation, New York

Smith E E, Kleiman G M 1979 Theoretical issues and instructional hints. In: Resnick L B, Weaver P A (eds.) 1979 Vol. 2, pp. 31–42

Snow R E 1980 Aptitude processes. In: Snow R E, Federico P A, Montague W E (eds.) 1980

Snow R E, Federico P-A, Montague W E (eds.) 1980 *Aptitude, Learning, and Instruction: Cognitive Process Analyses*, Vols. 1 and 2. Erlbaum, Hillsdale, New Jersey

Spada H 1978 Understanding proportionality: A comparison of different models of cognitive development. *Int. J. Behav. Dev.* 1: 363–76

Stein N L, Trabasso T 1982 What's in a story: An approach to comprehension and instruction. In: Glaser R (ed.) 1982 *Advances in Instructional Psychology*, Vol. 2. Erlbaum, Hillsdale, New Jersey

Sternberg R J 1977 *Intelligence, Information Processing, and Analogical Reasoning: The Componential Analysis of Human Abilities*. Erlbaum, Hillsdale, New Jersey

Sternberg R J, Detterman D K (eds.) 1979 *Human Intelligence: Perspectives on its Theory and Measurement*. Ablex, Norwood, New Jersey

Stevens A L, Collins A 1980 Multiple conceptual models of a

complex system. In: Snow R E, Federico P-A, Montague W E (eds.) 1980 Vol. 2

Svenson O, Broquist S 1975 Strategies for solving simple addition problems: A comparison of normal and subnormal children. *Scand. J. Psychol.* 16: 143–48

Svenson O, Hedenborg M L, Lingman L 1976 On children's heuristics for solving simple additions. *Scand. J. Educ. Res.* 20: 161–73

Thorndike E L 1922 *The Psychology of Arithmetic.* Macmillan, New York

Tobias S 1976 Achievement treatment interactions. *Rev. Educ. Res.* 46: 61–74

Tuma D T, Reif F (eds.) 1980 *Problem Solving and Education: Issues in Teaching and Research.* Erlbaum, Hillsdale, New Jersey

Vergnaud G 1981 A classification of cognitive tasks and opera-

tions of thought involved in addition and subtraction problems. In: Carpenter T P, Moser J M, Romberg T (eds.) 1982

Viennot L 1979 Spontaneous reasoning in elementary dynamics. *Eur. J. Sci. Educ.* 1: 205–21

Waern Y 1977a Comprehension and belief structure. *Scand. J. Psychol.* 18: 266–74

Waern Y 1977b On the relationship between knowledge of the world and comprehension of texts: Assimilation and accommodation effects related to belief structure. *Scand. J. Psychol.* 18: 130–39

Wertsch J V 1978 Adult–child interaction and the roots of metacognition. *Q. Newsl. Inst. Comp. Hum. Dev.* 2: 15–18

Wood D J 1979 Problem solving: The nature and development of strategies. In: Underwood G (ed.) 1978 *Strategies of Information Processing.* Academic Press, London

Task Analysis

P. W. Tiemann and S. M. Markle

Instruction planned for any educational or training context presumes some definition of valued outcomes, that is, some expression of the aims, goals, and objectives of the planned enterprise. There must also be some assemblage of resources, the personnel, materials, and logistics necessary to carry out whatever processes are planned, and some form of feedback to the system about how well the outcomes are being attained. In the academic world, the individual scholar cum professor may perform all of these functions, the development, transmission, and evaluation of instruction, exemplifying a small-scale instructional system. In contrast, several distinct roles are assigned among team members in large-scale instructional development projects. Such division of labor may be found in the Open University course teams (United Kingdom), in major industrial training organizations, in national curriculum projects such as Sesame Street's Children's Television Workshop (United States), and in government-funded organizations such as the Soviet Union's Academy of Pedagogical Sciences or the several laboratories of the National Institute of Education in the United States.

Among the roles generally assigned to separate individuals on these courses are those of task analyst and instructional designer. The task analyst will take as givens the valued outcomes established by consensus among management teams, curriculum committees, or some responsible individual. From these outcomes the analyst develops complete specifications of the skills and knowledge students must attain to satisfy the given objectives. Based on the analysis of criteria to be achieved and the expected population to be taught, the instructional designer constructs materials and develops procedures to bring about the skills and knowledge. This article discusses the methodology of task analysis and instructional design in the development of instruction.

1. Historical Development of Analysis Procedures

In its broadest sense, task analysis is a set of rational–empirical procedures applied after the decision on valued outcomes. Its product is a complete specification, to the level of detail required to develop instructional and evaluational procedures, of the components of mastery performance of a task. Where several tasks are part of a job, or where many tasks will be sequenced in a curriculum such as in mathematics, analysis will also seek logical hierarchical relations which will determine the sequencing of tasks during instruction. Analysis of some sort is central to any instructional planning but the emphasis of task analysis is a focus on student performance, with an eye to the student as a master performer, from which analyst and designer work back to the required instructional interactions and content coverage. The focus on mastery performance derives from its historical antecedents.

Early task analysis procedures were developed by academics interested in precise descriptions of tasks in order to rationalize job redesign for the sake of efficiency and to provide a basis for matching workers to job requirements. In the early 1950s, these procedures were adapted and widely applied in military and industrial training to describe the task components of jobs in sufficient detail to guide the training of personnel, most typically the skilled operator of complex equipment (Miller 1962). Task analysis procedures have also been used over the years to select skilled operators, to evaluate deficiencies in less skilled operators, and to suggest redesign of man–machine systems.

Several kinds of data collection techniques are employed by task analysts, including observation of master performers, interviews with supervisory and instructional personnel, questionnaires, and critical incident collection. The primary methodology has been observation of a sample of master performers each engaged in the task, a laborious and time-consuming technique. It is particularly applicable to sequential types of procedural tasks, those which impose a requirement for step-by-step completion of a series of discrete actions ordered in a particular sequence. The identifiable steps of such tasks are analyzed as three parts: the conditions which surround each step; the precise nature of the actions taken by the performer; and the consequences or feedback which signal to the performer completion of each step (Shoemaker and Short 1973).

Where the procedure being analyzed is essentially linear in its sequence, task analysis has adopted a tabular format for its documentation, with a column for the initiating conditions, a column for actions, and another for the feedback signaling completion. Where the procedure being analyzed contains branching points at which the next step differs depending on feedback, a flowchart format renders each decision point and its potential outcomes visible. The two formats conform somewhat to a distinction made by many analysts between tasks which are chains and those which are algorithms. Behavior chains are procedural sequences involving psychomotor manipulations, examples of which include surgical and dental procedures, athletic and artistic procedures, and many assembly tasks in the industrial area. Skilled coordinated motor performance is an important part of what must be learned (Tiemann and Markle 1978). Algorithms, on the other hand, are primarily cognitive operations involving information gathering and decision making, examples of which include diagnostic and trouble-shooting procedures in medicine and engineering, many mathematical and scientific calculations, and preparing one's income tax (Lewis and Horabin 1977).

2. Analysis and Design Relationships

The necessity for detailed analysis of actual performance before effective instruction can be designed has wide support. The gap between knowledge about and skill in some practical endeavor is a double-edged one. On the one hand, master performers of tasks may be unable to verbalize exactly the skillful aspects of their performance, that is, why they do what they do or especially what cues from the environment control their procedures. On the other hand, much of the verbalization that constitutes many training courses has had little relevance to performance of the task, so the trainee has been left to learn through experience on the job after the training. Complaints are frequent in the practical world about graduates with high levels of theoretical understanding and low levels of skill. There is however considerable evidence (Fitts 1962) that "intellectualization"—or verbalizing the cognitive components of complex skills—facilitates acquisition initially, although master performers may carry out the procedures with little or no conscious awareness of their decision processes. Analysis seeks to locate the communicable components of the skills in such a way that relevant verbalizations can be used to foreshorten training time and reduce the necessity for learning on the job.

That the investment of time and effort in task analysis can result in significant savings to industrial companies has been dramatically demonstrated in cost studies. In one course development project, the task analysis budget was about half of the US$400,000 cost. Training time was reduced from 45 to 9 days which saved the company over two million dollars a year, not by adopting more efficient training techniques but by making the training more relevant. "The old course taught one thing; the new course taught something else. This change in objectives was made possible by the task analysis. Therefore it is reasonable to attribute the largest part of the savings in training cost directly to the task analysis itself" (Short 1973 p. 65).

3. Learning Procedural Tasks

Instructional designers working from an analysis must deal with several components of the task. Anyone performing a procedure must remember the required order of steps. What to do next can be demonstrated by a live instructor or mediated by film, videotape, or a series of pictures or diagrams. In any step where skilled motor coordination must be acquired, sufficient practice must be provided with appropriate coaching feedback to the learner. And, most important and most frequently overlooked in demonstrations by master performers, instruction must call attention to the cues or signals coming out of the task which indicate a successful outcome for each step. For example, a skilled chef recognizes when cream has been whipped to the right consistency, a skilled dentist recognizes when all decayed material has been drilled from a tooth, or a skilled tennis player recognizes when the trajectory of the ball is right for a perfect serve. With appropriate simulation devices, such as might be found in driver education classes or many military training establishments, motor practice can be arranged without danger to the trainee. With appropriate visual aids, practice in discriminating the range of cues which arise from the task can be provided for those difficult discriminations or complex branching points without requiring the trainee to complete the whole task an interminable number of times in order to gain the broad experience required for mastery.

Trends in the design of recent self-instructional packages show an increased use of simple imperative prose and incisive visuals which reduce words to a minimum, a design feature attributable to the influence of Gilbert, Harless, Rummler, and other instructional designers in industry (Markle 1978). Recent emphasis on document simplification and graphic layout in the dissemination of information in government and legal documents (McDonald-Ross 1978) parallels this trend in instructional design. There is also an increasing trend toward the use of job aids, documents which enable a person to complete a complex sequence of steps without the necessity to commit the procedure to memory. (A cookbook is a classic job aid.) The training requirements are then reduced to instruction on the use of the job aid and key discriminations and motor responses that require more than a verbal instruction for mastery.

4. Multiplicity of Cognitive Tasks Implied by Content

The analysis of content covered in an ordinary academic year's work in a discipline presents challenges. The actual sentences that occur in texts, lectures, and other media do not clearly imply what potential tasks, beyond committing those particular words to memory, could be set for learners. Analysts find that text contains names of concepts in the discipline, statements of general laws and principles of the discipline, and the solutions to historic problems in the discipline arrived at by its scholars. Because mastery of concept classification schemes, of principle applying, and of problem-solving procedures requires time, analysts generally find that the typical course "covers" more material than can be mastered at an intellectual skill level in the time provided. Gagné (1974) argued that, rather than starting from text and determining what skills might be implied, one should start with a specification of the important intellectual skills to be mastered and work backwards to the content that must be included to facilitate these tasks. Such an approach puts verbal information or "knowledge" in a secondary position as an objective, and relegates to that position much of what the expert tends to talk about when covering the topic in a conventional lecture mode. An example illustrating Gagné's recommendations to concentrate upon intellectual skills is the extensive elementary-school curriculum, *Science: A Process Approach* (1968). Its objectives specify mastery of the problem-solving processes that scientists use with a de-emphasis on being able to state the knowledge that scientists have produced. That such a curriculum can be difficult for subject matter experts to generate was made stunningly clear by Lewis (1972) in his review of curriculum development at the Open University.

Subject matter experts create texts, select and assign them to students, and otherwise disseminate the content of instruction in their lectures, seminars, and discussions with students. One of the hallmarks of an expert in any field is a vast verbal repertoire of statable knowledge. It is not surprising that conventional instruction tends to emphasize telling about this knowledge. Many of the explicit objectives of the instruction require learners to state or restate what was told: to state verbatim or in paraphrase, to explain, to discuss, to list, to describe, and so forth. The key issue is the extent to which such observable behavior of learners reflects the complex conceptual schemata of the expert rather than uncomprehending verbal parroting. Recent research in cognitive science suggests that the sheer quantity of information that a learner is able to assimilate and retrieve from memory is strongly related to the elaborateness of the learner's conceptual structure (Calfee 1981, Resnick 1981). Therefore, the ability to verbalize knowledge, as in a lengthy essay test, may perhaps be an indicator of a significant level of comprehension and, thus, a valued outcome of instruction.

In a real sense, the range of possible outcomes suggested by the content of instruction confronts task analysts and, subsequently, instructional designers with the necessity for making judgments, usually in the absence of any tangible "job" to observe. For instance, in a music appreciation course, the term "sonata form" may be mentioned. As one possible outcome, learners may merely recognize (or state) that there is such a form in musical compositions; at a slightly higher level of complexity they may state the general design of a composition in sonata form. Still operating at a memory level, they may be able to state that certain compositions studied in the course exemplify the form, an objective that would pose different conditions on memory if the association is to be made when listening to the music itself or merely with the name of the composition or composer. Far more difficult would be an ability to identify the composition form in works not studied in the course, an objective at the conceptual level. This would not only involve prerequisite listening skills, which some learners may lack, but might also call into question the adequacy of standard definitions used by the subject matter experts.

As Gagné noted in his 1965 *Conditions of Learning*, such widely differing outcomes require widely differing instructional designs to bring about mastery. Higher cognitive outcomes require deeper levels of analysis of the tasks to be learned and require instructional designs which differ from those used in courses governed by content coverage. In his provocative series of papers on course development at the Open University, Lewis quipped: "It is no accident that programmed texts are usually *introductory* texts" (Lewis 1973 p. 196). Whether programmed in small steps or in larger chunks, designs aimed at memory objectives are simpler and more familiar to conventional instructors.

5. Committing Knowledge to Memory

Within any discipline there are a large number of facts to be committed to memory, including its vocabulary, symbol systems, dates, names, historical trends, and such. Whether the content is multiplication tables, Newton's Laws, the names and artists associated with important works of art or symphonic repertory, soliloquies from Shakespeare, or important dates and figures in history, association learning is a part of school learning. The design principles drawn from older studies by psychologists appear to remain valid (Fleming and Levie 1978) and can be seen in recent mediated instruction such as drill-and-practice routines in computer-assisted instruction. Principles such as active anticipatory responding, feedback, spaced practice, and drill to overlearning can be adapted by computers to individual acquisition rates but still resemble older flash card drills. In practical applications, efficiency of the instruction to be designed can be fostered by analysis of how the information is used on the job. Symbol systems can be both received as input and produced as output, with some tasks requiring activity (and therefore instruction) in only one direction. For example, Forest Service personnel must interpret terrain maps to carry out their duties in fighting fires, but the job does not require them to master map-making skills. To train in map-producing skills would increase training time unnecessarily. Similarly, a few courses have been designed in academic settings to train young scholars to read their discipline's literature in a foreign language without concurrent training in writing the language, a considerable saving in instructional time.

Where sets of items to be learned may be easily confused with each other, analysis of such multiple discrimination tasks (Tiemann and Markle 1978) can facilitate acquisition of the required discriminations. A set, such as any alphabet, is constructed of a few features, such as straight and curved lines in various configurations. Patterns in which highly similar components combine with only subtle differences will cause difficulty for learners. An analysis which identifies sets of easily confusible items enables a designer to group items for easy processing of the key differences. Sophisticated learners who have mastered many other symbol systems can be confronted with these difficult discriminations early in training, while unsophisticated learners must be gradually led to see the fine distinctions.

The model for memorizing that dominates present cognitive research in learning from prose provides limited assistance to instructional designers (Calfee 1981, Resnick 1981). There is a consensus on two points: the relatively small amount of information that the human processor can handle at one time in immediate memory and the necessity for rehearsal or active processing of information which is to be stored in long-term memory. A considerable body of research under the rubric "mathemagenics," a term coined by Rothkopf, has resulted in several useful principles for instructional designers working on comprehension and retention objectives (Rothkopf 1976). The insertion of occasional questions after, but relatively close to, the point at which to-be-retained information occurs in the prose passage facilitates retention. Research also suggests that higher level questions directed at principle applying and inferences will facilitate retention not only of the main ideas of a text but also of supporting details. Models of memory show that information in long-term memory is organized in networks and hierarchies, but how this organization is effected is not clear. Many of the texts developed for courses at the Open University exemplify mathemagenic practice, with occasional questions inserted into the text and with conceptual networks purportedly showing relations between terms being provided to students at the front of the book. As Lewis noted (1972), the questioning techniques parallel mathemagenic studies in that the text was prepared first and the questions added on the basis of the content

covered in the text, a procedure that contrasts with the order suggested by Gagné, as noted above. Mathemagenic principles are consonant with the underlying premise of early programmed instruction requiring continuous active responding from learners, although the recent materials have typically been sizable chunks of prose rather than the "small-step" chunks of the early heavily criticized programmed materials (Landa 1974, Markle 1978).

6. *Mastering Conceptual Schemes*

When objectives specify higher cognitive outcomes, such as mastery of concepts, principles, and problem-solving strategies, task analysts need techniques for generating a multiplicity of cases in a broad domain. In parallel with the observational technique of analyzing the step-by-step performance of master performers of complex procedures, analysis of the key conceptual structures in a discipline also involves probing the knowledge of its master performers, its subject matter experts. Formats such as those for concept analysis and for decision flowcharting guide the analyst's search. In spite of the mass of verbalization that accompanies most classroom instruction, task analysts frequently find unverbalized decision points in conceptual schemes and in problem-solving domains. These are points at which subject matter experts could show learners what the next step would be but, not unlike the master performers of procedural tasks mentioned before, could not verbalize the basis on which they know (Landa 1974, Tiemann and Markle 1978). Verbal knowledge and intellectual skill may be completely independent of each other, as exemplified by the heuristic skill of expert medical practitioners and electronic trouble shooters. A good analysis document resulting from such a probe of the subject matter expert's knowledge results in a prescription for the wide range of situations that learners must confront during acquisition of the concept or strategy.

The heuristic for concept analysis developed by Tiemann and Markle parallels a strategy for concept discovery described some years earlier (Bruner et al. 1956). The analyst concentrates on a central example of the class, changing a value of one of its attributes and observing whether such a change results in a different example or in a nonexample of the class. Where the change results in a different example, the attribute which has been changed is one of the variables which can be manipulated to generate a wide range of examples of the concept. Where the change results in a nonexample, the original value of the attribute is critical to class membership, and the nonexample generated by the change of that value is one that is easily confused with members of the class. In some disciplines, existing definitions may suggest an adequate set of critical attributes from which to generate nonexamples; in others, such as grammar (Landa 1974), the conventional definitions bear little relationship to the actual attributes subject matter experts use to classify cases. Few definitions in any discipline mention key variable attributes which enable analysts to generate a broad range of examples for teaching and testing. The result of a thorough analysis is a document which will enable a designer to prescribe a full range of needed examples and nonexamples both for teaching and testing (Tiemann and Markle 1978).

The primary purpose of conceptual instructional designs should be to give learners practice in classifying. During such practice, questions such as "Why is this a case of Class X?" may be used to prompt attention to attributes. In the absence of practice to determine whether a case is or is not a member of the class, such questions can only serve the function of memory drill, the goal of which is recall of a definition. The simplest level of overt classification is often naming ("That's a sonnet"). Where sets of concepts belong together, sorting cases into coordinate sets is appropriate. In other situations, applying appropriate rules to differing cases would show correct classification, as would be true in a translation exercise in a foreign language in which a set of rules are being practiced. Practice exercises on a single rule would not qualify, since learners would not have to determine whether the case was appropriate for the rule. For this reason many application exercises at the ends of typical textbook chapters do not practice the key discrimination, when to use the rule, a design deficiency that leads to student inability to solve wide-ranging problems on many rules on a final examination. Landa (1974) described cases in both geometry and language instruction in which learners could verbalize the theorems or state the indicative features (critical attributes) but could not apply the appropriate rules to solve problems. He found the skill deficit lay in the classifying skill itself, which led him to construct a lesson in how to determine whether a given case contained all the specified indicative features. The ability to recall a definition from memory is one outcome. Once remembered, the ability to apply that definition to classify cases correctly is a different outcome, requiring a different instructional design. If the latter skill is missing, the memorized definition is of scant use to the student who is required to solve problems.

These heuristic guidelines for conceptual designs have been available for a decade and have been subjected to much research (Klausmeier et al. 1974). Most of the studies have used a single concept from a well-defined discipline, with a few recent additions involving coordinate sets of concepts. The literature of instructional design still contains principles suggesting that instruction must proceed from the concrete to the abstract (Fleming and Levie 1978), but there is little evidence to determine whether subordinate concepts should be taught before the more general ones. Broad generic concepts (such as "animal") have equally as concrete instantiations as the narrower specific concepts (such as "ungulate"). Nor is there much evidence at present on how a designer should cope with "fuzzy" concepts

where experts within the same discipline cannot reach consensus on classification.

7. Acquiring Problem-solving Strategies

In the area of problem-solving, research and practical development efforts appear to be converging. In their 1969 review of instructional psychology, Gagné and Rohwer complained that cognitive research studies set tasks for the learner which "appear to cover a range from the merely peculiar to the downright esoteric" (p. 381). Resnick's (1981) review of instructional psychology included a heavy loading of research in reading, mathematics, science, and problem solving in academic subjects. Glaser's 1982 volume included several intensive analyses of generic problems of nonesoteric sorts, with definite instructional applications. In 1983, Gagné and Dick summarized several instructional design theories which derive prescriptions for teaching higher cognitive skills from such recent descriptive literature on cognitive strategies. Many recent publications in the field are task analyses of problem-solving heuristics bearing a strong resemblance in method and level of detail to the practical analyses of procedural tasks in industry. In the tradition of Piagetians, Landa (1974), Pask (1976), and others on the Continent, some American cognitive psychologists have begun to observe individual problem solvers at work, probing their thought processes as the thinkers search for appropriate strategies. Larkin and Reif in physics and Resnick and her colleagues in mathematics have compared the thinking strategies of experts with those of novices in the discipline. It is not always the case that the heuristics used by experts provide the best strategy for a novice to learn (Resnick 1981).

Prodded by data indicating severe deficiencies in formal thinking skills (the impetus came from a Piagetian orientation), some American science instructors have made major revisions of their course procedures to emphasize development of such skills along with subject matter knowledge (Renner et al. 1976). Others have developed special courses in thinking skills as prerequisites for courses in the disciplines (Lochhead and Clement 1979), using training problems that are "content free" (i.e., not requiring specific knowledge from the target scientific discipline). References to one or the other of these two approaches can be found worldwide as projects aimed at intellectual skill development proliferate at all levels from preschool to college. The development of logical thinking skills without intervention, as hypothesized by some developmental psychologists (Inhelder and Piaget 1958), does not seem to be inevitable.

Efforts to develop skill in generalizable thinking strategies confront a basic problem: will a student trained in a content-free situation or in a single-discipline situation apply the skill in a new discipline? Greeno (1978) surveyed the conflicting results in the literature on problem solving and hypothesized that the frequent failure to find transfer of training from one set of problems to a different set stemmed from a failure to recognize the existence of several categories of discrete thinking skills. Greeno suggested that there are at least three "pure" skills: inducing structure (rule finding, as required in solving analogy problems), transformation (means–ends analysis, as required in proving geometry theorems), and arrangement (as required in solving jigsaw puzzles). It is probable that few significant problems in any discipline represent one "pure" type as exemplified by the esoteric tasks of the psychological laboratory.

Analysis of problem-solving procedures in a discipline serves to indicate not only the steps to solution but also the prerequisite knowledge and skills, which provides a rational approach to sequencing instruction in tasks embedded in a curriculum. Skill hierarchies are well-established phenomena (White and Gagné 1974) validated in research studies as well as practice. While some of the analytical and empirical findings identify obvious dependencies (such as the prerequisite mastery of subtraction in order to perform long division), others have unearthed less obvious relations between skills. A previously mentioned illustration is the skill in using a memorized definition to classify cases for rule-applying activities described by Landa. Such intellectual skills are seldom the expressed intent of instruction in standard academic courses; rather, it is assumed that students will master them during their "intellectual development" without deliberate teaching. That some students have not is becoming apparent to many instructors.

One of the prime tasks of an instructional designer is to provide a logical order of learner activities. Skill hierarchies predetermine the plausible sequence with a rigidity that is not true of the conceptual structures which organize knowledge in a discipline (Reti 1978). There appear to be many paths to deep understanding, including choices that learners may make for themselves (Pask 1976). On the other hand, the sequence through which intellectual skill develops appears to have a linearity of a sort paralleling the developmental trends postulated by psychologists interested in intellectual growth. These skills are among the most important outcomes of education, justifying the sizeable efforts directed to their achievement.

Bibliography

Bruner J S, Goodnow J J, Austin G A 1956 *A Study of Thinking*. Wiley, New York

Calfee R 1981 Cognitive psychology and educational practice. *Rev. Res. Educ.* 9: 3–73

Fitts P M 1962 Factors in complex skill training. In: Glaser R (ed.) 1962 *Training Research and Education*. University of Pittsburgh Press, Pittsburgh, Pennsylvania, pp. 177–98

Fleming M, Levie W H 1978 *Instructional Message Design: Principles from the Behavioral Sciences*. Educational Technology, Englewood Cliffs, New Jersey

Gagné R M 1965 *The Conditions of Learning*. Holt, Rinehart and Winston, New York

Gagné R M 1974 Task analysis: Its relation to content analysis. *Educ. Psychol* 11: 11–18

Gagné R M, Dick W 1983 Instructional psychology. *Annu. Rev. Psychol.* 34: 261–95

Gagné 1969 Instructional psychology. *Annu. Rev. Psychol.* 20: 381–418

Glaser R (ed.) 1982 *Advances in Instructional Psychology*, Vol. 2. Erlbaum, Hillsdale, New Jersey

Greeno J G 1978 Natures of problem-solving abilities. In: Estes W K(ed.) 1978 *Handbook of Learning and Cognitive Processes*, Vol. 5. Erlbaum, Hillsdale, New Jersey, pp. 239–70

Inhelder B, Piaget J 1958 *The Growth of Logical Thinking from Childhood to Adolescence: An Essay on the Construction of Formal Operational Structures*. Basic Books, New York

Klausmeier H J, Ghatala E S, Frayer D A 1974 *Conceptual Learning and Development: A Cognitive View*. Academic Press, New York

Landa L N 1974 *Algorithmization in Learning and Instruction*. Educational Technology, Englewood Cliffs, New Jersey

Lewis B N 1972 Course production at the Open University. IV: The problem of assessment. *Br. J. Educ. Technol.* 3: 108–28

Lewis B N 1973 Educational technology at the Open University: An approach to the problem of quality. *Br. J. Educ. Technol.* 4: 188–204

Lewis B N, Horabin I S 1977 Algorithmics 1967. *Improving Hum. Perform. Q.* 6: 55–86

Lochhead J, Clement J (eds.) 1979 *Cognitive Process Instruction: Research on Teaching Thinking Skills*. Franklin Institute Press, Philadelphia, Pennsylvania

McDonald-Ross M 1978 Language in texts: The design of curricular materials. *Rev. Res. Educ.* 6: 229–75

Markle S M 1978 *Designs for Instructional Designers*. Stipes, Champaign, Illinois

Miller R B 1962 Analysis and specification of behavior for training. In: Glaser R (ed.) *Training Research and Education*. University of Pittsburgh Press, Pittsburgh, Pennsylvania, pp. 31–62

Pask G 1976 *Conversational Theory: Applications in Education and Epistemology*. Elsevier, New York

Renner J W, Stafford D G, Lawson A E, McKinnon J W, Friot F E, Kellogg D H 1976 *Research, Teaching, and Learning with the Piaget Model*. University of Oklahoma Press, Norman, Oklahoma

Resnick L B 1981 Instructional psychology. *Annu. Rev. Psychol.* 32: 659-704

Reti P G 1978 Integrative structural objectives. *Br. J. Educ. Technol.* 9: 27–35

Rothkopf E Z 1976 Writing to teach and reading to learn: A perspective on the psychology of written instructions. In: Gage N L (ed.) 1976 *The Psychology of Teaching Methods*, 75th Yearb. Natl. Soc. Stud. Educ., Part I. University of Chicago Press, Chicago, Illinois, pp. 91–129

Science: A Process Approach. 1968 American Association for the Advancement of Science, Washington, DC

Shoemaker H A, Short J (eds.) 1973 Task analysis: Special issue. *Improving Hum. Perform. Q.* 2: 1–75

Short J 1973 A case study of task analysis. *Improving Hum. Perform. Q.* 2: 60–67

Tiemann P W, Markle S M 1978 *Analyzing Instructional Content: A Guide to Instruction and Evaluation*. Stipes, Champaign, Illinois

White R T, Gagné R M 1974 Past and future research on learning hierarchies. *Educ. Psychol.* 11: 19–28

Learning from Textbooks

B. B. Armbruster and T. H. Anderson

Procedures for analyzing textbooks have been dominated by the use of readability formulas (Klare 1982). These formulas yield an index which supposedly makes it possible to match the reading demands of a textbook with the reading capabilities of the reader as determined by reading achievement scores. Two of the more well-known readability formulas, Dale and Chall (1948) and Fry (1977) use measures of word difficulty and sentence complexity to determine the appropriate reading level of the text.

In addition to readability formulas, an array of checklist instruments has been advocated as a potentially helpful way of analyzing textbooks. A sample of these checklists (Ball 1976, Jevitz and Meints 1979, Krause 1976) shows that they direct the textbook analyst to potentially important aspects of the textbook that are not necessarily measured by readability formulas. Checklist items direct the reader to consider such aspects of the textbook as the use of visual aids, cultural and sex biases, teacher's manuals or supplements, the quality of workmanship, the quality of materials, the costs, and the quality of writing. One checklist (Jevitz and Meints 1979) has 72 such items. In addition to the sheer magnitude of items to consider, many of them are stated so vaguely that the analyst may find it difficult to make the judgments required by them.

In this article some theoretical ideas and research findings are presented about how students read, understand, and remember ideas that can contribute to the process of analyzing textbooks. These ideas will enable the textbook analyst to set rational priorities on the potentially large set of criteria (such as those referenced above) and also help clear up the vagueness associated with some of the items.

Current theories suggest that learning from textbooks is a function of characteristics of the text itself and cognitive strategies used by the reader during reading.

1. The Text

One factor affecting learning from text is structure. Structure refers to the way ideas are connected together in logical organizational patterns. A few basic rhetorical structures appear to reflect fundamental patterns of human thought: (a) simple listing—a listing of items or ideas where the order of presentation of the item is not significant; (b) conclusion/evidence—a special case of simple listing, consisting of a proposition and a list of reasons serving as evidence for that fact; (c) comparison/contrast—a description of similarities and differences between two or more things; (d) temporal sequence—a sequential relationship between items or events considered in terms of the passage of time; (e) cause–effect—an interaction between at least two ideas or events, one considered a cause or reason and

the other an effect or result; and (f) problem–solution—similar to the cause–effect pattern in that two factors interact, one citing a problem and the other a solution to that problem. These basic structures can be subsumed in higher order structures that underlie particular text genres (e.g., narratives, newspaper articles) and content areas (e.g., biology, history) (Anderson and Armbruster 1984).

The structure of text can be conveyed in many ways: (a) words denoting relationships (because, before, for example, in comparison); (b) explicit statements of the structure; (c) previews or introductory statements, including titles; and (d) summary statements. Information in the text that points out aspects of structure has been called "signaling" (Meyer 1975). Research has shown that better organized text, and text that makes the organization clear to the reader (for example, through the use of signaling), increases the likelihood of the reader's understanding, remembering, and applying information learned from the text (Meyer 1979).

Another characteristic of text that influences learning outcomes is local coherence, also called cohesion by linguists (Halliday and Hasan 1976). Local coherence is achieved by several kinds of simple linguistic links or ties that connect ideas together within and between sentences. Among the most common links are various forms of reference (e.g., pronoun, anaphora, etc.) and conjunctions or connectives (e.g., and, or, but, because, however). Research has established the importance of cohesive ties in understanding and remembering text. For example, repeated references that help to carry meaning across sentence boundaries can decrease reading time and increase recall of text as an integrated unit (deVilliers 1974, Haviland and Clark 1974, Kintsch et al. 1975, Manelis and Yekovich 1976, Miller and Kintsch 1980). Also, children prefer to read, read faster, and have better memory for sentences connected by explicit conjunctions, particularly causal connectives, than sentences in which the conjunction is left to be inferred (Katz and Brent 1968, Marshall and Glock 1978–79, Pearson 1974–75).

Characteristics of the content itself also affect learning from reading. Kintsch and his colleagues have shown that one of these characteristics—idea density—contributes to reading difficulty. For example, Kintsch and Keenan (1973) kept text length constant while varying the number of propositions (ideas) in text. They found that reading time was more a function of the number of propositions than the number of words. Kintsch et al. (1975) showed that reading times were longer and recall less for texts with many different word concepts than for texts with fewer word concepts. In other words, it is easier for readers to process and retain in memory a proposition built from old, familiar elements than to process propositions which introduce new concepts into the text. In sum, the denser the text (the greater the number of new ideas per unit of text), the longer it takes to read and the less the likelihood of remembering it.

Another aspect of content that affects learning outcomes is the proportion of important to unimportant information, or main ideas to details. In a series of experiments by Reder and Anderson (1980), college students who read summaries one-fifth the length of original texts were better able to recognize important facts and learn new, related material than students who read the full version. Reder and Anderson (1980) conclude that text that helps students focus attention and avoid having to time-share between main points and details is an effective way to aid learning.

Another finding from research is that learning and memory are improved when people are given information clarifying the significance of facts that might otherwise seem arbitrary, particularly causal elaborations that establish a causal relationship between ideas (Bransford and Johnson 1973, Bransford et al. 1980). For example, in research on narratives, provision of information about the character's goal and events leading up to the goal has a significant effect on comprehension and memory (Kintsch and van Dijk 1978, Rumelhart 1977, Thorndyke 1977). Presumably, knowledge of the goal and the events leading up to the goal helps readers understand the significance of the character's actions and the consequences of those actions.

In sum, various features of the text itself—structure, local coherence, content—influence learning from reading. Characteristics of the reader, however, probably play an even more crucial role in learning from textbooks. Of particular importance are the cognitive strategies used during reading.

2. Cognitive Strategies

Cognitive strategies are what the students use to get the information from the text page into their heads. These information-processing strategies include not only the initial focusing of attention and the subsequent encoding of the information attended to but also an "executive level" aspect of these processes called metacognition. Metacognition refers to both the awareness and control that readers have over their own thinking and learning (Baker and Brown 1983). Research has demonstrated that several cognitive strategies (including the metacognition component) are associated with learning from text. Some of these strategies are discussed below. (For additional strategies of effective learners, see Baker and Brown 1983).

One beneficial strategy in learning from text is selective attention to, and processing of, the most important information in text as defined by the criterion task (that is, what students must do to demonstrate that learning has occurred; for example, answer questions at the end

of the chapter or take a test). Numerous studies have shown a clear relationship between learning outcomes and readers' knowledge of or expectations about criterion tasks. For example, one line of research has examined the effect on learning of questions inserted periodically in the text. These studies have shown that questions inserted in the text have a striking focusing effect on studying behaviors and learning outcomes. Students tend to spend more time studying the text that is relevant to the types of inserted questions they receive and they tend to perform better on posttest items testing the type of information tapped by the inserted questions they receive (Reynolds et al. 1979). The inserted questions establish expectations about the criterion task, which then guides cognitive processing.

A second strategy associated with effective learning from text is selective attention to, and processing of, the most important information in text as defined by the author's structure. Mature readers, at least, are able to detect the most important information from text and remember it. The ability to do this seems to develop gradually; immature or less competent readers are less likely to identify and process important information than more mature readers (Brown and Smiley 1977, 1978, Meyer et al. 1980). However, an encouraging line of research indicates that less mature students can be taught to identify and use text structure to facilitate learning. For example, Bartlett (1978) taught ninth graders (14-year-olds) to identify and use four common expository text structures as an aid to learning. Likewise, Dansereau (1983) has successfully trained college students to identify and use the inherent structure of text as an aid to learning.

Another strategy that can help students learn from text is to make use of their own prior knowledge to interpret and remember new information. Research has confirmed that what readers know already greatly influences what they learn and remember from text (Anderson et al. 1977, Spilich et al. 1979). One must not only have the relevant knowledge but also activate it at the appropriate time. In other words, readers must be able to "call up" appropriate prior knowledge when it is needed to understand new information. Research indicates that children often fail to spontaneously activate relevant prior knowledge when it could help them in learning from text, but that they can be trained to do so (Bransford et al. 1980, Bransford 1984).

Another important cognitive strategy is to encode information in such a way that it can be remembered. Research shows that some kinds of studying strategies or learning activities are particularly helpful. Studying strategies that involve the identification and manipulation of the author's structure (structuring strategies) appear to be especially helpful in learning, given that students know how to use the strategy. For example, students taught to outline can use outlining as a learning aid (Barton 1930), and students instructed in semantic mapping techniques (diagrammatic representations of text structure) can improve their memory for text (Armbruster and Anderson 1980, Dansereau 1983). Another studying technique that appears to promote processing is causal elaboration. Bransford and his colleagues (Bransford 1979, Bransford et al. 1980) have shown that people remember ideas better if they can establish a meaningful causal relationship between them. That is, in causal elaboration, readers use prior knowledge (information from the text or from their heads) to construct a significant connection between ideas that might otherwise seem unrelated. For example, readers might use prior knowledge of the function of an object to help them understand and remember the object's structure.

Selectively attending to and processing "important" information, engaging prior knowledge, and using high pay-off studying techniques are some of the cognitive strategies that research has shown to facilitate learning from text. Research has also shown that instruction in strategies can have a positive effect on learning outcomes. Research has already been mentioned in which instruction in identifying the author's structure and in using studying strategies has resulted in improved learning. Research has not only shown that instruction can be effective but has also suggested how teachers can best help students learn to learn from reading. The major practical implication from the research is that students should be taught to use cognitive strategies with awareness. That is, students should be informed about why, when, where, and how they should use particular strategies (Brown et al. 1981).

3. Implications for Practice

A prime reason for analyzing textbooks is to enable educators to make wise decisions when selecting textbooks for classroom use. As mentioned in the introduction, two techniques are rather widely used in analysis-for-selection. One is the use of readability formulas to index the general language complexity of the textbook prose. The other is checklist instruments which direct the analyst to various aspects of textbooks that are not indexed by the readability formulas. Both of these techniques can be helpful in deciding which textbooks are generally appropriate for classroom use.

In addition to these techniques, some questions are proposed that respond to the interpretation of what recent research on reading has to suggest about textbook evaluation. Answering these questions should add important information to the textbook selection decision. The first series of questions relate to the text:

(a) Does the textbook make a systematic effort to help the reader connect new ideas with ideas already learned? Does the author include well-written introductions, summaries to chapters, and questions that encourage students to use relevant prior knowledge?

(b) Are the texts coherent at a global level? Are they well-structured and is that structure readily apparent to the reader as evidenced by chapter titles, headings, outlines, introductions, conclusions, and topic sentences?

(c) Are the texts coherent at a local level? Do pronouns have clear referents and are the relationships between ideas explicit or obvious?

(d) Do the texts work toward some important purpose at an appropriate rate by introducing new, main ideas when they are needed? Are the intervening ideas between main ones the type that extend, elaborate, and make explicit the relationship between the main ones, or do the intervening ones simply introduce irrelevant detail?

The following questions concern student exercises.

(a) Do the student exercises at the end of chapters and in workbooks help students learn to locate and process important information from the text? If the students were to learn well the answers to questions at the end of the chapters, would they have an important body of knowledge to help them read and understand the next chapter, or next year's textbook?

(b) Do the student exercises at the end of chapters and in workbooks help students learn a variety of studying techniques? Are the when's, where's, how's, and why's of the studying techniques explained?

The final questions concern the teacher's materials.

(a) Do the teacher's manuals which accompany some textbooks explain to teachers the when's, where's, how's, and why's to teach students about some of the difficult studying aspects, such as text structure and what-to-do-when-something-is-not-well-understood?

(b) Do the teacher's manuals which accompany some textbooks explain to teachers the when's, where's, how's and why's students should be taught to become aware of and monitor their own cognitive processes while studying?

Bibliography

Anderson R C, Reynolds R E, Schallert D L, Goetz E T 1977 Frameworks for comprehending discourse. *Am. Educ. Res. J.* 14: 367–82

Anderson T H, Armbruster B B 1984 Content area textbooks. In: Anderson R C, Osborn J, Tierney R J (eds.) 1984 *Learning to Read in American Schools: Basal Readers and Content Texts.* Erlbaum, Hillsdale, New Jersey

Armbruster B B, Anderson T H 1980 *The Effect of Mapping on the Free Recall of Expository Text.* (Tech. Rep. No. 160). Center for the Study of Reading, University of Illinois, Urbana, Illinois

Baker L, Brown A L 1983 Cognitive monitoring in reading. In: Flood J (ed.) 1983 *Understanding Reading Comprehension.* International Reading Association, Newark, Delaware

Ball H G 1976 Standards for material selection. *J. Read.* 20: 208–11

Bartlett B J 1978 Top-level structure as an organizational strategy for recall of classroom text. Unpublished doctoral dissertation, Arizona State University

Barton W A 1930 *Outlining as a Study Procedure.* Teachers College, Columbia University, New York

Bransford J D 1979 *Human Cognition: Learning, Understanding, and Remembering.* Wadsworth Belmont, California

Bransford J D 1984 Schema activation and schema acquisition: Comments on Richard C. Anderson's remarks. In: Anderson R C, Osborn J, Tierney R J (eds.) 1983 *Learning to Read in American Schools: Basal Readers and Content Texts.* Erlbaum, Hillsdale, New Jersey

Bransford J D, Johnson M K 1973 Considerations of some problems of comprehension. In: Chase W (ed.) 1973 *Visual Information Processing.* 8th Symposium on Cognition, Carnegie-Mellon University, 1972. Academic Press, New York

Bransford J D, Stein B S, Shelton T S, Owings R 1980 Cognition and adaptation: The importance of learning to learn. In: Harvey J L (ed.) 1980 *Cognition, Social Behavior, and the Environment.* Erlbaum, Hillsdale, New Jersey

Brown A L, Smiley S S 1977 Rating the importance of structural units of prose passages: A problem of metacognitive development. *Child Dev.* 48: 1–8

Brown A L, Smiley S S 1978 The development of strategies for studying texts. *Child Dev.* 49: 1076–88

Brown A L, Campione J C, Day J D 1981 Learning to learn: On training students to learn from texts. *Educ. Res. AERA.* 10: 14–21

Dale E, Chall J S 1948 A formula for predicting readability. *Educ. Res. Bull.* 27: 11–20, 37–54

Dansereau D F 1983 Learning strategy research. In: Segal J, Chipman S, Glaser R (eds.) 1983 *Thinking and Learning Skills: Relating Instruction to Basic Research*, Vol. 1. Erlbaum, Hillsdale, New Jersey

de Villiers P A 1974 Imagery and theme in recall of connected discourse. *J. Exp. Psychol.* 103: 263–68

Fry E B 1977 Fry's readability graph: Clarification, validity, and extension to level 17. *J. Read.* 21: 242–52

Halliday M A K, Hasan R 1976 *Cohesion in English.* Longman, London

Haviland S E, Clark H H 1974 What's new? Acquiring new information as a process in comprehension. *J. Verb. Learn. Verb. Behav.* 13: 512–21

Jevitz L, Meints D W 1979 Be a better book buyer: Guidelines for textbook evaluation. *J. Read.* 22: 734–38

Katz E, Brent S 1968 Understanding connections. *J. Verb. Learn. Verb. Behav.* 1: 501–509

Kintsch W, Keenan J M 1973 Reading rate as a function of the number of propositions in the base structure of sentences. *Cognit. Psychol.* 5: 257–74

Kintsch W, van Dijk T 1978 Toward a model of text comprehension and production. *Psychol. Rev.* 85: 363–94

Kintsch W, Kozminsky E, Streby W J, McKoon G, Keenan J M 1975 Comprehension and recall of text as a function of content variables. *J. Verb. Learn. Verb. Behav.* 14: 196–214

Klare G R 1982 Readability. In: Pearson P D (ed.) 1982 *Handbook of Reading Research* Longman, New York

Krause K C 1976 Do's and don'ts in evaluating textbooks. *J. Read.* 20: 212–14

Manelis L, Yekovich F R 1976 Repetitions of propositional arguments in sentences. *J. Verb. Learn. Verb. Behav.* 15: 301–12

Marshall N, Glock M D 1978–79 Comprehension of connected discourse: A study into the relationship between the structure of text and information recalled. *Read. Res. Q.* 16: 10–56

Meyer B J F 1975 *The Organization of Prose and its Effects on Memory.* North Holland, Amsterdam

Meyer B J F 1979 Organizational patterns in prose and their use in reading. In: Kamil M L, Moe A J (eds.) 1979 *Reading Research: Studies and Applications.* 28th Yearbook of the National Reading Conference

Meyer B J F, Brandt D M, Bluth G J 1980 Use of top-level structure in text: Key for reading comprehension of ninth-grade students. *Read. Res. Q.* 16: 72–103

Miller J R, Kintsch W 1980 Readability and recall of short prose passages: A theoretical analysis. *J. Exp. Psychol: Human Learning and Memory* 6: 335–54

Pearson P D 1974–75 The effects of grammatical complexity on children's comprehension, recall, and conception of certain semantic relations. *Read. Res. Q.* 10: 155–92

Reder L M, Anderson J R 1980 A comparison of texts and their summaries: Memorial consequences. *J. Verb. Learn. Verb. Behav.* 19: 121–34

Rumelhart D E 1977 Understanding and summarizing brief stories. In: LaBerge D, Samuels J (eds.) 1977 *Basic Processes in Reading: Perception and Comprehension.* Erlbaum, Hillsdale, New Jersey

Spilich G J, Vesonder G T, Chiesi H L, Voss J F 1979 Text processing of domain-related information for individuals with high and low domain knowledge. *J. Verb. Learn. and Verb. Behav.* 18: 275–90

Thorndyke P W 1977 Cognitive structures in comprehension and memory of narrative discourse. *Cognit. Psychol.* 9: 77–110

Typographic Design

J. Hartley

This article is about the typographical design and layout of instructional materials, be they textbooks, manuals, handouts or worksheets. The article is relevant to both conventional and desk-top publishing, and five issues are briefly discussed. These are: (a) the choice of page size; (b) the spatial arrangement of the text on that page size; (c) the use of typographic cues to accentuate aspects of the text; (d) the use of "access structures" to help readers find their way around the text; and (e) the use of textual devices to help students learn how to learn. The purpose of this discussion is to remind readers and authors about the choices available to them, and about the possible consequences of making particular choices. More detailed treatments of the issues and additional illustrations can be found elsewhere (Hartley 1985a, Jonassen 1982, 1985, Miles 1987). Readers interested in the applications of this work to electronic text will find discussions in Galitz 1981, Hartley 1985a, 1987a Jonassen 1985 and Kerr 1985.

1. Choice of Page Size

Most people expect a review of typographic design to begin by considering issues such as typesizes, typefaces, and line-lengths. However, it is important to realize that the choice for each of these variables is already constrained by an earlier one—that of deciding on what size page to print the text. Clearly one does not expect to find large typesizes in a pocket dictionary, or single columns of print in a daily newspaper. These examples are extreme, but they illustrate a point. Text is printed on a page size which is appropriate to its use, and page size constrains what can be done.

The choice of appropriate page size is not always easy. Often large sizes are preferred because of the need to present detailed illustrations and tabular materials. But factors such as cost, preferences, ease of use, and what page sizes are available all have to be taken into account. In Europe choosing a page size is made somewhat easier because there is a set of standard page sizes—those recommended by the International Organization for Standards (see Hartley 1985a).

This first decision is crucial because it forms the baseline from which the remaining decisions are made. Once the decision on page size has been made then it is possible to choose the layout for that page, the width of the columns, the typefaces and typesizes to be used, and the interline spacing. Following these decisions come related ones about the positioning of illustrations, running headlines, page numbers, and so on.

2. The Spatial Arrangement of the Text

Unlike the prose of a novel—or even much of this Encyclopedia—instructional text often contains a wide variety of components. For example, there may be headings and subheadings, hierarchically developed and numbered arguments, lists of information, diagrams, tables, illustrations, captions, footnotes, appendices, and so on. Furthermore, much of this material will not be read continuously. A learner's focus of attention often ranges from a place on the page to somewhere else—to the teacher, to the task in hand, to other learners, and back again to the place on the page. The spatial arrangement of the text must support this situation by providing a consistent frame of reference from which the learner can move to and fro without confusion.

Yet if one inspects many textbooks it is hard not to come to the conclusion that these are often composed page by page during production—on a sort of "let's put this here" basis. Such a procedure produces inconsistency from page to page, particularly in terms of the spacing of the different components. The argument of this article is that if the instructional materials are to provide a consistent frame of reference for the reader,

then the layout of the text must be planned in advance of production.

One helpful device for planning the layout of the text is the typographic reference grid. Such a grid is a matrix of coordinates which "maps" the information area of the page horizontally in units of the typesize chosen and vertically in units of linefeed—or interline space (Hartley 1985a, Miles 1987). The amount of space to leave between the components in the text is determined in advance and this spacing is then adhered to throughout the text. Typographic grids are becoming more common in textbook production and, although subject to some debate, the more complex the text the more useful they seem to be. Indeed, some publishers of mathematical texts insist that authors type their copy on preprepared grids.

2.1 Horizontal Spacing

The legibility of a line is a function of, amongst other things, the typeface and typesize chosen, the amount of interline space between it and the next line, and its length. In printed text there may be one, two, three, or more columns of varying widths according to the page size chosen, the content of the text, and the use to which it will be put. Thus, any book which suggests optimal line lengths and typesizes without considering factors such as these can only provide helpful suggestions which might have to be reconsidered in specific contexts. Indeed, Tinker's (1965) "rules", which would suggest that a two-column structure is preferable to a single-column on an A4 (210 × 297 mm) page, do not apply in all situations. Research by Burnhill and his colleagues (Hartley 1985a p. 148) showed that such rules did not apply when the text contained large tabular inserts which cut across the columns. In this study 12 to 13-year-old schoolchildren had greater difficulty in retrieving information from the text when it was set in a two-column structure than they did from the same text set in a single-column one above and below tables on an A4 page.

One issue of particular interest when discussing line lengths is how to decide where to end a line within a given column width. In traditional printing (as in this Encyclopedia) the columns of text have straight left and right-hand edges. Technically this is called justified composition [see Fig. 1(a)]. If readers inspect the text of this Encyclopedia carefully they will see that justification is achieved by varying the spaces between the words and sometimes by using hyphenation. Indeed, sometimes the spaces between the letters forming the words are also varied in order to make the text fit a given length of line.

A different approach to setting text is to provide a consistent space between each word. Such a procedure results in unjustified composition, and the text has a ragged right-hand edge [see Fig. 1(b)]. Typescript provides a common example. Experiments have shown that there is little to choose between justified and unjustified

---

(a) *Justified text*

Now the sons of Jacob were twelve. The sons of Leah; Reuben, Jacob's firstborn, and Simeon, and Levi, and Judah, and Issachar, and Zebulun. The sons of Rachel; Joseph, and Benjamin: And the sons of Bilhah, Rachel's handmaid; Dan, and Naphtali. And the sons of Zilpah, Leah's handmaid; Gad, and Asher. These are the sons of Jacob, which were born to him in Padan-Aram.

(b) *Unjustified text*

Now the sons of Jacob were twelve. The sons of Leah; Reuben, Jacob's firstborn, and Simeon, and Levi, and Judah, and Issachar, and Zebulun. The sons of Rachel; Joseph, and Benjamin: And the sons of Bilhah, Rachel's handmaid; Dan, and Naphtali. And the sons of Zilpah, Leah's handmaid; Gad, and Asher. These are the sons of Jacob, which were born to him in Padan-Aram.

(c) *Unjustified text with the beginnings and endings of lines determined by syntactic considerations*

Now the sons of Jacob were twelve:
The sons of Leah;
   Reuben, Jacob's firstborn,
   and Simeon, and Levi, and Judah,
   and Issachar, and Zebulun:
The sons of Rachel;
   Joseph, and Benjamin:
And the sons of Bilhah, Rachel's handmaid;
   Dan, and Naphtali:
And the sons of Zilpah, Leah's handmaid;
   Gad, and Asher:
These are the sons of Jacob, which were born to him in Padan-Aram.

Figure 1
Different ways of setting text. The figure is based upon the *Washburn College Bible* and is reproduced with the permission of the President of Washburn College, Topeka, Kansas.

printed text in terms of legibility, reading speed or comprehension (Hartley 1987a), although there is some indication that unjustified text is helpful for less-able readers (be they young children or older adults).

A further advantage of unjustified composition is that it is more flexible than justified composition: one does not have to fill up each line with text. With unjustified text, for example, it is possible to specify that no line should end with the first word of a sentence, or that if the next to the last word of a line is followed by a punctuation mark then this last word can be carried over to the next line [see Fig. 1(c)]. Other rules about syntactic breaks can be developed and such rules are currently

being built into computer-assisted printing methods (Keenan 1984).

2.2 *Vertical Spacing*

The vertical units in a typographic grid are measured in units of linefeed or interline space, and by using a grid for the spacing above and below all the separate components in a text can be worked out in advance. Thus, for example, one might use two units of linefeed above a heading and one below it. Similarly, one might have two units of linefeed above a figure, one above its caption and two below it. Planning the vertical spacing in this way ensures that space is used consistently to group and relate separate parts of the text throughout the text. Too often in traditional text this is not done: the space between the components is arbitrarily changed in order to make the text fit a fixed depth on every page.

Research on vertical spacing provides a parallel with that on horizontal spacing. Work with adults reading a complex text has shown that they prefer new sentences to start on new lines within paragraphs separated by a line space rather than have the text run on in the usual manner (see Fig. 2). In addition, line spacing between paragraphs has been shown to aid retrieval from text compared with other methods of denoting paragraphs.

Consistent spacing between the vertical components requires a variable or "floating" baseline for every page. That is to say, instead of filling up the page to a fixed amount (as in this article) the stopping point on each column varies according to the groupings in the text. The argument here is parallel to that put forward for unjustified text. For example, it would seem better to stop rather than to finish a page with a heading or the first line of a new paragraph. Similarly, it would seem better to carry on and complete a paragraph rather than let the last few words be carried over to form the first few words of the next page. Thus, with consistent vertical spacing the depth of the text will vary slightly on different pages. Hartley 1987a describes research on horizontal and vertical settings of instructional text and work is proceeding with the development of computer-based layouts for the presentation of complex text (Sylla, et al. 1988).

3. *Typographic Cueing*

The first two sections of this article have concentrated on spacing and layout. There are, of course, additional devices that writers, designers, and printers can use to draw the reader's attention to specific points or important issues in the text. Such devices are generally known as "typographic cues". Typical examples of such cues are: underlining (especially in typescript); italics; bold typefaces; capital letters; and colour.

Hartley et al. (1980) reviewed over 40 studies on underlining and came to the conclusion that underlining did no harm, that it was sometimes useful, but that the conditions in which it was useful were not well-known.

(a) *Original setting*

All insulating gloves are made in the gauntlet style. There are four sizes: 9½, 10, 11, and 12. The size indicates the approximate number of inches around the glove across the palm. Each glove is about 14 inches long from the bottom of the gauntlet to the top of the second finger.

There are various kinds of insulating gloves. The first kind were originally just called Insulating Gloves. After that the B, C, D and E Insulating Gloves were developed. As described below, the D Glove replaced the original Insulating Gloves and the E Glove replaced the B and C Gloves.

(b) *Revised setting*

All insulating gloves are made
in the gauntlet style.
There are four sizes: 9½, 10, 11, 12.
The size indicates the approximate number
of inches around the glove across the palm.
Each glove is about 14 inches long
from the bottom of the gauntlet to the top
of the second finger.

There are various kinds of insulating gloves.
The first kind were originally just called
Insulating Gloves.
After that the B, C, D and E Insulating Gloves
were developed.
As described below, the D Glove replaced the
original Insulating Gloves, and the E Glove
replaced the B and C Gloves.

Figure 2

Typographic design of paragraphs. Readers generally prefer (b) to (a). Here new sentences start on new lines within paragraphs, and paragraphs are separated by a line-space. (Figures based on text supplied by Bell Telephone Laboratories, and reproduced with permission.)

In particular, and this seems true of all work on typographic cuing, cues can only work if the readers know what they signify. Furthermore, children have to learn to use the typographic cues that adults take for granted (Brown and Campione 1981).

There has been little research with italics or capital letters. Possibly this is because of the effectiveness of early studies in showing that passages set in italics or capitals were harder to read than passages set conventionally in lower-case letters. However, the effectiveness of these devices as typographic cues has not been adequately tested. One difficulty with such cueing systems in print is that the same cues are often used for different purposes. Bold faces, for example, can be used to indicate that a word will be defined elsewhere in a glossary, or to emphasize an important concept, or to indicate a heading. Similarly, italics can be used to draw attention

to a technical term, to emphasize a point, to indicate a heading, or to signify a book or journal title. It would probably be more helpful to the reader if a single cue were used for a single purpose. Certainly there is evidence that multiple-cueing can cause difficulties (Hartley 1987a).

In printed texts it is conventional for most of the text to be in a single typeface and size, and this is varied occasionally to help emphasize the organization of the text, or a particular point. This contrasts sharply with the output from poorly designed desk-top publishing where people seem to want to make use of the many available options open to them—just because they are there. Such enthusiasm needs restraining, for muddled typography can only convey the impression of muddled thinking.

Colour is used in printed instructional materials for two rather different purposes. Colour can be used functionally to aid instruction or for aesthetic and motivational reasons to make a text attractive. A classic example of the functional use of colour is that provided by the map of the London Underground railway system. Here each colour denotes a different route. It is often suggested that such a functional use of colour is a useful ingredient in line-drawings and illustrations (particularly technical ones). However, difficulties may arise in printed text from using too many colours, an inconsistent use of colour, and with using too few colours (if there are many different functions) (Waller et al. 1982).

4. Access Structures

In addition to typographic cues, authors and designers can use "access structures" to orient readers and to help them find their way around a text. Typical examples of such access structures would be: titles; summaries; headings and subheadings; numbering systems; contents pages; references and bibliographies; and indexes. The typography of these devices is greatly varied in style, and there is little research on the effectiveness of different designs.

It appears from research with printed text that summaries can aid the recall of salient facts, although there is some debate about whether they do this better if they are placed at the beginning or the end of a piece of text (Hartley and Trueman 1982). Some authors, of course, distinguish between and use different kinds of summaries. Thus, overview summaries presented at the beginning of a piece of text may contain a description of what is to follow in general terms, whilst review summaries, placed at the end, may summarize what has gone before using the more technical terminology introduced in the text itself.

Research on the effectiveness of headings suggests that headings can aid the recall of salient facts, and in addition, that they can help readers to find information from the text (Hartley and Trueman 1985). There is some debate over issues such as the frequency of headings, their length, their position (marginal or embedded), and their style (headings written in the form of statements versus headings written in the form of questions).

Numbering systems are often used to help sequencing in text. Headings and sections in technical materials are frequently numbered 1., 1.1, 1.1.1, 1.2, 2., and so on. Some numbering systems designed to aid retrieval can be confusing, especially when there are references in the text to other numbering systems—page numbers, chapter numbers, section numbers, table numbers, figure numbers, different appendices, and so on. Waller's 1977 paper (Hartley 1980) gives an illuminating example.

The research on the setting of contents pages, references, bibliographies, and indexes is characterized by the fact that each of these devices is a "list structure", that is to say, they all consist of a string of main elements, each of which contains a number of subelements. Thus a contents page for a journal will contain a list of authors, titles and page numbers, and a set of references will contain a list of authors, titles, and dates and places of publication. The task of the designer is to display the main elements and each of the subelements clearly, because different people will want to use the list in different ways. The way the designer solves this problem is to use a judicious mixture of spatial and typographic cues, so that the different elements each stand out in some way from each other.

The research in this area, however, indicates that the most important feature in the design of a list structure is its spatial arrangement. Whilst users like the combination of spatial and typographic cues to indicate each element in the structure, when given a choice between a spatial arrangement without typographic cues or a run-on display with typographic cues, users generally prefer the spatially arranged text.

5. Helping Students to Learn

Recent advances in cognitive psychology have posed an interesting problem for educational technology. So far it appears that technological devices can be used successfully to teach already known material, that is, they can pass on known information quite readily. The question being asked now is how far can such technological devices (including print) be used to help learners to develop their skills of learning, discovering and creating new knowledge.

Hartley 1987b reviewed a series of studies that examined the effectiveness of training pupils to use various study strategies thought to enhance their learning skills (for example, underlining, notetaking, creating headings, constructing summary tables, reading with questions in mind, and so on). A discussion then followed on how some of these strategies could be built into instructional text so that readers are obliged to carry them out in order to follow the exposition. Hartley's chapter in Branthwaite and Rogers (Hartley 1985b) illustrates this approach. Here the reader has to carry out brief experiments in order to follow the subsequent text. Readers will find a useful discussion of these issues by Pace (1985) but, unfortunately, there is virtually no research as yet on the typographic designs it is necessary to use to convey these strategies to readers.

Bibliography

Branthwaite A, Rogers D (eds.) 1985 *Children Growing Up.* Open University Press, Milton Keynes

Brown A L, Campione J C 1981 Learning to learn: On training students to learn from text. *Educ. Res.* AERA 10: 14–21

Galitz W O 1981 *Handbook of Screen Format Design.* Q.E.D Information Sciences Inc., Wellesley, Massachusetts

Hartley J 1985a *Designing Instructional Text*, 2nd edn. Kogan Page, London

Hartley J 1985b Developing skills of learning. In: Branthwaite A, Rogers D (eds.) 1985 *Children Growing Up.* Open University Press, Milton Keynes, pp. 112–21

Hartley J 1987a Designing electronic text: The role of print based research. *Educ. Commun. Technol. J.* 35: 3–17

Hartley J 1987b Typography and executive control processes in reading. In: Britton B K, Glynn S M (eds.) 1987 *Executive Control Processes in Reading.* Elbaum, Hillsdale, New Jersey

Hartley J, Bartlett S, Branthwaite J A 1980 Underlining can make a difference - sometimes. *J. Educ. Res.* 73: 218–24

Hartley J, Trueman M 1982 The effects of summaries on the recall of information from prose: Five experimental studies. *Hum. Learn.* 1: 63–82

Jonassen D (ed.) 1982 *The Technology of Text.* Educational Technology Publications, Englewood Cliffs, New Jersey

Jonassen D (ed.) 1985 *The Technology of Text*, Vol. 2. Educational Technology Publications, Englewood Cliffs, New Jersey

Keenan S A 1984 Effects of chunking and line-length on reading efficiency. *Vis. Lang.* 18: 61–80

Kerr S J 1985 Videotex and education: Current developments in screen design, data structure, and access control. *Machine Mediated Learn.* 1: 217–54

Miles J 1987 *Design for Desktop Publishing.* Gordon Fraser, London

Pace 1985 Learning to learn through text design: Can it be done? In: Jonassen D (ed.) 1985 *The Technology of Text*, Vol. 2. Educational Technology Publications, Englewood Cliffs, New Jersey, pp. 46–58

Sylla C, Dury C G, Babu A J G 1988 A human factors design investigation of a computerised layout system of text-graphic technical materials. *Hum. Factors* 30: 347–58

Tinker M A 1965 *Bases for Effective Reading.* University of Minnesota Press, Minneapolis

Waller R H W 1977 Notes on transforming No. 4: Numbering systems in text. In: Hartley J (ed.) 1980 *The Psychology of Written Communication: Selected Readings.* Kogan Page, London

Waller R H W, Lefrere P, MacDonald-Ross M 1982 Do you need that second color? *IEEE Trans. on Prof. Comm.* PC-25(2): 80–85

Perceptual Factors

M. L. Fleming

This is a highly selective summary of the findings from perception research, particularly vision research, which appear directly relevant to the design of instruction, whether by teachers or instructional developers. Also included are suggested ways of applying the perception findings. What follows is divided into two main sections: perceptual development and mature perception. (General references for what follows are Fleming and Levie 1978, Haber and Hershenson 1973, Neisser 1976, Rosenzweig and Porter 1986, and Schiff 1980.)

Because the concept of perception is changing in both psychology and education, it is difficult to define in a suitable way here. For psychology, perception is no longer a terminal product distinct from cognition but is increasingly seen as a dynamic process integral to cognition. For education, interest previously limited to special perceptual problems, for example reading, is beginning to broaden in the light of increasing evidence that some of the concrete residues of perception, for example visual imagery, are instrumental in other cognitive processes including memory, concept formation, and problem solving. Thus, though traditional perceptual terms will be employed, a more contemporary conception will be presented, including an interactive rather than contrastive relation between perception and other cognitive processes.

As will be exemplified in what follows, the human perceptual system both affords the educator a wide range of opportunities for development and utilization and presents the educator with certain constraints and limits. Knowledge of both is important to the practicing educator, influencing both the general expectations of administrators and curriculum planners and the specific practices of instructional designers (teachers and developers of materials and media).

1. Perceptual Development

Perceptual development, as presented here, is primarily a learning process, that is, learning efficient perceptual strategies for the various tasks and phenomena presented by the physical and cultural environments, including importantly the family and school environments.

In general, the perceptual apparatus is present at birth and, as recent research shows, is remarkably functional in early infancy. However, the perceptual data store accumulates throughout the life span, and the programs (perceptual skills and strategies) also continue to be developed and perfected, throughout childhood in particular, but during adulthood as well.

Research in recent years has increasingly revealed that the perceptual world of the infant is not as once described, one of booming, buzzing confusion. Rather, the infant possesses the essential structures and "prewired" programs necessary to give visual attention, to differentiate forms, to distinguish colors, and to focus an image, though the range of focus may be limited in the first month or two. Such initial responsiveness to changes in the visual environment forms the basis for the extraction of increasing amounts of perceptual data and, importantly, for the development of strategies for the more efficient and functional acquisition and use of perceptual information. Infants of 5 months can process and remember visual information well enough to recognize color pictures of a person whose face they had seen several times before (Dirks and Gibson 1977), and infants of 7 months can apparently form simple concepts (toy dog) based on a few visual features (Cohen 1979).

Thus the child entering school in kindergarten has for four to five years been an active perceptual learner. In general, though, the child at this point exhibits several deficiencies: he or she tends not to give systematic attention, tends to extract only partial information, tends not to adequately interrelate bits of information, tends to process information at a relatively slow rate, and does all with less deliberate, purposeful, or efficient strategies than adults.

Such a child is beginning to develop literacy—both verbal and visual. Earlier competence in perceiving and interpreting objects and events is being extended to signs (words and pictures) whose importance is not so much in what they are as in what they stand for or refer to. This transition from object to sign, iconic to symbolic, concrete to abstract, has been a point of controversy. Some, like Bruner et al. (1966), see this as a critical point in the child's intellectual development characterized by leaving the perceptual world of appearance (iconic) for the higher-order world of words and thought (symbolic). The effect is to denigrate perceptual factors and processes as childish, inimical to higher processes, and hence to be abandoned as a part of the intellectual maturation process fostered by schools.

Two recent lines of inquiry promise some moderation of this verbal/cognitive elitism. First, there is increasing evidence that the iconic and symbolic develop in parallel rather than iconic first and symbolic second. For example, perceptual discrimination and categorization behavior by infants less than a year old strongly suggests that higher conceptual processes are already at work and developing in harmony with perceptual learning. Further, the early childhood acquisition of oral verbal behavior (1 to 2 years) is almost universal, and is initiated without benefit of schooling, thus providing further evidence that the use of verbal signs (symbolic behavior) develops quite early and harmoniously with perceptual development.

Second, the understanding of one form of higher cognition, namely concepts, is changing. The work of Rosch (1975) suggests that many basic concepts are represented in memory not as an abstract list of features but as an image of a prototypic example. Further, the testimony of noted leaders from both science and art suggests that new concepts and theories frequently arise from mental imagery (Shepard 1978) and are subsequently communicated by diagram and analogy, all highly dependent on rich perceptual roots. Thus both iconic and symbolic modes of thought begin in infancy and continue through adulthood.

The present data on stages and sequences of perceptual development is voluminous but frustrating to interpret and integrate. Even where stages are agreed upon, the age of emergence differs between studies. Certain theoretical models of development, for example, Piaget (1960) or Bruner et al. (1966) have gained wide acceptance and are useful as means of ordering and understanding some aspects of the process. More pertinent here is the understanding of the general process of perceptual development that has emerged from recent research with sufficient clarity to help explain the apparent diversity of conclusions regarding the specifics of stage and sequence. A sketch of these follows.

The child from infancy is an ardent student of his or her environment. One aspect after another of the environment is scrutinized and explored repeatedly until it becomes familiar (learned, habituated). Then some other still-novel aspect will be selectively attended to. An important determinant of what is selected is what the environment offers. The readily observable regularities in a particular environment will predispose the child toward acquiring those perceptual attributes and related emergent concepts. One recent writer, Papert (1980), considers the possible effects of introducing responsive microcomputers into a child's environment. He cites case studies of children deficient in language or mathematics who have developed marked increases in interest and skill in these basic subjects by interacting with dynamic programs whose emergent, discoverable properties are fundamental to mathematics or language concepts.

This kind of interactive, child-with-environment model of perceptual development accommodates both the evidence of general trends and of marked individual differences. What is common to many childhood environments facilitates similar patterns, and what is variable favors divergent patterns. Thus, given awareness of the overall process, the educational practitioner can take account of widely differing experiential histories and act to qualitatively and quantitatively enrich the conceptual learning opportunities which the perceptual environment of the schools provides.

2. Mature Perception

"Mature" here does not mean maximum or fixed perception but only adequately adapted to a wide range of the adult's current needs and relatively stable. If the adult shifts vocation or location then a considerable amount of additional perceptual learning may be necessary.

Mature perception, of course, differs from the earlier description of the immature perception of a kindergartner, but more in degree than kind. The modern model of perception is not that of a passive video or audio recording system that receives and records all that occurs. Rather, perception is conceived as an active process of selection and construction from the available flux of a meaningful and useful reality for the individual. Thus perception is not a product but an interactive, two-directional process. The perceiver seeks information from the environment, feedforward, and as a result receives certain information back, feedback. For example, if the feedback suggests a lack of something desired, the feedforward may be to initiate a search strategy. Thus conceived, perception is a dynamic process which functionally modulates the amount and kind of information the person acquires.

One of the spinoffs of this conception is that perceptual processes become so intertwined with other cognitive processes that they may become indistinguishable or at least not separately understandable. The effect is to further erase the value distinction of many writers between perception and the so-called higher processes.

Because the intent here is to facilitate the understanding of certain perceptual processes and the application of this understanding to the design of instruction, the following has been organized into six main categories which have dual labels—one an instructional goal and the other an associated perceptual factor. Thus, there follow six instructional goals and six associated perceptual factors. Further, the instructional goals have been sequenced in an order that roughly simulates the time sequence of a unit of instruction, that is, from the learner's initial looking and listening to his or her learning and thinking. Under each instructional goal/perceptual factor will be a description of various designer moves which employ perceptual factors in the attainment of instructional goals. These designer moves can be applied by classroom teachers and by developers of instructional materials.

2.1 Goal: To Look/Listen—Perceptual Factor: Visual and Auditory Attention

Perception research reveals that people respond to novelty. Objects or events that are unexpected or unusual attract attention. Any change from what has been happening in the classroom will draw attention. Further, complexity holds attention, so long as the level of complexity is right, that is, more than the particular learner is familiar with but not so much as to discourage or frustrate.

The provision of novelty and complexity suggests designer moves useful in both getting the learner's attention and directing it to the relevant aspects of instruction. Such moves might make the critical attributes of a concept larger, brighter, moving, colorful, loud, more informative, or otherwise in contrast to the surrounding context.

Attention is strongly influenced by perceptual set, that is, an attitude or expectation toward what is being or will be experienced. Set strongly affects what is selectively perceived and how it may be interpreted, remembered, or applied. Set is powerful because of the goal-directed character of perception. For example, research evidence generally supports the efficacy of introductory information, that is, goals, objectives, or questions, which orient the learner to the instruction that follows (Melton 1978). These devices may take many forms (threats, appeals to interest, advance organizers, challenges, puzzles, questions), but from a perceptual point of view they influence the learner's feedforward processes which shape subsequent perceptual activity in that context.

A perceptual set induced by instruction can thus be seen as providing the learner with a kind of "image" of what to expect that can include both cognitive components (the subject or theme) and affective components (relevance, interest).

2.2 To Analyze (Search, Compare, Distinguish) — Perceptual Discrimination

Once the perceiver is set to receive certain kinds of information, several processes follow, often including an active search for the desired information as well as an analysis of it, once located, to a degree consistent with the operative goal or intent. This is perceptual discrimination.

The physiological evidence is that the visual perceptual apparatus is highly specialized to discriminate a variety of kinds of information, for example, the fovea of the eye for detail and color under high light levels; the periphery for gross figural information, brightness change, and vision under low light levels; eye movements to find the most essential information; and a receptor and analyzer system adapted to detect critical visual information including edges and lines, movement, and position and orientation. Skills in using these capabilities for perceptual discrimination are gradually developed, some learned by most people in a culture and some by only the most expert in a task or subject.

Psychologists make a distinction important to instructional designers, namely that between the nominal stimulus and the effective stimulus. The nominal stimulus is all the information available, for example on a textbook page, while the effective stimulus is that smaller portion of information which a certain learner discriminates or detects. The problem is that most who would learn do not know what information to select, and most who would teach select what is relevant so automatically that they often fail to provide the help the learner needs. All perceivers are discriminating, but they differ radically in what they discriminate or selectively perceive. The problem is to get the learner to see and hear what the expert and the designer see and hear.

Instructional strategies are many. The designer can eliminate all irrelevant information as in a topic sentence or abstracted picture. Alternatively, more information can be provided together with a strong set to discriminate certain parts and/or with appropriate perceptual aids, for example arrows, underlining, bold type, color codes, motion, contrast, and so on. Which approach to take is strongly influenced by developmental factors of several kinds. Essentially all perceivers are responsive to sizeable changes in brightness, motion, sound level. Other aids to perceptual discrimination are learned (arrows, underlinings, color coding, cross-sectional views, etc.). Designers using these with young children need to teach their meaning. Still other perceptual discriminations are subject matter specific and are gradually acquired.

Perceptual discrimination not only involves the cues selected but the strategy for selecting and relating them. The search and comparison strategies of kindergartners, for example, have been shown to be far too brief and unsystematic in same/different tasks involving pictures, not achieving adequacy until about 7 years (Vurpillot 1968). Further, the potentiality in adults for increasing particular discrimination skills with training and experience has been shown to be remarkable. The designer's problem is to assess the discrimination skills, both general and specific, of learners and arrange to use operative skills and/or train for others.

Perceptual discrimination is a fundamental precursor for other cognitive processes. For example, concept formation depends on the learner distinguishing the relevant attributes which define the concept from the irrelevant attributes which, if attention-getting, often interfere with accurate conceptualization. Also, problem-solving tasks are generally insolvable until the crucial aspects and relations of the situation are perceived.

2.3 To Synthesize (Combine, Relate, Generalize) — Perceptual Integration

It continues to be a challenging puzzle for researchers to understand how numerous elements discriminated by perceptual processes are integrated or synthesized into a smaller number of meaningful wholes or forms or figures. Physiological parallels for this are apparent in that neural activity from numerous sources converges at the retinal level, converges again at the thalamus, and again and again at the cortex.

Neisser's (1976) reference to the perceptual process as analysis-by-synthesis suggests the dynamic constructive nature of the process. Initial partial synthesis of a figure may be followed by further analysis of the details of that figure or by more synthesis of the several figures into a whole. Thus, depending on the available information and the operative goal, the perceiver intermixes analysis and synthesis processes as needed. A distinction is often made between the parallel processing of numerous inputs as in perceiving a picture and the sequential processing of one word after another in perceiving language, especially speech. Particular contingencies and constraints operate to influence differentially the synthesis in both cases. Synthesis of the information in a spoken sentence is strung out in time, depends on short-term memory, and is subject to interference from other sounds or from static or distortion in the audio reproducer, for example, tape recorder. Because of the perceptually more tenuous nature of such speech synthesis, the designer must maximize audio quality and build in redundancies so that the loss of a word or phrase is not crucial. Parallel processing and synthesis of pictorial information is less fragile in that the perceiver can repeat the analysis and synthesis processes as needed. Exceptions are fixed-pace media (film and television) where scenes may be too short or lacking in redundancy.

As with perceptual discrimination, perceptual integration improves with practice, and widely applicable strategies can be learned. A basic factor in synthesis is similarity. Perceptual discrimination separates differences while synthesis groups similarities. Another perceptual basis for synthesis is proximity. Events occurring close together in time or space are grouped.

Instructional designers have considerable control over both similarity and proximity factors. They can perceptually accentuate the relevant similarities across examples of a concept. They can also present examples close together in time, for example, the same sentence or paragraph, or close together in space, for example, the same picture or diagram. They can also facilitate memory as well as perception by making temporally and/or spatially proximate the name of something to be learned and the object, event, or idea to which it refers.

In general, what the learner observes to be regular, recurring, or interrelated facilitates the perceptual process of integration and the cognitive processes of generalization and concept formation. The environmental regularities which an instructional designer controls include both the character of the subject matter and the character of the presentation. Perceived order in both facilitates perceptual integration. An intrinsic order in the subject matter can be employed and accentuated to advantage, for example, the temporal order of a serial process or of historical events. Cause and effect relations, functional relations, as well as hierarchical relations between concepts and subconcepts can be the basis for ordering instruction. Where intrinsic order is lacking, the to-be-related elements can be incorporated into a readily perceived structure, for example, a sentence or picture. Both of these devices directly aid perceptual integration and have been shown to facilitate memory through elaboration processes such as mental imagery.

As perceptual discrimination and integration of a given situation (object, face) are repeated over and over again, the process becomes increasingly efficient. Further, as related situations are integrated there can develop a cognitive program, or schema, or strategy which becomes increasingly context free and functional as a general perceptual/cognitive strategy for processing and using information. Salomon (1980), for example, argues that frequent exposure to communication media (film, television) can prepare the learner not only to deal with such forms of information more effectively but can lead to more generalized ways of thinking. Further, perceptual/cognitive strategies can be taught, for example, mnemonic strategies, search strategies, discrimination skills, problem-solving skills, thinking skills, and so on.

2.4 To Decide, Choose (Judge, Estimate, Evaluate) — Perceptual Closure

In a dynamic perceptual process, feedback from each partial analysis and synthesis is repeatedly tested or evaluated against the operational goal, and decisions are made to proceed or terminate. A computer term, for example, test, exit, go to, might be more suitable, but perceptual closure at least captures the idea that a decision has been made, typically with partial information, and with reference to an expectation about the perceptual parameters of the situation.

Thus, at some point in the perceptual process a goal is satisfied or another becomes more pressing. The consequent decision may of course be deliberate or be driven by other inner or outer stimuli.

The processes of judging, evaluating, deciding are very real to practicing professionals of many kinds, including instructional designers who must often perform formative and summative evaluations. However, these processes seldom occur as something to be trained in school children. Exceptions may be in the areas of scientific or mathematical problem solving and aesthetic judgment or appreciation. However, in a world with no apparent reduction in the human capacity for conflict, it seems apparent that better skills of conflict management and resolution are imperative at all levels—interpersonal, community, international. One of the essential skills is the delaying of closure, or at least avoiding premature closure.

2.5 To Create (Innovate, Generate) — Perceptual/ Cognitive Imagination

The professional researcher must delay closure, that is, keep open; while the professional practitioner must achieve closure and keep functioning. As a consequence, neither appreciates the constraints under which the other operates. However, there appears to be consensus that in some contexts the avoidance or delay of closure is necessary, that is, where creative, innovative, generative processes are to be facilitated.

Much less is known about these, but there is ample self-report evidence that some of the same kinds of processes are involved as have been examined above, that is, goal, search, analysis, synthesis, and that the contents are often "perceptual" in character (Shephard 1978). The composer "hears" a chord, a novelist "sees" the characters interacting, the scientist manipulates variables (perhaps "seen" in a spatial model) and imagines interactions. The analogous process of "brainstorming" has been used in business and elsewhere. Eventually, some closure is reached, and selected imaginings are externalized and evaluated.

The perceptual aspects of the process appear to be: first, rich perceptual/cognitive input, then a period of incubation (imaginal exploration and manipulation), and finally (and hopefully) creation. Throughout this perhaps "highest" of all human cognitive processes the mutual interdependence of perceptual and cognitive processes is apparent, involving linear and simultaneous kinds of perceptions and thoughts, abstract signs and concrete representations, nonverbal images and verbal labeling.

2.6 To Develop Skill (Adapt, Learn, Perform) — Perceptual Learning

Much about the process of learning to perceive was considered earlier (see Sect. 1). Perceptual learning was also implicit in the discussion of the skill development aspects of perceptual search, discrimination, and integration.

Though the basic processes involved appear to be predominantly those of learning, for example, repetition, reinforcement, contiguity, meaning, and so on, it is clear that the perceptual apparatus and programs are remarkably fit for the process of developing increasingly vast reservoirs of perceptual knowledge and an increasingly functional repertoire of perceptual/cognitive skills.

Bibliography

Bruner J S, Oliver R R, Greenfield P M 1966 *Studies in Cognitive Growth: A Collaboration at the Center for Cognitive Studies.* Wiley, New York

Cohen L B 1979 Our developing knowledge of infant perception and cognition. *Am. Psychol.* 34: 894–99

Dirks J, Gibson E 1977 Infants' perception of similarity between live people and their photographs. *Child Dev.* 48: 124–30

Fleming M L, Levie W H 1978 *Instructional Message Design: Principles from the Behavioral Sciences.* Educational Technology, Englewood Cliffs, New Jersey

Haber R N, Hershenson M 1973 *The Psychology of Visual Perception.* Holt, Rinehart and Winston, New York

Melton R F 1978 Resolution of conflicting claims concerning the effect of behavioral objectives on student learning. *Rev. Educ. Res.* 48: 291–302

Neisser U 1976 *Cognition and Reality: Principles and Implications of Cognitive Psychology.* Freeman, San Francisco, California

Papert S 1980 *Mindstorms: Children, Computers and Powerful Ideas.* Basic Books, New York

Piaget J 1960 *The Psychology of Intelligence.* Routledge and Kegan Paul, London

Rosch E 1975 Cognitive representations of semantic categories. *J. Exper. Psychol.: General* 104: 192–233

Rosenzweig M R, Porter L W (eds.) 1986 *Annual Review of Psychology*, Vol. 37. Annual Revue, Palo Alto, California

Salomon G 1980 The use of visual media in the service of enriching mental thought processes. *Instr. Sci.* 9: 327–39

Schiff W 1980 *Perception: An Applied Approach*, Houghton Mifflin, Boston, Massachusetts

Shepard R N 1978 The mental image. *Am. Psychol.* 33: 125–37

Vurpillot E 1968 The development of scanning strategies and their relation to visual differentiation. *J. Exper. Child Psychol.* 6: 632–50

Media Selection

E. U. Heidt

It is one of the basic assumptions in instruction that different ways of teaching will influence the learning process and its result. In particular, media have been regarded as potentially effective instruments for the improvement of teaching and learning. Almost all publications on instructional design, curriculum development, educational technology, or on practical problems of school or university teaching deal with the problem of how to make best or better use of teaching aids, audiovisual equipment, learning materials, or—to use the most common term—of media. They try to help answer the question: given my present instructional task, which medium will be the most appropriate and effective to achieve the desired learning result? This article cannot give a comprehensive and exhaustive description of this substantial literature; but by condensing the great variety of individual approaches into six basic types, it describes a range of ways by which the selection problem is claimed to be solved. This first section on media selection models is followed by a second section

dealing with the factors on which selection is based and the differing contexts in which selection is made. A third section then summarizes instructional research on the relative effectiveness of different media and discusses its implications.

1. Media Selection Models: Types and Formats

This section will begin with the most simple common-sense approach and proceed to more formal and sophisticated procedures. This list includes examples of what have become known as media taxonomies, since without exception all media taxonomies so far have been devised with the selection problem in mind (for a critical appraisal of existing taxonomies see Heidt 1978). Although some approaches define media selection as only a suboperation, a single step in the instructional design process which begins with the definition of objectives, they still treat it as a process in its own right, for

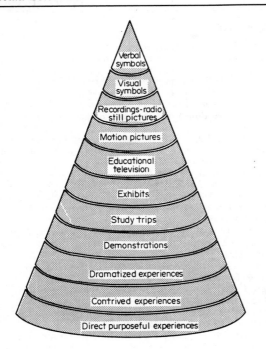

Figure 1
The Cone of Experience (Dale 1969)

which the considerations and results of preceding steps serve only as inputs.

1.1 Checklists of Questions to be Considered

Handbooks for teachers or instructors often contain questions to ask when evaluating a specific item of curriculum material. Up to 50 questions may be listed without any explicit theoretical basis or framework, and organized only into broad commonsense categories like "methodological aspects" or "technical aspects". Almost all such checklists ask the teacher to consider whether the medium meets his or her specific objectives, whether it is interesting, whether it is in accordance with the learners' level of development and knowledge, and whether its technical quality is satisfactory.

Some lists include affective criteria and ask whether the content and presentation meet contemporary standards of good taste or whether they show bias or propaganda. On the basis of the answers given and using good judgment, the teacher is then expected to select the appropriate medium and to reject unsuitable materials.

1.2 Media Description

Other authors take media categories like films, overhead transparencies, printed materials, audiotapes and so on as their starting point and give a detailed description of the capabilities, limitations, advantages, and disadvantages of each individual medium (Boucher et al. 1973, Heidt and Loser 1979). The problem is to identify and to compile a list of as many criteria as possible which

may be suitable as descriptive categories for media. While it is not important that these categories are on the same level of abstraction, it is essential that they permit as complete a description as possible of the medium under study, including its suitability for individualized instruction or self-directed learner activities, as well as information about maintenance costs and software availability or production time. These descriptions aim at enabling the teacher or developer to make a well-informed decision about what type of medium to look for or to develop for specific instructional purposes.

1.3 One-dimensional Taxonomies

While the models presented so far treat each medium as an independent unit, other models try to reveal the relation between media. They choose a criterion they consider educationally relevant, and devise a one-dimensional scale on which they mark the relative position of each medium. Figure 1 shows one of the best-known efforts in this field, Dale's Cone of Experience. Dale (1969) takes degree of abstraction as the basis of his classification. Thus the amount of immediate sensory participation decreases as one moves from the base of the cone to the top, that is from direct purposeful experiences over demonstrations and educational television to verbal symbols.

The hierarchical order of selected audiovisual instrumental media proposed by Duncan (1969) proceeds from the simplest to the most complex media. While one descends the order from duplicated notes of the lecturer or participant down to computer-based instructional systems and television broadcasts, the prime cost increases while the ease and flexibility of use decrease.

In setting out the various media in an orderly way, models of this type allow for an easy comparison between media although only according to a single criterion.

1.4 Matrices

Media matrices usually take the form of a two-dimensional array with gross media categories, like real objects, motion pictures, print and so on along one dimension and a list of selection aspects along the other. The media categories are linked to these aspects by a rating of "suitable—partly suitable—not suitable". Selection criteria used in these matrices are quite diverse. Some models draw their list of selection categories entirely from a theoretical educational framework, for example, the instructional functions as defined by Gagné (1965) or the educational aims of Bloom's "Taxonomy of Educational Objectives" (see Fig. 2, from Sparkes 1982). Others include practical factors, for example, group size, repeatability, and the necessity to darken the projection room (Briggs 1970).

A rather different approach is taken by Tosti and Ball (1969). They regard media only as carriers for the presentation form, for which they distinguish six dimensions, that is, stimulus and coding form, stimulus duration, response demand form, response demand frequency, management form or purpose, and management frequency. Only when the decisions with respect to all dimensions of the presentation form have been taken, can the instructor proceed to consider the most appropriate medium to carry it. This involves a specification of media with regard to the different dimensions of presentation. For a complete analysis of media selection possibilities a six-dimensional matrix would have to be used. Since this would be too complicated, Tosti and Ball suggest a series of matrices, in each of which two dimensions of presentation are linked by those media categories that meet the requirements of the respective presentation form.

By using a number of criteria for classifying media, these models aim at giving a lot of information in a very condensed form. Some authors try to counteract the danger of oversimplification by supplementing the very general suitability rating with extensive verbal explanations.

1.5 Flow Charts

Flow charts break down the selection process into an ordered series of steps, each marked by a question. As the instructor or designer answers one question after the other with "yes" or "no", he or she is guided through different branches of the graph. Each answer eliminates some media from the initial full list, and after the last question either a single medium or a group of media

remains which are considered appropriate for the instructor's purpose. Most flow charts require the teacher to analyse the learning task in terms of detailed objectives before he or she enters the decision process. Some models focus on a further breakdown of the necessary component of the learning task (e.g., Fig. 3, from Romiszowski 1974). Others use learner characteristics and factors of the instructional setting. Thus the geographical distribution of learners may influence the decision on whether to use broadcast media, low reading ability may rule out the use of print media, and the assumption that visuals will help recall may lead to the inclusion of visual media (Reiser and Gagné 1983). For the final decision on alternative media, authors usually recommend practical criteria like cost and convenience.

1.6 Algorithms

Cost–effectiveness studies often lead to algorithms for rational media selection which are based on the assumption that it is possible to quantify all relevant factors. Weiss and Klepzig (1981) give a subjective utility value to all factors, go through a series of calculations according to some formulas, compare the utility indices for the alternatives, and thus identify the most preferable medium. It is typical for this format that their model does not include any pedagogical factors but only expenditure, utilization characteristics, and organizational feasibility.

Aim \ Method	Lectures	Small group classes	Laboratory or workshop	Teaching text	Videotape	Audio vision	Broadcast, TV and radio	CAL	Teleconferencing	Home kit	Dial access	Projects	Assignments	Self-help group	Domain
1(a) Attitudes	ooo	⊕⊕			oo		ooo ooo		⊕⊕⊕	+++	+++ ++			+++ ++	Affective domain
1(b) Skills		⊕⊕⊕	⊕⊕⊕		ooo				⊕⊕	+++		⊕⊕⊕ ⊕⊕		++	
2(a) Knowledge	ooo ooo	⊕⊕⊕		ooo ooo	ooo ooo	ooo	oo oo	+++	⊕⊕⊕	+++	ooo oo				Cognitive domain
2(b) Understanding	oo	⊕⊕⊕ ⊕⊕⊕	++ ++	oo oo	oo oo	ooo	oo		⊕⊕⊕	++ ++	ooo	+++	⊕⊕⊕		
3(a) Techniques	o	⊕⊕⊕ ⊕⊕⊕	++	oo oo	o		oo oo	+++ +++	⊕			+	⊕⊕⊕ ⊕⊕⊕		
3(b) Analysis	o	⊕⊕⊕ ⊕⊕⊕		ooo	o		oo	+	⊕⊕ ⊕⊕	+++		⊕++	⊕⊕ ⊕⊕		Skills
3(c) Synthesis		⊕⊕ ⊕⊕		o	o		o	+++	⊕			⊕⊕+ +++	⊕⊕⊕ ⊕⊕⊕		
4 Manual			ooo ooo		oo oo		oo			++		++			

O In which the primary activity is one of teaching by the tutor

+ In which the primary activity is learning as a result of the students' own initiative

Figure 2
Media selection based on educational objectives (Sparkes 1982)

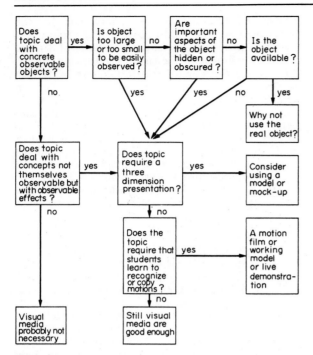

Figure 3
Decisions for selecting visual media (Romiszowski 1974)

2. Selection Factors and Contexts

2.1 Selection Factors

Although there is a considerable overlap of categories between models, each one uses its own set of selection criteria. For the following survey they have been ordered in six tentative groups, which are, however, interrelated in practical decision taking. The first three comprise genuine educational criteria, while the remaining three cover practical factors.

(a) Task factors: objectives, learning outcomes, learned capability, learning experience; content variables; type of stimuli, sense, or reception characteristics.

(b) Learner factors: group size and location; intellectual abilities, cognitive styles, student interests and preferences, age, learning experience.

(c) Instructional management factors: instructional strategy and method, response demand, degree of teacher control, instructional events.

(d) Economic factors: cost of hardware, software, production, maintenance, and staff training.

(e) Technical factors: technical quality, ease of handling, compatibility, flexibility of use, durability.

(f) Administrative factors: availability, management of media resources, school architecture and equipment.

The explanations and examples given for the different models show that under some circumstances each of these factors can be relevant for media decisions. However, apart from the more practical factors which can often be stated in exact and even quantitative terms, the application of these criteria depends on the subjective judgment of the individual teacher or designer.

2.2 Selection Contexts

What the selection procedures aim to identify depends largely on the purpose of the selector. One teacher may want to pick the best medium for his or her particular class here and now from an array of materials that are already available. Another instructor may have to select an appropriate medium for a new course which has yet to be developed and is aimed at several classes. A planner of educational policy may have to decide on the introduction of a media system on a nationwide level. Hence selection procedures lead to the identification of different categories of media:

(a) An individual item of software, for example, a specific film or book (this purpose is usually served by the format "List of Questions").

(b) The traditional gross media category, like film, print, audiotapes, and so on, treated as an undifferentiated hardware/software configuration.

(c) A set or combination of media as defined in (b).

(d) Stimulus characteristics, like visual, motion, colour, sound, and so on, which describe physical representational capabilities of hardware/software configurations.

(e) Idiosyncratic categories, often invented to refer to the function of media in the instructional process, for example, criterion visuals, simulated, and mediating visuals (Gropper and Glasgow 1971).

3. Instructional Media Research

Media selection is based on the fundamental assumption that there are instructionally relevant differences between media. However, a great number of research studies comparing two or more media in order to assess their relative effectiveness have either failed to detect significant differences or found contradictory results. The overall conclusion is that most media may be used effectively for the attainment of a great number of different objectives, but also that most objectives may be achieved through any of a variety of media. The reasons which have been put forward to explain those findings are also relevant for evaluating media selection models. The first point to be criticized has been the use of gross generic media categories, like film, print, audiotape, and so on. Since each of these terms covers a great variety of actual items, researchers suspect more variance within than between these categories. It has therefore been suggested that we should define media variables in terms of specific attributes, like the capability to present motion, colour, auditory stimuli, and so on. Investigations undertaken on this basis show, however, that no media attribute bears an inherent general advantage. They may enhance learning only when they serve an instructional function with regard to the learning task in hand. Finally, the learner has been identified as an important variable. Here again research, in particular the aptitude–treatment interaction (ATI) approach, has turned to more subtle descriptions, this time to psychologically defined personality characteristics, which are supposed to interact with task and media variables.

Although media studies have not resulted in any generally and easily applicable guidelines for media selection, the minimum specification of a selection approach which is in keeping with the trend of educational research may be summarized in the following question: given this kind of learning task and given a learner with these personality characteristics, which media attributes may be considered relevant?

4. Final Comment

Although no general and fundamental differences with respect to instructional effectiveness could be detected between the various media, researchers as well as media practitioners agree that there are differences, that these, however, are only relative and of a more subtle kind than hitherto expected. This view, which has led to more and more complex and sophisticated research designs, is hardly reflected in models for practical media selection problems, most of which still aim at the identification of media in gross categories of television, film, books, and so on, and with that, consider the selection problem as solved. These models seem to suggest that it does not matter *how* it is done as long as it is done with the help of the medium identified.

On account of the complexity and diversity of instructional situations and educational problems, many authors have warned against simple rules and recipes for media selection and even considered a deductive procedure, a sequence of logical steps to identify the best medium for a given situation, as not feasible. Nevertheless there are educational technologists who hold that the consideration of factors according to their specific model will "dictate" the final media choice. A closer look, however, reveals that even these authors specify only *what* to do but not *how* to do it. Their typical prescription "Having identified the objective (or learning difficulties or student characteristics, etc.), provide *appropriate* media" leaves that important question unanswered.

Concerning the use of psychologically defined personality characteristics of the learner as factors for media selection, it has to be admitted that although the ATI approach opens promising ways for future media research, its relevance for the media practitioner seems to be rather limited. Neither teachers nor developers usually know their target audience in exact psychologi-

cal terms. Hence there seems no direct way of applying findings from ATI research with its subtle distinctions of different mental abilities, cognitive styles, and other personality variables to practical selection problems.

In summary, none of the models developed to date can be regarded as an easy-to-handle satisfactory instrument. Some only identify factors, which should enter the decision-taking process, while others suggest procedures, in which usually a sequence of difficult operations ends in some commonsense decision. Research so far has not been successful in discovering how the factors commonly agreed upon as relevant should enter the selection process nor what the consequences of alternative media decisions really are. Because of the complexity of educational situations, the selection remains a matter of subjective good judgment based on the consideration of a large list of potentially relevant factors.

Bibliography

Boucher B G, Gottlieb M J, Morganlander M L 1973 *Handbook and Catalog for Instructional Media Selection*. Educational Technology Publications, Englewood Cliffs, New Jersey

Briggs L J 1970 *Handbook of Procedures for the Design of Instruction*. American Institute for Research, Pittsburgh, Pennsylvania

Cronbach L J, Snow R E 1977 *Aptitudes and Instructional Methods: A Handbook for Research on Interactions*. Irvington, New York

Dale E 1969 *Audio-visual Methods in Teaching*, 3rd edn. Dryden, New York

Duncan C J 1969 A survey of audiovisual equipment and methods. In: Unwin D (ed.) 1969 *Media and Methods: Instructional Technology in Higher Education*. McGraw-Hill, London, pp. 13–68

Gagné R M 1965 *The Conditions of Learning*. Holt, Rinehart and Winston, New York

Gropper G L, Glasgow Z 1971 *Criteria for the Selection and Use of Visuals in Instruction*. Educational Technology Publications, Englewood Cliffs, New Jersey

Heidt E U 1978 *Instructional Media and the Individual Learner: A Classification and Systems Appraisal*. Kogan Page, London

Heidt E U, Loser F 1979 Individualisierung und Differenzierung des Unterrichts durch eine Differenzierung von Medien. In: Dichanz D, Kolb G (eds.) 1979 *Unterrichtstheorie und Medienpraxis*. Klett, Stuttgart, pp. 30–152

Reiser R, Gagné R M Characteristics of media selection models. *Rev. Educ. Res.* 52(4): 499–512

Reiser R, Gagné R M 1983 *Selecting Media for Instruction*. Educational Technology Publications, Englewood Cliffs, New Jersey

Romiszowski A J 1974 *The Selection and Use of Instructional Media*. Kogan Page, London

Sparkes J J 1982 *On Choosing Teaching Methods* (ZIFF Papiere 39). Fernuniversität, Hagen

Tosti D T, Ball J R 1969 A behavioral approach to instructional design and media selection. *Audio-vis. Commun. Rev.* 17: 5–25

Weiss M, Klepzig H J 1981 Methodological aids to media evaluation and selection. *Program. Learn. Educ. Technol.* 18: 30–43

Media Attributes

W. H. Levie

Any instructional product can be epitomized by specifying (a) its message and (b) its message vehicle. The message is the instructional content of the product, and can be described by listing the skills, understandings, and affective responses that constitute the educational objectives associated with the product. Message vehicles are usually described in terms of media types. It is possible to speak of textbooks, motion pictures, audiotapes, slide sets, maps, models, and so forth. An alternative way to describe a message vehicle is by listing its media attributes. A media attribute is a characteristic that specifies the kinds of information the vehicle can provide and the kinds of learner responses the vehicle can accommodate. What benefits could result from describing message vehicles in terms of media attributes rather than in terms of media types? One situation in which this approach might be useful is during media selection in instructional development.

Given an instructional problem which has been specified by a set of instructional objectives, a group of learners, and an instructional setting, how can the instructional developer select the most appropriate medium or media mix through which to provide the instruction? Much early audiovisual research was devoted to this general question. Over and over researchers sought to determine the relative effectiveness of two or more media types (often television versus traditional classroom instruction). Usually the results showed that it made no difference. Reviewers such as Jamison et al. (1974) have concluded that this research provides no basis for making media-selection decisions. Indeed, it is now recognized that the methodology and basic paradigm of this media-comparison research are invalid and could never result in theoretically useful data (Salomon and Clark 1977).

In the absence of useful media-comparison research, several authors have offered guidelines based upon experience and intuition (for a survey, see Heidt 1976). A typical format for such guidelines is to construct a matrix consisting of media-types on one axis and types of instructional objectives on the other axis. Judgments are then offered about the probable effectiveness of each media type for facilitating the achievement of each type of objective. The rationale behind the judgments is rarely made explicit, and different authors come to different conclusions. Another problem with this approach is that the instructional products within a media type category exhibit considerable variation. For example, some motion pictures are silent films, and some are sound films. The visual might show continuous motion or a series of still pictures. The pictures might or might not be captioned or include titles. There might be stopping points for learner practice with an accompanying model or simulator. Random information access via videodisc technique might be possible. And so forth. So it may not be very informative to be told that for a particular purpose you should use a motion picture. What kind of motion picture? A more analytical approach to media selection is to analyze the objective, the learner, and the learning environment, and ask what media attributes are needed. Then the medium or media mix that provides these attributes can be identified. If alternative possibilities emerge, the further choice can be made on the basis of cost or other pragmatic determinants.

Not all attributes of instructional materials have importance for learning effectiveness. The smell and taste of the volume you are presently reading have no instructional significance. However, the fact that it is written in a language you can read is important. The fact that it cannot provide auditory stimuli is also important since it places limits on the kinds of content you can learn from this volume. Some classes of media attributes that are often important and that have been the subject of research are discussed below. Discovering how these attributes operate to influence learning should be of help in understanding instructional media.

1. Sensory Modality

The sensory modalities stimulated by a media presentation constitute one class of media attribute. Each sensory channel is capable of providing certain unique kinds of information. In teaching children to identify the sounds of orchestral instruments, there is no satisfactory substitute for the auditory modality. Color discrimination requires the visual modality. Simulators which provide learners with the opportunity to receive haptic stimulation or practice kinesthetic responses are critical in certain learning tasks. There are, however, cases in which the same information can be presented by more than one channel. An instructionally important case concerns reading versus listening to verbal material.

Research comparing reading versus listening to prose passages usually shows reading to be superior (e.g., Green 1981). Research on interactions of presentation modality with reading ability leads to the conclusion that since reading and listening involve many of the same cognitive processes, poor readers are also poor listeners. There is no strong support for the contention that many students can be reliably classified either as "auditory learners" or as "visual learners." Nevertheless, researchers such as Magoon and Raper (1977) point to a range of learning competencies and instructional applications where the learning modality may make a significant difference.

Are two modalities better than one? When is listening plus looking superior/inferior to listening alone or looking alone? Some broad generalizations are possible. (a)

When the information presented in the two channels is redundant, there is ordinarily no advantage for dual-channel presentation—for example, the simultaneous presentation of the same words in both channels is usually no better than visual presentation alone. (b) When the information in the two channels is unrelated, some information will be lost if the information load is too great to permit channel switching by the learner. Although this appears obvious, it is often violated in practice. Teachers continue to lecture while students attempt to read simultaneously from the chalkboard. (c) When the information presented in the two channels is related, as when spoken words are combined with relevant pictures, simultaneous presentation might enhance learning. Instances of such facilitation would include cases in which pictures provide concrete examples of abstract concepts stated orally. Thus the question of single versus multiple channel presentation resolves to an examination of what kinds of information are presented in the channels and how they are related.

2. Symbolic Modality and Symbol Systems

Another means of specifying the kinds of information that can be provided by a media presentation is to identify the symbolic modalities and symbol systems used. Table 1 (which was adapted from Paivio 1978) shows some types of stimuli that can be presented in the verbal and nonverbal symbolic modalities via three sensory modalities. The key distinction that has been made between the two symbolic modalities concerns the sequential presentation/reception of verbal information versus the simultaneous nature of nonverbal information. Memory research generally shows that presenting items in the verbal modality results in superior serial recall whereas nonverbal presentation produces a superior free recall (e.g., Paivio et al. 1975). Another important difference involves the relatively abstract nature of verbal information as contrasted with the concrete nature of nonverbal information.

An even more powerful analysis of the potentialities of a media presentation may result from identifying the symbol systems used. A symbol system consists of a presentational scheme and an associated domain of reference—a kind of content. For example, maps consist of a set of codes and conventions which are used "in correlation with" a field of reference—land forms. Thus symbol systems differ with respect to the types of

information they can carry. Some systems are quite limited. Numerical systems, for example, denote only quantities and mathematical relationships. Music is highly expressive—evoking emotional, affective responses—and is, generally speaking, void of denotation. Other systems such as printed language are relatively versatile in that they can represent, denote, and express a wide range of meanings. Each symbol system requires specialized mental skills on the part of the learner. While it is obvious that the interpretation of braille requires special skills, it may be less obvious that the understanding of line drawings requires skills that may be lacking in young children and in adults from remote cultures. Finally, it appears that extensive exposure to particular symbol systems may lead to the cultivation of related mental skills. Such outcomes may be thought desirable (for example, the continued use of the computer language LOGO may cultivate logical patterns of thought) or undesirable; (for example, extensive exposure to the symbol systems employed by commercial television results in preferences for shallow information processing). Thus, while research focusing on media-symbol systems has only just begun, this approach to understanding media seems to hold great promise (Olson 1974, Goodman 1976, Salomon 1979).

3. Design Cues and Codes

No matter which medium is chosen to provide instruction, the instructional developer has the choice of using or not using a variety of design cues. In pictorial media, such cues include color, motion, and aspects of pictorial detail such as shading, texture, and figural embellishment. In audio media, such cues include music, sound effects, and intonation in spoken prose. In printed text, a variety of typographic cues are available. (See Dwyer 1978 for a listing of such techniques.) What effects might such cues have on learning? The attribute of motion will be taken as an example.

Most research comparing motion presentations (such as film and television) with comparable static presentations (such as slides and filmstrips) has failed to produce differences in learning. In a few cases, however, when motion itself was a part of the context to be learned, differences were found (for a review, see Levie and Dickie 1973). Also, motion can be used to direct attention within a scene to critical learning cues, or to increase the relative salience of selected content. For example, Meringoff (1980) found that children seeing a film recalled more action content than those who read a comparable picture book. Finally, special techniques such as high-speed and time-lapse motion can be particularly effective in certain limited circumstances.

Hence, as with any media attribute, mere presence or absence is not the critical question. What does matter is how the cue is used. While particular design cues, due to their technical nature, have potentialities not shared by other cues, a few broad generalizations about the effective use of this class of media attribute seem warranted.

Table 1
To show stimuli that can be presented in the verbal and nonverbal modalities via three sensory modalities

Sensory modality	Symbolic modality	
	Verbal	Nonverbal
Visual	Printed words	Pictures
Auditory	Spoken words	Environmental sounds
Tactile	Braille	Feelable objects

(a) The presence of a design cue may be expected to facilitate learning when the content to be learned involves the nature of the cue itself. An obvious example would be the use of color when teaching color discrimination. (b) When a design cue functions to attract attention to an essential aspect of the learning stimuli that might otherwise go unnoticed, learning will be facilitated. When the cue functions to attract attention to unessential features, and hence, away from important learning cues, learning will suffer. (c) When cues are used as a coding devide (e.g., color coding) so that material is better organized and structured for the learner, the learning of these relationships may be facilitated. (d) Learning materials which include cues such as color, motion, and music are generally preferred by learners and are rated as more interesting and enjoyable.

4. Locus of Control Characteristics

This set of attributes concerns the degree to which users of instructional materials can control their access to information. Motion pictures and audiotapes are fixed in pace and sequence, allowing learners little control. Print materials may allow maximum learner control, although textbooks are sometimes used in very structured ways, and the design of some "programmed texts" thwarts ease of information access. In computer-assisted instruction, the learner is usually allowed to control the pace of instruction, frequently allowed to control some aspects of the sequence of instruction, and in rare cases given the choice of instruction goals (see *Computer-assisted Learning*).

When does it seem advisable to permit learning control? It is widely assumed that materials which force all learners to go through the program at the same rate are likely to be too slow and inefficient for some learners and too fast and ineffective for others. Indeed, it has been observed that in some self-paced programs, slower learners require five to six times as long as faster students to master a set of learning materials. Thus, providing for individualization in rate of instruction seems generally advisable—especially when the learner population is heterogeneous.

The case for learner control of sequence is much less clear. Although highly structured presentations have often been found to improve performance for low-ability learners, this inflexibility may be a hindrance for high-ability learners. Also, most learners appear to be poor judges of which instructional treatments will benefit them most. However, Tennyson (1981) has shown that when students receive continuous advice on their progress and current options in reaching instructional objectives, learner control can be effective.

Snow (1980) has observed that even though giving learners control of their instruction may be socially desirable, there is no clear evidence that learner control can accommodate (that is, compensate for the effects of) learner differences. He advises that one might "give control to all of the learners some of the time, and to some of the learners all of the time, but not . . . all of the learners all of the time" (p. 158).

5. Interactive Features

Do learners interact with the instructional program passively by just reading or listening, or are they given a more active role? In the early days of the programmed instruction movement, great importance was given to requiring frequent overt responses from learners and giving them "reinforcement" via immediate knowledge of results. Subsequent research has revealed this early conception to be too simple. Overt responding appears to be helpful only when the material to be learned is relatively new to the learner. When the learner is familiar with the material, overt responding is no better than covert responding, and may even be detrimental if the requirement to make repeated trivial responses leads learners to skim or to skip portions of the program which do present information new to them (Tobias 1982). Similarly, the role of feedback is more limited than was once thought. Feedback does not appear to serve an important reinforcing or motivating function and is of little value following correct responses. Feedback can facilitate learning by correcting errors. Generally, feedback is beneficial to the degree that it adds information. Computer technology is making dramatic advances in the potential for learner–program interaction. Collins et al. (1978), for example, found that students who were taught geography via tutorial interaction with a computerized map display performed much better than those who learned using a static map display.

In summary, analyzing instructional media in terms of media attributes rather than in terms of media types may help to clarify how media can be used effectively. Thinking in these terms focuses attention on the characteristics of media that have implications for instruction. The approach is, however, not trouble free. In many cases, neither research nor enlightened practice can provide certain guidance to the effects of particular attributes. Attributes used in various combinations can have markedly different effects from those same attributes operating in isolation. And, of course, the mere presence of an attribute hardly guarantees success. Media attributes enhance learning only when they are used to provide the information and when they activate the mental operations that are necessary for learning to occur.

Bibliography

Collins A, Adams M F, Pew R W 1978 Effectiveness of an interactive map display in tutoring geography. *J. Educ. Psychol.* 70: 1–7

Dwyer F M 1978 *Strategies for Improving Visual Learning: A Handbook for the Effective Selection, Design and Use of Visualized Materials.* Learning Services, State College, Pennsylvania

Goodman N 1976 *The Languages of Art*, 2nd edn. Hackett, Indianapolis, Indiana

Green R 1981 Remembering ideas from text: The effect of modality of presentation. *Br. J. Educ. Psychol.* 51: 83–89

Heidt E U 1976 *Medien und Lernprozesse: Das Problem einer Medienklassifikation im Zusammerhang Didaktischer Modelle und Lernpsychologischer Forschung.* Beltz, Weinheim [1978 *Instructional Media and the Individual Learner: A Classification and Systems Appraisal.* Kogan Page, London]

Jamison D, Suppes P, Wells S 1974 The effectiveness of alternative instructional media: A survey. *Rev. Educ. Res.* 44: 1–68

Levie W H, Dickie K E 1973 The analysis and application of media. In: Travers R M W (ed.) 1973 *Second Handbook of Research on Teaching: A Project of the American Educational Research Association.* Rand McNally, Chicago, Illinois, pp. 858–82

Magoon R A, Raper C C 1977 The effect of sensory modalities on learning. *Contemp. Educ. Psychol.* 2: 55–65

Meringoff L K 1980 Influence of the medium on children's story apprehension. *J. Educ. Psychol.* 72: 240–49

Olson D R (ed.) 1974 *Media and Symbols: The Forms of Expression, Communication, and Education.* 73rd Yearbook of the National Society for the Study of Education, Pt. 1. University of Chicago Press, Chicago, Illinois

Paivio A 1978 Dual coding approach to perception and cognition. In: Pick H L, Saltzman E (eds.) 1978 *Modes of Perceiving and Processing Information.* Erlbaum, Hillsdale, New Jersey

Paivio A, Philipchalk R, Rowe E J 1975 Free and serial recall of pictures, sounds, and words. *Memory and Cognition* 3: 586–90

Salomon G 1979 *Interaction of Media, Cognition, and Learning.* Jossey-Bass, San Francisco, California

Salomon G, Clark R E 1977 Reexamining the methodology of research on media and technology in education. *Rev. Educ. Res.* 47: 99–120

Snow R E 1980 Aptitude, learner control, and adaptive instruction. *Educ. Psychol.* 15: 151–58

Tennyson R D 1981 Use of adaptive information for advisement in learning concepts and rules using computer-assisted instruction. *Am. Educ. Res. J.* 18: 425–38

Tobias S 1982 When do instructional methods make a difference? *Educ. Res. AERA* 11(4): 4–9

Individualized Learning Systems

Individualized Instruction in Higher Education

D. J. Boud

Individualized instruction is the term used to describe those forms of teaching in which instruction takes place on an individual rather than a group basis. Almost all approaches allow students more flexibility in the pace of study and in the timing of study than do group-based approaches such as lectures or small-group teaching. The primary medium of communication is the written word supplemented by direct contact between teacher and student. The extent to which instruction is tailored to the needs of individual students varies according to the particular approach which is adopted. While some degree of adaptation is always present this is often achieved through the overall design of a course rather than through materials designed for specific individuals.

Individualized instruction developed in response to the recognition that any teaching method which treated all members of a group in a similar fashion could not address the differing needs of individual students. In particular, a teaching system based on the presentation of information to a group could not take into account the great variation in the rates at which students learn. As the range of students entering higher education became wider and more varied in performance and background, the problem became more pressing and the need for approaches which addressed this diversity became more apparent. The lock-step method of the lecture was not suitable in these circumstances.

The term "individualized instruction" is not used consistently by practitioners of individualized methods and is not in common usage in all countries. It is, however, the most common description of the group of teaching methods in which teaching is directed towards individual students rather than groups of students. The word "learning" is preferred to "instruction" in the United Kingdom, and "individualized" is commonly replaced by words which describe more precisely the approach used such as "self-paced", "resource based", or "contract learning". However, individualized instruction is not synonymous with independent learning or learning in isolation from other students. While individualized methods may encourage independence from the teacher this is not usually the main aim, nor do students necessarily work in isolation from their peers. Although almost all forms of distance learning through correspondence are forms of individualized learning, this account of individualized instruction refers only to on-campus activities.

It is difficult to frame a definition of individualized instruction which includes all those activities referred to by that term without also including other activities for which the term is not usually considered. For example, a definition could include individual one-to-one tutorials and individual supervision, although these are not representative of the methods normally included by the term. It is more common to restrict the use of the term "individualized instruction" to those developments that have occurred since the 1950s which are systems of individualized instruction. Goldschmid and Goldschmid (1974) have identified the characteristics of individualized instruction which are common to all approaches as: emphasizing learning rather than teaching, the use of clear goals, active student participation, a stress on feedback and evaluation, and individual pacing. These characteristics are manifest in many different forms.

1. Background

Following the introduction of programmed learning, a wide range of individualized instruction methods were developed in the 1960s. Many were based on similar behavioural principles, however, the idea of a simple instructional programme was broadened. The units into which a subject was divided were much larger than before and rather less control was exercised over the detailed presentation of information. Study guides were developed which led students through the study of textbooks and other media, provided a commentary on the content of these and included questions to enable students to test their own knowledge. Consideration of the total context of learning led to the development of teaching systems which incorporated the use of study guides and formal testing supplemented by lectures, tutorials, and practical work (see *Systems Approaches to*

403

Instructional Development). Among the best documented of these are the personalized system of instruction (PSI), the audio-tutorial approach and modular instruction.

Parallel to these developments in the use of structured written materials in teaching, and emerging from a different liberal tradition, the 1970s saw the appearance of another approach to the individualization of education. Unlike the methods already mentioned in which the mode of presentation was individual but with everyone studying the same material, learning contracts were used to tailor work to the unique needs of each individual. The aim of those who used learning contracts was to assist students to formulate their own learning plans in a particular area, to put this plan into practice, and to evaluate the outcomes of this learning. This was in significant contrast to many of the aims of the teaching systems mentioned earlier which were to make the learning of content specified by the teacher more effective.

At the time of writing both types of approach are in use in higher education around the world. In few institutions are these the main methods of teaching and learning although there have been some open learning institutions established in the United States which operate exclusively on the principles of contract learning. The penetration of individualized instruction into conventional institutions has been rather limited. However, some specific approaches have become quite common in particular subjects—PSI in psychology and physics, audiotutorial approach in the biological sciences—and it would be uncommon to find a major institution in which at least one example of individualized instruction was not to be found.

2. Methods

Different methods of individualized instruction vary greatly in their emphasis. Some are based explicitly on a learning theory while others are more pragmatic arrangements which have been adopted because they achieve certain desired outcomes. In all cases the schemes originally promoted have been modified and adapted by others and it is often difficult to classify any particular method in use today as it is likely to be a hybrid or a substantial variation on one of the major themes.

Each of the major approaches will be described in turn, beginning with the original version, discussing the principles on which each are based, the most common variations, and the findings of any research which has been conducted.

2.1 The Personalized System of Instruction

The personalized system of instruction is also known as the Keller Plan after Fred Keller, one of its founders. In a PSI course students are provided with a written study guide which is composed of a number of separate sections or units. For each unit of the course there is usually an introduction and a list of objectives. These are

followed by a suggested procedure for achieving these objectives which might involve students reading notes provided or referring to particular parts of textbooks. Problems, exercises, and practical work may be included to help the student achieve the objectives and there may be opportunities for students to test themselves by the use of self-tests to help them decide whether they have mastered the content of that unit. When students believe they have mastered the unit they can present themselves for a test during one of a number of scheduled test periods. During these periods students may take tests, study on their own or with their peers, or ask for tutorial assistance. The tests are usually quite short, perhaps taking 20 minutes to complete. When students have completed a test they take it to a proctor or tutor who marks it immediately and gives feedback to the student on his or her performance. If students demonstrate mastery of the unit through passing the test with very few errors they then proceed to the next unit. If they have been unable to demonstrate mastery they are instructed to study the unit further and retake an alternative version of the test.

In the original form of PSI, use is made of student proctors who have been chosen for their mastery of the course content. These are normally undergraduate students who have either progressed rapidly in the subject or who have successfully completed the course previously. These students may be paid or receive course work credit.

Lectures and demonstrations are used for purposes of enrichment, providing motivation and giving an overview of the course. These are far fewer than in a conventional course, attendance is voluntary, and they are not essential for mastery of the subject.

The key elements of the system are the requirements for progressive mastery and the self-pacing which necessarily follows. Students cannot progress unless they can demonstrate that they have mastered each unit. As different students learn at different rates the course proceeds at different rates for different students. Students are reinforced in their learning by receiving immediate feedback on their performance and they are not penalized if they are not successful at any stage. They can repeat the test until they are successful and the number of attempts does not count against them.

The personalized system of instruction has been the subject of probably more research and evaluation than any other approach to individualized instruction and a journal, the *Journal of Personalized Instruction*, has been established as a forum for such studies. Each of the elements of the method have been studied in detail (Robin 1976) and there have been a number of studies comparing the effects of PSI with conventional courses. Kulik et al. (1979a) undertook a meta-analysis of 75 comparative studies. Their findings were "that PSI generally produces superior student achievement, less variation in achievement, and higher student ratings in college courses, but does not affect the withdrawal rate or student study time in these courses." They found that the superiority of PSI could be demonstrated in a variety of course settings with a number of different research designs.

One of the most contentious aspects of PSI, and indeed all individualized methods using a mastery learning approach, concerns the resulting distribution of student grades. In conventional courses it is expected that the distribution of student performance will correspond approximately to that of a normal, bell-shaped, curve with similar numbers of students with high and low marks. However, the mastery principle is based on the assumption that all students can achieve at high levels if they are given sufficient time and favourable conditions. As mastery approaches to individualized instruction are designed to do just this, it is expected that the grade distributions which result will be considerably skewed towards the upper end of any scale. In other words it is a normal expectation in such courses that students who successfully complete all units will receive an "A" grade. In most respects PSI courses fit very easily into a programme which includes mostly conventional classes, however, it is with respect to the grade distribution that difficulties are to be found. Accommodations have been made, such as allowing for a mark to be awarded for a minimum number of units completed with additional marks for further units mastered, but there is a fundamental conflict of assumptions between the two systems of assessment. It should also be recognized that the concept of mastery is inapplicable in many important areas of learning and in these areas a mastery learning approach would not be appropriate.

There have been many variations on the basic PSI system, some of which do not retain the same basic principles as the original but still use the same name. The most frequent difference between PSI courses in the United States and the United Kingdom is in the use of student proctors. Unlike in the United States, there is no tradition in the United Kingdom of paying undergraduate students or allocating credit for peer teaching and it is therefore common to find more costly postgraduate students as tutors (Bridge and Elton 1977). Another variation is in the use of variable routes through course units and in the provision of optional units. This adds flexibility to the basic linear path and can allow for greater student choice in the selection of content (Melton 1981). Some adaptations have occurred to deal with one of the most frequently expressed problems of those who have adopted PSI, that of student procrastination. In a self-paced course, students are free to delay study, and if they are studying one self-paced course amongst a number of other teacher-paced courses workload demands get progressively greater through the year. Some practitioners have introduced in their courses minimum times for the completion of certain units and others have introduced incentive schemes which give bonus marks for completion of units in minimum time. Such adaptations are not always compatible with the principles on which the system is based and would be frowned upon by purists.

2.2 The Audiotutorial Approach

The audiotutorial or autotutorial approach was developed from 1961 onwards by Postlethwait and his colleagues in a biology course at Purdue University (Postlethwait et al. 1972). The main element of their system is the use of audiotape to provide students with individual guidance on how they should study a particular course. The audiotutorial takes place in a specially designed booth or carrel in which are available the taped instructions, a set of objectives for the unit, illustrative materials, laboratory manuals, and other audiovisual materials as appropriate. The taped instructions are a form of study guide rather than a lecture which is logically sequenced to enable students to learn effectively from the materials at hand. A number of booths are available in a learning centre which is open for an extended period of time and to which students can go at times convenient to themselves.

In addition to work in the learning centre there are what are known as general assembly sessions in which the kinds of activity best done in a large group take place. Lectures are given, films shown, and examinations conducted. Small-group sessions also take place. These terminate a week's work and students meet with an instructor to take a short oral and written test and engage in a structured discussion. Other activities can include short research projects and the preparation of papers.

Self-pacing can occur, but only within the confines of the week's activity. It is interesting to note that this approach was developed in a botany course in which the demands of the practical materials were such that often specimens could not be made available for extended periods. While written guides are used as in PSI, the use of the audiotape enhances the contact a student has with the instructor and enables students to feel a degree of personal contact which is missing from the written word.

Kulik et al. (1979b) have also conducted a meta-analysis of 48 studies which compared audiotutorial approaches with conventional instruction. Their findings are less positive than those for PSI. They found that audiotutorial instruction had a significant but small overall effect on student achievement in college courses and that it had little effect on withdrawal rates or on student course evaluations.

As the mastery concept is not central to the audiotutorial approach there are few reported problems with grade distributions and as far as this aspect of individualized instruction is concerned there is less conflict between this approach and conventional teaching and testing activities.

2.3 Modular Instruction

Modular instruction is a more recent development than either PSI or audiotutorial and it cannot be so clearly attributed to a particular person. Goldschmid and

Goldschmid (1973) are defined a module as "a self-contained, independent unit of a planned series of learning activities designed to help the student accomplish certain well defined objectives". Modular instruction can either take the form of a few modules inserted into an otherwise traditional course or it can form a complete course through a prescribed sequence or through student choice from a range of modules. It is therefore a more flexible arrangement than either PSI or audiotutorial, although it draws much from the experience of these approaches.

A module typically consists of a pretest which allows students to determine if they are ready to study the material of the unit or if they have previously mastered the content, a set of learning objectives, a variety of instructional activities such as reading textbooks and articles, viewing films or slides, examining demonstration materials, participating in experiments and projects, and a posttest to determine if the student has mastered the material. Testing procedures are not necessarily as formal as in PSI or audiotutorial methods. The instructor acts as a resource person who can be called upon for assistance when required. The provision of pretests aids in diagnosing the need for remedial study and they can be used to direct students to appropriate remedial sequences which may take the form of other modules.

Modular instruction has not been subject to as much research activity as its antecedents and that combined with the difficulty in being able to define what a modular course consists of—1 hour or 100 hours?—means that summative findings cannot be stated.

2.4 The Use of Computers

Most forms of individualized instruction in which the materials are developed by instructors for students can be regarded as falling within one of the categories mentioned above. The only major area not covered there is that which uses a particular device—the computer—to aid learning. In many cases computers have been used as components of PSI, audiotutorial or modular courses to either schedule sessions, provide tests, or act as teaching machines. However, there are a great many uses to which computers can be put in the individualizing of teaching. The main categories of use are in tutoring students by providing a variety of problems to solve and in guiding students through teaching sequences which have been programmed; in managing teaching by administering tests, diagnosing weaknesses, and directing students towards appropriate materials; in simulations by helping students to examine the relationships among variables in complex situations; and in programming studies in which the computer is used as a problem-solving tool which the student is required to programme. Many authors have extolled the virtues of the computer in learning and many sophisticated systems have been developed for educational purposes, but as yet in higher education their impact on learning is modest (Kulik et al. 1980). There is a high level of

activity in this area and this finding may well need to be modified in the future.

2.5 Learning Contracts

Learning contracts differ markedly from the approaches discussed previously, as learning activities are not designed in advance by a teacher. Learning contracts are a form of individualized learning and independent study in which students are responsible for planning what is to be learned, how they will learn it and for identifying how that learning is to be assessed. They may in this process draw upon self-instructional materials, but this is not an essential element of the approach. A learning contract is prepared by a student who then shows it to a teacher. Negotiation on the details of the contract takes place between the two parties and when they agree on the final version the student proceeds to study in the ways indicated in the contract document. Study may take any form whatsoever from participation in conventional classes to individual projects, community placements, or other forms of experiential learning. Assessment of learning takes place in the manner specified in the contract using the criteria which have been agreed.

Learning contracts may be used as one component of a subject, as a whole course, or for an entire programme of study for a degree. The key factors in learning contracts are that individualization occurs through students taking responsibility for directing their own learning, and that such learning is validated through a process of mutual negotiation which leads to a contract to which both parties are bound (Berte 1975). A scheme of learning contracts can be implemented in a variety of ways, with varying degrees of rigidity. Some practitioners stress the need for renegotiation of contracts on demand, others for the building of contracts through a sequence of short draft contracts before setting longer ones in order to assist students to develop the skills necessary for planning their own learning.

One of the main proponents of learning contracts is Knowles (1975). He has described their use in situations in which they are used as a substitute for teaching a particular course and he draws attention to the conditions which must surround the introduction of learning contracts to students unfamiliar with the idea. The first stage is to set a climate conducive to self-directed learning. This may be done by the use of simple tasks and exercises which help students to get to know each other as persons and as resources for mutual learning, introduces them to the ideas of self-directed learning and learning contracts, helps them understand the role of the facilitator (formerly the teacher), and begins to establish an atmosphere of support and cooperation. The next step is the diagnosing of needs for learning. This involves the identification of the competencies that the students wish to acquire and a self-assessment of current levels of performance with respect to these competencies. From this, students move to the formulation of a draft learning plan and consult with their peers, with the facilitator and with any other relevant parties about the plan. The plan is then redrafted and submitted for validation to the teacher. Once approved the students engage in the learning activities they have specified using the teacher as a resource to aid their learning. They then present evidence of their achievement which is assessed in whatever way has been agreed in the contract. Knowles uses four main headings for the written contract which students prepare: (a) learning objectives, (b) learning resources and strategies, (c) evidence of accomplishment, and (d) criteria and means of validating evidence.

Some forms of individualized learning are based upon the notion of student planning but do not proceed with the formalities of the contract, others use a form of contracting but do not use the term contract, preferring learning plan (Boud 1981). There is a great diversity of approaches to individualization through independent study and self-directed learning. These range from individual project work which is now commonplace in most courses to student participation in research and the all embracing approach which has developed in Western Europe since the early 1970s under the title of project orientation (Cornwall and Schmithals 1976).

To date there has been little research directed towards assessing the impact of learning contracts and other forms of student-planned learning. There is a fundamental difficulty in conducting comparisons between the outcomes of these approaches and those of conventional teaching; they are pursuing different aims. The proponents of student-planned learning do not regard this primarily as a means of making the teaching of present courses more effective, although this may result through students becoming more committed to learning those things which they have identified for themselves.

One of the main aims of student-planned learning is to involve students more fully in their education so that they may know what it is they study and develop the skills which they need in learning once they have departed from the educational institution. In conventional institutions these ideas are having a modest impact and elements of contracting or student planning in some advanced courses can be observed.

3. Issues

Any move to individualization has implications for staffing, for resources, and for policy within an institution. In some cases individualized instruction can be fitted into the conventional system with little disruption to the timetable or to other administrative arrangements; in others a profound change is required which forces a reappraisal of the educational goals of a programme or department. Depending on the nature of the individualization which is introduced, the implications can be very different. The issues raised by individualization will be considered for the role of the teacher, for costs and staffing, and for matters of implementation.

3.1 The Role of the Teacher

In all cases the role of the teacher is different in individualized instruction than in conventional teaching. Firstly, there is much less emphasis on instructing groups of students in a classroom. The main medium of communication is the written word, or in the case of the audiotutorial, the audiotape. Teachers need to develop the skills and sensitivities which will lead them to effective use of these media. For these approaches the teacher becomes an instructional designer, planning teaching in advance with less chance to respond to events as they arise, and with instructional material available in a permanent form. Secondly, the teacher becomes less of an instructor once the course has been established and takes on the role of a manager of learning resources and facilitator in the learning of others. Often these roles can be uncomfortable ones especially if the teacher is only familiar with normal classroom interactions. The teacher becomes necessarily less remote and is faced with counselling and often complex organizational tasks dealing both with students and with other people involved in the operation. Finally, in student-planned individualized learning the teacher becomes primarily a facilitator and loses much of the authoritative role which is basic to both conventional teaching and the design of intructional materials. The teacher has to respond to the varying needs of all students and is unable to set the agenda for learning. This is a role which some teachers find extremely difficult to accept.

3.2 Costs and Staffing

The implication for these are different for teacher-planned and student-planned approaches and will therefore be discussed separately.

Two main costs need to be considered: firstly, those of establishing the instructional system, of designing and preparing the resources which are needed; and secondly, the ongoing costs of keeping the system running once it has been designed. Developmental costs are greater in individualized instruction than conventional teaching. This is a consequence of requiring that materials be available in permanent form in advance of learning activities and therefore require greater care in preparation. The implication of this is that it is necessary for an individualized course to be used for a number of years if the initial costs are to be justified. It is also desirable for the same reasons for there to be relatively large numbers of students taking the course. The number of students required and the number of years of use to justify these costs depends greatly on the particular scheme adopted and the ongoing costs of the system. The magnitude of the ongoing costs and whether they are more or less than conventional teaching depend crucially on the level of staff support of the system as the staffing costs normally outweigh all other factors. If students can be used as tutors or proctors and rewarded with credit then the running costs will normally be less than conventional teaching. Similarly, if there is a large amount of self-testing or computer testing then costs can be lower.

Initial and ongoing costs need to be balanced if the costs of individualized instruction are to be acceptable or less than conventional teaching. It is commonly cited that a course needs to run for at least five years with only minor changes if the initial investment is to be justified. This implies that prestructured methods are not suitable for subjects in which the content is rapidly changing or situations in which it is not expected to be able to retain the same course for a number of years.

For student-planned courses the costs are more difficult to identify as they depend crucially on the level of support and facilitation which is provided for students. Students experienced in planning their own learning will need far less support than those meeting the task for the first time. However, most courses based upon contract learning are no more expensive to run than conventional teaching with classes of a modest size, say less than 40 students. Preparation time on the part of the teacher is normally no greater than that required for group-based instruction, but it is of course of a different type, focusing on the identification of resources and the planning of the initial climate setting and planning activities.

3.3 Adoption and Implementation

With few exceptions the implementation of individualized instruction has depended on the endeavours of enthusiasts. While many approaches have been accepted in universities and colleges, individualization is not normally to be found as part of most courses. In part this is due to the special demands such approaches make on teachers and the need for a reappraisal of the ways in which teaching responsibilities are viewed. It can be anticipated that there will be further new developments in individualized learning and there will be an increase in the number of individualized courses to be found. However, it is unlikely that the potential of these methods will be fully realized and have a major influence on established institutions of higher education. The main

barriers to this are: (a) the need in most cases for a higher initial investment of resources, (b) the need to retrain teachers to adopt new roles and ways of conceptualizing teaching, and (c) the rigidities imposed by the end of a period of expansion in most Western countries. In this, individualization is likely to suffer along with many other innovations in teaching.

Bibliography

Berte N R (ed.) 1975 *Individualizing Education Through Contract Learning.* University of Alabama Press, Alabama

Boud D J (ed.) 1981 *Developing Student Autonomy in Learning.* Kogan Page, London

Bridge W, Elton L (eds.) 1977 *Individual Study in Undergraduate Science.* Heinemann Educational, London

Cornwall M, Schmithals F (eds.) 1976 *Project-orientation in Higher Education.* University Teaching Methods Unit, University of London, London

Goldschmid B, Goldschmid M L 1973 Modular instruction in higher education: A review. *Higher Educ.* 2: 15–32

Goldschmid B, Goldschmid M L 1974 Individualizing instruction in higher education: A review. *Higher Educ.* 3: 1–24

Knowles M 1975 *Self-directed Learning: A Guide for Learners and Teachers.* Association Press, New York

Kulik J A, Kulik C-L C, Cohen P A 1979a A meta-analysis of outcome studies of Keller's Personalized System of Instruction. *Am. Psychol.* 34: 307–18

Kulik J A, Kulik C-L C, Cohen P A 1979b Research on audio-tutorial instruction: A meta-analysis of comparative studies. *Res. Higher Educ.* 11: 321–41

Kulik J A, Kulik C-L C, Cohen P A 1980 Effectiveness of computer-based college teaching: A meta-analysis of findings. *Rev. Educ. Res.* 50: 525–44

Melton R J 1981 Individualized learning methods in perspective. *Higher Educ.* 10: 403–23

Postlethwait S N, Novak J, Murray H T 1972 *The Audio-tutorial Approach to Learning, Through Independent Study and Integrated Experience.* Burgess, Minneapolis, Minnesota

Robin A L 1976 Behavioral instruction in the college classroom. *Rev. Educ. Res.* 46: 313–54

Individualized School Programs

J. O. Bolvin

For years educators have attempted to find means to individualize instruction. Grouping practices, tracking schemes, project work, independent study, nongraded systems, dual progress plans, continuous progress plans, and remedial systems have all been attempts to adapt to student differences. Cronbach (1967) has identified five patterns for describing education systems and their adaptability to the individual. His fifth pattern, establishing sets of goals and learning outcomes with a variety of instructional techniques and resources with time to reach the desired competencies varying from student to student, most closely represents the intent of most individualized programs currently in use. Most pro-

grams seem to have the following assumptions in common: (a) they can be adaptive to the abilities, interests, backgrounds, and needs of the student; (b) they can provide optional means for different students to achieve the same goals; (c) they can provide the opportunity for different students to pursue different goals and to differing degrees of attainment; and (d) the goals to be attained by the student are individually planned.

Among the many programs currently in use to adapt to the individual differences of students there are wide variations in their adherence to the assumptions stated above as well as in their approaches in providing for them. There are programs for individualizing single school subjects, such as math or reading, while there are others that include most, if not all, of the subjects offered by the school. There are programs that provide as a part of their system a core of instructional materials developed for a specific set of objectives while others provide suggested objectives and materials but leave the selection up to the user. There are programs that suggest adherence to mastery criteria while others do not. As a final example, there are individualized programs that suggest that new units begin with group instruction branching into individualized plans while there are others that begin all units with individualized plans.

In spite of these differences there are components of the various individualized systems which seem to be common to most (Bolvin and Glaser 1971, Glaser 1977). These are:

(a) A redefinition of school time to provide the opportunity to vary instructional time in order that students may complete tasks and reach planned outcomes.

(b) Well-defined and well-structured curricula which provide for necessary sequencing and multiple options for learning to facilitate student progress. For most subject areas there are a variety of ways of expressing the structure and even the most highly structured scope and sequence statements of a curriculum provide optional paths for the learner.

(c) Procedures for assessing student readiness, needs, characteristics, and accomplishments to assist in student and teacher decision making. Since the major focus of assessment instruments to meet these purposes is to provide information about "how much" or "how well" a student can perform a given task or set of tasks the instruments must provide criterion-referenced or performance-referenced scores.

(d) The availability of instructional materials and other resources to facilitate learning which are open and accessible to students and which can provide a variety of means to attaining the desired mastery. There is considerable variation among individualized instruction programs as to the number of alternative learning aides which are available to the learner.

(e) Individual lesson plans for each student that address the tasks to be accomplished, estimated time for accomplishment, materials and resources appropriate, and the criterion of accomplishments expected. Such plans are essential not only for communicating with the student but also for planning for the operation and management of the classroom(s).

(f) Strategies for information feedback to permit periodic monitoring of progress and to facilitate decision making. Programs vary from having to entirely rely on the student to compile the information on some predetermined form, to having clerks generate the information, or to computer storage of information.

(g) The reorganization of the school environment to permit greater flexibility in assignments of staff, utilization of facilities, and reallocation of time. Many individualized systems have moved to a "planning and instructional team" for organizing the staff since many decisions must now be shared ones.

The more closely a school begins to provide for the seven components outlined above, the more difficult it becomes for a teacher to provide the desired learning options needed for any one group of students. Instructional systems such as Individually Prescribed Instruction (Lindvall and Bolvin 1967), Primary Education Project (Resnick et al. 1975), Program for Learning in Accordance with Needs (Flanagan et al. 1975), Mastery Learning Plan (Block 1980), the Elementary and Middle School Program of the Korean Education Development Institute (Kim et al. 1973), and Individually Guided Instruction (Klausmeier 1976) have necessitated role changes for principals, teachers, and other staff. The one system that has gone the furthest in specifying organizational changes necessary is the Individually Guided Instruction System of the University of Wisconsin's Research and Development Center for Cognitive Learning (Klausmeier 1976). Each school is organized into multiage "units" responsible for the education of 100–500 students, coordinated by a unit leader and staffed by teachers, paraprofessionals, student teachers, or interns. The unit leader serves with the other unit leaders and the principal on a building Instructional Improvement Committee. This committee, working with the principal, is responsible for coordinating, planning, and managing the instructional program of the school. Although functions of all professionals change, the only new position within the structure is the unit leader. This individual is a teacher and an instructional leader of the unit (Sorenson et al. 1976).

The teacher's role in Individually Guided Instruction, as in most individualized instruction or adaptive education systems, changes from one who spends considerable amounts of time conveying and explaining information and ideas to a large group to one who guides and directs the learning which has been adapted to the needs of the learners. Teachers must spend time in organizing instruction (planning) for each student, assessing the student when she or he is ready, providing a variety of learning strategies in an attempt to relate specific strategies to specific students, establishing small groups for instruction as the need arises, and in planning with others for space, time, and instructional resources necessary to meet the short-term needs of a group of students.

Evaluation of the outcomes of individualized instructional programs is inconclusive whether conducted by the sponsors or by independent evaluators (Block et al. 1977, Resnick et al. 1975, Rosenshine 1976, Soar 1973, Stallings and Kaskowitz 1974). Generally, the results show no real differences in student achievement when different organizational patterns are compared. They indicate some improvement in students' attitudes toward school but no difference in attitude toward the teacher.

Due to the complex nature of most of the systems developed to adapt to learner differences, program developers have turned their attention to improving: learning materials; strategies for teaching; environments for learning; procedures to involve students in their own goal planning; and organizational arrangements to facilitate shared planning, decision making, and instruction. At the same time evaluators have turned their attention to developing better conceptual schemes for instructional evaluation including the study of factors related to student outcomes (Cooley and Leinhardt 1975, Rosenshine 1976).

Bibliography

Block G, Stebbs L, Proper E 1977 *Effects of Follow Through Models*, Vol. 4B. Abt Associates, Cambridge, Massachusetts
Block J H 1980 Promoting excellence through mastery learning. *Theory Pract.* 19: 66–74
Bolvin J O, Glaser R 1971 Individualizing instruction. In: Allen D W, Seifman E (eds.) 1971 *The Teacher's Handbook*. Scott, Foresman, Glenview, Illinois, pp. 270–79
Cooley W W, Leinhardt G 1975 *Application of a Model for Investigating Classroom Processes*. University of Pittsburgh, Learning Research and Development Center, Pittsburgh, Pennsylvania
Cronbach L J 1967 How can instruction be adapted to individual differences? In: Gagné R M (ed.) 1967 *Learning and Individual Differences: A Symposium of the Learning Research and Development Center, University of Pittsburgh*. Merrill, Columbus, Ohio, pp. 23–39
Flanagan J C, Shanner W M, Brudner H J, Market R W 1975 An individualized instructional system: Program learning in accordance with needs. In: Talmage H (ed.) 1975 *Systems of Individualized Education*. McCutchan, Berkeley, California
Glaser R 1977 *Adaptive Education: Individual Diversity and Learning*. Holt, Rinehart and Winston, New York.
Kim Y, Kwac S B, Park J, Park M, Song Y 1973 *Toward a New Instructional System: Summary Report of the First Small-scale Tryout*. Research Report No. 1. Korean Educational Development Institute, Seoul
Klausmeier H J 1976 Individually guided education. *J. Teach. Educ.* 27: 199–207
Lindvall C M, Bolvin J O 1967 Programmed instruction in the schools: An application of programming principles in "Individually Prescribed Instruction." In: Lange P C (ed.) 1967 *Programmed Instruction*. Sixty-sixth Yearbook of the National Society for the Study of Education. University of Chicago Press, Chicago, Illinois
Resnick L B, Wang M C, Rosner J 1975 *Adaptive Education for Young Children: The Primary Education Project*. University of Pittsburgh, Learning Research and Development Center, Pittsburgh, Pennsylvania
Rosenshine B 1976 Classroom instruction. In: Gage N L (ed.) 1976 *The Psychology of Teaching Methods*. Seventy-fifth Yearbook of the National Society for the Study of Education. University of Chicago Press, Chicago, Illinois, pp. 335–71
Soar R 1973 Final report. *Follow-through Classroom Process Measurement and Pupil Growth (1970–1971)*. University of Florida, College of Education, Gainesville, Florida
Sorenson J, Rossman P A, Barnes D 1976 The unit leader and educational decision making. *J. Teach. Educ.* 27: 224–25
Stallings J A, Kaskowitz D H 1974 *Follow-through Classroom Observation Evaluation 1972–1973*. Stanford Research Institute, Menlo Park, California. ERIC Document No. ED 104 969
Whitley T W 1979 The effects of individualized instruction on the attitudes of middle school pupils. *J. Educ. Res.* 72: 188–93

Programmed Learning

M. R. Eraut

Outside the field of education, the word programme has come to mean either (a) a listing of a series of events, such as the items in a concert or a show; or (b) the series of events themselves, considered collectively; or (c) a definite plan for an intended set of proceedings or performance. Something is said to be programmed if there is a predefined sequence of events that has been planned in advance. In particular, the term is used to describe distinctive segments of radio and television transmissions which have been separately scripted and are capable of being repeated in recorded form—these are called radio or television programmes, and distinct sets of instructions for computers to execute—these are called computer programs. In both broadcasting and computing contexts it soon became normal to distinguish

between hardware (machines, devices, instruments, etc.) which was the responsibility of engineers, and software (content, instructions, materials, etc.) which was the responsibility of communications specialists or information scientists. A program was a unit of software that was planned as a discrete entity and could be used independently of other programs.

When Skinner and Crowder began to experiment in the mid-1950s with different types of teaching machine, it was natural for them to describe the rolls of paper or film which carried their information for students as programmes, and the process of preparing these instructional sequences as programming. So, when Glaser et al. (1960) devised a means of presenting Skinnerian programmes in book format, they called their new product a "paper teaching machine" or, sensing that this term might cause some confusion, a programmed textbook. This new term did not resolve the definition problem because, according to the earlier definition, all textbooks could be regarded as programmed in some sense. But nevertheless the term stuck. Hence textbooks that resemble the early experimental products of Skinner, Glaser, and Crowder are called programmed texts, and most other textbooks are not so described. The collective term used to describe the whole of this newly developing field—the new kinds of teaching machine, the programmes that fed these machines, and the machine-independent programmed texts—was programmed instruction or programmed learning.

Later workers in the field of programmed learning have come to regret this early hardening of its terminology, but have been largely unsuccessful in their attempts to change it. The general public and, indeed, most educators have persisted in identifying programmed learning with its earliest, most experimental products (rather like identifying geometry only with Pythagoras and Euclid). Hence educational technologists have tended to drop the term and to use new names to describe innovations that incorporate many of the principles originally developed under the heading of programmed learning.

This article takes a historical approach. First it describes the early developments that gave programmed learning its "image". Then it explains how many of the early ideas were modified and new ideas introduced as a result of further research and practical experience. Finally, it discusses some of the innovations that grew out of the "programmed learning" field and indicates where they are covered elsewhere in the Encyclopedia.

1. Early Developments

Though there had been earlier work of relevance, the man who brought programmed learning into prominence was B. F. Skinner , whose publications between 1954 and 1968 commanded the attention of the scientific and educational communities and even the general public. Unlike many educational innovations, Skinner's work was based on a clearly articulated theoretical base—in his case the psychological theory of operant conditioning. According to this theory, behaviour is only learned if it is immediately reinforced, that is, followed by some pleasurable event such as food, praise, or attention. So the task of the programmer, or indeed any teacher, is to arrange the contingencies of reinforcement so that correct responses to some question or assignment are immediately rewarded whilst incorrect responses are not rewarded. Skinner strongly opposed punishment for creating a dysfunctional degree of anxiety, and even urged that incorrect responses be kept to a minimum so that there was no danger of developing a negative attitude towards the learning activity. His earlier work with rats and pigeons had shown that this theoretical prescription could be realized in practice by

breaking down a learning sequence into a large number of very small steps. This kept the error rate down to a minimum and allowed reinforcement to be frequent and immediate. Certain behaviours could be shaped by slowly refining the reinforcement contingencies, for example, rewarding almost any attempt at pronouncing a new word in the early stages and progressively becoming stricter about what would count as correct. With verbal material this shaping process could be accomplished by giving the student strong prompts at the beginning (hints, half-completed answers, etc.) then gradually weakening the strength of the prompts. Clearly, this whole process needs to be carefully controlled and it was for this purpose that Skinner invented his first teaching machine.

Skinner's early teaching machines shared certain common features. Only one step in the instructional sequence appeared at a time. This came to be called a frame, as it appeared in a "frame" or "window" on top of the machine; and was limited in length by the size of this window to about 30 words. Each frame demanded an overt response from the student (writing a word, punching a hole, or pressing a key, according to the type of machine) who then discovered if he or she was correct by comparing the answer with the correct one when he or she turned the roll or, in the case of punched responses, by the automatic presentation of the next frame. The student's responses are nearly always correct *if* the programme has been properly prepared by good design and testing and revision; and confirmation of this correctness is assumed to be reinforcing. The student can work at his or her own pace and gradually acquires the chunk of knowledge that the programme is designed to teach.

Early programmed texts simulated these machines in two important respects. First, they divided their presentation into frames of a similar size and used similar techniques of shaping and prompting to construct their learning sequences. Second, they sought to prevent students seeing the answer in advance of making their own response (a guaranteed feature of machine presentation) by printing successive frames on different pages, each new frame beginning with the answer to the previous frame. In a typical text of this kind, page 1 might contain frames 1, 6, 11, 16, and 21 while page 3 presented frames 2, 7, 12, 17, and 22, thus completing a 25-frame sequence on page 9 and leaving the even-numbered pages for a similar sequence working through the book backwards.

To summarize, then, the principle features of these Skinnerian or linear programmes (so-called because each student follows the same linear sequence of frames) are (a) division of the subject matter into a logical sequence of small steps, (b) revision of this sequence until the error rate is low, (c) overt responding by the student, (d) immediate presentation of the correct response, and (e) an individual mode of working which allows students to proceed at their own rate.

411

Thirty years earlier Pressey had designed a series of self-teaching devices based on different principles from those of Skinner, but these aroused little interest at the time. Pressey had noted that students can learn from the experience of taking tests, especially when provided with immediate feedback on their performance. So he devised a testing machine which required students to press keys to answer multiple-choice questions, and only presented the next question after the correct key had been pressed. The assumption was that, after students had been exposed to some initial instruction—either written material or a conventional lecture or lesson—they would consolidate their learning by going through an appropriate machine-presented test until they had mastered all the questions and ceased making any mistakes. The crucial distinction between Pressey and Skinner was that while Skinner treated errors as something to be avoided, Pressey regarded them as useful feedback to the student. A further development of Pressey's position was to use errors to direct the student to an appropriate explanation or remedial sequence; and this was initiated by Crowder.

Crowder's background was in training troubleshooters to find malfunctions in electronic equipment where he soon found that the "coach and pupil" method was the most successful. However, there was a scarcity of coaches; so Crowder attempted to automate the coaching procedure by devising a simulated tutor. This was achieved by giving the student some information, asking a multiple-choice question and then providing a different response for each answer chosen. Thus students proceeded through a programme along different routes or branches and care could be taken to see that they understood each point before they proceeded to the next. By adopting a fairly conversational style, the student could feel that he or she was talking to a remote tutor who paid special attention to diagnosing and remedying his or her own personal misunderstandings. Crowder called his machines Autotutors and used microfilm to present his programmes. The student's responses on the keyboard controlled the movement of the film, so that the appropriate next frame was shown. Soon, these branching programmes were also converted into a book format, with one frame on each page and a multiple-choice question directing the student to a different page for each answer. On reaching that page, the student gets feedback that he or she is correct or has made a particular kind of mistake. In the former case the next chunk of information is presented, while in the latter the student may either be sent back to answer the question again or routed through a short remedial sequence.

Typically, Crowder's frames were much longer than Skinner's and he presented new material a paragraph at a time. When he turned to education, he chose topics from secondary-school mathematics and computing. The approach to instruction was not shaping behaviour but explanation and reasoning. This appealed more to sophisticated adults and to brighter students for whom getting easy questions right was more tedious than reinforcing. One disadvantage, however, was that the provision of remedial loops lessened the burden on frame design, making it less likely that poorly written frames would get detected and revised while the programme was being developed.

From 1960 researchers embarked on experiments to compare linear with branching programmes and to investigate design variables such as step size, error rate, and response mode, while developers concentrated on training programmers and writing programmes. Implementing programmed learning in schools and colleges drew attention to the major problems of matching the right student to the right programme and managing classes where students did not all proceed as the same rate. After the initial excitement of the pioneering decade 1954–64, a more mature, reflective, and practical range of approaches developed; and it is these that form the substance of the next three sections.

2. Preparation for Programming

Skinner and Holland (1958) described the initial stages of preparing a programme to teach verbal knowledge in the following terms:

> *Specifications of a course.* The programmer must know what verbal behavior the student is to have in his repertoire after completing the course and how precisely and extensively he is to talk about the field.
>
> *Knowledge previously acquired.* The student is assumed to possess some verbal behavior in the area before he starts the course. This must be stated, and the programmer must not at any time appeal to material not included in the statement or not provided by earlier parts of the program...
>
> *Ordering the knowledge to be acquired.* At each step the programmer must ask, "What behavior must the student have before he can take this step?" A sequence of steps forms a progression from the initially assumed knowledge up to the specified final repertoire. No step should be encountered before the student has mastered everything needed to take it.
>
> *Listing the terms, etc.* Before writing frames for each set, the programmer should make lists of (a) the terms to be covered, (b) the processes or principles, (c) a wide range of illustrative examples.

Each of these stages was reconceptualized during the following decade, and a range of approaches developed to what was still recognized as essentially the same programming process.

What Skinner and Holland described as the intended "verbal behavior" of the student, was soon redefined in terms of learning objectives, thus introducing a term which was already familiar to training psychologists, curriculum specialists, and psychometricians without significantly changing the meaning. The notion of objectives was also given a tremendous boost by the popularity of Mager's (1961) *Preparing Objectives for Programmed Instruction* which argued the need for behavioural objectives in a short, witty, programmed book. Soon an explicit statement of objectives in behavioural terms became the standard form of course specification for all programmed learning sequences.

This was to be accompanied by a statement of student prerequisites, which indicated what knowledge a student would need to have previously acquired before starting the course. The careful step-by-step approach of a linear programme could only work if students possessed all the necessary prerequisites, and even branching programmes were limited in the number of remedial loops they could incorporate to cope with students who were not fully prepared for them. Sometimes this statement of prerequisites was replaced by a pretest, which a prospective student had to pass. But there was also another kind of pretest, covering the material taught in the programme, which students were expected to fail. Originally this was used for scientific reasons, that is, for measuring learning gain in terms of the difference in scores between a pretest and an identical or equivalent posttest. But later another, diagnostic, purpose for pretests was discovered. Some students were already competent in the area covered by the programme, and passing a pretest could enable them to skip it, and it was only a short step from this to design pretests which enabled knowledgeable students to skip some sections of a programme but not others (see *Task Analysis*).

These developments were relatively simple extrapolations from Skinner's original procedures, for it was not until the third and fourth stages of programme preparation that major problems arose. Here it was soon realized that Skinner's ideas about "ordering the knowledge to be acquired" and "listing terms" provided insufficient guidance for the programming of complex conceptual material. Nor could the stages be readily separated. The term "task analysis" was imported from the industrial training field to describe the difficult but crucial stage of programme preparation. Though some authors are prone to present their views without much modesty, task analysis remains an area where there is little general agreement on the appropriate approach, even today. Nevertheless, a range of concepts and strategies has been developed without which any instructional designer would have an impoverished repertoire of possible approaches. In particular, four main ideas have proved seminal—master performer, hierarchy, matrix, and classification by knowledge type.

The idea of a master performer had a double significance: on the one hand it linked with the training psychologists' tradition of job analysis, while on the other hand it was influential in the curriculum reform movements of the 1960s and early 1970s, where the goal of making students more like practising scholars in the disciplines was widely advocated. The job analysis approach proved useful to programmers working in industrial and military settings but was less directly applicable to education. Nevertheless, it drew attention to the importance of "knowing how" rather than "knowing that" and strengthened the behavioural focus of course specification by learning objectives. The approach through reanalysing the critical knowledge, skills, and attitudes of subject matter experts was more directly relevant to education, but often proved difficult to realize in practice where it usually conflicted with curricular traditions and conventional modes of assessment. Though some educators saw programmed learning as particularly inappropriate for a curriculum based on thinking processes, there has been some interesting work in this area.

The hierarchy approach comes closest to Skinner's original conception of sequencing. It assumes that each objective can be broken down into subobjectives. Each subobjective is dependent on the prior learning of other subobjectives to such an extent that it is appropriate to talk of a hierarchy of objectives, which the learner ascends level by level, one subobjective at a time, using each step as a basis for those that follow. This provides an additional theoretical reason for small steps and makes the seqencing of these steps a matter of crucial importance. Ideally, hierarchies need to be empirically verified, but it is generally assumed that programmers can discern them by careful analysis of the subject matter (White and Gagné 1974). Though the general notion of prerequisite knowledge is widely accepted, there is considerable dispute as to whether many areas of knowledge are in fact acquired in such a methodical piecemeal manner. However, this type of analysis provides a useful approach to the problem of sequencing even if some of the individual steps are later combined.

A more flexible, though some would argue less penetrating, approach to sequencing a series of subobjectives or teaching points is the matrix system (Thomas et al. 1963). This begins by listing what Skinner calls terms, principles, and examples along both the horizontal and the vertical axes of a two-dimensional matrix. Then linkages between any two items can be noted by colouring the appropriate square of the matrix. For example a red square might mean that A is an example of principle B, a green square that A and C are examples of the same principle, a blue square that principle B is a prerequisite for principle D, and so on. Careful interpretation of this matrix then suggests possible sequences for the programme, leaving it open for the programmer to choose, for example, between deductive (rule → example) and inductive (example → rule) sequencing.

Two quite distinct approaches have evolved to classification by knowledge type: one is based on Bloom's *Taxonomy of Educational Objectives* and various developments of it, many of them subject specific (Bloom et al. 1971); the other is based on the typologies of learning psychologists which seek to differentiate between such categories as discriminations, chains, concepts, and principles (Gagné 1977). Both are discussed in this Part of the Encyclopedia. There are a very large number of variations for each approach, so most programmers choose a category system that seems to suit the particular problem they are tackling, often introducing their own modifications to adapt it to each specific situation.

3. Frame Design

While task analysis, the identification and sequencing of teaching points, can still be regarded as part of the preparation process, the design of individual frames and the continuity between them is the central task of programme writing. So far two distinct approaches to programme writing have been identified—linear small-step programming and branching large-step programming—each with its own implications for frame design. But hybrids soon appeared as programmers developed alternative tracks within linear programmes and skip-forward arrangements for their more knowledgeable students, and branching programmes began to incorporate short linear sequences (Markle 1969). Pressey-type programmes were expanded to include short sequences of remedial instruction, and these were often called adjunct programmes because they were used after material had been introduced in a conventional lesson or lecture. However, when teachers began to use ordinary linear programmes in a similar way, this distinction became somewhat artificial.

The most notable change during the 1960s was the gradual removal of the original guiding principles of linear programming, sometimes with advantage and sometimes not. The first to go was the principle of the short frame, which was found to underestimate the cognitive capacities of many learners. Moreover, the original frame size was an artefact of the window size of the early teaching machines, a restriction which was removed as teaching machines were replaced in most educational contexts by cheaper and more flexible programmed texts. In the interests of efficiency it was argued that students should receive as much information at a time as they could handle. Master performers usually handled a lot of information at once, and dividing it up into too many pieces was delaying, if not actually preventing, the development of mastery in the student. If too much information was included, this would become apparent when the programme was tested and appropriate revisions could then be made. Large frames were particularly important when multiple discriminations were being developed, when passages of text were being analysed, when maps or diagrams were included, or when task analysis revealed procedural knowledge that could be represented in algorithmic form. They also made the task of frame design more difficult and more imaginative, because responses had to be created which required the student to actively process larger and more complex chunks of information. An influential early exponent of this approach was Gilbert who devised a complex system of task analysis and frame design called "mathetics" and produced some stunningly elegant programmes.

Gilbert paved the way for what came to be known as "lean programming", in which programmers tried to use some of the newer large-frame designs to maximize step size and produce programmes with as few frames as possible. One approach advocated by this group of programmers was to convert their preliminary list of teaching points into a small number of criterion frames. Each criterion frame, if correctly answered, indicated the achievement of a significant learning objective; so the full set of criterion frames should be, and usually was, similar to the posttest. Having designed these criterion frames, the programmer then attempted to get students to succeed on each of them with as little preliminary instruction as possible. Since sequences that proved to be "too lean" could easily be detected and revised, this was found to be a practical method of working, and it stimulated programmers' creativity much more than writing to a formula.

The process of shaping behaviour became more sophisticated as a range of techniques for prompting the correct response was developed (Markle 1969). However, some linear programmers abandoned the idea of shaping in favour of a simulated dialogue with the student which relied more on question-and-answer sequences than on the gradual withdrawal of prompts. This was more attractive to subject experts, but those who were untutored or inexperienced often failed to realize that information which was not needed for working out the answer to a frame was rarely learned. Programmers who indulged in teachers' natural tendency to talk too much were exposed by Holland's (1965) famous blackout technique, for he showed that if those parts of a frame that were unnecessary for finding the correct response were blacked out, the student usually learned just as much. Nevertheless, programmers who understood the importance of active responding were able to make much more use of question-and-answer sequences than Skinner had originally envisaged.

This principle of active responding was a modification of Skinner's original insistence on overt responding. When books were used instead of teaching machines, the benefit of students having to write their responses (and hence render the books nonreusable) was soon questioned. It was found that in many contexts active responding, in which the learner's mind had to process the necessary information in order to answer a question, was sufficient, and no overt manifestation of the response was necessary unless it was needed as evidence for making later modifications to the programme. Overt responding, however, was still superior (a) when the learners were young children, (b) when the material was difficult, and (c) when special terminology was being taught.

The related principle of providing knowledge of results has also been questioned, though evidence suggests it is usually an advantage. In particular, feedback enhances performance (a) if the learner is motivated, (b) if knowledge of results is informative, and (c) if the learner knows or is told what to do to correct his or her errors. Though no longer applied in so rigid a manner, the principles of active responding and feedback remain important for instructional design, and it is important to note that they are necessary for cognitive as well as for behavioural approaches to learning.

Two further assumptions that were common to both the linear and the branching paradigms were individualized learning and learner-controlled pacing. Neither has been abandoned as a result of research or practical experience, but both have been modified under certain circumstances. One alternative is for pairs of students to work through a programme together, the supposition being that they will challenge and assist each other and enjoy each other's company. Comparisons of pairs with individual working have usually given no significant difference (Hartley 1974). However, one would expect such findings to depend on the particular pairings chosen, previous experience of partners working together, and the learning milieu of each particular classroom.

Learner-controlled pacing is often relinquished when fixed-pace media, such as motion pictures or audiotape, are used to present a programme, though some programmes of this type stop moving whenever a question is asked, allowing the students to start them again as soon as they are ready. Large group presentation with fixed pairing may be necessary if there is insufficient equipment or space for individualized learning, and it has been argued that fixed-pace programming is more efficient on time as well. Once the initial novelty has passed, students who are not very highly motivated tend to follow Parkinson's Law, their rate of work adapts to fit the time available (Hartley 1974).

4. Developmental Testing

Though Skinner's reinforcement theory assigned special priority to maintaining a very low error rate, this particular principle soon diminished in importance, not because the theoretical debate was resolved but because errors acquired a much more practical significance. Skinner's (1958) comment that "an unexpected advantage of machine instruction has proved to be the feedback to the programmer" became the understatement of the decade. Since programmers were dependent on errors for information about where and how to revise, they were much more interested in their distribution pattern than in any overall rate. Particular attention, for example, was given to any error in a criterion frame and the prior sequence of responses would be scrutinized for clues to any mistake. But on less important frames, errors were ignored unless their frequency was high or some obvious improvement in frame design was readily apparent.

The greatest contribution of programmed learning was probably attitudinal. Programmers accepted that it was their responsibility to get their programmes to work for any student in their target population. Hence the focus of developmental testing was on course improvement, and it was not until a later validation stage that they sought firm evidence of the effectiveness of their final version (Markle 1967). Clues for revision were more important in the earlier stages than statistics, and programmers soon found that more useful feedback was gained from intensive work with individual students

than from large-scale testing. This allowed them to discuss mistakes and to try out alternative explanations on the spot. Indeed one group of "lean programmers" suggested changing the usual programme writing sequence to: (a) prepare a sequence of criterion frames, (b) tutor a few students through these frames, recording the dialogue on audiotape, (c) use this experience to write the first draft of the programme.

As people became more aware of the importance of developmental testing and less confident of the validity of the original programming paradigms, they sought to define programmed learning in terms of the developmental process rather than the features of the product. No doubt this change in preferred definition was hastened by the appearance on the market of large numbers of low-quality programmes which had not been properly developed but still bore a superficial resemblance to the early programmed texts. But it also represented a genuine change of opinion amongst programmers, albeit one which failed to convert educators in general away from their product-based image of programmed learning. Figure 1 summarizes the sequence of events which most programmers in the late 1960s were accepting as not only describing but also characterizing and defining the programming process.

5. The Move Towards Instructional Systems

When people tried to use programmes as part of larger instructional systems with ordinary teachers in ordinary classrooms, a host of new problems arose (Schramm 1964). First, programmes were only available for isolated topics, so it was difficult to construct a whole course from published programmed materials. This made them so much more inconvenient (and expensive) than the traditional textbook that only the most dedicated teachers were likely to take the trouble. Second, when whole programmed courses did appear, they showed little influence of the revolution in frame design described earlier and were uniformly dull. Third, teachers were quite unprepared for the difficult job of sifting out programmes of genuine quality which had been properly tested and validated from the crowd of poor imitations that flooded the market. While a bad textbook could be tolerated and adapted, a bad programme was a total disaster. Many teachers encountered such programmes in the 1960s and were effectively inoculated against programmed learning for life.

Even with good programmes, cultural and organizational factors hindered proper implementation. Most schools are not designed for individualized learning, either practically or attitudinally. Teachers find it difficult to manage students who finish early or to integrate programmes with group activities when all the students are at different stages. Considerable confusion was caused by the plethora of teaching machines and the debate about whether machines were needed at all. Pronouncements about the ineffectiveness of conventional education and talk of machines replacing teachers was

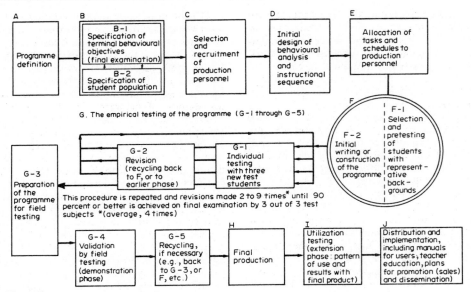

Figure 1
A generalized flow chart of programme development[a]

a Source: Lange (1967)

highly threatening, and the issue of the teacher's role in a programmed course was handled with an ambivalence that provoked even further anxiety.

It soon became apparent that there were two main alternatives. Programmes could be used as supplementary resources on an occasional basis, or the instructional systems which used them would have to be redesigned. The first was nonthreatening but unlikely to succeed. Though using programmes for occasional topics and occasional students was compatible with existing classroom practice, the problems of selecting, purchasing, and maintaining teacher awareness of what was available were considerable. There was little real incentive for any teacher who was not specially interested in programmed learning to give the matter any serious attention.

Increasing the scale of the operation from designing programmes to designing courses as instructional systems was a much more attractive proposition. The systems approach was becoming an important concept in educational technology and was capable of absorbing the kind of approach to programmed learning described in Fig. 1. Hence much of the effort of those who pioneered the field of programmed learning was redirected into what came to be called educational or instructional development. Most of the new types of instructional system invented during the late 1960s and early 1970s owed a great deal to programmed learning; but in each case some new name was invented to promote its special characteristics and to avoid association with some of the negative attitudes towards the early examples of programmed learning.

Many of the early instructional systems which evolved at school level in the late 1960s are described in Weisgerber (1971), while more recent work is summarized in other articles in this Part of the Encyclopedia. A system which retained the use of programmes that would still be recognized as such by the early pioneers is the Kent Mathematics Project (1978). This has divided the mathematics curriculum for the ages 9–16 into seven levels, evolved a clear teacher role in managing and supplementing its instructional materials, and developed a system for assigning students to appropriate tasks. The assignment system and a considerable variety of materials (programmed booklets, audiotapes, and games) have been gradually refined over a period of 10–15 years.

Similar developments in higher education are described in neighbouring articles. These include the Keller plan, the audiotutorial approach and modular instruction. The popular term "module approach" is often used to include both Keller courses and those originally described as "audiotutorial" because of their frequent use of audiotape. Audiotutorial courses originated independently of programmed learning but later incorporated some of its concepts and techniques. This exchange was mutually beneficial because programmers were encouraged to use a wider range of media and to programme practical work as well. Many of these college-level instructional systems built in roles for tutors, some of them managerial, some remedial, and some to involve students in discussion round the topic and to generally encourage intellectual enquiry. For example, a biology course developed at Sussex University, which contains some of the most intellectually demanding programmed texts, supplements these with audiovisual materials, simulations, and tutorials to assist students find connections between different aspects of the subject and to promote an inquiry-oriented approach to their studies (Tribe et al. 1975).

6. Alternative Paradigms

These aims of linkage and inquiry, and helping students to think for themselves and create their own personal maps of the subject matter are accorded special priority in a radically different approach to programming called structural communication (Egan 1976). This approach is modular like many of the instructional systems described above, with study units some 10 to 15 pages in length and suitable for about an hour of individual study. The construction of these study units, however, is quite unique. Each unit has six components linked together as in Fig. 2.

The intention provides a short orientation to the topic, while the presentation provides the bulk of the information—it often reads like a rather condensed version of a chapter from a textbook. The investigation then presents the students with four challenges, each designed to penetrate a different aspect of the topic. The student responds to these by selecting a group of four to eight items from a response matrix of 12-24 items. Each item consists of a short principle or statement, and the student has to decide which of them are most relevant and which are least relevant to the question posed by the challenge. Having made this selection, he or she consults the discussion guide—a set of decision rules leading to a set of discussion comments; for example it may include advice such as "If you included item 5 then read comment L" or "If you omitted item 9 or item 16 then read comment P". After reading and reacting to a few assigned discussion comments the student then proceeds to a concluding viewpoints section.

An unusual advantage of this approach is the way it forces students to synthesize a viewpoint of their own, while incidentally processing and remembering a considerable amount of information. It lends itself to use as an adjunct programme which can consolidate the teaching of a topic at a far more complex cognitive level than Pressey's multiple-choice testing system.

The idea of learning from multiple-choice testing is used in quite a different way in what came to be called a feedback classroom. In its more sophisticated form each student has a response board for answering multiple-choice questions wired to a master recorder at the teacher's desk, so a teacher can periodically ask a question of the class and receive immediate feedback on the distribution of answers. This keeps students actively involved and ensures that a teacher detects significant misunderstandings at an early enough stage for the lesson to be appropriately modified. An even simpler arrangement used pairs of cardboard discs. One disc is divided into five sectors, marked A, B, C, D, and E on one side and coloured on the other side; then a second disc of the same size with one sector cut out is pinned to it centrally. If each student is given a pair of discs he or she can use it to answer a multiple-choice question by putting the chosen sector at the top where the second disc has been cut out. When he or she holds the discs up the teacher will only see the colour appropriate to the student's choice, for example, blue, because the other colours will be masked by the rest of the cut-out disc. This enables the teacher to judge the approximate distribution of the students' answers by rapidly assessing the colour distribution held up. Used in this way, a planned series of multiple-choice questions, possibly presented by an overhead projector, could be said to constitute programmed teaching.

The most fully developed approach which builds on the notion of programmed teaching is a system called programmed tutoring. This is a one-to-one method of instruction in which a tutor teaches a student by following carefully structured printed instructions. Often the student will have some kind of workbook and the tutor will be programmed in an adaptive, branching style to respond to a variety of student behaviours. The system is particularly applicable to the teaching of reading and can be adapted to use a teacher aide, parent, or even another student as the tutor (Ellson 1976, Thiagarajan 1976). Sometimes it uses a sequencing technique called "brightening" in which an item is first presented in a relatively difficult form and then later made increasingly easier by the addition of prompts: this process will be familiar to the skillful classroom teacher, but is the exact opposite of the fading or withdrawal of prompting sequences developed by the early linear programmers.

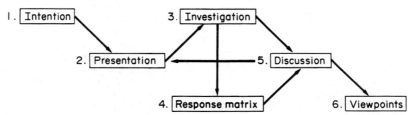

Figure 2
A structural communication study unit[a]

a Source: Egan (1976)

Finally, and probably of greatest significance for the future, come some of the new approaches being developed in computer-assisted learning (CAL) (see *Computer-assisted Learning*). Here, however, it should be noted that it is common for people preparing CAL sequences to be unaware of the developments in instructional design which were made by the more creative exponents of programmed learning. Computers offer great possibilities for new types of programme design, but many of the older ideas are still relevant. The same mistakes are being made in CAL as with programmed learning in the 1950s: a failure to realize that instructional design is a highly skilled and time-consuming activity, widespread marketing of low quality software, and lack of attention to the problems of implementation (see *Computer-managed Learning*; *Microcomputers in Schools*).

7. Conclusion

Many people now regard programmed learning as a historical curiosity. Yet some of its products still rank amongst the most useful and effective materials available. The term is still associated with the low-quality programmes that flooded the market in its early days, while many of its ideas have been incorporated into other "new" approaches to individualized learning. The corpus of literature on programmed learning is a major contribution to instructional design, and designers still have much to learn from careful inspection of some of its most successful products.

Bibliography

Bloom B S, Hastings J T, Madaus G F 1971 *Handbook on Formative and Summative Evaluation of Student Learning*. McGraw-Hill, New York

Davies I K, Hartley J (eds.) 1972 *Contributions to an Educational Technology*. Butterworth, London

Egan K 1976 *Structural Communication*. Fearon, Belmont, California

Ellson D G 1976 Tutoring. In: Gage N L (ed.) 1976 *The Psychology of Teaching Methods*. 75th National Society for the Study of Education (NSSE) Yearbook, Part 1. University of Chicago Press, Chicago, Illinois

Gagné R M 1977 *The Conditions of Learning*, 3rd edn. Holt, Rinehart and Winston, New York

Glaser R (ed.) 1965 *Teaching Machines and Programmed Learning: A Source Book*, Vol 2: *Data and Directions*. Department of Audiovisual Instruction, National Education Association, Washington, DC

Glaser R, Homme L E, Evans J L 1960 An evaluation of textbooks in terms of learning principles. In: Lumsdaine A A, Glaser R (eds.) 1960

Hartley J 1974 Programmed instruction 1954–74: A review. *Program. Learn. Educ. Technol.* 11: 278–91

Holland J G 1965 Research on programming variables. In: Glaser R (ed.) 1965

Kent Mathematics Project 1978 *Teachers Guide Levels 1–4*. Ward Lock, London

Lange P C (ed.) 1967 *Programed Instruction*. 66th National Society for the Study of Education (NSSE) Yearbook. University of Chicago Press, Chicago, Illinois

Lumsdaine A A, Glaser R (eds.) 1960 *Teaching Machines and Programmed Learning*. Department of Audiovisual Instruction, National Education Association, Washington, DC

Mager R F 1961 *Preparing Objectives for Programmed Instruction*. Fearon, Belmont, California

Markle S M 1967 Empirical testing of programs. In: Lange P C (ed.) 1967

Markle S M 1969 *Good Frames and Bad: A Grammar of Frame Writing*, 2nd edn. Wiley, New York

Schramm W L (ed.) 1964 *Four Case Studies of Programmed Instruction*. Fund for the Advancement of Education, New York

Skinner B F 1958 Teaching machines. In: Lumsdaine A A, Glaser R (eds.) 1960

Skinner B F, Holland J G 1958 The use of teaching machines in college instruction. In: Lumsdaine A A, Glaser R (eds.) 1960

Thiagarajan S 1976 *Programmed Instruction for Literacy Workers: A Guide for Developing Self-instructional Materials and Strategies for Adult Learners, Literacy Teachers and Discussion Leaders*. Hulton Educational, Amersham

Thomas C A, Openshaw D, Davies I K, Bird J B 1963 *Programmed Learning in Perspective: A Guide to Program Writing*. Educational Methods, Chicago, Illinois

Tribe M A, Eraut M R, Snook R K 1975 *Basic Biology Course, Tutors' Guide*. Cambridge University Press, Cambridge

Weisgerber R A (ed.) 1971 *Developmental Efforts in Individualized Learning*. Peacock, Itasca, Illinois

White R T, Gagné R M 1974 Past and future research on learning hierarchies. *Educ. Psychol.* 11: 19–28

Keller Plan

J. A. Kulik

The Keller Plan or Personalized System of Instruction (PSI) is an individualized teaching method developed for use in college-level instruction during the early 1960s by psychologist Fred Keller and his associates. Like other individualized teaching methods, PSI allows students to move through course material at their own rates, and requires that they show mastery of all major course objectives. What distinguishes PSI from other individualized approaches is its use of peer proctors as aides to a course instructor. The primary job of these proctors is to evaluate student performance on unit quizzes, but proctors also contribute to the interpersonal atmosphere in a classroom and provide some tutorial assistance for students.

Interest in PSI stems in part from its popularity as a teaching method. Thousands of teachers have offered courses using Keller's method since the early 1970s, and hundreds of thousands of students have taken such courses. The approach has been used by teachers in almost every discipline and in most parts of the world. But interest in PSI also comes from its record of success in evaluation studies and from its value as a tool in educational research. Few teaching innovations in the history of education have inspired so much research in so short a period of time. As previous articles in this Part have shown, the Keller Plan belongs to a long tradition of experiments in individualized instruction (Kulik 1982). Its formal history goes back to 1963 when two American psychologists, Fred Keller and J. Gilmour Sherman, and two Brazilian psychologists, Carolina Bori and Rodolfo Azzi, devised the method as a way of offering psychology courses at the newly established University of Brasilia. In 1964 Keller and his associates offered the first PSI course, and in 1968 Keller presented the first formal description of the method. The Keller Plan belongs to a long tradition of experiments in individualized instruction (Kulik 1982).

1. Description of PSI

In his 1968 paper "Good-bye, Teacher...," Keller identified five features that distinguish PSI courses from conventional ones. PSI courses are (a) mastery oriented and (b) individually paced courses that use (c) a few lectures to stimulate and motivate students, (d) printed study guides to communicate information, and (e) student proctors to evaluate quizzes. Together these five features form a "system." Given the goal of mastery—feature (a), the other features seem to follow directly. To achieve mastery in any part of a course, each student must be given the necessary time. Individual pacing—feature (b) thus seems necessary. Lecturing on required information to groups of students is incompatible with individual pacing, but optional lectures for "stimulation" are possible—feature (c). Required information must be packaged, usually in written form, for use at the student's individual rate—feature (d). Finally, since the teacher's time is limited, undergraduate proctors are needed to help with quiz evaluation and occasional one-to-one tutoring—feature (e).

To college students, Keller courses look different from other courses. The student beginning a PSI course first notes that the course is carefully divided into topics or units. In a simple case, the content of the units may correspond to chapters of a course textbook. At the start of a course, the student receives a printed study guide to direct work on the first unit. Although study guides vary, a typical one introduces the unit, states objectives, suggests study procedures, and lists study questions. The student may work anywhere—including the classroom—to achieve the objectives outlined in the study guide.

Before moving on to the second unit in the sequence, the student must demonstrate mastery of the first by perfect or near-perfect performance on a short examination. Students are examined on units only when they feel adequately prepared, and they are not penalized for failure to pass a first, second, or later examination. When the student demonstrates mastery of the first unit, the student receives the study guide for the next unit. Students thus move through PSI courses at their own rates. They may meet all course requirements before a term is half through, or they may require more than a term for completing a course.

The staff for implementing the Keller Plan includes the instructor and undergraduate proctors. The instructor selects and organizes material used in a course and usually writes study guides and constructs examinations for the course. PSI instructors give fewer lectures and demonstrations than do teachers in conventional courses (perhaps six during a semester), and these lectures are not compulsory and no examinations are based on them. Proctors evaluate readiness tests as satisfactory or unsatisfactory. Since proctors are chosen for their mastery of course content, they can prescribe remedial steps for students who encounter difficulties with course material. Proctors also offer support and encouragement for beginning students.

2. Evaluation

Evaluation studies that compare the educational outcomes of PSI and conventional classes provide important evidence about the effectiveness of PSI as an instructional system. Kulik et al. (1979) summarized results from 75 studies of this sort, reported in 72 different papers. This section is based on their findings.

2.1 Final Examinations

A total of 61 of these 75 studies compared the final examination averages of students taught the same content in PSI and conventional classes. In 57 of the 61 studies, final examination scores were higher in the PSI class; and in 48 of the studies, the examination difference in results from PSI and conventional classes was large enough to be considered statistically reliable. In no case was the examination average from a conventional class significantly higher than that from a PSI class.

In the typical PSI class, the average final examination score was 74 percent; in the typical conventional class, the average score was 66 percent. A difference of eight percentage-points may be large enough to have some practical significance. In statistical terms, it amounts to a separation of approximately one-half standard deviation unit. A difference of this size suggests that PSI raises the final examination score of a typical student in a typical class from the 50th to the 70th percentile.

The 61 studies differed from one another in many ways—in study design, setting, discipline, and so on. The reviewers classified the 61 studies according to such study features, and tried to determine whether PSI produced especially clear effects in studies of certain types. They reported that PSI added to instructional effectiveness in all types of studies. A few settings and research designs, however, produced especially sharp differences between PSI and conventional classes. Differences in results were very clear, for example, when different teachers taught PSI and conventional classes; differences were less clear when the same teacher taught the two types of classes. The discipline in which a course was given also influenced results; studies from the social sciences produced the clearest results.

2.2 Follow-up Examinations

Eight studies investigated student retention of what was learned. In these studies investigators looked beyond the final examination for effects of instruction by Keller's method. In each of the studies, PSI students performed better on follow-up examinations than did students from conventional classes, and in each study the difference between groups reached statistical significance. In most of the studies, differences were greater at the time of follow-up than at the time of the final examination. For the eight PSI classes in these comparisons, average performance was 77 percent on the final examination and 69 percent on the retention test; for the average conventional class, typical scores were 68 percent on the final examination and 55 percent on retention examination.

2.3 Student Attitudes

Evaluation studies also reported on student attitudes toward personalized instruction. Some of the studies asked students to compare their PSI class to the typical class that they had taken in college. In a representative study at the College of Engineering at the University of Texas at Austin, about 70 percent of the students in a PSI class considered this method to be superior to the lecture approach; about 20 percent considered the two methods about equal; and about 10 percent preferred the lecture method. Other studies compared student responses from PSI and conventional classes on items rating the overall quality of a course. PSI ratings were higher than conventional ratings in 10 of 11 studies that secured ratings of overall quality. In eight of the studies, the difference between PSI and conventional ratings was large enough to be considered statistically reliable.

2.4 Other Reviews

These findings are consistent with findings in seven other major reviews of the PSI literature cited by Kulik et al. (1979). Each of the seven reviews noted that the vast majority of evaluation studies report PSI outcomes that are superior to those from conventional teaching. Kulik et al. (1979) also noted that PSI effects are stronger than those usually reported for other alternative college teaching methods. Of five technologies examined by these reviewers, Keller's PSI had the strongest effects on student achievement and the most pronounced effects on student ratings of instruction.

3. Essential Components

Researchers have also tried to determine which features of PSI are necessary for its distinctive effects on student achievement. Four of the ingredients of PSI seem especially important. PSI seems to work well because it involves: (a) a mastery requirement; (b) small units of work; (c) immediate and specific feedback on quiz performance; and (d) a requirement for review work. Kulik et al. (1978) summarized research results on each of these features. This section presents their major findings.

3.1 Mastery

Most PSI teachers see the unit-mastery requirement as a cornerstone of the system. They feel that a mastery requirement inevitably leads to higher levels of student achievement since with this requirement, each student must answer correctly, at least once, each important type of question raised in a college course. Research studies tend to support this line of thought. In seven studies reviewed by Kulik et al. (1978), remediation was required for some students whenever unit-quiz performance failed to reach a predefined level of excellence (usually 90 percent); remediation was not required for other students when they failed to reach this level. In each of the seven studies, students for whom mastery was required scored at least slightly higher on final examinations; in four of the studies, students for whom mastery was required scored significantly higher on examinations. The evidence, therefore, seems good that the strong remediation requirement in PSI courses is one factor that contributes to superior student achievement.

3.2 Unit Size

In PSI courses, units are short in size but large in number, and students therefore must take many unit quizzes. At least three reasons are usually given for the use of short units in PSI courses. First, with short units, teachers can usually quiz students on every course objective; with large units, teachers are less likely to be comprehensive in their testing. Second, with short units, student study time is more likely to be evenly distributed over the term; with longer units and fewer quizzes, students are more likely to "cram." Finally, with short units and frequent quizzes, student errors can be corrected immediately before they propagate so that students in PSI courses always build on firm foundations. Research studies also tend to show that small units are more effective than large ones. Kulik et al. (1978) summarized results from three studies of short versus long units. Two of the studies reported that student achievement was significantly higher with short units.

3.3 Immediate Feedback

The main function of proctors in PSI courses is to provide immediate feedback on student performance on unit quizzes. Several researchers have provided convincing evidence of the importance of such immediate feedback. Kulik et al. (1978) summarized results from four studies comparing achievement of students who received immediate feedback with achievement of students who received delayed feedback. The studies showed that delaying feedback in PSI courses interfered with student learning of course material. It was not clear, however, why timing of feedback affected student learning so dramatically. The same mastery standard was required of students who received immediate and delayed feedback. Yet students who received delayed feedback performed less well on final examinations. The finding was especially perplexing because there is good evidence that for some kinds of learning tasks, delayed feedback is superior to immediate feedback.

3.4 Amount of Review

Many instructors feel that review is an important element in PSI courses. In arranging course material, therefore, they provide occasions for students to review and integrate what they have learned. Review materials are designed to show students what they know, to provide an overview of a subject, and to help students relate ideas covered separately in previous units. Some instructors put review materials into individual units, and write one review unit for every four or five regular units. Other instructors prefer to add a few review questions to each study guide and quiz in a PSI course. Kulik et al. (1978) summarized results from three studies on the importance of review units and review questions in PSI courses. Each of the studies reported that review procedures, either review units or review items on unit quizzes, enhanced student learning and retention.

3.5 Other Components

The more distinctive and controversial features of PSI have apparently played a less important role in its instructional successes. Amount of tutorial help available from proctors, for example, seems unrelated to overall student achievement. As long as quizzes are graded immediately, students perform at high levels in PSI courses. Additional actions taken by proctors—discussion of individual quiz answers, individual troubleshooting—seem not to add to the success of PSI courses. Restrictions can also be placed on self-pacing in PSI courses without affecting student achievement. Finally, lectures may be used for transmitting information in PSI courses without negative or positive effects on student achievement.

4. Theory of PSI Learning

The components that contribute most to PSI's effectiveness are the ones that increase the number of quiz items that students answer in college courses: short units, a high mastery requirement, and special review units or items. With short units, students usually have to take many quizzes and thus answer many quiz questions.

With a high mastery requirement, students take alternative forms of quizzes until they demonstrate mastery, and they thus have to answer additional quiz items. With review units, students answer still more quiz questions. Any change in PSI which reduces the amount of quizzing seems to reduce PSI's impact. Thus, it seems possible that amount of quizzing is the key variable in PSI's effectiveness.

Even if this is so, much more needs to be known about the effects of frequent evaluation of students. The important question is, how do frequent evaluations affect student performance? At least two types of influence are possible. First, the amount of evaluation in personalized instruction may affect student use of study time. The requirement of frequent evaluation and re-evaluation may affect how much and how often students study. Second, the requirement may affect the content that students attend to in college courses. The numerous evaluations in PSI courses may serve to direct students toward the content that teachers consider to be most important.

Examining how students use time in PSI courses seems especially appropriate today when many educational researchers emphasize the critical importance of time as a variable in school learning. Berliner (1979), for example, has proposed a general model relating the amount that classes learn to the amount of time that teachers and students in the classes spend on the learning task. According to Berliner's model, differences in the amount that students learn about a subject are closely related to differences in the amount of time their teachers allocate to the subject. The differences in amount learned are even more closely related to the amount of "engaged" time on a task, or the amount of time that students in a class actually spend working on the subject. Finally, differences in amount learned are most closely related to the amount of time students spend working on material of an appropriate level of difficulty. This model suggests that PSI students learn more because they spend more time engaged on relevant work.

Is this suggestion correct? Do students spent more time on PSI courses than on other courses? Early, self-report studies suggested that students did put more time and effort into PSI courses (Kulik et al. 1976). One early study, for example, reported that 90 percent of all students in a PSI class said that they were working harder than they did in comparable lecture classes. A more complex picture emerged from later, more carefully controlled studies. In one especially well-designed investigation, a teacher deposited in a special study center all the materials for a course in beginning psychology, and then monitored the amount of time spent on the course by students in PSI and lecture sections. The teacher found that students in the two groups spent the same amount of time on the course, but they spent their time differently. Students in the lecture group used about one-third of their time attending lectures and two-thirds of their time studying individually. Personalized System of

Instruction students spend nearly all of their time in individual study. Although total amount of time was about the same for the two groups, amount of "engaged" time may have been different.

Teachers have also reported other differences in the way students use time in PSI and conventional classes. First, student work may be more evenly distributed over time in PSI classes. With 15 to 20 quizzes to pass in a semester in a typical PSI class, work must necessarily be spread out. Students may cram for one or two major examinations in a conventional course; it is hardly possible to cram for the 15 to 20 separate quizzes in a PSI class. Second, in PSI classes, differences among individuals in study time may more accurately reflect differences among these individuals in aptitude and background for the course. Because of the requirement of mastery on short units of material in PSI classes, students with poor backgrounds may soon learn how much they have to study to overcome their deficiencies; students with strong backgrounds may soon learn that a small amount of work is sufficient for them. Thus, variation among individuals in study time may be greater in PSI classes than in other classes, and the correlation between student aptitude and amount of effort may also be different with the two types of teaching.

Another factor to consider in PSI classes is *what* is learned. Instruction by Keller's method is meant to keep student attention on course essentials and direct attention away from incidental and irrelevant matters. It is possible, of course, for teachers of conventional classes to publish lists of detailed course objectives and thus share with their students their ideas about course essentials. Some teachers of conventional classes and most PSI teachers, in fact, distribute lists of such objectives. But PSI teachers also do much more. They especially emphasize testing as a means of directing student attention. PSI teachers quiz students on every essential point,

again and again, until students reach the standard set by the instructor. Even after students reach this standard, PSI teachers ask students the same types of questions on review items. The result is that students in PSI classes learn very well those things that instructors consider important. On measures of incidental or irrelevant learning, PSI students may not do so well, but on tests that measure mastery of course essentials, PSI students show what they have learned.

Bibliography

Berliner D C 1979 Tempus educare. In: Peterson P L, Walberg H J (eds.) 1979 *Research on Teaching: Concepts, Findings and Implications.* McCutchan, Berkeley, California

Johnson K R, Ruskin R S 1977 *Behavioral Instruction: An Evaluative Review.* American Psychological Association, Washington, DC

Keller F S 1968 "Good-bye, teacher..." *J. Appl. Behav. Anal.* 1: 79–89

Keller F S, Sherman J G 1974 PSI: *The Keller Plan Handbook: Essays on a Personalized System of Instruction.* Benjamin, Menlo Park, California

Kulik J A 1982 Individualized systems of instruction. In: Mitzel H E (ed.) 1982 *Encyclopedia of Educational Research.* Macmillan, New York

Kulik J A, Jaksa P, Kulik C-L C 1978 Research on component features of Keller's personalized system of instruction. *J. Personalized Instruc.* 3: 2–14

Kulik J A, Kulik C-L C, Cohen P A 1979 A meta-analysis of outcome studies of Keller's personalized system of instruction. *Am. Psychol.* 34: 307–18

Kulik J A, Kulik C-L C, Smith B B 1976 Research on the personalized system of instruction. *Program. Learn. Educ. Technol.* 13: 23–30

Sherman J G 1974 PSI: *Personalized System of Instruction: 41 Germinal Papers.* Benjamin, Menlo Park, California

Mastery Learning Model

L. W. Anderson and J. H. Block

The Mastery Learning Model was introduced into the professional literature in the late 1960s (Bloom 1968). Since that time a great deal has been learned about mastery learning: what it is and isn't, how it works, and how well it works. The purpose of this article is to discuss what is currently known about mastery learning as well as what remains to be known.

The article begins with a definition of the model of teaching and learning called mastery learning. Subsequent sections detail the historical development of mastery learning, the basic tasks facing educators desiring to use mastery learning as a vehicle for improving teaching and learning, the effectiveness of such programs in producing desired learner outcomes, and the future of mastery learning as a model of school teaching and learning.

An extensive bibliography on mastery learning is available from Dr. Glenn Hymel, Clearinghouse on Mastery Learning, Loyola Center for Educational Improvement, Loyola University.

1. A Definition of Mastery Learning

What is mastery learning? Basically, it is two things. First, mastery learning is an old, optimistic philosophy about teaching and learning. Essentially this philosophy asserts that any teacher can help virtually all students to learn excellently, quickly, and self-confidently; the teacher can help "dumb," "slow," and "unmotivated" students to learn like "smart," "fast," and "motivated" students. Such learning, the philosophy contends, not only improves many students' chances for long-term social and personal prosperity, but many teachers' chances as well. In particular, the students acquire those basic personal competencies which ensure that they can and want to undertake lifelong learning, and the teachers acquire some basic professional competencies which ensure that they can and want to keep teaching.

Second, mastery learning is a set of old and new individualized instructional ideas and practices that consistently help most students to learn excellently, quickly, and self-confidently. These ideas and practices produce instruction that is systematic, provides help to students when and where they have learning difficulties, provides sufficient time for students to achieve mastery, and provides a clear criterion of what constitutes mastery (Bloom 1974 p. 6).

Two genotypic approaches to the use of these ideas and practices currently exist. The first is a group-based, teacher-paced approach. Students learn cooperatively with their classmates and the teacher controls the delivery and flow of instruction. The prototype for this approach is Bloom's Learning for Mastery (see, for example, Block and Anderson 1975). This approach has evolved from within the field of education and has had a major impact at the elementary and secondary levels of schooling.

The second approach is individual based and learner paced. Students learn independently of their classmates and each student controls the delivery and flow of instruction. Ideas and practices related to this latter approach lie at the heart of Keller's Personalized System of Instruction (PSI) and Postlethwait's Audio-tutorial Instruction (see Postlethwait et al. 1964). This second approach evolved from the fields of psychology and biology and has had its major impact at the college and university levels.

Both of these mastery learning approaches are similar to, yet different from, other individualized instructional approaches such as Individually Prescribed Instruction, Individually Guided Education, Program for Learning According to Needs, and the matching of learning styles with teaching styles. The major similarity lies in their attempts to provide instructional settings that will accommodate a diversity of students. They all attempt to modify the instructional setting so that students possessing a variety of entering abilities, skills, knowledge, attitudes, and values can succeed.

The major differences reside in the type and timing of the individualization. Four types of individualization exist: (a) matching learner aptitudes or learning styles with appropriate instructional settings and/or teaching strategies; (b) placing learners at appropriate points in a relatively fixed sequence of instructional units or objectives, and permitting them to progress at their own rates; (c) providing a variety of materials and activities related to particular goals or objectives and allowing the learner (often with teacher guidance) to select from among them; and (d) providing supplementary, alternative instruction so as to correct learner errors identified by short formative tests. The mastery learning model of school teaching and learning relies almost exclusively on the final two types of individualization. Quite typically the variety of materials and activities is introduced after the formative tests have been administered.

In addition to differing in the type of individualization, individualized instructional programs also differ in the timing of the individualization. Most approaches to individualized instruction (including the individual-based, student-paced approach to mastery learning—see Block and Burns 1976) provide individualized instruction all the time; that is, to the extent possible the instruction is responsive to the needs of individual learners. Put simply, the use of group-based, teacher-paced mastery learning implies that instruction will be individualized as needed; that is, when it becomes evident that certain students are experiencing difficulty in benefiting from the group-based, teacher-paced practices. After the individualization has occurred, however, the students are placed back into the more traditional group-based, teacher-paced practices.

The emphasis on individualized corrective instruction is a key element of mastery learning and is based on the following assumption. No matter how good the match is between learner and learning environment, no matter how exact the sequence of objectives might be, and no matter how large the variety of materials and activities that exist for each objective, it is likely that some learner errors and misunderstandings will occur. As a consequence, the provision of extra time and help to some learners so that errors and misunderstandings will be corrected before they accumulate and interfere with future learning seems necessary to ensure the success of any form that individualized instruction may take.

One final distinction between mastery learning and other individualized instructional approaches is worth noting. Unlike other individualized approaches, mastery learning approaches are designed for use in the typical classroom situation where teachers already possess curricula they must "cover" or complete in a fixed period of calendar time, where inordinate amounts of instructional time cannot be spent on testing, and where student learning must be evaluated and grades or marks must be assigned periodically. Moreover, mastery learning approaches rely primarily on human beings for their success rather than on machines and other technological devices. Teachers and students are responsible for ensuring that time is used productively and that available techniques and materials are employed as needed.

2. A Historical Perspective on Mastery Learning

While future historians of education may say otherwise, the evolution of mastery learning as a model of school teaching and learning seems to fall into two distinct periods. The first period, dominated by the writings of Bloom at the University of Chicago (hereafter called the Bloom period), spanned the years from 1968 to 1971. The second period, dominated by the writings of Bloom's students and colleagues (hereafter called the post-Bloom period), spanned the time from 1971 to the present. Each of these periods will be described briefly.

2.1 The Bloom Period

As noted briefly at the outset of this article, mastery learning as an idea—a belief system—is old. But as the idea was periodically introduced in schools over the centuries, it constantly floundered due to the lack of a practical sustaining technology (Block 1971). It was Bloom who first provided the theoretical and practical basis for such a technology.

Bloom's theoretical contribution to the evolution of mastery learning was to transform the conceptual model of school learning developed by Carroll into a working model for mastery learning. Central to Carroll's model were three propositions.

(a) A student's aptitude for a given subject could be defined in terms of the amount of time he or she needs to learn the subject to a given level, rather than the level to which the subject would be learned in a given amount of time. That is, aptitude could be viewed as an index of learning rate, rather than learning level.

(b) The degree of learning for any student in a school setting is a simple function of the time he or she actually spends in learning relative to the time he or she needs to spend. Thus, to the extent that each student is allowed sufficient time to learn a given subject to some prespecified level, and he or she spends the time needed to learn, the student will likely learn the subject to the specified level.

(c) In a school learning situation, the time a student actually spends learning a subject as well as the time he or she needs to spend will be determined by certain instructional and personal characteristics. The two major instructional characteristics are the student's opportunity to learn (that is, the amount of classroom time allocated to learning the subject), and the quality of instruction (that is, the degree to which the presentation, explanation, and ordering of the elements of the subject are optimal for the student). In addition to aptitude, the relevant personal characteristics are the student's ability to understand instruction and his or her perseverance.

Bloom synthesized these three propositions as follows. If aptitude is predictive of the rate at which, rather than the level to which, a student could learn, it should be possible to fix the degree of learning expected of students at some mastery level and to systematically manipulate the relevant instructional variables in Carroll's model such that all or almost all students attained mastery. Bloom argued that if students were normally distributed with respect to their aptitude for a subject and were provided uniform instruction in terms of both quality and time, then their achievement at the subject's

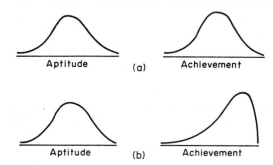

Figure 1
Instruction per learner
(a) Uniform
(b) Optimal

completion would be normally distributed. Furthermore, the relationship between aptitude and achievement would be high [see Fig. 1(a)].

If, however, students were normally distributed on aptitude but each received optimal quality of instruction and adequate learning time, then a vast majority of students could be expected to attain mastery. In addition, there would be little or no relationship between aptitude and achievement [see Fig. 1(b)].

Bloom's practical contribution to the evolution of the mastery learning approach to instruction was to outline a classroom teaching strategy that would systematically vary, as necessary, how and how long each student was taught. For this purpose, he returned to the earlier approach of Washburne (1922) called the "Winnetka Plan" and especially to the approach of Morrison (1926) at the University of Chicago's Laboratory School. And out of the similarities of these two approaches, he culled the basic elements of his own approach. Some of these elements have been summarized by McNeil (1969 p. 308).

(a) The learner must understand the nature of the task to be learned and the procedure to be followed in learning it.

(b) The specific instructional objectives relating to the learning task must be formulated.

(c) It is useful to break a course or subject into small units of learning and to test at the end of each unit.

(d) The teacher should provide feedback as to the learner's particular errors and difficulties after each test.

(e) The teacher must find ways to alter the time some individuals have available to learn.

(f) It may be profitable to provide alternative learning opportunities.

(g) Student effort is increased when small groups of two or three students meet regularly for as long as an hour to review their test results and to help one another overcome the difficulties identified by means of the test.

2.2 Post-Bloom Period

While Bloom turned his attention to theory (Bloom 1976), a number of his students and their colleagues devoted their attention to developing the practice of Mastery Learning. At first their efforts were concentrated on applying the theory and related practices to the improvement of classroom and then schoolwide practices. Soon it became apparent that interest in the evolving mastery learning approach had spread far beyond the classroom and school level. Entire local, regional, and even national school systems desired to plumb the potential of the evolving mastery learning approach for their particular problems (Block 1979). As a consequence the efforts of many individuals shifted to the improvement of systemwide practices. Since systemwide applications of mastery learning practices require the cooperative efforts of many individuals at many levels (e.g., university, faculty, school administrators, classroom teacher) a network of mastery learning practitioners was formed in the United States. This network, known as the Network of Outcome-based Schools, is affiliated with the American Association of School Administrators (Arlington, Virginia). Its primary purpose is to encourage the discussion, summarization, and dissemination of mastery-related strategies, practices, and materials. Through the network practitioners are spared the grief of rediscovering the wheel and instead can profit from the attempts and mistakes of others.

Also, since the mid-1970s, mastery learning has been applied to an ever-increasing variety of subject areas (many technical in nature) and extended beyond the secondary-school level. Subjects such as geography, biology, psychology, sociology, music, public speaking, allied health, nursing, pharmacy, and veterinary pathology have experienced the intrusion of mastery learning. Mastery learning programs have been implemented in community colleges as well as four-year colleges.

3. Basic Tasks Facing Developers of Mastery Learning Programs

Educators desiring to plan and implement mastery learning programs in their schools and classrooms must accomplish four major tasks. These tasks are (a) defining mastery, (b) planning for mastery, (c) teaching for mastery, and (d) grading for mastery. Each of these major tasks can be divided into several subtasks, the accomplishment of which is related to the accomplishment of the overall task.

Before moving to a discussion of the tasks and subtasks, two additional points must be made. First, if mastery learning programs are to be as successful as they might be, *all* of the tasks and related subtasks must be accomplished. That is, one cannot have a mastery learn-

ing program if one stops after defining mastery, for example.

Second, and somewhat related to the first point, *how* these tasks and subtasks are accomplished is less important than that they *are*, in fact, accomplished. Each of the tasks and related subtasks serves an important function within the context of mastery learning (Anderson and Anderson 1982). These functions should be understood by developers of mastery learning programs.

In light of the previous discussion the next four subsections will focus on the nature and function of the tasks and subtasks involved in the development of a successful mastery learning program. The majority of examples and illustrations will reflect the group-based, teacher-paced approach since this approach is the easiest and least costly to implement. The function of each major task will be presented at the beginning of each section. Following the presentation of the function of the task a sequence of subtasks will be described. Where appropriate the functions served by particular subtasks will be included in the discussion of the subtasks.

The focus on the nature and function of the tasks and subtasks at the expense of a discussion of the methods and techniques available for accomplishing these tasks is not meant to minimize the importance or availability of such methods or techniques. Indeed a vast, ever-improving technology has developed around many of the critical subtasks. A large number of papers and articles have been written on the topic of mastery testing, for example. Rather a focus on the nature and significance of the tasks and subtasks seems more appropriate for fostering a general understanding of mastery learning as a model of school teaching and learning.

3.1 Defining Mastery

As has been mentioned earlier, mastery learning programs are outcome based. Thus, the first task facing educators who want to employ mastery learning ideas and strategies is to define precisely what is meant by mastery. Such a definition includes the specification of long-term and short-term outcomes, and a specification of abstract outcomes (i.e., goals) and concrete representations of these abstract outcomes (i.e., tests and acceptable levels of performance on the tests). The major function of defining mastery by clearly specifying the goals, tests, and performance standards at both the course (long-term) and unit (short-term) level is the communication of learner and learning expectations to students, teachers, administrators, and parents.

The initial subtask related to defining mastery is the identification of the most essential, critical course outcomes or objectives. One of the major trade-offs involved in mastery learning is the substitution of excellent learning of a limited number of highly desirable objectives (which is called a "mastery" emphasis) for the mediocre learning of virtually all conceivable objectives with a course (which is called a "coverage" emphasis). If this trade-off is to be worthwhile, however, the objectives selected must be those with the greatest potential for transfer or applicability to future learning.

Once the objectives have been identified, a final, summative test is prepared. The functions of this test are to (a) assess the degree of student learning over the entire course, and (b) evaluate (i.e., grade) the overall quality of student learning.

Based on an examination of the objectives and related test items a standard of performance for the summative test is set that, when achieved, will be accepted as mastery of the course. Thus mastery can be defined as the answer to the question "What test evidence will be accepted that the desired type and degree of excellent learning has occurred?" Pragmatically, a standard is set which corresponds to the score typically attained or surpassed by the best students taught by traditional or nonmastery methods.

Next, the entire course is divided into a series of smaller learning units. A set of objectives for each unit, based on identified or hypothesized interrelationships, is delineated. Each unit is long enough to allow sufficient time for students to learn an interrelated set of facts, concepts, principles, skills, and appreciations. At the same time, however, the units are short enough to permit the close monitoring of each student's learning as the units and course unfold. The function of such units is to facilitate the teaching and learning of new objectives in a context (rather than in isolation).

Once the units have been formed they are sequenced or ordered so that the facts, concepts, principles, skills, and appreciations acquired in one unit are used over and over again in subsequent units. This approach to sequencing helps ensure that the things learned in one unit will not be forgotten by the students and, hence, will be available for later use. A second function of sequencing or order is to increase the likelihood that subsequent objectives will be at an appropriate level of difficulty for students who have mastered the objectives of the previous unit(s).

The final subtask of defining mastery involves deciding what will constitute mastery of each learning unit. Tests appropriate for the assessment of student learning vis à vis the unit objectives are designed. These tests, called formative tests, are intended to help teachers identify student errors and misunderstandings. Such information is to be used to improve student learning rather than to evaluate the quality of that learning. Once again, as in the case of the summative test, performance standards are set for each formative test. These mastery performance standards will aid the teacher in the determination of those students who have successfully mastered the unit and those who will require additional time and help if mastery is to be attained.

3.2 Planning for Mastery

Once mastery has been defined, the next task is to plan for mastery. Plans for helping students acquire the objectives of each unit are designed. These plans must be consistent with the way in which mastery has been defined. Specifically, the plans must include activities and materials related to the unit objectives and must include additional, supplementary activities and materials for those students failing to attain the performance standard on the unit formative test.

The function of planning for mastery is to permit teachers to be proactive in their classroom teaching. Rather than having to react to situations as they arise and having to manufacture solutions on the spot, proactive teachers are ready for such situations. They can anticipate likely problems and respond in one of a variety of appropriate, preplanned ways.

In essence, planning enables teachers to monitor student learning on a unit by unit basis. If the evidence gathered from the formative tests (and other sources such as homework) suggests that the learning is not proceeding as well as expected and/or desired, then steps can be taken to intervene so that, ultimately, the desired degree of learning is attained. If steps are not taken to overcome the errors and misunderstandings identified by the tests, then these errors and misunderstandings will probably accumulate and interfere with future learning.

The first subtask of planning for mastery is to design a general plan for helping all students master the unit objectives. Initial concerns for the development of such a plan focus on two important aspects of high quality instruction. First, the material relating to each objective should be presented in a way that is appropriate for the vast majority of students in the classroom. Second, the activities in which the relevant material is embedded should involve or engage the vast majority of students in the process of learning. This general plan is often referred to as the "original instructional plan" (Block and Anderson 1975).

The second subtask involves the preparation of methods for interpreting and using the information gathered from the formative tests. Quite typically, a set of alternative instructional materials and learning activities keyed to each objective on the unit's formative test is developed. These correctives, as they are called, are designed so as to reteach each unit's objectives, but to do so in ways that differ from the original instruction. Small-group study sessions, peer or cross-age tutoring, or alternative learning aids such as different textbooks, workbooks, and audiovisual materials are often used in this regard (Block and Anderson 1975).

If the correctives are to be used during regular class time, then plans for those students initially achieving mastery on the formative tests must be designed. Anderson and Jones (1981) suggest several options for use with these students. The options tend to develop, in the order to be presented, over the duration of a mastery learning program.

Option 1 involves using the initial "masters" as tutors for the "nonmasters." For this option to be entirely successful, however, the students must be willing to serve as tutors, they should have specific tutorial materials available, and they must be trained as tutors. Option 2 requires that the initial "masters" be permitted to complete work in other subject areas or engage in nonacademic work, such as recreational reading. Option 3 requires that the initial "masters" engage in structured independent study. Students specify (a) what they are to learn, (b) how they will learn, and (c) how they are to demonstrate they have learned. In many ways, such independent study reinforces the basics of mastery learning. Finally, option 4 allows the students to engage in "vertical enrichment." In one sense, student pacing permits "faster" students to engage in "horizontal enrichment." That is, students progress from unit to unit acquiring an increasing number of concepts, facts, and skills. In contrast with horizontal enrichment, vertical enrichment consists of materials and activities that allow students to probe more deeply into the content and ideas included in a learning unit by examining the relationships among the content and ideas within or across units. Examples of vertical enrichment are provided in Anderson and Jones (1981).

One aspect of planning which is often overlooked is the planning of time. Approximate amounts of time must be allocated to the original instruction, corrective instruction, and testing. Such time planning serves three functions. First, it provides the opportunity for realistic estimates of the amount of material and objectives that can be included in a course. Second, it increases the quantity of time that each student spends in learning. Essentially, each student is constrained to spend as much time as necessary to master the objectives of one unit before moving to another unit. Such constraints are the core of the Carroll model (see Sect. 3). Third, time planning helps to increase the quality of the time that each student spends in learning. This increase in quality stems from two sources. Students increasingly possess the knowledge and skills necessary to profit from each subsequent unit's instruction. In addition, students are exposed to several ways of presenting the material and involving them in learning. At least one of these ways is likely to be effective for virtually every student.

3.3 Teaching for Mastery

Following defining and planning, the next task is teaching. The focus when teaching for mastery is on managing learning rather than managing learners. Inside the classroom "the function of the teacher to specify what is to be learned, to motivate pupils to learn it, to provide them with instructional materials, to administer these materials at a rate suitable for each pupil, to monitor students' progress, to diagnose difficulties and provide proper remediation for them, to give praise and encouragement for good performance, and to give review and practice that will maintain pupils' learning over long periods of time" (Carroll 1971 pp. 29–30).

Since many students are not accustomed to learning for mastery or the possibility that they all might earn A's, the first subtask of teaching for mastery is the orientation of students. Students are informed of what they are expected to learn, how they will learn it, how they are expected to demonstrate their learning, and how the adequacy of their learning will be judged. They are told about the grading system (emphasizing that their learning will be graded relative to a predetermined performance standard, not relative to the learning of their classmates). Finally, they are told that they will receive extra time and help as needed in order to ensure their learning.

A series of subtasks occur in fairly rapid succession following this initial orientation of students. The second subtask involves teaching each learning unit in sequence using the original instructional plan. After the initial instruction has been completed, and before moving to the next unit, the next subtask, the administration of the unit's formative test, is performed. Based on the formative test results, those students who have achieved the performance standard are certified and those who have not are identified. Next, students initially classified as masters are free to engage in enrichment activities and/ or to serve as tutors for their "slower" classmates; the nonmasters move to the corrective stage of the mastery learning instructional model. The day on which initial instruction relative to the next unit will begin is announced. If teachers desire to postpone the start of the next unit students are given in-class as well as out-of-class time to complete their assigned or selected corrective activities and materials. If not, out-of-class time must be used.

Since formative tests provide information about the adequacy of instruction as well as learning, two phases of corrective instruction can be visualized. The first phase provides corrective instruction for those objectives not mastered by a substantial number of students. In all likelihood such massive nonmastery indicates an instructional problem. As a consequence, additional class time can be taken to provide whole-class or large-group corrective instruction relating to such objectives.

The second phase provides alternative activities and materials which are keyed to each objective and which can be used for corrective instruction. A sheet of paper identifying each objective, appropriate test items, and recommended activities and materials can be presented to each student. The objectives not mastered can be designated in some manner. Such a sheet becomes a "feedback/corrective" vehicle. Students are expected to explore these alternative ways of learning, to select, often with teacher guidance, those best suited to their individual needs and interests, and to spend sufficient time engaged in this relearning.

This cycle of original instruction, formative testing, and certification or correction is repeated, unit by unit, until all units have been completed. This cycle is paced by the teacher so that about as much material and as many objectives are covered as would be covered in the time available had traditional methods of instruction been used. Such pacing helps to ensure that all students, the "faster" as well as the "slower," are exposed to as much course material and as many course objectives as they would ordinarily encounter.

The teacher has two pacing options. If all the time for correctives and enrichment is available outside of the regular class period, then the pacing of the instruction proceeds as usual. If some part or all of the time for correctives (and enrichment) is available during the regular class period, the teacher can adjust the pace of the instruction. Such an adjustment can be made by allowing more time for the earlier units and less time for the later ones. Essentially, time that would ordinarily be spent on later units is "borrowed" and spent on the earlier units. The assumption underlying this borrowing is that the additional time spent early will yield great time benefits later. Students who learn for mastery at the onset of a course or program should learn more effectively and efficiently as the course proceeds than they would were they learning under more traditional methods.

3.4 Grading for Mastery

The final major task facing developers of mastery learning programs is grading for mastery. The function of grading in mastery learning programs is to reward students for the acquisition of the essential, critical course objectives. Thus grades are assigned to students based on their performance on the summative test relative to the predetermined performance standard, not based on their performance relative to the performance of other students.

Such mastery grading is designed to engage students in what White (1959) has called "competence motivation," that is, the desire to compete against oneself and the objectives to be learned, and to disengage students from what Block (1977) has termed "competition motivation," that is, the desire to compete against others. From the standpoint of developing the talents of all students, rather than the talents of a select few, competence motivation is preferable to competition motivation.

The first subtask of grading for mastery is the administration of the summative test. All students whose scores are at or above the mastery performance standard earn grades of "A" or equivalent. At least two options are available for the grading of students who score below the performance standard. The choice of an option constitutes the second subtask. A first option, one most consistent with the philosophy of mastery learning, is to assign grades of "incompletes" (or equivalent) to these students. From a mastery learning perspective these students have not yet spent sufficient time and/or received sufficient help. If this option is selected a so-called "open transcript" is required. An open transcript is one that allows students to demonstrate and receive credit for improved levels of performance at any time.

A second option is to assign the remainder of the traditional grades (that is, "B," "C," "D," and "F") to

scores at various gradations below the mastery performance standard. If this option is selected the grades assigned to these students should reflect the number of objectives acquired as evidenced by their performance on the summative test. Even a grade of "F" should indicate the acquisition of some number of objectives.

One issue related to grading for mastery must be raised. First, some teachers prefer to, or are required to, assign grades based on the results of several summative tests. The preference for this practice stems from the belief that sound evaluation of student learning is enhanced by multiple pieces of information, each test viewed as one piece of information. The necessity for this practice is based on the multiple marking periods which exist in many schools. To the extent that the length of a course is one academic year and that academic year is divided into, say, four marking periods, then a minimum of one summative test per marking period would be required for grades to be assigned each marking period. Course grades would be some composite of these four grades.

Some educators have expressed the desire to use formative test results as part of the grading process, rather than increasing the number of summative tests. Such a use of formative tests is contrary to their function. From a functional perspective, formative tests are intended to provide evidence that can be used to monitor (rather than evaluate) student learning so that quality of instruction decisions (not quality of learning decisions) can be made. As has been mentioned, summative tests are intended to gather cumulative information for use in grading students. In view of the different functions of the two tests the use of only summative tests for grading purposes is highly recommended. If this recommendation is followed, then multiple summative tests must be prepared when defining mastery. The preparation of such tests should be consistent with their intended functions as described in Sect. 3.1.

4. Research on Mastery Learning

Research on the mastery learning model of teaching and learning is abundant. Comprehensive reviews of the research have been conducted by Block and Burns (1976), Bloom (1976), Dolan (1977–78), Burns (1979), and Guskey and Gates (1985). The purpose of this section is to present what we consider the three major generalizations that can be derived from this research.

4.1 Mastery Learning is Effective

This generalization is evident to anyone who performs even a cursory examination of the research literature. Beginning with the early studies which were small-scale, used laboratory-like learning tasks, and occurred in rather contrived classroom settings (for example, programmed instruction) and continuing to the present studies which are large-scale (often involving entire school districts in the United States, or entire countries, such as the Republic of Korea and Indonesia), use school-related learning tasks, and take place in naturally occurring classroom settings, the effectiveness of mastery learning programs has been demonstrated repeatedly (about 90 percent of the time, in fact).

Recent reviews have begun to quantify this effectiveness. Burns (1979), for example, has estimated the average "effective size" of mastery learning programs compared to nonmastery programs. Based on this estimate, the research suggests that the average student enrolled in mastery learning classes would achieve better than 80 to 85 percent of the students in nonmastery classes.

Research on the effectiveness of mastery learning programs is not limited to studies of immediate achievement. Although not as numerous as those focusing on immediate achievement, several studies have examined the effectiveness of mastery learning programs in terms of students' retention and rate of learning, as well as students' attitudes and self-perceptions. In the vast majority of these studies students enrolled in mastery learning classes outperformed their nonmastery counterparts. That is, students learning under mastery-based conditions (a) retained a greater portion of what they learned, (b) learned to learn more efficiently, (c) were more positive in their attitudes toward the subject being learned, and (d) developed greater self-confidence in their ability to learn.

4.2 The Key to Effectiveness Lies Within the Feedback/Corrective Mechanism

At least two aspects of this generalization are worth noting and describing. The first is the level at which the mastery performance standard is set; the second is the provision and utilization of corrective instruction.

The level at which the performance standard is set is critical to the success of mastery learning programs. Block (1972) was the first to pursue the issue of the setting of mastery performance standards. Block examined the teaching of matrix arithmetic to eighth graders (13-year-olds). Based on his results, Block concluded that a mastery performance standard set at 95 percent correct produced maximal cognitive learning. Unfortunately, this 95 percent standard had somewhat negative effects on students' attitudes and interests. Setting the standard at 85 percent correct, however, produced maximal interests and attitudes and somewhat reduced, but acceptable, levels of cognitive achievement.

In a more recent study Chan (1981), using a mastery learning approach to the teaching of reading comprehension to third-grade students, partially replicated Block's findings concerning cognitive learning. Once again, the 95 percent correct mastery performance standard yielded maximal learning. Students required to attain a lesser standard (i.e., 75 percent correct) achieved no better than did students learning under the nonmastery approach. Unfortunately, Chan did not include a standard of 85 percent correct in her study.

The results of the research on standard setting suggest the standard must be set sufficiently high so as to ensure

that the desired learning has occurred. Capricious standard setting may result in no real, functional standards at all. The research suggests that standards somewhere between 85 and 95 percent are most appropriate.

As indicated earlier, the provision and utilization of corrective instruction is a second key to the effectiveness of mastery learning. The importance of corrective instruction was first hinted at in a study by Collins (1970) and established by Block (1970). A more recent study by Nordin (1980), however, provides greater details of the role that corrective instruction plays in the overall effectiveness of mastery learning. Nordin focused on three of the major components of Bloom's (1976) conceptualization of quality of instruction: cues (or the clarity of presentation of the material to the students), participation (or the extent to which students were actively engaged in the learning process), and feedback/correctives. Nordin formed five groups of Malaysian sixth-grade students. He provided enhanced cues to one group, enhanced participation to a second, enhanced cues and participation to a third, feedback and correctives to a fourth, and conventional group instruction to a fifth. In terms of both cognitive achievement and learning rate, the students in the feedback/corrective group outperformed the students in the other four groups. And, in terms of student interest, students in the feedback/corrective group were more positive than the students in three of the other four groups. The exception was the enhanced cues group whose students had levels of interest similar to the students in the feedback/corrective group.

Vivid graphical evidence of the improvement in student performance following the use of correctives is displayed in Soemarso et al. (1980). Furthermore, the importance of utilization (as opposed to mere provision) of correctives is shown in Jones et al. (1975).

The importance of the corrective instruction component of mastery learning can be attributed largely to the increase in time available for learning. Quite clearly, corrective instruction increases the amount of time available for learning. And there is some evidence to suggest that, following corrective instruction, students spend an increasing proportion of the available time involved in learning or on-task (Anderson 1976).

4.3 Mastery Learning is Differentially Effective for Different Types of Students

This generalization is derived from research on two student characteristics: ability and age.

(a) *Ability.* One of the questions posed to proponents of mastery learning is whether students at all ability levels benefit equally well from mastery learning or whether the increased learning of the lower ability students is purchased at the cost of decreased learning of high-ability students. The results from several studies have shed some light on this question.

Kim (1969) stratified his sample according to the students' general ability. Two strata of ability, above average and below average, were formed. Students were assigned to either a mastery learning or nonmastery class. Following completion of the study Kim examined the results of the summative test separately by ability stratum. Using 80 percent correct as the summative mastery performance standard, Kim found for the low-ability students that 50 percent of those in the mastery learning class as compared with only 8 percent in the nonmastery class achieved mastery. For the high-ability students 95 percent of the mastery learning students and 64 percent of the nonmastery students achieved mastery.

Detheux et al. (1974) used socioeconomic status as a proxy for entering ability level. Three levels of socioeconomic status were formed: underprivileged (60 percent), average (30 percent), and privileged (10 percent). The results of the Detheux et al. study suggested that while the mastery learning program was especially beneficial for the underprivileged students, all three groups benefitted from the program. The Detheux et al. study is important since a more elite group of high-ability students (10 percent) was included than in the Kim study (50 percent).

The results of studies which have examined students of different ability levels indicate that the lower ability students, do, in fact, benefit more from mastery learning than the high-ability students. At the same time, however, the high-ability students do not suffer. Either they also benefit somewhat from the mastery learning program or, at the very least, do not do any worse than their high-ability counterparts in nonmastery programs (Anderson and Reynolds 1979).

Some may attribute the comparable results of high-ability students in mastery learning and nonmastery classes to the ceiling effect of the test. A recent study (Chan 1981) tends to dispute this attribution. Chan devised three sets of reading comprehension items. The first set was targeted for grade 3, the second set for grade 4, and the third set for grade 5. These sets of items were "linked" together using techniques underlying the Rasch psychometric model. Since the students were enrolled in grade 3, the summative test was virtually "ceilingless." Chan found that the high-ability students in the mastery learning groups achieved at virtually the same level as their nonmastery counterparts.

(b) *Age*. Recent school-based evaluations of mastery learning programs have begun to examine the impact of these programs at different grade levels (Abrams 1981, Cohen 1981). Most frequently these programs have been implemented over a period of several years, typically in grades 1 through 8. A time-series design has been used to evaluate program effectiveness. The results suggest that mastery learning programs have their greatest impact on students in grades 5 through 8. Relatively little impact has been seen at grades 1 through 4.

These results are somewhat surprising given the assertion of both some proponents and critics of mastery learning that mastery learning is especially effective when (a) it is introduced very early in the schooling process, and (b) it is employed in the teaching of simple, "closed" subjects rather than more complex, "open"

subjects. Quite clearly subject matters become increasingly "open" and complex as students progress through the grades (Block and Burns 1976).

Taken as a whole, the research evidence suggests that the mastery learning model of school teaching and learning represents one of those major breakthroughs to the improvement of student learning and school teaching for which both the educational practitioner community and the educational research, development, and dissemination community have been searching. Indeed, this growing body of research strongly suggests that mastery learning strategies usually have met, wholly or in part, general research criteria usually unmet by most other innovative approaches to the improvement of school teaching and learning. Mastery learning strategies can be taught to teachers, are being used, and are effective for large numbers of students.

5. The Future of Mastery Learning Practice and Research

Having lasted for 15 years the mastery learning model of instruction can no longer be considered a fad or passing fancy. Rather it must be viewed as a legitimate attempt to improve the quality of teaching and learning in the schools. What does the future hold for mastery learning? This article concludes with several speculations.

5.1 Speculation 1

The number and variety of schools employing some type of mastery learning program will continue to increase. This increase will be greater in countries whose philosophy of education and/or societal needs are congruent with mastery learning as a philosophy and instructional strategy; countries in which the prevalent belief system is that virtually all students can learn and/or there is a societal need for an increase in the number of competent individuals.

However, two issues must be attended to if mastery learning programs are to expand and improve. First, key elements of the mastery learning model of teaching and learning should be included in the curriculum materials. Objectives should be clearly stated in meaningful (not necessarily behavioral) terms. Tests relating to each objective should be available and the relationship between test items and objectives clearly specified. Meaningful performance standards should be recommended. Such performance standards should be set on the basis of the application of some systematic procedure. The curriculum should be organized into learning units not book chapters. Criteria should be established for the development of such learning units. Multiple sets of teaching–learning activities and related materials should be available for each objective. These sets will be used to provide the initial and corrective instruction relative to the objectives. If possible, the types of students for which the different sets are likely to be particularly effective should be described. Finally, supplemental booklets of secure, summative tests should be included. The inclusion of these key elements will reduce the amount of time and effort needed by school personnel to define and plan for mastery. In essence, the first two major tasks described previously will have been accomplished.

Second, a strong staff development program needs to be prepared in order to teach teachers to teach for mastery. Many teachers must develop the skills needed to properly implement mastery learning programs. Specific teaching skills related to clarity of presentation, involving students in the learning process, providing knowledge of results, providing encouragement, using test results to make instructional decisions, prescribing appropriate corrective instruction, and monitoring student learning processes and outcomes are critical to the success of mastery learning programs.

To date attempts at large-scale implementation of mastery learning programs have tended to either (a) embed key elements into the curriculum and curricular materials, *or* (b) develop a strong staff development program. These two approaches have been identified and labeled as the curriculum/materials approach and the staff development approach. For mastery learning to be successful over the long haul, both the curriculum/ materials approach *and* the staff development approach must be employed.

5.2 Speculation 2

Educators will begin to explore the preventative power of mastery learning. To date the major use of mastery learning has been remedial rather than preventative. It is not uncommon in the United States, for example, to find mastery learning programs used in grades 11 and 12 to undo the learning problems accumulated by many students over the previous 10 or 11 years. Quite clearly, certain subjects, classes, teachers, and schools throughout the world already have many students, especially older ones, who have already failed to learn excellently, and educators must use approaches such as mastery learning in an attempt to discontinue this negative trend. At the same time, however, it may be possible to introduce mastery learning early in the grades to immunize students from future problems and failure. If such an immunization occurs it may be possible to eliminate mastery learning at the later grades because mastery learners have been produced.

6. Needed Research

Several areas of research require future attention if the full potential of mastery learning is to be realized and if a better understanding of mastery learning is to be gained. Additional studies of the overall effectiveness of mastery learning are simply not needed. Such studies already abound. Rather, it would be more profitable to turn attention to two related areas of research: (a) research which examines the conditions under which mastery learning is more and less effective, and (b)

research which examines the limits of student learning that are possible to achieve using the mastery learning approach to school teaching and learning. Each area will be considered briefly.

Are there conditions which are more and less conducive to the effective use of mastery learning programs? If so, do these conditions involve conditions of classrooms, teachers, administrators, and/or students? These two questions form the basis for this entire area of needed research. Replications of the research on student ability level and student age/grade level are needed. Research on the level or type of administrative support necessary for successful implementation of mastery learning programs would be useful. There is a need for research on the effectiveness of mastery learning programs in the hands of preservice and inservice teachers. Research focusing on the extent to which the effectiveness of mastery learning programs depends on classroom contextual characteristics such as the ability distribution of the students (homogeneous versus heterogeneous), classroom organization (open versus traditional), or class size seems important.

Finally, can empirically verified estimates of the limits of student learning be obtained under mastery learning conditions? Bloom (1968, 1976) has provided a theoretical estimate. He contends that approximately 95 percent of students can learn well what is taught in schools. Yet only a few studies have supported this theoretical estimate. These studies have been what Bloom (1976) labeled microlevel studies; that is, studies of relatively short duration, focusing on clearly defined learning tasks, and under relatively tight experimental control. The question remains: to what extent is it possible, under normal schooling conditions, to replicate the results of the microlevel studies and, as a consequence, to provide empirical support for Bloom's theoretical limits. If ways can be found to approach these theoretical limits the future of mastery learning is bright indeed. The only question remaining to be answered by educators is whether it is truly desirable to approach these limits.

Bibliography

Abrams J D 1981 Precise teaching is more effective teaching. *Educ. Leadership* 39: 138–39

Anderson L W 1976 An empirical investigation of individual differences in time to learn. *J. Educ. Psychol.* 68(2): 226–33

Anderson L W, Anderson J C 1982 A functional approach to the definition of mastery learning. Paper presented at the Annual Meeting of the American Educational Research Association, New York

Anderson L W, Jones B F 1981 Designing instructional strategies which facilitate learning for mastery. *Educ. Psychol.* 16(3): 121–38

Anderson L W, Reynolds A 1979 The effect of mastery learning on the achievement of high ability students and the academic self-concept of low achieving students. Paper presented at the Annual Meeting of the American Educational Research Association, San Francisco, California

Block J H 1970 The effects of various levels of performance on selected cognitive, affective, and time variables. (Unpublished Ph.D. dissertation, University of Chicago)

Block J H 1971 Introduction to mastery learning: Theory and practice. In: Block J H (ed.) 1971 *Mastery Learning: Theory and Practice*. Holt, Rinehart and Winston, New York, pp. 2–12

Block J H 1972 Student learning and the setting of mastery performance standards. *Educ. Horizons* 50: 183–91

Block J H 1977 Individualized instruction: A mastery learning perspective. *Educ. Leadership* 34: 337–41

Block J H 1979 Mastery learning: The current state of the craft. *Educ. Leadership* 37: 114–17

Block J H, Anderson L W 1975 *Mastery Learning in Classroom Instruction*. Macmillan, New York

Block J H, Burns R B 1976 Mastery learning. In: Shulman L S (ed.) 1976 *Review of Research in Education*, Vol. 4. Peacock, Itasca, Illinois

Bloom B S 1968 Learning for mastery. UCLA-CSEIP *Eval. Comment.* 1(2)

Bloom B S 1974 An introduction to mastery learning theory. In: Block J H (ed.) 1974 *Schools, Society, and Mastery Learning*. Holt, Rinehart and Winston, New York

Bloom B S 1976 *Human Characteristics and School Learning*. McGraw-Hill, New York

Burns R B 1979 Mastery learning: Does it work? *Educ. Leadership* 37: 110–13

Carroll J B 1971 Problems of measurement related to the concept of learning for mastery. In: Block J H (ed.) 1971 *Mastery Learning: Theory and Practice*. Holt, Rinehart and Winston, New York, pp. 29–48

Chan K S 1981 The interaction of aptitude with mastery versus non-mastery instruction: Effects on reading comprehension of grade three students. (Unpublished Ph.D. dissertation, University of Western Australia)

Cohen S A 1981 Dilemmas in the use of learner responsive delivery systems. Paper presented at the annual meeting of the American Educational Research Association, Los Angeles, California

Collins K M 1970 A strategy for mastery learning in modern mathematics (Unpublished study, Purdue University, Division of Mathematical Sciences)

Detheux M, Leclerq E, Paquay J, Thirion A M 1974 From compensatory education to mastery learning. *London Educ. Rev.* 3(3): 41–50

Dolan L 1977–78 The status of mastery learning research and practice. *Administrator's Notebook.* 26(3): 1–4

Guskey T R, Gates S L 1985 A synthesis of research on group-based mastery learning programs. Paper presented at the annual meeting of the American Educational Research Association, Chicago, Illinois

Jones E L et al. 1975 *Mastery Learning: A Strategy for Academic Success in a Community College (Topical Paper No. 53)*. ERIC Clearinghouse for Junior College Information, University of California, Los Angeles. ERIC Document No. ED 115 315

Kim H et al. 1969 *A Study of the Bloom Strategies for Mastery Learning*. Korean Institute for Research in the Behavioral Sciences, Seoul

McNeil J D 1969 Forces influencing curriculum. *Rev. Educ. Res.* 39: 293–318

Morrison H C 1926 *The Practice of Teaching in the Secondary School*. University of Chicago Press, Chicago, Illinois

Nordin A B 1980 Improving learning: An experiment in rural primary schools in Malaysia. *Eval. Educ.* 4: 143–263

Postlethwait S N, Novak J D, Murray H 1964 *An Integrated Experience Approach to Learning with an Emphasis on Independent Study*. Burgess, Minneapolis, Minnesota

Soemarso, Suharaini Arikunto, Moh. Said, Muhain Lubis 1980 *Dalam Bidang Studi: 1) Matematika Kelas IV, 2) Bahasa Indonesia Kelas IV, 3) Ilma Pengetahuan Alam Kelas VI*. Departemen Pendidikan dan Kebudayan, Jakarta

Washburne C W 1922 Educational measurement as a key to individualizing instruction and promotion. *J. Educ. Res.* 5: 195–206

White R W 1959 Motivation reconsidered: The concept of competence. *Psychol. Rev.* 66: 297–333

Self-planned Learning

A. M. Tough

Research in nine countries has shown that adults spend about 500 hours a year each at major learning efforts. Approximately 73 percent of these highly deliberate learning projects are planned by the learner himself or herself, while another 7 percent are planned by a friend, relative, or other nonprofessional. The remaining 20 percent of these deliberate learning projects are planned by a professional educator or guided by a set of materials.

Interest in self-planned learning has rapidly increased around the world during the 1980s. Various approaches to facilitating self-planned learning are being provided in noncredit settings as well as in programs for academic credit. These approaches include self-direction in a group, continued individual learning after a course finishes, sets of materials and resources from which the individual chooses, learning networks, learning contracts, self-help books and groups, competency-based programs, and individually chosen paths within an academic course.

1. Self-planned Learning Projects

Men and women are largely responsible for planning their own learning and change, according to studies in several countries. These studies will be summarized here. Details are available in the epilogue section of Tough (1979), in the updated bibliography of research that was added when Tough (1967) was reissued in 1981, and in Tough (1982).

Nearly 60 surveys of highly intentional learning projects have been conducted in Australia, the United Kingdom, Canada, Ghana, Israel, Jamaica, New Zealand, the United States, and Zaire. The basic picture is remarkably consistent from one nation or population to another. The numbers change a little, but the general pattern remains constant. In fact, the really large differences are within any given population, not between populations. About 90 percent of all interviewees have conducted at least one major learning effort during the year before the interview. Highly intentional learning is clearly a common natural human activity.

The typical or average adult learner conducts five distinct learning projects in one year: he or she learns five distinct areas of knowledge and skill. The person spends an average of 100 hours per learning effort. This is a total of 500 hours per year, or almost 10 hours a week.

Every study of adults finds a similar pattern of responsibility for planning what is learned, although the exact figures vary a little. About 73 percent of all adult learning projects are planned largely by the person himself or herself. Self-planned learning is clearly the most common form of highly intentional adult learning. In self-planned learning, the individual assumes the primary responsibility for planning, guiding, and conducting the learning project. Various terms have been used to describe such learning, including self-directed learning, self-teaching, self-instruction, self-education, self-culture, independent study, and individual study. People engaged in such learning have been called autodidacts, autonomous learners, and self-propelled learners.

About 14 percent of all adult learning revolves around a group: 10 percent in groups led by a person who is paid or is designated as the instructor and 4 percent in peer groups. In 10 percent of their learning efforts, people turn the responsibility for planning over to one other person, either a professional such as a sports instructor or music teacher (7 percent) or a friend or relative (3 percent). In only 3 percent of their learning projects do people primarily follow the sequence and instructions provided by nonhuman materials such as programmed instruction, a series of television programs, or a set of tapes or phonograph records.

In summary, about 20 percent of all learning projects are planned by a professional (someone trained, paid, or institutionally designated to facilitate the learning). The professional operates in a group (10 percent), in a one-to-one situation (7 percent), or indirectly through completely preprogrammed nonhuman resources such as programmed instruction or a television series (3 percent). In the other 80 percent of learning projects, the detailed day-to-day planning is handled by an amateur. This is usually the learner himself or herself (73 percent), but occasionally it is a friend (3 percent) or a democratic group of peers (4 percent).

If the entire range of the adult's learning efforts are represented by an iceberg, the extent of self-directed learning can be more easily seen. For many years adult educators paid attention mostly to the highly visible portion of the iceberg showing above the surface of the water. They focused their attention on professionally guided learning. They provided courses, classes, workshops, other learning groups, apprenticeships, tutorials,

correspondence study, educational television, programmed instruction, and so on. Virtually everyone still agrees that all of this professionally guided learning is an important phenomenon in the world today. At the same time, though, it turns out to be only 20 percent of the total picture, only the highly visible tip of the iceberg. The massive bulk of the iceberg that is less visible, hidden below the surface, turns out to be 80 percent of the adult's learning efforts. It consists largely of self-planned or self-directed learning, though some is planned by other amateurs such as friends or peers.

During their self-directed learning, men and women perform several of the major teaching tasks that might otherwise be performed by a professional teacher. They perform an average of nine tasks, such as choosing their goal, planning the learning activities, obtaining appropriate resources, and estimating their level of knowledge and skill (Tough 1967). In the typical learning project the person experiences difficulty with about three of these tasks. As a result, he or she seeks suggestions, information, encouragement, resources, or other assistance from an average of 10 people. About three-quarters of these people are friends, acquaintances, family members, and fellow learners; only one-quarter are approached on a business or professional basis (Tough 1967).

The most common motivation (about 70 percent) for learning projects is some anticipated use or application of the knowledge and skill. The person has a task—raising a child, growing vegetables, mending or sewing something, teaching a class, fixing or improving something around the home—and learns certain knowledge and skill in order to perform the task successfully. Less common (about 20 percent) is curiosity or puzzlement, or wanting to possess the knowledge for its own sake. Learning for credit toward a degree, diploma, driver's license, or other certificate is comparatively rare: about 5 percent of all learning projects.

In a national survey in the United States, Penland (1977) was interested in the reasons people have when they choose to learn on their own instead of taking a course. Their responses were surprising, and the traditionally cited factors of money and transportation were ranked last. Penland's rank order, beginning with the reasons most often selected as particularly important (p. 32): (a) desire to set own learning pace; (b) desire to use own style of learning; (c) keeping the learning style flexible and easy to change; (d) desire to put own structure on the project; (e) didn't know of any class that taught what was wanted; (f) wanted to learn this right away and couldn't wait until a class might start; (g) lack of time to engage in a group learning program; (h) didn't like formal classroom situation with a teacher; (i) didn't have enough money for a course or a class; (j) transportation to a class was too hard or expensive. In the four most common reasons, people wanted to retain control or retain their own natural process, not have a professional instructor intervene.

433

Penland did not find any large differences between the participation of different statistical groups such as different age groups, income, social class, race, or completed education. Differences did exist, but their magnitude was usually small. In participation in learning efforts during adulthood, at least in the United States, there does not seem to be any large imbalance, any grossly underrepresented group, nor any particular unfairness or injustice.

2. *Optimum Amount of Teacher Control*

Power or control is a significant recurring theme in various fields and professions. Many examples are provided by Rogers (1977), Gartner and Riessman (1977), Fischer and Brodsky (1978), and Tough (1982).

At one extreme the instructor or other professional helper can have 100 percent of the control and authority; he or she has total responsibility for choosing the learning objectives and planning the strategy for learning. The opposite end of the continuum might be called 100 percent freedom and autonomy, at which point the learner retains full control, turning none of it over to the teacher.

For a given teacher, learner, and content, there will be an optimum or ideal range on the continuum. If the teacher and learner stay within this range, the learning will be facilitated more effectively than if they move higher or lower on the continuum. In many learning situations the extreme ends of the continuum are ineffective: the most effective range is somewhere in the middle of the continuum. Teachers and other professional helpers commonly overcontrol, but occasionally they err in the other direction. The research cited in the previous section has shown that most men and women have a remarkably rich and successful natural process for choosing, planning, and conducting their learning. They largely handle the various tasks on their own, with some help from acquaintances and family. Some teachers ignore, distort, or interfere with the person's natural ongoing process. Instead of treasuring and fostering their natural process, they sometimes take over complete control and force the learner to fit into their teaching process. Many teachers, on the contrary, have recently been decreasing their amount of control. They have been shifting to a shared responsibility for planning the learning, and have been fitting into the learner's natural process in a light-handed manner. They are moving into the optimum range on the control continuum, maximizing their usefulness by avoiding overcontrol and undercontrol.

In both noncredit and credit programs for adults, some educational agencies and teachers are changing from high control to shared responsibility. Although the approaches of these two strategies are somewhat diverse, they all have in common the shift away from traditional high control by the teacher. The approaches are sometimes referred to by the general term "self-directed learning." Less commonly they are called "open learning" or "independent learning." The next two sections present examples of various approaches to self-directed learning and teaching.

3. *Self-planned Learning in Noncredit Adult Learning*

Various approaches to self-planning have recently been noted where adult learning is not being pursued for a degree, certificate, or other academic credit.

In workshops for managers or supervisors, some instructors have encouraged each participant to diagnose appropriate needs and objectives, and to choose individual learning methods as the workshop progresses. Such approaches have been used by Roger Harrison in the United States and Joffre Ducharme in Canada.

Any workshop or course, regardless of its format, can encourage the participant to continue the learning after the course is finished. Some organizations, in educational programs for their managers, provide a self-assessment instrument and form for listing learning to be continued after the course has finished.

Some approaches rely heavily on tape recordings, programmed instruction materials, and other nonhuman resources. Most of these preprogrammed materials shift at least two sorts of responsibility to the learner: when to learn and at what pace. Distance education is a well-known example of this approach, and is used also for credit programs. In Nancy, France, a person who wants to learn any aspect of English for any purpose is given an excellent range of options at the *Centre de Recherches et d'Application Pédagogiques en Langues*. (Centre for Pedagogical Research and Application in Languages). The person chooses his or her own combination of helper, outside help, simulation, task matching, peer matching, personal reading materials, cassettes, written texts, and a sound library.

Learning networks, such as The Learning Exchange serving Evanston and the greater Chicago area, are very close to the learner-control end of the continuum. They do not try to control either the goals or the methods of learning. Instead, they simply provide the names and telephone numbers of persons who can serve as helpers or teachers with whatever sort of learning the caller wishes. Thousands of learners and teachers have been matched by the successful learning networks.

Individual learning contracts are being used more and more for continuing professional development. A learning contract spells out the person's goals and strategies, and perhaps the methods for evaluating achievement, for one major learning project. In some professions, members of the profession must undertake continuing education in order to retain their professional license or certificate: sometimes recognition is given to individual self-directed learning (as well as courses and workshops) through approving learning contracts.

A few institutions are experimenting with group support and stimulation for self-planned learning projects.

Ronald Gross in the United States is establishing several centers for advanced scholars who are not working at a university or similar institution.

Several methods of psychotherapy encourage the relevant material or content to arise spontaneously: the therapist does not choose the content for a particular session. Examples of such approaches include free association, LSD therapy sessions, dream work, primal therapy, and the Diabasis approach of John W. Perry.

In many countries, peer self-help groups are rapidly becoming widespread for those with addictions, mental health problems, emotional crises, and various specific health problems. In these groups, peers are the source of information and advice, and each member not only receives help but also helps others. Professional helpers are involved at times with some of these groups, but are rarely permitted to control them. Professionals in several fields of practice are struggling to work out appropriate forms of interaction with self-help groups (Gartner and Riessman 1977).

Many self-help books provide suggestions, exercises, and techniques for use when appropriate. Most of these books leave the person free to incorporate these suggestions into the ongoing process of learning and change. Several self-help books help people to learn for themselves the various principles of behavioral self-control.

4. Self-planned Learning in Credit Programs

Various approaches to self-planning are evident in programs pursued for credit toward a degree, certificate, or other academic credentials. In recent years, various efforts to reduce instructor control have been implemented. Although somewhat diverse at first glance, these efforts have one thing in common: an attempt to shift from a high degree of control by the instructor, from an attitude of the instructor always knows best, to greater choice and control in the hands of the student. The responsibility for choosing what and how to learn is partially shifted away from the instructor. It may be shifted to a set of materials, to the individual learner, to small groups of learners, or to the whole class.

Several examples have a long history. Over the decades, some instructors have given their students a free choice of topic or focus for essays, projects, and other assignments. Many theses and dissertations have been examples of shared responsibility. On many campuses, students have had an option of taking one or two individual reading courses or independent study courses.

Competency-based degree programs have become common in recent years. The competencies required for the degree are spelled out, along with assessment procedures for judging when the student has gained each competency. Basing credentials and hiring on demonstrated competencies (rather than on the method used to gain them) is one step toward greater freedom in educational institutions. Some writers have urged that students be encouraged to write their own competence statements, which may differ from those of other students.

In a few colleges and universities, students are helped to learn how to set goals and plan their strategies, and generally "learn how to learn." This approach has been used by Laurie Thomas and Sheila Harri-Augstein at Brunel University in England, for example, and by Robert Smith at Northern Illinois University in the United States.

In Canada, Virginia Griffin has developed a highly effective self-directed approach to teaching in her graduate courses at the Ontario Institute for Studies in Education. Early in the course she brings differences in learning styles and philosophy to the surface through questionnaires and discussion. Throughout the course she increasingly leaves the decision making with the students. Her approach has been described in periodical articles, theses, and videotape recordings.

Malcolm Knowles (1975 pp. 44–58) has described his approach to a 15-session graduate course. Before and during the third session each student develops a learning contract, which can subsequently be revised or renegotiated as the student's interests change or become clearer. Certain knowledge and skill that most students have included in their contracts are handled by small groups ("enquiry teams"), who make class presentations during the eighth meeting through the thirteenth meeting. At the end of the course, each student is allotted up to 45 minutes to present evidence, to two peers, of having accomplished his or her objective.

Allen Tough (1982 Chap. 6) has described in detail his approach to teaching Canadian and American graduate students. He retains some control over what and how the students learn, but tries to keep the structure and requirements to a minimum. As a result of his research on self-directed learning and change, he has increasingly encouraged his students to have a large degree of freedom in what and how they learn. Each student in his courses is largely free to plan and modify an individual learning path. At the same time, his approach tries to ensure that students have adequate access to help and resources.

Scott Armstrong has experimented with time contracts in five marketing courses at the Wharton School of the University of Pennsylvania. The students who selected this option kept a daily diary on course activities, time spent, and knowledge and skill learned. Students who satisfied the instructor that they had spent between 100 and 124 hours on the course received a pass, those with 125-140 hours were graded as high pass, and those with over 140 hours were "distinguished." Armstrong's evaluations indicated that students using time contracts spent more time at learning, felt more responsible for their learning, and were more successful at changing attitudes and behavior, compared to their experiences under traditional teaching approaches.

In some colleges and universities, students take almost no courses in which a group of students begins on a certain date to learn within one subject matter area. Instead, each student (in consultation with a faculty adviser or mentor) develops individual objectives and learning activities for each course. If groups of students meet at all, they do so to help and encourage and perhaps evaluate one another, not to learn and discuss content. In Canada, examples are provided by the McMaster University program for health professionals (Boud 1981) and by Holland College (Prince Edward Island). In the United States, examples are provided by Empire State College, and by the Community College of Vermont.

Since the early 1940s, several schools and teachers have experimented with a shift from high teacher control to shared responsibility. In 1977 the Association for Supervision and Curriculum Development established a project on self-directed learning in the United States, and in 1979 published a book focusing specifically on that approach.

Bibliography

Boud D (ed.) 1981 *Developing Student Autonomy in Learning.* Kogan Page, London

Brookfield S 1985 *Self-Directed Learning: From Theory to Practice.* New Directions for Continuing Education, No. 25. Jossey-Bass, San Francisco, California

Fischer C T, Brodsky S L (eds.) 1978 *Client Participation in Human Services: The Prometheus Principle.* Transaction, New Brunswick, New Jersey

Gartner A, Riessman F 1977 *Self-help in the Human Services.* Jossey-Bass, San Francisco, California

Knowles M S 1975 *Self-directed Learning: A Guide for Learners and Teachers.* Cambridge Book Co., New York

Long H B et al. 1988 *Self-Directed Learning: Application and Theory.* Department of Education, University of Georgia, Athens, Georgia

Penland P R 1977 *Self-planned Learning in America.* University of Pittsburgh Book Store, Pittsburgh, Pennsylvania

Rogers C R 1977 *Carl Rogers on Personal Power.* Delacorte, New York

Tough A M 1967 *Learning Without a Teacher: A Study of Tasks and Assistance during Adult Self-teaching Projects.* Ontario Institute for Studies in Education, Toronto, Ontario

Tough A M 1979 *The Adult's Learning Projects: A Fresh Approach to Theory and Practice in Adult Learning,* 2nd edn. Books on Demand, University Microfilms International, Ann Arbor, Michigan

Tough A M 1982 *Intentional Changes: A Fresh Approach to Helping People Change.* Cambridge Book Co., New York

Evaluation

Formative and Summative Evaluation

A. Lewy

The terms formative and summative appeared first in the context of curriculum evaluation. Scriven (1967), who coined these terms, specified the differences between them, and stated that both formative and summative evaluation may examine the worth of a variety of entities such as products, processes, personnel, or learners. Nevertheless, for several years these terms were uniquely applied to describing various types of curriculum evaluation activities. Only later did they become generalized and employed in the context of learner evaluation (Bloom et al. 1971) and educational actions other than curricula (Cronbach et al. 1980). The distinction between formative and summative evaluation contributed to broadening the range of disciplined inquiries recognized as evaluation studies, by attributing scholarly significance and professional status to evaluation activities conducted in the course of program development. Prior to the emergence of these terms, program evaluation, insofar as it was carried out, typically meant the comparison of the outcomes of competing programs for the sake of advising the decision maker about selecting or continuing educational programs. The evaluators, taking a stance of impartial aloofness and employing some legitimate form of experimental design, made an attempt to compare the relative merits of neatly packaged or fully structured competing programs. The failure of studies of this type to provide conclusive results on the one hand, and the conviction of evaluators that they can, and should, contribute to the improvement of education programs at various stages of their development on the other hand, gave issue to relatively small-scaled studies focusing on particular aspects of programs in the course of their development. Such studies, which in many cases waived the demanding patterns of experimental design and frequently revealed little interest in comparisons, came to be labelled formative evaluation studies. At the same time, comparative studies examining the outcomes of finished programs, with the aim of providing recommendations about program selection and continuation, which up to that time had been considered the sole permissible genre of evaluation, were redefined as a particular type of evaluation study within the framework of a variety of summative evaluation studies.

Attempts at conducting evaluation studies of instructional programs in the course of their development had been made before the emergence of the formative–summative distinction (Markle 1967). But the introduction of these terms constituted a point of departure for systematically exploring and conceptualizing the differences between the two types, and for disseminating the idea that it is both permissible and highly desirable to conduct evaluation studies in the course of program development, with a design deviating from that of the classical comparison studies.

1. The Formative–Summative Dichotomy

Two decades after the emergence of these innovative terms, a full consensus had not been reached as to their precise meaning. Therefore some experts tend to disregard the summative–formative distinction and focus on other, in their view, more clearly defined evaluation study dichotomies, such as prospective versus retrospective, responsive versus preordinate, naturalistic versus experimental, holistic versus analytic, process versus outcome, and so on. Some of these have been erroneously interpreted as parallel to (if not fully identical with) the formative–summative distinction. In response to this confusion Scriven, the originator of these terms, provided definitions of formative and summative evaluations, which emphasize their orthogonality to the dichotomies mentioned above. According to Scriven (1980), formative evaluation is conducted during the development or improvement of a program or product (or person). It is an evaluation conducted for in-house staff and normally remains in house, but it may be done by an internal or external evaluator, or (preferably) a combination. Summative evaluation, on the other hand, is conducted after completion of a program (or a course of study) and for the benefit of some external audience or decision maker (e.g., funding agency or future possible users), though it too may be done either by an internal or an external evaluator or by a combination.

437

Scriven adheres to the view that there are no basic logical and methodological differences between formative and summative evaluation. Both are intended to examine the worth of a particular entity. Only timing, the audience requesting it, and the way its results are used can indicate whether a study is formative or summative. Moreover, the same study may be viewed by one client as formative and by another one as summative.

2. The Relative Importance of Formative and Summative Studies

While the scholarly status of formative evaluation studies was established only recently, they have swiftly dominated the field of program evaluation. Cronbach et al. (1980) claim that formative evaluation is more impactful and therefore more significant than summative evaluation. In their opinion, evaluation employed to improve a program while it is still fluid contributes more to the improvement of education than evaluation used to appraise a product already placed on the market. To be influential in course improvement, evidence must become available midway through program development and not in the home stretch, when the developer is naturally reluctant to tear apart a supposedly finished body of materials and techniques. Similarly, providing feedback to the teacher and learner about success or failure in mastering specific skills or components of the program constitutes an essential part of the teaching–learning process. It makes it possible to spot weak points of the program and to identify those learners who need corrective teaching. Formative information of this type contributes more to the improvement of learning than do results of end-of-course testing.

The superior usefulness of formative evaluation is so stressed in the writings of numerous evaluation experts that people dealing with specific programs often display no interest in conducting summative evaluation studies. Scriven deplores this attitude and points out that both types of study have unique and essential roles. Summative evaluation is an inescapable obligation of the project director, an obvious requirement of the sponsoring agency and a desideratum for schools.

3. Characteristics of Formative and Summative Studies

Despite the tremendous growth in the number of formative and summative evaluation studies published in the 1960s and 1970s, theoreticians have not produced rules as to the procedures appropriate for either type of study. An exception is within the field of formative and summative evaluation of students' learning. As to other targets of evaluation, Scriven plays down the differences between formative and summative studies. Nevertheless, several reviews of empirical studies have pointed out systematic differences.

Stake (1977) provides a series of terms which characterize differences in information sought by users of formative and summative evaluation. Formative evaluation focuses on relatively molecular analyses, is cause seeking, is interested in the broader experiences of the program users, and tends to ignore the local effect of a particular program, while summative evaluation focuses on molar analyses, provides descriptive information, is interested in efficiency statements, and tends to emphasize local effects.

Alkin (1974), analysing 42 evaluation reports, and questionnaires completed by the 42 project directors, lists additional characteristics of formative evaluation studies. Their design is characterized as exploratory, flexible, focusing on individual components of the program, and as emphasizing iterative processes. While not comparative, it seeks to identify influential variables. A formative evaluation study uses a great variety of instruments which are either locally developed or standardized; it relies on observation and informal data collection devices, mostly locally chosen. In contrast, summative evaluation studies tend to use well-defined evaluation designs, as unobtrusive and nonreactive as possible; they are comparative and concerned with a broad range of issues, for example, implications, politics, costs, competing options. The instruments used in summative evaluation are publicly accepted, reliable, and valid instruments, reflecting concerns of the sponsor and of the decision-maker.

The rules provided by Bloom et al. (1971) for conducting formative and summative evaluation of students' learning are more specific. For formative evaluation, it is first necessary to analyze the instructional materials, to map the hierarchical structure of the learning tasks, and to administer achievement tests after completing a short learning unit covering study materials for 6 to 10 periods of study. A sample of test items appearing in the formative tests, or equivalent items, should constitute the summative evaluation test to be administered at the end of the course, with the aim of providing a basis for grading or certifying the learner.

4. The Consequences of the Formative and Summative Distinction

The formative–summative distinction has increased the range of evaluation studies and contributed to the improvement of educational planning. But two decades of utilizing these terms produced little consensus concerning their distinct features. The allegation that they differ only from the point of view of decisions they are supposed to support, and that no distinction should be made between them from the point of view of design, methodology, etc., has been endorsed by many evaluators without its veracity having been empirically examined. At the same time, other evaluators have asserted that methodological rigor is required only in summative studies, while in formative ones the evaluator may rely on less rigorously validated data and analysis procedures. This claim has never been confirmed by evaluation experts, but nevertheless it, unfortunately, has lead to the burgeoning of sloppily designed formative evaluation studies.

To avoid such theoretical and empirical pitfalls, there is a need to conduct empirical studies to ascertain the characteristic method and design features of formative and summative evaluation. Such studies might facilitate the use of formative and summative evaluation, and enhance their quality.

Bibliography

Alkin M C 1974 *Evaluation and Decision Making: The Title VII Experience.* Center for Study of Evaluation, University of California, Los Angeles, California

Bloom B S, Hastings J T, Madaus G F 1971 *Handbook on Formative and Summative Evaluation of Students' Learning.* McGraw-Hill, New York

Cronbach L J et al. 1980 *Toward a Reform of Program Evaluation.* Jossey-Bass, San Francisco, California

Markle S M 1967 Empirical testing of programs. *Sixty-sixth Yearbook of the National Society for the Study of Education.* University of Chicago Press, Chicago, Illinois

Sanders J R, Cunningham D J 1973 A structure for formative evaluation in product development. *Rev. Educ. Res.* 43: 217–36

Scriven M 1967 The methodology of evaluation. In: Tyler R W (ed.) 1967 *Perspectives of Curriculum Evaluation.* Rand McNally, Chicago, Illinois

Scriven M 1980 *Evaluation Thesaurus*, 2nd edn. Edgepress, Inverness, California

Stake R 1977 Formative and summative evaluation. In: Hamilton D et al. (eds.) 1977 *Beyond the Numbers Game: A Reader in Educational Evaluation.* McCutchan, Berkeley, California

Program Evaluation

B. R. Worthen

As educational programs (and other publicly funded programs) have increased greatly in size and expense, taxpayers and public officials have increasingly urged that these programs be made more accountable to their publics. Indeed, "accountability" for expenditures of public funds has become the hue and cry of an ever-increasing number of social reformers. In several countries, policy makers at both national and local levels now routinely authorize funds to be used for the express purpose of evaluating educational programs to determine their effectiveness. Thus, "program evaluation" has come into being as both a formal educational activity and as a frequently mandated instrument of public policy. Many private educational enterprises have similarly turned to program evaluation as a means of answering questions about the benefits received from monies expended on various educational programs.

To define program evaluation, it is necessary to define its component parts. In an educational context, a program can be thought of as any educational enterprise aimed at the solution of a particular educational problem or the improvement of some aspect of an educational system. Such a program would typically be sponsored by public or private funds, possess specified goals, and exhibit some structure for managing the procedures, materials, facilities, and/or personnel involved in the program.

Evaluation can be defined most simply as the determination of the worth of a thing. In its simplest form, therefore, program evaluation consists of those activities undertaken to judge the worth or utility of a program (or alternative programs) in improving some specified aspect of an educational system. Examples of program evaluations might include evaluation of a national bilingual education program, a university's preservice program for training urban administrators, a ministry of education's staff development program, or a local parent education resource center. Evaluations may be conducted for programs of any size or scope, ranging from an arithmetic program in a particular school to an international consortium on metric education.

Curriculum evaluations may qualify as program evaluations if the curriculum is focused on change or improvement, as implied in the previous definition of "program." Program evaluations, however, often do not involve appraisal of curricula (e.g., evaluation of a computerized student record-keeping system or evaluation of the extent to which funds from a national program for the hearing impaired are actually used to provide services to children with hearing impairments). For this reason, the closely related but more specialized topic of curriculum evaluation is not discussed further in this section.

1. Purposes of Program Evaluation

Most program evaluators agree that program evaluation can play either a formative purpose (helping to improve the program) or a summative purpose (deciding whether a program should be continued). Anderson and Ball (1978) further describe the capabilities of program evaluation in terms of six major purposes (which are not necessarily mutually exclusive). They are:

(a) to contribute to decisions about program installation;

(b) to contribute to decisions about program continuation, expansion, or "certification";

(c) to contribute to decisions about program modifications;

(d) to obtain evidence to rally support for a program;

(e) to obtain evidence to rally opposition to a program;

(f) to contribute to the understanding of basic psychological, social, and other processes (only rarely can this purpose be achieved in a program evaluation without compromising more basic evaluation purposes).

2. The History of Program Evaluation

The informal practice of program evaluation is not new, dating back at least to 2000 BC, when Chinese officials were conducting civil-service examinations, and continuing down through the centuries to the beginnings of school accreditation in the late 1800s. The first clear evidence of formal program evaluation, however, appears to be Joseph Rice's 1897–1898 comparative study of the spelling performance of 33,000 students in a large United States school system. Few formal evaluations of educational programs were conducted in the next few decades, with Tyler and Smith's Eight-year Study of the 1930s being the next notable effort to evaluate the outcomes of an educational program. During the late 1950s and early 1960s (the post-Sputnik years), cries for curriculum reform led to major new curriculum development programs and to subsequent calls for their evaluation. The relatively few evaluation studies that resulted revealed the conceptual and methodological impoverishment of the field—or perhaps more accurately, the "nonfield"—of evaluation in that era. In many cases, the designs were inadequate, the data invalid, the analyses inaccurate, and the reports irrelevant to the important evaluation questions which should have been posed. Most of the studies depended on idiosyncratic combinations and applications of concepts and techniques from experimental design, psychometrics, curriculum development and, to a lesser extent, survey research. Theoretical work related to educational evaluation, per se, was almost nonexistent. Few scholars had yet turned their attention to the development of generalizable evaluation plans which could be adopted or adapted specifically to educational evaluation studies. In the absence of a "formal subject matter" or educational evaluation, evaluators of educational programs were left to glean what they could from other fields to help them in their work.

Since a large number of persons serving in evaluation roles during the late 1950s and 1960s were educational and psychological researchers, it is not surprising that the experimental tradition quickly became the most generally accepted evaluation approach. The work of Campbell and Stanley gave enormous impetus to the predominance of experimental or quasiexperimental approaches to program evaluation. Although some evaluators cautioned that correct use of the experimental model may not be feasible, the elegance and precision of this model led most program evaluators to view the experimental method as the ideal model for program evaluations.

Not all program evaluators were enamored with the use of traditional quantitative methods for program evaluations, however, and their dissatisfaction led to a search for alternatives. Qualitative and naturalistic methods, largely shunned by program evaluators during the 1960s as unacceptably "soft," gained wider acceptance in the 1970s and thereafter as proposals for their application to program evaluations were made by Parlett and Hamilton, Stake, Eisner, Guba and Lincoln, and others. Sharp disagreements developed between proponents of the newer qualitative approaches and adherents to the more broadly accepted quantitative methods and the 1970s were marked by polemics as the two schools of thought struggled for ascendancy. The late 1970s have, however, seen the dialogue begin to move beyond this debate as analysts have accelerated their discussions of the benefits of integrating both types of methods within a program evaluation (for instance see Cook and Reichardt 1979, Worthen 1981, and the especially useful summary by Madey 1982).

Concurrent with the program evaluators' struggle to sort out the relative utility of quantitative and qualitative methods, a separate but closely related development was taking place. Beginning in the late 1960s, several evaluation writers began to develop and circulate their notions about how one should conduct educational evaluations; these efforts resulted in several new evaluation "models" being proposed to help the practicing program evaluator. Although these seminal writings in educational evaluation (discussed in Sect. 3) were doubtlessly influenced by the quantitative–qualitative controversy and some proved more comfortable companions with one or the other methodological persuasion, several were broader in conceptualization, providing guidelines for conducting program evaluations that could use either quantitative or qualitative data. As these frameworks for planning evaluation studies were applied and refined, program evaluators began to turn to them as promising sources of guidance. Collectively, these writings, the so-called evaluation models, represent the formal content of program evaluation and are discussed in the following section.

3. Alternative Approaches to Program Evaluation

Because of space restrictions, only some of the more popular current approaches used in conducting program evaluations can be presented in this section. Many of these (and other) approaches to program evaluation are summarized in Worthen and Sanders (1973, 1987) and the work of authors mentioned but not referenced herein (and in other sections of this entry) can be found in that source. For convenience, these conceptual frameworks for evaluation are clustered into five categories, although some of the frameworks could appear in more than one category. Most of these "models" have focused broadly on program evaluation, although some are focused more specifically on curriculum evaluation. It should be noted that these frameworks deal with methods, not techniques; discussion of the many techniques which might be used in program evaluations is beyond the scope of this article.

3.1 Performance–Objectives Congruence Approaches

This approach to program evaluation was originally formulated by Ralph Tyler, who conceived of evaluation as the process of determining the extent to which the educational objectives of a school program or curriculum are actually being attained. He proposed a process in which broad goals or objectives would be established or identified, defined in behavioral terms, and relevant student behaviors would be measured against this yardstick, using either standardized or evaluator-constructed instruments. These outcome data were then to be compared with the behavioral objectives to determine the extent to which performance was congruent with expectations. Discrepancies between performance and objectives would lead to modifications intended to correct the deficiency, and the evaluation cycle would be repeated.

Tyler's rationale was logical, scientifically acceptable, readily adoptable by program evaluators (most of whose methodological upbringing was very compatible with the pretest–posttest measurement of student behaviors stressed by Tyler), and had great influence on subsequent evaluation theorists. Hammond's EPIC evaluation model followed Tyler's model closely, adding only a useful program-description "cube" which elaborates instructional and institutional variables often overlooked in previous evaluations. Provus' discrepancy model of program evaluation is clearly Tylerian and gains its name from the constant setting and juxtaposition of program standards against program performance to yield "discrepancy information" needed for program improvements. Popham's instructional objectives approach also clearly stems from Tyler's earlier conceptions.

Useful as this approach to evaluation is, viewed by its many adherents, critics such as Guba and Lincoln have noted that it lacks a real evaluative component (facilitating measurement and assessment of objectives rather than resulting in explicit judgments of worth), lacks standards to judge the importance of observed discrepancies between objectives and performance levels, and depends on a highly utilitarian philosophy, promoting a linear, inflexible approach to evaluation.

3.2 Decision–Management Approaches

The most important contributions to a decision-oriented approach to program evaluation are Stufflebeam's Context, Input, Process, and Product (CIPP) evaluation model and Alkin's Center for the Study of Evaluation model, which follows a similar logic to the Context, Input, Process, and Product model but distinguishes between program implementation and program improvement, two subdivisions of what Stufflebeam terms process evaluation. In both models, objectives are

eschewed as the organizer for the study and the decision to be made by program managers becomes pivotal. Stufflebeam (1971) has provided an analysis of types of decisions program managers are required to make and proposes a different type of evaluation for each type of decision. In both of these decision-oriented models, the evaluator, working closely with the program manager, would identify the decisions the latter must make and collect sufficient information about the relative advantages and disadvantages of each decision alternative to enable the decision maker to make a judgment about which is best in terms of specified criteria. Thus, evaluation became an explicitly shared function dependent on good teamwork between evaluators and decision makers.

This approach has proved appealing to many evaluators and program managers, particularly those at home with the rational and orderly systems approach, to which it is clearly related. It was viewed by others, however, as failing to determine explicitly the program's worth and being dependent on somewhat unrealistic assumptions about the orderliness and predictability of the decision-making process.

3.3 Judgment-oriented Approaches

This general approach to evaluation, which historically has been the most widely used evaluation approach, is dependent upon experts' application of professional expertise to yield judgments about a program being observed. For example, the worth of a program would be assessed by experts (in the view of the evaluation's sponsor) who would observe the program in action, examine its products or, in some other way, glean sufficient information to render their considered judgment about the program. Site visits initiated by funding agencies to evaluate programs they support and visits by accrediting agencies to secondary schools and universities are examples of judgment-oriented program evaluations. Scriven, in his *The Methodology of Evaluation* (Worthen and Sanders 1973), stressed judgment as the sine qua non of evaluation and, in his insightful examination of educational evaluation, did much to rescue this approach from the disrepute into which it had fallen in the headlong rush of evaluation to gain respectability as a science. He stunned orthodox objectives-oriented evaluators by his suggestion that evaluators might go beyond measuring a program's performance to also evaluate the program's goals and later compounded the shock still further with his suggestion that evaluators should do "goal-free" evaluations, in which they not only ignore the program's goals but actually make every effort to avoid learning what those goals are. Thus, judgments about programs were based on the actual outcomes of the program, intended or not, rather than on the program's objectives or on decisions faced by program managers.

Another important judgement-oriented evaluation model is Robert Stake's Countenance Model, in which he suggests that the two major activities of formal evaluation studies are description and judgment (the "two countenances") of the program being evaluated. Within the description phase, Stake follows Tyler's rationale of comparing intended and actual outcomes of the program. But in the judgment phase, he argued that standards and procedures for making judgmental statements must be explicated to ensure the publicness of evaluative statements, although he failed to provide any suggestions as to how to weight or combine individual standards into overall judgments about the program.

Eisner's "connoisseurship model" casts program evaluators as educational critics whose refined perceptual capabilities (based on knowledge of what to look for and a backlog of relevant experience) enable them to give a public rendering of the quality and significance of that which is evaluated (Eisner 1985). In this model, the evaluator is the "instrument," and the data collecting, analyzing, and judging that Stake tried to make more public are largely hidden within the evaluator's mind, analogous to the evaluative processes of art criticism or wine tasting.

Collectively, these judgment-oriented approaches to evaluation have emphasized the central role of judgment and human wisdom in the evaluative process and have focused attention on the important issues of whose standards (and what degree of publicness) should be used in rendering judgments about educational programs. Conversely, critics of this approach suggest that it often permits evaluators to render judgments that reflect little more than figments of fertile imaginations. Others have noted that the presumed expertise of the evaluators is a potential weakness and worse, strong arguments can be made that serious disadvantages can accrue if a program is evaluated only by content experts (Worthen and Sanders 1987). Finally, many program evaluators are disinclined to play the single-handed role of educational judge (which they feel smacks of arrogance and elitism) proposed by some of these approaches.

3.4 Adversarial Approaches

Adversarial evaluation is a rubric which encompasses a collection of divergent evaluation practices which might loosely be referred to as adversarial in nature. In its broad sense, the term refers to all evaluations in which there is planned opposition in the points of view of different evaluators or evaluation teams—a planned effort to generate opposing points of view within the overall evaluation. One evaluator (or team) would serve as the program's advocate, presenting the most positive view of the program possible from the data, while another evaluator (or team) would play an adversarial role, highlighting any extant deficiencies in the program. Incorporation of these opposing views within a single evaluation reflects a conscious effort to assume fairness and balance and illuminate both strengths and weaknesses of the program.

Several types of adversarial proceedings have been invoked as models for adversary evaluations in education, including judicial, congressional hearings, and debate models. Of these, most of the sparse literature in this area has focused on adaptations of the legal paradigm, providing insights into how concepts from the legal system (for instance, taking and cross-examination of human testimony) could be used in educational evaluations. Owens, Wolf, and others have adapted the legal model to educational evaluations, while Worthen and Rogers have described use of the debate model in an adversary evaluation and have discussed pitfalls and potentials of the legal and other forensic paradigms in conducting program evaluations.

Despite the publicity given this approach to evaluation, as yet there is little beyond personal preference to determine whether program evaluations will profit most from being patterned after jury trials, congressional hearings, debates, or other arrangements.

3.5 Pluralist–Intuitionist Approaches

House (1980) has used this descriptor to characterize several evaluation models, contrasting them with more "utilitarian" models. In this approach to evaluation, the evaluator is a portrayer of different values and needs of all the individuals and groups served by the program, weighing and balancing this plurality of judgments and criteria in a largely intuitive fashion. Thus, the "best program" is largely decided by the values and perspectives of whomever is judging (an obvious fact nonetheless ignored in most other evaluation approaches). Examples of pluralist–intuitionist evaluation "models" are those proposed by Stake's (1980) Responsive Evaluation, Parlett and Hamilton's (1976) Illuminative Evaluation, Rippey's (1973) Transactional Evaluation, and MacDonald's (1976) Democratic Evaluation. There are unique contributions of each of these proposals. Stake urges program evaluators to respond to the audience's concerns and requirements for information, in terms of their value perspectives, and argues that the evaluation framework and focus should emerge only after considerable interaction with those audiences. Parlett and Hamilton draw on the social anthropology paradigm (and psychiatry and sociology participant observation research) in proposing progressive focusing of an evaluation whose purpose is to describe and interpret (not measure and predict) that which exists within an educational system. Rippey focuses on the effects of programs on the program operators and views evaluation as a strategy for conflict management. MacDonald views evaluation as primarily a political activity whose only justification is the "right to know" of a broad range of audiences. Yet a common thread runs through all these evaluation approaches—value pluralism is recognized, accommodated, and protected, even though the effort to summarize the frequently disparate judgments and preferences of such groups is left as an intuitive process which depends heavily on the sagacity and impartiality of the evaluator.

Critics of this approach to program evaluation discount it as hopelessly "soft headed" and argue that few if any program evaluators are such paragons of virtue and wisdom as to be skillful in wielding the seductively simple, yet slippery and subtle tools that is required by this approach. Champions of pluralistic, responsive approaches reply that they can be readily used by any sensitive individual and that they are infinitely richer and more powerful than other approaches and, indeed, can subsume them, since they are flexible and do not preclude the use of other approaches within them, should that be desired by the evaluator's sponsor.

4. An Appraisal of Current Program Evaluation Models

Collectively, the writings reviewed briefly in Sect. 3, the so-called evaluation models, represent the formal content on which educational program evaluators draw. It is, therefore, appropriate to ask how useful they are.

The answer is "very useful, indeed," even though they collectively have not moved evaluation very far toward becoming a science or discipline in its own right (a dubious aspiration, nonetheless sought by many evaluators). An earlier analysis (Worthen and Sanders 1987) has shown that (a) the so-called evaluation models fail to meet standard criteria for scientific models, or even less rigorous definitions of models, and (b) that which has come to be referred to as the theoretical underpinnings of evaluation lack important characteristics of most theories, being neither axiomatic nor deductive, having no real predictive power, and being untested and unvalidated in any empirical sense. That same analysis, however, suggested that these conceptions about how evaluations should be conducted—the accompanying sets of categories, lists of things to think about, descriptions of different evaluation strategies, and exhortations to which one might choose to attend—influence the practice of program evaluation in sometimes subtle, sometimes direct, but always significant ways. Some program evaluators design evaluations which adopt or adapt proposed models of evaluation. Many evaluators, however, conduct evaluations without strict adherence (or even intentional attention) to any "model" of evaluation, yet draw unconsciously in their evaluation philosophy, plans, and procedures on that which they have internalized through exposure to the literature of program evaluation. So the value of the "models" lies in their ability to help us to think, to provide sources of new ideas and techniques, to serve as mental checklists of things we ought to consider, or remember, or worry about. Their value as prescriptive guidelines for doing evaluation studies seems much less.

5. Impediments to Improving Program Evaluation

Despite the advances made in program evaluation, there is obviously room for a great deal of improvement. In this section, four areas that need improvement for educational evaluation to reach its full potential are discussed briefly.

5.1 Evaluation Lacks an Adequate Knowledge Base

Since the early 1970s, Stufflebeam, Worthen and Sanders, Smith, and others have issued a call for evaluation to be researched to develop an adequate knowledge base to guide evaluation practice. That call is still largely unanswered, despite some promising research which has been launched on evaluation methods and techniques. A program of research aimed at drawing from other disciplines new methodological metaphors and techniques for use in educational evaluation has been in existence at the Northwest Regional Educational Laboratory for nearly eight years and has introduced program evaluators to promising new metaphors and techniques drawn from areas such as architecture, philosophic analysis, investigative journalism, and literary and film criticism. A second National Institute of Education-sponsored research effort at the University of California at Los Angeles has focused largely on descriptive studies of evaluation practices in educational agencies. In addition, a few research studies aimed at generating knowledge about either particular evaluation strategies and procedures or factors affecting evaluation utilization have begun to appear.

These positive developments notwithstanding, there is still little or no empirical information about the relative efficacy of alternative evaluation plans or techniques or many evaluation components germane to almost any model. For example, virtually no empirical information exists about the most effective way to conduct a needs assessment or weight criteria in reaching a summative judgment. Little is known about the extent to which various data collection techniques interfere with ongoing educational phenomena. Techniques for identifying goals are developed anew with every evaluation, since there is no evidence that any one way of conducting these activities is more effective than any other. Elaborate systems are developed for providing evaluative feedback, but there is no real knowledge base about the relative effectiveness of feedback under differing conditions and scheduling. One could go on to create an exhaustive list of phenomena and procedures in evaluation which badly need to be systematically studied, but the above should suffice to make the point. Smith (1981) has summarized the needs for research on evaluation as requiring more knowledge about (a) the contexts within which evaluation is practiced, (b) the nature of evaluation utility, and (c) the effectiveness of specific evaluation methods.

5.2 Evaluation Studies are Seldom Evaluated

The necessity of "meta-evaluation" is apparent and completion of the long-awaited *Standards for Evaluations of Educational Programs, Projects, and Materials* (Joint Committee on Standards 1981) marked a welcome milestone. Although many evaluation writers had proposed their own sets of meta-evaluation criteria, none carried the profession-wide weight reflected in the comprehensive standards so carefully prepared by the Joint Committee. These standards include criteria within each of the following categories: utility standards; feasibility standards; propriety standards; and accuracy standards.

Despite the wide acceptance and availability of these standards, however, there is no evidence that program evaluations are being subjected to any closer scrutiny than was the case before their publication. Even casual inspection reveals that only a small proportion of evaluation studies are ever evaluated, even in the most perfunctory fashion. Of the few meta-evaluations which do occur, most are internal evaluations done by the evaluator who produced the evaluation in the first place. It is rare indeed to see an evaluator call in an outside expert to evaluate his evaluation efforts. Perhaps the reasons are many and complex why this is so, but one seems particularly compelling—evaluators are human and are no more ecstatic about having their work critiqued than are professionals in other areas of endeavor. Indeed, it can be a profoundly unnerving experience to swallow one's own prescriptions. Although the infrequency of good meta-evaluation might thus be understandable, it is not easily forgivable, for it enables shoddy evaluation practices to go undetected and worse, to be repeated again and again, to the detriment of the profession.

5.3 Program Evaluators Fail to Understand the Political Nature of Evaluation

Cronbach and co-workers (1980) have presented the view that evaluation is essentially a political activity. They describe evaluation as a "novel political institution" that is part of governance of social programs. They assert that evaluators and their patrons pursue unrealistic goals of finding "truth" or facilitating "right" decisions, rather than the more pertinent task of simply enlightening all participants so as to facilitate a democratic, pluralist decision-making process. While some may reject this view as overstated, it underscores the fact that program evaluation is inextricably intertwined with public policy formulation and all of the political forces involved in that process. Evaluators who fail to understand this basic fact expend unacceptably large amounts of human and financial resources conducting evaluations that are largely irrelevant, however impeccably they are designed and conducted.

5.4 Program Evaluators are too Narrow in their Choice of Evaluation Approaches and Techniques

It may be that innocence about the political nature of the evaluation enterprise contributes to the naive hope that evaluation will one day grow into a scientific discipline. That day, if attainable, would seem far off. Education itself is not a discipline but rather a social process field which draws its content from several disciplines. It seems unlikely that educational program evaluation, which also borrows its methods and techniques from many disciplines will gain the coherence that would result in it becoming a discipline in its own right. Perhaps that is just as well, for much of the richness and potential of educational program evaluation lies in the depth and breadth of the strategies and tools it can employ and in the possibility of selectively combining them into stronger approaches than when used singly (Worthen 1981). Yet eclectic use of the evaluator's tools is a lamentably infrequent occurrence in program evaluations. Disciple-prone evaluators tend to cluster around their respective evaluation banners like vassals in a form of provincial bondage. For program evaluation to reach its potential, such intellectual bondage must give way to more mature and sophisticated approaches that draw appropriately on the richness and diversity of the many approaches, models, and techniques that characterize program evaluation today.

Bibliography

Anderson S B, Ball S 1978 *The Profession and Practice of Program Evaluation.* Jossey-Bass, San Francisco, California

Cook T D, Reichardt C T 1979 *Qualitative and Quantitative Methods in Evaluation Research.* Sage, Beverly Hills, California

Cronbach L J, Ambron S, Dornbusch S, Hess R, Hornik R, Phillips D, Walker D, Weiner S 1980 *Toward Reform of Program Evaluation: Aims, Methods and Institutional Arrangements.* Jossey-Bass, San Francisco, California

Eisner E W 1985 *The Art of Educational Evaluation: A personal view.* Falmer, Brighton

Guba E G, Lincoln Y S 1981 *Effective Evaluation: Improving the Usefulness of Evaluation Results through Responsive and Naturalistic Approaches.* Jossey-Bass, San Francisco, California

House E R 1980 *Evaluating with Validity.* Sage, Beverly Hills, California

Joint Committee on Standards for Educational Evaluation 1981 *Standards for Evaluations of Educational Programs, Projects, and Materials.* McGraw-Hill, New York

MacDonald B 1976 Evaluation and the control of education. In: Tawney D (ed.) 1976 *Curriculum Evaluation Today: Trends and Implications.* Macmillan, London, pp. 125–36

Madey D L 1982 Some benefits of integrating qualitative and quantitative methods in program evaluation, with illustrations. *Educ. Eval. Policy Anal.* 4(2): 223–36

Parlett M, Hamilton D 1976 Evaluation as illumination. In: Tawney D (ed.) 1976 *Curriculum Evaluation Today: Trends and Implications.* Macmillan, London, pp. 84–101

Rippey R (ed.) 1973 *Transactional Evaluation.* McCutchan, Berkeley, California

Smith N L 1981 Developing evaluation methods. In: Smith N L (ed.) 1981 *Metaphors for Evaluation: Sources for New Methods.* Sage, Beverly Hills, California

Stake R E 1980 Program Evaluation, particularly Responsive Evaluation. In: Dockrell W B, Hamilton D (eds.) 1980 *Rethinking Educational Research.* Hodder and Stoughton, London, pp. 72–87

Stufflebeam D L et al. 1971 *Educational Evaluation and Decision Making.* Peacock, Itasca, Illinois

Worthen B R 1981 Journal entries of an eclectic evaluator. In: Brandt R S, Modrak N (eds.) 1981 *Applied Strategies for Curriculum Evaluation.* Association for Supervision and

Curriculum Development, Alexandria, Virginia
Worthen B R, Sanders J R 1973 *Educational Evaluation: Theory and Practice.* Jones, Worthington, Ohio

Worthen B R, Sanders J R 1987 *Educational Evaluation: Alternative Approaches and Practical Guidelines.* Longman, New York

Evaluation of Learning Resources

M. R. Eraut

For this article, a learning resource will be defined as an identifiable physical object which carries information that can be used to promote learning. This includes printed, audio, and pictorial materials, and will also be taken to include computer programs and television programmes, since these can be stored and evaluated as distinct entities. It excludes physical objects such as scientific apparatus, communication equipment like a telephone, human resources, and resource-rich locations such as a museum or learning centre.

Learning resources range in significance from a complete curriculum package, through sets of booklets, to a single audiotape, film, slide, or worksheet. Hence, it is important to stress that the evaluation effort should be commensurate with the significance of the learning resource. If the resource is to be used for a long time or with a large number of students, then more than a token evaluation is called for. But if it is intended for only a few students for part of a lesson, the application of sophisticated evaluation techniques is clearly inappropriate. Since this article seeks to avoid the obvious and trivial, it will be mainly concerned with resources of sufficient significance to merit giving considerable attention to their evaluation. However, some of the methods discussed may also be useful for short quick evaluations of materials of lesser consequence.

Four main approaches to the evaluation of learning resources are reported in the literature.

(a) Evaluation by a panel or committee, whose inspection or viewing of the resource is followed by a discussion of its merits and weaknesses.

(b) Canvassing the opinions of users or potential users with a simple questionnaire, but without advice on techniques of resource evaluation. A simple popularity contest, with the proviso that certain types of criticism, for example, bias, will be seen as particularly important.

(c) Intrinsic evaluation, in which the learning resource is subjected to prolonged study in depth by reviewers and their reports are used as a basis for further discussion.

(d) Field testing in which the resource is tried out in one or more classrooms to assess its impact and its effects.

These four approaches may be combined in several ways. For example, in Japan, the textbook approval procedure involves intrinsic evaluations by specially appointed reviewers being passed on to a committee for discussion and recommendation; and in some districts of the United States, teacher members of a selection committee may briefly field test resources in their own classrooms. This article is mainly concerned with intrinsic evaluation and field testing, because these approaches are considered essential for improving the quality of learning resource evaluation.

First, however, let us distinguish the three main purposes which evaluation of learning resources may serve: (a) selection or purchase; (b) utilization planning; and (c) improvement, modification, or redesign. When a resource has been developed by a teacher for use in his or her own classroom, these purposes will overlap. Otherwise they are likely to be distinct. For each purpose is normally associated with a different context and with a different group of evaluators.

1. Evaluation for Selection or Purchase

Purchasing decisions for textbooks are made at national, provincial, district, or even school level. Such decisions may involve free choice by individual schools (as in the United Kingdom); central prescription at national (Kenya) or provincial level (Pakistan); or restricted choice from a list approved by a higher level of government (national in Japan, provincial in Canada and the Federal Republic of Germany). Above school level, decisions about approval or adoption are usually made by a system of committees with clearly specified procedures, and this is often extended to include supplementary materials as well. Supplementary materials, however, are likely to be approved rather than specified; and their purchase will be severely limited by cost in all but the wealthiest countries.

Large numbers of purchasing decisions are also made by the staff of libraries and resource centres. Their job is to develop and maintain collections of learning resources from which teachers or students may borrow. They are spared the burden of having to make a single absolute choice, but instead have to constantly consider the range and diversity of their collection as a whole and the needs of many potential users. New purchases have to take into account the resources that have already been assembled.

Finally, there is an important distinction between resources that are used in a single school or classroom, such as books and simple audiovisual materials, and resources that are too expensive to be allocated to a single site. Purchasing, production, and distribution systems for films, television, or computer-based learning are usually made by specialized agencies at the district or regional level. But it may still be left for the school to decide what use it makes of them. This pattern may well extend to other types of resource if electronic modes of distribution become more widely adopted.

The process of selection for purchase is usefully divided into four stages, though only the more elaborate evaluations will use all four.

Firstly, there is a descriptive analysis of the resource, which can vary in intensity from a cursory inspection by a potential user to a thorough intrinsic evaluation. Its purpose is (a) to discuss the main features of the learning resource, its structure, and its principal qualities; (b) to disclose the educational and pedagogic assumptions which explicitly or implicitly underpin its design; (c) to note any subsidiary features of special significance, for example, obscurities, inaccuracies, minor bias, creative treatment of a topic, and so on.

Secondly, there is a field testing of the resource in classrooms to ascertain its impact on pupils in various contexts and conditions.

Thirdly, there is evaluation by assembling arguments for and against choosing the resource. Each argument will need to be constructed by combining evidence from the descriptive analysis and the field testing with evaluative criteria derived from user opinion, consultation with interested parties, policy documents, or the education literature. Some of these arguments will be unproblematic, in the sense that all decision makers agree that a certain passage is inaccurate or that a certain characteristic is an asset. Other arguments will be contested because the same feature may be regarded positively by some people and negatively by others, according to their views about the curriculum and pedagogy of the area concerned. Eraut (1982) argues strongly that this kind of divergency should be mapped rather than hidden or removed.

Finally, decision making, the final stage, involves deliberation of the evidence, discussion, and eventually choice. Various approaches to purchasing and selection decisions are discussed in the methodology section below.

While there is now a growing body of prescriptive literature suggesting how selection and purchasing decisions ought to be made, there is very little research describing how such decisions are made. When systematic appraisal is used, it is usually only the procedures which are reported, not which factors were critical in determining the decision or which people's views prevailed. However, such systematic appraisal is itself still relatively rare. More often, appraisal amounts to little more than a cursory inspection; and it is perhaps unsurprising that so little attempt has been made to develop the necessary expertise.

2. Evaluation for Utilization Planning

The utilization of a learning resource can be planned at two levels, that of course design and that of lesson planning. When there is a detailed and elaborate teachers' manual, it could be argued that lesson planning is unnecessary: only preparation is needed. But such slavish adherence to a manual is unusual; and, though such manuals may appear to provide a complete specification of teaching, this is often illusory because utilization problems may not surface until the teacher is in front of the class. Indeed, many authors have argued that it is impossible to specify teaching in that degree of detail (Harris 1982).

Frequently, complete specification of teaching is not even attempted. The course design team recommends learning resources or sections of such resources for particular topics, but does not attempt to discuss how they might be used. Or there may be a general syllabus and a prescribed textbook without any course design. The teachers are left to plan the detailed lesson-by-lesson use of learning resources on their own; and for this purpose they need either to evaluate the resource themselves or to read an existing evaluation that conveys the right kind of information.

The approach to utilization planning can vary considerably, according to differences in the assumptions of teacher and designer and the degree to which each is prepared to accommodate the other. Figure 1 shows six possible outcomes, recognizing that discussions of curriculum implementation which assume a single teaching style or a single type of "correct" implementation can oversimplify. Even a fairly inflexible teacher will have more than one lesson-type in the repertoire though none may be very suitable for some kinds of resource. Similarly, resource designers may suggest several patterns of use, though some may deviate so far from common practice that even flexible teachers reject them as impractical. In theory, there is an important distinction between utilization planning which attempts to fit resources to existing practices, often without studying them sufficiently to even become aware of other possibilities; and utilization planning which attempts to maximize the potential of the resource by considering several patterns of use and choosing that which seems to offer the most benefit to pupils. In practice, research on

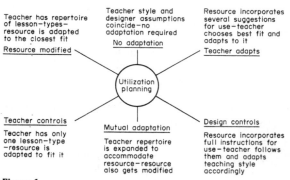

Figure 1

Outcomes of utilization planning

educational innovation suggests that the former is common and the latter unusual. Only when long-term classroom-based inservice education is provided is there a reasonable chance of teachers expanding their repertoire to include novel patterns of teaching; and then it is mutual adaptation rather than simple teacher adaptation which has the best chance of long-term survival.

In practice, evaluation by teachers is likely to merge with utilization planning, with early evaluation being influenced, possibly even terminated, by early utilization ideas and later evaluation being largely determined by the experience of use. Nevertheless it is useful to consider a three-stage model of evaluation for utilization planning even though the stages will normally overlap.

(a) Inspection and analysis of the resource.

(b) Generation of ideas for different patterns of use and possible modifications.

(c) Selection of the most appropriate idea, followed by detailed lesson planning.

A constructive use of the model would be to train teachers to approach learning resource evaluation in this kind of way, and to encourage the circulation among teachers of resource evaluation documents which incorporate the first two stages.

On the whole, good utilization of learning resources is not promoted by evaluations that either ignore the diversity of usage which most resources receive or regard such diversity only in terms of a mismatch between designer aspirations and teacher practice. However, empirical evaluations which gather data about the impact of a learning resource in a manner that takes into account variations in patterns and contexts of use, are an important contribution to the continuing professional development of teachers and the improvement of their resource utilization practice.

3. Evaluation for Improvement

Evaluation for improvement, modification, or redesign is perhaps the most advanced form of learning resource evaluation. Two traditions have contributed to our knowledge. "Developmental testing" was the term originally used by designers of programmed learning sequences, whose commitment to improving learning resources by cycles of testing and revision evolved during the 1960s. "Formative evaluation" was the term introduced by Scriven (1967) to describe the role of course improvement in curriculum evaluation.

Markle (1967), writing within the instructional technology tradition, describes three stages in the empirical testing of a learning resource: (a) developmental testing, during which early drafts or even short excerpts are tried out with several groups of students and immediate revisions are made; (b) validation testing, in which a later draft is tested with larger numbers of students under the designer's general supervisions; and (c) utilization testing, when designer supervision is abandoned,

variation in pattern of use is studied, and longer-term evidence of impact is collected.

Sanders and Cunningham (1974), writing within the curriculum evaluation tradition, identify and define four types of formative evaluation activity as follows:

(a) *Predevelopmental activities*—formative evaluation work that occurs before formal product development has started. Formative evaluation tasks related to the evaluation of needs, tasks, or other planning actitivies fall into this category.

(b) *Evaluation of objectives activities*—formative evaluation work directed at judging objectives in product development. The emphasis of work in this category is on the provision of reliable information about the worth of goal statements produced by the product developer.

(c) *Formative interim evaluation activities*—formative work dealing with the appraisal of early product development efforts.

(d) *Formative product evaluation activities*—formative evaluation work that focuses on the appraisal of a finished draft of the proposed product.

To this they added three main sources of information to obtain a two-dimensional matrix with 12 cells. These sources are:

(a) *Internal Information*—information that could be generated by inspecting the entity itself. Included in this category is descriptive information about and critical appraisals of the entity.

(b) *External Information*—information concerning the effects of an entity on the behaviours of relevant groups. Student achievement after using a product or parental attitudes toward the objectives of a product are examples of information placed in this category.

(c) *Contextual Information*—information concerning the conditions under which an entity is expected to function. Classroom environment, pupil characteristics, and time of year are three examples of information that fall into this category.

4. Intrinsic Evaluation Methodology

Techniques for intrinsic evaluation comprise both quantitative methods of content analysis and qualitative methods akin to those used in literary criticism and philosophy. This section begins with a review of techniques, both quantitative and qualitative, for the descriptive analysis of learning resources to reveal their content, structures, values, and communication style. It then focuses on how this and other evidence can be interpreted and presented during evaluation and decision-making. Its central assumption is that using checklists to collect reviewer opinions on either resource characteristics or resource quality is no substitute for a proper analysis. The methods by which reviewers arrive at their opinions cannot remain undiscussed and unexamined if our knowledge of learning resources and their potential is to progress. Such checklists can serve a useful reminder role to reviewers but cannot substitute for evidence and argument. Moreover, they are usually too vague for questions to have a common meaning for all reviewers, and there is a tendency for them to build in assumptions from theories that are by no means universally accepted.

Quantitative techniques of content analysis have been most fully developed in mass communications research. Although described below, in terms of written materials they are equally applicable, with appropriate modifications, to other media. Most quantitative techniques are based on (a) devising some system for classifying content along one or more dimensions; (b) defining the unit of analysis and a set of categorizing rules; and (c) applying the rules to each dimension in turn to obtain a series of profiles, which depict the distribution of communication units among the chosen sets of categories. The unit of analysis may be a chapter, a topic, a page, an assignable unit or a time interval such as a lesson or a given number of minutes. Each set of categories needs to have a coherent theoretical base for its characterization. For example, thematic categories indicate the selection and focus of thematic content. Categories based on classifications of objectives can indicate levels of thinking demanded of pupils, and other category systems can be devised to show the balance of pupil activities, the difficulty of the language, or the abstraction of the content. While some thematic categories may be based on existing theories, others may be specifically developed to suit the particular documents being analyzed. The most fully developed are probably those relating to the detection of bias against minority groups.

Analyzing the structuring and sequencing of content requires a rather different approach. The purpose is to show the relationships between different elements of content. Since this is rarely possible in linear form, some kind of diagrammatic presentation is usually needed. The term "content map" is often used, and several may be required in any one evaluation. For each map decisions have to be made about scale (book, chapter, or topic), the level of detail to be included, and the kinds of features which will be depicted. Chapter maps, for example, might include teaching points or pupils' assignments, while book maps may present more of a conceptual overview. In the most complex maps, different symbols may be used to depict different types of connection, for example, rule and example or concept and principle.

Other qualitative techniques found in most forms of critical writing include critical comment on selected extracts, the detailed discussion of particular examples, and the citation of examples to illustrate a general descriptive account. Where the purpose is to inform the reader about a resource's communication approach or language style, then it is useful to present extracts and comment on their salient features. Where one's concern is with the treatment of content, logical development, or value transmission, then it may be best to select a series of examples and discuss them in detail. A more general review of the design of pupil activities, bias, inaccuracies, or modernity may refer to several illustrative examples as evidence for the assertions being made.

All these qualitative techniques involve some form of sampling. Extracts and examples have to be chosen. Such sampling may be random, for example, every tenth unit theoretical unit e.g. one unit from each of a chosen set of categories. In either case it needs to be justified if the analysis is to be perceived as unbiased. The reader needs to be convinced that atypical examples have not been chosen, or where citations are atypical, as when pointing out inaccuracies or datedness, this should be clearly stated. The overall purpose of descriptive analysis is that both analysts and readers should be convinced that they have a reasoned and fairly objective understanding of the resource and the assumptions built into it, whether or not these assumptions are stated or intended by the authors. Werner (1980) addresses the important issue of validity and suggests three basic validation principles for curriculum criticism: an explicit methodological framework and purpose; public dialogue about the appropriateness of the framework and the validity of the critic's interpretations within it; and evidence that it has contributed to a better understanding of the curriculum. All three principles might usefully be applied to intrinsic evaluation in general.

Two distinctive approaches to the use of intrinsic analysis in evaluation and decision-making have been developed by the Educational Products Information Exchange in New York (EPIE 1974) and an Anglo–German research team based at the University of Sussex (Eraut et al. 1975). Both have been used in a number of countries, and have published sample analyses to illustrate their approaches. The Sussex report also reviews work undertaken in the Federal Republic of Germany, Sweden, and North America.

Central to the EPIE approach is the attempt to find the best fit between materials—as revealed by an instructional design analysis—and context—as revealed either by a needs analysis or by an analysis of an existing curriculum for which the materials are being considered. The various design features are grouped under four main headings: goals and objectives, scope and sequence of content, teaching–learning methods, and approaches to student evaluation. Then a direct comparison is made under each of these headings between alternative sets of materials and some preexisting programme or set of criteria. Additional information about teacher and student characteristics and community concerns may also be brought into the decision-making arena.

The Sussex scheme also begins by examining the curriculum strategy underpinning the design of the resource, and uses four similar constructs to describe it. Objectives and outcomes, subject matter, teaching–

learning and communication methods, and assessment patterns. But then it proceeds to explore different ways of using the resource and possible modifications. By expecting diversity rather than a single uniform pattern of use, it seeks to ascertain the potential of the resource under different implementation conditions and in different user contexts. External congruence is then handled through considering implications for implementation in different schools, with special attention to pupil, teacher, school, and community characteristics.

The approach to evaluation which follows is deliberately divergent and pluralistic. Before the decision-making stage is reached, it is argued that the strengths and weaknesses of the materials should be appraised from a range of different value positions. Otherwise important educational issues will be ignored and less powerful groups will feel that the process was biased against them from the start. Focusing is achieved by devoting attention in turn to aims, curriculum strategy, and quality of materials; and each is considered in terms of different patterns of use and implementation factors.

The other main difference between the EPIE and Sussex approaches is that EPIE either provides or recommends the development of checklists and rating scales for most sections of the analysis, while Sussex prefers a more open approach. The reasons are twofold. The EPIE analyses are much shorter than those produced by Sussex, and they appear to envisage selection from a large number of alternatives. They also expect learning resources to be based on coherent theoretical positions, which can easily be detected and discussed. Sussex sees theory more in terms of "ideal types" which influence but do not determine many crucial aspects of the design strategy. Materials evolve out of curriculum traditions and can usefully be criticized from several theoretical viewpoints without being completely identified with any. Alternative options are generated from considerations of practice in other schools or districts; and evaluation criteria can be derived from (a) critical differences between these options, (b) suggestions in the guide to the scheme, (c) the views of users, evaluators, and other interested parties, and (d) the education literature, especially that specific to the subject and age-group concerned. Trying to tidy up the decision-making process too much is dangerously reductionist, and useful analyses have to be fairly long.

5. Field-testing Methodology

Large-scale field testing of learning resources makes use of standard research techniques such as observations, interviews, and questionnaires, and, in general, models derived from curriculum evaluation are applicable. Small-scale field testing presents rather different problems, and these are discussed below. Two types of small-scale field testing are particularly important—student tryout in the early stages of resource development, and quick evaluations of small resources like films and audiotapes.

Small-scale developmental testing involves the designer or an associate trying out a prototype version of a learning resource with a relatively small number of students, either individually or in small groups. The purpose is to get quick feedback of sufficient quality (a) to improve the designer's understanding of student problems and perspectives, and (b) to suggest possible modifications. The students should be carefully chosen but are unlikely to be representative of the intended user population which will usually be more varied. With resources of short duration, it is sometimes possible for the designer to make small modifications on the spot or to give an alternative explanation which can subsequently be incorporated into a revised version of the resource. With larger resources it may still be possible for the designer to try out sections and modify or develop ideas at an early stage, before too much time and effort is committed to a particular approach.

Piloting of complex resources is discussed in considerable detail by Nathenson and Henderson (1980), with special attention to Open University courses. Their discussion of the use of in-text feedback questions for concurrent data collection, in addition to the usual posttests and interviews, is particularly helpful. They suggest collecting six types of tryout data and provide a checklist of questions under each of these headings: student performance, clarity of materials, level of materials, student actions (choice of routes, take-up of options, reaction to self-assessment, etc.), student attitudes, and student use of time.

Another agency using a qualitative, small-scale, interactive approach to field testing is the Media Center for Children in New York (Gaffney 1981). In this case the resource is in its published form, so the purpose is not to guide revision but to guide selection and utilization. There is a strong emphasis on children's rather than adult's responses to media; and priority is accorded to the affective rather than the cognitive. Their scheme for film evaluation comprises four sections. Section 1 notes children's behaviour during screening. Section 2 records children's responses in discussion to questions about the film, how it affected them, what they thought it was about, things they might change in it, and so on. Section 3 asks the teacher/evaluator to summarize the experience and interpret the children's response, and to answer questions about the film's appropriateness for various groups of children and different modes of utilization. Section 4 summarizes the overall impact of the film and the evaluation process. This approach could be adapted to other kinds of learning resource which generate emotional involvement or arouse children's curiosity, and makes an interesting contrast to the more usual custom whereby the teacher, evaluator, or designer asks all the questions.

This section has deliberately focused on small-scale qualitative approaches to complement the techniques discussed in much greater length elsewhere. It is also useful to be reminded that accounts of children's interaction with learning resources convey information that cannot be adequately summarized by other methods. Such information is vital for resource improvement, and probably equally important for utilization planning.

Bibliography

Educational Products Information Exchange (EPIE) 1974 *Selecting and Evaluating Beginning Reading Materials.* EPIE Report Nos. 62–63, New York

Eraut M 1982 Handling value issues. In: House E R, Mathison S, Pearsol J A, Preskill H (eds.) 1982 *Evaluation Studies Review Annual,* Vol. 7. Sage, Beverly Hills, California

Eraut M, Goad L, Smith G 1975 *The Analysis of Curriculum Materials.* Educational Area Occasional Paper 2. University of Sussex, Brighton

Gaffney M 1981 What's going on? Evaluating children's media. In: Brown J W, Brown S N (eds.) 1981 *Educational Media Yearbook 1981.* Libraries Unlimited, Littleton, Colorado

Harris I B 1982 Communication for guiding teachers: The impact of different conceptions of teaching and educational practice. Paper presented at the Annual American Educational Research Association Meeting, AERA, Washington, DC. ERIC Document No. ED 217 040

Markle S M 1967 Empirical testing of programs. In: Lange P C (ed.) 1967 *Programmed Instruction.* 66th National Society for the Study of Education Yearbook, Part 2. University of Chicago Press, Chicago, Illinois

Nathensen M B, Henderson E S 1980 *Using Student Feedback to Improve Learning Materials.* Croom Helm, London

Sanders J R, Cunningham D J 1974 Formative evaluation: Selecting techniques and procedures. In: Borich G D (ed.) 1974 *Evaluating Educational Programs and Products.* Educational Technology, Englewood Cliffs, New Jersey

Scriven M 1967 The methodology of evaluation? In: Tyler R W, Gagné R M, Scriven M (eds.) 1967 *Perspectives of Curriculum Evaluation.* American Educational Research Association, Curriculum Evaluation Monographs 1. Rand McNally, Chicago, Illinois

Werner W 1980 Editorial criticism in curricular analysis. *Curric. Inq.* 10: 143–54

Criterion-referenced Measurement

R. K. Hambleton

Criterion-referenced tests are constructed to permit the interpretation of examinee test performance in relation to a set of well-defined competencies (Popham 1978). In relation to the competencies, there are three common uses for criterion-referenced test scores: (a) to describe examinee performance, (b) to assign examinees to mastery states (e.g., "masters" and "nonmasters"), and (c) to describe the performance of specified groups of examinees in program evaluation studies. Criterion-referenced tests are presently receiving extensive use in schools, industry, and the military in the United States because they provide information which is valued by test users and different from the information provided by norm-referenced tests. This article will introduce basic criterion-referenced testing concepts, compare these tests to norm-referenced tests, consider some aspects of criterion-referenced test development, and describe several promising applications.

1. Basic Concepts

One of the first articles on the topic of criterion-referenced testing appeared in the *American Psychologist* (Glaser 1963). Over 700 papers on the topic have been published since then, and the scope and direction of educational testing has been changed dramatically. Glaser was interested in assessment methods that would provide necessary information for making a number of individual and programmatic decisions arising in connection with specific objectives or competencies. Norm-referenced tests were seen as limited in terms of providing the desired kinds of information.

At least 57 definitions of criterion-referenced measurement have been offered in the literature. Popham's definition which was introduced earlier in this article is probably the one which is most widely used. Several points about the definition deserve comment. First, terms such as objectives, competencies, and skills are used interchangeably in the field. Second, the competencies measured by a criterion-referenced test must be well-defined. Well-defined competencies make the process of item writing easier and more valid, and improve the quality of test score interpretations. The quality of score interpretations is improved because of the clarity of the content or behavior domains to which test scores are referenced. There is no limit on the breadth and complexity of a domain of content or behaviors defining a competency. The intended purpose of a test will influence the appropriate breadth and complexity of domains. Diagnostic tests are typically organized around narrowly defined competencies. End-of-year assessments will normally be carried out with more broadly defined competencies. Third, when more than one competency is measured in a test it is common to report examinee performance on each competency. Fourth, Popham's criterion-referenced test definition does not include a reference to a cutoff score or standard. It is common to set a minimum standard of performance for each competency measured in a criterion-referenced test and interpret examinee performance in relation to it. But, the use of test scores for describing examinee performance is common (e.g., the best estimate of student A's performance in relation to the domain of content defined by the competency is 70 percent) and standards are not needed for this type of score use. That a standard (or standards) may not be needed with a criterion-referenced test will come as a surprise to persons who have assumed (mistakenly) that the word "criterion" in "criterion-referenced test" refers to a "standard" or "cutoff score." In fact, the word "criterion" was used by Glaser (1963) and Popham and Husek (1969) to refer to a domain of content or behavior to which test scores are referenced.

Three additional points about criterion-referenced tests deserve mention: (a) the number of competencies measured by a criterion-referenced test will (in general) vary from one test to the next, (b) the number of test items measuring each competency and the value of the minimum standard will (in general) vary from one competency to the next, and (c) a common method for making mastery–nonmastery decisions involves the comparison of examinee percent (or proportion-correct) scores on competencies to the corresponding minimum standards. With respect to (c), when an examinee's percent score is equal to or greater than the standard, the examinee is assumed to be a "master" (M), otherwise the examinee is assumed to be a "nonmaster" (NM). There are however more complex decision-making models (for a review, see van der Linden 1980).

It is common to see terms like criterion-referenced tests, domain-referenced tests, and objectives-referenced tests in the psychometric literature. Popham's definition for a criterion-referenced test is similar to one Millman and others proposed for a domain-referenced test. There are no essential differences between the two if Popham's definition for a criterion-referenced test is adopted. The term "domain-referenced test" is a descriptive one and therefore it is less likely to be misunderstood than the term "criterion-referenced test." One reason for continuing to use the term, "criterion-referenced test," even though it is less descriptive and its definition has become muddled in the psychometric literature, is that there is considerable public support in the United States for "criterion-referenced tests." It would seem to be a waste of valuable time to mount a campaign for a new term.

Objectives-referenced tests consist of items that are matched to objectives. The principal difference between criterion-referenced tests and objectives-referenced tests is that in a criterion-referenced test, items are organized into clusters with each cluster serving (usually) as a representative set of items from a clearly defined content domain measuring an objective, while with an objectives-referenced test, no clear domain of content is specified for an objective, and items are not considered to be representative of any content domain. Therefore, interpretations of examinee performance on objectives-referenced tests should be limited to the particular items on the test.

2. Norm-referenced and Criterion-referenced Tests

Proponents of norm-referenced and criterion-referenced tests in the United States waged a battle in the 1970s for supremacy of the achievement testing world. A third group argued that there was only one kind of achievement test from which both criterion-referenced and norm-referenced score interpretations could be made when needed. It is now clear that there was no winner

although in the 10-year period the uses of criterion-referenced tests did increase substantially in the United States. Also, there was a reduction in the amount of norm-referenced testing taking place. There was no winner because it is clear that it is meaningful to distinguish between two kinds of achievement tests and both kinds of tests have important roles to play in providing information for test users. Norm-referenced achievement tests are needed to provide reliable and valid normative scores for comparing examinees. Criterion-referenced achievement tests are needed to facilitate the interpretation of examinee performance in relation to well-defined competencies.

Although the differences between norm-referenced tests and criterion-referenced tests are substantial, the two kinds of tests share many features. In fact, it would be a rare individual who could distinguish between them from looking at the test booklets alone. They use the same item formats; test directions are similar; and both kinds of tests can be standardized.

There are a number of important differences, however, between them. The first difference is test purpose. A norm-referenced test is constructed specifically to facilitate comparisons among examinees in the content area measured by the test. It is common to use age-, percentile-, and standard-score norms to accomplish the test's purpose. Since test items are (or can be) referenced to competencies, criterion-referenced score interpretations (or, more correctly, objectives-referenced score interpretations) are possible but are typically limited in value because of the (usually) small number of test items measuring any competency in the test. Criterion-referenced tests, on the other hand, are constructed to assess examinee performance in relation to a set of competencies. Scores may be used (a) to describe examinee performance, (b) to make mastery–nonmastery decisions, and (c) to evaluate program effectiveness. Scores can be used to compare examinees but comparisons may have relatively low reliability if score distributions are homogeneous.

The second difference is in the area of content specificity. It is common for designers of both test types to prepare test blueprints or tables of specifications. It is even possible that norm-referenced test designers will prepare behavioral objectives. But, criterion-referenced test designers must (typically) prepare considerably more detailed content specifications than provided by behavioral objectives to ensure that criterion-referenced test scores can be interpreted in the intended way. This point will be considered further in the next section. Thus, with respect to content specifications, the difference between the two types is in the degree to which test content must be specified.

The third difference is in the area of test development. With norm-referenced tests, item statistics (difficulty and discrimination indices) serve an important role in item selection. In general, items of moderate difficulty (p-values in the range 0.30 to 0.70) and high discriminating power (point biserial correlations over 0.30) are most likely to be selected for a test because they contribute substantially to test score variance. Test reliability and validity will, generally, be higher when test score variance is increased. In contrast, criterion-referenced test items are only deleted from the pools of test items measuring competencies when it is determined that they violate the content specifications or standard principles of item writing, or if the available item statistics reveal serious noncorrectable flaws. Item statistics can be used to construct parallel forms of a criterion-referenced test or to produce a test to discriminate optimally between masters and nonmasters in the region of a minimum standard of performance on the test score scale.

The fourth and final major area of difference between criterion-referenced tests and norm-referenced tests is test score generalizability. Seldom is there interest in making generalizations from norm-referenced achievement test scores. The basis for score interpretations is the performance of some reference group. In contrast, score generalizability is usually of interest with criterion-referenced tests. Seldom is there interest in the performance of examinees on specific sets of test items. When clearly specified competency statements are available and assuming test items are representative of the content domains from which they are drawn, examinee test performance can be generalized to performance in the larger domains of content defining the competencies. It is this type of interpretation which is (usually) of interest to criterion-referenced test users.

3. Content Specifications

Behavioral objectives had a highly significant impact on instruction and testing in the 1960s and 1970s. But, while behavioral objectives are relatively easy to write and have contributed substantially to the specification of curricula, they do not usually lead to clearly defined content descriptions defining competencies. Popham (1974) described tests built from behavioral objectives as "cloud-referenced tests." Several suggestions have been made for addressing the deficiency in behavioral objectives and thereby making it possible to construct valid criterion-referenced tests. These suggestions include the use of item transformations, item forms, algorithms, and structural facet theory. Possibly the most versatile and practical of the suggestions was introduced by Popham (1978) and is called domain specifications, item specifications, or expanded objectives. Domain specifications serve four purposes: (a) they provide item writers with content and technical guidelines for preparing test items, (b) they provide content and measurement specialists with a clear description of the content and/or behaviors which are to be covered by each competency so that they can assess whether items are valid measures of the intended competencies, (c) they aid in interpreting examinee competency performance, and (d) they provide users with clear specifications of the breadth and scope of competencies. Some educational measurement specialists have even gone so far as to suggest that the emphasis on content specification has been the most important contribution of criterion-referenced testing to measurement practice (Berk 1980).

Using as a basis the work of Popham (1978), Hambleton (1982) suggested that a domain specification might be divided into four parts:

(a) Description—a short, concise statement of the content and/or behaviors covered by the competency.

(b) Sample directions and test item—an example of the test directions and a model test item to measure the competency.

(c) Content limits—a detailed description of both the content and/or behaviors measured by the competency, as well as the structure and content of the item pool. (This section should be so clear that items may be divided by reviewers into those items that meet the specifications and those items that do not.) Sometimes clarity is enhanced by also specify-

Table 1
Steps for constructing criterion-referenced tests

Steps	Comments

1. Preliminary considerations
   (a) Specify test purposes.
   (b) Specify groups to be measured and (any) special testing requirements (due to examinee age, race, sex, socioeconomic status, handicaps, etc.).
   (c) Determine the time and money available to produce the test.
   (d) Identify qualified staff.
   (e) Specify an initial estimate of test length.
	This step is essential to ensure that a test development project is well-organized and important factors which might have an impact on test quality are identified early.

2. Review of competency statements
   (a) Review the descriptions of the competencies to determine their acceptability.
   (b) Make necessary competency statement revisions to improve their clarity.
	Domain specifications are invaluable to item writers when they are well-done. Considerable time and money can be saved later in revising test items if item writers are clear on what it is that is expected of them.

Table 1 *Continued*

Steps	Comments

3. Item writing
  (a) Draft a sufficient number of items for pilot testing.
  (b) Carry out item editing.
	Some training of item writers in the importance and use of domain specifications, and in the principles of item writing is often desirable.

4. Assessment of content validity
  (a) Identify a sufficient pool of judges and measurement specialists.
  (b) Review the test items to determine their match to the competencies, their representativeness, and their freedom from bias and stereotyping.
  (c) Review the test items to determine their technical adequacy.
	This step is essential. Items are evaluated by reviewers to assess their match to the competencies, their technical quality, and their freedom from bias and stereotyping.

5. Revisions to test items
  (a) Based upon data from 4(b) and 4(c), revise test items (when possible) or delete them.
  (b) Write additional test items (if needed) and repeat step 4.
	Any necessary revisions to test items should be made at this step and when additional test items are needed, they should be written, and step 4 carried out again.

6. Field test administration
  (a) Organize the test items into forms for pilot testing.
  (b) Administer the test forms to appropriately chosen groups of examinees.
  (c) Conduct item analyses, and item validity and item bias studies.
	The test items are organized into booklets and administered to appropriate numbers of examinees. That number should reflect the importance of the test under construction. Appropriate revisions to test items can be made here. Item statistics are used to identify items which may be in need of revision: (a) items which may be substantially easier or harder than other items measuring the same competencies, (b) items with negative or low positive discriminating power, and (c) items with distractors which were selected by small percentages of examinees.

7. Revisions to test items (a) Revise test items when necessary or delete them using the results from 6(c).	Whenever possible, malfunctioning test items should be revised and added to the pools of acceptable test items. When revisions to test items are substantial they should be returned to step 4.

8. Test assembly
  (a) Determine the test length, and the number of forms needed and the number of items per objective.
  (b) Select test items from the available pool of valid test items.
  (c) Prepare test directions, practice questions, test booklet layout, scoring keys, answer sheets, etc.
	Test booklets are compiled at this step. When parallel forms are required, and especially if the tests are short, item statistics should be used to ensure matched forms are produced.

9. Selection of a standard (a) Initiate a process to determine the standard to separate "masters" and "nonmasters."	A standard-setting procedure must be selected and implemented. Care should be taken to document the selection process.

10. Pilot test administration
  (a) Design the administration to collect score reliability and validity information.
  (b) Administer the test form(s) to appropriately chosen groups of examinees.
  (c) Evaluate the test administration procedures, test items, and score reliability and validity.
  (d) Make final revisions based on data from 10(c).
	At this step, test directions can be evaluated, scoring keys can be checked, and reliability and validity of scores and decisions can be assessed.

11. Preparation of manuals
  (a) Prepare a test administrator's manual.
  (b) Prepare a technical manual.
	For important tests, a test administration manual and a technical manual should be prepared.

12. Additional technical data collection (a) Conduct reliability and validity investigations.	No matter how carefully a test is constructed or evaluated, reliability and validity studies should be carried out on an ongoing basis.

Description

The student will identify the tones or emotions expressed in paragraphs.

Sample directions and test item

Directions: Read the paragraph below. Then answer the question and circle the letter beside your answer.

Jimmy had been playing and swimming at the beach all day. Now it was time to go home. Jimmy sat down in the back seat of his father's car. He could hardly keep his eyes open.

How did Jimmy feel?

A. Afraid   B. Friendly   C. Tired   D. Kind

Content limits

1. Paragraphs will describe situations which are familiar to grade 3 students.
2. Paragraphs should contain between three and six sentences. Readability levels should be at the third grade (using the Dale-Chall formula).
3. Tones or emotions expressed in the passages should be selected from the list below:

sad	mad	angry	kind
tired	scared	friendly	excited
happy	lucky	smart	proud

Response limits

1. Answer choices should be one word in length.
2. Four answer choices should be used with each test item.
3. Incorrect answer choices may be selected from the list above.
4. Incorrect answer choices should be tones or emotions which are familiar to students in grade 3 and which are commonly confused with the correct answer.

Figure 1

A typical domain specification in the reading area

ing areas which are not included in the content domain description.

(d) Response limits—a description of the kind of incorrect answer choices which must be prepared. The structure and content of the incorrect answers should be stated in as much detail as possible.

An example of a domain specification is shown in Fig. 1. Once properly prepared domain specifications are available, the remaining steps in the test development process can be carried out.

4. Criterion-referenced Test Development

It is essential to specify in as clear a form as possible the domain of content or behaviors defining each competency which is to be measured in the test being constructed. The mechanism through which the competencies are identified will vary from one situation to the next. For high-school graduation exams, the process might involve district educational leaders meeting to review school curricula and identifying a relatively

small set of important broad competencies (e.g., reading comprehension, mathematics computations). When criterion-referenced tests are needed in an objectives-based instructional program, it is common to define a curriculum in broad areas (and, sometimes into a two-dimensional grid). Then, within the cells of the grid the sets of relevant objectives, often stated in behavioral form, are specified, reviewed, revised, and finalized. With certification exams, it is common to first conduct a "role delineation study" with individuals working in the area to identify the responsibilities, subresponsibilities, and activities which serve to define a role. Next, the knowledge and skills which are needed to carry out the role are identified.

A set of 12 steps for preparing criterion-referenced tests adapted from Hambleton (1982) is suggested in Table 1.

5. Applications of Criterion-referenced Tests

Criterion-referenced tests (or domain-referenced tests, mastery tests, competency tests, basic skills tests, or certification exams as they are alternately called) are being used in a large number of settings in the United States to address many problem areas. Criterion-referenced tests are finding substantial use in US schools. Classroom teachers use criterion-referenced test score results to locate students correctly in school programs, to monitor student progress, and to identify student deficiencies. Special education teachers are finding criterion-referenced test scores especially helpful in diagnosing student learning deficiencies and monitoring the progress of their students. Criterion-referenced test results are also being used to evaluate various school programs. While it is less common, criterion-referenced tests are finding some use in higher educational programs as well (e.g., those programs based upon the mastery learning concept). Also, criterion-referenced tests are in common use in military and industrial training programs.

In recent years, it has become common for state departments of education and (sometimes) school districts to define sets of skills (or competencies) which students must achieve in order to be promoted from one grade to the next, or in some states, to receive high-school diplomas. The nature of these criterion-referenced testing programs varies dramatically from one place to another. For example, in some places, students are held responsible for mastering a specified set of skills at each grade level, in other states, skills which must be acquired are specified at selected grade levels, and in still other states, only a set of skills which must be mastered for high-school graduation is specified.

One of the most important applications of criterion-referenced tests is to the areas of professional certification and licensure. It is now common in the United States, for example, for professional organizations to establish entry-level examinations which must be passed by candidates before they are allowed to practice in their chosen professions. In fact, many of these professional organizations have also established recertification exams. A typical examination will measure the competencies which define the professional role and candidate test performance is interpreted in relation to minimum standards which are established. There are now hundreds of professional organizations, including most groups in the medical and allied health fields, which have instituted certification and recertification exams.

Bibliography

Berk R A (ed.) 1980 *Criterion-Referenced Measurement: The State of the Art.* Johns Hopkins University Press, Baltimore, Maryland

Glaser R 1963 Instructional technology and the measurement of learning outcomes. *Am. Psychol.* 18: 519–21

Hambleton R K 1982 Advances in criterion referenced testing technology. In: Reynolds C, Gutkin T (eds.) 1982 *Handbook of School Psychology.* Wiley, New York

Hambleton R K, Swaminathan H, Algina J, Coulson D B 1978 Criterion-referenced testing and measurement: A review of technical issues and developments. *Rev. Educ. Res.* 48: 1–47

Popham W J 1974 An approaching peril: Cloud referenced tests. *Phi Delta Kappan* 55: 614–15

Popham W J 1978 *Criterion-Referenced Measurement.* Prentice-Hall, Englewood Cliffs, New Jersey

Popham W J, Husek T R 1969 Implications of criterion-referenced measurement. *J. Educ. Meas.* 6: 1–9

van der Linden W J 1980 Decision models for use with criterion-referenced tests. *Appl. Psychol. Meas.* 4: 469–92

Part 5

Distribution and Organization of Knowledge and Resources

Part 5

Distribution and Organization of Knowledge and Resources

Introduction

The three central parts of this *Encyclopedia* have focused on the educational potential of various forms of mediated learning, and the design, development, and evaluation of learning resources. Access to these resources, however, cannot be taken for granted, for it depends on how they are distributed and organized. This final part examines three major traditions of resource distribution.

Curriculum Packages and Textbooks are distributed directly to schools for use by classes of children. They may be published by government agencies, private companies, or some combination of both. The tradition is still dominated by printed resources and the physical distribution of multiple copies. Decisions about which resources are to be distributed, approved, recommended, or purchased are typically regarded as curriculum decisions. Hence, the first section also carries articles on curriculum development and implementation. It should also be noted, however, that publishing is dominated by the private sector in many countries, and that many private publishers are not confined to the education market.

The Educational Broadcasting tradition is only partially influenced by educational concerns, because most broadcasting organizations regard education as a relatively minor part of their brief. Not only are the politics of educational broadcasting subordinate to those of national broadcasting for entertainment or information, but the norms, standards, and modes of thinking of broadcasters are largely shaped by those prevailing in the noneducational sector. For this reason, a regional approach has been used in this section with an additional article on transnational influences.

Libraries and Resource Centers rely mainly on published material for their intake, but may also stock recordings of broadcasts. Whereas curriculum packages and textbooks, even broadcasts, tend to be assigned learning for whole classes of students, library resources are organized with individual users very much in mind. Diversity rather than uniformity is the prevailing principle. As with broadcasting, many libraries also provide entertainment and information, and it is often difficult to decide whether a particular resource is educational or not. Both broadcasters and librarians would argue that many of their resources which are not specifically designed for formal educational use still serve important educational purposes, and advocates of adult education and nonformal education sometimes argue that these generally informative resources are at least as important as the others.

The final section of the *Encyclopedia* on Knowledge Organization and Knowledge Use takes a wider look at the distribution of knowledge, which is not confined to its incorporation into particular learning resources. It is concerned not only with school knowledge but also with professional knowledge and its dissemination among researchers and practitioners. Copyright issues are also addressed, before the *Encyclopedia* concludes with a review of *Electronic Publishing*, perhaps the major knowledge distribution system of the future.

1. Curriculum Packages and Textbooks

Within the formal education system, particularly in the schools sector, learning resources are designed to be used in particular curricular contexts. While there have been curriculum development projects that were able to produce textbooks and packages with some degree of freedom—this was particularly true in the United Kingdom and North America in the 1960s and 1970s—most learning resources have been designed to fit preexisting curriculum frameworks. The first article in this Section, *Curriculum Development*, discusses the nature of these frameworks and how they are derived, for it is these curriculum decisions which largely determine the knowledge to which pupils will be given access.

Gay begins her review of curriculum development by distinguishing it from curriculum design, that further process by which curriculum specifications are translated into learning resources and institutional strategies. The development of the curriculum framework is logically prior to curriculum design, and Gay discusses the main characteristics of this process, the likely participants, and the forces and factors which influence the resultant decisions. Some elements in the process are universal, others are dependent on the particular cultural and political context. First, curriculum development is an interpersonal process of decision-making, which is often highly political; but it is also a social, collaborative, and cooperative enterprise. Typically, decision-making is disjointed and incremental rather than carefully planned and rational. Decisions may be made at different levels—local, regional, and national—and in varying degrees of detail. A large number of people may influence this process, either through direct participation or by indirectly affecting the participants or the contexts in which they are working.

The more one understands the politics of curriculum development, the more one is surprised by the naivity of those who ignore it. Educational technologists have often been guilty of developing approaches for idealized worlds of their own which assume a ready-made consensus on curriculum objectives. More frustrating for them, however, is the continuing domination of the textbook as the principal form of learning resource, for writers of textbooks not only ignore the potential of other media, but fail to follow the principles of instructional design elaborated in Part 4 above. Westbury's article on *The Role of Textbooks* goes some way towards explaining this phenomenon. He argues that it is a mistake to see a textbook as a learning system on its own, for it is but part of the technology of schooling which evolved during the nineteenth and early twentieth centuries. The textbook is both the repository of the knowledge that schools communicate and the basic tool of the traditional teacher. Both the way schools are organized and teachers' conceptions of their role are dependent on the textbook. Abolish that, and everything else has to change as well. In addition to pointing out the paucity of research into how textbooks are used, Westbury discusses textbook content and textbook bias. He then concludes with a brief account of the publishing industry and the effect of poor distribution of textbooks on pupil performance.

Baker's short article on *Curriculum Packages* points out that in wealthier countries textbooks are sometimes supplanted by packages of learning resources. Often the textbook is still the central component, but other resources such as audiovisual software, games, workbooks, or even computer discs are also provided. The problem is usually the cost. However, where packages can be shared between more than one class, for example by being linked to topics or modules which can be taken in any order so that only one class needs the package at a time, the cost can become quite reasonable. The use of packages is also underresearched, particularly those which have not been developed by a sponsored curriculum project.

The consequences for developing nations of the rising costs of textbook development and the dominance of the Western publishing industry are discussed in Gopinathan's article on *Transnational Influences in Publishing*. He reviews the range of factors which continue to support a strong Western influence on textbooks in developing nations, including local adaptation projects, Western consultants, and scholarship schemes. Immediate commercial concerns tend to take priority over long term consideration of pedagogic effects and the appropriateness of Western curriculum frameworks and learning resources.

Many exported curriculum projects have not been very successful in their countries of origin, because they underestimated the problems and difficulties of implementation. Indeed this is now a well-established area of research and Fullan's review of *Curriculum Implementation* illustrates how much has been learned from the relative failure of many curriculum innovations in the 1960s and 1970s. That this research is still unheeded by many decision-makers is the educational tragedy of the 1980s. Fullan begins by pointing to the contrast between the "fidelity or programmed approach" and the "adaptive approach" to curriculum implementation, with research increasingly favouring the viability of the latter. At a more sophisticated level, it is useful to distinguish components of a curriculum change, some of which may be associated with a fidelity approach and some with adaptation. The main factors affecting implementation are divided into four categories: (a) characteristics pertaining to the curriculum change being attempted; (b) local contextual conditions at the district and school levels; (c) local strategies at the district and school levels used to foster implementation; and (d) external (to local) factors affecting the likelihood of implementation. Each of these is reviewed in some detail, before issues related to the evaluation of implementation and planning for implementation are discussed. The message that emerges strongly and consistently from this research is that the development and dissemination model is inappropriate for most educational innovations. Even the most promising products cannot just be disseminated. A planned process of implementation is required which may be even more complex and time-consuming than the original development.

2. Educational Broadcasting

This Section is primarily concerned with policies for educational broadcasting. Technical developments were discussed in Part 2 under *Distribution and Reception of Television Programs* and *Audio Production and Distribution*, while in the same part, Orivel's article

Economics of Educational Technology reviews research on the cost-effectiveness of educational broadcasting. The utilization and impact of broadcasts are discussed in Part 3 which includes articles on the *Use of Television in the Classroom*, *Children's Television*, *Mass Media in Adult Education*, and *Distance Learning Systems*. These articles also give some attention to the various roles which broadcasting can play, thus providing an essential background to the policy issues discussed below.

The Section is largely composed of regional reviews which cover *Africa* (Inquai), *Asia* (Hurst), *Australia and New Zealand* (Teather), *Latin America and the Caribbean* (McAnany), *North America* (Lyle), *The Pacific Region* (Hill), and *Western Europe* (Cathcart). These distinguished authors have interpreted their briefs in various ways, so that some themes are developed more in one article and some themes in another. This prevents too much replication, but also makes it advisable for interested readers to inspect more than one article if they want to encounter a full range of issues. Hence, this introduction is organized around themes rather than regions in order both to present the reader with an overview and to point to those particular articles where a theme is given the most thorough treatment.

Three forms of broadcasting agency are common: government departments, private companies, and independent public corporations. Eastern Europe and most African and Asian countries have government stations only. Other regions have mixtures of public and commercial channels in varying proportions. The commercial influence is strongest in the United States, and Central and South America, while in Western Europe the balance is fairly even. There is also a contrast between the governmental approach to noncommercial broadcasting in France and the public corporations of the United Kingdom and Canada. In all countries there is some regulation of the private sector, and in some countries commercial stations are required to provide airtime for educational programmes (Mexico) or even to produce them (United Kingdom).

Government sponsorship of educational broadcasts is heavily constrained by finance. As a result (a) radio is still the only medium widely used in poorer countries; (b) educational television production has declined as a result of recession; and (c) sponsored educational television projects in developing nations were abandoned when external funding ceased. Direct television teaching for use in schools has declined in most countries, partly for these financial reasons, but also because the shortage of teachers became less acute, teachers were resistant to using television that way, and evaluation studies cast doubt on its cost-effectiveness. At school level, therefore, the policy is usually to supplement and enrich the curriculum, with "core teaching" being left to classroom teachers. Usage is greatest at primary level, especially in those curriculum areas for which teachers are least well-prepared.

Broadcasts to children out of school provide another kind of service. These are particularly well-developed in Eastern Europe, Western Europe, Canada, and Japan, where the public broadcasting tradition accords them priority. Commercial interests are more dominant in the United States, though some of their techniques have been adopted by organizations such as the Children's Television Workshop, and successfully used to attract and maintain children's attention for explicit educational purposes. It is television rather than radio which is successful in capturing young audiences in the home, so broadcasting to children is largely confined to those richer countries where television sets are frequently found in the home.

During the late 1970s and the 1980s broadcasting policy-makers tended to shift their attention to adult education, where an initial emphasis on general informational programmes expanded to cover both basic adult education and vocational education. Radio and television are still used in many countries as media for governments to communicate with their people, but access to the media is unevenly distributed. Radio in particular is increasingly used in a carefully targeted manner to support specific developmental goals, especially in rural areas. Notable examples are the church-sponsored radiophonic schools of Latin America, the farm forums of India and Africa, and public health campaigns.

Finally, with the increasing development of open learning, formal courses for adults using television or radio have greatly expanded in number. Often the growth of distance education in the adult sector has occurred simultaneously with a reduction in broadcasts for pupils in formal education. These and other policy issues are given major attention by the authors indicated below.

(a) Balance between public and commerical needs in broadcasting (Cathcart, Hill, Lyle, Teather)

(b) Democratization of media use (Cruise O'Brien, Hill, McAnany)

(c) Teacher training in classroom use of broadcasts (Cathcart, McAnany)

(d) Cultural dominance of imported programmes (Cruise O'Brien, Hill, Lyle)

(e) Dominance of Western concepts of broadcasting policy and practice (Cruise O'Brien)

(f) Declining expectations of direct broadcasts to schools (Hurst, Inquai, McAnany)

(g) Involvement of user groups (Cathcart, Inquai)

(h) Use of multimedia packages (Cathcart, McAnany)

(i) Use of broadcasts in recorded form (Cathcart, Teather).

The final article in the section, that of Cruise O'Brien on *Transnational Influences in Broadcasting*, focuses not only on the more obvious effects of imported programmes but also on the more hidden influence of Western concepts of broadcasting and technological expectations.

3. Libraries and Resource Centres

Most library users are individuals, and it is through the provision of learning resources and information to individuals that libraries and resource centres support learning throughout the community. This distinguishes them from most other forms of educational support which are dependent on the formation of groups or classes for teaching. Even within formal education the best-known forms of individualized teaching, such as the tutorial system and individualized learning systems of the kind described in Part 4(d) are heavily dependent on the provision of appropriate libraries and learning centres. This commitment to individual clients makes prioritization particularly difficult when, as is usual, finance is extremely limited.

The term *resource centre* is sometimes used as an alternative to the term *library* within schools and occasionally at district level, when there is a desire to emphasize nonbook resources. However, a strong policy has developed in many countries and at many levels to integrate book and nonbook resources within a single organization and the onset of new technology is making this even more important. Therefore, the practice of using the term *library* to cover all collections of teaching and learning resources, whether or not they specialize in particular formats or media, is adopted in this section.

The first part of this section surveys four main types of library—*School Libraries/ Resource Centers, Public Libraries, College and University Libraries,* and *Special Libraries.* Each has a distinctive mission but there are also some common problems: the selection and organization of collections, staffing and staff development, access to and availability of resources, relationships with clients, and links with other libraries and information sources. Lowrie's article on *School Libraries/Resource Centers* examines patterns of organization and the role of standards and guidelines in addition to some of the more general issues. She argues that in a fully developed school library system there is a need for specialists in curriculum, information, production, utilization, and administration of learning resources. However, within individual buildings the immediacy of demand and lack of trained personnel are often the dominant constraints on sharing and developing resources and expertise.

In *Public Libraries,* there are particular problems in identifying and prioritizing the needs of a wide range of possible clients, some of whom demand attention while others have to be cajoled and enticed. Sullivan reviews services for a number of distinctive client groups: children, young adults, local businesses, partially literate adults, and those who are physically isolated by remote location, disability, or imprisonment. Both Lowrie and Sullivan discuss library services for minority groups which includes stocking material in minority languages and developing collections relevant to studying their traditions and culture.

College and University Libraries have well-defined but exceptionally demanding clients with an insatiable appetite for specialized information and expertise. Jackson discusses three possible approaches to organizing libraries to meet these needs based on function, subject, and format, and presents some typical examples. A particularly strong tension in higher education libraries is that between maintaining a core collection with multiple copies for undergraduates and developing specialized research collections, and this affects selection policy, bibliographic control, and staffing.

The client groups of *Special Libraries* are even more tightly defined, often being confined to quite small organizations. Some are educational, others entirely commercial. As Hewitt points out, they are particularly skillful in networking with other libraries and information sources; and they are usually able to be more preactive than other libraries in providing information to clients in advance of, rather than only in response to, specific requests.

All four articles mentioned above discuss the development of networking and the introduction of new technology—the main themes of Gorman's article on the *Processing of Library Materials.* Gorman concentrates on recent major developments in bibliographic networks and the automation of library processes. This has been aided by the international standardization of bibliographic data and the rapid growth of networks, such as OCLC in North America, to assist with library processing and bibliographic control. Gorman also discusses interlibrary loans and cooperative development of collections. The technical background to Gorman's article is more fully discussed in Part 2 under *Information Storage and Retrieval.*

The next two articles focus on nonprint media. Davis reviews *Film Libraries* whilst Thompson discusses the *Storage and Handling of Learning Resources* with particular attention to storage conditions, handling, and shelving.

The last two articles in this Section are particularly concerned with access and support for adult learners. Allred's review of *Libraries in Adult Education* covers historical developments, library support for adult education classes, libraries as locations for nonformal adult education, library involvement in distance learning systems, and library support for open entry to education for adults through provision of information about opportunities, appropriate learning resources, and even tutorial support. *Learning Centers* are a specialist facility for access to learning opportunities, located either in libraries or in formal educational institutions such as community colleges. They provide a suitable learning environment, resources, and tutorial support, and could be considered as intermediate in character between a library and formal education, combining the flexibility and open access of the library with the specialist teaching support of the college or school. Davies discusses various approaches to such centres, and the functions they fulfil. Some educators think we shall see much more of learning centres in the future, as they are consistent with many current trends. Others are rather more sceptical.

4. Knowledge Organization and Knowledge Use

This concluding section of the *Encyclopedia* takes a broader, more fundamental look at how knowledge is organized and used, which is distinct from its incorporation into resources for teaching and learning. There are two important reasons for this. First, it is important for educational technologists to consider how their own professional knowledge is created, organized, distributed, and used. While some attention was given to this question in Part 1, that discussion did not draw very fully upon relevant research into knowledge organization and use outside the educational technology field. Second, the development of new technologies and on-line information systems reduces knowledge users' dependence on distinct physical resources. So to concentrate attention on learning resources is to give undue weight to current formats. On-line distribution of knowledge still raises problems of selection, organization, access, and use of knowledge, but these need to be considered more generically.

The Section opens with Machlup's summary of his own pioneering research into *Knowledge Industries and Knowledge Occupations*. He begins by distinguishing knowledge from information, knowledge being the wider concept including both information and the thoughts and ideas which connect it up and organize it. Many kinds of knowledge are not of the kind associated with scholarship, nor is knowledge necessarily embodied in language. Knowledge industries can be classified under six main headings: education, research and development, artistic creation and communication, media of communication, information services, and information machines. Not all workers in these industries are knowledge workers, nor are knowledge workers only found in knowledge industries. Machlup then defines eight different classes of knowledge worker: transporters, transformers, routine processors, discretionary processors, managerial processors, interpreters, analysers and original creators of knowledge. Primary knowledge production industries accounted for 25 percent of the United States GNP in 1972, and knowledge occupations accounted for 40 percent of the total civilian labour force. Not only are these figures growing, but the character of much of the work is changing.

Research into *Knowledge Utilization* is reviewed by Dunn, Holzner, and Zaltman. They survey the rapid development of this new field and introduce important conceptual frameworks. They analyse knowledge systems in terms of functions (for example distributing knowledge), domains (for example education), and regions which have greater or lesser prestige or influence. Important questions are then raised about how knowledge claims are validated using ideas such as frame of reference, reality test, theory-in-use, and situated rationality. A section on research methodology pays particular attention to the distinction between conceptual use—changes in how users think—and instrumental use—direct changes in user behaviour. However, increasing evidence from studies of knowledge practice has shown how analytically distinct processes such as knowledge production and knowledge dissemination may be highly interdependent in practice. For example, involvement of practitioners in knowledge production has a positive effect on any subsequent dissemination. This can be explained in terms of the powerful influence of frames of reference and theories in use on the acceptance or rejection of new knowledge. Acceptable new knowledge has to come within the user's intellectual and social "comfort zone". For similar reasons data tend to be interpreted in accordance with preexisting frames of reference. Finally, the implications of the research are discussed for planned social change and the diffusion of innovations.

The third article in this group is specific to *Knowledge Diffusion in Education*. Keeves extends Dunn's distinction between conceptual use and instrumental use into a threefold categorization of the outcomes of educational research and development: those concerned with principle and paradigm, with policy and practice, and with products of immediate and direct application. He then discusses Weiss' typology of approaches to knowledge utilization and Havelock's four models of dissemination with particular attention to Havelock's linkage model. The article concludes with a review of practical approaches to the diffusion of educational innovations: publication programmes; abstracting services; information exchanges; research and development networks; research and development utilization centres; and school-based problem-solving programmes. One of these approaches, the educational database, ERIC, is separately reviewed by Ely.

The legal framework governing the distribution of learning resources and the diffusion of knowledge is provided by laws on *Copyright*. While educational users may grumble at the constraints it imposes on practice, some kind of framework is necessary for knowledge production to remain a viable occupation or business. Miller and Wynne describe the international copyright agreements, then review in greater detail the legal frameworks pertaining in the United Kingdom and the United States, with particular attention to educational usage and new media.

The section concludes on a forward-looking note with Kist's review of *Electronic Publishing*. Kist examines the total process of publishing from source to users, noting the new opportunities created by new technology. Given this greatly extended range of options, the publisher has to decide how to find, process, and manipulate information; how to store information; how to update the store; how to format the information for a user; and how to transport the information. One major change is the much more interactive relationship between author, publisher, and user. Kist examines the differing needs of user groups such as business executives, engineers, and social scientists. After discussing more fundamental concepts such as information, communication, and information centres, Kist concludes with a list of key factors affecting the progress of electronic publishing: user-group control, increasingly specialized marketing, market domination, pricing, distribution, size, and management.

Curriculum Packages and Textbooks

Curriculum Development

G. Gay

Professional literature and discourse are filled with examples of curriculum development being equated only with the technology of writing instructional objectives, content, activities, and evaluation procedures. Little or no systematic attention is given to the processes or dynamics which undergird this technology. This mistaken conception or oversight should be corrected. More attention needs to be given to the complex interactions, negotiations, and compromises surrounding questions of who makes curriculum decisions and how these decisions are made, in order to better understand the organization and emphases of given curriculum designs or plans.

Zais (1976) attempts to provide some clarity and precision in the various dimensions of the curriculum enterprise by distinguishing curriculum design or construction from curriculum development. According to him, "curriculum" is used typically by specialists to refer either to a plan for educating youth or as a field of study. When the intent is to identify the collective components of the substantive entity, that is, a plan for instruction, curriculum is being considered as "design." When the focus of attention is the people and operative procedures out of which the design or plan for instruction emerges, the reference ordinarily is to "curriculum development." Lawton (1975) makes a similar distinction between "the curriculum" and "curriculum planning." According to him, curricula are made up of those particular aspects of life, knowledge, attitudes, and values selected from the total culture of a society for transmission to future generations within the structure of educational systems. The ways in which educators make these selections and put them into practice is curriculum planning. Thus, curriculum development is the process, the syntactical structure, the interpersonal dynamics of decision making about instructional planning. By comparison, curriculum design is the product, the substantive entity, the end result of the decision-making processes. Curriculum development does not necessarily precede curriculum design or construction in a linear fashion. Instead, the two enterprises overlap and occur conjunctively.

Although helpful as a point of departure, a mere definitional distinction between curriculum development and curriculum design is not sufficient to capture the essence of the two dynamic enterprises. Rather, a detailed descriptive analysis of the two is required. The focus of attention in this discussion is curriculum development.

The purpose of this discussion is to explore some of the major dimensions of the interactive dynamics of the processes which produce curriculum plans. The issues discussed include: (a) the distinguishing characteristics of the curriculum development process; (b) who participates in curriculum decision making; and (c) the forces and factors that influence curriculum development and how. General principles related to each of these are discussed, as well as some specific examples of curriculum development dynamics in different countries. The purpose of these examples is twofold—to illustrate that some elements of the process of curriculum development are universal, and to demonstrate how the dynamics of the process are configured differently as a result of the particular cultural and political contexts in which they occur.

1. Nature of Curriculum Development

The essential elements of the curriculum development process involve issues of power, people, procedures, and participation. The critical questions are: Who makes decisions about curricular issues? What choices or decisions are to be made? and How are these decisions made and implemented? Invariably, these concerns lead to curriculum development being characterized as an interactional process that is political, social, collaborative, and incremental in nature.

First, curriculum development is an interpersonal process or system of operations for making decisions about where curriculum planning will take place (e.g., the political zone of influence according to legal stature), who will be involved in the planning, the selection and execution of working procedures, and how curriculum documents will be implemented, appraised, and revised (Beauchamp and Beauchamp 1972). It is a dynamic, vital complex network of interactions among people and forces, all of which occur in fluid settings or contexts that are in perpetual states of emergence. The particular contours of the process are shaped as much by the legal arenas in which curriculum decision making takes place as by the particular compilation of actors included, and by the substantive demands of the instructional issues under consideration. For example, while curriculum development at local and central governmental levels will encompass some of the same procedural dynamics, the people involved and the decisions to be made vary according to the societal and cultural contexts. Whereas in France education is a national function mandated by constitutional provisions, in the United States and Canada legal responsibility for curriculum belongs to regional governments (states and provinces respectively). Though England and Wales now have a national curriculum framework, considerable responsibility still remains with individual schools.

Second, curriculum development is a political process. Local, regional, and national governmental agencies regularly engage in policy making about instructional programming. In the United States, education is the province of state governments since it was not specifically delegated to the national government by the Constitution. Typically, states exert control over what schools teach by outlining general requirements of the curriculum. Illustrative of these are specifications about time allocations for the daily instruction of reading in the elementary grades, the number of credits required in particular subjects for students to graduate from high school, and the grade level intervals when minimum competency tests will be administered. Other mechanisms through which national governments become involved in curriculum decision making include: inspectors' reports in England and Wales, curriculum commissions appointed by the state Ministries of Education in the Federal Republic of Germany, policy regulations of the National Ministry of Education in Sweden, and the examination systems in Japan.

In Sweden, for instance, any one of three different national agencies—the Ministry of Education and Cultural Affairs, Parliament, and the National Board of Education—can initiate curriculum development. Generally, though,

> the Minister of Education and Parliament act in concert, i.e., Parliament may ask the Minister of Education and Cultural Affairs to come up with a needed curriculum proposal, or the minister may initiate a proposal for consideration by Parliament...most of the detail of curriculum planning work is done under the authority and direction of the National Board of Education.... In many cases curriculum decisions made at very high levels...include only decisions about overall objectives, range of subjects, and weekly time schedules for the subjects. The development of content into sequential organization in harmony with the objectives and the organizational plan of the school in question ... is done under the direct supervision of the National Board of Education. (Beauchamp and Beauchamp 1972 pp. 99–100)

As is true with other political processes, curriculum development also involves various constituent groups in power negotiations. These negotiations concern "a series of choices, often based upon values" (Saylor et al. 1981 p. 27), the "allocation of resources towards certain ends" (Pratt 1980 p. 111), and "the creation and distribution of benefits" (Hunkins 1980 p. 140). Moreover, "pressure groups of all kinds are always proposing competing values about what to teach" (McNeil 1977 p. 260). Simon (1980) contends that the political character of curriculum decisions becomes most apparent when the focus of attention is content about school customs and values, and when one interest group attempts to define the social character of society for others.

Obviously, then, the selection of curriculum objectives, content, activities, and evaluation are influenced as much by values and politics as by pedagogy. As Eggleston (1977 p. 23) suggests, these selections are essentially

> processes of conflict that give rise to a range of compromises, adjustments, and points of equilibrium of varying degrees of stability. In all of these negotiations an underlying concept is that of power...the power to make decisions that influence the work of students and teachers and...the control over the power that can be achieved by students or withheld from them by determining access to high or low status curriculum components and the evaluation and opportunities associated with them. Unquestionably curriculum determination is centrally concerned with both the use and the allocation of power.

Third, curriculum development is a social enterprise. It is a "people process" with all the attending potentialities and obstacles associated with humans engaged in social interactions. The interests, values, ideologies, priorities, role functions, and differentiated responsibilities form the contours of the interactional and dynamic contexts in which curriculum decisions are made. The personalities of curriculum developers, the structures of school systems, and the different patterns of group relations among members of school communities are significant determinants of power negotiations, resource allocations, and valuative conflict resolutions, which permeate curriculum determination.

Curriculum development implies the need for some kind of modifications in existing instructional systems. These modifications result from the interactional processes which occur among the people who have the power and authority to make these decisions. As Miel (1946 p. 10) suggests, curriculum development is

> something much more subtle than revising statements written down on paper. To change the curriculum of the school is to change the factors interacting to shape that curriculum. In each instance this means bringing about changes in people—in their desires, beliefs, and attitudes, in their knowledge and skill... In short, the nature of curriculum change

should be seen for what it really is—a type of social change in people. . . .

Zais (1976 p. 448) endorses Miel's analysis of the social character of curriculum development in his observation that "curriculum change is people change and cannot be brought about merely by fate or by organizational manipulation."

Furthermore, any kind of educational change always involves human, emotional, and valuative factors (Taba 1962). For this reason, Smith et al. (1957) equate changing the curriculum with social engineering. The school curriculum is inextricably interwoven into the patterns of relationships, social positions, expectations, and values of the different individuals, groups, and cultural ecologies that make up school communities. It cannot be separated from its social contexts and treated as if it were a totally independent entity existing in a vacuum. Rather, effective curriculum development requires concomitant change in the established normative structures of school communities, in existing patterns of interpersonal relationships, in people's attitudes towards what is most worthy of knowing, and in the perceptions of individuals and groups about educational roles, purposes, power, and procedures. In other words, "in order to change the curriculum, the social fabric must be changed. . . . Broadly conceived, then, the problem of curriculum change is a problem in social engineering" (Smith et al. 1957 p. 440).

Fourth, curriculum development, at any level, is a collaborative and cooperative enterprise. The fact that instructional planning involves a variety of technical and human relations skills, and must attend to many different priorities, perceptions, vested interests, and value commitments makes it virtually impossible for individuals, operating alone, to complete the task efficiently and effectively. Cooperation is essential in curriculum development. This does not mean that everyone involved in the process should participate indiscriminately in all aspects of curriculum determination. The technical complexities of curriculum construction, as well as its social and political character, require many kinds of competencies in different combinations at different points in the developmental process. Decisions about who participates when and how must be based upon the distinct function to be served, and the competencies of the participants. Thus, effective curriculum development must operate on the principles of cooperation, collaboration, and shared responsibility within the contextual framework of complementary and differentiated levels of involvement (Taba 1962).

Usually, curriculum decisions are made at three different levels of influence simultaneously. These are (a) the instructional level, or by classroom teachers; (b) the institutional level, or by school building and/or system personnel; and (c) the societal level, or by boards of education, governmental officials, and a plethora of interest groups (Kirst and Walker 1971). These decisions vary somewhat by zone or level of influence and

according to the position, power, and expectations of the participants, but all of them contribute significantly to shaping the overall character of the curriculum development process. Therefore, collaboration and cooperation are essential to ensure that all vested interests are sufficiently represented, that the various technical skills needed for qualitative curriculum planning are included, and that coherency and cohesion exist throughout the entire development process, from conception to completion.

Fifth, curriculum development is, according to Kirst and Walker (1971) a "disjointed incremental" system of decision making. It is neither a purely rational and scientifically objective, nor a neatly sequentialized and systematic process. Rarely are the various sets of decisions necessary in curriculum planning systematically coordinated throughout the entire cycle. Instead, "multiple starts are made and these efforts are scattered in several directions. A rule-of-thumb method still dominates, and often the persons involved do not know why they succeeded or why they failed" (Taba 1962 p. 454). Curriculum decisions are frequently made "through small or incremental moves on particular problems rather than through a comprehensive reform program" (Braybrooke and Lindblom 1963 p. 71). Macdonald (1971) describes curriculum development as an "historical accident" instead of a completely rational–technical process. By this he means that historically, curriculum planning has been "the outcome of a very long and dynamically complex process of social involvement and interaction. It is not something that has been deliberately chosen and rationally developed for a specific purpose it is intended to serve" (Macdonald 1971 p. 95).

These descriptions of curriculum development led Walker (1976 p. 299) to recommend a change in the image and ideal of the process. Rather than viewing it as a carefully planned and rational system of operations, he advises

we recognize that curriculum changes are necessarily subject to the operation of enormously powerful social forces that cannot possibly be brought under the control of any technical procedures or systematically designed process. The action of these powerful forces is influenceable at times and in some ways, and professional educators charged with responsibility for curricular maintenance and change need to learn how to cope with those forces as well as they can. The image of the technician at the control panel directing the entire operation needs to be replaced by a more realizable one, perhaps that of the mountaineer using all the tricks of modern science, together with personal skill and courage and an intimate study of the particular terrain, to scale a peak.

2. Participants in the Process

A key question to understanding the dynamics of curriculum development is, Who controls the decision making process, and how is this control exerted? Phillips and Hawthorne (1978 p. 365) answer these questions by saying "nearly any organization, at any level, that has a concern" determines school curriculum. According to

Saylor et al. (1981 p. 47), curriculum development involves "a cast of thousands." This cast of thousands can be grouped into two major categories—participants in the planning process (e.g., clients, critics, professionals, legislative groups, courts) and resources for the planners (e.g., authors, publishers, testers, accreditors, pollsters, lobbyists, media). Typically, "planners" make policy and determine the substantive details of curriculum designs while "resources" monitor the processes of planners, serve as quality controllers, and suggest alternative realities for consideration in curriculum planning.

From these observations and the preceding discussions it can be deduced that those who participate in curriculum development comprise a diversified and numerous lot. This is true irrespective of whether the societal context is the United Kingdom, the Soviet Union, United States, Israel, Japan, or Nigeria. However, the degree and kind of involvement vary according to the role functions and relationships of the actors and influences to the official structure of the school system, and the intensity of commitment and regularity of participation. For example, while some kind of specifically designated governmental agencies are involved directly and regularly in curriculum decision making in all countries, the authority for and extent of their involvement vary by the legal regulations governing control of education, and the political zone of influence in which curriculum development occurs. Conversely, the involvement of community-based pressure groups is indirect and sporadic. The extent and nature of their involvement is determined by the level of interest in particular issues and power of persuasion.

For purposes of analysis in this discussion the major actors and influences shaping curriculum decisions are classified as internal and external forces. The internal and formal determinants of curricula are those forces that are legally responsible for curriculum policy making and planning, and whose involvement is channeled through some regularized, structured arrangements. The external and informal forces exist outside governmental structures and the administrative bureaucracy of school systems. They influence curriculum planning through irregular patterns of pressure politics and powers of persuasion. These categories and relationships are summarized in Table 1. They prevail internationally; however, specific individuals and groups, as well as the particulars of their influence vary by country and culture. Invariably, though, in the actual operations of curriculum planning the two categories of participants and influences overlap significantly.

In acknowledging the diversity of internal and external, formal and informal, legal and extralegal forces involved in curriculum decision making, Kirst and Walker (1971, p. 488) assert that

a mapping of the leverage points for curriculum policy making...would involve three levels of government, and numerous private organization foundations, accrediting associations, national testing agencies, textbook–software companies, and interest groups.... Moreover, there would

be a configuration of leverage points within a particular local school system including teachers, department heads, the assistant superintendent for instruction, the superintendent and the school board. Cutting across all levels of government would be the pervasive influence of various celebrities, commentators, interest groups, and the journalists who use the mass media to disseminate their views on curriculum.

Nicholas (1980) attributes this plethora of participants involved in curriculum development to the normative features of the process. By nature of its existence and functions curriculum development invariably concerns questions of values, politics, control, and power. Even what appear to be consensus issues (such as teaching basic literacy skills)

raise several possible answers which are in turn contradictory or irreconcilable...some preferred answers are offered and canvassed by a variety of groups or individuals for a variety of motives from the ulterior to the altruistic. Examples of such groups abound, i.e., elected representatives of the central, regional, or local political structure, all perhaps in disagreement; employers' associations; trade unions; university authorities; groups of teachers and their associations; professional bodies; parent or community groups—and this list is by no means exhaustive. (Nicholas 1980 p. 153)

3. Perspectives on the Operations of the Process

Various levels of civic government, along with the governance structures of school systems, are the major determinants of formal curriculum policy and planning processes. Generally, governmental agencies establish general educational policies and curriculum guidelines. Specification of operational details is the responsibility of school system bureaucracies. The relative distribution of authority among governmental agencies and school system officials varies from nation to nation, as do the nature and extent of the external pressures which impinge upon the internal system of curriculum decision making. This is expected, given that schools and their programs are designed to perpetuate the cultures of which they are a part. They are, therefore, unavoidably culturally relativistic. Several examples of curriculum development in different countries are provided to illustrate how the dynamics of the process operate on different legal levels of decision making, and to demonstrate their similarities across nations irrespective of the official arenas of decision making.

3.1 Canada

In Canada the legal arena of curriculum decision making is regional. All official curriculum planning, as well as other education decisions, are the domain of provincial legislatures. In fact, "Canada has the distinction of being the only advanced nation in the world without a federal office of education" (Katz 1974 p. 7). This does not mean, however, that there are no national or local factors and forces operating which exert significant power and influence over educational matters. Other provincial departments of state often sponsor certain

Table 1
The web of forces influencing the curriculum development process[a]

	External		Internal	
	Formal	Informal	Formal	Informal
Forces influencing the process	(a) Testing bureaus and boards (b) Professional associations (c) Accrediting associations (d) Public opinion polls (e) Lobbyists (f) Student/parent/business (g) Labor organizations (h) Regulatory agencies of governments	(a) Special interest groups (b) Publishers of instructional materials (c) Mass media (d) Individual critics (e) Sociocivic crises (f) Customs and traditions (g) Philanthropic foundations (h) Pressure politics	(a) Governmental authorities (b) Advisory and administrative agencies (c) The law (legislative acts, court decisions, funding patterns) (d) School governance structures (e) District and building administrators and teachers (f) Bureaucratic style of school system (g) Resources and facilities (h) Decision-making system (i) Subjects taught	(a) Staff views of curriculum and instruction (b) Politics of the working of the formal structure (c) Customs and traditions (d) Sociology of group dynamics (e) Personalities and competencies of participants (f) Human relations skills (g) Arena of curriculum planning
	Curriculum decision			
Clients	Society Parents Employers Institutions of higher learning		The curriculum plan Teachers Students School systems	

a Adapted from Nicholas E J 1980 A comparative view of curriculum development. In: Kelly A V (ed.) 1980 *Curriculum Context.* Harper and Row, London, pp. 150–72 education programs. For example, the Department of Health and Welfare frequently initiates and sponsors athletic and physical activities; the Canadian Broadcasting Corporation helps prepare educational radio and television programs; and the Departments of Mining and Natural Resources, Trade and Commerce prepare information brochures on the Canadian economy for use in schools. In 1969 the central government announced plans to make funds available to those provinces willing to plan and implement bilingual education programs (Katz 1974).

The provincial ministries of education, official directors of Canadian education, are also susceptible to other internal and external, formal and informal forces which influence curriculum decisions. Typically, curriculum committees that are created to develop guidelines for curriculum planning are made up of representatives from schools, universities, business, industry, labor, and the community at large. Professional organizations, such as the Canadian Teachers' Federation and the Canadian Education Association, may create their own commissions to study different educational concerns and make recommendations pertinent to curriculum. Ethnic groups lobby for inclusion of their cultures and language in curricula and/or for the right to operate their own cultural studies schools. Mass media serves as a public forum for the debate of educational issues. Therefore, while the Canadian legal mechanisms of curriculum development may differ somewhat from those of other advanced nations, the pragmatic and operative dimensions of the process, in terms of individuals, groups, and circumstances that exert directional pressures upon it, are quite similar.

3.2 United States

The legal arena of curriculum decision making in the United States is similar to that of Canada. State governments are constitutionally responsible for education. They establish minimum requirements and general guidelines, but boards of education within local school districts make "the ultimate legal decisions about what shall be taught in the schools of that district" (Beauchamp and Beauchamp 1972 p. 137). The administrative personnel of the local school systems are responsible for executing board policy.

More often than not, a system of development committees and advisory councils is used to translate school board policies and state government guidelines into operational plans for instruction. A combination of political realities, educational practices, economic exigencies, legal mandates, and pressure politics determine the dynamics of how these committees address the task of curriculum planning. For instance, if a curriculum committee is operating in a local school system within a region which uses state-adopted textbooks, its functions may be restricted to selecting a textbook for use in the community schools. Frequently, this selection is made from a list that has already gone through preliminary

screening at the state level. The textbook adoption process is highly susceptible to the influence of publishers' advertising campaigns, mass media, and other various special interest pressure groups (e.g., parental, religious, ethnic, feminist, etc.). Public hearings on the books being considered for adoption are held at both the state and local level. These hearings provide opportunity for any interested person or group to publicly state its opinions on the suggested books. Also, all textbooks are examined by various sets of sociopolitical criteria (such as sexism, racism, classism, ageism, handicapism, and regionalism) to determine their levels of acceptability.

The task of local curriculum committees might be to write lists of minimum competencies, or performance criteria objectives, for a given grade level or subject area to bring the local school system in line with state mandates on minimum competency testing. Or, the composition and functions of local curriculum committees may be dictated by a school board's decision to solicit national government funds earmarked for specifically designated programs and populations, such as sex equality, desegregation, educating the handicapped, vocational education, bilingualism, and the gifted. Often, for these specially targeted programs, the national government stipulates, in the regulations governing the distribution of monies, who should participate in curriculum planning, and how these plans are to be structured. A case in point is the Education of the Handicapped Act of 1974. Commonly known as Public Law 94–142, this legislative act specifies that any school system, state or local, receiving national funds for educating handicapped youth must develop Individual Education Programs (IEP) for each student being served by the program. The IEP must use a minimum competency or performance criteria format in writing objectives, and must be developed collaboratively with different experts within the school who are familiar with the child's needs, and in consultation with the parents.

Periodically, the national government creates commissions to study specific education problems, and funds national curriculum development projects. Examples of the former are presidential commissions appointed to study functional literacy, drug abuse, employment trends, and violence and vandalism among high-school-age youth. The members of these commissions are reputable experts in different political, social, economic, and educational fields. Invariably, their official reports include recommendations of how school programs should be modified to help alleviate these social ills. The current emphasis on vocational education in the United States is a direct outgrowth of prestigious commission reports. The national government also, on occasion, gives financial support to national curriculum projects. The decade of the 1960s witnessed an unprecedented level of central government involvement in curriculum development through this mechanism. What began initially as governmental support of curriculum development efforts, directed by scholars, to improve the quality of mathematics, science, and foreign language instruction spread to the entirety of the high-school curricula before the trend ebbed. A plethora of inquiry science curriculum projects, conceptual-based mathematics, and new social studies curriculum projects emerged. Who directed these projects is another major force to be reckoned with in the process of curriculum development. In almost every instance, the project directors were scholars and academicians, not professional educators. United States schools, especially at the secondary level, have a long history of scholars dominating curriculum development. This tradition was exemplified in the curriculum reform movement of the 1960s.

In effect, then, state and local authorities in the United States still retain de jure responsibility for curriculum development, but more and more this function is being eroded by national influences. During the 1970s it seemed that national policy regulations and funding patterns were making curriculum development a de facto function of the central government (Della-Dora 1976, Sturges 1976). Then central government funding diminished, only to be succeeded by other centralizing tendencies.

Alarmist outcries from all segments of society about declining test scores, increasing rates of illiteracy, and deficiencies in basic intellectual skills have been instrumental in popularizing and institutionalizing demands for returning to "the basics," vocational skill development, and minimum competencies. Commercial publishers of instructional materials spend millions of dollars each year to produce, package, and publicize their products. Electronic media, through the use of advertisements, public announcements, and prime time programs are conveying convincing messages about such social issues as substance abuse, sex, teenage suicide, power of reading, and crimes against human nature. Some of these programs are even accompanied by study guides for teachers and students. Fundamentalist groups accuse schools of teaching "secular humanism," of destroying the sanctity of the family, and of using instructional materials and techniques that are anti-God and anticountry. Liberationists appeal to curriculum designers for the inclusion of more broadly based conceptions of humanity, sexuality, individual realizations, and life options. Private foundations and philanthropic organizations provide funds for the development of curriculum programs in certain subjects. Scholars and academicians continue to dominate teams assembled by commercial publishers to write textbooks and other instructional materials. Professional organizations of classroom teachers, school supervisors, counselors, and administrators sponsor conferences, resolutions, and study groups, and publish books and journals which suggest directions and priorities for educational programs. A case in point is the 1981 interorganizational statement on *Essentials of Education*, which carries the endorsement of 19 different professional associations. Censorship of instructional materials continues to plague the processes of curriculum development. The challenges of censors tend to focus on sex and

sexuality, unchristian attitudes and beliefs, objectionable language, unpatriotic sentiments, and criticism of United States history, and the more recent attacks of secular humanism, creationism versus evolution, values clarification, antiestablishment viewpoints, and moral relativism or situational ethics. A recent study on censorship (*Limiting What Students Shall Read* 1981) reports that challenges to textbooks increases as the school grade level increases, that a sizeable percentage of censors have not read or viewed in entirety the materials they are challenging, and that, consistently, the intent of censors is to limit or restrict the information and viewpoints made available to youth through instructional materials.

The magnitude of the pressures effecting curriculum development in the United States and other countries with respect to "who makes demands" and "what kinds of demands they make" gives validity to the observations of Saylor et al. (1981) that this enterprise includes "a cast of thousands," as well as to Phillips and Hawthorne's (1978) assessment that "any organization at any level that has a concern" can become involved in curriculum decision making. It also lends credence to Taba's caveats about extending the base of participation in curriculum development without a corresponding specification of the appropriate roles of different participants. She adds further that

Perhaps "being concerned" is too broad a criterion for participation in curriculum development. Some delineation is needed regarding the nature of that participation. Much grief has come from an indiscriminate participation of everyone in everything. . . . Clearly, there is a distinct function that all these groups can serve in the total job of curriculum development, and the decisions on participation must rest on who can best do what, and not on a sentimental concept of democratic participation. (Taba 1962 p. 252)

3.3 England

Until recently the English education system was based on considerable devolution of curriculum planning to individual schools. However, schools still worked within the framework of a national system of examinations at 16 and 18, strong curriculum traditions, parental expectations and a range of national government influences (Skilbeck 1984). Throughout the 1980s, however, the influence of national government was growing. The number of examination boards was reduced, national criteria were introduced for examinations at 16 and a series of reports from the Department of Education and Science and Her Majesty's Inspectors were published which were wide ranging in content and quite prescriptive in tone. Increasing politicization of education in general and the curriculum in particular came to a head with a new Education Act in 1988. This set up a National Curriculum Council for England and a Curriculum Council for Wales to keep the curriculum under review and advise the Secretary of State, who was given powers to establish a complete national curriculum. This curriculum is defined in terms of core subjects

(English, Mathematics, Science), foundation subjects (specified) and other subjects (not specified). Programs of study will be specified but not the time to be allocated to them. It is being assumed that there will be more local discretion outside the core and foundation subjects, at least in theory. But in practice national assessment targets at 7, 11, 14 and 16 are to be stipulated in core and foundation subjects, so there will be pressure to maximize the time accorded to the prescribed curriculum.

Within this framework, the new Act aims to place considerable responsibility on individual schools by giving them a great deal of financial autonomy and putting them into open competition for pupils with their neighbouring schools. This is intended both to improve school effectiveness and to subject schools to further local pressure. The government appears to be trying to channel this pressure into the arena of performance on national tests and examinations by requiring publication of these results. If successful, this would divert attention away from curriculum policy and have a powerfully conservative effect. Local groups who disagree with national curriculum policy will have to mobilize political pressure at national level and contend with a National Curriculum Council entirely appointed by the Secretary of State. Whether there will be a residual role for local education authorities in curriculum planning is not at all clear.

There is considerable concern that the long British tradition of school-based curriculum innovation will be stifled, and that teachers will be deprofessionalized. On the other hand, proponents of the new system argue that teachers have had too much influence on the curriculum and too little accountability. Even they remain worried that the new system will prove insensitive to local needs until new patterns of consultation have been properly developed.

Observers should not disregard, however, the extent to which national influences have already had a major impact on the British curriculum during the 1980s. The Science curriculum is undergoing a major transformation as a result of pressures from Her Majesty's Inspectors, centrally funded In-Service Training, changing examinations, and a major national curriculum project, the Secondary Science Curriculum Review. Ironically, the Review was predominantly led by teachers. Prevocational education has also rapidly developed during this period, though in this case there is doubt whether the trend will be confirmed by the new national curriculum.

An important side-effect of this strong local tradition, whether or not it survives in England, is the experience of school-based curriculum development which has been gained and to some extent embodied in publications. Given the increasing evidence of the role of local factors in curriculum implementation (see the final article of this section) much of this accumulated experience is likely to be relevant in the future.

3.4 National Curriculum Planning

The legal responsibility for curriculum development is a function of the central government in many nations. For instance, the national constitutions of Italy, Sweden, Spain, and France make explicit provisions for education. Agencies of the national government play very substantial roles in determining curriculum policy and plans. These curricula are expected to be the points of departure for instruction in all schools; however, opportunities are provided, in most instances, for them to be adapted to accommodate local needs. Consistent with these centralized systems of curriculum planning, the groups involved in the legal process are constituted by the national government. They include inspectors, standing committees that are subsidiaries of ministries of education, appointed committees of experts, and advisory committees of lay people (Beauchamp and Beauchamp 1972).

The observations made earlier that curriculum development does not occur in a vacuum, that it is a complex sociopolitical enterprise wherein conflicting interests compete for recognition, and that external, informal, and extralegal forces frequently penetrate the internal boundaries of legal decision-making structures are as valid for nationally based curriculum development as for planning at regional and local levels. A barrage of politicians, publishers, professionals, parents, interest groups, and socioecological elements participate informally, but nonetheless very significantly, in determining school curricula in Italy, France, Spain, and Sweden. Illustrative of these dynamics is Beauchamp's and Beauchamp's (1972 pp. 100–01) description of how curriculum development proceeds in Sweden:

> Although major curriculum change must be initiated or approved by Parliament, most of the detail of curriculum planning work is done under the authority and direction of the National Board of Education...[and] commissions....
> The composition of high-level commissions reflects the social and political dedication of the Swedes to integrate education and the realities of social life, and to democratically involve representatives of organized groups in their society in the decision making processes about public education. Commissions with large-scale curriculum assignments may be composed of representatives of the creating body (Parliament or the National Board of Education), specialists in education, and representatives of social groups such as labor, business, and professional organizations...the preliminary draft of a major curriculum proposal is sent to major outside organizations for their comment and support approval. Among the organizations are: national labor groups, business organizations, other professional organizations, parent organizations, student organizations, religious organizations...

Similarly, in Singapore and Malaysia where curriculum planning is also the responsibility of national ministries of education, the opinions and suggestions of heads of schools, parents, scholars, employment agencies, and various civic and special interest groups are solicited. In these countries the curriculum development process is also susceptible to influences which are particularly prominent in recently independent countries. These arise from the need to establish a stable government and a sense of national unity among very diversified populations, while developing a literate citizenry. The challenge is to build a nation out of people whose traditional allegiances have been to regional and/or tribal groups, and to imperialistic powers. Part of this challenge for the curriculum developer is to create a system of education that provides a common set of experiences for all youth. The same concerns are paramount in developing nations in Africa, South America, the Caribbean, and Southeast Asia as well. Establishing a viable education system is a natural extension of the political structures of these countries. Hence, general education aims and directions, as well as specific subject syllabi, textbook lists, and national examinations are produced or administered by agencies and subcommittees under the auspices of national ministries of education (Hoy Kee and Yee Hean 1971, Thomas et al 1968).

4. Conclusion

While the level and purpose of political participation in curriculum development in developing nations may be manifested somewhat differently than in advanced nations, the underlying operative principle is the same. That is, curriculum decision making, in any social or cultural context, has very strong political and valuative elements since it involves power negotiations about the allocation of resources and benefits toward the advancement of certain ends. In developing nations, the formal and legal structures regulating curriculum development are more directly determined and controlled by national governments, and the influences of extralegal, informal, and externally organized groups are not as diversified or powerful as in more developed nations. Still, the forces and the viewpoints they symbolize must be considered when curriculum decisions are made.

It therefore becomes patently clear that the dynamics of the curriculum development process are similar in most nations, regardless of whether curriculum planning is the legal responsibility of local, regional, or national governments. Curriculum decision making is inundated with social, political, and human factors. These stem from both formally constituted bodies with legal obligations for curriculum development, and community-based informal, often loosely structured, interest groups who claim the right and authority to participate in curriculum development by virtue of their representative voices and powers of persuasion. There also appears to be a growing erosion of the distinction between formal–informal, legal–extralegal, and internal–external determinants of curriculum policies and plans. Developments are underway in most nations which are expanding the roles and functions of everyone concerned about and involved with curriculum development. As the public becomes more actively involved in making its own decisions, and as economic conditions make governmental involvement in education an increasing and unavoidable

reality, curriculum development cannot help but become more politicized. Similarly, as the educational enterprise becomes more complex, the need for cooperation and collaboration among different constituencies and professionals within a society, as well as among societies, is essential. It is evident, then, that curriculum development is indeed a dynamic process of political, social, and personal negotiations that must occur in a cooperative and collaborative context if it is to produce viable education plans. These characteristics of the planning process are likely to become even more prominent in the future than they are today.

Bibliography

Association for Supervision and Curriculum Development 1981 *Limiting What Students Shall Read.* Association for Supervision and Curriculum Development, Alexandria, Virginia

Beauchamp G A, Beauchamp K E 1972 *Comparative Analysis of Curriculum Systems,* 2nd edn. Kagg, Wilmette, Illinois

Braybrooke D, Lindblom C E 1963 *A Strategy of Decision: Policy Evaluation as a Social Process.* Free Press, New York, New York

Della-Dora D 1976 Democracy and education: Who owns the curriculum? *Educ. Leadership* 34: 51–57

Eggleston J 1977 *The Sociology of the School Curriculum.* Routledge and Kegan Paul, London

Hoy Kee F W, Yee Hean G 1971 *Perspectives: The Development of Education in Malaysia and Singapore.* Heinemann Educational (Asia), Kuala Lumpur

Hunkins F P 1980 *Curriculum Development: Program Planning and Improvement.* Merrill, Columbus, Ohio

Katz J 1974 *Education in Canada.* David and Charles, Newton Abbot

Kirst M W, Walker D F 1971 An analysis of curriculum policy making. *Rev. Educ. Res.* 41: 479–509

Lawton D 1975 *Class, Culture and the Curriculum.* Routledge and Kegan Paul, London

Lawton D 1980 *The Politics of the School Curriculum.* Routledge and Kegan Paul, London

Macdonald J B 1971 Curriculum development in relation to social and intellectual systems. In: McClure R M (ed.) 1971 *The Curriculum: Retrospect and Prospect,* 70th Yearbook of the Society for the Study of Education, Part 2. University of Chicago Press, Chicago, Illinois, pp. 95–113

McNeil J D 1977 *Curriculum: A Comprehensive Introduction.* Little, Brown, Boston, Massachusetts

Miel A 1946 *Changing the Curriculum: A Social Process.* Appleton-Century-Croft, New York

National Council for Social Studies 1981 *Essentials of Education.* National Council for Social Studies, Washington, DC

Nicholas E J 1980 A comparative view of curriculum development. In: Kelly A V (ed.) 1980 *Curriculum Context.* Harper and Row, London, pp. 150–72

Phillips J A, Hawthorne R 1978 Political dimensions of curriculum decision making. *Educ. Leadership* 35: 362–66

Pratt D 1980 *Curriculum, Design and Development.* Harcourt Brace Jovanovich, New York

Saylor J G, Alexander W M, Lewis A J 1981 *Curriculum Planning for Better Teaching and Learning,* 4th edn. Holt, Rinehart and Winston, New York

Skilbeck M 1984 *School-Based Curriculum Development.* Harper and Row, London

Simon R I 1980 Editorial. *Curric. Inq.* 10: 1–2

Smith B O, Stanley W O, Shores J H 1957 *Fundamentals of Curriculum Development*. World Book, Yonkers-on-Harcourt, Brace and World, New York

Sturges A W 1976 Forces influencing the curriculum. *Educ. Leadership* 34: 40–43

Taba H 1962 *Curriculum Development: Theory and Practice*. Harcourt, Brace and World, New York

Thomas R M, Sands L B, Brubaker D L (eds.) 1968 *Strategies for Curriculum Change: Cases From 13 Nations*. International Textbook, Scranton, Pennsylvania

Walker D F 1976 Toward comprehension of curricular realities. In: Shulman L S (ed.) 1976 *Review of Research in Education*, Vol. 4. Peacock, Itasca, Illinois, pp. 268–308

Zais R S 1976 *Curriculum: Principles and Foundations*. Crowell, New York

The Role of Textbooks

I. Westbury

The books which surround and support teaching of all kinds at all levels of instruction are the central tools and objects of attention in all schooling. The information carried within books defines, for many, the tasks of education; books are the most important resources which teachers and schools have as they do their work of educating. Indeed, it may be that the core work of all schooling consists in developing the skills and attitudes associated with the mastery of the ideas and information carried by books without regard to their "ultimate" quality and social significance. Certainly, as given in particular situations (as a result of prescription or availability), the books which a teacher has are often the most significant limitation on the capacity of a school or teacher to work out his or her own purposes. Educational development and curriculum development thus go hand-in-hand with textbook selection and writing. Yet, in spite of the centrality of the book to education, and in spite of the attention that has been given to aspects of the book (design, readability, bias in text, etc.), the textbook itself and its use, seen in holistic terms, is an elusive component of schooling, at least from the viewpoint of conventional educational research and theory.

1. The Book as an Educational "Tool"

Any treatment of the book in the context of education must distinguish the book as a general repository of information and ideas and a general medium of thought and communication from the book (or textbook) as a tool used within situations of formal education. While there is no necessary difference in the character or form of the book when used in general (i.e., recreational or information seeking) or educational settings, the ways in which the book is used do differ. Gowin (1981), for example, stipulates that the defining condition of an educational event is a teacher teaching meaningful materials (typically book-based information or expressions) to a student who grasps the meaning of the materials. He suggests that the prerequisite of such teaching is an awareness on the part of the teacher of the meanings embedded in his/her materials which can be shared within teacher–pupil interactions. Such interaction may use books in any of the following roles:

(a) as vehicles of criteria of excellence of thought or sensibility;

(b) as records of prior events which have the potential for making new events happen;

(c) as authoritative records of ideas or procedures;

(d) as organizers of bodies of concepts or information;

(e) as stimuli for the multiplication of meaning and the enhancement of experience—through reorganization of what is already known, for thinking or feeling, or as invitations to explore new patterns of relationship.

Different educational tasks are, following Gowin, associated with different kinds of text materials. In each case there is a body of critical questions to be asked about potential and actual meanings, and the materials which can carry those meanings, to make them suitable for recovery within educational contexts. Thus, a teacher or text author must ask which Greek tragedy, or which speech within a given tragedy, has the most potential for illuminating these ideas for these students; he or she must ask how a topic like mathematical modeling or correlation can be most appropriately simplified for this or that instructional purpose.

Less expository roles are also very common. For example, within examination-based traditions of schooling the textbook may be a "crib" which outlines a body of standardized information to be learned for representation in examination format and under examination conditions. Within mathematics, the textbook's primary function may be to provide a convenient collection of problems. For the teacher who emphasizes ideational fluency as a basis for writing, the optimal textbook may be one that contains many competing sources of ideas presented in many ways. It is difficult, if not impossible in these circumstances, to offer any generalizable considerations which might apply to all types of textbook.

2. The Textbook in Educational Theory and Research

Given such a conception of the role of texts within education, it might be assumed that the discussion of the book as an educational medium, and the ways books

476

might be used, would be major themes within educational research and theory. This is not the case; in the main the research, and the associated expository literature within education, is accepting of the educational and pedagogical assumptions embedded in the materials conventionally used within schools and is indifferent to the educational, institutional, and rhetorical issues and developments associated with various traditions of textbook development and use.

The textbook is an integral part of all "modern" technologies and systems of schooling. Looked at from the perspective of history, these systems (a) assume that the book is the repository of the knowledge that schools communicate, (b) are built around the existence of the textbook as a basic instrument for organizing curricula and as a basic tool for teaching and learning. For most of its history, teacher education has focused on the preparation of personnel for work within the existing system and not on the questioning, and recovery, of the assumptions that lie behind those systems. Animation of teachers rather than reformation has been the socially sanctioned core undertaking of teacher education and its related research and theory building.

All systems of organized education presume social understanding of the goals and means of education. In many school systems these social understandings are incorporated into curriculum control structures which use the textbook as a vehicle for making such expectations explicit. The concern of such systems centers on the enactment of conventional educational interactions rather than the self-conscious search for materials which can support educating as an abstract goal. Of course, the effects of such forces differ depending on the firmness and directionality of the norms associated with given kinds of education; in graduate education, the books which might be used, how they might be used, and the adequacy of the given set of texts vis-à-vis ends and varying definitions of subjects and fields are typically more open issues than they are for teachers in elementary schools.

Given these constraints on the ways in which educational research has defined its problems, fundamental research on textbooks has more often been undertaken by scholars in other fields. Training, advertising, trade publishing, and elite higher education have offered better contexts than "education" as such for the consideration of the ways in which text materials might be used and conceived. And the contributions which have been made to the understanding of textbooks as social, institutional, and cultural forms have more often come from sociologists of knowledge, science, and culture, intellectual historians, psychologists working in industrial and military training, and typographers and designers working in "trade publishing" rather than "educational research." Bridge building from these areas of professional concern into educational research has emerged as a self-conscious scholarly preoccupation only since the early 1970s and only in a small number of centers.

Research on *Learning from Textbooks* and on *Typographic Design* is reviewed in the Instructional Development Part of this Encyclopedia. Thus, further attention here is confined to issues of textbook content and textbook bias.

3. Textbook Content

A school or university subject is, most typically, a body of information about a field that is thought appropriate for the education of students, and, implicitly at least, an organization of that field that defines what the field is and what should be emphasized within it. Successful textbooks typically offer both an effective rhetoric and a widely accepted treatment of the scope of their fields. And there are many "important" textbooks [for example, the Physical Sciences Study Commission (PSSC) (1960) *Physics*] which have not been successful in the marketplace over the long run but have derived their significance from their impact on the definition of the content of the "subjects." In the topics they treat and the ways in which they are discussed, such textbooks create a norm which other textbooks follow.

This quality of many "classical" school and university textbooks illustrates one of the most important continuing tasks of textbook writing and development within an educational system. Thus, while in one sense the textbook is a medium of presentation of a subject, it is also an ordering of a subject for purposes of teaching and, as such, operationalizes the social construct that is represented by such words as "sixth-grade arithmetic" or "sixth-form British history." And, typically, it is the appearance of an appropriate textbook which creates a subject or a new definition of a subject as its presentation penetrates the consciousness of teachers. Later textbooks tend to follow the patterns offered by such innovative textbooks. And the "subjects" which follow often develop a life of their own in the schools as they become the object of attention in teacher education and define for the public at large what the content of schooling is—and, often, should be. And in such subjects it is often the framework which was created by the first textbooks which creates the terms of all subsequent teaching. Thus, as Hodgetts (1968) has pointed out, it was the concerns of Canadian historians of the 1920s which were still dominating the teaching of Canadian history in the schools in the late 1960s by way of a textbook tradition—despite the fact that the issues which concerned Canadians and Canadian historians were far distant from issues which created the interpretation of Canada's history in the 1920s.

This issue becomes especially difficult analytically if it is posited, as it must be, that no-one can know a discipline or a subject at first hand but must instead rely on secondary sources to develop even a tentative synthesis of the kind required to know or teach a subject. From this perspective any "original" development of a textbook must be a work of scholarly synthesis—as it often was and is in the case of first textbooks in a field or in the case of fundamental revisions of previous textbook content and knowledge. But such concerns are characteristically far different from the concerns of both teachers who are interested in the here-and-now problems of teaching their subjects as they are conventionally understood and textbook writers who are seeking to meet the needs of those teachers. As a consequence there are many instances in which the seeming facts and interpretations of subjects presented in textbooks are, from the viewpoint of the research worker and the "advanced" scholar in a field, egregiously incorrect. Their status as facts and canonical interpretations comes from repetition in the textbook tradition rather than from disciplinary-embedded understanding.

Awareness of these kinds of issues about textbook content has been extended in a number of different directions by researchers. Sociologists of science have suggested that from the viewpoint of the socialization of students who work in routine scientific research, such issues are of little consequence. It is the task of students to learn the traditional content whatever it may be, with the implication that the social structures of such sciences only grant the freedom to question such interpretations to those who have passed the test of mastery of such interpretations. Schwab (1978), on the other hand, has suggested that the tentativeness of all knowledge must be communicated to students from the beginning of their study of a subject by means of treatments that convey firmly the revisionary character of all subjects.

Howson and Westbury (1980) have suggested that if it is assumed that most subjects are textbook based, there is a body of important research on the ways in which "new" understandings of what content should be treated in textbooks, and how that content should be treated, that emerges. Drawing on examples from mathematics they suggest that two different processes can be seen lying behind content revision or content invention within mathematics education: the translation of ideas from advanced mathematics into ideas which are amenable to treatment within schools by a process of "making accessible" (Kirsch 1976) and the development of embodiments by which mathematical ideas and classroom experiences are given form appropriate to classroom work. They suggest further that in all such processes of content invention there are important questions about the processes which determine the propensity of both individuals and groups to engage in authentic inventive activity.

Educational research has given little attention to the social processes which are associated with either content development and invention or the reception of content developments by teachers and schools. Both school systems and historical periods vary in their inventive capability, or, in other words, in their capacity to engage in content revision and content development and in the receptivity of schools or subsystems of schools to such content revision and development, but little research has been done on such issues. There are suggestions that in some fields at least the content found in the dominant school textbooks changes very slowly, but most such perceptions are speculative rather than firmly grounded in the analysis of actual textbook content.

4. Textbook Bias

The values and attitudes that are taught in schools are of obvious and central interest to the parents of schoolchildren, and to those who are concerned with the social futures that the patterns of schooling seem to foreshadow or with the world view that the schools seem to reflect at a given time. When the values that the schools reflect become inconsistent with the values that groups or individuals hold as important or critical to their futures, bias is often claimed. This charge reflects, however, the perspective of the person or persons making the charge: it can be made when schooling seems to threaten to reject or denigrate traditional values of religion and morality, nationality, race or ethnicity, sex roles and sexuality, and the like, or it can be made *because* schooling reflects these values.

The study of education finds its most typical starting points in the values represented by the idea of education itself and, as a result, the sustained study of the biases represented in schooling reflects liberal and cosmopolitan values and value systems. This article will describe some of the basic characteristics and dimensions of studies of textbook bias that have been undertaken within a broadly liberal framework. It should be remembered, of course, that perhaps the majority of those concerned with the forms of bias found within schooling would be indifferent to, and may even actively reject the assumptions of the work that will be discussed here. One 1972 opinion poll of United States school administrators found, for example, that 84 percent of the respondents did not think that a significant sex bias existed in elementary-school textbooks (Pottker and Fishel 1977). And in some countries at least, textbooks and other school materials are regularly removed from the schools because of their advocacy of "liberal" and "modern" values.

4.1 Textbook Bias and Textbook Revision: History

Beginning in the nineteenth century, European scholars have shown a continuing preoccupation with the extent to which school textbooks nurture and reflect crude nationalist and ethnocentric attitudes in their presentation of national histories and nationally oriented geographies. This has created a sustained concern for the specification of particular biases and distortions that might be found in texts, the revision of these texts, and the development of recommendations for future texts which might avoid the problems that had been identified. Research and dissemination activity within this tradition has been undertaken by national, bilateral, and multilateral working parties and has been given substantial institutional support by many national, regional, and international agencies, for example, UNESCO and the Council of Europe (Schüddekopf 1967).

Although an increasing variety of analytic methods are to be found in this work, the principal method is critical interpretation of the manifest content of texts, from the points of view both of omission and commission. The most distinctive characteristics are the strong normative concern and the concern for determining what an appropriate treatment of a particular topic should contain. The checklists of sources of distortion that have been developed within the tradition of possible sources of bias are one of the distinctive achievements of this field of study. Billington (1966), for example, in his discussion of the nationalistic biases of Anglo-American history textbooks identified the following sources of such distortion:

(a) The bias of inertia—the perpetuation of legends and half truths and the failure to keep abreast of scholarship.

(b) Bias by omission—the selection of information that reflects credit only on the writer's nation.

(c) Bias in use of language—the use of words with favorable connotations to describe one group and those with unfavorable connotations to describe another.

(d) Bias by cumulative implication—the tendency to give all credit to one nation or group.

4.2 Content Analysis of Textbooks

A parallel tradition of analysis of bias in textbooks has emerged in the years since the Second World War which draws on the methodologies of "content" and "propaganda analysis." This work builds on the assumption that the manifest and latent "messages" contained within texts and other communicative media penetrate the consciousness of readers as a result of their cumulative effect; research seeks to expose the character of this accumulation by measuring the frequency of given kinds of messages.

Content analysis proceeds by positing a universe of concerns and seeking indices which can be used to measure how a concern is treated in a particular set of messages. The universe can be defined in terms of the frequency with which a given attitude object appears in a text, the form of representation given the attitude object by its referential context (i.e., the quality of the activity in which different actors figure), and the strength or intensity of the term that links an attitude object with its referential context. All of the qualities that might be found associated with these components of a message system can be reliably measured.

In the recent past, many studies using one or another method of content analysis and one or another focus of analysis have been undertaken to explore gender and ethnic stereotyping with textbooks. The common outcome is the discovery of profound and pervasive stereotyping and bias in the textbooks used in many subjects and many nations.

5. Textbook Development and Distribution

In many nations, textbook development is the task of commercial textbook publishing companies. As such, the major factor that affects development practices is the marketability of the resulting textbook. While different traditions of textbook use within schools, different textbook adoption practices, and different curricular and instructional traditions open a variety of commercial possibilities for profitable textbook publishing, marketability and profitability are always the principal goals of commercial publishing (Broudy 1975, Goldstein 1978).

The other common mode of textbook development is through government or ministry-based centers or projects. These may have a monopoly over textbook production or there may be some form of mixed economy. In either case the cost of textbook development, production and distribution is a formidable barrier to wide content coverage, experiments with new approaches and regular updating. Not surprisingly, therefore, the influence of a Western commercial publishing industry is still strong in many nations. This is more fully discussed below in the article *Transnational Influences in Publishing*.

The distribution of textbooks has been shown to be a critical factor affecting successful learning in many less industrialized societies. Surveys have been conducted in 10 countries which included data on pupil achievement and access to reading materials in schools, and 15 of these studies, in areas as diverse as mathematics, science, reading, and language, have reported positive correlations between the availability of textbook materials and pupil achievement. This finding can be compared to parallel findings about the effects of variables like teacher training on academic achievement where the results of studies indicate more ambiguous effects. Heyneman et al. (1981) have concluded on the basis of such studies that the availability of a textbook to a student should be one of the central concerns of planners and administrators in such school systems; the provision of textbooks to students is a significant focus for efforts at school improvement on a systemwide basis. It also seems that textbook provision to lower social status students has significant effects in assisting the learning of such students.

Bibliography

Billington R A 1966 *The Historian's Contribution to Anglo-American Misunderstanding.* Hobbs, Dorman, New York

Broudy E 1975 The trouble with textbooks. *Teach. Coll. Rec.* 77(1): 13–34

Council of Europe 1974 *Religion in School History Textbooks in Europe.* Council of Europe, Strasbourg

Goldstein P 1978 *Changing the American Schoolbook.* Lexington Books, Lexington, Massachusetts

Gowin D B 1981 *Educating*. Cornell University Press, Ithaca, New York

Heyneman S P, Farrell J P, Sepulveda-Stuardo M A 1981 Textbooks and achievement in developing countries: What we know. *J. Curric. Stud.* 13(3): 227–46

Hodgetts A B 1968 *What Culture: What Heritage?* OISE Curriculum Series, No. 5. Ontario Institute for Studies in Education, Toronto, Ontario

Howson A G, Westbury I 1980 Creative activity in mathematics education: A first attempt at definition and problem-identification. *Comparative Studies of Mathematics Curricula: Stability and Change 1960-80*. Materialien und Studien Band 19. Institut für Didaktik der Mathematik, Universität Bielefeld, Bielefeld

Kirsch A 1976 Aspects of simplification in mathematics teaching. *Proceedings of the Third International Congress on Mathematics Education*. International Congress on Mathematics Education, Karlsruhe

Lorimer R, Long M 1979 Sex-role stereotyping in elementary readers. *Interchange* 19(2): 25–45

McDiarmid G, Pratt D 1971 *Teaching Prejudice*. Ontario Institute for Studies in Education, Toronto

Pottker J, Fishel A (ed.) 1977 *Sex Bias in Schools*. Associated University Press, Cranbury, New Jersey

Schüddekopf O-E 1967 *History Teaching and History Textbook Revision*. Council of Europe, Strasbourg

Schwab J J 1978 *Science, Curriculum and Liberal Education*. University of Chicago Press, Chicago, Illinois

Curriculum Packages

E. L. Baker

A curriculum package is a set of coordinated instructional materials designed to achieve particular goals. These materials may either provide for extended instructional time, for example, two weeks or a year, or be limited to a brief period. Often these materials consist of multiple activities, perhaps in different media. They consist at least of materials for the direct use by students, and adjunct materials to assist the teacher, or another instructor, such as the parent.

1. Two Types of Curriculum Packages

What distinguishes the curriculum "package" from curricula of the unpackaged type? The answer depends upon which type of curriculum package one means. The emergence of the idea of curriculum package came from two very distinct sources. One source was based on the revision of curriculum movements that occurred in the United States in the late 1950s and early 1960s, which strived to change both the content and the method of instruction. The focus of this effort was to improve and to update the content presented in public education. Courses were developed in social science, laboratory science, English language, and mathematics, and these courses were designed to present the most accurate view of the discipline in terms that children could understand. In addition to the reformation of content, the "new" curricula emphasized inquiry approaches. Students were encouraged to inquire about the nature of the discipline, to use discovery methods based largely on their autonomous application of the processes of the discipline, in contrast to earlier pedagogical styles that emphasized memory, drill, and practice. Curriculum packages answering the demands for changes of these types provided multiple options for students and teachers and emphasized outcomes focused on skill in using particular procedures, for example, observation and verification. Typically, such packages were designed to provide resources for a year, or even longer.

Almost concurrently, a second source of today's curriculum package was developing in the work of behavioral psychology. In this framework, instruction was conceived as the process of controlling learning through cues and feedback, and "programmed instruction" was the earliest school-oriented product of this line of research. Critical features of such packages were operationally stated objectives, criterion tasks, self-paced learning, gradually increasing difficulty, active participation, and feedback. Curriculum packages evolving from this line of development might be course length or as short as a 15 minute, single concept program (see Part 4(d) on Individualized Learning Systems).

2. Characteristics of Curriculum Packages

Despite having origins in the content reform movement and the operant learning movement, there are at least some common elements that define today's curriculum package, and while other curricula may share some of the features in combination they seem to circumscribe the universe of curriculum packages. First, a package is directed to a set of goals. These goals may be broadly focused on learning a process, for example, judgment, or directly tied to particular skills and content, for example, computational skills. Often, these goals are translated into behavioral skills, and component tasks (Gagné 1973) may be specified. A common set of goals may be specified for all learners, or differentiation of goals may occur as a function of individual differences, task complexity, or creativity. In many cases, particular activities and resources, or units of instruction, may be keyed to particular goals.

A second feature of curriculum packages is that they are self-contained, that is, they provide sufficient resources for instruction. In some cases, they may be used without extensive modification, improvisation, or instructional planning by the user. Materials presented to children directly may have a self-instructional flavor. They may offer a sequenced set of self-paced instruction to students. This sort of instruction derives from behavioral psychology and programmed instruction, especially the idea that learners should be given relevant practice on specified objectives. Other packages may be organized to present coordinated tasks for students using a variety of methods, cued, for example, by color-coded materials. For instance, in a set of materials designed to teach "main idea" in reading comprehension, students might be given the opportunity to read various paragraphs and to select the main idea from a list of choices. Additional tasks on the same general skill might include asking the student to provide the "best" title for a story, to write a brief story when given a title, or to draw a picture when given a particular topic. From a learning perspective, all these tasks might be considered relevant, particularly if a student's view of reading comprehension is atheoretical. Under specific learning theories, certain of the above tasks would be deleted. Other learning or curriculum packages, with stronger ties, perhaps, to the content reformation lineage, would not consist of particular instruction for students, but might present a wide range of resources, including simulated drafts of important historical documents, materials to conduct scientific experiments, and other manipulatives. These materials provide a library of resources for the learners that may be used in infinite ways.

In addition to the variety of particular activities provided for the student, the teacher may be provided with a set of coordinated, or at least compatible, options to use in teaching. These options may include directions for rearranging the group into teams for auxiliary games, providing information for students prior to their individual or team activity, suggestions for discussion, media presentations, or posters or drawings for display during the instructional unit. A wide range is found in the amount, type, and specificity of these instructions to teachers. In certain packages, they may be included in a teacher's edition of the major text. They may be provided as a separate volume or as a teacher's manual or leader's guide. In part, these decisions relate to the number of options suggested and the specificity of the suggestions. At the most general end of the continuum, the teacher may be merely presented with a list of references on the topic, with the assumption that the teacher will obtain the appropriate materials and extract from them ideas to augment the provided materials. At the other end of the continuum, certain manuals are provided with complete scripts for the teacher to use, with the assumption that compliance will lead to effective implementation of the package. Underlying this assumption was the general idea that materials can and should be made "teacher-proof," a notion which regards teacher contribution as a "noise" or interference in the system. Less severe versions of that notion result in the inclusion of lesson plans for the teacher to use. In either case, however, the intent is to provide instruction to the student with the teacher as adjunct mediator rather than

using the teacher's own experience, knowledge of setting, and intelligence as a principal organizing element. The choice of teachers' role may depend upon estimates of their familiarity with curriculum content, the quality of the teachers, and the evidence, or strength of belief, that instructional cues provided to the teacher result, in fact, in desired student performance.

Curricula need to be "packaged" when more than one artifact is provided. As implied above, a minimum package contains something for the student and something for the teacher. More frequently, however, a range of materials is provided. These materials may provide different instructional methods, different particular tasks, and may use different formats and media for instruction. For instance, one would have a package when the student is provided with a text, a workbook, or set of worksheets coordinated with the text, and a teacher's guide. More elaborate multimedia packages may contain games (with all necessary paraphernalia, such as board, tokens, scoring procedures), records, audiotapes, discs for the microcomputer, films, videotapes, or videodiscs.

In addition, other components may be included, particularly procedures for assessing student progress. Such procedures may be as simple as a tracking mechanism to monitor where the student is in a set of hierarchically structured materials, perhaps presented on a wall chart. Special grade books, or student-managed record sheets may provide the teacher and student with a clear sense of accomplishment.

More direct estimates of student accomplishment, that is, their actual performance, can be made from assessment materials that may be found in such packages. These procedures may include general ideas for testing, a list of suggestions for questions, or projects presented in the teachers' guide. In some cases, actual tests to be used for pretesting, progress assessment, and grading are included, either as prototypes, ready for local duplication and distribution, or in numbers appropriate for class administration. Quizzes, for either group or self-administration, may also be available, some with answer keys for the student. The quality and care with which these assessment instruments are developed represents another feature which varies greatly from package to package. Tests may cover only the information or the content provided and ignore the complex cognitive processes the student has learned. The tests may favor a particular format, for example, multiple-choice tests, without particular reference to the validity of the procedure or to the objectives as stated in the curriculum. If essay or project-based assessments are suggested, criteria are very rarely provided for the reliable scoring of student performance. By and large, these assessment devices are presented de novo with no technical information related to reliability and validity of the devices. This lack of information is unlikely to be an oversight and more probably results because no technical base exists for the assessment instruments.

3. Trends in Using Curriculum Packages

A critical question surrounding the use of these curriculum packages relates to their effectiveness. Although it was before the 1960s that standards for the assessment of curriculum packages were first provided (see Lumsdaine 1963 for a description), most curriculum packages distributed for school use do not receive any systematic validation, particularly extended trials with teachers and learners where student achievement is the principal criterion. In fact, these recommendations had more effect on the field of achievement measurement, leading to the field of criterion-referenced measurement (Glaser 1963) than on the field of curriculum (see *Criterion-referenced Measurement*). Even though a network of educational laboratories in the United States was specifically created to provide a model for the systematic design and revision of such packages based on their effects on student achievement, most curriculum packages do not go through this research and development process. The reason commonly provided is that the costs of such trials are too high. Another valid reason relates the differential goals of some curriculum packages, particularly those designed to serve as general resources or as a cache of activities for the teacher to use. The different processes of implementation, idiosyncratic to the teacher, make the use of a standard assessment difficult. However, the quality of projects or other "creative" work could be judged and evaluation of practicality, content accuracy, and satisfaction could provide sufficient information for an informed adoption to be made. At the present time, however, few curricula come with estimates of their effectiveness (see *Evaluation of Learning Resources*).

In view of the lack of information available about the quality of most curriculum packages, under what conditions should they be used? Packages of the highly structured sort requiring minimal contribution by teachers may be most appropriate when the content area is likely to be unfamiliar to the teacher or when the pool of teachers or the available teacher training is marginal, or when there is a need to differentiate instruction so that a subset of students can proceed, or review, with relative independence. For those curricular materials that provide resources for the teaching of processes or inquiry, it is important to ensure settings that include teachers and students with sufficient background, for example, in terms of reading comprehension for students, and subject matter familiarity for teachers. In either case, local educational agencies can make their own contribution to the utility of curriculum packages by documenting, in relatively simple terms, their usefulness and other performance information teachers can make available. At least, others in the same school system would have some basis for choice.

The future of curriculum packages will undoubtedly be linked with emerging technologies, particularly the personal computer. Curriculum packages must still be directed to educational goals and be based on sound pedagogy. Maintaining such concerns in the light of rapidly growing courseware markets and astounding advances in the visual technologies will require vigilence by those concerned with student learning.

Bibliography

Baker E L 1973 The technology of instructional development. In: Travers R M W (ed.) 1973 *Second Handbook of Research on Teaching: A Project of the American Educational Research Association*. Rand McNally, Chicago, Illinois, pp. 245–85

Gagné R M 1973 *The Conditions of Learning*. Holt, Rinehart and Winston, New York

Glaser R 1963 Instructional technology and the measurement of learning outcomes: Some questions. *Am. Psychol.* 18(8): 519–21

Lange P C (ed.) 1967 *Programmed Instruction*. The Sixty-sixth Yearbook of the National Society for the Study of Education, Part 2. National Society for the Study of Education, Chicago, Illinois, pp. 104-38

Lumsdaine A A 1963 Instruments and media of instruction. In: Gage N L (ed.) 1963 *Handbook of Research on Teaching: A Project of the American Educational Research Association*. Rand McNally, Chicago, Illinois

Transnational Influences in Publishing

S. Gopinathan

This article deals with transnational publishing and its impact on educational development in the Third World. The processes and effects of educational transfer and in particular the transfer of curricular models and materials are seen as poorly researched and understood. Links established on an official and bilateral basis for aid educational transfer serve to perpetuate Third World dependence and transnational publishers benefit from their links to home-based curriculum institutions and experts on loan. While transnational publishers gain considerable commercial benefit and help internationalize educational experiences and strategies, their activities are often detrimental to the development of indigenous publishing and intellectual capacity. Steps are now being taken to reduce this dependence.

The processes and problems inherent in the generation and international transfer of teaching materials have been one of the least studied aspects of the internationalization and diffusion of knowledge relevant to education. This has been ignored both in the few studies of international publishing and in the much larger corpus of writing on educational development and reform in the Third World. This lack of knowledge is indeed surprising considering that such a traffic is at least as old as colonialism—America's most popular arithmetic text in the 1770s was Thomas Dilworth's *The Schoolmaster's Assistant*, a reprint of an English text. Yet research in this field is important if the relationship is to be understood between the transfer of Western educational models and paradigms on the one hand, and Western curricula and teaching materials on the other. Studying such varied agencies as the Examination Syndicates in the United Kingdom, the Education Development Center in Boston (United States), national and international aid agencies, and transnational publishing houses should illuminate our understanding of patterns of ideological and commercial influence.

Part of the reason for a lack of scholarly attention may have been due to the assumption that pedagogy was neutral and therefore unproblematic and because attention was focused on school–society relations: gaining control over private sector education, expansion of facilities, and access for minorities were typically the problems that merited attention. Some attention was paid to medium of instruction issues but even here discussion dealt not so much with in-school issues such as poor achievement, relevance of policy, curriculum or methodology, and availability of materials as with questions of national integration and identity.

Several reasons may be advanced why studies of educational transfer and of international educational publishing may be considered of crucial relevance now. One reason is the continued dominance of the print medium in the classrooms in the Third World; indeed, faced with the enormous problems involved in producing teachers for still-expanding systems, some planners are hoping for "teacher-proof textbooks" to solve some of the problems. More positively, studies of cognitive achievement in the Third World show that textbook availability is an important factor (Heyneman et al. 1978). The World Bank, a major influence in promoting and internationalizing educational strategies, has projects in 10 countries worth US$38 million involving textbook purchase or development; in Indonesia the World Bank has embarked on an eight-year US$39 million project to develop curricula, train teachers, and produce 138 million textbooks in elementary-school core subjects for grades 1 through 6. Similar projects are underway in the Philippines, and in some African countries (Wagner 1979 p. 42). Finally, with the apparent failure of such curricular reforms as vocationalization and ruralization of curriculum to produce skills and improve opportunity, attention is once again focused on the means of enhancing cognitive development.

Recent scholarly work offers new perspectives with which to study educational transfer in the Third World. Apple (1979), for example, has explored the assumptions underlying the selection of curricular knowledge and transmission modes; and Altbach (Altbach and McVey 1976, Altbach and Rathgeber 1980) and Smith (1977) have discussed the role of publishing in an un-

equal system of intellectual relations. This enables us to treat pedagogic and curricular materials issues as significant and critical, and to place them firmly within a global perspective. If there are strong forces for internationalization, it is true as well that there is a counter pressure for a more conscious indigenization process especially in social science as a means of resisting the intellectual dependence that characterizes the Third World. This struggle is bound to leave its mark on how issues of curriculum and pedagogy are treated in the 1980s.

The continued influence of transnational publishing houses in the educational life of Third World nations is the cumulative effect of two sets of interrelated structures. The more important, since they provide the foundation, are the bilateral links established at an official level. These links give rise to programs for the enhancement of local expertise for curriculum and evaluation reform through training attachments and the loan of curriculum experts to Third World ministries of education; on another level it allows such institutions as the British Council via its scholarships, library and information services, and provision of experts and materials to have significant access to and influence on ministries of education, especially in the area of English language teaching. These linkages while an outgrowth of colonial experience—which explains why American publishers and curriculum innovations have less of an impact in ex-British territories—have in many instances been extended and strengthened, often on the initiative of Third World governments. The very real need for expertise, however, often leads to an uncritical reliance on experts willingly loaned and whose perceptions of the problems must of necessity be limited.

Indeed, it is a wonder that the objectivity of the foreign expert is so often taken for granted. The number of experts who were already authors, or who went on to write textbooks is legion; in a similar fashion, attachment of local experts to complex curriculum projects overseas has often led to subsequent adoption.

The structures which "deliver" the actual materials for classroom use are the transnational publishing houses; in British Commonwealth nations these would be the overseas branches of such publishers as Oxford University Press, Longmans, Macmillan, Heinemann Educational Books, Thomas Nelson, and Evans Brothers. It matters little that they are often locally incorporated, that they have local citizens as chief executives, or that much of their turnover comes from locally oriented publishing. These characteristics make it easier for governments to continue to deal with them. Though these publishing houses do have substantial backlists, financial resources, and production expertise to aid them, it is their access to the experts and the academic establishment back home, seen by local ministry of education officials as neutral and noncommercial, that is the most useful. While indigenous publishers can and do master the technical expertise required for publishing, the sort of intellectual inputs noted above remain beyond them;

where local academic expertise is available it tends to be attracted to the greater professionalism and better sales opportunities and prestige that transnationals offer. Indigenous publishers' inability, in a capital-intensive industry, to take the long view, to offer a series of textbooks, supplementary materials like workbooks and readers for a number of grade levels at one time, often means that even in more localized educational systems, transnational publishers will continue to dominate in secondary and postsecondary education (Gopinathan 1976). Where major national examinations are tied to overseas examination syndicates (Watson 1980) and the English language continues to be a major medium of instruction such dominance is intensified.

The reason for maintaining this dominance is simple enough for what is portrayed at one level as an intellectual exchange is on another a vital commercial one. Of all British books 37 percent are sold overseas; 20 percent of British book exports are of educational books. It is not an exaggeration to say that British educational publishing cannot survive without overseas markets. It has been estimated that the combined 1976–77 turnover of the six British publishers listed earlier is a total of £92.2 million of which £50 and £30 million came from Africa and the Far East respectively; sales in Nigeria alone accounted for £35 million.

Profit making can coexist with the enrichment of educational systems and the enhancement of indigenous capacity and expertise; in many instances transnational publishers were the only source for books and they have trained a whole generation of book industry personnel in Third World countries. It is also the case that it is often the desire of local administrators to imitate foreign models that keeps Third World educational systems captive. Nevertheless, it does seem fair criticism that many curriculum projects accepted by Third World nations have had little long-term impact on enhancing school achievement. At one time or another since the early 1970s, Third World countries have been offered innovatory programs and materials in science (BSCS, Nuffield), in mathematics (School Mathematics Project), in social studies (*Man—A Course of Study*), in English as a second language (language laboratories and accompanying software), and encouragement to invest in educational technology (educational radio and television). These have often been accepted as they seemed to represent development and progress; today many of these programs have been abandoned as unsuitable or drastically scaled back, victims both of pedagogical fashion and irrelevance to the most urgent educational problems in the Third World.

It has not very often been acknowledged that the transfer of curriculum materials poses real problems for pedagogy which have as yet not been adequately addressed. Adaptation of materials has often been suggested as an answer to the demands of relevance and while there are some examples of adequate adaptation, much of the adaptation practiced continues to be "scissors and paste" and the "purchase" of names of local experts to go on the covers of books to give them legitimacy. In the Far East in the 1970s one British publisher was able to use one English language textbook series to produce up to five versions for pupils in such diverse school systems as India and Hong Kong; on a smaller scale, this was to happen in mathematics, science, history, and geography as well. That this was possible at all in countries undergoing major social and educational change such as Hong Kong, Singapore, and Malaysia in the 1970s, says much for the progress made in internationalizing curricula. Nevertheless, this is only evidence that transnational publishers can and do contribute to internationalizing educational experiences and pre-empting effective indigenization. It leaves unanswered the question of whether the transfer has been pedagogically successful and that may only be answered when more is known about the norms of child development in different cultures, the effects of using a foreign language as a medium of instruction, the transferability of programmed instruction, open classrooms, and other strategies developed in a high-income, print-oriented culture.

One trend that will bear watching in the 1980s is the increasing attention being given to "learning packages," promoted as combining the best in print and nonprint techniques. This is in part a reflection of the increasing pressure for the inclusion of more and more technology into education, both on grounds of efficiency in enhancing cognitive development and as a less costly alternative to more schools and teachers. In much the same way and for the same reasons that some Western governments supported book subsidy programs like the English Language Book Scheme (ELBS) sponsored by the United Kingdom and the United States-run Indo-American Textbook Program (PL480), Third World nations are likely to be persuaded of the economy of technology. It may however be expected that such innovations are likely to produce as many problems as solutions. Technical solutions are not as neutral as they seem and are unlikely to solve problems inherent in the cultural and social context in which instruction takes place. Little systematic research exists on the merits of a technology-based approach for low-income countries. Indeed, it is probable that investment in such technology by locking Third World educational systems into those of developed countries will narrow options and the search for more viable alternatives and may thus prove ultimately more costly. It is necessary to be more aware of the ideological and commercial underpinnings of educational innovations.

One solution to the dependence upon transnational publishers can be the encouragement of state intervention in educational publishing. But as the experience of some African countries has shown, transnational publishers can exploit such a development and be the main beneficiaries of such intervention. But there have been more positive developments. A large number of countries in the Third World have established Book Development Councils to formulate and coordinate book policies and these can aid the growth and use of indigenously published materials. Following a change in the medium of instruction, institutions like Malaysia's Dewan Babasa and the various state textbook agencies in India have major educational roles to play in producing curricular materials in national languages. University presses being encouraged in Third World countries now provide academics a respectable alternative; there are encouraging signs too that academics are awakening to the need to write textbooks as well as publish the results of their research within the country. Such steps, if encouraged and developed, would contribute immensely to the evolution of an independent intellectual community in Third World nations.

Transnational educational publishers have in their possession a vast and rich array of material and expertise valuable to educational development in the Third World. Further, this is a resource that will be continually added to because of the research and financial resources available to transnational publishers. The solution to the problems outlined above lies therefore not in rejection but in understanding the ideological and commercial costs of such use and in gaining control over the processes by which Third World educational problems are defined and solutions attempted. Curriculum reformers will need in particular to learn to walk the tightrope between learning from educational exper-

iences elsewhere and of adopting uncritically these experiences; to use the foreign expert and to avoid being used by them. Only when such an understanding results in relevant and viable educational reform will indigenous publishing find for itself a productive and significant role in national educational development.

Bibliography

Altbach P G, McVey S (eds.) 1976 *Perspectives on Publishing*. Heath, Lexington, Massachusetts
Altbach P G, Rathgeber E-M 1980 *Publishing in the Third World*. Trend report and bibliography. Praeger, New York
Apple M W 1979 *Ideology and Curriculum*. Routledge and Kegan Paul, London
Gopinathan S 1976 Publishing in a plural society: The case of Singapore. In: Altbach P G, McVey S (eds.) 1976
Heyneman S P, Farrell J P, Sepulveda-Stuardo M A 1978 *Textbooks and Achievement: What We Know*. World Bank Staff Working Paper No. 298. World Bank, Washington, DC
Smith K B 1977 The impact of transnational book publishing on knowledge in less-developed countries. *Prospects* 7: 299–308
Wagner S 1979 Textbooks in Third World education: The World Bank's changing role. *Publishers Weekly* March 26, 1979
Watson K 1980 Influences and constraints on curriculum development in the Third World. *Can. Int. Educ.* 9 (2): 28–42

Curriculum Implementation

M. Fullan

Curriculum implementation is the process of putting a change into practice. It differs from the adoption of a change (the decision to use something new) in that the focus is on the extent to which actual change in practice occurs and on those factors which influence the extent of change. The idea of implementation and the factors affecting active use seem simple enough, but the concept has proven difficult to define. The following aspects of implementation are examined in order to identify the main issues: (a) implementation in perspective; (b) approaches to defining implementation; (c) components of implementation; (d) factors affecting implementation; (e) measurement and evaluation; and (f) planning for implementation.

1. Implementation in Perspective

There is no need to dwell on the fact that the vast majority of curriculum development efforts in the 1960s and 1970s did not get implemented in practice. Implementation is critically important because it refers to the means of accomplishing desired educational objectives. In perspective, most researchers see three broad, overlapping phases to the educational change process:

(a) initiation, development, or adoption; (b) implementation or use; and (c) institutionalization and other outcomes (Berman 1981). It can be seen that the amount and quality of change which occurs or fails to occur at (b) will significantly affect what outcomes are achieved in any given change effort.

It is also important to raise the question of whether implementation per se is always desirable. While change for the sake of change is not by definition good, neither is implementation. It depends on the answers to two questions: Are the objectives and goals which the particular change purports to address highly valued (by whichever criterion groups are used)? What is the technical quality of the change in relation to accomplishing the goals in question?

With the above perspective as context, various aspects of the implementation question can now be examined in more detail. It is necessary to recognize (a) that there are at least two different schools of thought or approaches to defining and researching implementation (see Sect. 2); (b) that actual use must be examined (involving different components—see Sect. 3); (c) that factors influencing use should be identified (see Sect. 4); (d) that measurement and evaluation issues arise at all phases and aspects of the change process (see Sect. 5); and (e) that no matter how adept people become at researching and explaining the implementation process, it is entirely another matter to develop effective planning procedures for bringing about better implementation (see Sect. 6).

Finally, while most of the references used in this article are from Canada and the United States, it is the case that interest in implementation problems is a worldwide phenomenon. [For some sources outside North America see Frey and Haft 1982, Lewy and Nevo 1981, and the international projects on educational implementation coordinated by the Centre for Educational Research and Innovation, the Organisation for Economic Co-operation and Development (CERI/OECD), and International Movements Toward Educational Change (IMTEC) in Oslo, Norway.]

2. Approaches to Defining Implementation

Implementation consists of putting into practice something which is new to the person who is attempting to bring about a change. Changes can be in the form of externally developed innovations or ones which are locally or self-developed. In either case, individual implementers are involved in a process of change. There are two distinct approaches to implementation in the research literature, one of which is labeled the "fidelity or programmed approach," the other the "mutually adaptive or adaptive approach." The two approaches are based on different assumptions and methodologies, and therefore it is necessary to separate clearly their main features.

The fidelity or programmed orientation as the label implies rests on the assumption that the main goal of implementation for selected changes is to bring about and assess the extent to which actual use corresponds "faithfully" to the kind of use intended by the developer or sponsor of the innovation. The assumption is that the change has certain program requirements established by its developer(s), which in turn can be installed and assessed for any group of users attempting to use the new practice. While minor variations might be tolerated, the emphasis is clearly on ensuring that practice conforms to the developer's intentions (Berman 1981, Fullan and Pomfret 1977, Crandall et al. 1982, Hall and Loucks 1977).

The adaptation approach on the other hand, assumes that the exact nature of implementation cannot and/or should not be prespecified, but rather should evolve as different groups of users decide what is best and most appropriate for their situation. There are different degrees of adaptation which might be envisaged ranging from minor adaptations (which is quite close to fidelity) through mutual adaptation (in which an external idea or innovation influences what users do while users more or less equally transform the idea for their situation), to evolutionary changes (in which the users evolve all sorts of uses according to their own interests, i.e., the adaptation is not mutual). Problems of mutual adaptation are discussed by Berman (1981), Fullan and Pomfret (1977), and Fullan (1981).

While there are different points on the fidelity–adaptive continuum, it is the case that different researchers and planners tend to stress one or the other approach. Those with a fidelity orientation formulate indicators to assess the degree of homogeneous implementation performance, while those with an adaptive orientation expect, encourage, and look for variations in practice. Fidelity emphasizes a priori specificity and structure, while adaptation is based on relatively unstructured, more open-ended premises (Fullan 1981). Berman (1981) suggests the interesting proposition that programmed (fidelity) approaches are appropriate under certain conditions (clear and consensual goals, well-worked out innovations, minor focused changes, etc.) while adaptive approaches are more effective under the opposite conditions (conflict over goals, incomplete development, major changes). Regardless of the situation however, the values of individual decision makers frequently determine whether a more structured (programmed) or more pluralistic (adaptive) approach is favored (see Fullan 1981 for some comparison of the United States and the United Kingdom in this regard).

Clearly, the assumptions and approach taken to implementation, influences to a great extent how research on implementation is conducted. Programmed changes have the advantage of being more clear, more specific, and easier to assess; but they also may be inappropriate for all or some situations and/or lead to rejection by individuals and groups who do not wish to use the particular version being advocated. Adaptive changes have the advantage of allowing for more individual choice, and development suited to a variety of situations; but they frequently create confusion about what should be done, and certainly from a research point of view are exceedingly difficult to assess (as the change is continually evolving, and varies across situations).

3. Components of Implementation

Components of implementation refer to what is meant by change in practice. Several researchers have stressed that change in practice is multidimensional, that is, there are a number of components of existing practice which are altered as a result of implementing something new. Leithwood (1981) spells out eight distinct dimensions of curricular implementation in describing changes in global conceptions, objectives, content, instructional material, teaching strategies, and the like. In a recent large-scale study of innovative practices in the United States, Crandall et al. (1982) have further developed the conceptual and methodological basis for measuring components of implementation in use.

In short, given curriculum changes whether they are externally or locally developed involve a number of changes in terms of what teachers (and others) think and do. Altering aspects of one's beliefs, using new curricular materials and technologies, employing new teaching strategies and learning diagnoses are all aspects of components of implementation. Further, the notion of components can be applied to both fidelity and adaptive approaches with the former consisting of identifying and measuring components contained in the developer's version, while the latter involves identifying and assessing what has changed in practice from what a person was previously doing regardless of other people's images of the change (Crandall et al. 1982).

4. Factors Affecting Implementation

Taken as a whole, implementation is a process over time by which people, events, and resources determine whether or not practice is altered when something new is attempted. Although the list of factors in any one situation can be quite large and variable, research since about 1965 has succeeded in identifying a number of factors commonly found to influence change in practice. These factors can be divided into four broad categories: (a) characteristics pertaining to the curriculum change being attempted; (b) local contextual conditions at the school district and school levels; (c) local strategies at the district and school levels used to foster implementation; and (d) external (to local) factors affecting the likelihood of implementation (Berman 1981, Fullan 1982). Research on each of these four sets of variables is reviewed briefly. In interpreting the role of these factors, two points should be borne in mind. First, the influence of any given characteristic is a function of how much impact it has on users. The meaning of change to those using it is a crucial aspect of effective implementation (Fullan 1982). Second, the factors cannot be understood in isolation from each other. It is the combination of characteristics occurring in specific settings which determines implementation outcomes.

4.1 Characteristics of the Change

Changes have different characteristics or attributes when perceived by those attempting to develop and/or those attempting to use them. These attributes can influence how likely real change is to occur in practice. In some pioneering work, Rogers and Shoemaker (1971) identified a number of attributes of innovation which they found contributed to adoption—relative advantage, compatibility, complexity, trialability, and observerability. Note, however, that their research synthesis was based on adoption outcomes (the decision to use, not actual use), and was by and large conducted on individual decision makers (e.g., farmers adopting a new technology) rather than on individuals in organizational contexts such as school systems.

Since Rogers and Shoemaker's work there has been some concentrated research on the relationship between attributes of curriculum changes and subsequent implementation. Four main factors identified in several major research studies are: need and compatibility, clarity,

complexity, quality and practicality of materials (Crandall et al. 1982, Emrick and Peterson 1978, Louis and Rosenblum 1981).

Curriculum changes, as with other social innovations are not always based on an assessment of need, especially as perceived by people responsible for working with the change. This is not to say that only changes which everyone agrees to should be attempted, but the research does suggest that the question of perceived need and compatibility makes a difference in terms of whether something happens.

Clarity (about goals and means) is another perennial problem in the curriculum change process. Even when there is some agreement that certain changes are needed, the adopted change may not be at all clear about what people should do differently. Problems related to clarity have been found in virtually every study of significant change. The role of clarity in the fidelity and adaptive approaches is particularly instructive for understanding the differences in the two approaches. In the fidelity approach, developers attempt to be highly specific, while in the adaptive approach there is much more open-endedness allowing for decisions to be made along the way (Shipman et al. 1974, Elliott 1976–77). In either case, the degree of clarity on the part of people attempting something new is related to the degree of change in practice which occurs. Further, even with highly programmed changes, research has found that clarity is not something which happens all at once. The development of clarity (or confusion) is a process which depends on the combination of factors and events discussed in this section. Nor is greater clarity an end in itself: very simple and insignificant changes can be very clear, while more difficult and worthwhile ones may not be amenable to easy clarification—a matter related to the third attribute, complexity.

Complexity refers to the difficulty and extent of change required of the individual involved in implementation. The actual amount depends on the starting point for any given individual or group. Many changes such as open education, systematic direct instruction, inquiry-oriented studies, involve an array of activities, diagnostic skills, teaching strategies, pedagogical understandings, and the like if effective implementation is to be achieved. While complex changes create more problems, they may result in more significant changes because more is being attempted.

The final factor associated directly with the nature of the change concerns the quality and practicality of the learning materials being used. Although it seems self-evident that quality is important, many curriculum changes fail to get implemented because the learning materials are insufficiently developed. The rather large-scale curriculum development efforts in the 1960s and early 1970s in the United States suffered because of inadequate attention to the quality, usability, and appropriateness of materials (Welch 1979). More recent research shows that many of the curriculum development efforts of the late 1970s are faring better. In an evaluation of the use of innovations in the National Diffusion Network (NDN), Emrick and Peterson (1978) found that "well-articulated adoption materials, which...are complete, well organized, comprehensive and detailed" and address "how-to" concerns are more effective at the implementation stage." The National Diffusion Network is a nationwide system in the United States to assist local districts and schools in selecting and using proven innovative programs. Using criteria of quality and effectiveness a panel screens potential programs for the purpose of selecting (validating) quality programs. Once validated they are disseminated through a system of state facilitators who help local decision makers select programs and who arrange for the developer of the programs to provide inservice training assistance to implementers.

More recent research has also found that perceived quality makes a difference in how likely and how well teachers implement a curriculum change (Crandall et al. 1982, Louis and Rosenblum 1981). Once again the difference between fidelity and adaptive approaches can be noted. In the former case, details of quality are attempted to be resolved at the developmental stage, while for the latter it is recognized that further development must be worked out by individuals and groups who are involved in implementing the particular change.

4.2 Local Conditions

It is necessary to distinguish between local conditions and local strategies relative to specific changes. Local conditions concern the climate and individual characteristics—at the county/district level, at the school level, and at the community level—which affect whether curriculum changes will be considered and under what conditions they are likely to be implemented. Some of the main factors found to influence change in practice are district leadership, school board and community support, the role of principals, school climate (e.g., professional collegiality among teachers), individual and collective emphasis on, and sense of efficacy about, instructional matters, and unanticipated critical events.

District leadership encompasses a number of variables which influence implementation. The nature of leadership sets the broad conditions for change in the district. Central office staff who show an active interest in determining which changes are needed, in supporting adopted changes during the initial implementation period, and in assessing their impact have an influence on the quality of implementation (see for example, Berman and McLaughlin 1977, Emrick and Peterson 1978). Through leadership in planning, through communication, and through decisions about resources, and selection and development of other leaders in the district, central administrators have an influence on the climate for change in the district as a whole.

If school districts are governed by local or regional boards of education as most are, such boards may have an indirect impact on implementation through the resource decisions they make, but there is not much evidence that they directly influence implementation, although there is some research which indicates that parent involvement in elementary schools can influence implementation (Fullan 1982). In any case, the large variety of organizational structures and cultural differences and the scarcity of research on the role of school boards in implementation does not put us in a position to draw clear conclusions.

On the other hand, there has been considerable research over the past few years on the role of the school principal. All major research on innovation and school effectiveness shows that the principal strongly influences the likelihood of change, but it also indicates that most principals do not play instructional leadership roles (Leithwood and Montgomery 1982). At the school level the principal frequently sets the climate of communication, support, and decision making which can foster or inhibit change in practice. Indeed, the next factor—school climate—brings together teacher–teacher and teacher–principal relationships. There is a good deal of evidence which says that interaction among users during attempts at change is the key to effective implementation. New meanings, new behavior, new skills depend significantly on whether teachers are working as isolated individuals or are exchanging ideas and support about their work (Rutter et al. 1979). While it is possible for teachers to develop such collegiality among themselves, the actions of the principal in relation to potential changes makes it more or less likely that school climate conducive to implementation will evolve.

It is not simply collegiality and school leadership per se which determine implementation outcomes, but also the question of the substance of concerns over which people interact. It is significant that two different bodies of research—that on school innovation, and that on school effectiveness—have made similar discoveries. Both found that better implementation and learning occurs when the principal and teachers set instructional matters as a high priority, and have a sense of efficacy that they can improve instruction through their efforts (see Edmonds 1979, Rutter et al. 1979).

Finally, there are a number of unanticipated events which occur with enough frequency to be cited as having a significant impact on the extent of change. These include teacher turnover, changes in leadership at the school or district level (e.g., through promotion), collective bargaining, strikes and other events which affect the quality of teacher–school board relationships (Berman 1981, Louis and Rosenblum 1981, Crandall et al. 1982).

4.3 Local Strategies

Local strategies refer to the planning and policy actions taken in relation to implementing specific curriculum changes. Two core aspects of implementation strategies involve choices about inservice or staff development activities, and communication–information systems. Since implementation (whether voluntarily sought or externally imposed) involves learning how to do something new, it follows that opportunities for inservice education in relation to specific changes are critical. There is a compelling body of research which demonstrates that little change in practice occurs when staff development activities are absent, or when they consist of one-time orientation sessions without follow-up; by contrast when staff development activities are conducted prior to and during implementation, significant change in practice can occur (McLaughlin and Marsh 1978).

Decisions about how to address communication problems are very complex. They range from questions about how much participation in decisions should occur (at each phase of adoption, implementation, continuation), whether and how to gather and use evaluative and other information on implementation problems as well as learning outcomes, and how to maintain a communication system among the different parties. There are too many variables and too many cultural differences at work to be able to draw firm conclusions. Lack of participation in initial decisions, for example, may not make a difference as long as the selected innovation meets a need, and there is intensive staff development support. Similarly, formal evaluation at the early stages of implementation may not be necessary or even helpful (see Sect. 5 below). However, it should be noted that other factors listed earlier address critical communication needs. Assessment of need, active leadership, principal and teacher–teacher interaction, staff development all serve to increase the communication between administrators and teachers about what should be done, and how to do it. Stated another way, while communication systems vary in their degree of formality, a regular, systematic exchange of information about implementation requirements is necessary for change in practice to occur (Fullan 1982).

4.4 External Factors

Factors external to the local school system can be seen as facilitating or inhibiting curriculum implementation. Three factors which illustrate this dilemma are policy change, financial or material resources, and technical assistance. The passage of a new piece of legislation or other government policy decisions in the curriculum/program area result in a certain amount of formal pressure for changes to be implemented, but the mere existence of the policy does not result in much implementation unless several of the other factors listed in this section are also conducive to change.

Similarly, the availability of financial or material resources does not guarantee curriculum change as there are a variety of opportunistic reasons why school systems seek additional resources (Berman and McLaughlin 1977). Forms of external assistance, depending on their characteristics can also be more or less helpful. External assistance (e.g., from government staff, project developers, etc.) given only at the orientation stage does not result in much change in practice, unless the local

conditions and strategies reinforce the external assistance. Two recent large-scale studies in the United States found that external training, given by a variety of consultants combined with follow through support which is coordinated with local consultants or staff represents a very effective combination in bringing about change in classroom practice (Crandall et al. 1982, Louis and Rosenblum 1981).

5. Measurement and Evaluation

There are three major components involved in assessing curriculum implementation as indicated in Fig. 1.

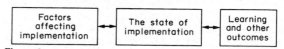

Figure 1
Components of implementation evaluation

In examining specific curriculum changes, it is possible to gather evaluative data on (a) factors affecting implementation (as outlined in Sect. 4), (b) implementation or the state of change in practice at any given time (Sect. 3), and (c) the impact of implementation on student learning, attitudes, organizational capacity, and other outcomes. Questions of measurement and instrumentation are discussed for each of the three components starting with outcomes. It can also be anticipated that the criteria of evaluation are more or less specific depending on whether one takes (and/or whether the innovation is conducive to) a fidelity or adaptive approach.

5.1 Outcomes

This article is not directly concerned with the evaluation of learning outcomes. However, the relationship to implementation should be understood. Implementation (or bringing about changes in practice) is the means to accomplishing desired outcomes. Several difficulties arise when an attempt is made to assess outcomes and relate them to implementation changes. First, learning outcomes will be considered, followed by some comments on other types of outcomes.

One of the first issues concerns the measurement of learning outcomes. Since the early 1970s there have been considerable developments in instrumentation for testing basic skills and knowledge (Lewy and Nevo 1981). Beyond this there is a great deal of controversy about how and whether to measure some of the higher cognitive development (e.g., problem-solving ability) and social development (e.g., ability to work in groups) objectives in education.

Even if valid information can be obtained on learning outcomes, the next question concerns what it indicates about implementation. Such information by itself tells very little. It indicates what students are learning and not learning, but provides no information on the source of the problem. For the latter information it is necessary to delve into the question of what changes in practice have in fact occurred, and in turn what factors affected these changes.

Two final issues remain: the question of other types of outcomes, and the matter of fidelity versus adaptive orientations to curriculum evaluation. In addition to learning outcomes, curriculum changes result in other individual and organizational changes. Crandall et al. (1982), for example, assessed the impact of specific program changes on teacher attitudes and benefits, organizational changes (e.g., increased or decreased communication, morale), and overall attitude toward engaging in school improvement activities (such as curriculum change). Louis and Rosenblum (1981) assessed a similar range of outcomes. Shipman et al. (1974) using a more open-ended approach uncovered a variety of outcomes in examining a major curriculum project in the United Kingdom. In brief, it is necessary to consider a number of intended and unintended consequences when examining the impact of curriculum change.

The final issue which complicates a researcher's ability to evaluate curriculum change relates to the fidelity/adaptive distinction. Obviously, the more that a curriculum change is amenable to clear, specific, a priori definition the more it is possible to measure instances of change in relation to corresponding outcomes. But, as has been seen, it is not appropriate or even possible to approach all curriculum changes with this orientation.

For all of the above reasons, the vast majority of the research literature does not contain studies in which both implementation and outcomes are assessed and their relationship examined. There are careful studies examining one or the other, but studies which investigate the relationship of implementation to outcomes are still in the early stages of development and face some intrinsically difficult problems.

5.2 Implementation

By contrast, there have been substantial developments in the direct measurement of implementation, that is, the extent of change in practice, especially from the fidelity perspective. In particular, the assessment of components of implementation, coupled with the measurement of levels of use vis-à-vis each component has received considerable attention. Hall and Loucks (1977) and colleagues at the University of Texas were responsible for many of the conceptual and methodological procedures for assessing the levels of use of innovations by individual users. They employ an eight-level distinction ranging from nonuse through mechanical use, to renewal. The procedures have been refined and applied to a large number of different program innovations. The separation of dimensions or components of implementation is a more recent phenomenon. Leithwood (1981) identified eight different dimensions of curriculum change (e.g., materials, teaching strategies, etc.). Hall and Loucks (1977), and Crandall et al. (1982) in building on this work, define components in relation to each innovation thereby allowing the number of components to vary depending on the innovation being assessed

(e.g., use of particular materials, use of a particular diagnostic test, using a certain question-asking technique, etc.). In all of these efforts researchers have refined methods involving interviews, questionnaires, and content analysis.

Using more open-ended procedures, researchers interested in adaptive or evolutionary patterns of implementation have also attempted to identify and describe what changes in practice have been happening. Shipman et al. (1974) explored some of these issues from "inside a curriculum project." In a collaborative research mode, Elliott (1976–77) worked with a group of teachers to develop a number of changes in classroom practice. Crandall et al. (1982) in addition to assessing implementation in relation to the developer's model, also described changes in practice regardless of the expectations of developers. Thus, whether interest lies in innovations from a developers perspective, or more broadly in what changes are occurring, it is possible to assess and describe the nature and extent of change in practice.

5.3 Factors Affecting Implementation

In Section 4, the list of factors found to affect the extent of implementation was divided into four broad categories. In evaluating implementation, it is important to include these types of factors in the evaluation design. It is necessary to understand the role of these local and external conditions and strategies in order to understand implementation outcomes. Researchers have used a combination of documentary or content analysis, observation, interview, questionnaire, and case-study methods to gather information on factors influencing implementation. Fullan and Pomfret (1977), and Fullan (1982) contain summaries of many of these studies. For large-scale projects, documentary, questionnaire, and interview instrumentation have been particularly comprehensively developed by Crandall et al. (1982), and Louis and Rosenblum (1981). One of the more intriguing methodological developments involves the use of the case study, especially multiple case studies to portray implementation processes more wholistically while at the same time struggling with problems of reducing and displaying the amount of information more concisely and explicitly.

6. Planning for Implementation

The topic of planning for more effective implementation is extremely complex. In this conclusion some of the main issues can be introduced. The first matter is that "understanding" the implementation process is not the same as being able to "influence" it for the better. Some factors may be unchangeable or a researcher may not have the authority to alter them. Planning for more effective implementation then, involves a new set of considerations. The second issue is that a good deal is known about the factors which make it more or less likely that change in practice will occur (see Sect. 4). By deriving implications from this knowledge some of the main planning goals and tasks can be identified. It is known that change in practice occurs when certain elements occur in combination: attention to the development of clear and validated materials; active administrative support and leadership at the district and especially the school level; focused, ongoing inservice or staff development activities; the development of collegiality and other interaction-based conditions at the school level; and the selective use of external resources (both people and materials).

This broad list can be used to generate a list of more particular strategies. Materials production and availability can be promoted through systems like the National Diffusion Network in the United States (Crandall et al. 1982). Leadership programs for district and school personnel can be used for long-term development of leadership capacity. Specific inservice activities can be designed and can significantly affect implementation provided that they are ongoing, specific, and combined with other factors.

The third complexity is that specific planning implications only make sense from the perspective of the situation and role of individuals. Therefore, there are many different planning guidelines that would have to be developed depending on whether one is a government official, a teacher, a parent, a principal, a consultant, and so on (Fullan 1982).

In conclusion, knowledge about curriculum implementation has increased substantially since the early 1970s. During this period, intensive research endeavors and accomplishments on a number of fronts have been made.

Bibliography

Berman P 1981 Educational change: An implementation paradigm. In: Lehming R, Kane M (eds.) 1981 *Improving Schools: Using What We Know*. Sage, Beverly Hills, California, pp. 253–86

Berman P, McLaughlin M W 1977 *Federal Programs Supporting Educational Change, Vol. 7: Factors Affecting Implementation and Continuation*. Rand, Santa Monica, California

Crandall D et al. 1982 *Master Report Series of the Study of Dissemination Efforts Supporting School Improvement*. The Network, Andover, Massachusetts

Edmonds R 1979 Effective schools for the urban poor. *Educ. Leadership* 37: 15–18

Elliott J 1976–77 Developing hypotheses about classrooms from teachers' practical constructs: An account of the work of the Ford Teaching Project. *Interchange* 7(2): 2–22

Emrick J, Peterson S 1978 *A Synthesis of Findings Across Five Recent Studies in Educational Dissemination and Change*. Far West Laboratory, San Francisco, California

Frey K, Haft H (eds.) 1982 *Compendium Curriculumforschung*. Universität Kiel, Institut für die Padagogik der Naturwissenschaften, Federal Republic of Germany

Fullan M 1981 The relationship between evaluation and implementation. In: Lewy A, Nevo D (eds.) 1981 *Evaluation Roles in Education*. Gordon and Breach, London, pp. 309–40

Fullan M 1982 *The Meaning of Educational Change*. Teachers College Press, New York

Fullan M, Pomfret A 1977 Research on curriculum and instruction implementation. *Rev. Educ. Res.* 47: 335–97

Hall G E, Loucks S F 1977 A developmental model for determining whether the treatment is actually implemented. *Am. Educ. Res. J.* 14: 263–76

Leithwood K A 1981 The dimensions of curriculum innovation. *J. Curric. Stud.* 13: 25–36

Leithwood K A, Montgomery D J 1982 The role of the elementary school principal in program improvement. *Rev. Educ. Res.* 53: 309–39

Lewy A, Nevo D (eds.) 1981 *Evaluation Roles in Education*. Gordon and Breach, London

Louis K, Rosenblum S 1981 *Linking R and D with Schools: A Program and its Implications for Dissemination*. National Institute of Education, Washington, DC

McLaughlin M W, Marsh D D 1978 Staff development and school change. *Teach. Coll. Rec.* 80: 69–94

Rogers E M, Shoemaker F F 1971 *Communication of Innovations: A Cross-cultural Approach*, 2nd edn. Free Press, New York

Rutter M, Maugham B, Mortimer P, Ouston J, Smith A 1979 *Fifteen Thousand Hours: Secondary Schools and their Effects on Children*. Harvard University Press, Cambridge, Massachusetts

Shipman M D, Bolam D, Jenkins D R 1974 *Inside a Curriculum Project: A Case Study in the Process of Curriculum Change*. Methuen, London

Welch W 1979 Twenty years of science curriculum development: A look back. In: Berliner D (ed.) 1979 *Review of Research in Education*, Vol. 7. American Educational Research Association, Washington, DC

Educational Broadcasting

Africa

S. Inquai

The communications revolution, unlike many other technological achievements of the West, found its way to the Third World relatively quickly and easily. There is no country in the world today without broadcasting facilities. All the African states have at least one, but often many, transmitting facilities. The first broadcasting station in Africa was introduced in Algeria in 1925 followed very closely by the introduction in Egypt in 1926 and in Kenya in 1928, and the latest is that in Equatorial Guinea established around 1968. Most of the radio stations were introduced by the colonial powers who saw some advantage in mass communication. Short-wave broadcasting was the first to be introduced. This was followed by medium wave (AM), and FM or VHF is now gradually spreading. Television on the other hand has been slow in making inroads in Africa: a number of countries have no facilities for television broadcasting, and many of those that do have only limited coverage. There is perhaps explained by the high cost of programme production and playback equipment or receivers. But, even if television broadcasts had wider coverage, they would still be underutilized because of the absence of electric power in most of rural Africa.

Africa still lags behind the rest of the world in all aspects of broadcasting. It has only 3 percent of the world's transmitters (27 percent for all developing countries) and only 7 percent of the population (18 percent for all developing countries) has access to broadcasts from these transmitters. This is a reflection of the low level of development which manifests itself in a low GNP and the poor purchasing capacity of the people. Most of rural Africa has no power supply and is thus cut off from television broadcasts. There is also the problem of the quality of radio signals which affects reception in those areas very far from the transmitters. Although Africa had 6.7 million television sets in 1979, most of these were concentrated in a few countries. The five North African countries of Morocco, Algeria, Tunisia, Libya, and Egypt together with South Africa account for 4.25 million of the television sets. This leaves the bulk of Africa with a thin distribution of sets. The number of television sets per 1,000 inhabitants differed widely from country to country with Egypt having well over 500 sets per 1,000 inhabitants, and Chad, Niger, and Mozambique having less than 5 sets (see Table 1).

When most of the African states attained their independence in the 1960s, the education that they inherited was inadequate. Most children had no access to school, and the population was largely illiterate. The quality of education was very poor because the colonial authorities did not consider it necessary to develop an educational system comparable to the systems in the metropolitan countries. This was usually reflected in the low level of expenditure on education, and the use of substandard or poorly trained teachers. It was felt perfectly adequate to recruit potential teachers from among primary-school leavers, and to give them a year or two of training. What was available was in no way comparable to what existed in the United Kingdom or France.

The newly independent African countries were thus faced with the mammoth task of providing education for all. They gave education top priority and saw it as the key to change and development. Already in 1960 at the African Ministers of Education Conference in Addis Ababa, long before many became independent, they had decided that their goal was to attain universal primary education by 1980. This was to happen while improving the quality of instruction, expanding secondary schooling, building new institutions for vocational and technical training, and creating tertiary institutions such as universities and polytechnics. All this was, for the most part, to happen from scratch. African states did not restrict their commitment to formal education only, although it remained their priority. Their aim was also for adult education to flourish, and to combat illiteracy. However, not all put the necessary resources into adult education; the effort was very often dependent on the political and ideological commitment of the state, the more "progressive" states putting more into it.

1. Educational Broadcasting

Most countries realized quite soon after independence that more than the conventional approach to education was needed to attain their goals. They appreciated the

Table 1
Media distribution by continent and regions—1979

	No. of radios per 1,000 inhabitants	No. of TV millions	TV per 1,000 inhabitants
Africa	77	6.7	15
North America	1,951	151.0	619
Latin America	252	37.0	103
Asia	108	50.0	32
Europe (and the Soviet Union)	450	219.0	294
Developing countries	97	64.0	29
Developed countries	801	407.0	353
World total	336	471.0	139

Source: UNICEF 1982 pp. 8–9

fact that it would be some time before they could train the required numbers of teachers to expand, diversify, and improve the quality of education; and recognized that it was almost impossible to do all that had to be done if they depended entirely on the conventional approach. Hence the idea was accepted that broadcasting could be beneficial in the democratization of education. A number of African states saw in broadcasting both the prospect of improving the quality of instruction in schools, and the possibility of reaching those sectors of society which otherwise remained outside the purview of the formal system of education and extension work. Broadcasting brought with it the promise of diversifying input in terms of content and subject matter, and also the potential for increasing the number of languages so as to reach as many people as possible, particularly in nonformal education. Several African states accepted almost from the outset the need, especially in adult education, to use the local languages in order to be effective with their message. It must however be underlined that not all African states are equally committed either to the democratization of education or to the exploitation of the broadcasting media.

Educational broadcasting covers a wide range of activities. It is easier to summarize what is taking place in the use of media in education by looking at education through a categorization into informal, formal, and nonformal. Educational broadcasting in Africa has been addressing itself to all three categories with mixed success. In the following paragraphs the role educational broadcasting is playing in each category will be discussed.

1.1 Informal Educational Broadcasting

It is not necessary to devote a great deal of space to this topic. Informal education is the least well-defined and least studied aspect of education. Many organizations and institutions that try to inform and enlighten the public use media a great deal. The most important and educationally relevant agencies are the ministries of agriculture and public health. These ministries have always been given airtime as their information broadcasts are considered vital to development and general social welfare. Much of their programming is not target

specific, nor is it monitored regularly. Programmes go out like commercial advertisements, with a vague hope that people will listen to them and learn. There has been very little variation over the years. The entire process is based on the assumption that the audience, for example farmers in the case of agricultural programmes, is interested and listens regularly. It is very difficult to assess their value, and little attention is paid to such questions as: Who would be interested in this specific subject or topic? Do they have access to a radio? However, given the linguistic complexity of much of Africa, and the low level of radio ownership, it is doubtful if they have a widespread effect. Nevertheless, programme originators point to the occasional letters they receive, and continue with the programmes. News and general public information, law and order topics are also included and no doubt are of interest to some. Many governments and public organizations have included important information as news items. This indicates that they have confidence that the people do listen to news broadcasts. However, it is perhaps the recognition of the ineffectiveness of such programmes that has led to more organized and systematic approaches, as will be shown below.

Radio has been successfully exploited by the business community, who have broadcast well-planned and well-produced advertisement programmes over the radio. Their effect is evident in the changing consumption pattern of both urban and rural Africa.

1.2 Schools Broadcasting

Perhaps the oldest and most widely spread application of broadcasting is in formal education. Most, if not all, African states have a schools' broadcasting department. This department is usually under the ministry of education and often works closely with the national broadcasting agency. Educational broadcasting in the formal education setting finds many uses. The most common use is to supplement or enrich the normal classroom teaching, but it is also used to introduce innovations in education at all levels, including postsecondary and teacher-training programmes. Broadcasting aimed to supplement classroom teaching commonly tries to emphasize those aspects of a subject which the classroom teacher is thought to be least capable of handling, for example, language teaching in primary schools, science and nature study, and social studies for secondary schools. The usual pattern is 15 minutes of broadcast followed by classroom discussion. In a number of countries the schools broadcasting is not fully exploited because (a) teachers do not understand its importance and fear that it might be used to replace them, or even think it is a waste of time, (b) there is constant equipment breakdown which is often not remedied in time, and (c) broadcast times and school timetables do not always coincide. However, many countries conscious of these problems have taken steps to remedy them. Many run short courses in integrating school broadcasting with classroom work and, where there are scheduling problems, distribute cassette tapes to schools so that they can listen when they are ready for them. The following paragraphs illustrate a few examples of school use of radio and television.

Ghana became the first African country to win its independence in 1957. The government launched almost immediately a plan for accelerated development of education. The Ghana Broadcasting Corporation (GBC) inaugurated the schools broadcasting programme. The programme was intended as supplementary enrichment to classroom teaching. Initially only radio was used, but television was introduced to schools broadcasting in 1965. Courses were aimed at both primary and secondary schools. In the 1970s, there were 11 subjects broadcast over the radio and seven over television. Supplemental radio courses included English, French, African history, science, teaching methods for primary-school teachers, and other courses for teacher-training programmes. Television offered English literature, geography, general science and mathematics, and teaching methods to secondary schools and teacher-training colleges. In addition to the broadcast material, the GBC prepared illustrated handbooks containing summaries of programmes content, and suggested exercises. This was sent in advance to all participating schools (Head 1974 p. 92).

Schools broadcasting in Ethiopia had a long gestation period. Very little was done until the introduction of television in 1964, which from the beginning was intended to be used mainly for educational purposes. After lengthy discussions between the Ministry of Information and Tourism, and the Ministry of Education and Fine Arts, the Educational Television Service came into being in 1965. Television transmission is limited to the immediate environs of Addis Ababa, the capital. Initially, the Educational Television Service (ETV) depended on Ministry of Information studio facilities to produce its programmes. However, it established its own studio with funds from government resources, and with British and American aid. The ETV was converted to the mass media centre with expanded premises. Courses covered were English (primary and secondary), French (secondary), geography (primary), biology (secondary), health (junior secondary), and physics (secondary). Initially, the British Council trained personnel at

the Council for Educational Television Overseas (CETO), and also sent technical advisers to Ethiopia, but by 1971 Ethiopia had developed its own training capabilities, and personnel were trained on the spot. Later the Germans also inaugurated training programmes for radio personnel in cooperation with the Ministry of Information. There were plans to have 10 regional radio transmitters, each with 1KW power. The first was installed at Sodo, and the rest are now to be installed after a delay of over a decade. The main purpose was to improve classroom instruction, but since there has been no formal evaluation, it is not possible to speak of its effect. What can be said is that the capital was already privileged, having well-equipped schools with qualified teachers. The need was most acute in schools much further afield from the capital and this is where television did not reach. Radio was introduced in 1972 on a limited basis. There were plans to inaugurate a much more comprehensive programme, but this was interrupted by the change in government in the mid-1970s.

The two former French colonies of the Ivory Coast and Niger decided to use television for direct teaching in order to introduce innovation, and to expand educational opportunity. Both these ventures in educational broadcasting have been considered a rather radical departure from the usual norm where educational broadcasting is used to enrich classroom teaching. Each country started with a massive and lengthy study (taking four years in Ivory Coast and two years in Niger) to establish the feasibility of teaching regular school subjects by television. They were assisted from bilateral and international sources, both in terms of finances and personnel.

In the Ivory Coast, ETV comes under the Ministry of Primary and Television Education. The directorate for educational television is based in Bouaké. Its aim, as stated earlier, was to expand primary-school enrolment, and to train teachers who will need to carry new responsibility. This means providing extensive inservice training. The Ivory Coast proceeded by producing courses at the rate of one a year. The initial intake was 200,000 in the first year and 60,000 in the second year. The ETV produced 7 to 8.5 hours of television programmes a week. There has been a great deal of research and evaluation of the Ivory Coast experience. Although the cost is high, the programme has been judged generally a success but with frequent negative reaction from teachers who want to do the actual teaching themselves, and resist the idea of becoming more dependent on the medium.

The Niger experience, although similar, differs in a number of specifics. To begin with, the Niger project is smaller in scale. Although it followed the procedure of developing one year's programme at a time, piloting in four classes and revising it in the light of experience, the total number of pupils was kept below 1,000, until it was finally expanded to reach 122 classes. This could by no means be considered large-scale evidence. Another important difference was that the Niger project did not use trained teachers; instead it used monitors who were given a three-month training and whose educational background was limited. All aspects of teaching were then done by the teleteacher.

Both countries point to a marked fall in the drop-out rate, and significant educational achievement. The achievement in spoken French of telestudents was especially impressive in Niger.

Reports indicate that the Ivory Coast has completely abandoned its ETV programme mainly for economic reasons. Similarly, the Niger experiment which in fact did not attain the magnitude of coverage achieved by the Ivory Coast, but remained stunted, has also met the same fate. The new Niger government that assumed power as a result of coups wanted to take over and use it for its own political end. This move was resisted by the French, who manned and financed the project, and no agreement could be reached on its continued operation.

1.3 Broadcasting in Nonformal Education

Many people in Africa are outside the reach of the formal school system. Many are illiterate, and the largest group of people live in rural areas, mainly as farmers. It has taken planners a long time to realize that nothing much will happen unless the rural people are involved directly in development projects. The belief that more schools will lead to more development is now strongly questioned. As a result, educators have been looking for alternative forms of "education" in a wider sense of the word. Such education, if it is to show results, has to be geared to the needs and interests of the rural majority. Broadcasting has found diverse uses in the field of nonformal education. Many countries have used radio in literacy campaigns, to inform adults about the programmes, to keep the motivation of learners high through regular reports and encouragement, and to hold discussions on topics related to the literacy lessons. Radio is also used to upgrade and inform the literacy teachers or leaders with the aim of making them more effective in their work.

The use of broadcasting in nonformal education has been shifting from open broadcasts aimed at individual listening, to programmes for group listening, whether these are already existing groups or whether the groups are specifically formed to follow a particular programme. Group listening, although it needs careful planning and administration, shows good results over a short period as is demonstrated by the number of decisions the people take and local projects they initiate. Furthermore, it is easier to monitor and to assess its effects. Such programmes are mainly aimed at people with a common interest, by virtue of the fact that they either belong to a community, or are engaged in a particular type of occupation and have common interests. However, with few exceptions, the scale of operation has not been commensurate with the need or the size of the potential target audience. This shortfall is usually explained by the shortage of funds and resources. In a

few instances, group listening has tended to reinforce existing social divisions and antagonisms within a community. This occurs when a village has a single group made up mainly of the privileged members of society.

Various approaches have been tried with different groups. As with everything in education, many of the programmes now seen in Africa have their origin in the West. Examples will be illustrated of the types of nonformal education available and how broadcasting is used. It is not possible to describe all known programmes in a short article but the following will concentrate on a selected few that best illustrate the role broadcasting is playing in nonformal education.

(a) *The radio farm forums.* Perhaps the most widespread nonformal programme in Africa is the forum. It has its origin in Canada in the 1930s from where it spread to India, and later on to Ghana and other parts of Africa. The forum in Canada was a winter project to be undertaken when the scattered farming communities had very little agricultural work to do. It helped, in those days, to fill a void in the farmers' lives and to inform them about farming techniques, government, and other civic and cultural matters. It used radio broadcasts coupled with printed materials and hints for discussion. People listened to the radio, read the printed material, and discussed the issues raised as they pertained to their daily lives, and those for whom it was appropriate, and who were sufficiently motivated, took a decision to do something about the issue. It was a pattern of listen/read, discuss, and decide.

Third World extension workers, perhaps through the intermediary of UNESCO, quickly grasped the idea as they considered it a useful means of teaching the mostly illiterate rural peasantry. Ghana was the first African country to adopt the farm forum programme. In 1964–65, UNESCO selected Ghana as an experimental country to analyse the applicability of forums for African rural development. Initially 40 villages were selected where 60 forums were organized, and another 40 villages were used as a control group. The experiment continued for 20 weeks with one programme a week. Not all the topics were related to agriculture. Since this was a well-planned experiment it was possible to see from the evaluation report that it was a successful undertaking. Pre- and post-programme surveys showed that there were considerable improvements in people's knowledge and understanding. People had taken steps to initiate self-help type programmes. Since then the forums have grown in number and the programme has continued to operate. After the initial success, however, it seems now to have reached a stage where it has ceased to be an effective programme, and has become just another regular radio feature. This is to a large extent due to lack of support and resources. The logical consequence of this lack is shrinkage.

Many countries in Africa have adopted the idea of radio forums, and have used it, again with mixed results. Forums seem to have lost their vitality and thus their usefulness as an approach. Examples of countries that have farm forum programmes are Malawi, Zambia, Kenya, Togo, and Dahomey.

(b) *Radio campaigns.* An interesting adaptation of the radio forum format is the radio learning group, or better, the radio campaign. Radio campaigns in Africa started in Tanzania in 1967. The approach is similar to the forums with a listening/reading, discussion, and action pattern. However, they differ in more than one fundamental way. The topics for a campaign are chosen with their practical or social importance in mind and they form a comprehensive unit. It has a sense of currency and immediacy. The group is temporarily organized for the duration of the campaign only. The campaign is normally kept short, 10 to 12 weeks long. The group leaders are given a short training of two to seven days, on discussion methods. The leaders are chosen from the ranks of the people themselves. They are enjoined in the training to be nondirective, nonassertive, and to leave the final decision to the participants. Finally each campaign is evaluated at the end.

The Tanzanian experience started with a pilot project involving only 15 groups, and was on "Government in Tanzania". That was in 1967. In 1969, two years after the first, another campaign, this time on development planning, "To plan is to choose", involving about 60 groups, was launched. These two small-scale operations led to the conclusion that the approach had merit and should be used from time to time to bring about desired changes in public knowledge and attitudes.

The approach was used in large-scale campaigns, in 1973 "*Mtu ni Afia*" ("Man is Health"), and the 1975 "*Chakula ni Uhai*" ("Food is Life") campaigns. The first was directed at the improvement of sanitary conditions and health practices, and the second at an increase in food production, and the improvement of nutrition. The success of these two campaigns has been variously discussed and documented (Grenholm 1975, Hall and Dodds 1974).

Radio campaigns are complex undertakings, requiring a long lead-in time, during which the campaign is planned in detail, radio programmes and the accompanying printed materials and posters, group leader manuals, and so on are produced, and the group leaders are trained. Since groups for each campaign are newly organized, a long promotion and publicity period is required to prepare the public psychologically and to organize the groups. Campaigns by their very nature are amenable to large-scale treatment, since personnel required for the duration of the campaign, usually about 10 weeks, could be either seconded from different departments or organizations, or recruited from students if the campaign coincides with school holidays. Campaigns also need careful planning from the point of view of timing, to ensure that it is the slack time, when the rural people are least busy, and thus able to attend, otherwise not much can be achieved.

The radio campaign approach has been adapted by Botswana which has run two successful campaigns. The first, "The People and the Plan" involved a limited number of groups, but the 1975/76 campaign "*Lefatse la rona*" ("The Land is Ours") which dealt with proposed government plans for land reform, involved some 5,000 groups throughout the length and breadth of the country, again to the satisfaction of everybody involved.

1.4 Other Forms of Educational Broadcasting

There are of course a number of formats and structures used for educational broadcasting in various parts of Africa. Botswana, as a result of "The Land is Ours" campaign, initiated a civic education programme based on the question and answer format. The programme "*Re Botseng*" ("Ask us") ran for a year. The community was asked to send questions to the then Botswana Extension College, now the Department of Nonformal Education, on government, national and international issues, religion, social and community problems, and so on. Each week, the college selected a group of questions and sought answers from the relevant organization in government and the community. The answer was either an interview in which case it was broadcast intact, or it came in written form and the radio producer put it together for broadcasting. "*Re Botseng*" was getting over 100 written questions a week at the height of its popularity, and had to be discontinued only for lack of personnel. The same college also ran a series on the history of Botswana which became quite popular. The project was a joint effort of the National Museum of Botswana, the History Department of the University College, and the Botswana Extension College which was responsible for its initiation and production.

One novel approach is the radio and television clubs found in Francophone Africa. The radio clubs trace their origin to the French tradition of group dynamics. Radio clubs, although not a large-scale operation, have proved to be useful educational tools. Schramm (1977) quotes Kahnert who claims the aims of the listening clubs are:

> ... to propagate government action throughout the country, to invite views of listeners on their day-to-day problems in any sphere such as health, agriculture, education, etc. and for this purpose to organise group listening in rural communities; to give those responsible for broadcast programmes a better knowledge of their audience, and to allow listeners under the direction of qualified leaders to express themselves and make known their ideas and suggestions about the programme. (pp. 252–53)

Each club is led by an "animateur" who is paid about US$20.00 a month. He or she is expected to assemble the group, lead the discussion, and take responsibility for the feedback to the station (Schramm 1977), like the group leaders of the forums and the radio campaigns. Subsequent themes are expected to come out of the feedback, as this is considered the expression of the community's needs and aspirations. Although clubs are basically centred around a radio programme, some francophone countries, Senegal and the Ivory Coast, for example, have experimented on a small scale with television.

Important users of broadcasting in education in Africa are the growing number of distance teaching institutions. Many of these were established after independence as purely correspondence colleges following the tradition popularized by commercial colleges, and print was the only medium used. However, many have diversified their work offering nonformal education as well as inservice and preservice training of teachers at a distance. Furthermore they have gradually moved to incorporate the use of radio, television, and face-to-face instruction in their work thus becoming users of multimedia. They use both radio and television either to reinforce the education through print, or as the main tools of instruction. The tendency is to use print, radio, and face-to-face teaching to differing degrees of centrality, depending on the kind of students and/or the subject to be taught. Colleges that have open admission, and that includes most African distance teaching institutions, are faced with the dilemma of how closely to link the radio programmes to the print medium. Their students, working at their own pace, are bound to be working on different lessons, which makes it difficult to find a common ground for radio programmes. In such a circumstance, a rather general programme, considered of "interest to all" is broadcast. In cases where there is strict pacing, radio and print are closely linked. This very often happens in teacher-training courses.

Educational broadcasting in Africa is limited mainly to radio. Although there is an increasing use of television throughout the continent, radio remains the true mass medium. There is ample evidence to suggest that its most productive application has been in nonformal education rather than in schools. Furthermore all existing evidence suggests that short, highly focused (specialized) programmes directed at groups of people and with the intention of informing and persuading, seem to produce a better result than open-ended broadcasts. However, despite the efficacy of certain programmes, the extent to which the medium is used remains limited. This is primarily due to financial and personnel shortages, and perhaps the level of national commitment. Similarly, since only a few African countries have broadcasting facilities primarily devoted to education, education programmes have to compete for prime airtime with music and other forms of light entertainment, and do not often come out well. The universal commitment to the use of media for popular music and light entertainment and not for education is baffling. Many African countries have yet to give the necessary prominence to nonformal education, and hence the necessary support. Short of this, not much growth and development can be envisioned. Finally, much of Africa is short of resources for the field of broadcasting. Over the years, UNESCO, and many friendly countries such as the United Kingdom, France, the Federal Republic of Germany have provided the initial per-

sonnel and the training of locals and since then many countries have developed their own training facilities. Yet the level and scale of personnel development is not commensurate with the needs and Africa still depends on foreign specialists for high-level personnel.

Bibliography

Anglo–Tanzanian Team Report 1979 *Educational Media in Tanzania*. British Council, London
Centre for Educational Development Overseas (CEDO) 1972 *Development of Education of Mass Media in Ethiopia*. CEDO, London
Crowley D, Etherington A, Kidd R, Hubbard P 1978 *Radio Learning Group Manual*. Friedrich Ebert Stiftung, Bonn
Dodds T 1972 *Multi-media Approaches to Rural Education*. International Extension College, Cambridge
Edington A B 1976 *Schools Broadcasts in Malawi*. The British Council, London
Eicher J-C, Orivel F 1980 *Cost Analysis of the Primary Instruction Television Programme in the Ivory Coast*. Academy for Educational Development, Washington, DC
Etherington A 1976 *Radio Programmes for 4B Clubs*. Education Unit, Botswana Extension College, Gaborone Evaluation Unit Botswana Extension College 1978 *Report on the Radio Programme Re-Botseng*. Botswana Extension College, Gaborone
Fraser C 1982 Radio listening clubs: The pros and cons. RRDC *Bull.* 16: 13–15
Grant S, Pierre S T 1975 *Visits to Twenty-three Villages to Determine the Impact of Water Series*. Produced by the out-of-school TV Department. Academy for Educational Development, Washington, DC
Grenholm L H 1975 *Radio Study Group Campaigns in the United Republic of Tanzania*. UNESCO, Paris
Guerri P 1980 *The Role of Support Media in Literacy Education in Botswana*. Department of Nonformal Education, Gaborone
Hall B L 1973 *Wakati Wa Furaha: An Evaluation of the Radio Study Campaign*. Scandinavian Institute for African Studies, Uppsala
Hall B L, Dodds T 1974 *Voices for Development: The Tanzanian National Radio Study Campaigns*. International Extension College, Cambridge
Hawkridge D G, Robinson J 1982 *Organizing Educational Broadcasting*. Croom Helm, London
Head S (ed.) 1974 *Broadcasting in Africa: A Continental Survey of Radio and Television*. Temple University Press, Philadelphia, Pennsylvania
Hornik R et al. 1978 *The Role of Communication in Education*. Institute for Communication Research, Stanford University, Stanford, California
Hungford B 1981 Forget the farm forum: A critical view of listeners' clubs. EBI 14: 70–71
Ingle H T 1974 *Communication Media and Technology: A Look at Their Role in Non-formal Education Programs*. Information Center on Instructional Technology, Washington, DC
Israel B (ed.) 1973 *New Paths to Learning*. International Council for Education, New York
Jamison D T, McAnany E G 1978 *Radio for Education and Development*. Sage, Beverly Hills, California
Katz E, Wedell G L 1977 *Broadcasting in the Third World: Promise and Performance*. Macmillan, London

Lenglet F 1976 *The Impact of 25 Television Programmes on "Water", Produced and Broadcast by the Out-of-school Education Project.* Academy for Educational Development, Washington, DC

Lenglet F, McAnany E G 1977 *Rural Adult Education and the Role of Mass Media: A Comparative Analysis of Four Projects.* Academy for Educational Development, Washington, DC

McAnany E 1972 *Rural Radio in Dahomey.* Praeger, New York

McAnany E 1972 *Radio Clubs of Niger.* Praeger, New York

McAnany E G 1980 *Communications in the Rural Third World: The Role of Information in Development.* Praeger, New York

Maddison J 1971 *Radio and Television in Literacy: A Survey of the Use of the Broadcasting Media in Combating Illiteracy among Adults.* UNESCO, Paris

Ministry of Education 1977 *Educational Broadcasting Services: Survey of Correspondence Students and Radio Listening.* Ministry of Education, Lusaka

Ministry of Rural Development *Radio Farm Forums, Literacy and Agricultural Broadcasts in Zambia.* Ministry of Rural Development, Lusaka

Minkkinen S 1978 *A General Curriculum Model for Mass Media Education.* UNESCO, Paris

Moulton J M 1977 *Animation Rurale: Education for Rural Development.* Center for International Education, University of Massachusetts, Amherst, Massachusetts

Postgate R et al. 1979 *Low Cost Communication Systems, for Educational and Developmental Purposes in Third World Countries.* UNESCO, Paris

Schramm W L 1977 *Big Media, Little Media: Tools and Technologies for Instruction.* Sage, London

Sock B 1977 Senegalese experience in using radio broadcasting for animating and educating basic communities with a view to development. Dartington Conference Paper

UNESCO 1978 *Educational Reforms and Innovations in Africa.* UNESCO, Paris

UNICEF 1982 On the people's wavelength: Communication for social change. UNICEF *News* 114 (whole issue)

Wagner L 1982 *The Economics of Educational Media.* Macmillan, London

World Bank 1981 *The Educational Use of Mass Media.* World Bank, Washington, DC

Young M 1973 Multi-media education in Swaziland. Mimeographed report (unpublished)

Young M, Perraton H, Jenkins J, Dodds T 1980 *Distance Teaching for the Third World: The Lion and the Clockwork Mouse: Incorporating a Directory of Distance Teaching Projects.* Routledge and Kegan Paul, London

Asia

P. Hurst

Educational broadcasting in Asia began in 1931 in Japan, with a series of experimental radio programmes broadcast in the Tokyo region. Regular broadcasts began in 1933 in Osaka, at about the same time as the United States and other industrialized countries were beginning their own educational broadcasting programmes (except the United Kingdom, which had started nine years earlier) (Nishimoto 1969). Since then, most countries in Asia have inaugurated educational radio broadcasting services, and many also have a television service. Some countries, such as Iran, India, and the Philippines, have about two decades' experience with educational television (ETV).

Yet despite this lengthy experience, the independent observer could scarcely claim that educational broadcasting has made a great deal of difference to educational systems in Asia, any more than it has done anywhere else. Those who work in educational broadcasting naturally tend to adopt an enthusiastic and optimistic view of the value of their contribution, and many writings on the subject are frankly propagandistic in tone, seeking to persuade the reader of the potential utility of broadcasting to education. In the present context however, a more dispassionate approach is appropriate. The purpose here will therefore be to review this past experience in order to learn some lessons from it.

Before doing so, it is necessary to stress two points. First, although educational broadcasting has had a more marginal impact than was anticipated throughout the world, this is not a uniquely Asian phenomenon.

Second, it has made a relatively greater contribution in industrialized countries—and some of those in the process of rapid industrialization—than in poor, developing ones. Asia, of course, comprises all three types of economy and there has been a much more extensive series of attempts to use broadcasting and associated media for educational purposes than in the other continents where developing countries are also concentrated (Africa and South America).

1. A Look at Some Systems

Asian countries which have had significant educational broadcasting services or have undertaken broadcasting experiments include Iraq, Iran, Israel, Jordan, Kuwait, Afghanistan, Pakistan, India, Sri Lanka, the People's Republic of China, Thailand, Malaysia, Singapore, Vietnam, Indonesia, the Philippines, Hong Kong, Korea, and of course Japan. The general pattern of development in these countries has been to begin with services for schools (sometimes with ETV started before radio) and to switch attention subsequently to nonformal educational broadcasting via radio, distance teaching institutions particularly in higher education, and—most recently—cassette distribution systems. Significant distance teaching schemes exist in Israel, Pakistan, Sri Lanka, the People's Republic of China, Thailand, and Japan, but in all of these the vast bulk of the work is by correspondence, and broadcasting plays only a minor part.

1.1 Iran

Iran has a long involvement with educational broadcasting, going back to the late 1950s. Television programmes for schools and general audiences were first broadcast at this time by the privately owned television station, but not long afterwards the Ministry of Education established its own ETV station and transmitter in Teheran. After some initial interest, stimulated by the gift of free receivers to a number of schools, enthusiasm died away and very few teachers could be found who regularly used the programmes. Nevertheless the station continued broadcasting for many years. There were a number of reasons why the ministry project failed to make a lasting impact on the Teheran schools, but one of the most obvious was that the whole scheme was grossly underfinanced and run on a shoestring budget. Consequently the locally made studio-based programmes looked poverty stricken, featured hastily and ill-written scripts by underpaid writers performed by underrehearsed performers, and were technically poor in execution. The programme schedule depended heavily on film imported from the United Kingdom, France, and the United States, which had only marginal relevance to the Iranian school system and its curriculum.

Meanwhile a state corporation took over television broadcasting and began some fairly successful adult education programmes in subjects like agriculture and foreign languages. When Iran's oil revenues escalated dramatically in the early 1970s pressure was applied by the Shah (a great fan of modern technology) to upgrade the use of educational broadcasting. This led to two major developments. The National Iranian Radio and Television Organization (NIRTO) took over responsibility for schools' broadcasts and hired a firm of American management consultants to design a comprehensive national system. A small army of university graduates was despatched to the United States to acquire higher degrees in educational technology, in order to run it. Second, the *Daneshgar-e-Azzad* (Free University) was set up to apply the techniques of the Open University of the United Kingdom to teacher and paramedical training. Cooperation between the Open University and the Free University was fairly modest however, partly because a substantial proportion of Open University faculty wanted nothing to do with the Pahlavi regime, and partly because of Iranian resentment of the attitudes of some of the British consultants. As with NIRTO, American influence came to predominate, and elaborate plans and systems designs were laid down for the establishment of the new institution. Unfortunately, very little of the grand scheme was realized in practice. As with similar institutions, the Free University of Iran was soon beset by problems of cooperation between the academics and the broadcasters of NIRTO, who were responsible for production and transmission of the programmes. Before long both the Free University and the schools' broadcasting system were engulfed by the Iranian revolution, and it is not yet clear in what form

educational broadcasting will be reestablished in that country. Islamic authorities were hostile to the use of television in schools before the revolution, but this may have been coloured by the association of television with the monarchy. NIRTO was run by a cousin of the Queen, and carried a great deal of pro-Shah propaganda. The potential use of the media in religious and moral education, much in evidence elsewhere in the Islamic world, may cause it to be viewed subsequently with much more sympathy.

1.2 Iraq

Of great interest here is the video cassette distribution system for inservice teacher training run by the Ministry of Education. Programmes are recorded and copied at a central studio complex in Baghdad, and distributed to some 20 regional teachers' centres. Here they may be used for individual viewing by teachers, or in inservice training courses. This project is most impressive and an imaginative and cost-effective use of the new media. Technical standards are high, and the scheme could obviously serve as the basis of a national system of cassette production and distribution for schools, as playback equipment becomes more widespread. Initially the format of the programmes was rather restricted, being confined largely to model lessons, but there is every reason to hope that a more flexible variety of formats will be developed.

1.3 India

India has had schools' broadcasting services for a number of years, and the problem of poor utilization is as common here as elsewhere, with the exception that in India at least it is openly acknowledged. For example Singh (1981) reports that even in an intensive educational project involving the use of radio in the classroom, only 11 percent, 12 percent, and 25 percent of the schools which had receiving facilities, made use of schools' broadcasts in Jaipur, Delhi, and Tamil Nadu respectively. And these figures do not indicate the level of use of broadcasts, that is the number of programmes listened to on average by the children (a common failing of educational broadcasting statistics).

Rather more successful have been the farmers' forum radio programmes broadcast by All-India Radio, and their success was partly behind the inspiration for India's most famous venture in educational broadcasting, the Satellite Instructional Television Experiment (SITE). No less inspirational was India's involvement in nuclear research and missile technology. Indeed the main impetus for the SITE project came from Professor V. A. Sarabhai, who created the Indian National Committee for Space Research within the Department of Atomic Energy, based at the Physical Research Laboratory (Dannheisser 1975). India's first space rocket was fired in 1963, and an earth station at Ahmedabad in Gujarat became operational in 1967, and later the hub of SITE.

For these reasons much more effort than before will go into nonformal applications, and there will be a greater interest in the use of radio, audio cassettes, and video cassettes. Above all, the media will, with luck, be integrated into the total learning system that is appropriate for any group of learners rather than the subject of independent, fragmented, and often underfinanced pilot projects. In education, the media have often been the victims of their own propaganda.

3. Some Useful Organizations

(a) Arab States Broadcasting Union
22a Hussein Street, Zamalek, Cairo, Egypt

(b) Asia-Pacific Broadcasting Union
NHK Broadcasting Centre, 2-2-1 Jinaan Shibuya, Tokyo 150, Japan

(c) Asia–Pacific Institute for Broadcasting Development
PO Box 1137, Pantai, Kuala Lumpur, Malaysia

(d) Asia Mass Communication Research and Information Centre
39 Newton Road, Singapore 1130

(e) Centre for Production and Training for Adult Education Television
Kay Siang Road, Singapore 1024

(f) Communication Foundation for Asia
4427 Int Old Sta Mesa Street
Sta Mesa, Manila, Philippines

Bibliography

Abu-Lughod I 1980 An open university for Palestinians: Tentative formulations. *Educ. Broad. Int.* 13: 22–26

Ahamed U 1981 Community development through local broadcasting: An experience among the hill tribes of Chiengmai, Thailand. *Educ. Broad. Int.* 14: 61–63

Akiyama T, Imaizumi S, Inoue M 1981 Broadcasting and school education in Japan. *Educ. Technol. Res.* 5: 15–40

Commonwealth Secretariat 1974 *New Media in Education in the Commonwealth: A Study.* Commonwealth Secretariat, London

Dannheisser P 1975 The satellite instructional television experiment: The trial run. *Educ. Broad. Int.* 8: 155–59

Epstein I 1982 Educational television in the People's Republic of China: Some preliminary observations. *Comp. Educ. Rev.* 26: 286–91

Hurst P 1980 Educational technology in the Middle East. *Educ. Broad. Int.* 13: 4–8

Larkin L H 1972 *Instructional Television in Asia.* Center for Educational Television, Quezon

McCormick R 1980 The Chinese Television University. *Educ. Broad. Int.* 13: 61–64

Mody B 1978 Lessons from the Indian satellite experiment. *Educ. Broad. Int.* 11: 117–20

Nippon Hoso Kyokai (NHK) 1967 *The History of Educational Broadcasting in Japan.* NHK Radio and TV Culture Research Institute, Tokyo

Nippon Hoso Kyokai (NHK) 1971 *Educational Broadcasts of NHK.* NHK, Tokyo

Nishimoto M 1969 *The Development of Educational Broadcasting in Japan.* Sophia University, Tokyo

Pitner N 1982 Radio broadcasting program for out of school education. *Eval. Educ.* 6(1)

Rogers E M 1980 Communication and development in the People's Republic of China. *Educ. Broad. Int.* 13: 51–57

Singh J 1981 Efficient management of educational radio for schools. *EPA Bull.* 4(2) National Institute of Educational Planning and Administration, New Delhi

Zaman R 1981 Battling with illiteracy. *Educ. Broad. Int.* 14: 117–21

Australia and New Zealand

D. C. B. Teather

A continent the size of mainland United States is the home of 15 million Australians; across the Tasman Sea, three million New Zealanders live in a country the size of the United Kingdom. Settled by Europeans only within the last 200 years, most of the population of both countries is urban, concentrated in the coastal cities. The dominant cultural forms are European, and institutions, in broadcasting and in education as elsewhere, are cast largely in a British mould. Despite economic reliance on primary industries, material standards of living are high and neither Australians nor New Zealanders have been slow to exploit technical innovations.

Indeed the oldest surviving radio station in the British Commonwealth, Pioneer Station 4XD, is in the New Zealand city of Dunedin. Links between broadcasting and education go back to the foundation of this station, for its principal founder was Robert Jack, Professor of Physics at the University of Otago. His original radio transmissions were from an aerial strung from the university clock tower! Pleading in 1921 for the right to transmit gramophone concerts from his apparatus, Jack asked "Why should the people of New Zealand not be allowed to hear the best things going?"

Bureaucracy was, it seems, alive and well in New Zealand in the 1920s; but Jack received his licence to transmit. In the early days of broadcasting the operation was small, and the regular broadcasts to schools provided in the 1930s by the Australian Broadcasting Commission were at first the responsibility of the Talks Department. The growth of the service led to the appointment, in 1937, of a Federal Controller of School Broadcasts, whose title was subsequently changed to that of Director of Education, ABC.

It is not entirely fanciful to suggest that these origins may go some way to explaining the definition of educationalbroadcasting adopted 40 years later by the (Australian) Commonwealth Education Broadcasting Conference:

Educational broadcasting is broadcasting with pre-determined educational objectives, normally planned in series which are designed to lead to the mastery of a body of knowledge or skill or to the acquisition of experience, which is normally accompanied by publications and planned in consultation with educational bodies where appropriate. (Gilmour 1979)

Compare, for example, the broader definition of Cathcart (1978):

Educational broadcasting is broadcasting which aims to educate, or to assist in the education of, its listeners or viewers. While educational transmissions may incidentally entertain or inform, they are primarily designed to instruct their audiences or at least to stimulate them to learn.

This article is concerned with four areas of educational broadcasting, distinguished on the basis of audience characteristics as follows:

(a) Broadcasts to schools: broadcasts designated as "school broadcasts" and with content relating to the school curriculum.

(b) Educational broadcasts to children and young people out of school: broadcasts with an educational intent, but designed for general listening or viewing by children and young people in the home.

(c) Broadcasts to adult students: broadcasting designed to be used in the course of their studies by adult students registered as such with a tertiary or other educational institution.

(d) Educational broadcasts to other adults: broadcasts with an educational intent but not requiring registration as a student of an educational institution.

Both radio and television will be considered under each head.

1. Broadcasts to Schools

Public service broadcasting in Australia is the responsibility of a federal body, the ABC. (Prior to 1932, ABC stood for the Australian Broadcasting Company, but between 1932 and 1983 this became the Australian Broadcasting Commission. In 1983 it became the Australian Broadcasting Corporation.) Schooling is, however, the responsibility of the individual states, each with its own educational bureaucracy. In New Zealand, which has a unitary rather than a federal political structure, there is a single Department of Education and nationwide public service broadcasting organizations.

ABC School Broadcasts Advisory Committees were established in each state in the early 1930s, and radio programmes for schools were produced in each state capital for broadcast to the schools in that state. Only in the mid-1960s, faced with mounting costs for more complex schools' television productions, was a concerted effort made to plan series of programmes for use nationwide. Now approximately 80 percent of all schools' television programmes produced in Australia are transmitted in all states.

When it was founded in 1932 the Australian Broadcasting Commission had no statutory requirement to broadcast to schools, but was given the broad duty of transmitting information. As Anders (1983) comments:

It must have seemed self-evident to the first members of the Commission...that a significant part of the resources at their disposal should be devoted to the provision of information for school children.

Indeed in the 1930s the ABC not only produced and broadcast radio programmes to schools, but also distributed to schools free copies of booklets to supplement the programmes and gave financial assistance for the purchase of radio receivers. In 1935, 21 percent of all Australian schools were making regular use of radio programmes. By the mid-1950s usage had risen to 90 percent, and 27 professional staff were employed in programme production (Australian Department of Education 1977).

Television was introduced in 1956 in Sydney and Melbourne and the first experimental educational programme, "Kindergarten Playtime", was screened on Christmas Day. Several series were broadcast to schools during 1957 and 1958, with the ABC drawing on its experience with schools' radio by producing programmes to "supplement the work of the teacher and provide experiences not readily available in the schools" (Gilmour 1979). Production facilities for educational television were considerably expanded in 1963, and by 1964 there were five television transmissions daily—two for primary schools and three for secondary schools—from transmitters which were by then capable of reaching 90 percent of the Australian population. Direct teaching programmes were introduced in science and mathematics to help implement new syllabi in these subjects and to overcome an acute shortage of maths and science teachers in the schools.

The decade 1965-75 saw a flowering of schools' television broadcasting in Australia. Production techniques were developed, and programmes were used with greater flexibility in the schools. By 1969 the education departments of South Australia and Queensland had begun to equip their schools with video recorders, and at the end of the period, 86 professional staff were employed in the production of radio and television schools' broadcasts (Australian Department of Education 1977). By 1972, over 90 percent of all Australian schools were making regular use of schools' television programmes.

Transmission figures from the early 1980s show that in South Australia, for example, 224 hours of original radio programmes and 334 hours of original television programmes were transmitted to schools in 1982. Comparable figures for Queensland were 175 hours of radio and 274 hours of television. Adding to these the hours of repeat broadcasts, an average of 260 hours of radio and 520 hours of television were transmitted to schools in these states. Of these broadcast hours, approximately half were aimed at primary and half at secondary pupils. For primary pupils the hours of television exceeded those of radio by 4:1; for secondary pupils the hours of television and of radio were approximately equal.

A very wide range of both enrichment and subject-specific material is presented. At the primary level, language arts, social studies, and (on radio) music and movement predominate; at the secondary level modern languages, social studies, and English. But the themes of recent schools' television series, for example, styles of life in Northern Australia, the effects of urbanization on rural landscape, the chemist's role in society, and dramatizations of detective stories to foster listening skills, evoke the breadth of the programme material. Some overseas material, for example the British Broadcasting Corporation's (BBC) series on French and German, is also broadcast.

Supplementary printed materials, for both teachers and pupils, are available for many of the radio and television schools' broadcasts. Special arrangements, such as the Queensland remote schools' videotape scheme, are made to supply audio- and video-cassette copies of broadcasts to schools in localities where the broadcast signal is poor or absent. Schools in South Australia can obtain, from the Educational Technology Centre of the Department of Education, a copy of any schools' programme broadcast in the state in exchange for a blank cassette.

Radio broadcasts to schools in New Zealand developed in a similar way to those in the Australian states. By 1973, 780 programmes were being produced annually. The following year discussions relating to the transfer of the production of schools' broadcasts from Radio NZ to the Department of Education began, but these were protracted. During the period 1974-79 the Schools' Broadcasts Section of RNZ was run down, and studios for the department's own audio production unit were not commissioned until 1981. This audio unit now produces programmes on audiocassettes for pupils of the Correspondence School (see below), programmes on audiocassettes for distribution to other schools, and master tapes for Correspondence School broadcasts. At present, Radio New Zealand's schools-related broadcasts comprise a 10-minute news programme (three times per week), a 15-minute programme for preschoolers (daily), and a 20-minute programme each day for the Correspondence School.

The policy of the New Zealand Department of Education has been to replace the schools' radio broadcasts by the distribution of materials on audiocassette. But

the necessary development of distribution facilities, in the National Film Library and in regional audiovisual libraries, has been severely curtailed by the lack of finance. For the same reason, those recommendations of the Williams Committee (1972) which advocated the introduction of broadcast television for schools have not been acted upon. Only small-scale experiments in broadcast television for schools have yet been attempted in New Zealand.

Thus far, "schools' broadcasting" has been regarded as broadcasting to classes in conventional schools. But the term takes on an additional dimension in Australasia. Between 1914 and 1924 the departments of education of the six Australian states, and that of New Zealand, established correspondence schools to teach pupils of primary-school age who were unable, because of the remoteness of their homes or because of illness, to attend school in person. Secondary teaching was added later, and today these schools provide by correspondence a very wide range of courses both for pupils of school age and for adults.

The New Zealand Correspondence School began broadcasting to its pupils in 1931, and its programmes are now carried by the Radio NZ Concert and Regional Networks for 20 minutes on each weekday of the school year. The 1982 broadcasts, 279 programmes, comprised 45 hours of original programming and 12 hours of repeats. In addition, 9,000 pupils received audiocassettes as part of their courses, particularly in language, music, English, and shorthand/typing; 70,000 cassettes are in circulation covering 650 titles. In 1982 the school ventured into television; the outcomes of broadcasting five hours of programming on this medium, comprising 25 lessons, are now being assessed.

The Correspondence School radio broadcasts are no longer designed as formal lessons but as enrichment materials, to stimulate the interest of the full-time school-age pupils in the subjects they are studying. In addition, however, radio is used to provide a sense of belonging to a nationwide school community—through broadcasts such as the fortnightly "principal's radio assembly"—and to make pupils familiar with as many of their correspondence teachers as possible.

The Australian "schools of the air", which have access to the flying doctor shortwave radio networks, use these to provide two-way interaction between pupils and teachers. Each school's pupils, who may be scattered over tens of thousands of square kilometers, study by correspondence. But they receive daily assistance, via radio, from a small group of teachers based at the broadcasting station (Fitzpatrick 1982).

2. Educational Broadcasts to Children and Young People out of School

Radio NZ has all but given up presenting programmes for young people. In Australia and New Zealand, as in other Western countries, most children spend more time watching television than undertaking almost any other single activity.

The habit starts early. Television New Zealand (TVNZ) caters for the under-5s with "Play School", a 25-minute programme presented twice daily. As in the case of some other series, the format is from overseas, but much of the content is written and produced in New Zealand. "Sesame Street", first broadcast in New Zealand in the early 1970s "primarily for its entertainment value" (Barney 1972), now has Maori language inserts. TVNZ's 60-90 minute late afternoon package, "After School", is broadcast each weekday and often contains 5-10 minute items on music, science, and similar topics. A children's news programme, excellent natural history documentaries, and "Spot On", a series designed to widen children's horizons through vicarious experiences, are all locally produced. For older teenagers a new series raises life-style issues.

While much of this programming falls outside a narrow definition of educational television, its existence is of the utmost importance. Arguably, it has a greater educational effect than much of what happens in the classroom. In recent years more attention has been paid to programming for young people—the result both of the appointment of Head of Children's and Young People's Programmes at senior level within TVNZ and of the activities of the pressure group, "Monitor". Even the New Zealand *Listener*, the mass circulation (readership 1.3 million out of a total population of 3 millions) journal of the Broadcasting Corporation of New Zealand now incorporates a junior section and attempts to involve young viewers in activities to complement the television series, for example, a recent national survey of thrushes and snails in connection with a natural history programme.

3. Broadcasts to Adult Students

There is no single institution in Australia or New Zealand exactly analogous to the Open University of the United Kingdom. At the time the Open University was founded there were, however, already four universities fulfilling in Australasia the essential function of the United Kingdom foundation, viz to provide opportunity for part-time university study by distance learning (Teather and McMechan 1980) (see *Distance Learning Systems*). Indeed Bewley (1982) pointed out that Massey University "reaches twice the proportion of New Zealand's national population that the Open University does in Britain". But Massey's external role, now some 12,000 students enrolled in several hundred courses, compares in absolute terms with an enrolment of 90,000 at the Open University in the United Kingdom.

In Australia approximately 35,000 students are enrolled externally in advanced courses (White 1982). These enrolments are spread over five universities and more than 30 colleges of advanced education. The economies of scale in the use of broadcast media, which characterize the Open University in the United Kingdom, are not available to its Australian counterparts. Comparatively small numbers of students, great distances, and the vested interests of institutions whose external studies provision was already well-established, led the Committee on Open University to report in 1974 to the Australian Universities Commission:

> . . .although broadcast radio and television may be of use in the programs of particular tertiary institutions over limited areas, it would be neither desirable on educational grounds, nor feasible on technical grounds to use simultaneous broadcasts over the whole continent. (Karmel 1975)

The use of radio to reach small, highly specialized audiences—"narrowcasting"—had been pioneered by the University of New South Wales. Radio VL2UV went on the air in May 1961 to broadcast lectures to adult, part-time students in their homes. At that time accommodation for evening classes on the university campus was in short supply.

The uphill battle which proponents of educational broadcasting have had to fight in recent years is graphically illustrated by the terms of the licence granted to VL2UV, the first radio station in Australia to be owned and operated by a university. Firstly, the transmission frequency allotted, 1750 kHz, was beyond the tuning range of an ordinary radio receiver, so students had to have their receivers modified. Secondly, power was limited to 300 watts, 0.6 percent of the power of the nearby ABC station, 2FC. Broadbent (1982) comments:

> At the outset, many students undoubtedly were put off by the contrast between what they heard from 2FC. . .and what they heard (or half-heard) from VL2UV.

Thirdly, the playing of music was prohibited; breaks between lectures were filled instead by poetry readings.

In 1962, the university established extension centres in Sydney suburbs where groups of students listened to broadcasts and held discussions afterwards. Groups of students beyond the range of VL2UV received copies of the broadcast tapes by mail. In 1966, the university began producing television programmes, transmitting these to the extension centres. By this time the courses comprised a multimedia mix of radio and television broadcasts, printed notes and diagrams mailed to the students in advance of the broadcasts, student-led discussions, and occasional live seminars on the university campus.

The radio and television operation of the University of New South Wales was developed by the Division of Postgraduate Extension Studies. By 1982, enrolments had grown to 2,300 students who registered for the broadcast courses and a further 2,700 who registered in small groups to study the same courses on audio- and video-cassettes. The 40 or so courses offered each year are highly specialized, from full master's or graduate diploma subjects in engineering, science, and human communication to short series of 5–10 lectures in computer programming, management, electronics, and pharmacy. The cost of using broadcasting technology to teach small numbers of adult students has been minimized by simplifying production techniques. At first the television "studio" was designed for operation by one person—the lecturer himself or herself. Since 1979 many programmes have been made with the television component comprising only the video output of a computer.

Ten years after the establishment of VL2UV, the University of Adelaide set up a radio station within its Department of Adult Education. This broadcast some courses obtained from VL2UV, some produced in Adelaide, and imbedded these in a larger framework of more general, educative programming for which formal enrolment in a course was not required. In recent years, a number of other Australian universities and colleges of advanced education have established radio stations, some broadcasting on AM and some on FM, with programming on the Adelaide model.

4. Educational Broadcasts to Adults

One of the success stories of recent years has been Radio New Zealand's Continuing Education Unit (Brook-White 1985). Established in 1975, this small unit produces series of radio programmes with the "distinct philosophy of using personal experiences to raise awareness on the part of the listener" (Crutchley 1983). The unit's current catalogue lists 45 series including, among others, a series on marriage breakdown, the effects of a heart attack, classical Maori oratory, science fiction, how trade unions work, starting school, and preparing for retirement.

Most of the unit's series are designed for and first broadcast on the RNZ National Programme. Each series typically comprises 3–7 programmes, each 15–30 minutes in length. But production spans the full spectrum of NZ radio stations, from the concert programme, (e.g., an hour-long discussion of new approaches to science teaching) to the commercial stations (e.g., a series of 18, 2–3 minute programmes on the early history of the Lake Taupo region). Booklets and reading lists are often prepared to accompany the series. These are available for the cost of post and packing only, and audiocassette copies of the programmes themselves are supplied to New Zealand residents for the cost of blank cassettes and postage.

A number of government departments, for example agriculture, have themselves produced radio programmes for public information. And in 1982 the University of Otago set up a radio unit to produce educational programmes for broadcast by RNZ and Pioneer Station 4XD. In that year Otago produced 54 half-hour programmes which went on the air; included in these were four six-programme series, copies of which have subsequently been sold to schools and colleges as components of multimedia kits.

Television New Zealand has as yet no counterpart to radio's Continuing Education Unit; the production and broadcasting of educational television programmes for adults is controlled by the head of general and special interest programmes. TVNZ, unlike RNZ, has no noncommercial channels; both television channels carry paid advertisements and current policy is to split the audience equally between the two. In Australia, public service (ABC) and commercial broadcasting are quite distinct, operated by different authorities and providing different networks—one national ABC television network, and up to three commercial television networks in the largest cities.

At present, TVNZ screens some series which encourage adults to learn. Examples are the locally produced "Money Programme" and the recently screened "Computer Programme" from the BBC. In addition, some series are designed to encourage the creative use of leisure; series on home renovations, gardening, exercise, and health are examples.

Currently TVNZ is formulating a policy on educational television, which, it is hoped, will lead to more effective liaison between television and educational interests (NCAE 1980). More lead time on programme scheduling is essential here. Since 1981, TVNZ has made available broadcast time not scheduled for other purposes (on Sunday mornings) to screen programmes for professional and other groups with the aim of developing the expertise of their members. Some 30 such programmes have been screened to date.

5. New Technology and Old Dilemmas

Distribution by satellite will play an important part in shaping the future of educational communications in Australasia. New Zealand, through a terminal at the Wellington Polytechnic, has been part of the PEACESAT network since its inception (Bystrom 1975), and as the footprint of the ATS-1 satellite has moved west, several Australian stations have joined the network.

Australian domestic communications satellites were launched in 1985 and 1986, and already educational networks are becoming established. However, Gough et al. (1981), pointing to the dangers of noncommercial users being squeezed out as the demands of paying customers grow, suggest that a fixed proportion (20 percent) of the capacity of the satellite should be reserved for noncommercial use.

This is but a new example of an old dilemma. Since the early 1950s, the institutional forms of broadcasting in Australia and New Zealand, drawing originally from the British public service model, have been reshaped under the influence of the dominant economic, and therefore the dominant cultural, force in the West—namely the United States. Commercial television and radio, in both Australia and New Zealand, respond to and promote commercial values. While there are politicians who regard commercial broadcasting as a free good, and public service broadcasting as an unfortunate drain on the public purse, there is little hope for the realization of the full educational potential of the media.

As Esslin (1982) and others have eloquently pointed out, because much of what is broadcast is trivial the broadcast media themselves tend to be regarded as trivial and their longer term effects on society are vastly underestimated. In the midst of today's commercial cornucopia, Professor Jack's plea for people to be allowed to hear (and to see) the best things going has even more relevance than when he made it in 1921.

Bibliography

Anders D J 1983 *The Beginning of Educational Radio and Television in South Australia.* Australian Broadcasting Commission, Adelaide

Australian Department of Education 1977 Research in educational television and radio in Australia. In: Bates T, Robinson J (eds.) 1977 *Evaluating Educational Television and Radio.* Proc. Int. conf., Milton Keynes, 9–13 Apr. 1976. Open University Press, Milton Keynes, pp. 31–35

Barney W D 1972 Research on Sesame Street. *N. Z. J. Educ. Stud.* 7: 80–92

Bewley D 1982 Correspondence as the core: The Centre for University Extramural Studies, Massey University. In: Teather D C B (ed.) 1982 *Towards the Community University: Case Studies of Innovation and Community Service.* Kogan Page, London, pp. 89–101

Broadbent D 1982 Radio and television universities in New South Wales. In: Teather D C B (ed.) 1982 *Towards the Community University: Case Studies of Innovation and Community Service.* Kogan Page, London, pp. 123–42

Brook-White V 1985 Broadcasting and the education of adults. *N.Z.J. Adult Learn.* 17: 77–82

Bystrom J W 1975 The application of satellites to international interactive service support communication. *Proc. Roy. Soc. London A* 345: 493–510

Cathcart H R 1978 Educational broadcasting. In: Unwin D, McAleese R (eds.) 1978 *Encyclopaedia of Educational Media Communications and Technology.* Macmillan, London, pp. 256–266

Crutchley N 1983 Community education and local radio: Working together in New Zealand. *N.Z.J. Adult Learning* 15: 30–38

Esslin M 1982 *The Age of Television.* Freeman, San Francisco, California

Fitzpatrick J 1982 The Australian schools of the air: The conundrum of who teaches. *Distance Educ.* 3: 183–97

Gilmour C 1979 *The Role of ABC Educational Broadcasting: A Report of a Sub-committee of the ABC Federal Education Broadcasts Advisory Committee.* Australian Broadcasting Commission, Sydney

Gough J E, Garner B J, Day R K 1981 Policy issues in planning for distance education using a domestic communication satellite. In: Gough J E, Garner B J, Day R K (eds.) 1981 *Education for the Eighties: The Impact of the New Communications Technology.* Deakin University Press, Geelong, pp. 21–29

Karmel P 1975 *Open Tertiary Education in Australia: Final Report of the Committee on Open University to the Universities Commission.* AGPS, Canberra

National Council of Adult Education (NCAE) 1980 *Report on Television and Continuing Education.* NCAE, Wellington

O'Dwyer B (ed.) 1981 *Broadcasting in Australia: Today's Issues and the Future.* Centre for Continuing Education, Australian National University, Canberra

Teather D C B, McMechan P 1980 Learning from a distance: A variety of models. In: Howe A (ed.) 1980 *International Yearbook of Educational and Instructional Technology 1980/81.* Kogan Page, London, pp. 53–71

White M 1982 Distance education in Australian higher education: A history. *Distance Educ.* 3: 255–78

Williams R M 1972 *Report of the Committee of Inquiry into the Uses of Television in Education.* Government Printer, Wellington

Latin America and the Caribbean

E. G. McAnany

Educational broadcasting in Latin America and the Caribbean must be understood in the broadest sense. Use of the various mass media, but especially radio and television, for purposes of informing and educating audiences of all types could be included in the discussion of educational media. The limitation of space, however, will mean that the discussion will be focused more on those uses of media that have an explicitly educational purpose, and to exclude other categories of programming like entertainment, sports, news, music, and advertisement. All of these latter have important cultural impacts on audiences but should be discussed in other contexts.

Educational media, then, would here include the variety of media used explicitly for educational purposes, such as radio, television, film, two-way radio or telephone, and such transmission means as cable and satellite. All of these media can carry educational messages between senders and receivers in a variety of formats of one-to-one (telephone or two-way radio), or one-to-many (broadcast radio and television, whether through microwave or cable systems and in combination with or solely by satellite).

This article will develop a brief historical overview of the development of educational media both in the United States and Latin America and the Caribbean by tracing the advance of technology and its use by the educational community. Other sections will discuss purposes, media, and audiences within education; institutions and costs of media; and finally a discussion of five critical issues for educational media in the region for the near future.

1. The Development of Educational Media

With the commercialization of radio broadcasting in the United States and Europe in the 1920s and 1930s, education began to look at the new medium as a potential pedagogical ally. There was a series of educational experiments with radio in the 1930s and 1940s in the United States, for example, that were almost forgotten when television began to capture the educators' attention in the 1950s (Madden 1968, Forsythe 1970, Jamison et al. 1974). During the 1950s and early 1960s, American educators turned their attention to the potential of teaching with television (Chu and Schramm 1968, Schramm 1977). It was in the early 1960s that television for schools began to have widespread use in America and promised a bright future for the growth of this sector. This coincided with the development and spread of programmed instruction and serious learning research that began to create the field of instructional design and learning systems; it was also reinforced by the passage of a series of federal education laws under the Johnson administration in the mid-1960s, and investment by major industrial interests in the development of hardware systems. Most of these activities subsided in the early 1970s for a variety of reasons: business pulled back, governments retrenched, and educators became disillusioned.

Finally, in the 1980s, there is renewed interest in the United States, Europe, and Japan in what the "new technologies" (generally including cable and satellite television, audio and video cassettes, computer and telecommunications systems for both office and home) may bring to education as a new generation of technology begins to take its place in the institutional structures of these societies (Council on Learning 1980).

In Latin America during these same 50 years (1930–1980), there was much slower development of interest in the use of educational media, but many of the same patterns can be observed. Radio as a commercial medium began only shortly after its counterpart in North America, but the major growth of the medium came in the 1940s and 1950s, while television began its real commercial growth only in the 1960s and 1970s.

One of the earliest and still continuing educational uses of radio was begun in 1947 by a Catholic priest in Sutatenza, Colombia. At first using it only to evangelize his scattered parish, he later built an educational institution of broadcasting and publishing that reached the entire nation. Known as *Accion Cultural Popular* (ACPO), this organization gave the name "radio schools" to its efforts to reach and educate rural poor people and helped to create what is now an international network of such radio schools in about 45 programs in almost all countries of the region (McAnany 1973, Jamison and McAnany 1978, Beltran et al. 1978, Morgan et al. 1980). The ACPO organization had a number of unique features that generally hold true today for it and the other radio schools: it was private (sponsored by the Catholic Church); it focused on rural illiterate adults; it taught practical knowledge of literacy, agriculture, health, and so on (usually without any school credit); it used volunteers for group study (thus the "schools" aspect of the title); it used a combined approach of radio, print, and face-to-face interaction for its

learning. Taken together, the radio schools are probably the single largest effort using educational media in the region [McAnany estimated about 250,000 enrolled students in 1973; Muhlman et al. (1977) report 62,365 students in ACPO alone].

In order to place radio schools in perspective, it is necessary to note that they grew [most began only in the early 1960s and changed directions as needs and circumstances changed throughout the subsequent years as White (1977) notes in the Honduran case] alongside other quite different educational media efforts in the public sector. Although there were cases of radio being used by ministries of education for various types of instruction (usually for enrichment of regular school topics) in the 1950s, the first major effort by the public sector seems to have come about the time television began to take its place as the primary medium for schools. [For example, in Schramm et al. (1967) case studies of educational media, there are only two cases of public media projects in Latin America.] With significant aid from the Ford Foundation and the United States government, Colombia began a major educational television effort for its primary schools in 1964 (Comstock and Maccoby 1966–1967). Although the effort reached as many as 250,000–300,000 students at one time, it did not spread to the entire system and soon became more of an enrichment than a core teaching instrument. During the later 1960s and early 1970s, a number of educational television projects were begun. [Tiffin (1978) notes that there were 14 by the mid-1970s.] Among such systems were the El Salvador junior secondary project begun in 1968 (Mayo et al. 1976), the Mexican Telesecundaria started in 1969 (Mayo et al. 1975), the Cuban system started about 1968 (Werthein 1977), and several instructional systems in Brazil begun in the early 1970s (Oliveira 1977, Oliveira and Orivel, 1982).

But even as major investments were being made in television for schools, doubts also began to be raised about costs, effectiveness, and the appropriateness of the technological transfer. Although Schramm had been an early advocate of educational media and television in particular (Schramm et al. 1963), he was also early in noting that television often did not make sense for many countries (1977). The "little media" that he suggested of radio, slides, audio cassettes, and portable video were not only cheaper and often as effective but also more under local control and more adaptive for local needs. More "appropriate technology" was advocated by many educators toward the end of the 1970s (*Revista de Technologia Educativa* 1978).

Three major developments in the 1970s regarding educational media were related to the changing circumstances of the region. The use of satellites for potential educational application was attempted in Brazil in 1972 with their SACI project (McAnany and Oliveira 1980) but, unlike India's year-long satellite experiment (SITE), the Brazilian project only used a satellite connection briefly. However, in 1972 to 1974, the United Nations Development Programme (UNDP) sponsored a serious regional review of the potential use of educational technology with special emphasis on television and satellites (UNDP 1975). The second major effort concerned nonformal education and rekindled the interest in the use of smaller media especially radio, to reach long neglected audiences (AED 1978, Evans 1976). The radio schools had been consistently focusing on these audiences since their beginning, but now public sector efforts were made in a number of countries including Brazil, Guatemala, Ecuador, and Colombia. Much of this effort was focused on farmers and others of the rural poor who were to be provided with information relevant to agriculture, health, nutrition, and family planning (Contreras 1980, O'Sullivan 1980). The third development in the 1970s was the popularization of a "distance learning" approach modeled after the successful British Open University (Kaye and Rumble 1981). The applicability of the idea that people could study on their own with printed texts and tutorial sessions and with the support of visual media to achieve certification at various levels in the educational system was taken up by various countries in the region (Escotet 1980, Perraton 1982, Mackenzie et al. 1975, White 1976, McAnany et al. 1983).

There were a number of problems facing Latin American education at the beginning of the 1980s (see Sect. 4), but during the previous three decades a great deal had been learned about the application of the media to education. Although large amounts of capital had been invested in experiments in radio, television, and other technology, there were no national systems operating (with the possible exception of El Salvador) as the 1980s began. A great deal of knowledge and sophistication had been acquired, but also a degree of scepticism about the appropriateness and efficacy of the media helped to temper the enthusiasm for large-scale investments.

Given this historical perspective for the region, it would be useful to sketch in a more logical way the various audiences and purposes that educational media serve.

2. Purposes, Media, Audiences

The media in education are simply "means" by which educational goals and objectives may be achieved. Ordinarily media are thought of as delivery systems with radio and television the outstanding examples, but more reflection would suggest that there are a variety of media including the most ancient such as chalkboards, pictures, and, most importantly, printed materials. The total plan for the implementation of educational content has grown more sophisticated and has been described as a total learning "system" while the process knowledge required to develop it has been called "educational technology." (see *Conceptual Frameworks and Historical Development*; *Systems Approaches to Instructional Development*).

Table 1 (Jamison and McAnany 1978) provides an overview for a communication system that might serve national development goals that include formal education and development communication (nonformal education). The variety of objectives that education undertakes is only hinted at in this table but the summaries under formal education (column one) and development communication (column two) are indicative of the main purposes of most media. Those dealing with formal education usually treat children and young adults in the primary, secondary, and higher education levels, but they also refer to audiences who study for certification at these levels in a variety of out-of-school or distance education endeavors. Perhaps this can be best illustrated by some examples from Latin America.

In the regular primary school a variety of broadcast media may be added to the traditional combination of face-to-face instruction, books, and sometimes other small classroom media. Colombia (Comstock and Maccoby 1966–67) used instructional television; Mexico used radio (Spain 1977); Nicaragua used radio to teach mathematics only (Suppes et al. 1978). In addition, however, a radio school in the Dominican Republic provided instruction by radio in a distance learning situation where students studied at home with considerable success (White 1976). In this last case, audiences were young adults in their teens, somewhat older than their regular school counterparts.

At the secondary level, there have been a variety of educational programs besides the traditional. El Salvador (Mayo et al. 1976), Cuba (Wertheim 1977), Maranhao, Brazil (Oliveira 1977), and Ceará, Brazil (Oliveira and Orivel 1982) have all added television to regular classroom instruction, but in each case it forms the core of the instruction and is not merely an enrichment added on to a teacher's work. In addition, Mexico's Telesecundaria (Mayo et al. 1975) helped parents establish their own "schools" in homes, churches, and town halls and provided instruction by television, a primary school monitor, and printed materials for secondary students who had no regular school available. Brazil has an even more open system with its *madureza* study (Oliveira and Orivel 1982) in which adults prepare to take equivalency exams by studying at home with a variety of print and electronic media. Colombia is attempting to create a national radio high school through which working adults would study at home and take exams to achieve an equivalent degree.

At the university level, several projects began around 1980 to provide training at a distance, either within the structure of a traditional university or by building a totally new institution similar to the British Open University. Of the former, Escotet (1980) refers to efforts in Mexico's UNAM and the University of Zulia in Venezuela. The independent universities are primarily the *Universidad Nacional Abierta* of Venezuela and the *Universidad Estatal a Distancia* of Costa Rica (see Kaye and Rumble 1981 for details on these and 10 other open universities throughout the world). There are, in addition, several efforts being focused on teachers to help them upgrade themselves for certification while still

Table 1
Services of a national communication system

	Formal education	Development communication	Interactive communication	Entertainment
Objectives Demand for service	(a) Basic education (reading and language skills, mathematics, basic science, socialization) (b) Vocational education (impartation of specific work skills–e.g., typing, accountancy, surgery)	(a) To motivate population (b) To inform population (e.g., local news, weather) (c) To teach adults (limited basic education, improved consumption and production efficiency) (d) To change behaviour (family planning, etc.)	To allow exchange of information, agreements, and directives for: (a) Industry and commerce (b) Public administration (c) Security (d) Financial intermediation and banking (e) Personal use (direct consumption)	Direct consumption
Delivery systems Supply of service	*Locale* (a) In-school (b) Distance learning (at home) (c) Apprenticeship (at work) *Media* (a) Face-to-face instruction (b) Books (c) Other printed materials (d) Radio (e) Television (f) Recorded audiovisuals	(a) Extension systems (b) Adult schools and listening groups (e.g., radiophonic schools of Latin America, farm forums of India and Africa) (c) Campaigns (intensive efforts of limited duration, like the Tanzanian health campaign) (d) Spot announcements in the mass media	(a) Telephony and telegraphy (b) Mail (c) Couriers (an important function of road, rail, and air systems is to transport couriers and mail) (d) Two-way radio	(a) Press (including books) (b) Radio (c) Television (d) Films (e) Recorded audiovisuals

Source: Jamison and McAnany 1978 p. 11

remaining in their classrooms. Brazil has tried this with their LOGOS system and Colombia's *Universidad Javieriana* has used television to do a similar job (Peña 1980).

3. Institutions and Costs

Two important factors in the successful use of educational media have emerged from the evaluations that have been undertaken in recent years (Bates and Robinson 1977). The first is the organizational structure and the institutional strength of media projects. The obvious distinction between private and public organizations has been made. Private organizations may be church-related or supported by foreign governments (with the permission of the host country). Church-supported radio schools have managed to survive on lean budgets through the 1970s. Projects within the public sector sponsored with outside funding often do not survive because their budgets do not become part of the regular ministry allocation. Funding from UNESCO, UNICEF, or other United Nations organizations, from the United States, and Western Europe (especially the German state foundations), and the Organization of American States have all seen projects blossom and fade through the cycle of funding. Even where indigenous organizations are internationally funded as in Mexico, Colombia, Brazil, and Chile, the strength of the educational efforts wax and wane with budgets. Two organizational types have emerged in the public sector: media organizations within ministries of education (El Salvador and Mexico) or separate organizations (Colombia, Chile, and Brazil). In some cases, broadcasting remains entirely in the hands of ministries of information or communications and close collaboration is needed with the ministries of education.

Institutions not included in the above are the four or five Centers for Educational Technology founded during the 1970s by the Organization of American States (OAS). The OAS trained a number of people at various levels in all aspects of educational technology. In addition, there have been a large number of educational researchers trained in and outside of Latin America who work in educational planning, research, and administration in public and private institutions. These groups have added to the already large educational establishments using media in the 1980s.

The other important factor that emerged in the area of educational media during the 1970s was the cost of technology systems. The gathering of historical costs (Jamison et al. 1974, UNESCO 1977, 1980, 1982) has helped in two ways: media systems can be compared with traditional systems for costs and effectiveness; different components within media systems can be identified, and cheaper alternatives sought (see *Economics of Educational Technology*). Newer methodologies for measuring costs have been developed at a time that is doubly fortuitous. First, educational systems throughout the world have begun to slow down investments since the early 1970s. Eicher and Orivel (1979) have demonstrated that as the economies of most countries contracted in the 1970s, so did educational budgets, especially in the developing countries. With better methods for assessing costs and with an accumulation of outcome evaluations on effectiveness of media, governments will use media. Secondly, as a new generation of technologies is developed in more advanced industrial societies and offered for purchase in Latin America, a sound economic as well as cultural and educational assessment will be needed.

4. Critical Issues for the 1980s in Latin America

At the beginning of the 1980s, the ministries of education in Latin America and the Caribbean met to discuss the future. Gonzales (1980) reflects on their official statements and suggests five challenges for education in the region: (a) democratization of opportunity and decentralization of educational structures; (b) incorporation of indigenous cultures into educational content; (c) better science education with special emphasis on transfer of technology; (d) training of new teachers;

(e) educational planning and research serving the administrator. These major themes might be slightly adapted to the educational media and serve as a guide to future development in the region.

(a) *Democratization/decentralization.* The media have had as a main goal reaching mass audiences. What was learned in the 1970s, however, was that the mass audience of the poor and unserved also tend not to be served by educational media either (McAnany 1980). If education is to be democratized and learning systems decentralized, better delivery and support systems will need to be developed (McAnany and Mayo 1980).

(b) *Participation/local cultural content.* The "little media" or "appropriate technology" that became widely used in the 1970s need to be examined to see how they can promote technology that is under local control and that can be adapted by users to local needs. The centralizing force that is found in most big technologies seems to militate against the decentralizing and localizing goals now current. Only smaller media like radio, portable video, two-way media, and so on will be easily adapted to these objectives, but even larger media may be used for such purposes if planning is careful (Hudson 1977).

(c) *New technologies/transfer problems.* The general problems of transferring technologies between countries began to be studied during the 1970s, and problems specific to educational technology were also discussed (*Revista de Tecnologia Educativa* 1978). But now with a whole new generation of advanced technologies bearing down on advanced countries and being adapted for education (Council on Learning 1980), it will not be long before Latin America must decide on the use of these same technologies for their own purposes. A clear approach to assessment must include educational, cultural, and economic factors among others.

(d) *New teachers.* It is clear that opportunities for using technology will affect teachers as well as school systems. There is evidence that teachers often react negatively to technology not only because it threatens jobs but because it changes relationships. There is an urgent need to innovate in education in the region, but the ability to do so will largely rest on the willingness and ability of teachers to implement these innovations.

(e) *Educational planning/research.* Media systems are attractive to many countries because of their promise of increased coverage and quality as well as lower costs. The major disappointment manifested in the media during the 1970s cannot be dispelled except by carefully planned and executed projects (Escotet 1980). Without better planning and research this is not possible. Latin America and the Caribbean have enough trained personnel to make sophisticated technological systems work for major educational goals, but there must be better institutional structures and sufficient rewards to draw these people into educational work and keep them there.

Bibliography

Academy for Educational Development (AED) 1978 *The Basic Village Education Project, Guatemala.* Academy for Educational Development, Washington, DC

Bates T, Robinson J (eds.) 1977 *Evaluating Educational Television and Radio.* Open University Press, Milton Keynes

Beltran L, Velez G, Fox E, Novoa A 1978 *Las Escuelas Radiofoncias de America Latina Una Resena Bibliografica* [Latin American Radio Schools, A Bibliographical Review]. International Center for Development Studies, Bogota

Chu G, Schramm W 1967 *Learning from Television.* National Association of Educational Broadcasters, Washington, DC

Comstock G A, Maccoby N 1966–67 *The Peace Corps Educational Television Project in Colombia: Two Years' Research* (12 vols). Stanford Institute for Communication Research, Palo Alto, California

Contreras E 1980 Brazil and Guatemala: Communications, rural modernity and structural constraints. In: McAnany E G (ed.) 1980

Council on Learning 1980 *The Communications Revolution and the Education of Americans.* Change Magazine Press, New Rochelle, New York

Eicher J, Orivel F 1979 *The Allocation of Resources to Education Worldwide.* UNESCO, Paris

Escotet M 1980 La Educación superior a distancia en Latinoamerica: Mito y realidad de una innovación [Higher distance education in Latin America: Myth and reality of an innovation]. *Revista de Tecnologia Educativa* 6(3–4): 239–51

Evans D R 1976 Technology in nonformal education: A critical appraisal. *Comp. Educ. Rev.* 20: 305–27

Forsythe R 1970 *Instructional Radio: A Position Paper.* Educational Resources Information Center (ERIC), Stanford, California

Gonzales J H 1980 Necesidades y perspectivas de la educación en la decada del 80 [Necessities and perspectives in education for the 80s]. *Revista de Tecnologia Educativa.* 6(2): 191–203

Hudson H 1977 Community use of radio in the Canadian North. In: Spain P L, Jamison D T, McAnany E G (eds.) 1977

Jamison D T, Klees S J, Wells S J 1978 *The Cost of Educational Media: Guidelines for Planning and Evaluation.* Sage, Beverly Hills, California

Jamison D T, McAnany E G 1978 *Radio for Education and Development.* Sage, Beverly Hills, California

Jamison D T, Suppes P, Wells S 1974 The effectiveness of alternative instructional media: A survey. *Rev. Educ. Res.* 44: 1–67

Kaye A, Rumble G (eds.) 1981 *Distance Teaching for Higher and Adult Education.* Croom and Helm, London

Leslie J 1977 Five nutrition projects that use mass media. *Development Communication Report.* Washington, DC

McAnany E G 1973 *Radio's Role in Development: Five Strategies of Use.* Clearinghouse on Development Communication, Washington, DC

McAnany E G (ed.) 1980 *Communications in the Rural Third World: The Role of Information in Development.* Praeger, New York

McAnany E G, Mayo J K 1980 *Communication Media in Education for Low-income Countries: Implications for Planning.* International Institute for Educational Planning, UNESCO, Paris

McAnany E G, Oliveira J 1980 *The SACI/EXERN Project in Brazil: An Analytical Case Study.* Reports and Papers on Mass Communication No. 89, UNESCO, Paris

McAnany E, Oliveira J, Orivel F, Stone J 1983 Distance education: Evaluating new approaches in education for developing countries. *Eval. Educ.* 6: 289–376

Mackenzie N, Postgate R, Scupham J 1975 *Open Learning: Systems and Problems in Post-secondary Education.* UNESCO, Paris

Madden R 1968 Educational radio bibliography. *Educ. Broad. Rev.* 2: 66–79

Mayo J K, Hornik R C, McAnany E G 1976 *Educational Reform with Television: The El Salvador Experience.* Stanford University Press, Stanford, California

Mayo J K, McAnany E G, Klees S 1975 The Mexican Telesecundaria: A cost-effectiveness analysis. *Instr. Sci.* 4: 193–236

Morgan R, Muhlman L, Masoner P 1980 *Evaluación de Sistemas de Comunicación Educativa* [Evaluation of Educational Communication Systems]. Accion Cultural Popular, Bogota

Muhlman L, Masoner P, Bernal H 1977 Accion cultural popular: Estudio de caso [Accion cultural popular: A case study]. *Revista de Tecnologia Educativa* 3: 461–94

Oliveira J 1977 ETV-Maranho: An effective case of endogenous growth. In: Bates T, Robinson J (eds.) 1977

Oliveira J, Orivel F 1982a The *Madureza* Project in Bahia, Brazil. In: Perraton H (ed.) 1982

Oliveira J, Orivel F 1982b The Minerva Project in Brazil. In: Perraton H (ed.) 1982

O'Sullivan J 1980 Guatemala: Marginality and information in rural development in the Western Highlands. In: McAnany E G (ed.) 1980

Peña L 1980 La Teleducación: Tecnologia o Communicación? [Teleducation: Technology or Communication?] *Revista de Tecnologia Educativa* 6(3-4): 309–22

Perraton H (ed.) 1982 *Alternative Routes to Formal Education.* Johns Hopkins Press, Baltimore, Maryland

Revista de Technologia Educativa 1978 Symposium on problems of transfer of educational technology. OAS journal, Santiago, Chile, Vol 4, No.1

Schramm W L 1977 *Big Media Little Media: Tools and Technologies for Instruction.* Sage, Beverly Hills, California

Schramm W L, Coombes P, Kahnert F, Lyle J 1967 *New Educational Media in Action: Case Studies.* Vols. 1–3. International Institute for Educational Planning, Paris

Schramm W L, Lyle J, Pool I 1963 *The People Look at Educational Television: A Report of Nine Representative ETV Stations.* Stanford University Press, Stanford, California

Spain P L 1977 The Mexican *Radioprimaria* Project. In: Spain P L, Jamison D T, McAnany E (eds.) 1977

Spain P L, Jamison D T, McAnany E G (eds.) 1977 *Radio for Education and Development: Case Studies.* (Staff Working Paper No. 266.) World Bank, Washington, DC

Suppes P C, Searle B, Friend J (eds.) 1978 *The Radio Mathematics Project: Nicaragua 1976–1977.* Institute for Mathematical Studies in the Social Sciences, Stanford, California

Tiffin J 1978 Problems in instructional television in Latin America. *Revista de Tecnologia Educativa* 4: 163–235

UNESCO 1977, 1980, 1982 *The Economics of New Educational Media.* UNESCO, Paris

United Nations Development Programme (UNDP) 1975 *Feasibility Study of a Regional System of Tele-education for Countries of South America.* UNESCO, Paris

Werthein J R 1977 A comparative analysis of educational television in El Salvador and Cuba (Unpublished Ph.D. dissertation, Stanford University) *Dissertation Abstracts International* 1977 38: 1183a–1184a (University Microfilms No. 77-18, 259)

White R 1976 *An Alternative Pattern of Basic Education: Radio Santa Maria.* (Experiments and Innovations in Education, No. 30.) UNESCO, Paris

White R 1977 Mass communication and the popular promotion strategy of rural development in Honduras. In: Spain P L, Jamison D T, McAnany E G (eds.) 1977

North America

J. Lyle

Canada, Mexico, and the United States have evolved three different systems of broadcasting although they share the philosophy that (a) all citizens have a right to receive numerous and uncensored broadcast signals; (b) users are not required to directly support the broadcast structure; and (c) the air waves are public domain or patrimony, and hence should be used for the general welfare and come under the supervision of central government.

The Canadian and Mexican systems have been influenced by the close proximity of their larger neighbor and its system. Both systems have some aspects which mirror the American system. But the governments of both nations have perceived a necessity to take actions to maintain the independent integrity of their own systems. Because they face different situations, their actions vary and the resulting systems are unique.

In all three nations use is made of both AM and FM for radio, and VHF and UHF for television.

1. The United States System

Broadcasting in the United States is dominated by the commercial system but there is a parallel "public" system which utilizes FM radio and television channels reserved for "noncommercial educational" use.

Most communities are served by television stations providing programs from three national commercial networks, the American Broadcasting Company (ABC), the Columbia Broadcasting System (CBS), the National Broadcasting Company (NBC), and from the noncommercial Public Broadcasting Service (PBS). In addition, most larger cities are served by one or more "independent" (nonnetwork) stations. Most stations broadcast from at least 6 a.m. to midnight. Radio and television sets are to be found in almost all homes.

Generally 90 percent or more of the viewing audience are tuned to the commercial stations. Most of the broadcast schedules of these stations come from the national networks who obtain a large proportion of their programs from independent production studios, located primarily in Los Angeles and New York. There are no restrictions on the importation of television programs. The commercial system makes little use of imported programs but foreign productions (especially from the United Kingdom) have been a prominent feature of the PBS schedule.

Since the advent of television, the nature of radio programming has changed. Most automobiles now contain radio receivers and listening while driving constitutes a large share of total time devoted to radio. Four national networks, ABC, CBS, Mutual, and NBC continue to operate, but their role has diminished. Residents of every community can choose from a multitude of both AM and FM channels. Individual stations tend to program for specialized audience interest such as different types of music, ethnic interests, sports, news, and so on. Most communities do have available the signal of a noncommercial station which provides programs from National Public Radio (NPR).

Cable television systems originated to provide off-the-air signals for residents in areas of bad reception but have become generally available, greatly expanding the variety of television services available to the public. These systems offer an increased number of "off-the-air" stations, including some from distant cities. Satellite distribution provides cable systems with nonbroadcast services, including programs of specialized interest as well as a variety of services such as interactive access to data services, financial reports, and shopping catalogs.

An international broadcasting service, the Voice of America (VOA), broadcasts programs in many languages. Its operations use 30 transmitters located in the United States and 70 located in foreign countries. They are administered by the United States Information Agency (USIA) in Washington, DC. In addition to the VOA, there are five high-frequency band stations licensed to private organizations for international broadcasting.

High frequency and satellite links, both radio and video, are used in some remote areas to provide basic telecommunications as well as broadcasting services to isolated populations in different parts of the nation. Instructional Television Fixed Services (ITFS) using 2500–2690 mHz have been made available on a local basis for distribution of school programs.

1.1 Regulation

A key factor in shaping the nature of American broadcasting was a 1912 decision giving the Department of Commerce responsibility for administering broadcasting activities. The potential of using the sale of air time for commercial messages to generate station income was recognized in the mid-1920s and this pattern of basic support was firmly established by the end of that decade.

The Federal Communications Commission (FCC) was created in 1934 as the sole agency regulating all interstate and foreign communication activities via wire and radio. The FCC consists of seven commissioners appointed by the President with the consent of the Senate.

The FCC regulates all domestic use of the frequency spectrum, including satellite signals, as well as telephony and cable. It also assigns frequency, power, and location of transmitters to provide a maximum spread of radio and television services throughout the nation. The number of channels for a given locale generally reflects the size of the population. Licenses for general radio and television stations are issued for three-year periods after which they are reviewed for renewal for a similar period. There are restrictions on the number of stations which any single ownership group may operate within and across markets to insure competitive ownership of mass media in any given market. Foreign ownership of any broadcasting management is limited to 20 percent.

Licensees are to operate broadcasting stations in the "public interest" but no definition of that concept has ever been set forth by the FCC. The Commission explicitly recognizes that each station management may vary programming to meet the individual needs of a given community. In actuality, there is little local television program production with the exception of news. Stations are required to do studies for the "ascertainment of needs" within their communities as part of the license application and renewal process.

The Communications Act specifies that the FCC cannot censor programs or do anything which interferes with the right of free speech. However, the FCC is authorized to regulate programming of a political nature. Station managements are permitted to broadcast editorial comment and to endorse candidates, but are required to be equitable in making time available to all legally qualified candidates for the same office. The "Fairness Doctrine" stipulates the right of reply for persons or institutions subjected to critical comment. Advertising content on the broadcast media is subject to review by the Federal Trade Commission.

Generally in the area of programming the FCC relies heavily upon "self-regulation" by broadcasters. The National Association of Broadcasters (NAB), to which almost all station managements belong, plays an important role in this area. It has promulgated a "Code," which includes limits for advertising (generally 18 minutes per hour for radio, 16 minutes per hour for television). However, the NAB has seldom invoked sanctions against members who violate the code.

It should be noted that networks are viewed as nonbroadcast entities and so are not regulated by the FCC.

1.2 Public Broadcasting

Since 1952, a noncommercial broadcasting structure has evolved. Confusion results from the use of the terms "public" and "educational" broadcasting in the American context. The terms refer to different types of content within the same system, which is generally referred to as "public broadcasting."

With the establishment of FM broadcasting in 1941, some frequency allocations were set aside for "noncommercial, educational" use. Since 1952 some television allocations have been similarly set aside. In 1966 the number of reserved television allocations was expanded from 242 to 615, providing an allocation for almost every community in the nation. Most of the "reserved" television channels are in the UHF band. Stations operating on these allocations, like commercial stations, are licensed to individual managements. Originally, most were operated by local or state educational authorities or universities to provide broadcasts to strengthen and enrich the instructional courses in schools. (Education in the United States is decentralized with authority vested in local boards of education.)

A significant number of stations are licensed to nonprofit local groups not related to the school authorities, but which may also broadcast "instructional" or "educational" programs. Some reserved FM channels are licensed to other private groups or religious organizations and these are not part of the "public broadcasting" structure. By 1980 the public system consisted of some 250 television and 220 FM radio stations and was still expanding.

The public stations tend to emphasize educational programming during the day. In the evening hours, the stations provide programs which are an "alternative" to those of the commercial stations. There is a heavy emphasis on cultural, informational, and ethnic programs.

The funding of the public broadcasting structure is diversified and varies considerably from one station to another. Major sources include local or state educational authorities, and grants from foundations and corporations. Although advertising is generally forbidden, corporations are allowed to "underwrite" programs and receive a brief acknowledgement at the beginning and end of the presentation. (In 1981, authorization was given to a small number of public stations to accept advertising on a limited, experimental basis.) There has been provision since 1962 for allocation of funds from the educational authorities of the federal government to finance capital investments to help build the public system.

In 1967, The Carnegie Commission, a panel of distinguished private citizens, recommended legislation to provide direct federal support to public broadcasting. Largely as a result of this report, the Public Broadcasting Act of 1967 came into being. The Act created the Corporation for Public Broadcasting (CPB) as a nongovernmental entity to receive and redistribute Federal money in support of public broadcasting, including direct allocation of funds to individual stations. A further result of the legislation was the creation of PBS and NPR to provide national programming services for both public television and radio.

The implied intention of the Public Broadcasting Act

was to create a system free of political interference. However, no provision was made to provide independent funding, leaving the system dependent upon periodic appropriation from The Congress with Presidential approval. This has made it vulnerable to political pressure generated by various groups dissatisfied with its programming.

1.3 Educational Broadcasting

Throughout the 1920s much emphasis was placed on the potential of broadcasting for developing education and culture. Attempts were made to have the Communications Act of 1934 "reserve" some radio channels for educational use. The attempts were unsuccessful and educational radio activities faded until 1941 when some FM allocations were set aside for this purpose.

In the 1950s, many school systems faced a shortage of teachers and physical facilities. Broadcast instruction was seen as a means of easing these pressures. Local and state educational authorities established stations using the reserved channels. These stations were used primarily in support of classroom instruction and most programs were locally produced using existing teaching staff. The use of evening hours for adult extension programs and "cultural" programming created a trend toward the concept of "public" broadcasting.

Expansion of educational broadcasting activity was facilitated by Title VII of the National Defense Education Act of 1958. This legislation made possible appropriations for support of educational broadcast projects starting in 1959. In 1962, provision was made for matching funds for capital programs to build or expand educational broadcasting stations.

By the mid-1970s, when school enrollments were declining and there was a surplus of teachers, several changes took place in the use of instructional broadcasting. Use of the medium for direct instruction declined. Use of video recorders, which make possible great flexibility in terms of both scheduling and program sources, increased.

Another change was a decrease in local production. In 1968, The Children's Television Workshop (CTW) came into being with the support of several foundations. Children's Television Workshop obtained substantial funding from the federal Office of Education to develop a television series to help prepare children, especially those from disadvantaged urban families, for entry into the primary-school programs. The success of this series, "Sesame Street," and CTW's series for older children, "The Electric Company," impressed upon school authorities the importance of production quality. Individual stations have limited resources and the quality of local production is problematic. To improve the quality of their schedules, managements have increased the acquisition of programs from entities such as CTW as well as commercial producers. Another strategy for improving program quality has been the pooling of resources through production consortia such as the Agency for Instructional Television (AIT).

In 1976–77 the first national audit of use of instructional television was jointly undertaken by CPB and the National Center for Educational Statistics (NCES). The survey reported that 72 percent of the nation's teachers had television available for in-class use and about 32 percent used at least one television series regularly in teaching some 15 million students. Over 40 percent of elementary-school teachers reported regular use, compared to 24 percent of intermediate and 21 percent of high-school teachers. Most of the program use, 58 percent, involved series provided by the public broadcasting stations. It was estimated that the nation's schools were spending between US$73 million and US$100 million annually to provide in-class televised instruction.

Several universities were among the first operators of radio stations in the early 1920s, and broadcast programs of university extension have existed ever since. Today, most college-level broadcast classes are on television. One of the earliest efforts was that of the Chicago Community College system which made it possible for viewers to complete a two-year certificate via televised instruction. Other pioneer college television courses included those provided by early morning broadcasts over CBS and NBC in the 1960s for which credit was arranged through cooperating universities.

A number of university and college systems have developed televised curricula both to expand opportunity in higher education more broadly for the public, and to attempt to reduce the pressure on physical plants. The SUN program of the State University of Nebraska is an example of such a program operated by a single system. There are also consortia through which a number of universities cooperate in televised courses. A 1979 survey by CPB and NCES found that 25 percent of the nation's colleges and universities offered courses for credit over television and 36 percent of them used broadcast television to supplement instruction.

The concept of a national university-level television program was advanced in 1981 when Walter H. Annenberg announced a gift of US$150 million over a 15 year period for this purpose. The Corporation for Public Broadcasting was selected as the agency to facilitate the planning and establishment of this operation.

2. The Canadian System

Canada is served by a dual system of broadcasting. The Canadian Broadcasting Corporation (CBC), a federal crown corporation, is required by statute to provide a comprehensive national service. It operates parallel national radio and television networks in English and French. There are also networks of private television stations providing programs in both languages.

As in the United States, most homes have both radio and television available and car radios provide a significant proportion of all radio listening time. Most communities have available the CBC radio and television services in both languages, stations of one or more private television networks, as well as one or more private radio stations. The latter do not have any national network organization.

Broadcasting stations are licensed by the federal government to service specific localities for which they are expected to provide programs of news, and current and community affairs. The CBC is licensed to operate stations in many communities, but in some areas its programs are carried by stations licensed to other groups.

Private stations are funded by the sale of time for advertising. The CBC obtains over a fifth of its budget through advertising, the rest through government grants voted annually by the Parliament.

Canada's situation is unique in several aspects. Firstly, a large Francophone population constitutes the majority in one province (Quebec) and a significant minority elsewhere. Political sensitivity related to this minority has resulted in a national policy requiring bilingualism, thus the mandate for CBC to provide parallel services in French and English.

Secondly, the vast majority of the nation's population resides in a narrow band adjacent to the border with the United States. Many Canadians live within the signal area of American broadcast stations. Because of their popularity, Canadian stations carried many American programs in order to be competitive. This situation created a national concern about "cultural colonialism." This concern has led to government willingness to provide the CBC with generous funding for production of high quality broadcast programs. It has also led to regulatory actions to restrict the importation of programs.

Thirdly, the remaining small minority of the population is widely dispersed over a vast area extending into the northern polar region. National policy stipulates that the entire population should have access to broadcast programs. Much effort has been given to attempts to implement that policy in these isolated northern communities. Many of these communities consist largely of indigenous populations, a factor which has provided yet another set of problems for the broadcasting services.

As a result of these factors, Canada has been in the forefront of experimental use of high frequency bands and satellite delivery in innovating communication programs. This includes provision of basic telecommunications services as well as broadcasting programs.

The CBC operates a multilingual Northern Service on the radio, as well as the Armed Forces Service, and Radio-Canada—the short-wave service for overseas listeners.

2.1 Regulation

Although radio broadcasting began in 1919, the first Royal Commission on Broadcasting was not convened until 1929. The stimulus for this commission was fear that the rapidly developing United States radio networks would dominate Canadian radio. It called for a crown corporation to assure the nation of its own national service and to provide service in areas which would not be serviced by commercial stations for economic reasons. In 1933, a Canadian Radio Broadcasting Commission was established by law, together with a Canadian network service. At this time, the precedent was set that such services should provide programs in both French and English. The CBC was established by law in 1936 to provide the national service and to regulate all broadcasting in Canada. Reaction from the private sector to this dual authority led to a 1958 action separating the regulatory authority but leaving the CBC as the national service in both radio and television. The Broadcasting Act of 1968 was a further revision and created the Canadian Radio–Television Commission (CRTC).

The CRTC is charged with the regulation and supervision of broadcasting. It mandates that all Canadians should be able to receive CBC services in both French and English and that programming should be balanced to reflect various tastes and interests. The CRTC and the CBC together implemented an Accelerated Coverage Plan to speed up the provision of broadcasting service with the result that radio is now available to 99 percent of households, television to 97 percent.

The regulation and control of technical aspects is vested in the minister of communications. In 1969, the Department of Communication was created to assist the minister in these matters. Advertising is subject to regulation under The Food and Drug Act and The Proprietory or Patent Medicine Act. Use of broadcast time for political purposes is also covered by law, primarily aimed at providing equity of access to all parties.

Much regulatory concern has focused on containing the influence of the United States broadcasting industry and programs. Canadian programs must constitute at least 60 percent of the schedule of all broadcasting entities. The resulting decrease of availability of popular United States television programs on Canadian stations provided a major stimulus to the spread of cable television services in Canada. This, in turn, resulted in CRTC regulations which guarantee full availability of Canadian stations on cable services before "importation" of United States services is allowed.

2.2 Educational Broadcasting

Canada developed one of the first programs to use interactive high frequency radio to provide educational services to isolated students in its northern areas. The pioneering has continued into the age of satellites, with government-sponsored experiments in using this technology for educational innovation. While much of this has focused on the problems of the isolated communities, attention has also been given to expanding the sharing of resources between campuses of institutions of higher education.

From its early days, the CBC has provided some programs intended for in-school use. The responsibility for education in Canada is vested in the provincial governments. As a precaution against offending the sensitivities of local authorities, the CBC programs have been primarily "enrichment" rather than "instructional" programs.

Provincial educational authorities have sought to develop their own broadcast programs. These are exemplified by the Ontario Educational Communications Authority (OECA) and the Alberta Educational Communications Corporation (ACCESS). These are crown corporations established within individual provinces and are funded by the legislatures of those provinces. Both operate their own broadcasting facilities as well as using leased time on CBC or other entities to provide a wide range of instructional and enrichment programs for both in- and out-of-school use. Both maintain active production units and market their programs for use elsewhere.

3. The Mexican System

Mexico has evolved a unique mix which combines private and government broadcasting, competitive and monopoly operations. In both radio and television, advertising-supported commercial stations predominate.

There is full coverage of the nation by radio and it is estimated that most families of the nation have receivers. However, there is a considerable concentration of stations in urban centers. The capital, Mexico City, is served by over 30 stations. Most stations are of low power, providing only local coverage. Although most do have some production capability, the vast majority of stations belong to networks which provide them with programs produced in the large cities. Mexico has no official overseas broadcasting service but there are a few stations with as much as 250 kW of transmitter power which are heard internationally.

Of the almost 700 AM and FM stations, only about 5 percent are noncommercial. Most of these are government owned, including those operated by universities, technical institutes, and the Ministry of Public Education. There are some 15–20 shortwave stations, most of them noncommercial.

Television coverage is estimated to reach over 70 percent of the nation's area and half of the population. Urban centers of the nation are fully covered by a highly competitive television system. Two major networks, *Telesistemas Mexicano* (TSM) and *Television Independiente de Mexico* (TIM) dominate the industry. Each network operates more than one station in the capital and some other cities. In 1977, these two organizations created a joint-venture company, *Televisa*, to pool production facilities and coordinate programming over four networks. These remain competitive although they have a policy of striving for complementary schedules to provide program diversity.

Concern about the lack of nonurban coverage led the government to establish *Television Rural de Mexico* (TRM) in 1977. It operates over 120 stations to provide signals to previously uncovered areas. By presidential decree, TRM has the right to rebroadcast any program of the commercial networks. The government also operates Channel 13 in Mexico City, which has become the center of a national network whose government subsidy is supplemented by advertising revenues. There is also noncommercial Channel 11 in the capital, operated by the *Comision de Operacion y Fomanto de Actividades Academicas* (Commission for the Promotion and Implementation of Academic Activities).

To expedite expansion of television reception throughout the nation, a massive program involving the installation of 1,000 satellite receiving antennae has been undertaken. Cable television is limited to a few urban areas.

3.1 Regulation

Experimental broadcasting began in 1921 and in 1923 the government authorized operation of commercial stations. This was a period of postrevolutionary political and social upheaval. Except for a 1926 law regulating technical aspects, the government paid little attention to broadcasting. However, by a 1931 law, the government laid claim to the right to exclusive jurisdiction over broadcasting.

During the 1930s, the United States networks became heavily involved in the development of stations and networks in Mexico. Concern over external control led to a 1940 law forbidding foreign ownership or control of broadcasting operations.

There had been government and party radio stations in the early years. However, the establishment of *La Hora Nacional* in 1937 was a major precedent through which the government made claim to access to broadcast time on all stations for purposes of promoting national development and unity.

In 1960, a major review and rewriting of broadcast legislation resulted in the Federal Law of Radio and Television. This law specifically states that the broadcast frequencies are public domain and are to be utilized in the public interest under franchise or license from the federal government. Considerable emphasis is placed by the law upon the social responsibility of broadcasters. The law stipulates there shall be no prior censorship of programs and guarantees freedom of expression and reception. The law also stipulates that all programs shall be in Spanish (unless special permission is obtained from the Ministry of the Interior) and that programs shall not corrupt the Spanish language. Broadcast of imported programs requires prior authorization (also from the Ministry of the Interior).

A presidential decree in 1968 stated that since broadcasters are benefitting from the use of the public domain, they should be taxed 25 percent of their total gross income. However, recognizing that such a tax would have a deleterious impact on the development of broadcasting, another presidential decree in 1969 established the concept of "fiscal time." In lieu of the 25 percent monetary tax, broadcasters are required to provide "fiscal time" to the government. This is a levy of 12.5 percent of each station's total broadcast time allocated throughout the day. If the government does not exercise the option of using any portion of "fiscal time," the broadcaster has an obligation to fill the time.

From the outset there has been less than full use of "fiscal time." To encourage greater use, the government has provided centralized production facilities. Since 1977, the *Direccion General de Radio, Television y Cinematographia* (RTC), attached to the Ministry of the Interior, has assumed responsibility for programmatic aspects of government broadcasting policy while technical aspects are vested with the Ministry of Communication and Transport. The RTC develops the overall plan regarding national radio and television operations, including determining programs and transmission schedules and enforcing "fiscal time" requirements. It also has the responsibility for the operation of the rural television network, TRM. The *Productora Nacion de Radio y Television* is a quasistate production company attached to the Ministry of the Interior to provide production services for agencies making use of "fiscal time." It is also allowed to do commercial production as a means of becoming self-supporting.

3.2 Educational Broadcasting

The Ministry of Public Education began operating a radio station in 1924. Closed in the 1940s, it was reactivated in 1969 as *Radio Educacion*. Its programming has placed more emphasis on programs of a cultural and informational rather than educational nature. The same is generally true for the several radio stations operated by national universities.

Direct instruction via radio was developed through the *Radioprimaria* program of the Ministry of Public Education to help improve classroom instruction. The Ministry of Public Education has also used radio in an attempt to teach Spanish to Indian populations. *Radiofonico Bilingue*'s daily programs are for in-school use. *Radio Tarahumara*, a program operated by the Jesuit order, has expanded educational opportunity for Indian children in one of Mexico's northern states.

Television Channel 11 in Mexico City is operated by the *Instituto Politecnico Nacional* (National Polytechnical Institute) primarily as a cultural channel. Under the Ministry of Education's *Direccion General de Educacion Audiovisual y Divulgacion* (DGEAD) a *Telesecundaria*

system has been developed to supplement the traditional school system much along the lines of Italy's pioneering *Telescuola*. The program uses television and classroom coordinators to provide secondary instruction where no secondary school has existed. The television instruction is prepared by DGEAD and the programs distributed via *Televisa*'s networks, using "fiscal time."

Televisa had created a *Fundacion Cultural Televisa* to cooperate with the *Universidad Nacional Autonoma de Mexico* (the nation's prestige university) in a project to create a *Universidad del Aire*. This operation was begun in 1975, using time on two of *Televisa*'s networks.

Bibliography

Barnouw E 1966 *A History of Broadcasting in the United States*, Vol. 1: *A Tower of Babel: To 1933*. Oxford University Press, New York

Barnouw E 1968 *A History of Broadcasting in the United States*, Vol. 2: *The Golden Web: 1933–53*. Oxford University Press, New York

Barnouw E 1970 *A History of Broadcasting in the United States*, Vol. 3: *The Image Empire: From 1953*. Oxford University Press, New York

Blakely R J 1979 *To Serve the Public Interest*. Syracuse University Press, Syracuse, New York

Broadcasting/Cable Yearbook 1981. Broadcasting Publications, Washington, DC

Cater D (ed.) 1976 *The Future of Public Broadcasting*. Aspen Institute, Program on Communications and Society. Praeger, New York

de Noriega L A, Leach F 1979 *Broadcasting in Mexico*. Routledge and Kegan Paul, London

Dirr P J 1979 *Uses of Television for Instruction 1976–77*. Corporation for Public Broadcasting, Washington, DC

Dirr P J 1981 *Higher Education Utilization Study Phase 1: Final Report*. Corporation for Public Broadcasting, Washington, DC

Hallman E S 1977 *Broadcasting in Canada*. Routledge and Kegan Paul, London

The Carnegie Commission on Educational Television 1967 *Public Television: A Program for Action*. Harper and Row, New York

The Carnegie Commission on the Future of Public Broadcasting 1979 *A Public Trust*. Bantam, New York

The Pacific Region

H. M. Hill

The Pacific Ocean covers an area roughly equal to one-third of the earth's surface yet its tiny islands have a population of less than 6,000,000 people. It is a region of immense cultural diversity, its inhabitants speaking no less than 1,200 indigenous languages and having been colonized by a variety of colonial powers, two of which, France and the United States remain. The region has communications problems not encountered in any other region. There are at least 20 separate political entities scattered over 12,000,000 square miles of oceans; most of them stretching over wide reaches of ocean with

poor air and surface transportation links between their constituent islands. In addition to the indigenous inhabitants of the islands, the Melanesians, Polynesians, and Micronesians, many Pacific territories have varying numbers of residents of Asian and European origin.

Although radio is of relatively recent origin in most of the island territories, its degree of penetration is high and it has become an extremely important medium (Hill 1982 pp. 20–21). In the South Pacific region are to be found models of broadcasting derived from British, French, and American origins. As yet it is only the

American and French territories which have broadcast television but video recorders are common in the independent Commonwealth countries (in regions with an electricity supply) and in at least two of these nations, Fiji and Papua New Guinea, the introduction of broadcast television has become a significant political issue (Seigel 1980).

The Pacific region is the home of several notable experiments in educational broadcasting, in particular educational television in American Samoa, and the use of the NASA satellite ATS-1 for educational experiments using low-cost ground stations and a number of networks throughout the region. But perhaps the most important form of educational broadcasting in the region is the use of national radio services by a variety of bodies involved in nonformal education, groups such as youth organizations, farmers' and women's groups.

1. History and Forms of Organization

When radio first came to the Pacific it was not to provide mass communications for the islanders but rather to enable colonial settlers to gain access to news from home, ships at sea to get weather forecasts, miners to hear the latest news from the London Metals Exchange, and plantation owners to keep up to date with the prices of copra. After the First World War, the governments of the United Kingdom, France, the United States, Australia, and New Zealand as administrators of island territories began to link up their administrative capitals with a point-to-point radio network. One legacy of this which still persists is the use of news broadcasts from the BBC World Service, Radio Australia, and the Voice of America on most of the national radio services of the English-speaking territories.

It was some decades after the introduction of radio into the Pacific islands, that improvements in technology and the availability of cheap transistor radio receivers began to give radio the importance it has today. While most Pacific islands, both independent and nonself-governing, have high literacy rates, due largely to the efforts of Protestant missionaries in the region from the early nineteenth century, the cultures remain predominantly oral. None—with the possible exception of Easter Island—had a written language before contact with the Europeans. Mastery of colonial languages by islanders also tends to be in oral rather than written form.

Radio has taken on an importance in the islands which cannot be underestimated. Lasarusa Vusoniwailala, a former broadcaster in Fiji, claims that in the rural areas of the country, radio is always regarded as the most reliable source of information and verification of events (Vusoniwailala 1975 p. 193). Edmund Carpenter observed in pre-independence Papua New Guinea that "when villagers ignore their leader the government may tape-record his orders. The next day the assembled community hears his voice coming to them from a radio he holds in his own hand. Then they obey him" (Carpenter 1973 p. 3). Anne Walker, in a study in three regions of Fiji found close to 100 percent ownership of radio receivers, even in rural areas (Walker 1976 p. 85). Waqavonovono (1981 p. 15) argues that radio is the only communications medium in the Pacific islands aimed at a truly mass market being the only one to use the vernacular to any extent.

The Pacific exhibits a variety of different forms of organization in broadcasting, in each case heavily influenced by the colonial power. With French, British, and American models in operation, the region is almost a textbook case study of the influences—philosophical, training, commercial, and institutional—posited by Cruise O'Brien (1975). In New Caledonia and French Polynesia (both overseas territories of France), the French public service model exists in the form of France Region 3 (FR 3), one of the networks which operates in France. The American commercial model operates (with investments from United States companies in many cases) in Guam, American Samoa, and the United States Trust Territory of Micronesia, while in the independent Commonwealth countries the BBC is clearly the model for broadcasting organizations which have developed as statutory authorities, albeit with some commercial advertising.

2. The Role of the South Pacific Commission in Broadcasting

In a region where islands are separated by vast distances and the population is sparsely distributed, regional cooperation is of utmost importance. The South Pacific Commission (SPC), a regional intergovernmental technical assistance body covering independent, French, and United States territories, has been active in the field of broadcasting since 1970 when a tape exchange was established. It included recordings of Pacific music, stories and legends, a news programme, and a series produced in cooperation with the Australian Broadcasting Commission to support the SPC's courses in English as a second language (Johnstone 1978). In the late 1970s, the SPC Radio Bureau moved towards a greater emphasis on training as many of the member countries were becoming independent and wished to replace expatriate personnel in their radio stations with nationals. Trainees now also experiment with video although many of their countries do not have a broadcast television service.

In 1973 Ian Johnstone, then Educational Broadcasts Officer of the SPC, wrote a paper in which he advocated that all Pacific territories introduce "closed TV", that is video-replay systems, in advance of "open" or broadcast systems in order to train people in production of local material and to ensure a more participative service. He also advocated a regional consortium to supervise the introduction of broadcast television in those countries which did not already have it, in order to reduce costs and dependency on foreign interests (Johnstone 1973). Although his recommendations were not implemented at the regional level, they have influenced some governments, for example that of Fiji which has recently extended the activities of the Fiji Film Unit to include the operation of a national video-cassette library service including full studio production and duplication facilities to make available to the public videorecordings of local projects and events, educational programmes geared to development needs, and good quality material from overseas. With commercial videoclubs now a reality in most of the island groups, governments are anxious to be able to make better use of video. A new SPC media centre is planned for Vanuatu which can pay attention to the needs of the French- as well as the English-speaking countries in this regard. (Vanuatu is the former Anglo–French Condominium of the New Hebrides where both languages are used.)

Short training workshops are also carried out in the independent countries of the Pacific by the Malaysian-based Asia–Pacific Institute for Broadcasting Development. Micronesian broadcasters from the Trust Territory often receive training with Voice of America in Washington or at the East–West Center Communications Institute in Hawaii. All broadcasters in the French territories are trained by their employer, FR3 in France.

3. *Educational Television in American Samoa*

Undoubtedly the largest and best documented experiment in educational broadcasting in the South Pacific has been educational television in American Samoa (Schramm et al. 1967 pp. 11–51, Schramm 1977, Richstad and McMillan 1978 pp. 30–35, Schramm et al. 1981). Inaugurated in 1964 by Rex Lee, the American Governor of the time, it was the largest and most ambitious attempt ever to restructure a whole school system by means of television. An official document described the aims of the television project in American Samoa as:

(a) To raise the educational achievement of the Samoan student at all grade levels to United States achievement standards.

(b) To raise the level of teaching competency of the Samoan teacher by developing a continuous in-service teacher-training programme in techniques making maximum use of television.

(c) To staff the schools with Samoan personnel wherever possible using only minimum specialized assistance from outside Samoa (Schramm et al. 1967 p. 17).

Using a US$2,579,000 appropriation from the United States Congress, Governor Lee contracted the Washington-based National Association of Educational Broadcasters to design and install a six-channel VHF television station with four studio production centres capable of producing 200 television lessons a week, and to recruit approximately 150 curriculum specialists, engineers, school principals, television teachers, researchers, producers, artists, photographers, and printers. With a further appropriation of US$3,173,750, 30 consolidated

elementary schools were built and the one existing high school remodelled. Television became the major form of instruction for the six elementary-school grades and a regular supplementary medium for the high-school grades. Television programmes were presented by a "studio teacher" with the assistance of a "research teacher" and a producer–director; a "classroom teacher" supervised the viewing of the televised lessons by the pupils while a "research teacher" was responsible for the preparation of written materials for use in the classroom. The decision to introduce television instruction to all levels at once, a decision taken for political not educational reasons, placed a severe strain on the teachers concerned, who at the peak of the operation were producing in excess of 6,000 live programmes a year, a level of production unmatched by any other educational television station anywhere in the world (Schramm 1977 p. 152).

In 1971, television was cut back to some 2,200 live programmes per year, a decision which, according to Schramm (1977 p. 163), "was a sign of maturity and rising standards, rather than a lack of confidence in the medium. Teachers, especially in the secondary schools, felt better able to teach their own classes without a crutch." However, there had been a great deal of criticism of television in the classroom, from parents, teachers, pupils, and political leaders. Surveys of student and teacher attitudes towards classroom television carried out between 1972 and 1976 showed a negative relationship between favourable opinions of instructional television and experience with it (Schramm et al. 1981 p. 95). In 1975 there were further cutbacks and the television service was transferred from the Department of Education to a new entity—the Office of Television Operations. This brought an end to live programming for the schools and completely removed television from the high-school curriculum. The three channels which remained came to operate "essentially as extensions of the US commercial networks" (Schramm et al. 1981 p. 186). The telecasts can also be received in Western Samoa, an independent country with no television service of its own. Seigel (1980 p. 18) has described how elders in Apia, the capital of Western Samoa have changed the time of their Sunday *lotu* (traditional religious ceremony) so as not to clash with their favourite television programme *All Star Wrestling*.

Studies of the educational achievement of American Samoan pupils are inconclusive in evaluating the precise role of television in learning. One problem is that no testing was done by the Samoan Department of Education before 1970 and no adequate baseline data are available for making comparisons. One of the aims of the introduction of television into the schools of American Samoa was to raise the level of English of both pupils and teachers. This has certainly been achieved in the case of spoken English but the gains do not seem to have led to corresponding improvements in reading and writing (Schramm 1977 p. 162).

Another question which is difficult to answer is, to what extent was academic improvement in American Samoan schools due to the presence of television in the classrooms and to what extent was it due to the better teacher training, improved lesson planning and achievement testing, or even the greatly improved school buildings and other facilities that were part of the package?

The educational television service in American Samoa attracted considerable interest among educationalists in other parts of the Pacific, and many visited Pago Pago in the early 1970s with a view to encouraging its replication in their own countries. However, it was beyond the financial reach of all of them. The Australian Administrator of Papua New Guinea in 1965 appointed a two-member team to enquire into the usefulness, technical feasibility, and costs of television in the territory. The consultants designed a system of instructional television very much along the lines of that they had seen in American Samoa. But Papua New Guinea has a very difficult terrain for television transmission and with over 700 vernacular languages, the cost of implementing the proposal would have beeen astronomical. Until now, successive governments in Papua New Guinea have decided to give priority to the development of a comprehensive network of national and local radio stations in English and 16 local languages (Mackay 1976). The introduction of a domestic satellite for Australia will create the technical possibilities for much cheaper communications, including television, in Papua New Guinea should the government desire it.

4. Use of Satellites for Educational Broadcasting

ATS-1 is a former weather satellite put into orbit by the National Aeronautics and Space Administration of the United States (NASA) in 1966. Its high power enables two-way voice communications with low-cost ground stations over a very wide distance. In 1969, when NASA had completed its weather experiments, a consortium of educational institutions in the Pacific proposed the Pan Pacific Educational and Communications Experiment by Satellite (PEACESAT) project; a network of ground stations which would use the satellite for interactive, noncommercial voice communications with educational, health, and community development related applications. PEACESAT first went on the air in 1971 and there are now 16 PEACESAT ground stations in 11 countries, (including Pacific rim countries, Australia, New Zealand, and the United States) (Bystrom 1978). Teleconferencing and the exchange of messages for scheduling or other administrative purposes are the main uses of time on the PEACESAT network. Regular PEACESAT sessions have been held on the network by widely separated agriculturalists, medical personnel, adult educators, ministers of religion, youth leaders, journalists, radio broadcasters, librarians, preschool teachers, women's interest officers, and members of organizations with regionwide membership, for example, YWCA and

Boy Scouts. The degree of success of PEACESAT meetings such as these usually depends on the amount of preparation which goes into planning the teleconference and the extent to which the participants know each other and have already participated in such exchanges (Plant 1979). The French-speaking territories have been largely unable to participate in PEACESAT. Although there is a terminal in Noumea, New Caledonia, it is at the SPC headquarters and largely used by SPC officials for communicating with the English-speaking Pacific. In 1974, the SPC established a regular News Exhange (in English) on PEACESAT for the use of islands media. It has not been as successful as it might have been (Brislin 1981 p. 25).

In 1973, the University of the South Pacific (USP), a founding member of PEACESAT, approached NASA for permission to operate its own network using ATS-1. The USP is a regional university established in 1968 by the administrations of all the then British and New Zealand administered territories in the South Pacific. (Australian-administered Papua New Guinea already had its own university and now has two.) The network, called USPNET, opened in 1974 with its headquarters on the main USP campus in Suva, Fiji and had terminals at each of the extension centres in the other member countries of the USP. The USPNET operates for 16 hours a week and is mainly used for administration and teaching of the USP introductory, foundation (7th form), degree, and vocational courses. The USPNET terminals can also be used to access the PEACESAT network (Wynne 1976). In 1978, slow scan television was added to the USPNET terminals in Fiji, Tonga, and Western Samoa which enables the transmission of still pictures and diagrams (Nettles 1981 p. 12).

It is not possible to complete a whole degree by extension study but it can minimize the number of years required in residence on the main campus in Fiji or the Agricultural Campus in Western Samoa thus enabling a great many people in employment to upgrade their qualifications. The enrolment of the USP is approx. 1,750 full-time internal students and 2,400 extension students. The USP uses a variety of media in its extension teaching including printed materials and audiocassettes. Many of the students live beyond easy reach of a satellite terminal. However, the experience of the university has been that the use of two-way voice transmission for administration, lecturing, tutorial discussions, and discussion of written work does have a marked effect on the overall success rate and has cut the dropout rate from extension courses (Wynne 1976, Miller 1981).

Distance education at the extension centres of the Community College of Micronesia does not involve satellite broadcasts although two networks are available; PEACESAT and the Department of the Interior Satellite Project, (DISP which has been renamed MICRONET). However the recently established Northern Marianas Community College has made use of the PEACESAT network in its courses. While the USP uses ATS-1 to bring the voices of centrally located lecturers to students in a number of far flung island locations, the Northern Marianas Community College uses it to enable students in Saipan to be taught by lecturers who can be anywhere in the Pacific, including Hawaii or the United States mainland (Porter 1981). The University of Papua New Guinea, which has an extension studies department cannot use ATS-1 as its needs are for a system which can reach students in isolated parts of the country, where there are no PEACESAT terminals. There is a possibility that with the Australian domestic satellite is launched, channels will be available for use in Papua New Guinea that could be used for two-way educational broadcasting (Priest et al. 1981 p. 44).

5. Broadcasting and Development

In most Pacific Islands there is but one, usually government-related, broadcasting authority and only one radio station. (An exception is Fiji which has a Fijian service and a Hindi service, both broadcasting simultaneously and each interspaced with English.) School broadcasts have a long history in the Pacific in both English- and French-speaking territories, yet evaluation of them is rare and debates as to whether they should be made by broadcasters or teachers seem to continue (Buik-Constable 1961, Reddy 1979). In addition, other government departments such as agriculture, cooperatives, health, and women's interest offices have a long history in broadcasting. Ian Johnstone pointed out in 1976 such broadcasts "are usually the product of expatriate initiative and imagination and . . . only rarely catch the imagination of those they are intended to help . . . they fail to accomplish their main purpose . . . they tend to the didactic; they are stilted and full of expertise and wisdom; they are too often counsels of perfection to people who have to make do with an imperfect world, they rely on old formulae because their producers have not had the chance to discover or experiment with new ones" (1976 p.70).

Anne Walker, in her research in Fiji in 1976, found a great desire, particularly among rural people, for participation in radio. Forty-one percent of her sample of urban residents and 74 percent of rural dwellers indicated that they would like to produce their own programmes, showing a marked preference for youth, women's, and agricultural programmes (Walker 1976 pp. 103–08). Most broadcasting authorities in the English-speaking Pacific do allow, and indeed encourage, some community access to the airwaves and it is here that some of the most interesting educational broadcasting is being done. For example, in Fiji the YMCA rural work programme has its own time slot on Radio Fiji where greetings, and news of past and forthcoming events are exchanged between members and staff throughout the country. According to leaders, the radio programme is important in helping group identity, motivating members towards improving life in their villages, and informing them about courses and so on which will be available in their district.

In the United States Trust Territory, the Catholic Church has considerable investment in personnel, training, and equipment for the production of radio programmes in the vernacular to broadcast on local radio stations throughout American Micronesia. The programmes, which for the most part are not religious, but concentrate on local activities in adult education, youth activities, cooperatives, and education for self-government, are often a marked contrast to the predominantly commercial fare heard in the Trust Territory.

Nutrition education, regarded as a high priority in all parts of the Pacific due to increases in malnutrition, obesity, tooth decay, high blood pressure, and diabetes, is being tackled by radio in a number of Pacific territories. The Fiji National Nutrition Committee has begun a series on gardening and cookery to encourage the use of local foods (Thomas 1981). In Micronesia, radio is used to debate the advantages of breast-feeding over bottle-feeding and to promote the drinking of fruit juices over soft drinks (Rody 1978).

In the French territories, broadcasting is still very much a government monopoly, although local organizations have found it easier to gain access to radio and television programmes since the election of the socialist government in France, for example to take part in debates on the economy or educational policy. This government has also introduced legislation making *radios libres* (free radios) legal, with the same guidelines as for those in France. However, only well-financed middle-class groups have been able to take advantage of this legislation and at present *radios libres* in New Caledonia and French Polynesia concentrate mainly on light entertainment and European music.

6. The Future

The South Pacific region, perhaps more than any other region, will be affected by the development of the next generation of communications satellites. ATS-1 will not last indefinitely and it is by no means certain at this stage what will take its place. Increased communications between the French, American, and Commonwealth territories are already taking place although colonial and neocolonial ties are strong. The decolonization of the French and American territories would certainly speed this process.

Several countries will make decisions about the introduction of television and what sort of systems to adopt. When these decisions are made they will be done with the lessons of American Samoa, the French Territories, and the Trust Territory to guide them. They have the possibility of being the most informed decisions ever taken anywhere on the introduction of television.

However, all this will mean that the fragile economies, ecosystems, and cultures of the islands will become even more subject to outside interference, a prospect which many Pacific leaders are not happy about.

Bibliography

Barney R 1978 Pacific islands. In: Lent J A (ed.) 1978 *Broadcasting in Asia and the Pacific: A Continental Survey of Radio and Television.* Temple University Press, Philadelphia, Pennsylvania

Brislin T 1981 Designing innovations for news exchanges among Pacific Island journalists via the PEACESAT experiment. *Pacific Islands Commun. J.* 10(2): 24–28

Broadcasting in the Pacific 1956 *South Pacific Commission Q. Bull.* 6(4): 41–45, 56

Buik-Constable L 1961 The history and use of radio education in the Pacific area. *Transactions Proc. Fiji Soc.* 8: 142–48

Bystrom J 1973 PEACESAT. *World Health.* January: 10–13

Carpenter E S 1973 *Oh, What a Blow that Phantom Gave Me!* Holt, Rinehart and Winston, New York

Cruise O'Brien R 1975 Domination and dependence in mass communications implications for the use of broadcasting in developing countries. *Institute of Dev. Studies Bull.* 6(4): 85–99

Hill H 1982 Horseless carriage and cracked mirror: The electronic media in the Pacific Islands. *Media Inf. Aust.* 23: 17–27

Johnstone I 1973 From closed to open television—A long term project for the South Pacific. *Asian Broadcasting Union Newsletter* 95: 5–9. Reprinted in *Pacific Islands Commun. J.* 1981 10(4): 9–17

Johnstone I 1976 Broadcasting in the Pacific. In: Lerner D, Richstad J (eds.) 1976 *Communication in the Pacific.* East–West Center, Honolulu, pp. 59–71

Johnstone I 1978 The South Pacific commission. In: Lent J (ed.) 1978 *Broadcasting in Asia and the Pacific.* Temple University Press, Philadelphia, Pennsylvania

Kingan S 1979 The PEACESAT experience in the Pacific. In: Deacon C (ed.) 1979 *DOMSAT '79: A Communications Satellite for Australia—Who Will Benefit?* Papers and Proc. of the 1st National Domestic Satellite Conf., Feb. 20–23, 1979. Centre for Continuing Education, Australian National University, Canberra, pp. 430–40

Mackay I K 1976 *Broadcasting in Papua New Guinea.* Melbourne University Press, Carlton

Miller J 1981 Media for distance education in the South Pacific. *Media in Educ. Dev.* 14(4): 173–75

Nettles P 1981 Slow-scan: Long-distance pictures by phone. *Dev. Commun. Report* 34: 5–12

Olkowski D 1976 Communication for the promotion of agricultural development in the Fiji Islands. M.Ed. thesis (Educational Communications), University of Hawaii, Hawaii

Plant C 1979 PEACESAT and development in the Pacific Islands. M.A. thesis (Communications), Simon Fraser University, Canada

Porter K 1981 Using satellites for teaching: A Northern Marianas experiment. *Pacific Islands Commun. J.* 10(3): 44–47

Priest M, Whippy H, Greenwood P 1981 A role for satellite communications educational projects in Papua New Guinea. *J. Engineering Educ. Southeast Asia* 11(2): 40–44

Reddy S 1979 Educational radio: Directions in the Pacific. *Directions* (Institute of Education, University of the South Pacific) 3: 18–24

Richstad J, McMillan M 1978 *Mass Communication and Journalism in the Pacific Islands: A Bibliography.* University Press of Hawaii, Honolulu, Hawaii

Rody N 1978 Things go better with coconuts—Program strategies in Micronesia. *J. Nutrition Educ.* 10: 19–22

Satellite: The PEACESAT Bulletin (Monthly) Wellington Polytechnic, New Zealand

Schramm W L 1977 *Big Media, Little Media: Tools and Technologies for Instruction.* Sage, Beverly Hills, California

Schramm W L, Coombs P, Kahnert F, Lyle J 1967 *New Educational Media in Action: Case Studies for Planners,* Vol. 1. UNESCO/IIEP, Paris

Schramm W L, Nelson L, Betham M 1981 *Bold Experiment: The Story of Educational Television in American Samoa.* Stanford University Press, Palo Alto, California

Seigel B 1980 South Pacific: Some enchanted prime time. *The Atlantic* 246(6): 18–22

Thomas P 1981 Communicating for nutritional development. *Review* (School of Social and Economic Development, University of the South Pacific) 2(5): 222–25

Vusoniwailala L 1974 The disc jockey and national policy: The role of radio in the South Pacific. *Pacific Perspective* 3(2): 29–37. Reprinted in: Tupouniua S, Crocombe R, Slatter C (eds.) 1975 *The Pacific Way: Social Issues in National Development.* South Pacific Social Sciences Association, Suva, pp. 193–201

Walker A S 1976 A study of relationships between mass media, community involvement and political participation in Fiji (Ph.D. thesis, School of Education, Indiana University, 1976). *Dissertation Abstracts International* 1977 37: 4680A–4681A (University Microfilms No. 77–1974)

Waqavonovono M 1981 Who manipulates Pacific media? Influences on newspapers and television. *Pacific Perspective* 10: 13–36

Wynne J G 1976 University teaching by satellite. *Int. Rev. Educ.* 22(1): 83–88

Western Europe

H. R. Cathcart

Broadcasting in Western Europe has a strong public service ethos so that even commercial broadcasting in the zone is affected by it. Most European broadcasters would endorse the view first expressed in 1922 by the great American pioneer, David Sarnoff: "Broadcasting represents a job of entertaining, informing, and educating the nation and should therefore distinctly be a public service." Within this threefold brief the task of "educating the nation" is open to two interpretations. There are those who believe it is most appropriately served by programmes in the general output. On the other hand, there are those who insist that in addition, specialized production is essential in order to meet the educational needs of the nation. Western European broadcasting organizations usually accept educational broadcasting in this stricter sense as a necessary aspect of their public service even when there is no statutory obligation imposed on them to do so.

When there is an obligation, programme production is usually financed in whole or in part by the ministry of education. The ministry exercises control but often shares programme policy making with other educational interests. The boards and advisory structures which then exist are not notably different from those which are created by more autonomous educational broadcasting services. The products of their deliberations, the educational broadcasts, are designed to assist the formal educational institutions and agencies in the state. Although the programmes may stimulate casual independent listeners or viewers to learn and may even teach them, most are intended for learners in classes or study circles. Inevitably, given this intention, educational broadcasting is addressed to minority audiences, many of them captive in schools and colleges. For this reason general broadcasters tend to think that educational broadcasting fails to realize broadcasting's potential and so relegate it to off peak and unsocial hours. They believe that broadcasting should strive for mass audiences and that success in achieving this objective does not preclude the possibility of providing the audiences with rewarding learning experiences. The distinction between the two types of production may be a fine one. Jacob Bronowski's "The Ascent of Man" was produced by the British Broadcasting Corporation (BBC) as a cultural series in the general output but when it was transmitted on the other side of the Atlantic by stations under the aegis of the Public Broadcasting Corporation it became an educational series. The programmes were closely integrated into award-bearing courses by institutions of higher education in the United States, as Bronowski himself intended.

1. Definitions

The recent disposition to regard any broadcast as educational which is used educationally reflects the tendency of educationalists and broadcasters in Western Europe to treat cultural and current affairs programming as a resource for learning no less than the strictly educational broadcasts. The context in which the programmes are received, which includes the motivation of the listener or viewer, determines whether they are considered as "educational" or not. Earlier definitions laid emphasis on the content of the programmes and the intentions of the producers. "A broadcast is *educational* if it is designed and executed for a didactic end and fits into place in a coherent and graduated whole" (Clausse 1949). This definition drawn from radio's golden times is echoed in a later one from the television age, when educational broadcasts were defined as "programmes arranged in series, and planned in consultation with appropriate educational bodies so as to contribute to the progressive mastery or understanding of some skill or body of knowledge" (Scupham 1976).

So long as educational broadcasts are received by motivated and/or captive audiences, the concept of an instructional series has validity and use. Students in educational institutions or attached to them are likely to

follow programmes through a series when this is formally required of them or the programmes prove to be a useful element in their courses. It is when the educational broadcasters reach out for a wider audience that they find the essential features of the traditional definition of their activity difficult to sustain. The mass audience prefers programmes which are entertaining or interesting to those which are overtly instructional. The educational producers have therefore to use their skills and the techniques of their medium to find an appealing format in which to offer their message. This becomes increasingly difficult in a series where the presumption is that the earlier programmes have been followed and understood. Unfortunately for the producer, evidence from research into patterns of television viewing suggests that: "Only about half the people who see a repetitive programme one week see the next episode in the following week. There is little difference in this by type of programme or demographic group...failure to repeat-view is generally a matter of social habits rather than a reaction to programme content" (Goodhardt et al. 1975). Such behaviour undermines the possibility of "progressive mastery" through series for many viewers. Educational broadcasting to a mass audience is like much adult education in that the clientele attend voluntarily and continue with a course only if it is convenient and if they are interested.

2. Schools' Broadcasting

Schools' broadcasting by contrast is received involuntarily in the sense that the students do not normally make the choice of whether to follow a series or not. The decision is the teacher's or that of the school administration. The educational broadcasters have to persuade the teachers and the administrators of the utility of their service. By 1975, subsequent to a survey of Western European countries, it was reported: "(a) the potential value of broadcasts has gradually been recognised by the teaching profession but it has also been found that if broadcasting's effectiveness is to be increased teachers should be better trained in the use of the media and feel themselves committed and involved; (b) there are still considerable obstacles to the maximum effective use of the programmes: lack of equipment, shortage of staff capable of recording the programmes and of building up a video-, or audio-tape library, legal restrictions on the right of recording and reproduction" (Daco 1976). This conclusion, although hedged about with reservations, may have been too sanguine. By 1981 in Scotland, for example, the level of video recording equipment in secondary schools ranked with that of Japan, yet only the most popular educational series reached over 50 percent of their potential audiences. Research also revealed that even when programmes were used it was often inadequately, because teachers lacked expertise in using them (Murray 1981). Perhaps, not surprisingly, the BBC threatened to cease local production of schools' programmes in Scotland in an economy drive. In Ireland, schools' programme production ceased in 1975 when the ministry of education withdrew the recurrent grant which covered the costs of production. While the Irish action was mainly due to economic recession, there is no doubt that a lack of conviction in official quarters that broadcasting is useful and effective may contribute to decline, if not cessation. France provides an example of decline. Educational programme production is there retained in the control of the ministry of education and transmission time is bought on the radio and television channels. The ministry has not increased its budget allocations to keep pace with rising costs. So the annual total of hours devoted to the transmission of the ministry's programmes on television and radio has fallen sharply. In 1973–74 it was 572 hours; in 1980–81 it was less than 150 hours (Treffel 1981). As early as 1973 an observer suggested that there was a more profound reason than the financial for the low level of educational broadcasting in France. He wrote that dialogue is difficult between "two monopolies, jealous of their prerogatives: the broadcasting monopoly versus the schools' monopoly". French broadcasters resent the incursions of the educational system on "their terrain" and consider the educational mission of broadcasting is properly fulfilled by general cultural and current affairs broadcasting. It is clear, however, that unlike its predecessors the government under President Mitterand favoured the expansion of educational broadcasting, although it would have wished to emphasize its educative rather than its instructional nature (Croissandeau 1981).

The political and social context within which educational broadcasting operates in Western Europe today is in striking contrast to that operating in the 1960s when broadcasting organizations were in the early stages of developing schools' television, and their schools' radio services were beginning to adjust to a subordinate role. The birth rate was then rising while it is at present falling. National economies were achieving prosperity and full employment in contrast to the present prolonged recession. Governments were launching major programmes of expansion in their educational systems. They were endeavouring not only to absorb the population increase but also to create greater educational opportunities for all. Democratization of the hitherto elitist systems was implemented for economic as well as for political reasons. Investment in education, with an emphasis on its technological and scientific aspects, was regarded as a precondition of economic growth. Governments found themselves confronted with a shortage of schools and teachers, with a teaching force whose knowledge and skills needed to be brought up-to-date. In 1960, a French consultant wrote in an Organisation for Economic Co-operation and Development (OECD) report, "It so happens—either by coincidence or design—that television is making its appearance in teaching at a particularly critical time in the history of teaching in Europe" (Dieuzeide 1960). Television

seemed to offer a means of easing the educational problems of Europe. Where there were no teachers, television could stand in for them; where there were inadequately trained teachers, highly skilled television teachers could teach the classes and the teachers at the same time. In so far as science and mathematics were the keys to technological and industrial development, these subject areas received priority and many Western European schools' television services were launched with series in these subjects. In 1958 in Italy, however, the most pressing problem had lain in the need to provide postprimary education in districts where schools had still to be built. *Telescuola* was founded to bring direct teaching to 12- to 15-year-olds without teachers. Its programmes prepared thousands for vocational colleges. Almost a decade later, in 1967, Bavarian Radio established *Telekolleg* for a similar purpose. It proved equally successful and *Telekolleg* went on to offer vocational courses itself. In the years between the foundation of *Telescuola* and that of *Telekolleg*, Western European countries all followed the lead of the pioneers, France in 1951 and the United Kingdom in 1957, and provided their schools with educational television.

The early years were a time of euphoria among educational broadcasters as it was realized how they were assisting in the democratizing and the modernizing of schools.

A further reason for the state of euphoria in the 60s was the novelty and attractiveness of the medium of television as a visual aid; television was only then developing into a mass medium. The idea that a message could be carried into every school and home led educationalists to believe that education could be transmitted in the same manner. Television appeared to be the ideal medium because it provided visual stimulus, "the basis of all understanding", according to Pestalozzi, and because in every learning process, visual perception must precede abstraction. (Simmerding 1977)

As television became a mass medium, school-going populations became avid viewers and began to spend as much time watching the small screen as attending school. The medium proved an alternative source of learning: the French called it "the parallel school". Its influence in the home spurred the development of schools' television. The nature and standards of production were affected. Programmes for transmission to schools had to become as sophisticated as general programmes or they lost impact. Overt didactic styles of presentation which were seldom encountered at home became increasingly unacceptable in school broadcasts.

Schools' television ceased to need to reproduce what went on in the classroom when there was no longer a shortage of schools and teachers. Instead, production concentrated on assisting the processes of curriculum reform and development. The programmes were received in schools which were experiencing a shift in emphasis from teaching to learning. The learner had to be assisted to learn rather than taught. This pupil-centred environment affected the significance of educational broadcasting. Programmes were assessed as a resource for learning rather than as a teacher's aid. Television was one means or medium among others, each of which had to be considered for the contribution it could make to an integrated-systems approach to learning.

In 1975 the heads of the schools' departments of the television organizations in the Federal Republic of Germany and West Berlin outlined the criteria which they apply to programme planning. The foremost criteria are: "(a) School television is to sustain the acceleration of curricular alternations, it is not to stabilise conventional teaching: *criterion of curricular innovation.* (b) It is to be used where it can provide the utmost of visualisation, not as a universal instrument for all occasions: *criterion of telegenity.* (c) School television programmes are not to be produced irrespective of other media in view of the necessity to supplement one-way communication: *criterion of multi-media systems*" (Bücker 1980).

The innovatory role of schools' television is important. In the United Kingdom, a Schools' Council survey into innovation in British schools revealed that next after their professional colleagues, teachers regarded schools' television as the most frequently useful source of information about curriculum innovation. Teachers everywhere, as well as their pupils, learn from school broadcasts. In the Federal Republic of Germany, teachers frequently view the programmes when they are transmitted outside school hours; quite a few do not in fact use them in class. In effect, the programmes are serving an inservice purpose. Many educational broadcasting departments and agencies in Western European countries produce inservice series for teachers. Initial training courses are rarely provided. Bavarian Radio, somewhat exceptionally, offered a comprehensive series in nursery education which, when successfully completed with examinations, gave the telestudents the status of recognized teachers.

The multimedia approach to learning today increasingly conditions the pattern of broadcasting production. It is not entirely new to schools' radio. Schools' radio producers from the beginning recognized the limitations of their medium compared to print. Its ephemeral and nonvisual nature prompted them to provide supportive literature which would consolidate and extend what was presented in the programmes. Schools' radio in the 1920s in the United Kingdom and in Sweden already offered printed information for teachers and pupils to accompany the broadcasts making up in effect a learning package designed to be fitted by the teacher into the classroom scene. The quality of what is produced today is much higher and the development of audio recording has given the package an increased usefulness. For some time too, radio has offered sets of coloured stills on film strip which can be shown simultaneously with the transmission or with playback. The success of radiovision, which got off the ground when monochrome sets were universal, has been impaired by the arrival of colour television.

Schools' radio played an important role through the years until it was overshadowed by schools' television. In broadcasting organizations where the production of programmes for both media has been closely associated, some attempt has been made to plan production with a view to using each medium for the purposes for which it is most suitable. Elsewhere, and that is in many Western European countries, schools' radio has continued to supply programme series covering the full range of curricula for all ages. Two fields have, however, been universally recognized as particularly suitable for radio productions, music education and the study of foreign languages (Sturm 1979).

Radio is by far the cheaper medium as regards costs of production. Scandinavian studies conducted in the early 1980s suggest a ratio of 10:1 in favour of radio. In times of recession this might be a significant factor in broadcast planning but expansion is hindered by lack of air time. There is no possibility of extending schools' time on national networks. In fact, the tendency is in the opposite direction. Schools' radio is now confined in some countries to VHF wavelengths. In the United Kingdom, arrangements have been completed to transmit many schools' programme series at night when the wavelengths are relatively free. This departure was proposed after a successful feasibility study which was followed with intense interest internationally. The widespread availability in schools and colleges of audio recording machines with time switches makes the operation possible. It may only be a matter of time before a similar fate overtakes schools' television.

3. Educational Broadcasts for Adults

The mass audiences which radio and television attract tempt adult educators in Western Europe as elsewhere. They represent fallow fields to be ploughed. Educational broadcasters know from experience and from research, however, that the conditions required to ensure that their programmes are educationally effective preclude mass audiences. Effectiveness depends on the programmes being "used in a suitable context of learning activities at the receiving end" and on commitment from the audience to follow the programmes. Producers are perpetually faced with a dilemma. If they exploit all the techniques of their medium to win the interest of the mass audience, they offend the committed members of that audience who find the inducements distracting— "entertainment is entertainment; learning is learning". So it is that producers may seek the many and lose the committed few or they may serve the committed few and lose the many (Van der Voort and Keekenkamp 1978, Cathcart 1982). While educational broadcasters are reluctant to renounce the mass audience, they frequently leave it, or are obliged to leave it, to the general producers.

Programmes in the general output may have an impact which leads to learning through the interest they stimulate. This is particularly true of cultural and natural science programmes. Their educational effectiveness is necessarily limited because it is impossible for the general broadcasters to arrange institutional backup as educational broadcasters often do. However, it has been discovered that books published to accompany series can have immense sales. Indeed, today many books on the best selling lists are related to broadcast series. The combination of a programme series and a book constitutes, in effect, a learning package even when the arrangement is not intended as such.

The situation is not very different when educational broadcasters produce series for the mass audience. They are obliged because of the size of the operation to limit their support for individual learners to a book or booklet. The popular topics handled by educational broadcasters in this way are usually chosen on the basis of research and experience. It has been found that the general public will watch educational programmes which deal with matters of immediate relevance to their daily lives. Series on aspects of the home, of the family, on leisure and holidays are all likely to win large audiences. Courses in cooking, for example, are universally successful.

Educational broadcasters usually attempt to ensure a greater measure of effectiveness for their productions by cooperating with adult agencies in the planning, design, and follow up of their programmes. Only in this way can they secure a basis of "learning activities at the receiving end". The adult education sector in Western European countries, however, consists of a wide variety of agencies with a diversity of interests and as such they cannot deliver audiences in the way the schools' sector can. Inevitably any topic chosen for a programme series will only interest some of the agencies and they alone will furnish audience support.

Even in the early days of radio, adult educators and the producers of adult education programmes realized that offerings on air were not enough in themselves. The programmes were modest: straight lectures and lessons. The style was that of the adult education movement at the time. Listeners were encouraged to improve themselves through the liberal arts. Courses to help them learn foreign languages were an important feature. Yet even in the 1920s it was considered important to furnish printed study guides to accompany the programmes, and the broadcasters set about establishing listening groups throughout the country. In the United Kingdom and Sweden such study circles became popular, as they remain in Scandinavia today.

The advent of television at first brought a perpetuation of the liberal arts style of broadcasting in most Western European countries. Yet in France and Italy new audiences were found from the start. The opportunity was seized in France of exploiting the situation which had arisen in the countryside. Rural communities had joined together in many places to purchase receivers for communal viewing. The television sets were frequently placed in the village schools. This permitted educational broadcasters not only to produce programmes for the school children but also to produce series for the peasants designed to encourage them to modernize their backward farming and to improve their lifestyle. Animateurs were trained to lead discussion of the programmes in the village teleclubs. They were often the local primary teachers and they were furnished with support literature. In Italy, many adults of limited education watched *Telescuola* and were allowed to take the examinations designed for the 15-year-olds. Having gained the final diploma they went on with the teenagers to the vocational colleges. The Italian educational authorities came to realize that *Telescuola* could be used directly in adult education. In the early 1960s a major national campaign was launched to eradicate adult illiteracy in the country. It proved remarkably successful.

The precedents established in France and Italy set one pattern for the future development of educational broadcasting in Western Europe. It was contrary to the conventional liberal arts pattern which, research revealed, chiefly benefited those who had already gained most from the educational system or who were at the time of listening or viewing actively involved in the system. Educational broadcasting could be used to provide greater educational opportunities for adults who hitherto had few of them. It was a role broadcasters in the 1960s and 1970s were increasingly required to play. Western European governments were obliged through economic necessity and political pressure to expand their provision for adult education. The educational standards of national workforces had to be raised if economic development was not to be inhibited. The vast majority of adults in European countries had received no more than an elementary education. They had a need which came to be regarded as an entitlement. There was a growing demand that all citizens should be enabled to fulfil their potential. The concept of permanent, or lifelong, education emerged which envisaged recurrent educational opportunities for all throughout the lifespan.

The challenge which expansion posed was received by educational broadcasters who had a realistic appraisal of the potentiality of their media. The euphoria of the television pioneers had passed. There was an acute realization that radio and television were two resources among several and that in responding to the needs of learners there had to be a critical assessment of what each medium could contribute. There were times when the broadcast media were distinctively useful in making up a multimedia system. There were times when they were not.

4. The Multimedia Approach to Learning

Ideally, multimedia systems and packages are created in circumstances where the vested interests of all media are tempered by the desire to facilitate the learner. Course teams plan on the basis of what are the best modes of presentation of materials for learning. Course teams, however, are normally required to work within constraints imposed by finance and limited air time. It is some consolation to them that experience and research suggest that the more carefully devised and integrated systems and packages are often educationally less effective than those which involve redundancy between the media used.

Among the most sophisticated multimedia systems and packages devised today are those produced by course teams in the Open University of the United Kingdom. Initially in 1965 it was intended that the institution should be called "the University of the Air", but very soon the advisory committee recognized the impracticality and the undesirability of using television and radio programmes as the basic resources for learning. Correspondence materials and textbooks are the prime resources but broadcasts are important, if not essential, dimensions of the University's courses. The advisory committee suggested that the university should be named after its outstanding characteristic, its open access to all adults who wished to enter on a course in higher education. Tens of thousands who had hitherto little or no chance of taking degrees have been enabled to do so from their homes since the Open University opened in 1971.

The Open University works in close association with the BBC. It pays all production costs from its own revenues which are chiefly derived from the government department of education and science. Originally, the commitment of the broadcasters was to 30 hours per week each of radio and television programming. The radio contribution has steadily declined being replaced by audio cassettes but the television production slightly exceeds the 30 hours per week during the academic year. In the beginning the BBC insisted that it must not be regarded as an outside agency and that its producers should play a creative role in the course teams. The contributions of the educational broadcasters are consequently thoroughly integrated into the university's courses.

The success of the experiment in the United Kingdom in distance learning for higher education prompted several Western European governments to examine the model and to consider establishing their own national open universities. The Spanish government in 1972 launched the *Universidad de Educación a Distancia* (UNED). The broadcast contribution to UNED's multimedia courses is made by radio. Television did not feature in the first decade.

Some countries have considered adopting the British model at a lower educational level. During the three-year period 1977–80 the Dutch government promoted the Open School project. Its principal aim was to provide a second chance for the considerable number of adults whose education did not extend beyond the second year of secondary school and in many cases terminated earlier. Multimedia courses were offered in Dutch, history, biology, geography, and arithmetic. Ninety

hours of network radio and 52 hours of network television were scheduled for each year. In the event the television and radio programmes were seldom used by the target groups. Their progress was achieved through their study circles. The broadcast media did, however, propagate the idea of the Open School throughout the nation and ensure that political support was won for the continuation of the Open School beyond the experimental stage.

In Norway a slightly different model has been tried with greater success as far as the broadcast media are concerned. In 1977 the Norwegian State Institute for Distance Education was established. The Institute's function is to coordinate the work of various agencies, the Norwegian Broadcasting Corporation, correspondence schools, adult education organizations, publishers, and libraries, in order to produce integrated multimedia courses on topics of national concern. The Institute has a small staff and no production facilities. It pays for the cost of most materials, including the broadcast productions.

In Norway the broadcast programmes are recorded and distributed on cassettes with the rest of the learning packages throughout the country. As this practice grows, less emphasis will be placed on the broadcasts and more on the materials, including the recordings, available in resource centres.

The development of the multimedia concept has tended to move educational broadcasting from centre-stage to the wings. In the examples quoted so far, the move has only affected one sector of a national educational system. In some countries in Western Europe, institutional consequences have been designed to affect and assist all sectors of national education. Sweden has the most advanced model. The Swedish government established *Utbildningsradion* which commenced operations in 1978. *Utbildningsradion* is responsible for the production of all audiovisual educational media and the preparation of multimedia learning systems. *Utbildningsradion* has broadcasting rights; it negotiates transmission times with Sveriges Radio for both its radio and television programmes; it pays for the air time. *Utbildningsradion* works with all educational agencies and aims to promote their activities and to help stimulate learning in and out of school. Its programme provision ranges from that for the preschool child to that for the retired pensioner. Priority has to be given to productions for disadvantaged groups, such as the physically and mentally handicapped and those with limited formal schooling. All its broadcast programmes are available on cassette along with the rest of the learning packages in resource centres all over Sweden. *Utbildningsradion* is state financed and is answerable directly to the ministry of education. The Danish answer to the changing technological situation is less comprehensive. The Danish National Centre of Educational Media set up in 1976 plans all media production, but production of both radio and television programmes remains with Danmark's Radio. The Danish ministry of education pays for all production. In the United Kingdom, the proposal that all radio and television production should be integrated and brought under the control of a National Educational Media Authority was considered by the government committee on broadcasting presided over by Lord Annan. The proposal was rejected in the committee's report in 1977 and existing arrangements were endorsed on the grounds that they sustained both the freedoms and the responsibilities of the educational and broadcasting authorities.

5. The Future

It is difficult to assess the prospects for educational broadcasting in Western Europe in the future. Clearly the pressures from general broadcasting, which have pushed educational broadcasting to the margins of schedules and even beyond, will continue. The pressures are dictated by the presumed appetite of the public for entertainment and information and by the prevailing limited air space. The pressures are growing at a time when questions are being asked about the need for educational broadcasting: it is now technologically possible to distribute all programmes over the surface in cassettes rather than over the air.

In the immediate future it is unlikely that the cost of surface distribution will fall sufficiently to make the abandonment of broadcasting a feasible proposition. There are, however, already instances where the target audiences for radio courses have been known to be so small that surface distribution has been preferred. The outlook for increased air space is good. The re-engineering of wavelengths and the advent of satellite television ought to ensure that new opportunities for educational broadcasting arise but the costs of production are escalating and governments will increasingly be pressed to decide, as they have always been, where educational broadcasting is to be placed among their educational priorities. If convinced of its value and effectiveness they may maintain an obligation on general broadcasting to allocate transmission time to educational broadcasting or they may even assign a complete channel to educational purposes. In either case, government departments will have to finance the service. It is obvious that public service broadcasting in Western Europe is increasingly unwilling to bear any of the costs.

Governments and their officials have varying perceptions of the effectiveness of educational broadcasting. In the Scandinavian countries they appear to be more convinced than elsewhere. Governments are not likely to be persuaded unless the teaching profession in all sectors of education, from nursery to adult, is convinced of the use and effectiveness of broadcasts. There is much evidence to show that very many teachers do not use programmes.

Research in the field of educational broadcasting in Western Europe has been quite extensive, although much of it is of indifferent quality. It has been designed to explore the issues: Where should provision be made, in what subject areas? How can programmes be made effective? Have the programmes been effective? In recent years questions have been investigated concerning the role of the broadcasting media in multimedia systems. Much of the research has been particular to specific programmes and the results have been of limited applicability to other programmes and programme areas. Yet, research and experience leaves no doubt that educational broadcasting can, particularly within multimedia systems, be an effective educational instrument. Decision makers in governments and the public need to be persuaded that this is so (Bates and Robinson 1977, Tulodziecki 1977).

Bibliography

Bates T, Robinson J (eds.) 1977 *Evaluating Educational Television and Radio*. Proc. of the Int. Conf. on Evaluation and Research in Educational Television and Radio, Milton Keynes, 9–13 April, 1976. Open University, Milton Keynes

Bates A 1984 *Broadcasting in Education: An Evaluation*. Constable, London

Bücker F J 1980 *Schulfernsehen*. Kösel, München

Cathcart H R 1982 *The Use of the Media in Adult Education*. European Bureau of Adult Education, Amersfoort

Clausse R 1949 *L'Education par la radio: Radio scolaire*. UNESCO, Paris

Croissandeau J M 1981 Les avatars de la télévision à l'école. *Le Monde de l'Education* 77: 55–58

Daco L 1976 Notes on some present trends in educational broadcasting in Western Europe. *Eur. Broadcasting Union Rev.* 27(3): 13–21

Dieuzeide H 1960 *Teaching Through Television*. Organisation for Economic Co-operation and Development, Paris

Goodhardt G J, Ehrenberg A S C, Collins M A 1975 *The Television Audience: Patterns of Viewing*. Saxon House, Farnborough

Harry K, Kaye A, Wilson K 1981 *The European Experience of the Use of the Mass Media and Distance Methods for Adult Basic Education*. Open University, Milton Keynes

Murray J F 1981 *The Future of Educational Broadcasting: A Discussion Paper*. Scottish Council for Educational Technology, Glasgow

Scupham J 1976 A future for educational broadcasting? *Listener Supplement on Educational Broadcasting*. British Broadcasting Corporation, London

Simmerding G 1977 *Educational Broadcasting: Its Philosophy and Practice*. Bayerischer Rundfunk, München

Sturm H 1979 *School Radio in Europe*. A documentation with contributions given at the European School Radio Conf., Munich, 1977. Saur, München

Treffel J 1981 *Présents et futurs de l'audiovisuel en éducation*. La Documentation Française, Paris

Tulodziecki G 1977 Educational television in the Federal Republic of Germany. *Prog. Learn. Educ. Technol.* 14: 108–16

Van der Voort T H A, Keekenkamp F 1978 *Edukative televisie voor volwassenen—een Researchoverzicht*. Netherlandse Omroep Stichting, Hilversum

Transnational Influences in Broadcasting

R. Cruise O'Brien

The capacity of industrialized countries to influence developing countries is greater now than at any time in the past. The rapidity with which countries are incorporated into the international economic system is complemented by the sociocultural influence of the flow of information throughout the world. The mass media in particular, as a techno-industrial mechanism for transmitting information and entertainment to a potential mass audience, are an element in this global process. Documenting the content of such flows is important, but it is equally important to understand the influences on media production in developing countries—in particular the sociocultural features of transferred models of professional training, and of the organization of communication structures.

The processes by which the mass media in developing countries are influenced by those in industrial countries are neither simple nor uniform, and they are subject to considerable regional variation. The influence of the United States in Latin America is one of relatively unimpeded market forces transferred through commercial audience-maximizing systems built around advertising. One effect of this has been to encourage, through advertising in particular, high consumption patterns and the creation of expectations which can only be met by the continual incorporation of these countries into the world economy. This makes it increasingly difficult to establish economic policies which correspond to the ability of these countries to foster locally conceived and based development strategies.

In Asia and Africa, by contrast, there is, in the 1980s, a more limited incorporation into the modern consumer economy. The model of institutional transfer in broadcasting is that of the state corporation, though this does not necessarily exclude the influence of the market. It is possible that a future rise in living standards will lead to greater incorporation into the modern consumer economy, and thus to the generalization of the Latin American model. But currently it is the influence of the European model of professionalism on the state broadcasting corporations which results in certain important characteristics of dependence being built into broadcasting policy and practice. Moreover, the organization of broadcasting in developing countries is bureaucratic, often as a consequence of the model imported from developed countries, although there is no necessity for this in terms of either technology or product. Structures and occupations are only partly shaped by transnational influence.

1. Technology, Structures, and Media Flows

Economists have mainly concerned themselves with the effects of different types of technology on employment and labour utilization. Other effects of technology transfer have rarely been considered. Yet it is questions about the effects of the transfer of technology on socialization, role relationships, and organizations, that are particularly pertinent to a consideration of broadcasting. The technology itself is very sophisticated and does not easily lend itself to experimentation in the development of appropriate technology. But the radio or television programme, in contrast, is a cultural product whose form and content are subject to local decisions, and whose influence goes beyond the simple consumption of goods and services.

The transnational influences carried through the mass media operate at two distinct levels: first, the direct influence on consumer patterns and lifestyles, of foreign programmes and advertising; second, the influence on standards and norms of training, professionalism, models of organization and media production which cause certain occupations to identify with their metropolitan counterparts, and ultimately draw the media away from the cultural base and resources of a poor country. Media technology and systems "can act as the chief cultural arm of the industrial order from which they originate".

Far from being a neutral feature in the process of industrialization or the transplantation of production processes, technology transfer necessitates certain types of social organization, role differentiation, and training. The technical aspects of broadcasting and their organization reflect this most obviously.

Electrical engineers trained in universities in Europe or North America will have a strong disposition towards the most sophisticated technology which is reinforced by close professional contacts with counterparts throughout the world, for instance through professional meetings and journals. Hence the system they would most like to have installed in their native countries reflects not necessarily local needs, but the standards and norms of the "transnational community". Engineers in broadcasting are as impressed as other members of the scientific and technical elite in developing countries with the ingenuity and sophistication of very expensive "gadgets". In addition, a source of their claim to authority as an occupation or profession may be based precisely on the sophistication of the equipment with which they work, and on which they have become dependent because of certain objectives of training or socialization in the wider sense. Considerations of this kind engender the choice of complex system design and costly equipment, while placing a heavy burden on the local service, which may have originally been intended to achieve low cost national coverage. Such a problem is indicative of the fact that the reorientation of cognitive categories achieved in the process of socialization may be at odds with the realities of local economic capacity. This is shown most dramatically in the technical side of broadcasting. The technology of broadcasting imported by developing countries, is, almost without exception, designed for production systems which emerged in relation to metropolitan needs and markets.

While the advanced and expensive technology of broadcasting is largely fixed, there is at least a possible choice between lightweight and heavy equipment. Unfortunately, like experimentation in terms of community participation in the mass media, the versatility and capacity of this lightweight equipment, which is cheaper and easier to use, is best known in international organizations (UNESCO seminars and FAO experiments on rural participation) or the leisure industries of developed countries. Even where it does come to the attention of engineers from developing countries, it is often resisted as being below "professional" standard. This especially limits the capacity for outside broadcasting, which is potentially so important in developing countries, to cumbersome purpose-built units.

This professional/nonprofessional distinction, a lynchpin of the engineers' stock in trade, has been called into question, in the 1980s, by experimental uses of broadcasting in major industrial countries. Yet news often travels slowly to the far corners of the world, and it does so in relation to transnational features of socialization combined with local social differentiation. One problem is the extent to which social relations of production or working methods and organizational structure can be made more flexible, even given the necessarily advanced nature of the technology required for production (whether lightweight or not).

Very important work has been done in the early 1980s, which documents the control of global news flows by a few predominant Western news agencies, or the volume of television entertainment programmes sold through a carefully constructed marketing structure. Documenting and analyzing the flows are important, but equally worthy of consideration is an understanding of the components of media production in the periphery and the transfer of the knowledge and organization necessary to sustain a communications structure.

Heads of government and ministers of information from developing countries have often made critical pronouncements on the effects of cultural imperialism, of which the media has become an acknowledged component. These pronouncements have served to call attention to some of the most obvious characteristics of dependence such as television programme imports and reliance on a few Western agencies for the circulation of news and information. More subtle processes, which are essentially structural and technological, have been hardly questioned. Such processes may be less apparent, but they are no less penetrating. While the percentage of locally produced programmes in proportion to imported television series is improving in many countries, thus satisfying at least the ephemeral characteristics of the

battle against cultural imperialism, the quality and relevance of local production remains heavily constrained by the organization, technology, and professional assumptions which go into its production.

2. The Role of Research

For a long time, scholarly research, which was mainly United States based, concentrated narrowly on the relationship between communications and other factors of modernization, on the diffusion of innovation within a given system, or on individual participation in the modernization process and its psychic effects. Such work concentrated on monitoring individual or group responses to the new stimulus of the mass media, regarding the process itself as an unquestioned catalyst of social change and therefore development. Looking at the media institutions themselves in this light went no further than reaffirming occupational differentiation familiar in other fields. The tenacity of this line of research reflected the implicit ideological bias in studies based on modernization and development which were pervasive in the 1960s. Such literature was designed to illustrate how rapidly the sociocultural or sociopolitical systems were exhibiting the qualities necessary to make less developed countries more like the industrial countries which preceded them. In the field of mass communications, such orthodoxies persisted alongside the most extraordinary growth of the power of transnational corporations which marketed the technical capability, the growth of advertising, and the volume of sale of United States entertainment programmes. And yet the studies continued to document and analyze development problems as if each country or process of social change existed in isolation from external influences and pressures for incorporation. This was perhaps most obvious in the mass media.

Those working on modernization as an aspect of communications growth, or diffusion of innovation, have made a rather disappointed reassessment of its progress, but continue either to ignore the features of domination and dependence implied in media growth, or attempt to relegate them to a separate field of study. At the very best, the somewhat more enlightened scholars have begun to concern themselves with the distribution of communications within developing societies noting, quite accurately, its tendency to inequality of access and its potential for reinforcing already existing social and economic inequalities. But this reformulation is still pursued without reference to the importance of external influences on this process. Yet to consider features of social differentiation in developing countries in isolation from such influences must surely be misleading.

A shift of interest, and a much more comprehensive approach to the role of the media which incorporates the global influences, came from two principal sources. In the political arena, the concern for cultural imperialism and in particular the dominance of major news agencies put information on the agenda of the New International Economic Order as early as 1976. This was an attempt to redress perceived imbalances in information. Yet the ideological pronouncements of government representatives largely ignored the more subtle and penetrating forces of dependence in the entertainment and features programmes in the media.

The second source of reinterpretation of the impact of the media in developing countries came from academic or para-academic research. The demand for a reinterpretation of media and development thinking is complemented by a serious reconsideration of the role of largely United States influenced media development in Latin America. Certain analyses focus on the interlocking power of transnational corporations to the information and entertainment business culture and advertising.

The documentation of flows of news and television programmes not only to developing countries but also to small European countries like Finland or Portugal, which are major importers of such programmes, is extremely important, for this work has begun to situate media marketing and the imitation of media forms in a global context. It will be most encouraging if more studies are done on the effects of this process in peripheral countries, which consider not only marketing forces and technological transfer, but also the more subtle and complicated features associated with organizational transfer and socialization, the transfer of knowledge, and the organization of media production. Sectoral studies on the development and use of the media in various countries may yield rich and fruitful material which could provide a more complete understanding of sociocultural processes in the international context.

Libraries and Resource Centers

School Libraries/Resource Centers

J. E. Lowrie

The variety of terms used to describe the school library in today's educational milieu are a result of changes in both content and concept. The traditional school library which contained primarily books and other printed materials often existed in a parallel structure with the audiovisual center — traditionally a collection of film-strips, slides, records, and so on. However, as graphics and production of materials as well as reprographic and video equipment and more recently minicomputers began to be used by both students and teachers, the phrase "media center" or "resource center" came into existence. Since both print and nonprint materials are included in the word media, and the pedagogical and economic soundness of merging all media in one center soon became evident, "school library/media (resource) center" became the accepted terminology. This article, therefore, is predicated on the current practice of presenting libraries and media centers as a unified service.

The purpose of the school library/media center is to aid the instructional goals and objectives of the school. It gives continuous support to the teaching and learning program; provides impetus to educational change; ensures maximum access to the widest possible range of resources and services; equips students with the basic skills to obtain and use a wide range of resources and services; and leads them towards a lifetime use of librar-ies for recreation, information, and continuing educa-tion (based on a resolution adopted by the School Library Section, International Federation of Library Associations and Institutions, Manila, August 1980).

The rapid growth of interest in school library devel-opment has led to a recognition of the need for stan-dards or at least guidelines for developing such units. It has likewise re-emphasized the need for constant evalua-tion of existing services in relation to changing needs and clientele. Many countries have now published manuals instructing in the development, maintenance, and maximum utilization of media centers (resource libraries). The UNESCO *Guidelines for the Planning and Organization of School Library Media Centers* (Carroll and Beilke 1979) provides an international tool for all

countries. Philosophy, personnel selection and acquisi-tion, and facilities are all discussed in detail. They must be adapted to meet the purposes of any school system/ educational program in any country. Even though resources may be meager to begin with, the initial effort will benefit children. The expansion of the centers comes with time and interest and results in the growth of materials-based learning for all children. International guidelines are an asset, but those designed for the spe-cific country or region by joint groups of educators and media specialists will be the most significant instruments of promotion.

Each school system (national or local) and each com-munity (from rural to metropolitan) will require certain decisions to be made regarding selection and organiza-tion of a collection, staffing, accessibility to, and availa-bility of, resources within a resource center. The resultant variations will be discernible to a small degree within the individual community, to a much larger degree at national level, and to an even greater degree when viewed from an international comparative position.

Not all variations can or should be discussed in this presentation, but there are significant variables which surface at any gathering of school library personnel and educational administrators which provide a useful focus. Among these are the relationship of collections to curriculum goals, standards, resource sharing and networking, public/school library relationships, regional centers, media format, local or national controls. A sur-vey of what is happening internationally in a few coun-tries will highlight some of these issues and present some of the policies being implemented.

1. Resource Sharing

Sharing of resources has become an item of some importance in the library profession. Research and aca-demic libraries and to a lesser degree public libraries have been involved in some aspect of resource sharing for many years. Such participation has now moved into the international arena with the many technological services now available for rapid transmission of information.

School librarians are beginning to realize that more effective use can be made of materials through sharing and that no one library can truly supply all user needs. Single and multitype cooperative programs as well as multitype networks are becoming increasingly visible. Typical examples of cooperative programs are interlibrary loans, union catalogs and lists, reciprocal borrowing, centralized processing, and cooperative surveys. School librarians have been slow to become involved in cooperative efforts and several reasons have been given for this: (a) schools are open only during the school days; (b) collections are chosen to support the curriculum; (c) interjurisdictional loans are sometimes prohibited by the systems; (d) lack of basic communications such as the telephone; (e) students and teachers have immediate needs which inhibit interlibrary loans; (f) lack of funds; (g) lack of incentive; and (h) negative attitudes of school personnel. Self-preservation and protection often appear to stifle the cooperative approach (American Library Association 1980 p. 500).

Another form of cooperation is the school–public library combination, that is services within the same facility. The Federal Republic of Germany, Australia, and Canada as well as the United States have recently been exploring this organizational pattern. The results of one study indicate quite clearly the hazards involved:

> It is unlikely that a community able to support or now supporting separate types of libraries will offer better school–public library resources...because the combination of factors required to promote a successful combined program seldom occurs. Further, when a community is unable to provide minimum library services through separate facilities and no option for improved services through system membership exists, the combined program presents alternatives to limited or nonexistent services under certain conditions. However, communities searching for a cheaper way to provide better library services should be aware that the study revealed no documented evidence that economy results from this organization pattern. (ALA 1980 p. 509)

One experiment being tried in some large suburban or geographical regions has been the creation of a unique position called "Children's Services/School Services Liaison Consultant." Such a person is responsible for working out a plan of action whereby school and public libraries can develop and implement policies and procedures which will aid in the transition of users and the exchange of resources, and which will develop expanded services and enhance general relationships. This person would be a catalytic agent helping to create meaningful change in the local community. The value of both types of libraries would be visible and respected (Drescher 1976).

A true network is the interfacing of more than one kind of system. Networks may take many forms but there are primarily two types, "electronic" and "people," although these are not mutually exclusive. Multitype networks which incorporate school, academic, public, special, and other types of libraries into a legal network are becoming more evident and more functional than the less formal cooperative programs. These may be regional or state networks and grant full rights in governance, responsibility, and participation to all librarians. They are particularly vigorous in the fields of classification, cataloging, and bibliographic sharing. Media professionals in schools are becoming more aware of the benefits of membership in such networks, and are seeking to determine how such services as resource sharing, coordinated purchasing and processing, and bibliographic access will be of special value to their particular school's clientele. "Equal opportunity to access" is as important for the school child as it is for the research or business patron.

2. Patterns of Organization

In both developed and developing countries, ministries of education have recognized since the early 1960s the need for library programs which will assist in the educational and literacy programs for their respective countries. In the early 1970s in the Federal Republic of Germany, specific projects were begun which brought together school and public libraries in cultural and educational activities and the first regulations for school libraries were developed. Here too experimentation in including both types of library services under one roof though in separate areas was begun.

Danish school library development started before the early 1920s but it has been accelerating since the early 1970s, particularly stimulated by legislation in 1975 which makes a school library in every school compulsory. Here one finds that students and parents are highly involved in the selection of materials for their respective library resource centers. The materials are processed by the centralized processing center for the country. The Danish Library Bureau and the Danish Binding Center serve both school and public libraries and the two kinds of institutions cooperate on tasks of joint interest. Under the Danish Ministry of Education there is a National Institute for Educational Media which has been given a series of coordinating tasks in the area of educational media (including cataloging and registration of educational materials), information for the consumer, coordination between producer and consumer, ordering and financing, processing, film distribution, and so on. Regional media centers are also part of the Danish program and many teachers come to them for what is called a "pedagogical workshop." Most of the schools have "pedagogical workshop apparatus" or hardware, but the regional workshop is better equipped, and there is both professional and technical assistance for individual production of educational materials. Regional center collections cannot supersede local school libraries and pedagogical workshops. Experience indicates that teachers in schools with well-equipped libraries use the regional center more frequently than the teachers from schools with poorly equipped libraries. New quantitative standards exist which must be followed (Lowrie 1978).

Pilot projects which can be models for expansion within a country have the potential to be significant methods for demonstrating the value of resource centers. The pilot program in Lagos State, Nigeria, which started as a UNESCO program, now includes an educational library for teachers, demonstration libraries for both primary and postprimary schools, a centralized school library service and training programs for teacher–librarians. The program has expanded beyond the immediate environs of Lagos into the suburbs and other communities of the state.

The Abadina Media Resource Center which is connected with the University of Ibadan (Nigeria) is not only a demonstration center for the teacher and library science training programs, it also serves the children of the immediate community. In addition, a workshop for teacher–librarians is an annual event. This has been upgraded into a teacher–librarian certification sandwich course lasting 12 weeks over a three-year period. The center also undertakes on request from other libraries short-term internship programs for training of staff.

Research is an important part of this center and the establishment of meaningful and relevant standards and specifications for school libraries in Nigeria has been of paramount interest. The first two years of the center's establishment were used to investigate, test, and establish such standards. These were then published in the *Manual for Nigerian School Libraries*. Local materials and local skills have been used in the design and production of suitable equipment so that meaningful and realistic costing can be recommended for school library operations and their establishment (Ogunsheye 1977).

Another device for sharing is a book depot such as that sponsored by the Bendel State Library Board, also in Nigeria. This center purchases and makes accessible books for library collections around the state and encourages many of the poorer and isolated communities to develop reading collections relevant to their needs.

Where there are problems of poverty and illiteracy, and inadequate incentives for indigenous authors and publishers to produce books and other media for educational purposes, then there is a need to explore networks of librarians, to experiment in resource sharing, and to develop innovative means of distribution such as book boxes on oxcarts, boats, trucks, and small planes and programs to "read and pass on." Though acceptance of the philosophy of resource centers provides the basic impetus, deciding how best to bring materials and school children together in a specific type of environment requires creative, innovative, and convinced persons. It is not always the most sophisticated, highly educated professional who can see the way ahead but the devoted and concerned individual who recognizes a

need and contrives, often in the most elementary fashion, a practical first step to finding it. But additional support—financial and philosophical—must come from the regional and national authorities so that the enriched services can be solidly implemented. Such an example is the Banco de Libro (Book Bank) in Venezuela.

In Venezuela, the systematic development of library services is very recent and is closely linked to the establishment of democratic government only 22 years ago, to the emergence of popular education, and to the process of urbanization and industrialization. Libraries have, in our country become the main instrument for democratization of information.

During these years the Book Bank, a private non-profit association free of bureaucratic and political bindings, has shown that it is not only possible but necessary to define common objectives, strategies, and procedures for the organization of library services for children and young people. The experimental and demonstration programs of this organization have shown that in an underdeveloped country, common elements are predominant in organizing and developing school and public libraries. The impact of such programs has created the favorable conditions for issuing a body of legislation which considers both types of libraries as complementary means to reach a common objective: the development of well-informed individuals, able to take a critical stand and to participate in society.

We have avoided the pitfall of competing for meager financial resources and have maximized the use of scant, specialized, human resources by centralizing, at a national level, planning, administration, and technical processes, and decentralizing operative functions at a local level through library networks.

These operative functions, besides backing formal learning processes, also take over the following activities: information on community resources and services; procuring and lending of hard-to-find material of local interest; organization of users as aides in running library services; stimuli to awaken or arouse community self-help groups.

Limited resources have been an encouragement to design an effective strategy which differs from our anarchic and individualistic tradition. We have integrated various disciplines in a permanent task force and have obtained technical and financial contributions from a variety of public and private agencies. Such an approach has oriented our activities since the onset of the Book Bank, and has continued in the subsequent stages of systematization and generalization taken over by the State.

The institutionalization of this process has taken place by:

(a) The establishment, in 1976, of a permanent Commission of the National Library and Information System (SINASBI) annexed to the National Planning Office, at a presidential level. The Commission coordinates the nuclei of the library, archives, documentary and statistical systems. This year for the first time the Commission incorporated in our National Master Plan a General Information Program for a five-year period (1981–1986).

(b) Three years ago, with support from all political parties, the National Congress approved a law which established an Autonomous Institute responsible for the coordination of the National Library System.

(c) Last year (1979) an executive decree was issued which established in the Ministry of Education, an agency responsible for the organization of a National Library System, founded on the 15 years of experience gained at the Guyana experimental library network.

Through visits to other countries we have shared and enriched our experience. We have also found that in Latin America, in spite of our cultural and economic differences, we must meet common challenges to organize library services oriented toward improving the quality of life of our people, especially of those most needed: political interven- tion in technical matters, lack of administrative continuity, lack of library tradition, authoritarian families, rigid school procedures, lack of high quality printed matter, and other programs derived from an unfair distribution of wealth.

Therefore, we are convinced of the need for agreements in this continent to share valid experiences at a technical and governmental level. We propose the elaboration and adoption of common principles and norms which will allow a demonstration effect on the community, specially of decision makers, and will stimulate the progressive institutionalization of library services and gain the necessary authority to defend the right of all children to have access to high quality books, magazines, and films, which meet their interests and needs, organized in efficient library services, dynamic, flexible, and closely immersed in their cultural reality.

This way we will contribute to develop future citizens able to participate actively and dynamically in the needed transformation to reach a more just and human society (Betancourt 1980 pp. 111–12).

3. Special Group Needs

The involvement of school libraries in providing cultural materials for migrant children and more recently refugee youngsters is increasingly important. There has been a lack of materials, particularly books, in the languages of these children. Publishing houses are now beginning to study the needs of these groups and are printing the same story in several languages, pertinent to the immigrant populations within their country. But it is not enough to provide books merely for the migrant child. It is even more important to help the native-born child to understand the culture and traditions of his or her fellow pupils and for migrant children to feel proud of their homeland. The social customs and family relationships of the migrant parents are often different from those of the native born. The school library can be an important factor in the integration of the various ethnic groups which now form part of the population in many countries. At the other end of the scale are the truly native persons—the Indians of North America, the Aboriginals of Australia, the Maori of New Zealand, and others. The rich cultures of these people is not a written one and too often the books written for children about these persons have been patronizing and inaccurate. School library/media specialists have a special responsibility to support publications and projects which promote better understanding of these cultures and people.

In isolated areas such as the Northern Territory of Australia, the Pacific Islands, the interior of Africa, or metropolitan poverty ghettos, the problems of literacy, and bilingual and multilingual groups demand special resource center programs. Reading materials in the vernacular must be produced. Adult education programs are as important as those for primary school children. Personnel must be especially trained to work with these groups. It has been suggested that stories handed down through oral communication be used as a basis for texts and that emphasis be placed on the vernacular prior to learning to read English or whatever the official main language of the country might be. School librarians having experience in such situations should share it through formal association or professional channels as well as through informal contacts. Administrators in educational planning offices will thus become aware of programs and materials which could be adapted to their specific situations.

4. Technological Influence

There is no question that communication devices such as minicomputers and videodiscs are rapidly becoming a part of teaching patterns in today's schools, along with older types of nonprint media. Again there is a difference in the rapidity at which this inclusion is taking place, but the international interest in computerized technology at all levels of business, government, culture, and education is undoubtedly one of the strongest influences in the world today. Hence all schools and particularly their resource centers are or will be involved in the utilization of these new tools. There are clear implications for school library/media specialists.

In addition to being prepared to introduce and incorporate technological advances into their school's instructional program, school library/media specialists will also have to involve themselves in efforts to more effectively make available the learning resources and instructional information which will be the heart of such transmission and delivery systems. They must assume an active role in shaping the future of education. Some of the activities will include:

(a) enlarging the quantity and quality of resources available to students through more cooperative lending procedures between libraries across school districts and geographic regions;

(b) improving the methods of bibliographic and media control that would allow for the creation of computerized union catalogs on a community or regional basis;

(c) training personnel and staff to become more aware of community resources and how to make them available to students and teachers;

(d) the establishment of networks of databases and retrieval mechanisms which will adequately meet the needs of students as well as the various instructional patterns that may be developed, whether they be controlled by the teacher, the media, or the learner;

(e) organizing learning resources to support interactive and learner-centered instruction as well as the traditional teacher-controlled approaches. (At minimum this means classification and indexing schemes must be developed to match learning resources with user needs.)

A projection of instructional needs suggests that future school library/media specialists will need to insure even greater efficiency and utilization of learning resources. The orientation and training of such media center personnel will need to take into account the shifting emphasis from collecting and controlling instructional resources to that of distribution, dissemination, and utilization. In addition, indexing and retrieval systems to allow for brief segments of sequentially presented materials in a variety of formats, must be developed. These formats could then be accessed randomly by teachers in classrooms or by students in home-learning centers on a demand basis. While the actual number of staff necessary to accomplish these tasks may vary with the needs and resources of the community, some of the more important areas of specialization that can be identified would allow for the following:

(a) Curriculum specialists—such as master teachers released from traditional classroom responsibilities and assigned to the school library/media center in order to become more familiar and knowledgeable with already available instructional resources, and who would suggest ways they could be more effectively introduced into the various curricular areas.

(b) Information specialists—responsible for the utilization of the databases relevant to the school's instructional needs as well as the development of computer-assisted instruction programs. Also important in this regard would be the transmission and dissemination of information in a wide range of presentation formats and learning levels to remote locations if necessary.

(c) Production specialists—responsible for the creation and validation of original learning materials as well as the modification and integration of already existing resources to meet changing informational and curricular needs.

(d) Utilization specialists—responsible for better use of all learning resources and function areas, but focusing on enrichment activities, recreational reading, listening, and receiving; research and study skills; concomitant learning; and other activities cross-disciplinary in nature.

(e) Administrators of learning resources—responsible for the overall administration and management of district or building level operations and for initiating such expanded services and activities. Involved at the highest level of decision making within the school and school district, such individuals could keep informed of the educational goals of the community and school and be ready to marshal the various learning resources and services necessary for their attainment (Fork and Weiner 1977).

To reiterate, the speed with which the development of such sophisticated centers moves ranges from happening immediately to happening within the next decade or two. But planning for this expansion, understanding of the way in which it may effect resource centers and education in general, and assessment of the appropriate technology must be a current part of the future goals and objectives in all countries.

5. Personnel Standards

Certification of personnel is a topic which demands continual attention in all countries. Although specific requirements vary from state to state, province to province, country to country, the minimum requirements include study in both education and library work. But here the variation begins. In the United States most school librarians must have a teaching certificate plus a minimum of library courses. The ideal is considered to be either a primary or a secondary teaching certificate plus a master's degree in librarianship and every effort is made to have this required by regional and state associations. In Denmark, the teacher–librarian is a teacher first and then a librarian and must be able to perform both activities during the school day. (It should be noted, however, that the school library is open the entire school day, continually manned by a teacher–librarian.) In Venezuela programs of certification and minimum librarian technicianship are just beginning. Special emphasis is placed on supplying initial information that was lacking for teachers.

Certification and guidelines or standards for school libraries cannot be considered mutually exclusive. The basic competencies needed by personnel responsible for the resource center will be tied in with the goals and objectives of the instructional program, with the minimum requirements of collection building, facilities, and staff support. Whenever school library persons gather, one of the major topics of discussion is the best method to achieve the highest standards or requirements possible for their particular branch of the profession. Education associations, as well as ministries of education and/or state boards of education, must be partners with the librarians in defining and achieving this goal. Tangential to certification is the growing use of volunteers. The use of volunteers is becoming more obvious, even in some cases essential, in this time of stringent economy. There has always been controversy about this particular type of staff assistance. In many instances it is the only way in which many of the clerical/housekeeping tasks can be accomplished. On the other hand, the volunteer too often has been coerced into serving as the librarian, there being no money for a professional. In this case, the concept of program and the relation to the school's instructional design is lost. Both faculty and students are deprived of the services which they should have. If a volunteer corps is necessitated because of economic problems some type of professional orientation and supervision should be developed, and the volunteers themselves must understand the necessity of being responsible both in attendance and for the tasks assigned. A special instruction program to bring them to the level of library technician is considered desirable. As additional assistants these volunteers can perform an important role. The correlation with certification requirements and professional competencies is obvious.

To successfully implement the current philosophy of a school library/media center, the librarian and the staff must work as a cohesive whole. The librarian as coordinator (building or system) must be a manager in the best sense of the word: he/she must be dedicated to the achievement of a flexible attitude and management position, maintenance of a strong philosophy, and the formulation of carefully developed objectives (Hicks 1981). The process of study, implementation, evaluation, and realignment is a constant one where the school library has moved beyond being a simple support agency to that of a real partner in the learning and teaching arena. The force behind this is the professional staff which "personalizes and humanizes" the services of the center. It is the librarian who is the energizing force, who utilizes the resources "wisely, creatively, and compassionately" for more permanent and satisfying experiences (Hicks 1981).

6. Conclusion

Presentations at annual conferences of the International Association of School Librarianship have over the years consistently emphasized the following items of concern, action on which must be undertaken in every country to a greater or lesser degree, if the concept of school library/resource centers is to be implemented and/or expanded.

(a) The need for a national plan either under a ministry of education (in most countries) or through a professional library or education association.

(b) The establishment of a minimum financial base to undergird the development of the plan.

(c) The designing of training programs for librarians, for paraprofessionals and for teachers introducing them to the information needed for developing those competencies pertinent to library utilization as well as to a staff's respective responsibilities.

(d) The publication of minimum guidelines for regional and local program development which will allow for flexibility in planning.

(e) The encouragement of indigenous publishing and writing programs which will produce materials relevant to the country, expanding the media which is currently being imported by the said country.

(f) The continuous evaluation by the ministry (or equivalent) to determine if goals are being met and where changes need to be made.

(g) The creation of a body of research relevant to the school and library program relationship as well as to user needs, including pilot projects and centers.

(h) The establishment of minimum certification requirements and the implementation of continuing education and inservice training programs for all personnel.

A corps of well-educated school library media specialists as leaders and consultants within a ministry of education, the establishment of a national school library/media association as a strong professional entity, and the education of teachers and administrators on the values of utilizing the services of resource centers is the tripod on which the future understanding, expansion, and viability of the service depends.

Bibliography

Aaron S L, Smith S O 1980 A study of the combined school public libraries. In: American Association of School Librarians 1980 *Focus on Trends and Issues*, Vol. 6. American Library Association (ALA), Chicago, Illinois

American Association of School Librarians and Association for Educational Communications and Technology 1988 *Information Power: Guidelines for School Library and Media Programs*. American Library Association (ALA), Chicago, Illinois

American Library Association (ALA) 1980 School libraries and media centers. In: Wedgwood R (ed.) 1980 ALA *World Encyclopedia of Library and Information Services*. American Library Association (ALA), Chicago, Illinois

Betancourt V 1980 National Library of Venezuela. IASL Annual Conference Proceedings, Ciudad Guyana, Venezuela, 1980

Canadian School Library Association 1967 *Standards of Library Service for Canadian Schools*. Ryerson, Toronto, Ontario

Carroll F L, Beilke P F 1979 *Guidelines for the Planning and Organization of School Library Media Centers*. PGI-79/WS/17. UNESCO, Paris

Commonwealth Secondary Schools Libraries Committee, Australia 1971 *Standards For Secondary School Libraries*. Australian Government Publishing Service, Canberra

Drescher J A 1976 What's the picture? The library administrator and children's services. *Ill. Libr.* 58: 784–86

Dyer E R 1978 *Cooperation in Library Service to Children*. Scarecrow, Metuchen, New Jersey

Falsone A M 1977 Participation of school libraries. In: Hamilton B A, Ernst W B (eds.) 1977 *Multiple Library Cooperation*. Bowker, New York

Fork D, Weiner M 1977 Educational technology: New trends and their implications in school libraries. IASL Annual Conference Proceedings, Ibadan, Nigeria, 1977

Frankowiak B 1977 Networks, databases and media programs: An overview. *Sch. Media Q.* 6: 15–20

Goedecke H 1975 School libraries in the Federal Republic of Germany. (Unpublished Paper)

Guidelines for Library Services in Primary Schools, 1974. Prepared by the Primary Schools' Libraries Committee of the Schools Commission, Canberra

Hall N (ed.) 1986 *Teachers, Information and School Libraries*, Paper prepared by International Federation of Library Associations and Institutions (IFLA) Section on School Libraries Working Group. PGI, UNESCO, Paris

Hannisdottir S (ed.) 1986 *Guidelines for the Education and Training of School Librarians*, International Federation of Library Associations and Institutions (IFLA) Professional Reports, No. 9 IFLA Section of School Libraries, The Hague

Hicks B 1981 Managing the building-level school library media program. In: American Association of School Librarians 1981 *Focus on Trends and Issues*, Vol. 7. American Library Association (ALA), Chicago, Illinois

Higgins J (ed.) 1983 *Getting Started: An Annotated Bibliography of Ideas and Procedures*. International Association of School Librarianship, Kalamazoo, Michigan

Holst A, Irgens K, Tølløse J (eds.) 1975 *School Libraries in Denmark*. Danish Association of School Libraries, Copenhagen

International Association of School Librarianship. Annual Conference Proceedings: Ciudad Guyana, Venezuela 1980;

Aberystwyth, Wales 1981; Red Deer, Alberta, Canada 1982; Bad Segeburg, West Germany 1983

International Association of School Librarianship (IASL) 1985 *Libraries and Information: Towards a Policy for Schools, Proc. Conf. IASL*, Kingston, Jamaica 1985. IASL, Kalamazoo, Michigan

International Association of School Librarianship (IASL) 1988 *Great Expectations: Standards, Innovative Programs and New Technology, Proc. Conf. IASL*, Kalamazoo, Michigan 1988. IASL, Kalamazoo, Michigan

Library service to isolated schools and communities 1981 IASL *Occasional Paper*, July 1981. Research Publications, Melbourne

Lowrie J E 1978 Margaret Scott Memorial Lecture. In: *Proc. Conf. IASL*, Melbourne, Australia, 1978

Media Programs: District and School 1975 Prepared by the American Association of School Librarians and the Association for Educational Communications and Technology. American Library Association (ALA), Chicago, Illinois

Obi D S 1977 *A Manual for School Libraries on Small Budgets*. Oxford University Press, Ibadan

Ogunsheye F A 1977 Abadina Media Resource Center. In: IASL Annual Conference Proceedings, Ibadan, Nigeria, 1977

Winslade B A J 1979 *Rancangan Pembangunan Perpustakaan Sekolah di Malaysia* [Blueprint for school library development in Malaysia]. Persatuan Perpustakaan Malaysia, Kuala Lumpur

Public Libraries

P. Sullivan

This article examines the goals, funding, functions, and organization of public libraries. School libraries, special libraries, and college and university libraries are covered elsewhere in this Section.

1. Scope and Mission

Public libraries are often created to meet the need for a general educational institution that would provide for those who are not, and may never have been, part of the student population of the community. Yet they must also recognize and respond to the interests of their actual users, who provide them with political justification and support. Hence, they can have the appearance of being thriving, successful places where many people find what they want and need, while there are many more people—certainly a majority of the population—who have no recognition of what public libraries are, and who may benefit from them in indirect ways without even being aware of their contribution. Their level of funding is rarely sufficient to allow major efforts to broaden their audience without incurring a reduction of services to existing users to a level that would be politically unacceptable.

In the 1980s, information flow is increasingly perceived as a major feature of society; and public libraries are part of this picture. Yet libraries have responsibilities assigned to them in which information and its provision are only a small part, and they are sometimes also seen as only a small part of the information provision effort. Public libraries provide access to more than information when they provide access to materials that are recreational or cultural, and when they offer space and environmental security to their users. When public library programs of service include classes and presentations in jails or mental institutions, for example, the message of concern may be as significant as any information they may provide.

Public libraries are almost universally recognized as being providers of reading materials as well as information, and as being free to all who wish to use them. Increasingly, they are taking on roles of more aggressive provision of information and materials, especially in countries where literacy is a high priority. This means not only developing countries, but also countries where new populations and/or a new recognition of the need to serve all people are calling attention to the need for concern for functional literacy for all. Reports which indicate that the achievement of literacy often occurs but is not sustained in the individual suggest that convenient provision of materials through public libraries could help to sustain newly literate people. The mission of the public library in literacy is not, however, clearly understood. In nations like Jamaica, where early and consistent links were made between the provision of a public library service and the maintenance of literacy, the library is a forceful part of the literacy effort, but there are public libraries and public librarians who seem to have the notion that the libraries will serve the illiterate if and when the people come to them. They do not see themselves as outreach oriented, nor are they. Public libraries are more often the sites for instructional programs than the initiators and providers of such programs. The educational mission of the public library, of course, does not have to limit itself to instructional efforts, but it is probable that greater concern about the maintenance of a literate population will result in increased efforts by public libraries to be significant parts of this effort.

Socially and politically, public libraries have been considered neutral by many. Often observed more in the breach than the promise, they have had as their goal the provision of materials on both sides of controversial issues. But there is scarcely a nation in the world that really provides, in widely disseminated formats, information on both sides of major political and social issues. Freedom of access in public libraries more typically means that materials are available to all, and that the individual user does not pay a specific fee for their use. However, as new formats or equipment are introduced, for example, computer-assisted reference services or automated databases, public libraries may provide them only to those who will pay for the time they are used. Pride in retaining all services as free is at odds with the need to make as many good services as possible available to as many people as possible.

2. Financial Support

Sources of funds for public libraries are, of necessity, becoming more diverse. Even governments that are relatively stable and affluent are often constrained in what they can provide for public libraries, and the libraries are competing for scarce funds with other longer recognized institutions, such as schools or health-care agencies. In developing countries, in general, it is the national government that is the major provider of public library support, and the services tend to be newer—in place since the Second World War—and more centralized. When identities of cities, states, or provinces are related to library development, the public library tends to receive support from such governments, sometimes with one unit of government requiring another to show evidence of its support and interest in order to be eligible for a share of the funding. Some libraries, usually those organized in districts or as entities of their own, have the right to levy and collect taxes, but it is much more common for them to receive a share of governmental funds based on their budgeted needs.

Funds from private sources of all kinds usually form only a small part of the public library's support, although such extensive efforts as the Carnegie Foundation's funding of public library buildings in the early years of this century are exceptions. Individual public libraries are usually eligible to receive funds from individuals and foundations by gifts and bequests, and

in many communities, the investment of time by volunteers, the gifts of books and other materials, and occasional contributions of money are the major kinds of gifts received by public libraries. When land and/or funds are donated for a new public library building or service, the donor may be commemorated in the name, but one need only review the names of libraries to note that cultural and political heroes are far more likely to be remembered in this way than are local donors.

Competition for funding, however, means that public libraries are often becoming involved in more organized and effective fund-raising efforts. Sometimes these are undertaken to secure new buildings or facilities, sometimes to initiate a new service, such as the lending of toys or the provision of special reference services for businesses. Many public libraries have groups of friends or patrons who may assist in such efforts, but more professionally based fund-raising efforts are likely to be needed as public libraries seek developmental assistance in the present and future.

3. Collections

The materials housed in public libraries and made available to users are probably easier to define and describe by purpose of use than by format. When public libraries are closely linked with federal government agencies, as in many developing countries, they are likely to include research collections, and extensive research collections—intended for use by scholars or others with scholarly related needs—can be found in many public libraries. Sometimes, these are inappropriate to the function and mission of the library but some historical accident and resultant inertia have caused their location in spite of limited use. It is also not unknown that a public librarian develops a kind of archival collection on the theory that it might come in handy someday, and it becomes a pseudo research collection. Even the process of retaining popular materials can lead to the establishment of a collection with research value, as when posters and publications of political or social movements or popular children's books are retained for their historical value. To judge that public libraries are somehow remote from the research purposes of other kinds of libraries is to make a considerable error in judgment.

Maintaining reference collections is a more generally acknowledged function of the public library, because standard sources of information such as encyclopedias and business directories need to be always available. Other information sources, however, may be needed in circulation. They may need lengthy study rather than short consultation; or their nature may require that they be used on site, as with books on auto repair. Hence public libraries usually try to circulate informational as well as recreational materials.

The goal of developing and maintaining a literate adult public requires access to a variety of materials. Some may relate to the everyday needs of life, such as books on household repairs, current news, or information on citizens' rights. Others may be purely recreational but still provide experience in reading and stimulate people to be readers. Thus, while information and recreation may be two different functions, the same parts of the collection may provide for them both.

School libraries have traditionally placed more emphasis on the need for a variety of formats for library materials than have public libraries, but many of the same characteristics occur in public libraries. Reluctant readers need to be able to use materials, such as films and filmstrips, that may stimulate them to read and/or provide them with information in formats they can learn from with greater success. Maps, periodicals, and realia are often the only ways some information can be acquired, so they, too, belong in the public library collection. Access to projectors, record players, and other media is undreamed of in some public libraries while very much taken for granted in others. More unusual still, but presumably becoming more frequent, are services such as loanable tools for household use or microcomputers that can be used in the library.

4. Services

Patterns of service in public libraries are usually planned according to various characteristics of users, both real and potential. Age level is traditionally the major basis on which groups of the public are identified and served. Even when public libraries have been established to respond to the needs of adults, there has usually been such demand for services to children in the same community that services to children are also provided. These may include activities, such as programs of films, storytelling, and dramatics, as well as provision of library materials. Young adults, defined with great variety in different libraries but usually including all those who are between 12 and 20 years old, often constitute another user group; but in many respects, young adults seek and need the same services and materials as adults: job-related requirements for information, recreational reading, the pursuit of hobbies, and access to space and services that welcome them and their interests.

Special concerns of the public library also include many individuals who are in some way isolated from customary services, for example, the physically disabled, the hospitalized, the imprisoned, and the geographically remote. Provision of materials by mail, scheduling of bookmobiles or book deposits in less accessible areas, provision of transportation to public libraries, telephone reference services, and information presentation by radio or other media are some of the means of reaching such isolated people.

There are parts of the public not usually recognized as disadvantaged who are not served effectively by the public library in many areas. Some developing countries have already identified the business community, for example, as a group to which special services need to be directed, because its needs for information and access to materials are not being met, even by long-established libraries. If a government responds to the needs of business with a more effective service for them, businesses may not need to develop their own special libraries to the same extent as in other settings.

Language can also be a major problem. Some languages suffer from a dearth of published material. Some countries' residents speak such a variety of languages that public libraries can scarcely hope to offer the range and quality of materials that the public needs. When large numbers of newcomers to a country create an audience for materials in their native languages, public libraries have usually tried to be responsive, but there are many difficulties. Publications in the desired languages may be hard or slow to acquire; there may be political and social differences between the newcomers and the native residents so that their interests are not well-matched to available reading materials, and their level of literacy in their native languages may be low.

As government-related institutions, public libraries are often expected to serve as facilities where government information can be disseminated. Especially when they are under ministries of culture, they may be located in complexes which also contain theaters, community meeting places, and other public rooms. Providing places for meetings or community groups, spaces for study, exhibit areas, interviewing and registration facilities, or even health testing areas, may be a significant function of the public library. Hence it needs to be located where people can find and use it as an ordinary part of their daily or weekly routine.

5. Organization

The external organization of the public library indicates which branch or agency of government has responsibility for it. Traditionally, departments or ministries of education have had the responsibility for public libraries, but it is not unusual for branches of government concerned with agricultural extension, military affairs, or institutions such as prisons or hospitals, to take on at least some responsibilities related to public library services. When public libraries are part of the educational establishment, their link with other parts of that establishment is likely to be clear, but this is not always an advantage, especially where finance is concerned. Recognizing that schools are probably going to receive priority in any allocation of resources, individuals whose prime concern is the public library have often championed the idea of a more separate status for it. However, given the likelihood of more, rather then less, centralization of governmental effort, the prospect of separate public library agencies at all levels of government is not promising.

What has happened, sometimes from the start of public library development in a country, is that public libraries have been placed under the same authority as museums and other cultural institutions. While this may combine more similar kinds of institutions, each with a broad-based audience in the population, and each with roughly similar claims on the public's support, it has sometimes meant that the overall authority itself is not as powerful as one with the responsibility for education and related programs. This may be weakening when the assignment of the public library to this agency exists from the beginning; it can be devastating when the shift of responsibility occurs after libraries are established, and when the best of the old scheme will be remembered to be compared with the worst of the new.

What affects public libraries and their external organization in an even more interesting way is that, often, they may be dealing with different kinds of ministries or departments at different levels of the governmental structure. Thus, a public library in a municipality may report directly to a city official as one of a number of fairly autonomous departments, but within its province or state, the liaison may be with a governmental department that is in the education unit, while the national government may have most public library programs in a cultural ministry.

Public libraries in the present day are usually parts of some library network or system. These range from loosely organized cooperative efforts in which library members agree to provide services and materials on request among themselves to more formally structured federations where some centralized services, such as purchasing of materials and/or provision of specialized reference collections and services, are available in return for assessments placed on the libraries. There is some irony in the fact that public libraries with limited budgets and other resources are sometimes reluctant or intimidated about joining in more organized structures, while established libraries with strong collections may be hesitant to enter into cooperative arrangements where they sense they may provide more services and materials than they will receive. True networks of information and service among all kinds of libraries and at all levels with use of fast, convenient transmission of information and resources are epitomes of library cooperation. While they are not limited to public libraries, they are usually developed with heavy reliance on the leadership and expertise of public librarians (see *Processing of Library Materials*).

The internal organization of public libraries is usually relatively simple. In areas where the administration of the public library is seen as a local responsibility, there is often a group of citizens with responsibility for administration. This can make it possible for two or more governmental units to unite in the administration of the library, with each one being represented in the decision-making, policy-setting process. Often, this group or board has a responsibility of advocacy for the library's missions, budgets, and policies with reference to the governmental unit of which the library is a part. Formidable as the responsibilities of such a part-time group sound when they are stated, they are often virtually totally assigned to a library director whose task it is to present plans of development for the board and to carry out the day-to-day administrative tasks of the library.

When public libraries are a part of the national government with no other levels of government taking responsibility for them, planning and development can be more unified, but there is also the possibility that the best service may be initiated in and around the capital city while other parts of the country receive comparatively little benefit.

6. Research

Research about public libraries has not been noted for its high quality. There are histories, reports of specific research projects, background statements for the development of mission statements, and evaluations of innovative developmental efforts. However, some of the most helpful research findings about public libraries and their use have come as minor parts of more extensive research. For example, when people responding to surveys about their life-styles indicate the role that the public library has played in their lives, their comments are considered free of the bias that occurs when public library personnel and researchers survey their own users or their community. There is, nevertheless, a need for the consistent acquisition of information about the public library's community and its expectations and needs. The context in which such user studies are conducted is important. The idea that if libraries knew more about their users and potential users and their needs and interests, they could develop collections and services to satisfy them, is basically sound. But, when public libraries are as undersupported as they typically are, it is reasonable to ask whether the implementation of recommendations from such studies is likely to be feasible. Public library personnel often claim that they do not have the resources to accomplish what they know should be done. So the searching out of new groups of the unserved and the raising of their expectations with regard to the public library may not be the most sensible way to proceed.

Efforts to establish standards for public libraries are similarly difficult. Quantitative standards that are based on sizes of buildings, numbers of people served, and numbers of items loaned are customarily a first step, but it is difficult enough to base them on similar measures within one region or country, without considering the variations across national boundaries. Qualitative standards may be more appealing, but they are even more difficult to establish in different localities, under different schemes of organization, and with different priorities of purpose.

7. Summary

Public libraries, perhaps partly because they are responsive and identify with the diverse communities they serve, are difficult to perceive and to evaluate in the aggregate. They are probably at their best when they stimulate their publics not be satisfied with them, because an informed, restless, and knowledge-seeking populace is what they were founded to help create and maintain.

Bibliography

Harrison K C (ed.) 1979 *Public Library Policy: Proceedings of the IFLA/UNESCO Pre-session Seminar*, Lund, 1979. Saur, Munich

International Federation of Library Associations, Public Libraries Section 1973 *Standards for Public Libraries*. Verlag Dokumentation, Pullach, Munich

Jackson M M (ed.) 1981 *International Handbook of Contemporary Developments in Librarianship*. Greenwood, Westport, Connecticut

Public Library Association, Goals, Guidelines, and Standards Committee 1979 *The Public Library Mission Statement and Its Imperatives for Service*. American Library Association, Chicago, Illinois

Robbins-Carter J (ed.) 1982 *Public Librarianship: A Reader*. Libraries Unlimited, Littleton, Colorado

Wheeler J L 1981 *Wheeler and Goldhor's Practical Administration of Public Libraries*. Harper and Row, New York

College and University Libraries

M. M. Jackson

Libraries are fundamental to study, research, and instruction in higher education. Their patterns of service tend to reflect the goals and purposes of the institutions they serve. Thus, in some instances national characteristics have made a distinctive impact on policy, but generally college and university libraries share a similar outlook. Therefore, it is possible to discuss significant trends in policies and problems on an international basis using commonly recognized terms. This article divides the discussion into the following areas: (a) planning; (b) organization of administration and resources; (c) services to users; (d) personnel and education; and (e) technology.

1. Planning

Library planning encompasses the setting of agenda through the use of detailed goals, policies, and procedures. Planning is an important function of library administration and it can involve staff, faculty, and students (Cargill and Webb 1988). Emphasis in planning is placed on decision making, commitment, and action aimed at the purposes of the library rather than the problems it might have.

College and university libraries use planning techniques for program activities that can include the establishment of operational policies for circulation and use of materials, collection development, selection of staff members, promotion of senior staff members, and the development and use of new library facilities. Library-related research studies utilizing social science research methodologies have emphasized planning in such areas as: (a) building facilities needs (Brookes 1970, Morse 1972); (b) acquisition of materials; (c) processing, which includes cataloging and classification; and (d) the storage of documents (Cox 1964, Booth 1969).

In English-speaking Africa, modern management techniques are responsible for those university libraries that are being efficiently operated. In many cases these are adequate and modern functional libraries that are providing high standards of service. Dean (1970) attributed the successful African university library system to sound planning. In Asia, with a few exceptions, library planning is hampered by the complete decentralization of library resources, services, and personnel. This condition exists because there is little or no coordination of faculties and curricula in colleges and universities (Harvey and Lambert 1971). In the case of college and university libraries in Latin America, there has been a movement to improve higher education and centralize administration of universities. Libraries have benefited by this movement to reform higher education. Some libraries have introduced standards adopted from those recommended by the American Library Association. In a few countries, such as Colombia, Mexico, and Brazil, library planning has resulted in technical services being centralized, a union catalog of holdings being formed, and interlibrary cooperation, including resource sharing, being established (Sabor 1966).

In Western Europe, planning has resulted in successful cooperation between university libraries and other types of libraries. For example, the Scandia Plan, in operation since the mid-1940s, attempts to provide access to all research materials available within Scandinavian countries. In Eastern Europe, where there is greater centralization, university libraries are mandated to plan and cooperate with other types of library. National plans are being implemented such as Poland's "Program of Development of Polish Librarianship until the year 1990" which will establish a nationwide information system that includes all the libraries in the country.

Trends point to libraries needing increased flexibility for problem solving and introducing change, especially the introduction of new technology. Strategic planning is increasingly being used to understand and control costs. This newer approach to planning is similar to

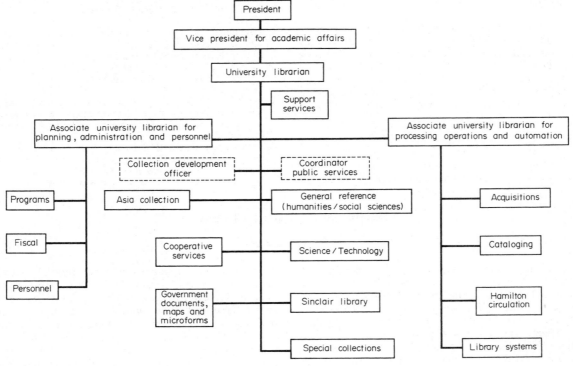

Figure 1
An example of administrative organization. After University of Hawaii 1988

other forms of planning activities discussed above. However, strategic planning differs in that there is a deliberate attempt to concentrate resources in those areas which can make a difference in a library's future performance and capabilities (Association of Research Libraries 1984). The emphasis in strategic planning is not on procedures as such, but rather on establishing a "frame of reference" or more importantly, "a way of thinking."

2. Administrative Organization

The academic library is a complex organization consisting of a conglomerate of specialized activities. Modern library administrative organization is based on the science of administration as developed by Fayol (1949), Gulick and Urwick (1937), and others. Their theories have been introduced into library administrative organization by such librarian writers as Shaw (1954), Wilson and Tauber (1956), Rogers and Weber (1971), Thompson (1979), and Cargill and Webb (1988).

Typically, academic libraries are organized in one or more schemes or a combination of schemes. These are: (a) along functional lines, that is, acquisitions, cataloging, or technical services; (b) subject, in many cases broad subject areas, that is, humanities, social sciences,

and sciences; and (c) form of materials, that is, serials, periodicals, archives, and documents.

The administrative organization illustrated in Fig. 1 is a combination of functional operations and subject divisions. Under functions, there are two associate librarians: one for (a) planning administration and personnel and one for (b) processing operations and automation. Subject divisions are divided into humanities/social sciences; science/technology; special collections; government documents; maps and microforms; and Asia collection. In Fig. 2 a typical functional organization is illustrated consisting of reference, circulation, and cataloging operations under the direct supervision of department heads who are responsible to the librarian. In both instances the lines of authority are clearly stated.

Efficient library administration utilizes a simple organization scheme. Centralization in its many forms is used to facilitate coordination and communication. Library administrative organization can vary from complete centralization to semicentralization, dependent upon local circumstances. However, there are certain activities that will operate more efficiently if the operation is centralized, that is, book ordering and cataloging.

A centralized university library system will have a central or main library, a professional school, and departmental and research institute libraries under one

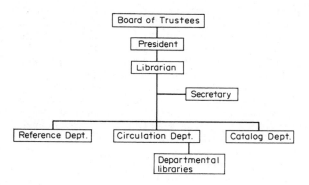

Figure 2
Example of typical functional organization of a library after
Lyle 1974

director (see Fig. 3). On the other hand, a decentralized
system will allow autonomy among professional school
libraries, research institute libraries, and other specialized collections. This latter system requires some duplication of materials and services, but there are several
distinct advantages to the decentralized arrangement.
These are: (a) faculty and students will have direct
access to materials; (b) services are more than likely pro-

vided by subject specialists; (c) stronger and more in-
depth collections will be possible; and (d) frequently
there is stronger financial support through grants and
endowments.

The typical university library, whether a highly centralized or semicentralized organization, is based on the
following broad program needs: (a) providing user
study areas; (b) providing access to documents within
the library; (c) providing access to documents in other
libraries vis-à-vis library networks; (d) providing aids in
locating and identifying documents in the building; (e)
promoting use of the library; and (f) providing general
administrative support services (Hamburg et al. 1974).

Since 1945, in many countries of the nonindustrialized world, the patterns of academic library administrative organization have been influenced by library
practices in Europe and North America. In the case of
North American influence it came largely when expatriate librarians were sent from such agencies as the Peace
Corps (US), the United States Agency for International
Development (USAID), Asia Foundation, Ford Foundation (US), Carnegie Corporation (US), Canadian University Service Organization (CUSO), and International
Development Research Center (IDRC) (Canada). From
the United Kingdom they came under the auspices of

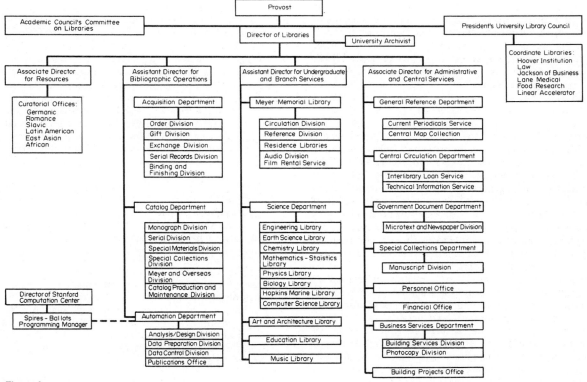

Figure 3
An example of administrative organization of a library after Rogers and Weber 1971 (p. 69)

the British Council or the Voluntary Service Overseas (VSO). Other countries such as France, Denmark, Sweden, Australia, and New Zealand have played some role in influencing library organization development in nonindustrialized countries.

3. Service to Users

One of the distinctive features of college and university libraries in North America is the emphasis on service to the user. Fundamental to good library service is the philosophy of "open stacks" or open access to all resources. In some other countries the "open stack" policy has not been adopted because the librarian is held financially responsible if any books are lost. This policy can still be found in many universities in the Middle East (Harvey and Lambert 1971).

Librarians are now beginning to recognize that they are the information experts. They have a vital role to play in guiding users through the maze of complex documentary sources of information. When major emphasis is placed on library service to users it requires a dedicated and highly competent staff. Increasingly, colleges and universities are channeling their services through at least two types of activities: formal instruction in the use of the library, and appointing subject specialists to the library staff (Martell 1983).

Formal instruction in library use is usually offered in three ways: (a) a single lecture or a series of lectures as part of a subject course—sometimes a library staff member is solely responsible for the instruction or shares it with the instructor of the course; (b) a separate course with credit; and (c) specialized subject or topic bibliographical lectures given in response to a request by the course instructor. Audiovisual aids are quite often used in conjunction with library use instruction (Fjällbrant and Stevenson 1978, Breviak 1972).

Subject specialists, it has been found, can render specialized library services to undergraduates, graduate and postdoctoral students, administrative officers, faculty, and research associates (Rogers and Weber 1971). Subject specialists in smaller academic libraries and college libraries are not generally used in information work mainly because of the need to have sufficient generalist staff members to meet the information needs of undergraduate students. The postwar growth in enrollments in higher education, coupled with the information explosion and growth of library collections prompted the establishment of undergraduate libraries at universities in the United States. These libraries were established as a way to relieve pressure on the universities' research libraries (Leide 1981). Collections range in size from 75,000 to 100,000 volumes. The collection is meant to be a "core" collection that meets the general needs of undergraduates rather than advanced or specialized needs. Because of the increasingly high costs of maintaining separate undergraduate libraries there has recently been less emphasis placed on them. In the United Kingdom the same problem exists—that of getting sufficient copies of books used on first-year courses, while still providing adequate specialized materials for research and final-year options. However, many British universities have only the one central library.

University and college libraries are increasingly finding it necessary to evaluate their services to users. There are at least three levels of evaluating library services: (a) effectiveness, which is concerned with determining user satisfaction. Research methodologies include mostly surveys of users by questionnaires or through interviews. (b) cost-effectiveness, evaluates a library's internal operating efficiency to meet user needs and (c) cost-benefit, determines whether the benefits received from a library justify costs (Lancaster 1977).

4. Personnel and Education for Academic Librarianship

The Williamson report of 1923 is the basic document that has guided library education in North America. This report, published in 1923, is considered the turning point in education for librarianship in the United States. Williamson, who was engaged by the Carnegie Corporation trustees to study existing library training programs, was highly critical of their emphasis on clerical and routine aspects of library work to the neglect of general and professional education. He therefore proposed two distinct levels of training: (a) a full college course providing for a general and broad education, followed by at least one year of postbachelor study in a library school to give thorough professional preparation; and (b) training for clerical work by completion of a four-year high-school course, followed by a short course of instruction on the mechanics and routine operations of a library. Today, in the English-speaking world as well as increasingly in many other countries, postdiploma/degree study of librarianship is the entry-level qualification for university librarianship. Typically, a graduate-level course will run from 12 to 18 months, but only in a few cases will it be specifically designed for academic librarians. The curriculum might be adjusted to suit their needs:

(a) A general thrust could be developed through the curriculum to give candidates all professional and psychological facilities needed for the assumption of an active role in their "partnership in study and research" with the academic user.

(b) Proficiency be required in at least one modern foreign language. The usefulness of this in the academic and research environment is undisputed. Schools could have a carefully coordinated, highly visible, and continuously monitored plan for the application of this hard-earned skill in such classes as cataloging, bibliography, history of books and libraries, comparative librarianship, indexing, and abstracting.

(c) Problems of higher education and the changing social patterns and attitudes, and their direct or indirect impact on college and university life and business, could become, by design, part of courses devoted to the social and educational role of the library.

(d) Courses in general national subject bibliography could go beyond the standard sources of the Anglo–Saxon world, and include African, Asian, and Latin American bibliography.

(e) Bibliographic methods and search strategy could be instilled by matching students with users and guiding them through all phases of such work—in a real-life situation.

(f) Direct encounters between advanced students and directors and staff members of academic libraries of all types could be arranged regularly. This would provide excellent opportunities to test theoretical knowledge and ideas acquired through classwork on the best possible sounding-board—the practicing professional librarian.

(g) Proficiency be required in understanding communications and information technologies in libraries.

5. Technology

Three important areas have been developed in library and information technology since the early 1950s: computer science, machine-readable technology, and microform technology. These new technologies made their mark on college and university libraries in the attempt to do something about the information explosion. Most college and university libraries in the world today are affected in one way or another by information technology. However, it is mostly the large university libraries that are using computers in library administration and services. Matthews and Brown (1969 p. 59) note that "automation of any existing process is a complex change, with many pitfalls, which must be approached with great care. The germane question is not how to automate, but rather what processes of libraries, if any, will be improved by automation."

Some of the early successful attempts at online retrieval of bibliographical data stored in computers were the Columbia–Harvard–Yale universities shared cataloging project; the New York Biomedial Communication Network; and Ohio University. Today, in North America most university libraries are using some type of computer application for library administration or service. Similarly, the majority of British university libraries have computerized some of their operations in the areas of cataloging, periodicals check-in, serials lists, circulation of documents, ordering and accounting, and data retrieval (Thompson 1979).

Increasingly, computerized databases, both bibliographical and full-text documents, are available to users through university and college libraries (Leide 1981,

Plaister 1981, Whyte 1981). In France in 1978, 14 scientific university libraries used on-line computerized information systems. The spread of Euronet, the principal network for scientific information in Europe, means European scholars will have increased access to computerized information systems (Baudin and Jackson 1981). However, until the mid-1980s in Eastern European countries there was a lack of modern computers for the full implementation of cooperative programs in acquisitions and cataloging.

In general, colleges and universities in the nonindustrialized countries have been slow in adding computers for their activities. This is explainable for several reasons: (a) the high cost of introducing computer technology; (b) the lack of highly skilled computer specialists; and (c) the absence of the technical infrastructure that is needed nationally and locally. However the cost factor may be diminished by the introduction of mini- and microcomputers, which are finding increasing use in North America. The use of a microcomputer with hard disc storage and the required software word processing can serve a college or university library adequately in most tasks (Swanson 1982).

In the mid-1980s university libraries in the industrialized countries have increasingly computerized library operations and services. When successful automation takes place the impact will usually be felt in work procedures and organizational structures. The most recent developments in compact disc (CD-ROM) storage will continue to revolutionize access to information.

Microfilm technology was slow in being received following the Second World War, especially by academic libraries and their users. However, this situation has changed and today microforms are recognized as viable formats for printed materials. Most libraries acquire microforms in four formats: microfilm or 35 mm film folls; microcard (opaque)—3 × 5 inches; microprint (opaque)—6 × 9 inches; and microfiche—4 × 6 inches, a film on a flat surface. A microcard holds approximately 50 pages of the original work while microprint and microfiche hold about 100 pages of the original work. Increasingly, books, documents, and journals are available only in microform; and a recent development has brought together the combination of computer technology and microfilm to produce COM (computer output microfilm). An alternative form of storage is CD-ROM (compact disc read-only memory) which is quickly revolutionizing information storage and retrieval.

In summary, libraries are vital units of the educational and research activities of colleges and universities. Their organizational structure, service orientation, and programs are predetermined by the goals and objectives of the institutions they serve. To cope with the information explosion, tertiary-level libraries are increasingly introducing computer technology in library operations.

Bibliography

Association of Research Libraries (ARL) 1984 *Strategic Planning in ARL Libraries*. ARL, Office of Management Studies, Washington, DC

Baudin F, Jackson M M 1981 France. In: Jackson M M (ed.) 1981 *International Handbook of Contemporary Developments in Librarianship*. Greenwood, Westport, Connecticut, pp. 405–11

Booth A D 1969 On the geometry of libraries. *J. Documentation* 25: 28–42

Breviak P 1972 *Planning the Library Instruction Program*. American Library Association, Chicago, Illinois

Brookes B C 1970 The viability of branch libraries. *J. Librarianship* 2: 14–21

Cammack F M, DeCosin M, Roberts N 1979 *Community College Library Instruction: Training for Self-reliance in Basic Library Use*. Linnet, Hamden, Connecticut

Cargill J, Webb G M 1988 *Managing Libraries in Transition*. Oryx, Phoenix, Arizona

Cline H F, Sinnott L T 1983 *The Electronic Library*. Lexington Books, Lexington, Indiana

Cox J G 1964 *Optimum Storage for Library Material*. Purdue University Libraries, Lafayette, Indiana

Dean J 1970 Organization and services of university libraries in West Africa. In: Jackson M M (ed.) 1970 *Comparative and International Librarianship: Essays on Themes and Problems*. Bingley, London

Fayol H 1949 *General and Industrial Management*. (Transl. by Constance Storrs) Pitman, London

Fjällbrant N, Stevenson M 1978 *User Education in Libraries*. Bingley, London

Gulick L H, Urwick L (eds.) 1937 *Papers on the Science of Administration*, 2nd edn. Institute of Public Administration, Columbia University, New York

Hamburg M, Clelland R C, Bonner M R W, Ramist L E, Whitfield R M 1974 *Library Planning and Decision-making*. MIT Press, Cambridge, Massachusetts

Harvey J F, Lambert B 1971 Librarianship in six southwest Asian countries. *Int. Libr. Rev.* 3: 15–34

Jackson M M (ed.) 1981 Africa. *International Handbook of Contemporary Developments in Librarianship*, Part 1. Greenwood, Westport, Connecticut, pp. 1–114

Kaldor I, Jackson M M 1974 Education for academic librarianship. In: Josey E J (ed.) 1975 *New Dimensions for Academic Library Service*. Scarecrow, Metuchen, New Jersey

Lancaster F W 1977 *Measurement and Evaluation of Library Services*. Information Resources Press, Washington, DC

Leide J 1981 Academic libraries. In: Jackson M M (ed.) 1981 *International Handbook of Contemporary Developments in Librarianship*. Greenwood, Westport, Connecticut, pp. 536–45

Lyle G R 1974 *The Administration of the College Library*, 4th edn. Wilson, New York

Martell C R 1983 *The Client-centered Academic Library: An Organizational Model*. Greenwood, Westport, Connecticut

Matthews M V, Brown S W 1969 Research libraries and the new technology. *On Research Libraries: Statements and Recommendations of the Committee on Research Libraries of the American Council of Learned Societies*. MIT Press, Cambridge, Massachusetts

Morse T M 1972 Measure of library effectiveness. *Libr. Q.* 42: 15–30

Plaister J M 1981 United Kingdom. In: Jackson M M (ed.) 1981 *International Handbook of Contemporary Developments in Librarianship*. Greenwood, Westport, Connecticut, pp. 441–58

Rogers R D, Weber D C 1971 *University Library Administration*. Wilson, New York

Sabor J 1966 Reconsiderations of the concept of library functions in Latin America. UNESCO *Bulletin for Libraries* 20: 108–16

Shaw R R (ed.) 1954 Scientific management in libraries. *Libr. Trends* 2: 359–483

Swanson D R 1982 Miracles, micro-computers, and librarians. *Libr. J.* 107: 1055–59

Thompson J 1979 *An Introduction to University Library Administration*, 3rd edn. Bingley, London

Whyte J P 1981 Australia. In: Jackson M M (ed.) 1981 *International Handbook of Contemporary Developments in Librarianship*. Greenwood, Westport, Connecticut, pp. 371–78

Wilson L R, Tauber M F 1956 *The University Library: The Organization, Administration and Function of Academic Libraries*, 2nd edn. Columbia University Press, New York

Special Libraries

V. D. Hewitt

It has been suggested that four characteristics distinguish special libraries from other libraries (Echelman 1976). A special library is:

(a) organized under the sponsorship of a parent enterprise or organization which provides the funds for its support and continuance;

(b) assigned the mission of acquiring, organizing, and providing access to information and knowledge so as to further the goals of its parent enterprise or organization (where the parent organization may not have direct library objectives);

(c) expected to assemble a physical collection of information, knowledge, and/or opinion limited to a single subject or group of subjects or to a single format or group of formats; and is

(d) administered by a librarian or a specialist in the subject(s) covered or format(s) included.

The first two characteristics are the most salient, according to Echelman, and all existing special libraries conform at least to these two. She notes in addition that libraries characterizing themselves as "special" generally also exhibit the last two characteristics as well.

Legislative reference libraries serving state and local governments were among the earliest modern special libraries, becoming models for intensive or "amplified" reference services. Special libraries in business and financial organizations emerged next to "manage" business and financial materials. These libraries also developed high levels of information service for a clientele relatively unfamiliar with the use of print.

The special library movement originated in the United States, where the Special Libraries Association was founded in 1909; and its pattern of development has been repeated around the world. Special libraries were established in the United Kingdom, France, Germany, and other industrialized nations in the first decades of the twentieth century, and their rate of growth, particularly in the scientific and technical fields, increased to meet the demand for support of increased research activities in the postwar periods. As developing nations begin to industrialize and increase their research efforts, special libraries are being established in their government agencies and industries and institutions. Van Halm (1979) gives a global picture of special libraries and special librarianship in some 100 countries in Africa, the Arabic world, Asia, Europe, Latin America, and Oceania.

Special libraries are located in many private businesses and industrial organizations such as banks, insurance companies, advertising agencies, public utilities, publishers, chemical and pharmaceutical manufacturers, petroleum producers, engineering firms, and the aerospace and automotive industries. Others serve federal, state, county, or municipal governments or quasigovernmental agencies. Still others exist in nonprofit institutions such as medical schools, hospitals, health agencies, philanthropic foundations, social and welfare organizations, museums, trade and professional associations, or subject branches or departments of a public library or university complex.

Special libraries, often described in relation to their subject orientation—transportation, communications, medicine, law, social sciences, and so forth, are further distinguished from other types of libraries in terms of format, that is, map libraries, picture, slide, film and record (audiovisual) libraries, or sometimes in terms of the parent organization—newspaper, museum, or hospital libraries. They serve a limited, well-defined clientele usually confined to the parent organization. Typically, the parent body may consist of doctors, lawyers, editors, chemists, researchers, economists, brokers, advertising personnel, musicians, or financiers.

Another predominant characteristic is size. Most are small in space, size of collection, and staff. It is estimated that at least half of all special libraries are one-or-two person libraries, though some industrial and technical libraries have hundreds of employees and thousands of volumes in their collections.

In three areas of responsibility—organization, acquisitions, and circulation control—the special librarian can be said to be much like fellow librarians who serve the general public. However, the special librarian's methods may be less formal, more experimental, with a greater tendency to use short cuts or adopt innovative techniques in order to collect the materials needed, and to organize them for the most efficient use. Also, special librarians may differ from their colleagues in general libraries in the greater breadth of information collected—not just printed information but the use of statistics and information from experts gathered by telephone or letter. They more often require primary source material rather than secondary to serve their clientele. For the special librarian, all these responsibilities, as vital as they may be to efficient library operation, are only the means to implement the fundamental responsibility—that of providing information services.

Because he or she is in the center of the flow of information, the special librarian must have a deep concern for helping the parent organization keep up to date with what is new and of interest. For this purpose, special librarians have developed a wide range of activities to keep their clientele informed. Most of them route regularly to various individuals in their organizations those journals, magazines, newspapers, newsletters, and reports that might offer worthwhile information. Some compile and distribute abstracts or news bulletins to serve the same purpose. At times their publications may be made available to other libraries, organizations, or individuals.

A more sophisticated current awareness service has been developed whereby incoming information is matched against an individual user's interest. This system, usually known as SDI, or selective dissemination of information, results in a more personalized service for the library's clientele. The service may be card file or computer based with services obtained by commercial abstract and index services (see *Information Storage and Retrieval*).

Special librarians have long known that they cannot restrict themselves to the collections, sometimes limited, within their own four walls. They have a long history of sharing resources among themselves. They have also recognized their dependence on other collections for in-depth subject background and for material peripheral to their major interests. The information needed may be in one of the nearby public or academic libraries, another special library, a law or medical library, a business institution or a government agency. The location of the material may be near or distant, it may even be overseas and in a foreign language. Wherever it is, whatever its form, the special librarian will seek it out and will not terminate the search until completely convinced that the material is either unavailable or the cost of obtaining it far exceeds its informational value.

Speed of access is vital to the clientele of special libraries. To accomplish this the special librarian may resort to the use of informal networks, messenger services, use of the telephone, teletype, computers, and so on.

One of the characteristics of special libraries' cooperative relationships has been an almost traditional pattern of informality. Some special libraries in physical proximity, ranging from a region of counties or states to an area as small as a complex of office buildings or an affinity group such as the Consortium of Foundation Libraries, New York City, develop relationships for sharing union lists, sharing of bibliographic utilities, cooperative acquisitions, and other library information facilities.

However, during the late 1970s, special libraries began to engage, through networking, in more sophisticated and formal forms of cooperation with other libraries, as well as amongst themselves. The special libraries' role in networks is still evolving, just as networks themselves are in the process of evolution; and as network experience accumulates, the special library's potential contribution is beginning to be recognized.

The Special Library Association's (SLA) *Getting into Networking* presents guidelines to assist in deciding whether to join an existing formal network or to establish a new one, while Gibson (1980) reported the proceedings of a conference which "discussed the current state of networking and worked to formulate a creative approach to special library involvement in network participation and management."

Continuing education, as a means of keeping up with ever changing methods and the new technologies, has become a prime concern of many special librarians. Many associations are concerned to provide courses of this kind for librarians. In a cooperative venture in June 1980, the Special Libraries Association joined with the Medical Library Association in offering a special continuing education program when both associations were meeting consecutively in Washington, DC. The SLA sponsors a nationwide regional education program throughout the year. It also cooperates in joint education programs with the American Society for Information Service.

In the United Kingdom, functions and activities similar to those of SLA are conducted by ASLIB. Founded in 1924 as the Association of Special Libraries and Information Bureaus, ASLIB has a very well-developed program of courses, workshops, visits, conferences, and meetings throughout the United Kingdom.

A discernible trend among special libraries is the increase of interest in new technology applications—computerization, miniaturization, telecommunications, and audiovisual applications. One reason for this interest in new technology is because special library patrons need the speediest, most up-to-date, complete information available, and are willing to pay for it.

Among the computerized online literature retrieval systems found in special libraries and information centers are Lockheed's DIALOG, SDC's ORBIT, Bibliographic Retrieval Services' BRS, and New York Times' The Information Bank. Subject matter in these systems ranges from multidisciplinary to the applied sciences and technology, and from the social services and humanities to business and economics.

Another computerized system is the Pictorial and Artifact Retrieval and Information System or PARIS, developed by Knowledge Based Services, Control Data Corporation (CDC), initially designed to index the holdings of the Hermitage Museum in Leningrad. Collections of ancient manuscripts, Indian pottery, Renaissance paintings, and medical drawings from the Mayo Clinic are among the reference sources included in this computer-based system for information management of museum and library collections. The Pictorial and Artifact Retrieval and Information System (PARIS) includes holdings from collections the world over. The PARIS program uses BASIC computer software and can be accessed through CDC's Cyber Net service network.

An acronym familiar to many special libraries is OCLC (Online Computer Library Center), a shared catalog of the holdings of over 2,200 member libraries in the United States, Canada, and other countries. The database contains over seven million catalog records of books, journals, and other library materials. Since each record includes a list of the libraries owning the item, the system can be used to facilitate interlibrary loans as well as cataloging. It can also help to answer reference questions dealing with bibliographic information.

Growth has been one of the outstanding characteristics of special libraries in the past, and the factors which gave rise to them are spreading in influence as new technologies and organizations evolve. *The American Library Directory* (34th edn. 1981) reports 8,571 special libraries including all law, medical, and religious libraries not affiliated with colleges and universities, while in Canada, 678 special libraries are reported. (ASLIB's *Handbook of Special Librarianship* has run into several editions and has fostered developments in this field.)

In 1976, recognizing the growth of special libraries throughout the world, the International Federation of Libraries and Associations (IFLA) adopted a new structure and changed the Special Libraries section into a fully fledged component, the Special Libraries Division. Several of IFLA's separate sections and round tables were brought together under one umbrella, including the Geography and Map Libraries Section, the Administrative Libraries Section, and the Social Sciences Library Section. New groups were added: an Art Librarians Round Table, a Music Librarians Round Table, a Science and Technology Libraries Section, and a Biological and Medical Sciences Libraries Section.

Bibliography

Batten W E (ed.) 1975 *Handbook of Special Librarianship and Information Work*, 4th edn. ASLIB, London

Echelman S 1976 Toward the new special library. *Libr. J.* 101: 91–94

Gibson R N (ed.) 1980 *The Special Library Role in Networks.* Conference Report, Special Libraries Association, New York

Jackson E B (ed.) *Special Librarianship: A New Reader.* Scarecrow, Metuchen, New Jersey

Koops W R H, Harvard-Williams P 1974 *Special Libraries— Worldwide.* IFLA, Verlag Dokumentation, The Hague

Special Libraries—all issues of Journal from 1909

Special Libraries Association 1977 *Getting Into Networking: Guidelines for Special Libraries.* State of the Art Review No. 5. Special Libraries Association, New York

Strable E G (ed.) 1976 *Special Libraries: A Guide for Management.* Special Libraries Association, New York

Tees M H 1981 *The Needs of the Special Librarian and the*

Library Association. The International Federation of Libraries and Associations (IFLA) Special Libraries Division, The Hague

van Halm J 1979 *The Development of Special Libraries as an International Phenomenon.* State of the Art Review No. 4. Special Libraries Association, New York

Processing of Library Materials

M. Gorman

This article defines the nature of modern library processing and describes the forces which are shaping and changing it. It discusses the question of bibliographic data exchange, the nature of machine-readable bibliographic formats, and the standardization of the content of those machine-readable records (especially the International Standard Bibliographic Description—ISBD). It describes an international bibliographic control system—the International Serials Data System and the largest national system—the United States OCLC. It further deals with the topic of resource sharing and interlibrary loan and borrowing. Some developments in the acquisition of library materials are noted.

1. Nature of Processing

To many people, the most important attributes of libraries are that they should be open and that the material thus made available should be that being sought. This view ignores another equally vital aspect of the practice of librarianship—the processing of materials received by the library and, to use the vogue term, the "bibliographic control" of those items. Most who are familiar with libraries will know of the activities of acquisitions and cataloging. The aim of the first of these activities is to acquire desired items as speedily and inexpensively as possible. The aim of the second is to control and make available bibliographic information which will enable the library to carry out its basic task—the connection of the users of the library with the material they seek. The extraordinary importance of these processes derives from the fact that most library users attempt to effect that connection without the assistance of the library's staff. That is, the speed and efficiency of the acquisition process and the comprehensiveness and excellence of the cataloging process are crucial to the success or failure of the library user's more often than not unaided search.

Both the fundamental processing tasks in libraries have undergone, and are undergoing, a sea change. They have been affected by forces which have affected the whole of society. These are the changing state of work in libraries, massive economic changes, and the effect of automation.

1.1 Labor

Traditionally, all library services have been heavily dependent on a continuous supply of cheap and little-skilled labor. Such tasks as the maintenance of card files (for books ordered, for periodicals, for binding, etc.), the retrieval and replacement of books from closed stacks, the marking of books, and other routine clerical tasks have always been carried out by large numbers of unskilled workers given minimal training and varying measures of supervision by paraprofessional and professional library workers. As everyone knows, such labor is no longer readily available. Whatever the ethics of such employment may be, the last is an ineluctable fact. The unavailability of cheap unskilled labor is a major impetus towards the automation of routine library processes.

1.2 Economics

Concurrently, libraries (as with all social services and arms of education) have been hit by comparative economic hardship. Personnel budgets and the costs of library materials have increased at a rate far greater than that of inflation—that is, in real money terms; the income and allocations which support those major expenditures have decreased in real money over the same period. The impact on the processing of library materials has been profound. All intelligent library administrators know that the materials budget is the last fund that should be cut and that the more direct forms of public service are in many cases irreducible. The obvious area in which economies can be made is that of processing.

1.3 Automation

The cumulative effect of the decline in the availability of cheap unskilled labor and the economically hard times afflicting libraries has been a growth of interest in the automation of library processes and in cooperative schemes based on computer systems. A necessary precondition for computer-based cooperation has been the promulgation and the implementation of standards, national and international, affecting both the data which are manipulated and the structures which hold that data.

The most prominent result of all these forces has been the rapid rise of networks within which library and library-related organizations cooperate on a range of activities aimed at increasing the cost-effectiveness of library processing either by decreasing the cost or by increasing the efficiency of a process, and, it is hoped, meeting both of these desirable aims eventually.

2. Bibliographic Data Exchange

The principle behind a bibliographic data exchange system is neither new nor complicated (Avram 1977). Libraries have been using bibliographic data supplied by others for many decades. Typically, these data were in the form of catalog cards supplied by a national agency (Giljarevski 1969). Probably the longest lived and certainly the most extensive system of this nature is the catalog card service of the Library of Congress. In addition to the use of catalog cards, libraries have for many years derived catalog data from printed catalogs such as the *United States National Union Catalog*, the *British Museum Catalogue*, the *Deutsche Bibliographie*, and the *Bibliographie de la France*. Thus, cataloging information was made available to libraries at costs far below those of professional cataloging done in the library. Though clumsy in execution, the sorting and filing of cards produced elsewhere or the transcription of data from existing sources was economically advantageous because it used cheap and relatively unskilled labor. The disadvantages, principally those of delay, the lack of availability of information, and the less than perfect matching of any single library's acquisitions to available cataloging data, meant that the system remained patchy. The system also possessed two important flaws. These were that libraries became dependent on a single source which increasingly became less and less able to provide all the needed data; and the lack of an advanced technology.

2.1 Formats

The use of computers in libraries, sporadic at best in the 1960s, became widespread in the North Americas and Europe in the 1970s. Several national library organizations in the United Kingdom, Canada, the Federal Republic of Germany, Belgium, the Netherlands, the Scandinavian countries, and elsewhere, devised plans for the use of computers to provide centrally produced bibliographic data. Most of these schemes were based on a "format" (a method of recording bibliographic data in machine-readable form) developed at the Library of Congress called MARC (Machine Readable Cataloging). The developed version of this system (MARC II 1968) was to form the basis for an international standard (ISO 2709) on which all machine-readable bibliographic data formats were to be based. The Library of Congress has been cataloging via MARC and making the resulting computer-readable tapes available since 1968. The total MARC database now comprises more than six million bibliographic records. As well as formats used for the transfer of information within countries, there have been a number of attempts to create formats for international exchange. Notable among these are UNIMARC (developed by the International Federation of Library Associations—IFLA), INTER-MARC (developed by a number of Western European countries), and the Council of Europe's EUDISED

format (designed for the exchange of information in the education field). The notable characteristic of all MARC (ISO 2709) formats is that the bibliographic information is held in numbered "fields" which are further subdivided into lettered "subfields." At the head of each record is a variety of coded information enabling computer programs to be written to locate and manipulate the data. Following the pattern set by the United States' MARC format, other formats are generally issued in subsets dealing with particular types of material (books, serials, films, maps, etc.).

2.2 International Exchange

The achievement of MARC has made a number of cooperative endeavors possible. National cataloging agencies can now issue their own, and receive other nations', current cataloging data with relative ease. Given agreement on the standards used in compiling the data held in the MARC records, they can use and disseminate those records within their country with little or no human intervention. A pioneering and well-developed bilateral exchange of this type is that between the Library of Congress and the National Library of Canada. The reason for the success of this example lies in the fact that they use the same conventions for recording bibliographic information (the *Anglo–American Cataloging Rules*, 2nd edn.) and subject information (the Library of Congress *List of Subject Headings* and *Classification* and the *Dewey Decimal Classification*). In this lies an important precondition for other international exchanges. The task of harmonizing the structures in which machine-readable data are stored and transferred is less by some degrees of magnitude than that of harmonizing the content of those records (Hickey 1977). The reason for the relative ease of the former is that such structures are new. The reasons for the difficulty of the latter are that cataloging practices are well-established, often fundamentally different, and do not translate readily from precomputer forms (cards, books, microforms) to computerized systems.

3. International Standard Bibliographic Description

One major advance in the international standardization of the content of machine-readable bibliographic records is the set of documents which together form the International Standard Bibliographic Description (ISBD) (Verona 1980). The ISBD stems from a research project sponsored by UNESCO in the late 1960s, and has been elaborated into a formula which has been approved by committees and meetings representative of a wide range of national and international interests. The ISBD is concerned only with the description of physical objects and not with the formulation of access points (names, subjects, classification numbers, etc.) by which those descriptions are retrieved. However, the descriptive data constitute both the core and the bulk of bibliographic records, and there are ways in which the computer manipulation can transcend the limits and inflexibilities of "traditional"access points. In essence, the ISBD assigns a fixed order to descriptive bibliographic data and a distinctive punctuation to those elements. This structure is very similar to the analysis behind the MARC formats (see above) and has been both heavily influenced by, and an important influence on, the development of MARC. Beyond its structure, the ISBD prescribes the data to be recorded, thus directly affecting the interchangeability of bibliographic records.

4. Standardization in Countries and Regions

Given a standard means of exchanging bibliographic data and a measure of international standardization in the content of those records, the way is open for effective cooperation and exchange and for the ability to put that cooperation to a variety of uses. In passing, it should be noted that the standardization of the content of data is near complete in many countries (within which all libraries use the same cataloging rules, subject descriptions, and the subject classification schemes) and internationally within linguistic groups. Instances of the latter are the English-speaking countries which use the *Anglo–American Cataloging Rules*, 2nd edn. (AACR 2) and the German-speaking parts of Western Europe which use the *Regeln für die Alphabetische Katalogisierung* (RAK).

5. International Serials Data System

An outstanding example of international cooperation in the field of bibliographic data is the International Serials Data System (ISDS). This ambitious endeavor began in 1973 and now embraces 44 countries and regions, each of which has a national or regional serials data center committed to the recording of information about serials published in that country. It also assigns two important means of identification to each serial—the International Standard Serial Number (ISSN) and the "key-title." The ISSN is an eight-digit number which identifies each title uniquely, and can thus be used in machine systems for, for example, purchase and control of serial publications. The "key-title" consists of the short title of the serial, enhanced, when necessary for unique identification, by such information as the place of publication, years of publication, and the form in which the serial is issued. Currently the International Center for ISDS in Paris is registering 30,000 serial titles a year (contributed by the national and regional centers) and estimates that its database now contains records for 80 percent of the world's serial literature. It is also estimated that 50 percent of the records stored relate to serial publications in the fields of science and technology. ISDS is a product of the UNESCO Unisist program which is dedicated to the universal availability and bibliographic control of the world's publications. The records compiled by the ISDS centers are made available by a variety of means, print and nonprint, and thus form an ever-increasing and increasingly valuable store of bibliographic information. The success of ISDS is based on computer technology. Using printed or typed data the current compilation and speedy dissemination of such a mass of data could not be contemplated. It is also a product of the desire of the world bibliographic community to rationalize their processes and make them more cost effective.

6. Networks

A crucial distinction must be drawn between bibliographic data networks and information networks. The former store and deal with bibliographic records relating to books and other examples of macrothought. The latter deal with the storage and delivery of information, typically in microthought documents (articles, abstracts, etc.). The one is concerned with records of documents, the other with the documents themselves.

6.1 OCLC

The most developed and extensive use of computer technology to assist bibliographic control and library processing in any one country is the OCLC system in the United States. It is both a paradigm for other countries and an indication that different social and library structures may lead to different solutions to the problems of bibliographic control in different countries. In most of the European countries, efforts towards the establishment of bibliographic networks have been led or actually carried out by government and quasigovernmental agencies (typically national libraries and national library agencies). In the United States and in Canada the most successful networks (OCLC in the United States and the University of Toronto Library Automation System—UTLAS in Canada) have been achieved by the endeavors of private corporations and academic institutions. The initials OCLC used to stand for Ohio College Library Center. It was founded in 1968 with the modest aim of bringing the benefits of automation and cooperation to some academic and college libraries in the state of Ohio. The foundation of the system, which even now remains unaltered, was the use of the MARC tapes produced by the Library of Congress to which were to be added MARC records produced by libraries in the system for items not cataloged by the Library of Congress. From these relatively humble and localized beginnings OCLC has spread all across the United States and, by way of a subsidiary—OCLC Europe—to Western Europe. The OCLC system now comprises more than 3,000 libraries of all kinds and operates on a database maintained at its headquarters near Columbus, Ohio, containing more than ten million machine-readable bibliographic records. A study done by OCLC in 1980 showed that about one-third of all records added originated in the Library of Congress, about a third in libraries which are members of the Association of Research Libraries (ARL)—the 100 or so largest research libraries in the United States, and about a third in non-ARL libraries—academic, college, public, and special libraries. This analysis shows one of the great strengths of OCLC—the range and diversity of its active membership. The way in which the cataloging system works is this: libraries check their new acquisitions, by means of a dedicated computer terminal, against the database; if a relevant record is found it is examined and, when necessary, modified; the record, modified and identified as being of an item belonging to the library, is added to an archival computer tape of that library's holdings; the computer record is also, in this transitional time, commonly used to generate sets of catalog cards to be sent to the library and added to its catalog. Less commonly, but increasingly, the computer tapes are used to generate microform catalogs or are added to the database of an online computer catalog. The economics of such a system are fairly simple. The library pays for each use of a record on the database and pays for the products (cards and archival tapes) derived from the records which it has identified. When an acquired item is not found on the database, the library catalogs it itself and adds the resulting information to the OCLC database. It pays no fee for doing this. Because of the wide range of members of OCLC this economic structure has proven satisfactory.

The members of OCLC range from very large libraries cataloging up to 10,000 titles a month of which up to 2,000 titles are contributed by the library, to small libraries with just tens of titles cataloged and contributing few or no records. Thus the model comprehends a small number of libraries taking (and paying for) a lot of titles individually and contributing many titles, and a large number of libraries taking (and paying for) little individually but being collectively a considerable economic force. It is this economic model which makes OCLC an example to be studied carefully. It is significant to note here that OCLC is the only national computerized bibliographic network in the world which is economically self-sufficient. All the others depend entirely or to a great extent on governmental or intergovernmental subsidy and/or gifts and loans from foundations and other scholarly and philanthropic institutions. The strength of OCLC derives from its breadth and depth and its flexibility in dealing with the vastly different needs of the vastly different sizes and kinds of library which make up its membership.

6.2 Quality Control

One important issue in the construction of bibliographic networks is that of quality control. When one has a broad range of libraries contributing cataloging to a jointly maintained database it is often difficult to ensure that all follow standard bibliographic practice. This was a problem in the early days of OCLC but has lessened. The increase in standardization and quality results from the increasing sophistication of the members of the network, the adoption of newer and better cataloging conventions, and the monitoring role of the network itself.

6.3 Other Networks in the United States

There are two other bibliographic networks in the United States. These are the Washington Library Network (WLN) and the Research Libraries Group's Research Libraries Information Network (RLIN). The former is a successful and sophisticated system located in the Pacific North West. The latter is a product of a consortium of around 20 academic libraries (some large, some not so large) which are geographically distributed but limited in number. That the embryonic RLIN is not at this time financially self-sufficient nor promises to be in the near future is a product of its lack of OCLC's broad base of membership.

6.4 Other Countries

Cataloging networks in other countries range from those which are well-established, as for example the United Kingdom's BLAISE system and Canada's UTLAS, to those which are either at an early stage or are still being planned.

7. Resource Sharing

7.1 Interlibrary Loan and Borrowing

When cataloging networks are fully operational—as in the case of OCLC and some European networks—their databases form a valuable resource for other purposes. They are in fact electronic union catalogs of their members' holdings (Gorman 1981). This electronic union catalog has a great advantage over those maintained in card form or in printed book form. The difference between such a database and its predecessors can most easily be summed up as one of currency and accuracy. The largest printed union catalog in the world, the *US National Union Catalog of Pre-1956 Imprints*, finally completed publication in 1981. This mammoth undertaking (consisting of 750 volumes of 600-plus pages each with 25–30 entries on each page) is a remarkable bibliographic resource. On the other hand, it records no book that is less than a quarter of a century old and records the holdings of libraries which were reported, in many cases, decades ago. In contrast the OCLC database, now aptly named the *On-line Union Catalog*, contains numerous current publications and holdings which can be as up-to-date as yesterday. Using the capabilities of the databases which have been constructed, in the first instance, for cooperative cataloging purposes, it is possible to identify speedily which libraries possess which books. Further, the capabilities of the links between terminals and the central database can be used to request electronically that the item be lent to the library at which the request originates. This is a quantum leap in the speed and efficiency of interlibrary loan and borrowing and, in some cases, is allowing libraries to cooperate in this manner for the first time.

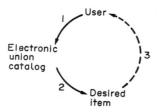

Figure 1
The interlibrary lending cycle

7.2 Cooperative Collection Development

Electronic union catalogs provide information about the holdings of other libraries and permit access to those collections by means of telecommunications. They are not, as yet, used for the electronic transfer of the items themselves. There is doubt whether, in many areas of interlibrary cooperation, such systems will ever be used to complete the interlibrary lending cycle (see Fig. 1).

In this diagram the electronic union catalog is used to complete parts 1 and 2 of the cycle. Part 3 is carried out by way of the mail or some other document delivery system. Devices such as electronic facsimile transmission of documents seem currently to be more suitable for the transfer of information in small packets (journal articles, abstracts, etc.) rather than the transfer of knowledge or culture in large packets (typically books). The distinction between information and knowledge/culture is too often blurred (Boorstin 1980). Devices which control and transmit one may be unsuitable for the control and/or transmission of the other.

Beyond interlibrary lending lies the question of cooperative development of library collections. One copy of a given work may be ample to fulfill the needs of the users of a number of libraries. In times when libraries had not the willingness, the economic imperatives, or the means to cooperate, the preceding sentence was a useless truism. Now, given the adverse economic climate and the electronic means it is perfectly feasible for a variety of cooperative endeavors to grow. These can range from formal agreements in which each library undertakes to buy in certain subject areas, to informal agreements in which a library may decide not to purchase an item which is available elsewhere.

8. Acquisition of Library Materials

Libraries acquire books and other materials to meet an expressed demand or to conform to an agreed acquisition policy. In recent years, they have increasingly used devices such as the blanket ordering of all publications from certain publishers or groups of publishers (e.g., university presses) or from certain areas of the world. These devices are designed to speed up the acquisition process and to ensure comprehensive coverage of subject areas. They attempt to control the document explosion by eliminating the need for individual decision on individual items. Increasingly, libraries work with commercial vendors of library materials who now quite commonly have computer systems of their own to provide for the immediate and long-term needs of the library collection and its users.

Bibliography

Avram H D 1977 Production, dissemination, and use of bibliographic data and summary of the conference. *Libr. Q.* 47: 347–69
Boorstin D J 1980 *Gresham's Law: Knowledge or Information? Remarks at the White House Conference on Library and Information Services, Washington, November 19, 1979.* Library of Congress, Washington, DC
Bouffez F, Grousseaud A 1978 Bibliographic control of serial publications. *UNESCO Bull. Libr.* 32: 154–56
Giljarevski R S 1969 *International Distribution of Catalogue Cards: Present Situation and Future Prospects.* UNESCO, Paris, pp. 1–84
Gorman M 1981 The electronic library. *Am. Libr.* 12: 273–74
Hickey D J 1977 The search for uniformity in cataloging: Centralization and standardization. *Libr. Trends* 25: 565–86
Massoneau S 1976 Technical services and technology. In: Jackson S L, Herling E B, Josey E J (eds.) 1976 *Century of Service: Librarianship in the United States and Canada.* American Library Association, Chicago, Illinois, pp. 192–207
Moore D M 1979–80 Library networks. *J. Educ. Technol. Systems* 8: 147–53
Perspectives on library networks and resource sharing. *Am. Soc. Inf. Sci. J.* 31: 403–44, November 1980
Verona E 1980 Decade of IFLA's work on the standardization of bibliographic description. *Int. Catalog.* 9: 2–9

Film Libraries

J. A. Davis

Comprehensive collections of educational films are too costly for many users to maintain. The purpose of film libraries is to centralize collections in order to circulate them to users. This article traces an historical and technological development of the educational resource centers.

1. Development of Film Libraries

Educational film distributing agencies began to appear in the early decades of the twentieth century. In the United States, films were circulated by state departments of education, extension divisions of land grant colleges, museums, and government agencies as early as

1910. The introduction of 16mm safety film in the 1920s encouraged widespread production of informational films which further spurred growth of film libraries. By the 1940s, encouraged by the landmark study by McDonald (1942) which provided needed guidelines, many public libraries in the United States expanded their services to include 16mm educational films.

The public acceptance and credibility won for educational films by their use in the Second World War for military and industrial training fostered greater post-War film use and further expansion of film libraries. A project in 1952, under the famed Marshall Plan, gathered and evaluated more than 6,000 United States films and filmstrips dealing with agricultural and industrial training, for distribution to nations of the world recovering from the war.

Nontheatrical film libraries were in no way limited to governmental and education agencies. "Sponsored" films produced by industries and trade associations circulated to schools, service clubs, and other audiences. Eventually this led to development of new services to gather, coordinate, and publish information for users of "free and inexpensive" educational materials. Additionally, specialized film libraries distributed feature-length entertainment films in 16mm format to noncommercial users throughout the world.

By 1980, increasing costs of films and distribution necessitated consolidations of many resource centers. In the United States, comprehensive university film centers serving regional or national constituencies evolved as the predominant pattern, supplemented by specialized libraries serving local constituencies. Distribution of educational films in other parts of the world was largely a function of governmental agencies such as ministries of education, science, or culture. Many Western nations were also served by independent film archives and distribution organizations. In many developing countries, however, the inherent instability of newly established educational systems restricted film use. Lack of knowledgeable personnel and adequate equipment in schools with primitive facilities has been a hindrance, even into the 1980s.

2. Technological Advances

In the late 1960s and early 1970s, notable efforts were made to standardize cataloging procedures for nontheatrical motion pictures. Cooperation among media personnel from throughout the English-speaking world led to general acceptance of cataloging rules for bibliographic control of educational films and other media. The protocols were designed to accomodate both mechanical and electronic implementation.

Technological improvements for film maintenance took much longer to develop than did the agreements about bibliographic standards. Hand inspecting and repairing of motion pictures was succeeded in the 1960s by high-speed film transport mechanisms with sensors

to detect damage and stop the film where repair was needed. Addition of automated cleaning and refurbishing capacities occurred in logical order. But distributors were frustrated by another serious problem—color fading. Badly faded color made films unacceptable to many users, despite the currency and validity of subject matter. In the 1970s, manufacturers of film stock introduced film bases which were highly resistant to physical damage and deterioration. But dye stability, especially in film prints intended for short life spans, continued as a problem. Many film industry sources advocated controlled atmosphere storage of films, or color separation negatives, both of which were prohibitive in cost to most educational film producers.

As film libraries moved to automated systems for maintenance of their materials, technological advances in scheduling, billing, and administration were also explored. Phillipson evaluated use of computers in educational film library management in the United States in 1978. Procedures to develop and integrate systems for management, circulation, and administrative functions were described in his paper at an International Colloquium on Economic Analysis for Educational Technology Decisions. By the 1980s, film libraries throughout North America were using automated systems for management of circulation and business operations. Programs were introduced which enabled customers to directly address the booking systems of major film rental centers.

Automation in the United States Postal Service introduced problems for film libraries, as package sorting equipment in bulk mail centers was unable to handle film shipping containers. Plastic film reels and containers in place of steel film reels, cans, and belted fibreboard boxes reduced weight but introduced new problems. The new containers had some "human engineering" shortcomings, did not fit into conventional film storage racks, and involved costly changeovers. Early in the 1980s, belted fibreboard shipping boxes holding steel cans of film were still the most widely used film shipping containers.

3. Alternative Motion Picture Formats

As technological advances in information handling developed, a progression of new formats for motion pictures received widespread attention, and then faded from view. In the 1960s and early 1970s, new formats for 8mm motion picture film were introduced, intended to reduce costs for duplication and distribution of educational films. 8mm formats with enlarged picture areas and sound capabilities were offered, but failed to gain widespread acceptance. The next challenge to 16mm motion pictures came from videotape recording (VTR), as helical scan systems became standardized and widely accepted. However, costly electronic distribution systems, marginal pictorial resolution, and small viewing screens discouraged widespread substitution of VTRs for

16mm films. In the late 1970s, smaller and cheaper video-cassette recordings (VCR) were introduced which had broad appeal. Major film distributors offered their products in both 16mm and video formats. Administrators in Rieck's (1987) survey of 204 rental film centers predicted that by 1996 collections will be primarily video, utilizing varied delivery methods (including electronic), serving a diverse clientele.

The advent of videodisc, an exciting new concept for motion picture storage, prompted a fresh look at the future for film libraries. In 1987, the National Information Center on Educational Media (NICEM) began marketing their database on compact disc (CD), a variant of the videodisc. New developments in high resolution television suggested that electronic media offer a viable alternative to the time-tested 16mm film. Forward-looking educational resource centers will meet these new challenges.

Bibliography

Directory of Film Libraries in North America 1971 Film Library Information Council, New York

A Directory of 16mm Film Collections in Colleges and Universities in the United States, 1974–75, 3rd edn. Educational Film Library Association, New York

Elsas D et al. 1977 *Third World Cinema*. Factfile No. 10. American Film Institute, Washington, DC

Kleinman J 1979 The impact of free loan film on educational budgets. *Technol. Horizons Educ.* 6(5): 48–49

McDonald G D 1942 *Educational Motion Pictures and Libraries*. American Library Association, Chicago, Illinois

Patterson R 1981 The preservation of color films. *Am. Cinematographer* 62: 694–97, 714–20, 792–99, 816–22

Phillipson W D 1978 *A Study of a Data Processing System for the Contemporary Film Library*. ERIC Document No. ED 184499 IR008032 Educational Resources Information Center, Washington, DC

Quinly W J et al. 1972 *Standards for Cataloging Non-print Materials*, 3rd edn. Association for Educational Communications and Technology, Washington, DC

Rieck D A 1987 Video format influences and trends in university film rental libraries: An investigation of selection and evaluation procedures. (Doctoral dissertation, Iowa State University), *Dissertation Abstracts International* 49:3, 443-A

Rose E D 1978 *World Film and Television Study Resources: A Reference Guide to Major Training Centers and Archives*. Friedrich-Ebert-Stiflung, Bonn

Storage and Handling of Learning Resources

A. H. Thompson

There are several types of learning resource materials, and more are under development. Print, consisting of a paper base containing textual or illustrative information or both, is used for books, periodicals, and other allied documents. Plastics are used to make long-playing audiodiscs and overhead transparencies. Combined with other materials, they are used to make compact discs, videodiscs, and other laser-read formats. Coated with a metal or metallic oxide powder, plastics are used to make magnetic recording tapes or discs to store both analogue and digital sound and video recordings and computer data. Photographic film, an acetate base coated with photographic emulsion, is used for microforms, cine films, slides and filmstrips. Real objects (*realia*), either full size or models, provide tactile information and real experiences.

1. Storage Conditions

In general, print and realia are more robust and less susceptible to deterioration in poor storage conditions. Magnetic tape, photographic film, and plastic discs, however, are more easily damaged and greater attention should be paid to correct storage conditions as they are affected by extremes of temperature and humidity.

1.1 Temperature and Humidity

Ideally all learning resource materials should be stored in temperatures of $21 \pm 3°C$, with a relative humidity of 50 ± 10 percent.

In temperate countries these conditions are reasonably easy to maintain, but in large resource collections in academic institutions and libraries where a long working life is required, temperature and humidity still need to be kept fairly constant throughout the year. A severe drop in temperature can cause condensation and the dampness so produced will cause damage, especially to photographic film or magnetic tape. Thus wherever possible the central heating should remain on in the area of the resource collection even when the rest of the building is not in use.

Learning resource collections in tropical and subtropical countries face much greater problems. Even the use of air-conditioning may not bring temperature and humidity down to the ideal levels. The normal solution is to store photographic film, magnetic tape, and plastic discs in separate areas of a building where air-conditioning can be maintained at all times, either by the use of an air-conditioning plant or by auxilliary units when the main plant is turned off and the building is not in use. In such situations, the nearer the temperature and humidity are to the stated ideal, the better. While photographic film and magnetic tape can be stored in temperatures up to 27°C, relative humidities above 60 percent, especially when combined with higher or extremes of temperature, will lead to fungus growth causing irreparable damage. Hence the storage of learning resources in tropical countries without air-conditioning, or where air-conditioning is only intermittent due to irregular electric power supply, is always a risk, so some degree of deterioration is inevitable.

1.2 Other Factors Affecting Storage Conditions

All learning resource materials should be kept out of the path of direct sunlight and at least one metre away from sources of heat, such as radiators or hot-air vents.

Dust can cause irreparable damage, to magnetic tape, photographic film, and plastic disc materials. These must be kept in dustproof containers when not in use—usually the container in which they are supplied will be sufficient.

The equipment in which these materials are played back also needs to be kept dust free by covering it when it is not in use and by regular maintenance and cleaning. Atmospheric pollution, especially of an acidic nature, can also damage learning resource materials over a period of time.

Exposure of magnetic tapes and discs, and magnetic sound tracks on cine film to strong magnetic fields such as those caused by large magnets, direct current electric motors, and some security systems in use in libraries and other buildings, can cause partial or complete erasure of the recorded information. A safety distance of between half to one metre for most electrical equipment is recommended.

All learning resource materials are open to damage by a variety of tropical insects, cockroaches, and other vermin.

2. Working Lifetimes

Some learning resource materials either have a limited natural lifetime or suffer a reduction in their useful lifetime each time they are used. For instance, colour photographic film will fade over a period of time, especially when constantly projected, due to the unstable nature of the colour dyes used in photographic emulsions. Cine film is inevitably damaged during projection, as are long-playing audiodiscs during playback and they will give only 30 to 60 presentations (approximately) before wear renders them less effective. Both film and disc formats can also suffer from warping during long-term storage.

Other materials, such as print and magnetic tapes and discs, can be expected to have much longer lifetimes in a normal use situation, whilst most real objects and laser-read materials should suffer little deterioration.

3. Handling

If learning resources are to last their expected working lifetime, then careful handling is required. While print and realia will stand most forms of reasonable handling, photographic film, magnetic tape, and plastic discs will not. These latter materials should not be touched on the surfaces containing the recorded information as fingermarks attract dust from the atmosphere, cause distortion on playback, and are very difficult to remove. Contact with any rough surface must also be avoided.

3.1 Photographic Film

Film should be handled by the edges only, except when approved film handling gloves are worn. This should always be the case when dealing with film materials for prolonged periods—for instance when preparing film materials for the resource collection, editing cine film, or mounting slides or filmstrips. For ease of handling it is recommended that filmstrips are cut up and mounted as slides. Glass mounting of slides is recommended for slides in reference collections, for slides used in group presentations, and for tape slide sequences.

3.2 Audiodiscs, Videodiscs, and Computer Discs

Audiodiscs, videodiscs, and computer discs should always be kept inside their dustproof containers except when in use. Long-playing audiodiscs, compact discs, and laser-read videodiscs should only be handled by the edges. Other videodiscs and magnetic computer discs should be handled by their containers; the recording or playing surfaces should never be exposed except by the disc equipment. The use of a groove and cleaner is recommended when playing long-playing audiodiscs and a static reducer will remove static charges from disc surfaces.

3.3 Magnetic Tapes

The recording surface of magnetic tapes should not be touched—the tape should only be handled by the coloured leader tape where it is provided or by the edges of the tape. Film handling gloves can be worn when tape editing.

4. Shelving

Ideally, learning resource materials should be shelved in such a way that they can be seen as complementing each other and their obvious presence in the collection will be an invitation to users to learn from them. Separation of some of the formats can have negative results, as those not on view or not seen to be in use in the main collection tend to be ignored and their value to the collection diminished. In temperate countries, the shelving of all the varied resources in one area is perfectly feasible for they all require similar storage conditions. In tropical countries, however, unless air conditioning is available throughout the year, it may be necessary to shelve photographic film, magnetic tape, and plastic discs in a separate area from the books and realia.

It is neither practically feasible nor necessary to attempt to shelve all the various formats into one single sequence. However, the various formats on the same subject should be shelved as close to each other as possible, advertising their existence to the user. In many resource collections the materials are placed on open access shelving, with magnetic tape and photographic film materials stored on shelves next to the shelves containing the print materials on the same subject. Plastic discs tend to be shelved separately because of their shape and fragility.

All learning resource materials can be shelved on generally available storage equipment—the book shelf will store books and allied documents, magnetic tapes, slide sets loaded into Kodak Carousel magazines in their boxes, cine films (film/computer tape racks can be placed on the shelf to stop the films rolling off), and a wide variety of smaller realia and multimedia packs. Vertical filing cabinets will contain smaller items such as overhead transparencies, plastic discs, filmstrips and notes, individual slides, maps, pamphlets, and newspaper clippings. In addition record browser boxes or record shelving may be necessary where large collections of discs exist. It is advisable to continue to use conventional storage equipment rather than purchase specially-designed audiovisual storage equipment, which is expensive, inflexible, and leads to segregation and confusion in the user's mind.

Learning resource packs which contain two or more formats, for example slides and printed notes or multimedia packs, should always be shelved as a single unit—splitting up the various items is unhelpful to staff and users.

5. Playback Equipment

Playback equipment for those learning resources that require it may be staff-controlled or user-controlled depending on the needs of the users of the collection, but should be close by the materials themselves and in the same area of the collection. The use of headphones permits the use of nearly all audiovisual equipment within the collection, rather than in separate areas where it has no advertising potential and gets less use as a result.

Bibliography

Kodak Limited 1967 *Storage and Preservation of Motion Picture Film*. Kodak, London

1983 Storage, handling and preservation of audiovisual materials. *Audiovisual Round Table Series: Audiovisuals in Action*, No. 3. International Federation of Library Associations, Nederlands Bibliotheck En Lektuur Centrum, Netherlands

Volkmann H 1965 *Film Preservation: A Report of the Preservation Committee of the International Federation of Film Archives*. British Film Institute, London

Libraries in Adult Education

J. Allred

This article covers the role libraries play in the support of adult learners whether or not the learner attends a formal education programme and whether or not the library is part of an educational institution. By adult education is meant the learning activities adults follow, after completing their full-time education, for recreation, personal development, or improvement in job skills. These learning activities occur in formal and informal education programmes but are distinguished by their emphasis on self-direction and independent learning strategies (see *Self-planned Learning*). These strategies are present, too, in conventional education with project work, reading, and research.

1. History

Libraries have long had connections with adult learners. As far back as the Middle Ages in Europe monks pursued their studies with the help of monastic libraries which maintained proficient systems for book production and location. The Reformation and the subsequent establishment of Protestant states and cities relied partly on libraries to implement educational programmes. The town libraries of Europe (Ipswich and Norwich in England, Hamburg in Germany) and in the United States (Boston and New Haven), and parish libraries, notably in Scotland under James Kirkwood's ideas in the eighteenth century, were resources of variable quality for adult independent learners.

In more modern times, industrial societies have faced the problem of an undereducated workforce. More schooling was an obvious solution. For adults this was impracticable and in some cases libraries had to be relied upon to fill the gap. Mechanics' institutes in the United Kingdom were forerunners of public libraries providing, alongside class programmes, libraries for the self-education of the artisan. The rate- (local tax) -supported public library was established in the United Kingdom in 1850 as an educational agency in the vacuum created by parliamentary dispute over the provision of state schooling. The government's Select Committee of Inquiry was told, at that time, that reading would "add a softening and expanding influence to the great practical education the Englishman received from incessant intercourse between man and man in trade".

Public libraries were promoted as an educational force in both the United Kingdom and the United States, not by popular demand, but by the efforts of a few enlightened and philanthropic individuals who believed in the virtues of "self-help" and in the value of access to carefully chosen bookstocks. In practice, their impact upon adult education was limited by the conservatism of their stocks and by the librarian's preoccupation with the mechanics of collection and conservation (Lee 1966, Johnson 1938).

Adult education through libraries was not always in the interests of the government of the time. In Russia, the adult education movement of the Kul'turniki after the Crimean War relied upon educational centres, societies, and public libraries and was linked to the postrevolutionary educational programmes of the Communist governments working through the same agencies (Raymond 1981). Adult education in the Eastern Bloc is seen as a cooperative effort, which includes all libraries, working in the direct interests of the state's own philosophy.

Western Europe and the United States did not take such a directive approach. Adult education in these countries was served by libraries working with, for example, the university extramural movement in the United Kingdom. University lecturers travelled to give courses of a high standard to people who had little chance of going to a university. Some universities built up large extramural libraries of their own (London, Birmingham) with specialist staff to supply students of these courses with reading matter. These libraries now provide a wide range of teaching materials for university extramural programmes. The Central Circulating Library for Students was founded in 1916 from the Workers' Educational Association's Central Library for Tutorial Classes with help from the Carnegie United Kingdom Trust to provide books for students either directly or through public libraries. It became the National Central Library and is now part of the British Library Document Supply Centre.

After the First World War, both the United Kingdom and the United States included adult education in their programmes of reconstruction. The Ministry of Reconstruction's Adult Education Committee report in the United Kingdom provided the impetus for the 1919 Public Library Act, which put public libraries under local education authorities and presented them as places for "self-development in an atmosphere of freedom" contrasted with schooling as "training in an atmosphere of restraint or discipline". In 1924 the American Library Association's Commission on Libraries and Adult Education reinforced the role of the reader's advisor in public libraries whose job it was to plan personalized reading programmes. This meant close involvement between the librarian and the library user. Historians have remarked upon the disappearance of this role after the 1930s when help for adult learners became much more an assumed role of the general library service. This continued until the 1960s and 1970s when a renewed concern for people, underprivileged by lack of education and information, caused librarians to develop community information services and services for adult independent learners.

2. Role of the Library

A distinction might be made between the library's support for other providers of adult education (for example book box supplies to evening classes) and "library learning" itself where the librarian might provide a course of directed reading. Librarians are not usually trained as teachers and therefore more easily see themselves as supporting other educational providers. There have been moves in several countries to ensure that public libraries are placed under government departments responsible for education. Though many library laws recognize the educational role of libraries, education laws commonly do not. The Norwegian Libraries Act 1971 stressed the importance of public libraries in adult education but the 1976 Adult Education Act did not.

A study of United Kingdom public libraries (Allred and Hay 1979) attempted to discover the extent to which they offered special services to adult learners. Their findings were as follows.

(a) *The general library service.* Access to general library stocks with special borrowing privileges in a few cases. Problems arose when materials were not available at the time required or for the length of time required. Sometimes materials would be delivered to adult education classes. Material includes books, audio and video tapes, film, and specially prepared teaching packs, for example on local history. Adult classes were held in the library as a convenient and relaxed setting. In Sweden grant-aided "study circles" often met in public libraries and, as in the United Kingdom and other countries, the libraries showed films, and held concerts and exhibitions, all of which might be considered as part of adult learning (Griffiths 1971).

(b) *The provision of educational information and advice (educational brokering).* In the late 1970s this was a rapidly growing activity. The expansion of educational opportunities and retraining needs increased the demands for such services. In the United Kingdom these were established in colleges and as independent services [Hatfield's Educational Guidance Service for Adults (EGSA), Northern Ireland's EGSA, Wigan's Contact for Learning and Educational Opportunities (CLEO)]. Libraries provided educational information themselves, but the staff were not trained to advise and counsel. Some public libraries assisted these services by sharing premises (Birmingham), by acting as a referral link (Newcastle-upon-Tyne had a direct telephone line), and by compiling indexes and information sheets. Databases of information about education and training are now common in Europe and America. In many cases (for example, the United Kingdom's Training Access Points project) librarians are involved in both the provision of terminals for user access and in the development of indexes and standard record formats. Both are crucial to reliable retrieval of the complex information that these databases hold. In the United States, the Educational Information Center projects funded first by Federal funds and now by the Kellog Foundation promote public libraries, among other places, for information and guidance about educational opportunities.

Many educational providers placed their publicity in libraries and some libraries collaborated in educational "fairs" or information weeks (Leicestershire County Council, Guildford in Surrey).

Learning exchanges (an idea of Illich and others in the United States) are an extension of educational information services where prospective learners and "tutors" (who do not need to be trained teachers) are matched to facilitate less formal, but not independent, learning. In New Zealand such an exchange became part of the services of Wellington City Library. In the United Kingdom an experimental service was started in Orton, at the Cambridgeshire County Library.

(c) *Instruction in library use*. A most useful service provided by librarians was that of the instruction of adult learners in the use of the library. Competent library use is a major part of study skill and such instruction is commonplace in colleges and universities. East Sussex County Library and Norfolk County Library staff taught evening classes in public library use in connection with local history and genealogy and were surprised by their popularity.

Guides to library services in some regions were published by the Open University and other educational providers. Many public libraries had adult education liaison staff to maintain contacts with tutors. A well-developed service was provided by Derbyshire County Library with a current awareness bulletin on the subject of adult education and with participation in tutor training programmes. A similar information service based on nine educational libraries but on a larger scale and computerized is operated in Austria called *Das Dokumentationssystem Erwachsenenbildung* (DOKEB) or Documentation System for Adults.

Specialist library services for professionals and others working in adult education exist in most countries. For example Syracuse University in the United States operates a Clearing House of Resources for Educators of Adults. In the United Kingdom the National Institute of Adult Education in Leicester maintains a library and a register of research.

3. Library Programmes

3.1 Developing Countries

The important Malmö Seminar (Houle 1951) had one of its three groups devoted to this subject. In countries where resources are scarce and educational systems limited, libraries provide a valuable extension of educational provision. In the 1970s, the Indian government's National Education Programme was urged to recognize the need of adults for access to books and to realize the help that public libraries can provide through discussion groups and reading aloud groups, with visual aids and drama activities. In Tanzania it is the job of the Tanzania Library Service to help people

to participate in national development. Where the government has failed to emphasize the role of the library as in Zambia, the library profession has drawn attention to this.

3.2 Adult Basic Education

In 1955 in Brooklyn in the United States, the public library started a reading improvement programme in collaboration with Brooklyn College, which continues to this day. Librarians are trained to teach adults at all levels. The American Library Association Adult Services Division published its *Service to Adult Illiterates* in 1964 and libraries such as Kalamazoo, the Free Library of Philadelphia, Enoch Pratt Free Library, and many others were soon providing adult reading centres and discussion groups, as well as materials. Libraries had to cooperate with other agencies and this was not always easy. A common problem was a lack of appropriate reading materials for adults.

A major project in the United States was that promoted by the Appalachian Adult Education Center of Morehead (Kentucky) State University in 1972, which involved 77 libraries in 10 states by 1976. The library profession in the United States more readily accepted responsibility for adult illiterates than that in the United Kingdom (Lyman 1977), but the concern for illiteracy did spread to the United Kingdom where libraries, public and academic, cooperated in the Adult Literacy Campaign.

3.3 Distance Learning: Broadcasting

The United Kingdom literacy programme of the 1970s was considerably reinforced by the participation of the British Broadcasting Corporation (BBC), and public libraries played a part, though a variable one. The activity brought about a much closer relationship between broadcasting and libraries. Programmes such as Yorkshire Television's *Disraeli*, the BBC's *Roadshow*, and *Speak for Yourself* drew the public library into the systematic provision of back-up materials for the audiences of these programmes.

Broadcast educational programmes have been initiated by libraries. In the 1940s, Louisville Public Library in the United States ran a radio station and later used television in its "neighbourhood college", run in conjunction with the university. The Open University of the United Kingdom is an important example of a worldwide movement. Its own librarians are members of the course production teams and its course materials are stocked by many libraries. Prince George's County Library in Maryland provides Open University and other material for its university's independent students. Public libraries in Quebec supported their local tele-university. In practice, students have little time to use anything other than the learning materials supplied direct to them but the adoption of project-based work by the Open University has resulted in fresh demands being made on libraries.

Dependence upon libraries by adult learners may be more a function of the learning style than of the distance from the educational provider. New learning media are finding their way into libraries, particularly college libraries. Interactive video, CD-ROM and other media are increasingly common with the rapid extension of "open learning". They present radical problems of organization and use.

Some major developments in distance education fail to include libraries. The Norwegian Distance Education Institution set up in 1978 to coordinate television, the National Film Centre, and the University Press made no mention of the place of libraries, but the National Library Office now takes part in all planning discussions.

3.4 Open Entry to Education

Adults should not be debarred from education because of a lack of formal entry qualifications, and provision should be easily accessible. These principles have provided another reason for "library learning". Between 1972 and 1976 a major project was undertaken by the United States College Entrance Examination Board's (CEEB's) Office of Independent Study and Guidance Projects. Nine library systems across the United States were involved in providing library-based guidance and tutorial support for learners wishing to gain credits for university courses or to learn for any other reason. The work was based on the researches of Allen Tough, which demonstrated that adults undertake a great number of learning projects but often with unsatisfactory guidance and resources. The public library staff were trained, not to teach, but to make available suitable resources, to support and encourage, and to refer when necessary. Great emphasis was placed on evaluation of the outcomes for the library and for the learners (Mavor et al. 1976, Boles and Smith 1979). The idea has been paralleled and copied in other libraries and in other countries. Philadelphia Free Library created a "Lifelong Learning Center" in 1976. The Netherlands has an Open School, in which libraries cooperate in adult education by providing tours of the library, instruction in library use, and reading lists. Simple devices like OPACs (on-line public access catalogues) are opening the way to greatly enhanced exploitation of library materials by learners. Catalogue entries, already searched on combinations of keywords, will be able to contain the contents pages and indexes of books.

4. The Future

The high costs of formal education, the need for adults to retrain and adapt to change, and the emphasis on lifelong learning have resulted in alternative and more flexible learning systems. New teaching methods in sec-

ondary schools have trained people in independent study skills. All learning resource centres, often integrated with libraries, are under great pressure (de la Court 1974). College libraries are asked to allow adult independent learners access to their collections. Public libraries are expected to support broadcast learning. Professional training for librarians incorporates "user needs" in general and sometimes the needs of adult learners in particular. Their needs are for more than information; they need encouragement, clarification, motivation, and review. Special groups of learners claim the librarian's attention. In Oud-Gastel, in the Netherlands, the public library provided a course in social awareness for women, which resulted in greater use of the library's information services. The CEEB project referred to above attracted many older adults.

Research shows that it is important for librarians to concern themselves with the intentions of those who use their libraries and not simply with delivery of material. New technologies are likely to replace librarians for many of the mechanical tasks of collection and delivery. The future will tell how far libraries as resource centres for adult learners will be replaced by electronic resources delivered direct, and how far librarians will supply the need adult learners have for experienced and sympathetic guidance to the multiplicity of resources and systems available to them.

Bibliography

Allred J, Hay W 1979 *A Preliminary Study of the Involvement of Public Libraries with Adult Learners.* Leeds Polytechnic Public Libraries Management Research Unit, Leeds

Birge L E 1981 *Serving Adult Learners: A Public Library Tradition.* American Library Association, Chicago, Illinois

Boles S, Smith B D 1979 The learner's advisory service. *Libr. Trends* 28: 165–78

de la Court W 1974 *Openbare Bibliotheek en Permanente Educatie* [Public libraries and permanent education]. Tjeenk Willink, Groningen

Griffiths T E 1971 Adult education and libraries in Sweden. *Libr. Assoc. Record* 73(6): 105–07

Houle C O 1951 *Libraries in Adult and Fundamental Education.* The Report of the Malmö Seminar. UNESCO, Paris

Johnson A S 1938 *The Public Library: A People's University.* American Association for Adult Education, New York

Lee R E 1966 *Continuing Education for Adults Through the American Public Library, 1833–1964.* American Library Association, Chicago, Illinois

Lyman H H 1977 *Literacy and the Nation's Libraries.* American Library Association, Chicago, Illinois

Mavor A S, Toro J O, De Prospo E R 1976 *The Role of the Public Libraries in Adult Independent Learning.* College Entrance Examination Board, New York

Raymond B 1981 Libraries and adult education: The Russian experience. *J. Libr. Hist.* 16(2): 394–403

Learning Centres

W. J. K. Davies

The term "learning centre" has arisen as an outcome of three, often conflicting trends in the individualization of learning during the 1960s and 1970s. These were the urge towards the "discovery" or "resource-based learning" approach; the development of programmed learning techniques of self-instruction; and the belief by media specialists and librarians that their communications and information retrieval skills should have an increasing part to play in the educational process. Learning centres were seen by all these groups as an essential part of their work and their ideas had one thing in common—the concept that a student should be enabled to work individually and to learn largely by his or her own efforts rather than through direct face-to-face teaching. Otherwise they differed widely according to their particular perspectives (see *Conceptual Frameworks and Historical Development*).

1. Different Approaches

The "discovery" enthusiast, mainly at primary-school level and particularly in the United Kingdom, saw the learning centre essentially as a cornucopia of resources which the liberated child would feast on with minimum guidance. Simple exposure to an appropriate environment would be sufficient. From this developed the resource-based learning movement in which the resources—defined as information and teaching materials—were seen as supplementing and even occasionally substituting for the teacher as a stimulus to learning. The learning resources centre was thus envisaged as a place where the individual could not only be exposed to such stimuli but helped to pick out those items needed for his or her work. This idea was taken up especially by secondary schools and higher institutions in various countries and was welcomed particularly by those agencies such as libraries which felt their contribution to learning could thereby be increased.

The third thrust came from the programmed learning movement composed mainly of teachers and trainers who wanted to make their teaching more effective. Programmed learning generated a wide variety of highly structured, self-instructional learning materials which almost guaranteed success for their users. The availability of these, and the ability to produce them for specific needs, resulted in the first true learning centres where individuals could confidently expect by their own efforts to achieve predetermined goals. The vogue for "learning by appointment" stemmed from this approach (see *Programmed Learning*).

In practice, while proponents of all these approaches have made some progress, none has proved successful enough for its learning centres to be assimilated into the mainstream of education. Learning centres to date have generally been regarded as an interesting extra when money was plentiful but as something that can be dispensed with when economies are needed.

2. The Ideal Learning Centre

This is seen by all its advocates as a place where any individual can come at will and learn what he or she wishes. Its exact characteristics differ with the views of its promoter(s) but in general it is seen as having four elements:

(a) A physical base where a student can work or from which he or she may obtain support when working elsewhere. This is envisaged as something akin to a very good library fitted with study facilities and generously equipped with various media of presentation such as videocasettes and synchronized slide–tape devices controlled from a central point (see *Learning Environments*).

(b) A wide variety of materials, at least some of which are sufficiently structured to support the student's learning rather than just to act as sources of information. A variant perception is that the materials themselves may be largely unstructured, guideline assignments being provided where needed to help individuals.

(c) Provision of tutorial help as and when required. The ideal is seen as being the immediate availability of an appropriate specialist but the practical necessity of an advance booking system is generally acknowledged.

(d) An organization which will enrol, communicate with, and monitor the progress of the student as required. This is normally envisaged as being one component of an existing educational institution rather than an organization set up specifically to run an autonomous centre.

As can be seen, the provision of all this would required considerable and continuing expenditure. As a consequence, most learning centres have specialized in one or two fields of work. An interesting development, however, is the renewed stimulus for such centres provided by recent open learning initiatives. These have all the requirements listed above.

3. The Learning Centre in Practice

In practice, learning centres have tended to specialize to some degree and to fall into one of four categories.

3.1 The Learning Laboratory

More common in the United States than in Europe, this often sprang from an urge to individualize a single course or related courses in a single subject area; its background is firmly in programmed learning. Its title has deliberate links with the language laboratory and it has many of the latter's characteristics (see *Language Laboratories*). Thus it is frequently media based, usually with some form of slide and audiotape equipment; expects to put all its students through basically the same course; relies heavily on specially prepared packages often designed to fit the existing media devices irrespective of whether the presentation method is the most appropriate one. Its proponents are usually enthusiasts for a certain approach who appear satisfied with what they achieve but the concept has only limited application. Little evidence is available as to what happens if the initiator(s) leave.

3.2 The Learning By Appointment Centre

This is a structure which offers learning on demand in a wide range of subjects, theoretically to anyone who cares to come and learn. The concept enjoyed a considerable vogue in the United Kingdom especially during the 1960s and early 1970s owing to the availability of many programmed, self-instructional learning materials and was taken up mainly by institutions of further and higher education. Responsibility was firmly with the student. Several such centres still operate but the development of this concept has suffered from two related problems. First the supply of self-instructional material dried up when programmed learning lost its impetus. This meant that centres had to use only partly structured materials such as those prepared for correspondence courses and this, in turn, required additional tutorial assistance which increased costs and complicated the organization. Such centres are, therefore, tending to become workshop or tutorial based. The concept has not been applied much to school level though some success was achieved in Hertfordshire, UK in developing independent learning centres funded by and serving a group of primary and secondary schools. The idea has proved sound but requires additional resources and is, therefore, not likely to develop further in times of economic stringency.

3.3 Learning Workshops

These can be considered as a hybrid between learning laboratories and learning by appointment. They are normally restricted to one subject or skills area and their materials are therefore specialized. At the same time most learning workshops provide a wide range of materials and tutorial guidance within that area and may serve the local community as well as the host institution. Typical examples of such workshops are in mathematics (Bradford College, UK is probably the best known) and in remedial work, many schools in the United States and the United Kingdom having their remedial provision organized in this way. An interesting development of this is the so-called learning room, where a variety of prestructured courses in related subjects are available to mature students on a self-study

basis. A recent example is the initiative in business studies at Redditch, UK.

3.4 The LRC

Variously translated as "learning resource centre" or "library resource centre", this is normally conceived as being within a single institution to service that institution. Its origin was in the need felt by librarians and media specialists to contribute more actively to the educational process. The concept has been widely adopted in Europe and the United States and in countries within their influence. The LRC is most commonly seen as a physical place well-stocked with resource materials and staffed by professionals who are there to help its clients. The exact nature of the materials, professionalism, and service are seen differently by their providers depending on the background of the people concerned. Thus a library-based centre is likely to be basically an information retrieval environment, with students expected to carry out their own learning tasks. In secondary schools such centres were often generated initially by one faculty to service its own work and frequently contained large quantities of homemade assignments largely in print medium.

In practice, in the United States some LRCs have developed into genuine individualized learning units, in many ways paralleling the United Kingdom developments noted under learning by appointment. In other countries, however, the trend has been for them to become teaching support services and outside the scope of this article.

4. Future Developments

The overall concept of tutorially guided individualized work is now firmly established, though provision is more often within existing institutions than in the grandiose centres advocated in the early 1970s. Specialist learning laboratories and workshops will probably continue on a small scale where they can be justified economically. The main development, however, is likely to be in the open learning field, following on the initiatives of the United Kingdom Open University and its disciples, whose local study centres have some claim to be considered as models for student support. This urge towards open and distance learning, coupled with the economic climate, will tend to encourage provision for individuals rather than conventional class groups, at least in adult education. It should be possible to see, therefore, more and more development of institutionalized centres which will provide a support service to students working elsewhere but will also provide study facilities within their institution(s). The development is likely to be reinforced by initiatives in various countries toward open learning at subdegree level. It seems likely that the development of specialized materials and procedures for these schemes may in turn provide the basis for a revival of the learning by appointment idea.

Bibliography

Albrecht A, Spencer D C 1976 *Flexastudy: The Professional Tutorial System Operated at Redditch College*. Coombe Lodge Further Education Staff College Paper No. 1119, Blagdon, Bristol

Clarke J, Leedham J (eds.) 1976 *Aspects of Educational Technology*, Vol. 10: *Educational Technology for Individualized Learning. Proceedings of the 10th Annual Conference of the Association for Programmed Learning and Educational Technology, Dundee, April 1976*. Kogan Page, London

Davies W J K 1980 *Alternatives to Class Teaching in Schools and Colleges*. Council for Educational Technology, London

Davies W J K, Needham M 1977 Individualized learning cen-
tres. In: Mills P, Gilbert J (eds.) 1977 *Aspects of Educational Techology*, Vol. 11: *The Spread of Educational Technology*. Kogan Page, London

Foster J 1967 *The Napier Experiment*. Proceedings of the 1967 Scottish National Conference on Educational Technology, Glasgow

Mackenzie M 1978 Deciding to individualize learning: A case study. In: Mills P, Gilbert J (eds.) 1977 *Aspects of Educational Technology*, Vol. 11: *The Spread of Educational Technology*. Kogan Page, London

Mackie A 1975 Consumer-orientated programmed learning in adult education. In: Mills P, Gilbert J (eds.) 1977 *Aspects of Educational Technology*, Vol. 11: *The Spread of Educational Technology*. Kogan Page, London

Knowledge Organization and Knowledge Use

Knowledge Industries and Knowledge Occupations

F. Machlup

Knowledge industries and knowledge occupations are convenient terms to denote the total activities in an economy undertaken with the intentions to create, transmit, and receive knowledge. The purpose of these activities may be to sharpen and enrich people's minds; to inform, enlighten, advise, and entertain; to improve the understanding of nature and society; to increase the efficiency of work and of production processes; or to serve any other aims. There are two approaches to the economic analysis and statistical measurement of these activities: (a) the industry approach, which focuses on the output of groups of people, and (b) the occupations approach, which focuses on the labor input of individuals engaged in producing knowledge.

The groups in the knowledge industries may be organizations (agencies, institutes, business firms) or parts of organizations (departments or teams within firms) whose major output is knowledge or some instrument for the reception, processing, or transmission of knowledge. The individuals in knowledge occupations are members of the labor force whose input consists chiefly receiving, processing, creating, or transmitting knowledge.

In these contexts the terms knowledge and knowledge production are used in the widest senses of the words, limited only by the requirement that the organizations in the various branches of the knowledge industry incur measurable or estimable costs for the creation, reception, and dissemination of knowledge and that the workers in the various knowledge-producing occupations receive, or could receive, measurable or estimable incomes for their labor. This limitation is required by the economic point of view, because economics deals with the use of scarce and therefore valuable inputs for the production of valuable outputs. Hence, an economic investigation of knowledge industries and knowledge occupations must be confined to those kinds of knowledge that somebody regards as worth spending money for or incurring costs that can be expressed in money. No moral judgment is involved here, only a methodological decision.

1. Information or Knowledge?

A question of terminology may be answered before proceeding with the discussion: is it better to use the word "information" instead of "knowledge"? Many people are so inclined, because there is so much talk about information systems and information theory. Both nouns have their root in verbs: to inform and to know. The first means an action or process, the second means a state. This difference could also be applied to the nouns but, in the usual vagueness of language, the nouns mean also the subject or contents of information and of knowledge. Thus, useful information means not only that the act of informing but also the content of the message is useful. Likewise, useful knowledge refers to what is known, not only to the state of knowing. As far as the subjects or contents of informing and knowing are concerned, the word "information" is usually applied more to disconnected or particular facts or events, and the word "knowledge" to interconnected or general thoughts, usually of enduring value.

In any case, information is always a kind of knowledge, whereas not all knowledge can be called information. Since it is the wider concept, the term knowledge is used here, and the word information is restricted to those contexts where the process of informing is essential, as for example with regard to information services.

2. Types of Knowledge

The distinction between knowledge as that which is known and knowledge as the state of knowing is fundamental, but production of knowledge is concerned with both the increase in what is known and the increase in the number of people who know. There is no way of measuring knowledge. One cannot even say whether more knowledge is produced when a few people learn to know more things previously unknown to anybody or when more people learn to know what has already been known to others. The total contents of the brains of the entire population cannot be counted, weighed, or estimated. Precisely for this reason, for the sake of economic and statistical analysis the following aspects were chosen because they could be measured: (a) the annual total gross revenue received or cost incurred in knowledge industries and (b) the number of persons engaged in knowledge occupations and the total annual incomes they earned.

For these purposes, the definition of knowledge production has to be wide enough to comprise both the creation of socially new knowledge and the dissemination of existing knowledge to more people. Thus we define knowledge production as any human or human-induced activity effectively designed to create, alter, or confirm in a human mind—one's own or another person's—a meaningful apperception, awareness, cognizance, or consciousness of whatever it may be.

Philosophers and other scholars have proposed various classifications, distinguishing sometimes two, sometimes three classes of knowledge. For example, they have contrasted scientific and historical knowledge; scientific and artistic; general and particular; abstract and concrete; analytical and empirical knowledge; or instrumental, intellectual, and spiritual knowledge. Most of these categories, however, are confined to types of knowledge with which scholars deal, and they provide no place for the mundane kind of knowledge relevant to the ordinary people, knowledge that may be of enduring or of merely transitory interest to them but is too trivial to have occurred to a philosopher. Yet a considerable portion of the total cost of knowledge production may be for information of this rather crude or simple type.

An all-inclusive classification distinguishes at least five types:

(a) practical knowledge (professional, business, workman's, political, household, and other practical knowledge);

(b) intellectual knowledge (satisfying intellectual curiosity, humanistic and scientific learning, knowledge acquired in active concentration with an appreciation of cultural values);

(c) pastime knowledge (small talk, satisfying the desire for light entertainment and emotional stimulation, including local gossip, stories, jokes, games, knowledge acquired in passive relaxation from serious pursuits);

(d) spiritual knowledge (religious instruction about God and the salvation of the soul); and

(e) unwanted knowledge (knowledge outside the recipient's interests, perhaps accidentally acquired and aimlessly retained).

Strictly speaking, the application of these categories in particular instances would require awareness of the knower's motivations and intentions; but by thinking of typical recipients of the various types of information one may use the categories to describe the composition of the output of some of the knowledge industries.

The concept of truth is not a part of the definition of knowledge used here. This becomes immediately clear when one remembers that knowledge is not always embodied in language but includes paintings, sculptures, and music; and in linguistic expression it includes literature (fiction and poetry) that does not pretend to convey literal truth. Even scientific knowledge is always subject to revision and amendment; it never pretends to be more than a tentative approximation to the truth. Only for practical knowledge does it really matter that it be true and accurate enough to enable those who use it as a basis for action to get what they want.

3. The Demand for Knowledge

Only a part of the nation's production of knowledge is guided by the market mechanism. Much, perhaps most, of the knowledge produced is not purchased by the consumer at a price but is offered to him free of charge. The largest item in most countries is the expenditure for schools and universities, paid for largely by government, with smaller portions defrayed by philanthropists, parents, and the students themselves; the content of the teaching is determined partly by a political process and partly by professional educators.

Another large item, though only in a few countries, is the cost of research and development; the projects are often selected by the government, which usually pays for a large percentage. Radio and television are paid for by government in many countries, but by commercial sponsors in some countries, including the United States; the programs are chosen on the basis of either what the masses of the audience seem to like best or what is thought to be good for them. For large parts of the output of the knowledge industry there can be much controversy regarding what the people want and what they ought to want or would want if they were better prepared to make their choices.

4. The Difference Between Knowledge Industries and Knowledge Occupations

A knowledge industry is defined as a group of firms, institutions, or any other organizations, or of departments or teams within them that incur or induce costs, explicit or implicit, to create or disseminate knowledge of any type. Since the supply of information is sometimes inseparably connected with the supply of other goods or services, we count among the knowledge industries only those suppliers who provide information not merely as a minor by-product of other activities but as one of their major functions. But we include not only those knowledge suppliers who sell their services but also those who distribute them free of charge, financed by the taxpayer, by philanthropists, or by business.

Not all workers employed in a knowledge industry are knowledge workers. For example, schools and universities in the education industry employ cleaning personnel, janitors, and mechanics whose work is physical, not mental. The publishing industry employs not only writers, reporters, editors, printers, and proofreaders, all of whom perform chiefly mental work, but also chauffeurs, truck loaders, warehouse personnel, bookbinders, and many others whose work is chiefly manual; it has the journals and books printed on paper produced in mills that employ mainly physical workers, use machines made of steel and copper, and fabricate pulp from wood that was cut by lumber workers. Thus, while the output of the publishing industry is designed to transmit knowledge, a large component of the input is the labor of workers who are not in knowledge occupations. Likewise, the industry manufacturing computers and other information machines employs a majority of manual workers. In other words, to be employed in a knowledge industry does not transform a manual worker into one who performs knowledge work.

On the other hand, not all workers in knowledge occupations are employed in knowledge industries. Many such workers are employed in industries producing physical goods. No industry, whatever it produces, can be operated without some workers whose chief task is mental. To mention a few examples, the chemical industry employs chemists for research, development, and testing; it employs stenographers, typists, accountants, and other clerical workers, a sales staff that never has to do any physical labor, and many others whose work is mental, not physical. Likewise, the textile industry employs designers and again the nonphysical workers in the sales department, accounting department, secretariat, and so forth. Moreover, no firm can be without management, and managers are knowledge producing in that their task is to receive and evaluate information, to make judgments and decisions, to give orders and instructions, and direct the operations of the firm.

Now that the difference between knowledge industry and knowledge occupation has become clarified, one may raise the question whether the number of non-knowledge-producing workers employed in knowledge industries is greater or smaller than the number of knowledge-producing workers in nonknowledge industries. The answer, however, depends to a large extent on arbitrary classifications. For example, if one regards all research and development as a knowledge industry even where the work is undertaken not in separate firms or institutions but in departments or teams within firms engaged in manufacturing physical products that have nothing to do with knowledge production, one has arbitrarily lifted parts of nonknowledge branches of industry and transferred them into the column headed "knowledge industry."

The statistical decision to regard all research and development as a separate knowledge industry has suggested itself by the availability of statistical measurements that included both types of research and development: not only that performed by agencies, firms, and institutions specialized in research and development, but also that performed within firms (or other organizations) for internal use, as part of an integrated industry. There is a justification for this manipulation of statistical data. If an automobile manufacturer operates a steel mill, it makes good statistical sense to report steel production separately from output of automobiles and include it with the output of the steel industry. Likewise if a steel producer operates coal and iron ore mines, it is sensible for the statistician to disintegrate the output of the firm and transfer the respective data to the coal mining and iron ore mining industries. The analogous treatment of research and development transforms integrated operations by thousands of firms in a large variety of industry branches into a separate industry. The procedure still remains arbitrary; for example, we could with equal justification show an accounting industry that would include, besides the information services provided by specialized auditing and accounting firms and by independent accountants and tax counselors, all the accounting departments of large corporations and even the bookkeeping performed with the smallest firms.

As long as this statistical disintegration (for the purpose of an aggregation serving a different purpose) is done only for some and not for all production of knowledge for "internal use," the question of the relative magnitudes of the total knowledge industry and of the total knowledge labor force is not really meaningful. What is meaningful, however, is a comparison of growth rates of the two magnitudes.

5. Knowledge Industries Enumerated

In a statistical survey of the output produced by knowledge industries, the following six industry groups may be included: education; research and development; artistic creation and communication; media of communication; information services; and information machines. These groups are subdivided in the following branches:

5.1 Education

(a) Education in the home.

(b) Training on the job.

(c) Education in the church.

(d) Education in the armed forces.

(e) Elementary and secondary schools (monetary expenditures and implicit costs).

(f) Colleges and universities (monetary expenditures and implicit costs).

(g) Commercial, vocational, and residential schools.

(h) Government programs for education not elsewhere counted.

5.2 Research and Development

(a) Basic research.

(b) Applied research and development.

5.3 Artistic Creation and Communication

(a) Literary arts: poetry, fiction, playwriting.

(b) Music: vocal music, instrumental music, symphonic music.

(c) Performing arts: theatre, opera, dance.

(d) Motion pictures and cinema.

(e) Visual arts: drawing, painting, sculpting.

(f) Architecture.

(g) Museums and art galleries.

5.4 Media of Communication

(a) Printing and publishing: books and pamphlets, periodicals, journals, magazines, newsletters, newspapers, stationery and other office supplies, commercial printing and lithography.

(b) Commercial photography and phonography.

(c) Oral and visual communications: from the podium and screen, spectator sports.

(d) Electronic media of communication: radio stations revenue, television stations revenue, radio and television sets and repairs, radio and television stations investment.

(e) Other advertising.

(f) Addressed communications: telephone, telegraph, postal services.

(g) Conventions and conferences.

5.5 Information Services

(a) Libraries.

(b) Science and technological information.

(c) Professional services: medical services (excluding surgical), legal services, engineering and architectural services, accounting and auditing.

(d) Other specialized information services.

(e) Business information services.

(f) Information joint with financial services: deposit banking and money market funds, securities exchanges, brokers, dealers and analysts, insurance agents.

(g) Information joint with trade: real-estate agents, wholesale agents, miscellaneous business services.

(h) Management as an information process.

(i) Government: legislature, judiciary, executive, regulatory agencies.

5.6 Information Machines

(a) Printing machines.

(b) Musical instruments.

(c) Motion picture apparatus and equipment.

(d) Telephone and telegraph equipment.

(e) Signaling devices.

(f) Measuring and controlling instruments.

(g) Typewriters.

(h) Electronic computers.

(i) Other office machines.

(j) Office machine parts.

The statistical data for these branches of knowledge production can be broken down by the source of funds paying for the activity—government, business, or consumers—and by the character of the output, either intermediate product or final product (the latter being either consumption or investment). Regarding the second breakdown, it proves necessary to dissent from some of the characterizations made in the official statistics of gross national product (GNP). For example, the GNP statistics of the United States Department of Commerce regard research and development as final product when the expenditures are paid by the government, but as intermediate product when paid by business; it is more reasonable to treat these outlays uniformly as investment (even if business firms, in computing their taxable incomes, include them as current cost of producing whatever product they sell). For analogous reasons, broadcasting over radio and television is more properly characterized as final product—as consumption, not investment—even where business pays for it as a tax-deductible advertising expense. The largest part of the cost of education is the income that employable students over 14 or 15 years of age forgo by studying rather than taking jobs; this does not appear in the GNP, but may properly be regarded as investment, social as well as private.

6. Statistics of Knowledge Industries

A computation for the United States (Machlup 1962) yielded the findings given in Table 1 for the total cost of knowledge production in 1958. Total knowledge production in the United States was, in 1958, 29 percent of GNP, after the latter was adjusted for the various changes appropriate for the purpose.

No analogous statistics have been prepared for other countries, probably because it is difficult to obtain the relevant data from the conventional national income accounts. From these accounts one may at best obtain the output of so-called "primary" knowledge industries, that is, those that sell "final" product to the market or distribute it to consumers. The output of the so-called "secondary information sector," which produces information chiefly for internal use within the firm or within the same industry, is much more difficult to estimate. Porat and Rubin (1977) estimated outputs of both primary and secondary information sectors in the United

Table 1
Costs of production of knowledge in the United States, 1958

Classified by industry branches (%):	
Education	44.1
Research and development	8.1
Media of communications	28.1
Information services	13.2
Information machines	6.5
Classified by source of funds (%):	
Government	27.8
Business	30.9
Consumers	41.3
Classified by character of product (%):	
Intermediate (current cost)	20.0
Final (consumption or investment)	80.0

States for 1967. Their estimate for the primary sector was 25.2 percent and for the secondary sector 21.2 percent of GNP, together 46.4 percent. This tallies reasonably well with Machlup's estimate of 29 percent for the year 1958, accounting for growth during the nine years.

Estimates for the primary information sector have been supplied by the Organisation for Economic Cooperation and Development (OECD) for several industrial countries. Relative to gross domestic product the primary information sector accounted for 24.8 percent in the United States in 1972 (a little less than in 1967), 22.0 percent in the United Kingdom in 1972, 18.5 percent in France in 1972, 18.8 percent in Japan in 1970, 16.9 percent in Sweden in 1970, and 14.6 percent in Australia. The share of the cost of education (excluding implicit costs, such as forgone earnings) in these estimates of the primary information sector varied between less than one-sixth and almost one-third.

7. Knowledge Occupations

Knowledge workers are engaged in producing effects on their own minds or on the minds of others. Activities of the former type include watching, listening, reading, experimenting, inferring, intuiting, discovering, inventing, interpreting, computing, analyzing, judging, and evaluating. Activities of the second type include talking, writing, typing, printing, gesturing, signalling, drawing, painting, sculpturing, singing, and performing. All these activities may serve different purposes; for example, one may talk as a teacher, actor, priest, supervisor, manager, counselor, legislator, physician, and in many other types of knowledge occupations.

One may classify knowledge workers according to the degree to which messages which they deliver or transmit differ from the messages which they have previously received. Eight such classes or levels can be distinguished:

(a) transporters,

(b) transformers,

(c) routine processors,

(d) discretionary processors,

(e) managerial processors,

(f) interpreters,

(g) analyzers, and

(h) original creators of knowledge.

The transporter of information delivers exactly what he has received. The transformer changes the form of the message, but not the contents (example: stenotypist). The processor changes both form and contents either by routine practices following fixed rules or instructions (example: accountant) or by discretionary or managerial decision making. The interpreter has to use his or her imagination to create in a new form effects equivalent to those intended by the message received (example: translator of poetry in a foreign language). The analyzer uses much of his or her own judgment and intuition besides accepted procedures, so that what he or she transmits is quite different from the message received. The original creator, though drawing on a rich store of information received in the past, adds so much personal inventive genius and creative imagination that only weak and indirect connections can be found between what he or she has received and what he or she communicates.

8. Statistics of Knowledge Occupations

To permit numerical estimates of the numbers of persons in these eight classes or levels, very detailed statistical information is required. American census data permit the sorting from broader categories the occupations engaged chiefly in knowledge production. Thus, after eliminating all occupations that include a large component of manual work, the percentage breakdown given in Table 2 was found for the civilian labor force in the United States in 1960 and in 1970.

In interpreting these percentages one must bear in mind that several of the first five categories in the official statistics contain occupations which we have transferred into the class of occupations not producing knowledge. For example, we have so transferred certain groups of

Table 2
Percentage of the total civilian labor force in knowledge occupations in the United States

	1960	1970
Professional and technical workers in nonmanual work	9.0	11.8
Managers, officials, and proprietors (excluding farm)	5.8	6.5
Clerical workers	14.9	17.9
Sales workers in nonmanual work	3.1	3.2
Craftsmen and foremen in nonmanual work	0.5	0.5
Total in nonmanual work	33.3	39.9
Occupations not producing knowledge	66.7	60.1

professional and technical workers such as dentists and pharmacists, proprietors of small shops, more than one-half of sales workers, and almost all (97 percent) of the craftsmen and foremen. This explains why the statistics of white-collar labor in the United States come to larger percentages than those shown here for knowledge-producing workers. However, considerably higher percentages of knowledge workers are obtained if one includes students from the ninth grade upward, and hence of employable age, among the knowledge occupations and among the potential labor force: the percentages of persons producing knowledge (including knowledge in their own minds) were 44.3 percent in 1960 and 53.1 percent in 1970.

The Organisation for Economic Co-operation and Development (OECD) supplied estimates of the "information labor force" as a percentage of the total labor force in nine industrial countries, but not for the same year. The percentage for 1970 or 1971 was 41.1 in the United States, 39.9 in Canada, 35.6 in the United Kingdom, and 28.0 in Austria; for 1975 (evidently higher than 4 or 5 years earlier) it was 34.9 in Sweden, 32.1 in France, 29.6 in Japan, and 27.5 in Finland. The OECD also estimated the shares of "information producers," "information processors," "information distributors," and "information infrastructure operators." Educators are regarded as information distributors. The lack of linguistic sensitiveness in characterizing education as intending to distribute information instead of to develop cognitive and artistic skills and to implant knowledge of enduring value is regrettable.

9. Growth of Knowledge Industries and of Knowledge Occupations

The rates of growth observed in knowledge industries have exceeded those of the GNP, and the rates of growth observed in knowledge occupations have exceeded those of the total labor force. This was true for both Japan and the United States—at least until 1970—and probably also for other developed countries.

The highest growth rates are always found in new industries. Thus, in the 4 years from 1954 to 1958 American sales of electronic computers increased at a compounded rate of 104.4 percent per year. Similarly, in the 11 years from 1947 to 1958 the revenues of American television stations increased at a compounded rate of 77.2 percent per year. These growth rates are typical of all new industries, not just of knowledge industries. But the growth of all knowledge industries together was fast enough to suggest a trend. In the United States, the weighted average of the annual rates of increase of 36 branches of the knowledge industry for which data covering a period of 11 years ending in 1958 were available was 10.6 percent, which compares with a 5.9 percent rate of increase of GNP at current prices and with a 4.1 percent rate of increase of goods and services other than those produced by the knowledge industry.

A detailed breakdown of growth rates for various classes of knowledge industries in Japan shows that in the 5 years from 1960 to 1965 expenditures for education increased at a compound annual rate of 19.5 percent, research and development at 18.4 percent, free professions at 24.8 percent; "package knowledge" at 17.2 percent; and telecommunications at 14.7 percent. The weighted average of these growth rates was 18.1 percent, which may be compared with the annual growth rate of Japan's GNP (at current prices) of 14.8 percent. Again, the knowledge output increased faster than the total output of the nation.

The growth in the number of persons in knowledge occupations can be observed over a much longer period, at least in the United States. The percentage of workers in knowledge occupations increased from 10.7 percent of the labor force in 1900 to 18.3 percent in 1920, 23.4 percent in 1940, to 33.6 percent in 1960, and to 39.9 percent in 1970. The percentage of workers plus students of employable age increased from 13.5 percent of the potential labor force in 1900 to 23.9 percent in 1920, to 34.4 percent in 1940, to 44.3 percent in 1960, and to 53.1 percent in 1970. But not only did the ratio of mental to manual workers increase so sharply, but within the categories of knowledge occupations one can observe a trend from lower level to higher level knowledge work. Looking over a span of 70 years, from 1900 to 1970, clerical workers showed the largest percentage increase; during an intermediate period of 20 years from 1940 to 1960 the group of managers and officials had the largest increase; but over the period from 1940 to 1970 the professional and technical workers increased fastest.

Similar developments can be seen in Japan, though the statistical data go back only to 1952. Taking all professional and technical workers, all managers, officials, and proprietors (excluding farm proprietors), all clerical workers, and half of the sales workers, we find that their share in the total labor force increased from 20.1 percent in 1952 to 27.0 percent in 1965, and to 29.1 percent in 1969. These changes in the composition of the labor force in Japan are due to differences in the rates of growth of the various categories of work. Clerical workers were the fastest growing group in Japan over the 17 years from 1952 to 1969, when its compounded annual growth rate was 4.8 percent, but no longer over the 9 years from 1960 to 1969, when its annual growth rate was down to 4.5 percent and the category of managers and officials had reached a growth rate of 5.3 percent. Over these two periods the total labor force increased only by 1.8 percent and 1.3 percent, respectively.

10. The Outlook for the Future

Projections into the future can be misleading. Many economists expect that the knowledge industries will for some years continue to grow faster than the economy as a whole. Some are convinced that many of those alive today may in their lifetime see society devote more than 50 percent of its total measured economic activity to the production of knowledge. Among the branches of knowledge industries that social reformers wish to grow especially fast is education.

At least three reasons have been given to support the view that the growth of the production of knowledge will continue for some time at a rate faster than that of the economy as a whole. Firstly, knowledge production increases productivity; individuals, business firms, and governments recognize it as an investment yielding a high rate of return. Secondly, partly as a result of these investments, technology changes from processes using much physical labor to processes using more mental labor; thus knowledge is an increasingly productive intermediate product in many industries, and productivity increases most rapidly where the ratio of what Adam Smith and Karl Marx used to call "productive labor" declines relative to what they called "unproductive labor." Thirdly, the demand for knowledge as a consumer good, for entertainment or for the enrichment of our lives, has been increasing at a fast rate; this demand may continue to rise more than proportionally with the consumers' incomes.

At the same time there will be a steady increase in the educational levels attained by the people. This permits a constant upgrading in the occupational composition of the labor force. With both the supply of knowledge input and the demand for knowledge output rising, the trend may continue for some time; one should not be surprised, however, if the proportion devoted to knowledge production levels off before long.

Bibliography

Machlup F 1962 *The Production and Distribution of Knowledge in the United States*. Princeton University Press, Princeton, New Jersey

Machlup F 1982 *Knowledge: Its Creation, Distribution, and Economic Significance*, Vol. 2: *The Branches of Learning*. Princeton University Press, Princeton, New Jersey

Machlup F, Kronwinkler T 1975 Workers who produce knowledge: Steady growth, 1900 to 1970. *Weltwirtschaftliches Arch.* 3: 752–59

Machlup F, Leeson K 1978–80 *Information Through the Printed Word: The Dissemination of Scholarly, Scientific, and Intellectual Knowledge*. Praeger, New York

Organisation for Economic Co-operation and Development 1981 *Information Activities, Electronics and Telecommunications Technologies: Impact on Employment, Growth, and Trade*. OECD, Paris

Porat U, Rubin M R 1977 *The Information Economy*. Office of Telecommunications, Washington, DC

Knowledge Utilization

W. Dunn, B. Holzner, and G. Zaltman

The study of knowledge utilization is concerned with understanding and improving the utilization of scientific and professional knowledge in settings of public policy and professional practice. The field itself is a product of the historic rise in reflective awareness of the importance of knowledge in contemporary societies and has been accompanied by the emergence of professional roles and practices for knowledge utilization in such fields as agriculture, mental health, and education (Cernada 1982, Lehming and Kane 1981). This article describes the major research traditions on which contemporary work draws and describes available conceptual frameworks, methodology, and practice.

1. The Research Traditions

The field of knowledge utilization has emerged from several different research traditions, including the history and philosophy of science (Laudan 1977) and the sociology of knowledge (Remmling 1967). There has been a call for a sociology of knowledge applications, a classic sociology of knowledge "turned upside down" (Holzner 1978). A convergent program has emerged in the psychology and economics of knowledge applications in the major efforts of Campbell (1977) and Machlup (1980, 1982).

Another origin of present perspectives is the research tradition of applied social science, as exemplified by the Bureau of Applied Social Research at Columbia University under Lazarsfeld. Late in his career Lazarsfeld turned explicitly to the study of the social and intellectual processes of knowledge application, culminating in his conceptualization of the "utilization cycle" (Lazarsfeld et al. 1975). An even earlier source stemmed from the work of Lewin in the style of "action research" (Marrow 1969), which became influential as one model for the interlinking of research and practical action.

Most empirical studies of knowledge utilization were not based on these conceptual perspectives. They tended to be practice-oriented investigations, often responsive to urgent administrative information needs. Investigators drew on conceptual resources from research on planned social change, marketing, and the communication of innovations. Much of this work has been oriented to the translation of social science knowledge into guidelines for the improvement of practice. There has been a lag in developing the needed empirical base for a better understanding of knowledge-use processes.

Since the early 1960s there has been a great increase in applied and practice-oriented studies of this kind. Glaser (1976) estimates that there are as many as 20,000 items in the research literature on knowledge use and planned change. This figure may well double by the mid-1980s. The field has its own scholarly journal, *Knowledge: Creation, Diffusion, Utilization*, established in 1979. Since the early 1970s many investigations were carried out in such domains as education, mental health, criminal justice, community development, information management, program evaluation, policy analysis (Glaser 1976, Weiss 1977, Rich 1981, Ciarlo 1981), and technology assessment.

Some of the more active centers of current research in North America are the Knowledge Transfer Institute at the American University, the Center for Research on Utilization of Scientific Knowledge at the University of Michigan, and the Program for the Study of Knowledge Use at the University of Pittsburgh. Major research programs on knowledge utilization have been sponsored by several national and international agencies, including the Mental Health Services Branch of the National Institute of Mental Health, the Research and Educational Practices Unit of the National Institute of Education, and the Organisation for Economic Co-operation and Development.

2. Conceptual Frameworks

A prominent metaphor for knowledge utilization as a cognitive process is the image of the "two cultures" drawn from Snow's *The Two Cultures and the Scientific Revolution* (1959) and his recommendations for bridging the gap. This notion of "gaps" has brought forth ideas about bridging them, as in the new roles of "linkers" (Havelock 1969), "translators" (Lazarsfeld et al. 1975), and "brokers" (Sundquist 1978). It also focuses attention on knowledge transformations, as in Lazarsfeld's idea of the gap between the formulation of a practical problem and the structure of a research problem, or the gap between research findings and policy recommendations.

A methodological and conceptual review of the extant literature on knowledge utilization with a focus on education (Dunn and Holzner 1982) concludes that the following four propositions provide an integrative framework:

(a) Knowledge use is interpretive. This means that potentially transferable knowledge products, whether research based or experiential, do not "speak for themselves." They are, rather, interpreted by the various stake holders in terms of their own frames of reference.

(b) Knowledge use is socially constrained. The interpretive processes of knowledge utilization themselves are located in social structure and are constrained by role responsibilities, networks, and other institutional arrangements and the "situated rationalities" they engender.

(c) Knowledge use is systemic. Problems of knowledge utilization are rarely decomposable into discrete parts, since knowledge utilization involves typically a whole system of problems in the production, organization, storage, retrieval, transfer, and utilization of knowledge (Holzner and Marx 1979).

(d) Knowledge use is transactive. Knowledge cannot really be said to be "exchanged," "marketed," or "transferred"—terms which suggest a one-directional process of moving discrete pieces of information among parties who share an a priori common definition of what constitutes "knowledge." On the contrary, knowledge is in fact transacted among parties engaged in symbolic or communicative acts of negotiating the adequacy, relevance, and cogency of knowledge claims (Dunn 1982).

Given this framework, an array of conceptual tools for the analysis of knowledge utilization becomes necessary (Holzner and Salmon-Cox 1982). These concepts permit the analysis of social knowledge systems, of the construction of knowledge and practice, and the identification of strategic foci in the analysis of knowledge utilization processes.

Knowledge-related activities are differentially distributed in society and often occur in highly specialized social frameworks (Gurvitch 1972). As the economist Machlup (1962, 1963, 1969) has shown, it is fruitful to view a society from the point of view of the structured distribution of knowledge-related activity. This aspect of a social system is called the social-knowledge system. It encompasses a complex array of institutions and organizations as well as social roles and positions. The social structure of knowledge systems is in complex ways related to the creation and use of knowledge, but it is also limited to a society's moral culture and sense of identity (Robertson and Holzner 1980). Processes of knowledge creation and utilization now can be seen in their interdependence. It should be emphasized that such interdependence is not always beneficial—as illustrated by the vigorous utilization of Lysenko's "findings" by the Communist Party of the Soviet Union and the resulting constraints for Soviet biology at the time.

The diffuse (that is, nonspecialized) knowledge systems of simple societies have long since been replaced in the advanced industrial countries by highly specialized and often formally institutionalized structures. In complex modern knowledge systems, the scientific community and the science-based professions, while they constitute the core, do not exhaust the system (Mendelsohn et al. 1977, Knorr et al. 1980, Elias et al. 1982, Mendelsohn and Elkana 1981, Agassi 1981, Merton 1968, 1973).

Knowledge systems can be analyzed in terms of knowledge functions, institutional domains, and frameworks for knowledge, as well as in terms of the centrality or peripherality of system components or "regions." The major knowledge functions can be described under the following five headings:

(a) producing knowledge, for example, in scientific research and scholarship;

(b) organizing and structuring knowledge as in the construction of theories, but also of texts, curricula, and the like;

(c) distributing knowledge, for example, through journals or through linkage agents;

(d) storing knowledge in archives as well as in the memory of individuals and collectivities; and

(e) using knowledge, with varying kinds of feedback relations to any of the other functions.

The analytical distinctiveness but empirical interpenetration of activities and structures serving these functions is emphasized in the third section of this article.

Major institutional domains, such as agriculture, education, medicine, or other domains of public policy may evolve into specialized social knowledge systems of their own. The established professions are good examples of this (Freidson 1970).

Finally, the distinction between center and periphery (Shils 1975) points to the fact that these systems are not only differentiated, but also ordered along a dimension of higher and lower degrees of prestige, influence, and, in some instances, formal authority. Further, the regions of the knowledge system are variously limited or peripheral to the center of political power.

The knowledge system constitutes a society's most important resource for a collective learning capacity. Societies, like individuals, live in a reality which is often harsh and dangerous, but they can only come to terms with their realities by what they learn about them, that is with the manner in which they socially construct what is taken to be real.

This raises the question of the definition of knowledge. It is undeniably true that different societies, regions within one knowledge system, and different historical epochs exhibit vast differences in what is taken to be valid knowledge. Is the student of knowledge utilization therefore to conclude that "knowledge" is whatever is socially taken to be knowledge? The answer is no. There needs to be a critical assessment of knowledge. Throughout history there has been a quest for valid knowledge, recently vastly accelerated. Such validity was at times established on the basis of traditional authority, or religious revelation, or the dictates of conscience, or rationally guided empirical inquiry, or formal, logical, or mathematical calculation, or in still other ways. It is quite clear that not all such modes of validation of knowledge claims are of equal merit. Indeed, we are living in the context of an historical process striving for ever more "adequate" knowledge claims.

Yet there is not now and will never be a single algorithm for the determination of ultimate knowledge. This position, which is that of a constructivist and evolutionary epistemology, accentuates the importance of certain conceptual tools for the analysis of processes within and across regions of the knowledge system.

They are the concepts' frame of reference, reality tests, theories-in-use, and situated rationality.

A frame of reference is the structure of assumptions and implicit or explicit decision rules in inquiry which provides the framework for the construction of meanings. It provides a perspective that focuses attention, but it also sets boundaries for what is to be considered the field of relevant information (Holzner et al. 1977, Weiss and Bucuvalas 1980, Holzner et al. 1976).

Reality tests are important components of frames of reference. In knowledge-use studies and practice, it is of crucial importance to discover empirically in what ways knowledge claims are scrutinized and on what grounds they are accepted or rejected.

The concept of theories-in-use will be dealt with especially in the section on knowledge-utilization practice. It refers to the working theories of practitioners that, embedded in their frames of reference, actually guide their actions. The surfacing of these often tacit theories and their formalization and critique is an important tool in knowledge-utilization practice.

Situated rationality refers to the fact that actors often attempt to proceed rationally within their frames of reference, even as they are tied into situations which pose for them certain more or less inescapable predicaments.

3. Methodology

Empirical research on knowledge utilization has been variously criticized by the research community itself (Weiss 1977, Dunn 1983a, Dunn and Holzner 1982). This section of this article is primarily a description of the methodology employed in a large sample of knowledge-utilization studies scrutinized in a multiyear project supported by the United States National Institute of Education (Dunn and Holzner 1982, Dunn 1983a, 1983b).

A key decision in knowledge-utilization research is the selection of an appropriate unit of analysis. In studying the impact of knowledge use on collective decisions it is often essential to obtain data about a respondent's relationship with other individuals. Aggregations of individual responses may provide an inaccurate or actually misleading picture. However, in the actual set of empirical studies almost all dealt with individuals as units of analysis. For example, questionnaires are often used to assess the concerns of individual users and nonusers about the implementation of particular educational innovations.

Available studies reflect a diversity of research designs ranging from case studies and cross-sectional analyses to quasi-experiments conducted in representative contexts of practice. Some case studies are based on prior theory, while others are not. A few knowledge-use studies are based on quasi-experimental designs, including real-time field experiments where research-based ideas, suggestions, or recommendations are actively introduced into practice settings. Cross-sectional or longitudinal studies exploring factors affecting the utilization of research include research on the sources of information used by congressional staff members and studies of the uses of social science research by federal, state, and local policy makers.

The prevailing method for obtaining data in knowledge-use studies is the self-administered questionnaire. The use of content analysis, naturalistic observation, and interview schedules is relatively rare, while few studies are qualitative in the specific sense that they seek to capture the underlying contextual meanings attached to knowledge and its uses. Knowledge-use studies, while they can be based heavily on the use of questionnaires whose reliability may be readily assessed, are frequently based on procedures with unknown or unreported reliability and validity. Given that knowledge-use studies are intimately related to the assessment of cognitive (subjective) properties of many kinds, the absence of information about the reliability of procedures and the validity of constructs represents a serious unresolved problem of most research in the field.

A central problem of knowledge-use studies is defining what is meant by use. The most widely used definition in the field is one that distinguishes between conceptual and instrumental uses of knowledge (Rich 1975, Caplan et al. 1975, Weiss 1977). Generally, conceptual use refers to changes in the way the users think about problems, while instrumental use refers to changes in behavior, especially changes that are relevant to decision making. While many unresolved difficulties continue to plague this two-fold distinction (Dunn 1983a), many knowledge-use studies continue to employ it. Instrumental use, for example, tends to imply that respondents are single decision makers, notwithstanding the collective or systemic nature of organizational decision making. Given these and related difficulties it is striking that most studies define use in primarily instrumental terms, with the remainder stressing uses that are conceptual (Weiss and Bucuvalas 1980), symbolic, or affective (Anderson et al. 1981).

Available research yields little consistent empirical support for claims that particular classes of factors — economic, political, social, organizational, behavioral, attitudinal—affect the creation, diffusion, and utilization of knowledge in decisive and practically significant ways. There are many reasons for the inconsistency or instability of research findings, many of which stem from conceptual and methodological problems documented by Downs and Mohr (1976), Weiss (1977), Berman (1981), Miles (1981), Larsen (1981), Dunn and Holzner (1982), and Huberman and Miles (1982). The most important of these problems are reviewed below.

3.1 The Problem of Criteria

In terms of what criteria should knowledge use be defined? Answers to this basic question assume a variety of forms. Knowledge use may be viewed as principally conceptual, defined and measured in terms of mental processes of various kinds, and it may be represented and measured in terms of overt behavior. The distinction between conceptual and instrumental use, while it provided an initial focus for early studies, conceals a number of important dimensions according to which knowledge and its uses may be classified and measured. Instrumentally focused definitions of use, for example, generally neglect properties related to the expected benefits, purposes, and underlying assumptions of knowledge and its uses. Even those studies based on a conceptual definition of use often focus on surface properties of knowledge, taking for granted the meaning of knowledge, research, or information.

3.2 The Multiattribute Problem

Why does knowledge vary in perceived relevance, adequacy, and cogency? This question calls attention to the fundamentally interpretive character of processes of knowledge use. Processes of knowledge use are structured by the ways that policy makers, practitioners, and social scientists anticipate or predict events, such anticipation being a function of collective and individual reference frames and of the coordinative social contexts in which they are established, maintained, and changed. The specification of these subjectively meaningful contexts is frequently a product of the meanings of researchers, and not of those to whom such categories are applied. What is needed are procedures for identifying criteria actually employed to assess knowledge, as distinguished from criteria that are imposed on research contexts by investigators.

3.3 The Transactional Problem

How can knowledge transactions be conceptualized and measured? Research on individual frames of reference, while important for mapping the meanings surrounding processes of knowledge use, does not necessarily deal with the distribution of various reality tests or with changes in the structure of individual and collective frames of reference over time. A recognition of the contextual, relational, and generative properties of knowledge use has prompted many researchers to discard the terms interaction, exchange and transfer, replacing these with the concept of transaction. While research on communication networks recognizes the importance of distinguishing contextual and referential meanings (Rogers and Kincaid 1981), it has been difficult to preserve subjectively meaningful dimensions of knowledge transactions.

4. Knowledge Practice

Practice refers to processes whereby data are given meanings that pass certain reality tests and are incorporated into a frame of reference, consequently reinforcing or changing existing beliefs and/or behaviors. For example, at an individual level a set of research results may be interpreted as supporting court-mandated school busing. Reality tests applied by the individual may certify this meaning as being both socially and technically valid. This may reinforce the individual's assumptions and decision rules about the merits of court-ordered school busing. Such reinforcement may be expressed through more vigorous social actions on the part of the individual whose sociopolitical beliefs have now been heightened.

4.1 Knowledge Application in Relation to Production and Dissemination

Traditionally social processes related to knowledge production have been studied relatively independently of the social processes of dissemination and knowledge application. More recent thinking is taking a somewhat different perspective (Zaltman 1983). This perspective suggests that knowledge production, dissemination, and application are interactive in nature or, more accurately, that they are not separable constructs. Knowledge production occurs during application and dissemination. Similarly knowledge dissemination may occur during its production and application. To borrow a metaphor from statistics, rather than focusing on so-called "main" effects it may be more helpful to concentrate on so-called "interaction" effects. A kind of dialectic may also characterize the three processes. That is, while substantial pressures encourage the production of knowledge, equally powerful, though less well-understood, pressures "forbid" the production and dissemination of knowledge, keeping significant social events "hidden" and hence difficult to study or inform others about (Nelkin 1982, Westrum 1982, Peters and Ceci 1982). Also, while there is significant motivation to apply knowledge there are equally significant and prevalent motivations to prevent knowledge application or to even disavow the presence of knowledge. Thus, while it is conceptually convenient to separate the different knowledge functions, it is also necessary to remember that they comingle to the degree that one process may contain the others.

4.2 Theories-in-use and Frames of Reference

The assumptions, expectations, and decision rules which constitute frames of reference set the context for ideas guiding action. Such sets of ideas represent theories which individuals as well as complex social units such as government bureaucracies use in dealing with their internal and external environments. These causal maps or theories have been labelled theories-in-use (Argyris and Schön 1974). This concept has developed in the context of knowledge applications (Zaltman 1979, 1983).

Research findings concerning the impact of theories-in-use on knowledge practice include the well-documented finding that knowledge developed without consideration of theories-in-use among practitioners is unlikely to pass their reality tests (Rogers and Shoemaker 1971). Research about the value of prevention in mental health, if conducted with an understanding of the dominant curative orientation of mental health practitioners, is more likely to be accepted than the same research ideas developed without this sensitivity to practitioner theories-in-use. Moreover, when practitioners are actively involved in the development of knowledge as reverse consultants the resulting research is generally judged by all parties to be of higher technical quality and greater relevance to practice. Finally, the more that practitioners share researcher frames of reference about the conduct of research, the more likely that research will be accepted independently of the researcher's sensitivity to practitioner concerns. Thus, shared frames of reference with respect to knowledge-production issues affect knowledge applications.

The more consonant a set of research findings are with practitioners' theories-in-use the more likely their acceptance and application. The more divergent these findings are the more likely they are to be rejected or to be adapted in a way the originators of the research would themselves reject. These processes of knowledge rejection and knowledge adaptation have received considerable attention. They pertain not only to practitioners' behaviors but to the behaviors of agents active in knowledge production and dissemination systems. Knowledge which is perceived as surprising—as contrary to expectations—is likely to be rejected even if the surprise is in a positive direction. Frames of reference establish a kind of intellectual and social "comfort zone" and an item of information whose meaning could cause an agency to operate outside this comfort zone will tend to be rejected. This is partially described by the notion of group think (Boje and Murningham 1982). Group dynamics often present evidence which runs contrary to an existing or emerging consensus. Individuals and groups will often stop short of the point in their information-acquisition activities at which they might encounter information falling outside their comfort zones and which might require a major alteration in their theories-in-use. This is reflected by the term "half-knowledge" (Lazarsfeld cited in Marin 1981): enough is known about a situation that the organization realizes that there is a possibility that if more were known a difficult decision or action may be required. The notion of hidden events is also relevant here (Westrum 1982). A hidden event is a social phenomenon whose existence is either seriously doubted or simply not known about at all. Events may be hidden for several reasons: fear of ridicule keeps individuals from reporting phenomena and hence multiple experiences of the event go uncorrelated; arrogance with respect to evidence, for example, "If it existed I'd know about it"; misclassification (Greaves 1980); the absence of and/or the inability of accepted methodology to study the event (Charman 1979); restricted or "forbidden" access to information collection and application opportunities (Nelkin 1982); and so forth.

The meanings assigned to data by those who originate or create them may not be congruent with the meanings assigned or developed by those who disseminate and apply the data. More precisely, the meanings which are enacted by users of a research report may be at substantial variance with the meanings disseminators felt they were conveying. Moreover, both disseminators and users may have interpretations which are not shared by knowledge producers. Data are assimilated into frames of reference in ways which are biased toward reinforcing existing theories-in-use (Ross and Lepper 1980, Nisbett and Ross 1980). These tendencies have been observed not only at the level of the individual but among informal groups and formal organizations as well. The mechanisms whereby this occurs cannot be treated here. The important point is that a given set of statistics or a given verbal reporting of an event can give rise to very different "productions" of knowledge. These productions may be so divergent that the stake-holder group originating the data, when observing practitioners' behaviors based on the latter group's assigned meaning of these data, would conclude that a very different set of data were being acted upon. Of course practitioners often do agree with meanings assigned by producers and disseminators. However, the social realities of the context of application might require giving greater or lesser emphasis to certain concepts or sets and omitting some concepts altogether while adding yet others. In effect, a somewhat different theory is required and hence developed even if unwittingly by practitioners as a result of the realities of the implementation context.

4.3 Planned Social Change

A second major approach for viewing knowledge-use practices utilizes planned social-change concepts (Havelock 1969, Zaltman 1979, Rich and Zaltman 1978, Rothman 1980, Cernada 1982, Glaser 1981). This approach argues that new information may result in new social constructions or interpretations which are innovations. These innovations may exist only as ideas or as practices and products. If these innovations pass the reality tests applied by key stake holders and are adopted they may result in changes in the structure and functioning of social systems. Thus the application of knowledge may result in social change.

If knowledge "products" can be regarded as innovations resulting in social change then strategies for promoting product innovations such as medical drugs, solar energy technology, and instructional tools might be usefully applied to achieve more complete dissemination and use of other types of innovations such as scientific research intended for use by research scientists or practice innovations intended for other practitioners (Fine 1981, Larsen 1981, 1982). This is consistent with the view of knowledge practice as transactional and knowledge as a social construct. That is, the field of planned social change considers the diffusion of innovations as exchange processes between different communities which may have different frames of reference. Thus

there is an emphasis on researcher understanding of the needs and requirements of potential users prior to the production of knowledge and in the design of knowledge products. The communication behaviors of potential users as well as their adoption decision processes are considered in the design of dissemination strategies. The role of linking agents (Havelock et al. 1973) and linking systems (Holzner and Salmon-Cox 1982) become central concepts when knowledge use is viewed as planned social change. Moreover, formal management information systems assume greater prominence as user-initiated linking systems within this view of knowledge applications.

4.4 Conclusions

As a field of inquiry and professional practice, knowledge use is a distinctively modern enterprise. Until recently the field has not been consciously shaped by theory and research in the sociology, economics, and psychology of knowledge applications or, more broadly, by a basic interdisciplinary social science that seeks to examine the practical consequences of applying scientific and professional knowledge. Instead, the field of knowledge use has been mainly oriented towards the translation of social science knowledge into guidelines for the improvement of practice. While this applied research orientation has created greater sensitivity to the costs and benefits of the social sciences, this same orientation has contributed less to the resolution of basic theoretical, conceptual, and methodological issues. A basic social science of knowledge utilization still needs to be constructed.

Bibliography

Agassi J 1981 *Science and Society: Studies in the Sociology of Science.* Reidel, Dordrecht
Anderson C, Ciarlo J A, Brodie S 1981 Measuring evaluation: Induced change in mental health programs. In: Ciarlo J A (ed.) 1981 pp. 97–123
Argyris C, Schön D 1974 *Theory in Practice: Increasing Professional Effectiveness.* Jossey-Bass, San Francisco, California
Berman P 1981 Educational change: An implementation paradigm. In: Lehming M, Kane M T (eds.) 1981 pp. 253–86
Boje C, Murningham C 1982 Group confidence pressures in interactive decisions. *Manage. Sci.* 28(10): 1187–96
Campbell D T 1977 *Descriptive Epistemology: Psychological, Sociological and Evolutionary.* Preliminary Draft of the William James Lectures. Harvard University, Cambridge, Massachusetts
Caplan N S, Morrison A, Stambaugh R J 1975 *The Use of Social Science Knowledge in Policy Decisions at the National Level: A Report to Respondents.* University of Michigan Institute for Social Research, Ann Arbor, Michigan
Cernada G P 1982 *Knowledge into Action: A Guide to Research Utilization.* Baywood, Farmingdale, New York
Charman W N 1979 Ball lightening. *Physics Reports* 54: 261–306
Ciarlo J A (ed.) 1981 *Utilizing Evaluation: Concepts and Measurement Techniques.* Sage, Beverly Hills, California

Downs C W, Mohr L B 1976 Conceptual issues in the study of innovation. *Admin. Sci. Q.* 21: 700–13

Dunn W N 1980 The two-communities metaphor and models of knowledge use: An exploratory case survey. *Knowledge: Creation, Diffusion, Utilization* 1(4): 515–36

Dunn W N 1981 If knowledge utilization is the problem, what is the solution? Working Paper KU-109. Program for the Study of Knowledge Use, University of Pittsburgh, Pittsburgh, Pennsylvania

Dunn W N 1982 Reforms as arguments. *Knowledge: Creation, Diffusion, Utilization* 3(3): 293–326

Dunn W N 1983a Measuring knowledge use. *Knowledge: Creation, Diffusion, Utilization* 1(5): 120–33

Dunn W N 1983b Qualitative methodology. *Knowledge, Creation, Diffusion, Utilization* 4(4): 590–97

Dunn W N, Holzner B 1982 *Methodological Research on Knowledge Use and School Improvement.* Final Report. US Department of Education, Washington, DC

Elias N, Martins H, Whitley R (eds.) 1982 *Scientific Establishments and Hierarchies.* Sociology of the Sciences Yearbook, Vol. 6. Reidel, Dordrecht

Fine S H 1981 *The Marketing of Ideas and Social Issues.* Praeger, New York

Freidson E 1970 *Profession of Medicine: A Study of the Sociology of Applied Knowledge.* Dodd, Meade, New York

Glaser E 1976 *Putting Knowledge to Use: A Distillation of the Literature Regarding Knowledge Transfer and Change.* Human Interaction Research Institute, National Institutes for Mental Health, Los Angeles, California

Glaser E 1981 Knowledge transfer strategies. Paper presented at Conference on Knowledge Use. University of Pittsburgh, Pittsburgh, Pennsylvania

Greaves G B 1980 Multiple personality, 165 years after Mary Reynolds. *J. Nervous and Ment. Disease* 168: 577–96

Gurvitch G 1972 *The Social Frameworks of Knowledge.* Harper and Row, New York

Havelock R G 1969 *Planning for Innovation Through Dissemination and Utilization of Knowledge.* Center for Research on Utilization of Scientific Knowledge, University of Michigan, Ann Arbor, Michigan

Havelock R G, Havelock M C, Markowitz E A 1973 *Educational Innovation in the US,* Vol. 1: *The National Survey: The Substance and the Process.* Center for Research on Utilization of Scientific Knowledge, University of Michigan, Ann Arbor, Michigan

Holzner B 1978 The sociology of applied knowledge. *Sociol. Symposium* 21: 8–19

Holzner B, Marx J 1979 *Knowledge Application: The Knowledge System in Society.* Allyn and Bacon, Boston, Massachusetts

Holzner B, Salmon-Cox L 1982 Knowledge systems and the role of knowledge synthesis in linkages for knowledge use. In: Beal G M, Dissayankae W, Konoshima S (eds.) 1982 *Knowledge Generation, Exchange and Utilization.* East-West Center, University of Hawaii, Honolulu, Hawaii

Holzner B, Fisher E, Marx J 1977 Paul Lazarsfeld and the study of knowledge applications. *Sociol. Focus* 10(2): 97–116

Holzner B, Mitroff I, Fisher E 1976 An empirical investigation of frames of reference, case studies in the sociology of knowledge. Unpublished working paper. University of Pittsburgh, Pittsburgh, Pennsylvania

Huberman M, Miles M 1982 Drawing valid meaning from qualitative data: Some techniques of data reduction and display. Paper prepared for a symposium on Advances in the Analysis of Qualitative Data. Annual Meeting of the American Educational Research Association, New York, March 1982. American Educational Research Association, Washington, DC

Knorr K D, Krohn R, Whitley R (eds.) 1980 *The Social Process of Scientific Investigation.* Sociology of the Sciences Yearbook. Reidel, Dordrecht

Larsen J 1981 Knowledge utilization: Current issues. In: Rich R F (ed.) 1981 *The Knowledge Cycle.* Sage, Beverly Hills, California

Larsen J 1982 *Information Utilization and Nonutilization.* American Institutes for Research in the Behavioral Sciences, Washington, DC

Laudan L 1977 *Progress and Its Problems: Toward a Theory of Scientific Growth.* University of California Press, Berkeley, California

Lazarsfeld P, Reitz J, Weiss C 1975 *An Introduction to Applied Sociology.* Elsevier, New York

Lehming R, Kane M (eds.) 1981 *Improving Schools: Using What We Know.* Sage, Beverly Hills, California

Machlup F 1962 *The Production and Distribution of Knowledge in the United States.* Princeton University Press, Princeton, New Jersey

Machlup F 1963 *Essays on Economic Semantics.* Prentice-Hall, Englewood Cliffs, New Jersey

Machlup F 1969 If matter could talk. In: Morgenbesser S, Suppes P, White M (eds.) 1969 *Philosophy, Science and Method: Essays in Honor of Ernest Nagel.* St. Martin's Press, New York, pp. 286–305

Machlup F 1980 *Knowledge: Its Creation, Distribution, and Economic Significance,* Vol. 1: *Knowledge and Knowledge Production.* Princeton University Press, Princeton, New Jersey

Machlup F 1982 *Knowledge: Its Creation, Distribution, and Economic Significance,* Vol. 2: *The Branches of Learning.* Princeton University Press, Princeton, New Jersey

Marin B 1981 *Knowledge: Creation, Diffusion, Utilization.* Sage, Beverly Hills, California

Marrow A J 1969 *The Practical Theorist: The Life and Work of Kurt Lewin.* Basic Books, New York

Mendelsohn E, Elkhana Y (eds.) 1981 *Sciences and Cultures: Anthropological and Historical Studies of the Sciences.* Reidel, Dordrecht

Mendelsohn E, Weingart P, Whitley R (eds.) 1977 *The Social Production of Scientific Knowledge.* Reidel, Dordrecht

Merton R K 1968 *Social Theory and Social Structure.* Free Press, New York

Merton R K 1973 *The Sociology of Science: Theoretical and Empirical Investigations.* University of Chicago Press, Chicago, Illinois

Miles M B 1981 Mapping the common properties of schools. In: Lehming R (ed.) 1981 *What We Know.* Sage, Beverly Hills, California, pp. 42–114

National Institute of Education 1973 *Building Capacity for Renewal and Reform.* National Institute of Education, Washington, DC

Nelkin D 1982 Forbidden research: Limits to inquiry in the social sciences. In: Beecham T L, Faden R (eds.) 1982 *Ethical Issues in Social Science Research.* Johns Hopkins University Press, Baltimore, Maryland

Nisbett R E, Ross L 1980 *Human Inference: Strategies and Shortcomings of Social Judgment.* Prentice-Hall, Englewood Cliffs, New Jersey

Peters D P, Ceci S J 1982 Peer review practices of psychological journals: The fate of published articles submitted again. *Behav. and Brain Sci.* 5: 187–95

Remmling G W 1967 *Road to Suspicion: A Study of Modern Mentality and the Sociology of Knowledge.* Appleton-Century-Crofts, New York

Rich R F 1975 Selective utilization of social science related information by federal policymakers. *Inquiry* 13(3): 239–45

Rich R F 1981 *Social Science Information and Public Policymaking: The Interaction Between Bureaucratic Politics and the Use of Survey Data.* Jossey-Bass, San Francisco, California

Rich F, Zaltman G 1978 Toward a theory of planned social change: Alternative perspectives and ideas. *Evaluation* (Special issue)

Robertson R, Holzner B (eds.) 1980 *Identity and Authority: Explorations in the Theory of Society.* St. Martin's Press, New York

Rogers E M, Kincaid D L 1981 *Communication Networks: Toward a New Paradigm for Research.* Free Press, New York

Rogers E M, Shoemaker F F 1971 *The Communication of Innovation: A Cross-cultural Approach*, 2nd edn. Free Press, New York

Ross L, Lepper M 1980 The perseverance of beliefs: Empirical and normative conclusions. *New Directions for Methodology of Social and Behavioral Sciences* 4: 17

Rothman J 1980 *Using Research in Organizations: A Guide to Successful Application.* Sage, Beverly Hills, California

Shils E A 1975 *Center and Periphery: Essays in Macrosociology.* University of Chicago Press, Chicago, Illinois

Snow C P 1959 *The Two Cultures and the Scientific Revolution.* Cambridge University Press, New York

Sundquist J 1978 Research brokerage: The weak link. In: Lynn L (ed.) 1978 *Knowledge and Policy: The Uncertain Connection.* National Academy of Science, Washington, DC, pp. 126–44

Weiss C H (ed.) 1977 *Using Social Research in Public Policy Making.* Heath, Lexington, Massachusetts

Weiss C H, Bucuvalas M 1980 Truth-tests and utility tests: Decision makers' frames of reference for social science. *Am. Sociol. Rev.* 45(2): 302–12

Westrum R 1982 Social intelligence about hidden events. *Knowledge: Creation, Diffusion, Utilization* 3(3): 381

Zaltman G 1979 Knowledge utilization as planned social change. *Knowledge: Creation, Diffusion, Utilization* 1(1): 82–105

Zaltman G 1983 Theory-in-use among change agents. In: Seidman E (ed.) 1983 *Handbook of Social and Community Intervention.* Sage, Beverly Hills, California, pp. 289–312

Knowledge Diffusion in Education

J. P. Keeves

This article is concerned with the transmission of knowledge about education from those who are involved in research and development to those who must employ that knowledge in their daily work. Just as knowledge in many fields of human endeavour has increased greatly, so too, in education as a consequence of the very significant growth in expenditure on research and development since the early 1960s, has there been a substantial increase in the knowledge about the educational processes for diffusion or dissemination to all those who have use for such knowledge. However, as Huberman and his colleagues have pointed out (Huberman et al. 1981), it is evident that the dissemination of knowledge in education is far more complex and far less manageable than in other fields which would superficially appear similar, such as agriculture or public health.

Related to the increase in knowledge in education and in other fields, there has been widespread recognition of a need for research and investigation into the processes of transmission of knowledge. While diffusion research is emerging as an area of study which is attracting research workers from several disciplines in an attempt to form a single integrated body of concepts and generalizations about the diffusion process, it is important to recognize that the overall area is still very fragmented because of the wide range of disparate elements associated with the creation and utilization of knowledge in different fields of endeavour. One important source of this fragmentation is associated with the different disci-

plinary perspectives from which the knowledge under consideration has been created. Rogers and Shoemaker (1971) classified the 2,750 items in their diffusion bibliography in seven major and seven minor disciplinary traditions, but they noted that a transfer of ideas was taking place across disciplines in many of the studies under survey. From this review Rogers and Shoemaker were able to revise previous work on the identification of factors which affected the rate of adoption of an innovation. They noted that adoption was not the only outcome, since in reality rejection was also likely to occur; that evaluation of innovations took place either formally or informally at all stages; and that even after adoption had occurred, further evaluation might lead to subsequent rejection. In addition they noted four stages in the innovation–decision process which are as follows: (a) knowledge—the individual is exposed to the innovation's existence and gains some understanding of how it functions; (b) persuasion—the individual forms a favourable or unfavourable attitude towards the innovation; (c) decision—the individual engages in activities which lead to a decision to adopt or reject the innovation; and (d) confirmation—the individual seeks reinforcement for the innovation–decision which has been made, but a previous decision may be reversed if conflicting information about the innovation is received (Rogers and Shoemaker 1971 p. 103).

From research into the diffusion process there has started to emerge a conceptual paradigm related to the transmission of knowledge that is relevant to many disciplines. Since most social scientists, including educators, are interested in social change, the broad area of diffusion research offers a convenient framework within which to develop such understandings, because a general approach to diffusion has something to offer each discipline. It is necessary before examining the processes of transmission of knowledge in the field of education to consider first the particular characteristics of both the creation and utilization of knowledge in education and how these relate to the processes of diffusion.

1. Creation of Educational Knowledge

It is important to recognize that in the field of education, by and large, the body of knowledge that has the most profound influence on policy and practice is derived not from research or from scholarly analysis but from the accumulated wisdom of teachers and administrators working in schools and administrative units throughout the world. Systematic and cumulative research and development in education is a relatively recent phenomenon, commencing only during the twentieth century and only gaining sufficient strength to make a substantial contribution on a worldwide basis during the late 1960s and the 1970s. It has, however, been possible to document the impact of research and development on education through a series of case studies which establish beyond doubt the contribution that research has made during this century to educational policy and practice (Suppes 1978)

Educational research and development yield outcomes that are of three distinct types. Rich (1977), from a study of the use of social science information by administrators in the United States, found it of value to differentiate between the instrumental and the conceptual utilization of knowledge: between what he termed knowledge for action and knowledge for understanding. Likewise, Fullan (1980) has suggested that there are two main types of knowledge available for use. The first refers to knowledge that can be applied to a particular problem and is derived from a specific research study or from a collection of studies. The second refers to cumulative knowledge.

From these perspectives it can be seen that there is firstly knowledge together with the use of knowledge in the field of education, which has been derived from research and study in education, that is associated with principles, broad conceptions, and fundamental paradigms, and that provides a basis for an understanding of the educational process. It must be recognized that such knowledge which is largely of a theoretical nature, is nevertheless important, even if it does not appear to have any immediate application. Contrary to common belief, one of the major outcomes of the very substantial investment in educational research that has taken place since the early 1970s has been the gradual assembling of a considerable body of knowledge about schools and

how they function that is only now being built into a coherent conceptual framework.

Secondly, there are findings arising from educational research that have direct applications in educational policy and practice. Nevertheless, it is rare for an individual research study to yield findings that can be used alone to change either policy or practice. The complexity of most educational activities and of the settings in which such activities are carried out will restrict the applicability of the findings derived from a single investigation. However, if several similar studies have been undertaken in a variety of situations, there frequently emerges a more general finding that gains are to be made through the implementation of a new policy or practice.

A third and important type of outcome of educational research and development is the preparation of a tangible product that incorporates the findings of research and has a direct use in schools and classrooms. The marked increase in research and development that occurred in many parts of the world during the late 1960s and the 1970s resulted in the production of a number of educational materials for classroom use, each of which was derived from a particular body of research. The acceptance of these materials varied according to the quality of the research, the quality of the materials, and, in particular, the extent to which the ideas underlying the development of the materials were disseminated to the teachers using particular materials in their classrooms.

These three types of outcome of educational research and development, concerned with principle and paradigm, with policy and practice, and with products that have immediate and direct application in schools are different in kind. They are also associated with different types of utilization and with different approaches to diffusion and dissemination.

2. Utilization of Educational Research

As a consequence of the increased body of research-based knowledge in education it has become clearer how such knowledge might be used in the making of policies, the development of practice, and the introduction of tangible products. Weiss (1979) has identified seven ways of utilization of social science research, and all seven approaches would seem to apply in the field of education. What is envisaged is a classification of type of knowledge or product combined with an approach to utilization in the form of a two-way matrix with the three types of knowledge along one axis and the seven approaches to utilization along the other. While not all cells of this matrix will be associated with a specific application, this systemization of the creation of knowledge with the utilization of knowledge would appear to be an appropriate framework within which to consider in detail the mediating process of diffusion or transmission. Moreover, it would seem likely that certain models of the diffusion process will relate to either specific categories of creation of knowledge, or categories of utilization of knowledge, or possibly to a specific cell within the creation–utilization classificatory grid. The seven approaches to utilization of knowledge are considered below.

(a) *Knowledge-driven approach.* Underlying this approach is the view that basic research reveals some findings that have direct application in practice. While this approach would seem highly applicable in the fields of the natural and medical sciences, it is less relevant to education. However, the findings relating to the teaching of subtraction and division have influenced the methods of instruction used in schools in both the United Kingdom and the United States. They provide clear examples of how specific knowledge can be applied in the field of education.

(b) *Problem-solving approach.* In educational policy and practice, a commonly held view of research utilization envisages research as providing empirical evidence and conclusions to help to solve a particular policy problem. In this approach the problem exists and is identified and a decision has to be made to solve the problem, but information and understanding are lacking on how the problem might be solved. Under these circumstances it is appropriate to recognize that research could provide the missing knowledge and understanding.

(c) *Interactive approach.* In this approach neither the researcher involved in the creation of knowledge, nor the practitioner with a problem to be solved, work independently of the other. They interact with one another in a manner that involves both a search for knowledge as well as a solution to a problem. Sometimes the necessary knowledge is obtained through a search for and reconceptualization of findings already available and sometimes the need to obtain an appropriate solution leads to a substantial programme of research and development. The creation of new knowledge, however, is only one component of an interactive process that also involves the utilization of knowledge.

(d) *Enlightenment approach.* Probably the most common way in which knowledge derived from educational research is used for policy making or practice is through the cumulative effects from a substantial number of research studies each of which contributes to a change in thinking about certain educational questions. In this approach there is no assumption that decision makers or practitioners seek out research-based knowledge to assist them, but rather they are influenced by an enlightenment that has come to them as a result of the cumulative findings derived from research, often without an awareness of the origins of the knowledge.

(e) *Political approach.* Recognition that policy and practice are influenced by an accumulated body of research findings has led many educational policy makers and practitioners to resolve to make certain changes, and then to seek legitimation from research. This can occur through a search in the research literature to find support for the proposed change; a task that is not as difficult as would seem at first because of the often contradictory nature of the results of research studies in the same area. Alternatively, it can occur through the commissioning of research, particularly of an evaluative kind, to find evidence to legitimate a decision that has already been made but perhaps not been publicly or explicitly stated. Some of the research in recent years into open-plan schooling was of this kind.

(f) *Tactical approach.* Related to the political approach is a tactical approach where certain decisions which were made have subsequently come under challenge. In these circumstances it is a common ploy to commission research as a delaying action to enable the new policy or practice to become more thoroughly established. The implications of the findings of the research may have to be faced at a later stage.

(g) *Research-oriented approach.* Underlying this approach to the utilization of research-based knowledge is the view that the process of inquiry is of value in itself. It is assumed that if policy makers and practitioners are directly engaged in the research enterprise they will not only facilitate the utilization of research findings but they will also promote wider diffusion and acceptance of research-based knowledge. This approach emphasizes the unity of the three components of creation, diffusion, and utilization of knowledge rather than the distinctiveness of each component process. In part this is an underlying theme in action research and in the teachers as researchers or the teachers as evaluators movements that were advocated in the early twentieth century and which have gained acceptance once more in recent years.

3. The Diffusion Process

The theoretical framework that has helped to guide much of the thinking about the diffusion process in education, although of relatively recent development, has come to be called the "classical diffusion model". A detailed statement of this model is provided by Rogers and Shoemaker (1971). The four main elements of this model are: (a) an innovation defined as an idea perceived as new by an individual, (b) is communicated through certain channels, (c) over a sustained period of time, (d) among the members of a social system. This classical model in one form or another is still the most popular for the study of diffusion or for an understanding and use of the diffusion process. There are many other models that differ in their degree of comprehensiveness, such as the suggestion made by Hood (1973) that there are three models for the study of change in education: the organizational improvement model, the extension network model, and the research, development, and marketing model. However, the most extensive treatment of models of the diffusion process has been undertaken by Havelock and his colleagues and their models provide a sound basis for the consideration of the transmission or dissemination of knowledge in

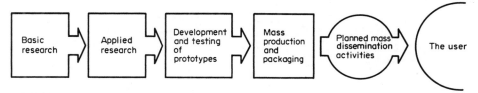

Figure 1
The research, development, and diffusion model

Source: Havelock R G 1971

education. In this article the models developed by Havelock will be described in some detail, because with these models it is possible to investigate the diffusion process in education in a coherent way. In addition, it is possible to consider the planning of a range of services for the transmission of knowledge in education in terms of various combinations of the Havelock models. It is also important to note the interrelations between the Havelock models and the various categories of knowledge creation and utilization considered in the previous sections of this article.

4. The Havelock Models

In the mid-1960s, Havelock undertook a major review of the literature in the diverse fields of medicine, agriculture, industrial technology, and education and, in 1970, a national survey of school districts in the United States, to learn what research workers and practitioners said about the processes of dissemination and utilization of knowledge from research. From the review he concluded that there were three existing perspectives or models which described the transmission of knowledge from the research centres to the user.

4.1 Research, Development, and Diffusion Model

In this model it was assumed that there was a rational and orderly sequence from basic research, to applied research, to the development and testing of a prototype, the preparation and packaging of a product, and the planned dissemination to the user (Havelock 1971). This model is presented diagrammatically in Fig. 1. In it, the user is seen to play a relatively passive role. While this model gained wide acceptance in the 1960s, experience would appear to indicate that it involves a gross over-simplification of the manner in which knowledge about education and the products of research actually spread. It should be noted that the model relates directly to one of the approaches to utilization of knowledge advanced by Weiss (1979).

4.2 Social Interaction Model

This second perspective is seen to apply widely in the spread of knowledge both in agriculture and in medicine. In this model individuals are seen as interacting with colleagues within a reference group or through membership of an association, and these colleagues

influence whether or not the individuals accept the research findings and the practices advocated, or adopt particular products. Informal personal contacts within the reference group provide the opportunity for the transmission of ideas. This model is portrayed in Fig. 2. Some educational innovations spread in this way, but the operation is dependent on the leaders of the reference groups and associations gaining access to the necessary information from research sources.

4.3 Problem-solving Model

A third approach, that is widely accepted as applying in education, is the problem-solving model. Again it relates to one of the categories of knowledge utilization advanced by Weiss (1979). In this model each user identifies a need, diagnoses a problem, undertakes a search for a solution, and tries possible alternative solutions to the problem. In education, this model would appear to be particularly applicable to the solving of organizational problems. Consultation with a research worker or person outside the system engaged in solving a problem is not necessarily part of the process, and when one is consulted it is customary for a nondirective or advisory role to be adopted. This approach involves an emphasis on a local initiative and the development of a local solution that in all probability would not apply in another setting. The nature of this problem-solving model is shown in Fig. 3.

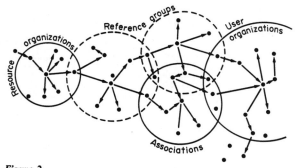

Figure 2
The social interaction model

Source: Havelock R G 1971

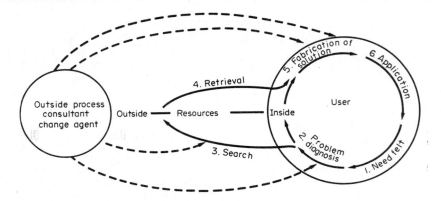

Figure 3
The problem-solver model

Source: Havelock R G 1971

4.4 Linkage Model

Subsequently, Havelock (1973) attempted to combine the best documented features of each of the previous models in order to account for a two-way flow of information between the source and the user. This led to the development of a fourth model, which is presented in simplified form in Fig. 4. The user and the resource system are involved in a reciprocal and collaborative interaction, and each reacts to assimilate the ideas that the other can provide. Thus there is a linkage established between the two systems and the model is known as the linkage model. An important component of the linkage model is the presence of a linkage medium, since direct face-to-face contact is rarely possible in educational work between the users and the resource system. It should be noted that the linkage model has three major components; the resource system, the linkage medium, and the user system. Within the user system are the schools, their teachers and students, the parents of the students, the regional and state education boards or authorities, and the administrative staff serving those

boards or authorities. The linkage medium comprises the linkage agents, linkage instruments, and linkage institutions. The linkage institutions include the colleges of education and teachers' colleges, curriculum centres, inservice education centres, teachers' centres and resource centres, and the regional offices or district offices as these institutions are variously called in different parts of the world. The linkage agents are, in the main, the persons who work within the linkage institutions, and include college lecturers, education officers, advisory officers, school district officers, supervisory and inspectorial officers, and curriculum consultants. The linkage instruments consist of published reports, journals, video programmes, pamphlets, and the like. All three components are used in one way or another for the two-way communication between the two systems. There remains the resource system which necessarily includes the research institutions, the universities, and their research centres, curriculum development centres, and other research and development centres. It is important to recognize that in the linkage model there is not

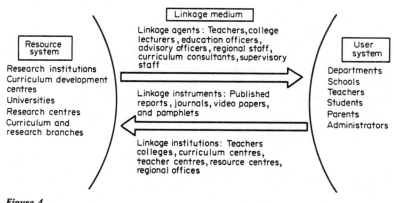

Figure 4
The linkage model

just a one-way transmission of information from the resource system to the user system. There is in addition a necessary transmission of information from the user system to the resource system. Without this communication of issues and needs for research and development, the resource system would be operating largely in a vacuum. Huberman et al. (1981) have examined the operation of the linkage model in terms of knowledge transfer theory and organizational theories. They have emphasized that very few real-world knowledge transfer situations involve only one resource system and only one user, and the linkage paradigm presented above must be enlarged to provide for these complexities. In addition they suggest that the term "network" must be employed to refer to relations among individuals, and the term "interorganizational arrangements" to refer to the more formal relations that must necessarily be established between organizations or institutions. Not only are networks and interorganizational arrangements built up among the members of a resource system and among the members of a user system, but they must also be built up between the user system, the linkage agents and linkage organizations, and between these agents and organizations and the resource system. Huberman et al. (1981) have begun to explore the nature of the transactions that occur between and within these systems.

4.5 A Study of the Linkage Model

Owen (1979) has carried out a significant study to investigate the applicability of the linkage model to the adoption and implementation of the Australian Science Education Project materials by Australian secondary schools. The research undertaken by Owen has found that elements of all three models: the research, development, and diffusion model; the problem-solving model; and the social interaction model operate in a complex way within the linkage model in a manner that is consistent with the perspective advanced by Havelock (1973). The contribution made by Owen has been not only to identify in the Australian setting the characteristics of the user system but also to investigate the dimensions of the linkage medium. The user system was viewed by Owen in terms of five characteristics: knowledge of research findings; openness to innovation and change; interaction with other users, and with the linkage medium; organization within the user unit, so that resources available are effectively displayed; and cooperation within the user unit, so that individual users share with each other experiences gained during the introduction of the innovation. In addition, Owen identified four linkage mechanisms which were associated with a high level of adoption and maintenance of an innovation. These were: participation within the research and development enterprise; contact with the charge agent; engagement in relevant teacher education programmes; and the examination of appropriate dissemination material. Adoption and effective utilization of innovative practices in the Australian setting appeared to require

not only possession of a high degree of several of the user characteristics, but also the effective operation of several of the linkage mechanisms. Possession of one characteristic alone by a user, or the operation of one mechanism alone within the linkage medium was not enough.

Owen did not investigate directly how the resource system could act most effectively in the diffusion and dissemination of its research findings and products. However, the account that he has provided of the way in which and the degree to which one innovation spread across Australia gives some picture of how a resource system should operate to ensure that maximum gains are made in the use of findings and products of educational research and development. Nevertheless, it is clear that a one-way flow from the resource system to the user system is not considered an appropriate or effective account of the processes of dissemination or diffusion of the products of research and development in education. Furthermore, the chance interactions within a social network or interorganizational arrangement as envisaged within the social interaction model, or the passive wait for the users to identify a need as envisaged in the problem-solving model are clearly not efficient approaches to the diffusion and utilization of knowledge in education. Nevertheless, there are situations operating in practice in which Owen and his colleagues have been able to show that one of the three component models is operating largely in isolation and without interplay with either of the other two models as is envisaged within the linkage model. Hence all four models are required to give a complete account of the real-world situation.

5. Approaches to Planned Diffusion

There is no single method or procedure which alone can be recommended to carry out the effective transmission of useful knowledge in education. Rather there would seem to be many approaches that should be used when and where they are considered appropriate. It is clearly necessary to identify different approaches and promote and develop their use in ways judged to be most effective. Nevertheless, it is important to recognize that not only should the resource system be planning to ensure that the maximum benefits flow from its research and development work, but the user system should also be planning to ensure that it receives maximum benefit from the research and development work that is carried out. This latter is accomplished both by ensuring that knowledge is disseminated in appropriate ways as well as by ensuring that the research being undertaken takes cognizance of the perceived needs of the users.

Thompson (1981) in an account of the programmes sponsored by the National Institute of Education in the United States, saw these dissemination programmes lying along a continuum from the Educational Resources Information Centre (ERIC) at one end to local problem-solving work at the other. This view of

Research, development, and diffusion orientation

— Programmes of publication

— Indexing and abstracting services

— Research and development information exchanges

— Research and development networks

— Research and development utilization centre

— School-based problem-solving programmes

Problem-solving orientation

Figure 5
The diffusion continuum

dissemination may be extended to suggest that most dissemination activities in education may be considered to lie along a similar continuum ranging from a research, development, and diffusion orientation at one end to an orientation towards problem solving at the school and classroom levels at the other. While this view is perhaps an oversimplified one, the two orientations do take cognizance of the perspectives of the resource system and the user system respectively. Thus to consider diffusion programmes and activities as lying along a continuum is helpful in ordering thinking about such programmes. This framework, the diffusion continuum, which is represented in Fig. 5, may be used to give a brief account of the major types of formal programmes or planned activities that are operating in the transmission of knowledge about education. It must be recognized that there are informal activities which occur as well to assist in the diffusion of knowledge. These are covered, in the main, by the social interaction model where it operates at an informal level. This model can, however, be used in a more deliberate way through the establishment of networks among individuals.

5.1 Programmes of Publication

Perhaps the most obvious form of dissemination of information is through planned programmes of publication in the form of books, research monographs, journals, microfiche documents, summary reports, and newsletters. The major problems encountered are associated with the need to write for different audiences. Reports providing full technical detail are necessary in order for an assessment to be made of the quality of the research, but such reports are largely incomprehensible

to practising teachers and administrators. On the other hand, summary reports can receive widespread publicity, but be based on poor quality work that is effectively concealed by skilful writing and lack of detail. It is important to note that while some of the costs of production of publications can be reduced through the increased use of technology in typesetting and preparation, the overall costs of printing and distribution might be expected to rise to such an extent that much important material may become lost or buried through lack of resources for publication.

5.2 Indexing and Abstracting Services

A second approach to dissemination is the systematic compilation of an index and the provision of an abstracting service in the field of education. In the late 1970s and early 1980s significant steps were taken through the introduction of new technology to improve both the quality of such services and their accessibility. Access can now be provided to indexing and abstracting services by means of computer-based systems across countries linked by satellite, through microfiche copies of reports, and through videographic procedures. It must be recognized, however, that such systems based on advanced technology are costly to install.

5.3 Research and Development Information Exchanges

Both the profusion and diffuseness of much of the reporting in the field of educational research makes it difficult for individual users to select directly from the publications available, or through an abstracting service, the more general ideas that could influence their thinking on specific issues, or that could assist with the solving of particular problems. However, there are increasing numbers of newsletters and similar publications which provide both summaries of research that is reported more fully elsewhere, as well as discussions of current problems and issues. At the present time the programmes and activities in this area and the information available are perhaps too far towards the research, development, and diffusion end of the continuum in Fig. 5. They do not present as fully information on the problems being encountered by schools that would be helpful to the research system in its thinking about research studies which might be planned and conducted. Moreover, there is a need for such exchanges to promote the widespread adoption of validated innovations as opposed to simply disseminating information from research or from the evaluation of particular programmes.

5.4 Research and Development Networks

The establishment of research and development networks is based on the assumption that the exchange of information can take place in ways other than those provided by printed documents. In the main, networks rely on social interaction between individuals, and operate at an informal level. The functions of the networks are: (a) to select, synthesize, and interpret the findings of educational research for practitioners in the schools and for policy makers, (b) to identify validated innovations and to spread information about such practices, (c) to provide information to consumers on products together with evidence of their effectiveness, (d) through discussion and debate to communicate the needs of practitioners and policy makers to research workers, and (e) to collect information on the experiences of practitioners and to add this information to the accumulated body of knowledge about education. In general, networks are loosely structured and rely on informal contacts and the social interaction between members of the network to achieve the goals set within the network, rather than through the adoption of clearly defined policies and programmes. It is, however, possible for change agents to be appointed to develop such networks and so to fulfil a mission to effect the widespread adoption of particular innovations or products rather than to merely supply information regarding new practices and policies.

5.5 *Research and Development Utilization Centres*

From the time of the setting up of the Schools Council in the United Kingdom in the mid-1960s there has been an increase in the establishment and growth of a range of centres and units, both in that country and more recently elsewhere, whose activities are directed towards: (a) the enhancement of problem-solving capabilities, (b) the supply of appropriate research and development resources, (c) the promotion of an awareness of the existence and nature of problems, and (d) the stimulation and motivation of personnel within schools and districts to meet the conditions necessary for change and innovation. In general, the centres which have been established are of two types, differing in the extent to which they focus on more specific but widely occurring problems, or on more general issues relating to the common problems of schools and teachers in an area. The former more specific problems are catered for in resource centres, which commonly provide services and facilities to assist with the resolution and treatment of particular problems. The latter more general problems are catered for in teachers' centres that have far greater flexibility of operation in order to meet the specific needs of the teachers and school administrators served by the centres. Since many of the centres that have been established are self-governing, there has been marked variation in their stated aims and the ways in which they function. As a consequence, the impression is often gained of an amorphous collection of small centres and units serving many different purposes. Nevertheless, since such centres are located more at the problem-solving end of the continuum presented in Fig. 5 than at the research, development, and diffusion end it is not surprising that such differences in purpose and function should appear since, in the main, these research and development utilization centres have been set up to help solve the problems of a specific group of educational

practitioners, rather than to fulfil a highly specified role or to promote a highly specific programme or product.

5.6 *School-based Problem-solving Programmes*

During the 1970s there was an increased emphasis and a widespread acceptance in many parts of the world of school-based evaluation programmes. Stemming from this work the practice has developed of examining specific problems of a curricular or organizational kind within schools without conducting a full-scale evaluation exercise. There is clearly a growing interest in the identification and analysis of specific problems in schools, together with attempts to find solutions to those problems. The effectiveness of such programmes may, in part, depend on their capacity to draw on the knowledge and expertise available from research and development enterprises. While there may be little cause to doubt that a great deal of value is being achieved by such programmes, there would sometimes appear to be a lack of appropriate structures and strategies by which guidance and assistance could be obtained from resource systems to provide the knowledge and understanding which can be derived from research and development in education.

6. *Some Issues in Dissemination in Education*

The models of the diffusion process advanced above expose some of the weaknesses in current dissemination programmes. The research, development, and diffusion approach is deficient in so far as it assumes relatively passive consumers and a linear sequence of activities. The problem-solving perspective has limitations as a strategy in so far as it involves responding only to local initiatives, and makes no provision for the planning and promotion of change through the dissemination of knowledge about improved practice. The social interaction approach pays little attention to the nature of the knowledge or innovation to be diffused or to how implementation takes place after adoption. The linkage perspective, in so far as it combines the most appropriate features of the three earlier models is the most useful. It permits a diagnosis of need and a planned organization of the resources whether in the form of knowledge or innovatory practice and product, to ensure their relevance to the user. However, as Raizen (1979) has pointed out, unless those responsible for the implementation of proposed changes are involved at an early stage in the process of identification of the problem, and in the consideration of alternative strategies for its solution, it is unlikely that effective implementation will occur after the adoption of a proposed improvement. It is clear that future research in the field of diffusion needs to focus on the implementation process and the subsequent history of an innovation once it has been introduced. In the planning of strategies for widespread programmes of diffusion it would appear important to give full consideration to the range of alternatives that lie along the continuum extending from research, development, and diffusion at one extreme to specific problem-solving programmes at the other. However, it is necessary to recognize the need for full cooperation between the individuals and agencies involved, rather than to depend on programmes originating solely from the resource system or from a centralized bureaucracy.

Furthermore, recognition must also be given to the need to provide information in forms that are appropriate to the specific audience receiving the information. In addition, it is necessary to acknowledge both the difficulty and the importance of combining and condensing the information available so that a coherent and consistent message is presented. Following a decade or more of intensive research and development in the field of education during the 1970s, the major task in the diffusion of knowledge is the finding of ways of synthesizing the evidence that is available and presenting the findings in a manner that is meaningful to audiences who conduct school systems and who implement change in systems, schools, and classrooms. Following the synthesis of the evidence available, the next major development would appear to be the formation of dissemination centres in which linkage agents would work to promote educational policies and practices that would incorporate the best of what is known from research about the educational process.

Bibliography

Fullan M 1980 An R & D prospectus for educational reform. In: Mack D P, Ellis W E (eds.) 1980 *Interorganizational Arrangements for Collaborative Efforts: Commissioned Papers.* Northwest Regional Educational Laboratory, Portland, Oregon, pp. 29–48

Havelock R G 1971 The utilisation of educational research and development. *Br. J. Educ. Technol.* 2: 84–98

Havelock R G (ed.) 1973 *Planning for Innovation through Dissemination and Utilization of Knowledge.* Center for Research and Utilization of Scientific Knowledge, Ann Arbor, Michigan

Hood P D 1973 How research and development on educational roles and institutional structures can facilitate communication. *J. Res. Dev. Educ.* 6(4): 96–113

Huberman A M, Levinson N S, Havelock R G, Cox P L 1981 Interorganizational arrangements: An approach to educational practice improvement. *Knowledge: Creation, Diffusion, Utilization* 3: 5–22

Husén T, Kogan M (eds.) 1984 *Educational Research and Policy: How do they Relate?* Pergamon, Oxford

Kosse G B (ed.) 1982 *Social Science Research and Public Policy Making.* National Foundation for Educational Research, Slough; Nelson, Windsor

Owen J M 1979 The Australian Science Education Project: A study of factors affecting its adoption and implementation in schools. Doctoral Thesis, Monash University, Monash

Raizen S A 1979 Dissemination programs at the National Institute of Education: 1974–1979. *Knowledge: Creation, Diffusion, Utilization* 1: 259–92

Rich R F 1977 Uses of social science information by federal bureaucrats: Knowledge for action versus knowledge for understanding. In: Weiss C H (ed.) 1977 *Using Social Research in Public Policy Making.* Heath, Lexington, Massachusetts, pp. 199–211

Rogers E M, Shoemaker F F 1971 *Communication of Innovations: A Cross-cultural Approach,* 2nd edn. Free Press, New York

Suppes P (ed.) 1978 *Impact of Research on Education: Some Case Studies.* National Academy of Education, Washington, DC

Thompson C L 1981 Dissemination at the National Institute of Education: Contending ideas about research, practice and the federal role. Paper presented at the 1981 Annual Meeting of the American Educational Research Association, Los Angeles, California

Weiss C H 1979 The many meanings of research utilization. *Public Admin. Rev.* 39: 426–31

Educational Resources Information Center (ERIC)

D. P. Ely

The Educational Resources Information Center (ERIC), an information system established in 1966, is sponsored by the National Institute of Education, within the United States Department of Education. Through a network of 16 subject-specialized clearinghouses, educational documents are acquired, reviewed, and processed into the database. Journal articles are selected and indexed as well. Access to documents is through *Resources in Education* (RIE), a monthly abstract journal, and microfiche. Citations for journal articles appear monthly in the *Current Index to Journals in Education,* but ERIC does not make the text of these copyrighted materials available through the database. The *Thesaurus of ERIC Descriptors* facilitates access to the printed abstract journals and the database, which can be searched online by computer.

1. Information Available

The Educational Resources Information Center (ERIC) collects primarily English-language documents which are not published or made available through normal channels, that is, publishers. Almost all the information is directly relevant to some aspect of education: counseling; management; elementary, early childhood, handicapped, gifted, and higher education; library and information science; educational technology; junior colleges; languages and linguistics; reading; rural education; science, mathematics, and environmental studies; social studies; teacher education; testing and evaluation; and urban education.

Types of material include such items as: research reports, project descriptions, position papers, speeches, evaluation studies, instructional materials, syllabi, curriculum guides, conference papers, bibliographies, tests, glossaries, statistical compilations, and taxonomies. At the end of the first 15 years, there were 198,624 documents in ERIC.

The Educational Resources Information Center (ERIC) selects and indexes articles from about 700 English language journals in the content fields noted above. At the beginning of 1982, there were 250,663 citations in ERIC.

2. Access to Information

Documents in the ERIC system are listed in the monthly abstract journal, *Resources in Education*, published for ERIC by the United States Government Printing Office. There are approximately 2,700 locations worldwide which subscribe to RIE. Documents are listed by subject, title, author, and institution, and an abstract is provided for each title. The *Thesaurus of ERIC Descriptors* is a basic tool for locating specific information by using key words.

The Educational Resources Information Center (ERIC) obtains permission from authors to reproduce approximately 95 percent of the documents announced in RIE. These items are available in microfiche or paper copy. For those items not available in this form, sources are always given. The microfiche and paper copies may be purchased directly from the Educational Document Reproduction Service (P.O. Box 190, Arlington, Virginia 22210, USA) or they may be found and used at any of the more than 900 depositories, mostly libraries, worldwide. The biannual *Directory of ERIC Information Service Providers* is a geographically arranged reference tool which includes address, telephone number, contact person, collection status, services provided, and access hours. There are 111 collections in 22 countries in addition to the 780 in the United States and its territories. The directory is available from the ERIC Processing and Reference Facility, 4833 Rugby Road, Suite 301, Bethesda, Maryland 20814, USA.

The periodical literature from journals is indexed by subject and author in *Current Index to Journals in Education* and is published by Oryx Press (2214 North Central Avenue, Phoenix, Arizona 85004, USA). The articles can be found in the designated journal or copies from about 65 percent of the journals may be obtained from University Microfilms International, Article Reprint Service, 300 N. Zeeb Road, Ann Arbor, Michigan 48106, USA.

Both *Resources in Education* and *Current Index to Journals in Education* can be searched online by computer through online retrieval services or by purchasing ERIC tapes from the ERIC Facility. Searching requires a computer terminal which can be linked by telephone to a central computer source. Arrangements for use must be made with the organization which handles the central computer. Computer searching provides responses in real time, permitting users to make complex logical demands and obtain immediate responses. It is possible to interact with the computer so that search requirements can be adjusted. The increased efficiency of computer searching is usually at some cost to the user. More than 700 locations in 18 countries which provide computer search services are listed in the *Directory of ERIC Information Service Providers*. It is available from the ERIC Facility.

The *Thesaurus of ERIC Descriptors* is the master list of approved terms used by the ERIC system, with a complete cross-reference structure and rotated and hierarchical displays. It is available from Oryx Press.

3. Special Information Sources

Beyond access to information in the system, there are two major services provided by ERIC: question answering and information analysis.

(a) Within the ERIC system, subject expertise resides primarily within the various specialized ERIC clearinghouses. Questions that involve substantive matters can be directed to the appropriate clearinghouse. Such requests may be for a specific document or for matters closely associated with the specialty of the clearinghouse.

(b) In addition to collecting the literature of education for announcement in RIE and CIJE, the ERIC clearinghouses analyze and synthesize the literature into research reviews, state-of-the-art reports, interpretative essays on topics of high current interest and similar publications. These publications are designed to compress the vast amounts of information available and to make it more easily accessible for users.

4. Submitting Documents to ERIC

The Educational Resources Information Center (ERIC) actively solicits documents concerned with any aspect of education. The user audience is broad and therefore all information which can be placed in the public domain is considered. Each document is reviewed by a specialist in the content area and selected (or rejected) on the basis of its utility to educators.

Bibliography

Educational Resources Information Center (ERIC) 1981 *Pocket Guide to ERIC*. ERIC Processing and Reference Facility, Bethesda, Maryland

Copyright

J. K. Miller and M. W. Wynne

There is no universally accepted definition of copyright, but it may be possible to describe it as a system of statutory laws (laws passed by legislative bodies) and common laws (laws evolving from court decisions) which offer a balancing of interests in literary, artistic, and other works between the creator and the user. The creator has almost absolute control over his or her unpublished works and limited control over works after they have been published, performed, distributed, or transmitted. The creator's rights include the right to control translations, new editions, new formats, and the like. The creator also has the right to withhold a work from the market or resist access to it. Thus, an author may refuse permission to have his or her book translated or refuse permission to have a companion educational filmstrip made from it. Most authors use this right to regulate the quality of the derivative work and the royalties derived from it. The chief limitations on the creator's rights are: the duration of copyright protection (in most nations, life plus 50 years) and the rights granted to users to copy, perform, or display all or part of a work for educational or scholarly purposes; copying for purposes of review, criticism, or parody; and other forms of copying, display, or performance sanctioned by law or custom which do not seriously injure the creator's interest.

1. Historical Developments

Copyright originated in the Renaissance from efforts of kings and city councils to regulate businesses, including book sellers and printers. In time, patents or charters gave favourite printers and book sellers exclusive rights to print or vend certain types of books, and even certain titles. This process was carried further in England when Henry VIII and Mary Tudor employed the royal licensing power to censor political and religious works. This combination of copyright and censorship ended in Britain with the expiration of the Stationers' Company charter in 1695. It was replaced in 1710 by the Statute of Anne, the first statutory copyright law. Under this act, copyrights were limited to 14 years, renewable for an additional 14 years, and the copyright was vested in the author, not the printer. The printers' hereditary monopoly was effectively broken, as copyrights were then available to everyone.

In 1790, the United States enacted the second national statutory copyright act, based on the Statute of Anne and earlier state copyright laws. France adopted the third national statutory copyright law in 1793 and most other nations adopted statutory copyright laws in the early nineteenth century. As new nations developed in the twentieth century, almost all of them adopted copyright statutes and ratified international copyright agreements.

2. International Copyright Agreements

International cooperation in copyright affairs began with bilateral agreements between nations to respect copyrights in the works of each other's nationals. Bilateral agreements are still widely used but they lack the power and convenience of multinational copyright agreements. International copyright agreement began in 1886 with the Berne Copyright Union. Signatories to the Berne Union granted reciprocal protection to each other's copyrighted works, so that works protected under the laws of one nation are protected in all of the signatory nations. Unfortunately, some nations, especially the United States, cannot participate in the Berne agreement because of registration and deposit requirements, protectionist printing laws, and the like.

This problem was resolved by the creation of the Universal Copyright Convention (UCC) in 1952 under the sponsorship of UNESCO. The UCC's requirements are less stringent than those of the Berne Union, so almost any nation that favours international copyright agreements may participate. Some 50 nations are signatories to both the Berne and UCC agreements. The United States and the Soviet Union subscribe only to the UCC. It is the UCC that requires the symbol ©, followed by the year of publication and the owner's name, to be appended to all published copies of a work in order to establish the copyright.

The Rome Convention of 1961, with about 30 signatories, protects makers of phonograms (gramophone records and audiotapes) and performers and broadcasting organizations. Other conventions include the Council of Europe's agreement on television broadcasts and the Satellite Convention of 1974 on satellite transmissions of broadcasts.

3. Current National Positions

Copyright law is complex and a short article cannot cover all its ramifications, even within a single country. But is it important for educators to be aware of the issues and to attempt to protect the interests of the education sector. In order to illustrate the major issues that concern education, two accounts of current national positions follow. These articles are accurate only for the United Kingdom and the United States in 1988, but the views they discuss are likely to remain relevant for some considerable time. Not all countries have resolved them in precisely the same way, but most have found some similar kinds of compromise between the various interests. The impact of new communication technology, however, has led to a review of current practice; and many new issues have still to be resolved.

4. Copyright in the United Kingdom

4.1 The General Position

4.1.1 The law of copyright 1709–1988

The first Act of Parliament dealing with copyright, the Statute of Anne 1709, entitled "An Act for the Encouragement of Learning...", was concerned with the protection of printers' rights. In the present century legislation has catered for those who create and those who perform, who have been protected respectively by the Copyright Acts of 1911 and 1956 and by the Dramatic and Musical Performers' Protection Acts of 1925 and 1958, followed by the Performers' Protection Acts of 1963 and 1972.

It has long been recognized that copyright law in the United Kingdom is complex, difficult to understand, unable to adapt to rapid technological change, slow in operation, and sometimes unenforceable. Progress towards reform has been tardy and cumbersome, although prompt action can be taken if the need is urgent, as happened when, early in 1982, piracy in videotapes had become a public scandal. Within weeks a Copyright Amendment Act was passed, making it a criminal offence to be in possession of an infringing copy of a sound recording or cinematograph film by way of trade.

Meanwhile, in 1977, a committee under the chairmanship of Judge Whitford, after an exhaustive inquiry, recommended a number of changes. This was followed by two government Green Papers (consultative documents) and in 1986 by a White Paper (policy document) and finally by the 1988 Copyright Act.

4.1.2 The Copyright, Designs, and Patents Act 1988

The Act reforms the law of copyright and provides the substantive law in this field. It restates the basic law and introduces the concept of moral rights in response to the 1971 Paris revision of the Berne Copyright Convention of 1886. It supersedes the Performers' Protection Acts. It provides for the control of licensing schemes and sets up the Copyright Tribunal, replacing the Performing Right Tribunal which was created by the 1956 Copyright Act. It also deals with designs and patents, which are not discussed in this article.

The Act will not be retrospective in its operation, nor will all its provisions come immediately into force. Account must therefore still be taken of the Copyright Act 1956, the Performers' Protection Acts 1958–1972, and other intermediate legislation.

4.1.3 Definitions

In the United Kingdom, copyright means the exclusive right to reproduce a work, to publish it, adapt it, perform it in public, broadcast it, or diffuse it by cable to subscribers, or to authorize others to do any or all of these things.

Copyright is concerned with the product of certain kinds of labour, skill and capital. There is no copyright in ideas but copyright does cover the expression of ideas in material form. There are three categories of copyright works: (a) original literary, dramatic, musical, or artistic works; (b) sound recordings, films, broadcasts, or cable programmes (transmissions by satellite are generally classed as broadcasts); and (c) the typographical arrangement of published editions. A compilation is also copyright, so that the creator of a multimedia package for educational or other purposes has a copyright of his or her own whether the material collected is copyright or not.

The Copyright (Computer Software) Amendment Act 1985 classes computer programmes as literary works, with copyright vested in the author. Storing a programme in a computer counts as copying and is therefore illegal without the owner's permission.

Not all the terms relevant to the law of copyright are defined by statute, and some definitions, as well as the interpretation of the Act itself, depend upon judicial decisions. Case law can settle such questions as what is meant by copying a "substantial part" of a work. Recently a learned judge was required to determine whether the trade name "Exxon" is an original literary work—which may appeal to one's sense of the ridiculous, but decisions like these may establish important precedents. (His Lordship decided that it was not a literary work.) Interpretation can be assisted by nonjudicial professional bodies, though their pronouncements do not have the force of law.

4.1.4 Ownership

The first owner of copyright is the author or creator of the work, unless the work is made under a contract of service (that is in the course of regular employment), in which case the employer owns the copyright. A special rule applies to work made under a contract of service for publication in a newspaper or periodical. Here the employer has the copyright in its publication in that medium, but the author has it when the work is transferred to another medium. A person who commissions a portrait, engraving, or photograph for payment is the owner of the copyright unless the parties agree otherwise. The copyright in photographs which have not been commissioned belongs to the photographer him or herself. Under the 1956 Act, it resided, curiously enough, in the owner of the material on which the photograph was taken.

Ownership of copyright materials varies according to the nature and the sponsorship of the process involved. The copyright in a sound recording, film, or videotape rests with the person who makes the necessary arrangements, that is the producer (or employer), and the contracts of all who contribute to its creation usually contain a term giving their copyright to the producer. The copyright on a broadcast belongs to the BBC (British Broadcasting Corporation) or the IBA (Independent Broadcasting Authority), or any other independent company or organization responsible for the broadcast. Finally, the copyright in a particular edition of a work belongs to the publisher of that edition.

4.1.5 *Plural copyright*

The reproduction of a work may involve more than one copyright. For instance, a broadcaster making use of a recording requires the permission of the author of the work (unless the copyright has expired) and of the maker of the recording, and a third copyright will accrue to the broadcasting authority as the maker of the broadcast. A contrary example would be a tape-recording of bird song which will obviously be protected by only one copyright, that of the maker of the recording. Whether the owner of a cage-bird has an interest in a recording of that bird's song has not, to the author's knowledge, been tested in the courts.

4.1.6 *Duration of copyright*

Most material which has neither been published nor performed enjoys copyright without limit of time. Otherwise, copyright normally subsists during the lifetime of the author and for 50 years from the author's death or, if publication is posthumous, for 50 years from the year of first publication, reckoning from the last day of the year in all cases. Copyright in recordings, films, broadcasts, or cable programmes lasts for 50 years from the year in which the material was made. The copyright in a particular published edition lasts 25 years from the year of publication of that edition.

4.1.7 *Infringements and remedies*

An infringement of copyright is the exercise without permission of one or more of the exclusive rights belonging to the owner or maker of the work or material. There are a number of exceptions and dispensations. It should be stressed, however, that the one complete defence against any allegation of infringement is proof that the permission of any persons who may have an interest in the product has been obtained. To secure these permissions may be slow, difficult, and sometimes impossible, and consequently many small infringements occur which are overlooked or pass unnoticed.

The five "restricted" acts which, unless done with the copyright owner's permission, constitute "primary infringements" are: (a) copying; (b) issuing copies to the public; (c) performing, showing, or playing the work in public; (d) broadcasting the work or transmitting it by cable; and (e) making an adaptation of the work. "Secondary infringements" are: (a) importing, except for private and domestic use, possessing or dealing with material known or believed to be an infringing copy; and (b) making, importing, or dealing with an article for the purpose of making infringing copies.

The remedies for infringement are as follows. A copyright owner may sue for damages, may require an infringing copy, or equipment for making it, to be forfeited, and may even enter premises and seize the copy or the equipment, provided that the person infringing copyright knows or has reason to believe that the work is copyright. The owner may also obtain an injunction to prevent further infringement. A person who without the owner's permission makes, imports, or deals with infringing articles commits a criminal offence. A court may award aggravated damages in cases of flagrant infringement, and for a criminal offence it may impose a fine or up to two years' imprisonment, or both.

4.1.8 *Moral rights*

The author or maker of a work has the right to be identified whenever the work is published, performed or broadcast, or transmitted by cable, not to have the work adapted or modified to an unjustified extent, nor to have a work falsely attributed to him or her. The author or maker must assert these rights in advance—a provision which presumes an awareness and a vigilance hardly to be expected of most of those affected.

The concept of moral rights gained statutory sanction for the first time in the United Kingdom under the Copyright Act 1988. Previously the copyright owner could only sue for damages if, without his/her permission, his/her work had been adapted or altered to his/her detriment, or he/she could seek a civil remedy against "passing off".

4.2 *Special Arrangements*

4.2.1 *Permitted exceptions*

The Copyright Act allows the following exceptions: (a) fair dealing, which covers only original works, and which specifically excludes research for commercial purposes; (b) use for educational purposes; (c) special provision for libraries and archives; (d) a public reading or recitation, with sufficient acknowledgement, of a reasonable extract from a published work; (e) a photograph or film of a building or work of artistic craftsmanship (for example, sculpture) already on public display; (f) a sound recording or film if used only for a club or society not run for profit, and with generally charitable objectives; (g) recording for private purposes a radio or television broadcast or cable programme; (h) showing or playing in public a broadcast or cable programme if there is no admission fee nor any indirect payment; and (i) copying a broadcast or cable programme for subtitling for the deaf and hard of hearing.

4.2.2 *Fair dealing*

The Copyright Act allows fair dealing with a literary, dramatic, or musical work for purposes of private study or noncommercial research, for criticism or review, or for reporting current events. But, what is "fair dealing"? The Act does not define it, and it may be for a court to decide whether an apparent infringement can be justified as fair dealing. To constitute an infringement, the amount copied must be "substantial"—again undefined, but the Society of Authors and the Publishers Association have suggested not more than 8,000 words nor more than 10 percent of a whole work. The courts have ruled that content is a more important criterion than volume. Copying for private study or research has been strictly interpreted to mean copying by an individual for his or her own study or research, not for general private use.

4.2.3 Copyright and education

Of the various exceptions and concessions made under the Copyright Act, several affect educational use. Education provides a very considerable market for work and material protected by copyright, and it is not to be presumed that copyright owners will forgo their rights in a philanthropic spirit. On the other hand, there are educational needs whose nature and extent justify some relaxation of copyright, and this is provided in sections 6, 7, and 41 of the 1956 Act. A balance has to be struck between the claims of the owner and those of the user. A practising teacher or lecturer, who writes a textbook or research paper and thus finds himself or herself on both sides of the fence, will be especially appreciative of the problems involved. Consequently, there is a code of practice issued by the University Grants Committee which suggests reciprocal arrangements between universities for the use of internally produced material.

Use for educational purposes is precisely defined, though there are questions, yet to be determined, such as what institutions other than schools are classed as places of education. For example, may a teacher take a lawfully recorded educational broadcast and play or show it for an educational purpose to hospital patients? The following are permitted uses:

(a) A work may be copied "in the course of instruction or of preparation for instruction...by a person giving or receiving instruction". Photocopying, however, is limited, with the special exception of examination questions, to one per cent of a work in any quarter of the year (for example, 1 January to 31 March).

(b) Short passages of literature or drama (unless published expressly for educational use) may be included in an anthology for educational purposes, but only two excerpts from the same author may be put, within five years, into anthologies published by the same publisher.

(c) A work may be performed "by a teacher or pupil in the course of the activities of an educational establishment, or at an educational establishment by any person for the purposes of instruction", and a sound recording, film, broadcast, or cable programme may be "played or shown at an educational establishment for the purposes of instruction" before an audience limited to teachers and pupils and "other persons directly connected with the activities of the establishment". This definition does not include parents.

4.2.4 Libraries and archives

Public nonprofit-making libraries are "prescribed" (privileged), and this includes university and school libraries. Public archives are also prescribed. Librarians of prescribed libraries may copy and supply, for an appropriate payment, to individual students or researchers for private study or noncommercial research an article in a periodical or part or the whole of a published literary, dramatic, or musical work. They may also supply copies to another library. If the copyright owner is known or can be identified, his or her permission must be obtained to do these things. A librarian or archivist may copy a lost or damaged item for replacement.

4.2.5 Photocopying

Copying by an individual under the fair dealing rules and, in these cases, reprography (a bastard word meaning the use of a mechanical duplicating process) is permitted. Librarians of schools, colleges, and universities may also use reprography in cases where copying is allowed, however, a teacher may only photocopy examination papers.

Multiple photocopying without permission is normally an infringement of copyright. Therefore, neither a teacher nor a "prescribed" librarian on the teacher's behalf may, without prior consent of the owner, make photocopies for distribution among students for their work as a group, but the laborious process of writing on a blackboard or dictating material for students to copy is permissible. This anomalous situation probably reflects the view that only mechanized copying could make a serious dent in the potential market for published material and ultimately dry up the source of supply. However, the use of a single copy with an overhead projector is permitted.

4.2.6 Language laboratories

Copying from a master tape to students' tapes may be an integral part of a language teaching course and a copyright problem inevitably arises. This problem is solved by the owner consenting to waive his or her copyright in return for part of the proceeds of the sale of the master tape, which is priced higher to meet this charge.

4.2.7 Performing rights

Before 1988 performers were protected by the Performing Rights Acts 1958–1972, but these provided neither a copyright nor a property right to the actual performance. The Act of 1988 breaks new ground in giving to a performer, or to anyone who has an exclusive recording contract with the performer, the copyright to his or her performance, making it possible to give or withhold consent to the recording, except for private purposes, or the filming or broadcasting of a performance.

This protection covers a dramatic performance, dance or mime, a musical performance, a formal speech or lecture (though these are not specified), a reading or recitation, a variety act "or any similar presentation". Recording without consent includes making a film or videotape or sound recording of the whole or a substantial part of a live public performance, of a broadcast or cable programme or of another recording. The Act may therefore be invoked to deal with "bootleg" recordings made at concerts or festivals.

The Act does not define a public performance, but any performance for profit before a number of people with or without a charge for admission may be assumed to be a public performance. The definition would thus cover an engagement with a concert society or a performance for a fee in a works canteen but not a private performance before family and friends. The rights in a performance last for 50 years from the end of the year of the performance. Infringement of these rights—unless there was good enough reason to believe that consent had been given—is actionable as a breach of statutory duty. Civil and criminal remedies, including damages, forfeiture, power to enter and search, fine, and imprisonment, correspond closely (where applicable) with the infringements described in Section 4.1.7.

4.2.8 Recording educational broadcasts

The development of the audiotape and videotape has greatly increased the variety and extent of the possible uses of broadcasts in schools and in educational institutions generally. Most recording is done for "time-shifting", but material can also be recorded for selective or repeated use, and teachers can study broadcasts before presentation to the class. Initially these activities constituted a breach of copyright, but agreement has been reached with the BBC, IBA, and other interested parties whereby any broadcast, whether radio, television, or radiovision, if designed for use in schools, may be recorded, stored, and played back for up to three years, and broadcasts planned for further or continuing education for up to one year, without infringing copyright, provided that the whole operation takes place within the school or some other place of education. A closed circuit system does not earn this exemption, for its use would involve a rebroadcast.

It may be convenient for a teacher to record a school broadcast at home and take it to school for use there—especially now that certain radio series are broadcast after midnight solely to be recorded and stored for later use. This, however, would be a contravention, because the whole operation must be contained within the school. Colleges of education (teacher training colleges) and university departments of education, which share these privileges in relation to school or continuing education broadcasts, may also take tapes into schools or colleges for use in teaching practice. Recordings made under this dispensation must be destroyed within the permitted period (three years or one year) from the date when the recording was made. Open University broadcasts are designed for domestic use and are not included in these arrangements. Separate agreements have nevertheless been reached with the Open University and also with the independent television channel, Channel 4, and various independent programme companies for the recording of certain broadcasts for use in educational institutions. In most cases a special licence or registration fee is required.

In the light of new legislation, this whole area of activity is expected to come under review by the bodies concerned, and may possibly be brought under a licensing scheme (see Section 4.3.2).

4.3 The Administration of Copyright

4.3.1 Professional organizations

Internationally, copyright is regulated principally by the Berne Copyright Convention and the Universal Copyright Convention, to one or both of which most countries belong. Within the United Kingdom authors, artists, musicians, film makers, broadcasters, and the like have their own professional organizations which represent their interests. Some of these also assist in the administration of copyright through collective licensing, by one of two methods. One is the system of "blanket licensing", which conveys the rights in practically the whole of a repertoire, of musical performance for example. Such a scheme is administered by the Performing Right Society (PRS), which issues a blanket licence to proprietors of places of entertainment where music is to be played, and to broadcasting authorities, all of whom provide periodic lists of works performed, whereupon the PRS collects and distributes the appropriate fees. The other method is centralized licensing per item. This is operated by the Mechanical Copyright Protection Society (MCPS), which licenses the mechanical recording rights in musical works.

4.3.2 Licensing schemes and the Copyright Tribunal

A person or an organization owning a copyright or acting as agent of the owner may grant a copyright licence permitting one or more of the restricted acts, subject to conditions and subject, if desired, to a charge. The Copyright Tribunal, which is to have a legally qualified chairman, two deputy chairmen, and up to eight members, will approve licensing schemes and settle disputes. It may refer questions of law to the High Court (in Scotland the Court of Session). The Secretary of State (that is, the responsible minister of the Crown) also has a part to play. He or she may, for instance, set up an inquiry into whether a new licensing scheme is required for reprographical copying by educational establishments, and may, if need be, order a statutory licence. He or she may also, if application is made, certify a scheme for the educational recording of broadcasts or cable programmes, or reprographic copying of published works.

4.4 Perspective

4.4.1 Copyright under the new Act

Copyright law needs to be simple in structure, comprehensive in scope, and flexible in operation. How does the 1988 Act measure up to these requirements?

Simplification is difficult in this complex area and, though there are major changes, much of the copyright law has been left unchanged. There seems to be an attempt to steer a course between the Scylla of protection and the Charybdis of free access. A proposal in the White Paper for a levy on the purchase of all blank tapes, adopted in West Germany and contemplated elsewhere, offered a form of rough justice to deal with the widespread practice of illicit recording. This plan was abandoned and the right to record at home for private and domestic use, with its potentialities for abuse, remains. However, the penalties for illegal exploitation are stiffer than before. The licensing schemes are complicated, and how they will work out remains to be seen. The rules for recording broadcasts and other audiovisual material for educational use are still problematic; this appears to be one of the areas of ministerial discretion. The broadcasting organizations will no doubt try to rationalize existing practice.

A serious attempt is being made to cover the whole field of intellectual property and innovation, and the new law should provide a basis for effective practice for at least a decade. Innovation travels fast and unpredictably, and no law can anticipate it all. The Act does, however, offer something of the third requirement, flexibility, for it gives the Copyright Tribunal and the Secretary of State a measure of discretion and the capacity, if need be, to compel.

4.4.2 The future of copyright

Article 27 of the Universal Declaration of Human Rights claims, on the one hand, free participation for all in the life of the community and in the enjoyment of its benefits and, on the other hand, protection of the moral and material rights accruing to authorship. This is the classic conflict between protection and access, the theme with which this article began. The problem for the future is to strike a proper balance between the two.

"The underlying arguments in favour of copyright contain elements of thought which appeal to governments and legislators of almost every political complexion. Copyright can be seen as beneficial both to public policy and to private profit; as a boon to individual freedom and as an aid to state intervention; either as an expression of natural justice or as an assertion of property rights". So wrote Michael Freegard in the Performing Right Yearbook of 1977. As general manager of the Performing Right Society he naturally believed in copyright, but he was increasingly aware of the challenges to it, technological, economic, and social, and he even wondered whether in the long run there was a future for authors' copyright at all.

It is argued in some quarters that copyright is entrenched beyond the limit of reasonable need for protection and that the public interest has been neglected. To take a somewhat parochial example, there is, at present, a three year limit to the retention of recordings of school broadcasts, but who ever heard of a school librarian having to burn all his/her books every three years and start again? Even the market economy argument in favour of copyright has been challenged on the grounds that it has not been proved that without copyright the creative impulse would fail.

Has copyright a future? It faces that triple challenge—technological, through new means of reproduction, transmission, and use; economic, with increasing state intervention and the formation of international trading blocks which tend to ignore the rights of the individual; and a social challenge in the demand for the free flow of information, especially on behalf of developing countries which depend on it for teaching, study, and research. This last need was declared by the General Conference of UNESCO as long ago as 1966.

To sum up, information and culture are marketable commodities which carry proprietary rights. But they are also resources which are essential to any society in transition, especially at a time of rapid technological and social change such as the present. What, then, is the position of the United Kingdom in this ideological conflict of protection versus access? The traditional British view is that copyright is a form of property and that a principal function of the law is to protect property. This view, however, is being challenged: the tide of opinion seems to be running against copyright. The White Paper of 1986 referred to the availability of information as being generally in the public interest. There is a public campaign to promote and extend freedom of information, and there is a growing fear that the inventiveness for which Britain has been notable in the past is being thwarted not only by underfunding but by restrictive practices which are driving talented researchers abroad to seek better working conditions and richer rewards. Copyright law, in so far as it impedes the free exchange of information and ideas, contributes to this dangerous situation, but protection is a legitimate right in the United Kingdom, and its hold on the law is still strong. The White Paper, with its title "Intellectual Property and Innovation", aptly expressed the inherent opposition between protection and development.

5. Copyright in the United States

The United States copyright laws are similar to the United Kingdom copyright laws, but they also demonstrate unique features. The Statute of Anne nominally applied to the British North American Colonies, but the American printers were advocates of "freedom of the press", which served to justify reprinting popular English and Scottish publications without permission. During the 1780s, 12 of the 13 American states enacted ineffective copyright laws which were superseded in 1790 by the Federal Copyright Act. The federal act protected books, periodicals, maps, and navigation charts published in the United States by American citizens and resident aliens. This enabled the American printers to continue printing foreign works without permission. The copyright law was amended several times to extend the duration of copyright protection, to extend copyright protection to additional materials (e.g. plays, photographs, music, and films), and to make other changes. Copyright protection for works published abroad was not added until 1891. The United States began participating in bilateral copyright agreements that year and signed its first multilateral copyright agreement, the Mexico City Convention, in 1902.

5.1 The Copyright Revision Act of 1976

The Copyright Revision Act of 1976 marked a major change in United States copyright legislation. It removed the printed media orientation in earlier acts in favour of copyright protection for all media formats. It also removed the author–publisher orientation of earlier laws in favour of a balancing of interests between the creators and users of copyrighted materials. Under this act, all media now known or developed in the future are capable of copyright protection, including computer programmes, computer databases, and teaching machine programmes. Copyright protection for computer programmes was withheld from the 1976 Act, as that topic was still under consideration by the National Commission on the New Technological Uses of Copyrighted Works (CONTU). The commission's recommendation that copyright protection be extended to computer programmes was embodied in a 1980 amendment.

Copyright laws have traditionally emphasized the authors' rights. Users' rights developed slowly through the British and then the American courts under the rubric of "fair use", "fair quotation", and "fair dealing", but the application of these rights was ambiguous. The ambiguity was reduced by incorporating the fair use concept into the law. The fair use section is so brief it deserves inclusion here:

> Sect. 107. Limitations on Exclusive Rights: Fair Use.
>
> Notwithstanding the provisions of section 106, the fair use of a copyrighted work, including such use by reproduction in copies or phonorecords or by any other means specified by that section, for purposes such as criticism, comment, news reporting, teaching (including multiple copies for classroom use), scholarship, or research, is not an infringement of copyright. In determining whether the use made of a work in any particular case is a fair use the factors to be considered shall include:
>
> (1) the purpose and character of the use, including whether such use is of a commercial nature or is for nonprofit educational purposes;
>
> (2) the nature of the copyrighted work;
>
> (3) the amount and substantiality of the portion used in relation to the copyrighted work as a whole; and
>
> (4) the effect of the use upon the potential market for or value of the copyrighted work.

The four criteria must be met in each application of fair use. The first criterion indicates that the application of fair use depends on the purpose of the copying. Few rights are given to copying for commercial gain but greater latitude is given to copying for nonprofit purposes. The second criterion indicates that the nature of the work influences the degree of acceptable copying. Materials vulnerable to injurious copying, especially sheet music, play scripts, newsletters, standard examinations, and student workbooks, should not be copied. The third criterion centres on both amount and substantiality. Although the law does not include numerical limits on copying, the official literature suggests that a teacher may copy up to 10 percent of a work as a fair use, if the other criteria are met. The substantiality test hinges on the value of the portion to be copied; it infrequently applies to printed materials, but it must be considered in copying unusual, irreplaceable, or costly scenes in audiovisual materials. Even a small amount of copying from key scenes can injure the copyright proprietor, which is not a fair use. The last criterion, "the effect of the use on the potential market for or value of the copyrighted work", is frequently considered the most important criterion. If one or several acts of copying deprive a publisher or distributor of a sale, lease, or rental, it is not a fair use.

The fair use section of the law was written in vague terms so the four criteria could be applied to a broad variety of situations, including the work of journalists, students, scholars, critics, and the like. This means it will not have to be rewritten to reflect each new technological development.

5.2 Fair Use Guidelines

Educators, publishers, and producers were not entirely pleased with the vague terms in the fair use section of the law and sought specific guidelines. Three fair use guidelines have been written and recognized by the appropriate Congressional committees. They are: "An Agreement on Guidelines for Classroom Copying in Not-for-profit Educational Institutions", "Guidelines for Educational Uses of Music", and "Guidelines for Off-air Recording of Broadcast Programming for Educational Purposes". The first two guidelines were included in the Congressional reports accompanying the Copyright Revision Act of 1976. The "Guidelines for Off-air Recording of Broadcast Programming for Educational Purposes" was finished in October 1981, approved by the House of Representatives Subcommittee on Courts, Civil Liberties, and Administration of Justice, and read into the *Congressional Record* of October 14, 1981. None of the guidelines has the force of law, but they are respected as reflections of the intent of the legislative body that wrote the law. Although the courts are not bound to observe the guidelines in resolving copyright infringement cases, it seems unlikely that a court could ignore these official documents.

The "Agreement on Guidelines for Classroom Copying in Not-for-profit Educational Institutions" provides minimum fair use guidelines for teachers to use in copying materials for lesson planning or for classroom distribution. These minimum guidelines suggest that a teacher may copy a chapter, an article, a short story, a poem, or an illustration for lesson planning. The teacher may also make multiple copies of any of these items for classroom distribution, so long as the copying meets the tests of brevity, spontaneity, and cumulative effect. Brevity limits the amount that can be copied. Spontaneity suggests that the copying must be at the inspiration of the teacher and not at the direction of higher authority, and that the teacher did not have time to obtain permission to make the copies. Cumulative effects limits the number of items that may be copied from a single source, and the number of instances of copying in a semester. Many school administrators employ this guideline as a definition of the outer limit of fair use copying, although it is clearly labeled as a minimum standard and states that copying in excess of these guidelines may be a fair use.

The "Guidelines for Educational Use of Music" give music teachers some latitude in copying sheet music for school use. This includes copying a small part of a work in multiple copies for class use, copying out-of-print music for class use, and emergency copying of a missing piece which could not be obtained prior to a performance.

The "Guidelines for Off-air Recording of Broadcast Programming for Educational Purposes" permit videotaping programmes off-the-air for classroom use. The recording may be used in the classroom for the first 10 school days after the broadcast and may be retained for 45 calendar days for evaluation. Each recording may be used by a number of teachers, but it can only be used twice in any class. The recordings may also be delivered or transmitted to homebound students.

The fair use section of the law and its four criteria may be more liberal than similar legislation in other parts of the world, but the use of the three fair use guidelines is unique. American teachers are not impressed with this apparent liberality and frequently object to the limits the guidelines place on their work. Copying in excess of the guidelines is a common practice in United States schools. Publishers and media producers sometimes obtain out-of-court settlements with infringing schools, but there is little organized effort to pursue infringers. Because of confusion over the application of the fair use guidelines and concern about legal actions for copyright infringements, many colleges and school districts are adopting copyright policies and copyright manuals to help educators observe the law.

5.3 Library Photocopying

The traditional concept of fair use is incorporated in Section 108 of the 1976 Copyright Act which grants libraries and archives the right to duplicate copyrighted materials for their patrons. Libraries may copy a chapter from a book, an article from a periodical, or a small part of another work for a patron if the request is initiated by the patron, the copy is for the patron's personal use, and the act of copying is not part of a "systematic" scheme of copying. Libraries are also permitted to copy all or part of "damaged, deteriorating, lost, or stolen" work from their collection for purposes of replacement, so long as "an unused replacement cannot be obtained at a fair price". Section 108 also authorized the use of self-service photocopying machines in libraries. If a copyright warning notice is displayed at each machine, the library is not responsible for the patrons' use of the machines. Libraries and archives are also permitted to videotape television news programmes off-the-air and

retain them indefinitely for archival use. These recordings are not available for classroom use.

5.4 Interlibrary Loan

One of the most controversial aspects of the 1976 Copyright Act was the authorization in Section 108 permitting libraries to respond to interlibrary loan requests by sending a photocopy of a chapter or an article in lieu of sending the book or periodical. Libraries that meet certain requirements may send up to five photocopies per year, per book, or five photocopies per year, per journal volume in response to interlibrary loan requests. The requests received by most libraries fall below this limit. Libraries having greater demands for copying may pay for copies in excess of the five item limit through the Copyright Clearance Center, a nonprofit agency operated by United States publishers.

5.5 Reception and Copying from Satellites

Many schools and colleges in the United States are purchasing satellite reception antennae to show or record television programmes distributed by satellite. This is a questionable practice under the copyright law and clearly infringes the Communications Act (Title 47, *US Code* Sect. 101 et seq.). Educators who wish to show or record programmes transmitted via satellite should obtain a licence from the satellite agency.

Bibliography

Cable and Broadcasting Act 1984 (C. 46). Her Majesty's Stationery Office, London

Committee of Vice-Chancellors and Principals 1982 *Copyright: Response on the Consultative Document.* Committee of Vice-Chancellors and Principals, London

Copyright Act 1956 (C. 74). Her Majesty's Stationery Office, London

Copyright Act 1988 (C. 48). Her Majesty's Stationery Office, London

Copyright (Amendment) Act 1982 (C. 35), 1983 (C. 42). Her Majesty's Stationery Office, London

Copyright (Computer Software) Act 1985 (C. 41). Her Majesty's Stationery Office, London

1985 *A User's Guide to Copyright*, 2nd edn. Butterworth, London

Great Britain Department of Trade 1981 (Green Paper) *Reform of the Law Relating to Copyright, Designs and Performers' Protection: A Consultative Document.* Her Majesty's Stationery Office, London

Great Britain Department of Trade 1985 (Green Paper) *The Recording and Rental of Audio and Video Copyright Material*, Cmd. 9445. Her Majesty's Stationery Office, London

Great Britain Department of Trade 1986 (White Paper) *Intellectual Property and Innovation*, Cmd. 9712. Her Majesty's Stationery Office, London

Laddie H I L, Prescott P, Vitoria M 1980 *The Modern Law of Copyright.* Butterworth, London

McFarlane G 1986 *Copyright Through the Cases.* Waterlow, London

Miller J K 1979 *Applying the New Copyright Law: A Guide for Educators and Librarians.* American Library Association, Chicago, Illinois

Miller J K 1981 *US Copyright Documents: An Annotated Collection for Use by Educators and Librarians.* Libraries Unlimited, Littleton, Colorado

Miller J K 1987 *Using Copyrighted Videocassettes in Classrooms, Libraries, and Training Centers.* Copyright Information Services, Friday Harbor, Washington

Nimmer M B 1981 *Nimmer on Copyright: A Treatise on the Law of Literary, Musical and Artistic Property, and the Protection of Ideas.* Bender, New York

Performers' Protection Acts 1958 (C. 44), 1963 (C. 53), 1972 (C. 32). Her Majesty's Stationery Office, London

Performing Right Yearbook 1977. Performing Right Society, London

Skone James E P, Mummery J F, Rayner James J E, Latman A, Silman S 1980 *Copinger and Skone James on Copyright,* 12th edn. Sweet and Maxwell, London

UNESCO 1981 *The ABC of Copyright.* UNESCO, Paris

Vlcek C W 1987 *Copyright Policy Development: A Resource Book for Educators.* Copyright Information Services, Friday Harbor, Washington

Whale R F, Phillips J J 1983 *Whale on Copyright,* 3rd edn. ESC, Oxford

Whitford Committee 1977 *Copyright and Designs Law: Report of the Committee to Consider the Law on Copyright and Designs.* Her Majesty's Stationery Office, London

Electronic Publishing

J. Kist

Electronic publishing could be defined as the issuing of a written work of an author by electronic means (particularly by computer) either directly or over a communications network.

This definition can be broadened to include as "publishing", the process by which the written word is "captured, shaped and stored". There is a definite distinction between (a) the use of electronics in publishing (e.g. the manufacturing process of source data capture, database management, computerized typesetting, and even laser-printing) together with optical or nonelectronic technologies, and (b) electronic publishing itself, which is really the issuing, or the dissemination, or the putting into circulation of the written word by electronic or electro-optical means. If one incorporates both the manufacturing and dissemination aspects into a single definition, then the broad definition of electronic publishing should read as follows: Electronic publishing is the application by publishers of computer-aided processes, by which they find, capture, shape, store, and update informational content in order to disseminate it to a chosen audience.

1. The Opportunities Created by New Technology

Until the 1960s, publishing techniques evolved gradually, based on the assumption that the demands of readers and the nature of the publisher's products would remain more or less the same. Since then, however, new technologies have generated many changes and even more fundamental changes are now in store (see Fig. 1). Besides existing media such as books, newspapers, and journals, information delivery can also occur through a variety of new electronic and optical media, in whose development the rapid advance in computer memory capacities has played a central role. It is anticipated that during the next few years these new delivery systems will be integrated with, replace, or—and this seems most likely—supplement the current information carriers.

In electronic publishing, basic material—data and information—must be captured and organized in such a way that it is entirely independent of requirements connected to any single output product. All the material, moreover, must be conserved so that any part that is needed to create other outputs or products remains available.

Publishers who apply the above principles will find themselves controlling: (a) the means of distributing folio products; (b) the means of data capture and print production; and (c) the technologies for electronic distribution.

Mainly because of the broad range of information products handled by most publishers (from journals to information files, from looseleaf products to directories, etc.), and the manner in which modifications generally affect the publishing industry, the change will be relatively long-term.

The integrated process of electronic publishing is illustrated in Fig. 2. Raw material for the information

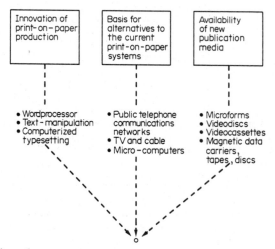

Figure 1
Convergence and integration of new delivery media and technologies

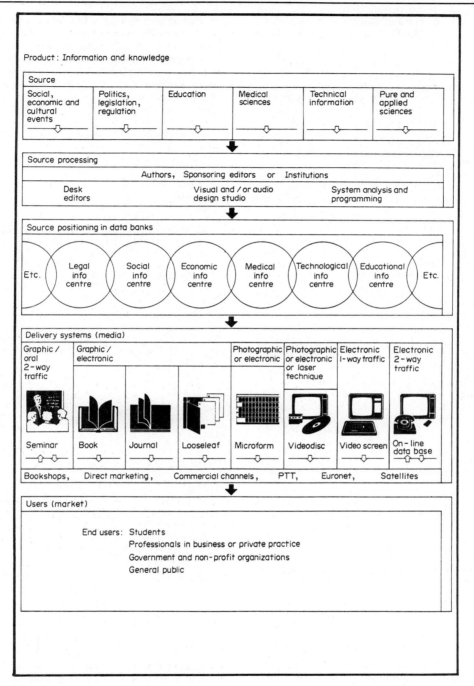

Figure 2
The integrated process of electronic publishing

product is found and captured at the source by authors and/or editors and then processed, shaped, and formatted.

Even at this stage the computer plays a vital role in tracing sources and new developments (e.g. through bibliographies or early warning systems). Authors and editors use computers with wordprocessing facilities to capture and process the informational content, which is the real product of electronic publishing. The next logical step in the integrated electronic publishing process is to store the "refined" informational content in a databank. Intellectual information technology helps to decide how the storage and continuous updating of this databank can best be effected. It should be mentioned here that, in electronic typesetting, a databank can be an automatic by-product of modern print technology.

At this stage in the electronic publishing process, publishers can really assume their role as information providers. With the backing of their databases, publishers are able to select and integrate the most suitable media in order judiciously to distribute and disseminate the informational content (one-way or interactive) to their chosen audiences: their users in the market.

This judicious delivery of content with the assistance of a computer is the most vital function of electronic publishers. It distinguishes them from other agents in the information market who dump information as a by-product or an afterthought.

From this description it becomes clear that in the process of electronic publishing, computers are much more than storage and distribution tools. They grant publishers the power of selection. Computers can be used to organize—and reorganize—all kinds of information for easy manipulation in processing printed as well as electronic delivery and, moreover, to repackage information in multiple forms, formats, and modes: online, on a disc, tape, fiche, or paper.

2. Main Considerations for Electronic Publishers

In view of the aforementioned factors, an electronic publisher's main considerations are:

(a) how to find, process, and manipulate information—using computers, minis, micros, and mainframes;

(b) how to store information—using storage devices such as discs;

(c) how to update the database—adding to the store of knowledge at the moment of creation;

(d) how to format information for a user—using interface systems such as television sets, terminals, microcomputers, or paper printouts;

(e) how to transport information—using communication networks or postal delivery.

The devices and software are merely the means which enable electronic publishers to offer their clients content:

data, information, and/or knowledge. The real revolution in publishing is not simply in the technology; the dramatic difference is that the power of the new technology is forcing the integration of human resources into the publishing process in previously unknown ways. For the first time users interact directly with publishers and with authors. Academics can interact with researchers, teachers with students, business executives with clients, and so on, in a manner that was previously beyond the publishing process but which can now be an integral part of it.

3. A Quantum Leap Through Electronic Publishing

Undoubtedly, new systems and delivery mechanisms will continue to appear in the market. These innovations, however, will most likely only add greater facility, capability, and ease of use to the existing systems and mechanisms. A drastic change in the creation, organization, and transfer of knowledge is brought about, however, by integrating human resources—the quantum leap in electronic publishing—which is achieved through: (a) author/user interaction; (b) user-driven publishing; (c) accessing dynamic knowledge banks; and (d) unifying the information exchange process.

Electronic publishing dramatically alters the relationships in the author/publisher/user spectrum, moving from a linear relationship to a circular one. The author's and publisher's roles tend to merge, driven by the need for greater knowledge and expertise in the creation and updating of electronic files and databanks for specific users.

Author and publisher together become information providers, "narrowcasting" to selective, segmented audiences: a welcome development in an age of increasing specialization. Users, in turn, become more than just buyers of titles. Through their use of the databases, they signal their interests; through user-driven publishing or desk-top publishing they themselves become publishers in their own right.

Successful electronic publishers are in tune with their users' needs to a far greater degree than in traditional publishing; in other words, theirs is a more direct and personal commitment to the market.

4. The Requirements for Electronic Publishing

Except for the widely publicized online, videotex and CD-ROM (Compact Disc Read Only Memory) projects, electronic publishing has yet to arrive in full strength. The reason for this is paradoxical. Initially, technology pushed too hard and in too undifferentiated a manner. The overawed potential customers waited for solutions to their specific information problems but waited in vain; the market had not been properly researched and the real user needs had not been addressed. In the late-1980s, however, the situation is changing. This is mainly due to the breakthrough in microcomputing, which has made computer power available on every desk and which has started a market demand for simple, user-friendly electronic publishing products.

Meanwhile, appropriate technology is available and in search of employment; the requirements for electronic publishing are known and can now be clearly defined. They are:

(a) machine-readable text (words/characters which can be processed by a computer);

(b) low-cost computer facilities;

(c) sophisticated word-processing software for desktop computers;

(d) low-cost and high-speed mass storage devices capable of accommodating vast quantities of data, text, images, and sound;

(e) low-cost, dependable telecommunications for the link between users and computers;

(f) availability of reliable and inexpensive personal computers;

(g) pump-priming calls for electronic publishing proposals from government, the European Community, and industry; and

(h) the opportunity to choose from the wide range of professional hardware, software, and uncomplicated operational methods which demand minimal user expertise.

5. Data, Information, and Knowledge

That data consists of numbers, and information consists of letters, would be too simplistic a definition but the comparative approach does help to distinguish the two. With data signifying collections of raw facts, information stands for selection, organization, and intelligent interpretation of those raw facts. Data collections represent that which is recorded serially, while information imposes order, dictates categorization, and represents ideas. Knowledge, of course, represents judgment and expertise. An added complication is that *information* is often used as an umbrella term for data, information, and knowledge.

5.1 Concepts of Information and Communication

It is also important to recognize the manner in which different users perceive a piece of information (using the word as an umbrella term). One could illustrate this point by describing three men out on a walk.

Walking down a path, Mr A inadvertently bumps his toe on a rock. In the moment of discomfort he makes a mental note to watch his step. For Mr A the event signified short-term *data*.

Mr B strolls along the same path and stumbles over the same rock. He stops, looks at it, and mentally notes that it is a curious piece of stone: brown and oval. For

Mr B the happening produced a bit of *information* he might use in the future.

Mr C, along the same path and confronted with the same stone, stops, studies it, and recognizes it as being a Stone Age artifact. He picks it up and takes it with him for further study, whereby he augments his current body of *knowledge*.

As these examples show, data, information, and knowledge are not always fixed concepts for the user. Nor is there any general indication that Mr B would be willing to pay more for a product that provides him with information than Mr A for short-term data (e.g. share prices on the stock market on the screen of his terminal).

5.2 Three Information Concepts

Two distinct information concepts can now be identified, namely: (a) syntactic information (characters, sounds, electric waves); and (b) semantic information (meanings in relation to signals).

Although computers are capable of processing large quantities of data, to a receiver such data merely constitutes syntactic information or, in other words, information carriers that must be interpreted and processed before the semantic meaning can be comprehended. Semantic information, therefore, is derived from syntactic information. Semantic information, moreover, involves knowledge. It demands a response to the question of what the facts and data tell about the world.

Along with syntactic and semantic information is a third information concept, namely, pragmatic information. This concept deals primarily with the function of information and the effects data and/or facts have on (a user's) behaviour. Pragmatics might be regarded as the ultimate purpose of an information transfer, as facts or data which do not result in an ultimate effect barely deserve to be called information.

Information and communication are closely related: as communication is a process of social exchange, information is the object of the exchange. Communication usually starts with an idea, a thought, or message which a sender wishes to convey to others; it also implies transfer of information from a sender to a receiver via a particular channel. To accomplish that, a thought or message must be worded, made comprehensible, and coded. Thus semantic information becomes syntactic information.

Communication ends at the receiver's semantics and pragmatics: the signals must be decoded. If the receiver can handle the syntactic information, it becomes semantic information that may, in turn, be converted into pragmatic information. If generally accepted and stored over a longer period of time, pragmatic information evolves into knowledge.

5.3 Are There Differences in the Users' Information Needs?

Analogous to Maslow's understanding of the hierarchy of psychological needs, electronic publishers must understand the hierarchy of information needs. Individuals in different positions need different quantities, qualities, and values of information, particularly if that information is transmitted electronically. Studies by the National Science Foundation in the United States and others have shown that there are substantial differences in information-seeking behaviour between professional groups and, consequently, differences in their use of information.

The various distinctions that were identified are the result of the differences in education and training, personality characteristics, professional requirements, or the professional mission.

Looking at some of these professional groups vis-à-vis their information-seeking behaviour, certain characteristics are easily identifiable. Starting with the professionals for whom the original electronic business machines were developed—the *business executives* (and among these the policy makers in particular)—it is known that as information seekers, they:

(a) seek options rather than answers;

(b) rely heavily on quantified, evaluated information;

(c) make a variety of short-, middle-, and long-term decisions on the basis of a good deal less than 100 percent information (in business circles 75 percent information is considered a high availability level);

(d) want their information today and want it on their desks.

Engineers, as information seekers:

(a) have as their primary goal the production of results or products;

(b) seek reliable answers to their immediate questions (which precludes guides to source literature as they seldom use bibliographies);

(c) require focused, objective information.

Medical Specialists slightly resemble engineers in their information-seeking behaviour but their needs extend to analogies, comparable cases, and examples.

Social scientists, for example:

(a) produce documents and thus contribute to the information flow as well as draw from it;

(b) are involved in work that usually progresses over a long(er) period of time;

(c) are interested in theory and source data, that is, full text material, preferably on paper so that they can pencil in remarks or put in markers, and so forth;

(d) tend to browse through literature for idea exploration and formulation; and

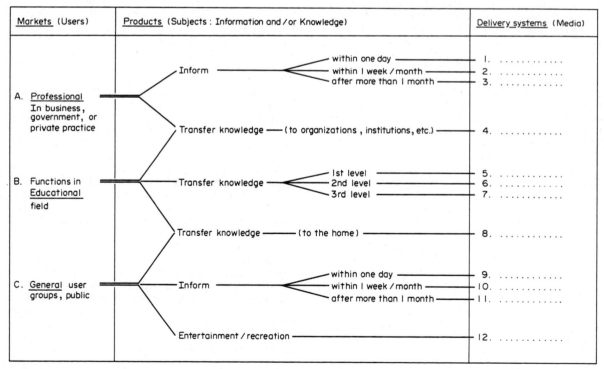

Figure 3
Market product delivery system analysis

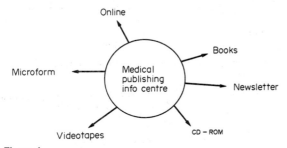

Figure 4
The information centre concept

(e) want 100 percent information and find bibliographies in particular exceedingly helpful.

Undoubtedly, many additions and exceptions to the rule could be made to these listings. Defining the various characteristics, however, can serve to create an awareness of the fact that each group does have very specific information needs in quality, quantity, value, price, delivery time, and user-friendliness.

6. *The Role of the Publisher*

Before entering the electronic publishing marketplace, publishers should sharply (re)define their current business, their markets (users), their products (the informational content) and their current delivery systems (e.g. books, newsletters), and should identify and analyse the factors which influence their publishing activities in the present and future. A diagram (Fig. 3 for example) can be used as a guide to describe current activities and to analyse in which product/market segments traditional delivery systems could be replaced by new systems (new media, electronics). For instance a publisher might consider replacing a newsletter service by a videotex system if customers insisted on quicker delivery. Another example could be the introduction of one optical disc instead of a multivolume encyclopedia.

7. *Information Centres*

The integration of publishing activities can take several forms. With legal journals, professional books, and jurisprudence on CD-ROM, for instance, integration in the search for authors or in the delivery of informational content to user groups is favourable. Some publishers refer to the information centre concept (Fig. 4); and this form of organization according to subject area is making headway in scientific and business publishing. In traditional publishing, but even more so in electronic publishing, an information centre contains the information (re)source from which users are served through different delivery systems.

An information centre is in fact an electronic or folio database which enables a subject area publisher to organize delivery of data, information and knowledge

products, and services to the selected user group. Putting together all available delivery systems, old and new and modern technology in one diagram, one could produce a picture of the most advanced kind of integrated electronic publishing (Fig. 5). Indeed, systems of this kind are already in existence within publishing houses where computerized typesetting and databases are used to handle informational content.

For the most part, the publisher's product is basically information that is generally accessible and/or easily obtainable; a publishing company's strength, therefore, must stem from its products' added value. The result is often, especially in the case of electronic publishing, that the demand for end-products and/or services is an extremely individual matter and largely dependent on the added value a user attributes to those products.

8. *Key Factors for the Organization of Electronic Publishing Activities*

Although each sector of publishing is unique, whether it involves folio or electronic publishing, there are common threads which run throughout all sectors. The factors that appear critical for successful electronic publishing are described below—but not necessarily in order of importance.

8.1 *User Group Control and Backlist of Products*

Of crucial importance is control over a user group through the possession (or acquisition of) a subscription service, a solidly established journal, or a dependable list of looseleaf titles.

An important condition is that these titles will continue to sell well for a long time and that relatively slight additional expense is needed for new product or content creation, market acquisition, and so on. Up-front money, in the sense of advance payment, is an essential element for survival in the modern publishing business.

As described, computerized typesetting of folio subscription products offers a good opportunity for the creation of a machine-readable databank that could lead to parallel electronic products. These products, however, must be (re-)edited and compressed; full text electronic derivatives of a folio product will seldom be successful in the electronic publishing marketplace. Here only malleable elements—or in other words, compact bursts of information—are acceptable in the sense of electronic updates and current awareness services, either alone or complementary to folio products.

A fundamental rule which should be applied in this process is: attain and maintain full integrity of data. However tempting last-minute modifications may be, manual revisions should not be permitted. All changes and corrections must be made at the database level so that the full integrity remains consistent throughout the whole scale of repackaged information products.

8.2 Increased Specialization in Marketing

Because of its scarcity, time is highly valued by most of us. Consequently, users are more interested in special information categories than in access to alternative or general information carriers. As a result, they are liable to devote more time to special subjects—for which they are willing to pay a good price—at the expense of general interest information products. This trend is most evident in newsletter fields and the journal and tabloid publishing industry where it has led to renewed overall growth.

Marketing specialization is essential and in electronic publishing, it is demonstrably superior when: (a) the information offered is time-sensitive; (b) the information offered is volume-sensitive; (c) the information can and is intended to be manipulated or combined with other kinds of information.

Marketing an electronic product is much more costly than any of the simple advertising/direct mail activities involved in putting a folio product on the market. Electronic publishers, upon entering the electronic publishing marketplace, not only have to refine their marketing and management skills, they also have to educate the prospective customer/end-user during the marketing process (see Fig. 6).

Many electronic publishers start their activities in sector C of the diagram. A stumbling block in this sector is that, during their marketing efforts, the technological aspects often receive too much emphasis and the information uses of the database are neglected.

Practical experience has shown that a start is much more effective when the first step is taken in the direction of Section B, where current as well as prospective clients are approached with folio products which reflect certain editorial aspects of the electronic service. For example, if newsletters or other periodical "fast fact" folio products are formatted in such a way that they resemble the usual concise, extremely structured nature of information projected on a terminal, the client

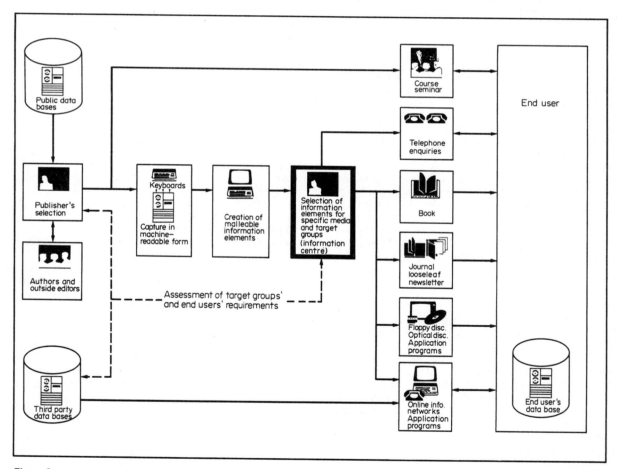

Figure 5
The electronic publisher of the future

A	B
–traditional folio product	–new folio product
–traditional customer	–traditional customer
	–new customer

C	D
–electronic service	–electronic service
–traditional customer	–new customer

Figure 6
Product/market options

becomes accustomed to the new manner in which information is transferred. The next step—from B to C—is much easier to take than going directly from A to C and moreover, there is the advantage of the stepping stone to D. The information, after all, is already edited for the terminal.

Another possibility is providing clients with the newly formatted information through information providers already established in Section D.

At each step, the end-users must be told why they need the electronic service. One way of doing so is to offer them an extremely modern, user-friendly folio product and, subsequently, demonstrate how electronic updating could beat the combination of print and postal delivery.

8.3 Market Domination

If expenses can be met by an affluent customer group, a publisher can successfully dominate a diminutive market by publishing the leading newsletter, looseleaf system, or information service for an insurance or health care target group, for example. In that way, a publisher dominates an information sector first and the product sector second. Dominance, therefore, is not measured by the size of a market share in a broad or general market such as textbook publishing but by dominance of a specific subject/user category. This holds especially true for electronic products and services.

8.4 Pricing

Generally speaking, because of dominance in a market, a publisher can choose between selling many items—or connect minutes—at a low price or a few items at a much higher price. Folio publishing permits both possibilities as most of the traditional publishers tend to price their products on the basis of average costs.

With only a few competitors in a small market, prices will be high; with many competitors in a large market, prices will be low. Successful traditional publishers will acquire their profits through volume and lowered relative expenses.

This is only partly true for electronic publishing, where pricing is much more complex. Electronic products cannot be managed in the same manner as print

products. Moreover, the buyers/users perceive the value of new electronic products differently and unpredictably. Rather than overwhelming a customer with a flood of information, it is a wise policy to withhold small morsels of—possibly superfluous—information. Adages such as, for instance, "Less is more" or "The half is better than the whole" are especially true of electronic products.

8.5 Distribution

Some marketing efforts, such as those for encyclopedias and textbooks, are geared directly to consumer groups. Others use retailers, retailers and wholesalers, or even more complicated delivery channels. In general, successful traditional publishers maintain a certain control over distribution and/or delivery channels. In electronic publishing, control is much more difficult due to the monopoly positions held by national post/telegraph/telephone agencies, major telecommunication companies, and hosts or vendors. Here, concerted action between publishers—a united stand—could help to gain some control over prices and quality of service.

8.6 Size

By itself, a publishing company's size is not a guarantee for success; a larger company, however, benefits from the following opportunities:

(a) ability to influence distribution/delivery;

(b) overhead reduction in integrated operations;

(c) more leverage to attain better production and service contracts or terms;

(d) the financial capacity to use the latest technologies (e.g. in-house composition, computer manipulation of data and closer control of subscribers);

(e) sufficient financial resources to promote autonomous development in costly new media products and services as well as to acquire support activities.

8.7 The Most Crucial Factor: Management

Publishing was, is, and always will be a labour-intensive business. Royalties to authors, commissions, salaries, and a significant part of the text-processing and computer costs can all be relegated to labour costs. Therefore, an integrated group of dedicated people is more important in publishing than in most industries. As established authors, by definition, tend to sell better than newcomers and unknowns, they must be cultivated and held. Editors become efficient only after a period of some years and have to develop a sense of their marketplace's needs and desires—depending on the life cycles of the products—from the next six months to 10 years or more into the future.

Like advertising, this is a business in which most of the assets go home every night. By the same token, it is a business which requires managers who lead rather than manage groups of independent, creative, and well-educated individuals, simultaneously attaining adherence to time schedules and budgets.

A characteristic of good managers is an ability to formulate the future that they envisage for themselves and for their industry; poor managers are seldom able to see beyond the present. In sum, people with vision and experience, who understand both the product lines and marketplaces of publishing and who can consistently achieve good bottomline records are the kind of managers needed. Good management is the most critical factor in folio and in electronic publishing.

9. Fact and Fantasy

For outsiders or for investment analysts in the electronic publishing scene, it is difficult to distinguish between facts and futuristic dreams or between financial success and fantastic losses. This might be explained by the propensity for wishful thinking among some players of the game. The computer and software industries seldom seem to understand sufficiently the real needs of information users, readers who are expected to switch to other delivery systems and media. Traditional publishers as well as the multifeathered flock of new information providers pretend an understanding of user needs but usually do not fathom the multidimensional financial aspects of this new delivery/communications technology; some even close their eyes to economics because they are so enraptured by the boundless possibilities (e.g. in on-line scientific research).

Last but not least, there is the trade press, a press with a penchant for publishing science fiction-type fantasies. There are exceptions, however, in the magazines and newsletters which bravely defy that temptation, and accurately report electronic publishing developments.

In electronic publishing fact leads to success, while fantasy leads only to disaster.

Bibliography

Brinberg H R 1981 Tailor specific data to specific needs: New thrust of information management. *Manage. Rev.* 8–11

Compaine B M (ed.) 1984 *Understanding New Media: Trends and Issues in Electronic Distribution of Information.* Ballinger, Cambridge, Massachusetts

Electronic Publishing: An Introductory Guide. 1981 Publishers Association, London

Electronic Publishing Review 1983 Vol. 3(4), 1984 Vol. 4(4) (issues devoted to Impact of Electronic Publishing)

Kist J 1980 *Many Roads to Electronic Publishing.* International Publishers Association, Stockholm

Kist J 1987 *Electronic Publishing: Looking for a Blueprint.* Croom Helm, London

Kist J, Krüger M 1988 *Electronisches Publizieren.* Raabe, Stuttgart

Look H E 1983 *Electronic Publishing: A Snapshot of the Early 1980s.* Learned Information, Oxford

Proc. 22nd Congress Int. Publishers Association. Mexico City, 1984

Strategies in the Online Database Marketplace. 1978 Link Resources Corporation, New York

Contributors Index

Contributors are listed in alphabetical order together with their affiliations. Titles of articles which they have authored follow in alphabetical order, along with the respective page numbers. Where articles are co-authored, this has been indicated by an asterisk preceding the article title.

† deceased

† deceased

Name Index

The Name Index has been compiled so that the reader can proceed either directly to the page where an author's work is cited, or to the reference itself in the bibliography. For each name, the page numbers for the bibliographic citation are given first, followed by the page number(s) in parentheses where that reference is cited in text. Where a name is referred to only in text, and not in the bibliography, the page number appears only in parentheses.

The accuracy of the spelling of authors' names has been affected by the use of different initials by some authors, or a different spelling of their name in different papers or review articles (sometimes this may arise from a transliteration process), and by those journals which give only one initial to each author.

Subject Index

The Subject Index has been compiled as a guide to the reader who is interested in locating all the references to a particular subject area within the Encyclopedia. Entries may have up to three levels of heading. Where the page numbers appear in bold italic type, this indicates a substantive discussion of the topic. Every effort has been made to index as comprehensively as possible and to standardize the terms used in the index. Given the diverse nature of the field and the varied use of terms throughout the international community, synonyms and foreign language terms have been included with appropriate cross-references. As a further aid to the reader, cross-references have also been given to terms of related interest.